Revised Second Edition

Masterplots

1,801 Plot Stories and Critical Evaluations of the World's Finest Literature

Revised Second Edition

Volume 1
A – Ber
1 – 614

Edited by
FRANK N. MAGILL

Story Editor, Revised Edition
DAYTON KOHLER

Consulting Editor, Revised Second Edition
LAURENCE W. MAZZENO

SALEM PRESS

Pasadena, California   Englewood Cliffs, New Jersey

96-274

Editor in Chief: Dawn P. Dawson
Consulting Editor: Laurence W. Mazzeno   Managing Editor: Christina J. Moose
Project Editors: Eric Howard   Research Supervisor: Jeffry Jensen
Juliane Brand   Research: Irene McDermott
Acquisitions Editor: Mark Rehn   Proofreading Supervisor: Yasmine A. Cordoba
Production Editor: Cynthia Breslin Beres   Layout: William Zimmerman

Library of Congress Cataloging-in-Publication Data
Masterplots / edited by Frank N. Magill; consulting editor, Laurence W. Mazzeno. —
Rev. 2nd ed.
p.   cm.
Expanded and updated version of the 1976 rev. ed.
Includes bibliographical references and indexes.
1. Literature—Stories, plots, etc. 2. Literature—History and criticism. I. Magill,
Frank Northen, 1907-   . II. Mazzeno, Laurence W.
PN44.M33   1996
809—dc20   96-23382
ISBN 0-89356-084-7 (set)   CIP
ISBN 0-89356-085-5 (volume 1)

Revised Second Edition
First Printing

PUBLISHER'S NOTE

Masterplots: Revised Second Edition is an expanded and updated version of the 1976 *Masterplots: Revised Edition*, which was itself a culmination of the four previous *Masterplots* sets published at intervals since 1949. This new twelve-volume edition retains the original purpose of the Masterplots concept, that of providing fundamental reference data, plot synopses where applicable, and critical evaluations of a comprehensive selection of world literature that is available in English. In accordance with previous practice, the articles are in alphabetical order by title. As a new feature, each article now concludes with an annotated bibliography that gives the reader direction for further study.

The 1,801 articles (3.5 million words) in this set have been either newly written or revised and edited as part of the continuing *Masterplots* updating process, which reflects the results of recent research and new critical understanding of the works in question; sexist, dated, and ethnically biased language was expunged. All the titles in the 1976 set were carefully reviewed for currency, accuracy, and quality of critical analysis. Of the titles dropped from that edition, by far the majority were at one time considered important works—often contemporaneous with their original inclusion in *Masterplots* in the 1940's, 1950's, and 1960's—but are today rarely addressed in schools or recognized critically. Of the retained titles, 110 were completely rewritten, twenty-five received a new *The Story* section, and about 530 received a new *Critical Evaluation* section; nearly thirty of the essay-review type articles were updated and expanded. To all titles a brief annotated bibliography was added. In adding 425 new titles to this new edition, Consulting Editor Laurence W. Mazzeno of Ursuline College and other editors considered classroom curricula at both the high school and the college level, as well as the broader context of literary culture within and outside North America. It was their purpose to add classics that had been previously overlooked and contemporary classics that represent a range of cultural identities and diverse modern experiences.

Although the editors realize that the definition of what constitutes a literary classic or masterwork shifts over time, they have attempted to create a collection of important literary texts drawn from as many sources as are accessible in English. The core of the *Masterplots* collection remains the canon of English and American literature, but this has been significantly augmented with contemporary literature and with works representing a wide range of cultures, peoples, and politics. Contemporary Latin America, for example, is represented by approximately fifty articles, Russia and the former Soviet Union by about sixty, and Asian and Asian American writers by about twenty-five. The chronological range of the set extends from antiquity to the 1990's, with the main emphasis being on the literature of the nineteenth and twentieth centuries. There are approximately 700 works of British and U.S. fiction, 300 works of European fiction, 400 dramatic works, 240 works or collections of poetry, and 160 works of nonfiction. Nearly 400 new titles were drawn from contemporary and non-English literature.

Because *Masterplots* articles are intended to be efficient reference sources, they have been formatted to provide the available factual information about a work at a glance. All articles open with a succinct compilation of carefully researched reference data on the type of work, the author, and the date of first publication and, where applicable, first English translation. The category *Type of work* indicates whether a work of fiction is a novel, short fiction, drama, or poetry; for nonfiction the specific genres—including, but not limited to, autobiography, history, social criticism, travel and nature writing, and essays—are indicated. Information on the *Author* line includes the given name in cases where the writer is known by a pseudonym; pseudonyms under which the writer published; and the years of birth and death. The *First published* category provides a range of information that depends on the work, including alternative titles under which the work may have been published or, for foreign-language works, the original title; the date of first publication or transcription (in rare cases, where this is greatly at variance with the time of creation, a *First written* date will be given); dates of serial publication; and dates of publication for the individual volumes of multivolume works. For plays, the dates of first performance and first publication are given, and for foreign-language works the date of the first English translation (in cases where the title of the first translation differs from that used in this series, the first title is also indicated). For all works of fiction, the opening section also provides information on the *Type of plot*, which indicates the genre of the work, and *Time of plot* and *Locale*, which give the time frame and places in which the story takes place. These categories can prove useful for comparative and historical literary research. In addition, there is for all works of fiction a section entitled *Principal characters*, which lists the work's more important characters, along with brief descriptions.

Also retained from the previous *Masterplots* edition is the use of two types of format for the articles, that of the synopsis review and that of the essay review. The roughly 1,400 synopsis reviews, which treat works that have an identifiable narrative line, provide five categories of information: the opening reference data already described above; *Principal characters*; *The Story*, a straightforward summary of the plot; *Critical Evaluation*, an incisive, critical analysis that discusses significant aspects of the work's artistry and history; and, finally, *Bibliography*, a brief, annotated list of the most important English-language secondary sources that are readily accessible to the general reader and will be able to provide more in-depth information and interpretation of the work in question. The approximately 400 essay reviews cover collections of poetry and short stories, as well as the various forms of nonfiction. In this format, the article has three subdivisions: the reference data described above; the analytical essay; and an annotated bibliography. Occasionally, as for some autobiographical and travel writing, there will be the inclusion of an additional category entitled *Principal personages*, a list and brief descriptions of all historical figures mentioned in the work.

For all ancillary works of literature, music, or art referred to throughout the text of the individual articles, the dates of first publication, performance, or creation are provided in parentheses; as a rule, titles, except in the case of some extremely long, cumbersome examples from eighteenth century fiction, are not abbreviated. All historical persons are referred to at first mention by their full name. Other reference aids in *Masterplots: Revised Second Edition* include four comprehensive indexes at the conclusion of volume 12: a *Chronological Index* of titles, a *Geographical Index* that includes the writers' countries of origin and activity, an alphabetical *Title Index*, and an *Author Index*. All indexes are cross-referenced with alternative author names and work titles.

Hundreds of scholars have contributed their expertise and creativity to the preparation of this work. Their names are given in two lists: those whose critical evaluations for the 1976 *Masterplots: Revised Edition* were retained for this volume; and those who contributed new material written expressly for this set (this list also mentions the contributors' academic affiliations). In most cases bylines are given for whole articles or for the specific *The Story* or *Critical Evaluation* section that was revised or rewritten. Scholars who supplied only a bibliography have not been separately credited except in the new contributor list. Salem Press extends sincere thanks to all the scholars and writers who helped compile *Masterplots: Revised Second Edition*. Most particular thanks go to Consulting Editor Laurence W. Mazzeno.

ORIGINAL CONTRIBUTORS OF CRITICAL EVALUATIONS

V. Addington
Phyllis E. Allran
Kenneth John Atchity
Nancy G. Ballard
Laurence Behrens
Judith Bolch
Timothy E. Bollinger
Peter A. Brier
Larry K. Bright
John J. Brugaletta
Sally Buckner
David B. Carroll
James Thomas Chiampi
Eric H. Christianson
Constance A. Cutler
Robert Dees
Terrence R. Doyle
Glenn M. Edwards
Robert A. Eisner
Mary Peace Finley
Edward E. Foster
Jan Kennedy Foster
Bonnie Fraser
William Freitas

E. N. Genovese
Leslie E. Gerber
William E. Grant
Max Halperen
Stephen Hanson
Lodwick Hartley
Wayne E. Haskin
Vera Lucia de Araujo Haugse
Mary H. Hayden
Howard Lee Hertz
Katharine Bail Hoskins
James Marc Hovde
Muriel B. Ingham
Joanne G. Kashdan
Henderson Kincheloe
Patricia Ann King
David L. Kubal
Michael Levine
Eileen Lothamer
Margaret McFadden-Gerber
Willis E. McNelly
Phyllis Mael
Brian L. Mark
Jean G. Marlowe

Elaine Mathiasen
Frank Joseph Mazzi
Walter E. Meyers
Leslie B. Mittleman
Catherine E. Moore
Patrick D. Morrow
Keith Neilson
Benjamin Nyce
Vina Nickels Oldach
Kenneth Oliver
Roberta L. Payne
Audrey C. Peterson
Bruce D. Reeves
Ann E. Reynolds
Michael S. Reynolds
Steven C. Schaber
Clifton M. Snider
Gayle Steck
Charles Johnson Taggart
John G. Tomlinson, Jr.
R. David Weber
James Weigel, Jr.
Janet Wester

CONTRIBUTORS TO MASTERPLOTS: REVISED SECOND EDITION

Laurence W. Mazzeno, Consulting Editor
Ursuline College

Michael Adams
Fairleigh Dickinson University

Patrick Adcock
Henderson State University

C. M. Adderley
University of South Florida

Amy Adelstein
Independent Scholar

Linda Adkins
University of Northern Iowa

A. Owen Aldridge
University of Illinois

Betty Alldredge
Angelo State University

Diane Almeida
University of Massachusetts, Boston

Candace E. Andrews
San Joaquin Delta College

Scott Andrews
University of California, Riverside

Jeanette Angeletti
Independent Scholar

Raymond M. Archer
Indiana University at Kokomo

Stanley Archer
Texas A&M University

Gerald S. Argetsinger
Rochester Institute of Technology

David B. Arnett
Independent Scholar

Heidi Aubrey
Independent Scholar

Mary C. Bagley
Missouri Baptist College

Jim Baird
University of North Texas

JoAnne Balingit
Independent Scholar

Jane Lee Ball
Wilberforce University

Henry J. Baron
Calvin College

David Barratt
Chester College, England

Melissa E. Barth
Appalachian State University

Dana Reece Baylard
Mount San Jacinto College

Paulina L. Bazin
Loyola University, New Orleans

L. Elisabeth Beattie
Elizabethtown Community College

Cynthia S. Becerra
Humphreys College

Carol F. Bender
Alma College

Chris Benson
Clemson University

Joe Benson
A&T State University

Richard P. Benton
Trinity College

Charles Merrell Berg
University of Kansas

Gordon N. Bergquist
Creighton University

Donna Berliner
Southern Methodist University

Dorothy M. Betz
Georgetown University

Cynthia A. Bily
Adrian College

Margaret Boe Birns
New York University

Nicholas Birns
La Guardia Community College and The New School for Social Research

Carol Bishop
Indiana University Southeast

Robert G. Blake
Elon College

Kevin J. Bochynski
Independent Scholar

Pegge Bochynski
Salem State College

Edra Charlotte Bogle
University of North Texas

Sarah A. Boris
Boston University

Brinda Bose
Boston University

Bradley R. Bowers
Barry University

Beth Adams Bowser
Independent Scholar

Gerhard Brand
California State University, Los Angeles

Glen Brand
University of Northern Iowa

Chris Breyer
Independent Scholar

Jennifer Costello Brezina
University of California, Riverside

Ludger Brinker
Macomb College

Wesley Britton
Grayson County College

David Bromige
Sonoma State University

Diane Brotemarkle
Aims Community College

Keith H. Brower
Dickinson College

Stephen G. Brown
University of South Florida

CONTRIBUTING REVIEWERS

Earle V. Bryant
University of New Orleans

Faith Hickman Brynie
Independent Scholar

Jeffrey L. Buller
Georgia Southern University

Judith Burdan
James Madison University

Susan Butterworth
Independent Scholar

Ann M. Cameron
Indiana University at Kokomo

Edmund J. Campion
University of Tennessee

Carmen Carrillo
Los Angeles Harbor College

Emmett H. Carroll
Seattle University

Sharon Carson
University of North Dakota

Ron Carter
Rappahannock Community College

Tara Y. Carter
University of Northen Iowa

Catherine Cavanaugh
College of Saint Rose

Kathleen R. Chamberlain
Emory & Henry College

C. L. Chua
California State University, Fresno

Jarrell Chua
California State University, Fresno

Julian W. Connolly
University of Virginia

Alan Cottrell
University of Missouri at Kansas City

Howard Cox
Magnolia Bible College

Theresa L. Crater
Metropolitan State College of Denver

Su A. Cutler
Kalamazoo Valley Community College

Marsha A. Daigle-Williamson
Spring Arbor College

Richard Damashek
Independent Scholar

Delmer Davis
Andrews University

Jane Davis
Fordham University

Jo Culbertson Davis
Williams Baptist College

Linda Prewett Davis
Charleston Southern University

Mary Virginia Davis
California State University, Sacramento

Frank Day
Clemson University

Dennis R. Dean
Independent Scholar

Mary Jo Deegan
University of Nebraska, Lincoln

Bill Delaney
Independent Scholar

Francine Dempsey
College of Saint Rose

Scott Denham
Davidson College

Carolyn F. Dickinson
Columbia College

Frank Dietz
Independent Scholar

Matts Djos
Mesa State College

Kim Dolce
Independent Scholar

Barbara Drake
Linfield College

William Ryland Drennan
University of Wisconsin Center, Baraboo/Sauk County

Margaret Duggan
South Dakota State University

Charles Freeman Duncan
Clark Atlanta University

Joyce Duncan
East Tennessee State University

K Edgington
Towson State University

Janet Mason Ellerby
University of North Carolina, Wilmington

Robert P. Ellis
Independent Scholar

Thomas H. Falk
Michigan State University

B. K. Faunce
Mary Washington College

James Feast
Baruch College

Joseph A. Feustle, Jr.
University of Toledo

John W. Fiero
University of Southwestern Louisiana

Jack Finefrock
Kenyon College

Edward Fiorelli
Independent Scholar

Sandra K. Fischer
State University of New York at Albany

Bonnie Flaig
Kalamazoo Valley Community College

Thomas C. Foster
University of Michigan, Flint

Robert J. Frail
Centenary College

Carol Franks
Portland State University

Thomas B. Frazier
Cumberland College

Michelle Fredette
Loyola University, New Orleans

Raymond Frey
Centenary College

Patricia H. Fulbright
Clark College

Kelly Fuller
Claremont Graduate School

Constance M. Fulmer
Pepperdine University

Jean C. Fulton
*Maharishi International
University*

Robert L. Gale
University of Pittsburgh

M. E. Gandy
*Bishop State Community
College*

Ann Davison Garbett
Averett College

Marie M. Garrett
*Patrick Henry Community
College*

Marshall Bruce Gentry
University of Indianapolis

Bishnupriya Ghosh
Utah State University

Jill B. Gidmark
University of Minnesota

Howard Giskin
Appalachian State University

Beaird Glover
Independent Scholar

Diana Pavlac Glyer
College of the Ozarks

Vibha Bakshi Gokhale
Independent Scholar

Marc Goldstein
Independent Scholar

Sidney Gottlieb
Sacred Heart University

Karen Gould
Independent Scholar

Lewis L. Gould
University of Texas at Austin

James Green
Arizona State University

John L. Grigsby
*Tennessee Technological
University*

M. Katherine Grimes
Ferrum College

M. Martin Guiney
Kenyon College

Kenneth E. Hada
Bartlesville Wesleyan College

Angela Hague
*Middle Tennessee State
University*

James Hale
Independent Scholar

Elsie Galbreath Haley
*Metropolitan State College of
Denver*

Jay L. Halio
University of Delaware

Gavin R. G. Hambly
University of Texas at Dallas

Barbara J. Hampton
Independent Scholar

Katherine Hanley
St. Bernard's Institute

Tina L. Hanlon
Ferrum College

Judith E. B. Harmon
Lake Forest College

Natalie Harper
Simon's Rock College of Bard

Gregory Harris
Independent Scholar

Suzan Harrison
Eckerd College

Jack Hart
University of Rio Grande

Stephen M. Hart
University of Kentucky

A. Waller Hastings
Northern State University

John C. Hawley
Santa Clara University

Barbara Heavilin
Taylor University

Terry Heller
Coe College

Joyce E. Henry
Ursinus College

Susan Henthorne
White Pines College

Angela D. Hickey
Adrian College

John Higby
Appalachian State University

Michael R. Hill
University of Nebraska, Lincoln

Richard A. Hill
Taylor University

Susan E. Hill
University of Northern Iowa

Rebecca Stingley Hinton
Clermont College and *Indiana
East University*

Tom E. Hockersmith
Independent Scholar

James L. Hodge
Bowdoin College

Roseanne L. Hoefel
Alma College

Dennis Hoilman
Ball State University

John R. Holmes
*Franciscan University of
Steubenville*

Yasuko Honda
Loyola University, New Orleans

Roberta M. Hooks
Potsdam College

Glenn Hopp
Howard Payne University

Pierre L. Horn
Wright State University

William L. Howard
Chicago State University

Anne Howells
Occidental College

E. D. Huntley
Appalachian State University

Michael Hurd
East Tennessee State University

Archibald E. Irwin
Indiana University Southeast

John Jacob
Northwestern University

Mary Dalton Jamieson
*Broward Community College—
North*

Helen Jaskoski
*California State University,
Fullerton*

CONTRIBUTING REVIEWERS

Shakuntala Jayaswal
University of New Haven

David Johansson
Brevard Community College

Jeff Johnson
Brevard Community College

Sheila Golburgh Johnson
Independent Scholar

Yvonne Johnson
Central Missouri State University

Eunice Pedersen Johnston
North Dakota State University

Douglas A. Jones
Andrews University

Jane Anderson Jones
Manatee Community College

Richard Jones
University of Kansas

Sharon Lynette Jones
University of Georgia

Michael Scott Joseph
Rutgers University Libraries

Mitchell Kalpakgian
Simpson College

Ludmila Kapschutschenko-Schmitt
Rider University

Daven M. Kari
California Baptist College

Milton S. Katz
Kansas City Art Institute

Susan E. Keegan
Mendocino College

Richard Keenan
University of Maryland—Eastern Shore

Heidi Kelchner
Independent Scholar

Steven G. Kellman
University of Texas at San Antonio

Richard Kelly
University of Tennessee at Knoxville

Viktor R. Kemper
Western Illinois University

W. P. Kenney
Manhattan College

Donna J. Kessler
Embry-Riddle Aeronautical

Cassandra Kircher
University of Iowa

Susan S. Kissel
Northern Kentucky University

Grove Koger
Boise Public Library

Stephen W. Kohl
University of Oregon

Tom Koontz
Ball State University

Kenneth Krauss
College of Saint Rose

Linda L. Labin
Husson College

Janet M. LaBrie
University of Wisconsin Center, Rock County

Jon W. La Cure
University of Tennessee

Gari Laguardia
State University of New York at Purchase

Carole J. Lambert
Azusa Pacific University

David W. Landrum
Cornerstone College

David H. J. Larmour
Texas Tech University

Craig A. Larson
Trinidad State Junior College

Eugene Larson
Pierce College

Dorie LaRue
Louisiana State University, Shreveport

Jon Lavieri
Independent Scholar

John M. Lawless
Providence College

Linda Ledford-Miller
University of Scranton

L. L. Lee
Western Washington University

Richard M. Leeson
Fort Hays State University

Leon Lewis
Appalachian State University

Anna Lillios
University of Central Florida

Thomas Lisk
North Carolina State University

Richard Logsdon
Community College of Southern Nevada

R. M. Longyear
University of Kentucky

Janet M. Luehring
University of Northern Iowa

Janet McCann
Texas A&M University

Joanne McCarthy
Tacoma Community College

Barbara McCaskill
University of Georgia

Sandra C. McClain
Georgia Southern University

Andrew Macdonald
Loyola University, New Orleans

Gina Macdonald
Loyola University, New Orleans

Ron McFarland
University of Idaho

Robert Kuhn McGregor
Sangamon State University

S. Thomas Mack
University of South Carolina at Aiken

Richard McKirahan
Pomona College

Nancy A. Macky
Westminster College

Peter W. Macky
Westminster College

Joseph McLaren
Hofstra University

John L. McLean
Shawnee State University

A. L. McLeod
Rider University

xi

Jim McWilliams
*Southern Illinois University—
Carbondale*

Paul Madden
Hardin-Simmons University

Gordon Robert Maddison
Broward Community College

Maria Theresa Maggi
University of Idaho

Annette M. Magid
Erie Community College

Philip Magnier
*Maharishi International
University*

Mary Mahony
*Wayne County Community
College*

Cherie Maiden
Furman University

Edward A. Malone
University of Missouri at Rolla

Anne B. Mangum
Bennett College

Barry Mann
Independent Scholar

Lois A. Marchino
University of Texas at El Paso

Kathryn Dorothy Marocchino
California Maritime Academy

Chogollah Maroufi
*California State University,
Los Angeles*

Cynthia L. Marshall
*Community College of Beaver
County*

Catherine Gimelli Martin
University of Memphis

Hubert M. Martin, Jr.
University of Kentucky

R. A. Martin
Laussane Collegiate School

Beverly J. Matiko
Andrews University

H. A. Maxson
Nash Community College

Charles E. May
*California State University,
Long Beach*

Laurence W. Mazzeno
Ursuline College

Kenneth W. Meadwell
University of Winnipeg

Muriel Mellown
*North Carolina Central
University*

Vasa D. Mihailovich
University of North Carolina

Jane Ann Miller
Dartmouth College

Paula M. Miller
Biola University

Craig A. Milliman
*Northwestern State University
of Louisiana*

Christian H. Moe
*Southern Illinois University at
Carbondale*

Robert A. Morace
Daemen College

Bernard E. Morris
Independent Scholar

Charmaine Allmon Mosby
Western Kentucky University

Roark Mulligan
Christopher Newport University

C. Lynn Munro
Independent Scholar

Russell Elliott Murphy
*University of Arkansas at
Little Rock*

N. Samuel Murrell
The College of Wooster

Michele Mock Murton
*Indiana University of
Pennsylvania*

John M. Muste
Independent Scholar

D. Gosselin Nakeeb
Pace University

Richard A. Nanian
Salem State College

William Nelles
*University of Massachusetts,
Dartmouth*

Elizabeth R. Nelson
Saint Peter's College

Terry Nienhuis
Western Carolina University

Emma Coburn Norris
Troy State University

Herb Northcote
Independent Scholar

George O'Brien
Georgetown University

Rafael Ocasio
Agnes Scott College

Stephen C. Olbrys
Independent Scholar

Lawrence J. Oliver
Texas A&M University

Bruce Olsen
Independent Scholar

James Norman O'Neill
Bryant College

Max Orezzoli
Florida International University

William Osborne
Honda International University

Coílín D. Owens
George Mason University

Geert S. Pallemans
*Southern Illinois University at
Edwardsville*

Lucille Izzo Pallotta
Onondaga Community College

Janet Taylor Palmer
Caldwell Community College

Matthew Parfitt
Boston University

David B. Parsell
Furman University

David Patterson
Oklahoma State University

Jay Paul
Christopher Newport University

Pamela Pavliscak
University of North Carolina

Craig Payne
Indian Hills Community College

D. G. Paz
Clemson University

CONTRIBUTING REVIEWERS

David Peck
California State University,
Long Beach

Pamela Peek
Charleston Southern University

Ted Pelton
Lakeland College

Leslie M. Pendleton
Independent Scholar

Thomas Amherst Perry
East Texas State University

Thomas D. Petitjean, Jr.
University of Southwestern
Louisiana

Marion Boyle Petrillo
Bloomsburg University

R. Craig Philips
Michigan State University

Lela Phillips
Andrew College

Allene Phy-Olsen
Austin Peay State University

H. Alan Pickrell
Emory & Henry College

Mary Ellen Pitts
Western Kentucky University

Francis Poole
University of Delaware

Clifton W. Potter, Jr.
Lynchburg College

John Powell
Pennsylvania State University,
Erie

Julie D. Prandi
Illinois Wesleyan University

Andrew B. Preslar
Lamar University at Orange

Verbie Lovorn Prevost
University of Tennessee at
Chattanooga

Cliff Prewencki
Independent Scholar

Victoria Price
Lamar University

Karen Priest
Lamar University at Orange

Charles Pullen
Queen's University

R. C. S.
Independent Scholar

Josephine Raburn
Cameron University

Gregary J. Racz
Princeton University

R. Kent Rasmussen
Independent Scholar

Abe C. Ravitz
California State University,
Dominguez Hills

Rosemary M. Canfield
Reisman
Independent Scholar

Janine Rider
Mesa State College

Claire J. Robinson
Independent Scholar

Susan M. Rochette-Crawley
University of Northern Iowa

Kim Dickson Rogers
Independent Scholar

Mary Rohrberger
University of Northern Iowa

Carl Rollyson
Baruch College

Paul Rosefeldt
Delgado Community College

Joseph Rosenblum
Independent Scholar

Natania Rosenfeld
Duke University

Robert L. Ross
University of Texas at Austin

Susan Rusinko
Bloomsburg University

Murray Sachs
Brandeis University

Chaman L. Sahni
Boise State University

Gregory Salyer
Huntingdon College

James David Schiavoni
Hiwassee College

Gary D. Schmidt
Calvin College

Beverly E. Schneller
Millersville University

Noel Schraufnagel
Alcorn State University

James Scruton
Bethel College

Kenneth Seib
Heartland Community College

John Sekora
North Carolina Central
University

David Seyle
Andrew College

D. Dean Shackelford
Concord College

Elizabeth B. Sharpe
Miami University

Suzanne Obenauer Shaut
Caldwell Community College
and *Appalachian State*
University

Agnes A. Shields
Chestnut Hill College

Wilma J. Shires
Cisco Junior College

R. Baird Shuman
University of Illinois,
Urbana-Champaign

Charles L. P. Silet
Iowa State University

Armand E. Singer
West Virginia University

Carl Singleton
Fort Hays State University

Jan Sjåvik
University of Washington

Genevieve Slomski
Independent Scholar

Nick David Smart
College of New Rochelle

Marjorie Smelstor
University of Wisconsin—
Eau Claire

Pamela J. Olubunmi Smith
University of Nebraska at
Omaha

xiii

Traci S. Smrcka
*University of Southwestern
Louisiana*

Jean M. Snook
*Memorial University of
Newfoundland*

A. J. Sobczak
Independent Scholar

Stephen F. Soitos
Independent Scholar

George Soule
Carleton College

Madison U. Sowell
Brigham Young University

Hartley S. Spatt
*State University of New York
Maritime College*

Brian Stableford
Independent Scholar

James Aaron Stanger
*University of California,
Riverside*

Isabel B. Stanley
East Tennessee State University

Karen F. Stein
University of Rhode Island

Tiffany Elizabeth Stiffler
*Randolph-Macon Woman's
College*

Ingo R. Stoehr
Kilgore College

Louise M. Stone
Bloomsburg University

Gerald H. Strauss
Bloomsburg University

Geralyn Strecker
Ball State University

Trey Strecker
Ball State University

Michael Stuprich
Ithaca College

James Sullivan
*California State University,
Los Angeles*

A. Tatiana Summers
Loyola University, Chicago

David Sundstrand
Independent Scholar

Charlene E. Suscavage
University of Southern Maine

Catherine Swanson
Independent Scholar

Alice L. Swensen
University of Northern Iowa

Glenn L. Swygart
Tennessee Temple University

James Tackach
Roger Williams University

Thomas J. Taylor
University of Akron

Charlotte Templin
University of Indianapolis

Terry Theodore
*University of North Carolina,
Wilmington*

Julie Thompson
Independent Scholar

Lou Thompson
Texas Woman's University

Jonathan L. Thorndike
Lakeland College

Susan Schoenbauer Thurin
University of Wisconsin—Stout

Karen Tracey
University of Northern Iowa

Richard Tuerk
East Texas State University

Linda J. Turzynski
Rutgers University

Dennis Vannatta
*University of Arkansas at
Little Rock*

Albert Wachtel
Pitzer College

Kelly C. Walter
Southern California College

Gordon Walters
DePauw University

Qun Wang
*University of Wisconsin—River
Falls*

Kate Carnell Watt
*University of California,
Riverside*

Thomas Whissen
Wright State University

Lana A. Whited
Ferrum College

Julia Whitsitt
Lander University

Albert E. Wilhelm
*Tennessee Technological
University*

Thomas Willard
University of Arizona

Philip F. Williams
Arizona State University

Scott G. Williams
University of Texas at Austin

Tyrone Williams
Xavier University

Judith Barton Williamson
Sauk Valley Community College

Michael Witkoski
Independent Scholar

Susan Wladaver-Morgan
Independent Scholar

Pat M. Wong
Binghamton University

Shawn Woodyard
Independent Scholar

Qingyun Wu
*California State University,
Los Angeles*

Jennifer L. Wyatt
Civic Memorial High School

Robert E. Yahnke
University of Minnesota

Clifton K. Yearley
*State University of New York
at Buffalo*

Mary Young
The College of Wooster

Laura M. Zaidman
*University of South Carolina
at Sumter*

Laura Weiss Zlogar
*University of Wisconsin—
River Falls*

LIST OF TITLES IN VOLUME 1

Revised Second Edition

ABRAHAM AND ISAAC

Type of work: Drama
Author: Unknown
Type of plot: Mystery play
Time of plot: Antiquity
Locale: Beersheba
First performed: Fifteenth century

Principal characters:
ABRAHAM
ISAAC, his son
DEUS, God
ANGELUS, the angel
THE DOCTOR, a commentator

The Story:

Abraham, offering a prayer of thanksgiving to God, counted his blessings—his land, his peaceful life, his children—and told of his delight in his favorite child, Isaac. He stood praying in a field near his home in Beersheba. After the prayer, he called to Isaac to return to their home.

God, in Heaven, summoned an angel and told him that he intended to test Abraham's steadfastness by asking him to sacrifice Isaac, and he ordered the angel to announce his wish to Abraham. Meanwhile, Abraham prayed again, asking God what gift or offering might please him most. The angel then appeared and told Abraham that God had commanded the sacrifice of Isaac as an indication of Abraham's love for the Lord. Abraham immediately experienced great inward conflict. He kept repeating that Isaac was the most loved of all his children, that he would rather sacrifice anything else of his, including his own life, than to offer up Isaac. At the same time, he was aware that God's will must be obeyed and that the sacrifice, no matter how painful, must be made. Abraham then called Isaac, who had been praying, and told him that they must perform a sacrifice for the Lord. Isaac declared his willingness to help. Abraham felt his heart breaking as they walked toward Mount Vision to make the sacrifice.

On their arrival at the mountain, Isaac asked why Abraham seemed so concerned. The boy began to quake at the sight of the sharp sword in his father's hand because, aware of his father's acute misery, he guessed that he was to be the offering in the sacrifice to the Lord. Abraham then tried to explain to Isaac that they must follow God's commandment, having no other choice. Isaac prayed to his father, asking him to spare his life and wishing his mother were there to intercede for him. Isaac also wondered what crimes he had committed that his life should be demanded by God. Abraham, in his misery, explained that God's will must simply be obeyed. At last, Isaac understood and yielded to God's will. He asked, however, that Abraham not tell his mother he had been killed. Instead, she was to believe that he had gone into another land.

Resigning himself to death, Isaac asked for his father's blessing. Abraham gave his blessing, lamented further, and proceeded to bind Isaac's hands. Abraham then repeated his hope that he could be sacrificed in Isaac's place, but the brave Isaac reminded him that God must be obeyed and asked that the killing be done quickly. Abraham covered Isaac's face with a cloth and made ready to lift his sword. Just as Abraham was about to strike Isaac, the angel appeared and took the sword from Abraham's upraised hand. The angel said that Abraham had proved his willingness to obey God's command, an act that fully displayed Abraham's mind and heart.

Therefore, the angel continued, Abraham would not be compelled to sacrifice his son, but might substitute a young ram, tied nearby, for the offering. Abraham was overjoyed and, after the angel's departure, gave thanks to God for Isaac's deliverance. Isaac welcomed his reprieve, but only after Abraham had assured him that God would regard the ram as a worthy substitute. Isaac, at his father's bidding, ran to bring the ram. Returning with it, Isaac expressed his happiness that the beast, rather than he, was to be sacrificed. When Abraham offered up the ram, Isaac still showed a great fear of Abraham's sword and did not wish to look at it.

After the sacrifice, God again spoke to Abraham, acknowledging his goodness and promising that his family would multiply. Abraham then returned with Isaac to their home, recounting on the way his pleasure that his favorite child had been spared. Isaac was also grateful, but he mentioned his fear and stated that he never wanted to see the hill again. Abraham and Isaac thanked God and showed great relief to be returning home together. Abraham praised the gentleness and understanding of his young son.

The play's commentator, the Doctor, then appeared on the scene to make explicit the moral of the story: that one should follow God's commandments without quarreling. The Doctor asked how many in the audience would be willing to smite their children if God so commanded. He thought that several might do so, although the children's mothers would wail and protest. The Doctor then said that God would mend everything for those truly willing to follow his commandments—those who served God faithfully would be certain to benefit from their loyalty.

Critical Evaluation:

One of the fifteenth century mystery plays performed by guild members in various towns in England, *Abraham and Isaac* tells the biblical story of Abraham's willingness to sacrifice his son. The Brome version is distinguished from others by its greater length and its fuller development of the characters of Abraham and Isaac. The mystery plays, although often simple in both plot and design, helped to provide the background and tradition from which Elizabethan drama later emerged. The play is in verse, sometimes written in five-line stanzas rhyming *abaab*, sometimes in eight-line stanzas with alternate rhymes, these stanzas often ending in a shortened line; sometimes with no clear rhyming or stanzaic pattern. It is difficult to determine whether the play was originally written in a more careful poetic pattern, now lost through successive copyings and oral repetition, or whether it was originally written in a form close to the present version.

Abraham and Isaac is a type of work that could have been created only in an age of faith. Dealing as it does with the ultimate subject of human duty to God, it depends for its effectiveness on a set of shared assumptions between playwright and audience about the omnipotence and omnipresence of God, humanity's relationship to God, and God's justice. The slightest hint of skepticism or rationalistic questioning of values—for example, asking why God's commandment should be obeyed blindly when it appears so arbitrary and unjust, or how one can be sure that this is truly the word of God—would be fatal. As it is, the playwright handles his subject not only with a perfect consistency of tone, but also with great clarity, dramatic power, and, most important, with considerable insight into the human dimension.

The central issue of the play is made clear at the outset when God says, "I shall assay now his good will,/ Whether he loveth better his child or me./ All men shall take example by him my commandments how to keep." This issue never deviates thereafter. The play is an exemplum, or moralized tale, as shown by the Doctor's appearance on stage at the end to reinforce the moral and to make the personal application to the audience explicit. The dramatic power of *Abraham and Isaac* derives largely from the manner in which the degrees of ignorance of father and son become knowledge. The audience, from God's first speech and also from its own knowledge of the Bible, knows the significance of the events to come, making dramatic irony possible. Abraham is ignorant of God's will for an appropriate sacrifice until the angel partially discloses it to him. His knowledge makes him heavy with grief, and so he tries to keep Isaac ignorant of the dire event to come until it is no longer possible to conceal it. When Isaac becomes aware of God's will, he acquiesces immediately, and the plight and subsequent behavior of father and son in their state of partial knowledge become poignant in the extreme. Finally, this partial knowledge of God's purpose is revealed as true ignorance when the angel stays Abraham's hand and informs him of God's real purpose in demanding the sacrifice of Isaac. The full knowledge thus acquired provides characters and audience with new insight not only into God's power and authority, but also into his beneficence.

If the play were merely an exemplum, it would no longer interest us except on the level of didacticism and as an indication of medieval attitudes toward God. This play, however, is an intensely personal work; the playwright is not simply a dramatic preacher, but a man who shares and makes his audience share the agony of Abraham and Isaac. Abraham's love for his son is one of the first dramatic facts established in this play. The loving father's anguish and near despair as he is torn between his reverence for his God and his love for his son is powerful even on the printed page. Isaac does even more to create audience sympathy. By turns he shows us his innocence, his filial love, his devoutness, his trustingness, his anxiety at the sight of Abraham's sword, his fear, his resignation to the will of God, his courage (even exceeding his father's), his mildness under sentence of death, his concern for his mother, his plea for a quick death, and finally his joy at his deliverance. He also displays his lingering fear of the knife and the hill on which he so narrowly escaped slaughter. All of these psychologically sound changes of mood, material for a play of far greater length, are handled with a dramatic skill that is economical, convincing, and moving.

Bibliography:
Collier, Richard. "Poetry and Instruction." In *Poetry and Drama in the York Corpus Christi Play*. Hamden, Conn.: Archon Books, 1978. Collier shows that the moral is explicitly drawn in the Abraham and Isaac plays by the Brome play's Doctor, the Chester play's Expositor, and in the dialogue of the York play.

Mills, David. "Religious Drama and Civic Ceremonial." In *Medieval Drama*. Vol. 1 in *The Revels History of Drama in English*. New York: Methuen, 1983. Discusses the way in which the verisimilitude of the Brome *Abraham and Isaac* threatens the exemplary quality of the drama. He also notes that the play was probably not part of a cycle.

Rendall, Thomas. "Visual Typology in the Abraham and Isaac Plays." *Modern Philology* 81, no. 3 (February, 1984): 221-232. Focuses on the way in which medieval staging underlined the typological overtones in the plays. Rendall points out the parallel staging between the Old Testament and New Testament plays.

Williams, Arnold. "The Literary Art of the Cycles." *The Drama of Medieval England*. East Lansing: Michigan State University Press, 1961. Shows how scriptural exegesis is needed to understand the mystery plays' use of biblical material. As an example of this, Williams notes that the Abraham and Isaac play is one of the types of the sacrifice of the cross.

Woolf, Rosemary. "Types and Prophecies of the Redemption." In *The English Mystery Plays*. Berkeley: University of California Press, 1972. Compares the Abraham and Isaac plays with the Noah and Moses plays of the mystery cycles. She considers the Brome, Chester, and *Ludus Conventriae* Abraham and Isaac plays the most accomplished among the cycles.

ABRAHAM LINCOLN

Type of work: Biography
Author: Carl Sandburg (1878-1967)
First published: Abraham Lincoln: The Prairie Years, 1926; *Abraham Lincoln: The War Years,* 1939

Carl Sandburg's six-volume *Abraham Lincoln* is a monumental work on a monumental theme: the life, works, and times of a symbolic American of history and legend. Sandburg sets Lincoln against a tremendous movement of history as he tells simultaneously, on different levels, the story of a man, a war, an age, and a people. In the end the qualities that set this work apart seem appropriate and significant. Lincoln, that ungainly, complex, humorous, melancholy, and sadly serene man, was also one of the great solitaries.

When *Abraham Lincoln: The War Years* appeared in 1939, more than one reviewer commented on the happy conjunction of the perfect writer and the perfect subject. In Sandburg's case there is more truth in this critical generalization than in most, for he brought to his tremendous task a greater familiarity with the regional and folk aspects of Lincoln's life than anyone had possessed since Lincoln's day. In the late nineteenth century there was still no wide gap between Sandburg's boyhood in Galesburg, Illinois, and Lincoln's growing years in the Sangamon River country. Familiar with New Salem, Vandalia, Springfield, and other landmarks of Lincoln's early life, the Swedish immigrant's son had known the men and women of Lincoln's day and had listened to their stories. Poet, fabulist, folklorist, and singer of the American Dream, Sandburg felt in time that the Lincoln story had become a part of himself, not in the sense of blind hero worship but as evidence of the believable reality and fulfilled promise of American life.

More than thirty years of preparation, research, and writing went into the two divisions of *Abraham Lincoln.* At first Sandburg had in mind a history of Lincoln as the prairie lawyer and politician, but as Sandburg's investigations continued he realized that his book was outgrowing its projected length and purpose. His increasing desire to tell all the facts of Lincoln's life as they existed in books already published, documentary records, or in the memories of men and women finally led him to divide his material into two parts, the first the story of the country boy and lawyer-politician, the second an account of Lincoln in the White House.

The Prairie Years was published in 1926. In these two volumes Sandburg deals with the more legendary aspects of the Lincoln story: boyhood days and backwoods life; a young man's journeys down the Mississippi; Lincoln's education, mostly self-taught, in grammar, mathematics, surveying, debate, and law; the years of clerking in grocery stores and working at odd jobs; military service in the Black Hawk War; his relations with Ann Rutledge, Mary Owens, and Mary Todd; his law practice; and his early political career. This material is presented with a wealth of anecdote—stories about Lincoln and by him—so that it resembles at times an anthology of Lincoln lore. This period of Lincoln's life lends itself at times to fabulous or lyric treatment of which Sandburg the poet takes full advantage. There are passages that read like poetry, sentences and paragraphs that celebrate the beauty of nature and the mystery and wonder of life. Yet these occasional flights of poetic fancy are held within bounds by realistic portrayal and strict regard for fact. In these volumes Sandburg's Lincoln emerges as a man of the people but no hero in the ordinary sense. Circumstances had shaped him into a man of vision and resource, but he was also a troubled, threatened, doubted man when he left Springfield in 1861 on the eve of his inauguration as president of the United States.

Abraham Lincoln: The War Years was published in four volumes thirteen years later. In the meantime Sandburg had traveled widely to gather material from every available source, read extensively in histories, biographies, newspapers, pamphlets, diaries, letters, and handbills, looked at pictures and cartoons, collected memorabilia of every sort, and written steadily while he studied, pondered, and re-created—in effect, relived—Lincoln's life during the Civil War period. The result, in the opinion of historians and critics, is a biography not likely soon to be surpassed of a man linked inseparably to his country's history and folk imagination.

Sandburg makes no attempt to gloss over the dark years of 1861-1862. Lincoln, who had incurred ridicule by arriving in Washington, D.C., in a military cape and a Scotch plaid cap—in disguise, his enemies jeered—found himself hated in the South, handicapped by his cabinet and the Congress, and faced with the crisis of Fort Sumter. Having taken over the leadership that William Henry Seward, secretary of state, had tried at first to withhold from the chief executive, Lincoln then proceeded to display a temporizing attitude that history finds hard to explain. His declaration at the end of 1862—"Fellow-citizens, we cannot escape history"—is open to various interpretations. Lincoln was to ride out of the storm of public disfavor. The Emancipation Proclamation, the turn of the tide at Gettysburg, the appointment of Ulysses S. Grant to the high command, and the Gettysburg Address mark what Sandburg calls the "Storm Center" of the war years. Although the mid-term elections of 1863 were against Lincoln and his own party was prepared to abandon him for the sake of political expediency, he won the campaign of 1864 in the face of the bitterest opposition of his enemies and the apathy of his party. From this time on Sandburg shows the tide in full flood—the aggressive final phase of the war, Sherman's march to the sea, the passing of the Thirteenth Amendment, the surrender at Appomattox, and the night at Ford's Theater on April 14, 1865. The end of the story is starkly, movingly, eloquently told with a poet's power of words and the historian's respect for truth.

In handling the massive reportage of *Abraham Lincoln*, Sandburg never pretends to be more than a storyteller, a recorder. Ever since the publication of *Abraham Lincoln: The Prairie Years* critics had tried to find a term to describe Sandburg's method as a biographer, since his work could not be judged by any of the accepted schools of writing history. *Abraham Lincoln: The War Years*, with all its vast accumulation of fact piled on fact, detail on detail, gave them the answer. Sandburg's method is the way of the old chronicles and sagas in telling the stories of folk and tribal heroes. This biography is a work that expands within the consciousness of the reader because of its continuous addition and multiplication of concrete and evocative details— battle summaries, character sketches, anecdotes, letters, quotations of every kind—all presented without analysis or interpretation so that in the end they shape themselves to their own pattern and carry their own weight of meaning.

Nothing is too vast or too commonly known to be glossed over without patient attention to every living detail; nothing is too trivial to be included. Never has there been such a summoning of witnesses to testify to a man and his age. Foreign diplomats, members of the Cabinet and the Congress, military men of the North and the South, Leo Tolstoy, Henrik Ibsen, Nathaniel Hawthorne, Mrs. Mary Chesnut, and hundreds of obscure men and women appear briefly, make their gestures or have their say, and then disappear. Lincoln's enemies make their insults and accusations; his detractors voice their ridicule; his friends speak in his praise. All leave behind them something that adds to the readers' understanding of Lincoln, something more important than the opinions of politicians or the decisive outcomes of battles and accounts of military campaigns in creating the illusion of life.

These details, great and small, are the background setting against which Lincoln casts his shadow. Against this backdrop of history he appears as a man with human weaknesses and failures, just as he appears greater than other men in the strength, wisdom, and sad serenity of his last months. "Unfathomable" is the adjective Sandburg most frequently applies to him. Many writers have tried to analyze Lincoln. It remained for Sandburg simply to show the man, letting him speak and act for himself. This also was the method of the anonymous writers of the ancient sagas.

Abraham Lincoln: The War Years, more somber in tone, offers less opportunity than *Abraham Lincoln: The Prairie Years* for bardic song. Occasionally, however, the poet breaks in on the biographer and historian. One such passage occurs after the account of the Gettysburg Address when Lincoln, a wet towel over his tired eyes, was on his way back to Washington, and a moonlit hush had fallen over the battlefield and the new-made graves. Then in Whitmanesque measures Sandburg speaks his requiem for the buried dead in the silent cemetery as he looks out over the land and into the homes where the son, the husband, or the father is missing from his familiar place and the clocks of time and destiny tick on. Again, at the beginning of the chapter titled "The Calendar Says Good Friday," he employs another poetic passage to set the mood for coming tragedy. Nowhere, however, is he more moving than in the solemn intensity of the three simple sentences that bring the Lincoln story to its close.

Sandburg's *Abraham Lincoln* is the biography of an American whose true story lends itself to the spirit of legend, a pageant of history, a poet's dream, a national myth. It is a story that is vast and at times contradictory. It is the stubborn, time-defying stuff of life itself, a story in which Sandburg finds in Lincoln's life the meaning of America. *Abraham Lincoln* is a poet's biography only in the sense that every true poet is a biographer providing insights to human experience. Unfortunately, not all biographers are poets. Carl Sandburg, to the readers' enrichment, is the rare writer who is both. If America has an epic, it is this story of a national hero re-created from the testimony of the men and women of Lincoln's time.

Bibliography:

Allen, Gay Wilson. *Carl Sandburg*. Minneapolis: University of Minnesota Press, 1972. Brief but useful introduction to Sandburg's life and creative career. Includes references to the poet's biographical studies of Abraham Lincoln.

Callahan, North. *Carl Sandburg: His Life and Works*. University Park: Pennsylvania State University Press, 1987. Provides an overview of Sandburg's career and critical readings of his poems and offers a complete discussion of Sandburg's works on Lincoln. See pages 121-172.

_____. *Carl Sandburg: Lincoln of Our Literature*. New York: New York University Press, 1970. A critical biography of Sandburg that focuses, in large part, upon the nature of the poet's interest in and writings on Abraham Lincoln.

Crowder, Richard. *Carl Sandburg*. New York: Twayne, 1964. Excellent overview of Sandburg's life and literary career. The chapters "Lincoln and America" and "The People and the Union" recount and interpret the development of the poet's publications on Abraham Lincoln. Notes the author was as interested in Lincoln the myth as he was in the historical personage, which accounts for the unique power of Sandburg's biographical works on the president.

Niven, Penelope. *Carl Sandburg: A Biography*. New York: Charles Scribner's Sons, 1991. First-rate critical biography of Sandburg. Includes a section titled "The Lincoln Years." Discusses the nature of the poet's interest in and identification with Lincoln. Perhaps the best single work to date on Sandburg and his literary career.

ABSALOM, ABSALOM!

Type of work: Novel
Author: William Faulkner (1897-1962)
Type of plot: Psychological realism
Time of plot: Nineteenth century
Locale: Mississippi
First published: 1936

Principal characters:
THOMAS SUTPEN, owner of Sutpen's Hundred
ELLEN COLDFIELD SUTPEN, his wife
HENRY and
JUDITH, their children
ROSA COLDFIELD, Ellen's younger sister
GOODHUE COLDFIELD, Ellen's and Rosa's father
CHARLES BON, Thomas Sutpen's son by his first marriage
QUENTIN COMPSON, Rosa Coldfield's young friend
SHREVE MCCANNON, Quentin's roommate at Harvard

The Story:

In the summer of 1909, when Quentin Compson was preparing to go to Harvard, old Rosa Coldfield insisted upon telling him the whole infamous story of Thomas Sutpen, whom she called a demon. According to Miss Rosa, he had brought terror and tragedy to all who had dealings with him.

In 1833, Thomas Sutpen had come to Jefferson, Mississippi, with a fine horse and two pistols and no known past. He had lived mysteriously for a while among people at the hotel, and after a short time he had disappeared from the area. He had purchased one hundred square miles of uncleared land from the Chickasaws and had had it recorded at the land office. When he returned with a wagonload of wild-looking blacks, a French architect, and a few tools and wagons, he was as uncommunicative as ever. At once, he set about clearing land and building a mansion. For two years he labored, and during all that time he rarely saw or visited his acquaintances in Jefferson. People wondered about the source of his money. Some claimed that he had stolen it somewhere in his mysterious comings and goings. Then, for three years, his house remained unfinished, without windowpanes or furnishings, while Thomas Sutpen busied himself with his crops. Occasionally he invited Jefferson men to his plantation to hunt, entertaining them with liquor, cards, and savage combats between his giant slaves—combats in which he himself sometimes joined for the sport.

At last, he disappeared once more, and when he returned, he had furniture and furnishings elaborate and fine enough to make his great house a splendid showplace. Because of his mysterious actions, sentiment in the village turned against him. This hostility, however, subsided somewhat when Sutpen married Ellen Coldfield, daughter of the highly respected Goodhue Coldfield.

Miss Rosa and Quentin's father shared some of Sutpen's revelations. Because Quentin was away in college, many of the things he knew about Sutpen's Hundred had come to him in letters from home. Other details he had learned during talks with his father. He learned of Ellen Sutpen's life as mistress of the strange mansion in the wilderness. He learned how she discovered her husband fighting savagely with one of his slaves. Young Henry Sutpen fainted,

7

but Judith, the daughter, watched from the haymow with interest and delight. Ellen thereafter refused to reveal her true feelings and ignored the village gossip about Sutpen's Hundred.

The children grew up. Young Henry, so unlike his father, attended the university at Oxford, Mississippi, and there he met Charles Bon, a rich planter's grandson. Unknown to Henry, Charles was his half brother, Sutpen's son by his first marriage. Unknown to all of Jefferson, Sutpen had got his money as the dowry of his earlier marriage to Charles Bon's West Indian mother, a wife he discarded when he learned she was part black. Charles Bon became engaged to Judith Sutpen. The engagement was suddenly broken off for a probation period of four years. In the meantime, the Civil War began. Charles and Henry served together. Thomas Sutpen became a colonel.

Goodhue Coldfield took a disdainful stand against the war. He barricaded himself in his attic and his daughter, Rosa, was forced to put his food in a basket let down by a long rope. His store was looted by Confederate soldiers. One night, alone in his attic, he died. Judith, in the meantime, had waited patiently for her lover. She carried his letter, written at the end of the four-year period, to Quentin's grandmother. Sometime later, Wash Jones, the handyman on the Sutpen plantation, came to Miss Rosa's door with the crude announcement that Charles Bon was dead, killed at the gate of the plantation by his half brother and former friend. Henry fled. Judith buried her lover in the Sutpen family plot on the plantation. Rosa, whose mother had died when she was born, went to Sutpen's Hundred to live with her niece. Ellen was already dead. It was Rosa's conviction that she could help Judith.

Colonel Thomas Sutpen returned. His slaves had been taken away, and he was burdened with new taxes on his overrun land and ruined buildings. He planned to marry Rosa Coldfield, more than ever desiring an heir now that Judith had vowed spinsterhood and Henry had become a fugitive. His son, Charles Bon, whom he might, in desperation, have permitted to marry his daughter, was dead.

Rosa, insulted when she understood the true nature of his proposal, returned to her father's ruined house in the village. She was to spend the rest of her miserable life pondering the fearful intensity of Thomas Sutpen, whose nature, in her outraged belief, seemed to partake of the devil himself.

Quentin, during his last vacation, had learned more of the Sutpen tragedy. He now revealed much of the story to Shreve McCannon, his roommate, who listened with all of a northerner's misunderstanding and indifference. Quentin and his father had visited the Sutpen graveyard, where they saw a little path and a hole leading into Ellen Sutpen's grave. Generations of opossums lived there. Over her tomb and that of her husband stood a marble monument from Italy. Sutpen himself had died in 1869. In 1867, he had taken young Milly Jones, Wash Jones's granddaughter. After she bore a child, a girl, Wash Jones had killed Thomas Sutpen.

Judith and Charles Bon's son, his child by an octoroon woman who had brought her child to Sutpen's Hundred when he was eleven years old, died in 1884 of smallpox. Before he died, the boy had married a black woman, and they had had an idiot son, James Bond. Rosa Coldfield had placed headstones on their graves, and on Judith's gravestone she had caused to be inscribed a fearful message.

In the summer of 1910, Rosa Coldfield confided to Quentin that she felt there was still someone living at Sutpen's Hundred. Together the two had gone out there at night and had discovered Clytie, the aged daughter of Thomas Sutpen and a slave. More important, they discovered Henry Sutpen himself hiding in the ruined old house. He had returned, he told them, four years before; he had come back to die. The idiot, James Bond, watched Rosa and Quentin as they departed. Rosa returned to her home, and Quentin went back to college.

Quentin's father wrote to tell him the tragic ending of the Sutpen story. Months later, Rosa sent an ambulance out to the ruined plantation house, for she had finally determined to bring her nephew, Henry, into the village to live with her so that he could get decent care. Clytie, seeing the ambulance, was afraid that Henry was to be arrested for the murder of Charles Bon many years before. In desperation she set fire to the old house, burning herself and Henry Sutpen to death. Only the idiot, James Bond, the last surviving descendant of Thomas Sutpen, escaped. No one knew where he went, for he was never seen again. Miss Rosa took to her bed and died soon afterward, in the winter of 1910.

Quentin told the story to his roommate because it seemed to him, somehow, to be the story of the whole South, a tale of deep passions, tragedy, ruin, and decay.

Critical Evaluation:

Absalom, Absalom! is the most involved of William Faulkner's works, for the narrative is revealed by recollections years after the events described have taken place. Experience is related at its fullest expression; its initial import is recollected, and its significance years thereafter is faithfully recorded. The conventional method of storytelling has been discarded. Through his special method, Faulkner is able to re-create human action and human emotion in its own setting. Sensory impressions gained at the moment, family traditions as powerful stimuli, the tragic impulses—these focus in the reader's mind so that a tremendous picture of the nineteenth century South, vivid down to the most minute detail, grows slowly in the reader's imagination.

This novel is Faulkner's most comprehensive attempt to come to terms with the full implications of the Southern experience. The structure of the novel, itself an attempt by its various narrators to make some sense of the seemingly chaotic past, is indicative of the multifaceted complexity of that experience, and the various narrators' relationship to the material suggests the difficulty that making order of the past entails. Each narrator has, to begin with, only part of the total picture—and some parts of that hearsay or conjecture—at his disposal, and each narrator's response is conditioned by individual experience and background. Thus, Miss Rosa's idea of Sutpen depends equally upon her Calvinist background and her failure to guess why Henry Sutpen killed Charles Bon. Quentin's father responds with an ironic detachment, conditioned by his insistence upon viewing the fall of the South as the result of the workings of an inevitable fate. As Quentin and Shreve do, the reader must attempt to coordinate the various partial histories of the Sutpen family into a meaningful whole—with the added irony that the reader must also deal with Quentin's romanticism. In effect, the reader becomes another investigator, one whose concern is with the entire scope of the novel rather than only with the Sutpen family.

At the heart of the novel is Thomas Sutpen and his grand design, and the reader's comprehension of the meaning of the novel depends upon the discovery of the implications of this design. Unlike the chaos of history the narrators perceive, Sutpen's design would, by its nature, reduce human history and experience to a mechanical and passionless process that he could control. The irony of Sutpen's failure lies in the fact that he could not achieve the design precisely because he was unable to exclude such human elements as Charles Bon's need for his father's love and recognition. Faulkner, however, gains more than this irony from his metaphor of design. In effect, Sutpen's design is based upon a formula of the antebellum South that reduces the South to essentials. It encompasses the plantation, the slaves, the wife and family— all the external trappings of the plantation aristocracy that Sutpen, as a small boy from the mountains, saw in his first encounter with this foreign world. Sutpen, who never really becomes one of the aristocracy that his world tries to mirror, manages, by excluding the human element from his design, to reflect only what is worst in the South. Unmitigated by human emotion and values, Southern society is revealed to have at its heart the simple fact of possession: of the land, of the slaves, and of the wife and children. Thus, Faulkner demonstrates that the urge to possess is the fundamental evil from which other evils spring. Sutpen, trying to insulate himself from the pain of rejection that he encountered as a child, is driven almost mad by the need to possess the semblance of the world that denies his humanity, but in his obsession, he loses that humanity.

Once the idea of the design and the principle of possession in *Absalom, Absalom!* are established, Sutpen's treatment both of Charles Bon and Bon's mother is more easily understood. In Sutpen's distorted mind, what is possessed can also be thrown away if it does not fit the design. Like certain other Faulkner characters—Benjy of *The Sound and the Fury* (1929) being the best example—Sutpen is obsessed with the need to establish a perfect order in the world into which he will fit. His first vision of tidewater Virginia, after leaving the timeless anarchy of the mountains, was the sight of perfectly ordered and neatly divided plantations, and, like a chick imprinted by its first contact, Sutpen spends his life trying to create a world that imitates that order. He also seeks to establish a dynasty that will preserve that order. His rejection of Bon is essentially emotionless, mechanical, and even without rancor because Bon's black blood simply excludes him from the design. Similarly, the proposal that Rosa have his child to prove herself worthy of marriage and the rejection of Milly when she bears a female child are also responses dictated by the design. Thus, Sutpen, and all whose lives touch his, ultimately become victims of the mad design he has created. Sutpen, however, is not its final victim: The curse of the design lives on into the present in Jim Bond, the last of Sutpen's bloodline.

Sutpen's rejection of Charles Bon and the consequences of that rejection are at the thematic center of *Absalom, Absalom!* In the fact that Charles is rejected for the taint of black blood, Faulkner very clearly points to the particularly Southern implication of his story. Bon must be seen, on one level, to represent the human element within Southern society that cannot be assimilated and will not be ignored. Faulkner implies that the system, which inhumanely denies the human rights and needs of some of its children, dehumanizes all it touches—master and victim alike. In asserting himself to demand the only recognition he can gain from his father—and that only at second hand through Henry—Charles Bon makes of himself an innocent sacrifice to the sin upon which the South was founded. His death also dramatizes the biblical admonition relevant to *Absalom, Absalom!*: A house divided against itself cannot stand.

Sutpen's history is a metaphor of the South, and his rise and fall is Southern history written in one man's experience. The Sutpens, however, are not the only victims in the novel. The narrators, too, are the victims of the Southern experience, and each of them seeks in Sutpen's history some clue to the meaning of his own relationship to the fall of the South. Their narratives seek to discover the designs that will impose some order on the chaos of the past.

"Critical Evaluation" by William E. Grant

Bibliography:
Blotner, Joseph. *Faulkner: A Biography.* 2 vols. New York: Random House, 1974. A lengthy biography of William Faulkner's life and work. Shows how *Absalom, Absalom!* evolved to become what Blotner considers Faulkner's most important and ambitious contribution to American literature.

Brooks, Cleanth. *William Faulkner: Toward Yoknapatawpha and Beyond.* New Haven, Conn.: Yale University Press, 1978. The appendices are an especially valuable aid. One essay discusses Brooks's answer to the question of how typical Thomas Sutpen is of the "Southern planter." Another focuses on the narrative structure of the novel.

Leary, Lewis. *William Faulkner of Yoknapatawpha County.* New York: Thomas Y. Crowell, 1973. Chapter 5 describes *Absalom, Absalom!* as disclosing the way history is made and legends develop. Cites examples of how Thomas Sutpen's story emerges as a jigsaw puzzle, as various narrators' contributions finally fit together to disclose a design.

Minter, David. *William Faulkner: His Life and Work.* Baltimore: The Johns Hopkins University Press, 1980. Provides a context for the writing of *Absalom, Absalom!* Identifies the force of the novel as emerging from entangled relationships among generations of "doomed" families, races, and sexes. Discusses relationships between the narrators' stories and their lives.

Volpe, Edmond L. *A Reader's Guide to William Faulkner.* New York: Farrar, Straus & Giroux, 1964. An earlier treatment of Faulkner's novels, this volume remains valuable. Sections on narrative structure and technique as well as on key characters. Contains a genealogy and a helpful chronology of events.

ABSALOM AND ACHITOPHEL

Type of work: Poetry
Author: John Dryden (1631-1700)
Type of plot: Satire
Time of plot: Late seventeenth century
Locale: London
First published: 1681

> *Principal characters:*
> DAVID, king of Israel
> ABSALOM, his illegitimate son
> ACHITOPHEL, chief of the rebels

The Story:

The political situation in Israel (England), had much to do with David's (Charles II's) virility, which though wasted on a barren queen, produced a host of illegitimate progeny, of which by far the fairest and noblest was Absalom (Duke of Monmouth). David's kingly virtues were equally strong but unappreciated by a great number of Jews (Whigs), who because of a perverse native temperament, wanted to rebel. Although David had provided no cause for rebellion, as the wiser Jews (Tories) pointed out, a cause was found in the alleged Jebusite (Catholic) plot to convert the nation to the Egyptian (French) religion. The plot miscarried, but it did create factions whose leaders were jealous of David and opposed his reign.

Achitophel was the chief of these leaders (the Earl of Shaftesbury, leader of the Whigs), and he made efforts to persuade Absalom to seize the throne. Achitophel was a brilliant wit touched by the madness of ambition. Unwilling to be remembered only for his distinguished career as a judge, he "Resolv'd to ruin or to rule the State," using the king's alleged sympathy for the Jebusites as an excuse for rebellion. Achitophel first used flattery to win over Absalom, proclaiming that the nation was clamoring for him—a "second Moses." At first Absalom resisted, pointing out that David was a wise and just king, and that David's brother (the Duke of York) was the legal heir. These half-hearted objections Achitophel met with sophistry. David's mildness, he claimed, had deteriorated into weakness; the public good demanded Absalom's strength; the rightful heir was planning to murder Absalom; David himself secretly wanted Absalom to be king and would support his claim as heir to the throne. To these specious arguments Absalom succumbed, whereupon Achitophel proceeded to organize all the Jewish malcontents into a single seditious party.

Among these misguided patriots were opportunists, republicans, and religious fanatics. Zimri embodied the fickleness and "extremity" of Buckingham, Shaftesbury's lieutenant in the Whig Party. Shimei represented the Sheriff of London, who had betrayed the king's interests, and Corah, the notorious Titus Oates, who had fabricated many of the details of the Catholic plot.

Absalom made a nationwide tour, planned by Achitophel to gauge the extent of the people's support for their plan to exclude the legal heir from the throne and to establish Absalom's right to the succession by law. Traveling up and down the land, Absalom craftily represented himself as the people's friend, opposed to Egyptian domination, the Jebusite plot, and a senile king, but powerless to act because of his loyalty to the crown and the lawful succession. The Jews, always easy to delude, proclaimed Absalom a new messiah.

The speaker of the poem attacked the Jews' naïve support of Absalom and their willingness

12

to overthrow legally instituted authority. He feared that the government would quickly deteriorate into anarchy if the people were given the power to make and break kings at will by changing the order of the succession.

Next came portraits of David's supporters—the Tory leaders. Barzillai (the Duke of Ormond) was lavishly praised as the noblest adherent to David's cause and one of Israel's true heroes. Two members of the clergy, namely Zadoc (the Archbishop of Canterbury) and the Sagan of Jerusalem (the Bishop of London), were commended for their services to the crown. Other loyalists, praised for their services in Sanhedrin (Parliament), include Adriel (the Earl of Mulgrave), Jotham (the Marquis of Halifax), Hushai (Laurence Hyde), and Amiel (Edward Seymour). These loyal chieftains who defied the powerful rebel faction ultimately convinced David that concessions to the people would but feed their leaders' ambition, and that Absalom was being used as a tool by the treacherous Achitophel.

David finally reasserted the royal prerogative. Realizing that his enemies had been scoffing at his moderation and clemency as a sign of weakness and fear, he resolved to show his strength. David, regretting that Absalom would be compelled to suffer, expressed his willingness to forgive at the sign of repentance, but he refused to condone disloyalty. The Sanhedrin's attempt to change the line of succession David denounced, scorning their deceitful claim that they were trying to protect him from a scheming brother. Finally David stated his reluctance to resort to force but declared his readiness to use it to defend the supremacy of established law over both Sanhedrin and king. Heaven clapped its thunder in approval of David's words and the new era that they heralded.

Critical Evaluation:

Dryden claimed that *Absalom and Achitophel* was carefully planned to promote political reform. To gain this end, Dryden used satire, the true aim of which he defined as "the amendment of vices by correction." The particular vices he wanted corrected were those of the Whigs of his day, who were seeking to secure the succession of the Duke of Monmouth, illegitimate son of Charles II, to his father's throne. Second, realizing that direct satire might defeat its purpose by incurring resentment, Dryden chose to attack the Whigs by casting them as characters in the biblical story of Absalom's revolt against David. Third, to increase his satire's effectiveness, he cast it in verse, "for there's a sweetness in good verse, which tickles even while it hurts."

Written in heroic couplets, *Absalom and Achitophel* is often called John Dryden's best poem. It is one of the most famous political satires ever written. Its direct literary influence reaches from Dryden's contemporaries to Alexander Pope and Charles Churchill in the eighteenth century and to George Gordon, Lord Byron in the nineteenth century. In the poem, Dryden indicates similarities between the biblical story, which tells how the wicked Achitophel urged King David's illegitimate son Absalom to rise up against his father, and events in England between 1678 and 1681, when Anthony Ashley Cooper, Earl of Shaftesbury, a leader of the Whiggish opposition to the king, was accused of persuading James Scott, Duke of Monmouth and illegitimate son of Charles II, to rebel against his father.

Perhaps Dryden intended his poem, published in November, 1681, to help in convicting Shaftesbury, on trial for treason for his part in the rebellion. If so, Dryden was not successful: The jury, friendly to Shaftesbury, declared that they did not have sufficient evidence for a conviction and acquitted Shaftesbury. Dryden's devastating satire probably helped to create an atmosphere so hostile to the Earl that soon after the trial he fled to Holland, where he remained until his death several years later.

The poem is difficult reading for those unaccustomed to satire, unversed in the Bible, and unacquainted with late seventeenth century English history. It presented no problems to readers in Dryden's day, who, vitally interested in contemporary politics and well read in the Bible, were able to correlate King David's situation with that of Charles II. The Bible not only gave Dryden's satire a ready-made, well-known reference; it also provided heavenly authority for condemning the actions of Shaftesbury, Monmouth, and their allies. It enabled Dryden to use the outcome of the biblical story of David to show that Monmouth's rebellion would be useless and that the king's divinely sanctioned victory would be inevitable.

In the poem, which is 1,031 lines long, the putative speaker suits the tone to the rhetorical purpose in telling the story of the rebellion. The first part (lines 1-227) begins with a good-humored account of the father-son relationship, in which Absalom (the Duke of Monmouth), although illegitimate and therefore unable to succeed to the throne, is David's (Charles II's) beloved son, whose every fault is forgiven. The tone becomes condemnatory when the speaker accuses David of too much leniency. David is too lenient toward his grumbling subjects, the Jews (the English), whom "No king could govern, nor no God could please"; toward the inhabitants of his own city, the Jebusites (the Londoners); and particularly toward their depraved leader, the "false Achitophel" (Shaftesbury). Achitophel is a Satanic tempter who looks for and finds in Absalom a likely victim. Achitophel's appeals to Absalom's ambition (lines 229-302) soon prove convincing. Absalom, of course, fails to realize that "They who possess the prince, possess the laws" applies not just to his mastery of his own father but also to Achitophel's mastery over him. Next (lines 491-681), readers are told how Achitophel collected other malcontents, named in the poem after evil men of the Bible. They include several noblemen, the Lord Mayor of London, the Sheriff of London, members of Parliament, and others important in the opposition to Charles II. First is Zimri, the notoriously indecisive Duke of Buckingham, who "in the curse of one revolving moon,/ Was chemist, fiddler, statesman, and buffoon." Dryden was so proud of that jab that he compared his own satiric skill with the artistry of the executioner Jack Ketch, whose deft axe strokes left his victims with their heads still sitting on their necks.

After Absalom is applauded for his hypocritical lament on the necessity of rebellion (lines 682-810), a few alarmed defenders of the king, bearing the names of virtuous men in the Bible, appear to warn the king that he must act to save his throne (lines 816-938). These include such members of the high nobility as the Duke of Ormonde and the Marquis of Halifax and churchmen such as the Archbishop of Canterbury.

The climax of the narrative, when the king is about to invoke the law, is intended to evoke the situation in England in the autumn of 1681, when royalists hoped that Charles II would assert his rights (lines 939 and following). The king's soliloquy shows that reluctantly he has put aside geniality for sternness. In so doing, he has become like Zeus the Thunderer and like Jehovah the Judge in condemning the rebels to the fate they themselves have chosen (lines 1005-1011). The poem ends with the putative speaker's announcement of the simultaneous end of rebellion and disappearance of all discord—an abrupt but appropriate conclusion because it corresponds to the king's decisive action. The ending, with its promise of "a series of new time," is a prophecy that recalls both Greek myths of renewal and Hebrew accounts of how Jehovah made fresh starts possible.

Most important in the historical context is that the ending of the poem is a warning to rebels not to persist. If events in England are really parallel to biblical events, then, as Dryden strongly hints, Monmouth's end will be like that of Absalom, who was killed despite David's pleas that he be spared. Monmouth's fate, it turned out, was like Absalom's. In 1685, soon after the death of his father, Monmouth led an army rebellion against his uncle, James II, the new king. Monmouth was caught, tried, convicted, and executed.

"Critical Evaluation" by Margaret Duggan

Bibliography:
Griffin, Dustin. "Dryden's Charles: The Ending of *Absalom and Achitophel.*" *Philological Quarterly* 57 (Summer, 1978) 359-382. Argues that the end of the poem can be connected to the way Charles II himself behaved during the Exclusion crisis of 1678-1681—he waited for a right moment to act.
Lewalski, Barbara K. "The Scope and Function of Biblical Allusion in *Absalom and Achitophel.*" *English Language Notes* 3 (1965): 29-35. Concerned with the range and importance of biblical allusion in *Absalom and Achitophel* and with its use in structuring the poem. Suggests the poem's epic dimension.
McKeon, Michael. "Historicizing *Absalom and Architophel.*" In *The New Eighteenth Century: Theory, Politics, English Literature,* edited by Felicity Nussbaum and Laura Brown. New York: Methuen, 1987. Argues that, "In *Absalom and Achitophel,* Dryden proposes a model for a new sort of poetry, which draws power and value from the realms of religious faith, political allegiance, and historic factuality while evading subservience to them all."
Schilling, Bernard. *Dryden and the Conservative Myth.* New Haven, Conn.: Yale University Press, 1961. Discusses Dryden's role as spokesman for royalism and as creator of myths that justify and defend kingship. Shows how the myth appears in the structure, style, and content of *Absalom and Achitophel.*
Thomas, Walter K. *The Crafting of "Absalom and Achitophel": Dryden's "Pen for a Party."* Waterloo, Ontario, Canada: Wilfred Laurier University Press, 1978. Investigates political conditions in England from 1678 to 1681. Discusses Dryden's responses to them in *Absalom and Achitophel.*

THE ABSENTEE

Type of work: Novel
Author: Maria Edgeworth (1767-1849)
Type of plot: Social realism
Time of plot: Early nineteenth century
Locale: England and Ireland
First published: 1812

Principal characters:
    LORD CLONBRONY, an absentee landlord
    LADY CLONBRONY, his affected, ambitious wife
    LORD COLAMBRE, their son
    GRACE NUGENT, a cousin
    MISS BROADHURST, an heiress
    ARTHUR BERRYL, Lord Colambre's friend
    COUNT O'HALLORAN, an Irish gentleman
    SIR TERENCE O'FAY, an impecunious nobleman
    LADY DASHFORT, a designing noblewoman
    LADY ISABEL, her daughter
    MR. MORDICAI, one of Lord Clonbrony's creditors
    MR. BURKE, an honest estate agent
    NICHOLAS GARRAGHTY, a dishonest estate agent

The Story:

Lord Clonbrony was an absentee landlord who owned large but encumbered Irish estates. He lived in England because his wife, an extravagant, ambitious woman, would have nothing to do with Ireland or the Irish. People of wealth and position laughed at her and the silly determination with which she aped English manners and speech, and they totally ignored Lord Clonbrony. A respected peer in Dublin and a good landlord when he had lived on his own estates, he was a nobody in his wife's fashionable world. As a result, he associated with such questionable and dissipated companions as Sir Terence O'Fay. Little was known about their son and the Clonbrony heir, Lord Colambre, except that he was a student at Cambridge and a young man of considerable expectations from a distant relative. A cousin, Grace Nugent, was well thought of because of her beauty and good manners.

Lady Clonbrony was anxious to have her son marry Miss Broadhurst, a young woman of much sense and large fortune. Although Lady Clonbrony and Mrs. Broadhurst did their best to promote the match, the young people, while friendly, were not drawn to each other. Lord Colambre was attracted by Grace's amiability and charm, and Miss Broadhurst respected his feelings for his cousin.

In execution of a commission for Arthur Berryl, a Cambridge friend, Lord Colambre went to the establishment of Mr. Mordicai, a coachmaker and moneylender. There he overheard that his father's financial affairs were not in good order. When questioned, Lord Clonbrony admitted that his situation was grave but that he relied on Sir Terence, often his intermediary with his creditors, to prevent legal action against him. The father reflected with some bitterness that there would be no need for such expediency if landowners would live on their own estates and kill their own mutton.

Lord Colambre saw for himself the results of reckless borrowing when Sir John Berryl, the father of his friend, was taken suddenly ill. Mordicai, demanding immediate payment of a large debt, attempted to have the sick man arrested and thrown into prison. Only Lord Colambre's presence and firm words of rebuff kept the moneylender from carrying out his intention. Mordicai left with threats that Lord Colambre would someday regret his insults. Sir John Berryl died that night, leaving his family almost penniless.

Deeply concerned for his own family's welfare, Lord Colambre decided to visit Ireland to see for himself the state of his father's affairs. Lady Clonbrony used every possible argument to dissuade her son, and Sir Terence suggested that the young man could best help his father by marrying a woman as wealthy as Miss Broadhurst. When Lord Colambre left suddenly for Ireland, his mother, refusing to give up her matrimonial plans for her son, allowed her friends to believe that he had gone to attend to private business in connection with his marriage settlement. Since many people expected him to marry Miss Broadhurst, that story satisfied the Clonbrony creditors for the time being.

Arriving in Dublin, Lord Colambre met Sir James Brooke, a British official who was well informed on Irish affairs, and the two men became good friends. The young nobleman, pleased with everything he heard and saw, was unable to understand his mother's detestation of the Irish. He tried to meet Nicholas Garraghty, his father's agent, but the man was away on business. Instead, he was entertained by the agent's sister, a silly, affected woman named Mrs. Raffarty.

He also met Lady Dashfort, who saw in him a possible husband for her widowed daughter, Lady Isabel. Although he heard no favorable reports of Lady Dashfort or her daughter, he became a frequent visitor in their home. At last, interested in securing an alliance for her daughter, Lady Dashfort proposed that he accompany her to Killpatrickstown, where she was going to visit Lord and Lady Killpatrick. It was her intention to show him Irish life at its worst so that he would have no desire to live on the Clonbrony estates after his marriage to Lady Isabel. Aware of his affection for Grace, Lady Dashfort arranged matters so that Lady Killpatrick asked her to exhibit her genealogical table, which had been prepared as evidence in a lawsuit. She did so with seeming reluctance, on the grounds that she was ashamed of her remote connection with the scandalous St. Omars. She then revealed that Grace's mother had been a St. Omar.

Lord Colambre wrote to his mother to ask the truth. She replied that the girl's mother had been a St. Omar but that she had taken the name Reynolds after an affair with a gentleman of that name. When the Reynolds family refused to acknowledge her child, she had married Mr. Nugent, who had generously given the daughter his own name. The young man realized that this disclosure put a barrier between Grace and him.

Through the Killpatricks, Lord Colambre met Count O'Halloran, who was regarded by his neighbors as an oddity because of his learning, his fondness for animals, and his liking for the Irish. When the count returned the visit, Lady Dashfort took issue with him because he criticized the improper conduct of an English officer with whom both were acquainted. Lady Dashfort's lack of good manners and moral sense and the further revelation of Lady Isabel as a malicious flirt showed the two women to Lord Colambre in their true light. He decided to leave the Dashforts and continue his tour alone.

Count O'Halloran prevailed on Lord Colambre, however, to accompany him to Oranmore. There Lord Colambre found a family of taste and breeding, interested in affairs of the day and the welfare of their tenants. Stimulated by the example of Lord and Lady Oranmore, he planned to go immediately to his father's estate, but incognito, so that he could observe more accurately the conditions of the tenantry and the conduct of the estate agents.

He found the village of Colambre neat and prosperous, well looked after by Mr. Burke, the agent. After a dinner with the Burkes, the agent showed him around the estate with evident pride in all he had accomplished. He regretted, however, that the absentee owner took no interest in the land or the tenants, aside from the revenues derived from them. Burke's fears that Lord Clonbrony was displeased with his management were confirmed by the arrival of a letter in which his lordship dismissed the agent and directed him to turn over his accounts to Nicholas Garraghty.

Lord Colambre went on to Clonbrony, where he learned from a driver that the tenants hated and feared Nicholas Garraghty, the factor, and Dennis Garraghty, his brother and assistant. When his carriage broke down, Lord Colambre spent the night with Mrs. O'Neill, a widow whose niece had been named after Grace Nugent. The next day, the young nobleman was present when Dennis Garraghty refused to renew a lease promised to Mrs. O'Neill's son Brian. The arrival of Mrs. Raffarty and her identification of Lord Colambre caused Garraghty to change his mind quickly. Disgusted by the man's methods of doing business and by the unkempt, poverty-stricken appearance of the village, Lord Colambre wrote to his father and asked him to have no further dealings with the Garraghtys.

During the voyage back to England, Lord Colambre's ship was delayed by a storm, so that the Garraghtys arrived in London ahead of him. He returned, however, in time to confront the agent and his brother with a report on their transactions. Hearing his son's story, Lord Clonbrony would have dismissed them on the spot if he had possessed the cash necessary to settle their entangled accounts. Lord Colambre then asked his father and Sir Terence for a full accounting of the distressed nobleman's obligations. In return, he proposed to settle the debt with the inheritance he would receive when he came of age, a date only a few days off, if his father would end all business relations with the Garraghtys and go to Ireland to live. Lord Clonbrony welcomed the proposal, but his wife, when she heard of it, treated the idea with scorn. She was already displeased with her son because he had not pressed his suit with Miss Broadhurst, who was now to marry his friend, Sir Arthur Berryl. When Lord Colambre expressed pleasure over his friend's good fortune, Lady Clonbrony retired in disgust.

Under persuasion by every member of her family, Lady Clonbrony at last ungraciously agreed to return to Ireland. Meanwhile, Lord Colambre, busy with his father's accounts, discovered that many of the London bills had been deliberately overcharged and that Nicholas Garraghty was, in reality, his lordship's debtor, not his creditor, as the agent had claimed. With ready money sent by Lady Berryl, the former Miss Broadhurst, through her husband, Lord Colambre was able to settle his father's most pressing debts, and Sir Terence was able to reclaim Mordicai's bond at a discount. After Garraghty was dismissed in disgrace, Mr. Burke was appointed agent of the Colambre and Clonbrony estates.

On the day he came of age, Lord Colambre's first duty was to execute a bond for five thousand pounds in Grace's name, to repay her the inheritance that had been lent to her guardian years before. The young man's secret regret was that he could not offer his heart with his cousin's restored property.

Arriving in London, Count O'Halloran called on Lord Colambre. When the young nobleman confided his true feelings for Grace and told his friend something of her story, the count recalled Captain Reynolds, whom he had known in Austria. Dying, the officer had told of his secret marriage with Miss St. Omar and had entrusted to the count a packet of private papers, among them a marriage certificate. The count had given the papers to the English ambassador, and they had passed in turn into the keeping of Sir James Brooke, the executor of the ambassador's estate. Acting on this information, Lord Colambre went to Sir James and obtained the papers, which had never been carefully examined. When he presented them to the dead officer's father, old Mr. Reynolds accepted the proof of his granddaughter's legitimacy with delight and declared his intention to make her his heiress. Because Grace had never known of the shadow cast on her birth, Lady Berryl was delegated to tell her the whole story, a task that young woman performed with great delicacy and tact.

Acquainted with the true state of affairs, Lady Clonbrony offered no objections to her son's marriage to Grace. Lord Clonbrony and his wife returned to Ireland and there, in due time, Grace became Viscountess Colambre, much to the satisfaction of Lady Clonbrony, who saw so happily fulfilled her hopes that her son would marry an heiress.

Critical Evaluation:

The Act of Union of 1800, which brought Ireland under the direct rule of the British, was a significant influence on the conception, execution, and reception of The Absentee. Some of the act's direct implications may be gathered from the depiction of the Dublin that Lord Colambre encounters on his arrival in Ireland. The city that had asserted parliamentary independence about twenty years earlier is a shadow of its former self. The prospect of independence had been part of the public atmosphere in which Maria Edgeworth grew up. Beyond that, the kind of juridical and administrative independence conceived by the Dublin parliament was one with which Edgeworth's family of enlightened landowners readily identified.

The Act of Union dislocated the landowning class's sense of where their interests lay, dividing their sources of identity between the control they had over their land and the judicial and parliamentary sanction for that control, which was now lodged explicitly in the organizations of the British state. The condition of dislocation was lived out literally by many Irish landlords who spent the rents earned by their land in a manner exemplified by Lady Clonbrony in *The Absentee*. This subset of landlords was known as absentees, and while their absence had been a feature of Irish life long before the Act of Union, the new political order made their dereliction of duty even more difficult to overlook.

Edgeworth's sense of the significance of the various problems deriving from the new institutional and administrative arrangements forms the narrative core of *The Absentee*. Because it belongs to the two series of novels and novellas known by their collective title as *Tales from Fashionable Life*, this novel may be considered representative of the so-called silver-fork school of fiction. There is, however, a great deal more explicit cultural and political awareness in *The Absentee* than in most other works of that type. Silver-fork novels concentrate on fashionable life to the virtual exclusion of other concerns. Although it is extremely difficult to depict fashionable life without being aware of its economic and ideological underpinnings, such an awareness is typically merely latent. In the case of *The Absentee*, however, it is Colambre's heightened awareness of the insufficiency of fashionable life that provides both narrative and plot with their momentum and moral insight.

Thus *The Absentee* is not merely a search for a responsible agenda for Irish landlords and, by extension, Irish social and economic life. It may also be considered as a critique of some of the vulgar consumerist excesses in early nineteenth century England. The freedom without responsibility that Lady Clonbrony exhibits is understandably embarrassing to her son. Yet Edgeworth is also careful to note that she perpetrates her spendthrift excesses in order to gain credibility as an equal member of the society putatively enlarged by the Act of Union. The fact that she will never be accepted as an equal by the matrons who patronize her parties makes the point. Parliamentary independence may have been surrendered because of the Act of Union, but Edgeworth shows that there is no need for self-respect to vanish also. Colambre's decision to return to to Ireland and to a responsible role there as landlord implies that the situation cannot be rectified by exclusively parliamentary means.

By going to Ireland, Colambre forsakes the metropolis for the rural life, the fashionable for the unprepossessing, the self-denying mimicry of the salon for the self-empowering possibility to learn through experience. The strangeness of Ireland and the fact that Colambre does not bring with him all the moral resources and ideological self-consciousness necessary for him to live the life for which birth and fortune have equipped him are vital to the didactic purpose that here, as always, underlies Edgeworth's fictional preoccupations. Colambre's experiences in Ireland register the country's distinctive and frequently disturbing difference, and they challenge him to confront that difference.

The importance of his capacity to sustain such a confrontation is not merely to authenticate Colambre by virtue of his personal adaptability to change. In addition, Edgeworth implies that if Colambre can adapt to Irish conditions and intervene in them productively, he will be well on the way to becoming a model landlord. With commitment, control, and maturity, he can redress the social and moral ills of absenteeism. The Act of Union will take its place among the statutes without having impinged on the integrity of the new generation represented by Colambre. As a result, the integrity of relations between landlord and tenant can be restored, an act of union far more significant than its parliamentary counterpart because of the demonstrable social contract that is its premise.

Edgeworth grounds these social and cultural concerns in a series of challenges that Colambre has to overcome before he arrives at the appropriately mature identity. Although Edgeworth's significance as a novelist derives in part from the fact that she never shirks the large question, that question is shown here to have an unsuspected number of facets. Among the more noteworthy of these are the state of Irish culture, with which Colambre engages through his acquaintance with Count O'Halloran, and the young lord's emotional integrity, which is exemplified by his relationship with Grace Nugent. The fact that there is a link between these two areas suggests that Edgeworth is aware of the significance of providing Colambre not only with property and moral intelligence but with an extensive inner life, the existence of which distinguishes him from his hollow and defeated parents. It is the combination of the various elements of Colambre's experiences that distinguishes Edgeworth's *The Absentee*.

"Critical Evaluation" by George O'Brien

Bibliography:
Butler, Marilyn. *Maria Edgeworth: A Literary Biography*. Oxford, England: Clarendon Press, 1972. The standard biography, providing comprehensive information on all aspects of Maria Edgeworth's life, work, and family. The sources, intentions, and reception of all of Edgeworth's writings are discussed. Contains a thorough account of *The Absentee*'s social, artistic, and political contexts.
Davie, Donald. *The Heyday of Sir Walter Scott*. London: Routledge, 1961. A pioneering study of Scott's influence on English and European literature. The distinctive place of Edgeworth's fiction in this overview is clearly established. *The Absentee* receives concise and pertinent treatment.
Dunne, Tom. *Maria Edgeworth and the Colonial Mind*. Dublin: National University of Ireland, 1985. An influential study of Edgeworth's work, to which subsequent considerations of Edgeworth's politics and culture colonialism are indebted. Dunne's discussion is directly relevant to the concerns addressed in *The Absentee*.

Edgeworth, Maria. *The Absentee.* Edited by W. J. McCormack and Kim Walker. Oxford, England: Oxford University Press, 1988. Contains a scholarly introduction, bibliography, and explanatory notes. Also reprints material on the connotations of the name Grace Nugent and Edgeworth's notes for an essay on Edmund Burke.

McCormack, W. J. *Ascendancy and Tradition in Anglo-Irish Literary History from 1789 to 1939.* Oxford, England: Clarendon Press, 1985. Contains a section on *The Absentee,* which is appraised in the light of Edgeworth's reading of the writings of Edmund Burke. A path-breaking contribution to Irish cultural history.

THE ACHARNIANS

Type of work: Drama
Author: Aristophanes (c. 450-c. 385 B.C.E.)
Type of plot: Satire
Time of plot: 431-404 B.C.E.
Locale: Athens
First performed: Acharnēs, 425 B.C.E. (English translation, 1812)

> *Principal characters:*
> DICAEOPOLIS, a peace-loving citizen
> AMPHITHEUS, his friend
> EURIPIDES, the playwright
> LAMACHUS, a general
> AMBASSADORS TO THE ALLIES OF ATHENS
> THE ACHARNIANS, a chorus of charcoal burners

The Story:

Dicaeopolis, waiting for the assembly to convene, sat musing, making figures in the dust, pulling out his loose hairs, and longing for peace. He was fully prepared to harass and abuse the speakers if they talked of anything but peace with Sparta. Immediately after the citizens had gathered, his friend Amphitheus began to complain of hunger because of the wartime diet. He was saved from arrest only by the intervention of Dicaeopolis.

The assembly then listened to a series of fantastic claims made by the pompous ambassadors to Athens' allies, each speech punctuated by a scoffing aside from Dicaeopolis, who knew full well that the entire alliance was wasting away from the effects of the Peloponnesian War. The high point of absurdity was reached when the last of the ambassadors ushered in a few scraggly, miserably dressed troops, introducing them as a Thracian host sent to assist in the war. Dicaeopolis, knowing of the assembly's willingness to adjourn upon the slightest provocation, then brought about the end of the session by claiming to have felt a drop of rain.

Finding himself unable to bring about the end of the war, Dicaeopolis determined to effect a personal, separate peace. Amphitheus, his own ambassador, returned from the enemy with three bottles of wine—the first five years old, the second ten years old, and the third thirty years old. The first two tasted vile, but the last was rich with a bouquet of nectar and ambrosia. Drinking it down, Dicaeopolis personally accepted and ratified a thirty-year peace. The Acharnians, whose vineyards had been ravaged by the enemy, having got wind of this traitorous act, arrived in pursuit of Amphitheus just as Dicaeopolis was leaving his house to offer up a ritual prayer to Bacchus in thanks for the peace that allowed him to resume once more a normal existence with his wife. Upon hearing his prayer, the Acharnians began to stone him as he tried in vain to persuade them that peace was good. Threatened with further violence, Dicaeopolis seized a covered basket of coals and announced that it was an Acharnian child, a hostage, which he would disembowel if he were not permitted to plead his cause. When the Acharnians agreed, he asked further to be allowed to dress properly for the occasion.

Dicaeopolis then went to the house of Euripides to borrow the costume of Telephus, the most unfortunate and pathetic of all the heroes of Euripides' tragedies. The great playwright, in the midst of composing a new tragedy, was hardly in the mood to be disturbed, but Dicaeopolis

22

could not resist the opportunity to tease him about his wretched heroes and about the fact that his mother had sold vegetables. Finally the irate Euripides gave him the miserable costume and turned him out.

The eloquent plea for peace that Dicaeopolis delivered to the Acharnians was so moving that the chorus was divided on the issue. At that moment Lamachus, a general dressed in full armor, arrived on the scene. He declared that nothing could dissuade him from eternal war on the Spartans and their allies. Dicaeopolis countered with a proclamation that his markets were henceforth open to all the enemies of Athens, but not to Lamachus.

Shortly thereafter a starving Megarian appeared in Dicaeopolis' marketplace with his two daughters, who had agreed with their father that it would be better to be sold than to die of hunger. After disguising them as pigs by fitting them with hooves and snouts, the Megarian stuffed them into a sack and offered them to Dicaeopolis as the finest sows he could possibly offer to Aphrodite. Dicaeopolis, aware of the deception, nevertheless accepted them in exchange for a supply of garlic and salt. The next trader was a fat, thriving Boeotian with a tremendous supply of game birds, animals, and fish. All he asked in exchange was some item of Athenian produce not available in Boeotia. Careful bargaining revealed, however, that the only such item was an informer—a vessel useful for holding all foul things, a mortar for grinding out lawsuits, a light for looking into other people's accounts. At last the bargain was made, and the next meddling informer to enter the marketplace and threaten Dicaeopolis with exposure to the authorities was seized, bound, and carefully packed in hay for the Boeotian to carry home.

Suddenly General Lamachus was ordered to take his battalions to guard the borders against invasion during the forthcoming Feast of the Cups. At the same time the priest of Bacchus ordered Dicaeopolis to prepare for joyous participation in the feast. The chorus wished them both joy as Lamachus donned his heavy armor and Dicaeopolis dressed in festival clothes, as Lamachus unhooked his spear and Dicaeopolis unhooked a sausage. After the feast Lamachus was carried in, hurt in a fall in a ditch before encountering the enemy; and Dicaeopolis entered, hilariously drunk and supported by two voluptuous courtesans. The blessings of peace were emphasized by the fact that, in the end, Lamachus the militarist was carried off to the surgeon while Dicaeopolis was conducted before the judges to be awarded the wineskin of victory.

Critical Evaluation:

Thematically, *The Acharnians* is the most inclusive of Aristophanes' plays; in it audiences find his powerful wit and satire against militarism and war, his contempt for petty politicians and informers, his delight in earthy sex play, and his spirited spoofing of Euripides—qualities which make it the most personal of Aristophanes' works. When Dicaeopolis speaks directly to the audience, he does so with the voice of Aristophanes, eloquently asserting his intellectual honesty and independence and declaring that he will always fight for the cause of peace and justice. Aristophanes directed the play and acted in it, taking the part of the protagonist.

Presented in 425 B.C.E., *The Acharnians* is the earliest surviving play of Aristophanes, who began his career as a dramatist in 427. The play is set in the sixth year of the Peloponnesian War (431-404 B.C.E.), which was fought by Athens and Sparta. The conflict had already inflicted grave hardship on Athens. Some Athenians apparently wished to pursue the war more aggressively to exact revenge on Sparta. The protagonist of *The Acharnians*, Dicaeopolis, takes a different approach and concludes a private peace treaty with the Spartans. Much of the play depicts the opposition to Dicaeopolis' treaty and the way in which the hero thwarts his opponents and sets about enjoying the rewards of his private peace.

Most plays of Aristophanes are built around some great idea, which is a plan undertaken by the main character to remedy some unsatisfactory political or private situation. This fantastic project is the main character's way of setting things right, and he or she usually encounters strong opposition to the proposal. Overcoming this opposition, the protagonist eventually implements the plan, and the good (or bad) consequences follow. The role of the great idea in *The Acharnians* is somewhat different: Dicaeopolis achieves his object—a private peace treaty with Sparta—very early in the play. For the remainder of the play he rebuffs his opponents and enthusiastically enjoys the benefits of his treaty. The result is an apparently lopsided dramatic structure. Aristophanes bypasses the usual dramatic struggle regarding implementing the plan and indulges instead in broad satire of leading Athenians of his day, such as Cleon, Lamachus, and the poet Euripides. Another consequence of this design is a lingering impression of the protagonist's selfishness. Dicaeopolis' peace treaty is for himself and his family alone. The implicit message is that peace is good for everyone. Through the greater part of the play Dicaeopolis extravagantly enjoys the benefits of his treaty and refuses (with one exception) to share his wineskin of peace with anyone else.

The private nature of Dicaeopolis' peace should also constitute a warning against reading *The Acharnians* simply as a political tract. The central concern of Dicaeopolis is to achieve peace and to end the personal hardships caused by the protracted struggle with Sparta. Although *The Acharnians* may therefore seem to advocate a political program, the dramatist's message is clearly different from that of a political pamphlet. On the one hand, like many Athenians, Aristophanes probably believed that conflict among Greeks was foolish and wasteful. The gist of the argument that Dicaeopolis presents to the chorus is that the causes of the war are trivial. This viewpoint should not be confused with pacifism, or opposition to all war, since in the opening scenes of the play there are suggestions of greater military threat from outside Greece, that is, Persia. There is no evidence that an organized peace movement at Athens existed at the time of the play's first production, and the play generally depicts the war more as a nuisance than as something unjust.

Aristophanes has a reputation for conservatism in politics and social mores. He was, however, no enemy of democracy, only of its abuse in the hands of leaders such as Cleon. After all, it was the famous free speech and democracy of the Athenians that allowed the poet to speak in support of peace with Sparta in the midst of war. As for Aristophanes' championing old-fashioned virtues, it is to be noted that the Acharnians, who violently oppose Dicaeopolis, represent the older generation and its values. They are staunch advocates of war with Sparta. It is possible that as an artist Aristophanes was primarily interested in depicting the great polarities of Athenian life such as the old and the new, city and country, and peace and war. The political content of his plays should be understood more as a dramatic opposition of competing ideas than as advocacy of a specific political program.

Parody is one element that gives *The Acharnians* its special appeal, and the objects of parody range from the political and social to the literary and artistic. Using the power of slapstick parody, Aristophanes creates a broad satire of Athenian politics, society, and art. Although the figure of Cleon lurks in the background, it is the soldier Lamachus who is specifically held up for ridicule. He is depicted as the typical braggart soldier and militarist, although the historical Lamachus appears to have been a brave and admirable soldier, who actually helped to negotiate the Peace of Nicias in 421 B.C.E. Yet it is the tragic poet Euripides who is Aristophanes' favorite object of satire. Aristophanes apparently resented the political message of some of Euripides' plays that contain anti-Spartan sentiments, but he also has a literary argument with the dramatist who experimented with technical innovations and depicted new kinds of characters (beggars like Telephus) on the tragic stage. Still, Aristophanes' criticism of Euripides, in this play and elsewhere, shows intimate familiarity with his tragedies. One cannot escape the impression of grudging admiration for the tragic poet's work.

Aristophanes' play won first prize in the dramatic competition of 425 B.C.E., taking precedence over works by the veteran poets Cratinus and Eupolis. Although we never know on what explicit basis the judges of the festival made their verdicts, it is probable that the fantasy of Dicaeopolis, with his private peace, was a great success with its Athenian audience.

"Critical Evaluation" by John M. Lawless

Bibliography:
Aristophanes. *Acharnians*. Edited and translated by Alan H. Sommerstein. 2d ed. Warminster, Wiltshire, England: Aris & Phillips, 1984. Provides scholarly introduction, bibliography, Greek text, facing English translation, and commentary keyed to the translation. Sommerstein's translation supersedes most earlier versions.

Dover, K. J. *Aristophanic Comedy*. Berkeley: University of California Press, 1972. Useful and authoritative study of the plays of Aristophanes. Chapter 6 provides a synopsis of the play, a scholarly discussion of problems of its theatrical production, and an examination of the themes of peace and war. An essential starting point for study of the play.

Harriott, Rosemary M. *Aristophanes: Poet and Dramatist*. Baltimore: The Johns Hopkins University Press, 1986. A recent study of Aristophanes. The plays are discussed not in individual chapters but as each illustrates the central themes and techniques of Aristophanes' work.

Spartz, Lois. *Aristophanes*. Boston: Twayne, 1978. A reliable introduction to the comedy of Aristophanes for the general reader. Chapter 2 summarizes the problems of the play and discusses the central themes of peace and prosperity.

Whitman, Cedric. *Aristophanes and the Comic Hero*. Cambridge, Mass.: Harvard University Press, 1964. A standard work on the characterization of the Aristophanic protagonist. Chapter 3, "City and Individual," offers a valuable study of Dicaeopolis and of the motifs and imagery in this play.

96-27 4

ADAM BEDE

Type of work: Novel
Author: George Eliot (Mary Ann Evans, 1819-1880)
Type of plot: Domestic realism
Time of plot: 1799
Locale: England
First published: 1859

Principal characters:
ADAM BEDE, a carpenter
SETH, his brother
MARTIN POYSER, the proprietor of Hall Farm
MRS. POYSER, his wife
DINAH MORRIS, her niece and a Methodist preacher
HETTY SORREL, another niece
CAPTAIN ARTHUR DONNITHORNE, the young squire
PARSON IRWINE, the genial vicar of Hayslope

The Story:

In the village of Hayslope at the close of the eighteenth century, there lived a young carpenter named Adam Bede. Tall and muscular, Adam was respected by everyone as a good workman and an honest and upright man. Even the young squire, Captain Arthur Donnithorne, knew Adam and liked him, and Adam in turn regarded the squire as his best friend.

Adam was, in fact, so good a workman that his employer, Mr. Jonathan Burge, the builder, would have welcomed him as his son-in-law and partner. Adam, however, had no eyes for Mary Burge; his only thoughts were of distractingly pretty Hetty Sorrel, niece of Mrs. Poyser, whose husband, Martin, ran Hall Farm. Hetty, however, cared nothing for Adam. She was interested only in Captain Donnithorne, whom she had met one day in her aunt's dairy.

No one in Hayslope thought Hetty would make a good wife for Adam, least of all Adam's mother, Lisbeth, who would have disapproved of any girl who threatened to take her favorite son away from her. Her feelings of dependence upon Adam were intensified after her husband, Matthias Bede, drowned in Willow Brook while on his way home from the village inn.

Adam's brother Seth had fallen in love with the young Methodist preacher, Dinah Morris. Dinah was another niece of Mrs. Poyser, as unlike her cousin Hetty as Adam was unlike Seth. Hetty was as soft and helpless as a kitten, but Dinah was firm and serious in all things. One evening, while she and Seth were walking home together from the village green, he had proposed marriage. Dinah sadly declined, saying she had dedicated her life to preaching the gospel.

When funeral services for Matthias Bede were held in Hayslope Church on the following Sunday, the thoughts of the congregation were on many events other than the solemn occasion they were attending. Adam's thoughts of Hetty blended with memories of his father. Hetty's thoughts were all of Captain Donnithorne, who had promised to make his appearance. She was disappointed, however, for Donnithorne had already departed with his regiment.

When Donnithorne returned on leave, the young squire celebrated his twenty-first birthday with a great feast to which nearly all of Hayslope was invited. Adam was singled out as a special guest to sit at Donnithorne's table, which made Adam's mother both proud and jealous, since her son seemed to be getting more and more out of her reach.

One August night three weeks after the Donnithorne party, Adam was returning home from his work on the Donnithorne estate when he saw Donnithorne and Hetty Sorrel in close embrace. When Adam's dog barked, Hetty hurried away. Donnithorne, embarrassed, tried to explain that he had met the girl by chance and had stolen a kiss. Adam called his friend a scoundrel and a coward. They came to blows, and Donnithorne was knocked senseless. Adam, frightened that he might have killed the young squire, revived him and helped him to a nearby summerhouse. There he demanded that Donnithorne write a letter to Hetty telling her that he would not see her again.

The next day, Donnithorne sent the letter to Hetty in Adam's care, thus placing the responsibility for its possible effect on Adam himself. Adam gave Hetty the letter while they were walking the following Sunday. When she read the letter in the privacy of her bedchamber, Hetty was in despair. Her dreams shattered, she thought only of finding some way out of her misery.

In November, Adam was offered a partnership in Mr. Burge's business, and he proposed to Hetty. Mr. and Mrs. Poyser were delighted to find that their niece was to marry the man they so much admired. The wedding had to be delayed, however, until two new rooms could be added to the Bede house. In February, Hetty told her aunt that she was going to visit Dinah Morris at Snowfield. Actually, she was determined to find Donnithorne. When she arrived at Windsor, where he was supposed to be stationed, she found that his regiment had been transferred to Ireland. In complete despair, Hetty roamed about, ending up in a strange village in the house of a widow named Sarah Stone, where her child by Donnithorne was born. Confused and frightened, Hetty wandered on, leaving her baby to die in the woods. Later, tortured by her conscience, she returned to find the child gone.

When his grandfather died, Donnithorne returned to Hayslope to discover that Hetty was in prison, charged with the murder of her child. He did everything in his power to free her, and Dinah Morris came to her prison cell and prayed with her to open up her heart and tell the truth. Finally, poor Hetty broke down and confessed everything that had happened since she left Hayslope. She had not intended to kill her baby; in fact, she had not actually killed the child. She had considered taking her own life. Two days later, Donnithorne, filled with shame and remorse, brought a reprieve. Hetty's sentence was commuted to deportation. A few years later, she died on her way home. Donnithorne went to Spain.

Dinah Morris stayed with the Poysers often now. Gradually she and Adam were drawn to each other, but Dinah's heart was still set on her preaching. She left Hall Farm and went back to Snowfield. Adam Bede found his only satisfaction in toiling at his workbench. Then one day, when his mother again mentioned Dinah and her gentle ways, Adam went to find her.

Critical Evaluation:

This novel of English pastoral life probably shows George Eliot's quality as a novelist better than any other of her works, with the possible exception of *Middlemarch* (1871-1872). When Eliot was writing about peasants, artisans, yeomen, clergy, and the squires of Warwickshire, she was writing out of memories of her own childhood; her characters come to life as people she had known. She modeled the Methodist preacher Dinah Morris after her own aunt, Mrs. Samuel Evans, who was an enthusiastic supporter and preacher in the movement begun by John Wesley; Wesley's Methodism had led to the Evangelical movement to which Eliot belonged in her childhood. Her depiction of the stalwart carpenter Adam Bede included many of the characteristics of her own father. These real-life parallels were recognized by contemporary critics, who felt that the novelist had successfully practiced the tenets of realism expounded by her narrator in chapter 17.

Although Eliot was pleased that the novel was so well received, she was concerned that many readers did not seem to take to heart the moral truths she had embodied in the novel. She wanted the sympathies of her readers to enlarge as they responded to the suffering of the characters and wanted them to learn the significance of the individual in the interconnected web of society. Throughout the novel, the major characters grow in sympathetic understanding as they suffer the consequences of their deeds and those of their fellows.

Adam Bede, who is faithful to duty and responsibility, comes to realize that he has been very hard and unfeeling in his judgments of his father and his beloved Hetty as well as of Arthur, the young squire who leads Hetty astray. In the first of two significant meetings with Arthur in woods that are reminiscent of the Garden of Eden, Adam bitterly accuses Arthur and knocks him down. In the second encounter, Adam has learned to recognize his own egotism, and the two men bond as he accepts the management of Arthur's estate.

In the days in "the upper room" before Hetty's trial, he learns to identify with the sufferings of others from his communion with Parson Irwine and Bartle Massey. He supports and stands by Hetty as she is sentenced, and he consequently becomes a more caring son and brother, as well as a fit husband and father. He thus emerges as a Venerable Bede who embodies the moral earnestness of the Hebraic tradition. Once Adam has tempered his harsh judgments, he becomes sensitive to his mother's admonitions and to the promptings from within himself to realize that he is in love with Dinah Morris.

In contrast to Adam, Arthur Donnithorne has the white hands of an Olympian god and represents the Hellenistic tradition. His passion and sense of his own infallibility cause him to use Hetty, which eventually leads to her death. From the guilt that pricks his self-image and tempers his egotism, he learns that he cannot control his own destiny or the destinies of others. His coming of age morally does not occur at the celebration of his twenty-first birthday but only after he has witnessed the suffering his selfishness has caused. He acknowledges his recognition of having sinned by sending his gold watch to Dinah Morris and exiling himself to a life of military service.

As the novel opens, Hetty is a pretty round-faced child in whose large dark eyes there is a roguishness that intrigues both Arthur and Adam. She is the orphaned niece of Mr. Poyser and works in the Poysers' dairy yet entertains aspirations to become a ladies' maid. Both her innocence and her delusions about rising in status make her vulnerable to Arthur's gifts and attentions. When she discovers that she is pregnant, she leaves home to look for Arthur; miserable and alone, she gives birth to his baby, which she leaves in the woods beside a Wordsworthian thorn bush. She confesses her sin and repents, but even Arthur's reprieve cannot keep her from being banished, and she is dead by the end of the novel.

The opening scene of the novel also portrays the serious and otherworldly Dinah Morris preaching on the village green. In a chapter that describes Hetty and Dinah in their adjacent bedrooms at the Hall farm, Hetty gazes admiringly at her own reflection in her mirror while the ethereal Dinah gazes out the window and consults her Bible to guide her in giving comfort and assistance to Hetty. In giving support to Hetty throughout her trial, Dinah is softened and humanized, and her growth in sympathetic understanding leads her to give up her public role as a Methodist preacher and become a wife and mother.

The major events of the novel take place in 1799, the year after the publication of William Wordsworth's *Lyrical Ballads*, which Arthur recommends to Parson Irwine. Critics have noted the many Wordsworthian echoes throughout the novel that accompany Eliot's ordinary people as they learn that their deeds carry wider and more significant consequences than they had imagined. When the novel opens, Parson Irwine is reading Aeschylus and practicing the simple practical lessons of everyday kindness that he preaches, but even he grows in sympathetic understanding along with the other members of the community whose lives are touched and changed by Hetty's suffering and death.

"Critical Evaluation" by Constance M. Fulmer

Bibliography:
Fulmer, Constance M. "Contrasting Pairs of Heroines in George Eliot's Fiction." *Studies in the Novel* 6, no. 3 (Fall, 1974): 288-294. Examines Hetty and Dinah as one of a series of heroine pairs that Eliot uses to define moral maturity and levels of egotism and to preach the broadening, positive effects of sympathetic understanding.

Higdon, David Leon. "*Sortes Biblicae* in *Adam Bede.*" *Papers in Language and Literature* 9, no. 4 (Fall, 1973): 396-405. Higdon suggests that Dinah's practice of "opening the Bible" for guidance individualizes her character and develops historical and thematic structure in the narrative.

Homans, Margaret. "Dinah's Blush, Maggie's Arm: Class, Gender, and Sexuality in George Eliot's Early Novels." *Victorian Studies* 36, no. 2 (Winter, 1993): 155-179. Argues that the euphemistic manner in which Eliot treats her heroines communicates their universal womanhood without regard to class.

Lefkovitz, Lori Hope. "Delicate Beauty Goes Out: *Adam Bede*'s Transgressive Heroines." *Kenyon Review* 9, no. 3 (Summer, 1987): 84-96. Suggests that Eliot uses both delicate health and healthy delicacy in creating her heroines.

Miller, J. Hillis. *The Ethics of Reading: Kant, de Man, Eliot, Trollope, James, and Benjamin.* New York: Columbia University Press, 1987. Reprinted in *George Eliot*, edited by K. M. Newton. New York: Longman, 1991. In his discussion of Eliot's "economic-ethical-religious-affective-performative theory of realism," Miller points out the use of figurative language to depict human experience in art, nature, love, and religion.

THE ADMIRABLE CRICHTON

Type of work: Drama
Author: Sir James M. Barrie (1860-1937)
Type of plot: Satire
Time of plot: Early twentieth century
Locale: Loam House, Mayfair, England; a desert island
First performed: 1902; first published, 1914

Principal characters:
THE EARL OF LOAM
LADY MARY,
LADY CATHERINE, and
LADY AGATHA, his daughters
THE HON. ERNEST WOOLLEY, his nephew
WILLIAM CRICHTON, his butler

The Story:

Once every month, the philanthropic Earl of Loam gave expression to his views on human equality by forcing his servants to have tea with him and his family in the great hall of Loam House in Mayfair. It was a disagreeable experience for everyone concerned, especially for his butler, Crichton, who did not share his master's liberal views. Lord Loam alone enjoyed the occasion, for he was the only one who remained in his station. He ordered his daughters and his nephew about and treated them exactly as he treated his servants on the other days of the month.

Lady Mary, his oldest daughter, was a spirited young woman who resented her father's high-handed methods with his family. Her indignation reached a climax one day when Lord Loam announced that his three daughters were to have but one maid among them on a yachting trip on which the family was about to embark. Lady Mary was furious, but she assumed that her maid, Fisher, would go along. When Fisher learned that she was expected to look after the two younger sisters in addition to Lady Mary, she promptly resigned, and the two maids attending Catherine and Agatha followed suit. Lord Loam was left without any servants for his projected cruise, for his valet also resigned. Although it hurt his pride deeply, Crichton finally agreed, out of loyalty to his master, to act as his valet on the trip. Moreover, he persuaded Tweeny, the housemaid upon whom he had cast a favorable eye, to go along as maid to Lord Loam's daughters.

The cruise ended unhappily when the yacht was pounded to pieces during a violent storm in the Pacific, and the party was cast away on a tropical island. All reached shore except Lord Loam. The other survivors had watched him throw away his best chance at safety in a frantic but vain attempt to get into the lifeboat first.

On the island all tried to preserve as much as possible the class distinction that had prevailed in England, but the attempt was unsuccessful. Crichton alone knew exactly what he was doing, and it was upon him that the others had to depend. So Crichton, the servant, became on the island the natural leader, and he ruled his former superiors with a gentle but a firm hand. For example, he found the epigrams of the Hon. Ernest Woolley, which had seemed so brilliant in England, a bit trying; as a consequence, Crichton adopted the policy of submitting Ernest to a severe ducking whenever he came forth with an epigram. The aristocrats worried over the rising authority of their former butler and the decline in their own prestige. When Lord Loam appeared, after washing ashore with some wreckage, they urged him to take a stand of authority. Lord Loam's only recourse was to remove his little party to another section of the island apart from Crichton. Hunger, which the aristocrats by their own efforts could not assuage, brought them meekly back. Crichton became the acknowledged leader of them all.

Crichton took full advantage of his newly acquired authority. Having none of the earl's ideas about equality, he found no necessity for pretending that on the island his former betters were his equals in any sense. Each was kept in his place and required to do his own work according to the needs of the camp.

Under Crichton's rule the aristocrats were happy for perhaps the first time in their lives. The hard physical labor made something approaching a man out of Ernest, and the task of helping to prepare Crichton's food and waiting on him at the table turned Lord Loam's snobbish daughters into attractive and useful women. Lord Loam, dressed in animal skins, was merely a harmless and rather genial old man with no particular talents, whom everyone called Daddy. The greatest change occurred in Lady Mary. She alone realized that in any environment Crichton was superior to them all, and that only the conventions of so-called civilized society had obscured that fact. Consequently she fell in love with the butler and did everything in her power to make herself his favorite. Crichton, attracted to the beautiful Lady Mary, considered making her his consort on the island. He indulged in the fancy that in some past existence he had been a king and she a Christian slave. When a rescuing ship appeared on the horizon, Crichton realized that his dreams were romantic nonsense. On their return to England he again would be a butler, and she would be Lady Mary.

It was as Crichton had expected. After the rescue Lord Loam and his family returned to their old habits of thought and behavior. Crichton was again the butler. The Hon. Ernest wrote a book about their experiences on the island and made himself the hero of their exploits. Crichton was barely mentioned. Lady Mary reluctantly renewed her engagement to the rather asinine Lord Brocklehurst, whose mother was greatly worried over what had happened on the island and not sure that a daughter of Lord Loam was a fit wife for her son.

Lady Mary still recognized Crichton's superiority, and told him so frankly. Crichton was shocked. Her views might have been acceptable on the island, he said, but not in England. When she expressed the radical view that something might be wrong with England, Crichton told her that not even from her would he listen to a word of criticism against England or English ways.

Critical Evaluation:
One of the best of Barrie's comedies, *The Admirable Crichton* contains a more definite theme than Barrie generally put into his plays. His satirical portrait of an English aristocrat with liberal ideas is the most skillful that has been done. Lord Loam, like many liberals, is a kind of social Jekyll and Hyde, accepting the doctrine of the rights of humanity in theory, but holding tightly to his privileges in practice.

The immediate inspiration for *The Admirable Crichton*, as for its successor *Peter Pan* (1904), was Barrie's relationship with the four sons of Arthur Llewellyn Davies, whom Barrie "adopted" as almost his own. *Peter Pan* was based in the stories Barrie made up for the boys, and *The Admirable Crichton* was based in the make-believe games he played with them, in which fantasies of being cast away on a deserted island played a major part. The games were fueled by his memories of Daniel Defoe's *Robinson Crusoe* (1719) and of such boys' books derived from Defoe's work as J. R. Wyss's *The Swiss Family Robinson* (1812-1813) and R. M. Ballantyne's *The Coral Island* (1858). In all these tales the resourcefulness of the heroes invariably allows them to establish a very comfortable lifestyle, thereby demonstrating the superior nature of British civilization. The skeptical Barrie probably used the make-believe games to teach the four boys that lighting fires and building huts is not quite as easy as such stories make out—a lesson that Lord Loam learns the hard way.

The title of the play is as ironic as its contents. The reputation—what kind of reputation is a matter of interpretation—of the original Admirable Crichton, a sixteenth century Scots adventurer who died in a brawl at the age of twenty-two, is immortalized in Sir Thomas Urquhart's *Ekskubalauron* (1652), for example. The play's contrasting of the English aristocracy and its servant class is rooted in Barrie's awareness of the difference in outlook between the wealthy but airy-fairy English and the poor but hard-headed Scots. As a Scotsman from a poor background, Barrie was acutely aware of the delusions of the well-off Londoners among whom he had come to live, and the temptation to subject their affectations to the hypothetical test of castaway life must have been irresistible. The silliness that moves the plot along is not as casually satirical as it seems; there is a depth of bitter feeling in it that becomes increasingly apparent as the play progresses.

The blue-blooded Lord Loam poses as a believer in the equality of men, although he only sets aside one day a month for the elevation of his servants' status. Crichton, on the other hand, makes an obsession out of knowing his place and insisting that one's rank reflects one's worth. How ironic this insistence is depends on how the part is played—Barrie's notes to the cast are relentlessly sarcastic—but Crichton's keen awareness that worth depends on context indicates that he harbors carefully concealed resentments.

While it is society that determines his worth, Crichton is a dutiful servant, but when the castaways are cut off from society, his true self emerges. When Lady Mary asks him who made up the rule that those who do not work do not eat, he explains that he "seems to see it growing all over the island." Unlike the rules governing London society, it is no arbitrary invention: It is the way things are. This ability to see things as they are, and to apply his common sense to them—which fits Crichton for the leader's role on the island—is exactly the same ability that fit him to be a butler in Mayfair. On the island this ability receives the approval of nature. His common sense sends him straight back to his former station when the party returns to Mayfair, but he is determined that it will be a temporary measure. Having lived for a while as his true self, he can no longer be content with a lie.

A last inversion in the plot is Lady Brocklehurst's interrogation of Crichton, who contrives to answer all her questions truthfully while giving a completely false picture of what had actually transpired on the island. The result of this deception is that Lady Mary's promise to marry Crichton does not compromise her engagement to the young Lord Brocklehurst. Afterward, Lady Mary asks Crichton whether he despises her for allowing it to remain uncompromised. This question makes a very subtle point. Instead of having Crichton reply to Lady Mary's question, Barrie inserts a gratuitous (and inaccurate) note that "the man who could never tell a lie makes no answer." Shortly thereafter, Lady Mary asks Crichton to tell her that he has not lost his courage; the man who could and did tell several lies calls down the curtain with an assertion that he has not. The author carefully leaves it to the audience to make up its mind what he means by that remark. He clearly cannot mean that he intends to resume his interrupted courtship of Lady Mary—he has just exerted himself to ensure that she can marry Lord Brocklehurst—but he must mean that he considers that his obligations to the family are now finally and fully discharged.

Crichton, as an honorable and admirable man, could not have refused to fire the beacons that enabled his companions to be restored to their place in society, but now that he has seen Lady

Mary's marriage prospects safely restored, everything is back in its "proper" place except for him. Whatever his proper place may be, he must leave in order to find it. The audience is likely to wish Crichton good luck—but one does have to bear in mind the fate of the man after whom Crichton is named.

"Critical Evaluation" by Brian Stableford

Bibliography:
Birkin, Andrew. *J. M. Barrie and the Lost Boys.* London: Constable, 1979. Discusses the way in which Barrie, playing castaways with the Llewellyn Davies boys, was inspired to write *The Admirable Crichton.*
Blake, George. *Barrie and the Kailyard School.* London: Barker, 1951. Places Barrie's work in its social and literary context.
Darlington, W. A. *J. M. Barrie.* London: Blackie, 1938. An appreciation of Barrie's work by a noted drama critic.
Roy, James A. *James Matthew Barrie: An Appreciation.* London: Jarrolds, 1937. A useful commentary on Barrie's works.
Walbrook, H. M. *J. M. Barrie and the Theatre.* London: F. V. White, 1922. The first detailed survey of Barrie's dramatic work.

ADOLPHE

Type of work: Novel
Author: Benjamin Constant (1767-1830)
Type of plot: Psychological realism
Time of plot: Late eighteenth and early nineteenth centuries
Locale: Germany and Poland
First published: 1816 (English translation, 1816)

> *Principal characters:*
> ADOLPHE, the narrator
> ELLÉNORE, his mistress

The Story:

Having creditably completed his studies in Göttingen in spite of a somewhat dissipated life, Adolphe was expected, after a preliminary period of travel, to take his place in the governmental department of which his father, the minister of a German electorate, was the head. His father had great hopes for his son and was inclined to be lenient about his indiscretions, but because of an inherent timidity shared by father and son—a timidity combined, on the part of the father, with a defensive outward coldness—no real sympathy was possible between the two. The constraint generated by this relationship had a considerable effect on Adolphe's character, as did a period he spent as the protégé of a much older woman whose strong and unconventional opinions made an indelible impression on him. This period, spent in long, passionately analytical conversations, had ended with the woman's death.

Upon leaving the university, Adolphe went to the court of a small German principality of D——. At first, he was welcomed, but he gradually attracted resentment for his mannered frivolity, alternating with scathing frankness, which stemmed from his profound indifference to the society of the court. The woman who had formed his mind had bequeathed to him an ardent dislike of mediocrity and all of its expressions, and he found it difficult to reconcile himself with the artificiality of society and the necessity for arbitrary convention. Moreover, his only interest at that time was to indulge in passionate feelings that led to contempt for the ordinary world.

One thing that did impress him was to see the joy of a friend at winning the love of one of the less mediocre women of the court. His friend's reaction not only developed in Adolphe the regrets connected with piqued vanity but also other, more confused, emotions related to newly discovered aspects of his desire to be loved. He could discover in himself no marked tastes, but soon after making the acquaintance of Count P——, Adolphe determined to attempt to establish a liaison with the woman who had shared the count's life for ten years and whose two illegitimate children the count had acknowledged. Ellénore was a spirited woman from a good Polish family that had been ruined by political troubles. Her history was one of untiring devotion to the count and constant conflict between her respectable sentiments and her position in society—a position that had gradually become sanctioned, however, through the influence of her lover.

Adolphe did not consider himself to be in love but to be fulfilling an obligation to his self-esteem; yet, he found his thoughts increasingly occupied with Ellénore as well as his project; unable to make a verbal declaration, he finally wrote to her. His inner agitation and the conviction he sought to express rebounded, however, and his imagination became wholly entangled when Ellénore refused to receive him. That convinced him of his love, and he finally succeeded in overcoming her resistance to his suit. When the count was called away on urgent business, Adolphe and Ellénore basked for a few weeks in the charm of love and mutual gratification. Almost immediately, however, Adolphe began to be annoyed at the new constraint imposed on his life by this attachment, rewarding though he found it. The idea that it could not last calmed his fears, and he wrote to his father upon Ellénore's urging, asking permission to postpone his return for six months. When his father consented, Adolphe was immediately confronted again by all the drawbacks involved in his remaining at D——. He was irritated at the prospect of prolonging the deceptions required by his affair; of continuing the profitless life he led under Ellénore's exciting domination; and, above all, of making her suffer by compromising her position, for upon his return, the count had become suspicious.

Adolphe's resentment led to a quarrel with Ellénore in which were made the first irreparable statements that, once spoken, could not be recalled. The quarrel and the forced intimacy that followed it only increased Ellénore's anxiety and ardor, and she decided to break with Count P—— when he ordered her not to see Adolphe. Adolphe could not summon the courage to reject her sacrifice, although it caused him great anguish and destroyed in a moment the social respect that Ellénore had acquired after years of effort. His sense of duty increased as his love weakened; he was willing to fight a duel at the slightest disparaging remark about her, yet he himself wronged her in inconsequential social conversation. When the time came for him to leave, he promised to return, fearing her violent grief. Moreover, he discovered that the arrival of the break he had longed for filled him with keen regret, almost with terror. He wrote regular letters to her, each begun with the intention of indicating his coldness but always ended with words calculated to restore her confidence in his passion. At the same time, he relished his regained independence.

When Ellénore understood from Adolphe's letters that it would be difficult for him to leave his father, she decided to join him. He wrote to advise her to postpone her coming, with the consequence that she became indignant and hastened her arrival. Adolphe had resolved to meet her with a show of joy that concealed his real feelings, but she sensed the deception immediately and reproached him, putting his weakness in such a miserable light that he became enraged. In a violent scene, the two turned on each other.

When Adolphe returned to his father's house, he learned that his father had been informed of Ellénore's arrival and had taken steps to force her to leave the town. His father's concern with Adolphe's future was undoubtedly genuine, but it unfortunately took the form of adherence to the standard values of a corrupt society and could only have the effect of strengthening the bond between the lovers. Adolphe made hurried arrangements and carried Ellénore off precipitately, smothering her with passion. Always astute, she detected contradictions in his actions and told him that he was moved by pity rather than love—thereby revealing something he would have preferred not to know and giving him a new preoccupation to conceal.

When the two reached the frontier, Adolphe wrote to his father with some bitterness, holding him responsible for the course he had been forced to take. His father's reply was notable for its generosity; he repeated everything Adolphe had said and ended by saying that although Adolphe was wasting his life, he would be allowed complete freedom. In the absence of the necessity to defend Ellénore, Adolphe's impatience with the tie became even more pronounced. They settled for a time in Bohemia where Adolphe, having accepted the responsibility for Ellénore's fate, made every effort to restrain himself from causing her suffering. He assumed an artificial gaiety and with the passing of time once again came intermittently to feel some of his feigned sentiment. When alone, however, his old unrest gripped him, and he made vague plans to flee from his attachment.

At this point, Adolphe learned of a fresh sacrifice that Ellénore had made, the refusal of an offer from Count P—— to settle her again in suitable circumstances. Adolphe, grasping at this opportunity, told her that he no longer loved her; at the sight of her violent grief, however, he pretended that his attitude had been a ruse. Another possibility of escape occurred after Ellénore's father was reinstated in his property in Poland: She was notified that he had died and that she had been made the sole heir. Because the will was being contested, Ellénore persuaded Adolphe to accompany her to Poland. Their relationship continued to deteriorate.

Adolphe's father wrote, pointing out that since Adolphe could no longer be considered Ellénore's protector there was no longer any excuse for the life he was leading. The father had recommended Adolphe to his friend, Baron T—— (the minister from their country to Poland), and suggested that Adolphe call on him. When the young man did so, Baron T—— assumed the father's role and attempted to separate the lovers. Adolphe spent a night wandering in the country, engaged in confused meditations in which he told himself that his mind was recovering from a long degradation.

Ellénore made another futile effort to penetrate the closed sanctuary of his mind, but a new alignment of forces emerged as Adolphe succumbed more and more to the influence of Baron T——. He continued to procrastinate about ending the relationship. When the baron forwarded some of Adolphe's incriminating letters to Ellénore, she became fatally ill. Adolphe was finally freed by her death, which produced in him a feeling of great desolation.

Critical Evaluation:

Although Benjamin Constant was recognized by his contemporaries as what we would call a polymath—he was a religious and literary scholar, an astute politician and political writer, a cosmopolitan socialite, and a novelist—it is the last activity that accounts for his modern reputation. *Adolphe*, the only important literary work Constant published during his lifetime, is a short, intense novel carefully constructed on pairs of opposites. The circumstances of his early life suggest, for example, that Adolphe's character was formed by forces beyond his control and that he was therefore not responsible for his later behavior; yet he himself acknowledges that in his affair with Ellénore he should not have acted as he did. Ellénore too is prey to contradictory tendencies. She leads an irregular life as mistress first to Count P—— and then to Adolphe, yet she attempts to maintain the high standards of a married, wholly virtuous woman. While Adolphe exhibits the characteristics traditionally thought to be male, Ellénore to a great extent acts out the traditional female role. Finally, each finds that love turns to ashes when acceded to. Constant's subtle orchestration of these contradictory forces accounts for the success of his novel.

Adolphe explains that the coldness and diffidence with which he and his father treated each other during his childhood, and the influence of the strong-willed older woman with whom he had an early affair, turned him into an analytical, overly calculating young man. At the same time, Adolphe assures the reader that he is not "seeking to make excuses." In a sense he is doing just that, but he also makes clear that he very much regrets his actions. The framework that Constant establishes for his novel—allowing an older, wiser Adolphe to comment on the callous actions of his younger self—may in effect let Adolphe have it both ways, but it also endows his character and the novel with greater complexity.

The portrait Constant paints of Ellénore is almost equally complex, although we see her entirely through Adolphe's eyes. As he remarks, "Ellénore was continually fighting against her destiny"—an observation that to a large extent might apply to Adolphe himself. Ellénore is so conscious of her socially ambiguous status that she makes every effort to act modestly and virtuously. Because religion condemns her way of life, she sets great store by religion. This overcompensation results in the emotional instability that eventually kills her.

Adolphe and Ellénore play out the differing, opposing roles that tradition expects of participants in an affair. Adolphe pursues Ellénore relentlessly until she capitulates, after which he soon tires of her. Ellénore, on the other hand, warms to Adolphe only slowly but she ultimately gives herself to him completely. The more she now pursues him in return, the more Adolphe resents her control and regrets his loss of freedom. *Adolphe* remains the classic literary embodiment of this conventional scenario.

Benjamin Constant's life and character bear many resemblances to Adolphe's, and for years critics endeavored to link the novel's characters and events to Constant's own experiences. His relationship with his father was emotionally barren, and he had had a long affair with an older writer, the socialite Madame de Charrière, who died in 1805. Subsequently, he met and married Charlotte von Hardenberg and carried on an affair with Anna Lindsay, both of whom shared traits with his fictional Ellénore.

Works of fiction cannot be considered as accounts that fail or succeed according to their adherence to "real" events but must be considered on their own terms. Scholarship has revealed that Constant carefully shaped *Adolphe* to achieve artistic coherence and that the novel differs in important aspects from the specifics of the author's own life. After finishing a first version in 1807, Constant spent the next nine years polishing the work and reading it to friends before he published it in 1816.

Adolphe emerges as one of the masterworks of French literature. Although it is the story of four years of love and suffering and was written at a time when novels tended to be lengthy and diffuse, it is remarkably brief. Constant distills the essence of the story into ten short chapters and endows the plot with the unity achieved in drama by such French writers as Jean-Baptiste Racine and Pierre Corneille. Like the works of these dramatists, *Adolphe* unfolds with tragic inevitability. The first-person narrative concentrates its action and mood still further. Among later writers, the novel attained the status of a "novelist's novel," a work that repays the close study of fellow writers.

Adolphe's final note is timeless, for the novel's protagonist is the ultimate personification of the frustrations of gratified desire, a victim of that most profound pair of opposing tendencies. As soon as Ellénore is his, Adolphe retreats from her; upon her death he experiences utter desolation. However much today's readers may reject some of the conventions on which *Adolphe* is based, the central dilemma it portrays remains ever contemporary.

"Critical Evaluation" by Grove Koger

Bibliography:
Cruickshank, John. *Benjamin Constant*. New York: Twayne, 1974. One of the best introductions in English to the wide range of Constant's literary, biographical, political, and religious works. Includes a good chronology and selected bibliography.
Fairlie, Alison. *Imagination and Language: Collected Essays on Constant, Baudelaire, Nerval, and Flaubert*. Cambridge, England: Cambridge University Press, 1981. Approximately one-fourth of Fairlie's volume consists of essays on *Adolphe*, which Fairlie calls "that most quietly disruptive of all French novels." Treats the book's style, structure, and characterization, as well as its reception by other French novelists such as Honoré de Balzac. Two of the eight essays are in French.
Nicolson, Harold. *Benjamin Constant*. Westport, Conn.: Greenwood Press, 1985. A sympa-

thetic biography by a noted writer and diplomat. The most readily available biography in English, but one based on secondary sources and not reflecting later scholarship. Places Constant clearly in the context of his tumultuous period.

Turnell, Martin. *The Novel in France*. Freeport, N.Y.: Books for Libraries, 1972. Turnell considers Constant and *Adolphe* in a tradition that extends from the seventeenth century novelist Madame de La Fayette to the twentieth century novelist Marcel Proust, and declares Constant's protagonist to be "the ancestor of the heroes of innumerable modern novels."

Wood, Dennis. *Benjamin Constant: Adolphe*. Cambridge, England: Cambridge University Press, 1987. An essential, sharply focused volume. Includes a useful chronology of Constant's life, chapters on the novel's biographical and intellectual context, and a detailed analysis of the book's first three chapters. Wood concludes by highlighting the novel's impact on future generations of writers.

THE ADVENTURES OF AUGIE MARCH

Type of work: Novel
Author: Saul Bellow (1915-   )
Type of plot: Picaresque
Time of plot: 1920-1950
Locale: Primarily Chicago
First published: 1953

Principal characters:
> AUGIE MARCH, the narrator and protagonist
> SIMON MARCH, Augie's older brother
> CHARLOTTE MAGNUS, Simon's wife
> GEORGIE MARCH, Augie's feeble-minded younger brother
> WILLIAM EINHORN, Augie's friend and employer
> MRS. RENLING, a woman who wants to adopt Augie
> THEA FENCHEL, Augie's sometime mistress
> STELLA CHESNEY, Augie's wife

The Story:

Born and reared in Chicago, Augie March never knew who his father was. Grandma Lausch, who was not related to Augie but boarded with the Marches, dominated the household, teaching Augie manners and how to lie to people in authority. As a child, he got involved in petty crime, stealing from a department store where he worked as one of Santa Claus's helpers and participating in a robbery. At Grandma Lausch's insistence, Georgie, Augie's retarded brother, was institutionalized. Grandma Lausch eventually went to a home for the aged, and Augie's mother went to a home for the blind.

For a while, Augie did odd jobs for a paraplegic named William Einhorn, whom Augie called the "first superior man" he knew. Shortly after graduating from high school, Augie attended college at night and worked in a downtown clothing store where his brother Simon worked. Then he quit his job and school to work for Mr. and Mrs. Renling, selling articles associated with dude ranches to an aristocratic clientele in Evanston, Illinois. Augie learned to ride horses. On Mrs. Renling's summer vacation, Augie accompanied her to Benton Harbor. There, he fell in love with Esther Fenchel, and her sister Thea fell in love with him. Esther rejected Augie, and Augie rejected Thea, but Thea vowed that she would see him again.

Returning to Evanston, Mrs. Renling decided to adopt Augie, so Augie left the Renlings and worked at odd jobs in Chicago. He stole books and almost got caught in an illegal scheme to bring immigrants out of Canada.

Meanwhile, Simon married Charlotte Magnus, daughter of a wealthy family, and entered the coal business in which her family worked, soon getting his own coal yard. Augie worked for him. Simon became wealthy. Augie became engaged to Lucy Magnus, Charlotte's cousin. Helping Mimi Villars, his friend and neighbor, get an abortion, Augie was spotted by one of Lucy's relatives, who told Lucy's family. Lucy's father forced her to break off her relationship with Augie. Simon fired Augie, saying he wanted nothing more to do with him.

Augie worked then as a union organizer and started an affair with Sophie Geratis, a chambermaid in a hotel Augie was trying to organize. While Augie was in bed with Sophie, Thea Fenchel knocked on his door. Augie left Sophie for Thea, whom he came to believe he loved.

Thea wanted Augie to help her train an eagle to hunt giant iguanas in Mexico. Thea provided the money. In Texarkana, they bought the eagle, which they named Caligula. Driving south, they trained Caligula. When they reached Thea's house in Acatla, Mexico, they started training the bird with lizards. He did well with little ones, but when a medium-sized one bit him, the eagle became furious, killing the lizard but refusing to eat it. The first giant iguana Caligula attacked bit him, and Caligula flew from it. During the encounter, Augie's horse threw him and he fractured his skull. While Augie recovered, Thea sold Caligula and started hunting snakes.

In Acatla, Augie met Stella Chesney, who was with a man who was running from the Treasury Department. One day the man threatened Stella with a gun. She got Augie to help her get away from him. Seeing Augie leaving town with Stella, Thea tried unsuccessfully to stop him. The car broke down in the mountains, and Stella and Augie spent the night together. The next day, Augie lent Stella some money, and she went to Mexico City. Augie returned to Thea, who broke up with him.

While Augie was in Acatla, Leon Trotsky, Russian revolutionist and commissar of war who had quarreled with Joseph Stalin, the Soviet dictator, came to see the cathedral. Augie went to Mexico City, where he got involved in a plan to pretend he was Trotsky's nephew, so the Russian could travel incognito in Mexico and thus elude Stalin's secret police, who were trying to assassinate him. Trotsky, however, rejected the plan. Augie then returned to Chicago, where he and Simon became friends again. Augie worked for a millionaire named Robey and went to school to become a teacher. He dreamed of running a school for foster children and having children of his own.

Then the United States entered World War II. When Augie tried to enlist, he discovered that he had an unhealed inguinal hernia from falling off the horse in Mexico, so he had an operation. He still was rejected by the Army and Navy, so he joined the Merchant Marine. He took a training cruise on the Chesapeake Bay. On his first liberty, he visited Stella in New York. When he later graduated from Purser's and Pharmacist's Mate School, he and Stella got married. After a two-day honeymoon, Augie shipped out on the *Sam McManus*, which was torpedoed. Augie spent many days on a lifeboat with one other man from the ship, who wanted to go to the Canary Islands, where he could be interned and do research for the rest of the war. He tried to keep Augie from signaling for help. Augie did signal, and they were picked up by a British ship that took them to Naples.

After six months, Augie returned to New York. During the war he made three more voyages. After the war ended, he and Stella lived in Europe. Stella worked in motion pictures. Augie made large amounts of money doing illicit dealing with a man he met through Stella. He learned some unpleasant things about Stella's past and discovered that she "lied more than average." He would, he wrote, prefer to be in America having children, but Stella refused to leave Europe. Augie traveled around Europe on business and wrote his memoirs.

"The Story" by Richard Tuerk

Critical Evaluation:

Saul Bellow's *The Adventures of Augie March* is a novel that must be read and understood at several levels. Each of these levels is completely meaningful in itself yet unmistakably intertwined with the others.

At the simplest level of reading, the novel is in the picaresque tradition, telling the adventures, often comic, of a rascal born out of wedlock to a charwoman, reared in the poverty of a down-at-heels Chicago neighborhood, and early addicted to taking life as it comes. Augie

March the adult, thus seen, is a ne'er-do-well hanger-on to people of wealth and, at times, a thief, even a would-be smuggler. As a child of poverty, he learns from the adults about him and from his experience that a ready lie told with a glib tongue and an air of innocence is often profitable. Growing older, he learns that many women are of easy virtue and hold the same loose reins on their personal morality as Augie does himself. Love of a kind and easy money seem, at this level, to be Augie's goals in life. Although he may dream of becoming a teacher, take a few courses at the University of Chicago, and read widely in an informal way, Augie stays on the fringes of the postwar black market, where he finds the easy money he needs to live in what he regards as style.

When viewed at the literal level, *The Adventures of Augie March*, like Bellow's earlier fiction, is largely in the naturalistic tradition. In his choice of setting, in his pessimistic choices of detail and character, in his use of a wealth of detail, and in the implicit determinism apparent in the careers of Augie March, his relatives, and his friends, one notes similarities to the fiction of the giants of the naturalistic tradition in literature. One notes also a kinship with the novels of Nelson Algren and James T. Farrell. At times, Augie March seems little more than a Jewish boy from Chicago's Northwest Side who is one part Farrell's Studs Lonigan and one part the same author's Danny O'Neill from Chicago's South Side Irish neighborhood. With Farrell's characters, Augie March shares an immigrant background, little or no sense of meaning in life, degrading poverty, and a grossly hedonistic view of life.

Unlike many naturalistic novelists, however, Saul Bellow seeks meaning in facts; he is not confined to the principle that the novelist is simply an objective, dispassionate reporter of life as he finds it, a recorder of life among the lowly, the immoral, and the poverty-stricken. Nor does he permit his character Augie March to be merely a creature of environment, molded by forces outside himself, or within himself, over which he has no control. *The Adventures of Augie March* can be read at a deeper level than environmental determinism. Augie is capable of intellectual activity of a relatively high order, of knowing what he is struggling with and struggling for. Throughout his life, he learns that other people want to make him over. Grandma Lausch, an elderly Russian Jew of fallen fortunes who lives with the Marches, tries to form the boy, and he rebels. Later Mr. and Mrs. Renling, well-to-do shopkeepers in a fashionable Chicago suburb and Augie's employers, want to make him over, even adopt him, but he rebels. Augie's brother Simon, who achieves wealth and considerable respectability, tries to make a new man of Augie and finds Augie rebellious. Various women in Augie's life, including Thea Fenchel, Augie's mistress (whom he follows to Mexico to hunt iguanas with an eagle), try to recast Augie's character. They, too, fail, because above all, Augie refuses to be molded into someone else's image of what he ought to be.

What does Augie want to be, that he refuses to be cast in any mold suggested by the people about him? He wants to become something, but he never seriously accepts any goal. He wants always to be independent in act and spirit, and some sort of independence he does achieve, empty though it is. He wants to be someone, to achieve all of which he is capable, but he never finds a specific goal or pattern. By refusing to commit himself to anything, he ends up accomplishing virtually nothing. It is a sad fact of his existence that he comes to be a bit envious of his mentally deficient brother Georgie, who has mastered some of the elements of shoe repairing. Saul Bellow seems to be saying through Augie that it is possible to have a fate without a function, but as he presents the character the result is, ironically, to show that without a function no one, including Augie March, can have a fate. Whether or not the irony is intentional, the reader cannot be sure.

Another view of the novel that is both logical and fruitful is to regard it at the level of social comment. Most remarkable at this level is the section of American society in which Augie March moves. Augie is a Jew; that fact is literally beaten into him by neighborhood toughs, including those among the Gentiles he thought his friends, while he is a child. As he grows up, takes jobs, finds friends and confidants, seeks out women to love, Augie moves almost always in the company of Jews. The respectability toward which he is pushed is always the respectability of the Jewish middle classes, particularly that of the Jews who have lost their religion and turned to worshiping success in moneymaking, which is mirrored in their passion for fleshy women, flashy cars, and too much rich food. While in one sense Bellow's novel is a novel of an adolescent discovering the world, it is a restricted world in which Augie makes his discoveries. He seems never to understand the vast fabric of American culture that lies about him. If his is a sociological tragedy, and many readers will find it so, it is not an American tragedy in the broad sense. Rather, it is the tragedy of a Jewish child who sees only the materialism of Jews who have forsaken their rich tradition and who have found nothing to replace it.

While some readers will most readily grasp the tragic elements in *The Adventures of Augie March*, others will grasp more readily the comic aspects. Following as it does in some ways the picaresque tradition, the novel has a wide strain of the comic. Neither Augie nor his creator takes some of the character's deviations from conventional standards of conduct very seriously. Augie bounds in and out of crime and sin with scarcely a backward glance. If his loves seem empty, his women unfaithful, Augie accepts the results with comic aplomb. If to be unheroic, to give in with little or no struggle, to be weak and ineffectual is comic (and thus it has long been viewed), Augie is a comic protagonist and the novel a comic work. The comic spirit, however, is also used traditionally for serious, often satiric, purpose. It is here that the reader well may be puzzled. While the comic elements are undeniably in the novel, adding to the richness of its texture, one wonders at their purpose. The novel seems at times to be offering satiric comment on the foibles of humanity, but such comment seems alien, if not contradictory, in the framework of Bellow's work, unless it is there to show that the creator of Augie March shares the character's belief in the irrational nature of the individual, of society, and of the universe.

Augie seems at times to be a symbol of the irrational; this symbolic value is mirrored by the eaglet that Augie and Thea Fenchel train to hunt. The young bald eagle, fierce in appearance, proves to be an apt pupil; he seems marvelously equipped, with powerful wings, beak, and claws, to be an instrument of destruction, and he learns well how to attack a piece of meat tendered by his trainers. Yet, when a live creature, even a tiny lizard, puts up resistance, the eagle turns away from the attack. He refuses to do what he is capable of doing, defying his nature. Like the eagle, Augie March fails, too. Young, handsome, charming, and intelligent, Augie refuses to face life, always seeing it as something someone else wants him to do. When life hits back at him, Augie turns away from what he was prepared to do. He strikes the reader as being without purpose. Like the eagle, he exists to exist, to be looked at, and to be fed. That the character sees this as living is perhaps the greatest irony of all. Augie is an antihero; he is not so much comic as pathetic. As narrator, he realizes, however vaguely, that while he has denied the traditional goals which people have held up for him, he has failed to find a goal for himself that he can regard as worthwhile. In trying to live, he has found little but a meaningless existence.

Bibliography:
Clayton, John Jacob. *Saul Bellow: In Defense of Man*. 2d ed. Bloomington: Indiana University Press, 1968. An early book-length study of Bellow. Says the novel is about reaching after

personal uniqueness and the way each person tries to convince others that he has "captured reality."

Cohen, Sarah Blacher. *Saul Bellow's Enigmatic Laughter*. Champaign: University of Illinois Press, 1974. Argues that in this "comedy of character," Augie is a kind of Columbus exploring America and Americans. He is "the picaresque apostle" who hears all confessions and forgives all sins.

Dutton, Robert R. *Saul Bellow*. Rev. ed. Boston: Twayne, 1982. Treats the novel on three levels: as a picaresque, as a "fictional history of American literature," and as a comment on the "contemporary human condition." Augie turns out to be a "fallen angel" and "artist of alienation."

Pifer, Ellen. *Saul Bellow Against the Grain*. Philadelphia: University of Pennsylvania Press, 1990. Describes how Augie travels through "a New World Babylon" on a pilgrimage to discover what is "uniquely meaningful" in his life. He refuses to yield to the authority of people who claim to be authorities but instead seeks his own truth.

Wilson, Jonathan. *On Bellow's Planet: Readings from the Dark Side*. Rutherford, N.J.: Fairleigh Dickinson University Press, 1985. Augie's main conflict is internal. For him, growing up does not bring with it control over the self. Instead, he struggles between the will to freedom and the need to be controlled.

ADVENTURES OF HUCKLEBERRY FINN

Type of work: Novel
Author: Mark Twain (Samuel Langhorne Clemens, 1835-1910)
Type of plot: Satire
Time of plot: Nineteenth century
Locale: Along the Mississippi River
First published: 1884

Principal characters:
HUCKLEBERRY FINN
TOM SAWYER, his friend
JIM, a black slave
PAP FINN, Huck's father
THE DUKE and
THE KING, con men
THE WIDOW DOUGLAS, Huck's guardian

The Story:

Tom Sawyer and Huckleberry Finn had found a box of gold in a robber's cave. After Judge Thatcher had taken the money and invested it for the boys, each had the huge allowance of a dollar a day. The Widow Douglas and her sister, Miss Watson, had taken Huck home with them to try to reform him. At first, Huck could not stand living in a tidy house where smoking and swearing were forbidden. Worse, he had to go to school and learn how to read. He did, however, manage to drag himself to school almost every day, except for the times when he sneaked off for a smoke in the woods or to go fishing on the Mississippi River.

Life was beginning to become bearable to him when one day he noticed a boot print in the snow. Examining it closely, he realized that it belonged to his worthless father, whom he had not seen for more than a year. Knowing that his father would be looking for him when he learned about the money, Huck rushed to Judge Thatcher and persuaded him to take the fortune for himself. The judge was puzzled, but he signed some papers, and Huck was satisfied that he no longer had any money for his father to take from him.

Huck's father showed up one night in Huck's room at Widow Douglas' home. Complaining that he had been cheated out of his money, the old drunkard later took Huck away with him to a cabin in the Illinois woods, where he kept the boy a prisoner, beating him periodically and half starving him. Huck was allowed to smoke and swear, however, and before long he began to wonder why he had ever liked living with the widow. His life with his father would have been pleasant if it had not been for the beatings. One day, he sneaked away, leaving a bloody trail from a pig he had killed in the woods. Huck wanted everyone to believe he was dead. He climbed into a canoe and went to Jackson's Island to hide until all the excitement had blown over.

After three days of freedom, Huck wandered to another part of the island, and there he discovered Jim, Miss Watson's black slave, who told Huck that he had run off because he had overheard Miss Watson planning to sell him down south for eight hundred dollars. Huck swore he would not report Jim. The two stayed on the island many days, Jim giving Huck an education in primitive superstition. One night, Huck paddled back to the mainland. Disguised as a girl, he called on a home near the shore. There he learned that his father had disappeared shortly after the people of the town concluded that Huck had been murdered. Since Jim had disappeared just after Huck's apparent death, there was now a three-hundred-dollar reward posted for Jim's capture, for most people believed that he had killed Huck.

Knowing that Jackson's Island would soon be searched, Huck hurried back to Jim, and the two headed down the Mississippi on a raft. They planned to sell the raft at Cairo, Illinois, and then go on a steamboat up the Ohio River into free territory. Jim told Huck that he would work hard in the North and then buy his wife and children from their masters in the South. Helping a runaway slave bothered Huck's conscience, but he reasoned that it would bother him more if he betrayed a good friend. One night, as they were drifting down the river on their raft, a large steamboat loomed before them, and Huck and Jim, knowing that the raft would be smashed under the hull of the ship, jumped into the water. Huck swam safely to shore, but Jim disappeared.

Huck found a home with a friendly family named Grangerford, who were feuding with the nearby Shepherdson family. The Grangerfords treated Huck kindly and left him mostly to himself, even giving him a young slave to wait on him. One day, the slave asked him to come to the woods to see some snakes. Following the boy, Huck came across Jim, who had been hiding in the woods waiting for an opportunity to send for Huck. Jim had repaired the broken raft. That night, one of the Grangerford daughters eloped with a young Shepherdson, and the feud broke out once more. Huck and Jim ran away after the shooting and set off down the river.

Shortly afterward, Jim and Huck met two men who pretended they were European royalty and made all sorts of nonsensical demands on Huck and Jim. Huck was not taken in, but he reasoned that it would do no harm to humor the two men to prevent quarreling. The Duke and the King were clever schemers. In one of the small river towns, they staged a fake show, which lasted long enough to net them a few hundred dollars. Then they ran off before the angered townspeople could catch them.

From a talkative young man, the King learned about the death of Peter Wilks, who had left considerable property and some cash to his three daughters. Wilks's two brothers, whom no one in the town had ever seen, were living in England. The King and the Duke went to the three nieces, Mary Jane, Susan, and Joanna, and presented themselves as the two English uncles. They took all of the inheritance and then put up the property for auction and sold the slaves. This high-handed deed caused great grief to the girls, and Huck could not bear to see them so unhappy. He decided to expose the two frauds, but he wanted to ensure Jim's safety first. Jim had been hiding in the woods waiting for his companions to return to him. Employing an ingenious series of lies, subterfuges, and maneuverings, Huck exposed the Duke and King. Huck fled back to Jim, and the two escaped on their raft. Just as Jim and Huck thought they were on their way and well rid of their former companions, the Duke and King came rowing down the river toward them.

The whole party set out again, with the Duke and the King planning to continue their schemes to hoodwink people in the towns along the river. In one town, the King turned Jim in for a reward, and he was sold. Huck had quite a tussle with his conscience. He knew that he ought to help return a slave to the rightful owner, yet on the other hand he thought of all the fine times he and Jim had had together and how loyal a friend Jim had been. Finally, Huck decided that he would help Jim to escape.

Learning that Silas Phelps was holding Jim, he headed for the Phelps farm. Mrs. Phelps ran up and hugged him, mistaking him for the nephew whom she had been expecting to come for a visit. Huck wondered how he could keep Mrs. Phelps from learning that he was not her nephew. Then to his relief, he learned they had mistaken him for Tom Sawyer. Huck rather liked being Tom for a while, and he was able to tell the Phelps all about Tom's Aunt Polly and Sid and Mary, Tom's brother and sister. Huck was feeling proud of himself for keeping up the deception. Tom Sawyer, when he arrived, told his aunt that he was his own brother, Sid.

At the first opportunity, Huck told Tom about Jim's capture. To Huck's surprise, Tom offered to help him set Jim free. Huck could not believe that Tom would be a slave stealer, but he kept his feelings to himself. Huck had intended merely to wait until there was a dark night and then break the padlock on the door of the shack where Jim was kept; but Tom said the rescue had to be done according to the books, and he laid out a highly complicated plan. It took fully three weeks of plotting, stealing, and deceit to get Jim out of the shack. The scheme resulted in a chase, however, in which Tom was shot in the leg. After Jim was recaptured, Tom was brought back to Aunt Sally's house to recover from his wound. There, he revealed the fact that Miss Watson had died, giving Jim his freedom in her will. Huck was greatly relieved to learn that Tom was not really a slave stealer after all.

When Tom's Aunt Polly arrived unexpectedly, she quickly set straight the identities of the two boys. Jim was given his freedom, and Tom gave him forty dollars. Tom told Huck that his money was still safely in the hands of Judge Thatcher, and when Huck moaned that his father would likely be back to claim it again, Jim told Huck that his father was dead; Jim had seen him lying in a derelict house they had seen floating in the river. Huck was ready to start out again because Aunt Sally said she thought she might adopt him and try to civilize him. Huck thought that he could not go through such a trial again after having tried to be civilized once before under the care of Widow Douglas.

Critical Evaluation:

Little could Mark Twain have visualized in 1876 when he began a sequel to capitalize on the success of *The Adventures of Tom Sawyer* (1876) that *Adventures of Huckleberry Finn* would come to be regarded as his masterpiece and one of the most significant works in the American novel tradition. His greatest contribution to the tradition occurred when, with an unerring instinct for American regional dialects, he elected to tell the story in Huck's own words. The skill with which Mark Twain elevates the dialect of an illiterate village boy to the highest levels of poetry established the spoken American idiom as a literary language and earned for Mark Twain the reputation, proclaimed for him by Ernest Hemingway, William Faulkner, and many others, as the father of the modern American novel.

Mark Twain maintains an almost perfect fidelity to Huck's point of view in order to dramatize the conflict between Huck's innate innocence and natural goodness and the dictates of a corrupt society. As Huck's story, the novel centers around such major themes as death and rebirth, freedom and bondage, the search for a father, the individual versus society, and the all-pervasive theme of brotherhood. Huck's character reflects a stage in Mark Twain's own development when he still believed human beings to be innately good though increasingly corrupted by social influences that replaced their intuitive sense of right and wrong. This theme is explicitly dramatized through Huck's conflict with his conscience over whether or not to turn Jim in as a runaway slave. Huck, on the one hand, accepts without question what he has been taught about slavery by church and society. In his own mind, as surely as in that of his Southern contemporaries, aiding an escaped slave was both legally and morally wrong. Thus Huck's battle with his conscience is a real trauma for him, and his decision to "go to Hell" rather than give Jim up is made with a certainty that such a fate awaits him for breaking this law of society. Mark Twain compellingly establishes the irony that Huck's "sin" against the social establishment affirms the best that is possible in the individual.

Among the many forms of bondage that permeate the novel—including the widow's attempt to "civilize" Huck, the "code of honor" that causes Sherburn to murder Boggs, and the law of vendetta that rules the lives of the Grangerfords and Shepherdsons—slavery provides Mark Twain his largest metaphor for both social bondage and institutionalized injustice and inhumanity. Written well after the termination of the Civil War, *Adventures of Huckleberry Finn* is not an antislavery novel in the limited sense that *Uncle Tom's Cabin* (1852) is. Rather than simply attacking an institution already legally dead, Mark Twain uses the idea of slavery as a metaphor for all social bondage and injustice. Thus, Jim's search for freedom, like Huck's own need to escape both the Widow and Pap Finn, is as much a metaphorical search for an ideal state of freedom as it is flight from slavery into free-state sanctuary. It is almost irrelevant that Mark Twain has Huck and Jim running deeper into the South rather than north toward free soil. Freedom exists neither in the North nor in the South but in the ideal and idyllic world of the raft and river.

The special world of raft and river is at the very heart of the novel. In contrast to the restrictive and oppressive social world of the shore, the raft is a veritable Eden away from the evils of civilization. It is here that Jim and Huck can allow their natural bond of love to develop without regard for the question of race. It is here on the raft that Jim can become a surrogate father to Huck, and Huck can develop the depth of feeling for Jim which eventually leads to his decision to imperil his soul. While the developing relationship between Huck and Jim determines the basic shape of the novel, the river also works in other structural ways. The picaresque form of the novel and its structural rhythm are based on a series of episodes on shore, after each of which Huck and Jim return to the peaceful sanctuary of the raft. It is on shore that Huck encounters the worst excesses of which "the damned human race" is capable, but with each return to the raft comes a renewal of spiritual hope and idealism.

The two major thrusts of Mark Twain's attack on the "civilized" world in *Adventures of Huckleberry Finn* are against institutionalized religion and the romanticism he believed characterized the South. The former is easily illustrated by the irony of the Widow's attempt to teach Huck religious principles while she persists in holding slaves. As with her snuff-taking—which was all right because she did it herself—there seems to be no relationship between her fundamental sense of humanity and justice and her religion. Huck's practical morality makes him more "Christian" than the Widow, though he takes no interest in her principles. Southern romanticism, which Mark Twain blamed for the fall of the South, is particularly allegorized by the wreck of the steamboat *Walter Scott*, but it is also inherent in such episodes as the feud, where Mark Twain shows the real horror of the sort of situation traditionally glamorized by romantic authors. In both cases, Mark Twain is attacking the mindless acceptance of values that he believed kept the South in its dark age.

Many critics have argued that its ending hopelessly flaws *Adventures of Huckleberry Finn*; others argue that the ending is in perfect accord with Mark Twain's themes. Nevertheless, all agree that the substance of Mark Twain's masterpiece transcends the limits of literary formalism to explore those eternal verities on which great literature rests. Through the adventures of an escaped slave and a runaway boy, both representatives of the ignorant and lowly of the earth, Mark Twain affirms that true humanity is of humans rather than institutions.

"Critical Evaluation" by William E. Grant

Bibliography:
Adams, Richard P. "The Unity and Coherence of *Huckleberry Finn*." In *Huck Finn Among the Critics: A Centennial Selection*, edited by M. Thomas Inge. Frederick, Md.: University

Publications of America, 1985. Summarizes previous critical opinion about the novel's structure and argues that its organization of imagery results in symbolic patterns that include the organic ending.

Blair, Walter. *Mark Twain and Huck Finn*. Berkeley: University of California Press, 1960. Elegantly written classic essay on the writing of *Adventures of Huckleberry Finn*. Still valuable as an exploration of the novel's background of characters and ideas.

Doyno, Victor. *Writing "Huck Finn": Mark Twain's Creative Process*. Philadelphia: University of Pennsylvania Press, 1992. The most nearly definitive essay on the creation of *Adventures of Huckleberry Finn*.

Quirk, Tom. *Coming to Grips with "Huckleberry Finn": Essays on a Book, a Boy, and a Man*. Columbia: University of Missouri Press, 1993. Explores issues in the novel and presents factual contexts for them. Examines Twain's attitude toward race.

Rasmussen, R. Kent. *Mark Twain A to Z: The Essential Reference to His Life and Writings*. New York: Facts On File, 1995. Contains the most detailed published synopsis of the novel, cross-referenced to analytical essays on all characters and places mentioned in the text.

Twain, Mark. *Adventures of Huckleberry Finn*. Edited by Walter Blair. Berkeley: University of California Press, 1985. The major corrected edition. Includes hundreds of pages of explanations and notes.

Williams, Kenney J. *"Adventures of Huckleberry Finn*: Or, Mark Twain's Racial Ambiguity." In *Satire of Evasion? Black Perspectives on "Huckleberry Finn,"* edited by James S. Leonard, Thomas A. Tenney, and Thadious M. Davis. Durham, N.C.: Duke University Press, 1992. Offers a balanced analysis of racial ambiguity in the novel. Finds that Mark Twain satirized romanticized attitudes toward race problems. Includes bibliographies.

THE ADVENTURES OF RODERICK RANDOM

Type of work: Novel
Author: Tobias Smollett (1721-1771)
Type of plot: Picaresque
Time of plot: Eighteenth century
Locale: England
First published: 1748

Principal characters:
RODERICK RANDOM, an adventurer
TOM BOWLING, his uncle
STRAP, Tom's friend and companion
MISS WILLIAMS, an adventuress
NARCISSA, Roderick's sweetheart

The Story:

Although Roderick Random came from a wealthy landowning family in Scotland, his early life was beset by vicissitudes. Soon after Roderick's birth, his mother died. When Roderick's father thereupon married a servant in the household, he was disowned by his own father. Heartbroken and penniless, he disappeared, leaving his son Roderick in the care of his grandfather, who was prevailed upon to send the lad to school for the sake of the family reputation.

At school, Roderick, although a great favorite with the boys his own age, was the butt of the masters. His whippings were numerous, for he could be used as a whipping boy whenever something had gone wrong and the real culprit could not be determined. In Roderick's fourteenth year, however, there was a change in his fortunes. His mother's brother, Tom Bowling, a lieutenant in the navy, came to visit his young nephew.

Lieutenant Bowling remonstrated with his nephew's grandfather over his treatment of Roderick, but the old man was firm in his refusal to do anything beyond what necessity dictated for the offspring of the son whom he had disinherited. When the grandfather died, he left Roderick nothing. Tom Bowling sent the lad to the university, where Roderick made great progress. Then Tom Bowling became involved in a duel and was forced to leave his ship. This misfortune cut off the source of Roderick's funds and made it necessary for him to leave the university.

Casting about for a means of making a livelihood, Roderick became a surgeon's apprentice. He proved to be so capable that before long his master sent him to London with a recommendation to a local member of Parliament, who was to get Roderick a place as surgeon's mate in the navy. Securing a place on a man-of-war was a difficult task. To keep himself in funds, Roderick worked for a French chemist in London. In the shop, he met and fell in love with Miss Williams. Much to his chagrin, however, he discovered one day that she was a prostitute trying to better her fortune. Soon afterward, Roderick was accused of stealing and was dismissed by his employer. While he was leading a precarious existence, waiting for his navy warrant, he learned that Miss Williams lived in the same lodging house. He won her everlasting gratitude by acting as her doctor while she was ill.

One day, while walking near the Thames, Roderick was seized by a press-gang and shanghaied aboard the man-of-war Thunder, about to sail for Jamaica. Roderick found friends on board the ship and was made a surgeon's mate. The voyage to Jamaica was terrible. The commanding officer, Captain Oakhum, was a tyrant who came very close to hanging Roderick and another surgeon's mate because one of the ship's officers claimed he had heard them speaking ill of the surgeon and the captain. The captain thought that Roderick's Greek notebook was a military code, and he threatened again to hang him as a spy.

After seeing action against the Spanish at Cartagena, Roderick secured a billet as surgeon's mate aboard the *Lizard*, a ship returning to England with dispatches. On the way, the captain died and Lieutenant Crampley, an officer who greatly disliked Roderick, took command of the ship. Crampley, a poor officer, ran the ship aground off the Sussex coast. The crew robbed and tried to kill Roderick when they reached the shore, but an old woman befriended him, cured him of his wounds, and found him a place as footman with a spinster gentlewoman who lived nearby.

Roderick spent several months in her service. He found his way into his employer's goodwill by his attention to his duties and by showing a knowledge of literature, even to the extent of explaining passages from Torquato Tasso's Italian poetry to her. The spinster had a niece and a nephew living with her. Narcissa, the niece, was a beautiful girl of marriageable age to whom Roderick was immediately attracted. Her brother, a drunken, fox-hunting young squire, was determined that she should marry a wealthy knight in the neighborhood.

One day, Roderick prevented the girl's brutal suitor from forcing his attentions on her and beat the man severely with a cudgel. While he was deliberating on his next move, he was taken prisoner by a band of smugglers who for their own safety carried him to Boulogne in France. There Roderick found his uncle, Tom Bowling, and assured him that he would be safe if he returned to England, for the man Bowling believed he had killed in a duel was still alive.

Roderick set out for Paris in company with a friar who robbed him one night and left him penniless. Roderick then met a band of soldiers and enlisted in the army of King Louis XIV. He saw service at the battle of Dettingen. After the battle, his regiment went into garrison, and Roderick unexpectedly met a boyhood companion, Strap, who was passing as Monsieur d'Estrapes and who was friendly with a French nobleman. Strap befriended Roderick and secured his release from onerous service as a private in the French army.

Strap and Roderick schemed for a way to make their fortunes. They finally hit upon the idea of setting up Roderick as a wealthy gentleman. They hoped that he would soon marry a wealthy heiress. The two men went to Paris, where Roderick bought new clothes and became acquainted with the ways of a man about town. Then they went to London. There Roderick quickly became acquainted with a group of young men who were on the fringe of fashionable society.

Roderick's first attempt to become intimate with a rich woman was a dismal failure, for she turned out to be a prostitute. On the second attempt, he met Melinda, a young woman of fortune, who won many pounds from him at cards and then refused to marry him because he did not have an independent fortune of his own. Finally, one of Roderick's friends told him of a cousin, Miss Snapper, who was a wealthy heiress. The friend promised that he would help Roderick in his suit in return for Roderick's note for five hundred pounds, due six months after the marriage.

Roderick agreed to this suggestion and immediately started out for Bath in company with the young woman and her mother. On the way, he saved them from being robbed by a highwayman, a deed that established him in the good graces of both mother and daughter. At Bath, Roderick squired the young woman about day and night. Although she was crippled and unattractive, her fortune was more important to him than her appearance. Besides, she was an intelligent and witty young woman.

All went well until Roderick caught sight of Narcissa. Realizing that he was in love with her, he deserted Miss Snapper. Narcissa soon revealed to Roderick that she returned his love. Her brother had no objections to Roderick because he thought that Random was a wealthy man. Unfortunately, Roderick's former sweetheart, Melinda, arrived in Bath and caught the attention of Narcissa's brother. At a ball, she spread evil reports about Roderick because he had left her. The result was that Roderick first fought a duel with Lord Quiverwit, one of Narcissa's admirers, and then saw his Narcissa being spirited away by her brother. The only thing that kept Roderick's hope alive was the fact that he knew Narcissa loved him and that her maid, the Miss Williams whom Roderick had long before befriended, was eternally grateful to him and would help him in any way she could.

Roderick returned to London and again met his uncle, Tom Bowling, who had been appointed to take a merchant ship on a mysterious trip. He proposed to take Roderick with him as ship surgeon, and he gave Roderick one thousand pounds to buy goods to sell on the voyage. He also made out a will leaving all of his property to Roderick in case he died.

The mysterious trip proved to be a voyage to the Guinea Coast to pick up black slaves for the Spanish American trade. The slaves and the cargo, including the goods shipped by Roderick, were sold at a handsome profit. While their ship was being prepared for the return voyage, Roderick and his uncle spent several weeks ashore, where they were entertained by new friends and business acquaintances. One of their acquaintances was a wealthy Englishman known as Don Rodrigo, who invited them to visit him on his estate. During their stay, it was discovered that the man was Roderick's father, who had gone to America to make his fortune after having been disinherited.

The voyage back to England was a happy one. Roderick was full of confidence, for he had made a small fortune out of the voyage and had expectations of a large fortune from the estates of his father and his uncle. He immediately paid his addresses to Narcissa, who accepted his offer of marriage despite her brother's opposition. They were married shortly afterward and went to live in Scotland on the Random estate, which Roderick's father had bought from his bankrupt elder brother.

Critical Evaluation:

The Adventures of Roderick Random is among the most adventure-ridden episodic novels of the eighteenth century. Innumerable incidents befall Roderick as he roams in every conceivable direction on land and sea, driven by necessity. It is a novel written in the best picaresque tradition, with a hero who is at once roguish and (up to a point) virtuous, resilient in the face of adversity yet often despairing, honorable in some matters but underhanded in a great many others. He is by turns whimsical, deliberate, sensitive, vengeful, petulant, gracious, and whatever else Tobias Smollett finds occasion for him to be. Structurally *The Adventures of Roderick Random* also fits easily into the picaresque tradition, not only in the obvious influence of Alain-René Lesage's *Gil Blas* (1715-1735), which Smollett translated into English in 1749, but also in its plot deficiencies. There are several such weaknesses—most of them sudden, unconvincing turns in the narrative—which betray the picaresque fondness for overemphasizing action and character.

The novel is marked above all by its glittering wit and caustic social satire. There are many delightful touches in the book (the repartee of Miss Snapper, for example) that show off Smollett's comic skills and these, added to the author's ribaldry, make for highly diverting passages. Perhaps the most engaging parts of the novel are its scenes of London life: the card sharps, the wags, the floozies and fops, the poverty, the stench, the cruelty. Readers meet every imaginable species of human creature, ranging from prissy lords and lavender-trousered ship captains to lascivious priests and penitent whores. Smollett depicts not just the sins of a sin-worn world but also the need to match good nature with plain animal cunning. Part of the controlling idea in *The Adventures of Roderick Random* is that education is best obtained not in schoolrooms but in living and learning to adapt to harsh realities.

This theme is a favorite of eighteenth century British fiction. Henry Fielding's *The History of Tom Jones, a Foundling*, published just a year after *The Adventures of Roderick Random*, is a well-known reiteration of it. Because Tom, like Roderick, lacks wisdom and self-control (the age would have called it prudence), he is repeatedly victimized by individuals with a crueler nature than his own. In Smollett's book, readers see the same pattern: A young man with a basically good nature (to echo Fielding) is forced into a world of duplicity where his kindness and trust are manipulated by others. The "knavery of the world," as Smollett dubs it, everywhere demands that the hero learn to be worldly-wise; his main difficulty is to do this without losing his fundamental goodness. Often Roderick appears on the verge of such a fate. He is ungracious to his faithful friend Strap, he is at times unconsciously cruel in his schemes for revenge, he gravitates too easily toward unsavory rakes (Banter is a good example), and he himself is at times tainted with affectation. He does, however, remain good at heart and in the end is rewarded with Narcissa much as Tom Jones, having gained prudence, is allowed to possess Sophia.

It can be said that the novel employs its main character as a moral exemplum for preaching and illustrating the traditional values of the age, among them temperance, virtue, fortitude, and honesty. It can also be said that the book's emphasis on sensibility reinforces the efficacy of human goodness, for if the reader is moved to applaud virtue and hate vice, to upbraid the hero's ingratitude despite his attractiveness, then Smollett has in large part proved his point.

Even a quick reading of the novel makes it plain how much Smollett relies on the theme of disguise to develop not only the concept of prudence but also a number of other concerns. One notable example is clothing imagery, which abounds in the book in such scenes as Beau Jackson's appearance before the medical examiners. Wildly costumed as an old duffer, Jackson is a literal application of the adage that "the clothes make the man." He is found out, naturally, and thereby Smollett prepares readers for one of the dominant themes of the novel: Pretension, subterfuge, and hypocrisy are all penetrable. An individual with experience and a sharp eye can see through them.

The question as to who that individual may be is usually answered by eighteenth century writers as "the satirist." It is a commonplace observation that the satirist strips away the coverings of things, that after creating disguises for his characters he tears them away in order to reveal what lies beneath. This is unquestionably so in the case of Smollett. The clothing imagery fits well with his satiric purposes, for everywhere his intent is to bare human morals as well as physical nature. An understanding of this commonplace in part elucidates Smollett's dislike of romantic novels and other such writings. His attack on romance in the preface owes much to the satiric spirit that prevailed in the Augustan age, for there are few modes so different in philosophy as the romantic and the satiric. Romances—or "novels" as they were often called in Smollett's day—are in a sense departures from this world; they are fantasies, unrealities, idealizations. Satire, on the other hand, is fully committed to the world as it is; therefore, it both eschews the improbable and dissolves the apparently real in order to plumb life's deepest recesses.

It should also be mentioned that *The Adventures of Roderick Random*, Smollett's first novel, is interesting simply for its biographical and historical inclusions. Smollett was a surgeon and, as is to be expected, the book offers plenty of commentary on eighteenth century medical practices. Like his main character, the author served in the Royal Navy as a surgeon's mate and was present at the disastrous attack on Cartagena (this is discussed at length in the novel); he thus had a firsthand knowledge of seamanship as well as medicine. The story of Molopoyn, which occurs near the end of the book, is a thinly disguised account of Smollett's endeavors to promote his tragedy, *The Regicide* (1749).

"Critical Evaluation" by David B. Carroll

Bibliography:
Bold, Alan, ed. *Smollett: Author of the First Distinction.* London: Vision, 1982. A collection of essays designed to review and revive Smollett's literary reputation. Deals with his work in the context of his Scottish heritage and tradition and discusses the author's urgency of pace, use of language, and selection of themes.

Bouce, Paul-Gabriel. *The Novels of Tobias Smollett.* Translated by Antonia White. London: Longman, 1976. Begins with brief biography and attempts to show autobiographical injection throughout the author's novels. Addresses Smollett as a moralist rather than the usual picaresque designation but notes the influence of Alain-René Lesage and Miguel de Cervantes on his work.

Bruce, Donald. *Radical Doctor Smollett.* Boston: Houghton Mifflin, 1965. One of the definitive works on Smollett, which gives a historical survey of Smollett's critical reputation as a novelist. Addresses his use of medicine, sex, crime, and wealth as themes for social criticism. Discusses whether or not the work should be categorized as picaresque and ultimately classes the author as pessimistic and belligerent.

Giddings, Robert. *The Tradition of Smollett.* London: Methuen, 1967. Discusses Smollett as a standard-bearer of the picaresque tradition and compares him to Henry Fielding. Also discusses Smollett as evolutionary predecessor for all rogue novels up to the work of John Barth.

Spector, Robert Donald. *Tobias George Smollett.* Rev. ed. Boston: Twayne, 1989. Discusses Smollett's five novels as masterpieces of the picaresque form and shows how each led to and perfected the next. Repudiates previous critical analysis of the author.

THE ADVENTURES OF TOM SAWYER

Type of work: Novel
Author: Mark Twain (Samuel Langhorne Clemens, 1835-1910)
Type of plot: Adventure
Time of plot: 1840's
Locale: St. Petersburg, Missouri
First published: 1876

Principal characters:
TOM SAWYER
AUNT POLLY, his deceased mother's sister
HUCKLEBERRY FINN and
JOE HARPER, his friends
BECKY THATCHER, his sweetheart
INJUN JOE, a murderer
MUFF POTTER, the village ne'er-do-well

The Story:

Tom Sawyer lived securely with the knowledge that his Aunt Polly loved him dearly. When she scolded him or whipped him, he knew that inside her breast lurked a hidden remorse. Often he deserved the punishment he received, but there were times when he was the victim of his tattletale half brother, Sid. Tom's cousin Mary was kinder to him. Her worst duty toward him was to see to it that he washed and put on clean clothes, so that he would look respectable when Aunt Polly took the children to Sunday school.

When a new family moved into town, Tom saw a pretty, blue-eyed girl with lacy pantalettes. Instantly the fervent love he had felt for Amy Lawrence fled from his faithless bosom to be replaced by devotion to this new girl. At Sunday school, Tom learned that her name was Becky Thatcher. She was in school the next day, sitting on the girls' side of the room with an empty seat beside her. Tom had come late to school that morning. When the schoolmaster asked Tom why he had been late, that empty seat beside Becky Thatcher caught his eye. Recklessly he confessed he had stopped to talk with Huckleberry Finn, son of the town drunk. Huck wore cast-off clothing, never attended school, smoked and fished as often as he pleased, and slept wherever he could. For associating with Huckleberry Finn, Tom was whipped by the school-master and ordered to sit on the girls' side of the room. Amid the snickers of the entire class, he took the empty seat next to Becky Thatcher.

He first attracted Becky's attention with a series of drawings on his slate. At length, he wrote the words, "I love you," and Becky blushed. Tom persuaded her to meet him at lunch. Sitting with her on a fence, he explained to her the possibilities of an engagement between them. Innocently, she accepted his proposal, which Tom insisted must be sealed by a kiss. In coy resistance she allowed Tom a brief chase before she yielded to his embrace. Tom's happiness was unbounded. When he mentioned his previous tie with Amy Lawrence, however, the brief romance ended, and Becky left with a toss of her head.

That night, Tom heard Huck's whistle below his bedroom window. Sneaking out, Tom joined his friend, and the two went off to the cemetery, Huck carrying a dead cat. They were about to try a new method for curing warts. The gloomy atmosphere of the burial ground filled the boys with apprehension, and their fears increased still more when they spied three figures—Injun

Joe, Muff Potter, and Doctor Robinson. Evidently they had come to rob a grave. When the two robbers had exhumed the body, they began to quarrel with the doctor about money. In the quarrel, the drunken Potter was knocked out. Then Injun Joe took Potter's knife and killed the doctor. When Potter recovered from his blow, he thought he had killed Robinson, and Injun Joe allowed him to believe himself guilty. Terrified, Tom and Huck slipped away from the scene they had just witnessed, afraid that if Injun Joe discovered them he would kill them too.

Becky Thatcher had not come to school since the day she had broken Tom's heart. Rumor said she was also ill, and Tom lost all interest in life; he also brooded over what he and Huck had seen in the graveyard. Convinced that Tom was ill, Aunt Polly dosed him with a quack pain killer and kept him in bed, but he did not seem to recover. When Becky finally returned to school, she cut Tom coldly. Feeling that there was nothing else for him to do, he decided to run away. He met Joe Harper and Huck Finn. Together they went to Jackson's Island and pretended to be pirates.

For a few days they were happy on the island and learned from Huck how to smoke and swear. They were beginning to get homesick when they heard a cannon being fired over the river from a steamboat. Then the boys realized that the townspeople were searching for their bodies. This discovery put a new aspect on their adventure; the people at home thought they were dead. Gleeful, Tom could not resist the temptation to see how Aunt Polly had reacted to his death. He slipped back to the mainland one night and into his aunt's house, where Mrs. Harper and Aunt Polly were mourning the deaths of their mischievous but good-hearted children. When Tom returned to the island, he found Joe and Huck tired of their game and ready to go home. Tom revealed to them an attractive plan which they immediately decided to carry out.

With a heavy gloom overhanging the town, funeral services were held for the deceased Thomas Sawyer, Joseph Harper, and Huckleberry Finn. The minister pronounced a lengthy eulogy about the respective good characters of the unfortunate boys. When the funeral procession was about to start, Tom, Joe, and Huck marched down the aisle of the church into the arms of the startled mourners.

For a while, Tom was the hero of all the boys in the town. They whispered about him and eyed him with awe in the schoolyard. Becky, however, ignored him until the day she accidentally tore the schoolmaster's anatomy book. When the irate teacher demanded to know who had torn his book, Tom confessed to save Becky from a whipping. Becky's gratitude and forgiveness were his reward.

After Muff Potter had been jailed for the murder of the doctor in the graveyard, Tom and Huck swore to each other they would never utter a word about what they had seen. Afraid that Injun Joe would murder them for revenge, they furtively sneaked behind the prison and brought Muff food and other cheer; but Tom could not let an innocent man be condemned. At the trial, he appeared to tell what he had seen on the night of the murder. While Tom spoke, Injun Joe, a witness at the trial, sprang through the window of the courtroom and escaped. For days Tom worried, convinced that Injun Joe would come back to murder him. As time went by and nothing happened, he gradually lost his fears. With Becky looking upon him as a hero, his world was filled with sunshine.

Huck and Tom decided to hunt for pirates' treasure in an old abandoned house. One night, they watched, unseen, while Injun Joe—who had returned to town disguised as a mute Spaniard—and a companion unearthed a chest of money buried under the floorboards of the house. The two frightened boys fled before they were discovered. The next day, they began a steady watch for Injun Joe and his accomplice, for they were bent on finding the lost treasure.

Becky Thatcher's parents gave a picnic for all the young people in town, after which Becky was supposed to spend the night with Mrs. Harper. One of the biggest excitements of the merrymaking came when the children went into the cave by the river. The next day, Mrs. Thatcher and Aunt Polly learned that Tom and Becky were missing, for Mrs. Harper said that Becky had not come to spend the night with her. No one remembered having seen Tom and Becky after the picnickers had left the cave. Tom and Becky had lost their bearings and wandered through the cave's labyrinthine passages until their last candle burned out beside a freshwater spring. To add to Tom's terror, he discovered that Injun Joe was also in the cave.

Meanwhile, Huck had kept his vigil at Injun Joe's lodgings in town until the disguised murderer emerged. He then followed Injun Joe and his accomplice and overheard them planning to assault the Widow Douglas. After warning a neighbor named Jones in time for the man and his sons to save the widow and chase away her would-be attackers, Huck collapsed in a fever. He later recovered to learn that he was a public hero.

After Tom and Becky had been inside the cave for five days, Tom found a way out—at a spot five miles from the main entrance. He and Becky then miraculously reappeared in town, where he was again acclaimed a hero. To prevent others from getting lost in the cave, Judge Thatcher had a heavy iron door installed at its entrance. When Tom recovered from his exhausting ordeal two weeks later and heard about the iron door, he announced that Injun Joe was inside the cave. Townspeople then rushed to the cave, where they found Injun Joe lying behind the new door, dead of starvation.

Using the secret entry that he had discovered, Tom later took Huck back to the cave, where they found the treasure chest hidden by Injun Joe. It contained twelve thousand dollars in gold coins. Huck, who now had an income of a dollar a day for the rest of his life, was informally adopted by the Widow Douglas. He never would have stayed with the Widow or consented to learn her prim, tidy ways if Tom had not promised that he would form a pirate gang and make Huck one of the bold buccaneers.

Critical Evaluation:

Mark Twain, who began his writing career as a frontier humorist and ended it as a bitter satirist, drew on his experiences growing up with little formal schooling in a small Missouri town and on his life as printer's apprentice, journalist, roving correspondent, silver prospector, world traveler, Mississippi steamboat pilot, and lecturer. He was influenced by Artemus Ward, Bret Harte, and Joel Chandler Harris. Beginning with the publication of his short story "Jim Smiley and His Jumping Frog" (1865; later published as "The Celebrated Jumping Frog of Calaveras County") and proceeding through novels and travel books—*Innocents Abroad* (1869), *Roughing It* (1872), *The Gilded Age* (1873), *The Adventures of Tom Sawyer* (1876), *Life on the Mississippi* (1883), *Adventures of Huckleberry Finn* (1884), *A Connecticut Yankee in King Arthur's Court* (1889), and *The American Claimant* (1892)—Mark Twain developed a characteristic style that, while uneven in its productions, made him the most important and representative nineteenth century American writer. His service as delightful entertainment to generations of American youngsters is equaled by his influence on such twentieth century admirers as Gertrude Stein, William Faulkner, and Ernest Hemingway.

Mark Twain's generally careful and conscientious style was both a development of the tradition of humor of Augustus Baldwin Longstreet and Joel Chandler Harris and a departure from the conventions of nineteenth century literary gentility. It is characterized by the adroit use of exaggeration, stalwart irreverence, deadpan seriousness, droll cynicism, and pungent commentary on the human situation. All of this is masked in an uncomplicated, straightforward narrative distinguished for its introduction of the colloquial and vernacular into American fiction that was to have a profound impact on the development of American writing and shape the world's view of America. Mark Twain, according to Frank Baldanza, had a talent for "paring away the inessential and presenting the bare core of experience with devastating authenticity." The combination of childish rascality and innocence in his earlier writing gave way, in his later and posthumous works, to an ever-darkening vision of man that left Mark Twain bitter and disillusioned. This darker vision is hardly present in the three Tom Sawyer books—in addition to *The Adventures of Tom Sawyer*, Twain wrote *Tom Sawyer Abroad* (1894) and *Tom Sawyer, Detective* (1896)—and in his masterpiece, *Adventures of Huckleberry Finn*.

Mark Twain's lifelong fascination with boyhood play led to the creation of *The Adventures of Tom Sawyer*, a book of nostalgic recollections of his own lost youth that has been dismissed too lightly by some as "amusing but thin stuff" and taken too analytically and seriously by others, some of whom seek in it the complexities of carefully controlled viewpoint, multiple irony, and social satire found in *Adventures of Huckleberry Finn*. Beyond the fact that *The Adventures of Tom Sawyer* is a delicate balance of the romantic and realistic, humor and pathos, innocence and evil, the book defies analysis. In fact, Mark Twain's opening statement in *Adventures of Huckleberry Finn* is, ironically, more applicable to *The Adventures of Tom Sawyer*: "Persons attempting to find a motive in this narrative will be prosecuted; persons attempting to find a moral in it will be banished; persons attempting to find a plot in it will be shot." The book is purely, simply, and happily "the history of a boy," or as Mark Twain also called it, "simply a hymn, put into prose form to give it a worldly air." It should be read first and last for pleasure, by both children and adults.

As even Mark Twain admitted paradoxically, *The Adventures of Tom Sawyer* is also for those who have long since passed from boyhood: "[It] is not a boy's book at all. It will be read only by adults. It is written only for adults." Kenneth S. Lynn explicates the author's preface when he says that *The Adventures of Tom Sawyer* "confirms the profoundest wishes of the heart." Christopher Morley called the book "a panorama of happy memory" and made a special visit to Hannibal because he wanted to see the town and house where Tom lived. During that visit, Morley and friends actually whitewashed Aunt Polly's fence. Certainly there can be no greater testimony to the effectiveness of a literary work than its readers' desire to reenact the exploits of its hero.

Tom is the archetypal all-American boy, defining in himself the very concept of American boyhood, as he passes with equal seriousness from one obsession to another: whistling, glory, spying, sympathy, flirtation, exploration, piracy, shame, fear—always displaying to the utmost the child's ability to concentrate his entire energies on one thing at a time (as when he puts the treasure hunt out of his mind in favor of Becky's picnic). Tom is contrasted to both Sid, the "good boy" who loses the reader's sympathies as immediately as Tom gains them, and to the outcast, Huck. In contrast to Huck's self-reliant, unschooled, parentless existence, his passive preference for being a follower, and his abhorrence of civilization, Tom is adventurous, shrewd in the ways of civilization, and a leader. He comes from the respectable world of Aunt Polly and has a literary mind coupled with a conscious romantic desire for experience and for the hero's part, an insatiable egotism that assists him in his ingenious schematizations of life to match his heroic aspirations. The relationship between the two boys may be compared to that between the romantic Don Quixote and the realist Sancho Panza. It was Mark Twain's genius to understand that the games Quixote played out of "madness" were, in fact, those played by children with deadly seriousness. Lionel Trilling summarizes Mark Twain's achievement when he says that "*The Adventures of Tom Sawyer* has the truth of honesty—what it says about things and feelings is never false and always both adequate and beautiful." Mark Twain's book is an American classic, but a classic that travels well as an ambassador of American idealism.

Bibliography:

Blair, Walter. "Tom Sawyer." In *Mark Twain: A Collection of Critical Essays*, edited by Henry Nash Smith. Englewood Cliffs, N.J.: Prentice-Hall, 1963. A leading Mark Twain scholar traces autobiographical and literary influences in *The Adventures of Tom Sawyer*. Shows how Mark Twain adapted real people, places, and events into this early novel.

Fields, Wayne. "When the Fences Are Down: Language and Order in *The Adventures of Tom Sawyer* and *Huckleberry Finn*." *Journal of American Studies* 24, no. 3 (December, 1990): 369-386. A valuable comparison of the two novels. Images of fences place Tom Sawyer within an ordered community, while Huck explores a disordered, insecure world outside the fences.

Norton, Charles A. *Writing "Tom Sawyer": The Adventures of a Classic*. Jefferson, N.C.: MacFarland, 1983. The most complete analysis of how Mark Twain wrote the novel.

Rasmussen, R. Kent. *Mark Twain A to Z: The Essential Reference to His Life and Writings*. New York: Facts On File, 1995. Contains a detailed synopsis of the novel, cross-referenced to analytical essays on every character and place mentioned in the text, as well as other related subjects.

Robinson, Forrest G. "Social Play and Bad Faith in *The Adventures of Tom Sawyer*." *Nineteenth-Century Literature* 39, no. 1 (June, 1984): 1-24. Defends the novel's reputation by asserting that its coherence relies on a dominant character with "a dream of himself as a hero in a world of play."

Twain, Mark. *The Adventures of Tom Sawyer, Tom Sawyer Abroad, and Tom Sawyer, Detective*. Edited by John C. Gerber, Paul Baender, and Terry Firkins. Berkeley: University of California Press, 1980. The definitive, corrected edition of all three Tom Sawyer novels, prepared by the Mark Twain Project at Berkeley. Heavily annotated, with citations to many specialized sources.

THE AENEID

Type of work: Poetry
Author: Vergil (Publius Vergilius Maro, 70-19 B.C.E.)
Type of plot: Epic
Time of plot: After the Trojan War
Locale: The Mediterranean
First transcribed: c. 29-19 B.C.E. (English translation, 1553)

Principal characters:
 AENEAS, a Trojan hero destined to found the Roman race
 DIDO, Queen of Carthage, in love with Aeneas
 ANNA, her sister
 ASCANIUS, son of Aeneas
 ANCHISES, father of Aeneas
 VENUS, goddess of love and beauty, mother of Aeneas
 JUNO, queen of the gods and enemy of the Trojans
 CUMAEAN SIBYL, prophetess who leads Aeneas to Hades
 LATINUS, king of the Latins, whom Aeneas defeats in battle
 LAVINIA, his daughter
 TURNUS, Latin hero ambitious for the Latin throne and hand of Lavinia
 EVANDER, Arcadian king, ally of Aeneas
 PALLAS, his son

The Story:

Aeneas, driven by storm to the shores of Libya, was welcomed gladly by the people of Carthage. Because Carthage was the favorite city of Juno, divine enemy of Aeneas, Venus had Cupid take the form of Ascanius, son of Aeneas, so that the young god of love might warm the heart of proud Dido, and Aeneas come to no harm in her land. At the close of a welcoming feast, Aeneas was prevailed upon to recount his adventures.

He described the fall of his native Troy at the hands of the Greeks after a ten-year siege, telling how the armed Greeks had entered the city in the belly of a great wooden horse, and how the Trojans had fled from their burning city, among them Aeneas, with his father, Anchises, and young Ascanius. Not long afterward, Anchises had advised setting sail for distant lands. Blown by varying winds, the Trojans had at length reached Buthrotum, where had been foretold a long and arduous journey before Aeneas would reach Italy. Having set sail once more, they had reached Sicily. There Anchises, who had been his son's sage counselor, had died and had been buried. Forced to leave Sicily, Aeneas had been blown by stormy winds to the coast of Libya. Here he ended his tale, and Dido, influenced by Cupid disguised as Ascanius, felt pity and admiration for the Trojan hero.

The next day, Dido continued her entertainment for Aeneas. During a royal hunt, a great storm drove Dido and Aeneas to the same cave for refuge. There they succumbed to the passion of love. Aeneas spent the winter in Carthage and enjoyed the devotion of the queen, but in the spring, he felt the need to continue his destined course. When he set sail, the sorrowing Dido killed herself. The light of her funeral pyre was seen far out at sea.

Again on the shores of Sicily, Aeneas bade his men refresh themselves with food, drink, and games. First, there was a boat race in which Cloanthus was the victor. The second event was a

59

foot race, won by Euryalus. Entellus engaged Dares in a boxing match, which Aeneas stopped before the clearly superior Entellus achieved a knock-out. The final contest was with bow and arrow. Eurytion and Acestes made spectacular showings, and each was awarded a handsome prize. Following the contests, Ascanius and the other young boys rode out to engage in war games. Meanwhile, the women were grieving the lost guidance of Anchises, and, at the instigation of Juno, set fire to the ships. Aeneas, sustained by the gods, bade his people repair the damage. Once more, the Trojans set sail.

Finally, they reached the shores of Italy, at Cumae, which was famous for its sibyl. The sibyl granted Aeneas the privilege of visiting his father in the underworld. After due sacrifice, Aeneas and the sibyl began their descent into Hades. At length, they reached the river Styx and persuaded the boatman, Charon, to row them across. Aeneas saw the spirits of many people he had known in life, including the ill-fated Dido. Then they came to the beginning of a forked road. One path led to the regions of the damned; the other led to the land of the blessed. Following this latter road, they came at last to Anchises, who showed Aeneas in marvelous fashion all the future history of Rome, and commanded him to found his kingdom at the place where he would eat his tables. On his return to the upper regions, Aeneas revisited his men and proceeded to his own abode.

Again the Trojans set sail up the coast of Italy, to the ancient state of Latium, ruled over by Latinus. On the shore, they prepared a meal, laying bread under their meat. As they were eating, Ascanius jokingly observed that in eating their bread they were eating their tables. This remark told Aeneas that here was the place Anchises had foretold. The next day, the Trojans came to the city of King Latinus on the Tiber. Latinus had been warned by an oracle not to give his daughter Lavinia in marriage to any native man, but to wait for an alien, who would come to establish a great people. He welcomed Aeneas as that man of destiny.

A Latin hero, Turnus, became jealous of the favor Latinus showed Aeneas, and stirred up revolt among the people. Juno, hating Aeneas, aided Turnus. One day, Ascanius killed a stag, not knowing that it was the tame favorite of a native family. From this incident, there grew such a feud that Latinus shut himself up in his house and ceased to control his subjects. Aeneas made preparations for battle with the Latins under Turnus.

In a dream, he was advised to seek the help of Evander, whose kingdom on the Seven Hills would become the site of mighty Rome. Evander agreed to join forces with Aeneas against the armies of Turnus and to enlist troops from nearby territories as well. Now Venus presented Aeneas with a fabulous shield made by Vulcan, for she feared for the safety of her son.

When Turnus learned that Aeneas was with Evander, he and his troops besieged the Trojan camp. One night, Nisus and Euryalus, two Trojan youths, entered the camp of the sleeping Latins and slaughtered a great many of them before they were discovered and put to death. The enraged Latins advanced on the Trojans with fire and sword and forced them into open battle. When the Trojans seemed about to beat back their attackers, Turnus entered the fray and put them to flight. The thought of Aeneas inspired the Trojans to such bravery that they drove Turnus into the river.

Aeneas, warned in a dream of this battle, returned and landed with his allies on the shore near the battlefield, where he encountered Turnus and his armies. Evander's troops were being routed when Pallas, Evander's beloved son, began to urge them on and himself rushed into the fight, killing many of the enemy before he was slain in combat with Turnus. Aeneas sought to take the life of Turnus, who escaped through the intervention of Juno.

Aeneas decreed that the body of Pallas should be sent back to his father, with appropriate pomp, during a twelve-day truce. The gods had watched the conflict from afar; now Juno relented at Jupiter's command, but insisted that the Trojans must take the Latin speech and garb before their city could rule the world.

Turnus led his band of followers against Aeneas, in spite of a treaty made by Latinus. An arrow from an unknown source wounded Aeneas, but his wound was miraculously healed. The Trojan hero reentered the battle, was again wounded, but was able to engage Turnus in personal combat and strike him down. Aeneas killed his enemy in the name of Pallas and sacrificed his body to the shade of his dead ally. No longer opposed by Turnus, Aeneas was now free to marry Lavinia and establish his long-promised new nation. This was Rome, the greatest power of the ancient world.

Critical Evaluation:

Publius Vergilius Maro, better known as Vergil, is the greatest poet Rome has produced. His finest work, the *Aeneid*, became the national epic and, when Rome collapsed, it survived to become the most influential book Rome contributed to Western culture. Dante Alighieri drew direct inspiration from book 4 for *The Divine Comedy* (c. 1320), allowing the spirit of Vergil to guide him through the Inferno and up the heights of Purgatory.

Vergil was a modest, retiring man who preferred the seclusion of his country estate to life in the bustling metropolis of Rome. He was much liked and esteemed by important people, including the poet Horace and the Emperor Augustus. He won the patronage of the great, secured the wealth and leisure necessary to write, composed three supreme poems—the *Georgics* (36-29 B.C.E.), the *Eclogues* (42-37 B.C.E.), and the *Aeneid*—and died revered and honored. In his lifetime, he saw the closing years of the Civil War that destroyed the Roman Republic, and the establishment of the Roman Empire under Augustus. To celebrate the Pax Romana and the leadership of Augustus, Vergil wrote the *Aeneid*, his patriotic epic dealing with the mythical Roman past.

According to legend, the Trojan hero Aeneas came to Italy after escaping the fall of Troy and became the ancestor of the Romans through his descendant, Romulus. Vergil took this material and, borrowing his structure from Homer, fashioned an epic of it. The first part of the poem, dealing with Aeneas' wanderings, resembles Homer's *Odyssey* (c. 800 B.C.E.) in form and content; the second half, which treats Aeneas' war in Latium and its surroundings, imitates in some ways the *Iliad* (c. 800 B.C.E.). Certain poetic devices, such as the repeated epithet, are taken from Homer, as well as the way the gods interfere on behalf of their favorites. Yet the *Aeneid* is wholly original in concept, possessing a unique unity of its own.

The originality lies in its presentation of Aeneas, a hero who struggles and fights, not for booty, personal fame, or any existing country, but for a civilization that will exist in the distant future, that of Rome and Augustus. He sacrifices his personal comforts, leaving home after home because of the prodding of his inner sense of destiny. He knows that he is to be the founder of a new nation, but the details are revealed to him gradually in the course of his journeying. Chronologically, the pattern is one of revelation and sacrifice, and each new revelation about his destiny imposes a greater burden of responsibility on him. The final revelation—when Aeneas descends with the sibyl into the cavern of death and is shown the coming glory of Rome by his father, Anchises—prepares him spiritually and physically for the greatest fight of his life. Finally, he is something greater than a man. In fulfilling his grand fate, he becomes a monument, an unstoppable force, an instrument of the gods, like the Roman Empire itself as Vergil visualized it.

When the poem opens and Aeneas and his men are shipwrecked at Carthage, the hero already knows two things: that he has an important mission to accomplish and that his future home lies on the western coast of Italy. This knowledge ensures, on his part, a limited commitment to Dido, whereas she falls completely in love with him, giving herself freely even though it ruins her as a woman and a queen when Aeneas is ordered by Jupiter to sail on to Italy. In the coldness of his parting, the founder of Rome draws upon himself all the wrath of Dido, the founder of Carthage, which points forward to the Punic Wars between those cities.

Aeneas is not hardhearted, however. He feels pity for those who are crushed in trying to prevent him from accomplishing his aim—Dido, Lausus, the son of Mezentius, even Turnus. The entire epic is weighted with the sadness of mortality. Aeneas' sense of destiny gives him courage, fortitude, patience, determination, and strength; yet it also makes him humorless, overbearing, and relentless. Still, without that inner conviction in the future destiny of his line and of his fellow Trojans, he would be nothing. Pity is the most that a person who knows he is doing right can feel for those who oppose him. Aeneas has a noble character, although somewhat inhuman, and he seems to embody the best traits of the Roman people.

The crux of the *Aeneid* comes, as Dante rightly perceived, in book 4, where Aeneas enters the realm of Death to gain enlightenment about his future. From the fall of Troy, where the ghost of Hector warns Aeneas, to this point, the dead are associated with revelation. In the underworld Aeneas must purify himself ritually, enter the cavern of death, brave all the terrors of hell, meet dead comrades, and finally, with a rite, enter the realms of the blessed to learn the truth about himself and his fate. Like Dante's hell, Vergil's has various places assigned for various acts, sins, and crimes, but punishment there purges the soul to prepare it for the Elysian Fields, from which it may reincarnate.

In this section, Vergil delineates his view of the meaning of life and death. There is a Great Soul that gave birth to all living spirits, which incarnated themselves in flesh as assorted creatures, including people. The desires of these spirits hindered them from living up to their true purpose in bodily form, so that they must be cleansed after death, only to take on flesh again until they learn their rightful end and achieve it. Thus, death purifies and life tests one on the long road to perfection. This occult view is, in Vergil's case, a mixture of Pythagorean reincarnation, Stoic pantheism, and Platonic mysticism. That view gives credence to everything Anchises shows Aeneas about his illustrious descendants and the rising power of Rome. Aeneas sees the souls of the future waiting their turn, and he knows how much responsibility he really bears. Anchises' judgment of Aeneas is a fitting comment on Rome itself:

> But yours, my Roman, is the gift of government,
> That is your bent—to impose upon the nations
> The code of peace; to be clement to conquered,
> But utterly to crush the intransigent!

In those lines, Vergil summed up the particular genius of Rome, together with its greatness and its terrors.

"Critical Evaluation" by James Weigel, Jr.

Bibliography:
Cairns, Francis. *Virgil's Augustan Epic*. Cambridge, England: Cambridge University Press, 1989. An outstanding piece of criticism that opens the poem to the reader. Explains the role of games in the narrative, the significance of numerous characters, and geographical and mythological references. Accessible and pleasantly written.

Gransden, K. W. *Virgil: The "Aeneid."* Cambridge, England: Cambridge University Press, 1990. Stresses the character of Aeneas, his moral burdens, his ambition, and his suffering. Also useful in understanding Vergil's epic ambition and the political goals of his poem within the context of Augustan Rome.

Johnson, W. R. *Darkness Visible.* Berkeley: University of California Press, 1976. Reassesses the temper of the poem, seeing it not as imperial and stately but pessimistic and skeptical. Controversial among Vergil scholars, but probably the most important book on the *Aeneid* published in the last quarter of the twentieth century.

Lyne, R. O. A. M. *Words and the Poet: Characteristic Techniques of Style in Vergil's "Aeneid."* Oxford, England: Clarendon Press, 1989. Occasionally difficult, but excellent stylistic analysis of the *Aeneid.* Especially provocative in its discussion of the technique of epic simile and the way in which epic simile helps the poem define itself as a narrative.

Slavitt, David. *Virgil.* New Haven, Conn.: Yale University Press, 1991. Pays particular attention to the craft of the poem and the personal sensibility of the poet. Comments on and critiques the quality of various English translations of the *Aeneid.*

AESOP'S FABLES

Type of work: Short fiction
Author: Aesop (c. 620-c. 560 B.C.E.)
Type of plot: Fable
Time of plot: Antiquity
First collected: Aesopea, fourth century B.C.E. (English translation, 1484)

The fables attributed to Aesop were actually composed over the course of many centuries. Aesop is a semilegendary figure, about whom various stories have been told. All that can be known with any certainty about Aesop is that he was a Phrygian slave who was later freed by his Greek master because of the wit and charm of Aesop's stories. All other details about Aesop's life appear to have been invented after his death. For example, it is said that Aesop served under two masters, Xanthus and Iadmon, on the island of Samos. After being freed by Iadmon, Aesop is reported to have traveled as far as the Lydian city of Sardis, where he became a favorite of King Croesus (c. 600-546 B.C.E.). Another legend reports that the citizens of Delphi were outraged by Aesop's description of them as mere parasites, living off the wealth of others. To punish Aesop for this insult, the Delphians are said to have hidden a golden bowl among his possessions just before he left the city. When the bowl was discovered, Aesop was convicted of theft and executed by being thrown from a cliff. None of these incidents is likely to have occurred. While the historian Herodotus (c. 484-c. 425 B.C.E.) does describe Iadmon as Aesop's master and says that the former slave was murdered by the Delphians, it must be remembered that Herodotus is not always reliable. In the fourth century B.C.E., the comic poet Alexis wrote a play, *Aesop*, now lost. Some of the episodes included in later biographical sketches of the author may actually have been derived from this comic work.

The stories told by the historical Aesop appear to have been a mix of legends, myths, and political parables. Even in antiquity, however, it was the fable—and, in particular, the animal fable—with which Aesop became most closely associated. More than a hundred animal stories are now attributed to him. Aesop himself was probably responsible for few of the tales that bear his name. He never wrote a book. His stories belonged to the oral tradition. Even as late as the Renaissance, numerous moral fables were still being attributed to Aesop. Many of the fables that later ages believed were written by Aesop were actually the work of Demetrius of Phalerum (c. 350 B.C.E.), Phaedrus (c. 15 B.C.E.-c. 50 C.E.), Babrius (second century C.E.), Avianus (c. 400 C.E.), and Jean de La Fontaine (1621-1695). Manuscripts of stories said to have been written by Aesop include legends that vary widely by date, are sometimes composed in Greek and sometimes in Latin, and are arranged not by subject but alphabetically by the first word in the story, hardly a likely categorization system for a storyteller.

In most examples of Aesop's fables, each animal symbolizes a different human virtue or vice. The fox represents cunning, the ass stupidity, the lion ferocity, the ant industry, the grasshopper laziness, the crow vanity, and so on. By placing these creatures in different combinations, the fables comment upon the varieties of human nature and criticize common human foibles. For example, in "The Ass, the Fox and the Lion," a fox offers to betray his friend the ass to the lion provided that the lion promises never to harm the fox. The lion agrees to this proposal and the ass foolishly falls into the trap that the fox has prepared. Once the ass is safely ensnared, however, the lion turns and attacks the fox, proving that those who act with treachery are themselves often betrayed.

In a similar tale, "The Lion, the Ass, and the Fox Go Hunting," the same three animals agree to help one another by forming a hunting party. Since each contributes his own particular skills, they are very successful and, at the end of the day, there is a great heap of booty. The ass proceeds to divide their profits into three equal parts and asks the lion which share he would prefer as his own. Instead of answering, the lion simply attacks the ass and gobbles him up. Then the fox proceeds to divide the booty, claiming only a tiny morsel for himself and granting his comrade the "lion's share." "Why did you divide our goods in that way?" the lion asks. "I'm no fool," the fox replies. "I needed no other lesson than the ass's fate."

Frequently, the fox is depicted as using his cleverness to the detriment of others. In "The Fox and the Crow," for example, a crow has stolen a piece of cheese which she holds in her beak high in the branches of a tree. The fox sees her and begins to flatter her great beauty. "What a pity," the fox concludes, "that a creature with such a beautiful beak and feathers does not have an equally lovely voice!" The crow wishes to prove the fox wrong out of vanity and, opening her beak to sing, drops the piece of cheese. The fox leaps on the cheese at once, proving both the shallowness of false flattery and the foolishness of conceit.

At times, however, even cunning is not enough to win the fox what he wants. In "The Fox and the Grapes," for instance, a fox sees a bunch of grapes ripening in the sun high up on a vine. Despite his repeated efforts, the fox is unable to leap high enough to reach the grapes. "Never mind," the fox mutters as he walks away, "the grapes were probably sour anyway." From this story comes the expression "sour grapes," a phrase used to describe a person's denigrating something that the person wants but cannot have. In a similar story, "The Fox and the Bramble," the fox is about to fall from a hedge when he catches hold of a bramble for support. The thorns of the bramble wound the fox severely and he accuses the bramble of being inhospitable to those in need. "You were foolish," the bramble replies, "to cling to one who usually clings to others." The moral of the story is that no one should expect aid from those who usually seek it.

In the fable of "The Ant and the Grasshopper," a grasshopper is hungry during the winter and begs an ant for a share of the food that it has in its store. "Why did you not do what I did and spend the summer storing up grain?" the ant asks. "Because I preferred to sing all summer," the grasshopper replies. "Well," the ant says as it walks away, "if, instead of working, you sang all summer, then you must dance hungry all winter." The moral of the story is that the person who works hard will be rewarded while the person who wastes time in idleness will suffer when times are lean.

Not all of the stories attributed to Aesop are animal fables. "Zeus, Poseidon, Athena, and Momus" is a traditional Greek myth with the Olympian gods as central characters. Zeus, Poseidon, and Athena decide to have a contest to see which of them can produce the most perfect creation. Zeus makes a man, Athena makes a house, and Poseidon makes a bull. The god Momus, who personifies fault-finding and is never happy with anything, is then appointed by the gods to choose the winner of their contest. Momus, however, refuses to award the prize to any of the participants: The man was poorly made, Momus says, because the man does not have a window in his breast so that all can see what is hidden in his heart; the house was poorly made because it has no wheels to roll it away from unpleasant neighbors; and the bull was poorly made because he has to lower his eyes when he charges. In frustration at this reply, Zeus drives Momus from Mount Olympus forever, accusing him of being one of those critics who can only find flaws but never create useful things themselves. Other stories by Aesop also deal with other gods from Greek mythology, including Hermes and Heracles.

Even inanimate objects occasionally appear as the subjects of Aesop's fables. In "The Two Pots," for example, a bronze pot and an earthenware pot are carried off by a stream. The bronze pot urges the earthenware pot to remain close to him so that his strength can protect the weakness of the clay pot. "That is just what I am afraid of," the earthenware pot replies. "If I keep my distance from you, we may both be safe. If I get too close to you, your very strength may do me damage." This story suggests that humble people should not associate too closely with the mighty since, when trouble comes, the weak will suffer from having risen above their place.

The typical Aesop's fable seeks, therefore, to make its point through a homely and easily understood parable. Few of the legends attributed to Aesop are much longer than a paragraph. They teach a lesson simply and not through elaborate detail. The author draws character by introducing broad types of personalities rather than by creating highly differentiated individuals. According to tradition, the historical Aesop told stories to comment upon political events of his day. For example, he is said to have created the fable "The Frogs Who Wanted a King" because he wanted to suggest to the Athenians that they were better off under the tyrant Peisistratus (d. 527 B.C.E.) than they would be under a ruler whose faults they did not yet know. The majority of the tales that survive bearing Aesop's name are not political in nature. They deal with general personality types and draw broad conclusions that relate to all people.

Jeffrey L. Buller

Bibliography:

Aesop. *Aesopica*. Edited by Ben Edward Perry. Champaign: University of Illinois Press, 1952. The most thorough and scholarly collection of Aesopic texts. Contains the fables themselves and texts relating to the life of Aesop. The best place to begin for those who wish to undertake advanced study of the Aesopic canon.

Babrius and Phaedrus. *Babrius and Phaedrus*. Edited by Ben Edwin Perry. Cambridge, Mass.: Harvard University Press, 1975. Original texts and English translations of all Aesopic fables by the authors Babrius and Phaedrus. Includes a valuable historical introduction and a comprehensive survey of all Greek and Latin fables in the Aesopic tradition.

Blackham, Harold John. *The Fable as Literature*. Mineola, N.Y.: Dover, 1985. Blackham does not confine himself to Aesop, but this is the best introductory study to the literary use of fable. Includes an index and a bibliography.

Halliday, William Reginald. *Indo-European Folk-Tales and Greek Legend*. Cambridge, England: Cambridge University Press, 1933. Although somewhat dated, Halliday's discussion of Greek legend and its origin in Indo-European folklore is still a valuable survey of the origins of myth, saga, and fable.

Keidel, George Charles. *A Manual of Aesopic Fable Literature*. Geneva, Switzerland: Slatkine Reprints, 1974. Useful reference on the sources of Aesopic animal fable from antiquity to 1500.

Patterson, Annabel M. *Fables of Power: Aesopian Writing and Political History*. Durham, N.C.: Duke University Press, 1991. An extensive and highly readable study of Aesop's influence and of the imitations of his fables in English literature during the sixteenth and seventeenth centuries. Discusses the continuing role that Aesop's fables have played in European society.

THE AFFECTED YOUNG LADIES

Type of work: Drama
Author: Molière (Jean-Baptiste Poquelin, 1622-1673)
Type of plot: Comedy of manners
Time of plot: Seventeenth century
Locale: Paris
First performed: 1659; first published, 1660 as *Les Précieuses ridicules* (English translation, 1732)

Principal characters:
LA GRANGE and
DU CROISY, young men of Paris
MAGDELON and
CATHOS, the romantic ladies
THE MARQUIS DE MASCARILLE, La Grange's valet
VISCOUNT JODELET, Du Croisy's valet
GORGIBUS, Magdalon's father and Cathos' uncle

The Story:
 Gorgibus had brought his daughter Magdelon and his niece Cathos from their country home for a stay in Paris. There La Grange and Du Croisy, calling on them to propose marriage, were greatly disgusted by the affectation displayed by the young ladies, for the girls had adopted a manner prevalent everywhere in France, a combination of coquetry and artificiality. With the help of their valets, La Grange and Du Croisy determined to teach the silly young girls a lesson. One of the valets, Mascarille, loved to pass for a wit; he dressed himself as a man of quality and composed songs and verses.
 Gorgibus, meeting the two prospective suitors, inquired into their success with his niece and his daughter. The evasive answers he received made him decide to discuss the affair with the two ladies. He had to wait for them while they painted their faces and arranged their hair. When they were finally ready to receive him, he was enraged by their silly conversation.
 He had expected them to accept the two young men, who were wealthy and of good family, but the affected young ladies explained that they would spurn suitors who were so direct and sincere. Much to their disgust, the young men had proposed at their first meeting. They wanted lovers to be pensive and sorrowful, not joyful and healthy, as La Grange and Du Croisy had been. In addition, a young lady must refuse her lover's pleas in order to make him miserable. If possible, there should also be adventures: the presence of rivals, the scorn of fathers, elopements from high windows. Another fault the girls found with the two young men was that they were dressed simply, with no ribbons or feathers on their clothing. Poor Gorgibus thought that his daughter and niece were out of their minds, especially when they asked him to call them by other names, for their own were too vulgar. Cathos was to be called Aminte and Magdelon Polixene. Gorgibus knew only one thing after this foolish conversation—either the two girls would marry quickly or they would both become nuns.
 Even their maid could not understand the orders the girls gave her, for they talked in riddles. She announced that a young man was in the parlor, come to call on the two ladies. The caller was the Marquis de Mascarille, in reality La Grange's valet. The girls were enchanted with Mascarille, for he was a dandy of the greatest and most artificial wit. His bombastic puns were

67

so affected that the girls thought him the very soul of cleverness. He pretended to all sorts of accomplishments and acquaintances. On the spot, he composed terrible verses and songs, which he sang out of key and in a nasal tone. He claimed to have written a play that would be acted at the Royal Theater. He drew their attention to his beautiful dress, complete with ribbons, feathers, and perfume. Not to be outdone, the ladies boasted that although they knew no one in Paris as yet, a friend had promised to make them acquainted with all the fine dandies of the city. They were a perfect audience for the silly valet. They applauded each verse, each song, each bit of shallow wit.

The Viscount Jodelet, in reality Du Croisy's valet, joined the group. He claimed to be a hero of the wars, in command of two thousand horsemen, and he let the girls feel the scars left by deadly wounds he had received. The two scoundrels were hard put to outdo each other in telling the foolish girls ridiculous tales. When they talked of their visits with dukes and countesses, the girls were fascinated by their good connections. Running out of conversation, the two valets then asked the girls to arrange a party. They sent for musicians and other young people in order to have a proper dance. Mascarille, not being able to dance, accused the musicians of not keeping proper time, and Jodelet agreed with him.

The dance was in full swing when La Grange and Du Croisy appeared and fell upon the two impostors, raining blows on them and calling them rogues. Mascarille and Jodelet tried to pretend it had all been a joke, but their masters continued to beat them. When other servants appeared and began to strip the clothes from the two pretenders, the girls screamed in horror. La Grange and Du Croisy berated them for receiving servants better than they received their masters. They told the girls that if they loved the two scoundrels so well, they must love them without their masters' finery. Taking all the outer apparel from the rogues, La Grange and Du Croisy ordered them to continue the dance.

Gorgibus, having heard of the scandal on the streets of Paris, soundly berated the pranksters for the disgrace they had brought on his house. All Paris, all France even, would laugh at the joke, for the young people at the dance were now spreading the news up and down the streets and in the cafés. Gorgibus was furious with La Grange and Du Croisy for their trick, but knew the stupid girls deserved the treatment they had received. He sent the two valets packing and ordered the affected young ladies to hide themselves from the world. Then he cursed folly, affectation, and romantic songs, the causes of his horrible disgrace.

Critical Evaluation:

The Affected Young Ladies was first performed only one year after the author's permanent establishment in Paris; it was an enormous success and secured his reputation as the capital's foremost dramatist. The play is significant as a curious blend of the particular and the universal, for it not only ridicules a specific group in the Parisian society of Molière's day but also satirizes human foibles common to every time and place.

In the second quarter of the seventeenth century, there grew up in Paris, in reaction to the prevalent coarseness of manners in French society, a group known as the Précieux. This group centered on the literary salon of Madame de Rambouillet and was devoted to the cultivation of dignified speech and manners and the study, discussion, and patronage of literature. What began as a sort of cultural club, however, evolved in the hands of Madame de Rambouillet's successors into a fad distinguished only by its absurdity. These later Précieux, who met to gossip and act out scenes from popular romantic novels, spoke in a highly affected style that became for a time the rage in salons all over Paris. It was the craze led by this later circle that Molière lampooned in *Les Précieuses ridicules* (which is also frequently translated as *Two Precious Damsels*

Ridiculed). Madame de Rambouillet herself, realizing that Molière's barbs were aimed not at her but at her successors, was one of the play's ardent admirers and invited Molière to stage three performances at her home.

Given the specificity of the play's target, it is easy to imagine its success with Molière's contemporaries. They understood all the references and recognized the follies of the characters. They laughed at Cathos' and Magdelon's assumption of romantic pseudonyms ("The names Polixene and Aminte are far more graceful, you must agree") and their avowal to live their lives as romantic heroines; they sympathized with the down-to-earth Gorgibus and his bewilderment in the face of his daughter's and niece's "gibberish" ("No doubt about it; they're over the edge"). If audiences have continued to laugh over this play for more than three centuries, the answer lies in the universality of Molière's comedy. The impulse toward preciosity is not exclusively a seventeenth century French phenomenon, but rather a constitutional weakness common to all people. Every time and place has its précieux because the desire for distinctiveness and novelty of expression seems to be part of human nature. Thus it is that people laugh at Cathos and Magdelon, at Mascarille and Jodelet, even as they recognize some of their folly and affectation as their own.

Molière found the perfect vehicle for making audiences laugh at human folly in plays such as *The Affected Young Ladies*. In the development of this style, he drew heavily on two sources: traditional French farce and Italian *commedia dell'arte*. Using and creatively transforming features from each, he molded the kind of dramatic comedy for which he became famous. Masks, for example, which date back to ancient times and which had been revived in Italian drama, were thereupon adopted by French neoclassicists, who used them to characterize types such as scheming valets, jealous husbands, unscrupulous liars, misers, prudes, braggarts, coquettes, libertines, and pedants. Molière developed his own character types on the basis of old stock figures; two of his most famous types were Sganarelle and Mascarille. He became a master of the device of the mask and developed the art of relying on gesture and posture rather than facial expression to convey meaning. After expanding, modifying, and exploring all the theatrical possibilities of masks, however, Molière went on to do what the *commedia dell'arte* never attempted: He depicted through his characters all the social relationships and class conditions within French society, exposing the vices of high and low alike with his wit.

In an early play such as *The Affected Young Ladies*, the masks are still of standard farcical types. In the play's original performances, Molière himself played Mascarille, wearing a mask, while Jodelet, a widely popular slapstick comedian, performed under his own name, wearing the white powder mask for which he was famous. The figures of Mascarille and Jodelet—valets who have a talent for parading about, passing for what they are not—represent the folly of affectation and falseness. They are the agents through which Molière ridicules the representatives of the Précieux, Cathos and Magdelon; they are brought to humiliation through their gullible acceptance of the valets' deception. The message in *The Affected Young Ladies* is basically the same as in all of Molière's plays: Excess, whether of vice or virtue, leads to downfall. Molière, a constant and thorough observer of life, early concluded that people who become dominated by a single passion, idea, or obsession lose their common sense. Because the two young ladies in this play have been carried beyond all bounds of reason by their passion for romances, they are easily duped by the valets.

The plot in *The Affected Young Ladies*, as in all of Molière's comedies, is minimal; it is merely a vehicle to allow characters their full comic play, which is the playwright's primary purpose. Molière was a master of all the verbal laugh-getting devices, including double entendre, echo-dialogues, and malapropisms, but above all he was the supreme farceur. Some fine examples of traditional, rollicking French farce in this play include Mascarille's entrance with the sedan-chair bearers; the drubbing of the valets by La Grange and Du Croisy; and Jodelet's stripping of his countless layers of garments. For this reason, a play such as *The Affected Young Ladies* must be seen performed for full effect. Molière's greatness lies in his ability to fuse astute criticism of the follies and absurdities of human behavior with unsurpassed comedy. Ironically, perhaps his greatest and most lasting tribute came from one of his contemporaries who, in a malicious attempt to slander him, called Molière "the first jester of France."

"Critical Evaluation" by Nancy G. Ballard

Bibliography:
Backer, Dorothy. *Precious Women.* New York: Basic Books, 1974. A historical study that shows that preciousness (*préciosité*) was an early feminist literary movement. Explains that Molière made fun only of the pretentious and not truly creative precious writers who were his contemporaries.
Lawrence, Francis L. *Molière: The Comedy of Unreason.* New Orleans: Tulane University Press, 1968. Explores conflicts between rational and irrational characters in Molière's comedies, and examines parody and comic representations of love in *The Affected Young Ladies.*
Wadsworth. Philip A. *Molière and the Italian Theatrical Tradition.* 2d ed. Birmingham, Ala.: Summa Publications, 1987. Analyzes the profound influence on Molière of Italian actors and playwrights. Discusses the importance of nonverbal gestures and wordplay in *The Affected Young Ladies.*
Walker, Hallam. *Molière.* Rev. ed. Boston: Twayne, 1990. Contains an excellent introduction to Molière's comedies and an annotated bibliography of important critical studies on the playwright. Also examines the role of parody and social satire in *The Affected Young Ladies.*
Yarrow, P. J. *A Literary History of France.* Vol. 2 in *The Seventeenth Century: 1600-1715.* London: Ernest Benn, 1967. A general history of seventeenth century French literature that includes one chapter with a very clear introduction to Molière's plays. Yarrow discusses role reversal and the conflict between illusion and reality in *The Affected Young Ladies.*

THE AFTERNOON OF A FAUN

Type of work: Poetry
Author: Stéphane Mallarmé (1842-1898)
First published: L'Après-midi d'un faune, 1876 (English translation, 1958)

Stéphane Mallarmé's *L'Après-midi d'un faune* is first and foremost poetry, but its origins link it to the theater. At the time of its composition, Mallarmé described it as a "heroic interlude," a fragment of a dramatic presentation. In the same letter, however, he also refers to its lines as "verses," and when the text was ready for publication, he submitted it for inclusion in the third collection of *Le Parnasse contemporain* in 1874. Rejected for inclusion in this volume, the poem finally appeared in its own limited edition in 1876.

Mallarmé's subtitle calls the work an "eclogue," a word derived from the idea of a poetic fragment that in later usage came to designate a work with a bucolic setting. While both senses of the word fit the text that follows, that alone does not prepare the reader to understand the first lines on an initial reading.

In the manner of the French classical theater, the faun's speech draws on events that have already begun and translates past action into dramatic discourse. The first line, "These nymphs, I want to perpetuate them," indicates from the initial descriptive adjective a need to refer to circumstances that the faun knows but that the reader must intuit. The French phrase "je les veux perpétuer," uses archaic word order and links the speech to past time, underlining both the dramatic conventions and the mythological persona that define the faun.

As with much of Mallarmé's poetry, the reader must imagine the action. Here, however, Mallarmé supplies more obvious clues than he does in his more difficult poems. Idyllic images immediately lead the reader into a reverie resembling that of the faun. Given the reader's participation in the creation of the poem, the experience is all the more likely to touch the reader personally.

The faun has apparently just awakened from a dream in which he saw the nymphs. Mallarmé immediately forces the reader to exert his interpretive faculties by the use of nontraditional language to describe this experience. When the nymphs appear in "leur incarnat léger," the pale rosy color that might normally be a descriptive adjective takes on the substance of a noun. The faun himself is "drowsy with bushy sleep." The adjective "touffus" may allude to the woodland setting in which the faun slept, but its other possible use in describing an involved style of writing suggests the faun's confused state of mind. He asks, after a pause, whether he has loved a dream, since the empty woods around him suggest that he has been alone. As he reflects on his memory, however, a number of specific details attest to the reality of the experience. There were clearly two nymphs. The first, he recalls, had the cold blue eyes of chastity. The other was defined by the music of her sighs. The faun expands on the musical sound, similar to the tone he can produce on his panpipes, and on the breath that produced it, warm as a summer breeze.

Emboldened by these specific memories, the faun invokes the "Sicilian shores" that his vanity would "pillage" to tell him what actually happened. Here Mallarmé introduces the first of three italicized segments of the poem in which the faun, playing both parts of the still theatrical dialogue, seems to answer his own question. Yet the answer remains incomplete. The faun recalls only that he was cutting reeds to play music when he suddenly saw an "animal whiteness" that could have been either swans or naiads.

Then the memory, along with the italics, disappears. The faun remains alone under a hot sun, thinking that his own sexual longing may have inspired the fantasy. As he awakens, presumably

71

returning to the present, he finds himself beneath an "ancient flood of light." The light of the sun, constant over time, represents to him a link with the past and recalls the state in which he had awakened in the first lines of the poem troubled by a doubt that came from "old night." Both images suggest the hold the past still has upon him. Still contemplating his memories, the faun finds evidence of a kiss in the mark of a tooth that has bitten his breast. Still he hesitates, knowing that beauty can deceive and that he seems to have confused it with his own "credulous song." Perhaps all that happened was that he had a banal glimpse of the two fleeing creatures.

Even if the vision led to an imagined encounter, the faun knows how to relive the event. He addresses his panpipes, "the instrument of flight," asking them to make the lakes "flower again." The pipes may evoke the flight of the nymphs, but they also enable the faun's imagination to take flight in the sense that the images of the nymphs will bloom through his artistic re-creation. This imaging of the nymphs draws on important analogies between Mallarmé's work and the poems of Charles Baudelaire. In *Les Fleurs du mal* (1857), Baudelaire developed a vision of a female figure as muse that both inspired and tormented the poet. Similarly, Mallarmé's faun says that he will "speak at length of goddesses," whom he seems to dominate (he "removes the belts from their shades" to reveal their physical being) at the same time that he allows them to dominate him. In a further association with Baudelaire, the vision of the nymphs reminds the faun of intoxication. He will reveal the intimate picture of them just as he saw light through the empty skins of grapes when he had spent a long afternoon "sucking out the brightness" of their apparently intoxicating juice. The fusion of images of bright light, fruits of nature, and the female figures emphasizes the role of woman as muse. She inspires the faun's visions that are linked to his music and provides an analogy to the creation of the poet's songs.

The inspiration provided by the nymphs leads to Mallarmé's second italicized section, much more explicit than the first, in which the faun recalls finding the two nymphs asleep and ravishing them. Nature images in this section reinforce the sensuality of the experience. At first, the faun sees only fragments of the nymphs' bodies as his eye pierces the reeds. Then he runs toward them as toward a mass of blooming roses. More Baudelairian themes occur as he likens the light reflected in their hair to jewels and evokes the secret perfume of the flowers.

Between this and the final italicized section, the faun pauses to reflect on the "wrath of virgins" that he has provoked. The nymphs' resistance increased his desire, but apparently they did not continue to resist long, as fear "abandons their innocence." Despite references to their trembling and tears, the passage ends with emotions that are "less sad." The nymphs seem moved by the desire of the faun. Whereas the nymphs awaken to desire, the faun begins to see the harm of his attack. The final italicized section begins with his reference to "my crime." Devoted to pleasure as he is, however, the faun cannot think of seduction in negative terms. A number of positive references seek to justify his action as he "gaily vanquished their fears" with an "ardent laugh under the happy folds" of the nymphs. He even sees a divine sanction for the seduction in that "the gods had kept their kisses so well mingled."

By the end of this scene a reversal has taken place. The nymphs, no longer blushing, are inspired to passion by the faun's advances. Yet the encounter ends. The nymphs, whom the faun now describes as his "prey," free themselves, leaving "without pity for the sob still intoxicating" him. The faun may have sought to exploit the nymphs, but he now sees himself as the victim of the emotions he has released. The faun does not remain emotionally engaged for long. Immediately after the italicized memory ends, he looks to the future and to others who will bring him new happiness, "knoting their tresses around the horns on my forehead." Each passionate encounter, far from representing a unique event, forms a part of the lascivious pattern of nature.

The faun sees his passion as resembling a ripe pomegranate surrounded by bees that represent "the eternal swarming of desire."

The faun's erotic insouciance echoes the traditions linked to such creatures in classical times. The faun invokes this past tradition as the setting of the festival of nature that will take place on "Etna, visited by Venus." The goddess arrives to touch the mountain's lava with her "naïve heels." Thus she recalls the innocence of the nymphs, but her hovering light, as she barely touches the ground, parallels that often attributed to the muse by the Romantic poets. Ethereal though the nymph may be, the faun sees her as yet another woman because, when sleep finally extinguishes the flame of his desire, he concludes this section with the exclamation, "I hold the queen!" This declaration of possession, almost as if he were referring to the queen in a deck of cards, reasserts the faun's dominance.

The poem asks whether the fatigued sleep is a punishment for the faun's actions, to which he answers that it is not, but that he merely "succumbs to the proud silence of noon" for a mid-day nap, his mouth open to the sun, the producer of wine. In the last line of the poem, an adieu to the nymphs before the faun goes to sleep, he declares, "I will see the shadow that you become." He will sleep and dream, again, of his vision of the nymphs. The time invoked by this final section seems to conflict with the title of the poem. If, after the major events described, the faun falls asleep in the noon sun, the "afternoon" of the title has not yet begun. The question arises what the true subject of the poem actually is. The faun will probably spend the afternoon re-creating the events in his dream. If the afternoon is the true subject, the major importance attaches not to the event but to its re-creation, the element evocative of the composition of the poet.

Dorothy M. Betz

Bibliography:

Fowlie, Wallace. *Mallarmé*. Chicago: University of Chicago Press, 1953. The first part of this study analyzes the dominant themes in Mallarmé's work. In the second part, Fowlie discusses specific texts. Chapter 5 is devoted to a discussion of the genesis of the poem *The Afternoon of a Faun* as well as to a close reading and interpretation.

Gill, Austin. *The Early Mallarmé*. 2 vols. Oxford, England: Clarendon Press, 1979. Two chapters in volume 1, discussing Mallarmé's early compositions, focus on his use of the god Pan and provide background to *The Afternoon of a Faun*.

St. Aubyn, Frederic Chase. *Stéphane Mallarmé*. Rev. ed. New York: Twayne, 1989. Discusses *The Afternoon of a Faun* in chapter 5, "The Secret Terror of the Flesh," and provides a close and accurate reading of the text.

Shaw, Mary Lewis. *Performance in the Texts of Mallarmé: The Passage from Art to Ritual*. University Park: Pennsylvania State University Press, 1993. In chapter 8, Shaw analyzes *The Afternoon of a Faun* with an emphasis on its theoretical elements. An examination of the evolution of Mallarmé's text reveals the work's distinctly theatrical genesis.

Woolley, Grange. *Stéphane Mallarmé: 1842-1898*. Madison, N.J.: Drew University, 1981. Begins with a lengthy biographical sketch followed by short essays on various poems. The discussion of *The Afternoon of a Faun* provides information on the poem's sources and critical reception and concludes with a narrative analysis.

AGAINST THE GRAIN

Type of work: Novel
Author: Joris-Karl Huysmans (1848-1907)
Type of plot: Character study
Time of plot: Late 1800's
Locale: Paris
First published: À rebours, 1884 (English translation, 1922)

Principal character:
JEAN DES ESSEINTES, an aesthete

The Story:

The Des Esseintes were an old family. In the Château de Lourps, the portraits of the ancestors were those of rugged troopers and stern cavalrymen. The family, however, had followed a familiar pattern; through two hundred years of intermarriage and indulgence, the men had become increasingly effeminate. Now the only remaining Des Esseintes was Jean, a man of thirty. By a kind of atavism, Jean's looks resembled his first grandsire. The resemblance, however, was in looks only.

Jean's childhood had been unhappy. His father, living in Paris most of the time, visited Jean briefly at school once in a while when he wished to give moral counsel. Occasionally, he went to see his wife at the château. Jean was always present at those hushed interviews in which his mother took little interest. Jean's mother had a strange dread of light. Passing her days in her shaded boudoir, she avoided contact with the world. At the Jesuit school, Jean became a precocious student of Latin and acquired a fair knowledge of theology. At the same time, he was a stubborn, withdrawn child who refused all discipline. The patient fathers let him follow his own bent, for there was little else they could do. Both his parents died while he was young; at his majority, he came into complete control of his inheritance.

In his contacts with the world, Jean went through two phases. At first, he lived a wild, dissolute life. For a time, he was content with ordinary mistresses. His first love was Miss Urania, an American acrobat. She was strong and healthy; Jean yearned for her as an anemic young girl might long for a Hercules. Nevertheless, Miss Urania was quite feminine, even prudish in her embraces. Their liaison prematurely hastened his impotence.

Another mistress was a brunette ventriloquist. One day, he purchased a tiny black sphinx and a chimera of polychrome clay. Bringing them into the bedchamber, he prevailed on her to imitate Gustave Flaubert's famous dialogue between the Sphinx and the Chimera. His mistress, however, was sulky at having to perform offstage.

After that phase, Jean began to be disgusted with people. He saw that men reared in parochial schools, as he was, were timid and boring. Men who had been educated in the public schools were more courageous but even more boring. In a frantic effort to find companionship, he wildly sought out the most carnal pastimes and the most perverted pleasures.

Jean had never been strong, and from childhood he had been afflicted with scrofula. Now his nerves were growing weaker. The back of his neck always pained him; his hand trembled when he lifted a light object. In a burst of despairing eccentricity, he gave a farewell dinner to his lost virility. The meal was served on a black table to the sound of funeral marches. The waitresses were nude black women. The plates were edged in black; the menu included dark bread, meat with licorice sauce, and wine served in dark glasses.

At thirty years old, Jean decided to withdraw from the world. Having concluded that artistry was much superior to nature, he vowed that in his retreat he would be completely artificial. He found a suitable house in a remote suburb of Paris and made elaborate preparations for his retirement. The upper floor was given over to his two elderly servants, who had to wear felt coverings on their shoes at all times. He reserved the downstairs for himself. The walls were paneled in leather like book binding, and the only color for ceilings and trim was deep orange. In his dining room, he simulated a ship's cabin and installed aquariums in front of the windows. The study was lined with precious books. With great art, he contrived a luxurious bedroom that looked monastically simple.

Among his paintings, Jean treasured two works of Gustave Moreau that depicted Salomé and the head of John the Baptist. He pondered long over the meaning of the scenes. History being silent on the personality of Salomé, Jean decided that Moreau had re-created her perfectly. To him, she was the incarnation of woman.

His library was his chief concern. Among the Latin writers, he had no love for the classicists: Vergil, for example, he found incredibly dull. Nevertheless, he took great delight in Petronius, who had brought to life Roman decadence under Nero. He ardently loved a few of the French sensualists, Paul Verlaine and Charles Baudelaire among them. He also had a small collection of obscure Catholic writers whose refinement and disdain for the world suited his own temperament.

For months, his life was regular and satisfying. He breakfasted at five and dined at eleven. About dawn, he had his supper and went to bed. Because of his weak stomach, he was most abstemious in his diet. After a time, his old ailments came back to plague him. He could eat or drink very little, and his nerves pained him. After weeks of torture, he fainted. When his servants found him, they called a neighborhood doctor who could do little for him. At last, Jean seemed to recover, and he scolded the servants for having been so concerned. With sudden energy, he made plans to take a trip to England.

After his luggage had been packed, he took a cab into Paris. To while away the hours before train time, he visited a wine cellar frequented by English tourists and had dinner at an English restaurant. Realizing afresh that the pleasure of travel lies only in the anticipation, he drove himself home that same evening and thus avoided the banality of actually going somewhere. At one stage of his life, Jean had loved artificial flowers. Now he came to see that it would be more satisfying to have real flowers that looked artificial. He promptly amassed a collection of misshapen, coarse plants that satisfied his aesthetic needs.

Jean's energy, however, soon dissipated. His hands trembled, his neck pained him, and his stomach refused food. For weeks, he dreamed away his days in a half-stupor. Thinking of his past, he was shocked to realize that his wish to withdraw from the world was a vestige of his education under the Jesuits. Finally, he became prey to hallucinations. He smelled unaccountable odors, and strange women kept him company.

One day he was horrified to look into his mirror. His wasted face seemed that of a stranger. He sent for a doctor from Paris. After the physician had given him injections of peptone, Jean returned to something like normal. Then he mistook a prescription for a dietary supplement for a recipe for an enema. For a while, Jean was entranced with the notion of getting all his sustenance through enemas. One more activity, eating, would therefore be unnecessary.

Then the doctor sent his little artificial world crashing; he ordered Jean to leave his retreat and go live a normal social life in Paris. Otherwise, his patient would be in danger of death or at least of a protracted illness with tuberculosis. More afraid of his illness than he was of the stupid world, Jean gave the necessary orders and glumly watched the movers begin their work.

Critical Evaluation:

Against the Grain became the central document of the French Decadents, partly because its elaborate description of Des Esseintes' tastes in art and literature established a frame of reference for Decadent writers and painters and partly because the characterization of Des Esseintes helped to define the Decadent sensibility. The novel instructed the acolytes of the movement in what to read, how to appreciate what they read, and how to pass cynical judgment on the affairs of a world, which they were fully entitled to despise. It sent people forth in search of new ways to experience the world, and it offered philosophical arguments to justify all manner of self-indulgent fetishisms. Its most attentive readers were doubtless careful to bear in mind that the whole thing was a joke, but it has to be admitted that not everyone noticed that.

As the story begins, Des Esseintes has already given up the kinds of activity that most people think of as decadent. He has abandoned all his mistresses and concluded his experiments in unnatural passion. His experiments with drugs never really got far, because drug-taking only made him vomit. His one desire is to seek solace in well-furnished isolation. He isolates himself in carefully designed luxury, like a castaway on an island infinitely better in its equipment than that on which Robinson Crusoe found himself. Incidentally, Jean-Jacques Rousseau, the champion of the essential goodness of nature and the human spirit, to whose ideas Huysmans and the Decadents were diametrically opposed, recommended *Robinson Crusoe* (1719) as the only book that a boy needed by way of education.

It is important to notice that Des Esseintes does not see this process of careful isolation as an abandonment of human relationships. He craves contact with the minds of men, as others do, but he desires to refine that contact into a peculiar kind of perfection by restricting his contact to the works of art that are the finest product of human endeavor and the best medium of human communication.

Unlike many who retreat from society, Des Esseintes is not intent upon private communion with God or nature. He acknowledges the contribution made by nature to the hothouse flowers and perfumes of which he is a connoisseur, but insists that they are essentially products of human artifice. He loves the exotic because, for him, exoticism is the ultimate manifestation of human imagination and human artistry. His antipathy to the natural is reflected in antipathy to the realistic; he despises representative works of art, preferring those that attempt to transform and transcend ordinary experience. This is one reason why he has retired from the company of actual human beings. In the flesh, people cannot rise above their essential ordinariness; their artwork offers something more.

The character of Des Esseintes is to some extent a caricature. Some of his tastes and mannerisms are borrowed, tongue-in-cheek, from the most famous of contemporary Parisian men-about-town, Count Robert de Montesquiou. Des Esseintes is also a fantastic self-projection of the author, and there is an unmistakable depth of feeling behind the calculatedly absurd mask. The character's final decision to throw himself into the arms of the Church—not because its doctrines are true but rather because they are fantastic—anticipates the direction the author was to take in real life. Huysmans' account of a man who ardently desires to do everything in stark opposition to the way things are conventionally done is based on his authentic and wholehearted rejection of the tyranny of normality.

Against the Grain never tries to deny that an uncompromisingly Decadent worldview cannot actually work as a practical, or better yet impractical, way of living. Experiments in the building of private utopias are always doomed to failure. The narrative is content to insist that the Decadent's view of life and art is clearer and more logical, aesthetically and morally, than anything that passes for common sense or orthodox faith. The pose that Des Esseintes adopts is not entirely sincere, and contains a strong element of self-mockery, but its insincerity and irony are the velvet glove that overlies the iron determination of Des Esseintes' condemnation of the world. The moral parables he derives by comparing barmaids with prostitutes, and by throwing crusts of bread to a mob of street urchins, have a sharp satirical bite.

The key to Des Esseintes' entire enterprise is that he is sick, in body, mind, and heart. The treatment of his sickness eventually leads to the most absurd and most brutal of all his inversions of normality, when he begins to take his daily nourishment by enema. His doctor leaves him in no doubt that if he continues to nurture his sickness instead of trying to cure it, he will die. At this point, Des Esseintes capitulates to the tyranny of fate and gives up his experiment. He never surrenders the conviction, however, that his sickness has allowed him to step outside the world of the commonplace and look back at it objectively, thus giving him a clearer insight into the condition of the world than what is contained in the self-satisfied illusions of healthy, normal people.

Huysmans does not ask or expect his readers to sympathize with Des Esseintes, or to accept his conclusions. The text is designed to provide a challenge rather than be a guidebook. It intends to make its readers take a step back from the moral and aesthetic judgments that they take for granted, and to wonder whether such judgments might profitably be inverted. Huysmans scrupulously leaves the verdict open, and is careful never to forsake his sense of humor while summing up the evidence.

"Critical Evaluation" by Brian Stableford

Bibliography:
Antosh, Ruth B. *Reality and Illusion in the Novels of J.-K. Huysmans*. Amsterdam: Rodopi, 1986. Rejects the opposition of realism and decadence, which has dominated criticism of Huysmans. Sees the entire work as presenting the tension between the real and the imaginary. Excellent analysis of memory in *Against the Grain*.

Baldick, Robert. *The Life of J.-K. Huysmans*. Oxford, England: Clarendon Press, 1955. Still the most authoritative biography of Huysmans available in English. Contains valuable information about the writing of *Against the Grain*.

Ellis, Havelock. Introduction to *Against the Grain*, by J.-K. Huysmans. Translated by John Howard. Mineola, N.Y.: Dover, 1969. A fascinating reaction to Huysmans' novel from an important English psychologist.

Friedman, Melvin J. "The Symbolist Novel: Huysmans to Malraux." In *Modernism*, edited by Malcom Bradbury and James McFarlane. Atlantic Highlands, N.J.: Humanities Press, 1978. Defines the Symbolist novel as being more concerned with words than with reality. As such, *Against the Grain* has great significance in the development of the modern novel.

Lloyd, Christopher. *J.-K. Huysmans and the Fin-de-Siècle Novel*. Edinburgh, Scotland: Edinburgh University Press, 1990. Defines the *fin de siècle* period as it applies to literature, and charts in detail the influence of *Against the Grain* on other writers.

THE AGE OF ANXIETY

Type of work: Poetry
Author: W. H. Auden (1907-1973)
First published: 1947

W. H. Auden was one of the outstanding poets of the twentieth century. He had not only the vision and skill of a major poet but the necessary luck, or perspicacity, to create poetry that many of his contemporaries felt spoke for them. He spoke their language, he had the "sound" of the 1930's, and he found that sound early. He played a part in shaping the decade because his words and ideas had helped shape many of the people who helped influence the course of events. Auden went on composing poetry for another thirty years and more, but he made his mark when barely thirty years old himself.

Auden was born in 1907 in England, where he continued to live until emigrating to the United States in 1939 just before World War II broke out in Europe. He studied at Oxford, published his first book of poems in his early twenties, and several more in the next decade. He also published plays, some of which were given radio performance, and he supported himself by teaching school; once in America, he took temporary positions at a number of colleges.

Although Auden never stopped challenging his readers, his work began to lose currency during the 1940's. His career peaked early, and while his early success guaranteed him a substantial readership for the remainder of his days, many felt that his career was on a downward slope in later years.

Auden wrote *The Age of Anxiety* right after World War II. Its setting recalls the poem he had written on the outbreak of that war, which begins

> I sit in one of the dives
> On Fifty-Second Street
> Uncertain and afraid
> As the clever hopes expire
> Of a low dishonest decade.

It is as though the poet were completing a circuit after a six-year hiatus, but there is little other similarity between "September 1, 1939" and *The Age of Anxiety*. The former is driven urgently by the need to respond to the impending cataclysm after Germany had invaded Poland. *The Age of Anxiety*, on the other hand, although it too is set during World War II, was actually written a year and more after the war's end. The poem contains many passages that are amusing, entertaining, and instructive, but overall the work feels desultory and under-motivated. Many critics agree that it is not among Auden's finer achievements.

To understand the attractiveness of Auden's earlier work it needs to be seen against the backdrop of its immediate precursors, principal among them the poems of T. S. Eliot, Ezra Pound, H. D., Marianne Moore, and Edith Sitwell among the modernists, and Robert Graves, John Betjeman, and W. B. Yeats among those who opposed the modernist temper. The figure of the long-lived Thomas Hardy, born in 1840 but still writing poems during the 1920's, also looms large in this configuration. Auden took it upon himself to make a poetry that tried to reconcile these various camps.

Auden's innovations were characteristically paradoxical. He kept up with the innovators of the previous generation by returning innovation to traditional measures. He resuscitated many old forms and gave them a contemporary aspect. He was particularly fond of, and adroit with,

Anglo-Saxon, or Old English, verse techniques, bringing its heavy alliteration and paucity of articles into play while presenting a modern landscape or theory. *The Age of Anxiety* shows this technique, as in the passage with Auden's rendering of a radio bulletin during World War II:

> *Now the news. Night raids on*
> *Five cities. Fires started.*
> *Pressure applied by pincer movement*
> *In threatening thrust. Third Division*
> *Enlarges beachhead. Lucky charm*
> *Saves sniper. Sabotage hinted*
> *In steel-mill stoppage. Strong point held*
> *By fanatical Nazis. Canal crossed*
> *By heroic marines.*

Auden uses four "n" sounds in the first of these lines, two "f" sounds in the second, three "p" sounds in the third, and so on. He combines the Anglo-Saxon tendency to do without articles, with an up-to-date telegrammatic manner appropriate to news headlines. Like many other poems by Auden, there is a good deal of contemporary slang from the 1940's, as well as topical references to such objects as juke-boxes and radios. Auden thus spans the entire history of the English language.

The Age of Anxiety is called a Baroque eclogue; traditionally, an eclogue is a pastoral dialogue between bucolics who are really erudite and sophisticated persons playing at being bucolics. They go—or pretend to go—to the country for refreshment and relaxation, then return to town renewed. Auden's eclogue is baroque insofar as it resembles a style in art and architecture from the sixteenth, seventeenth, and early eighteenth centuries in Europe, a style marked by strict forms and elaborate ornamentation.

The bucolics in *The Age of Anxiety* are four people who meet in a bar one evening during World War II. They are Quant, an older man and an Irish emigré; Malin, also older and a medical intelligence officer on leave from the Canadian Air Force; Rosetta, who is probably in her thirties, was raised in Britain, and is now a successful buyer for a U.S. department store; and Emble, a young and handsome U.S. sailor. In part 1, the first, prose part of the prologue, Auden provides a historical frame (World War II) that is also timeless (wartime). During a war, Auden tells us, bar-business booms, and "everyone is reduced to the anxious status of a shady character or a displaced person, and becomes a worshiper of chance." So they seek out "an unprejudiced space in which nothing particular ever happens"—a bar.

It is All Hallows Eve. First one character, then the next, speaks to himself or herself his or her thoughts. When the radio delivers a wartime news bulletin, memories of the war revive in the four characters. Rosetta then speaks, permitted to do so by the common topic of the news. The others respond, and shortly they are engaged in a discussion of the present. Another radio bulletin, and they decide to share a round of drinks. Malin begins to wax metaphysical—"Let us then/ Consider rather the incessant Now of/ The traveller through time. . . ." The alcohol makes them convivial, and they move from bar-stools to a booth.

Part 2, "The Seven Ages," does not have much to do with war but consists of the quartet's various responses to, and reflections upon, human fate as seen through its seven stages: childhood, adolescence, early adulthood, the struggle to succeed, success and recognition, the beginning of senescence, and old age sliding into death. (Of course, the fact of war casts its shadow over the entire recitation.)

Sobered and scared by the picture they have jointly conjured, they turn to Rosetta, the only woman, for consolation, but she can offer only the comfort of the "regressive road to Grandmother's House." Part 2 ends with the bucolics getting drunker, seeking out "that state of prehistoric happiness which, by human beings, can only be imagined in terms of a landscape bearing a symbolic resemblance to the human body." In their separate fantasies, although this is not clear to the reader at the time, they imagine themselves together encountering what ensues.

Part 3, "The Seven Stages," consists of their imaginary wanderings—alone, all together, or in various pairings—across a countryside and through a city, commenting upon the symbolism of the mythic landscapes. The stages of the title are the episodes of this journey but also the settings where their journey plays itself out. Finally, they find themselves facing the last half of the seventh stage, a desert of Joshua trees and giant cacti, and anxiously ask themselves if they are, against all odds, about to succeed in completing this dream quest. Their fears are confirmed: "For the world from which their journey has been one long flight rises up before them now." They come to themselves; the bartender is flicking the lights on and off, as it is closing time. Rosetta invites them back to her place for a snack and a nightcap, and they all accept.

Part 4, "The Dirge," occurs as the quartet shares a cab uptown. It is a stately, highly alliterative poem in dancing measures for whoever had spared them from the dangers of the wilderness, of praise and lament "for such a great one who . . . has always died or disappeared."

Part 5, "The Masque," plays out at Rosetta's apartment. Quant and Malin sing; Rosetta and Emble dance, feeling their casual attraction grow. Later, sitting, they kiss, and exchange vows in stychomythic alternation. After some high-spirited interchanges among the four, Quant and Malin decide that the time has come to depart. Rosetta escorts them to the elevator. When she returns, Emble has passed out on her bed. Rosetta, half sad, half relieved, soliloquizes above his sleeping body, to the effect that it is all for the best and that their encounter will remain forever a lovely dream, safe from the slow erosion of suburban reality. In Part 6, "Epilogue," Quant and Malin bid each other goodnight and each goes home alone with his thoughts, returned to his solitary condition.

W. H. Auden begins his Baroque eclogue not in some grand European park but in a setting that recalls the bar-life of midtown Manhattan, a life Auden knew well. He loved New York, and became an American citizen (he is, in fact, often classified as an American poet), but of course he remained more British than not. In *The Age of Anxiety*, for example, written six years after he had emigrated, three of his four characters are not native Americans, and the landscapes are often British; moreover, the use of Americanisms accords uneasily with the prevailing English diction.

Through its very pervasiveness, Auden's heavy use of alliteration, which in this work brings along with it a diction that suggests the Anglo-Saxon origins of modern English, overwhelms distinctions between characters. Yet, this is not a play in the dramatic sense of the term, but rather an "entertainment," where the pretense of the actors should be allowed to show.

Part 3 aside—which is confusing and unnecessarily mystifying as characters hop in and out of airplanes, boats, and trains—*The Age of Anxiety* contains many delights for the fans of Auden. The work features many of his familiar devices, his logical reversals, clever puns, philosophical nuggets, and irreverent asides. For the student of verse-forms, it offers a wide variety of formal techniques that Auden had either revived or invented.

David Bromige

Bibliography:
Bloomfield, Barry, and Edward Mendelsohn. *W. H. Auden: A Bibliography, 1924-1969.* 2d ed. Charlottesville: University Press of Virginia, 1972. Excellent and thorough bibliography.

Callan, Edward. *Auden, a Carnival of Intellect.* Oxford, England: Oxford University Press, 1983. Full, sound study of Auden's life and works. Views Auden as a "professional" poet rather than one seeking constant inspiration. Discusses the wide range of Auden's forms and techniques and defines his "perennial themes" to be consciousness and the human condition.

Carpenter, Humphrey. *W. H. Auden, a Biography.* Boston: Houghton Mifflin, 1981. Gives a detailed account of the poet's life and situates the works in relation to it. Good primary and secondary bibliographies.

Spears, Monroe K., ed. *Auden: A Collection of Critical Essays.* Englewood Cliffs, N.J.: Prentice-Hall, 1964. A somewhat uneven but highly useful collection of essays.

Spender, Stephen, ed. *W. H. Auden: A Tribute.* New York: Macmillan, 1975. Essays by those who knew him in England—Stephen Spender, Geoffrey Grigson, Sir John Betjeman, Cyril Connolly, and Christopher Isherwood—and those who knew him principally in America—Chester Kallman, John Hollander, Oliver Sacks, and others.

Wright, George T. *W. H. Auden.* New York: Twayne, 1969. Makes rather too much of the "mystification" of Auden's verses, but a sound discussion of Auden's appeal to society, his distinctions between the private and public, and his philosophical progress.

THE AGE OF INNOCENCE

Type of work: Novel
Author: Edith Wharton (1862-1937)
Type of plot: Social realism
Time of plot: Late nineteenth century
Locale: New York City
First published: 1920

Principal characters:

NEWLAND ARCHER, a young attorney
MAY WELLAND, his fiancée
COUNTESS ELLEN OLENSKA, her cousin

The Story:

Newland Archer, a handsome and eligible young attorney engaged to lovely May Welland, learned that the engagement would be announced at a party to welcome his fiancée's cousin, Countess Ellen Olenska. This reception for Ellen constituted a heroic sacrifice on the part of the many Welland connections, for her marriage to a ne'er-do-well Polish count had not improved her position so far as rigorous and straitlaced New York society was concerned. The fact that she contemplated a divorce action also made her suspect, and, to cap it all, her rather bohemian way of living did not conform to what her family expected of a woman who had made an unsuccessful marriage.

Newland Archer's engagement to May was announced. At the same party, Archer was greatly attracted to Ellen. Before long, with the excuse that he was making the cousin of his betrothed feel at home, he began to send her flowers and call on her. To him she seemed a woman who offered sensitivity, beauty, and the promise of a life quite different from the one that he could expect after his marriage to May. He found himself defending Ellen when the rest of society was attacking her contemplated divorce action. He did not, however, consider breaking his engagement to May but constantly sought reasons for justifying what was to the rest of his group an excellent union. With Ellen often in his thoughts, May Welland's cool beauty and correct but unexciting personality began to suffer in Archer's estimation.

Although the clan defended her against all outsiders, Ellen was often treated as a pariah. Her family kept check on her, trying to prevent her from indulging in too many bohemian acts, such as her strange desire to rent a house in a socially unacceptable part of town. The women of the clan also recognized her as a dangerous rival, and ruthless Julius Beaufort, whose secret dissipations were known by all, including his wife, paid her marked attention. Archer found himself hating Julius Beaufort very much.

Convincing himself that he was seeing too much of Ellen, Archer went to St. Augustine to visit May, who was vacationing there with her mother and her hypochondriac father. In spite of her cool and conventional welcome and her gentle rebuffs to his wooing, her beauty reawakened in him a kind of affection, and he pleaded with her to advance the date of their wedding. May and her parents refused because their elaborate preparations could not be completed in time. Archer returned to New York. There, with the aid of the family matriarch, Mrs. Manson Mingott, he achieved his purpose, and the wedding date was advanced. This news came to him in a telegram sent by May to Ellen, which Ellen read to him just as he was attempting to advance the intimacy of their relationship. Archer left Ellen's house and found a similar telegram from

May to him. Telling his sister Janey that the wedding would take place within a month, he suddenly realized that he was now protected against Ellen and himself.

The ornate wedding, the conventional European honeymoon that followed, and May's assumption of the role of the proper wife soon disillusioned Archer. He realized that he was trapped, that the mores of his society, helped by his own lack of courage, had prepared him, like a smooth ritual, for a rigid and codified life. There was enough intelligence and insight in Archer, however, to make him resent the trap. On his return to New York, he continued to see Ellen. The uselessness of his work as junior attorney in an ancient law firm, the stale regimen of his social life, and the passive sweetness of May did not satisfy that part of Archer that set him apart from the rest of his clan.

He proposed to Ellen that they go away together, but Ellen, wise and kind, showed him that such an escape would not be a pleasant one, and she indicated that they could love each other only as long as he did not press for a consummation. Archer agreed. He further capitulated when, urged by her family, he advised Ellen, as her attorney and as a relative, not to get a divorce from Count Olenska. She agreed, and Archer again blamed his own cowardice for his action. The family faced another crisis when Julius Beaufort's firm, built upon a framework of shady financial transactions, failed, ruining him and his duped customers. The blow caused elderly Mrs. Mingott to have a stroke, and the family rallied around her. She summoned Ellen, a favorite of hers, to her side. Ellen, who had been living in Washington, D.C., returned to the Mingott house to stay. Archer, who had not met Ellen since he advised her against a divorce, began seeing her again, and certain remarks by Archer's male acquaintances, along with a strained and martyrlike attitude that May adopted, indicated to him that his intimacy with Ellen was known among his family and friends. The affair came to an end, however, when Ellen left for Paris, after learning that May was to have a baby. It was obvious to all that May had triumphed, and Archer was treated by his family as a prodigal returned. The rebel was conquered. Archer made his peace with society.

Years passed. Archer dabbled in liberal politics and interested himself in civic reforms. His children, Mary and Dallas, were properly reared. May died when Archer was in his fifties. He lamented her passing with genuine grief. He watched society changing and saw the old conservative order give way, accepting and rationalizing innovations of a younger, more liberal generation.

One day, Archer's son, Dallas, about to be married, telephoned him and proposed a European tour, their last trip together. In Paris, Dallas revealed to his father that he knew all about Ellen Olenska and had arranged to visit her apartment. When they arrived, however, Archer sent his son ahead, to pay his respects, while he remained on a park bench outside. A romantic to the end, incapable of acting in any situation that made demands on his emotional resources, he sat and watched the lights in Ellen's apartment until a servant appeared on the balcony and closed the shutters. Then he walked slowly back to his hotel. The past was the past; the present was secure.

Critical Evaluation:

Edith Wharton's *The Age of Innocence* is probably one of her most successful books because it offers an inside look at a subject the author knew very well, that is, New York society during the 1870's. That was her milieu, and her pen captures the atmosphere of aristocratic New York as its inhabitants move about in their world of subtleties, innuendoes, and strict adherence to the dictates of fashionable society. Wharton describes those years for herself as "safe, guarded, and monotonous." Her only deviation as a young adult consisted in frequent journeys abroad and summers in Newport. Her marriage to Edward Wharton, a prominent Bostonian, assumed the same character as her own early life until it became apparent that he suffered from mental illness and would have to be hospitalized. During World War I, Wharton worked for the allies and received the French Cross of the Legion of Honor for her work with the Red Cross in Paris. Most critics agree that her best years as a novelist were from 1911 to 1921, during which time she produced *Ethan Frome*, a grim New England study, and *The Age of Innocence*, for which she was awarded the Pulitzer Prize.

Wharton's most successful theme (like that of her friend Henry James) was the plight of the young and innocent in a world which was more complicated than that for which they were prepared. Newland Archer and Ellen Olenska found the society of New York intricate and demanding and, as such, to be an impediment to their personal searches for happiness and some degree of freedom. *The Age of Innocence* is a careful blending of a nostalgia for the 1870's with a subtle, but nevertheless inescapable, criticism of its genteel hypocrisies and clever evasions.

With respect to Wharton's style, it can be generalized that she was not a particularly daring writer nor an experimenter in form. Rather, she wrote in a comfortable, fixed, formal style that was closely layered. In some instances, her narrative becomes heavy, and the intricate play and counterplay of the characters' motives can lose all but the most diligent reader. The author's presence is never forgotten and the reader feels her control throughout the story, as the narrative view is quickly established from the beginning. Wharton's characters are portrayed through their actions. Since *The Age of Innocence* so carefully fits a historical niche, its scope is limited and its direction narrow. That is not to say that the drama is limited or lacking. On the contrary, in detailing such a small world, the drama is intense, even if it is found beneath a sophisticated, polished surface.

Three figures are projected against the historical background of New York society. May Welland, the beautiful betrothed of Newland Archer, is completely a product of the system she seeks to perpetuate. Newland observes, after their marriage, that May and her mother are so much alike that he sees himself being treated and placated just as Mr. Welland is by his wife and daughter. There is no doubt that May will never surprise Newland "by a new idea, a weakness, a cruelty or an emotion."

Ellen Olenska, on the other hand, has freed herself from the restraints of society by her experiences abroad and through her subsequent separation from her husband, the Polish count. Madame Olenska not only is more cosmopolitan but also is a character of more depth and understanding than the other women in the novel. She suggests by her presence as well as by her past experiences a tragic and emotionally involved element in the story. Ellen definitely does not conform to the rules of accepted behavior. She moves in a cloud of mystery that makes her an intriguing personality to those who observe her, if even only to criticize. As soon as she and Archer are aware of their feelings for each other, Archer tries to convince Ellen, in a halfhearted way, that one cannot purchase freedom at the expense of another. He has given her an idea by which to live and, in so doing, destroys his opportunity to find freedom for himself.

Newland Archer is, in many ways, a typical Wharton masculine figure. He is a man set apart from the people he knows by education, intellect, and feeling, but is lacking the initiative and courage to separate himself physically from the securities of the known. The movement of the plot in *The Age of Innocence* is established by the transition from one position to another taken by Archer in his relations with May and with Ellen. Archer's failure to break the barriers of clan convention leads him to an ironic abnegation, for in the last pages of the novel readers see Newland retreating from the opportunity to meet with Ellen—an opportunity his eager son Dallas is quick to arrange. Dallas is anxious to meet Ellen, because he heard from his mother, shortly before she died, that Archer had given up the thing he had most wanted (namely, Ellen) for her. It is sad to see that Archer, the object of two loves, has never been able to satisfy or be satisfied by either. The tragedy in the novel rests with May; it is she who appears to be the most innocent and naïve; yet in the end, she is perhaps the most aware of them all. She has suffered quietly through the years, knowing that her husband's true desires and passions were elsewhere. Dallas' generation observes the whole situation out of context, as "prehistoric." He dismisses the affair rather casually, because his contemporaries have lost that blind adherence to social custom that the Archers, Wellands, and the rest knew so well.

The novel is an incisive but oblique attack on the intricate and tyrannous tribal customs of a highly stratified New York society. Wharton's psychological probing of the meaning and motivation behind the apparent façade of her characters' social behavior shows her to be of the same school of fiction as her friend Henry James. The method is that of James, but Wharton's style is clearer and less involved. The novel is the work of a writer for whom form and method are perfectly welded, and the action results inevitably from the natures of the characters. *The Age of Innocence* is a novel of manners that delineates a very small world with great accuracy. Under the surface of wealth, readers see a world of suffering, denial, and patient resignation—a situation that deserves more attention and reflection than one might give at first reading.

"Critical Evaluation" by Constance A. Cutler

Bibliography:
Ammons, Elizabeth. *Edith Wharton's Argument with America*. Athens: University of Georgia Press, 1980. Comprehensive study of Wharton's fiction, with particular focus on the issue of freedom for women in the early years of the twentieth century. Wharton's criticism of patriarchy in *The Age of Innocence* is seen in the contrast between May Welland, the fair child-woman, and Ellen Olenska, the dark-haired intruder who is ultimately banished.

Fryer, Judith. *Felicitous Space: The Imaginative Structures of Edith Wharton and Willa Cather*. Chapel Hill: University of North Carolina Press, 1986. An important inquiry into the meaning of actual and imagined spaces in the works of the two women writers. Explores Wharton's anthropological knowledge in the structure and characterizations of *The Age of Innocence*.

Lewis, R. W. B. *Edith Wharton: A Biography*. New York: Harper & Row, 1975. This biography of Wharton's life won a Pulitzer Prize. Enormously detailed, beginning with a discussion of Wharton's English and Dutch colonial ancestors and tracing her life and artistic development.

McDowell, Margaret. *Edith Wharton*. Boston: Twayne, 1976. An excellent introduction to Wharton's life and work. Interprets *The Age of Innocence* as satirical portrait of a society that Wharton also respected. Annotated bibliography of secondary sources.

Wolff, Cynthia Griffin. *A Feast of Words: The Triumph of Edith Wharton*. New York: Oxford University Press, 1977. An exceptional psychological study of Wharton's life and artistic career that complements the Lewis biography. *The Age of Innocence* is read as Wharton's most significant *Bildungsroman*, tracing Newland Archer's struggle to mature.

THE AGE OF REASON
An Investigation of True and of Fabulous Theology

Type of work: Religious
Author: Thomas Paine (1737-1809)
First published: part 1, 1794; part 2, 1795

In *The Age of Reason*, Thomas Paine is driven by the same impulses that energize such earlier works as the pamphlet *Common Sense* (1776) and series of papers gathered under the title *The Crisis* (1776). In *The Rights of Man* (1791-1792) he expresses his hatred of enslavement and his belief that all people have the natural right to be free of all tyranny—physical, mental, and spiritual. Benjamin Franklin once said, "Where liberty is, there is my country." Paine replied, "Where liberty is not, there is mine." This idealistic altruism motivated him to give his writings to the world without hope of financial remuneration.

In approach and style *The Age of Reason* is similar also to the earlier works. The author is direct, candid, and simple; he appeals to common sense, and presents what to him is over-whelming evidence for his arguments. The author is at times ironic, jeering, or sarcastic. He never writes down to his audience or forgets for whom he is writing.

It is one of the ironies of the literary and theological world that *The Age of Reason*, which, although written to express the author's doubts regarding traditional religion, was intended primarily to save the world from atheism, brought against Paine the charge of atheism. Paine, in *The Age of Reason*, seeks to combat atheism. As a result of this book the great reputation he had earlier enjoyed as one of the prime movers in the Revolutionary War was blackened. Paine became feared throughout America because of his alleged atheism.

Paine's doubts about conventional religion were deep. John Adams said that Paine had them in 1776, and Paine says in *The Age of Reason* that he had entertained such ideas for many years. Paine's ideas grew out of his idealistic view that the human condition could be better. They were strengthened by the influences of his Quakerism, by his Newtonian bent toward science, by the examples of classical antiquity in the teachings of such people as Aristotle, Socrates, and Plato and the great society in which they lived, and by the revelations of research into Eastern religions. Paine was one of the early comparative religionists.

The Age of Reason is subtitled *An Investigation of True and of Fabulous Theology*. In the dedication to his "Fellow-Citizens of the United States of America," Paine insists that the views he is about to express are his alone, and he reaffirms his belief in the right of all to form their own opinions, for to deny the right of all to their own beliefs leads to slavery. He would therefore, he says, examine all aspects of life, especially religion, with reason.

Paine's own position is made clear from the start. He believes in one God and, like all Newtonians, he professes the Deistic hope for happiness in another world because, contrary to the Calvinistic doctrines that he detested, Deism affords a happiness not found in other religions. Paine states explicitly that he does not believe in the creeds professed by any churches, for his own mind is his tabernacle. All national institutions of faith and dogma have been instituted to rule over the lives of people, he opines.

The universal purpose of churches—to beguile or deceive the people—is strengthened by another characteristic churches all have in common, the pretense of some special mission from God communicated to certain individuals: Moses to the Jews, Jesus Christ to the Christians, Mahomet to the Turks. These revelations must be accepted on faith because there is never any pragmatic truth vouchsafing their validity.

Paine has no criticism of Jesus. He was, Paine feels, a virtuous and amiable man. Jesus, Paine notes, wrote nothing about his so-called special mission on earth. Thus, all accounts about him were written by others, many long after his death. For this reason they are open to suspicion. That Jesus existed is an unquestionable historical fact, and that he preached morality is certain. That he claimed to be the Savior of the world, however, is suspect. Further, most of the writings about Jesus as Savior, the bases of Christianity, differ very little from the writings of other mythologies. Such writings, written by limited and particular human minds, calumniate the wisdom of the Almighty.

Paine examines in detail the whole structure of Christianity. He investigates the books of the Old Testament. He seizes upon the Apocrypha, rejected by those who established the biblical canon, and concludes that all books were chosen arbitrarily; had others been chosen or rejected, the present basic structure of Christianity would have been altered. The books that were chosen are filled with "obscene" stories, "voluptuous debaucheries," and "cruel and torturous executions" which constitute a "history of wickedness that has served to corrupt and brutalize mankind." Paine detests these stories, as he despises all cruelty. The Proverbs, attributed to Solomon, are inferior to the proverbs of the Spaniards and are less wise and economical than those of Benjamin Franklin. Here, as elsewhere, Paine demonstrates his great respect for the wisdom and general goodness of Franklin, who had been instrumental in getting Paine to come to America in 1774.

The New Testament, Paine claimed, is likewise spurious. Had Jesus been truly the Savior of humanity, he surely would have arranged to have this knowledge transmitted to the world during his lifetime. He was in fact a Son of God only in the way all people are children of God, and the falsehoods about his divinity were written after his death. Like scholars interested in comparative mythologies, Paine notes that it is curious that all leaders of religions come from obscure or unusual parentage: "Moses was a foundling; Jesus was born in a stable; Mahomet was a mule driver."

Having destroyed the sanctity of the Bible as a basis of religion, Paine asks if there is no word of God, no revelation. A Deist, his response is without equivocation. The true theology is nature, and the "word of God is the Creation we behold," and only in the Creation are united all of humanity's "ideas and conceptions of a word of God." God to Paine is a first cause. Here, with an adroitness and wit more characteristic of his earlier works, he turns the Christian's own assertions against him. The Christian "system of faith," he says, seems to be a "species of atheism," a kind of "denial of God," for it believes in a man rather than in the true God and interposes "between man and his Maker an opaque body, which it calls a Redeemer." All such beliefs run counter to Deism, the belief in one Deity who is wise and benign and which imitates him in all things moral, scientific, and mechanical.

The Christian belief in miracles brings forth from Paine his bitterest tirades, almost as fiery and heated as they had been in his earlier works. Mysteries, he says, run counter to true religion. He jeeringly examines the miracle of the whale swallowing Jonah and concludes that although it approaches the marvelous it would have been much more marvelous if Jonah had swallowed the whale. He derides especially the "most extraordinary" of all miracles of the New Testament, that of Satan flying Jesus to the top of a high mountain and promising him all the kingdoms throughout the world. Paine wonders why both then did not discover America; he questions whether "his sooty highness" was interested only in kingdoms.

One of Paine's more amusing refutations of biblical lore is found in part 2. His book is clearly serious in intent, but he delights in poking fun wherever possible. He attacks the wisdom of Solomon as claimed in Ecclesiastes. Paine affirms that Solomon should have cried out that "All

87

is vanity," for with seven hundred wives and three hundred concubines, how could any man in retrospect conclude anything else? Then Paine contrasts Solomon with Benjamin Franklin, whom he glorifies almost to deification; he claims that Franklin was wiser than Solomon, for his "mind was ever young, his temper ever serene; science, that never grows gray, was always his mistress."

Between the writing of part 1 and part 2 Paine spent eleven months in a French prison. Believing that part 1 had been written in too great haste without a Bible handy for reference, Paine attempts in part 2 to buttress his former statements with details. He directs part 1 against the "three frauds, mystery, miracle, and prophecy," and he intends to blast revelation in part 2, for although all things are possible with God, he is against the use of "pretended revelation," which is "the imposition of one man upon another." He feels that most of the wickedness, the greatest cruelties and miseries that have broken the human race, have originated in the hoax called revelation. Whereas Deism teaches without any possibility of deceit, Christianity thrives on deceit. Religion becomes form instead of fact, "of notion instead of principle," and morality is replaced by faith, which had its beginnings in a "supposed debauchery."

Part 2 is an attack on the Bible as an imperfect collection of words, not as a statement of religion. Except in details, in more evidence, and in more direct examination and refutation, part 2 advances Paine's thesis little beyond its points in part 1. Paine ends part 2, as he generally ends his works, with a challenge to the reader. He has shown, he says, that the Bible is filled with "impositions and forgeries," and he invites readers to refute him if they can. He hopes that his ideas will cause readers to think for themselves, for he is certain that when opinions are allowed to thrive in a free air "truth will finally and powerfully prevail."

Paine's style and technique are uniquely his. He is candid in approach and unrelenting in carrying out his thesis. His style is simple, honest, direct, and free of all cant and reverence. His subject matter and his approach led to his being accused of being unscientific and vulgar. When it was first announced that Paine was going to write on the subject of religion, many Americans approved. As the work appeared, reprinted far and wide in newspapers, approval turned to disapprobation. His reputation was so blackened that after his return to the United States in 1802 he found himself virtually without friends. Paine's pen was always his most important weapon, but the reputation that his earlier writings had created was what *The Age of Reason* destroyed.

Bibliography:
Aldridge, Alfred Owen. "*The Age of Reason*." In *Man of Reason: The Life of Thomas Paine*. London: Cresset, 1960. Provides an excellent summary of the argument developed in *The Age of Reason*. Describes the work's publication history and critical reception.
Davidson, Edward H., and William J. Scheick. *Paine, Scripture, and Authority: "The Age of Reason" as Religious and Political Idea*. Bethlehem, Pa.: Lehigh University Press, 1994. Discusses Paine's subversiveness and notes how *The Age of Reason* appears to authorize a world order that depends on the traditions it criticizes.
Faulk, Robert P. "Thomas Paine: Deist or Quaker." *The Pennsylvania Magazine of History and Biography* 62 (1938): 52-63. Although somewhat dated, this essay provides a solid basis for understanding the degree to which Quakerism played a part in defining the social ideas in *The Age of Reason*.
Popkin, Richard H. "*The Age of Reason* versus *The Age of Revelation*: Two Critics of Tom Paine: David Levi and Elias Boudinot." In *Deism, Masonry, and the Enlightenment*, edited by J. A. Leo Lemay. Newark: University of Delaware Press, 1987. Shows how Paine's humanistic Deism was opposed to orthodoxy.

Wilson, Jerome D., and William F. Ricketson. "Reaction to Organized Religion." In *Thomas Paine*, edited by Patricia Cowell. Boston: Twayne, 1989. Describes the historical and social contexts of *The Age of Reason* and notes how the essay stands as a remarkable example of classic eighteenth century Deism.

AGNES GREY

Type of work: Novel
Author: Anne Brontë (1820-1849)
Type of plot: Domestic realism
Time of plot: Mid-nineteenth century
Locale: England
First published: 1847

> *Principal characters:*
> AGNES GREY, a young governess
> EDWARD WESTON, a curate and later Agnes' husband
> MARY GREY, Agnes' sister
> RICHARD GREY, Agnes' father
> MRS. GREY, Agnes' mother
> MRS. MURRAY, the owner of Horton Lodge and Agnes' second employer
> ROSALIE MURRAY, Mrs. Murray's older daughter
> MATILDA MURRAY, Mrs. Murray's younger daughter
> MR. HATFIELD, the rector at Horton and Rosalie's suitor
> SIR THOMAS ASHBY, later Rosalie's husband
> HARRY MELTHAM and
> MR. GREEN, Rosalie's other suitors
> NANCY BROWN, an old widow at Horton
> MRS. BLOOMFIELD, the owner of Wellwood and Agnes' first employer
> TOM BLOOMFIELD, her oldest child
> MARY ANN BLOOMFIELD, her older daughter
> FANNY BLOOMFIELD, her younger daughter
> UNCLE ROBSON, Mrs. Bloomfield's brother

The Story:

Mrs. Grey, a squire's daughter, had offended her family by getting married only for love to a poor parson in the north of England. She bore him six children, but only two, Mary and Agnes, survived. Nevertheless, the Greys were happy with their humble, educated, pious life in their small house and garden. Mr. Grey, never wholly at his ease because his wife had been forced to give up carriages and fine clothes in order to marry him, attempted to improve their fortunes by speculating and investing his patrimony in a merchant's sea voyage; but the vessel was wrecked, everything was lost, and the Greys were soon left penniless. In addition, Mr. Grey's health, never robust, began to fail more perceptibly under the strain of his guilt for bringing his family close to ruin. Mary and Agnes, reared in the sheltered atmosphere of a clergyman's household, had spent their time reading, studying, and working in the garden. When the family situation became desperate, however, Mary began to try to sell her drawings to help with the household expenses, and Agnes, the younger daughter, decided to become a governess.

Overcoming the qualms her family felt at the idea of her leaving home, Agnes found employment and, on a bleak and windy autumn day, arrived at Wellwood, the home of the Bloomfield family. She was received coldly by Mrs. Bloomfield and told that her charges, especially Tom, a seven-year-old boy, were noble and splendid children. She soon found that the reverse was true. Tom was an arrogant and disobedient little monster whose particular delight was to pull the legs and wings off young sparrows. Mary Ann, his six-year-old sister, was given to temper tantrums and refused to do her lessons. The children were frightened of their father, a peevish and stern disciplinarian, and the father, in turn, blamed Agnes when the children frequently got out of control.

Agnes found it impossible to teach the children anything because all her efforts to discipline them were undermined by Mrs. Bloomfield, who felt that her angels must always be right. Even four-year-old Fanny lied consistently and was fond of spitting in people's faces. For a time, Agnes was heartened by Mr. Bloomfield's mother's visit, but the pious old lady turned out to be a hypocrite who sympathized with Agnes verbally and then turned on her behind her back.

Matters became a great deal worse with the visit of Uncle Robson, Mrs. Bloomfield's brother, who encouraged young Tom to torture small animals. One day, after he had collected a whole brood of young birds for Tom to torture, Agnes crushed them with a large stone, choosing to kill them quickly rather than to see them suffer a slow, cruel death. The family felt she had deprived Tom of his normal, spirited pleasure. Shortly after this incident, she was told that her services would no longer be required; the Bloomfields felt that she had not disciplined the children properly or taught them very much.

Agnes spent a few months with her family at home before taking up her next post. She found the Murrays, the owners of Horton Lodge, more sophisticated, wealthier, and less bleak and cruel than the owners of Wellwood; but they were still hardly the happy, pious, warm family that Agnes had hoped to encounter. Her older charge, Rosalie, was sixteen years old, very pretty, and interested only in flirting and in eventually making the most suitable marriage possible; her younger charge, Matilda, fourteen years old, was interested only in horses and stables. Although they treated her with politeness, neither girl had any respect for the learning and piety that Agnes had to offer. If Agnes' work was less unpleasant than it had been at Wellwood, it was equally futile.

After living at Horton Lodge for nearly a year, Agnes returned home for a month for her sister's wedding. During this time, the Murrays had given Rosalie a debutante ball, after which she began to exercise her charms on the young men at Horton. When Agnes returned, she was shocked to find Rosalie flirting with all the men and summarizing the marital possibilities of each with a hardened and materialistic eye. In the meantime, a new curate had come to Horton. Edward Weston was a sober and sincere churchman, neither climbing nor pompous like the rector, Mr. Hatfield. Mr. Weston and Agnes, attracted to each other, found many opportunities to meet in their sympathetic visits to Nancy Brown, an old widow who was almost blind. At first, Rosalie found Mr. Weston both dogmatic and dull, but Agnes found him representative of the true piety and goodness that she believed were the qualities of a clergyman. Rosalie, continuing to play the coquette, first conquered the unctuous rector, Mr. Hatfield, and then after he had proposed and been quickly rejected, she turned her charms on Mr. Weston. Although Agnes was fiercely jealous of Rosalie's flirtation, she never really acknowledged her own growing love. Finally, Rosalie accepted Sir Thomas Ashby; his home, Ashby Park, and his fortune were the largest in the vicinity of Horton.

Shortly after Rosalie's marriage, before Agnes had the opportunity to see much of Edward Weston, she was called home by the death of her father. She and her mother decided to start a school for young ladies in the fashionable watering place of A——. Although Agnes returned to Horton Lodge for another month, she did not see Mr. Weston before she resignedly left to rejoin her mother. Although the school began to prosper after a few months, Agnes still seemed weary and depressed, and she welcomed an invitation from Rosalie, now Lady Ashby, to visit Ashby Park. She found Rosalie disappointed in her marriage to a grumbling, boorish man who ignored her and who, after a honeymoon on the Continent, had forbidden her the frivolous pleasures of London and European society. Agnes also learned from Rosalie that Mr. Weston had left Horton a short time before.

A few days after Agnes returned to her mother and the school, she was walking along the waterfront one morning when she unexpectedly encountered Mr. Weston. He had secured a position as a minister in a nearby village. He promptly began calling on Agnes and her mother, who soon came to hold him in high esteem. One day, while walking with Agnes to the top of a high hill, Mr. Weston proposed marriage to Agnes. As husband, father, clergyman, and manager of a limited income, he was in later years the perfect mate for virtuous and worthy Agnes.

Critical Evaluation:

Written around 1846, *Agnes Grey* expresses ideas on women and their capacity for a life based on reason similar to those of Mary Wollstonecraft in *A Vindication of the Rights of Woman* (1792). Its feminism predates that of the novels by Charlotte Brontë, Elizabeth Gaskell, and George Eliot, yet only recently has it come to be recognized as a notable achievement, distinguished for its pervasive realism, its significant themes, and its innovative literary techniques.

The work of Anne Brontë, long dismissed as insipid compared to that of her sisters Charlotte and Emily Brontë, is in fact simply different in kind from theirs. In *Agnes Grey*, Brontë eschews sensational events and strong passions in favor of a restrained portrayal of actual life. The opening sentence, "All true histories contain instruction," suggests both her goal and her method: a demonstration, through sustained realism, of the heroine's spiritual and moral growth. Drawing heavily on her own experiences, Brontë convincingly presents the governess' life and the factors which often made it unbearable. She takes for her heroine and hero ordinary people struggling to cope in difficult situations. Numerous details of travel, weather, food, customs—all the circumstances of Victorian life—increase the verisimilitude.

The underlying theme, that women are rational beings who should be accorded the means and opportunity for independence and fulfillment, is expressed primarily in Agnes' life story. Seeking employment, Agnes accepts the only occupation available to middle-class women, and she embarks on her career as a governess exhilarated by the prospect not merely of earning money but of broadening her horizons. Yet her excited optimism is naïve, based on ignorance of the world. The novel concerns her education and growth toward maturity. Despite her trials as a governess, she perseveres, determined to adopt a logical, rational approach to her unruly charges. She enlarges her understanding of human nature, making shrewd character evaluations and learning to penetrate hypocrisy. Although she suffers many humiliations, she gains self-assurance, and, at certain points, she openly challenges authority.

At Horton Lodge, she makes further progress toward understanding others and learning to control herself. Her consistent attempts to inculcate firm moral principles in her charges eventually win her some measure of respect. Moreover, even in situations which emphasize her social inferiority, she remains cognizant of her own worth and moral superiority. Love for Mr. Weston does not diminish her self-control and judgment. Pained as she is by Rosalie's flirtation with him, she never loses her composure in public; she steadily attempts to view her situation with reason and objectivity.

Finally, at the school she establishes with her mother, she achieves a position in which she is a decision maker instead of a subordinate. Here, while she does not overcome what appears to be a hopeless love, she gains command of her feelings and experiences an upsurge of energy, physical well-being, and a sense of freedom. It is a confident, self-reliant woman who strolls along the sands at the dawn of a new day and unexpectedly meets Mr. Weston. Their declaration of love, denuded of glamour and the trappings of romance, is the prelude to a union which is an equal partnership, founded on sincere feelings, mutual respect, and shared moral principles.

These feminist themes are reinforced by the other female portraits. Agnes' mother is an accomplished woman, possessed of spirit and energy. She has defied her parents in her marriage, and she defies convention in her determination to support herself after her husband's death. She is the opposite of the gentle but ineffective Mr. Grey, and if she has a fault, it is that of trying to control too much in the home, a fault occasioned by the narrow sphere in which she is forced to exercise her considerable organizational abilities.

By contrast, Mrs. Murray and Rosalie reveal the emptiness and misery experienced by women who have no meaningful activity. Mrs. Murray's life is centered on parties, fashion, and unfortunate matchmaking for her daughters. Rosalie is the victim of such a lifestyle. Not trained or disciplined, she is guided by her ambitious mother into a bitterly unhappy marriage to Sir Thomas Ashby, and when Agnes visits her at Ashby Park, Rosalie's situation underlines the advantages which the poorer, but more purposeful, woman possesses.

A secondary theme concerns the corrupting effects of the economic system. The novel presents different gradations of wealth, ranging from the Bloomfields, who acquired their money from trade, to the Murrays, who represent the country gentry, to the Ashbys, who belong to the titled aristocracy. At all levels, the pernicious consequences of the leisured life of the moneyed classes are shown. The cruelty and viciousness of Mr. Robson and Tom Bloomfield are only the most obvious instance. Mr. Bloomfield's snobbery, the Murray daughters' mockery of the cottagers, Mr. Hatfield's ingratiating ways with the rich and neglect of his poorer parishioners, and Sir Thomas Ashby's dissipation are all the result of an economic system that fosters idleness, self-indulgence, and lack of good judgment.

Brontë's innovations, however, extend beyond themes to narrative technique. The first-person female narration recounts experiences and opinions very close to the author's own. While author and female narrator are not identical, the link between them establishes an entirely female perspective enhanced by direct address to the "Reader." This original manipulation of female point of view adds authenticity and conviction.

Equally significant is the style. Lucid and restrained, the style never draws attention to itself but presents persons and events with an air of controlled objectivity. The cool, unimpassioned voice of the female narrator is perfectly adapted to the theme of woman's rational nature. Yet, the quiet tone is enlivened by a mild and sometimes comic irony. Agnes is skilled in deflating human affectation and gently mocking human foibles. Typical is her quiet response to Rosalie's query about whether her sister's husband is rich, handsome, and young: "Only middling," comes the calm reply.

In comparison with most Victorian novels, *Agnes Grey* is subdued. However, if it lacks the dramatic, it also avoids the melodramatic, the sensational, and the sentimental. In its sober way, it gives a telling picture of women in Victorian England and utilizes a technique and style consonant with that subject. It deserves recognition as a significant contribution to nineteenth century feminism.

"Critical Evaluation" by Muriel Mellown

Bibliography:
Bell, A. Craig. *The Novels of Anne Brontë*. Braunton, England: Merlin Books, 1992. A critical study providing a general introduction to Brontë's work. Includes discussion of the novels under the headings "Sources," "Style and Structure," and "Characters."

Chitham, Edward. *A Life of Anne Brontë*. Cambridge, Mass.: Blackwell, 1991. This biography reexamines sources of previous biographies and guards against indiscriminate use of novels and poems for the purpose of biographical study. Explains the composition of *Agnes Grey* and distinguishes its autobiographical and fictional elements.

Eagleton, Terry. *Myths of Power: A Marxist Study of the Brontës*. New York: Barnes & Noble, 1975. A significant reading by a major Marxist critic. Analyzes social implications of *Agnes Grey* and its triadic structure of pious heroine, morally lax upper-class man, and principled hero. Maintains that the novel connects social and economic issues with moral principles and inculcates bourgeois virtues of piety, plainness, duty, and sobriety.

Langland, Elizabeth. *Anne Brontë: The Other One*. Totowa, N.J.: Barnes & Noble, 1989. The best book-length critical study of Anne Brontë. Examines Brontë's innovations in theme and technique, identifies her literary precursors, and analyzes the relationships between the novels of all three Brontë sisters. Treats *Agnes Grey* as a novel of female development and stresses its feminist principles and realism.

Scott, P. J. M. *Anne Brontë: A New Critical Assessment*. Totowa, N.J.: Barnes & Noble, 1983. Analyzes themes and characters with particular emphasis on moral issues and on Agnes' learning to cope with the realities of life. Includes close reading and explication of a number of passages.

AJAX

Type of work: Drama
Author: Sophocles (c. 496-406 B.C.E.)
Type of plot: Tragedy
Time of plot: Trojan War
Locale: Phrygia, before Troy
First performed: Aias, early 440's B.C.E. (English translation, 1729)

> *Principal characters:*
> AJAX, a Greek warrior
> ODYSSEUS, a Greek leader
> TECMESSA, Ajax's female captive
> TEUCER, Ajax's half brother
> EURYSACES, son of Ajax and Tecmessa

The Story:

Odysseus, chosen by Greek leaders in the Trojan War to replace the dead Achilles as the chief warrior of the Greek forces, paced up and down before the tent of Ajax, who had been slighted by the selection of Odysseus. The goddess Athena, appearing above the tent, told Odysseus that Ajax, covered with blood, was in his tent. Her words confirmed Odysseus' suspicions that it had indeed been Ajax who had slaughtered all of the Greeks' livestock and their shepherd dogs. Athena explained that she had cast a spell over Ajax, who, in his hurt pride, had vowed to murder Menelaus and Agamemnon, the Greek commanders, as well as Odysseus. Under her spell Ajax had committed the horrible slaughter in the belief that the animals he slew were the hated leaders who had opposed his election to the place of the late Achilles.

When Tecmessa, Ajax's Phrygian captive, revealed to his followers what the great warrior had done, they lamented his downfall and questioned the dark purposes of the gods. Certain that Ajax would be condemned to die for his transgressions, his warriors prepared to retire to their ships and return to Salamis, their homeland.

Ajax, recovered from the spell, emerged from his tent and clearly revealed to his friends that he was a shamed and broken man. Sick in mind at the thought of the taunts of Odysseus, he wished only to die. Even in his abject misery, however, he was sure that had Achilles personally chosen his successor he would have named Ajax. The despairing man tried to find some means of escape from the consequences of his deed. The alternative to death was to return to Salamis and his noble father, Telamon; but he knew that he could never shame Telamon by facing him. His friends, alarmed at his deep gloom and sensing tragedy, advised him to reflect; Tecmessa urged him to live for her sake and for the sake of their little son, Eurysaces. At the mention of the name of his beloved son, Ajax called for the boy. Solemnly he gave Eurysaces his great shield and directed that the child be taken to Salamis, so that he might grow up to avenge his father's disgrace. After dismissing Tecmessa and his son, he remained in his tent alone to clear his troubled thoughts. His followers, meanwhile, resumed their lament over their disgraced leader.

Apparently reconciled to his fate, Ajax emerged at last from his tent and declared that he was ready to recognize authority, to revere the gods, and to bury his sword with which he had brought disgrace and dishonor upon himself. His decision, he said, had been dictated by his affection for Tecmessa and Eurysaces. This apparent change brought forth cheers of rejoicing from his countrymen; they thanked the gods for what appeared to be Ajax's salvation.

95

In the meantime the Greeks taunted Teucer, Ajax's half brother, for his kinship with one demented. Calchas, the Greek prophet, warned Teucer that unless Ajax were kept in his tent a full day, no one would again see Ajax alive, since the proud warrior had twice offended the goddess Athena in the past. Ajax, however, had already left his tent in order to bury his sword. Teucer and the men of Salamis, in alarm, hastened in search of their leader.

Ajax planted his sword, a gift from Hector, the great Trojan warrior, hilt down in the earth. After he had asked the gods to inform Teucer of his whereabouts so that he might receive a proper burial, he fell upon his sword. Heavy underbrush partly concealed his body where it lay.

Tecmessa was the first to discover her dead lord; in sorrow she covered him with her mantle. Teucer was summoned. Tecmessa and the men of Salamis could not refrain from mentioning the dire part played by Athena in the tragedy of Ajax and the pleasure Menelaus and Agamemnon would feel when they heard of Ajax's death. Fearing foul play, Teucer ordered Tecmessa to bring Eurysaces immediately. Teucer himself was in a dilemma. He knew that the Greeks detested him because of his kinship with Ajax. He feared also that Telamon would suspect him of being responsible for Ajax's death, so that he might be Telamon's heir.

While Teucer pondered his own fate, Menelaus appeared and told him that Ajax could not receive proper burial because he had been a rebel, offensive to the gods. Teucer maintained that Ajax had not been subject to Spartan Menelaus, nor to anyone else, for he had come to Troy voluntarily at the head of his own men from Salamis; therefore he deserved burial. Seeing that Teucer held firm, Menelaus went away. Teucer dug a grave while Tecmessa and Eurysaces stood vigil over the body. The men of Salamis sang a dirge over their dead leader.

Agamemnon, King of Mycenae, appeared and rebuked Teucer, the son of a slave, for his audacity in defying the will of Menelaus. Agamemnon insulted the memory of Ajax by saying that he had been stronger than he was wise. Teucer, bitterly recalling Ajax's many heroic deeds in behalf of the Greek cause, reminded Agamemnon of the many blots on the escutcheon of the Atridae, Agamemnon's royal house. Teucer defended his own blood by pointing out that although his mother, Hesione, was a captive, she was nevertheless of noble birth.

Odysseus resolved the dispute by declaring that no Greek warrior should be denied burial. He himself had hated Ajax, but he admitted that Ajax had been both noble and courageous. He shook hands with Teucer in friendship, but Teucer, lest the gods be offended, refused his offer to assist in the burial. Thus Ajax, whose pride had brought him to an early death, received proper burial and the death ceremonies of a warrior hero.

Critical Evaluation:

The problem of individual versus group prerogative is masterfully presented in this play. One finds it tempting to sympathize with Ajax for his devotion to his consort and his son, the love and admiration he commands from his followers, and the courage he displays before the walls of Troy. It is inevitable, however, that his ungovernable pride should bring about his ruin. His downfall is one of the most touching and disturbing in literature.

Ajax is considered the earliest of Sophocles' plays that have survived, first produced about 442 B.C.E. The playwright was in his middle fifties at that time and had already had a successful dramatic career of about twenty-five years. Thus *Ajax* was the work of a fully mature writer, and one who had considered life deeply. Whatever problem the play may present structurally, its strengths are remarkable.

Sophocles was the most accomplished poet among the three great Athenian dramatists. His style is marked by smoothness, simplicity, and clarity. It is at once beautiful and lofty; and it has an august dignity that Aeschylus and Euripides could not equal. With Sophocles even the most intense passions are revealed in a stately, logical, well-polished manner that can be surprisingly moving. For all the formality of his poetry, it never impresses one as being artificial. He actually created the classical style of writing, and he remains unsurpassed in it.

An accomplished athlete, an honored public dignitary, and the most successful tragedian of the Periclean Age, Sophocles lived to be ninety with his full creative and intellectual vigor intact. His good luck did not blind him to the suffering of others. His extant plays explore the problem of human misery with a rare honesty and thoroughness. He saw Athens reach its finest moment in the Persian Wars and then devolve into a ruthless imperial power embarking on a suicidal war. He knew very well the instability of life, and how greatness can be the source of calamity.

Ajax is a case in point. Next to Achilles, Ajax was the most formidable fighter in the Greek army at Troy. A huge, headstrong bull of a man, his pride was bitterly offended when the Greeks voted to give Achilles' armor to Odysseus. To avenge himself he tries to massacre the Greeks, but madly butchers their livestock instead in a god-induced frenzy. Thus, in one night he turns from a hero into an outcast and a laughingstock. The humiliation is too much for him, and he commits suicide. This is the heart of the story, but what is interesting is the way Sophocles develops it.

The key to Sophocles' treatment of the legend is balance. The action moves by antithesis, by the juxtaposition of opposites, in the revelation of Ajax's character and heroism. At the end of the play the audience has arrived at a complete assessment of this tragically flawed man, and the impersonal verdict is that he is to be buried as a hero rather than left to rot like a renegade. The decision is close, for Sophocles has shown Ajax at his very worst, in total degradation.

At the beginning, when Athena calls Ajax from the tent to reveal his shame to Odysseus, Ajax is insane. He is vindictively slaughtering and tormenting helpless animals in his delusion. Odysseus is appalled and touched by pity. Athena is merciless, however, because Ajax in his own mind is savagely murdering the Greeks. Ajax himself is pitiless in his wounded pride.

When his sanity returns his pain is excruciating because he failed to kill his enemies and because he made a fool of himself. He thinks of himself as a hero, and public disgrace is unbearable. As he talks to his soldiers, or to Tecmessa and Eurysaces, he shows himself to be self-centered, hard, concerned only with his damaged honor. Yet this portrait is relieved by the pity and the love these dependent people feel for him. An ignoble man could not command such loyalty.

The audience is further softened to his plight when he seems piously resolved to live with his shame out of concern for Tecmessa and his son. Then the audience realizes he has simply been putting on an act to avoid a scene. He is still intent on suicide. Beyond that, the audience learns the reason for Athena's hostility to Ajax. He deliberately affronted her in his arrogant pride by twice refusing her assistance, desiring all the glory for himself. Athena, then, operates by the same vengeful morality that Ajax does. She, however, merely supervises Ajax's destruction—it is actually his own pride that forces him to commit suicide. He is proud to the last, calling upon Zeus to ruin his enemies and arrange a means of burial.

Sophocles goes further and points up the desolation caused by Ajax's stubborn vanity and death. Tecmessa, Teucer, and the Salaminian warriors are utterly bereft of comfort: friendless, unprotected, subject to ridicule, and exiled from home. Ajax has betrayed them all in his inhuman pride.

This situation makes the debate over Ajax's right to burial doubly forceful, because Teucer is defending a man who has violated every human trust, a man who has cut him off from his own father. Menelaus' argument that Ajax put himself before the good of the community has special validity in this context. Ajax even put himself before the gods. Teucer's assertion that, on the other hand, Ajax prevented a complete defeat of the Greek army is also true. He was a hero no matter how monstrous he became. Neither the Atridae nor Teucer is allowed to make the final judgment. The Atridae want Ajax unburied out of vindictiveness, while Teucer wants him buried out of brotherly loyalty. Neither is impartial. It is Ajax's enemy, Odysseus, who decides that Ajax is to have a decent burial. Odysseus, who was capable of pity when Ajax was mad, is also capable of forgiving him in death. So Ajax receives his burial by sheer grace.

Sophocles demonstrates in this play the hairbreadth line between criminality and heroism. The very pride that motivates the hero to surpass everyone else can also degrade him into the vilest bestiality. Heroes do not feel the demands of others; they live by some imperious demand within their own breast. Heroes can call forth extraordinary loyalty from their followers—a loyalty that persists after heroes betray their followers—but heroes can also conjure up terrible hatred in their pride. At the last it is grace alone that pronounces the verdict. *Ajax* is a profound and moving study of the nature of the hero.

"Critical Evaluation" by James Weigel, Jr.

Bibliography:

Kirkwood, Gordon MacDonald. *A Study of Sophoclean Drama.* Vol. 31 in *Cornell Studies in Classical Philology.* Ithaca, N.Y.: Cornell University Press, 1958. Analyzes Sophocles' structures and methods of dramatic composition. Compares the plays of Sophocles. Focuses on the characters, irony, illustrative forms, use of diction, and oracles in each. Excellent coverage of *Ajax.*

Scodel, Ruth. *Sophocles.* Boston: Twayne, 1984. Focuses on the historical and mythological significance of the character Ajax. Discusses the plot and compares it to Homer's *Iliad.* Includes information on Sophocles' seven plays. Includes a chronology of Sophocles' life, a bibliography, and an index.

Seale, David. *Vision and Stagecraft in Sophocles.* Chicago: University of Chicago Press, 1982. An excellent starting point. Distinguishes Sophocles from other playwrights of his time and demonstrates his influence on later ones. Considers the theatrical technicalities in many Sophoclean plays, including *Ajax.* Includes an extended explanation and notes regarding *Ajax.*

Segal, Charles. *Tragedy and Civilization: An Interpretation of Sophocles.* Cambridge, Mass.: Published for Oberlin College by Harvard University Press, 1981. Compares *Ajax* to the other plays by Sophocles in terms of structure and theme. Traces and explains the plot.

Woodard, Thomas, ed. *Sophocles: A Collection of Critical Essays.* Englewood Cliffs, N.J.: Prentice-Hall, 1966. A collection of essays, including writings by Friedrich Nietzsche, Sigmund Freud, and Virginia Woolf. Draws connections between *Ajax* and later literary works.

THE ALBANY CYCLE

Type of work: Novel
Author: William Kennedy (1928-   )
Type of plot: Psychological realism
Time of plot: 1930's
Locale: Albany, New York, and environs
First published: 1985: *Legs*, 1975; *Billy Phelan's Greatest Game*, 1978; *Ironweed*, 1983

> *Principal characters:*
> JACK DIAMOND, a gangster, known as "Legs"
> MARCUS GORMAN, his lawyer
> ALICE, Jack's wife
> MARION (KIKI), Jack's mistress
> BILLY PHELAN, a young man
> MARTIN DAUGHERTY, a journalist
> PATSY MCCALL, the political boss of Albany
> FRANCIS PHELAN, Billy's father, a hobo
> HELEN ARCHER, Francis' companion
> ANNIE PHELAN, Francis' wife

The Story:

Albany was a wide-open town in the 1930's. The capital of the state of New York, it was also the wholly owned property of the corrupt and apparently omnipotent Democratic machine headed by Patsy McCall. Although the notorious gangster Jack "Legs" Diamond concentrated most of his criminal activities outside the city itself, it was a fitting place for him to be shot to death, as he was at 67 Dove Street early in the morning of December 18, 1931.

In 1948, however, Marcus Gorman still was not sure that Jack Diamond was dead. Marcus had been Jack's attorney and, at the time of the shooting, had just won him an acquittal on a charge of kidnapping. In the months leading up to these events, Marcus, after a casual meeting with Diamond in a speakeasy in the summer of 1930, found himself drawn more and more into the gangster's orbit. At first, Marcus' personal and professional relationship with Jack remained within clearly defined boundaries. Marcus was able to avoid any complicity in the criminal life of his client. "Legs" Diamond, however, was the object of a national obsession. It was hard for Marcus, a lapsed Catholic whose hierarchy of values was shaky to begin with, to resist this man who so fascinated a nation.

Marcus knew, for example, that sailing to Europe with Jack could compromise an attorney's professional standing, but he went. On the voyage, he resisted the proposal that he carry stolen jewels, and when Jack, accepting Marcus' decision, cast the stones in the ocean, Marcus was impressed. Jack seemed to be a man of integrity; he continued to respect the boundaries defined by Marcus. Jack also had flair; throwing those valuable jewels over the side was a grand gesture.

Marcus either underestimated Jack Diamond or overestimated himself. Before long, Marcus was wearing a money belt; the money it concealed was money Jack had stolen from other gangsters. It was not surprising that by the time of the kidnapping trial, Marcus' defense strategy included constructing a false alibi for a client of whose guilt he had no doubt. Like the women who loved "Legs" Diamond—Alice, his wife, and Kiki, his mistress—and like the country that was fascinated by him, Marcus Gorman had been seduced.

Looking back seventeen years after Jack was fatally shot, Marcus was still not convinced the gangster was dead. Had he simply been transformed from the mortal man of flesh and blood to the mythic man of collective memory and imagination?

Jack Diamond was a force, a man who could take on a place like Albany, to some extent even shape it. His kind were few. More commonly, the people of Albany were shaped by the place and its institutions. The most powerful of these, even more powerful than the Church in this largely Irish Catholic community, was the local Democratic machine, dominated by Patsy McCall. A young man like Billy Phelan might think that Patsy McCall's organization played no significant role in his life. Billy had a genius for games; his bowling score of 299 had been celebrated in the local press by Martin Daugherty, an eminent local journalist. Billy was not involved in politics. When Patsy McCall's nephew was kidnapped, suspicion fell on Morrie Berman, a friend and occasional backer of Billy, and Billy was summoned into the presence of McCall himself. Billy was a man who played by the rules and beyond them, and he knew that the rules by which he lived meant he could never betray a friend, no matter what the circumstances. For his refusal to become Patsy McCall's instrument, Billy found himself declared an unperson, unable even to buy a drink in his own town.

Martin Daugherty had troubles of his own. He found it hard to accept his son Peter's decision to enter the priesthood, and he also was working out the still-unresolved tensions of his relationship with his own father, including the complex relationship he had with his father's mistress. The two conflicts were emotionally related. Coming to terms with his father's memory, which involved going to bed with his father's mistress, enabled Martin to accept with a better grace the decision of his son. Another column by Martin made McCall lift the curse on Billy. In managing to survive while remaining true to his code, Billy had played his greatest game.

During this already difficult time, Billy's life was complicated by the return to Albany of his wandering father, Francis Phelan. Once a major league ballplayer, Francis was now a bum who hoped to earn a little money voting for the Democratic machine, at five dollars a vote, on election day.

Francis had lived with violence. A rock he threw with a ballplayer's skill at the head of a scab in a strike years before had killed the man and sent Francis into hiding; he had killed again in his time on the road; and he would be forced to kill one more time during this visit to Albany. Scarring him more deeply than any of these killings was the accidental death of Gerald, his infant son. The infant, slipping from Francis' grasp, had broken his neck. Guilt and shame led Francis to abandon his family.

Over the course of three days sacred in the Christian calendar—Hallowe'en (All Saints' Eve), All Saints' Day, and All Souls' Day—Francis worked his way toward a kind of redemption. The process began with a visit to the cemetery where Gerald was buried. From the grave, Gerald told Francis that he would have to perform acts of expiation for abandoning his family, even though he would not recognize his acts as expiatory. When these acts were complete, Gerald promised, Francis would stop trying to die because of Gerald.

During those days, Francis worked as a gravedigger and rag collector. He looked after his fellow hoboes, Rudy and Helen, to the best of his ability. He shared what he had with others. Above all, he faced the family he had abandoned. For Billy, acceptance of his father was easy. Billy's sister Peg resisted longer; old resentments had to be overcome. Annie, Francis' wife, had long since moved beyond forgiveness. She welcomed him. What Francis could never have imagined, but somehow was not surprised to learn, was that Annie had never told anyone that it was he who was holding Gerald when the accident occurred.

When Francis had to kill once more, in defense of another hobo's life, he could take refuge in the Phelan home. Or was this the fantasy he carried with him as, a fugitive once more, he rode a freight out of Albany? Either way, Francis Phelan had come home.

Critical Evaluation:

The idea of referring to the three novels *Legs, Billy Phelan's Greatest Game*, and *Ironweed* by the collective title of *The Albany Cycle* was apparently not William Kennedy's; reportedly, it was dreamed up as a marketing device by an editor at Viking, Kennedy's publisher. Nevertheless, it is true to his perception early in his career that Albany, the city in which he grew up, would become his great subject. His first novel, *The Ink Truck* (1968), is set in Albany, although not in the 1930's. *Quinn's Book* (1988), although set in the nineteenth century, places much of the action in Albany. In *Very Old Bones* (1992), Kennedy returns to the period and some of the characters, including several Phelans, of the earlier *Albany Cycle*. There is no place, Kennedy realizes, that he will ever know as he knows Albany. He further understands that he is the sort of writer for whom the sense of place is crucial. Abstract novels of psychological analysis do not interest him. His interest in place, specifically in Albany, is by no means primarily sociological. Rather, he wants to explore how the inner lives of human beings are shaped by the experience of living in a particular time and a particular place. Because all people are shaped by such forces, Kennedy's examination of these particulars as they manifest themselves through highly individual characters is equally an examination of what may be most universal in human experience.

The protagonist of *Legs*, the first novel of *The Albany Cycle*, was an actual historical figure who operated around Albany and was finally shot to death there in 1931. Kennedy thoroughly researched Diamond's life, and, as far as the external events are concerned, the novel does not deviate significantly from the established facts. A documentary account of a killer's life, however, was not the author's goal. His Jack Diamond transcends the historical record to enter the realms of legend and myth. Why, Kennedy asks, are people so fascinated with Diamond and with others like him? An important structural pattern is the seduction and moral collapse of Marcus Gorman. Since he is not predominantly evil, but a man of middling moral stature, Gorman's inability to resist Diamond's charisma symbolizes the hold a man such as Diamond can have on the imagination of ordinary, moderately decent people. Some critics have felt that the author, not merely the character, has been seduced by Jack Diamond. These critics argue that Kennedy, fascinated by Diamond as some kind of life force, fails to place him within a coherent moral vision. Kennedy would respond that by watching a character such as Diamond go to extremes of charisma and cruelty, one may be stimulated to explore one's own hierarchies of value.

Billy Phelan, protagonist of the second novel, *Billy Phelan's Greatest Game*, is a character whose hierarchies of value bring him close to destruction at the hands of Patsy McCall, the political boss of Albany. Kennedy modeled this character on Dan O'Connell, who was Albany's political boss for more than forty years. The key event in Kennedy's plot, the kidnapping of McCall's nephew, is based on the actual kidnapping of O'Connell's nephew in the 1930's. Once again, Kennedy is anything but a documentarist. He wants to explore the consequences for the self of living in the shadow of a corrupt and omnipotent political machine. This is the most political novel of the three, but Kennedy's primary concern is with the inner life.

Some critics have found that *Billy Phelan's Greatest Game* fails as a novel because its parts, although often impressive in themselves, fail to cohere. The secondary plot involving Martin Daugherty may seem extraneous to the main plot focusing on Billy. In fairness to Kennedy, his purposes require that the reader know Albany in order to know Billy. Whether the secondary plot provides the sort of knowing that best illuminates Billy, however, remains a legitimate critical question.

Ironweed, the third novel of *The Albany Cycle*, is, for many critics, the finest novel in the trilogy, perhaps the most impressive achievement of Kennedy's career. Initially rejected by publishers on the grounds that it was depressing, that readers did not care about bums, even that real bums were not as eloquent as Kennedy's creations, the novel's publication won its author not only widespread critical acclaim, but an audience. Excited by *Ironweed*, readers discovered the simultaneously reissued earlier novels, which had hitherto been relatively neglected.

As is customary with Kennedy, the strength of this novel rests on its eloquent evocation of place, but it is even more impressive in its exploration of the soul of its protagonist, Francis Phelan. As he confronts the past and its many pains, Francis moves toward a redemption that is presented entirely without sentimentality. His circumstances have altered only slightly. As before in his life, he is being pursued for killing a man, but he has confronted his demons and taken his own measure as a man. Above all, against the odds, he has survived, not physically only, but in his soul.

As the third novel of *The Albany Cycle*, *Ironweed* illuminates the first two in a number of ways. Francis becomes a touchstone for understanding "Legs" and Billy, and Francis' struggles deepen one's sense of the Albany one meets in the other novels. One consequence is that the earlier novels improve in the light of the later one. Features that had been troublesome, now find their place in the larger whole. The structural problems of *Billy Phelan's Greatest Game* no longer seem so important. The moral ambiguities of *Legs* become acceptable as part of a more inclusive design. Ultimately, *The Albany Cycle* adds up to a whole greater than the sum of its parts.

W. P. Kenney

Bibliography:
Edinger, Claudio. *The Making of Ironweed.* New York: Penguin Books, 1988. A detailed look at the 1987 film made from the third novel of *The Albany Cycle* and the process of its production. Kennedy himself wrote the script, and the book illuminates a number of aspects of the novel, as does a viewing of the film itself.

Kennedy, William. *Riding the Yellow Trolley Car.* New York: Viking Press, 1993. The first section of this collection of pieces by Kennedy includes many of the author's reflections on the novels that make up *The Albany Cycle*. The fifth section contains his account of the making of the film *Ironweed*.

McCaffery, Larry, and Sinda Gregory. *Alive and Writing: Interviews with American Authors of the 1980's.* Urbana: University of Illinois Press, 1987. Probing, engaging interview with Kennedy. Provides a concentrated supplement to the materials in *Riding the Yellow Trolley Car.*

Reilly, Edward C. *William Kennedy.* Boston: Twayne, 1991. Introduction to Kennedy's life and works for the general reader. Broadly useful critical study. Includes bibliography.

Van Dover, J. K. *Understanding William Kennedy.* Columbia: University of South Carolina Press, 1991. Asserts that Kennedy moves toward his true subject in the process of writing *The Albany Cycle*. Heavy emphasis on the role of place in Kennedy's work.

ALCESTIS

Type of work: Drama
Author: Euripides (c. 485-406 B.C.E.)
Type of plot: Tragicomedy
Time of plot: Antiquity
Locale: Pherae, in ancient Greece
First performed: Alkēstis, 438 B.C.E. (English translation, 1781)

> *Principal characters:*
> APOLLO, god of the sun
> ADMETUS, the king of Pherae
> ALCESTIS, his wife
> THANATOS, Death
> HERCULES, son of Zeus and friend to Admetus

The Story:

Phoebus Apollo had a son, Asclepius, who in time became a god of medicine and healing. Asclepius transgressed divine law by raising a mortal, Hippolytus, from the dead, and Zeus, in anger, killed Apollo's son with a thunderbolt forged by the Cyclops. Apollo then slew the Cyclops, a deed for which he was condemned by Zeus to leave Olympus and to serve for one year as herdsman to Admetus, the king of Pherae in Thessaly.

Some time after Apollo had completed his term of service, Admetus married Alcestis, the daughter of the king of Iolcus, Pelias. On his wedding day, however, he offended the goddess Artemis and so was doomed to die. Apollo, grateful for the kindness Admetus had shown him in the past, prevailed on the Fates to spare the king on the condition that when his hour of death should come, they accept instead the life of whoever would consent to die in his place.

None of Admetus' kin cared to offer himself in his place, but Alcestis, in wifely devotion, pledged herself to die for her husband. The day arrived when she must give up her life. Concerned for the wife of his mortal friend, Apollo appealed to Thanatos, who had come to take Alcestis to the underworld. Thanatos rejected his pleas, warning the god not to transgress against eternal judgment or the will of the Fates. Apollo declared that there was one powerful enough to defy the Fates who was even then on his way to the palace of Admetus. Meanwhile Alcestis prepared for her approaching death. On the day she was to die, she dressed herself in rich funeral robes and prayed before the hearth fire to Vesta, goddess of the hearth, asking her to be a mother to the two children she was leaving behind, to find a helpmate for the boy, a gentle lord for the girl, and not to let them follow their mother's example and die before their time. After her prayers, she placed garlands of myrtle on each altar of the house and at each shrine prayed tearlessly, knowing that death was coming. In her own chamber she wept as she remembered the happy years she and Admetus had lived together. Her children found her there, and she said her farewells to them. The house was filled also with the sound of weeping servants, grieving for the mistress they loved. Admetus too wept bitterly, begging Alcestis not to leave him. While he watched, however, her breath grew fainter, and her cold hand fell languidly. Before she died, she asked him to promise that he would always care tenderly for their children and that he would never marry again.

At that moment, Hercules arrived at the palace of Admetus, on his way to slay the wild horses of Diomedes in Thrace as the eighth of his twelve labors. Admetus concealed from Hercules the news of Alcestis' death so that he might keep the son of Zeus as a guest and carry out the proper rites of hospitality. Hercules, ignorant of what had taken place before his arrival in Pherae, spent the night carousing, drinking wine, and singing, only to awaken in the morning to discover that Alcestis had died hours before he came and that his host had purposely deluded him in order to make his stay in Pherae as comfortable as possible. In gratitude for Admetus' thoughtfulness and in remorse for having reveled while the home of his friend was deep in sorrow, he determined to ambush Thanatos and bring Alcestis back from the dead.

Since no labor was too arduous for the hero, he set out after Thanatos and Alcestis. Overtaking them, he wrestled with Thanatos and forced him to give up his victim. Then he brought Alcestis, heavily veiled, into the presence of sorrowing Admetus, and asked the king to protect her until Hercules returned from Thrace. When Admetus refused, Hercules insisted that the king at least peer beneath the woman's veil. Great was the joy of Admetus and his household when they learned that the woman was Alcestis miraculously returned from the grave. Pleased with his efforts, doughty Hercules continued his travels, firm in the knowledge that with him went the undying gratitude of Admetus and the gentle Alcestis.

Critical Evaluation:

Alcestis, the earliest extant tragedy by Euripides, was written when the dramatist was in his forties. It is therefore the work of a fully matured man. First staged in 438 B.C.E., the play is in part a product of Athens' Age of Pericles, that period between the end of the Persian Wars and the onset of the Peloponnesian War. This play shares some of the piety and optimistic confidence of that golden era when Athens reached its greatest power and achieved its finest cultural successes, including the great tragedians Aeschylus, Sophocles, and Euripides.

In *Alcestis*, Euripides reworked an old legend that had earlier been dramatized by the tragic poet Phrynichus. The work bears Euripides' inimitable stamp in the keen psychological portraiture, in the rare mixture of comic and tragic elements, and in the *deus ex machina* ending. Presented as the fourth drama in a tetralogy, which was traditionally a satyr-play, *Alcestis* is best described as a tragicomedy.

The opening confrontation between Apollo and Thanatos, or Death, sets forth the opposition that is the play's main underlying theme. Apollo is a radiant god, the representative of light, health, and life, whereas Thanatos is a dark, dismal underworld divinity with an awesome power over all living creatures. Both deities have a claim on Admetus and Alcestis, yet because they belong to different supernatural spheres a compromise between them is impossible. However, Apollo, with his prophetic gift, foresees a resolution in the arrival of Heracles, who will rescue Alcestis from Death.

From that point on, the action proceeds on purely human terms. All the characters are recognizable as persons, with private attitudes, emotions, and choices. Euripides reveals the feelings of Alcestis, a woman who freely sacrifices her life so that her husband may live; of Admetus, who has asked for and accepted such a sacrifice; of the child of such a marriage; of Admetus' old father, Pheres, reviled by his only son for refusing to lay down his life; and of Heracles, who accepts hospitality from the grieving Admetus, drunkenly amuses himself, and then wrests Alcestis from Death to redeem his honor. These are not mere puppets of Fate but men and women acting of their own volition. They are, however, torn between life and death—between Apollo and Thanatos—by the choices they make.

Alcestis chooses the heroic role in laying down her life for Admetus. She knows well what she will leave behind: the joy of her marriage bed, her small children, and the pleasures of living. Her sacrifice is all the greater because she is also aware of the terrors of death. She loves her husband, but Alcestis is also thinking of her children and of what would happen to them if the kingdom passed to a stranger. Her final restoration dramatically suggests the biblical paradox that whoever loses his life for love's sake will gain new life.

Admetus suggests the complementary paradox, that whoever seeks to save his life will lose it. He turns weak in the face of death and chooses to let another die for him. His remorse while his wife is still alive is sheer sentimentality, for at heart he is an egoistic coward. Yet when she is dead he must confront his ignoble shame and live a deathlike existence of perpetual mourning.

His moment of self-recognition occurs in the bitter meeting with his father, Pheres. Admetus blames Pheres for Alcestis' death, because the old man chose to live when he might have died for his son. Pheres exhibits the same cowardice that afflicts Admetus, but he speaks the truth when he condemns Admetus and declares that no one should ask another to die in his place. Pheres in clutching life loses the only thing that mattered to him—the respect of his son—and so his life has become a curse.

If Admetus has damned his father, he has also damned his children to a motherless desolation and damned himself. He performs one generous act by admitting Hercules as a guest and disguising the cause of his mourning. It is dramatically necessary that Hercules be ignorant of Alcestis' death so that he makes a drunken fool of himself. Euripides ingeniously retains the sober mood of the play in this scene, for Hercules in his intoxicated solemnity discourses on death's inevitability. This leads to Hercules' discovery of the truth and of his own shame. To every man in this play there comes a moment when he must face personal shame. In Hercules' case, shame motivates him to a noble act. The final scene, where Hercules restores Alcestis to Admetus, is perfectly integrated with the pattern of the whole play and with the themes of sacrifice, loss, and redemption.

The view of life behind this drama is psychologically coherent. It shows the heroic nature of a total sacrifice, the base nature of asking and accepting such a gift, and the path of salvation through a full realization of personal degradation and through acts of unsolicited generosity. Hercules, in entering Admetus' home, becomes involved in his degradation and must save himself by this same path. Baseness is a form of death, Euripides seems to say, but redemption is life, true life. In *Alcestis*, Euripides revives an old myth in a way that probed the basis of human experience.

"Critical Evaluation" by James Weigel, Jr.

Bibliography:
Euripides. *Alcestis*. Edited by Desmond J. Conacher. Warminster, England: Aris & Phillips, 1988. Greek text and English translation. Conacher's introduction sets the play in context and discusses problems of interpretation. The commentary emphasizes structure and themes.
_____. *Alcestis*. Edited by A. M. Dale. Oxford, England: Oxford University Press, 1954. Contains a Greek text and a valuable introduction and line-by-line commentary. An indispensable starting point for serious study.
Grube, G. M. A. *The Drama of Euripides*. London: Methuen, 1941. A general treatment of Euripides, still highly regarded. Contains chapters on the structural elements of Euripides' plays, the chorus, the gods, and contemporary issues; also provides penetrating analysis of individual plays, including *Alcestis*.
Pickard-Cambridge, Arthur W. *The Dramatic Festivals of Athens*. Rev. ed. Oxford, England: Clarendon Press, 1968. A magisterial work, closely based on ancient sources, treating the

religious festivals at which tragedy and comedy were performed. Includes chapters on the actors, costumes, chorus, audience, and guilds of performers.

Wilson, John R., ed. *Twentieth Century Interpretations of Euripides' "Alcestis."* Englewood Cliffs, N.J.: Prentice-Hall, 1968. A useful collection of ten critical essays on *Alcestis* that were originally published between 1940 and 1965, as well as ten "Points of View," brief, thought-provoking extracts from larger works.

THE ALCHEMIST

Type of work: Drama
Author: Ben Jonson (1573-1637)
Type of plot: Comedy of manners
Time of plot: Early seventeenth century
Locale: London
First performed: 1610; first published, 1612

> *Principal characters:*
> FACE, a butler
> SUBTLE, a swindler posing as an alchemist
> DOL COMMON, their partner
> LOVEWIT, owner of the house and Face's master
> SIR EPICURE MAMMON, a greedy knight
> DAME PLIANT, a young widow

The Story:

Master Lovewit had left the city because of plague. His butler, Jeremy, known as Face to his friends of the underworld, invited Subtle, a swindler posing as an alchemist, and Dol Common, a prostitute, to join him in using the house as a base of operations for their rascally activities. Matters fared well for the three until a dispute arose between Face and Subtle over authority. Dol, seeing their moneymaking projects doomed if this strife continued, rebuked the two men and cajoled them back to their senses.

No sooner had Face and Subtle become reconciled than Dapper, a gullible lawyer's clerk given to gambling, called, by previous arrangement with Face. Dapper wanted to learn from the eminent astrologer, Doctor Subtle, how to win at all games of chance. In the hands of the two merciless rascals, Dapper was relieved of all his ready cash, in return for which Subtle predicted that Dapper would have good luck at the gaming tables. In order to gull Dapper further, Subtle told him to return later to confer with the Queen of Fairy, a mysterious benefactress who could promote Dapper's worldly success.

Abel Drugger, an ambitious young druggist who had been led on by Face, was the next victim to enter the house. To his delight, he learned from Subtle, who spoke mostly in incomprehensible pharmaceutical and astrological jargon, that he would have a rich future.

Next arrived Sir Epicure Mammon, a greedy and lecherous knight, with his friend Pertinax Surly, a man versed in the ways of London confidence men. Having been promised the philosophers' stone by Subtle, Mammon had wild visions of transforming all of his possessions into gold and silver, but he was completely taken in by the duplicities of Subtle and Face. Subtle further aroused Mammon's greed by describing at length, in the pseudoscientific gibberish of the alchemist-confidence man, the processes that led to his approximate achievement of the mythical philosophers' stone. Surly, quick to see what was afoot, scoffed at Subtle and at the folly of Mammon.

During the interview, Dol appeared inadvertently. Mammon caught sight of her and was fascinated. Thinking quickly, Face told Mammon that Dol was an aristocratic lady who, being mad, was under the care of Doctor Subtle but who, in her moments of sanity, was most affable. Before he left the house, Mammon promised to send to the unprincipled Subtle certain of his household objects of base metal for the purpose of having them transmuted into gold.

The parade of victims continued. Elder Ananias of the Amsterdam community of extreme Protestants came to negotiate for his group with Subtle for the philosophers' stone. Subtle, with Face as his assistant, repeated his extravagant jargon to the impressionable Ananias, who, in his greed, declared that the brethren were impatient with the slowness of the experiment. Subtle, feigning professional indignation, frightened Ananias with a threat to put out forever his alchemist's fire.

Drugger reappeared to be duped further. Subtle and Face were delighted when he told them that a wealthy young widow had taken lodgings near his, and that her brother, recently come into an inheritance, had journeyed to London to learn how to quarrel in rakish fashion. The two knaves plotted eagerly to get brother and sister into their clutches.

Ananias returned with his pastor, Tribulation Wholesome. The Puritans managed to wink at moral considerations as Subtle glowingly described the near completion of the philosophers' stone. Prepared to go to any ends to procure the stone, Ananias and Tribulation contracted to purchase Mammon's household articles, which, Subtle explained, he needed for the experiment; the proceeds of the sale would go toward the care of orphans for whom Subtle said he was responsible.

Subtle and Face also plotted to sell these same household articles to the young widow, who, having just moved to London, was probably in need of such items. In the meantime, Face met in the streets a Spanish Don—Surly in clever disguise—who expressed a desire to confer with Subtle on matters of business and health.

Dapper returned to meet the Queen of Fairy. At the same time, Drugger brought to the house Master Kastril, the angry young man who wanted to learn to quarrel. Kastril was completely taken in. Subtle, promising to make him a perfect London gallant, arranged to have him instructed by Face, who posed as a city captain. Kastril was so pleased with his new acquaintances that he sent Drugger to bring his sister to the house.

Kastril having departed, Dol, Subtle, and Face relieved Dapper of all of his money in a ridiculous ritual in which Dapper was to see and talk to the Queen of Fairy. During the shameless proceedings, Mammon knocked. Dapper, who had been blindfolded, was gagged and hastily put into a water closet at the rear of the house. Mammon entered and began to woo Dol, whom he believed to be a distracted aristocrat. Face and Subtle, in order to have the front part of the house clear for further swindles, shunted the amorous pair to another part of the house.

Young Kastril returned with his widowed sister, Dame Pliant; both were deeply impressed by Subtle's manner and rhetoric. When the Spanish Don arrived, Subtle escorted Kastril and Dame Pliant to inspect his laboratory. By that time, both Subtle and Face were determined to wed Dame Pliant. Face introduced the Spaniard to Dame Pliant, who, in spite of her objections to Spaniards in general, consented to walk in the garden with the Don.

In another part of the house, Dol assumed the manner of madness. Subtle, discovering the distraught Mammon with her, declared that Mammon's moral laxity would surely delay completion of the philosopher's stone. Following a loud explosion, Face reported that the laboratory was a shambles. Mammon despondently left the house, and Subtle simulated a fainting spell.

In the garden, Surly revealed his true identity to Dame Pliant and warned the young widow against the swindlers. When, as Surly, he confronted the two rogues, Face, in desperation, told Kastril that Surly was an impostor who was trying to steal Dame Pliant away. Drugger entered and, being Face's creature, insisted that he knew Surly to be a scoundrel. Ananias came to the house and all but wrecked Subtle's plot by talking indiscreetly of making counterfeit money. Unable to cope with the wily rascals, Surly departed, followed by Kastril.

Glad to be rid of his callers, Subtle placed Dame Pliant in Dol's care. They were thrown once more into confusion when Lovewit, owner of the house, made an untimely appearance. Face, quickly reverting to his normal role of Jeremy, the butler, went to the door in an attempt to detain his master long enough to permit Subtle and Dol to escape.

Although warned by his butler that the house was infested, Lovewit suspected that something was amiss when Mammon and Surly returned to expose Subtle and Face. Kastril, Ananias, and Tribulation confirmed their account. Dapper, having managed to get rid of his gag, cried out inside the house. Deciding that honesty was the only policy, Face confessed everything to his master and promised to provide him with a wealthy young widow as his wife, if Lovewit would have mercy on his servant.

In the house, meanwhile, Subtle concluded the gulling of Dapper and sent the young clerk on his way, filled with the belief that he would win at all games of chance. Subtle and Dol then tried to abscond with the threesome's loot, but Face, back in Lovewit's good graces, thwarted them in their attempt. They were forced to escape empty-handed by the back gate.

Lovewit won the hand of Dame Pliant and, in his good humor, forgave his crafty butler. When those who had been swindled demanded retribution, they were finally convinced that they had been defrauded as a result of their own selfishness and greed.

Critical Evaluation:

The Alchemist marks the peak of Ben Jonson's artistic career. Despite a somewhat muddled denouement, the play is a masterpiece of construction. As far as is known, the plot was original with Jonson. In this play, Jonson the artist supersedes Jonson the moralist: A highly entertaining and dramatic satire on human greed, *The Alchemist* displays none of the sermonizing that marks, to some extent, Jonson's other plays.

For anyone interested in learning how to take in the gullible, Ben Jonson's *The Alchemist* is a fundamental text. "Cony-catching" was a popular practice in Elizabethan England, and Jonson, an intimate of London's jails, taverns, theaters, and places of even less repute, reveals in this play the techniques involved in several of the most amusing and lucrative ploys. His protagonist, it should be noted, is not punished for his misdeeds.

The complexities of life in London during the Elizabethan era, coupled with limited general scientific understanding, help account for the widespread faith in astrology and alchemy of the time. This faith in such branches of knowledge helped make them leading gimmicks for swindles. Commerce thrived and new continents were explored, but people were not far from believing in the dragons slain by King Arthur's knights. Many believed also that the dawning age of science would discover a "philosophers' stone" that would transmute dross into gold. Jonson's London, the London of *The Alchemist*, was growing and glittering and slightly hysterical, and cozening was easy, widespread, and immensely successful.

The critical response to the play has been intriguing. Samuel Taylor Coleridge, presumably impressed by the play's adherence to the classical unities, praised it as having one of the three best plots in literature, the other two being Sophocles' *Oedipus Tyrannus* (c. 429 B.C.E.) and Henry Fielding's *Tom Jones* (1749). Several modern commentators have contended that, although *The Alchemist* does cleave to the classical ideals, it is not a proper comedy, has no plot at all, and consists merely of a series of linked incidents. Romantic and Victorian critics particularly, understandably enchanted by Jonson's contemporary and diametric opposite, William Shakespeare, were put off by Jonson's classical forms, his satiric manner, and his coarseness. They also disliked his unemotional tone, controlled plots, and intellectual detachment. Although *The Alchemist* lacks none of these features, they do not render it deficient.

The classical ideals are so well met in *The Alchemist* that the play is, in its own way, a small classical masterpiece. Jonson observes unity of time, in that the dramatic situation is enacted in the same amount of time that it would take in real life. Unity of place is maintained because the scene, Lovewit's house in the Friars, is specific and limited. The discrete beginning, middle, and inevitable conclusion of the play provide for unity of action. The characters are "types" who behave consistently, doing nothing unexpected, and thus the ideal of decorum, the paramount classical precept, is met: Jonson's prostitute is bawdy, his churchmen sanctimonious.

Faithfulness to classical concepts, however, is not the only virtue of *The Alchemist*. A talented actor as well as a writer of poetry, masques, criticism, and tragic and comic plays, Jonson was a masterful manipulator of theatrical effects. The opening argument of *The Alchemist*, presented in antic verse, catapults the play headlong into a rollicking, boisterous, bawdy life of its own. The simple yet ingenious plot provides for the multiplicity of incident dear to the Renaissance heart; costume, disguise, and transmutation of identity are similarly exploited.

The internal development is more complex than some critics suggest. The characters are introduced in approximate order of their social status and rapacity. As these advance, so does the degree of cozening inflicted by Face and Subtle, and this progression reinforces the cohesiveness of the play. Although the fates of the characters are not contingent, since all are frauds or dupes, they interact in complex and amusing ways. These interactions, which become so dense that eventually Face and Subtle have their victims cozening each other, engender organic unity and dramatic tension simultaneously. As the play advances, the number of characters on stage increases, the pace quickens, and the scenes grow shorter. The climax is predictable but impressive, the entire proceeding animated by a genuine and hearty spirit.

Despite its qualifications as a well-wrought, clever, and entertaining play in the classical mode, *The Alchemist* owes much of its literary interest and charm to Jonson's rhetorical flourishes. The underworld slang and alchemical jargon used by the protagonists lend color and authenticity. Double entendres, and simultaneous dialogue, which originated with Jonson, add to the effect. Most impressive, perhaps, is the way Subtle and Face use a debased eloquence in perpetrating their frauds. One of Subtle's elegant, highly rhetorical, pseudo-rational arguments, for example, seems unequivocally to establish the propensity of all metals to turn into gold. Surly's calm and earnest reasoning with Dame Pliant, on the other hand, seems but a pale counterfeit of Subtle's spirited equivocation.

The Alchemist dramatizes what might happen when moral order is suspended by plague in London. Lovewit, representing responsible society, jettisons civic responsibility and flees the city, leaving behind only knaves and fools. Although the reader is reminded early that order will be restored eventually, society in the hands of the unscrupulous degenerates into chaos. The servant supplants the master, science is overthrown by alchemy, reason is toppled by rhetoric, nature's secrets are transcended, and moral order is subverted as churchmen become swindlers.

Jonson's vehicle, satire, was quite popular in Elizabethan England, and in *The Alchemist* its effect is intensified by the plague in the background. Jonson intended to be instructive, even if it meant instructing by ridicule. The classicist in him wanted to restore to England some of the glory of Augustan Rome. To this end, Jonson adhered in his works to Cicero's famous dictum, "a copy of life, a mirror of custom, a representation of truth." Accordingly, he anchors his play in contemporary London and reflects the speech, behavior, and attitudes of its citizens. The Renaissance saw a shift in emphasis from the world of the Church to the world of experience, but while Jonson set an extremely worldly stage, his morality was severe and almost medieval. His moral values, clear from the first scene on, are constantly reiterated as *The Alchemist* indicts vain and wishful thinking and directs the mind to the contemplation of virtue. It is a sign of Ben Jonson's genius that he does it unequivocally and entertainingly.

"Critical Evaluation" by Michael Levine

Bibliography:

Barton, Anne. *Ben Jonson: Dramatist.* Cambridge, England: Cambridge University Press, 1984. In addition to its introduction to *The Alchemist*, offers an essential discussion of the meaning and use of names and naming in Jonson's plays—an almost obsessive interest of Jonson's throughout his work—in the context of Western discussions of language from Plato to historian William Camden, Jonson's contemporary and teacher.

Donaldon, Ian. "Language, Noise, and Nonsense: *The Alchemist.*" In *Seventeenth Century Imagery*, edited by Earl Miner. Berkeley: University of California Press, 1971. Focused discussion of the thematic significance of the play's concern with language, including meaningless language. Places the play in the context of seventeenth century ideas about language.

Knights, L. C. *Drama and Society in the Age of Jonson.* London: Chatto & Windus, 1937. Starting point for discussions of Jonson's plays as social sets. The first attempt to discuss Jonson's dramatic works in the context of early seventeenth century London society, politics, and economics.

Partridge, Edward B. *The Broken Compass.* London: Chatto & Windus, 1958. The first extended study of Jonson's imagery. Excellent introduction for readers unfamiliar with Jonson's sometimes difficult language.

Wayne, Don E. "Drama and Society in the Age of Jonson: An Alternative View." *Renaissance Drama*, n.s. 13 (1982): 103-129. Criticizes Knights's thesis. Offers a more sophisticated, historical view of how the plays operated in and gave expression to Jonson's society.

ALCOOLS

Type of work: Poetry
Author: Guillaume Apollinaire (Guillaume Albert Wladimir Alexandre Apollinaire de Kostrowitzky, 1880-1918)
First published: 1913 (English translation, 1964)

The son of a Polish adventuress and an Italian officer, Guillaume Apollinaire spent most of his childhood in Monaco and the South of France. By 1899, when he was nineteen, he had come to Paris, where he became one of the most remarkable leaders of the young intellectual movements in the capital. In one way or another he contributed to fauvism, to cubism, and even to Surrealism. He helped, moreover, to establish the reputation of the painter Henri Rousseau.

Apollinaire's *Alcools*, a collection of poems published in 1913, contains works that span the years 1898 to 1912. There is little thematic or formal unity within this collection, and the title expresses the poet's thirst for vivid sensation and experience, as well as his remarkable impressionability.

The rather long poem "Zone" was not Apollinaire's original selection as the first in the 1913 collection. Its themes and aesthetic are scarcely characteristic, but perhaps an explanation may be sought in the very element of surprise, which was an essential part of Apollinaire's poetic technique.

"Zone" and several other pieces in *Alcools* may justifiably be compared with cubist paintings by artists such as Robert Delaunay. There is the same prismatic view of the world, the juxtaposition of apparently disparate elements, and the attempt to offer several views from different angles simultaneously. A contrapuntal or polyphonic effect in "Zone," as in other pieces, is furthered by Apollinaire's complete suppression of punctuation from the collection. This effect introduces a constant element of ambiguity and necessitates a careful reading, and often a rereading, which helps to immerse the reader in the atmosphere of the poem. Apollinaire, when he used punctuation, showed himself to have a faulty knowledge of it; he was later to become skilled in not using it. The reader always has the impression of helping to re-create the poem when he or she reads it.

The opening lines of "Zone" situate its mood, if not its true time or location. The poem is ostensibly a lament for excessive devotion to the past, and Apollinaire's introduction of the Eiffel Tower, automobiles, and precise, proper names is pointedly topical. There is, however, a much deeper theme and unity in the form of the poet's quest. Unhappy in love, he searches in vain for some consolation. The mood remains nostalgic, even unhappy. Walking through Paris, the poet has the impression that he is cast in the role of unhappy lover and as if this unhappiness has developed into a pattern, a consciousness of a life lived in frenzy and waste. With a technique very similar to that of the flashback in the cinema, the language dissolves into a series of images as the poet reviews the places he has visited. Viewing himself as object, then speaking as the subject of the description, passing from second to first person, then combining the two, the poet achieves a remarkable fusion of past and present, the overall effect of which is a sense of complete failure.

Apollinaire's influence on the later Surrealist movement cannot be doubted. "Zone," like many other pieces, suggests the presence of beauty and poetry as a latent quality in the most unconventional objects. Street scenes in Paris with cafés and streetcars, the Eiffel Tower, police thrillers: These are a few of the manifestations of the French scene in Apollinaire's day around which he could shape his poetry.

The Surrealist poet André Breton was later to assert that poetry was contained within objects that up to his time had been held to be alien to art. Apollinaire would have agreed. He did not hesitate to intersperse snatches of conversation with a nostalgic lament or part of a popular song. In at least one poem, "The Pretty Redhead," Apollinaire's stated ambition is no less enormous than that of André Breton and indeed could easily find a place inside one of the Surrealist manifestos.

It would be quite wrong to cast Apollinaire simply as a poet-explorer or a virtuoso playing with words. Many critics would even claim that his essential talent is lyrical, and it is true that there is a peculiar poignancy about his laments for love lost or the passage of time, two of the permanent subjects of poetry.

In "Mirabeau Bridge," Apollinaire offers the reader the simplest of situations: a bridge over the Seine, with someone looking into the water. Though the external description is slight, almost everything in the poem suggests movement, and the flow of the river evokes the moods of love and of the passing of time. When the poet tries to establish a parallel between the bridge and the lovers, to suggest a possible permanence in love, the attempt fails. Love is shown to disappear, like the waters of the river.

The third piece in *Alcools* is a long poem in several movements entitled "The Song of the Ill-Beloved." In it Apollinaire displays his ready acceptance of the world and his openness and receptiveness to it, as well as his vulnerability. The poem is often ambiguous. It has love as its theme, but love made noticeable through its absence and the poet's memory of it rather than through any form of fulfillment. The opening stanza prepares the reader for the mysterious, unreal atmosphere of the poem, similar here to that conjured up in the thrillers of the period. In the image of a young hoodlum appearing in the fog of a London evening Apollinaire creates an aura of mystery which makes anything seem possible. He communicates a sense of immediacy, so that each description comes vividly to life. For each mood, each idea, the poet immediately offers an image. A memory is no sooner called up than it fills the poem, temporarily changing its direction. Yet there is a single threat running through the poem, a strain of melancholy involving a return to present reality from memories of springtime and love. The final stanza reasserts the poet's awareness of his role as the one who captures memories and sings them, who makes of his experience a pattern, a ritual, a song that can be passed on to others.

Better, perhaps, than any other poet in the early twentieth century, Apollinaire was able to translate the eclectic, anxious consciousness of his time, which combined the awareness of tradition and the desire for change. In Apollinaire, the Romantics' rediscovery of the dual nature of human beings—angel and beast, body and soul, the *homo duplex* of Christian terminology— gives way to a more complex concept. Apollinaire reveals the *homo multiplex*, the human beings of manifold aspirations and moods that often coexist simultaneously. The apparent disorder of this consciousness is reflected in the poems.

Bibliography:
Bates, Scott. *Guillaume Apollinaire*. New York: Twayne, 1967. A detailed, exhaustive study of Apollinaire's poetic art, tracing characteristic themes and sources.
Davies, Margaret. *Apollinaire*. Edinburgh: Oliver & Boyd, 1964. A well-grounded life-and-works study in the British tradition, rich in documented anecdote if somewhat short on literary analysis. Davies examines in detail the "riddle" of Apollinaire's paternity, a major theme in his literary art.
Shattuck, Roger. *The Banquet Years*. Rev. ed. New York: Vintage Books, 1968. A pioneering work of cultural history. Although trained as a scholar of literature, Shattuck ranges freely

and knowledgeably across disciplinary boundaries in search of the modernist spirit and its origins, concentrating on the figures of Henri Rousseau, Alfred Jarry, Apollinaire, and Erik Satie. Treats both Apollinaire's poetry and his role as critic and publicist of modern art.

Stamelman, Richard Howard. *The Drama of Self in Guillaume Apollinaire's "Alcools."* Chapel Hill: University of North Carolina Department of Romance Languages, 1976. Offers insightful commentary and criticism in clear, often memorable prose.

Steegmuller, Francis. *Apollinaire: Poet Among the Painters.* New York: Farrar, Straus, 1963. Written by one of the best-known and most effective English-language translators of Apollinaire, Steegmuller's volume complements Shattuck's discussion of Apollinaire as poet and art critic. Also provides a useful re-creation of artistic life in turn-of-the-century Paris.

ALECK MAURY, SPORTSMAN

Type of work: Novel
Author: Caroline Gordon (1895-1981)
Type of plot: Social realism
Time of plot: Late nineteenth and early twentieth centuries
Locale: Virginia, Tennessee, Mississippi, and Missouri
First published: 1934

Principal characters:
ALECK MAURY, a Southern sportsman
JAMES MORRIS, his uncle
VICTORIA, his aunt
JULIAN, his cousin
MR. FAYERLEE, the owner of Merry Point
MRS. FAYERLEE, his wife
MOLLY FAYERLEE, their daughter and Aleck's wife
RICHARD and
SARAH or SALLY, Aleck's and Molly's children
STEVE, Sarah's husband

The Story:

Aleck Maury's love for hunting and fishing began in childhood. At the age of eight, Aleck went coon hunting with Rafe, a black handyman at the Maury household. Not long after, a mill owner named Jones took the boy fishing and encouraged his lifelong love for that sport. Aleck was always happiest when he was out in the fields. One of five children, he was reared by his oldest sister after his mother died. Until he was ten years old, he was educated at home by his father, who put great stress upon the classics and taught his children nothing else.

At the age of ten, Aleck went to live at Grassdale with his Uncle James and Aunt Victoria Morris and their son, Julian. There, his education was to be broadened under the tutelage of Aunt Victoria, who was a learned woman. Aleck's life at Grassdale was pleasant, centering chiefly on sport.

When Aleck was graduated from the University of Virginia, he had a classical education but no plans for making a living. He tried several jobs. He cleared out a dogwood thicket for a set sum of money; he worked on a construction project on the Missouri River, in the city engineer's office in Seattle, and as a day laborer on a ranch in California. While working at the ranch, he contracted typhoid fever and was sent back east, as far as Kansas City, to stay with some relatives there. At last, through the efforts of his family, Aleck became a tutor at Merry Point, the home of Mr. Fayerlee, near Gloversville, Tennessee.

Aleck, living with the Fayerlees, became the local schoolmaster for the children of most of the landowners in the area. Aleck's first interest, however, was not in the school or the students he taught but in the possibilities for fishing and hunting.

During his stay with the Fayerlees, Aleck fell in love with Molly Fayerlee, and in 1890, they were married. They continued to live with the Fayerlees, and Aleck continued to teach school. During his first year of marriage, Aleck acquired the pup Gyges, a small but thoroughbred bird dog. He trained Gy from a puppy and became greatly attached to him. The next fall, Aleck's son, Richard, was born. Two years later, Sarah, nicknamed Sally, was born. They all continued to live at Merry Point.

When Richard was seven, Aleck was offered the presidency of a small seminary in Mississippi, and over the protestations of the Fayerlee family, the Maurys left Merry Point. On the way, while spending the night in Cairo, Aleck lost Gy. The dog was never heard of again. They continued their journey to Oakland and the seminary. When Aleck arrived, he found that the school was running smoothly under the able direction of Harry Morrow, his young assistant, who was interested in administration rather than teaching. A few months after arriving at Oakland, Aleck acquired an untrained two-year-old pointer named Trecho from his friend, William Mason. Once again Aleck started the slow, arduous training of a good hunting dog.

When Richard was fifteen, Aleck tried to interest him in the joys of his own life, hunting and fishing, but his son, although he was a splendid swimmer and wrestler, had little interest in his father's fondness for field and stream. That summer, Richard, while swimming in the river with a group of his companions, was drowned. The boy had been Molly's favorite and his loss was almost more than she could bear. Aleck thought it would be best for all concerned to leave for different surroundings.

He decided after some correspondence with friends that he would start a school in Gloversville, and the family moved back there. Settled in the small Tennessee town, Aleck found much time for fishing and hunting. He met Colonel Wyndham and from him learned a great deal about casting, flies, and the techniques to be used for catching various fish. Finally, he began to grow tired of the same pools and the same river, and it was with pleasure that he accepted Harry Morrow's offer of a job on the faculty of Rodman College at Poplar Bluff, Missouri, of which Morrow had just been made president.

Aleck's main reason for accepting the position was the possibility it offered for fishing in the Black River. Thus once again, after ten years in Gloversville, the Maury family was on the move to newer fishing grounds. Sally, however, did not accompany them but went to a girls' school in Nashville. The faithful Trecho was also left behind, for he had been destroyed at the age of twelve because of his rheumatism.

At Rodman, Aleck had only morning classes, a schedule which left him free to fish every afternoon. This pleasant life—teaching in the morning, fishing in the afternoon—continued for seven years. Then Molly died after an emergency operation. Mrs. Fayerlee and Sally arrived too late to see her alive. The three of them took her back to be buried in the family plot at Merry Point.

Aleck returned to Poplar Bluff and continued teaching there for several years, but he at last resigned his position and went to live at Jim Buford's, near Gloversville, where he spent the next two years restocking Jim's lakes with bream and bass. Later, he decided to go to Lake Harris in Florida to try the fishing; but he found it disappointing because of the eel grass, which kept the fish from putting up a fight. About that time, he received a letter from Sally, who had married and gone touring abroad with her husband. The letter informed him that she and her husband were soon to return home and that they hoped to find a quiet place in the country on some good fishing water, where Aleck would go to live with them. Aleck wrote and suggested that they start their search for a house near Elk River.

Four weeks later, he met Sally and Steve at Tullahoma, only to learn that Steve and Sally, who had arrived the day before, had already discovered the place they would like to own. They told him it was the old Potter house, close to the river. When Aleck saw the big, clapboard house, however, all his dreams about a white cottage disappeared, and when he looked at the river, he decided that it would probably be muddy about half the year. Seeing his disappointment, Steve and Sally promised to continue their attempt to find a more ideal house, but at the end of the day's search, they decided that they still liked the old Potter house the best. That night Aleck boarded a bus bound for Caney Fork, the place where he really wanted to live, and he went to stay at a small inn located there. The fishing was always good at Caney Fork.

Critical Evaluation:

Caroline Gordon's second novel, *Aleck Maury, Sportsman* marks her first experiment with a first-person narrator. Seventy-year-old Alexander Gordon Morris Maury reminisces about his life, from his lonely childhood in Virginia to the solitary future he envisions on Caney Fork in Tennessee. The narrative, divided into eight chapters, seems episodic because in each chapter the focus is upon Aleck's hunting and fishing experiences, with the accounts of his family life relegated to a comparatively minor role. Gordon's original title was *The Life and Passion of Aleck Maury*, and she always preferred the title of the English edition, *Pastimes of Aleck Maury: The Life of a True Sportsman*.

Caroline Gordon claimed her father provided the background material for this novel, as she induced him to tell her stories about his hunting and fishing experiences. Clearly Aleck Maury and his family are closely modeled upon the Gordon family. Aleck's name reflects his similarity to James Maury Morris Gordon, Caroline Gordon's father. Classically educated by an inattentive father, Aleck is hired to tutor the children of the large Fayerlee clan, all of whom live at or near Merry Point, a family estate similar to Merrimont, the Meriwether estate near Clarksville, Tennessee. Aleck marries Douglas Fayerlee's daughter Molly, just as James Gordon married Nancy Minor Meriwether. Their first child, a handsome, blond son named Dick, is his mother's favorite, as Caroline's older brother, Morris Meriwether Gordon, was Nancy's special pet. The second child, a daughter named Sarah but called Sally, inherits her father's dark coloring and "Maury features." The novel's final chapters gently poke fun at the intellectual Sally and her scholar husband, Stephen Lewis, obvious parallels to Caroline Gordon and Allen Tate.

At the time of the novel's debut, its popularity was attributed to its vivid accounts of hunting and fishing, and Caroline Gordon was criticized for the almost photographic detail of her descriptions. *Aleck Maury* can be read solely for its description of fishing and hunting in the early twentieth century South. Before long, however, critics discerned the author's impressionistic style and the novel's symbolism. Interpretation then focused upon Aleck Maury as a modern epic hero, resembling Ulysses in his restless search for new experiences and fresh challenges, but also possessing Aeneas' single-minded dedication to fulfilling his destiny and Davy Crockett's capacity for boasting about his skills and accomplishments. Such criticism customarily links Miss Gordon with the Southern agrarians in her use of the hunt as a ritual that establishes order and meaning in a chaotic world.

Initially, Aleck's perseverance appears heroic, and for much of his life, he seems to find sacramental value in his sport. As an eight-year-old boy on his first hunt, he experiences a mystic "delight" when he looks into the golden, glowing eyes of a possum just before its death. His life is devoted to recapturing that excitement in new hunting grounds and fishing holes. Aleck does not measure success in terms of career advancement; he chooses to be a teacher because that occupation leaves his afternoons free for fishing. The only possessions he values are his hunting dogs, his guns, and his fishing rod.

According to the sportsman's code, death in the hunt is heroic. For his favorite dog, Aleck provides the ideal death in the field: a shot through the head while the dog is on point. This code also demands that Aleck respect the birds he shoots and the fish he catches. He believes that he

117

must thoroughly know his prey in order to take full pleasure in the life-and-death struggle. Thus, he devotes his life to studying these creatures, and generally he can anticipate their behavior, but he prefers to fish alone because he is unwilling to share his hard-won knowledge with others.

Gradually, however, Caroline Gordon demonstrates the limitations of the sportsman's code, and Aleck's failures of comprehension are seen to be an integral part of the novel's meaning. In middle age, Aleck receives a symbolic warning: His vision becomes unreliable and he has difficulty seeing his targets. Still, he rarely considers the effects of time. The ritual deaths of birds and fish allow Aleck to ignore his own mortality until Molly dies. He then must confront death as the ultimate enemy, and for two years he merely "goes through the motions" of fishing, becoming increasingly aware that his lifestyle is as obsolete as the classical Greek and Latin he teaches. For the first time he suspects that, though he may heroically battle time's changes, probably time, in the form of the modern world, ultimately will defeat him. Actually, despite the fact that *Aleck Maury, Sportsman* ends with a temporary victory as Maury escapes to his newest fishing hole, a later short story, "The Presence," portrays the elderly Maury forced to watch younger men enjoy the sports in which he can no longer participate.

Aleck draws emotional sustenance from what critic Louise Cowan calls "the secret life of joy and danger" in the rituals of his sport: Hunting provides him an escape from stress when Molly is in labor and from grief when Richard dies. Nevertheless, pursuit of his sport isolates him from his family, whom he repeatedly uproots as he pursues new fishing grounds. Aleck never manages to live up to Molly's expectations, and he cannot understand a son whom he cannot teach to hunt, fish, or read Latin. Finally his preference for Caney Fork separates him even from Sally. In fact, Aleck needs the emotional distancing his sporting rituals provide; he comments that keeping in touch with family and friends has become too painful for him.

Ultimately, then, Aleck's sporting code proves inadequate. First, it fails to link him with society. Although Aleck admires legendary hunters and fishermen, he scorns the group ritual of the fox hunt, calling it an immature form of the sport. Thus, he becomes the solitary man, lacking any tie with his personal or regional past. Moreover, Aleck's code is not strong enough to counterbalance the inherent selfishness of his nature. For example, when he wants a boat to travel up the Black River, he abandons his own principles and catches spawning bream to pay the rental fee. Likewise, he treats his superior casting skill as a subject for gloating; and, deciding that he deserves an excellent line more than Harry Morrow does, he steals Morrow's one-hundred-foot black enameled fly line.

Thoroughly grounded in the classical tradition, Caroline Gordon based her critical stance upon Aristotelian principles of unity. As Gordon explains in *How to Read a Novel* (1957), she considers form important: For her, complication and resolution are essential plot elements, and the author's role is to impose form upon complex human experience. In *Aleck Maury, Sportsman*, the title character's experiences as a sportsman constitute the complication, and the resolution is the reader's recognition that Maury's life has been pleasant but ultimately inconsequential. Gordon adheres to her belief that a novel must present the complexity of life, as she portrays a character who seems both self-effacing and self-centered. Lamenting the absence of heroism in the modern world, Miss Gordon turns to the classics to highlight humanity's archetypal patterns. Ultimately, then, the key to Aleck Maury's character may be pride, the tragic flaw he shares with the heroes of Greek tragedy.

"Critical Evaluation" by Charmaine Allmon Mosby

Bibliography:
Brinkmeyer, Robert H., Jr. "The Key to the Puzzle: The Literary Career of Caroline Gordon." In *Three Catholic Writers of the Modern South*. Jackson: University Press of Mississippi, 1985. Discussion of the book in terms of Caroline Gordon's emphasis upon the classical literary tradition.

Cowan, Louise. "Aleck Maury, Epic Hero and Pilgrim." In *The Short Fiction of Caroline Gordon: A Critical Symposium*, edited by Thomas H. Landess. Dallas: University of Dallas Press, 1972. Interpretation of Aleck as an Odysseus figure, in the novel and especially in the short stories.

Fraistat, Rose Ann C. *Caroline Gordon as Novelist and Woman of Letters*. Baton Rouge: Louisiana State University Press, 1984. Consideration of Aleck as an example of Caroline Gordon's lifelong concern with the artist's role, which, she thought, was to create a code of honor that can combat society's disintegration.

McDowell, Frederick P. W. *Caroline Gordon*. University of Minnesota Pamphlets on American Writers 59. Minneapolis: University of Minnesota Press, 1966. Discussion of *Aleck Maury, Sportsman* as an account of an outwardly uneventful life that is actually the story of "a Ulysses figure, always seeking the new and untried."

Makowsky, Veronica A. *Caroline Gordon: A Biography*. New York: Oxford University Press, 1989. A feminist interpretation of *Aleck Maury, Sportsman* as a balance between a man's potential for heroic action and "his tendency to desert it all at a whim and leave women to suffer the consequences."

Stuckey, W. J. "The Sportsman as Hero." In *Caroline Gordon*. New York: Twayne, 1972. Sympathetic appraisal of Aleck Maury as a candid and reliable narrator, set apart from other people by his exceptional responsiveness to nature. Praises the novel's lightly ironic tone, dramatic structure, and comic resolution.

THE ALEXANDRIA QUARTET

Type of work: Novel
Author: Lawrence Durrell (1912-1990)
Type of plot: Psychological realism
Time of plot: Before and during World War II
Locale: Alexandria, Egypt
First published: The Alexandria Quartet, 1962: *Justine,* 1957; *Balthazar,* 1958; *Mountolive,* 1958; *Clea,* 1960

> *Principal characters:*
> L. G. DARLEY, an Anglo-Irish schoolteacher and an aspiring writer
> JUSTINE HOSNANI, Darley's second lover and wife of Nessim
> NESSIM HOSNANI, a Coptic banker and conspirator
> NAROUZ HOSNANI, his younger, hairlipped brother and a religious fanatic
> S. BALTHAZAR, a Jewish doctor and mystic
> DAVID MOUNTOLIVE, a British diplomat
> CLEA MONTIS, a golden blonde painter, Darley's third lover
> MELISSA ARTEMIS, a pale, sick Greek dancer and prostitute, Darley's first lover
> PAUL CAPODISTRIA, an ugly, rich lecher and a conspirator
> PERCY PURSEWARDEN, an erudite, ironical English writer
> LIZA PURSEWARDEN, the writer's blind sister
> MEMLIK PASHA, the Egyptian Minister of Interior

The Story:

Justine. A young Anglo-Irish writer, L. G. Darley, was reflecting on his life in Alexandria, Egypt, around the time of World War II, and on his three great loves: Melissa, Justine, and Clea. Darley resided on a Greek island and was writing and gaining perspective on his love affairs.

He first recalled Melissa, a poor cabaret dancer who sometimes engaged in prostitution. They had begun their love affair as "fellow bankrupts": He was a writer who could not write and she, a dancer with no talent. They had nothing in common, except that they had both been through Alexandria's "winepress of love."

While living with Melissa, Darley met his second great love, Justine, who attended one of his lectures on Alexandria's famous poet, Constantine Cavafy. Justine, "solitary student of the passions and the arts," was a modern incarnation of Cleopatra. She captivated men with her esoteric searchings into the nature of knowledge and with her magnificent body. After the lecture, Justine invited Darley to her home, so that he could meet her husband, Nessim, a fabulously wealthy Coptic banker, who also shared in her metaphysical speculations.

Although Darley respected Nessim, he could not refrain from falling into an affair with Justine. She ruled his mind to such an extent that Darley sought insight into her nature from the novel *Moeurs,* written by Justine's ex-husband, Arnauti. In *Moeurs,* Arnauti had created an emotionally complex character like Justine, who had been sexually abused by an uncle. Arnauti failed to unravel Justine's secrets and Darley, too, was tormented by the decline in Justine's affections and by his belief that Nessim had learned of the affair. Tensions reached a climax at a duck shoot that Nessim arranged at Lake Mareotis. Darley feared that he would be murdered by the jealous husband. Instead, another body was found floating in the lake. The corpse turned out to be Capodistria, the relative who had abused Justine. When the hunters returned to shore, they discovered that Justine had fled. Darley felt as if the whole city had crashed around about his ears. Later, Darley heard through Clea that Justine was working on a Jewish kibbutz in Palestine and that Capodistria was still alive.

Darley took a job teaching English at a school in Upper Egypt for two years and kept in only limited contact with Melissa, who was in a clinic trying to cure her tuberculosis. Melissa died before Darley could see her for a last time. He agreed to adopt her child, who was the outcome of Melissa's brief liaison with Nessim after Justine's departure.

By the end of the novel, Darley had drawn closer to Clea, a lovely artist who was recovering from a lesbian affair with Justine. Together Clea and Darley analyzed the events that had transpired, recalling the wisdom of their enigmatic literary friend, Percy Pursewarden, who had recently committed suicide.

Balthazar. On the Greek island, Darley completed his manuscript, presumably *Justine*, and mailed it to his friend, Balthazar. Balthazar knew the secrets of his fellow Alexandrians. After reading Darley's book, Balthazar traveled to the island to set Darley straight and present him with his own commentary—the Interlinear—penned between the lines of Darley's manuscript. The Interlinear provided Darley with new information regarding the characters about whom he had written. One revelation was that Justine's true love was Pursewarden. Darley was stunned. He was forced to take a new perspective on his reality, an essential task for one who aspired to be a writer. After Balthazar departed, Darley picked up an old photograph and stared at the images of his friends. He was ready to begin the torturous process of reassessment by examining the many facets of his friends' personalities.

There was a wild carnival attended by Narouz Hosnani, Nessim's brother. Narouz, a rough-hewn religious fanatic, managed the family's country estate. He attended the carnival because he hoped to see his great secret love, Clea, who loathed him. Instead, he murdered a man, in the guise of Justine, who had made lecherous advances to him.

This volume closes with a letter that Pursewarden wrote to Clea just before his suicide. He proposed "a new way of living with joy" and called for relationships based on loving-kindness.

Mountolive. The British ambassador to Egypt was David Mountolive. The omniscient narrator chronicled Mountolive's life—how he began his diplomatic career in Egypt as a guest at the Hosnani estate and rose through the ranks to become ambassador. The Hosnanis, particularly Leila, Nessim and Narouz's mother, gave the young Mountolive his education in Egyptian mores. Mountolive fell in love with Leila and carried on a passionate affair with her out of sight of her disabled husband. When he was posted elsewhere, they stayed in touch through letters. With the passage of years their ardor faded. Their meeting, after Mountolive had been appointed ambassador, was a disaster. He was repulsed by how much she had aged, and she was disappointed in his lack of character.

More knowledge was gained regarding Justine's true affections. She was in fact Nessim's devoted wife. She shared Nessim's political goal: to conspire against British interests in Palestine. She became involved with Darley and Pursewarden, both minor functionaries in the British legation, in order to spy for Nessim. The plot though fell apart when Melissa inadvertently stumbled onto its details and informed Pursewarden during the one night of passion they shared. He, in turn, faced a dilemma, torn between his friendship with Nessim and his official duties. His suicide appeared to be a way out of the quandary; before dying he let both Nessim and Mountolive know that he had uncovered the conspiracy.

Retribution arrived swiftly. Nessim had been bribing the minister of the interior, Memlik, to overlook his activities; but, learning of the plot, Mountolive forced Memlik to suppress it. Memlik decided to spare Nessim and sent his agents to kill the other leader, Nessim's fanatical brother, Narouz. Narouz suffered an agonizing death. His last request was to see Clea again. She reluctantly went to his deathbed, but arrived too late.

Clea. Darley left his island retreat to return to Alexandria and was nervous about seeing Justine again. She was much changed. The collapse of the conspiracy had made her a recluse, and a slight stroke had diminished her beauty. Darley realized he had grown beyond her narcissistic type of loving. He was more in tune with the gentle Clea, who, like him, was struggling to become an artist. Clea and Darley began a love affair amid the shelling of World War II.

Inexplicably, Clea and Darley drifted apart. They decided to separate, but, before doing so, they went on one last excursion. Accompanied by Balthazar, they traveled by boat to a nearby island. As Clea was swimming underwater, Balthazar accidentally released a harpoon which went through Clea's hand and pinned her underwater. Darley sprang to save Clea's life by hacking off her hand.

Although the two separated, they seemed likely to reunite. Both resolved their artistic problems: Darley was able to start writing and Clea was painting extraordinary paintings with her artificial hand. She wrote to Darley that she was "serene and happy, a real human being, an artist at last." Darley too felt as if "the whole universe" had given him "a nudge."

Critical Evaluation:

Beginning with the publication of Durrell's first serious novel, *The Black Book* in 1938, perceptive readers recognized his innovative genius. T. S. Eliot praised *The Black Book* as "the first piece of work by a new English writer to give me any hope for the future of prose fiction." *The Alexandria Quartet* marks a turning point in the development of the twentieth century novel. In its pages, modernism makes the transition into postmodernism. Modernist concerns with the privileged role of art, the mythic quest, and the hero's search for meaning give way to postmodern concerns: indeterminacy, relativity, and hero's unstable ego.

The Alexandria Quartet is experimental in style and metaphysical in content, so readers are often confused by the lack of narrative structure. Durrell is a meticulous craftsman; the novel is based on what he calls an n-dimensional structure, based in turn on Albert Einstein's theory of relativity. The theory of relativity, Durrell believed, accurately defines the reality of time. Einstein destroyed the old Victorian material universe. Science has shattered any coherent view of the cosmos, Durrell points out in the preface to *Balthazar*. Modern literature therefore offers no unities either. The book's relativity in its point of view is a reflection of the central advance made in human understanding in the twentieth century. Thus, the first three novels of *The Alexandria Quartet* present three dimensions of space, and the last novel, *Clea*, moves the story ahead in time. How the reader should, ideally, read such a novel is illustrated by a cartoon, which appeared around the time of *The Alexandria Quartet*'s publication. A man is shown reading *The Alexandria Quartet* by means of a machine that allows him to read all four volumes simultaneously.

In addition to incorporating relativistic ideas into his novel, Durrell incorporates the idea that Sigmund Freud destroyed the idea of the stable ego. Describing such a personality in fiction or in love is complicated by the fact that many perspectives can be taken on the subject. Balthazar points out this notion to Darley: "Each psyche is really an ant-hill of opposing predispositions. Personality as something with fixed attributes is an illusion—but a necessary illusion *if we are to love!*"

By focusing on love relationships in *The Alexandria Quartet*, Durrell addresses issues raised by Sigmund Freud and Alfred Einstein. The central topic of the novel is an investigation of modern love. Durrell believed that "the sexual act becomes identified with all knowledge." In other words, eros is the "motive force in man." Eros awakens the "psychic forces latent in the human being." Durrell's characters are interesting in their own right, but they are also metaphysical pawns in the search for metaphysical knowledge. Such knowledge must take into account the cosmology of the age: Personality is not fixed, and space and time are relative. Thus, Darley's adventures in love are the key elements in his progression toward greater self-awareness and knowledge not only of himself but also of the world around him.

His first lover, Melissa Artemis, encounters him at his lowest point of self-awareness. They meet at a party. Melissa has passed out, from exhaustion and from the ingestion of Spanish fly. Darley takes her home and nurses her back to health. They begin a relationship based on the fact that they are "fellow bankrupts," without a "taste in common."

During this period with Melissa, Darley gives a lecture on Constantine Cavafy. After the lecture, a beautiful society woman approaches him with questions. This woman is Justine, who becomes his second great love. Justine is married to the immensely wealthy Coptic Christian banker Nessim Hosnani. Darley is instantly intrigued by the dark Justine, who has the remarkable ability to expel "people from their old selves." Darley is willing to be led and follows after Justine, despite the fact that he meets her husband and strikes up a friendship with him. When Justine abruptly leaves both of them, Darley is forced to re-evaluate the relationship and himself; this act increases his awareness of self and others.

Darley seeks solace in his third and most important relationship, with the painter Clea Montis, who has also suffered through a sexual relationship with Justine. Darley and Clea work together as they attempt to determine the right way to live as artists and as human beings. Rejecting the ego-dominated, narcissistic concerns of their past lives, they try to live a more tender existence, which their mentor, Pursewarden, claims exists in the "primal relation between animal and plant, rain and soil, seed and trees, man and God."

Before Clea and Darley reach this state of being, however, they must pass through a terrible trial. When Clea is accidentally shot by a harpoon, Darley must suddenly transform himself from a man sunk in passivity to a man of action. In saving Clea's life, he transforms himself as well. By the end of *The Alexandria Quartet*, his self-awareness and confidence allow him to take his place in the community of authors.

Durrell's goal in the novel is twofold: First, he attempts to address the major philosophical questions regarding the nature of reality and the right way to live and love. Second, he believes that there is an ideal spiritual realm in which to live. Durrell believes in an existence that abandons selfish cravings and ambitions and that enters a state of oneness with the universe. His characters begin their journeys in Alexandria, but metaphorically become reflections of their age.

Anna Lillios

Bibliography:
Begnal, Michael H., ed. *On Miracle Ground: Essays on the Fiction of Lawrence Durrell.* Cranbury, N.J.: Bucknell University Press, 1990. In a transcript of a 1986 lecture, Durrell explains his life and art. Other essays in this volume give mythological, Buddhist, and narratological perspectives on *The Alexandria Quartet.*
Durrell, Lawrence. *A Key to Modern British Poetry.* Norman: University of Oklahoma Press, 1952. In the context of the book's subject, Durrell presents the philosophical, artistic, and scientific ideas that underlie *The Alexandria Quartet.*

Friedman, Alan Warren, ed. *Critical Essays on Lawrence Durrell*. Boston: G. K. Hall, 1987. Contains the most comprehensive selection of essays on Durrell's work. Included are early reviews of *The Alexandria Quartet*.

_____. *Lawrence Durrell and the Alexandria Quartet: Art for Love's Sake*. Norman: University of Oklahoma Press, 1970. Shows that love presents "an endless potential for variations on a theme."

Pine, Richard. *Lawrence Durrell: The Mindscape*. New York: St. Martin's Press, 1994. The first book-length study of Durrell's work to appear in the past twenty-five years. Based on Durrell's diaries and notebooks.

Unterecker, John. *Lawrence Durrell*. New York: Columbia University Press, 1964. A brief, incisive explanation of *The Alexandria Quartet*'s themes, such as love, the nature of reality, and the role of the artist.

Weigel, John A. *Lawrence Durrell*. Boston: Twayne, 1989. A good summary of Durrell's life and work. Selected bibliography.

ALICE'S ADVENTURES IN WONDERLAND

Type of work: Short fiction
Author: Lewis Carroll (Charles Lutwidge Dodgson, 1832-1898)
Type of plot: Fantasy
Time of plot: Victorian era
Locale: The dream world of an imaginative child
First published: 1865

Principal characters:
ALICE
THE WHITE RABBIT
THE DUCHESS
THE QUEEN OF HEARTS

The Story:

Alice was quietly reading over her sister's shoulder when she saw a White Rabbit dash across the lawn and disappear into its hole. She jumped up to rush after him and found herself falling down the rabbit hole. At the bottom, she saw the White Rabbit hurrying along a corridor ahead of her and murmuring that he would be late. He disappeared around a corner, leaving Alice standing in front of several locked doors.

On a glass table, she found a tiny golden key that unlocked a little door hidden behind a curtain. The door opened upon a lovely miniature garden, but she could not get through the doorway because it was too small. She sadly replaced the key on the table. A little bottle mysteriously appeared. Alice drank the contents and immediately began to grow smaller, so much so that she could no longer reach the key on the table. Next, she ate a piece of cake she found nearby, and soon she began to grow to such enormous size that she could only squint through the door. In despair, she began to weep tears as big as raindrops. As she sat crying, the White Rabbit appeared, moaning that the Duchess would be angry if he kept her waiting. He dropped his fan and gloves, and when Alice picked them up, she began to grow smaller. Again she rushed to the garden door, but she found it shut and the golden key once more on the table out of reach.

Then she fell into a pool of her own tears. Splashing along, she encountered a mouse who had stumbled into the pool. Alice tactlessly began a conversation about her cat Dinah, and the mouse became speechless with terror. Soon the pool of tears was filled with living creatures— birds and animals of all kinds. An old Dodo suggested that they run a Caucus Race to get dry. Having asked what a Caucus Race was, Alice was told that the best way to explain it was to do it, whereupon the animals ran themselves quite breathless and finally became dry. Afterward, the mouse told a "Tail" to match its own appendage. Alice was asked to tell something, but the only thing she could think of was her cat Dinah. Frightened, the other creatures went away, and Alice was left alone.

The White Rabbit appeared once more, this time hunting for his gloves and fan. Catching sight of Alice, he sent her to his home to get him a fresh pair of gloves and another fan. In the Rabbit's house, she found the fan and gloves and also took a drink from a bottle. Instantly, she grew to be a giant size and was forced to put her leg up the chimney and her elbow out of the window to keep from being squeezed to death.

She managed to eat a little cake and shrink herself again. As soon as she was small enough to get through the door, she ran into a nearby wood where she found a caterpillar sitting on a mushroom. The caterpillar was very rude to Alice, and he scornfully asked her to prove her worth by reciting "You Are Old, Father William." Alice did so, but the words sounded very strange. Disgusted, he left her, after giving her some valuable information about increasing or decreasing her size. She broke off pieces of the mushroom and found to her delight that she could become taller by eating from the piece in her left hand, shorter by eating from the piece in her right hand.

She came to a little house among the trees. There a footman, who looked very much like a fish, presented to another footman, who closely resembled a frog, an invitation for the Duchess to play croquet with the Queen. The two amphibians bowed to each other with great formality, tangling their wigs together. Alice opened the door and found herself in the chaotic house of the Duchess. The cook was stirring a large pot of soup and pouring plenty of pepper into the mixture. Everyone was sneezing except the cook and a Cheshire cat, which sat on the hearth grinning. The Duchess herself held a sneezing, squalling baby and sang a blaring lullaby to it. Alice, in sympathy with the poor child, picked it up and carried it out into the fresh air, whereupon the baby gradually turned into a pig, squirmed out of her arms, and trotted into the forest.

Standing in bewilderment, Alice saw the grinning Cheshire cat sitting in a tree. He was able to appear and disappear at will, and after exercising his talents, he advised Alice to go to a tea party given by the Mad Hatter. The cat vanished, all but the grin. When that, too, finally disappeared, Alice left for the party.

There, Alice found she had to deal with the strangest people she had ever seen—a March Hare, a Mad Hatter, and a sleepy Dormouse. All had been too lazy to set the table afresh, and dirty dishes from preceding meals lay next to clean ones. The Dormouse fell asleep in its teacup; the Mad Hatter told Alice her hair needed cutting; the March Hare offered her wine and then told her there was none. They asked her foolish riddles that had no answers. Then they ignored her completely and carried on a ridiculous conversation among themselves. She escaped after the Dormouse fell asleep in the middle of a story he was telling.

Next, she found herself in a garden of rose-trees. Some gardeners appeared with paintbrushes and began to splash red paint on a white rose. Alice learned that the Queen had ordered a red rose to be planted in that spot, and the gardeners were busily and fearfully trying to cover their error before the Queen arrived. The poor gardeners, however, were not swift enough. The Queen caught them in the act, and the wretched gardeners were led off to be decapitated. Alice saved them by shoving them down into a large flowerpot, out of sight of the Queen.

A croquet game began. The mallets were live flamingos, and the balls were hedgehogs which thought nothing of uncurling themselves and running rapidly over the field. The Duchess cornered Alice and led her away to the seaside to introduce her to the Mock Turtle and the Gryphon. While engaged in a Lobster Quadrille, they heard the news of a trial. A thief had stolen some tarts. Rushing to the courtroom where a trial by jury was already in session, Alice was called upon to act as a witness before the King and Queen of Hearts, but the excited child upset the jury box and spilled out all of its occupants. After replacing all the animals in the box, Alice said she knew nothing of the matter. Her speech infuriated the Queen, who ordered that Alice's head be cut off. The whole court rushed at her, and Alice defiantly called them nothing but a pack of cards. She awoke from her dream as her sister brushed away some dead leaves blowing over her face.

Critical Evaluation:

One summer afternoon in 1862, the Reverend Charles Lutwidge Dodgson, an Oxford friend of his, and three little girls set out on a boat trip. Somewhere along the way, *Alice's Adventures in Wonderland* was created. Although it was not the first story that Dodgson had told the daughters of Henry George Liddell, the dean of Christ Church in Oxford, it was one that immediately captivated Alice Liddell, the prototype for the fictional seven-year-old heroine. Her later requests for Dodgson to "write it down" led to his becoming one of the world's favorite authors; his work was eventually translated into more than forty-five languages and became part of the heritage of most literate people growing up in Western culture.

Dodgson, who transposed his first two names into the pen name Lewis Carroll, was a shy and seemingly conventional Oxford mathematician who could relate most easily with children, particularly young girls. Later ages regarded his seemingly innocent affinity for children as the sign of a possible neurosis and an inability to grow up. Alice Liddell was only one of many young girls who shared with him the secret world of childhood in which he spent much of his adult life.

Lewis Carroll's attraction to fantasy expressed itself in many ways, among them his love of whimsical letters, gadgets, theatricals, toys, and, of course, fantasy stories. The Alice stories were first prepared for Alice Liddell in a handwritten manuscript and initially given the title *Alice's Adventures Under Ground*; the book was published in its present form in 1865 and was an almost immediate popular success. Adding to its originality were the illustrations by Sir John Tenniel (for his model, he did not use the real Alice who unlike the pictured child, had short dark hair and bangs).

The book—which was followed in 1871 by the even more brilliant sequel, *Through the Looking-Glass and What Alice Found There*—has always been enjoyed on several levels. It is a children's story, but it is also a book full of interest for adults and specialists like mathematicians, linguists, logicians, and Freudians. It may be the suggestion of a philosophical underpinning that gives the work its never-ending appeal for adults.

Viewed as children's literature, the book offers its young readers a charming new outlook that dispenses with the moralistic viewpoint then so prevalent. Alice is neither continuously nice nor thoroughly naughty; she is simply a curious child whose queries lead her into strange situations. In the end, she is neither punished nor rewarded. A moral, proposing that she do this or that, is absent. Indeed, Carroll pokes fun at many of the ideas with which Alice, a well-bred English child, has been imbued. The Mock Turtle, for example, chides the sacred subject of learning by terming the branches of arithmetic Ambition, Distraction, Uglification, and Derision. Children who read the book are permitted to see adults quite unlike the perfect beings usually portrayed. It is the story's adults rather than Alice who are rude, demanding, and ridiculous.

As a work for the specialist, *Alice's Adventures in Wonderland* touches on many puzzles that are subsequently even more thoroughly presented in *Through the Looking-Glass and What Alice Found There*. The playfulness with language, for example, involves puns, parodies, and clever phrasing but does not deal as fully with the basic nature of language as does its sequel. Even in *Alice's Adventures in Wonderland*, however, Carroll's casual amusement with words often has deeper meaning. When he parodies the well-known poems and songs of his day, he is clearly questioning their supercilious platitudes. When he makes a pun (the Gryphon tells the reader that boots and shoes under the sea are "done" with whiting rather than blacking and are, of course, made of soles and eels), Carroll asserts the total logic of illogic. When he designs a Cheshire cat, he was taking a common but unspecific phrase of his time—"Grin like a Cheshire cat" referred either to inn signs in the county of Cheshire depicting a grinning lion or to Cheshire cheeses modeled in the shape of a smiling cat—and turning it into a concrete reality. Logicians also find a multitude of tidbits. The Cheshire cat "proves" it is not mad by adopting the premise that if a dog is not mad, anyone who reacts in ways opposite to a dog must be so. The March Hare offers a nice exercise in logic and language with his discussion of taking "more" versus taking "less" and his challenge as to whether "I mean what I say" is the same as "I say what I mean."

For mathematicians, Carroll presents the Mad Hatter's watch, which tells the day of the month rather than the hour. The watch does not bother with the hour, since from the center of the earth, the sun would always look the same, whereas the moon's phases would be visible. For the Freudians, the book is also a mass of complicated mysteries. Freudians see significance in most of the characters and incidents, but the fall down the rabbit hole, the changes in size, the great interest in eating and drinking, the obnoxious mature females, and Alice's continual anxiety are some of the most revealing topics, all of them possibly suggesting Carroll's neuroses about women and sex.

The larger philosophical questions raised by Alice center on the order of life as readers know it. Set in the context of the dream vision, a journey different from a conscious quest, the book asks whether there is indeed any pattern or meaning to life. Alice is the curious innocent who compares so favorably with the jaded, even wicked, grown-ups. Always sensible and open to experience, she would seem the ideal messenger of a true concept, yet her adventures hint that there is only the ridiculousness of logic and reality and the logic of nonsense. Readers see that Wonderland is no more incomprehensible—but no more comprehensible, either—than Victorian England, that the Mad Duchess lives next door, that as the Cheshire cat says, "We're all mad here."

Alice brings to Wonderland certain acquired concepts and a strong belief in order. When Wonderland turns her views askew, she can withstand only so long, then she must rebel. The trial, which is the last refuge of justice in the real world, is the key factor in Alice's rejection of Wonderland, for it is a trial of Wonderland itself, with many of the earlier-encountered creatures reassembled to assert forcefully that expectations and rules are meaningless. Like the child of the world that she is, Alice (and Carroll) must deny the truth that there is no truth. She must shout "Nonsense" to it all. As one critic has pointed out, she rejects "mad sanity in favor of the sane madness of the ordinary existence." The reader faces the same confusion and, frightened by what it implies, must also rebel, though with laughter.

"Critical Evaluation" by Judith Bolch

Bibliography:
Blake, Kathleen. *Play, Games, and Sport: The Literary Works of Lewis Carroll*. Ithaca, N.Y.: Cornell University Press, 1974. Wittily argues that the *Alice* books create a world of games spinning out of control. Firmly establishes their author in a Victorian context.

Carroll, Lewis. *The Annotated Alice: Alice's Adventures in Wonderland and Through the Looking-Glass*. Edited by Martin Gardner. New York: Clarkson N. Potter, 1960. Martin Gardner's notes in the margin alongside the text help to clarify jokes and conundrums and explain contemporary references.

_____. *More Annotated Alice: Alice's Adventures in Wonderland and Through the Looking-Glass*. Edited by Martin Gardner. New York: Random House, 1990. Based on letters from readers of the original *The Annotated Alice*, as well as new research, this sequel supplements rather than revises the first book. Reprints for the first time Peter Newell's illustrations and includes Newell's essay on visually interpreting *Alice in Wonderland*.

Guiliano, Edward, ed. *Lewis Carroll: A Celebration*. New York: Clarkson N. Potter, 1982. A collection of fifteen essays, most referring to the *Alice* books, written to commemorate the 150th anniversary of Lewis Carroll's birth. Provides many photographs and illustrations, including Lewis Carroll's original renderings for *Alice in Wonderland*.

Kelly, Richard. *Lewis Carroll*. Boston: Twayne, 1977. A broad critical survey of Carroll's work. Emphasizes the humor in the *Alice* books.

Phillips, Edward, ed. *Aspects of Alice: Lewis Carroll's Dreamchild as Seen Through the Critics' Looking-Glasses, 1865-1971*. New York: Vanguard Press, 1971. A wide-ranging and often entertaining omnibus. Includes a comprehensive bibliography.

ALL FALL DOWN

Type of work: Novel
Author: James Leo Herlihy (1927-1993)
Type of plot: Bildungsroman
Time of plot: Late 1950's
Locale: Cleveland, Ohio
First published: 1960

> *Principal characters:*
> CLINTON WILLIAMS, a boy
> RALPH WILLIAMS, his father
> ANNABEL WILLIAMS, his mother
> BERRY-BERRY, his older brother
> ECHO O'BRIEN, a girl loved by Clinton and destroyed by Berry-Berry
> SHIRLEY, a young prostitute

The Story:

Clinton Williams was fourteen years old. His brother, Berry-Berry, was away "on his travels," begun shortly after his twenty-first birthday. The Williams family had recently moved into a house in a different section of Cleveland. Clinton was afraid that Berry-Berry would not be able to find the new house if he should return, and as a gesture of quiet protest he stayed away from school for fifty-seven consecutive days. In the daytime, he loafed in the Aloha Sweet Shop, recording in his notebooks everything he saw or overheard. At home he eavesdropped on his parents' conversations, which he recorded into his journals as well, along with copies of letters he opened on the sly. During the time he was skipping school, he filled twenty-five notebooks. His entries were naïve, funny, boring, and revealing. His romantic view of Berry-Berry was the first interest of Clinton's life. The second was his tremendous curiosity about people and the nature of experience; hence, his effort to put down everything he knew and learned in order that he might solve some of life's mysteries.

In many ways, Clinton was his father's son. Ralph Williams had been a politically active liberal before he was trapped by marriage and a family. Theoretically he was in business, but he spent most of his time in the cellar with a jigsaw puzzle in front of him and a bottle of bourbon within reach. He had simplified his life to two convictions: that Christ had founded the Socialist Party and that Berry-Berry would turn out all right in the end. His wife, Annabel, was nervous, querulous, and tearful, constantly wishing for Berry-Berry's return without ever realizing that he hated her.

The memory of the absent son was all that held the strange family together. Ironically, Berry-Berry was unworthy of his family's love or their hopes for his return. A bum, a pimp, and a sadist, he turned up first in one section of the country, then in another, in jail or out, either living off one of his women or else calling on his family for money to get him out of his latest escapade. Most of these facts were unknown to Clinton, however, during the time when he was working in an all-night eating place and saving his money for the day when he might join his brother. The opportunity came when Berry-Berry wrote asking his father for two hundred dollars to invest in a shrimping venture in Key Bonita, Florida. Ready to offer the money, Clinton took a bus to Key Bonita, to find on his arrival that Berry-Berry had already skipped

130

town after mauling one of his lady loves. This knowledge came to Clinton during the night he spent with a prostitute, and the realization of his brother's true nature was almost more than he could stand. He returned home, fell sick, and even contemplated suicide. He was saved when he fell shyly in love with Echo O'Brien, older than he and the daughter of one of his mother's friends, who came to visit in Cleveland.

Berry-Berry returned and all was forgotten, or at least forgiven, and the Williamses were reunited by love. Berry-Berry made a play for Echo O'Brien. His parents hoped that the affair would cause Berry-Berry to settle down at last. Clinton accepted the fact of Echo's romance with his brother out of gratitude for the atmosphere of family happiness in which he shared. Berry-Berry, however, could not be reclaimed from the moral rot that infected him. Refusing to accept responsibility for Echo's pregnancy, he callously discarded her, and Echo committed suicide. Clinton at first intended to kill his brother, but in the end, he decided that Berry-Berry's knowledge of his own corruption was punishment enough. Berry-Berry took to the road again. Clinton began writing in his notebooks once more, with the difference that, he felt, he had grown up.

Critical Evaluation:

The route by which one travels from the cradle to the grave is no broad highway but a road with many ups and downs, sudden turnings, and strange byways. To many modern novelists, no route is more interesting or significant than the downward road to wisdom. In much modern fiction, the beginning of knowledge is the loss of innocence.

The fable of innocence confronted by evil and gaining a sad kind of wisdom in the encounter is the theme of James Leo Herlihy's *All Fall Down*. The fact that its youthful hero makes a long journey in the geography of his own soul puts him into some rather interesting literary company: Huck Finn on his raft, Holden Caulfield exploring an adult world of hypocrisy and sham, Frankie Addams willing herself into becoming a member of the wedding. Although *All Fall Down* is a book that invites comparisons, to note them is not to say that Herlihy is in any way imitative. Quite the opposite: His ability to present the emotional adventures of youth as a difficult passage between childhood and maturity, and to tell the story as if it had never been written before, is striking proof of his imaginative force and dramatic control.

Clinton Williams, his hero, is a boy as free-wheeling in his character as J. D. Salinger's Holden Caulfield in *The Catcher in the Rye* (1951), but in a vastly different way. Caulfield is an uncomplicated realist whose quickness of mind enables him to identify pretense wherever he finds it. Clinton, on the other hand, grows up pursuing an illusion, the glamour that his romantic imagination throws about his older brother, whom Caulfield would have recognized at once. Ironically, while Caulfield the realist suffers a nervous breakdown as a result of his disillusioning experiences, Clinton the romantic experiences emotional liberation through his painful epiphany. Although Clinton wants to be a writer, he cannot produce anything but verbatim transcriptions of other people's speech and correspondence, because he has not yet learned how to synthesize his experience. This *Bildungsroman*, or coming-of-age novel, mainly concerns Clinton's liberation from bondage to his illusions. This liberation comes through his insight into his brother Berry-Berry's true character. There is a strong suggestion that Clinton's adoration of Berry-Berry has homosexual overtones and that the story, like Herlihy's *Midnight Cowboy* (1965), is really about the disenchanted protagonist's attaining the freedom to form a wholesome heterosexual relationship when he finds an appropriate love object.

Ralph Williams, Clinton's father, who was a political activist and dynamic personality in his youth, seems to have been emasculated by a dull marriage and his effort to maintain middle-class respectability. He deals in real estate but does not do well at it, because of his anticapitalist sentiments and his chronic depression. He is a heavy solitary drinker. He feels despised and rejected because both Clinton and Annabel have directed all their love toward the rebellious, charismatic Berry-Berry. In this carefully orchestrated novel, Ralph stands in sharp contrast to Berry-Berry, who has no respect for convention or middle-class morality.

Annabel Williams, Clinton's mother, a drab, unimaginative housewife, has an unhealthy emotional attachment to her older son. There is a strong suggestion that she may have even had an incestuous relationship with Berry-Berry. At any rate, he loathes and fears her. She is the most symbolic of all the characters in the novel; she represents Herlihy's unfavorable view of American middle-class women in general. Annabel's unwholesome possessiveness is largely responsible for Berry-Berry's cruelty toward women and his dread of forming a permanent relationship with a woman. Clinton escapes the same destructive influence, because most of his mother's affection is directed at his older brother, who can be regarded as a victim as well as a victimizer.

Berry-Berry Williams, Clinton's handsome, predatory older brother, is about twenty-three years of age when most of the events of the novel take place. His unusual first name suggests "beriberi," which is a serious and often fatal disease. Psychologists would diagnose him as a psychopath, a totally self-centered person who is incapable of realizing that other people have feelings or exist as independent entities. Like most psychopaths, Berry-Berry can be very likable and can project an illusion of human sympathy and affection. It is precisely because he is totally lacking in normal human emotions that he is so fascinating to women: He has learned to mimic affection and sympathy through a natural flair for imitation common to psychopathic personalities. Although Berry-Berry is not the hero or the viewpoint character in this cleverly constructed novel, he is the sun around whom all the other characters revolve—or a "disease" with which all the other characters are infected.

Echo O'Brien is a virgin in her early thirties. She has lived a sheltered life as her invalid mother's nurse and constant companion; she has remained sweet and innocent. She is clearly heading for tragedy because of her alarmingly childlike trust in the essential goodness of everyone she encounters. Her wholesomeness provides a striking contrast to the sickness of the members of Clinton's dysfunctional family. Her first name, Echo, suggests that she possesses the instinctive responsiveness, the authentic ability to relate to other people, that Berry-Berry only projects through mimicry. She is a mirror in which the other characters view their own hypocrisy and unworthiness. Most important, she is the catalyst directly responsible for the change in the relationship between Clinton and Berry-Berry.

Shirley is a young prostitute who introduces Clinton to sex and begins the boy's long process of disillusionment with Berry-Berry by telling him cold facts about his older brother's parasitical and sadistic behavior. This gentle, generous young woman serves as the novel's only concrete example of the kind of women Berry-Berry habitually exploits.

All Fall Down is a story expertly told, dramatically convincing, and oddly comic. For his novel's epigraph, Herlihy uses a passage from Sherwood Anderson's *Winesburg, Ohio* (1919), the section telling of people who seize upon some particular truth, try to make it their truth only, and become grotesques as a result. The quotation is relevant to Herlihy's novel for the book is, on one level, a story of grotesques. For a long time, the Williamses have lived apart and according to their own concerns. It is not until they share love that they really come alive. The use of the grotesque also is in keeping with the modern view that its image, antiromantic and antitragic alike, provides the most effective means of expressing both the irrationality of things and the moral evil that is also the devouring, obsessive evil of modern society, the isolation of the loving and the lonely. Herlihy sees moral isolation as one of the conditions of being, but he does not make it, as some of his contemporaries have done, a reason for fury or despair. His novel ends on a note of hope.

Bibliography:
Hicks, Granville. "Within the Shadow of Winesburg." *Saturday Review* 43 (August 6, 1960): 14. Compares Herlihy to his "literary ancestor" Sherwood Anderson, who drew his material from grotesques and social misfits. Mentions other Anderson followers, such as John Steinbeck, William Saroyan, and Erskine Caldwell.

Levin, Martin. "Young Man on the Lam." *New York Times Book Review*, August 21, 1960, 30. Complimentary and influential review of *All Fall Down*. Compares it to a Tennessee Williams play with its mixture of "incest, infantile regression, impotence and sadism overlaid with quaintness."

"Odd but Human." *Time*, August 15, 1960, 76. Compares Clinton Williams to J. D. Salinger's Holden Caulfield. Defines theme of *All Fall Down* as the universal need for love. Asserts that the characters are odd, but important because of their kinship with humanity.

Pratley, Gerald. *The Cinema of John Frankenheimer*. New York: A. S. Barnes, 1969. Chapter 6 of this study of the filmmaker who directed the 1962 film adaptation of *All Fall Down* presents John Frankenheimer's interpretation of the story and his analysis of the characters' motivations.

Quirk, Lawrence J. *The Films of Warren Beatty*. Secaucus, N. J.: Citadel Press, 1979. Contains an analysis of the 1962 screen adaptation of *All Fall Down*. Screenplay was written by William Inge; cast included Karl Malden, Eva Marie Saint, Brandon De Wilde, and Angela Lansbury. Illustrated.

ALL FOOLS

Type of work: Drama
Author: George Chapman (c. 1559-1634)
Type of plot: Comedy
Time of plot: Sixteenth century
Locale: Italy
First performed: 1604; first published, 1605

> *Principal characters:*
> RINALDO, a young gentleman
> VALERIO, his friend
> GOSTANZO, Valerio's father
> MARC ANTONIO, Rinaldo's father
> FORTUNIO, Rinaldo's brother
> CORNELIO, a jealous husband
> GRATIANA, Valerio's wife
> BELLANORA, Valerio's sister, loved by Fortunio
> GAZETTA, Cornelio's wife

The Story:

Gostanzo fancied himself a man of true worldly wisdom. He loved money, relished his neighbor's misfortunes, and was unhampered by any petty scruples about honesty. Aware of the temptations that might lead a young man to become a wastrel, he had taken great care in rearing his son Valerio. He had lectured the boy on the importance of thrift and, to teach him responsibility, made him an overseer.

Valerio was also a man of worldly wisdom. He put on the appearance of industry and innocence in front of his father, and he was well acquainted with the gentlemanly activities of dicing, drinking, and wenching. He had, as the result of these pursuits, accumulated a respectable number of debts. To cap his sins, he had now married Gratiana, a woman with beauty but no dowry. Fortunio was a young man of quite different character. Without parading his virtue, he led an upright life and was a dutiful son. In love with Valerio's sister Bellanora, he was not permitted to court her because Gostanzo was seeking a wealthier son-in-law. Fortunio's brother Rinaldo, having experienced the fickleness of women, was through with love and now devoted himself exclusively to conning others.

One day, when Rinaldo, Fortunio, Valerio, and Gratiana were together talking, they sighted Gostanzo coming their way, and all but Rinaldo rushed off. In answer to Gostanzo's questions, Rinaldo said that Gratiana was the wife of Fortunio, who dared not tell his father of the marriage; Gostanzo believed the lie. Although he promised to keep it secret, he nevertheless revealed it the minute he was alone with Marc Antonio, the father of Fortunio and Rinaldo. Acting on Rinaldo's suggestion, Gostanzo recommended that Fortunio and Gratiana be installed in his home. Marc Antonio accepted this offer, not because he was angry with his son, but because Gostanzo had convinced him that Fortunio was in danger of falling victim to greater evils. With the restraining influence of the strict Gostanzo and the good example of Valerio, he might still be saved.

Rinaldo's scheming thus enabled Valerio and his wife to live in the same house, and it also gave Fortunio a chance to pursue his courtship of Bellanora. When Gratiana was brought to

Gostanzo's home, the old man told Valerio to kiss her, but the crafty youth feigned shyness. The father, gratified by this manifestation of a strict upbringing, congratulated himself on being a much better parent than the easygoing Marc Antonio.

Later, however, Gostanzo found Valerio embracing and kissing Gratiana. The old man, still not suspecting the true state of affairs, thought merely that his son was a fast learner. He decided that, to avoid mischief, Gratiana and Fortunio would have to leave his house. When he told Rinaldo of this development, Rinaldo suggested that his father be told that Gratiana was really Valerio's wife and that Marc Antonio now take her into his house. Rinaldo further advised that, in order to make the ruse effective, Valerio be permitted to visit her there. The plan met with the ready assent of Gostanzo, who, being gulled, was happy in the thought that he would be gulling Marc Antonio.

Meanwhile, Rinaldo, encouraged by his success in this project, had been directing his genius to a new endeavor, a plan intended to gull Cornelio, an inordinately jealous husband who was an easy mark for a trickster and whose wife, Gazetta, complained that he brought home gallants and then upbraided her for being in their company. Rinaldo's accomplice in his scheme was Valerio, who had been angered at Cornelio for making fun of his singing. Valerio had little difficulty in awakening the jealousy in Cornelio. With the help of a page who defended Gazetta on the grounds that women's wantonness was a result of weakness and not design, he so infuriated Cornelio that the jealous husband attacked and wounded his wife's supposed lover.

When Marc Antonio was told that Valerio, not Fortunio, was married to Gratiana, he made merry with Gostanzo for his blind pride. The latter, unable to tolerate gloating other than his own, declared that the plot had been contrived for entertainment. When they met Valerio, Gostanzo feigned extreme anger with him and threatened to disown his son. Valerio, playing the penitent, protested his devotion to his father and avowed his love of Gratiana. Gostanzo, believing the whole affair a joke, dissembled an appearance of being softened and gave his blessing to the match.

Cornelio, meanwhile, had procured a notary and was proceeding with the divorce of his wife. A nosebleed, which he took as an omen, caused him to suspend action just as he was preparing to sign the final papers. After the notary left, a friend explained to him that he had been tricked into his jealousy by Rinaldo and Valerio. Cornelio resolved to repay them with a deception of his own.

When Cornelio found Rinaldo, he told this master trickster that Valerio had been arrested for debts. Since Valerio had been dodging the officials for some time, Rinaldo believed the lie and, having gone on bond for Valerio, he felt that some immediate action was unnecessary. At Cornelio's suggestion, he took Gostanzo with him to the Half Moon Tavern, where Cornelio said Valerio was being held before being taken to prison. Valerio was at the tavern, but not as a captive. Instead, he was engaged in his usual pursuits of drinking and playing dice.

When Gostanzo saw his son's true nature and also learned that Valerio really was married to Gratiana, he threatened, this time in earnest, to disown the boy and to settle his estate on his daughter. This plan was rejected when he discovered that Bellanora had married Fortunio. The old man, frustrated in his efforts to control events, decided to accept them. Finally, when Cornelio revealed that his jealousy had been feigned in order to restrain his wife's high spirits, the reconciliations were complete and happiness reigned in the Half Moon Tavern.

Critical Evaluation:

The English poet and critic Algernon Charles Swinburne considered *All Fools* to be George Chapman's best comedy. Having proven successful with sophisticated and popular audiences, it was notably revived for performance before King James I on New Year's Eve night, 1604. *All Fools* remains one of Chapman's most skillfully constructed plays, with well-rounded, realistically established characters and a plot that transcends the contrivance of much of Jacobean comedy.

All Fools is based on elements taken from three separate plays by the Roman dramatist Terence, a favorite source of playwrights of the Elizabethan and Jacobean period. The main plot, contrasting two fathers, Gostanzo and Marc Antonio, and their two sons, Valerio and Rinaldo respectively, was adapted from the comedy *The Self-Tormentor*. Substantial additional material was also taken from two other plays by Terence, *The Adelphi* and *The Eunuch*. In addition, Chapman freely added to his plot, introducing figures of contemporary satire such as the notary and the doctor, in order to skewer the types so prevalent in the comedies of the period.

Chapman did more than simply translate and adapt the classical Roman comedies. He substantially revised and expanded his original sources, making the major individual characters more rounded and providing them with additional motivations. While this has the effect of making the comedy more believable and substantial, it also allows Chapman to introduce a moral dimension to the play that is lacking in Terence.

The stock figures of the Roman comedy were guided by simple and often base motivations, in particular lust and avarice. Chapman's characters, on the other hand, are imbued with the wealth of the Christian and humanist traditions, which makes them more honorable, attractive, and sympathetic. For example, Rinaldo, younger brother of Fortunio, is based on the scheming slave who sets into motion and then continues through his machinations the dizzying round of events in *The Self-Tormentor*. In the Roman play, the slave is an essentially stock character rather than an individual; he is an amoral trickster, witty and clever, whose purpose is to advance the plot in a fairly predictable fashion. In *All Fools*, on the other hand, Rinaldo is elevated to the status of family member. He is an accomplished scholar and has a complex moral code which, while it allows him to fool others, does so in the service of love and family affection. His tricks allow the pair of lovers to live together despite the disapproval of their fathers. In Chapman's play, there is a substance to Rinaldo that, ultimately, has a moral basis. He is much more than a trickster, and if he is at times a con man, he is usually in the service of morally laudable goals.

This same higher degree of motivation in Chapman's play is also seen in Valerio, Rinaldo's friend. Although Valerio initially appears to other characters and to the audience as only a dandy, given to music, poetry, dancing, and flirting, he also comes to express, in his speeches and in his actions, a sincere neo-Platonic idealism. Valerio believes that devotion to love is a ladder by which human beings can transcend their mortal limitations and gain greater knowledge and excellence.

Chapman makes outstanding use of language and theatrical staging in establishing these characters and presenting the action of the play. In Terence's original, the humor was derived mainly from the plot, which was complex to the point of confusion and complicated beyond either rationality or realism. By grounding his comedy on sympathetic characters, Chapman makes the multiple tricks and deceptions practiced in the play understandable, humorous, and believable. At the play's end, for example, Gostanzo, Valerio's father, learns at last that Valerio is really married to Gratiana and Fortunio has wed Bellanora. Gostanzo's learning that what he has believed throughout the play is actually false is a comedic revelation that leads to a final thematic and moral development. Gostanzo realizes that he is unable to control the young lovers; he must simply accept them with the full measure of his love. Such an ending transcends the moral frame of Terence's original drama and raises Chapman's play to a different level.

As typical with Chapman, the language of *All Fools* is flowing and fluent, easy to grasp. Some critics have objected to this quality in Chapman's other plays, noting that while his verse carries the sense of meaning remarkably well, it lacks any outstanding or distinctive touches. Such, however, is not the case with *All Fools*, for the play, although set in Italy, makes extensive use of Elizabethan figures of speech. These bring a strength and sense of immediacy to the dialogue that is sometimes lacking in Chapman's other dramas. Chapman displays an impressive command of the possibilities of colloquial speech of his times.

Ultimately, it is the combination of all of these qualities of characterization, plotting, staging, and language that raises *All Fools* to its acknowledged level as being among the best, if not the best, of Chapman's comedies.

"Critical Evaluation" by Michael Witkoski

Bibliography:
Bradbrook, M. C. "George Chapman." In *British Writers*, edited by Ian Scott-Killert. New York: Charles Scribner's Sons, 1979. Fine overview of Chapman and his work. Presents a measured view of his plays.

Lewis, C. S. *English Literature in the Sixteenth Century, Excluding Drama*. Oxford, England: Clarendon Press, 1954. The discussion of Chapman, while relatively short, is excellent, and evaluates him as a writer of his times rather than as an isolated figure.

Sanders, Andrew. *The Short Oxford History of English Literature*. Oxford, England: Clarendon Press, 1994. Concise and to-the-point. Useful for gaining an appreciation of Chapman's career and achievements.

Spivack, Charlotte. *George Chapman*. Boston: Twayne, 1967. Introductory survey volume to Chapman's life and writings, with a generous and sympathetic study of *All Fools*. Bibliography.

ALL FOR LOVE
Or, The World Well Lost

Type of work: Drama
Author: John Dryden (1631-1700)
Type of plot: Tragedy
Time of plot: First century B.C.E.
Locale: Alexandria, Egypt
First performed: 1677; first published, 1678

>   *Principal characters:*
>   MARK ANTONY, one of the Roman triumvirate
>   VENTIDIUS, his faithful general
>   DOLABELLA, Antony's friend
>   OCTAVIA, Antony's wife
>   CLEOPATRA, Queen of Egypt
>   ALEXAS, Cleopatra's eunuch

The Story:

After his humiliating defeat at Actium, Mark Antony retired to Alexandria, Egypt, where he remained in seclusion for some time in the temple of Isis. He avoided meeting his mistress, Cleopatra, the Queen of Egypt, whose cowardice had largely caused the defeat. Meanwhile the Romans, under Octavius, Maecenas, and Agrippa, had invaded Egypt, where, having laid siege to Alexandria, they calmly awaited Antony's next move. Serapion, a patriot and a priest of Isis, became alarmed at a sudden rising of the Nile and by prodigious disturbances among the royal tombs; these events seemed to presage disaster for Egypt.

Ventidius, Antony's trusted and highly successful general in the Middle East, came at this time to Alexandria to aid his commander. Alexas, Cleopatra's loyal, scheming eunuch, and Serapion tried to encourage citizens and troops with a splendid birthday festival in Antony's honor. Ventidius, in Roman fashion, scorned the celebration. He told Antony's Roman soldiers not to rejoice, but to prepare to defend Antony in his peril. Antony, clearly a ruined man, at last came out of his seclusion. While he cursed his fate and lamented the day that he was born, Ventidius, in concealment, overheard the pitiful words of his emperor. Revealing his presence, he attempted to console Antony. Both men wept; Antony marveled that Ventidius could remain faithful to a leader who had brought a large part of the Roman Empire to ruin through his love for Cleopatra.

Ventidius offered to Antony his twelve legions, which were stationed in Lower Syria, but his stipulation that these legions would not fight for Cleopatra plunged doting Antony into renewed gloom. When Ventidius mentioned the name of Cleopatra lightly, Antony took offense and cursed the general as a traitor. After this insult Antony, his mind filled with misgivings, guilt, and indecision, hastened to assure Ventidius of his love for him. He promised to leave Cleopatra to join the legions in Syria.

The word that Antony was preparing to desert her left Cleopatra in a mood of anger and despair. Meanwhile Charmion, her maid, went to Antony and begged the Roman to say farewell to her mistress. Antony refused, saying that he did not dare trust himself in Cleopatra's presence. Not daunted by this refusal, Alexas later intercepted Antony as he marched out of Alexandria. The eunuch flattered the Romans and presented them with rich jewels from Cleopatra. As

138

Antony was with difficulty clasping a bracelet around his arm, Cleopatra made her prepared appearance. Antony bitterly accused her of falseness and of being the cause of his downfall. The two argued. In desperation, Cleopatra told Antony that as her friend he must go to Syria, but that as her lover he must stay in Alexandria to share her fate. Antony wavered in his determination to leave when Cleopatra told him that she had spurned Octavius' offer of all Egypt and Syria if she would join his forces, and he elected to stay when she represented herself as a weak woman left to the mercy of the cruel invaders. Antony declared, in surrendering again to Cleopatra's charms, that Octavius could have the world as long as he had Cleopatra's love. Ventidius was overcome with shame and pity at Antony's submission.

Cleopatra was triumphant in her renewed power over Antony, and Antony himself seemed to have recovered some of his former magnificence when he was successful in minor engagements against the troops of Octavius. While Octavius, biding his time, held his main forces in check, Ventidius, still hopeful of saving Antony, suggested that a compromise might be arranged with Maecenas or with Agrippa.

Dolabella, the friend whom Antony had banished because he feared that Cleopatra might grow to love the young Roman, came from Octavius' camp to remind Antony that he had obligations toward his wife and two daughters. Then Octavia and her two young daughters were brought before Antony, Octavia, in spite of Antony's desertion, still hoping for reconciliation with her husband. When Antony accused her of bargaining with her brother Octavius, Octavia, undismayed, admitted that Octavius was prepared to withdraw from Egypt at the news that a reconciliation had been effected between his sister and Antony. Octavia's calm dignity affected Antony greatly, and when his two small daughters embraced him, he declared himself ready to submit to the will of Octavia. Cleopatra, entering upon this family reunion, exchanged insults with the momentarily triumphant Octavia.

Still afraid to face Cleopatra for the last time, Antony prevailed upon Dolabella to speak his farewell to Cleopatra. Dolabella, aspiring to Cleopatra's favors, accepted the mission with pleasure. Alexas, knowing of Dolabella's weakness and ever solicitous of the welfare of Egypt, advised Cleopatra to excite Antony's jealousy by pretending to be interested in Dolabella. After Ventidius and Octavia had secretly overheard the conversation between Dolabella and Cleopatra, Ventidius, now unwittingly a tool of Alexas, reported to Antony Cleopatra's apparent interest in the young Dolabella. Octavia confirmed his report, and Alexas suggested to the raging Antony that Cleopatra was capable of perfidy. Antony's passionate reaction to this information convinced Octavia that her mission was a failure and she returned to the Roman camp. Antony, meanwhile, accused Cleopatra and Dolabella of treachery. Ignoring their earnest denials, he banished them from his presence.

Cleopatra, cursing the eunuch's ill advice, attempted unsuccessfully to take her own life with a dagger. Antony ascended a tower in Alexandria harbor to watch an impending naval engagement between the Egyptian and Roman fleets. To his horror he saw the two fleets join and the entire force advance to attack the city. Antony realized now that his end was near; furthermore, his heart was broken by the belief that Cleopatra was responsible for the treachery of the Egyptian fleet. When Alexas brought false word that Cleopatra had retired to her tomb and had taken her life, Antony, no longer desiring to live, fell on his own sword. The faithful Ventidius killed himself. Cleopatra came to the dying Antony and convinced him, before he died, that she had remained steadfast in her love for him. Then, to cheat Octavius of a final triumph, she dressed herself in her royal robes and permitted herself to be bitten by a poisonous asp. Her maids, Iras and Charmion, killed themselves in the same manner. Serapion entered to find that Cleopatra had joined her Antony in death.

Critical Evaluation:

Dryden, the premier poet of his age, is honored primarily as a satirist and controversialist in the political and religious skirmishes of the Restoration. It was in drama, however, that he honed the fine poetic skills of his later poems. Between 1667 and 1678, he wrote a series of comedies and tragedies that provided him with the opportunity to develop the authority and control that distinguish his major poetry. Dryden was never a truly successful comic dramatist, perhaps because the prospect of a foolish or flawed man's getting better than he deserved was at odds with Dryden's essentially satiric sensibility. He did, however, create a series of memorable tragedies, including *Aureng-Zebe* (1675) and *Tyrannic Love: Or, The Royal Martyr* (1669), which set the norm for heroic drama in the period.

The Restoration was an exciting period in the history of the drama, with the introduction of women playing female roles. The heroic drama, the dominant serious form, was an exaggerated and stylized presentation of themes of epic proportions. Large heroes and heroines confronted dastardly villains with a great deal of bombastic rhetoric, usually in heroic couplets. Through his tragedies, Dryden had been building toward a greater control of the excesses of the genre and, in *All for Love*, he abandoned the couplet for blank verse and managed his highly romantic subject matter with distance and restraint.

All for Love is a retelling of the story of Antony and Cleopatra, but, despite Dryden's great admiration for Shakespeare, it is in no sense an adaptation of Shakespeare's version. Dryden's play lacks the panoramic sweep of Shakespeare's *Antony and Cleopatra*, which ranges broadly over the civilized world. As a devotee of a more rational kind of theater based on a strict interpretation of Aristotle, Dryden was much more concerned about the unities of time, place, and action. The whole drama unfolds in Alexandria and is narrowly limited to the period after the defeat of Antony at the battle of Actium.

The play does not have a climax in the usual sense of the term. The climax of a drama is ordinarily a focal point toward which the conflicts and complications build. It is true that in some Shakespearean plays the climax is early, as in *Macbeth* (1606), in which the murder of Duncan is accomplished in the second act so that the audience may concentrate on the consequences of Macbeth's crime. Dryden went a step further. If *All for Love* has a climax at all, it occurs before the beginning of the action on stage. The play traces the complex chain of results of the battle of Actium, which changed the course of history, sealed the fate of Antony, and doomed Egyptian civilization.

Such a context is the natural element of Restoration heroic drama: a hero larger than life, worthy of the grandest exploits, is thrust into a moribund civilization. Heroic drama of the Restoration is fashioned by a poetics of the terminal. The overreacher, the hero who monumentally represents all that is best in a nation and who tests the justice and the restraining limits of the universe, is gone from the moral universe of the Restoration. Instead, the audience has heroes, noble beyond reproach, who are cast into a twilight world, the world of the terminus, or end. Dryden's images of sunsets and twilight reinforce the impression of finality. The optimism of Renaissance drama has been replaced, if not by despair, at least by resignation to a world in decline. Antony had challenged the world, but that time is now past. He is left to examine his passions in a series of after-the-fact confrontations.

New attitudes about what is efficacious social behavior emerged from the Restoration's predilection for order and stability. The heroic drama is a transposition of the daring hero into a more subdued context. Dryden's play may be considered a reflection of the time in which he lived in its lack of belief in the social utility of the hero. Dryden establishes a new kind of tragedy that recognizes the limitations of the hero and searches out what is beyond.

Unlike Shakespeare, Dryden does not use setting as a premise for characterization. Dryden takes pains to remove his characters from the particularities of any specific time or place, to isolate them in a world free of extraneous distractions. In this context Antony, his great exploits over, is free to confront himself. It is probably a limitation of the dramatic form that these complications seem to be thrust externally upon Antony, but the fact remains that he must face a series of trials, each of which is designed to challenge another facet of his sorely burdened moral identity. As Antony faces his troubles, he is no more a passionate drunkard than he is any longer the potent hero. He is not a weak man. The conflict is no longer a simple dichotomy of passion and responsibility. Rather it is a matter of Antony, through the blandishments of Ventidius and Cleopatra, trying to decide who he is by discovering where his true loyalties lie.

It is typical of this oddly muted tragic world that its passions are manipulated and stage-managed by the eunuch Alexas. Octavius, the hero in the ascendant, never appears on stage. It is Antony's descent from godhead to humanity, rather than the drama of war, that is the source of the special tragedy of *All for Love*. Antony's experience brings him to a self-perception and an understanding of passion, loyalty, and power that are beyond the hero at the height of his success. Heroic perception of this diminished sort is the appropriate insight for an age of reason and skepticism.

"Critical Evaluation" by Edward E. Foster

Bibliography:

Kirsch, Arthur. *"All for Love."* In *Twentieth Century Interpretations of "All for Love,"* edited by Bruce King. Englewood Cliffs, N.J.: Prentice-Hall, 1968. Discusses the play's relationship to heroic tragedy. Maintains that in the play, heroism is replaced by sentimentality and domesticity. The introduction by Bruce King is also illuminating.

Milhous, Judith, and Robert D. Hume. *"All for Love."* In *Producible Interpretation: Eight English Plays, 1675-1707.* Carbondale: Southern Illinois University Press, 1985. Examines the play in terms of staging. Provides discussion that includes the nature of its tragedy, character analysis, rhythm, settings, time, costumes, casting, and effects.

Novak, Maximillian E. "Criticism, Adaptation, Politics, and the Shakespearean Model of Dryden's *All for Love.*" In *Studies in Eighteenth-Century Culture,* edited by Roseann Runte. Vol. 7. Madison: University of Wisconsin Press, 1978. Discusses the relationship of *All for Love* to Shakespeare's *Antony and Cleopatra.* Explores how, where, and why Dryden made his play different from Shakespeare's.

Waith, Eugene. "The Herculean Hero." In *Twentieth Century Interpretations of "All for Love,"* edited by Bruce King. Englewood Cliffs, N.J.: Prentice-Hall, 1968. Examines Antony's character. Claims that he is a "Herculean hero" because he is brave, generous, passionate, and indifferent to public opinion.

ALL HALLOWS EVE

Type of work: Novel
Author: Charles Williams (1886-1945)
Type of plot: Allegory
Time of plot: October, 1945
Locale: London
First published: 1945

Principal characters:
> LESTER FURNIVAL, a dead young wife
> RICHARD FURNIVAL, her husband
> EVELYN MERCER, her dead friend
> BETTY WALLINGFORD, another friend
> LADY SARA WALLINGFORD, Betty's mother
> JONATHAN DRAYTON, Betty's artist fiancé, friend of Richard
> SIMON THE CLERK, the leader of a religious group

The Story:

To Lester Furnival, standing on Westminster Bridge at twilight, the lights of the city and the drone of a friendly plane overhead were symbols of the peace, a return to the natural order of life. Lester slowly became conscious, however, of a silence that was unnatural. Lester realized that she was dead.

A vital and passionate young woman killed in a plane crash, she first found herself alone in the city with Evelyn, the friend who was killed with her. She realized that theirs was never a true friendship. As the two dead women tried to establish a genuine relationship in the afterlife, they became involved in the affairs of the living. Lester's husband Richard had an artist friend, Jonathan, who was in love with Betty, a school friend whom Lester and Evelyn had never liked. Betty was completely dominated by her mother, Lady Wallingford, who was a disciple of a mysterious faith healer who called himself Simon the Clerk.

Lady Wallingford and Betty called to see a portrait of Father Simon commissioned from Jonathan. Jonathan, a Christian, had without realizing it revealed in the portrait the essence of evil, which Simon represented. Lady Wallingford, infuriated, called off Betty's engagement to Jonathan and took Betty away. Jonathan called on Richard for help. The conflict between mother and lover for possession of Betty became the conflict between the God of love and the power of darkness for the human soul.

Surrounded by a band of zealous converts, preaching to a mesmerized audience in his shabby backstreet headquarters, Simon was the reembodiment of Simon the Magus, of the Jew who rejected Christ. Simon was, in fact, the Antichrist. Exploiting the devotion of Lady Wallingford, he conceived Betty to be his agent and feared that his power over his daughter was threatened by her love for Jonathan. Simon decided that the time had come for the final magical operation that would separate her human soul from her body and substitute his will in its place. He was thwarted by love in action. At each crisis, he made a mistake, because his magic powers could not perceive what love can do. When Simon went to Betty's bedroom to perform the final operation of magic, Lester was there, having gone to ask Betty's forgiveness for rejecting her friendship. Betty's forgiveness of Lester released Lester's spirit; Lester's love sustained Betty and became Betty's substitute to receive Simon's magic. Lester was already dead, so Simon's magic had no effect on her, and Betty was released from his spell to rebel against her mother and rejoin Jonathan. The defeated Simon then turned his attention to the wretched soul of Evelyn, who had sought his aid to regain her power of persecuting Betty. Lester tried to rescue Evelyn, as she had rescued Betty, by joining her within Evelyn's miserably deformed physical body, which Simon created for her with his magic powers. Simon attempted to control Evelyn's body and use it to trap Betty, Jonathan, and Richard. Lester, however, exercised a greater control through the power of love and warned them in time for them to expose Simon and bring his work and his house to ruins.

The climax of the action took place on a gray, rainy Halloween, All Hallows Eve, when the deformed body, containing the souls of Lester and Evelyn, moved through the streets of London and kept a rendezvous at Jonathan's flat. The engaged couple had invited the bereaved Richard to join them for dinner. When Lester wanted to warn Richard of the approach of the magical body, she thought of the telephone. Having begged two pennies from a passerby, she went into a telephone booth opposite the Charing Cross underground station. When Richard came to the phone, he heard Lester's voice as clearly as he had seen her form several times in the last few days. She gave him the message that they had to wait at the flat until the old woman came. Instead of going out to dinner, they spread a meal of bread, cheese, cold cuts, and wine, and thus prepared themselves for the crisis of All Hallows Eve. After meeting, the three living friends took the deformed body with them in a taxi through the rainy midnight streets of London to the darkened house where Simon and Lady Wallingford were stalled in their last desperate act of magic. Love triumphed over evil; Lester disappeared in a blaze of white light.

Critical Evaluation:

Charles Williams' last novel is set in the locale he knew best, central London, but in a time that he did not live to appreciate: the first autumn of the peace after World War II. The novel removes the barrier between the natural and the supernatural worlds. Lester is the central character in a drama that illustrates Williams' mystical and imaginative interpretation of Christian doctrine. The plot traces the triumph of love over evil during Lester's period of purgatory. She is a modern version of the figure of Beatrice, the spiritual guide of Dante Alighieri's *The Divine Comedy*. Her love for her husband, which has survived her death, leads to his conversion, to the defeat of evil, and to her own salvation. The story combines natural and supernatural elements with a realism that is not merely a matter of literary technique but also an expression of Williams' belief that the material and the spiritual, and the temporal and the eternal, are equally real. This tenet of faith is basic to the creative imagination for Williams. The novel is not intended as a fantasy or as allegory; the novel form is used simply for its traditional purpose of revealing life's reality. Williams believed that a person who loves can bear another's burdens in a way that he considered physical as well as spiritual. This ability involves not simply praying for the burdened one but also loving that one so deeply that the burden of suffering is transferred from the loved one to the person who loves. As the human form of Christ on the cross suffered for all humanity, so the central character of this story saves a victim by substituting herself.

From the moment when Lester finds herself alone on Westminster Bridge to the climax of her disappearance from Simon's house, there is always a strong sense of London as the background to the action. At first, Lester can see only the city, but as her spirit develops, she hears all the familiar noises of people and traffic, feels the pavement under her feet, and smells the river and the October rain.

The literalness of London sights, sounds, and locations is not merely a device to root the supernatural story in the natural world. For Williams, London is an image of the City of God, the Holy City, the community of the saints. When the city is first mentioned, the term indicates the ancient borough of London, site of St. Paul's, as distinguished from Holborn, where Simon's headquarters are. Through Lester's developing spiritual perception, however, the spiritual reality of the eternal city is revealed. Its identity is hinted to mortal eyes on the fateful afternoon when Lady Wallingford and Betty call to look at Jonathan's portrait of Simon. Lady Wallingford is equally antagonized by another painting that Jonathan and Richard consider the best that Johnathan has done, a painting of a part of London after a raid, a scene of desolation bathed in living light.

This city, emerging from war and night, is the setting in which Richard meets his wife again with a deeper understanding of their love. At the end of the novel, Jonathan and Betty give Richard the painting, and Lester disappears into light. Although the plot of the novel centers on the conflict over Betty, considerable thematic interest is focused on the dead Lester and the living Richard as they move through the city, at first absolutely separated, then gradually reunited as each comes to understand the reality of love, and finally separated when the understanding is complete. These two characters are developed with a psychological depth, dramatic sensitivity, and humor that make them as fully credible as the protagonists of a more traditional novel. Jonathan and Betty are less fully delineated and are seen more from the outside, through the eyes of their friends, than from the inside. The dead Evelyn is no longer a human personality but merely the epitome of egocentric peevishness, which was her dominant trait.

In descending scale, Simon and Lady Wallingford are agents of evil, as much puppets as the bodies that Simon can create. These differing degrees of characterization reflect Williams' belief that only love can make a human being whole. Jonathan and Betty, in their initial stages of love, cannot be as fully developed as Lester and Richard are. In characterization, as in every aspect of the novel, Williams' story is perfectly integrated with his doctrine. Final assessment of his achievement requires the resolution of a basic dilemma: whether the credibility of the story makes the doctrine convincing or whether the credibility of the story depends on conviction about the doctrine.

Bibliography:

Anderson, Angelee Sailer. "The Nature of the City: Visions of the Kingdom and Its Saints in Charles Williams' *All Hallows Eve.*" *Mythlore: A Journal of J. R. R. Tolkien, C. S. Lewis, Charles Williams and the Genres of Myth and Fantasy Studies* 57, no. 3 (Spring, 1989): 16-21. This quarterly periodical regularly contains articles on Williams' work. Two other periodicals that offer information on Williams' work are *Inklings* and *Seven.*

Eliot, T. S. Introduction to *All Hallows Eve,* by Charles Williams. Grand Rapids, Mich.: Wm. B. Eerdmans, 1981. Eliot was an important literary friend of Williams.

Howard, Thomas. *The Novels of Charles Williams.* New York: Oxford University Press, 1983. Discusses Christian doctrines of forgiveness and judgment as portrayed in the novel.

Sibley, Agnes. *Charles Williams.* Boston: Twayne, 1982. In addition to a summary and insightful commentary on *All Hallows Eve,* Sibley's work contains a useful bibliography.

Williams, Charles. *The Image of the City and Other Essays.* Edited by Anne Ridler. New York: Oxford University Press, 1958. Williams expounds his theories himself; in addition, the critical introduction contains a brilliant analysis of Williams' major themes.

ALL MEN ARE BROTHERS

Type of work: Novel
Author: Unknown; associated with Shih Nai-an (c. 1290-1365)
Type of plot: Adventure
Time of plot: Thirteenth century or earlier
Locale: China
First published: Shui-hu chuan, possibly the fourteenth century (English translation, 1933; also
translated as *Water Margin*)

Principal characters:

SHIH CHIN, the Nine Dragoned
LU TA, later LU CHI SHEN, the Tattooed Priest
LING CH'UNG, the Leopard Headed
CH'AI CHIN, the Little Whirlwind
YANG CHI, the Blue-Faced Beast
CHU T'UNG, the Beautiful Bearded
LEI HENG, the Winged Tiger
CH'AO KAI, the Heavenly King
WU YUNG, the Great Intelligence
KUNG SUN SHENG, Dragon in the Clouds
SUNG CHIANG, the Opportune Rain
WU SUNG, the Hairy Priest
WANG THE DWARF TIGER
TAI CHUNG, the Magic Messenger
LI K'UEI, the Black Whirlwind
LU CHUN I, the Jade Ch'Lin

The Story:

To escape the persecution of evil Commander Kao, a military instructor fled to the borders.
On the way, he instructed a village lord's son, Shih Chin, in warlike skills. Later, Shih Chin
became friendly with the robbers of Little Hua Mountain. Discovery of this alliance forced Shih
Chin to flee. He fell in with Captain Lu Ta, who, after killing a pig butcher who was persecuting
a young woman, escaped capture by becoming priest Lu Chi Shen. His violence and intemper-
ance, however, forced the abbot to send him to another temple. On the way, he made peace
between a village lord and the robbers of Peach Blossom Mountain.

Shih Chin joined the robbers of Little Hua Mountain. Lu Chi Shen went on to his temple,
where he became a friend of military instructor Ling Ch'ung. Commander Kao's son lusted for
Ling Ch'ung's wife, so Ling Ch'ung was falsely accused of murder, branded, and exiled to
Ch'ang Chou. His guards were prevented by Lu Chi Shen from carrying out their secret orders
to kill Ling Ch'ung. Again on his way, Ling Ch'ung was hospitably received by Lord Ch'ai
Chin.

In Ch'ang Chou, Ling Ch'ung accidentally escaped a death trap and killed his three would-be
assassins. Again, he encountered Ch'ai Chin, who sent him to take refuge in Liang Shan P'o, a
robbers' lair headed by the ungracious Wang Lun. Warrior Yang Chi, after killing a bully, was
branded and sent to be a border guard. His skill delighted Governor Liang of Peking, who kept

and promoted him and even selected him to transport rich birthday gifts to Liang's father-in-law. To rid the way of robbers, Chu T'ung and Lei Heng were sent out ahead of the party that was carrying the treasures. Lei Heng captured drunken Liu T'ang and took him to Lord Ch'ao Kai, but the lord arranged his release on privately discovering that Lei Heng had come to seek him; Lei Heng brought the news of the birthday gifts, which he, Ch'ao Kai, and a teacher, Wu Yung, then plotted to steal. Magician Kung Sun Sheng and the three Juan brothers joined them.

The plotters cleverly drugged Yang Chi and his disguised soldiers and stole the treasure. In despair, Yang Chi left the others, who resolved to pin the blame on him. Yang Chi fell in with Lu Chi Shen; they went to Double Dragon Mountain and, overcoming the robber chief who refused to admit them, became the leaders of the band.

When Ch'ao Kai was discovered to have been one of the robbers, plans were made to catch him; but with the aid of scribe Sung Chiang and robber-catcher Chu T'ung, Ch'ao Kai and the others escaped to Liang Shan P'o. Ling Ch'ung killed the ungracious Wang Lun, and Ch'ao Kai was made the chief. Ling Ch'ung discovered that his wife had killed herself to escape the advances of Commander Kao's son. The robbers vanquished two groups sent against them.

Sung Chiang's connection with the robbers was discovered by his unfaithful mistress. Enraged at her blackmail threats, he killed her and escaped to Ch'ai Chin's village. There he met Wu Sung, who was on his way to see his older brother after a long absence.

Wu Sung killed a tiger and he was greatly celebrated. He was of heroic size; his brother was puny and small. The latter's wife tried unsuccessfully to seduce Wu Sung. In Wu Sung's absence, she took a lover and, with his help, killed her husband. Wu Sung returned and killed the pair. Although generally pitied, he was branded and exiled.

After an eventful journey, Wu Sung defended his jailer's son against a usurper and so offended the tyrant that he plotted with General Chang to accuse Wu Sung falsely of a crime. Wu Sung killed the plotters and joined those at Double Dragon Mountain.

While on a visit to military magistrate Hua Yung, Sung Chiang was captured by the robbers of the Mountain of Clear Winds, but they recognized and welcomed him. One of them, lustful Wang the Dwarf Tiger, captured the wife of a civil magistrate, Liu Kao. Hoping to please Hua Yung, Sung Chiang persuaded Wang to release her. Later the woman, a troublemaker, identified Sun Chiang as one of the robbers. Sung Chiang and Hua Yung escaped to the Mountain of Clear Winds, and Liu Kao was killed.

General Ch'ing Ming came against these robbers and was captured. Their plot to force him to join their band was successful. Liu Kao's wife was recaptured and executed. Sung Chiang promised to get a wife for the disappointed Wang the Dwarf Tiger. The whole band decided to join those at Liang Shan P'o, but Sung Chiang was summoned home for the burial of his father. The report of his father's death, however, turned out to be a trick to keep Sung Chiang from turning outlaw. Persuaded to stand trial for his mistress' murder, he was branded and exiled. The trip was very eventful, involving many near escapes in encounters with robbers who later proved friendly. At his destination, Sung Chiang became a friend of his jailer, Tai Chung, who possessed magic enabling him to walk three hundred miles a day. Another friend, violent but loyal Li K'uei, caused much trouble, which Sung Chiang was able to smooth over. One day, Sung Chiang became drunk and wrote revolutionary verses on a wall. Tai Chung, sent to a distant city to get execution orders, went instead to Liang Shan P'o, where a letter was forged, freeing Sung Chiang. A mistake made in the seal, however, also resulted in Tai Chung's death sentence. Both were freed from the execution grounds by the robbers. All went back to Liang Shan P'o, enlarging their group with additional robbers recruited along the way.

Sung Chiang set out to bring his father and brother to the robbers' lair. He was miraculously saved from capture by a temple goddess who gave great prophecies. The robbers took the Sung family to the lair. Kung Sun Sheng and Li K'uei went out to get their old mothers. On his journey, Li K'uei killed a false robber who pretended to be himself, but the impostor's wife escaped. On the return journey, Li K'uei's mother was killed by tigers. Li K'uei killed the tigers, but when he went to receive the reward money, the impostor's wife identified him, and he was captured. Another of the band freed him, however, and they returned to Liang Shan P'o.

Shih Hsiu opened a meat shop with the help of official Yang Hsiung. Shih Hsiu discovered adultery between Yang Hsiung's wife and a priest. They killed the adulterers and escaped. Later, they fell in with a thief, Shih Ch'ien, who caused a row and was captured in the village of Chu. In Liang Shan P'o, the robbers planned warfare against the Chu village; the others were, at last, victorious. Li K'uei, ignoring a pact between the robbers and the Hu village, killed all the members of the Hu household except the female warrior, The Ten-Foot Green Snake, who had previously been captured by the robbers. Later, she joined the robbers and married Wang the Dwarf Tiger.

Robber-catcher Lei Heng, after killing a courtesan, was allowed to escape to Liang Shan P'o by robber-catcher Chu T'ung, who was, consequently, exiled. He pleased the magistrate, however, who wanted Chu T'ung to look after his little son. By killing the little boy, the robbers forced Chu T'ung to join them.

Li K'uei and Ch'ai Chin went to right a wrong; Ch'ai Chin was captured, and the robbers attempting to free him were repelled by their enemies' magic. Kung Sun Sheng, now a hermit, was summoned; his magic finally enabled the robbers to overcome the enemy and free Ch'ai Chin.

A fresh advance planned by Commander Kao against the robbers resulted in many useful additions to Liang Shan P'o when enemy leaders were captured and persuaded to change allegiance. The robbers of Double Dragon, Peach Blossom, and Little Hua Mountains, after some difficulties of capture and escape, joined those at Liang Shan P'o.

A stolen horse intended for Sung Chiang had been stolen again by the Chun family. Instructor Shi Wen Kung, who now possessed the horse, boasted that he would destroy the robbers. While leading his men, Chief Ch'ao Kai was mortally wounded. Before he died, he asked that whoever captured Shi Wen Kung be named the new chief. A long period of mourning followed.

Rich and respected Lu Chun I was enticed to Liang Shan P'o in the hope that he would join them. Returning, he was arrested and imprisoned as a robber. His steward, now in possession of his wife and goods, plotted to have Lu Chun I killed. Many events followed, including the near death of Sung Chiang, but finally the city was taken. The prisoners were freed and the adulterers killed. Lu Chun I refused Sung Chiang's offer to make him the chief.

The robbers captured additional soldiers sent against them and added many of the leaders to their ranks. Ch'ao Kai's death was finally avenged in the conquest of the Chun family and of Shi Wen Kung, whose actual captor was Lu Chun I, who still refused to become the chief. Since all the robbers wished Sung Chiang to remain the leader, he prepared a test. He and Lu Chun I each led a group against one of the two cities remaining to be taken. The first to take his city would be the chief. After some reverses, Sung Chiang was successful. He then went to the aid of Lu Chun I, who had been twice vanquished by warrior Chang Ch'ing. This general, finally overcome, was persuaded to join the outlaws. Sung Chiang received a heavenly message in the form of a miraculous stone tablet that listed all thirty-six greater and seventy-two lesser chieftains who made up the robber band. All swore undying loyalty, wishing to be united forever, life after life.

Critical Evaluation:

The stories that make up the plot originated many years before the novel as a whole was composed and probably have some basis in fact. The translation of the shortest version of the novel runs to more than twelve hundred eventful pages. One hundred and eight named chieftains form the band at the close of the book. The plot outline given above conveys only a little of the extraordinary bloodthirstiness of these "good fellows," who slaughter entire households of their enemies, who occasionally indulge in cannibalism, and whose reasons for becoming outlaws are not always noble. The characters, however, are vividly portrayed, the story is always interesting, and all is presented with the greatest realism and vigor. Long attributed to Shih Nai-an, the novel, many scholars claim, may be the work of Lo Kuan-chung or of another author whose identity is unknown.

All Men Are Brothers was translated into English in 1933 by noted author Pearl S. Buck. Buck, the daughter of U.S. missionaries and the wife of a missionary, was familiar with the Chinese people and culture. Buck titled her translation *All Men Are Brothers* because she thought the literal translation of the title (water margin novel) was too remote for the sensibilities of Western readers. Her title comes from the *Analects* of Confucius (fl. fifth century B.C.E.) and is intended to capture the novel's human spirit.

There are many more versions of this novel than of other Chinese novels. This may be the result of the vastness of its scope and characterization, or the suitability of the novel to shorter versions.

Readers may wish to distinguish one bandit from another by means of the vividness of their characterizations and the uniqueness of their stories, but readers should not expect to keep the identity of the myriad bandits straight, beyond some exceptional personalities and incidents. Perhaps not every leader of the bandit gang is meant to be identifiable; the text, unlike the average Western novel, has many inconsistencies, errors, and improbabilities. For example, none of the 108 chieftains dies in the numerous fights and battles before the assembly at the end.

Perhaps, to Western sensibilities, these imperfections flaw the novel as a conscious literary creation. Given the early date of this novel, and the fact that it is probably a compilation of the work of multiple storytellers, weaving fiction in and out of some probable historical events, complications, errors, and improbabilities are to be expected. Also, Chinese readers have exhibited tolerance for error, incongruity, implausibility, and lack of completeness, especially when the vitality, energy, spirit, and underlying psychological truthfulness are as evident, as they are in *All Men Are Brothers*. The truth of a Chinese novel lies more in its insight into and sympathy with its characters than in its crafted, careful exposition. Portraying a world of emotions, sensibilities, feelings, and actions is often, to the Chinese reader, in opposition to, or subtly at odds with, a strictly factual, totally explainable, plausible world.

Broad generalizations are often used to discuss this complicated, highly episodic, and well-peopled novel, when few generalizations can be accurate for the novel as a whole, beyond that of a compendium of Robin Hood-like, best-loved bandit stories, renowned in Chinese literature for their variety, inventiveness, dramatic surprise, and knowledge of human nature. Even these generalizations are not always applicable to the text: The bandits often have little socially redeeming value, help only themselves, and often are unnecessarily violent.

Despite the fact that the novel was probably composed after a period of storytelling, its incidents and moods are surprisingly consistent and uniform in narrative structure, and almost always captivating, enlivening, thrilling, adventurous, spontaneous, and varied, with much of the appeal of the unseen endings of modern Western mystery stories.

Seen at various times as a textbook for outlaws and an actual sourcebook for the nicknames of real bandits, it has also been seen as a political metaphor for the actions of Chinese Communists after 1949 by some, and as a glorification of peasant revolutionaries by others. It could be argued that nearly any use or misuse could be made of a novel so large and various. *All Men Are Brothers*, however, has a unique popularity in Chinese literature, transcending use or even explanation of a band of bandits who see themselves as mostly generous-spirited, but have been forced by the oppressions of life and government into banditry and outlaw life, and now glorify in a marginal life in the boundaries of the safe swamps that they make their hideout, headquarters, and refuge. That so much life, liveliness, inventive incident, and devilish and repugnant charm should issue from the least likely, and perhaps least deserving, of characters is one of the great unexplainable fascinations of this highly popular novel.

"Critical Evaluation" by Jack Finefrock

Bibliography:
Buck, Pearl S. *The Chinese Novel.* New York: John Day, 1939. Her 1938 Nobel Prize lecture discusses the vividness of characterization in *All Men Are Brothers*, the folk mind, and the freedom and flexibility of the Chinese novel. Includes her philosophy of translation and a brief discussion of the instincts of Chinese fiction.
Hsia, C. T. *The Classic Chinese Novel.* Bloomington: Indiana University Press, 1980. Introduction discusses the importance of the work as one of six major Chinese novels. General discussion and excellent commentary on the text; well-selected quotations from the text.
Irwin, Richard Gregg. *The Evolution of a Chinese Novel: "Shui-hu chuan."* Cambridge, Mass.: Harvard University Press, 1953. Discusses the novel in its most complete form, and shorter forms and translations. Conclusion has helpful chapter-by-chapter plot summaries.
Plaks, Andrew H. *The Four Masterworks of the Ming Novel.* Princeton, N.J.: Princeton University Press, 1987. Chapter on deflation of heroism in *All Men Are Brothers*. Argues that the models in the novel can serve for serious historical writing, although the characters are largely products of the imagination and not true historical figures.
Rolston, David L., ed. *How to Read the Chinese Novel.* Princeton, N.J.: Princeton University Press, 1990. General introduction to Chinese fiction criticism; chapter on how to read *All Men Are Brothers*.

ALL MY SONS

Type of work: Drama
Author: Arthur Miller (1915-   )
Type of plot: Psychological realism
Time of plot: Mid-twentieth century
Locale: An American town
First performed: 1947; first published, 1947

> *Principal characters:*
> JOE KELLER, a middle-aged businessman
> KATE, his wife
> CHRIS, their son
> ANN DEEVER, a former neighbor
> GEORGE, her brother

The Story:

The night Ann Deever returned to her old neighborhood to visit Chris Keller and his family, a tree in their backyard blew over in a storm. The tree had been planted as a memorial to the older Keller son, Larry, a fighter pilot who was lost in World War II. The morning after the storm, family members and neighbors gathered in the yard to chat, to read the newspaper, and to discuss Ann's return.

Ann's father, who had been Joe Keller's partner in a wartime business, was in the penitentiary for having allowed cracked cylinder heads to be shipped, which had caused the deaths of twenty-one pilots. (Joe Keller had been jailed, too, but was later exonerated for his part in the incident.) After the neighbors left and while Ann was still inside the Keller house eating breakfast, Joe Keller and Chris—a father and grown son who obviously admired each other—discussed Larry's tree and the effect it would have on Kate, the mother. Chris also told his father that he had asked Ann to visit because he wanted to ask her to marry him; Joe responded that his mother would not like the news because she still thought of Ann as Larry's girl. Chris explained that if he was to stay with the family business, he would need his father's support in convincing Kate that Larry was not coming back from the war and that Ann and he had the right to be happy.

When she entered the backyard, Kate tried to downplay the significance of Larry's destroyed tree, but she noted the coincidence of Ann's return. She reminded the two men that she was sure Larry was not dead and that Ann must share that sentiment. Chris tried to reason with her, but she insisted that it was possible that Larry was still alive. She mentioned that a neighbor was working out Larry's horoscope to establish whether or not Larry's plane crash could have occurred on one of Larry's "lucky" days.

Once Ann joined the Keller family in the yard, the talk turned to old times and ultimately to Larry. Ann made it clear that she was not waiting for Larry, but Kate told her that she should listen to her heart, "because certain things have to be, and certain things can never be." Their talk also turned to Ann's father in prison, and Ann revealed that her sympathy for him had come to an end once she heard of Larry's crash. Joe explained that Steve—Ann's father—was not a bad man, just the type of weak man who buckled under pressure. Joe went on to say that in spite of Steve's claim that he, Keller, had approved the damaged shipment, he would be willing to let Steve come back to the business, not as a partner but as a worker. Ann marveled at Joe's magnanimity, and Chris agreed that he was "a great guy."

After the group made plans to go out for a celebratory dinner, Chris and Ann talked seriously together. Chris explained his feelings for her, and Ann assured him that she wanted to marry him. Chris also confided his guilt in having survived the war, explaining that in combat he had realized his responsibility for others. He wondered whether there was any meaning to all the suffering and destruction and whether his actions and participation in his father's business since the war were admirable or self-serving.

Ann's brother George called after having visited their father in prison, and he announced that he needed to come to the Kellers. He did not say why, and Joe began to worry that he might want to stir up old trouble. In anticipation of George's return, Kate made his favorite grape drink and told her husband: "Be smart now, Joe. The boy is coming. Be smart."

Ann challenged Chris's complete acceptance of his father's innocence, and Chris asked: "Do you think I could forgive him if he'd done that thing?" Later that afternoon, George arrived. He told Chris and Ann that his father had charged Joe with having given him the go-ahead to ship the defective cylinder heads and with lying about his role in the crime when he claimed to have been home, sick in bed.

Chris and Ann were able to calm George, and once Kate greeted him and reminded him of all the good times in the old neighborhood, George accepted the Kellers' dinner invitation. Joe appeared in the backyard and greeted George, and eventually the conversation turned to Joe's remarkable good health. Kate offhandedly mentioned that he had not been sick a day in his life. Joe interjected with a reminder that he had had the flu during the war, but George had caught the Kellers in the discrepancy and he openly charged Joe with having let his father take the blame.

George stormed out, and Chris confronted Joe, asking him what he had done with the one hundred and twenty cracked engine heads. Joe explained that a slowdown in production would have been costly for the business and that he had let the shipment go, but that he had not thought the defective parts would be installed. He concluded by saying that he had done it for Chris. Chris yelled back at him and pounded on his father's chest before he left.

At two o'clock the following morning, Kate and Joe discussed the situation and wondered what their son would do with their secret. Ann entered the backyard where they sat and said that she would do nothing about Joe but that Kate must accept that Larry was dead so that she and Chris could marry. Kate balked and Joe went into the house. Ann produced a letter from Larry written on the day he crashed, in which he told of knowing about his father's part in the shipment of defective engine parts and that it was his intention to crash his plane.

When Chris returned, he announced that he was going to leave home and asked his parents what they were going to do to make the situation right. Joe, still unable to comprehend, asked why he was considered "bad," to which Chris responded, ". . . you're no worse than most men but I thought you were better. I never saw you as a man. I saw you as my father."

Chris read Larry's letter aloud to his father and asked him if he understood his moral obligation. Just before going back into the house, Joe haltingly admitted that the deaths of the twenty-one pilots were his responsibility: ". . . they were all my sons." A few minutes later, inside the house, Joe shot himself.

Critical Evaluation:

Regarded by critics as Arthur Miller's first successful play, *All My Sons* presents a narrow slice of American middle-class life. The play's context is limited: A manufacturer sells defective parts to the military and then covers up the crime by forcing his partner to take the blame. The ensuing situation, however, is where the scope of the play enlarges, culminating in the moment when the American Everyman must take a moral stand.

The drama's spatial confines underscore the theme of the play. The Kellers' backyard is enclosed by hedges and arbors and offers only a glimpse into the adjoining neighbors' yards. The focus is on the individual family and its moral limitations. While the story's premise is specific, the everyday, down-home setting of a backyard in a middle-class neighborhood in a nameless American town offers the audience a common ground of experience and relatedness.

A major theme of *All My Sons* is that of responsibility. Before the play's action begins, Joe Keller had ducked moral responsibility by allowing cracked cylinder heads to be shipped out of his factory. He covers up and blames his partner, but he is able to justify his actions as a consequence of his obligation to his family. At the end of the play, he accepts responsibility for his crime only after his dead son Larry's letter has indicted him.

Kate Keller, too, bears responsibility for the cover-up, but she participated in it primarily as a way to keep Larry alive in her mind. If she had acknowledged Joe's guilt, she would have acknowledged that Larry had actually crashed. Kate represents the intuitive and the irrational. Her responsibility to her family defies—and defines—moral obligation.

The son Chris is the idealist who must come to grips with his parents' human weaknesses. It could be said that in idolizing his father he set up a barrier to the truth and to exploring the notion of his father's guilt, a possibility that must have occurred to him. Chris feels a larger responsibility. Where Joe had his family in mind, Chris sees something bigger than family. It is Chris's responsibility to make his father see that larger arena. In doing so, he brings about his father's ultimate acceptance of responsibility and his father's decision to take his own life in expiation for his crime.

All My Sons also addresses the material aspect of the American Dream and its effects on the soul. When Joe Keller says that he acted as he did for Chris and his family, he represents the tension between the need to succeed materially and the responsibility of behaving ethically. Because the American economy flourished as a result of World War II, a sense of guilt could be overpowering. Chris lives this tension, and by the end of the play Keller, too, is forced to confront it. The sentiments of the play are rooted in a prewar era, but the emotional power defines the angst of postwar American society.

All My Sons, which prepares the way for Miller's masterpiece, *Death of a Salesman* (1949), continues a tradition in twentieth century American drama that was established by Eugene O'Neill in *Ah, Wilderness!* (1933) and *Long Day's Journey into Night* (1940), and by Thornton Wilder in *Our Town* (1938). In these plays, as in Miller's *All My Sons*, the authors explore the complex dynamic between individual responsibility and family relationships.

Douglas A. Jones

Bibliography:
Bigsby, C. W. E. "Drama from a Living Center." In *Arthur Miller*, edited by Harold Bloom. New York: Chelsea House, 1987. Initially discusses *All My Sons* as a play of moral didacticism and then probes a subtext that explores the guilt of the idealist. Maintains that the play has a well-constructed plot development and contrivances.
Huftel, Sheila. *Arthur Miller: The Burning Glass*. New York: Citadel Press, 1965. The chapter dedicated to *All My Sons* provides a significant overview of the play along with a careful analysis of the main and peripheral characters. The influence of Henrik Ibsen, the Norwegian dramatist, on Miller is discussed, as is *All My Sons* in relation to Miller's adaptation of Ibsen's play *An Enemy of the People* (1882).

Miller, Arthur. Introduction to *Arthur Miller's Collected Plays*. New York: Viking Press, 1957-1981. Miller devotes many pages to *All My Sons*, explaining that it is a social play of relationship and responsibility. He discusses the inspiration for the drama and gives context for the play's underlying philosophies.

Stambusky, Alan A. "Arthur Miller: Aristotelian Canons in the Twentieth Century Drama." In *Modern American Drama: Essays in Criticism*, edited by William E. Taylor. DeLand, Fla.: Everett/Edwards, 1968. The first part of this chapter discusses classical tragedy and Miller's adherence to the literary archetype. Stambusky argues that *All My Sons* falls short of tragedy in plot development, dialogue, and characterization.

Wood, E. R. Introduction to *All My Sons*, by Arthur Miller. London: Heinemann, 1971. Probes the relationship between commerce and war. Explicates the play's dramatic qualities and the three main characters' motivations and actions.

ALL QUIET ON THE WESTERN FRONT

Type of work: Novel
Author: Erich Maria Remarque (Erich Paul Remark, 1898-1970)
Type of plot: Political
Time of plot: World War I
Locale: Western front and Germany
First published: Im Westen nichts Neues: serial, 1928; book, 1929 (English translation, 1929)

> *Principal characters:*
> PAUL BÄUMER, a young german soldier, a private
> KROPP,
> MÜLLER, and
> KEMMERICH, several of his young comrades
> TJADEN,
> HAIE WESTHUS, and
> DETERING, slightly older draftees, also Bäumer's comrades
> STANISLAUS KATCZINSKY (KAT), the group's forty-year-old leader
> CORPORAL HIMMELSTOSS, the recruits' antagonistic training instructor
> KANTOREK, the younger soldiers' former high school teacher

The Story:

Paul Bäumer was a typical German soldier in World War I. He joined up, fought, experienced the horrors and madness of war, saw his comrades killed, and was finally killed himself. He told his own story in vignettes that do not follow chronologically, until finally an outside narrator reported his death on a day when the army report said only, "All quiet on the western front."

Bäumer and his comrades were somewhere behind the lines of the western front late in the war. They had just been relieved from a grueling stint as sappers at the front and were pleased to find that the terrible loss of nearly half their company had the pleasurable consequence of double rations. They ate well, those who were still alive to do so, and later they enjoyed a long game of cards, deploying several portable wooden latrine boxes in a tight circle. Paul spoke often throughout his tale of how soldiering intensified the simple pleasures of eating and defecating. Following this renewing pause, the group of soldiers went to visit their friend Kemmerich, whose leg would have to be amputated because of a battle wound. The friends—Paul Bäumer, Müller, and Kropp—saw that Kemmerich was near death; after leaving him they discussed the matter of his fine boots: Following his death they would be of no use to him, they knew. This was a fact. Kemmerich, also practical, passed his boots on to Müller just before his death. The boots, though good to wear, soon brought death to their wearer, it turned out.

Paul, along with his school chums, had been encouraged to join up by a typically enthusiastic, nationalistic high school teacher named Kantorek. Upon joining the army, Paul was first subjected to the rigors and trials of boot camp at the sadistic hands of Corporal Himmelstoss. His young group of volunteers met new draftees, generally somewhat older North German farmers. Paul's group, back in camp after devastating losses, watched new recruits arriving. Although Paul and his comrades had been soldiers themselves for no more than a few months, they felt like ancient, hardened veterans. Camp and drill life had taught them about the petty and pointless aspects of the army; but at the same time they had learned to fend for themselves, to view the officers and drill sergeants with suspicion, and to let themselves become indifferent to emotions, pain, and exhaustion. Himmelstoss met Paul and his comrades behind the lines in camp. By now they had experienced the horrors of battle and knew a great deal more than their old tyrant. One fine evening, as Himmelstoss returned alone from a bar, they ambushed and beat him. Their revenge for all his spiteful tortures in months past was pure and sweet, and they felt no remorse.

Back at the front, Paul's sapper detail once again experienced the horrors of modern trench warfare: artillery barrages, gas attacks, long hours in damp, dark dugouts, death and loss. The convulsed earth was the only refuge for the soldiers, though the screams of wounded horses pierced even the relative safety of their dugouts and caused the survivors even more pain. During the next respite behind the lines, the soldiers spent time killing their lice, stealing and roasting geese, and plotting another round of revenge against Himmelstoss, who had been assigned to their fighting unit. Some of the older soldiers took special pleasure in insulting Himmelstoss; it got them three days' arrest, which they regarded as a welcome furlough from duty. The next stint at the front, the most gruesome yet, entailed a great deal of hand-to-hand fighting, broken only by artillery barrages and the distractions of corpse-eating rats. New recruits always died at a much faster rate than the veterans like Paul, Kat, and their friends, and the old circle of soldiers saw the folly of sending in barely trained boys. They began to criticize the planners' conduct of the war, which was resulting in a lost generation. Himmelstoss encountered his former trainees again when Paul found him cowering in a dugout at the front. Upon returning to the rear again, Paul's company had only thirty-two men, one-fifth of its original number.

Two important episodes followed this devastating mission, an erotic encounter with local French-speaking women, and Paul's home leave. The meeting with beautiful women only seemed lighthearted, for actually they traded their bodies only because they were nearly starving; a melancholy fog lay over the whole adventure. During Paul's subsequent home leave he discovered the chasm which from then on would separate him from his past. His mother treated him still as a child and could understand nothing of his changed personality. His father thought he was a war hero and forced him to endure the company of the local armchair generals, who were hopelessly out of touch. No one at home could begin to understand Paul's loss and the profundity of his change. The tragic state of Russian prisoners of war whom Paul saw at home impressed him with the hopelessness and tragedy of war and his victimization by it. Things were even more painful back at the front. Paul stabbed a French soldier and remained pinned down by the body overnight in a shell crater. Paul retrieved his victim's wallet and saw his pictures and letters, his life and humanity. Knowing his victim's name, Paul was nearly crushed by his own deed, which had suddenly become personal. The frequency of death increased; Paul's comrades were killed off until only he and his best friend Kat were left. Then Kat was shot, first wounded, then killed while being carried to safety. After more death, loneliness, and hopelessness, Paul, too, was killed, another insignificant soul devoured by the war machine.

Critical Evaluation:

Although it is not the first war novel of the "war novel boom" of the late 1920's and early 1930's, Erich Maria Remarque's book is by far the best known. Within its first year of publication more than one and a half million copies were in print in twelve languages, and about forty million copies were sold in Remarque's lifetime, making it one of the best-selling German books of all time. Despite—or perhaps because of—its unparalleled popularity, *All Quiet on the*

Western Front received relatively little serious critical attention. The work continued to be considered popular literature by most critics, even though Remarque received many literary awards and was nominated for the Nobel Prize in Literature. The novel's popularity is in part due to its omnibus message. Though eventually seen by most as the antiwar book that it is, in the politically and socially chaotic climate of the late Weimar Republic the novel spoke to readers on both the pacifist left and the militarist right. In condemning the war's needless carnage and attributing that to the officers, Remarque served the pacifist agenda; at the same time, however, the book was seen to glorify the simple patriotic soldiering of Paul and his comrades and, in so doing, to confirm the good memories many soldiers had of the war.

Early reviewers debated the book's authenticity, many treating it as a memoir or diary rather than as a fictional creation. Others chose to attack the book for what they perceived as its pacifist, antiauthoritarian message by impugning the author and questioning his personal war record. Remarque did indeed serve on the western front briefly in the summer of 1917; though he was not a decorated officer, he was wounded on the first day of the battle of Flanders. In fact, the source of an iron cross pinned to his uniform in one 1918 photograph is suspect. Remarque's dandified airs—the altered spelling of his name from the original Remark, his high society contacts, and love for auto racing and famous actresses—allowed conservative critics to cast further doubt on the realism of his portrayal of war. It is missing the point, however, to try to tie Remarque's novel directly to actual war experiences. More than anything else, the novel represents the emotional impact of the war on the young generation of recruits who fought it. Gertrude Stein called these men the "lost generation": They could no longer have faith in the elders who had thrown them into the trenches, nor did they have anything meaningful to go home to. This was a generation made lonely by the war; as Paul Bäumer put it, "We will be superfluous even to ourselves."

Copies of *All Quiet on the Western Front* were burned by the Nazis in May, 1933, along with works by Jewish writers, pacifists, socialists, and others they believed were enemies of the state or of the German people. The Nazis burned Remarque's works because of what they called his "literary betrayal of the soldiers in the world war." Remarque emigrated, first to Switzerland, then to the United States, and Nazi Germany revoked his citizenship in 1938. He returned to Switzerland after World War II.

Scholars continue to find the novel interesting because of its immense impact on the popular understanding of World War I. The novel also has much to offer artistically, however. Like many works of the Weimar Republic period (1919-1933), it shows remnants of literary expressionism. Remarque presents a version of the generational conflict, especially between fathers and sons, which had been pointed out so clearly by many of his contemporaries, and there are passages of lyrical organicism, such as those in which Paul seeks safety in the earth or solace in a tree-lined vista, as well as, in certain key passages, an exultant, declarative style. *All Quiet on the Western Front* tells a tragic story of loss and helplessness, yet it also contains important moments of life-affirming energy.

Scott Denham

Bibliography:
Barker, Christine R., and R. W. Last. *Erich Maria Remarque*. New York: Barnes & Noble, 1979. An accessible biography, with a great deal of material that is relevant to *All Quiet on the Western Front*. Good, brief coverage of the novel's popular and scholarly reception. The best place to start further study.

Firda, Richard Arthur. *"All Quiet on the Western Front": Literary Analysis and Cultural Context.* New York: Twayne, 1993. Contains much biographical information, as well as a somewhat pedantic but solid discussion of the novel. Useful annotated bibliography.

Pfeiler, Wilhelm K. *War and the German Mind: The Testimony of Men of Fiction Who Fought at the Front.* New York: Columbia University Press, 1941. An excellent study of German World War I novels. The chapter on *All Quiet on the Western Front* treats the novel in the context of contemporary war novels; especially good on political background and reception.

Taylor, Harley U., Jr. *Erich Maria Remarque: A Literary and Film Biography.* New York: Peter Lang, 1989. Four brief chapters supply a very basic, even journalistic treatment of the novel and the fascinating story of the 1930 American film based on it. Useful chronology.

Wagener, Hans. *Understanding Eric Maria Remarque.* Columbia: University of South Carolina Press, 1991. The best starting point for further general study, a basic text that treats all of Remarque's works. In one long chapter, *All Quiet on the Western Front* receives a thorough analysis. A basic biographically and historically grounded presentation.

ALL THAT FALL

Type of work: Drama
Author: Samuel Beckett (1906-1989)
Type of plot: Absurdist
Time of plot: Twentieth century
Locale: County Dublin, Ireland
First performed: 1957

> *Principal characters:*
> MADDY ROONEY, a woman in her seventies
> DAN ROONEY, Maddy's husband
> MR. BARRELL, a stationmaster
> MISS FLITE, a lady in her thirties

The Story:

It was a fine summer Saturday in Boghill, a community in rural Ireland. In most respects, it was an ordinary day. Trains were expected to run on time. Things had remained unchanged in the enigmatic home of the widow which Maddy Rooney passed on her way to the railroad station to meet her husband Dan, who was returning at midday from work. This was a time when it was customary to work a five-and-a-half-day week. Everything that Maddy had learned about the condition of the spouses and dependents of those she encountered on her walk to the station had remained, painfully, unchanged.

Yet, in other respects, it was by no means an ordinary day. One difference was that a race was to be held locally. Although this event was not greeted with a great deal of exuberance by Mrs. Rooney and the majority of the other characters, including Mr. Slocum, the clerk of the course, it did alleviate the boredom of the station-hand, Tommy. Each of the old, familiar acquaintances whom Mrs. Rooney met in the course of her walk to the station offered to give her a helping hand. Although well meant, these offers varied only in the degree of their preposterousness. Today, as on every other day, it was enough for Mrs. Rooney to try to keep her feet on the ground. Therefore, in response to the offers of assistance, she insisted on her desire to make every effort to maintain her elementary means of locomotion. The offers ranged from a ride on Christy's manure cart to a ride in Mr. Slocum's car. Mrs. Rooney accepted the latter offer, but its results proved as humiliating as if she had taken the former. Her walk to the station, however, was not taken up by questions of transportation alone. On her way, Mrs. Rooney mused in a fashion that was alternately desultory and fretful about various experiences and perceptions. The most prominent of these was the death of her daughter Minnie.

Her journey did not quite end once she arrived at the station. She also needed assistance to climb the stairs to the platform. It was when she asked for help, however, that it turned out not to be readily forthcoming. Eventually, Miss Flite helped her. Although she had suspected while she made her way to the station that something was amiss, it was only when she got there that her suspicions were confirmed. Her husband's train had been delayed. Such a state of affairs was previously unknown. In due course, however, the train arrived, and Dan Rooney alighted accompanied by his guide, Jerry, a necessary presence because of Dan's blindness. The weather changed for the worse as the Rooneys made their way home, and the miserable conditions overshadowed the conversation between husband and wife. Their conversation covered many topics, including Dan's thoughts on his retirement, particularly relevant as his birthday fell on this very day. Their homeward path took them past the church at which they regularly worshiped. Here they noted with uncharacteristic amusement the text for Sunday's sermon: "The Lord upholdeth all that fall and raiseth up all those that be bowed down."

As they walked along, Maddy was also quite interested to discover the cause of the train's delay, but Dan remained rather uncommunicative about that. Oddly, however, just as the stormiest interludes of their conversational exchanges seemed to have passed, they were hailed by Jerry. He had been sent after them by the stationmaster in order to return to Mr. Rooney something he had dropped. It was a child's ball. To satisfy her curiosity about the late arrival of the train, Maddy asked Jerry if he could tell her anything. Jerry replied that the delay was caused by a child falling out of a carriage and under the wheels of the train. Nothing further was said, but the impression irresistibly remained that this accident was Mr. Rooney's doing, and that perhaps there was little difference in either his or his wife's mind that such an act was to be meaningfully differentiated from the early, and presumably unjustifiable, death of their daughter.

Critical Evaluation:

First broadcast by the British Broadcasting Corporation on January 13, 1957, *All That Fall* is Samuel Beckett's first and, arguably, most substantial radio play. Quite apart from the insights it provides into this controversial and significant author's overall output and imaginative vision, the play also represents a comparatively rare conjunction of an avant-garde artist and a mass medium. As such, it represents both a milestone in the history of radio drama—a literary form taken much more seriously in European artistic circles than in American—and in the diversification of Beckett's aesthetic range.

What ultimately gives the play substance is the same distinctive approach that distinguishes all this artist's works: the manner in which it challenges—and even satirizes—the medium through which it is being produced. Yet, on a superficial level, the play seems to be a departure for Beckett. Despite its unprepossessing name, the setting of Boghill bears a recognizable relationship to Foxrock, the community in County Dublin, Ireland, where Beckett grew up. This relationship is to some degree strengthened by the proximity of a racecourse in the play. Foxrock is quite close to the premier racing venue of Leopardstown. Although commentators have strongly discouraged neat and exclusive identifications of Beckett characters with real-life counterparts, Beckett's father did commute to the city by train. Protestantism looms large in a number of the characters' existences, including the Rooneys, and Beckett's background was Protestant.

Another distinctive feature of *All That Fall* is that it is an uncharacteristically populist work for Beckett. While the range of characters is comparatively narrow, it suggests a more common social world and the roles, mannerisms, and equipment used in order to represent oneself within it. These roles—the stationmaster, the clerk of the racecourse, and so on—are clearly identified. Other nominally realistic features of the play include weather, sound effects, a superficially conventional sense of time, and a marked use of colloquial and idiomatic English as it is spoken in Ireland. Like all Beckett plays, *All That Fall* also appears to be structured in terms of the Aristotelian unities of time, place, and action.

At the same time, however, the play subverts these ostensibly reliable, and essentially commonplace, elements. The name of Boghill is an oxymoron. Two types of terrain are contained in it, each of which, in its own distinct and opposite way, makes forward movement difficult. While the name may indeed convey Irish resonances, its evocative relationship to the Rooneys' progress seems more to the imaginative point. This relationship may be further appreciated by considering the familiar Irish name Rooney, with its echoes of "ruin," which is commonly pronounced in Ireland as "rune." The second syllable of the Rooney name acts as a diminutive of those echoes, muffling them and diminishing them lest they provide too facile an interpretative opening. These minor facets of the work both are and are not what they seem. Perhaps the most significant instance of this is the play's Christian dimension. While the Rooneys may attend church, and while Maddy might be subjected to various parodic instances of Good Samaritanism on her way to the station, their acquaintance with the Christian message may be more a matter of habit than of profundity, as their blasphemous laughter at the phrase from the Psalms which gives the play its name suggests.

The play's minor characters act as a chorus which articulates the opposite of the dual perspective embodied by the Rooneys. Unlike the chorus in Greek tragic drama, however, these characters do not act in concert, nor are they intended to function as mediators between action and audience. On the contrary, the state of privileged knowledge that such functioning implies is the very opposite of the quality of consciousness embodied by a Christy or a Mr. Slocum. Each of the minor characters represents a point on a scale of ineffectuality the highest point of which is denoted by Maddy Rooney and Dan. This highest point may also, without contradiction, be termed the lowest point. It is the point of maximum pain, denoted by Maddy in her inability to confine her discourse to mundane pleasantries and connoted by Dan in his blindness. Compared to them, the other characters are nothing if not one-dimensional. While a case may be made for the Aristotelian unities being observed, the fact that the most important action—the death of the child—takes place outside the dramatic framework of the play seriously compromises any such case. It is not clear what kind of action the death is, since Dan's involvement with it is, to say the least, obscure. The time of the accident is not clear. The place of the accident is unfixed in two senses: The train is moving, and the event has to be viewed in the context of that emptiness in which all falls take place.

Rather than develop a plotline in which variously conflicting interests collide and are resolved, the conflict of *All That Fall* exists between the irreconcilable duality of its various elements. The nature of this duality extends to the conditions under which the play is produced, and the work exploits many of the apparent contradictory production values of radio drama. Thus, for example, the play places an emphasis on sensory experience—particularly hearing and seeing—which is unusual for a Beckett drama. Paradoxically, the naturalistic detail of the sensory material evokes for the audience an imaginary landscape. This paradox in turn draws attention to the gap that exists between audience and performance, a gap which is obviously endemic to radio plays. The play's formal and aesthetic reality is based on what transpires in the emptiness between the radio and the listener. The integrity of that emptiness is what the play addresses.

Despite the scrupulous integration of its formal elements, *All That Fall* is far from being a hollow organizational exercise. Like all of Beckett's works, the formal order serves ultimately to crystallize that which cannot be ordered. Dan's mathematical summation of his work and days cannot allay the uncertainty of whether he will be alive when Jerry comes to fetch him for another week's work. Open as Maddy is to her own awareness of the vicissitudes of existence, she cannot hear that the music coming from the widow's house—the "Death and the Maiden" quartet by Franz Schubert—has themes which are unnervingly close to her own home. The discrepant representation of Christian ideas in the play does not reduce the relevance of such motifs as pilgrim and Via Dolorosa. As though to demonstrate that form is finally negated by its own requirements, the two deaths which underlie the play's pedestrian and repetitive action—those of Minnie and of the child—take place outside the course of the day.

George O'Brien

Bibliography:

Alspaugh, David J. "The Symbolic Structure of Samuel Beckett's *All That Fall*." *Modern Drama* 9 (December, 1966): 324-332. An overview of the play's features. Discussion focuses on the work's plot, and on such themes as paternity and Christianity. The idea of movement in the play is also examined.

Fletcher, John, and John Spurling. *Beckett the Playwright*. Rev. ed. New York: Hill and Wang, 1985. A helpful introductory study of all of Beckett's dramatic works, with a chapter on *All That Fall*. Discussion focuses on the work's motifs of love and loss and on the wit of its complicated verbal play.

McWhinnie, Donald. *The Art of Radio*. London: Faber, 1969. The author produced the first broadcast of *All That Fall*. As well as general thoughts about radio as an artistic medium, detailed information regarding the play's production is included. Of particular interest are the insights regarding the challenges of Beckett's script.

Van Laan, Thomas F. "*All That Fall* as 'a Play for Radio.'" *Modern Drama* 28 (March, 1985): 38-47. An analysis of how the play uses radio as an artistic idea. The ways in which language and action in *All That Fall* are significantly reshaped by the medium are discussed. The relationship of the play to the overall preoccupations of Beckett's work is also explored.

Zilliacus, Clas. *Beckett and Broadcasting*. Abo, Finland: Abo Akademi, 1976. The definitive account of Beckett's artistic and professional involvement with radio and television. Beckett's thoughts about the various productions of his broadcast works are included. Detailed accounts of the productions are provided, including some illuminating commentary on the use of sound effects in *All That Fall*.

ALL THE KING'S MEN

Type of work: Novel
Author: Robert Penn Warren (1905-1989)
Type of plot: Social realism
Time of plot: Late 1920's and early 1930's
Locale: Southern United States
First published: 1946

> *Principal characters:*
> JACK BURDEN, a journalist and political lackey
> WILLIE STARK, a political boss
> SADIE BURKE, his mistress
> ANNE STANTON, a social worker
> ADAM STANTON, her brother
> JUDGE IRWIN

The Story:

When Governor Willie Stark tried to intimidate old Judge Irwin of Burden's Landing, the judge stood firm against the demagogue's threats. As a result, Willie ordered Jack Burden to find a scandal in the judge's past that could ruin the elderly man.

Jack had met Willie back in 1922, when Willie, the county treasurer, and Lucy Stark, his schoolteacher wife, were fighting against a corrupt building contractor who was constructing the new schoolhouse. Sent by his newspaper, *The Chronicle*, to investigate, Jack found that both Willie and Lucy had lost their jobs but were still fighting graft. Two years later, when the fire escape of the school collapsed during a fire drill, Willie became a hero.

He thereupon ran for governor in the Democratic primary race, in which there were two factions. Jack covered the campaign. Because it was expected to be a close race, someone from one side, that supporting Harrison, proposed that Willie be used as a dummy candidate to split one group of rural voters who supported MacMurfee. Tiny Duffy and others convinced Willie that he could save the state. By then, Willie had become a lawyer and politically ambitious. Supporting him was Sadie Burke, a clever, energetic woman with political skill. Inadvertently she revealed Harrison's plan to Willie. Crushed at this news, Willie rallied and offered to campaign for MacMurfee, who was elected. Willie practiced law until 1930; he then ran for governor with the assistance of Sadie Burke, who became his mistress, and Tiny Duffy, who was Willie's political jackal.

Meanwhile, Jack had quit his job on *The Chronicle*. Reared by a mother who had remarried after Ellis Burden had deserted her, Jack had become a faithless, homeless cynic who practiced his profession without believing in its higher aims. He had, in his youth, played with Anne and Adam Stanton, the children of the governor. Adam was now a famous surgeon, and Anne, still unmarried, had become a welfare worker. Jack was in love with Anne, but time had placed a barrier between him and the girl with whom he had fallen in love during the summer after he had come home to Burden's Landing from college. He had been twenty-one then, she seventeen. Even then, however, Jack's youthful cynicism had damaged him in Anne's eyes. When Jack went to work for Governor Willie Stark, Jack's mother was deeply pained and Judge Irwin was disgusted, but Jack cared little for their opinions.

By 1933, Willie was on the verge of losing his wife, who could no longer tolerate her husband's political maneuvers and his treatment of their son, Tom. Willie assured Jack that Lucy knew nothing about Sadie Burke. Lucy remained with Willie through his reelection, in 1934, and then retired to her sister's farm. She appeared with Willie in public only for the sake of his reputation.

When Jack began to dig into Judge Irwin's financial transactions during the time when he was attorney general under Governor Stanton, he learned that the government had sued a power company for a large sum. The company had bribed the attorney general by firing one of its men and giving the highly paid job to Irwin. Later, the man who had been fired, Littlepaugh, committed suicide after writing the facts in a letter to his sister. Miss Littlepaugh told Jack the story.

Willie Stark's six-million-dollar hospital project made it necessary to use the scandal Jack had uncovered. Willie told Jack that he wanted Adam Stanton to head the new hospital. It would, Jack knew, be a ridiculous offer to the aloof and unworldly young doctor, but he made an effort to convince Adam to take the post. Adam flatly refused. A few days later, Anne sent for Jack. She, too, wanted Adam to take the position. Jack showed Anne the documents proving that Judge Irwin had accepted a bribe and that Governor Stanton had attempted to cover up for his friend. Knowing that Adam would want to protect his father's good name, Anne showed the evidence to him, after which he agreed to head the hospital.

Later, Jack wondered how Anne had known about the plans for the hospital, because neither he nor Adam had told her. Jack's suspicions were confirmed when Sadie Burke, in a torrent of rage, told him that Willie had been betraying her. Jack knew then that Anne Stanton was the cause. Disillusioned, he packed a suitcase and drove to California. Once he had completed the journey to the West and back, Jack had his torment under control and went back to work for Willie.

One of MacMurfee's men tried to bribe Adam to select a man named Larson as the builder of the medical center. Adam, outraged, decided to resign, whereupon Anne phoned Jack for the first time since he had learned of her affair with Willie. Anne and Jack decided to persuade Adam to sign a warrant against the man who had tried to bribe him. Jack warned Anne, however, that as a witness she would be subject to public scrutiny of her relationship with Willie, but she said she did not care. Jack asked her why she was associating with Willie. She said that after learning about Governor Stanton's dishonesty in the past, she did not care what happened to her. Later, Jack persuaded Adam not to bring suit.

After Willie's political enemy, MacMurfee, tried to blackmail him because of a scandal concerning Tom Stark, Willie ordered Jack to use his knowledge to make Judge Irwin throw his weight against MacMurfee's blackmail attempt. When Jack went to Burden's Landing to confront Judge Irwin with the evidence that he had obtained from Miss Littlepaugh, the old man shot himself. In the excitement following the suicide, Jack's mother told him that he had caused his father's death. Belatedly, Jack discovered the reason for Ellis Burden's desertion. In his will, Judge Irwin left his estate to his son, Jack Burden.

There seemed to be only one way left to handle MacMurfee. Willie decided to give the building contract for the hospital to MacMurfee's man, Larson, who in turn would suppress the scandal about Tom. Duffy made the arrangements. Tom Stark was a football hero. One Saturday during a game, his neck was broken. Adam reported that Tom would remain paralyzed for life. When he heard this, Willie told Duffy that the hospital deal was off. He broke things off with Sadie Burke and Anne Stanton and turned back to Lucy.

Duffy, driven too far by Willie, telephoned Adam and told him that Anne had been responsible for his appointment. Adam had known nothing of his sister's relationship with the governor. He went to her apartment to denounce her. After that, in the hall of the state building, Adam shot Willie and was killed immediately afterward by Willie's bodyguard.

Piece by piece, the tangled mess of Jack's life began to take on new meaning. He separated himself from every particle of his past with the exception of two people: his mother, whose devotion to Judge Irwin over all the years had revealed a new personality to Jack's eyes, and Anne Stanton, whom he married.

Critical Evaluation:

One of the richest and most powerful of twentieth century American novels is Robert Penn Warren's *All the King's Men*. In its pages can be traced a multitude of fascinating subjects ranging from politics to religion, from sociology to philosophy. There is an equally wide scope to the thematic questions posed by the work. The novel's complexities arouse various responses in its readers. Some, for example, praise it as Christian, while others revile it as nihilistic on exactly the same grounds. The book is generally regarded as the masterpiece of a novelist who was also a respected poet, critic, and professor.

Warren, a Kentucky native, had a special affinity for the South, and much of his work suggests the traditions and problems of this region. *All the King's Men*, while exploring issues that are universal as well as regional, has an unmistakable Southern flavor in areas other than mere setting. An immediate query regarding this Pulitzer Prize-winning book usually touches on the relationship of Willie Stark and Huey Long. Governor of Louisiana from 1928 to 1931, Long led a career that parallels what Warren designs for Stark, and Long presented a similarly powerful and paradoxical personality. The product of a poor background, Long became a lawyer at twenty-one after completing the three-year Tulane University course in eight months. Three years later, aggressive and determined, he sought and won the one state office open at his age, a seat on the Railroad Commission. An unorthodox champion of the little man, Long in his 1924 race for governor was unsuccessful when he tried to remain moderate on the Ku Klux Klan issue. His 1928 try for the office was a triumph, however, and at thirty-five, the outspoken country boy was a governor who almost single-handedly ruled the state. Using patronage as his lever, Long talked the legislature into a thirty-million-dollar bond issue to finance farm roads, hospitals, free schoolbooks, and other programs popular with the poor but infuriating to his opponents. Like Stark, Long soon found himself impeached and charged with bribery, plotting the murder of a senator, misusing state funds, and various other crimes, some of which this strange mixture of demagogue and selfless public servant no doubt had committed. Yet his promises and threats kept Long in office after a sufficient number of senators signed a round robin promising not to convict him no matter what the evidence.

Long's career, which included the unprecedented move of becoming a United States senator while still serving as governor, as well as plans to seek the presidency, was halted by assassination. In a 1935 scene almost re-created in *All the King's Men*, a man stepped from behind a pillar at the capitol and shot once. Felled by sixty-one bullets from Long's bodyguards, the assassin, Dr. Carl A. Weiss, died within seconds. Thirty hours later, Long, the "Kingfish," was also dead. Weiss's motivations were never satisfactorily explained, but some claimed that he was angry because Long's maneuvering had cost his father a judgeship.

Despite the overwhelming similarities between Long and Stark, Warren denied having attempted merely to create a fictional counterpart of a political figure. He admitted, however, that the "line of thinking and feeling" in the book did evolve from the atmosphere of Louisiana he encountered while teaching at Louisiana State University, an atmosphere dominated and directed by Long's tenure as governor.

Central to the book is the primary theme of human beings' search for knowledge; all other facets are subordinate to and supportive of this theme. Knowledge includes both objective and subjective comprehensions, with the end goal being self-knowledge. "Life is Motion toward Knowledge," as Warren writes in *All the King's Men*. Elsewhere, the author asserts that the right to knowledge is the human being's "right to exist, to be himself, to be a man." Humans define themselves through knowledge, and the book's pivotal incident demands accumulation of knowledge. Jack, assigned to "dig something up" on the judge, does indeed uncover the judge's dishonor, but the information precipitates a far greater understanding.

For each of the characters, it is a lack of knowledge or an incomplete knowledge that constitutes the chief problem, and those who eventually blunder forward do so only when they see what has previously been hidden from them. The narrator, Jack Burden, is, for example, allegedly telling Willie Stark's story. Yet the reader senses that as he relates the events, Jack is clarifying their meaning mostly for his own benefit. The product of an aristocratic background, Jack in essence eschews knowledge throughout most of the story, for he exists in a vacuum, refusing to be touched or to feel. At moments of crisis, he seeks oblivion in The Great Sleep or by adhering to a belief in The Great Twitch: "Nobody has any responsibility for anything." He is a man of reflection only until those reflections become painful.

Willie seems to be the book's most knowing character. Yet his knowledge is questioned, at first only occasionally, then fully. Unlike Jack, who drops his idealism for inertia, Stark is always a man of action, though that action is sometimes based on only partial knowledge. His innocence, lost by the knowledge that he has been betrayed, is replaced by a willingness to use evil if it is necessary for his purposes. He can justify blackmail or protection of a crook on this basis. For a time, Willie maintains and understands the balance between good and evil, but "obsessed with the evil in human nature and with his power to manipulate it," he is drawn completely onto the side of this dark force.

Jack ignores both ideals and the world; Willie ignores the ideals. The third important character, Adam Stanton, ignores the world. Make good out of evil, says Willie, for the bad is all you have to work with. Horrified by such a philosophy, Adam denies that honor, purity, and justice can commingle with evil. When his preconceptions of the state of the universe prove false, he repudiates not his ideas but the universe. He is the man of idea untainted by fact or action; thus, his knowledge is also faulty and weak, a situation that leads him to tragedy.

Through his investigation of the judge, Jack inadvertently stumbles on the greater truth for himself and for the novel. He discovers his true father, but, even more important, he learns what he is: an imperfect being who must accept imperfection in himself and others and lovingly make what he may out of that state. He learns that human beings cannot be separated from other human beings, that no action or idea exists alone, that past, present, and future are entangled in the web. He realizes what Willie initially knew, then forgot, but reclaimed at the end of the novel. When he tells Jack that all might have been different, Willie implies that his fate might have been different had he remembered that both good and evil exist and influence each other, but that they are not the same.

Closely aligned with the knowledge theme is the Humpty Dumpty motif. The title hints at multiple meanings, for on one level Willie is the king (the boss), and the characters "all the king's men." Yet even greater significance arises when Willie is interpreted as Humpty Dumpty, who falls to his doom and cannot be repaired. In this view, the king is God, and the king's men represent humankind. The fall becomes The Fall because Willie ruins himself by his knowledge of evil unbalanced by a corresponding ability to overcome its effects. Jack too could be interpreted as Humpty, but one whose breakage is not irrevocable because his understanding and knowledge of evil ultimately correspond to an appropriate conception of the nature of good.

"Critical Evaluation" by Judith Bolch

Bibliography:

Bohner, Charles. *Robert Penn Warren.* Rev. ed. Boston: Twayne, 1981. A good general introduction to Warren's writings. Views the novel as the story of Jack Burden's philosophical growth. By examining the past, Jack comes to recognize the paradoxical nature of human isolation and simultaneous kinship through the oppressions of sin that bind all humankind.

Chambers, Robert H., ed. *Twentieth Century Interpretations of "All the King's Men."* Englewood Cliffs, N.J.: Prentice-Hall, 1977. The best collection of criticism on the novel. Discusses such topics as point of view, character studies, significance of the title, the centrality of the Cass Mastern episode, and the search of Jack Burden for a father.

Guttenberg, Barnett. *Web of Being: The Novels of Robert Penn Warren.* Nashville, Tenn.: Vanderbilt University Press, 1975. An existentialist reading of Warren's novels. Asserts that the greatness of *All the King's Men* results from Warren's decision to make Jack Burden the narrator of and a chief participant in Willie Stark's story.

Justus, James H. *The Achievement of Robert Penn Warren.* Baton Rouge: Louisiana State University Press, 1981. Examines the entire body of Warren's work and in that context views *All the King's Men* as both a moral fiction and a political novel.

Watkins, Floyd C., and John T. Hiers, eds. *Robert Penn Warren Talking: Interviews 1950-1978.* New York: Random House, 1980. Contains brief but valuable comments by Warren on the relationship of *All the King's Men* to the dramatic versions, the significance of the epigraph, and various other aspects of the novel.

ALL'S WELL THAT ENDS WELL

Type of work: Drama
Author: William Shakespeare (1564-1616)
Type of plot: Comedy
Time of plot: Sixteenth century
Locale: France and Italy
First performed: c. 1602-1603; first published, 1623

Principal characters:
THE KING OF FRANCE
BERTRAM, the Count of Rousillon
THE COUNTESS OF ROUSILLON, his mother
HELENA, the Countess' ward
PAROLLES, a scoundrel, Bertram's follower
A WIDOW OF FLORENCE
DIANA, her daughter

The Story:

Bertram, the Count of Rousillon, had been called to the court to serve the King of France, who was ill of a disease that all the royal physicians had failed to cure. In the entire country the only doctor who might have cured the king was now dead. On his deathbed he had bequeathed to his daughter Helena his books and papers describing cures for all common and rare diseases, among them the one suffered by the king.

Helena was now the ward of the Countess of Rousillon, who thought of her as a daughter. Helena loved young Count Bertram and wanted him for a husband, not a brother. Bertram considered Helena only slightly above a servant, however, and would not consider her for a wife. Through her knowledge of the king's illness, Helena at last hit upon a plot to gain the spoiled young man for her mate, in such fashion as to leave him no choice in the decision. She journeyed to the court and, offering her life as forfeit if she failed, gained the king's consent to try her father's cure on him. If she won, the young lord of her choice was to be given to her in marriage.

Her sincerity won the king's confidence. She cured him by means of her father's prescription and, as her boon, asked for Bertram for her husband. That young man protested to the king, but the ruler kept his promise, not only because he had given his word but also because Helena had won him over completely.

When the king ordered the marriage to be performed at once, Bertram, although bowing to the king's will, would not have Helena for a wife in any but a legal way. Pleading the excuse of urgent business elsewhere, he deserted her after the ceremony and sent messages to her and to his mother saying he would never belong to a wife forced upon him. He told Helena that she would not really be his wife until she wore on her finger a ring he now wore on his and carried in her body a child that was his. He then stated that these two things would never come to pass, for he would never see Helena again. He was encouraged in his hatred for Helena by his follower, Parolles, a scoundrel and a coward who would as soon betray one person as another. Helena had reproached him for his vulgar ways, and he wanted vengeance on her.

Helena returned to the Countess of Rousillon, as Bertram had commanded. The countess heard of her son's actions with horror, and when she read the letter he had written her, restating his hatred for Helena, she disowned her son, for she loved Helena like her own child. When

Helena learned that Bertram had said he would never return to France until he no longer had a wife there, she sadly decided to leave the home of her benefactress. Loving Bertram, she vowed that she would not keep him from his home.

Disguising herself as a religious pilgrim, Helena followed Bertram to Italy, where he had gone to fight for the Duke of Florence. While lodging with a widow and her daughter, a beautiful young girl named Diana, Helena learned that Bertram had seduced a number of young Florentine girls. Lately he had turned his attention to Diana, but she, a pure and virtuous girl, would not accept his attentions. Then Helena told the widow and Diana that she was Bertram's wife, and by bribery and a show of friendliness she persuaded them to join her in a plot against Bertram. Diana listened again to his vows of love for her and agreed to let him come to her rooms, provided he first gave her a ring from his finger to prove the constancy of his love. Bertram, overcome with passion, gave her the ring, and that night, as he kept the appointment in her room, the girl he thought was Diana slipped a ring on his finger as they lay in bed together.

News came to the countess in France and to Bertram in Italy that Helena had died of grief and love for Bertram. Bertram returned to France to face his mother's and the king's displeasure, but first he discovered that Parolles was the knave everyone else knew him to be. When Bertram held him up to public ridicule, Parolles vowed he would be revenged on his former benefactor.

When the king visited the Countess of Rousillon, she begged him to restore her son to favor. Bertram protested that he really loved Helena, though he had not recognized that love until after he had lost her forever through death. His humility so pleased the king that his confession of love, coupled with his exploits in the Italian wars, won him a royal pardon for his offense against his wife. Then the king, about to betroth him to another wife, the lovely and wealthy daughter of a favorite lord, noticed the ring Bertram was wearing. It was the ring given to him the night he went to Diana's rooms; the king in turn recognized it as a jewel he had given to Helena. Bertram tried to pretend that it had been thrown to him in Florence by a high-born lady who loved him. He said that he had told the lady he was not free to wed, but that she had refused to take back her gift.

At that moment, Diana appeared as a petitioner to the king and demanded that Bertram fulfill his pledge to recognize her as his wife. When Bertram tried to pretend that she was no more than a prostitute he had visited, she produced the ring he had given her. That ring convinced everyone present, especially his mother, that Diana was really Bertram's wife. Parolles added to the evidence against Bertram by testifying that he had heard his former master promise to marry the girl. Bertram persisted in his denials. Diana then asked for the ring she had given to him, the ring which the king thought to be Helena's. The king asked Diana where she had gotten the ring. When she refused to tell on penalty of her life, he ordered her taken to prison. Diana then declared that she would send for her bail. Her bail was Helena, now carrying Bertram's child within her, for it was she, of course, who had received him in Diana's rooms that fateful night. To her Diana gave the ring. The two requirements for becoming his real wife being now fulfilled, Bertram promised to love Helena as a true and faithful husband. Diana received from the king a promise to give her any young man of her choice for her husband, the king to provide the dowry. Thus the bitter events of the past made sweeter the happiness of all.

Critical Evaluation:

All's Well That Ends Well is one of William Shakespeare's plays that defies easy genre classifications and is often grouped under such categories as dark comedy or problem play. Though more comic than tragic, these plays contain troublingly dark aspects or resolutions whose very glibness causes unease. Some of these plays received very little attention until the twentieth century, when the unflagging interest in Shakespeare caused critics to turn to the less familiar works in his canon. The modern interest in these more difficult plays is also quite natural because modern literature often focuses on uncertainty, ambiguity, irony, unstable characters, and mixed moods. Those aspects of Shakespeare's plays which may have puzzled his contemporaries and repelled even his greatest fans invite creative attention from modern readers and audiences.

Among such plays, *All's Well That Ends Well* presents several distinctive problems of interpretation. The history of the critical reception of this play, though covering many other aspects, identifies fairly clearly three key subjects of controversy: the active character of Helena, the suprisingly ungracious character of Bertram, and the bed-trick to which the heroine turns in order to win back her reluctant husband, a trick which raises grave questions about the moral center of the play.

One way that scholars have tried to ease their discomfort about issues in the play is to consider the folk tradition underlying the plot. Several have noted that tales of women who endured much hardship for love and of wives who were sorely tested were extremely popular. Stories about women who manipulated events in order to get what they wanted often presented such women in a favorable light. That Shakespeare might have wanted to preserve this point of view for those in his audience not familiar with the folk tradition seems likely, given his depiction of the older characters in the play. Unlike traditional comedies, where the older people are obstructions to the younger ones, in *All's Well That Ends Well*, Helen has the support of the Countess and of the King. Such support serves two purposes. Within the plot, it allows Helena to concentrate her efforts on winning Bertram, and the approval of the older characters places Helena in a positive light, subtly persuading the audience to accept her desires and actions favorably.

These differences from other comedies give rise to controversies in interpretation. On the one hand, Helena can be seen as the agent of a double healing action in the play. She effects the physical cure by healing the King and then spiritually "cures" Bertram of his immaturity and brings about his acceptance of responsibility as an adult male. This interpretation is not far from the love-conquers-all scenario found in most romantic comedies. It may be considered merely a pleasant change that the woman, rather than the man, is the active pursuer who resorts to doing all that is necessary to achieve her desire. The basic underlying plot of traditional comedy remains intact.

A closer scrutiny of this, however, reveals that the gender change creates a much messier play. Innumerable questions about Helena's motivations and behavior come to mind. In the first act alone, Helena mentions several times, in her soliloquy and in speaking to the Countess, that she is deeply conscious of the class difference between Bertram's position in society and her own. Yet she decides to try to win him anyway. Having used her personal knowledge and skill inherited from her physician father to get Bertram, only to find that he does not want her, she then exacerbates her initial mistake in judgment by continuing to pursue him. She lies to those who care about her, pretending to take a pilgrimage when she is actually on her way to find Bertram in Italy. When she gets there, she is willing to pay to degrade herself to substitute for Diana. Though it is quite conventional for comic characters—and more often, their servants— to resort to all manner of guile and deception to overcome obstacles, it has seemed troubling to some critics over the years that it is a woman who determines the man she wants and then sets out to get him by any means available.

The object of all her travails is another source of unease in the play because Bertram is such an unattractive male character. Granted that his position in the beginning is pitiable, since he is forced by the King into a marriage he does not want, his subsequent actions seem both reprehensible and inconsistent. He behaves in a hateful manner, taunting Helena with two impossible tasks, running away to war, and abandoning his mother, estate, and country to escape his wife. He seduces young women, and then, as in the case of Diana, denies responsibility for his behavior, casting aspersions on their characters. His repentance and newfound love for Helena upon hearing of her death is, at the very least, patently insincere, and, at best, a mysteriously sudden and inconsistent change of heart. This young man, with so few discernible attractive personality traits, seems to have little but noble birth to recommend him. Helena's determination to have him anyway is sometimes interpreted to mean that she is a social climber. This motivation links her to Parolles, one of Shakespeare's great comic creations, morally questionable but theatrically vital to the comic atmosphere of the play. This viewpoint alone makes the play unusual, for though other characters in Shakespeare's plays have attempted to move up in class, Helena is the only one who succeeds, to general approval.

From being a simple comic tale of sturdy and faithful love surviving all obstacles, the meaning of *All's Well That Ends Well* thus begins to shift and waver, starting with the ambivalence of the title. The play can only ironically be said to end well, when the heroine has tricked the hero into staying with her. That the hero cannot distinguish between Diana, the woman he obstensibly desires, and Helen, the wife he has rejected, is unromantic, at the very least. Instead of sounding like a simple exclamation of relief that troubles have been success-fully endured, the title can take on a more morally ambiguous shade: that all—including the means—is justified by the end.

The concept that merit, as in the case of Helena's independent and courageous spirit, counts as much as or more than the inherited position of Bertram seems startlingly modern. That and the combination of comic and puzzling characterizations make *All's Well That Ends Well* one of Shakespeare's more thought-provoking plays.

"Critical Evaluation" by Shakuntala Jayaswal

Bibliography:
Adams, John F. *"All's Well That Ends Well*: The Paradox of Procreation." *Shakespeare Quarterly* 7, no. 3 (Summer, 1961): 261-270. Includes a discussion of the human worth and the nature of honor in the play. Stresses the importance of the bed-trick in understanding the play.

Charlton, H. B. "The Dark Comedies." In *Shakespearian Comedy*. London: Methuen, 1938. Approaches the comedy from the point of view of the older people and their role in the play. Useful for discussions of characters.

Cole, Howard C. *The All's Well Story from Boccaccio to Shakespeare*. Urbana: University of Illinois Press, 1981. A unique source for tracing the different versions of the basic story, starting with Giovanni Boccaccio's *Decameron* (1348-1353). Detailed discussions include a chapter on Shakespeare's handling of the tale.

Lawrence, William Witherle. *"All's Well That Ends Well."* In *Shakespeare's Problem Comedies*. London: Macmillan, 1931. One of the earliest, and most influential, studies to connect the play with the narrative and dramatic traditions preceding it. Explains the basic folktale underlying the plot.

Zitner, Sheldon P. *All's Well That Ends Well*. New York: Harvester Wheatsheaf, 1989. An excellent critical introduction to many aspects of the play. Considers the stage history, critical reception, sources, and the main critical issues of the play. A good starting point for study.

ALMAYER'S FOLLY
A Story of an Eastern River

Type of work: Novel
Author: Joseph Conrad (Jósef Teodor Konrad Nałęcz Korzeniowski, 1857-1924)
Type of plot: Social realism
Time of plot: Late nineteenth century
Locale: Dutch East Indies
First published: 1895

Principal characters:
ALMAYER, an unsuccessful trader of Dutch ancestry
MRS. ALMAYER, his Malay wife
NINA, his half-caste daughter
DAIN MAROOLA, Nina's Malay lover
LAKAMBA, rajah of Sambir and Almayer's enemy

The Story:

By marrying Lingard's adopted Malay daughter, Almayer had inherited that prosperous merchant's business and his plans for amassing a huge fortune in gold from rich mines up the Pantai River. Almayer and his wife had one daughter, Nina, a beautiful girl, who had been sent to Singapore, where for ten years she was educated as a European. She returned home to Sambir unexpectedly at the end of that time, for she could not bear to be treated as a half-caste in a white community. Unsuccessful in business, Almayer nursed dim hopes that he could find a gold mine and, his fortune made, take Nina to Amsterdam to spend his last days in prosperous retirement.

News that the English were to seize control of the Pantai River caused Almayer to begin building a new house in his compound, not far removed from the one in which he was living. He wanted a house fine enough to receive the British. When the project was abandoned and the Dutch were left in nominal power, Almayer stopped work on his new house. A company of Dutch seamen christened the structure "Almayer's Folly."

Lakamba, the native rajah, had a compound across the river from Almayer's home. There he lived with his women, his slaves, and his principal aide, Babalatchi. Lakamba kept close watch on Almayer when he would leave for several days at a time with a few of his men. After a time, Almayer gave up his trips and settled down to empty daydreams on his rotten wharf. His native wife despised him.

Nina's presence in Sambir offered another problem for Almayer, for the young men of the settlement were eyeing her with interest. One day, Dain Maroola, the handsome son of a Malayan rajah, came sailing up the river in a brig to trade with Almayer. After conversations with Lakamba and long conferences with Almayer, Dain got the gunpowder he had been seeking. Meanwhile, he had fallen passionately in love with Nina. One night, she came into the women's room in her father's house and discovered her mother counting out the money Dain had been giving her in payment for Nina. Mrs. Almayer had been arranging meetings between Nina and Dain and giving them warning at the approach of Almayer. Mrs. Almayer wished her daughter to remain native. She had a deep distrust of white men and their ways.

Dain went away, promising that he would return to help Almayer in locating the hidden gold mine. When he did return, he saw Almayer for just a moment and then hurried to see Lakamba. He told the rajah that his brig had fallen into the hands of the Dutch and that he had narrowly escaped with one slave. Most of his men had been killed, and in a day or two, the Dutch would be up the Pantai looking for him.

After this interview, Lakamba told Babalatchi he must poison Almayer before the arrival of the Dutch. Now that Dain knew where the gold treasure was located, Almayer was no longer needed. If allowed to live, he might reveal his secret to the white men.

Next morning, the body of a Malay was found floating in the river. The corpse was beyond recognition, but it wore an anklet and a ring that had belonged to Dain. Almayer was overcome with grief, for Dain was his last hope of finding the gold. The Dutch officers who came looking for Dain told how he had escaped. As the Dutch approached his brig, the gunpowder it carried ignited and blew up the boat, killing two of the Dutch. Almayer promised his visitors that after they had dined he would deliver Dain into their hands.

Meanwhile, Babalatchi was telling Lakamba the true story of Dain. Nina had been waiting for the young Malay on the night of his conference with Lakamba, and she had taken him to a secluded clearing farther up the river. He was now hiding there. The corpse that had floated down the river was that of his slave, who had died when the canoe overturned. Mrs. Almayer had suggested that Dain put his anklet and ring on the body and let it float down the river. Lakamba and Babalatchi planned Dain's escape from his Dutch enemies. Knowing that Dain would not leave without Nina, Babalatchi and Mrs. Almayer plotted to get her away from Almayer, who was drinking with the Dutch. After some persuasion, Almayer did lead his guests to the grave of the man recovered from the river. The Dutch took the anklet and ring as proof that Dain was dead. Then they left for the night.

Nina, willing to go with Dain, felt an urge to see her father once more before she left, but her mother would not let her go into the house where her father lay in a drunken sleep. Nina went to the clearing where Dain was hiding. Soon afterward, a slave girl awakened Almayer and told him of Nina's whereabouts. Almayer was panic-stricken. He traced Nina to Dain's enclosure and begged her to come back to him, but she would not. She did not want to run the risk of insults from white people. With Dain she would be a ranee, and she would be married to a Malay, a brave warrior, not a lying, cowardly white man. Almayer threatened to send his servant to tell the Dutch of Dain's hiding place.

While they argued, Babalatchi approached and cried out that the slave girl had revealed Dain's hiding place to the Dutch, who were now on their way to capture the young Malay. Babalatchi, astounded when Dain announced that he would stay with Nina, left them to their fate. After he had gone, Almayer said he would never forgive Nina, but he offered to take the two to the mouth of the river. In heavy darkness, the fugitive lovers escaped their pursuers.

On an island at the mouth of the river Dain, Nina, and Almayer awaited the canoe that would take the lovers to Lakamba's hidden boat. After the two had gone, Almayer covered up Nina's footprints and returned to his house up the river. His compound was deserted.

Mrs. Almayer and her women had gone to Lakamba for protection, taking Dain's gift of money with her. Almayer found the old rusty key to his unused office. He went inside, broke up the furniture, and piled it in the middle of the room. When he came out, he threw the key into the river and sat on his porch until the flames began to billow from his office. He burned down his old house and lived out the rest of his days in "Almayer's Folly." Eventually, he began the practice of smoking opium in an effort to forget his daughter, Nina. When he died, the opium had given his eyes the look of one who indeed had succeeded in forgetting.

Critical Evaluation:

In *Almayer's Folly*, his first novel, Joseph Conrad blends together several of the characteristic themes that would pervade his later and more powerful works: the conflict between two mutually uncomprehending civilizations, western and eastern; the fearsome and nearly unconquerable power of human sexuality, especially as embodied in the female; and his harsh, dismal belief that all human beings are condemned to live out their lives in isolated worlds of individual illusion. In this early work, Conrad is also exploring and refining his distinctive methods of presenting these themes through setting, characterization, and style. Since *Almayer's Folly* can be seen as a precursor to such later tales as *Heart of Darkness* (1899) and *Lord Jim* (1900), it has the double value of being an important work in itself and the first step in Conrad's development as one of English literature's most powerful writers.

The conflict between European and eastern cultures underlies the novel. Sambir, the setting for the tale, is the prize in an interlocking series of conflicts for power between forces ranging from the imperial to the domestic. Nominal control of Sambir is disputed between the Dutch, who initially claim the territory as part of their possessions, and the British, who as the more dynamic and progressive imperial power seem poised to exert their influence over the deceptively sleepy tropical site. It is in response to what he perceives as an imminent change of rule that Almayer begins construction of the house that, never completed, becomes a "new ruin" and is dubbed "Almayer's Folly." Almayer's house fits the traditional architectural sense of the word "folly," in that it is an expensive but useless building that serves no practical purpose. More significant, however, is Almayer's true folly: that he neglects the true politics of Sambir, which center not on distant empires but on local domestic concerns. The rajah of Sambir, Lakamba, is Almayer's implacable enemy not least because he believes that the European knows of a rich source of gold. Lakamba commands Almayer's native wife to leave him by playing on the disgust she feels at her white husband's sloth and failure. Almayer, convinced of his innate superiority—after all, he is a European—hardly notices, much less combats, his decline. In this sense, he prefigures Kurtz of *Heart of Darkness*, who becomes more savage than the natives among whom he lives.

Almayer is betrayed twice by women close to him. His wife and his half-caste daughter, Nina, both abandon him and reject European ways for the native Malay culture. Through his dense, highly rhetorical prose, Conrad heavily implies that this rejection is more than cultural; it is in large part a condemnation of Almayer's inadequate sexuality, bound by centuries of European repression and therefore incapable of the natural expression found among the Malay people, characters such as Nina's lover, Dain Maroola.

The distinctive trait of all the major figures in *Almayer's Folly* is self-delusion; no one, European or Malay, truly understands his or her situation or character. All of them are to some extent exiles. Lakamba, although he is a powerful figure on the local scene, is only a pawn in the larger game of the great powers. He has been marginalized and made, to a great degree, irrelevant—the politician's final exile.

Almayer is cut off from his European heritage by distance and from his own dreams by his indolence and lack of ability; at the end of the novel, through the destructive powers of opium, he exists only in a dream world, truly isolated. His wife, on the other hand, has been exiled from her native culture through her marriage to Almayer; she can end her isolation only by betraying her husband and fleeing to his archenemy, Lakamba. Nina, Almayer's daughter, is perhaps the most pitiful exile of all. A half-caste, she will never be accepted as European (although she was educated as one in Singapore), yet her return to her Malay roots is accomplished only by renouncing her father and all his dreams and escaping into the jungle with Dain Maroola.

These themes, which occur repeatedly in Conrad's writings, are expressed in an early and sometimes fumbling form of the narrative style that became uniquely his. When the novel opens, the reader is forced to navigate through a series of flashbacks and interior monologues until the outlines of the situation and story begin to resolve themselves. In a sense, this pattern is a structural representation of the moral confusion in which the characters find themselves, but it is also a foreshadowing of Conrad's technique in works such as *Lord Jim*, where the plot progresses in a psychological rather than chronological fashion.

The eastern setting of *Almayer's Folly* becomes—another typical Conrad trait—almost a character itself. The dangerously lush and exotic landscape is more than a backdrop to the actions of the human characters, and the setting becomes partly an expression, partly a cause, of the characters' actions. In such a location, all emotions, especially the more primal ones, are intensified and natural inclinations are emphasized and exaggerated. Sambir is an early version of the nonhuman, even demonic landscape that Conrad creates in *Heart of Darkness*, and the river in *Almayer's Folly*, the Pantai, is an early study of the Congo River that winds through the later story. In Conrad's prose, tropical vegetation comes to represent both the primal force of life and life's inevitable and implacable decay.

Stylistically, the novel is characteristic of Conrad in its heavy reliance on adjectives and a tendency toward rhetorical excess. The descriptions of the Malay landscape and the portraits of the novel's characters are often lengthy and involved, most often with the purpose of establishing a psychological and artistic frame in which the story and its meaning can take shape. At times convoluted in its syntax, the language of *Almayer's Folly*, like its setting, mirrors the complex, complicated, and often self-contradictory nature of its characters and their motivations and actions. It was with this novel that Conrad staked out territory that remained very much his own throughout his works.

"Critical Evaluation" by Michael Witkoski

Bibliography:

Gordon, John D. *Joseph Conrad: The Making of a Novelist*. Cambridge, Mass.: Harvard University Press, 1940. An early but still valuable study of Conrad's artistic development as a novelist. Although the discussion is weighted toward the more well-known books, it sheds informative light on *Almayer's Folly*.

Hampson, R. G. *Joseph Conrad: Betrayal and Identity*. New York: St. Martin's Press, 1992. In the chapter "Two Prototypes of Betrayal: *Almayer's Folly*," the author examines the psychologies of the major characters and the tension created within them by their ideal selves at war with their actual personalities.

Karl, Frederik R. A. *Reader's Guide to Joseph Conrad*. Rev. ed. New York: Farrar, Straus & Giroux, 1969. An introduction that provides a clear review of the essential features of *Almayer's Folly* and its place in the Conrad canon.

Schwarz, Daniel R. *Conrad: "Almayer's Folly" to "Under Western Eyes."* Ithaca, N.Y.: Cornell University Press, 1980. An excellent discussion of Conrad's psychology during the period he conceived and composed the novel. Schwarz also discusses the connections and relationships between *Almayer's Folly* and *An Outcast of the Islands* (1896).

Sherry, Norman. *Conrad's Eastern World*. London: Cambridge University Press, 1966. Places the novel within the context of Conrad's early and continuing interest in settings and plots involving the Far East. Helpful in understanding the nuances of Malayan politics and culture.

ALTON LOCKE
Tailor and Poet

Type of work: Novel
Author: Charles Kingsley (1819-1875)
Type of plot: Social realism
Time of plot: 1840's
Locale: London and Cambridge
First published: 1850

Principal characters:
ALTON LOCKE, a poor tailor, self-taught poet, and political radical
SAUNDERS (SANDY) MACKAYE, a philosopher and bookseller who encourages Locke's writing
JOHN CROSSTHWAITE, a fellow tailor who introduces Locke to working-class radicalism
LORD LYNEDALE, a paternalistic aristocrat seeking to improve the laborers on his estates
ELEANOR STAUNTON, his wife, who believes in reconciliation among the classes
GEORGE LOCKE, Alton's ambitious, conscienceless, middle-class cousin
LILLIAN WINNSTAY, Alton's vain, selfish, beautiful love interest

The Story:
Alton Locke was a poor, Cockney retail tradesman's son. His father had invested all his money in a small shop that failed; by contrast, his uncle had prospered and now owned several grocery stores. Desperately poor, Alton's widowed mother asked the uncle to find Alton a position as a tailor's apprentice. The tailor's establishment was Alton's first experience of the world outside his mother's strict Baptist household. The workroom was close, stinking, and filthy, and most of the other tailors were gross, vulgar, and irreverent. Alton was, however, drawn to a coworker, John Crossthwaite, who was more thoughtful than the others. Locke wanted to improve himself by reading. Having exhausted his mother's few narrow Calvinist theological tomes, he discovered a used-book shop. The shop owner, Sandy Mackaye, befriended him, lent him books, and gave him a place to live after his mother evicted him for reading secular books.

One morning, Alton was summoned to his uncle's office for an interview, during which he met his cousin George, who was about to enter Cambridge University. Together, they visited an art gallery, where Alton saw the beautiful Lillian Winnstay, her father Dean Winnstay, and her friend Eleanor Staunton. Alton instantly fell in love with Lillian, and spent the following year looking for her in London and feeling bitter toward the gentlemen who could visit her because of their rank in society. His frustration found release in poetry. At first, he wrote mannered, Byronic trash until under Sandy Mackaye's guidance he found his poetic voice in poetry that described the lives of the poor workers of London.

Meanwhile, Alton's employer, wanting to increase his profit margin, changed to the "show-trade"—cheap, flashy, ready-to-wear clothing—and ordered his workers to do piecework at home for much lower wages. John Crossthwaite organized a protest, which Locke joined, but they lost their jobs when Jemmy Downes, one of their number, reported them to the employer. Angered at this injustice and under Crossthwaite's influence, Alton joined the Chartist movement, which advocated the vote for workingmen. Sandy Mackaye thought that Alton was too young to become involved in politics; he advised him to visit his cousin George in Cambridge and ask him for help in finding a publisher for his poetry.

Alton's stay at Cambridge was memorable for several reasons: He came to know his cousin better and was at last introduced to the people he had seen at the gallery so long before. George had decided to become an Anglican priest, despite his lack of either preparation or belief, in order to obtain security. Being self-centered, George made little effort to help Alton, but he did introduce him to Lord Lynedale, another Cambridge student. Lynedale proved to respect Alton's abilities, despite their difference in rank, and he was interested in improving the agricultural workers on his family estates and helpful in finding a publisher. He introduced Alton to Dean Winnstay, who arranged for publication of the poetry. The dean, however, asked Alton to omit certain crucial passages that he thought politically subversive. Alton agreed, as it was the only way to see his work in print. Through the dean, Alton met Eleanor Staunton. Eleanor was sympathetic to the plight of the working classes but argued that workers and clergy should be reconciled. The cause of the hostility between the two, she averred, was the workers' lack of self-discipline and self-restraint. Once workers improved their behavior, she said, they would win the clergy's confidence.

Feeling guilty about having betrayed his poetry, Alton returned to London and made his living with hack writing for the popular press, especially for Feargus O'Flynn's Weekly Warwhoop, while waiting for his book of poetry to appear in print. When at last it did, Alton resumed contact with his upper-class acquaintants. He learned that his cousin George was pursuing ordination and planned to marry Lillian and that Eleanor and Lynedale had married, but that the latter had died in an accident. Alton also continued his Chartist activities. Although O'Flynn turned against him, Alton represented the London Chartists at a rally; when the rally turned into a riot, he was arrested and sentenced to three years in jail. He was released just in time to help present the People's Charter (a petition calling for enactment of the Chartist movement's democratic goals) to Parliament on April 10, 1848.

Sandy Mackaye had long warned Alton and Crossthwaite that the Chartist movement was too influenced by rogues and demagogues like Feargus O'Flynn and that the Charter itself was filled with false signatures; with his dying breath, he predicted that the attempt to present it would prove a disaster. Meanwhile, Crossthwaite and Alton dreamt of revolution and prepared for streetfighting. When April 10 arrived, Mackaye was proven correct. The Chartist leaders, fearing arrest, fled the rally, the London workers ignored the presentation, and the meeting broke up in disarray. As Alton, despairing, walked the streets, he met the betrayer Jemmy Downes, now living in poverty. Jemmy's wife and children, dead of fever and starvation, lay covered by the coats they had been sewing. Alton called for help, but it came too late to prevent Jemmy from committing suicide.

Alton's despair deepened into illness and delirium. Nursed back to health by Eleanor and Crossthwaite, Alton became convinced that the Bible was the true Charter, that workers should earn their rights by reforming their characters, and that class cooperation rather than class conflict was the prerequisite for bringing God's kingdom to pass. Alton also learned that the coats that had shrouded Jemmy's family had infected George and Lillian, killing the former and destroying the latter's beauty. As he came to learn of Eleanor's charitable activities among the London poor, Alton realized that he had loved the wrong woman, but he found the opportunity for redemption. Sandy Mackaye had bequeathed him money on condition that he and Crossthwaite emigrate. Eleanor could not go with them, for her health was declining, so Alton and the Crossthwaite family set sail for Texas. The night their ship arrived on the American shore, Alton died. His last written words were a poem, calling for a day of hope between workers and gentlemen.

Critical Evaluation:

Charles Kingsley's *Alton Locke* is solidly rooted in the events of the 1840's. In 1848, Kingsley had made a tour of Jacobs Island in Bermondsey, one of the worst of London's slums, and had made it the basis of both *Yeast* (1848), his first novel of social criticism, and *Alton Locke*. Kingsley also drew on his social observation for his description of working conditions among the London tailors. Before writing *Alton Locke*, he published an inflammatory and powerful pamphlet, *Cheap Clothes and Nasty* (1850), that described the sweated tailors' trade.

The Chartist movement of the 1840's also provides background for the novel. Chartism took its name from the People's Charter, a petition to Parliament that called for universal suffrage for men, the secret ballot, and other political reforms that would have turned Britain into a democracy with working-class participation in government. The Chartist movement ended in a somewhat anticlimactic attempt to deliver the People's Charter to Parliament on April 10, 1848. Kingsley used real-life characters for *Alton Locke*. Feargus O'Flynn and the *Weekly Warwhoop* represent the Chartist leader Feargus O'Connor and his *Northern Star*. Alton Locke himself is based on two Chartist tailors: Thomas Cooper, who was likewise a poet, and Walter Cooper, who converted to Anglicanism.

Although Kingsley was sympathetic to the economic plight of British workers during the 1840's, he clearly did not approve of the main strand of Chartism, which called for political rights for the working classes. Rather, Kingsley believed in what was called "moral force" Chartism—the belief that the ruling classes would give the workers their rights once the latter had shown by self-education that they were worthy of those rights.

Kingsley's main ideological influence came from the Scottish essayist Thomas Carlyle (1795-1881). Sandy Mackaye is a Carlyle-like figure, and Eleanor Staunton is explicitly described as being a vehicle for Carlyle's ideas. Carlyle believed that a strong, heroic leader was the main cause of social progress. Hence he thought that only such heroes as Oliver Cromwell or Frederick the Great could solve the problem of mass poverty that existed alongside increasing middle-class wealth. In response to the Chartist movement, Carlyle rejected electoral reform and a democratic political system. Kingsley shared these views and gave expression to them in the novel.

Two other nineteenth century themes appear in this novel. The love interest between Alton and Lillian was doomed to tragedy because the two were of different social classes. The theme of love across class lines appears frequently in Victorian literature, although authors more commonly wrote of working-class women loving upper-class men. Kingsley resolved the novel's conflict by sending the protagonists abroad, a method of resolving conflict also frequently seen in Victorian literature.

Alton Locke shows more of the strengths than of the weaknesses that characterized Kingsley's later works. The novel has many vivid, descriptive passages, among which those depicting Alton's tailor's workshop, the London slums, and Jemmy Downes's dead family are especially noteworthy. Kingsley wrote an unusual dream sequence to describe Alton's delirium, a hallucination in which Alton imagines himself evolving from a sea creature to a Stone Age tribesman. Kingsley's most serious failing as a novelist—his habit of interrupting the narrative with long, didactic lectures—is not as noticeable in *Alton Locke* as in some of his later novels (especially *Hypatia*, 1851). *Alton Locke* is Kingsley's most readable novel. It is the one novel that he took pains over in both writing and revising. Moreover, it is important as a social document of working-class life in mid-Victorian Britain.

D. G. Paz

Bibliography:
Chitty, Susan. *The Beast and the Monk: A Life of Charles Kingsley*. London: Hodder and Stoughton, 1974. This innovative biography, which draws on unpublished documents, illuminates the place of physical love in Kingsley's thinking and private life. The chapter on *Alton Locke* discusses the London scenes that inspired Kingsley to write the novel.
Horsman, Ernest Alan. *The Victorian Novel*. Vol. 13 in *The Oxford History of English Literature*, edited by John Buxton and Norman Davis. New York: Oxford University Press, 1990. This authoritative survey discusses minor as well as major novelists, and includes a good bibliography of secondary works for further reading. Horsman compares Kingsley's *Alton Locke* with the works of Elizabeth Gaskell.
Martin, Robert Bernard. *The Dust of Combat: A Life of Charles Kingsley*. New York: W. W. Norton, 1960. This standard biography of Kingsley focuses more on his public life than on his private thoughts. Includes an extensive analysis of the background of social observation that led to the novel.
Uffelman, Larry K. *Charles Kingsley*. Boston: Twayne, 1979. A brief, clear overview of Kingsley's works. In the chapter devoted to the three novels of social criticism, Uffelman relates the characters in *Alton Locke* to figures in British life during the 1840's.
Williams, Raymond. *Culture and Society, 1780-1950*. London: Chatto & Windus, 1960. This is a classic analysis of modern British culture from a Marxist perspective. The chapter on *Alton Locke* focuses on the conflict among different conceptions of Chartism.

AMADÍS OF GAUL

Type of work: Novel
Author: Attributed to Vasco de Lobeira (c. 1360-c. 1403)
Type of plot: Romance
Time of plot: First century
Locale: France, England, and the rest of Europe
First published: Amadís de Gaula, 1508 (English translation, 1619)

> *Principal characters:*
> AMADÍS OF GAUL
> KING PERIÓN, his father
> PRINCESS ELISENA, his mother
> GALAOR, another son of King Perión
> LISUARTE, king of Great Britain
> BRISENA, his queen
> ORIANA, their daughter
> URGANDA, an enchantress
> ARCALAUS, a magician

The Story:

Not many years after the passion of Christ, there lived in Lesser Britain a Christian king named Garinter. His older daughter was married to the king of Scotland. The younger daughter, Elisena, found none of her suitors attractive until the day her father brought home King Perión of Gaul, whom Garinter had watched defeat two powerful knights and kill a lion. The scheming of Elisena's attendant, Darioleta, allowed the young people to meet secretly in the royal garden. King Perión departed ten days later without knowing the results of their nights of love.

When Elisena's son was born, Darioleta concealed her mistress' indiscretion by putting him into an ark, along with his father's sword and ring, and a parchment declaring the boy to be "the timeless Amadís, son of a king." She set the ark afloat in the river beside the palace; it drifted out to sea, where it was found by a knight, Gandales, who was on a voyage to Scotland. Gandales, who reared the foundling with his son Gandalin, called the boy "Child of the Sea."

Gandales, riding through the woods when the boy was three years old, rescued Urganda, an enchantress who was being pursued by a knight. The grateful witch, after prophesying that the adopted boy would become the flower of knighthood, the most honorable warrior in the world, promised to aid him should he ever need her help.

When the boy was seven years old, King Languines of Scotland and his queen saw him and offered to bring him up at court. Five years later, King Lisuarte and Queen Brisena paused in Scotland on their way to claim the throne of England. Until all was safe, they asked permission to leave behind their daughter Oriana. King Languines appointed the "Child of the Sea" to be her squire.

The two children fell so deeply in love with each other that never again did they fall out of love, but they dared not let others know of their feelings. To be worthy of Oriana, Amadís determined to be knighted, and when King Perión visited Scotland to seek help against his enemy, King Abies of Ireland, Oriana asked her father's old friend to knight Amadís. The young knight then rode away in search of fame through adventures.

Urganda met him in the forest and gave him a lance with which he rescued King Perión from Irish knights. Although neither was aware of the blood relationship between them, Amadís swore always to aid King Perión in time of danger. Then followed a series of fantastic and extraordinary adventures, among them the encounter with haughty Galpano, whose custom was to stop and rob all who passed through his realm. Amadís defeated the bully and his two brothers, although he was so severely wounded in the battles that he had to be nursed back to health by a friendly noble.

Meanwhile, King Perión had married Elisena. Although they lamented their lost son, they took pleasure in a second son, Galaor. When King Abies sent an expedition against Gaul, Amadís overcame the Irish champion. In the celebration festivities at King Perión's court, the identity of Amadís was discovered through the ring he wore, and King Perión proudly acknowledged his long-lost son.

Amadís remained melancholy, thinking himself unworthy to aspire to wed the daughter of the king of England. He did briefly visit her at Vindilisora (Windsor), only to be called away to rescue his brother Galaor. That summons was a trick of the enchanter Arcalaus, who cast a spell over the knight and disarmed him. When the villain appeared in the armor of Amadís and riding his horse, Oriana almost died. Only the timely news of further feats of arms by Amadís told her that he was still alive, and so she was restored to health.

Tireless in his villainy, Arcalaus caused King Lisuarte to disappear and abducted Oriana. Amadís and his brother, knighted by Amadís, rescued the princess, but in the absence of the king, the traitor Barsinan tried to seize Brisena and usurp the throne. Dressed in rusty armor, Amadís defeated the rebel, and when Oriana's father reappeared, twelve days of feasting followed. Amadís, however, was no nearer to winning the hand of his beloved despite his great service to the king.

Continuing to seek knightly fame, Amadís and his friends sailed for Firm Island, settled by Apolidon, son of the king of Greece, who had taken refuge there after eloping with the daughter of Emperor Siudan of Rome. In Firm Island was an enchanted arch through which only faithful lovers could pass. Beyond it was a marriage chamber guarded by invisible knights. After his arrival in that land, Amadís received a note from Oriana, who had believed the lying charges of unfaithfulness made against him by a malignant dwarf. She had signed herself as a damsel pierced through the heart by the sword of Amadís.

His ecstasy of grief upon reading the note and his withdrawal, under the name of Beltenebros (The Fair Forlorn One) to the hermitage at the Poor Rock, convinced Oriana that she had wronged him. There was nothing she could do, however, to right matters, for King Lisuarte had given her in marriage to the emperor of Rome.

When a fleet from Rome took her away, Amadís, calling himself the Greek Knight, defeated it and returned Oriana to her father, asking only that she be protected against further misalliances. King Lisuarte decided to punish such effrontery by an attack on Firm Island, a decision that ranged the knights of the world on two sides. King Lisuarte enlisted the help of the emperor of Rome. Amadís visited the emperor of Constantinople and sent a messenger to the king of Bohemia. Arcalaus hated both Amadís and King Lisuarte and encouraged King Aravigo to march with his army and prey on both sides.

When the hosts assembled for the battle, King Gasquilan of Sweden sent a personal challenge to Amadís to meet him in single combat between the lines. The king's overthrow was the signal for a general onslaught that lasted for two days, until at last the death of the emperor of Rome disheartened and routed his army.

Out of affection for Oriana, Amadís did not pursue the defeated host, but King Aravigo took this opportunity to plunder the followers of King Lisuarte. A hermit, who had been trying to bring about peace among the combatants, sent the youthful Esplandian to take the news of King

Lisuarte's distress to Amadís. The hero marched at once to the rescue of King Lisuarte, a kindness that wiped out the enmity between them. The marriage of Oriana and Amadís was solemnized on Firm Island. Afterward, the couple passed under the Arch of True Love into the magic bridal chamber.

Critical Evaluation:

If one can speak of there being a single original at all to this text, such an original has been lost. What most modern English readers have is an abridged 1803 translation by the poet Robert Southey of a Spanish work published in Saragossa in 1508 by Garcia Rodríguez de Montalvo. Southey's work superseded an earlier English translation by Anthony Munday, dating from the Elizabethan era, while Montalvo claimed to have derived his version from a work by the Portuguese writer Vasco de Lobeira. This attribution is dubious because Vasco de Lobeira was active in the latter part of the fourteenth century and the earliest references to the text date from the first half of that century.

If the work did originate in Portugal a more probable author might be Juan Lobeira, who was active in the latter part of the thirteenth century and who is credited elsewhere with the composition of a song whose Spanish translation can be found in the Montalvo version, but Vasco de Lobeira might conceivably have done a later version of it. There is no way of knowing for sure where the original version of the story was written down, by whom, or when. Montalvo does tell his readers, however, that in translating Lobeira's work he has considerably modified its supposedly outmoded style, and modern commentators believe that the fourth volume of his version consists of material added by him.

In its form and content *Amadís of Gaul* is an imitation of the tradition of French chivalric romances concerning the exploits of Charlemagne and his knights, which had expanded to take in such figures as Alexander the Great and the English King Arthur and such motifs as the quest for the Holy Grail. Like many such romances *Amadís* begins in "Lesser Britain" (Brittany), at the interface of Anglo-Norman and Gallic culture. Amadís, the son of Perión of Gaul, is brought up on the barbarous fringe of the Norman sphere of influence but must eventually seek his fortune on a hypothetical island which has been settled by a prince of Greece and the daughter of the emperor of Rome. In this manner the plot bridges the whole spectrum of imagined European traditions and values (tacitly extended to include the eastern domains of Constantinople and Bohemia). The central figure, Amadís, symbolizes, among other things, the union of all Christendom. His natural nobility must perforce be hidden under various guises—most notably that of the Green Knight—but it nevertheless causes him to remain absolutely faithful to his ideal, Oriana. Oriana is primarily a romantic ideal, but she is also a political and spiritual ideal.

Montalvo's version of the story is important in several ways. As a robust product of a vernacular language it embodied something of the spirit of the Renaissance. It was enormously popular not only as an adventure story but also as a guide to morals and manners, and it made a substantial contribution to the sense of cultural rebirth which boosted progressive ideas and ideals. It also wrought a subtle but vital revision of the Medieval mythology of courtly love, in which the women idealized by knights had traditionally been the wives of their liege-lords, and thus permanently unattainable. The substitution of a marriageable heroine changed the story's ideal ending, and hence its whole direction. The most perfect knights of traditional romance had been those who remained utterly chaste; the ultimate prize of beholding the holy grail was withheld from any who had ever harbored a lustful thought. Montalvo refuses to indulge such fervent asceticism; the symbolic Arch of True Love which grants Amadís and the conveniently eligible Oriana passage into their bridal chamber grants a significant license to physical passion. This conclusion probably did not exist in the accounts of Amadís' adventures which circulated before Montalvo's, and may mark the story as it exists currently as a true product of the early sixteenth century.

Although the supernatural plays a muted role in Montalvo's story—at least by comparison with later tales of adventure penned by his many imitators—the mode of its operation contrasts with the pious supernaturalism of the grail romances, more closely resembling the fanciful supernaturalism of the French romances featuring the conveniently pre-Christian Alexander. *Amadís of Gaul* cannot be regarded as a wholeheartedly secular work but much of Amadís' knight errantry is conducted in a forthright spirit of adventure that finds a Christian conscience relatively unburdensome. This aspect of the work is probably not original to Montalvo, but is nevertheless significant of an important shift in values.

The genre for which *Amadís of Gaul* served as an archetype flourished during the sixteenth century. The genre was one of the most popular forms of literature ever. Its ruthless satirization in Miguel de Cervantes' *Don Quixote de la Mancha* (1605) signified that it had become ridiculous. Although the genre of chivalric romance faded away throughout Europe in the seventeenth century, certain key elements of it retained their potency and continued their evolution. *Amadís of Gaul* provided a vital stepping-stone in the evolution of the modern mythology of romantic love, and modern "romantic fiction" still retains within its formula that final passage through the arch of true love to the bridal chamber. Even more spectacularly, the revived genre of "heroic fantasy" brought back into favor exactly the kind of plot that *Amadís of Gaul* lays out, with an astonishing abundance of misplaced heroes embarking upon lengthy quests, beset by all manner of magical and monstrous perils before they finally achieve their proper station in a confused world. The strong similarities between these modern genres and a work which few modern writers can possibly have read are testimony to the sturdiness of the literary traditions. The survival of such forms of literature is tribute to the extent to which modern culture is rooted in the intellectual achievements of the Renaissance.

"Critical Evaluation" by Brian Stableford

Bibliography:

Green, Otis H. *Spain and the Western Tradition.* 4 vols. Madison: University of Wisconsin Press, 1963. A discussion of *Amadís of Gaul* in the context of the mythology of courtly love appears in volume 1 on pages 104-111.

Moorcock, Michael. *Wizardry and Wild Romance: A Study of Epic Fantasy.* London: Victor Gollancz, 1987. Chapter 1 discusses *Amadís of Gaul* as the primary ancestor of the modern genre of fantasy.

Northup, George Tyler. *An Introduction to Spanish Literature.* 3d ed., revised by Nicholson B. Adams. Chicago: University of Chicago Press, 1960. Describes the origins of chivalric romance, discussing the authorship and influence of *Amadís of Gaul.*

Place, Edwin B., and Herber C. Behm. *Amadís of Gaul: A Romance of Chivalry of the Fourteenth Century Presumably First Written in Spanish.* 2 vols. Lexington: University Press of Kentucky, 1974. A full English translation of the work from the earliest available source; the introduction offers a brief history of the text.

Williams, Grace S. "The *Amadís* Question." *Revue Hispanique* 21 (1909): 1-167. A comprehensive discussion of the origins of the story and its various versions.

THE AMBASSADORS

Type of work: Novel
Author: Henry James (1843-1916)
Type of plot: Psychological realism
Time of plot: c. 1900
Locale: Paris, France
First published: 1903

>   *Principal characters:*
>   MRS. NEWSOME, a wealthy American widow
>   CHADWICK "CHAD" NEWSOME, her son and an American expatriate
>   LAMBERT STRETHER, his friend
>   MARIA GOSTREY, an acquaintance of Strether
>   COMTESSE DE VIONNET, a woman in love with Chadwick Newsome
>   MRS. POCOCK, Chadwick's married sister
>   MAMIE POCOCK, Mrs. Pocock's husband's sister

The Story:

Lambert Strether was engaged to marry Mrs. Newsome, a widow. Mrs. Newsome had a son, Chadwick, whom she wanted to return home from Paris and take over the family business in Woollett, Massachusetts. She was especially concerned for his future after she had heard that he was seriously involved with a Frenchwoman. In her anxiety, she asked Strether to go to Paris and persuade her son to return to the respectable life she had planned for him. Strether did not look forward to his task, for Chadwick had ignored all of his mother's written requests to return home. Strether also did not know what hold Chadwick's mistress might have over him or what sort of woman she might be. He strongly suspected that she was a young girl of unsavory reputation. Strether realized, however, that his hopes of marrying Mrs. Newsome depended upon his success in bringing Chad back to America, where his mother could see him married to Mamie Pocock.

Leaving his ship at Liverpool, Strether journeyed across England to London. On the way he met Miss Gostrey, a young woman who was acquainted with some of Strether's American friends, and she promised to aid Strether in getting acquainted with Europe before he left for home again. Strether met another old friend, Mr. Waymarsh, an American lawyer living in England, whom he asked to go with him to Paris. A few days after arriving in Paris, Strether went to Chad's house. The young man was not in Paris, and he had temporarily given the house over to a friend, Mr. Bilham. Through Bilham, Strether got in touch with Chad at Cannes. Strether was surprised to learn of his whereabouts, for he knew that Chad would not have dared to take an ordinary mistress to such a fashionable resort.

About a week later, Strether, Miss Gostrey, and Waymarsh went to the theater. Between the acts of the play, the door of their box was opened and Chad entered. He was much changed from the adolescent college boy Strether remembered. He was slightly gray, although only twenty-eight years old. Strether and Chad Newsome were pleased to see each other. Over coffee after the theater, the older man told Chad why he had come to Europe. Chad answered that all he asked was an opportunity to be convinced that he should return. A few days later, Chad took Strether and his friends to a tea where they met Mme and Mlle de Vionnet. The former, who had married a French count, turned out to be an old school friend of Miss Gostrey. Strether was at a loss to understand whether Chad was in love with the comtesse or with her daughter Jeanne.

Since the older woman was only a few years the senior of the young man and as beautiful as her daughter, either was possibly the object of his affections. As the days slipped by, it became apparent to Strether that he himself wanted to stay in Paris. The French city and its life were much calmer and more beautiful than the provincial existence he had known in Woollett, and he began to understand why Chad was unwilling to go back to his mother and the Newsome mills.

Strether learned that Chad was in love with Mme de Vionnet, rather than with her daughter. The comtesse had been separated from her husband for many years, but their position and religion made divorce impossible. Strether, who was often in the company of the Frenchwoman, soon fell under her charm. Miss Gostrey, who had known Mme de Vionnet for many years, had only praise for her and questioned Strether as to the advisability of removing Chad from the woman's continued influence. One morning Chad announced to Strether that he was ready to return immediately to America. The young man was puzzled when Strether replied that he was not sure it was wise for either of them to return and that it would be wiser for them both to reconsider whether they would not be better off in Paris than in New England.

When Mrs. Newsome, back in America, received word of that decision on the part of her ambassador, she immediately sent the Pococks, her daughter and son-in-law, to Paris along with Mamie Pocock, the girl she hoped her son would marry. They were to bring back both Strether and her son. Mrs. Newsome's daughter and her relatives did not come to Paris with an obvious ill will. Their attitude seemed to be that Chad and Strether had somehow drifted astray, and it was their duty to set them right. At least that was the attitude of Mrs. Pocock. Her husband, however, was not at all interested in having Chad return, for in the young man's absence, Mr. Pocock controlled the Newsome mills. Mr. Pocock further saw that his visit was probably the last opportunity he would have for a spirited time in the European city, and so he was quite willing to spend his holiday going to theaters and cafés. His younger sister, Mamie, seemed to take little interest in the recall of her supposed fiancé, for she had become interested in Chad's friend, Mr. Bilham.

The more Strether saw of Mme de Vionnet after the arrival of the Pococks, the more he was convinced that the Frenchwoman was both noble and sincere in her attempts to make friends with her lover's family. Mrs. Pocock found it difficult to reconcile Mme de Vionnet's aristocratic background with the fact that she was Chad's mistress. After several weeks of hints and genteel pleading, the Pococks and Mamie went to Switzerland, leaving Chad to make a decision whether to return to America. As for Mr. Strether, Mrs. Newsome had advised that he be left alone to make his own decision, for the widow wanted to avoid the appearance of having lost her dignity or her sense of propriety.

While the Pococks were gone, Strether and Chad discussed the course they should follow. Chad was uncertain of his attitude toward Mamie Pocock. Strether assured him that the girl was already happy with her new love, Mr. Bilham, who had told Strether that he intended to marry the American girl. His advice, contrary to what he had thought when he had sailed from America, was that Chadwick Newsome should remain in France with the comtesse, despite the fact that the young man could not marry her and would, by remaining in Europe, lose the opportunity to make himself an extremely rich man. Chad decided to take his older friend's counsel.

Waymarsh, who had promised his help in persuading Chad to return to America, was outraged at Strether's changed attitude. Miss Gostrey, however, remained loyal, for she had fallen deeply in love with Strether during their time together in Paris. Strether, however, realizing her feelings, told her that he had to go back to America alone. His object in Europe had been to return Chad Newsome to his mother. Because he had failed in that mission and would never marry Mrs. Newsome, he could not justify to himself marrying another woman whom he had met on a journey financed by the woman he had at one time intended to marry. Only Mme de Vionnet, he believed, could truly appreciate the irony of his position.

Critical Evaluation:

In Henry James's *The Ambassadors*, plot is minimal; the story line consists simply in Mrs. Newsome's sending Lambert Strether to Europe to bring home her son, Chad. The important action is psychological rather than physical; the crucial activities are thought and conversation. The pace of the novel is slow. Events unfold as they do in life: in their own good time. Because of these qualities, James's work demands certain responses from the reader, who must not expect boisterous action, shocking or violent occurrences, sensational coincidences, quickly mounting suspense, or breathtaking climaxes: These devices have no place in a Henry James novel. Rather, the reader must bring to the work a sensitivity to problems of conscience, an appreciation of the meaning beneath manners, and an awareness of the intricacies of human relationships. Finally, and of the utmost importance, the reader must be patient; the power of a novel like *The Ambassadors* is only revealed quietly and without haste. This is why, perhaps more than any other modern author, James requires rereading—not merely because of the complexity of his style, but also because the richly layered texture of his prose contains a multiplicity of meanings, a wealth of subtle shadings.

In *The Ambassadors*, which James considered his masterpiece, this subtlety and complexity is partially the result of his perfection of the technique for handling point of view. Departing from traditional use of the omniscient narrator, James experimented extensively with the limited point of view, exploring the device to discover what advantages it might have. He found that what was lost in panoramic scope and comprehensiveness, the limited viewpoint more than compensated for in focus, concentration, and intensity. It was the technique perfectly suited to an author whose primary concern was with presenting the thoughts, emotions, and motivations of an intelligent character, and with understanding the psychological makeup of a sensitive mind and charting its growth.

The sensitive and intelligent character through whose mind all events in the novel are filtered is Lambert Strether. The reader sees and hears only what Strether sees and hears; all experiences, perceptions, and judgments are his. Strictly adhered to, this device proved too restrictive for James's purpose; therefore, he utilized other characters—called confidants—who enabled him to expand the scope of his narrative without sacrificing advantages inherent in the limited point of view. The basic function of these "listening characters" is to expand and enrich Strether's experience. Miss Gostrey, Little Bilham, Waymarsh, and Miss Barrace—all share with him attitudes and insights arising from their widely diverse backgrounds; they provide him with a wider range of knowledge than he could ever gain from firsthand experience. Maria Gostrey, Strether's primary confidante, illustrates the fact that James's listening characters are deep and memorable personalities in their own right. Miss Gostrey not only listens to Strether but also becomes an important figure in the plot, and as she gradually falls in love with Strether, she engages the reader's sympathy as well.

Lambert Strether interacts with and learns from the environment of Paris as well as from the people he meets there; thus, the setting is far more than a mere backdrop against which events in the plot occur. To understand the significance of Paris as the setting, the reader must appreciate the meaning that the author, throughout his fiction, attached to certain places. James was fascinated by what he saw as the underlying differences in the cultures of America and

Europe and, in particular, in the opposing values of a booming American factory town such as Woollett and an ancient European capital such as Paris. In these two places, very different qualities are held in esteem. In Woollett, Mrs. Newsome admires practicality, individuality, and enterprise, while in Paris, her son appreciates good food and expensive wine, conversation with a close circle of friends, and leisure time quietly spent. Woollett pursues commercialism, higher social status, and rigid moral codes with untiring vigor; Paris values the beauty of nature, the pleasure of companionship, and an appreciation of the arts with studied simplicity. Thus, the implications of a native of Woollett, such as Lambert Strether, going to Paris at the end of his life are manifold; it is through his journey that the theme of the novel is played out.

The theme consists of a question of conscience: Should Strether, in his capacity as Mrs. Newsome's ambassador, be faithful to his mission of bringing Chad home once he no longer believes in that mission? That he ceases to believe is the result of his conversion during his stay in Paris. He is exposed to a side of life that he had not known previously; furthermore, he finds it to be good. As a man of noble nature and sensitive conscience, he cannot ignore or deny, as Sarah Newsome later does, that life in Paris has vastly improved Chad. Ultimately, therefore, he must oppose rather than promote the young man's return. The honesty of this action not only destroys his chance for financial security in marriage to Chad's mother but also prevents him from returning the love of Maria Gostrey. Although Strether's discovery of a different set of values comes too late in life for his own benefit, he at least can save Chad. The lesson he learns is the one he passionately seeks to impart to Little Bilham: "Live all you can; it's a mistake not to. It doesn't so much matter what you do in particular, so long as you have your life. . . . Don't, at any rate, miss things out of stupidity. . . . Live!"

If, in reading *The Ambassadors*, readers' expectations are for keenness of observation, insight into motivations, comprehension of mental processes, and powerful characterizations, they will not be disappointed. If Henry James demands the effort, concentration, and commitment of his readers, he also—with his depth and breadth of vision and the sheer beauty of his craftsmanship—repays them a hundredfold.

"Critical Evaluation" by Nancy G. Ballard

Bibliography:

Bell, Millicent. *Meaning in Henry James*. Cambridge, Mass.: Harvard University Press, 1991. Examines James's novels in reference to narrative theory. Analysis of *The Ambassadors* focuses on narrative techniques and shows the relationship between narrative and meaning.

Edel, Leon. *Henry James: A Life*. Rev. ed. New York: Harper & Row, 1985. A classic biography. Places *The Ambassadors* in the context of James's biography, showing its place in James's life and in his stylistic development. Good for those interested in biographical criticism.

Fussel, Edwin Sill. *The French Side of Henry James*. New York: Columbia University Press, 1990. A good analysis of James's novels set wholly or partly in France. Discussion of *The Ambassadors* shows the importance of place to the theme in James's work. Explains specific French concepts and images in the novel.

Grover, Philip. *Henry James and the French Novel*. New York: Barnes & Noble Books, 1973. Introduces the French portion of the James canon. Traces the influence of French Impressionism and other French elements on *The Ambassadors*.

Wagenknecht, Edward. *The Novels of Henry James*. New York: Frederick Ungar, 1983. Excellent basic study of James's novels. The chapter on *The Ambassadors* presents an enlightening reading of the novel and places it at the highest point of James's achievement.

AMELIA

Type of work: Novel
Author: Henry Fielding (1707-1754)
Type of plot: Domestic realism
Time of plot: 1740's
Locale: England
First published: 1751

> Principal characters:
> CAPTAIN BOOTH, a soldier
> AMELIA, his wife
> ELIZABETH HARRIS, her sister
> SERGEANT ATKINSON, her foster brother
> DR. HARRISON, Booth's benefactor
> MISS MATTHEWS, a woman of the town
> COLONEL JAMES, Booth's former officer

The Story:

One night, the watchmen of Westminster arrested Captain William Booth, seizing him as he was attempting to rescue a stranger being attacked by two ruffians. The footpads secured their own liberty by bribing the constables, but Booth was brought before an unjust magistrate. His story was a straightforward one, but because he was penniless and shabbily dressed, the judge dismissed his tale and sentenced him to prison. Booth was desperate; there was no one he knew in London to whom he could turn for aid. His plight was made worse by his reception at the prison. His fellow prisoners stripped him of his coat, and a pickpocket stole his snuffbox.

He was still smarting from these indignities when he saw a fashionably dressed young woman being escorted through the gates. Flourishing a bag of gold in the face of her keepers, she demanded a private room in the prison. Her appearance and manner reminded Booth of Miss Matthews, an old friend of questionable background whom he had not seen for several years; but when the woman passed him without a sign of recognition, he believed himself mistaken.

Shortly afterward, a guard brought him a guinea in a small parcel, and with the money, Booth was able to redeem his coat and snuffbox, but he lost the rest of the money in a card game. Booth was once again penniless when a keeper came to lead him to Miss Matthews, for it was indeed she. Seeing his wretched condition as he stood by the prison gate, she had sent him the guinea. Reunited under these distressing circumstances, they proceeded to relate the stories of their experiences. Miss Matthews told how she had been committed to await sentence for a penknife attack on a soldier who had seduced her under false promises of marriage.

Booth, in turn, told this story. He had met Miss Amelia Harris, a beautiful girl whose mother at first opposed her daughter's marriage to a penniless soldier. The young couple eloped but were later reconciled with Amelia's mother through the efforts of Dr. Harrison, a wise and kindly curate. Shortly before a child was to be born to Amelia, Booth's regiment was ordered to Gibraltar. Reluctantly he left Amelia in the care of her mother and her older sister, Elizabeth. At Gibraltar, Booth earned the good opinion of his officers by his bravery. Wounded in one of the battles of the campaign, he became very ill. Amelia, learning of his condition, left her child with her mother and sister and went to Gibraltar to nurse her sick husband. Then Amelia, in her turn, fell sick. Wishing to take her to a milder climate, Booth wrote to Mrs. Harris for money, but in reply he received only a rude note from Elizabeth. He hoped to get the money from his army friend, Major James, but that gentleman was away at the time. Finally, he borrowed the money from Sergeant Atkinson, his friend and Amelia's foster brother, and went with his wife to Montpelier. There the couple made friends with an amusing English officer named Colonel Bath and his sister.

Joy at the birth of a second child, a girl, was dampened by a letter from Dr. Harrison, who wrote to tell them that old Mrs. Harris was dead and that she had left her property to Amelia's sister. The Booths returned home, to be greeted so rudely by Elizabeth that they withdrew from the house. Without the help of Dr. Harrison, they would have been destitute. Harrison set Booth up as a gentleman farmer and tried to help him make the best of his half-pay from the army. Booth, however, made enemies among the surrounding farmers because of several small mistakes. Dr. Harrison was traveling on the Continent at the time, and in his absence, Booth was reduced almost to bankruptcy. He came to London to try his fortunes anew. He preceded Amelia, found modest lodgings, and wrote her of his location. At this point, the latest misfortune had landed him in prison. At the end of Booth's story, Miss Matthews sympathized with his unfortunate situation, congratulated him on his wife and children, and paid the jailer to let Booth spend the next few nights with her in her cell.

Booth and Miss Matthews were shortly released from prison. The soldier wounded by Miss Matthews had completely recovered and dropped his charges against her. Miss Matthews also secured Booth's release, and the two were preparing to leave prison when Amelia arrived. She had come up from the country to save him, and his release was a welcome surprise. The Booths established themselves in London. Shortly afterward, Booth met his former officer, now Colonel James, who had in the meantime married Miss Bath and grown quickly tired of her. Mrs. James and Amelia resumed their old friendship. Booth, afraid that Miss Matthews would inform Amelia of their affair in prison, told Colonel James of his difficulties and fears. The colonel gave him a loan and told him not to worry. Colonel James was also interested in Miss Matthews, but he was unable to help Booth by his intercession. Miss Matthews continued to send Booth reproachful, revealing letters, which might at any time have been intercepted by Amelia.

While walking in the park one day, the Booths met Sergeant Atkinson. He joined their household to help care for the children, and soon he started a mild flirtation with Mrs. Ellison, Booth's landlady. Mrs. Ellison proved useful to the Booths; a lord who also came to visit her advanced money to pay some of Booth's debts. Meanwhile, Miss Matthews had spitefully turned Colonel James against Booth. Colonel Bath, hearing his brother-in-law's poor opinion of Booth, decided that Booth was neither an officer nor a gentleman and challenged him to a duel. Colonel Bath strongly believed in a code of honor, however, and when Booth had vanquished him in the duel without serious injury, the colonel was so impressed by Booth's gallantry that he forgave him and brought about a reconciliation between James and Booth.

During this time, Mrs. Ellison had been trying to arrange an assignation between Amelia and the nobleman who had given Booth money to pay his gambling debts. Amelia was innocently misled by her false friends. The nobleman's plan to meet Amelia secretly at a masquerade, however, was thwarted by another neighbor, Mrs. Bennet. This woman, who had been a boarder in Mrs. Ellison's house, had also met the noble lord, encountered him at a masquerade, and drunk the drugged wine he provided. To prevent Amelia's ruin in the same manner, Mrs. Bennet came to warn her friend. Then she informed Amelia that she had recently married Sergeant

Atkinson, whom Amelia had thought in love with Mrs. Ellison. Amelia's joy at learning of the plot, which she now planned to escape, and of the marriage, was marred by the news that Booth was again in prison for debt, this time on a warrant of their old friend Dr. Harrison.

Amelia soon discovered that Dr. Harrison had been misled by false rumors of Booth's extravagance and had had him jailed to stop his rash spending of money. Learning the truth, Dr. Harrison allowed Booth to be released from prison.

On the night of the masquerade, Amelia remained at home but sent Mrs. Atkinson dressed in her costume. At the dance, Mrs. Atkinson was able to fool not only the lord but also Colonel James. There were many complications of the affair, and almost every relationship was misunderstood. Booth fell in with an old friend and lost a large sum of money to him. Again, he became worried about being put in jail. Then he became involved in a duel with Colonel James over Miss Matthews, whom Booth had visited only at her insistence. Before the duel could take place, Booth was again imprisoned for debt, and Dr. Harrison was forced to clear his name with Colonel James. Finally James forgave Booth, and Miss Matthews promised never to bother him again.

Called by chance into a strange house to hear the deathbed confession of a man named Robinson, Dr. Harrison learned that Robinson had at one time been a clerk to a lawyer named Murphy who had made Mrs. Harris' will. He learned also that the will, which had left Amelia penniless, was a false one prepared by Elizabeth and Murphy. Dr. Harrison had Robinson write a confession so that Amelia could get the money that was rightfully hers. Murphy was quickly brought to trial and convicted of forgery.

Booth's troubles were now almost over. He and Amelia returned home with Dr. Harrison to confront Elizabeth with their knowledge of her scheme. Elizabeth fled to France, where Amelia, relenting, sent her an annual allowance. Booth's adventures had finally taught him not to gamble, and he settled down with his faithful Amelia to a quiet and prosperous life blessed with many children and the invaluable friendship of Dr. Harrison and the Atkinsons.

Critical Evaluation:

As Henry Fielding stated in his introduction to *Amelia*, he satirized nobody in the novel. Amelia, the long-suffering wife of every generation, is charming and attractive; the foibles of her husband still ring true; and Dr. Harrison is a man any reader would like to know. Some of the interest of the novel lies in Fielding's accurate presentation of prison life and the courts. Having been a magistrate for many years, he was able to present these scenes in a most realistic way, for aside from presenting the virtuous character of Amelia, Fielding wanted to awaken his readers' interest in prison and legal reform. The novel lacks the extravagant humor of his earlier novels, but the plot presents many amusing characters and complex situations.

Amelia was intended to appeal to a psychological and social awareness rather than to an intellectual consciousness. Between the publication of *The History of Tom Jones, a Foundling* (1749) and *Amelia*, the nature of Fielding's moral feelings deepened and with it the means and techniques by which he expressed his ethical purposes. Impressed by the social problems he encountered daily in the world around him, he felt the need to promote virtue and to expose the evils that infected England. He abandoned his satirical comic mode and such traits as impartiality, restraint, mockery, irony, and aesthetic distance. Instead, he adopted a serious, sentimental, and almost consciously middle-class tone.

The characters in *Amelia* give strong indications of Fielding's intensified moral purposes. They are more fiery and vehement, and clearly intended to embody his beliefs more so than was the case in his earlier works. Abandoning the aesthetic distance between himself and his characters, he seems, in *Amelia*, to live and act directly in them. This results in a new kind of immediacy and closeness between the novel's characters and the writer's psychological concerns. The cost of this immediacy is the rejection of almost all formal conventions of characterization. The description of the heroine is typical of this. On a number of occasions, she is described by the emotions that are reflected in her face or by her physical reactions to situations that bring pain or joy; but in contrast to Fielding's elaborate descriptions of the beauty of the heroines of his earlier works, Amelia's beauty is never delineated. Rather, her beauty is embodied in the qualities she represents. The same might be said for the other characters in the novel. Fielding is more concerned with the moral makeup of each one than in their physical appearance. In *Amelia*, the author does not segregate the reader and the characters, who reveal themselves to the reader through their own words and deeds. The characters thereby appear as individuals rather than types.

The central theme of Fielding's portrait of a marriage concerns not so much the issue of adultery as it does the tragic irony of marital distrust that accompanies it. Although Booth's infidelity with Miss Matthews strains the marriage and seems disgusting when contrasted with Amelia's steadfast loyalty, what almost destroys the marriage is that Booth, throughout most of the novel, cannot bring himself to confess his adultery out of fear and pride. He does not trust in his wife's understanding and love for him. Amelia, who is beset almost from the beginning of her marriage by amorous advances, fails to confide to her husband the real motive behind James's pretense of friendship because she fears Booth will lose his temper and attack James. Husband and wife, therefore, work unconsciously to the detriment of their marriage because they will not trust in each other.

In *Amelia*, the reader cares more about the heroine, but the action turns on Booth. It is on the adequacy or inadequacy of Booth that the novel succeeds or fails for the reader. Amelia is the stable character. Booth constantly poses the problems of marriage, while she endures and solves them. Booth's ordeal reflects Fielding's own increasing despair with social conditions. The grim social picture of this novel is Fielding's solemn warning that society may destroy itself on the larger plane, as it very nearly destroys the Booths on the smaller plane. The placement of a woman of Amelia's moral character within a society that preys on her effectively points up the evils of that society in relation to the constant moral Christianity of the heroine. It is Fielding's most emphatic statement of Christian morality through the treatment of the subject within marriage. The loss of faith in individual morality, as portrayed in this novel through the assaults on Amelia's virtue and the setbacks suffered by Booth, is easily transferred from the plane of individuals to reflect criticism of society as a whole.

Amelia was published to much rancor and ridicule on the part of the majority of critics. The characters were reviled as being low and the situations as too sordid. Enemies gleefully pounced on Fielding's oversight in failing to mend his heroine's broken nose. Earlier victims of Fielding's satire, notably Samuel Richardson, author of *Pamela* (1740-1741), were gleeful over the adverse reception of this novel and joined in denouncing it. The novel's later success was based on the gradual recognition of the work as a serious denunciation of, as Fielding himself said, "glaring evils of the age."

"Critical Evaluation" by Patricia Ann King

Bibliography:
Dircks, Richard J. *Henry Fielding*. Boston: Twayne, 1983. An introduction to Fielding, with an emphasis on the major novels, including *Amelia*. Includes brief but useful biographical

information, a chronology, and an annotated bibliography. With few notes and references, and a clear, accessible style, this is a good tool for students.

Fraser, Donald. "Lying and Concealment in *Amelia*." In *Henry Fielding: Justice Observed*, edited by K. G. Simpson. Totowa, N.J.: Barnes & Noble Books, 1985. Shows how Fielding uses lying, deception, and concealment as a theme and as a device to force the reader to pay close attention to details and explanations within the story.

Johnson, Maurice O. *Fielding's Art of Fiction: Eleven Essays on "Shamela," "Joseph Andrews," "Tom Jones," and "Amelia."* Philadelphia: University of Pennsylvania Press, 1961. Three of the essays in this study deal directly with *Amelia*, which Johnson sees as a moral work exalting the "good life." Little biography or historical context, but excellent explications of specific passages and structural effects.

Smallwood, Angela J. *Fielding and the Woman Question: The Novels of Henry Fielding and Feminist Debate, 1700-1750.* New York: St. Martin's Press, 1989. Argues that Fielding's novels, including *Amelia*, actively engage in the eighteenth century debate about gender roles. As important as his concern with national politics is Fielding's concern with sexual politics.

Wright, Andrew. *Henry Fielding: Mask and Feast.* Berkeley: University of California Press, 1965. Explores the relationships in Fielding's work between art and life, with a strong focus on the influence of comic theater. Wright looks at three Fielding novels and considers *Amelia* as a domestic epic.

THE AMERICAN

Type of work: Novel
Author: Henry James (1843-1916)
Type of plot: Psychological realism
Time of plot: Mid-nineteenth century
Locale: Paris
First published: 1877

    Principal characters:
        CHRISTOPHER NEWMAN, an American
        MR. TRISTRAM, a friend
        MRS. TRISTRAM, his wife
        M. NIOCHE, a shopkeeper
        MLLE NIOCHE, his daughter
        MADAME DE BELLEGARDE, a French aristocrat
        CLAIRE DE CINTRE, her daughter
        MARQUIS DE BELLEGARDE, her older son
        VALENTIN DE BELLEGARDE, her younger son
        MRS. BREAD, her servant

The Story:

In 1868, Christopher Newman, a young American millionaire, withdrew from business and sailed for Paris. He wanted to loaf, to develop his aesthetic sense, and to find a wife. One day, as he wandered in the Louvre, he made the acquaintance of Mlle Nioche, a young copyist. She introduced him to her father, an unsuccessful shopkeeper. Newman bought a picture from Mlle Nioche and contracted to take French lessons from her father.

Later, through the French wife of an American friend named Tristram, he met Claire de Cintre, a young widow, daughter of an English mother and a French father. As a young girl, Claire had been married to Monsieur de Cintre, an evil old man. He had soon died, leaving Claire with a distaste for marriage. In spite of her attitude, Newman saw in her the woman he wished for his wife. An American businessman, however, was not the person to associate with French aristocracy. On his first call, Newman was kept from entering Claire's house by her elder brother, the Marquis de Bellegarde.

True to his promise, M. Nioche appeared one morning to give Newman his first lesson in French. Newman enjoyed talking to the old man. He learned that Mlle Nioche dominated her father, who lived in fear that she would leave him and become the mistress of some rich man. M. Nioche told Newman that he would shoot his daughter if she did. Newman took pity on the old man and promised him enough money for Mlle Nioche's dowry if she would paint more copies for him.

Newman left Paris and traveled through Europe during the summer. When he returned to Paris in autumn, he learned that the Tristrams had been helpful; the Bellegardes were willing to receive him. One evening, Claire's younger brother, Valentin, called on Newman and the two men found their opposite points of view a basis for friendship. Valentin envied Newman's liberty to do as he pleased; Newman wished himself acceptable to the society in which the Bellegardes moved. After the two men had become good friends, Newman told Valentin that he wished to marry his sister and asked Valentin to plead his cause. Warning Newman that his social position was against him, Valentin promised to help the American as much as he could.

Newman confessed his wish to Claire and asked Madame de Bellegarde, Claire's mother, and the Marquis for permission to be her suitor. The permission was given, grudgingly. The Bellegardes needed money in the family. Newman went to the Louvre to see how Mlle Nioche was progressing with her copying. There he met Valentin and introduced him to the young lady. Mrs. Bread, an old English servant of the Bellegardes, assured Newman that he was making progress with his suit. He asked Claire to marry him, and she accepted. Meanwhile, Valentin had challenged another man to a duel in a quarrel over Mlle Nioche. Valentin left for Switzerland with his seconds. The next morning, Newman went to see Claire. Mrs. Bread met him at the door and said that Claire was leaving town. Newman demanded an explanation. He was told that the Bellegardes could not allow a commercial person in the family. When he arrived home, he found a telegram from Valentin stating that he had been badly wounded and asking Newman to come at once to Switzerland.

With this double burden of sorrow, Newman arrived in Switzerland and found Valentin near death. Valentin guessed what his family had done and told Newman that Mrs. Bread knew a family secret. If he could get the secret from her, he could make them return Claire to him. Valentin died the next morning. Newman attended the funeral. Three days later, he again called on Claire, who told him that she intended to enter a convent. Newman begged her not to take this step. Desperate, he called on the Bellegardes again and told them that he would uncover their secret. Newman arranged to see Mrs. Bread that night. She told him that Madame de Bellegarde had killed her invalid husband because he had opposed Claire's marriage to M. de Cintre. The death had been judged natural, but Mrs. Bread had in her possession a document proving that Madame de Bellegarde had murdered her husband. She gave this paper to Newman.

Mrs. Bread left the employ of the Bellegardes and came to keep house for Newman. She told him that Claire had gone to the convent and refused to see anyone, even her own family. The next Sunday, Newman went to mass at the convent. After the service, he met the Bellegardes walking in the park and showed them a copy of the paper Mrs. Bread had given him.

The next day, the Marquis called on Newman and offered to pay for the document. Newman refused to sell. He offered, however, to accept Claire in exchange for it. The Marquis refused. Newman found he could not bring himself to reveal the Bellegardes' secret. On the advice of the Tristrams, he traveled through the English countryside and, in a melancholy mood, went to some of the places he had planned to visit on his honeymoon. Then he went to America. Restless, he returned to Paris and learned from Mrs. Tristram that Claire had become a nun.

The next time he went to see Mrs. Tristram, he dropped the secret document on the glowing logs in her fireplace and told her that to expose the Bellegardes now seemed a useless and empty gesture. He intended to leave Paris forever. Mrs. Tristram told him that he probably had not frightened the Bellegardes with his threat, because they knew that they could count on his good nature never to reveal their secret. Newman instinctively looked toward the fireplace. The paper had burned to ashes.

Critical Evaluation:

One of Henry James's achievements is that he developed the international novel. *The American*, his first major book, portrays a typical post-Civil War American and delineates his differences from Europeans. Although ultimately a tragic story, *The American* uses irony and humor in its depiction of some of the incongruities between the two cultures.

The hero's name strongly hints at James's purpose. Christopher Newman, we are told, was named after the explorer Christopher Columbus. Thus, as he returns to Europe for the culture and civilization that he has not had time previously to pursue in his moneymaking career, this new man becomes a discoverer in reverse. Whereas Columbus brought the Old World to the New, Newman is a representative of the New World who seeks to discover the Old.

Besides visiting museums, Newman seeks a wife who embodies culture. In his pursuit, he strikes against rigid European traditions. The new man is confronted with the old ways. Those old ways include the exercise of unearned privilege. Newman underestimates the power and prejudice of his French adversaries. In his New World innocence, he does not anticipate their sinister machinations. He achieves some small victories and attracts the approbation of the finest Europeans—Mrs. Bread, Valentin de Bellegarde, and the incomparable Claire de Cintre—but ultimately Newman discovers something that he had not experienced in America. He is denied an opportunity to reap the rewards of his own endeavors. Through no fault of his own, but rather through the injustice of others, he loses the prize for which he has longed.

Part of the frustration that the American experiences is that, with his native capaciousness, he believes that he can incorporate into his own character the best of other cultures, and so improve himself. Indeed, Valentin and Claire, brother and sister of the old Bellegarde family, are willing to join Newman's wide embrace. Their good natures are stronger than their aristocratic prejudices. James, however, does not allow the best members of the Bellegarde family to prevail. He ends the novel unhappily. In answer to the objections of his editor, William Dean Howells, James explained that a happy ending would have been unrealistic and would have been pandering to his readership. Claire and Christopher would have been, in James's words, "an impossible couple."

In exploring the contrasting outlooks of the democratic Americans and the aristocratic Europeans, James utilizes humor. This novel is sometimes reminiscent of Mark Twain's *The Innocents Abroad* (1869), a hilarious account of Americans in Europe and the Middle East. James's boorish Mr. Tristram, for example, wonders whether the pictures hanging in the Louvre are for sale. Subtler irony lies in Newman's failure to realize that his having manufactured washtubs jeopardizes his efforts to win the approbation of the French aristocracy. Like Twain, James was keenly aware of differing cultural values and their humorous potential.

James's biographer suggests that the portrait of Newman as a national type is filled with ambiguity. Newman could not have met with James's total admiration. He is too obtuse and self-satisfied with his material success, and he has the audacity to believe that he can buy culture, including a cultured wife. The new man has fine qualities and deplorable ones. He does not deserve the wrong he receives, but then again, does he really deserve to gain the hand of Claire de Cintre?

Some romantic elements in the novel were deplored by critics and by James himself later in his career. The mystery of Monsieur Bellegarde's death, the implications of foul play lying behind the medieval walls of the Bellegarde's home, and the horrible prospect of Claire de Cintre's impending "burial" in a convent are all melodramatic. James became, in spite of this beginning, one of the major figures of the realistic movement. His attention was on verisimilitude, as his choice of a common man for a protagonist and his interest in the pragmatic philosophy of the protagonist attest. Usually regarded as inferior to masterpieces such as *The Ambassadors* (1903) and *The Portrait of a Lady* (1880-1881), *The American* nevertheless exhibits many of the qualities that made James one of the major novelists of his time.

"Critical Evaluation" by William L. Howard

Bibliography:

Cargill, Oscar. *The Novels of Henry James.* New York: Hafner Press, 1971. An analysis of the sources of the novel, including Ivan Turgenev, French theater, and James's own inspiration. Defines the international novel in which a character possessing one set of cultural values is confronted with a different set of values.

James, Henry. *The American.* Edited by Gerald Willen. New York: Thomas Y. Crowell, 1972. Includes the text of the later, revised version of the novel, a preface by James, the ending from the original version of the novel, a letter from James to his editor William Dean Howells, and ten interpretative essays by different critics on subjects as diverse as the revision, point of view, romantic elements, and the American self-image.

Lee, Brian. *The Novels of Henry James: A Study of Culture and Consciousness.* New York: St. Martin's Press, 1978. Argues that James was interested in the concept of consciousness and its response to culture. Thematically, *The American,* with its confrontation between an innocent American and sophisticated Europeans, opposes moral consciousness and social consciousness. Lee notes James's own later assessment of the novel: that it violated the reader's sense of how things really happen.

Long, Robert Emmet. *Henry James: The Early Novels.* Boston: Twayne, 1983. Places *The American* in the context of James's early career. Provides basic information about the novel's magazine serialization, James's subsequent revision, and the novel's influences. The roles of romance, melodrama, and realism are discussed.

Powers, Lyall H. *Henry James: An Introduction and Interpretation.* New York: Holt, Rinehart and Winston, 1970. Discusses the theme, nomenclature, humor, gothic elements, and characterization regarding Christopher Newman.

THE AMERICAN COMMONWEALTH

Type of work: Social criticism
Author: James Viscount Bryce (1838-1922)
First published: 1888; final revised edition, 1922-1923

James Bryce served in several capacities that qualified and trained him to write on American political and social institutions. A professor of history at Oxford and a member of Parliament, he also served in numerous political posts and was ambassador to the United States from 1907 to 1913. His monumental work The American Commonwealth grew out of five visits to the United States and extensive reading about the country.

The book is a shrewd analytical study of the American scene designed for a European audience and obviously written by a man who was prejudiced in favor of America. In Bryce's opinion, regardless of the many flaws and weaknesses (especially on the local and state levels) in the American political system and institutions, the sum total of American hopes and aspirations had created a system of rule that was the best to date, one that offered hope to the world.

The American Commonwealth is divided into six parts. The first concerns the national government, the Constitution, the presidency, the two houses of Congress, the federal courts, the federal system of government, and the relations of the federal government with the state governments. Bryce emphasizes the organic growth of the American political system. He believes that the happy combination of events and thinking that resulted in the system, and especially in the Constitution, stemmed from the fact that the predominant race in America in the eighteenth century was Anglo-American. This race was directly responsible for the Constitution, which, though by no means a perfect instrument, merits the veneration that Americans generally bestow on it. Bryce believed that the greatness of the Constitution derives from the fact that there is nothing new about it, that like all good political documents and all things that deserve to win and hold the obedience and respect of citizens, it has its roots deeply planted in the past and grew slowly through changing periods of history. The men who drew up the Constitution were practical politicians who wanted to walk the paths trodden by former successful governments. The path was made easy and its progress assured by the fact that in America during those days there were no reactionary conspirators threatening the nation. The most remarkable feature of the American governmental system, Bryce believes, is the preeminence of the Constitution and the fact that the Constitution can be altered only by the people.

The creation of a president to head the American government was fortuitous. In outlining his role and power, the framers of the Constitution, fearing the monarchical system and a strong centralized government, nevertheless modified existing offices of leaders; that is, they created the office as one that enlarged the role of the state governor, whose office resembled that of the British king but on a smaller and improved scale. There are many disadvantages to this office and the method of electing its holder, but in practice the responsibility of the position and the realization that the president represents the nation as a whole sobered and controlled the holders of the office. With a few exceptions, the presidency has not been filled by men of brilliance, but the office does not demand intellectual brilliance but rather common sense and honesty.

In fact, political offices in America are not filled by outstanding citizens, few of whom take up a career in politics. Even the Senate and the House of Representatives are not constituted of the nation's best minds, although the Senate draws to itself the best talent in politics and has established its authority in the American political system by its dignity and six-year tenure in office. It faithfully fulfills the intentions of the founders of the nation in resisting change and yielding to it only gradually.

In comparison to the Senate, the House of Representatives is chaotic and lacks the dignity and the power of the upper chamber. It also lacks the men of ability claimed by the other chamber, but what it lacks in these aspects it makes up for in the worthiness of its purpose and its real accomplishments.

Those who drafted and signed the American Constitution were especially wise in establishing such complex legal institutions. Bryce believed that few American institutions deserved closer study than the intricate system of the judiciary, which deserves great admiration because it operates smoothly and contributed to the peace and prosperity of America. The weaknesses in the American legal system, in fact, flow not from their makeup but from human frailties.

The second part of *The American Commonwealth* discusses state and local governments. The state constitutions in general grew out of the royal charters, but in being changed and rewritten they cast out the worst aspects of their models. A state constitution is a law passed directly by the people at the polls and is an example of popular sovereignty directly exercised. As such, it has few parallels in modern Europe. State governments are more subject to local pressures than is the federal government, and they are more widely influenced by political parties. Some of the weaknesses of the state governments are exaggerated in lower local groupings, especially in city governments. Universal suffrage has many serious weaknesses, and all become evident and important in a city, where foreign immigrants swell the population. Though there are obviously serious problems in the American city, probably no other system of government could have been devised that would have worked as well, and American cities have made progress in solving their problems.

Part 3 concerns itself with "Political Methods and Physical Influences." It is a detailed study of the American political machinery, nominating conventions, and public opinion and its power. Bryce considers that of all American experiments in politics the most worthy of serious study is this governing by public opinion, which towers above all other aspects of American political life as a source of power. Yet it is a power used well: Individuals are reckless, but the mass of people are restrained. As a result, public opinion becomes gradually more temperate, mellow, and tolerant.

The very size, strength, and potential of the United States give Bryce great pause for contemplation. Can a nation so immense in size, so varied in population, and with such immense wealth remain one nation and control itself? Given his own tentative and conservative disposition, Bryce hesitates to answer his own question, but his conclusions almost assert themselves. His prophecies are in fact somewhat optimistic. Never before, he claims, has a nation had such golden opportunities for defensive strength and material prosperity. He concludes that the nation will probably remain unified in government and in speech, character, ideas, and action.

In all aspects *The American Commonwealth* is exhaustive. One of its great strengths derives from the background of its author. Deeply read in European and other governments, Bryce gives his study of the American government an unusual breadth and depth, which inform the reader profoundly. His book becomes essentially a study in comparative governments and therefore remains as informative today as at the time of its composition. Only in the study of some of the detailed aspects of American government—in cases where the institutions he describes or aspects of those institutions have been changed by custom, act of legislature, or amendment—is the work dated. In general, Bryce's comments on the American character and his belief that America is the nation pointing toward the future constitute stimulating and interesting reading.

Bibliography:

Graubard, Stephen R. "Presidents: The Power and the Mediocrity." *The New York Times Book Review* 94 (January 15, 1989): 1, 36-37. An examination of Bryce's hypothesis as to why great men are not elected president of the United States and whether his analysis applies to contemporary occupants of the office.

Ions, Edmund S. *James Bryce and American Democracy, 1870-1922.* New York: Humanities Press, 1970. A British scholar uses Bryce's personal papers to trace his interaction with the United States. Contains much useful information about the writing and impact of *The American Commonwealth* and Bryce's subsequent career as ambassador between 1907 and 1913.

Keller, Morton. *Affairs of State: Public Life in Late Nineteenth Century America.* Cambridge, Mass.: The Belknap Press of Harvard University Press, 1977. A late twentieth century historian looks at the period that Bryce's book examined. Useful for a comparative perspective on what Bryce wrote.

_____. "James Bryce and America." *The Wilson Quarterly* 12 (Autumn, 1988): 86-95. Keller considers Bryce's work a century after it was written and finds it "a vivid, affectionate, informed portrait" of the United States and its government during the 1880's. The best short analysis of Bryce's contribution to the study of American culture.

Shaughnessy, D. F. "Anatomy of the Republic: On Bryce's Americans." *Encounter* 73 (July/August, 1989): 31-37. An interesting analysis of Bryce's view of the United States and the accuracy of his assessments. Shaughnessy argues that Bryce's judgments held up very well and that his comments about American political institutions retain contemporary relevance.

THE AMERICAN NOTEBOOKS

Type of work: Diary
Author: Nathaniel Hawthorne (1804-1864)
First published: 1932

Nathaniel Hawthorne's *The American Notebooks* review the writer's recurrent themes of isolation, sin, the degeneration of families, and the subjugation of one person to another. Hawthorne was one of the originators of the American short-story form, and he was a leading novelist of nineteenth century American letters. He began the observations, story ideas, and character sketches that make up *The American Notebooks* in 1835, when he was an unknown college graduate living in isolation in Salem, Massachusetts. The last entry of the notebooks is that of June, 1853, by which time Hawthorne had traveled in the northeastern United States and had married and had children. By then Hawthorne had also published his most successful works. *The American Notebooks* show Hawthorne's development as a writer; as such, they are an invaluable contribution to an understanding of his literary development. Some of the collection's entries contain ideas that are important in his most famous fictional works.

The American Notebooks follow a chronological order, tracing Hawthorne's development over a period of eighteen years. The individual entries, however, are quite random in their makeup and contain adages, animal folklore, and biblical references that captivated Hawthorne. Observations of people whom he saw in the streets of nineteenth century Salem, Boston, and North Adams, Massachusetts, are mixed with flights of fancy that occurred to Hawthorne as he labored at his writing. Quotations from early eighteenth century newspapers and church books chronicle Hawthorne's lifelong interest in New England history. In this sense, the notebooks provide not only a glimpse of Hawthorne's close observation as a writer but also a picture of New England in the early-to-mid-nineteenth century.

The production of the novels, essays, and tales took up much of the winter months in Hawthorne's adult life; the notebook entries were made mainly during the summer months as he traveled to and from Boston, out to western Massachusetts, and through the towns of Maine. The freer time of summer may account for the relatively unfocused form of the notebooks; however, the unfocused form shows the creative imagination of Hawthorne at work.

When he began *The American Notebooks*, Hawthorne was a recent graduate of Bowdoin College. He had confounded his family by returning to the family home in Salem, Massachusetts, to use his time to read and practice the craft of writing. These early entries show Hawthorne at work on descriptions of long nature walks; these entries reflect his sadness, preoccupations, and fantasies. A particular entry notes an idea for a story—never to be produced—of "the fantasy of a man taking his life by installments, instead of at one payment,—say the years of life alternately with ten years of suspended animation." This was an odd but fitting idea for an artist who would later write novels that fused the fantastic with the mundane and the real. The early entries also hint at the major themes that Hawthorne would actively explore for all of his writing life. He recorded entries on decaying, degenerate families, and he made notes on the evil in every human heart. He also planted the seeds for future fiction on the diseases of the soul.

By July, 1837, however, the notebooks had begun to tell a different story. Hawthorne had gone on an extended summer visit to Horatio Bridge, a Bowdoin College classmate who lived in bachelor's quarters in Augusta, Maine. In these early entries, Hawthorne records his walks through the streets of Augusta and his visits to the Irish and Nova Scotian shantytowns with his friend Bridge. Hawthorne makes detailed observations of the houses with sod roofs and an Irishwoman washing her clothes in a river. Hawthorne was still an unknown author with one book, *Twice-Told Tales* (1837), to his credit when he wrote the long descriptive passages of fishing for sturgeon, drinking brandy and rum in a dimly lit store, and riding to Augusta past mowers pausing along the roadside with their scythes. Hawthorne was emerging from his years of solitary living in Salem, Massachusetts, however, and was contemplating a new stage in life.

In the second phase of *The American Notebooks*, Hawthorne demonstrates his capacity to link thematic interests to the places he sees in geographical landscapes. On a trip to view the Maine mansion of General Henry Knox, the secretary of war in President George Washington's cabinet, Hawthorne links his preoccupation with the degeneration of families over time with the house which he carefully observes: His notebook chronicles his thought that in less than forty years since the mansion had been built, "now the house is all in decay." This observation underscores his obsession with the decline of the fortunes of a family, represented by the decay of a mansion. As a writer primarily interested in ideas such as sin, the estrangement of the individual from society, and the degeneration of families over time, Hawthorne appears to have used the notebooks to review those themes: Repeatedly, he sketches characters and places that illustrate his ideas; equally important, he uses the notebooks to set out his ideas regarding the conflicts of life.

The American Notebooks also record some of the changes which took place in Hawthorne's life. By 1841, he had experimented with different ways of life. He resided at Brook Farm, a Utopian agricultural commune in Massachusetts. Then he married in 1842 and took up residence at the old Manse in Concord, Massachusetts. There he was able to have a relationship and important conversations with Ralph Waldo Emerson, the Transcendentalist American philosopher and writer. Although Hawthorne does not record the actual conversations, *The American Notebooks* contain invaluable descriptions of Emerson. Hawthorne characterizes Emerson—and, perhaps, Emerson's Transcendentalist philosophy, as well—as "that everlasting rejector of all that is, and seeker for he knows not what." For his part, Emerson valued Hawthorne's friendship, while placing little value on his writing. Equally important to Hawthorne's development were his discussions with the writers Henry David Thoreau, Margaret Fuller, and others.

In contrast with the journal entries of earlier years, which reflect solitude and preoccupation with sin and death, his later journals, while never completely leaving those issues aside, do record a different side of Hawthorne as a man who exchanges ideas with his contemporaries in the fields of literature and art, and as a husband who revels in his newfound home life and marriage. In the entries of the early 1840's, Hawthorne compiles descriptions of his home in his notebooks; these descriptions later served as material for some of his essays. In one such entry he notes: "My business is merely to live and to enjoy; and whatever is essential to life and enjoyment will come as naturally as the dew from Heaven."

These entries, filled with the daily activities of the two children born to him at this time, and Hawthorne's obvious enjoyment of them, gave Hawthorne material for *The Scarlet Letter* (1850); some of the elaborate descriptions of their childhood play served as background material for that novel, especially in the characterization of little Pearl. These entries also give the reader a broader perspective of a more settled, cheerful, indeed rapturous Hawthorne as a recorder of his children's lives.

The record of his son's laughter is interspersed with story ideas that reflect a darker reality. In part, *The American Notebooks* serve to record the dual nature of life as Hawthorne saw it.

One story idea written by Hawthorne during the 1840's reflects the duality this way: "In a grim, weird story, a figure of gay, laughing, handsome youth, or young lady, all at once, in a natural, unconcerned way, takes off its face like a mask, and shows the grinning bare skeleton face beneath." Such individual entries show Hawthorne's mixture of fantasy with reality in his work and in his notebook. Fantasy is always an important element throughout the notebooks; these entries convey Hawthorne's lifelong obsession with the darker sides of life.

Recurrent themes, story ideas, tantalizing conflicts, and character sketches, many of which appeared later in his fiction, provide a rich canvas of ideas in the notebooks. One entry notes the following: "The life of a woman, who, by the old colony law, was condemned always to wear the letter A, sewed on her garment, in token of her having committed adultery." This entry in *The American Notebooks* refers to a law passed in the New England colonies in 1696; its record in the notebooks shows the seed of an idea to which Hawthorne would return much later in his writing of *The Scarlet Letter*. In that novel, Hawthorne's heroine, Hester Prynne, must struggle with a community that has condemned her for the act of adultery. Isolated and punished, she is sentenced to wear an "A" on her chest as an eternal announcement of her crime. Throughout *The American Notebooks*, Hawthorne struggles with the themes of guilt, redemption, and sin.

A final entry in June, 1851, after Hawthorne completed his major works, including *Twice-Told Tales*, *The Scarlet Letter*, *The House of the Seven Gables* (1851), and *The Blithedale Romance* (1852), ends on a curious, tantalizing note. In this last entry, Hawthorne records having burned great quantities of his letters and personal papers in preparation for an extended journey to England. He records: "What a trustful guardian of secret matters is fire! What should we do without fire and death!" This entry surely alerts the reader to the fact that *The American Notebooks* are not intended as a completely candid and factual chronicle of Hawthorne's personal life. Indeed, many personal milestones of his life are left out. Hawthorne makes no effort to review the contents of *The American Notebooks*, which were an important professional resource for him as a writer, and which have preserved an intimate portrait of his creative, keen, and active mind.

R. C. S.

Bibliography:
Hawthorne, Julian. *Hawthorne and His Circle*. New York: Harper & Row, 1903. Reminiscences and notes on Hawthorne's life and the times recounted in *The American Notebooks*. An illuminating second look at the individuals and ideas chronicled by Nathaniel Hawthorne.
Hawthorne, Nathaniel. *The Heart of Hawthorne's Journals*. Edited by Newton Arvin. Boston: Houghton Mifflin, 1929. Contains entries in Hawthorne's journals that extend beyond the time period of *The American Notebooks*. Notes Hawthorne's journal observations up to his time in England in 1866.
Matthiessen, F. O. *American Renaissance: Art and Expression in the Age of Emerson and Whitman*. Oxford, England: Oxford University Press, 1941. Critical interpretation of the mid-nineteenth century and Hawthorne's place in it. The treatment of Hawthorne and his relation to American fiction is of particular merit for the reader of *The American Notebooks*.
Mellow, James R. *Nathaniel Hawthorne in His Times*. Boston: Houghton Mifflin, 1980. A complex and comprehensive investigation into Hawthorne's development as a major writer of nineteenth century America. Essential to an understanding of the historical context behind *The American Notebooks*.

Stewart, Randall, ed. *The American Notebooks*. New Haven, Conn.: Yale University Press, 1932. Examines Hawthorne's notebooks as they appear in manuscript form in the Pierpont Morgan Library. Points out the recurrent themes and character types in Hawthorne's notebooks. Offers extensive historical notes on persons and places discussed in the notebooks.

AN AMERICAN TRAGEDY

Type of work: Novel
Author: Theodore Dreiser (1871-1945)
Type of plot: Naturalism
Time of plot: Early twentieth century
Locale: Kansas City, Chicago, and Lycurgus, New York
First published: 1925

> *Principal characters:*
> CLYDE GRIFFITHS
> ROBERTA ALDEN, his mistress
> SAMUEL GRIFFITHS, Clyde's wealthy uncle
> GILBERT GRIFFITHS, his son
> SONDRA FINCHLEY, a society girl whom Clyde loves

The Story:

When Clyde Griffiths was still a child, his religious-minded parents took him and his brothers and sisters around the streets of various cities, where they prayed and sang in public. The family was always very poor, but the fundamentalist faith of the Griffithses was their hope and mainstay throughout the storms and troubles of life. Young Clyde was never religious, however, and he always felt ashamed of the life his parents were living. As soon as he was old enough to make decisions for himself, he went his own way. At age sixteen, he got a job as a bellboy in a Kansas City hotel. There the salary and the tips he received astonished him. For the first time in his life he had money in his pocket, and he could dress well and enjoy himself. Then a tragedy overwhelmed the family. Clyde's sister Hester, or "Esta," ran away, supposedly to be married. Her elopement was a great blow to their parents, but Clyde did not brood over the matter. Life was too pleasant for him; more and more, he enjoyed the luxuries that his job provided. He made friends with the other bellhops and joined them in parties that revolved around liquor and women. Clyde soon became familiar with drink and brothels.

One day, he discovered that his sister was back in town. The man with whom she had run away had deserted her, and she was penniless and pregnant. Knowing his sister needed money, Clyde gave his mother a few dollars for her. He promised to give her more; instead, he bought an expensive coat for a girl in the hope that she would yield herself to him. One night, he and his friends went to a party in a car that did not belong to them. Coming back from their outing, they ran over a little girl. In their attempt to escape, they wrecked the car. Clyde fled to Chicago.

In Chicago he got work at the Union League Club, where he eventually met his wealthy uncle, Samuel Griffiths. The uncle, who owned a factory in Lycurgus, New York, took a fancy to Clyde and offered him work in the factory. Clyde went to Lycurgus. There his cousin, Gilbert, resented this cousin from the Midwest. The whole family, with the exception of his uncle, considered Clyde beneath them socially and would not accept him into their circle. Clyde was given a job at the very bottom of the business, but his uncle soon made him a supervisor.

In the meantime, Sondra Finchley, who disliked Gilbert, began to invite Clyde to parties that she and her friends often gave. Her main purpose was to annoy Gilbert. Clyde's growing popularity forced the Griffithses to receive him socially, much to Gilbert's disgust. In the course of his work at the factory, Clyde met Roberta Alden, with whom he soon fell in love. Since it was forbidden for a supervisor to mix socially with an employee, they had to meet secretly.

Clyde attempted to persuade Roberta to give herself to him, but the girl refused. At last, rather than lose him, she consented and became his mistress. At the same time, Clyde was becoming fascinated by Sondra. He came to love her and hoped to marry her and, thus, acquire the wealth and social position for which he yearned. Gradually, Clyde began breaking dates with Roberta in order to be with Sondra every moment that she could spare him. Roberta began to be suspicious and eventually discovered the truth.

Roberta also discovered that she was pregnant. Clyde went to drugstores for medicine to terminate the pregnancy, which did not work. He attempted to find a doctor of questionable reputation. Roberta went to see one physician, who refused to perform an operation. Clyde and Roberta were both becoming desperate, and Clyde saw his possible marriage to the girl as a dismal ending to all his hopes for a bright future. He told himself that he did not love Roberta, that it was Sondra whom he wished to marry. Roberta asked him to marry her for the sake of her child, saying she would go away afterward, if he wished, so that he could be free of her. Clyde would not agree to her proposal and grew more irritable and worried.

One day he read an item in the newspaper about the accidental drowning of a couple who had gone boating. A plan began to form in his mind. He told Roberta that he would marry her and persuaded her to accompany him to an isolated lake resort. There, as though accidentally, he lunged toward her. She was hit by his camera and fell into the water. Clyde escaped, confident that her drowning would look like an accident, even though he had planned it all carefully. He had been careless, however, and letters that he and Roberta had written were found. When her condition became known, he was arrested. His uncle obtained an attorney for him. At his trial, the defense built up an elaborate case in his favor. Yet, in spite of his lawyer's efforts, he was found guilty and sentenced to be electrocuted. His mother came to see him and urged him to save his soul. A clergyman finally succeeded in getting Clyde to write a statement—a declaration that he repented of his sins. It was doubtful if the religious statement was sincere. Clyde died in the electric chair, a young man driven to betrayal, murder, and his own destruction by desire for luxury and wealth.

Critical Evaluation:

Theodore Dreiser was one of the primary practitioners of American naturalism, a school of writing that, like its counterpart in France, sought to convey realistically and almost clinically the effects of social conditions on individual lives. All of Dreiser's characteristics are most clearly reflected in *An American Tragedy*, the masterpiece of an author who had earlier published three important novels: *Sister Carrie* (1900), *Jennie Gerhardt* (1911), and *The Financier* (1912). In this book, Dreiser the naturalist asserts the doctrine that the individual is struggling endlessly to survive in an uncaring world. The individual is also a victim of heredity, environment, and chance, all of which leave one with little room for free choice. Dreiser's theory of life is largely mechanistic, and for *An American Tragedy*, he invented the term "chemism" to explain the chemical forces that he believed propelled people to act the way they did. Humanity, according to Dreiser, is a "mechanism, undevised and uncreated and a badly and carelessly driven one at that." Such a poor creature is Clyde Griffiths, the central character of *An American Tragedy*. The book, which is full of scientific imagery, shows readers how Clyde is driven to his final destruction.

Dreiser chooses to concentrate on one's struggle against one particular force: society and its institutions. In each of the novel's three sections, Clyde strives not against a malign God or a malevolent fate but against the unyielding structure of his culture. In other times, people have defined themselves by other touchstones (religion, honor, war), but Clyde can answer his craving for meaning in only one way. To matter in America means, in the book's terms, to be masterful, to have material goods and status. Clyde's America tempts him with its powerful businesses, its glittering social affairs, and its promises that anyone who is deserving can share in its riches. That is a false promise; the American tragedy is the gap between the country's ideals and its reality.

Doomed to failure in his quest, Clyde, whose story has been called a parable of the U.S. experience, cannot be blamed for desiring what he sees all about him. Nor can he be blamed for the weaknesses and handicaps that assure his end. Immature and shallow, offering a "gee" on all occasions, uneducated and poor, Clyde is willing to compromise in any necessary fashion in order to become materially successful. His lack of moral or intellectual distinction, when coupled with the intensity of his desires, makes him representative of a culture in which achievement is gauged by material and social success. In the novel (inspired by a 1906 murder case involving Chester Gillette, who killed an inconveniently pregnant girlfriend for reasons much like those in the book), Clyde's attorney calls him a "mental as well as a moral coward—no more and no less," but he later adds that Clyde cannot help this state.

The list of what created Clyde includes poor parents who were as inept as he. Impractical and ineffectual, the Griffithses offer him only their God, who, as Clyde can plainly see, has brought them none of the things he or they want. Religion is one obstacle Clyde can and does overcome when he ignores his parents' protests and responds instead to his environment and inner urgings. His adaptability is exploited in the hotels in which he works, places where luxury alone is vital, and kindness and honesty mere trifles. When, in the second part of the novel, Clyde finds himself in Lycurgus, he once again gravitates helplessly toward the surrounding values. Named after the Spartan who initiated that society's rigid rules, Lycurgus is just as tantalizing as the hotels. It is a "walled city" that, as one of the novel's major symbols, allows outsiders to peek at its glories but rarely permits them to enter its gates. Clyde, fascinated and overwhelmed, abandons the simple pleasures he has found with Roberta and attempts to climb its walls.

Whenever Clyde struggles free of his environmental influences, he is frustrated by the accidents and coincidences that haunt him. He unwillingly leaves Kansas City because of the car accident, and he leaves Chicago because of a seemingly happy encounter with his uncle. His chance meeting with Sondra begins their relationship, and Roberta's unplanned pregnancy obstructs his dreams. Even his murder scheme is derived from a chance newspaper article, and the murder itself, in a sense, happens by accident, for Clyde, in a failure of nerve, allows rather than forces Roberta's drowning.

Other characters in the novel are equally victims of the roles in which they find themselves. While many of them are compellingly presented, their main importance is to provide background and stimuli for Clyde. He rarely sees others as people but rather as either impediments (his family, Roberta) or as exciting objects (Sondra); the reader too (in an act of complicity that Dreiser's narration skillfully elicits) is for the most part interested in the other characters in the same ways that Clyde is. The book belongs almost entirely to the decidedly unsympathetic Clyde.

In *An American Tragedy*, Dreiser, a former newspaperman and editor of women's publications, watches Clyde's world and its foibles and is moved by humanity's helplessness. He shows readers how useless moral judgment is in solving such dilemmas as the existence and acts of Clyde. Dreiser insists, as he does in all of his works, that all that people may expect of one another is compassion for common plights. Although he offers little encouragement, Dreiser does hint that perhaps the human condition may improve. The final scene—"Dusk, of a summer night"—closely resembles the opening. A small boy once again troops reluctantly with a group of street missionaries—the Griffithses. Yet Mrs. Griffiths responds to Esta's child as she had never done to Clyde. She gives the child money for an ice cream cone. This child, she promises herself, will be different.

"Critical Evaluation" by Judith Bolch

Bibliography:
Bloom, Harold, ed. *Theodore Dreiser's "An American Tragedy."* New York: Chelsea House, 1988. One of America's leading literary critics updates Salzman's collection (listed below).
Gerber, Philip L. "Society Should Ask Forgiveness: *An American Tragedy.*" In *Theodore Dreiser Revisited.* Boston: Twayne, 1992. A structural analysis that also examines Dreiser's sources, his progression through early drafts, and the novel's effect on his career. Annotated bibliography.
Lehan, Richard. *"An American Tragedy."* In *Theodore Dreiser: His World and His Novels.* Carbondale: Southern Illinois University Press, 1969. Discusses Dreiser's identification with Clyde Griffiths, particularly his fundamentalist religious background and the techniques Dreiser uses to mitigate Clyde's culpability.
Pizer, Donald. "American Literary Naturalism: The Example of Dreiser." In *Realism and Naturalism in Nineteenth-Century American Literature.* Rev. ed. Carbondale: Southern Illinois University Press, 1984. One of the foremost authorities on naturalism in American literature defends Dreiser against critical antagonism toward naturalism and illustrates the principles of determinism in *An American Tragedy.*
Salzman, Jack, comp. *The Merrill Studies in "An American Tragedy."* Westerville, Ohio: Charles E. Merrill, 1971. A critical casebook on the novel, containing essays on topics such as naturalism, materialism, and Dreiser's sources for the novel.

AMORES

Type of work: Poetry
Author: Ovid (Publius Ovidius Naso, 43 B.C.E.-17 C.E.)
Type of plot: Erotic
Time of plot: Augustan Age
Locale: Rome
First transcribed: c. 20 B.C.E. (English translation, c. 1597)

Principal characters:
THE LOVER, the speaker of the poems
CORINNA, the beloved of the speaker

The Story:
Book 1. The speaker, prepared to sing of heroic deeds, arms and war, was struck by Cupid's arrow. He turned to the poetry of love. The speaker tossed sleepless at night, enthralled by love and suffering. He prayed that the lady would favor him; he in return would immortalize her in verse. A monologue addressed to the lady explained how at a party she could dupe her husband and send signals to the speaker.

The first assignation of the lovers, on a sultry summer afternoon, took place. There followed a sorrowful complaint as the speaker spent a long solitary night outside the locked door of Corinna's house. Next he felt guilt and remorse for a moment of anger in which he disheveled her hair. He overheard a conversation between Corinna and Dipsas, a bawdy old hag who gave the lady cynical advice on milking her lovers of gold and gifts. The speaker scolded his lady for her cupidity and tried to persuade her that love can only be given, never sold. He sent a letter to her, in hopes of a meeting, and felt despair when it was returned with a refusal.

Next, the lovers spent a night together, and the speaker complained of the inexorable coming of day, when they would have to part. A crisis happened: From too-frequent applications of the curling iron, Corinna's hair fell out. The poet chided and commiserated with her.

Book 2. Opening with a stout denial that he would be a better poet if he tried more serious subjects, the speaker harangued Corinna's guard about how easy and profitable he might find it to smuggle the speaker past the door and into her house. A similar plea was made to her eunuch. The speaker boasted about his ability to love any woman in town; but as if for punishment, the next poem related his agonies when he suspected a rival.

Accused of dallying with Corinna's slave girl, the speaker denied the charge vehemently, with injured dignity, and in the next poem chided the slave for having blushed at the accusation, proving it true. A general complaint to Cupid came next, on the theme that love is hell but heaven too. The lover boasted to a friend of his great capacity for lovemaking; he hoped he might die in bed.

When Corinna went on a voyage, the lover bemoaned their separation, charged the seas to be calm, the winds favorable, the trip safe and short. The lover then experienced another successful meeting with his love. Immediately following, the lover discovered Corinna had performed an abortion on herself and endangered her life, and the poet was shocked and worried. She recovered and he gave her a ring as a love token.

Another separation occurred. The lover, visiting his native village, Sulmo, missed Corinna deeply. The poet explained how hard it was to write seriously when Cupid laughs and the ladies distract him. In poetry, he predicted, love would triumph over war. The last poem of book 2 advised Corinna's husband during an imagined meeting. Since forbidden fruits are sweetest, the poet would have the husband be jealous and watchful of his wife, to make the cuckolding more satisfying.

Book 3. The affair was on the wane. The muse of tragedy called to the poet for a great work, but he asked for a short delay while he finished his *Amores.* The poet discovered that Corinna's vows of love had been broken. He was bitter and blamed himself for ever having believed her protestations. At last he decided to let her lie if she must, but let her not swear false vows by his eyes.

Addressing the husband, the poet pointed out how silly it was to set guards on his wife: The faithful wife does not need them and the unfaithful wife will always find ways to get around them. Next was an account of a dream the poet had of a bull deserted by a heifer. A seer interpreted this as a forecast that Corinna would leave the poet. The speaker, however, was still eager for her. On his way to visit her, he was blocked by a flood-swollen stream, which he cursed and raged at in his thwarted desire.

Matters continued to go wrong: Once with her, he found, ironically, that he was impotent, and he raged even more mightily at himself. The lady was furious, thinking he had worn himself out with other women. She smiled on a new lover, and the poet, neglected, was left to wonder how she could prefer a parvenu and a soldier to him, a great poet.

The following poem was in a more serious tone. It was a funeral elegy on the death of a poet and friend, Tibullus. Next came a poem in autumnal mood in praise of Ceres, goddess of the harvest, and of lament for his unhappy love affair. The poet tried unsuccessfully to renounce his love for the false Corinna. She was too beautiful, and he had to love her. Wryly he realized that it was his celebration of Corinna in poetry that spread her fame and attracted other men to her. He said they should have known he exaggerated, and that she could not be perfect, as he had painted her.

In a last confrontation with his cruel lady, the poet begged her at least to pretend she still loved him, even though he knew she was deceiving him. Let her deny that she strayed, he argued, so that he could continue to persuade himself that she loved him. In the last poem the poet announced that he had given up writing love poetry. He was ready to turn to a grave and serious subject. He hoped that all his writing would immortalize him.

Critical Evaluation:

Ovid read publicly from his *Amores* in 25 B.C.E., when he was about eighteen, and they proved immediately popular in Augustan Rome, despite, or perhaps because of, Augustus' efforts to promote morality, particularly marital fidelity, at court. The tradition of romantic and erotic elegies had been established by Catullus, who died in 54 B.C.E., and Propertius, who died no later than 2 C.E. Ovid's elegies are often examined in the context of the work of these two predecessors. The poems of Propertius in particular are often compared to those of Ovid, who appears to have imitated and in some cases parodied Propertius. In general, Ovid undermines serious, romantic love in favor of fun.

Typical marriages for free and literate Roman patricians or aristocrats, those most likely to be Ovid's audience, were arranged. Adulterous relationships for both husband and wife appear to have been the rule rather than the exception. The male speaker in the forty-nine poems that make up the three books of the *Amores* takes this condition for granted and assumes his audience will be sympathetic. It is not surprising, therefore, that the first-person speaker and the mistress (sometimes Corinna and other times apparently not) are playful and promiscuous.

Most critics now agree that there was no model in Ovid's life for Corinna, who appears by name in about one-fourth of the poems, but Ovid gives her realistic features. She has auburn hair, as readers discover in 1.14, in which her hair is ruined by being restyled, and she is attended by various servants. She appears to be married, although she could be a concubine.

The speaker is a poet from Sulmo (as was Ovid) who believes in the power of his art to win and sustain the affections of his mistresses. More specifically in several "programmatic" poems (1.1, 1.15, 2.1, 2.18, 3.1, 3.8, 3.15) the poet argues his confidence in the elegy as opposed to either tragedy or epic when it comes to assuring his fame. This argument constitutes one theme of the *Amores*. In effect Ovid argues for poems other than those that are filled with pathos or profundity. In 2.1, he says he would like every young man who is in love to be able to recognize his symptoms in these poems, "and ask himself in amazement 'How does this poet know/ about me and my personal problems?'" Perhaps this is the goal of most poets.

The perspective throughout is distinctively male. Not well-off financially, the speaker depends on his art and its appeal to his mistress' vanity (her desire for eternal fame) to get by. As a lover he is at odds with men of affairs, whether businessmen or soldiers, but he makes use of their language in the process of presenting his case. For example, in 1.9, he argues that all lovers are soldiers, and they must use military tactics to avoid the guards and night patrols set out by sleeping husbands.

Of course the lover is jealous and suspicious, but the cause may have less to do with his mistress' infidelity than with his own. In 2.7, for example, he uses metaphors drawn from the law in describing himself as a defendant unjustly accused of an affair with his mistress' hairdresser, Cypassis. He insists no true gentleman would carry on with a mere maid, but in the next poem he smooth-talks Cypassis with an argument from Homer, pointing out that, after all, "Achilles adored his maid Briseis." Clearly, the fun of the *Amores* requires the setting aside of conventional moral and ethical standards, and perhaps of the rules of logic as well.

It could be said that the premise of the *Amores* is hedonistic, that the poems are founded upon the simple human drive to avoid pain and seek pleasure, even at great cost. Certainly the languid sexuality of 1.5, and the morning song 1.13, in which the lover pleads with the sun not to rise, are examples. In 2.15 he imagines himself as his girlfriend's ring slipping inside her dress and fondling her breast, and in 3.4 he pleads to her husband to be more alert and more possessive, as the challenge will make their affair more exciting. The speaker's most embarrassing moment is celebrated in 3.7, when he confesses his inability to achieve an erection, despite the professional efforts of his mistress (not Corinna, in this case, as he mentions her for having "inspired" his "record" of nine times "in one short night").

One might argue that in the *Amores* Ovid offers comic relief to a society that tended to be stifling in its commitment to business and affairs of state and increasingly puritanical in its moral outlook. As studies of supposedly proper Victorians have revealed, repressive societies tend to force sexual play underground, not to eradicate it. Some critics have suggested that Ovid himself, who was married three times, may not have enjoyed the self-indulgent escapades of his speaker, but the poems remain an invitation to erotic love. In 2.4 the speaker says he offers no excuse for his "weak character" or lack of discipline, for he loves all types of women: "I admire a girl in make-up for what she is/ and a girl without for what she could be."

There is a price to be paid for the unleashing of the libido, however, and occasionally Ovid reveals it. For example, in 1.7 he shows remorse for having beaten his mistress, and in 2.13 and 2.14 he shows his concern when she nearly dies after a self-inflicted abortion and then anger over the act itself. The third book of the *Amores* involves a sort of cooling off, as Ovid prepares his audience for other kinds of poetry. Poems such as 3.6, on rivers, and 3.10, on sexual abstinence practiced during the feast of Ceres, concern mythological tales rather than personal erotic adventures. The third book also includes a moving elegy to the poet Tibullus (3.9) and a dream allegory (3.5) that most critics think is not Ovid's work.

Poems 3.11 through 3.15, the last five of the book, include an angry farewell to the bondage of love, a lament that the speaker has lost Corinna because his poems made her too popular, an account of the legend of his wife's hometown, and a plea to his mistress to deceive him if she does not really love him. The poet, who is supposed to be the master of illusions, now begs to be deluded.

"Critical Evaluation" by Ron McFarland

Bibliography:
DuQuesnay, I. M. le M. "The Amores." In *Ovid*, edited by J. W. Binns. London: Routledge & Kegan Paul, 1973. Conjectures on Corinna and comments on style and technique. Sees the speaker as parody not really directed at Propertius but at Ovid and notes that Ovid takes playful jabs at Augustan society.
Lyne, R. O. A. M. *The Latin Love Poets.* Oxford, England: Clarendon Press, 1980. The chapter on Ovid's *Amores* reflects on the kind of society that reads the poems, on the character of Corinna, and on connections with poems by Propertius and Tibullus. Notes Ovid's antiromantic wit, playful cynicism, and opposition to "the moral earnestness of Augustan Rome," arguing that what Ovid believed in was fun and poetry.
Mack, Sue. *Ovid.* New Haven, Conn.: Yale University Press, 1988. Notes the conventionality of the lover, the mistress, and the situations in the poems. Finds that Ovid distinguishes between poet and persona and creates a "constantly changing interaction between himself and the audience."
Morgan, Kathleen. *Ovid's Art of Imitation.* Leiden, The Netherlands: E. J. Brill, 1977. Examines Ovid's "creative imitation" and parody of Propertius in the *Amores.* Useful bibliography of works on the *Amores.*
Wilkinson, L. P. *Ovid Recalled.* Cambridge, England: Cambridge University Press, 1955. The chapter on the *Amores* emphasizes the "pleasing shocks of blasphemy" in the poems, several of which are translated by the author. More appreciation than analysis.

AMORETTI

Type of work: Poetry
Author: Edmund Spenser (c. 1552-1599)
First published: 1595

Edmund Spenser's sonnet sequence, the *Amoretti* (meaning "little love gifts" in Italian), ranks among the most notable of the collections produced during the golden age of English poetry, also the heyday of the English sonnet. Beginning in fourteenth century Italy with Petrarch's tributes, in sonnet form, to his beloved Laura, the sonnet cycle describing the lover's pangs and the inamorata's remote beauty quickly became a poetic standard. The introduction of this poetic form to England is generally credited to Sir Thomas Wyatt, who brought it from France and adapted it to the English taste and tongue. Although the prestige of the sonnet had begun to decline by the time Spenser produced his sequence, no notable poet of the period could afford to ignore the sonnet or the sonnet cycle. As had William Shakespeare and Sir Philip Sidney before him, Spenser used the sonnet cycle as part of his claim to literary fame.

The *Amoretti* differs from Sir Philip Sidney's *Astrophil and Stella* (1591) sequence and from Shakespeare's sonnets in ways that have too often led to comparisons unfavorable to Spenser. Not only does Spenser use a more labored rhyme scheme (adapted from the French), but also his subject matter is subtler and less dramatic. Shakespeare and Sidney address their rhymes to amorous objects presented in a highly fictionalized and formalized context. Spenser, on the other hand, blends traditional elements of idealization of the love object with elements of the actual courtship of his future wife. For this reason, the *Amoretti* wavers somewhere between the dramatic outpourings of emotion typical of Shakespeare and the elegantly crafted tributes to the lady's charms typical of Sidney. As a result, Spenser's reader must look beneath the "artificial" elements of the sonnets to see their "natural" appeal. They record the vagaries of real courtship, with all its alternating moments of doubt, despair, hope, tenderness, elation, and joy sketched with characteristic Spenserian delicacy and tact.

This delicacy may create problems for the reader who demands more straightforward vigor; it can best be appreciated by noting how the sonnets' unusual rhyme scheme produces a graceful modulation between and within lines. Although each of Spenser's sonnets closes with a ringing couplet, traditional in the sonnet in English, its scheme as a whole is tighter and subtler than that of the more ordinary form. Ending each quatrain with the rhyme that will begin the next, Spenser achieves a remarkably smooth, graceful, and highly unified effect. While some critics have criticized this rhyme scheme as overly artificial, it is very well suited to the fine modulation of emotions expressed by a forty-year-old poet seeking the hand of a beautiful and socially superior young lady. Similarly, while the character of this lady tends toward the ideal, Spenser ably sketches the personality of a real woman. His Elizabeth Boyle was not the inaccessible mistress of Petrarchan tradition, nor was her lover its traditional victim. Each partner to this courtship exhibits strengths and weaknesses, each ultimately being referred back to the perfecting grace of God. Spenser's sonnet sequence is a remarkable achievement: It is one of the first fully realized attempts in lyric poetry to represent an actual, rather than an ideal, human relationship. The *Amoretti* creates one of the earliest and greatest tributes to the Protestant virtues of married love and domestic tranquillity.

The sequence also is unique in charting a real time sequence, the period between late 1592 and June 11, 1594, the day on which Spenser's wedding was finally solemnized, and which his famous *Epithalamion* (1595) celebrates. The New Year's Days of 1593 and 1594 are observed in the sequence, as are the occasions of Easter, the couple's betrothal, and their separation for a brief period before their wedding. Along with these time markers, many purely conventional elements are included, as in the first sonnet, a traditional dedication to love, to poetry, and to the muse. Characteristic of Spenser, this classical theme is Christianized by the poet's asking his book to testify to "that angels blessed look,/ My souls long lacked food, my heavens bliss." Yet instead of merely borrowing the language of religion to praise the ecstatic "bliss" of the lady's beauty, the poet uses it to consecrate the institution of holy matrimony, which will in turn prepare the couple for their heavenly home. This theme is reiterated with new emphasis in sonnet 3, in which the poet speaks of his beloved's beauty as having kindled heavenly fire

> In my frail spirit, by her from baseness raised:
> That being now with her huge brightness dazed,
> Base thing I can no more endure to view;
> But looking still on her, I stand amazed
> At wondrous sight of so celestial hue.

Even in this sonnet, however, some customary aspects of the poet's praise are apparent. Drawing upon the Neoplatonic conception of the relationship between light, beauty, and virtue, the poem praises a conventionally fair lady, a golden-haired ideal of Elizabethan loveliness. More than a compendium of Christian virtues, then, she is also celebrated for her classically aristocratic "virtue" of pride. In sonnet 5, Spenser associates her pride not only with nobleness of spirit and mind but also with chastity:

> For in those lofty looks is close implied
> Scorn of base things, and disdain of foul dishonor;
> Threatening rash eyes which gaze on her so wide,
> That loosely they ne dare to look upon her.
> Such pride is praise, such portliness is honor.

This theme is continued with variations throughout the sequence. The poet also argues that women are like trees even while he laments the suffering that their "hardness" inflicts upon him. His protests of the suffering caused him by the hardness and remoteness of the love object rank among the most conventional devices of the *Amoretti*. Comparing his lady's eyes to blinding darts or beams capable of inflicting life or death, he eventually grows outraged in sonnet 10 at "the huge massacres which her eyes do make"; at how, in sonnet 11, a warrior has taken him hostage without ransom; and at how like a huntress she seeks to despoil his poor "hart." The pun on the human heart and the tender "hart," or deer (with an additional pun on "dear"), is conventional. Such techniques date back to Petrarch, although Spenser uses them with a characteristically personal emphasis. For example, he begins sonnet 15 with a traditional metaphor of love as a form of journey, courtship as a labor of exploration, and his beloved as a precious mine: her lips are rubies, her teeth pearls, her skin ivory, her hair gold, and her hands silver. Rather than extending the metaphor and making this blazon or ceremonial poetic device culminate in an ultimate jewel or setting, the poet unexpectedly declares that her true worth is as immeasurable as the invisible beauty of "her mind." A series of metaphors that are concrete and particular culminate not in a summary of the concrete and particular aspects of the loved one's beauty but rather in an abstraction. Spenser's characteristically Protestant emphasis falls on the inner self, the invisible realm of human and divine perfection.

This mixing of Petrarchan convention and a more individual approach persists throughout the sequence, with the innovative approach ultimately triumphing. As the poet's love prospers, so does the originality of his inspiration. This triumph is foreshadowed by Spenser's continual refusal, even in despair, to regard his beloved as merely the trite goddess of lyric tradition. What he wants is a companion and a virtual equal. Although her feminine beauty is a predictably perfect blend of "Nature and Art," its true purpose is not only to humble her suitors but also to "train and teach" her lover, in sonnet 21, with "such art of eyes I never read in books." Spenser combines the literal eye of beauty with the metaphoric "mind's eye" of Platonic tradition. Spenser's vision of the lady amplifies her human completion: Neither her beauty nor her pride can be reduced to earthly treasures of art or nature; both must be seen as spiritual treasures, on earth as in heaven. This thought, lacking in the Petrarchan tradition, constitutes Spenser's most remarkable contribution. Even when lamenting the lady's cruelty, the speaker continually encourages her to examine and refine her motives. In sonnet 30, for example, his comparison of her to ice and of himself to fire is resolved into a kind of "miracle" in which each becomes capable of taking on the properties of the other.

Once the lady graciously accepts him (this is also a significant departure from convention), both lady and lover are free to develop their personal characteristics in a new context. The turning point in the sequence and the courtship appropriately concurs with the arrival of the new year in sonnet 62. The passing of the solstice and the "storms and tempests" of winter in sonnet 63 are sealed with a kiss as sweet as all the gentle blooms of spring in sonnet 64. Some doubts remain in her heart, however, so the poet reassures his lady that her miraculous gift will increase rather than diminish her liberty: She will free them both to each other. The most successful sonnets of the sequence surround this turning point, which culminates with Spenser's praise of the "lord of life," whose example, at Eastertide in sonnet 68, teaches the lovers the lesson of rebirth by means of self-sacrifice. Marriage is celebrated as a "sweet prison" of freedom and "eternal peace" in sonnet 71.

The final sonnets of the *Amoretti* rank among the most elevated and moving examples of the Renaissance sonnet tradition. They sometimes merely rewrite Petrarch by way of Wyatt (the metaphor of the huntsman, for example, in sonnet 67), but examples of the sonnets' considerable originality (which, in the poet's time, was not as important in poetry as it has been since the Romantic era) include the poet's personal admiration, in sonnet 71, of his love's "drawn work." He characteristically interprets her drawing as signifying the reign of an "eternal peace." His celebration of her "thrice happy" name in sonnet 74 and his denunciation in sonnet 85 of a gossip who threatens their relationship are other examples of Spenser's original use of personal experience in actual courtship. Interspersed with these personal reflections are some of Spenser's loftiest spiritual sonnets, such as 79. Perhaps the most successful sonnet of the sequence incorporates the mundane and the lofty. Sonnet 75 begins with the poet's unsuccessful attempt to write Elizabeth's name on the sand. The tide erases her name and speaks to the poet, mocking him for his efforts. The sonnet ends with a meditation on how in the poet's praise of her "virtues rare," "Our love shall live, and later life renew." Conventional as this theme is, Spenser's complex reflection on the tides of time and of human life produces a timeless work of art.

Catherine Gimelli Martin

Bibliography:
Dasenbrock, Reed Way. "The Petrarchan Context of Spenser's *Amoretti*." *PMLA* 100, no. 1 (1985): 38-50. The best comprehensive statement of the case for the originality and vigor of the *Amoretti*. Bibliography.
Gibbs, Donna. *Spenser's "Amoretti": A Critical Study*. Aldershot, Hants., England: Scolar

Press, 1990. The single best sourcebook on the poetic structure, personas, and philosophical background of the *Amoretti*, as well as current critical reception. Excellent bibliography and index.

Lewis, C. S. *The Allegory of Love: A Study in Medieval Tradition.* London: Oxford University Press, 1967. A classic study of the *Amoretti* in the context of Western culture's evolving ideas about love and marriage.

Martz, Louis L. "The *Amoretti*: "Mostly Goodly Temperature." In *Form and Convention in the Poetry of Edmund Spenser*, edited by William Nelson. New York: Columbia University Press, 1961. A generally sympathetic treatment of the *Amoretti* from the perspective of the sonnets' emotional and literary development.

Spiller, Michael R. G. "The Elizabeth Sonnet Vogue and Spenser." In *The Development of the Sonnet: An Introduction.* London: Routledge & Kegan Paul, 1992. An invaluable and highly perceptive guide to the place of the *Amoretti* in the sonnet tradition.

AMPHITRYON

Type of work: Drama
Author: Plautus (c. 254-184 B.C.E.)
Type of plot: Farce
Time of plot: Heroic Age
Locale: Thebes
First performed: Amphitruo, c. 185 B.C.E. (English translation, 1694)

> Principal characters:
> AMPHITRYON, a Theban general
> ALCMENA, his wife
> JUPITER, and
> MERCURY, Roman gods
> SOSIA, Amphitryon's slave

The Story:

Amphitryon, a Theban, joined the army of Thebes to fight against the Teloboans. When he left for the wars, his wife Alcmena, daughter of Electryon, was pregnant. Nevertheless, in the absence of Amphitryon, Jupiter fell in love with Alcmena and decided that he must enjoy her favors. Disguising himself as Amphitryon, Jupiter appeared to Alcmena as her husband, just returned from a battle with the Teloboans. Alcmena was unable to recognize the impostor and welcomed Jupiter as her husband. Because Jupiter wished to enjoy Alcmena as long as possible, he had the sun, moon, and stars remain fixed, and so the night he spent with Alcmena was long enough for her to conceive and be ready to bring forth a child by Jupiter at the same time she gave birth to the child by her husband.

In the meantime Amphitryon's ship returned to Thebes. It was still night, so Amphitryon's slave, Sosia, fearfully walking the streets of the sleeping town, tried to console himself with the pleasantness of the news he was bringing to its citizens. He thought how well his master, Amphitryon, had handled the war with the Teloboans, how the enemy had refused to arbitrate the dispute over lands, how the battle had been joined, and how Amphitryon had been awarded the golden cup of Pterela as a token of the valor displayed in the battle.

While Sosia soliloquized, Mercury, disguised as Sosia, was listening to every word. Mercury had assumed the disguise to aid his father, Jupiter, in the latter's scheme to make love to Alcmena. As Sosia came through the streets to Amphitryon's house, Mercury, in the guise of Sosia, was guarding the house and the inmates against any disturbance. When Sosia saw Mercury he was afraid, but he went up to the door and tried to enter. Mercury, as Sosia, told him to be gone and beat him with his fists. When Sosia cried out that he was a slave named Sosia who belonged to the household, he received another drubbing.

Sosia, confused, then asked the stranger who he was. Mercury replied that he was Sosia, a slave of the household. Looking closely, Sosia saw that the person in front of him was dressed and looked exactly like himself. When Sosia went on to ask questions about the household, Mercury answered each one satisfactorily. Sosia asked about his own conduct during the battle; Mercury replied that he had been drinking. Knowing that the answer was correct and sure that someone had stolen his identity, Sosia ran off to the ship, leaving Mercury to chuckle over the ruse that would prevent Amphitryon from spoiling Jupiter's night with Alcmena.

Eventually Jupiter took leave of Alcmena, after telling her that he had to return to his army,

215

lest the men become bitter because their leader absented himself while they could not. When she grew sad at the thought of his departure, the god, to propitiate her, gave her the golden cup of Pterela that Amphitryon had received as a token of merit in the war. As he left, Jupiter ordered the night to move on in its regular course.

Amphitryon was furious when Sosia returned to the ship. He thought that the slave must be mad or, at the very least, drunk, and he refused to believe that anyone could have stolen the identity of Sosia, as the slave declared. Amphitryon, anxious to discover what was happening, set out for his home immediately, taking Sosia with him. By the time the real Amphitryon and Sosia arrived at the house Jupiter and Mercury had departed. Alcmena was surprised to see her husband return in so short a time. She feared that he was simply testing her fidelity.

Amphitryon, greeting his wife as a husband would after an absence of months, was unable to understand what Alcmena meant when she rebuked him for leaving her a short time before on a pretext of returning to his army. When she told Amphitryon that he had spent the night with her, Amphitryon became suddenly and decidedly angry. Then she mentioned the golden cup of Pterela, which she had received from Jupiter during his visit in disguise. Amphitryon declared she could not have the cup, for he had it under seal in his possession. When Amphitryon opened the chest in which he had put the cup, however, it was missing; the gods had stolen it to give to Alcmena.

In spite of the evidence produced to show that it was he who had been with his wife, Amphitryon was exceedingly angry and accused his wife of losing her honor by breaking her marriage vows. Alcmena, entirely innocent of any such intent and still believing that her husband had visited her earlier, was hurt and furious at the charges he made. Amphitryon, wishing to be fair but wanting to get to the bottom of the matter, went to get Alcmena's kinsman, Naucrates, who had been with him all night on board the ship. He also told Alcmena that he would divorce her unless she could prove her innocence.

Alcmena was upset at the charges heaped upon her by Amphitryon and made plans to leave the house. Jupiter, sorry for the trouble he had caused, prepared to help her. He appeared to Alcmena in disguise and softened somewhat her anger against Amphitryon. Speaking as Amphitryon, he apologized for the charges made against Alcmena's honesty and virtue.

Amphitryon was unable to find Naucrates and returned to his home. Warned by Mercury, Jupiter appeared as Amphitryon, and a riotous scene, with both men seeming to be Amphitryon, followed, an argument broken off when word came that Alcmena was about to give birth to a child. As Amphitryon prepared to leave, Jupiter struck him unconscious with a thunderbolt. With Jupiter's aid Alcmena painlessly gave birth to two sons, one by Amphitryon and the other by Jupiter. One child was so active that he could hardly be held on his cot to be bathed, and the waiting-women reported that within a few minutes of his birth the baby had strangled two large snakes that entered the room. The voice of Jupiter called out to Alcmena and told her that the lusty lad, Hercules, was his and the other child Amphitryon's.

After the waiting-women had gone, Jupiter himself appeared to Amphitryon and told the husband what had happened. When he warned Amphitryon not to be harsh toward his wife for producing a child by a god, Amphitryon, faced with no other choice, promised to obey all that the god commanded.

Critical Evaluation:

When the Roman writers adapted Greek comedies, as Plautus almost certainly did in the case of this play, they eliminated the chorus completely, thereby making the action continuous. They also made song and dance an integral part of the play, much like contemporary musical comedies. Tradition says that Plautus learned stagecraft early in life, put his earnings into trade, went bankrupt, had to work in a flour mill, and there began writing his comedies, of which more than a hundred were attributed to him. Twenty have survived, and from these readers can see that Plautus was very experienced in stage technique. He knew the value of timing, of comic repetition, of puns, of double entendre, of idiomatic speech, and of varying his poetic meters. His humor was suggestive rather than lewd. He was a master at simply being funny. In reading his plays it is essential to visualize the action as taking place on the stage in front of a backdrop of a house or two. Imagination is necessary to re-create the humor of Plautus. Otherwise, his jokes seem stale, particularly in translation. His plays were performed outdoors at public festivals in a carnival atmosphere, and they had to compete with other entertainments. The audiences were restive, unsophisticated, and straitlaced in that period of Roman history. Under such conditions a dramatist had to be continuously interesting, and a comic dramatist had to be amusing at all costs. Plautus knew his audience thoroughly. He took the threadbare formulas of Greek New Comedy and inspirited them with his own vivacity.

Amphitryon is the only extant Roman comedy to treat Greek mythology. The story derives from a myth in which Zeus (Jupiter) lengthened a night into seventy-two hours and, disguised as Amphitryon, made love to Amphitryon's wife Alcmena. The supreme god did this in order to engender the great hero Herakles (Hercules). In this play, however, the effect is to make Jupiter appear as an insatiably lecherous and troublemaking bully who would do anything to satisfy his whims. He and Mercury are rogues playing a rather nasty practical joke on three decent people. It is a joke that gets out of hand and threatens to become tragic when Amphitryon intends to divorce Alcmena for adultery. Yet Jupiter unravels the mystery, restoring an equilibrium, when he has had enough amusement at their expense. Thus the play blends two of Plautus' favorite plots—the comedy of mistaken identity and the comedy of deliberate deception.

The structure is surprisingly well done for Plautus, who usually took few pains to construct a sound plot. He makes excellent use of dramatic irony in the confusions of the human characters balanced against the knowledge of the divine characters, which the audience shares. The audience is given an Olympian viewpoint from which to witness the befuddlement of human beings as they encounter their exact duplicates and are bested at every turn. Much of the humor lies in the way Plautus exposes the discrepancy between perplexed humans and clear-sighted, interfering immortals. It is very funny when Sosia comes to doubt his own identity, having been displaced in his household by another Sosia who is identical in every respect. He thinks he has somehow twinned himself. The joke is still good later when Amphitryon and Jupiter ask Blepharo the pilot to decide who is the real Amphitryon. The theme of twins, the *Doppelgänger*, is carried through right to the end, when Alcmena gives birth to twins, one of human and the other of divine origin.

Yet the play becomes serious where Alcmena is accused of adultery because she found no difference between Amphitryon and Jupiter playing Amphitryon. Her husband comes to seem like an utter lunatic vacillating wildly between tenderness and incomprehensible jealousy. She genuinely loves Amphitryon and is deeply hurt by his accusations. Plautus gives a sympathetic portrayal of her as the duped wife. Amphitryon, although he loves Alcmena, seems like a proud, hot-tempered stuffed shirt who deserves, to an extent, his humiliation at Jupiter's hands. Plautus lifts both of these characters above the farcical level to reveal two people tricked and thwarted by the gods. Their love endures these buffetings.

Amphitryon has had a great influence on modern drama throughout the Western world, and there have been numerous translations, adaptations, and imitations. Such great dramatists as

John Dryden, in England, and Molière, in France, made use of its theme and structure. A production of the story as adapted by Jean Giraudoux was successful as a stage play under the title *Amphitryon 38* (1929).

"Critical Evaluation" by James Weigel, Jr.

Bibliography:

Anderson, William S. *Barbarian Play: Plautus' Roman Comedy.* Toronto: University of Toronto Press, 1993. Focuses on what the author calls the playwright's deconstruction of Menander, the ways in which he alters elements in his source to make his plays Roman instead of Greek. Good notes, thorough index, comprehensive bibliography.

Duckworth, George E., ed. *The Complete Roman Drama.* 2 vols. New York: Random House, 1942. General introduction provides an excellent summary of Roman drama and its cultural setting. Introduction to the *Amphitryon* is extremely helpful; combines facts with interpretation and includes some comments on later influence.

Hunter, R. L. *The New Comedy of Greece and Rome.* Cambridge, England: Cambridge University Press, 1985. Lucid discussion of forms, motifs, and themes in New Comedy, with numerous references to Plautus and *Amphitryon.* Extensive notes and a bibliography.

Sandbach, F. H. *The Comic Theatre of Greece and Rome.* London: Chatto & Windus, 1977. Both the chapter "Drama at Rome" and the chapter devoted to Plautus provide excellent overviews. Insists that Plautus was less dependent on Greek sources than is generally assumed. Essential Greek and Roman terms are defined in a glossary, which includes a thorough discussion of meter. Brief bibliography. Illustrated.

Segal, Erich. *Roman Laughter: The Comedy of Plautus.* Harvard Studies in Comparative Literature 29. Cambridge, Mass.: Harvard University Press, 1968. Shows how Plautus' works reflect Roman culture and literary traditions. References to *Amphitryon* appear throughout the text and the notes. Carefully indexed.

AMPHITRYON 38

Type of work: Drama
Author: Jean Giraudoux (1882-1944)
Type of plot: Mock-heroic
Time of plot: Antiquity
Locale: In and about Amphitryon's palace, Thebes
First performed: 1929; first published, 1929 (English translation, 1938)

> *Principal characters:*
> JUPITER, master of the gods
> MERCURY, a god
> AMPHITRYON, a general of Thebes
> ALKMENA, his wife
> SOSIE, their servant
> LEDA, Queen of the Spartans

The Story:

Basking on a cloud and spying on Alkmena, Jupiter and Mercury laid plans for the seduction of Alkmena as if preparing for a tasty banquet. In order to remove Amphitryon from his bedchamber, Mercury suggested that Jupiter have the Athenians declare war on Thebes. Amphitryon, a stalwart general of the Theban army, would hurry to engage the enemy. Mercury could then take the place of Sosie, a servant, and tell Alkmena that Amphitryon would momentarily desert the battle and return to her bed that night. Jupiter could impersonate Amphitryon and partake of the delectable Alkmena. They began to carry out their plan.

Jupiter arrived before the palace of Alkmena amidst a great clanging noise, for he had forgotten the laws of gravity in his descent. With the help of Mercury and with some difficulty, Jupiter transformed himself from his state as a god to that of a mortal.

Mercury had already prepared the faithful wife for the return of Amphitryon, to whom she had promised fidelity or suicide if she knowingly deceived him. Jupiter whetted his appetite for love by demanding admission to her bed as a lover, not as a husband. It was not enough to love within the union of marriage—the added fillip was to be the tantalizingly illegal husband-seducer. With guileless logic, Alkmena swore fidelity to her vows and refused to open her gates and admit the false husband to her chambers as a lover. As her husband, however, he gained easy entry through the gates, which had been unlocked all the while.

Mercury thoughtfully held back the dawn until Jupiter consummated the union, and he took the precaution of informing the universe that Jupiter had made another mortal conquest so that the proper celestial eruptions would signify the seduction. He also practiced a caprice of his own and had the real Amphitryon leave the battle and return to Alkmena the next day. This was only fair, since Jupiter, as had been his practice, would reveal his true identity to Alkmena with the coming of dawn and take leave of her in a burst of ego-satisfying, celestial glory.

Mercury and Jupiter, however, had underestimated the power of Alkmena. Alkmena, because she was a woman, was more than a match for Jupiter. When dawn finally arrived, she was on her patio placidly eating breakfast fruit, while Jupiter, the traditional ravisher of innocent womanhood, lolled in the drowsy sensuality of her bed. When he joined her, he tried to reveal his true identity, but he was thwarted at every turn by Alkmena's charming and unclouded humanistic approach to divinity. She possessed a clarity and lack of religious fervency that perhaps resembled naïveté, although in truth her attitude was more indicative of admirable simplicity and faithfulness in the gods.

Jupiter, having satisfied his desires, and knowing that if his true identity was revealed Alkmena would kill herself and his unborn child, wished to stroke his holy ego by paying a formal celestial visit to Alkmena, thereby legalizing their secret union. Mercury made the official proclamation of the impending visit, and Leda, Queen of Sparta, who had had some previous knowledge of heavenly unions, paid a call on Alkmena. Leda described her encounter with the heavenly swan.

Alkmena, having discovered that Leda longed for another encounter with Jupiter, persuaded the queen to take her place in the bedchamber. Jupiter would visit her in the form of Amphitryon, for he had a habit of appearing in the form most desired by his earthly mates. Leda agreed, and the real Amphitryon arrived. He was mistaken for Jupiter, and was sent into the palace. Only when Jupiter himself appeared to Alkmena did she realize her mistake.

The resolution of the provocative situation was brought about by the resourceful Alkmena. She asked if perhaps Jupiter would forgo the celestial visit for which she was so evidently unprepared, and remain only friends with her. Jupiter quickly agreed to this strange relationship and assured the suspicious Alkmena that he had never visited her before—as her lover. Jupiter then gave his blessing to Alkmena and Amphitryon and bid them name their unborn child Hercules. As an afterthought, he offered to be "godfather" to the child.

Critical Evaluation:

Jean Giraudoux began his writing career with the Paris newspaper *Le Matin*, for which he wrote many stories. It was a job that introduced him to a number of figures in the literary world. Next, he launched a career as a novelist, but it was not until 1928, with the performance of his play *Siegfried*, that his name became widely known. He followed up this success a year later with a greater one when *Amphitryon 38* was presented. Popular as these plays were, however, Giraudoux was not taken seriously by the intellectual audience until the production of his 1935 play, *Tiger at the Gates*. The major theme concerns the inevitability of war, and the possibility of another war with Germany was much on the minds of Giraudoux's French audience—of people throughout the world—in 1935.

Giraudoux's other employment, as an inspector general of diplomatic posts abroad, did not prevent him from continuing to turn out plays and novels, and his drama *Electra* (1937), as the title suggests, continued his practice of using ancient Greece for the setting, a distancing device to help his audience see themselves more clearly. In his 1939 play, *Ondine*, he availed himself of a German legend concerning a water nymph.

A number of Giraudoux's plays and stories were published and presented posthumously. Critical acclaim waxed throughout the 1950's and later, and Giraudoux's plays have been performed many times in all parts of the world. His major theme, the reconciliation of the ideal with the real, has proven popular in decades of rapid social change, decades that have required continual readjustment on the part of those who have had to live through them. One of his favorite devices—putting contemporary sentiments and expressions in the mouths of figures from ancient legends—provides the pleasures of incongruity. This device is well illustrated by *Amphitryon 38*. The number presumably signifies that the author is aware of the fact that many writers before him have made use of this legend, although there may have been more or fewer than thirty-seven precursors. Gods and mortals alike give the impression that they are acting in roles, rather than being themselves; they take themselves either too seriously or not quite seriously enough; they insist too much on their identities, or they are too offhand with them. They may bear the names and wear the costumes of the gods and heroes of ancient Greece, but they appear to suffer some impairment of memory about who they are and how they should act. Another way of saying this is to point out that they appear to be what they are in truth: contemporary people dressed up as, and pretending to be, ancient Greeks. This incongruity encourages readers to think that, superficial (and amusing) distinctions aside, the ancients were not much different from people today, and there is a human nature whose relationship to the cosmos and to the divine transcends social change. Another effect of this technique is to bestow some of the dignity of the old myths upon the contemporary world, turning what would otherwise be a 1920's drawing-room comedy into something loftier, an embodied disquisition upon man, woman, and the divine. Giraudoux's interest in the institution of marriage drives the drama. For a man of his day, Giraudoux was something of a feminist, and Alkmena evinces his feminism. It is necessary to exempt her character from most of the preceding generalities. Seriousness has its home in her, in this play. None of the other characters can match her for depth and variety. She is not without flaws, but these only serve to enhance her credibility; for example, having persuaded Jupiter not to insist on making love with her, she worries that she is losing her sex appeal. Beside her, even Mercury, a glib and witty figure, and certainly Amphitryon and Jupiter, look flat and two-dimensional.

The play concerns the irrational forces that bring about passionate love and lust and that cause wars to be fought, won, and lost. The gods rule over these—or are people's creations, on whom people lay the blame for their irrationality. As mere mortals, what can people do when taken over by divine madness? What can people do, as sometimes rational creatures, to regulate their lives, to spare pain to themselves and to others, to live at one with the cosmos? The answers mostly lie with Alkmena. She has none of Leda's giddy lust and vanity; Alkmena would rather not lie with Jupiter. She does not wish for immortality; she has no envy of the gods. She loves her husband, and she wants only their faithfulness to each other. If, nevertheless, she commits adultery with Jupiter, and she contrives affairs so that Amphitryon is adulterous with Leda, and if she is pregnant with Hercules, Jupiter's son, still, none of these deeds or results are within her capacity to prevent or avoid. In this way, Giraudoux's play exudes an air of forgiveness, of tolerance and acceptance. Mortals have limits, and ignorance and forgetfulness can prove to be happy failings. Deceit, where it offers and intends no harm, may be preferable to the truth; it can certainly be kinder.

"Critical Evaluation" by David Bromige

Bibliography:
Lemaître, Georges. *Jean Giraudoux: The Writer and His Work*. New York: Frederick Ungar, 1971. Usefully incisive analysis of many of the plays; particularly sound on *Amphitryon 38*.
LeSage, Laurent. *Jean Giraudoux: His Life and Works*. University Park: Pennsylvania State University Press, 1959. Another of the basic studies. Good on the relationship of technique and style to content.
Raymond, Agnes. *Jean Giraudoux: The Theatre of Victory and Defeat*. Amherst: University of Massachusetts Press, 1966. Political analysis of the plays, including their relationship to war.
Reilly, John H. *Jean Giraudoux*. Boston: Twayne, 1978. One of the better studies in the Twayne series, this book examines each work, whether dramatic or literary, in chronological order, and offers an engaging discussion of the role that predestination plays in *Amphitryon 38*, and also of the harmful effects of the ideal upon humans, and the possibly beneficent effects of deceit. Notes the influence of the German playwright Heinrich von Kleist's play, *Amphitryon* (1807), in turn based on Molière's *Amphitryon* (1668).

ANABASIS

Type of work: Poetry
Author: Saint-John Perse (Alexis Saint-Léger Léger, 1887-1975)
Type of plot: Allegory
Time of plot: Indeterminate
Locale: The East
First published: Anabase, 1924 (English translation, 1930)

> *Principal characters:*
> THE SPEAKER, the poet
> THE LEADER, an unidentified man who tells the story
> THE STRANGER, an unidentified man
> THE WOMEN, a group of young women met by the Leader and his troops

The Story:

In the opening song, the Leader, unidentified, described the foaling of a colt under bronze tree leaves. A passing Stranger placed bitter berries in the Speaker's hands. The Speaker's exclamations evoked far-off provinces, the call of a trumpet, and winged movement. From the bronze tree came a great noise, forces of life and death expressing themselves, as the Stranger beckoned to roads leading to unknown destinations.

In canto 1, the Leader recounted how, with honor and dignity, he founded his law and built a primitive society in a coastal region, not yet knowing the name of the sun but realizing the potential of humanity to dream of achieving glory. The Leader declared that he would spend one more year among his followers, not because he wished to trace towns along the sloping landscape but because he desired to live in the community he had created. The Leader communicated the aspirations of his people, spiritual and eternal, to strive to discover the unknown, to uncover the cosmic forces that feed humanity's desires. He repeated his intent to stay for one more year among his own, although recognizing that his glory was upon the seas.

In canto 2, the Leader and his followers walked along slopes covered in the linen of the Greats, exposed to the air. The Leader spoke of a man's desire for a woman and her daughter, a primordial impulse liberated by a sea breeze that blew inland, scattering the linen like a priest torn into pieces.

In canto 3, at barley harvest, the Leader recounted how visiting foreign dignitaries ate at a table at his door. The Assayer of Weights and Measures, with the remains of insects and bits of straw in his beard, returned after surveying the flora and fauna of the region. A society that was no longer nomadic was being founded. Illuminated by the Sun's power, the natural order was challenged by the newly organized forces of civilization. The Leader spoke of the danger of illusion, of questioning the reality of things. As a man of action, the Leader condemned idle contemplation of one's sadness and began to specify the members of this new society: princes, ministers, captains, priests, grammarians, and tailors. Finally, the Leader, enveloped by the strong smells of the world around him, condemned the contemplation of death in the present.

The founding of the City, built of stone and bronze, was described by the Leader in canto 4. No longer surrounded by encampments on the hills, the unidentified port city received tall ships laden with grain. However, in the midst of the bustling activity, a dead ass floated in the port's dead water, a sign of the stagnation and destruction that might befall this civilization. Blacksmiths, mules, bankers, the druggist's wares, festivals, and tumults were contrasted to those who, keeping watch on the hillside, refused to become part of the City. A dealer in flasks like his father, a sole man strode forth toward the beginning of the desert.

Following the foundation of the City, the Leader felt the need of solitude and the desire to depart in canto 5. Squadrons of stars beckoned to him, and at dawn the Stranger of the opening song reappeared, and the colt, born in the opening song, nuzzled its chin into the hands of a child. The sudden presence of the Stranger, embodiment of transcendental forces, suggested the imminent departure of those wishing to continue their nomadic discoveries.

The Leader, now a powerful military governor, enjoyed omnipotence and triumph against invading forces. In canto 6, a call to the horsemen, now dismounted among the crops, was heard. Future expeditions to impoverished, weakened countries were near at hand.

The Leader described the ephemeral nature of civilization. In canto 7, all was transient; of this the Leader was acutely aware. Like camels, hills marched in silence toward this civilization, kneeling at the plains as a beckoning force. Evoking deserts, they invited nomadic wanderings. Voices proclaimed the erection of protecting walls as the shadow of a great bird, a symbol of life and movement, passed over the Leader's face.

Canto 8 recounts the long march of humanity, begun once again. Nomads' laws and visions of swaying grass and horsemen on the move: these were the fundamental elements of this voyage whose Leader remained an eternal wanderer, committed to the quest, not for personal glory but for the progress of civilization.

Moving westward through the desert in canto 9, having forsaken the temporal nature of his own society, the Leader was addressed by one of a group of young women who greeted the expedition and announced great blessings. The woman spoke of the vine of the womb, the fecundity of the female body, and earthly pleasures. A union between men and women created a new order.

In the final canto, the tenth, this new union was celebrated. Sacrifice of colts on the tombs of children, purification of widows, consecration of monuments and flags, and a general rebuilding of this formerly ruined society were the first activities. Diverse vocations were enumerated to show the array of duties and interests among the citizens, from the toll gatherer to the man with the falcon to he who dwelt in a country of great rains to the man learned in science. Finally, the Leader, who incarnated the conquering spirit of humanity, remained conscious of the call from faraway lands in dream, of the eternal beckoning from exotic, fertile countries.

In the song which closes *Anabasis*, the Leader and his horse stopped by a tree full of turtledoves. The young colt of the introductory song had been carried forward by time toward maturation. The Leader, supremely fulfilled, whistled sweetly and wished peace to the dying.

Critical Evaluation:

In 1960, Saint-John Perse, career diplomat and poet, received the Nobel Prize in Literature. In 1916, he had been posted to the French legation in Peking and, during his China years, which lasted until 1921, traveled in Korea, Manchuria, Mongolia, and the Gobi Desert. The composition of *Anabasis* dates from this period. He is said to have written this work, his best known, in a Taoist temple overlooking the caravan routes leading to the northwest. T. S. Eliot published his English version of the poem, the first English translation of it, in 1930.

Perse explained that the poem, whose title means "military expedition" in the tradition of such mighty military Leaders as Alexander the Great, depicts the loneliness of action and the breadth of human potential. A prose poem, it is allegorical; the action is seen through the deeds and words of the nameless Leader, who recites the text. Leader of a nomadic people, he remains faceless throughout the entire work, revealing his innermost thoughts as he speaks but never identifying his ancestry or the elements of his personal life. A similar lack of detail is noticed in all the other characters as well as in the time and place of the poem. Perse's travels in Asia inspired the sweeping images he depicts of nomadic movement and conquest, although the geographical setting, apart from references to maritime and desert areas, is without identifying detail. The historical period is depicted with equal ambiguity for, although the peoples evoked in *Anabasis* live in a relatively complex society, as seen in allusions to agriculture, architecture, blacksmithing, and libraries, a precise time frame in world history is not conveyed to the reader. Perse's objective is to capture the essence of human action in the process of realization and, in doing so, compensate for the lack of precise spatial and temporal references by creating sweeping epic verses that carry the reader along with the Leader on his conquests and discoveries.

Perse's encyclopedic vocabulary, the use of somewhat obscure words—*anabasis* for example—is characteristic of his unique style. While his vocabulary conveys extreme precision, and in the contexts of botany and zoology is almost scientific in its specificity, the structure of individual cantos in *Anabasis* is often elliptical and sometimes difficult to follow. Perse does not guide the reader by means of a simple, straightforward style. Rather, his complex images at times produce cryptic meanings that do not always reveal themselves to the reader but that add to the mystery that emanates from the poem. The characters, for example, receive little realistic differentiation, allowing them to convey more than individual personalities; they express the essence of pioneers, adventurers, and nomads. More important than the characters themselves is the ultimate action of the poem: the foundation and organization of a society. The captivating rhythm of *Anabasis* is built on symmetries, alliterations, assonances, and internal rhymes that carry the reader along in the same majestic and expansive movements that characterize the anabasis. Human movement is, therefore, at the core of the poem's imagery. The use of language is often elliptical, reflecting the idea of movement and omitting linking elements that follow a standard language usage that renders a text easily understandable. Perse's style, lyric and evocative, follows an internal logic different from standardized usage, but that conveys, for example, the urgency of movement or an act in progress.

Skillful translations of *Anabasis* exist in Russian, Italian, and German. The fact that the poem is so widely read is testimony to the manner in which its grandeur captivates the reader through the portrayal of humanity's collective history, of its epic aspirations to establish modern civilization, and of the constant yearning to surpass the here and now. The universal appeal of Perse's work is undoubtedly the presence of allegory and symbolism, elements that unite us in a shared cultural experience that transcends time and space.

Saint-John Perse is the poet of humanity's struggle to surpass itself. His gift of poetic language achieves its apotheosis in complex and exotic images: "Like milch-camels, gentle beneath the shears and sewn with mauve scars, let the hills march forth under the scheme of the harvest sky." His poetry functions as myth in a modern world, paradoxically subject to fragmentation and disunity, for it expresses a vision of history that reminds one of the cohesive influence of collective action, of our past, and of a future that will forever loom on the horizon of the human imagination.

Kenneth W. Meadwell

Bibliography:
Galand, René. *Saint-John Perse.* New York: Twayne, 1972. A complete general introduction to

Saint-John Perse's poetry. Includes a concise study of *Anabasis* as well as a short, annotated bibliography of the major critical studies (mostly in French) of his work.

Knodel, Arthur. *Saint-John Perse: A Study of His Poetry*. Edinburgh, Scotland: Edinburgh University Press, 1966. An excellent study of all of Saint-John Perse's poetry. Includes some biographical details and in-depth analyses of *Anabasis*.

_____. "Towards an Understanding of *Anabasis*." *Publications of the Modern Language Association of America* 79 (June, 1964): 329-343. An excellent and in-depth study of the structure and recurring elements of *Anabasis*.

Little, Roger. *Saint-John Perse*. London: Athlone Press, 1973. A brief overview of Saint-John Perse's work, including some comments on *Anabasis*. Includes a short biographical sketch.

_____. *Saint-John Perse: A Bibliography for Students of His Poetry*. London: Grant and Cutler, 1971. An excellent list of studies of all of Saint-John Perse's work.

ANABASIS

Type of work: History
Author: Xenophon (c. 431-c. 354 B.C.E.)
First transcribed: Kurou anabasis, between 394 and 371 B.C.E. (English translation, 1623)

> *Principal personages:*
> XENOPHON, the narrator
> CYRUS, son of King Darius of Persia
> ARTAXERXES, the older son of Darius
> TISSAPHERNES, a Persian general
> CLEARCHUS, a Spartan exile, a general under Cyrus
> CHIRISOPHUS, a Spartan mercenary captain
> AGASIAS, a Stymphalian captain in the Greek army
> PROXENUS, a Theban mercenary captain under Cyrus

For centuries, the *Anabasis* has been recognized as a stirring piece of historical narrative, but dismissed as lacking in intellectual substance because of what some have seen as overzealousness on Xenophon's part toward self-justification. Unquestionably, the portrait of Xenophon the military leader that emerges from the text is exceedingly flattering. The tone often shows great objectivity and restraint, but the stirring record of the Greeks rising to the many challenges they faced in struggling to survive against both military and political obstacles can hardly be called impartial. Unfortunately, the propagandistic qualities of the story have often overshadowed the literary and intellectual merits of a work important in its own right.

One must remember, however, that historiography had a different meaning for the Greeks than it does for later scholars. Like most historians of antiquity, including his predecessor and model Thucydides, Xenophon takes great liberty with speechmaking, inventing lengthy speeches to place in the mouths of characters who represent various types of those whom he respects or reviles. One has a sense, however, that he represents the major actions he describes with great accuracy, and his analysis of motives sets his story apart from mere chronicles. Xenophon also examines larger moral and social issues important to his countrymen. Through his analysis of character and motive, and through his careful structuring of events to present his readers clear parallels which highlight comparisons and contrasts, Xenophon elevates his narrative to an analysis of moral qualities, revealing something of the nature of his society and its values. In *Anabasis,* Xenophon offers a valuable lesson to readers about the impact of practicing virtue, especially in times of crisis.

The *Anabasis* is Xenophon's personal account of one of the most amazing marches in history, the march of a Greek army numbering ten thousand men from Babylon to the Black Sea. Xenophon played a leading role in the march and was, in effect, supreme commander of the army, although he refused the actual title. This account of the Persian expedition begins with the recital of Cyrus' effort to wrest the Persian throne from his brother Artaxerxes, but its principal part is concerned with the march from Babylon after the death of Cyrus at the battle of Cunaxa.

After the death of King Darius of Persia, his son Artaxerxes took possession of the throne. Cyrus, the younger son, with the support of his mother, Parysatis, began to build up an army to wrest control of Persia from his brother. By pretending to need troops to fight the Persian general Tissapheres and the Pisidians, Cyrus acquired armies from the Peloponnese, the Chersonese (under the Spartan exile Clearchus), the Thessalians (under Aristippus), the Boeotians (under Proxenus), the Stymphalians (under Sophaenetus), and the Achaeans (under Socrates, the mercenary).

Cyrus marched form Sardis to Tarsus, gathering the elements of his army. At Tarsus the troops under Clearchus refused to move forward, arguing that they had not been hired to fight against the king. Clearchus dealt with the mutiny by first enlisting the loyalty of the men to himself (by pretending he would stay with them and not with Cyrus) and then by supporting Cyrus' claim that the enemy was not the king, but Abrocomas, one of the king's commanders.

By marches averaging fifteen miles a day Cyrus brought his army from Tarsus to Issus, the last city in Cilicia, where he was joined by ships from the Peloponnese. The march continued through the gates of Cilicia and Syria without opposition.

When Cyrus arrived at the city of Myriandrus, Xenias the Arcadian and Pasion the Megarian deserted the army. Cyrus refused to pursue or punish them, declaring that they had served him well in the past.

The army moved on to the Euphrates and the city of Thapsacus. Here the word was finally given to the Greek soldiers that the campaign was to be against King Artaxerxes. At first the soldiers refused to go further without more pay, but when Menon led his forces across the Euphrates in order to set a good example and to win Cyrus' favor, and when Cyrus promised to give each soldier additional pay, the Greeks crossed the river in force, making the crossing on foot. Since the Euphrates was usually too high for such a passage, the army was encouraged by this good sign.

When they reached the Arabian desert, Cyrus forced the troops to long marches in order to bring them to water and fodder. He kept discipline by ordering important Persians to help with the wagons when the road was difficult. A quarrel between the soldiers of Menon and Clearchus was halted by Cyrus' warning that they would all be destroyed if they fought among themselves.

Orontas, a Persian under Cyrus, attempted to transfer his army to the king's forces, but Cyrus learned of the plan by intercepting a letter from Orontas to the king. At a trial held in Cyrus' tent Orontas was condemned to death. He was never seen again.

Cyrus moved through Babylonia and prepared for battle with King Artaxerxes, but when the king's forces failed to take a stand at a defensive ditch which had been dug, Cyrus proceeded with less caution.

The two armies met at Cunaxa, and the Greeks put the opposing Persian forces to flight. Cyrus, with six hundred Persian cavalry, charged the center of the Persian line in order to reach the king; but after wounding King Artaxerxes, Cyrus was himself killed by a javelin blow. The cavalrymen with Cyrus were killed, except for the forces under Ariaeus, who hastily retreated.

While the main Greek armies under Clearchus and Proxenus were pursuing the Persians, the king's troops broke into Cyrus' camp and seized his mistresses, money, and property. Tissaphernes then joined the king's force and attacked the Greeks, but again the Greeks put the Persians to flight.

Phalinus, a messenger from King Artaxerxes, attempted to force Clearchus to surrender, but the Spartan, regarding the Greeks as victors, refused. The Greeks then allied themselves again with Ariaeus, who had been second to Cyrus, and pledged their support of him. When Ariaeus refused to attempt further battle against the king, the joint decision was to take a longer route back, putting as much distance as possible between their forces and the king's army.

The Greeks began their march and by accident came close to the king's army, frightening it into retreat. A truce was then arranged, and the king transferred supplies to the Greeks. Finally a treaty was made which provided safe conduct for the Greek army, with Tissaphernes as escort.

Many of the Greek leaders suspected Tissaphernes of treachery, but Clearchus, reassured by a conference with the Persian general, went to Tissaphernes with four of his generals and twenty of his captains in order that those who had been slandering the Persian commander could be named. Then, at a signal from the treacherous Tissaphernes, the Persians massacred the captains and took the generals as prisoners. The generals—Clearchus, Proxenus, Monon, Agias, and Socrates—were taken to the king and beheaded. Ariaeus was discovered to have been involved with Tissaphernes in this act of treachery.

After the capture of the generals, Xenophon, who had accompanied the Greek army at the urging of his friend Proxenus, bolstered the courage of the Greeks and urged that new generals and captains be appointed. The army responded to this decisive act of leadership.

Mithridates, a Persian commander who had been with Cyrus, returned to the Greeks and pretended to be friendly, but he suddenly attacked them and had to be driven back. The Greeks were then pursued by Tissaphernes and harassed by attacks from the Carduchi as they crossed the mountains to Armenia. Hearing that Tiribazus, the governor of Western Armenia who had promised the Greeks safe passage, planned to attack them, the Greek generals ordered a raid on Tiribazus' camp and then quickly resumed the march across snow-covered plains. The soldiers suffered from snow blindness and frostbite.

To encourage the soldiers, Xenophon often worked and marched with the men. He arranged to procure guides from the Armenians and conceived the idea of capturing the mountain pass beyond the Phasis River by climbing it at night. Chirisophus and Xenophon were the principal leaders of the march.

In the country of the Taochi the Greeks were delayed by an attack from a fortification out of which large boulders were rolled down a hill, but when the stones were exhausted and as the opposing forces—including women and children—began to leap from the walls, the Greeks took possession. Finally, after fighting the Chalybes, the Greeks came within sight of the sea on their arrival at Trapezus.

Chirisophus was sent to secure ships, and the Greeks, now numbering eighty-six hundred troops of their original ten thousand, went on plundering expeditions for supplies. When Chirisophus was delayed, the available ships were loaded with the sick and wounded and with women, children, and baggage, while the rest of the army continued by land. After battling their way through the country of the barbarous Mossynoici, the Greeks arrived in the Euxine. There Xenophon considered founding a city, but he rejected the idea when the others opposed him. Some of the generals were critical of Xenophon's disciplinary measures, but he was able to defend himself against their charges.

The Greeks bought food and also plundered supplies from the Paphlagonians. During their stay in that territory the captains went to Xenophon and asked him to be commander-in-chief of the army, but after reflection and sacrifices to the gods he decided that it would be better both for himself and the army if the command were either kept divided or given to some other man. When Chirisophus was elected commander-in-chief, Xenophon willingly accepted a subordinate position.

By this time the Greeks had enough ships to carry all of their men, and they sailed along the Paphlagonian coast from Harmene, the port of Sinope, to Heraclea, a Greek city in the country of the Maryandyni. The army then split into three parts because of a disagreement about demanding supplies from Heraclea. The Arcadians and Achaeans, who favored the demand, formed one body; Chirisophus, no longer in supreme command, headed a second body of troops; and Xenophon commanded the remainder. The Arcadians landed in Thrace and attacked some villages. When they got into difficulties, they were rescued by Xenophon and his force. At Port Calpe the three armies were reunited.

Many Greeks were killed by the Bithynians while hunting for supplies, but the Greek forces finally achieved victory. A quarrel involving Cleander, the Spartan governor of Byzantium, and Agasias, a Greek captain who had rescued one of his men from arrest by Dexippus, a traitorous Greek acting by Cleander's order, was settled by Xenophon's diplomacy.

Eventually the army crossed the straits from Asia to Byzantium. After some difficulty with Anaxibius, a Spartan admiral at Byzantium, the Greeks joined forces with King Seuthes of Thrace and participated in numerous raids on Thracian villages for supplies. When King Seuthes withheld pay from the Greeks, Xenophon was blamed, but after a long inquiry, during which Xenophon was accused of being too much concerned with the welfare of the ordinary soldier, King Seuthes finally gave the Greeks the money due them.

Xenophon then led the army out of Thrace by sailing to Lampsacus, marching through the Troad, and crossing Mount Ida to the plain of Thebes. When the army reached Pergamon in Mysia, Xenophon conducted a partially successful raid against the Persian Asidates. He then turned the Greek army over to Thibron, the Spartan commander, who used the Greeks to war against Tissaphernes and Pharnabazus, a Persian governor.

Updated by Laurence W. Mazzeno

Bibliography:

Anderson, J. K. *Xenophon*. New York: Charles Scribner's Sons, 1974. Complete and scholarly study of Xenophon's life and works. Judges the *Anabasis* as the work of a reporter, not of a historian. Twelve pages of plates, a list of important dates, suggestions for further reading, and concise footnotes enrich this study.

Livingstone, R. W. *The Pageant of Greece*. Oxford, England: The Clarendon Press, 1923. A scholarly history of the literature and culture of classical Greece, with a broad introduction followed by excerpts from the major writers and commentary on them. Characterizes Xenophon as "a man of action" and praises his "natural, unaffected style."

Murray, Augustus Taber. Introduction to *The Anabasis of Xenophon*, by Xenophon. Boston: Scott, Foresman, 1914. An invaluable introduction covers the main topics in Xenophon's life, sketches the literary qualities of the *Anabasis*, and traces Cyrus and his expedition with care.

Nussbaum, G. B. *The Ten Thousand: A Study in Social Organization and Action in Xenophon's "Anabasis."* Leiden, The Netherlands: E. J. Brill, 1967. A scholarly study that addresses basic questions about military organization. Separate sections study the common soldiers, the captains, the generals, the assembly. Others treat the public and the leadership.

Xenophon. *The Persian Expedition*. Translated by Rex Warner. New York: Penguin Books, 1972. Excellent paperback edition, with a map and an informative introduction by George Cawkwell. A six-page glossary of names is useful, as is the comprehensive index. The complicated historical context is spelled out in detail.

THE ANATOMY OF MELANCHOLY

Type of work: Psychology
Author: Robert Burton (1577-1640)
First published: 1621

In the seventeenth century, ideas and theories, old and new, clamored for attention and consideration; rational thought and science had not yet begun to classify, assimilate, accept, and reject the great mass of learning that had accumulated over the centuries since ancient times. More than that, each scholar attempted, in that age before specialization, to master all human knowledge. Such was the age in which Robert Burton, who styled himself Democritus, Jr., wrote *The Anatomy of Melancholy*, which in many ways exemplifies the times in which it was written.

Burton was more than an educated man; he gave his life to learning, and much of his vast hoard of erudition found its way into his book. Ostensibly a study on melancholy, his work, before it was finished, absorbed into its pages most of the learning of Burton's time, either through his examination of everything he could associate with melancholy or through his many digressions.

The Anatomy of Melancholy is difficult to categorize. Its organization is complex, almost incoherent. An outline for each of the three "partitions" of the book, complicated though each is, does not indicate all that Burton manages to cram into the pages. The device seems really to be Burton's way of following a pseudoscientific convention, a style of his times. Perhaps the best way to categorize the book is to regard it as an informal and heterogeneous collection of essays on human dissatisfaction with the universe, as people of the seventeenth century understood the universe, and on ways in which that dissatisfaction could be cured. In that sense, at least, the book is a treatise on psychology, although the digressions Burton made are so numerous and involved that the reader sometimes wonders whether the author may not have lost his way.

Burton assuredly has no special theme or thesis he is attempting to prove. One critic has said that all *The Anatomy of Melancholy* proves is that a seventeenth century classical education could produce an astounding amount of recondite learning. Burton presents no set of principles, scientific or otherwise, to be proved, but he does bring to his work a tremendous zest for learning. This sense of gusto often puts the contemporary reader at a disadvantage, for Burton lards his paragraphs heavily, perhaps no English writer more so, with tags of Latin prose and poetry. Too few contemporary readers have enough knowledge of Latin to enable them to read tags in that language. The quotations are from countless authorities, many of them long since forgotten. A typical page, for example, cites Leo Afer, Lipsius, Zuinger, Seneca, Tully, Livy, Rhasis, Montaltus, Celsus, and Comesius. This host of references, allusions, and quotations makes Burton's style seem heavy. Actually, he wrote in the tradition of Francis Bacon, studiously striving for a plain, even colloquial and racy, style. Like Bacon, too, he frequently begins a topic with an allusion, an anecdote, or a quotation as a springboard and from such a start often moves to whimsy and humor.

Sections of *The Anatomy of Melancholy* are famous for various reasons. The opening letter, a foreword to the reader, is well known for its satirical tone and its catalog of the follies of humanity. Humor and whimsy account for the popularity of the sections on marriage and bachelorhood, on the "love of learning or overmuch study," and on the nature of spirits. The last "partition," ostensibly on melancholy growing out of love and religion, has many short synopses of world-famous stories. One contemporary critic has shown that if Elizabethan literature had somehow been lost during the intervening centuries, scholars could reconstruct a good bit of its nature from a study of *The Anatomy of Melancholy* alone.

The pervading tone of the book is satirical, but Burton's satire is always realistic, reflecting the point of view of an objective, even detached, observer of human folly. He begins the first "partition" with a contrast between people as they were in the Garden of Eden and people as they have been since the Fall. The result of human transgression, according to Burton, is that humanity has since suffered a universal malady, a melancholy that affects mind and body. Since he regards the individual as a whole, from a humanistic point of view, he proceeds to mingle sympathetically both religion and science. Much of the learning and many of the notions and theories which found their way into the book are nowadays of historical interest only, such as the analysis of the four bodily humors, the discussion of the understanding and the will (as the seventeenth century used those terms), and the discussion of the nature of angels and devils. Still amusing, however, are his discussions of old age, diet, heredity, exercise, and constipation. While admitting that none is a panacea, Burton offers various cures for melancholy, including prayer, practice of the arts, the study of geography, coffee, traditional games, and moderate amounts of wine and other drink.

Like many another learned man in history, the writer often found himself discoursing on subjects on which there is perhaps no answer. Thus it is in his critique on marriage, which he delivers under the heading of "Cure of Love-Melancholy," that Burton, who himself never married, first quotes twelve reasons in favor of marriage, taking them from Jacobus de Voragine. Those arguments in favor of marriage include statements that a wife is a source of comfort and assistance in adversity, that she will drive away melancholy at home, that she brings an additional supply of the "sweet company of kinsmen," and that she enables a man to have fair and happy children. Immediately following these arguments, Burton himself adds an equal number of contrary arguments. He suggests that a wife will aggravate a man's misery in adversity, will scold a man at home, bring a host of needy relatives, and make him a cuckold to rear another man's child. At the last, all Burton can say is that marriage, like much of life, is filled with chance: "'Tis a hazard both ways I confess, to live single or to marry."

A sound observer of human nature, Burton also shows sympathetic understanding for his fellow beings. Living in an age when religious beliefs maintained a strong hold on men's and women's emotions, reinforced by fears of Satan and by Calvinistic doctrines of predestination and the depravity of humanity, Burton advocates that people afflicted by religious melancholy turn from contemplation of the more awful aspects of God and religion to such aspects of God as his infinite mercy and love. Burton also advocates recreation of an honest sort as an antidote to too much religion. In this, as in other ways, Burton stands out as being ahead of his time.

Bibliography:
Chapple, Anne S. "Robert Burton's Geography of Melancholy." *Studies in English Literature 1500-1900* 33, no. 1 (Winter, 1993): 99-130. Examines the influence of the contemporary proliferation of maps and charts (for which Burton had a natural affinity) on the *Anatomy*, a work that Burton compared to an explorer's task in its examination of uncharted territories.
Dewey, Nicholas. "Robert Burton's Melancholy." *Modern Philology* 68 (1971): 292-293. Notes the early shift in the preferred abbreviation of the title, from *Melancholy* to *Anatomy*. Dewey sees this shift as a move away from scholarly interest in the psychological and toward antiquarian delight in miscellaneous learning.
Mueller, William R. "Robert Burton's Frontispiece." *PMLA* 64 (1949): 1074-1088. Reproduces

the original illustration which introduced the work and examines each of its block pictures and their verses as representations of Burton's themes—the introduction of the philosopher Democritus Junior, melancholy qualities such as jealousy and solitude, and victims of melancholy.

Patrick, J. Max. "Robert Burton's Utopianism." *Philological Quarterly* 27, no. 4 (1948): 345-358. Regards the Utopia described in the introduction to *The Anatomy of Melancholy* as the earliest such vision written in English; analyzes its components and its developing style.

Renaker, David. "Robert Burton's Tricks of Memory." *PMLA* 87 (1972): 391-396. Examines the means by which Burton was able to quote, though often inaccurately, from memory or from sketchy notes. Renaker examines the errors.

AND QUIET FLOWS THE DON

Type of work: Novel
Author: Mikhail Sholokhov (1905-1984)
Type of plot: Historical realism
Time of plot: 1913-1918
Locale: Tatarsk, Russia
First published: Tikhii Don, 1928-1940 (*And Quiet Flows the Don*, 1934; *The Don Flows Home to the Sea*, 1940; complete translation, *And Quiet Flows the Don*, 1967)

Principal characters:
GREGOR MELEKHOV, a Cossack
PIOTRA, Gregor's brother
NATALIA, Gregor's wife
AKSINIA ASTAKHOVA, Gregor's mistress
BUNCHUK, a revolutionary leader

The Story:
The Melekhov family lived in the small village of Tatarsk, in the Don river basin of czarist Russia. Gregor, the oldest son, had a love affair with Aksinia, wife of his neighbor, Stepan Astakhov. Stepan was away serving a term in the army. In an effort to make his son settle down, Gregor's father arranged a marriage with Natalia Korshunov. Gregor never loved Natalia, and their relationship was a cold one. Soon Gregor went openly to Aksinia, and the affair became the village scandal.

When he heard the gossip, Gregor's father whipped him. Humiliated and angry, Gregor left home. With Aksinia, he became the servant of the Listnitsky family, well-to-do landowners who lived outside the village of Tatarsk. When Aksinia bore him a daughter, Gregor's father relented enough to pay a visit before Gregor left for the army.

In the meantime, Gregor's wife, Natalia, tried to commit suicide because Gregor did not return her love. She went back to her own home, but the Melekhovs asked her to come to them. She was glad to do so. When Gregor returned to Aksinia on his first leave from the army, he discovered that she had been unfaithful to him with Eugene Listnitsky, the young officer-son of his employer. Aksinia's daughter had died, and Gregor felt nothing but anger at his mistress. He fought with Eugene and whipped Aksinia as well. Then he returned to his own home, and there he and Natalia became reconciled. During the time he served in the army, Natalia bore twins, a boy and a girl.

In the war against the Central Powers, Gregor distinguished himself. Wounded, he was awarded the Cross of St. George, and so he became the first Chevalier in the village. While in the army, he met his brother, Piotra, and his enemy, Stepan Astakhov, who had sworn to kill him. On one occasion Gregor nevertheless saved Stepan's life during an attack.

Discontent was growing among the soldiers. Bolshevik agitators began to talk against the government and against a continuation of the war. In Eugene Listnitsky's company, an officer named Bunchuk was the chief agitator. He deserted before Listnitsky could hand him over to the authorities.

Then the provisional government of Kerensky was overthrown, and a Soviet Socialist Republic was established. Civil war broke out. The Cossacks, proud of their free heritage, were

233

strongly nationalistic and wanted an autonomous government for the Don region. Many of them joined the counterrevolutionists, under such men as Kornilov. Many returned to their homes in the Don basin. Gregor, joining the revolutionary forces, was made an officer of the Red Army.

Meanwhile, the revolutionary troops in Rostov were under attack. Bunchuk, the machine gunner, was prominent in the battle and in the administration of the local revolutionary government. He fell in love with a woman machine gunner, Anna Poodko, who was killed during an attack. The counterrevolutionary troops were successful, and the Red Army troops had to retreat.

Gregor returned to the village and resumed the ordinary life he had led before the war. News soon came that revolutionary troops were advancing on the village. When his neighbors prepared to flee, Gregor refused to do so. Stories of burning, looting, and rape spread throughout the countryside. A counterrevolutionary officer attempted to organize the villagers against the approaching enemy troops. He named Gregor as commander, but the nomination was turned down in anger because all the village knew that Gregor sympathized with the Reds, had fought with them. Instead, Gregor's brother Piotra was named commander.

The village forces marched out, and Gregor went with them. When they arrived at their destination, they found that the revolutionary troops had already been defeated and that the leaders had been captured. When Gregor asked what would happen to them, he was told they would be shot. Then Gregor came face-to-face with Podtielkov, his old revolutionary leader. When his former leader accused him of being a traitor and opportunist, all of Gregor's suppressed feelings of disgust and nationalism burst forth. He reminded Podtielkov that he and other Red leaders had ordered plenty of executions, and he charged that Podtielkov had sold out the Don Cossacks. The revolutionists died prophesying that the revolution would live. Gregor went back to his Cossack village.

Critical Evaluation:

And Quiet Flows the Don is Mikhail Sholokhov's main work, comprising four parts, and it is largely for this novel that Sholokhov won the Nobel Prize in 1965. Its title in the original means simply "the quiet Don," and it was published in English in two volumes (in 1934 and 1940) under two different titles: *And Quiet Flows the Don*, containing the first two parts, and *The Don Flows Home to the Sea*, containing the latter two parts).

The novel is of truly epic proportions. It starts sometime in the first decade of the twentieth century in the Don region of rural Russia and follows the fortunes of the Melekhov family through peacetime, World War I, and the revolution and civil war in Russia, concluding with the victory of the Bolsheviks in that civil war. Within that broad framework, the entire life of a nation within a nation—the Don Cossacks—is depicted: at peace and war, at work and play, through joys and sorrows, weddings, births, love, hatred, death, murder, even incest. The historical, sociological, and ethnographical aspects of the novel are not to be underestimated, although *And Quiet Flows the Don* is not truly a historical novel. Many events, places, and names are historical, to be sure, but there are also fictitious events and characters that make the novel a fictional creation.

As a result of circumstances beyond their control, the Cossacks were called upon toward the end of World War I to decide their future in a situation beyond their understanding. They had been living a secluded life for centuries, always regarding Moscow with suspicion and disapproval. Their only bond with the rest of Russia was their inexplicable love and veneration for the czar; when they had to live without him after his abdication, they were left adrift. Although Russians themselves (but mixed with other nationalities, especially those from Asia), they considered the outside world as intruding. Not well informed about the world's happenings and yet forced to participate in them, they were thrust into turbulent events and made numerous mistakes, yet the survival instinct kept them afloat. When the years-long upheaval ended, they found themselves bidding farewell to a life they had been living for centuries and adapting to a new life under the Bolsheviks, facing an uncertain future. No one exemplifies the fate of the Cossacks better than the protagonist of the novel, Gregor Melekhov.

At the beginning of the novel Gregor is a carefree, playful youth, whose only desire is to work on the farm and get as much as possible out of life, including amorous pleasures. After years of fighting for causes he does not fully understand, he loses almost all members of his family and faces an uncertain future himself. During those years he changes his allegiance from the czarist army to the revolutionaries, to the Whites, to the separatist Cossacks, back to the revolutionaries or Reds, to the outlaws, and finally comes to terms with the Bolsheviks. He thus becomes a hero in search of himself. Throughout these ordeals, Gregor possesses an uncanny sense of right and wrong, and every time he changes sides he follows his conscience. Although an uncommonly brave and fierce soldier, he is happiest working on his land in peace. He is not the positive hero of the kind required by the official Soviet literary standard in the 1920's and 1930's, because he does not "see the light" at the end and "change for the better." He cannot be called an antihero either, because of his basically healthy and constructive outlook. The closest classification is that of a Greek tragic hero, his tragic flaw being ignorance of the forces shaping his life—a flaw he shares with his entire nation.

Sholokhov succeeds in eschewing potentially didactic, politically overloaded subject matter through genuine artistry. His straightforward realism is sprinkled with poetic outbursts, especially when describing nature. His closeness to nature is expressed also in the employment of all senses when describing human action. Nearly all the action in the novel occurs on the surface of the narration; there is hardly any symbolism, and philosophical themes, if it may be said that they are there at all, are implied. The author keeps himself in the background, creating superb characters and letting them speak and act. The powerful dramatic quality of the action is underscored by the extraordinary time in history of the setting and the excessive amount of fighting and killing throughout the book. The story between Gregor and his neighbor's wife, Aksinia, adds love to the story. The striking objectivity in the presentation of the Russian Revolution makes *And Quiet Flows the Don* one of the outstanding novels of twentieth century literature.

"Critical Evaluation" by Vasa D. Mihailovich

Bibliography:
Ermolaev, Herman. *Mikhail Sholokhov and His Art.* Princeton, N.J.: Princeton University Press, 1982. One of the best studies of Sholokhov and his works by a native scholar trained in the West. *And Quiet Flows the Don* is treated extensively, especially the historical events and sources and Sholokhov's use of them.

Hallet, Richard. "Soviet Criticism of *Tikhy Don*, 1928-1940." *The Slavonic and East European Review* 46, no. 106 (1968): 60-74. A brief but substantive treatment of Sholokhov's difficulties with the authorities in publishing the novel. They did not like his objective presentation of the revolution.

Klimenko, Michael. *The World of Young Sholokhov: Vision of Violence.* North Quincy, Mass.: Christopher Publishing House, 1979. A useful study of Sholokhov's early works, with emphasis on *And Quiet Flows the Don*.

Medvedev, Roy. *Problems in the Literary Biography of Mikhail Sholokhov*. Cambridge, England: Cambridge University Press, 1977. A leading former Russian dissident discusses the controversy about the accusations of Sholokhov's plagiarism in writing *And Quiet Flows the Don*.

Muchnic, Helen. "Mikhail Sholokhov." In *From Gorky to Pasternak*. New York: Random House, 1961. Extensive essay on Sholokhov, the first part of which is devoted to *And Quiet Flows the Don*.

Simmons, Ernest J. *Russian Fiction and Soviet Ideology: Introduction to Fedin, Leonov, and Sholokhov*. New York: Columbia University Press, 1967. Evaluates Sholokhov within an ideological and political context. Simmons is one of the leading American scholars of Russian literature.

Stewart, D. H. *Mikhail Sholokhov: A Critical Introduction*. Ann Arbor: University of Michigan Press, 1967. A solid introduction to Sholokhov, with emphasis on *And Quiet Flows the Don*.

ANDERSEN'S FAIRY TALES

Type of work: Short fiction
Author: Hans Christian Andersen (1805-1875)
Type of plot: Fairy tales
Time of plot: Indeterminate
Locale: Denmark
First published: Eventyr, at intervals 1835-1872 (English translation, 1946)

Principal characters:
KAREN, the owner of the red shoes
THE UGLY DUCKLING
THE SNOW QUEEN
KAY, a little boy
GERDA, a little girl
THE SHEPHERDESS, a china figure
THE CHIMNEYSWEEP, her lover
THE EMPEROR
A TIN SOLDIER
A POOR SOLDIER

The Stories:

The Red Shoes. Karen was such a poor little girl that she had to go barefoot in winter. An old mother shoemaker felt sorry for her and made Karen a clumsy pair of shoes out of pieces of red felt. When Karen's mother died, the girl had to wear the red shoes to the funeral. An old lady, seeing Karen walking forlornly behind her mother's coffin, pitied her and took the child home. The old lady thought that the red shoes were ugly, and she burned them.

One day, Karen saw the queen and the little princess. The princess was dressed all in white, with beautiful red morocco shoes.

When the time came for Karen's confirmation, she needed new shoes. The old lady, almost blind, did not know that the shoes Karen picked out were red ones just like those the princess had worn. During the confirmation, Karen could think of nothing but her red shoes.

The next Sunday, as Karen went to her first communion, she met an old soldier with a crutch. After admiring the red shoes, he struck them on the soles and told them to stick fast when Karen danced. During the service, she could think only of her shoes. After church, she started to dance. The footman had to pick her up and take off her shoes before the old lady could take her home.

At a ball in town, Karen could not stop dancing. She danced out through the fields and up to the church. There an angel with a broad sword stopped her and told her she would dance until she became a skeleton, a warning to all other vain children.

She danced day and night until she came to the executioner's house. There she tapped on the window and begged him to come out and cut off her feet. When he chopped off her feet, they and the little red shoes danced off into the forest. The executioner made Karen wooden feet and crutches and taught her a psalm, and the parson gave her a home. Karen thought she had suffered enough to go to church, but each time she tried she saw the red shoes dancing ahead of her and was afraid. One Sunday, she stayed at home. As she heard the organ music, she read her prayer book humbly and begged help from God. Then she saw the angel again, not with a sword but with a green branch covered with roses. As the angel moved the branch, Karen felt that she was being carried off to the church. There she was so thankful that her heart broke, and her soul flew up to heaven.

The Ugly Duckling. A mother duck was sitting on a clutch of eggs. When the largest egg did not crack with the rest, an old matriarchal duck warned the setting fowl that she should let that egg alone; it would probably turn out to be a turkey. The egg, however, finally cracked, and out of it came the biggest, ugliest duckling ever seen in the barnyard. The other ducklings pecked it and chased it and made it so unhappy that it felt comfortable only when it was paddling in the pond. The mother duck was proud only of the very fine paddling the ugly duckling did.

The scorn heaped on his head was so bitter that the duckling ran away from home. He spent a miserable winter in the marsh. When spring came, he saw some beautiful white swans settle down on the water. He moved out to admire them as they came toward him with ruffled feathers. He bent down to await their attack, but as he looked in the water he saw that he was no longer a gray ugly duckling but another graceful swan. He was so glad then that he never thought to be proud but smiled when he heard some children say that he was the handsomest swan they had ever seen.

The Snow Queen. A very wicked hobgoblin once invented a mirror that reflected everything good as trivial and everything bad as monstrous; a good thought turned into a grin in the mirror. His cohorts carried it all over the earth and finally up to heaven to test the angels. There many good thoughts made the mirror grin so much that it fell out of their hands and splintered as it hit the earth. Each tiny piece could distort as the whole mirror had done.

A tiny piece pierced Kay through the heart, and a tiny grain lodged in his eye. Kay had been a happy little boy before that. He used to play with Gerda in their rooms high above the street, and they both admired some rosebushes their parents had planted in boxes spanning the space between their houses. With the glass in his eye and heart, however, Kay saw nothing beautiful, and nothing pleased him.

One night, he went sledding in the town square. When a lady all in white drove by, he thought that she was so beautiful that he hitched his sled behind her sleigh as she drove slowly around the square. Suddenly, her horses galloped out of the town. The lady looked back at Kay and smiled each time he tried to loosen his sled. Then she stopped the sleigh and told Kay to get in with her. There she wrapped him in her fur coat. She was the Snow Queen. He was nearly frozen, but he did not feel cold after she kissed him nor did he remember Gerda.

Gerda did not forget Kay; at last, she ran away from home to look for him. She went to the garden of a woman learned in magic and asked all the flowers if they had seen Kay, but the flowers knew only their own stories. She met a crow who led her to the prince and princess, but they had not heard of Kay. They gave her boots and a muff and a golden coach to ride in when they sent her on her way. Robbers stopped the golden coach. At the insistence of a little robber girl, Gerda was left alive, a prisoner in the robber's house. Some wood pigeons in the loft told Gerda that Kay had gone with the Snow Queen to Lapland. Since the reindeer tethered inside the house knew the way to Lapland, the robber girl set him free to take Gerda on her way.

The Lapp and the Finn women gave Gerda directions to the Snow Queen's palace and told her that it was only through the goodness of her heart that Kay could be released. When Gerda found Kay, she wept so hard that she melted the piece of mirror out of his heart. Then he wept the splinter from his eye and realized what a vast and empty place he had been in. With thankfulness in her heart, Gerda led Kay out of the snow palace and home.

The Shepherdess and the Sweep. In the middle of the door of an old wooden parlor cupboard was carved a ridiculous little man with goat's legs, horns on his head, and a beard. The children called him Major-general-field-sergeant-commander-Billy-goat's-legs. He always looked at the china figure of a Shepherdess. Finally, he asked the china figure of a Chinese man, who claimed to be her grandfather, if he could marry the Shepherdess. The Chinese man, who could nod his head when he chose, nodded his consent. The Shepherdess had been engaged to the china figure of a Chimneysweep. She begged him to take her away. That night, he used his ladder to help her get off the table. The Chinese man saw them leave and started after them.

Through the stove and up the chimney went the Shepherdess and the Chimneysweep. When she saw how big the world was, the Shepherdess began to cry, and the Chimneysweep had to take her back to the parlor. There they saw the Chinaman broken on the floor. The Shepherdess was distressed, but the Chimneysweep said the Chinaman could be mended and riveted. Although the family had the Chinaman riveted so that he was whole again, he could no longer nod his head. When the Major-general-field-sergeant-commander-Billy-goat's-legs asked again for the Shepherdess, the Chinaman could not nod, and so the Shepherdess and the Chimneysweep stayed together and loved each other until they were broken to pieces.

The Emperor's New Clothes. Once there was a foolish Emperor who loved clothes so well that he spent all the kingdom's money to buy new ones. Two swindlers, who knew the Emperor's weakness, came to town with big looms. They told the people that they wove the most beautiful cloth in the world but that it had a magical property. If someone unworthy of his post looked at it, the cloth became invisible.

The Emperor gave them much gold and thread to make him a new outfit. The swindlers set up their looms and worked far into the night. Becoming curious about the materials, the Emperor sent his most trusted minister to see them. When the minister looked at the looms, he saw nothing; but, thinking of the magical property of the cloth, he decided that he was unworthy of his post. He said nothing to the swindlers and reported to the Emperor, praising the colors and pattern of the cloth as the swindlers had described it.

Others, looking at the looms, saw nothing and said nothing. Even the Emperor saw nothing when the material was finished and then was made into clothes, but he also kept silent. He wore his new clothes in a fine procession. All the people, who also knew of the cloth's supposed property, called out that his new clothes were beautiful—all the people except one little boy, who said that the Emperor did not have on any clothes at all.

Then there was a buzzing along the line of march. Soon everyone was saying that the Emperor wore no clothes. The Emperor, realizing the truth, held himself stiffer than ever until the procession ended.

The Steadfast Tin Soldier. A little boy had a set of twenty-five tin soldiers made out of the same tin spoon. Since there was not quite enough tin, one soldier had only one leg, but he stood as solidly as those with two legs. The one-legged soldier stood on a table and looked longingly at a paper castle, at the door of which stood a paper dancer who wore a gauze dress. A ribbon over her shoulder was held in position by a spangle as big as her face.

One morning, the little boy put the one-legged soldier on a windowsill. When the window opened, the soldier fell three stories to the ground. There he stuck, head down between two stones, until some boys found him. They made a paper boat for the soldier and sailed it down the gutter. After a time, the boat entered a sewer. Beginning to get limp, it settled deeper into the water. Just as the soldier thought he would fall into the water, a fish swallowed him.

When the fish was opened, the soldier found himself in the same house out of which he had fallen. Soon he was back on his table looking at the dancer. For no reason, the boy threw him into a roaring fire. Suddenly, a draft in the room whisked the dancer off the table and straight to the soldier in the fire. When the fire burned down, the soldier had melted to a small tin heart. All that was left of the dancer was her spangle, burned black.

The Tinder Box. A soldier was walking along the high road one day when a witch stopped him and told him that he could have a lot of money if he would climb down a hollow tree and bring her up a tinder box. Thinking that was an easy way to get money, he tied a rope around his waist and the witch helped him to climb down inside the tree. He took along the witch's apron, for on it he had to place the dogs that guarded the chests of money. The first dog, with eyes as big as saucers, guarded a chest full of coppers. The soldier placed the dog on the apron, filled his pockets with coppers, and walked on.

The next dog, with eyes as big as millstones, guarded silver. The soldier placed the dog on the apron, emptied his pockets of coppers, and filled them with silver. The third dog had eyes as big as the Round Tower. He guarded gold. When the soldier had placed the dog on the apron, he emptied his pockets of silver and filled them, his knapsack, his cap, and his boots with gold. Then he called to the witch to pull him up.

When she refused to tell him why she wanted the tinder box, he cut off her head and started for town. There he lived in splendor and gave alms to the poor, for he was good-hearted.

He heard of a beautiful princess who was kept locked up because of a prophecy that she would marry a common soldier. Idly he thought of ways to see her. When his money ran out and he had no candle, he remembered that there was a piece of candle in the tinder box. As he struck the box to light the candle, the door flew open and the dog with eyes like saucers burst in, asking what the soldier wanted. When he asked for money, the dog brought it back immediately. Then he found that he could call the second dog by striking the box twice, and the third dog by striking it three times. When he asked the dogs to bring the princess, she was brought to his room.

The king and queen had him thrown into prison when they caught him. There he was helpless until a little boy to whom he called brought the tinder box to him. When the soldier was about to be hanged, he asked permission to smoke a last pipe. Then he pulled out his tinder box and hit once, twice, three times. All three dogs came to rout the king's men and free the soldier. The people were so impressed that they made the soldier king and the princess his queen.

Critical Evaluation:

Hans Christian Andersen was a dreamy little boy whose thoughts were very much like those of many of the characters in his fairy tales. When his father died and his mother remarried, he asked to go to Copenhagen to make his fortune. A soothsayer had told his mother that Hans would be Denmark's pride, so she let him go. When he tried to enter the theater, he had little success. Some influential men, however, realized that he was a poet and helped him until his publications began to attract attention. By the time Hans Christian Andersen died, he was Denmark's most beloved countryman. His tales may be fantastic, running through many moods, but they merely reflect his own character, which was equally fantastic, though lovable.

The 168 tales written by Andersen may be classified in two general groups. The first group comprises the traditional European folktales retold by Andersen and includes selections such as "Little Claus and Big Claus," "The Wild Swans," and "The Three Little Pigs." These are excellent versions in which the spirit of the source is maintained while the tale is enhanced by the author's gift for storytelling. The majority of the tales, however, belong to the second group, composed of Andersen's original stories; among these one finds a great variety, ranging from stories imitative of the folktale style, to moral allegories, to stories that seem to foreshadow modern fantasy tales. Despite their diversity, however, all of Andersen's tales are marked by common features in both their content and their style.

To a greater or lesser degree, almost all the tales directly reflect the author's personal experiences. Perhaps the most striking example of this is "The Ugly Duckling," which may be read as both a literal and a spiritual autobiography. Similarly, Karen in "The Red Shoes" directly parallels the young Andersen, who at his confirmation was more thrilled with his leather shoes, so new that they squeaked, than with the religious ceremony. In addition to occasional fictionalized accounts of the author's past, readers find a multitude of tales that are more subtly sprinkled with the author's childhood experiences and with the rich lore and colorful traditions of Odense, the provincial town in Denmark where he was reared. The appearance of benevolent grandmothers in so many of the stories, for example, is owing to Andersen's own kindly grandmother, who not only gave the boy sympathy and support but also fed his imagination with peasant tales and reports of the eerie happenings in the insane asylum near which she worked. The many portraits of witches in the fairy tales owe their vividness to the author's terrifying memories of the local "witches" for whom his mother sent when he was ill; towns like Odense in the early nineteenth century were still steeped in medieval beliefs, and mothers of peasant background might still trust in a witch's potion rather than turn to a doctor's prescription to cure their children. Still other tales in the collection are built around recollected daydreams rather than the actual experiences of the author. Such is the case in the beautiful story "The Nightingale," inspired by Andersen's fanciful habit as a boy of singing in the evening to the emperor of China, reputed by the peasants to reside directly under the Odense River.

Perhaps the single most important feature of Andersen's tales is the meaning or significance with which they are charged; a tale is rarely told solely for the sake of a catchy or entertaining plot. This certainly is not to say that the plots are dull—they are never that—or that the stories are heavily didactic, but rather that all of Andersen's work is illuminated (unobtrusively, for the most part) by a moral outlook on life. Sometimes this outlook takes the form of sharp social criticism, as in "The Emperor's New Clothes," which satirizes the pompousness and vanity of court life through its portrait of the unscrupulous weavers, the ridiculous emperor, and the hypocritical courtiers. Similarly, "The Swineherd" attacks the artificial and materialistic values that blind people to the true worth of things. Occasionally, a tale will be particularly frightening in its harsh presentation of a moral lesson; "The Red Shoes," in which a girl's amputated feet go dancing off, leaving her a cripple in punishment for her vanity over a new pair of shoes, is an especially grim and severe illustration. This type of story, however, is the exception rather than the rule; for the most part, Andersen's humor is gentle rather than scathing, and his moral viewpoint is characterized by its subtlety and sensitivity, its kindliness and concern for others.

One distinctive device which Andersen developed as a highly effective way of presenting his ideas was the transformation of inanimate objects into creatures with personalities. Perhaps most memorable is the steadfast tin soldier whose struggles to remain fearless through all of his trials for the sake of his beloved paper ballerina exemplify the spirit of true devotion. In "The Old Streetlamp," Andersen uses a worthy (and very human) old lamppost to weave a symbolic tale about how fear of death robs the soul of its tranquillity, and about the hope that leads to inner peace. Interspersed with these tales peopled by tin soldiers and lampposts, drops of water and darning needles, candles and inkstands, are others containing the more traditional talking animals and trees, which are also used to convey various themes. "The Three Little Pigs" illustrates the superiority of brains over physical strength; while in "The Buckwheat," a wise old oak tree weeps over a proud stalk of wheat that is destroyed because he refuses to take advice from his neighbors. Andersen's ability to create such vivid and sympathetic characters, be they humans, animals, or objects, is the result of his exceptional handling of dialogue. His interest in dialogue began early in his childhood, when, with the aid of a polyglot dictionary, he wrote whimsical stories in which each character spoke a different language. By the time he came to write the fairy tales, his characters all spoke the same language, but he had mastered the secret of revealing their personalities and motives through their speech. Rather than describing what a character is like, Andersen lets the characters expose themselves. Therefore, in "The Shepherdess and the Sweep," the Shepherdess shows both her frivolity and petulance— "I'll never be happy until we are out in the big, wide world"—and her flightiness and shallowness: "I followed you faithfully out into the world, and if you love me the least bit you'll take me right home." The chimneysweep's speech shows him to be sensible yet devoted: "Have you thought how big [the wide world] is, and that we can never come back here?"

Andersen saves his descriptive passages for presenting scenery and landscape, and at this, too, he is masterful. He reproduces with loving detail the inside of a humble cottage kitchen or brings a towering mountain range before the reader's eyes with equal skill. In this excerpt from "The Ice Maiden," one of the longer tales, the author's descriptive power is at its best:

> Often the clouds hang around the towering peaks like thick curtains of smoke, while down in the valley dotted with brown wooden houses, a ray of the sun may be shining brightly, throwing into sharp relief a brilliant patch of green, until it seems transparent.

Toward the end of his life, Andersen made the statement, "I have imagined so much and had so little." He was referring in part to his frequent romantic attachments to women who eventually married other men, and to his long life spent as a bachelor. Still, coming from a man, beloved by his fellow Danes, whose friendship was valued by great writers of his age, and whose society was sought after by nearly all the courts of Europe, the words "so little" seem incongruous. With the "so much," however, no one who has read Andersen's tales will quarrel, except to call the phrase an understatement.

"Critical Evaluation" by Nancy G. Ballard

Bibliography:
Blegvad, Erik. *Hans Christian Andersen: From an Artist's Point of View*. Washington, D.C.: Children's Literature Center, Library of Congress, 1988. Critique of Andersen's fairy tales from a noted Danish illustrator. Describes visual qualities of Andersen's tales that are rarely noted. Originally a talk, is casual about references; the reader needs to have some familiarity with Andersen's works.

Dahl, Svend. *A Book on the Danish Writer, Hans Christian Andersen, His Life and Work*. Copenhagen: Berlingske Bogtr., 1955. An introductory approach to Andersen's life and work. Includes coverage of his story themes and relates them to events in his life.

Gronbech, Bo. *Hans Christian Andersen*. Boston: Twayne, 1980. Treats Andersen's fairy tales in depth, primarily as literary compositions. Extensive bibliographical references.

Mortensen, Finn. *A Tale of Tales: Hans Christian Andersen and Danish Children's Literature*. Minneapolis: Center for Nordic Studies, University of Minnesota, 1989. Considers the original quality of some of the writer's best-known tales and their importance to the national literature.

Nojgaard, Morten, et al., eds. *Telling of Stories, Approaches to a Traditional Craft: A Symposium*. Odense, Denmark: Odense University Press, 1990. Conference proceedings that include essays looking at Andersen's fairy tales from the perspective of the storyteller. Selected tales are examined from the point of view of drama, audience, voice, and cultural notions of continuity and disruption.

ANDRIA

Type of work: Drama
Author: Terence (Publius Terentius Afer, c. 190-159 B.C.E.)
Type of plot: Comedy
Time of plot: Second century B.C.E.
Locale: Athens
First performed: 166 B.C.E. (English translation, 1598)

> *Principal characters:*
> SIMO, a wealthy Athenian
> PAMPHILUS, Simo's son
> GLYCERIUM, beloved of Pamphilus
> DAVUS, slave of Pamphilus
> CHREMES, another wealthy Athenian, friend of Simo
> CRITO, a traveler from Andros
> CHARINUS, a suitor for the daughter of Chremes

The Story:

One day Simo confided in a servant that he had been pleased with his son Pamphilus until that very afternoon, when Simo had discovered that his son was in love with Glycerium, the sister of a courtesan who had recently died. Simo, who wished to marry his son to the daughter of his friend Chremes, saw in his son's love for Glycerium a threat to his plans.

Later Simo encountered his son's slave, Davus, and threatened him with severe punishment. Simo was afraid that Davus, a clever fellow, would help Pamphilus thwart his father's plans for his future. Davus immediately saw that some scheme would have to be put into action quickly if the love between Pamphilus and Glycerium were to end in marriage. Glycerium was already pregnant by Pamphilus.

Pamphilus' own scheme was to acknowledge the expected infant and then claim that Glycerium was actually an Athenian whose father had been shipwrecked on Andros and who had been reared by the family of the courtesan as a foster child. Davus laughed at the story and felt that no one would believe it.

Pamphilus, warned that his father wanted him to marry that day, was greatly troubled. He was put at ease, however, when Davus heard that the approaching marriage to Chremes' daughter had been refused by the young woman's father. Chremes had also learned of the affair between Pamphilus and the courtesan's sister. Davus told Pamphilus to agree to the marriage for the time being. Before long, he reasoned, some way out of the predicament might be found.

Charinus met Davus and Pamphilus and told them that he was in love with Chremes' daughter. Pamphilus said he had no desire to marry the woman and that Charinus was welcome to her. Not knowing the true reason for Pamphilus' assent, Charinus was thrown into despair later when he heard Pamphilus agree to marry Chremes' daughter.

Later, while Simo, the father, and Davus stood before the door of Glycerium's residence, they heard the servants send for a midwife. Simo was angry, thinking that Davus was trying to trick him into believing that Glycerium was having a child by his son. A short time later Glycerium was delivered of a baby boy. When Simo heard the news, he still thought Davus was trying to trick him and refused to believe what he heard.

Meanwhile Pamphilus waited patiently, believing that no marriage with Chremes' daughter had been arranged. While he waited, however, Simo met Chremes on the street, and they agreed once more to marry their children to each other. When Davus reported the latest development to Pamphilus, the young man was furious. It now seemed certain he would never be able to marry the woman he loved. Glycerium, from her confinement bed, sent for Pamphilus to learn what progress he was making in his plans to marry her.

Davus, to prevent the marriage between Pamphilus and Chremes' daughter, had Glycerium's maidservant lay the infant on a bed of verbena in front of Simo's door. Chremes came up the street and saw the child. Davus, pretending that he did not see Chremes, began to argue with Glycerium's servant. During the argument the fact that the child was the son of Pamphilus and Glycerium was shouted aloud. Chremes stormed into Simo's house to withdraw again his offer of marriage between Pamphilus and his daughter.

Soon afterward Crito, a cousin of the dead courtesan, came looking for the house of his dead cousin. As soon as he found it, he asked the maidservant if Glycerium had found her parents in Athens. Davus, looking after Pamphilus' interests, overheard the conversation and entered the house after them.

When Davus left the house a few minutes later, he met Simo, who ordered the slave chained and thrown into a dungeon. While Chremes and Simo were talking over the delayed wedding, Pamphilus also left the house. After some argument the young man convinced his father that Crito had proof that Glycerium was an Athenian, and Pamphilus would have to marry her because they had had a child. Pamphilus reentered the house where Glycerium was lodged and emerged presently with Crito.

Chremes immediately recognized Crito as an acquaintance from Andros. Simo was finally convinced that Crito was an honorable man from that island. Crito then told how Phania, a citizen of Athens, had been shipwrecked on Andros and had died there. With the man had been a little girl, whom the dying man said was his brother's daughter. Chremes then broke into the story to exclaim that Glycerium must be his own daughter, because Phania had been his brother. When Chremes asked what the girl's name had been, Crito said that her name had been changed to Glycerium from Pasibula, the name of Chremes' daughter.

Everyone congratulated Chremes on finding his long-lost child. Pamphilus reminded his father that there could be no barrier to the marriage since Glycerium, too, was a daughter of Chremes and, according to the law, Pamphilus would have to marry her as her seducer. Chremes, overjoyed, declared that he would give a dower of ten talents to the bride.

Davus was freed from the dungeon, and Pamphilus told him all that had occurred. While they spoke, Charinus entered, happy that the other daughter of Chremes was now free to be his bride. The father gave ready consent to Charinus' suit and said that his only objection had been a desire to have his family united with Simo's. In addition, he promised that Charinus would receive a large dowry as well as a wife.

Critical Evaluation:

Although *Andria* was Terence's first play, it shows those characteristics for which this dramatist was noted throughout his career. As in all his plays, the action is closely knit, with no digressions, and the comedy is of a more serious turn than popular slapstick humor. The language is natural.

The plot was not new. Terence admits in his prologue that he adapted his drama from two plays (*The Lady of Andros* and *The Lady of Perinthos*) by Menander, a Greek dramatist who wrote in the fourth century B.C.E. The story turns, as it does in so many Greek and Latin comedies, on the theme of mistaken identity. The modern reader will be inclined to compare the play to William Shakespeare's *Comedy of Errors* (c. 1592-1594), which in turn was freely adapted from *The Menaechmi* (third century B.C.E.) of Plautus. Nor have modern authors ceased to adapt from Terence's *Andria*. It was the basis of Richard Steele's *The Conscious Lovers* (1722) and Thornton Wilder's novel *The Woman of Andros* (1930).

As Terence's first play, produced in 166 B.C.E. when the author was in his early twenties, *Andria* shows the direction and concerns of the playwright's later work. Like each of Terence's dramas, this was adapted from the Greek New Comedy, Menander in particular. Among critics there is wide variance of opinion as to how much Terentian comedy owes to the original sources, and since the original sources have been lost, there is no way of settling the dispute. It seems likely, however, that the tone and the use of the double plot are distinctly Terence's.

If one compares Terence to his only predecessor whose plays have survived, Plautus, there is striking dissimilarity in these two comic playwrights, even though both adapted from Menander and his contemporaries. Plautus is preeminently a man of the stage; ebullient, funny, always ready to sacrifice the logic of plot for the sake of humor and interest. Terence is more the writer than the playwright; a careful craftsman, he is concerned with polished style, character delineation, and a smooth and elegant plot. If he lacks Plautus' vivacity, he is always agreeably humane.

Terence's career itself was remarkable. Born in North Africa, he was brought to Rome as a slave while still a child. His master, Terentius Lucanus, educated him and eventually freed him, which allowed Terence to develop his interest in drama. He was admitted into the aristocratic circle of the Scipios, which was interested in disseminating Greek culture in Rome. As a youthful member, he achieved early success with his plays and encountered the envious spite of the elderly dramatist Luscius Lanuvinus, whom he took pains to answer in his prologues. His career was cut short at about the age of twenty-eight when he mysteriously disappeared on a trip to Greece. Tradition says that he was lost at sea.

The dramas of Terence, then, are the work of a young man, and they reflect the interests and assumptions of youth. The two primary subjects with which he deals are romance and the relations of sons and fathers, both of these being related in his plots. Generally, his stories center on a double love affair, each of which is thwarted or clandestine usually because of fatherly opposition, and each tends to be resolved satisfactorily. Often there is a clever slave who complicates matters by his deceptions, acting on behalf of one of the young men and against the will of the father.

In *Andria* readers see Terence's initial development of this subject matter. Later works would handle the double plot with greater virtuosity, but this play is fresher and livelier, and shows considerable maturity. The reader finds natural, idiomatic dialogue, use of the neat maxim, and appealing, if misguided, characters. *Andria* is the first romantic comedy to come down to modern readers from antiquity and is a precursor of Shakespearean comedy. One thinks of all the double romances in Shakespeare's comedies and one is struck by the similarities to Terence.

The basic problem in *Andria* is that of getting Simo to consent to Pamphilus' marriage to Glycerium, when Simo has become intent on having his son marry Chremes' daughter, Philumena. The difficulty is that Simo, a forceful old man, believes what he wishes to believe, and he interprets what he sees in terms of his self-delusion. Thus, he pretends a forthcoming marriage between Pamphilus and Philumena to test his son's feelings, but also because he wants it to occur in actuality, since Philumena has birth, wealth, and status, whereas Glycerium has none of these. Threatening the slave Davus, Simo gets support in his mistake, which results in an actual marriage-to-be. This is a calamity for both Pamphilus, who loves Glycerium, and

Charinus, who loves Philumena. Having lied successfully, Davus is forced to tell the truth to extricate Pamphilus, and no matter what Davus does, Simo refuses to believe him, insisting obsessively on the marriage. The trouble becomes grave when Simo disowns his son for visiting Glycerium. Everything is settled, however, by a *deus ex machina* ending in which Glycerium's parentage, citizenship, status, and wealth are established. In this plot Simo is the center of the action. His character determines the fates of Davus, Pamphilus, Charinus, and Glycerium. Finally, it is his wish to have his son marry well that must be appeased by the arbitrary ending.

The other characters, while peripheral to Simo, are clearly delineated. Chremes is a sensible old man who wants his daughter to marry happily, in contrast to the deluded Simo, who wants his son to marry, even if unhappily. Pamphilus has a passionate nature like his father, and he ardently cares for Glycerium. Charinus, on the other hand, is theatrical, and one has the impression that his love is make-believe, founded on a desire to marry into status and money. Davus at first secures his own safety by lying and getting Pamphilus to pretend compliance to Simo, but when that backfires, he risks and receives punishment in order to reveal the truth. None of these characters, not even the stubborn ones, is unsympathetic.

In *Andria* age must be respected, no matter how mistaken a father may be. As Terence continued to write, it increasingly becomes youth that must be served, although Terence felt some restraints must be exercised on the whims of young men. *Andria* has influenced many writers, who borrowed its plot without dissimulation. A great borrower himself, Terence would have felt honored.

"Critical Evaluation" by James Weigel, Jr.

Bibliography:

Butler, James H. *The Theatre and Drama of Greece and Rome*. San Francisco: Chandler, 1972. Discusses Terence's defense of plays he wrote; Terence's works were better received after his lifetime and severely criticized during it. Shows *Andria* in context of other works by Terence. Compares the plays of Terence to those of Plautus.

Copley, Frank O. "Terence." In *Latin Literature: From the Beginnings to the Close of the Second Century A. D.* Ann Arbor: University of Michigan Press, 1969. Describes the circumstances in which *Andria* was written and how it was first presented to playwright and critic Caecilius.

Hadas, Moses. *A History of Latin Literature*. New York: Columbia University Press, 1952. Examines how *Andria* was created from two plays of Menander, a classical playwright. Gives a helpful plot line and offers criticism of *Andria*. Discusses circumstances in which the play was presented and produced.

Norwood, Gilbert. *The Art of Terence*. Oxford: Basil Blackwell, 1923. Examines the success of the play and whether Terence received help from other sources. Allows for a comparison of *Andria* to the other comedies by Terence. Helpful for finding early twentieth century criticism on Terence.

Terence. "A Poet Defends Himself: *Andria* I-27." In *Ancient Literary Criticism: The Principal Texts in New Translations*. Edited by D. A. Russell and M. Winterbottom. Oxford: Clarendon Press, 1972. Discusses Terence's prologue of *Andria*. Claims Terence uses this prologue for literary defense—Terence often used his prologues to defend his works and not merely for an introduction of the plot.

ANDROMACHE

Type of work: Drama
Author: Euripides (c. 485-406 B.C.E.)
Type of plot: Tragedy
Time of plot: About a decade after the Trojan War
Locale: The temple of Thetis in Thessaly
First performed: Andromachē, 426 B.C.E. (English translation, 1782)

Principal characters:
ANDROMACHE, Hector's widow and slave to Neoptolemus
HERMIONE, the wife of Neoptolemus and daughter of Menelaus
MENELAUS, the king of Sparta
PELEUS, Neoptolemus' grandfather
MOLOSSUS, the son of Andromache and Neoptolemus
ORESTES, Agamemnon's son
THETIS, a goddess and the dead wife of Peleus
CHORUS OF PYTHIAN MAIDENS

The Story:

After the death of Hector and the fall of Troy, Andromache had been given as a special prize to Neoptolemus, son of Achilles. As his slave and concubine, she had borne a son, Molossus, thereby arousing the jealous wrath of Hermione, Neoptolemus' barren wife. Fearing Hermione's hatred and sensing her doom, Andromache sought sanctuary in the sacred grounds of the temple of Thetis, after secretly sending her son to a neighbor for safekeeping.

Hermione appeared at the temple and accused Andromache of seeking to oust her, taunted her for bearing a son to Hector's slayer, and threatened her with death. Andromache protested that as an aging woman and a helpless slave she would be mad to compete with Hermione and that she herself had gracefully accepted Hector's illegitimate children rather than let herself be corrupted by jealousy. Hermione, unmoved by these arguments, left the temple, threatening to find the bait that would lure Andromache from her sanctuary.

She was true to her word, for soon afterward Menelaus arrived leading Molossus by the hand. The Spartan king warned Andromache that he would kill the boy on the spot if she did not emerge and offer up her own life instead. Andromache argued with him, pointing out that murder would surely pollute his reputation and that Neoptolemus would never condone the death of his only son. Menelaus was adamant, however, and Andromache emerged from the sanctuary to learn that both she and her son were marked for slaughter. Before the order for execution could be carried out, the aged Peleus appeared and in response to her supplication commanded that her bonds be loosened. Peleus, furious with Menelaus, denounced Spartan cowardice and treachery; he ordered the king to leave Thessaly at once and to take his barren daughter with him. Menelaus, however, announced that he was leaving with his army only in order to vanquish a city hostile to Sparta, after which he would return to confront Neoptolemus himself and settle the matter of his daughter's status in Thessaly.

After everyone had left the temple, a terribly distraught Hermione entered carrying a sword with which she intended to commit suicide. When her nurse wrested the sword from her, Hermione, in great anguish, lamented the horrible deed she had plotted and spoke of her fear that Neoptolemus would banish her. Suddenly Orestes appeared, claiming that he was merely

247

passing through on his way to the oracle at Dodona. Hermione threw herself at his feet. Orestes had once been betrothed to Hermione and had always loved her, and he now revealed that he had come to carry her off and was prepared to murder her husband even if the deed involved sacrilegious treachery. Hermione's taunts at Andromache were now ironically turned upon herself.

After the desperate pair had fled, Peleus appeared, but before he could question the chorus about the fearful rumors he had heard, a messenger brought the sad news that his grandson, Neoptolemus, was dead; he had been horribly murdered and mutilated by Orestes and his brigands while praying to the gods in the temple of Phoebus. Neoptolemus' body was then carried in on a bier. The bereaved old Peleus lamented the end of his line now that the only son of his only son was dead. Throwing his scepter on the ground, the distraught king resolved to grovel in the dust until his death. At that moment the dim form of the divine Thetis, the goddess who had once been his wife, appeared hovering in midair. She commanded her husband to cease his mourning and take the body of Neoptolemus to be buried at the Pythian altar as a reproach to the Spartans. She further commanded that he take Andromache and Neoptolemus' son to Helenus, whom Andromache would marry so that the line of Peleus could continue. After this mission, Peleus himself would be converted into a god and live with Thetis in the halls of Nereus forever. Peleus consented, moralizing that every prudent man should take heed to marry a wife of noble stock and give his daughter to a good husband.

Critical Evaluation:

The problem with Andromache on which critics have focused their attention is Andromache's complete disappearance from the story midway through the play. The action falls basically into three stages that are only connected by the slenderest of threads. In the first stage, Andromache provides the focus, as her life and the life of her small son are imperiled by Hermione's jealous hatred; in the second, Hermione, beside herself with fear after her plot fails, is rescued by her old lover, Orestes. In the last stage, after Neoptolemus has been brutally murdered by Orestes, his aged grandfather Peleus mourns his death until his divine mate, Thetis, appears to comfort him.

Critics have complained of the discontinuous plot structure, but not all have been strong in their criticism. Some have proposed that the play's episodic plot is compensated for by a unity of theme and characterization. It has been suggested, for example, that Andromache is a bitter attack on the Spartan national character, particularly on its qualities of arrogance, treachery, and ruthlessness. This theory is certainly supported in the first two parts of the play when Andromache, generalizing from the individual wrongs committed against her, denounces all Spartans as liars and cheats, and Hermione's vengefulness and Menelaus' cowardly, bullying, bragging nature seem to confirm her judgment. The interpretation is much less convincing, however, when applied to the last portion of the play, since it is never made clear that Orestes is meant to represent Spartan villainy. Other readings have seen the play variously as a denunciation of slavery, as a dramatization of the political failure of Greek alliances, and as a warning against forced or inadvisable marriages.

Perhaps more convincing than these views, as well as more consistent with the values Euripides expressed in his other dramas, is the interpretation of Andromache as a portrayal of the tragedy of war. The theme of war—its trivial causes, horrible course, and disastrous aftermath—is everywhere present. Although the Trojan War ended ten years earlier, it continues to dominate the lives of the characters, either directly or indirectly. Andromache combines within herself all the tragic ills suffered by victims of war: She is not only widowed and orphaned but enslaved in the enemy's land. Menelaus, who represents the victors, is shown as worthless and self-serving; having left the fighting and dying to men such as Achilles, he returned to strut about and reap a hero's reward. Even Orestes, who was not personally involved in the war, is presented as someone whose character has been warped by the evil circumstances surrounding the conflict.

"Critical Evaluation" by Bruce D. Reeves

Bibliography:

Aldrich, K. M. *The "Andromache" of Euripides*. Lincoln: University of Nebraska Press, 1961. A detailed analysis of the play. Aldrich makes an argument for the work's unity of plot and theme.

Grube, G. M. A. *The Drama of Euripides*. London: Methuen, 1941. A learned, traditional, close reading of the play. Accepts the anti-Spartan tone of the work at face value and sees the characters as lively but not subtle.

Kitto, Humphrey Davy Findley. *Greek Tragedy: A Literary Study*. London: Methuen, 1939. A classic study of classical tragedy. Argues that *Andromache* is unified in theme but not in plot and that Hermione, Menelaus, and Orestes embody negative Spartan qualities of "arrogance, treachery, and criminal ruthlessness." Expresses admiration for the work's action and characterization.

Kovacs, Paul David. *The "Andromache" of Euripides*. Chico, Calif.: Scholars Press, 1980. Argues against the view that Euripides' tragedies are antiheroic and that they attack traditional attitudes. Instead, Kovacs sees *Andromache* as conventional and close to Sophocles' view of the tragic. Kovacs also disputes the claim that Euripides sides with the Sophists in this play.

Vellacott, Philip. *Ironic Drama: A Study of Euripides' Method and Meaning*. London: Cambridge University Press, 1975. Sees *Andromache* as an indictment of cruelty to women and the horrors of war. Vellacott rejects the view that the play's early episodes are irrelevant to the outcome, maintaining instead that these scenes are essential.

ANDROMACHE

Type of work: Drama
Author: Jean Baptiste Racine (1639-1699)
Type of plot: Tragedy
Time of plot: Shortly after the end of the Trojan War
Locale: Epirus
First performed: 1667

> *Principal characters:*
> ANDROMACHE, the widow of Hector and captive of Pyrrhus
> PYRRHUS, the king of Epirus and son of Achilles
> ORESTES, the son of Agamemnon and spurned suitor of Hermione
> HERMIONE, the daughter of Helen and affianced bride of Pyrrhus
> PYLADES, Orestes' friend and companion

The Story:

Orestes, son of the Greek leader Agamemnon, journeyed to Epirus to tell Pyrrhus, king of Epirus, that the Greeks were fearful of Astyanax, the young son of Hector and Andromache, who might someday try to avenge the fall of Troy. Because of the Greeks' fear, they had sent Orestes to request that Pyrrhus put Astyanax to death.

Pyrrhus had fallen in love with Andromache, however, and, at first, afraid of losing her love, he refused to grant the request. To Orestes, who had long loved Hermione, betrothed of Pyrrhus, the news of Pyrrhus' love for Andromache was welcome. Orestes thought he saw in the situation a chance for him to win Hermione for his wife. Orestes' friend Pylades was amazed, for Orestes had previously sworn that his love for Hermione had degenerated into hate because she spurned him.

When Pyrrhus refused to kill Astyanax or turn the child over to the Greeks, Orestes threatened him. Pyrrhus swore that he would make Epirus a second Troy before he permitted the death of Astyanax. Pyrrhus, hoping that his decision would lead her to forget her dead husband, told Andromache what he had done, but she made no response to his overtures. Angered, Pyrrhus told her that unless she married him the child would die.

Meanwhile Hermione, spurned by Pyrrhus, was trying to decide whether she loved or hated the king, and whether she wanted to flee with Orestes. When Pyrrhus, rebuffed by Andromache, went to her, they decided that they were still in love. Reconciled to Hermione, Pyrrhus promised to love only her and to give Astyanax to the Greeks.

Hermione, however, changing her mind, prepared to flee with Orestes to inflict punishment on Pyrrhus, after Orestes told her that Pyrrhus had renewed his suit of Andromache. Pyrrhus returned while they spoke and announced that he was ready to give the boy to the Greeks because Andromache had again spurned his love and aid.

Convinced that Pyrrhus had decided to marry Hermione only to keep her from her Greek lover, Orestes plotted to flee with the girl. Pylades, his friend, agreed to help in the abduction. When Hermione met Orestes, she spoke only of her approaching marriage to Pyrrhus, whom she still loved. While they talked, Andromache entered the room and begged Hermione to protect Astyanax, whom Pyrrhus had determined to kill. Andromache reminded Hermione that Hector had championed Helen, Hermione's mother, when the Trojans had wished to murder her. Hermione refused to listen and scorned Andromache's request.

Andromache then pleaded with Pyrrhus, but he told her that her plea came too late. At last, when Andromache vowed to kill herself, her vow and tears moved the vacillating Pyrrhus, who once again told her that he would marry her instead of Hermione and champion the boy against the Greeks. Andromache, however, refused to save her son by marrying her captor and former enemy. After a conference with her waiting-woman, she decided to consult her husband's ghost. The result of that conference was a decision to marry Pyrrhus, thus bringing Astyanax under Pyrrhus' protection, and then to kill herself.

Hermione, furious when she learned that on the following day Pyrrhus intended to marry Andromache, sent for Orestes and told him that she wanted his help in avenging herself on the king. Without promising herself to Orestes, she asked him to kill Pyrrhus during the wedding ceremony.

At first Orestes demurred. Not wishing to become an assassin, he wanted to declare war on Pyrrhus and earn glory on the battlefield. At Hermione's urging, however, he finally agreed to the murder. She told him that it would be easy to commit the crime because the king's guards had been sent to watch over Astyanax and none had been ordered to guard the nuptial ceremonies. She finally added that after the murder she would become Orestes' bride.

After Orestes left, Pyrrhus came once more to Hermione. Hoping that the king had changed his mind again, she sent her serving-woman to tell Orestes not to act until he had further word from her. Pyrrhus, however, had come to tell her only that he intended to marry Andromache, come what would. Hermione vowed she would have revenge. This was her message to Orestes. Finally Orestes arrived to inform her that the deed was done; Pyrrhus had died at the hands of Orestes' soldiers.

Hermione, turning on Orestes, declared that she disowned such savagery and would have no more to do with him because he had killed the man she loved. When Orestes argued with her that she had persuaded him to commit the murder for her sake, her only defense was that she had been distraught at having her love spurned by Pyrrhus and that Orestes should not have listened to her. When she rushed out of the room, Pylades came with the Greek warriors to warn Orestes that if they were to escape the wrath of Pyrrhus' subjects they must take ship and sail away from Epirus at once. The people, they said, were obeying Andromache as their queen. Hermione, too, was dead; she had run into the temple and thrown herself on Pyrrhus' body, after stabbing herself with mortal wounds. Hearing that news, Orestes turned mad and fainted in his agony. His men quickly took him away and made their escape from Epirus.

Critical Evaluation:

Andromache, with its interplay of human passions, its frenzied picture of love turning to fierce jealousy and then to hatred and finally to madness and crime, began the main cycle of Jean Baptiste Racine's dramas. Although his earlier plays, *La Thébaïde* (1664) and *Alexandre le Grand* (1665), established Racine's reputation as a dramatist, *Andromache* is clearly a more sophisticated and mature work. The French theater of the seventeenth century accepted, on what it thought was the authority of Aristotle, the three unities of time, place, and action. Racine's predecessor, Pierre Corneille, deliberately accepted the principle that the action of the play must take place in a single day, that it must be concerned with a single situation in one circumscribed locality. Corneille found it difficult to confine himself to these limitations, but Racine's plays, concentrating on the moment more than the story, fit into this mold more easily and with great dramatic force. *Andromache* showed what could be done within these conventions.

Racine's tragedies are of a different type than William Shakespeare's; there is not the rich variety, the comedy mingled with tragedy, the breathless sweeping from scene to scene, the mad beauty of language thrown out almost recklessly. Instead, in the meticulously worded tragedies of *Andromache* and *Phèdre* (1677) there burns a peculiar, if rather decorous, beauty. The action is concentrated, and it is less important than the mental reactions of the characters. In *Andromache*, the room in the Palace of Pyrrhus mentioned in the stage directions is, in a sense, any room anywhere, a place where tortured souls display their agony, their inner conflict, and their ultimate strength. The narrowness of the scene actually helps to concentrate the attention of the audience upon Racine's psychological analysis. The characters are not only Homeric Greeks, but man and woman in the most universal sense. The neoclassic tragedy of *Andromache* moves with a feverish intensity, exposing as seldom done on the stage the moment of passion and its consequences.

Racine theorized less about the neoclassic rules than Corneille, but he followed them more closely. He was a disciple of reason, as was Corneille, his teacher and later rival, but he saw reason more as a guide for the author than for the character. To Racine, this meant that his plays must be free from fantastic or irrational characterizations, that he must avoid complicated and impossible plots or climaxes that had nothing to do with what had gone before in the plays. He sought, within his conventions, a naturalness in drama. *Andromache* is probably the play in which Racine most perfectly achieved the combination of passionate concentration and reasonable naturalness.

Andromache launched Racine into his greatest period. It was the time of Molière's masterpieces *Tartuffe* (1664), *Don Juan* (1665), and *The Misanthrope* (1666), and Corneille's greatest plays were already behind him. Racine struck out for himself in *Andromache*, attempting a realistic portrayal of human passion. Hermione is shown as a jealous and neglected woman seeking revenge. In a sense, the problem of the play is the *crime passionnel* always so popular in French newspapers. Even in Racine's day, such cases were well known. French literature was filled with such people, but this was the first time that the psychology of such a character had been put upon the stage.

Racine took his characters from the Homeric tales and transformed them into Frenchmen and Frenchwomen. Andromache, in spite of her intense fidelity to Hector's memory, understood the power of her sexuality over King Pyrrhus. Racine interpreted the drama more as a battle between the sexes than had ever been attempted previously. The universality of the playwright's vision brought the characters from the dignity of history to the fire of human passion, thus creating realistic men and women.

Pyrrhus, king of Epirus, is one of the most interesting characters in the play and in all of Racine's works. A fierce barbarian of a man, the son of Achilles, he is yet curiously at home within the walls of his palace, ever analyzing emotions and mental conditions. This dual nature almost strikes the audience as contradictory, perhaps even unlikely. In 1667, however, Racine had to defend his complex portrait of Pyrrhus from the charge of brutality. Such a virile, dominant man, with the warrior's blunt nature, had never before appeared so nakedly on the stage. Racine covered new ground in this play with his male characters as well as with the now more famous female characters.

The plot of *Andromache* depends more upon inner action expressed in words than upon external action such as can be found in the more romantic Shakespearean drama. Racine was the great psychological poet and analyzer of character, the beginning of a long line of such writers in French literature, leading up to Guy de Maupassant, Sidonie-Gabrielle Colette, and finally, in the twentieth century, André Gide. Racine's men and women might step out of their period costumes and don the clothes of any other age. The plot of the play, through which these men and women subtly maneuver, develops logically and precisely to its inevitable and tragic conclusion. The audience's reaction to *Andromache* must be more mental than emotional, more one of admiration than sympathy.

The world Racine shows the audience in *Andromache* is a world in which honor is still a way of life. In this realm, men and women are responsible for their own conduct. Nothing, not love or even life, is as important as honor. Today this seems a strange and old-fashioned code, but it is fundamental to the tragic point of view, and the heart of all of Racine's dramas. The character of Andromache alone emerges from the play with her honor—in the broadest conception of the word—intact. The others have compromised their honor and have paid the price. Modern audiences, accustomed to a world in which everybody denies responsibility for everything, may find it difficult to understand this code by which the characters of *Andromache* must live and die, yet they cannot help but find it impressive and possibly inspiring. The morality upon which the conduct of these men and women is based is universal, reaching back to classical antiquity and forward to the future.

"Critical Evaluation" by Bruce D. Reeves

Bibliography:
Cloonan, William J. *Racine's Theatre: The Politics of Love*. University, Miss.: Romance Mono-graphs, 1977. Examines the profound unhappiness of the four principal characters in *Andromache*. Explores the destructive nature of Pyrrhus' egotistical desire to dominate Andromache and the violence and irrational behavior of Orestes and Hermione.
France, Peter. *Racine's Rhetoric*. Oxford, England: Clarendon Press, 1965. An insightful analysis which examines Racine's skill in using classical rhetorical devices in order to create many effective psychological tragedies. Discusses the portrayal of passion and solitude in *Andromache*.
Lapp, John C. *Aspects of Racinian Tragedy*. Toronto: University of Toronto Press, 1955. Explores Racine's artistry in using the conventions of French classical theater in order to compose psychologically powerful and aesthetically pleasing tragedies. Examines the heavy weight of the past on Andromache, whose suffering continues long after the end of the Trojan War.
Mourgues, Odette de. *Racine or the Triumph of Relevance*. London: Cambridge University Press, 1967. Examines Racine's creative imitation of classical writers and his tragic vision of the world. Applies Aristotle's theory of catharsis or purgation to Racine's tragedies.
Turnell, Martin. *Jean Racine: Dramatist*. London: Hamish Hamilton, 1972. Contains a very good introduction to Racine's eleven tragedies and also includes a lengthy bibliography of major critical studies on Racine. The chapter on *Andromache* examines representations of love and violence and the psychological complexity of its four principal characters.

ANGELS IN AMERICA
A Gay Fantasia on National Themes

Type of work: Drama
Author: Tony Kushner (1956-   )
Type of plot: Political
Time of plot: Mid-1985 to 1990
Locale: New York
First performed: Part 1, *Millennium Approaches*, 1991, first published, 1992; part 2,
   Perestroika, 1992, first published, 1994

Principal characters:
   PRIOR WALTER, a man with AIDS
   LOUIS IRONSON, Prior Walter's lover, a Marxist
   ROY M. COHN, an unscrupulous right-wing lawyer
   JOSEPH "JOE" PORTER PITT, chief clerk of a Federal Appeals Court, a
      Mormon
   HARPER AMATY PITT, Joseph's wife
   HANNAH PORTER PITT, Joseph's mother
   BELIZE, a nurse and former drag queen
   THE ANGEL, also known as the CONTINENTAL PRINCIPALITY OF HEAVEN

The Story:
   Roy Cohn offered Joe Pitt a job in Washington with the Reagan Justice Department but Joe
had to discuss it with his wife, Harper. Harper hid in her home consumed by fantasies and fears.
When she wanted to travel, Mr. Lies, a travel agent, magically appeared and offered to take her
to anywhere. When Joe returned, he and Harper fought about going to Washington, her
emotional problems, and the secrets he kept from her.
   Prior Walter revealed to his lover, Louis Ironson, that he had a cancerous lesion, a sign of
advancing AIDS. Prior joked about it, but he feared that Louis might leave him. In truth, Louis
did not know if he could stay and watch Prior die. Joe found Louis crying in the bathroom at
the Brooklyn Federal Courthouse. Louis thought Joe was gay and was surprised when Joe
denied it.
   Prior and Harper were in each other's dreams. Prior told Harper that her husband was a
homosexual. Harper told Prior that deep inside he was free of disease. For the first time, Prior
heard a mysterious angelic voice call to him. When Harper asked Joe if he was homosexual,
Joe insisted he fought all his indecent desires. His behavior was correct, and that was all that
mattered.
   Told that he had AIDS, Roy threatened to destroy his doctor if he said that Roy Cohn was a
homosexual. For Roy, "homosexual" did not mean what it seemed to mean. It did not explain
who had sex with whom, but rather it described one's status and one's power. Homosexuals had
no clout but Roy Cohn had clout. He could talk to the president or the president's wife at any
time. Roy Cohn had sex with men, but Roy Cohn was not a homosexual. Therefore, he did not
have AIDS. The doctor advised Roy that an experimental drug, AZT, might help him, but there
was a two-year waiting list for it. Roy would have to call the president for help.
   When Prior became violently ill, Louis, hysterical, took Prior to the hospital, and then, afraid,
ran away. When Joe told Roy about his marital problems, Roy, who revealed he was dying,

passed this wisdom on to Joe: Love is a trap, responsibility is a trap, and Joe should not be afraid to live alone.

Roy, threatened with disbarment, wanted Joe to take a job at the Justice Department so that Joe might protect Roy from his enemies. Roy's enemies included the fancy lawyers with corporate clients who needed the goodwill of the Justice Department. At the Justice Department, Joe could pressure these lawyers to leave Roy alone. Joe knew that this would be unethical. Angry, Roy told Joe that in politics, ethics did not matter.

Joe and Louis fell in love. They felt that they were caught between their duty to love and their duty to themselves. Both feared and wanted freedom. They were children of the age: selfish, greedy, loveless, and blind. They became lovers. Louis left Prior, saying he had to be free, and Joe told Harper that he had no sexual feeling toward her. Harper, heartbroken, asked Mr. Lies to take her to Antarctica.

Late at night, Joe called Hannah Pitt, his mother in Utah, and told her he was homosexual. Angry, she told him to go home to his wife. Hannah immediately sold her house and went to New York. Two of Prior's dead ancestors told him he had been chosen by The Angel and Prior saw a huge book drop from the heavens. More and more he felt doomed, as if something were following him.

Roy called Joe a sissy when he refused the Washington job. Joe wanted to be nice, but he had to choose between being nice and being effective, as Roy had been in getting Ethel Rosenberg executed. As Roy collapsed in pain, the ghost of Ethel Rosenberg appeared to watch him suffer. Roy raved at her, refusing to give in.

With great fanfare, The Angel appeared to Prior. God, fascinated by humanity's ability to evolve, change, and progress, had become bored with angels and had abandoned heaven. Prior was to tell humanity to stop moving and changing, so that God might perhaps return.

Harper's fantasy of Antarctica eventually ended and, back in reality, she was rescued by Hannah Pitt, who, after being lost in the Bronx, had found Harper's apartment.

Hospitalized, Roy insulted Belize, but the nurse fought back. Belize gave Roy medical advice, and when Roy asked why he should trust Belize, the nurse answered that unlike Roy's doctors, Belize was gay. When Roy got his AZT, he shared it with Belize, but only after goading the nurse into insulting him.

At the Mormon center, Prior and Harper watched a diorama of a pioneer Mormon family. The father looked just like Joe. When they saw Louis enter the diorama and take Joe away with him, Harper and Prior felt they were going crazy. Harper asked the Mormon woman in the diorama how people change; she answered that God slit them open, squeezed their insides, and left them to heal themselves.

At Jones Beach, Louis told Joe about gay life and sex before AIDS. Although Joe said he loved Louis, Louis missed Prior and Joe felt guilty about Harper. Louis admitted that he never accounted for love in his theories. Joe suggested that being selfish is sometimes the most generous thing one can do.

Louis asked Prior for forgiveness, but Prior refused. Angry that Louis had abandoned him and betrayed him with a Mormon Republican, Prior told Louis to come back when he had visible wounds. Roy, remembering the Bible stories his mother told him, gave Joe his blessing. When Joe confessed his homosexuality, Roy ordered him to go back to his wife and never speak of it again.

Belize told Louis that Joe was Roy's protégé. Louis could not accept it: Roy was, to Louis, the most evil man in the world. Belize hated Louis' idealistic notions about America. For him, Roy Cohn was America: terminal, crazy, and mean.

Hannah had no sympathy for her son. Joe had been running away all his life, and he was still running. Joe and Harper try to reconcile, but Joe could not hide his sexuality. Harper knew that she would leave Joe.

Joe tried to return to Louis, but Louis, who had researched the legal decisions Joe had written, attacked Joe for the immoral way he had manipulated the law. Joe tried to defend his politics but finally became so angry that he beat Louis.

The ghost of Ethel Rosenberg brought Roy the news of his disbarment. Having long hated him, Ethel relished his defeat. Roy, pretending to be delirious, tricked Ethel into singing him a Yiddish song. Mocking her, Roy claimed victory even as he died.

Prior, on Hannah's advice, wrestled The Angel. When he won, The Angel took him to Heaven, to the council of angels. Prior told them that humanity cannot stop changing, for that is what living things do. He could not bring God back. If God did come back, Prior believed, humanity should sue him for abandoning them and for all the horrible things that had happened in the terrible twentieth century. Although the angels said that the future would be terrible, Prior wanted more life. Humanity was addicted to life, no matter how painful.

Belize insisted that Louis say the Kaddish for Roy, that their enemy be forgiven. Louis did not know the Hebrew prayer, but Ethel Rosenberg gave him the words. Roy, in the afterlife, offered to defend God, who was being sued, although God was guilty and had no case. Prior woke up wondering if all that had happened was a dream. Louis again asked if he could come back even though he had failed at love. Prior loved Louis but could never take him back.

Flying to San Francisco, Harper had a vision: She saw the souls of the dead rising, hands clasped together, forming a protective shield for the earth.

Four years later, Prior, Louis, Belize, and Hannah were in Central Park, beneath the statue of the angel Bethesda. Prior was still alive and with AIDS. Many had died, but the gay men were not going away, nor would they die secret deaths.

Critical Evaluation:

When the thirty-three-year-old Tony Kushner began writing *Angels in America* in 1989, he was the respected but not famous author of two little-known plays. When *Angels in America* arrived on Broadway four years later, it was the most eagerly anticipated and highly publicized theatrical event in decades. Tony Kushner's play was almost universally hailed for its epic scope and daring subject. Running almost eight hours, *Angels in America* takes its audience from earth to heaven. It mixes reality and fantasy, comedy and deep pain, low politics and mysticism, personal dramas and world history, and ideas and poetry to produce a dazzling theatrical work. Kushner's eclectic style is common in the drama of his time, but rarely have theatergoers experienced such extravagant, thematically ambitious, and daring theater. With wit, passion, and rage, Tony Kushner attacks an astounding number of provocative issues: sex, race, religion, gay rights, the politics of AIDS, leftist ideals and the success of capitalism, selfish individualism, love, the absence of God, and the meaning of America.

A rich, complex, and provocative play, *Angels in America* may have to wait some time before critics and scholars can come to terms with it. There is no doubt that Tony Kushner has a brilliant gift for theatrical language and for creating fascinating characters. It is less clear whether the play's sprawling narrative and, more important, its abundance of ideas and themes create a completely coherent vision. Despite the playwright's explicitly didactic intentions, he offers less a moral than a passionate account of conflicting desires and ideals that are central to life.

The central image of the play is The Angel. Perfect, but static and unchanging, The Angel's fear of change, of chance, of striving, and of evolution represents modern conservative philosophy. The play undermines right-wing nostalgia for what America used to be. For Kushner, America has abandoned its ideals and the struggle for justice and democracy. Every character in the play struggles to evolve and, clearly, society too must embrace progress. Change is hard, but, as Prior tells the angels, it is what living things do.

Angels in America explicitly addresses the gay community's response to the AIDS crisis. A socialist and political playwright, Tony Kushner urges the gay community to political action and to resist The Angel's call of nostalgia and passivity. Kushner is torn between confronting and attacking mainstream, heterosexual America and creating a political vision that may unite all of America.

Many of the play's conflicting impulses collide in the demonic but fascinating figure of Roy Cohn, who embodies the corrupt values Tony Kushner wishes to criticize and who represents a power and vitality Kushner admires. Kushner rejects the traditional notion of the individual and the selfish philosophies that justify hurting and exploiting others. Roy Cohn lives to use and dominate, to win and exploit, and he tells Joe Pitt not to fear being alone to fulfill his ambitions. Despite all that, Kushner admires Roy Cohn: He is a daring, vital, political animal who is willing to break the rules and who never stops fighting. For all his talk of selfishness, Cohn believes in loyalty, even love. Cohn is a gay man who never asks to be tolerated, but rather demands power. Louis, the leftist thinker, is ineffectual and ambivalent, but Cohn is a man of action. Cohn's challenge to Joe Pitt, that one can either be nice or be effective, haunts Kushner's dream of an idealistic politics. *Angels in America* is a milestone in American theater. Grand and ambitious, full of ideas and theatrical extravagance, it reminds its audience that theater can be both great entertainment and great art.

Chris Breyer

Bibliography:

Brustein, Robert. "On Theater: *Angels in America*." *The New Republic*, May 24, 1993, 29. One of America's finest theater critics provides an excellent overview of the play.

Kushner, Tony. "Playwright of Pain and Hope." Interview by Bob Blanchard. *Progressive* 58, no. 10 (October, 1994). Tony Kushner talks about *Angels in America*.

Olson, Walter. "Winged Defeat." *The National Review*, January 24, 1994, 71-73. A revealing discussion of how Tony Kushner tries to combine Marxism, mysticism, and transgression in his work.

Posnock, R. "Roy Cohn in America." *Raritan* 13, no. 3 (Winter, 1994): 64-77. A study of how Tony Kushner uses the real history of Roy Cohn.

Tucker, Scott. "A Storm Blowing from Paradise." *The Humanist* 53, no. 6 (November/December, 1993): 32-35. A provocative examination of Tony Kushner as gay militant and as a writer whose vision includes the mainstream.

ANGLE OF REPOSE

Type of work: Novel
Author: Wallace Stegner (1909-1993)
Type of plot: Historical realism
Time of plot: 1860-1970
Locale: California, the Dakotas, Colorado, Idaho, and Mexico
First published: 1971

> *Principal characters:*
> LYMAN WARD, the narrator
> ELLEN HAMMOND WARD, Lyman's estranged wife
> RODMAN WARD, their son
> SUSAN BURLING WARD, Lyman's grandmother
> OLIVER WARD, Susan's husband
> AUGUSTA DRAKE HUDSON, Susan's close friend
> THOMAS HUDSON, Augusta's husband
> ADA HAWKES and
> ED HAWKES, Lyman's neighbors and caregivers
> SHELLY RASMUSSEN, daughter of Ada and Ed

The Story:

Fifty-eight-year-old Lyman Ward had been a history professor at the University of California at Berkeley, where his research had won for him a Bancroft Prize. Following his retirement, Lyman, a partial invalid since he lost a leg to a bone disease, moved to Grass Valley, California. He lived in Zodiac Cottage, which had been built and inhabited for many years by his paternal grandparents, Oliver and Susan Burling Ward. There he found the letters from which he reconstructed the story of his grandparents' lives.

Oliver, a self-taught engineer and a cousin of Henry Ward Beecher, dropped out of Yale after two years because of failing eyesight. He met Susan at a reception in Brooklyn; shortly thereafter, he left for California, seeking his fortune. Susan, a twenty-one-year-old art student who mixed freely in New York's artistic and literary society, corresponded with Oliver but was not romantically attached to him.

Her lifelong friend was Augusta Drake, with whom Lyman suggested his grandmother may have had a lesbian relationship during the first five years of their friendship. Susan, not actively seeking a husband, developed a strong platonic attachment to Thomas Hudson, the brilliant editor of Scribner's and later *The Century*. Thomas, Susan, and Augusta became an inseparable trio. Then Thomas and Augusta married. Their marriage left Susan feeling excluded.

Coincidentally, Oliver returned after half a decade in the West, and spent a week with Susan and her family in Milton, New York. During that week, Susan fell in love with and decided to marry Oliver, agreeing to join him in the West for a short sojourn before they returned to the East to live permanently.

Two weeks after the two married in Milton, Oliver returned to California, where he worked as a mining engineer in New Almaden. He prepared a house for Susan, spending so much money on renovation that he had nothing left to send her for the railroad tickets she needed to get herself and her servant, Lizzie, across the continent. Susan paid for the tickets, setting out for what became a lifelong adventure.

Oliver's work was extremely demanding. He had a knack for invention, but lacked the business acumen that would help him to profit from such inventions as hydraulic cement or flood control valves, which he developed, failed to patent, and lost to opportunists. Early in their marriage, Oliver sometimes lived apart from Susan because the places where he worked lacked suitable accommodations for her.

Susan continued to draw and write, regularly selling her work to significant publishers in the East, always nurturing the dream of returning to eastern society. Susan remained ever the eastern snob; Oliver remained the kindly, gentle, unassuming engineer and inventor. When Susan was thirty-seven years old, and Oliver thirty-five, their marriage crumbled. Infatuated with Oliver's assistant, Frank Sargent, Susan conspired to go into the Idaho countryside with him, saying that she was taking five-year-old Agnes for a walk. She did not pay sufficient attention to Agnes, whose lifeless body was found floating in a canal. The day after Agnes' funeral, Frank Sargent committed suicide.

Grief-stricken, Oliver left for work in Mexico, while Susan remained in Idaho. After two years, the two were reunited, but Oliver never forgave Susan's infidelity. Through more than half a century, they lived together with forbearance rather than love, never touching each other. Susan remained the snob she always had been, the celebrity she received for her writing feeding her sense of superiority. Oliver continued to be the gentle, patient man he had always been. Oliver died at the age of eighty-nine. Susan, ninety-one years of age, died two months later.

Lyman Ward was a distinguished historian who commented darkly about the Berkeley of the revolutionary 1960's. His invalidism forced an early retirement. Ellen, his wife, was unable to cope with Lyman's disability and ran off with his surgeon and divorced her husband. Rodman, Lyman and Ellen's only child, was a sociology professor at the University of California at Santa Cruz. He had little respect for history and was unimpressed by Lyman's academic accomplishments. His chief goal was to get his father into a nursing home.

Lyman not only resisted Rodman's pressures but also calculatedly documented his routine activities so that Rodman had no grounds for declaring him incompetent. Ada and Ed Hawkes lived on the property with their daughter, Shelly Rasmussen, who had dropped out of Berkeley. The Hawkeses and Shelley attended to Lyman's needs. Lyman, living alone, asserted his independence in every possible way. One night, Lyman had a nightmarish dream in which Ellen returned and attempted to care for him. She and Shelly fought over who would give him his bath, a nightly ritual usually performed by Ada who, in the dream, was suddenly hospitalized.

Critical Evaluation:

In the late 1940's, Wallace Stegner, professor of creative writing at Stanford University, arranged for the university's library to acquire the papers of U.S. writer and illustrator Mary Hallock Foote. Foote lived from 1847 until 1938, roughly the period during which Susan Burling Ward lived and, like Susan, married a self-educated mining engineer. Using the Foote papers as his base, Stegner wrote the Pulitzer Prize-winning novel, *Angle of Repose*.

The novel, although detailed and based on much fact, is essentially a fiction. Stegner, as a creative artist, felt free to distort history to his own artistic ends. The book is realistic and, because it is based on history, can be labeled historical realism.

Recognized as a preeminent writer about the West, Stegner is sometimes compared to William Faulkner, because both use locale to express universal truths that extend far beyond their compressed geographies: Stegner, the West; Faulkner, the South and his fictional Yoknapatawpha County. Stegner, however, ranges farther geographically than Faulkner usually did; the story in *Angle of Repose* centrally involves three parts of California, as well as Colorado, Idaho, and Mexico.

Angle of Repose is, to a large extent, a study in contrasts between East and West. One major distinction between the two is that of scale, as Stegner demonstrates in the scene in which Susan, on an outing along the Hudson River with Oliver, falls in love with him. Susan leans over a precipice to see a waterfall; Stegner notes that at about the same time, John Muir was doing the same thing to look at Yosemite Falls in California. He comments that Muir had much farther to look and that the rush of water was much greater than what Susan was looking at.

In building this contrast, Stegner sets up the sort of dichotomy that, throughout the novel, defined Susan, an easterner who, despite living for seventy years in the West, could never be a westerner. Perhaps the vastness of scale intimidated her, forced her retreat into herself, into her world of words and drawings.

The most salient East-West distinction Stegner makes, however, is that the West lacks the sense of community and tradition the East has. There is, in the West, a sense always of moving on, of impermanence.

Susan is the more distinguished of Lyman Ward's grandparents. Oliver, however, emerges as the admirable character. He lacks Susan's imagination and abilities, although he has his own abilities firmly grounded in the world that he inhabits. The differences between the two probably are what first attracted them to each other, Stegner implies, but these differences also eventually drove them into their own separate worlds. Stegner uses the geological term "angle of repose," the slope at which rocks cease to roll, as a metaphoric description of their relationship. Their angle of repose, however, was merely an unhappy accommodation.

The story Stegner tells might have been told in half the space he uses for its unraveling. Had he compressed it, however, he would have compromised the novel's relaxed, episodic quality. In this book, which spans the period from 1860 to 1970, he explores the complex theme of how people interact with each other over time. He also explores how people deal with their wounds. When Oliver and Susan lose their daughter, the pain is too great for them to speak of her again within the family. Although Lyman's father never speaks of his lost sister, he expends considerable time and great energy perfecting a hybrid rose that he names "The Agnes Ward." Through this device, Stegner shows that, although people refrain from talking about the injuries that haunt their souls, the memory of these injuries remains with them.

Tied into this theme is the novel's final, surrealistic dream, in which Ellen comes to Zodiac Cottage. This chapter brings together many of the novel's disparate threads, answering some questions the rambling narrative posed and suggesting, however feebly, that perhaps people did, with difficulty, finally achieve their angles of repose.

Ellen has presumably come to effect some sort of reconciliation with Lyman. Lyman, however, is no longer a part of Ellen's life, Ellen no longer a part of his. He has constructed quite carefully the society he wants and needs: the Hawkeses, Shelly Rasmussen, and Al Sutton, his old friend from junior high school. When Ellen intrudes into this society, she threatens the structure that Lyman has devised and that suits him well. His dream becomes a nightmare as he is left alone with Ellen, who finally has to fix his meal because Ada has suffered an arrhythmia that requires Ed and Shelly to take her to the hospital. Al Sutton has long since departed.

After dinner, when the subject of Lyman's bath is raised, Shelly has returned, planning to bathe Lyman. She goes into the bathroom with him, draws a hot bath, takes off her blouse (her pendulous breasts transfix him), and then proceeds to strip him. Lyman becomes an object in a struggle between his former wife and his caregiver, thereby revealing his subconscious fears generated by his son's desire to control his father's life.

R. Baird Shuman

Bibliography:
Abrahams, William. "The Real Thing." *Atlantic Monthly*, April, 1971, 96-97. Penetrating evaluation of *Angle of Repose*. Applauds Stegner for making this fictional connection with an important past.
Proffitt, Steve. "Wallace Stegner: An Interview." *Los Angeles Times*, June 7, 1992, M3. This interview, published a year before Stegner's death, focuses on some of the writer's most central concerns. Reveals a great deal about Stegner's approach to the West as a literary setting.
Robinson, Forrest G., and Margaret G. Robinson. *Wallace Stegner*. Boston: Twayne, 1977. Offers an extended analysis of *Angle of Repose* and interesting insights into Stegner's creative production generally. Useful chronology and well-constructed index.
Streitfeld, David. "Wallace Stegner and the West Years of His Life." *The Washington Post*, April 15, 1993, C1-C2. This appraisal of Stegner's writing, published shortly after his death, makes brief but cogent statements about his major work, including *Angle of Repose*. Credits Stegner with considerable artistic integrity.

ANIMAL FARM

Type of work: Novel
Author: George Orwell (Eric Arthur Blair, 1903-1950)
Type of plot: Satire
Time of plot: Mid-twentieth century
Locale: England
First published: 1945

Principal characters:
MR. JONES, a human, owner of Manor Farm
OLD MAJOR, a pig, the first to speak of rebellion
BOXER, a cart horse
MOLLIE, a white mare
BENJAMIN, a donkey
MOSES, a tame raven
SNOWBALL, a pig, coleader in the rebellion, with
NAPOLEON, a pig, later ruler of Animal Farm
SQUEALER, a pig, a brilliant talker

The Story:

Old Major called a meeting as soon as Mr. Jones went to sleep. Jones, who was cruel to his animals, had been drinking excessively of late. When all the animals were gathered, Major began to speak. He had had a dream in which he remembered the song *Beasts of England* from his distant past. He taught it to the others and told them they should rise up to defeat Jones and do their work for themselves, for their own benefit. He said that all men were evil and that all animals were good and equal.

Three days after telling his dream, Major died. Snowball, Napoleon, and Squealer developed Major's teachings into a system called Animalism. The rebellion came quickly and suddenly after Jones had been drinking in town. When he returned home, the animals ran him and the other humans off the farm. The animals could hardly believe their good fortune. Napoleon led them back to the barn, where everyone was served extra food to celebrate.

In preparation for the rebellion, the pigs had learned to read and write. One day, the pigs wrote the seven commandments of Animalism on the wall of the barn. It was realized that since the rebellion, the cows had not been milked. The pigs managed to do it but the five buckets of milk vanished while the other animals were out working.

The animals set forth to harvest the hay crop. They did this faster than had ever been done, but the pigs did not do any actual work, they held a supervisory position. Boxer, the cart horse, was the hardest worker and the quickest to follow the rules set up by the pigs. "I will work harder," was his maxim and his motto; under any difficult circumstance, he always repeated it. Benjamin, the donkey, was the only animal that was unchanged since the rebellion. He worked in the same obstinate way that he always had, doing his share and no more. Napoleon and Snowball opposed each other at every juncture at which decisions were made. Snowball began committees for the adults while Napoleon took puppies away from their parents, to educate them and keep them in a special loft of the barn where no one else was allowed to go.

Jones and other humans attempted to take Animal Farm back again but they were unsuccessful. In the battle, Snowball led the forces and was wounded by a shotgun. Snowball managed to rid Jones of his gun, and Boxer kicked a boy. This was named the "Battle of the Cowshed" and was a success for the animals.

The winter drew near and at the meetings held every Sunday, Napoleon and Snowball still opposed each other. No matter what was in question, they always held different views. Snowball was a brilliant speaker at the meetings and won support through his eloquent speeches, while Napoleon was better at drumming up support for himself in sly conversations between the meetings. Napoleon trained the sheep to bleat "Four legs good, two legs bad" at crucial moments in Snowball's speeches, which served to negate anything of relevance that Snowball might say.

The worst argument was the one over the windmill. Snowball wanted the animals to build a windmill because with it, and the electricity it would provide, the animals would only have to work three days a week. Napoleon was against it, and said they should spend their time producing more food. Benjamin was the only one who did not side with either Snowball or Napoleon. Windmill or no windmill, he said, life would go on as it had always gone on—that is, badly. When the meeting at which the question of the windmill would be decided, Snowball gave an eloquent speech and Napoleon said nothing. Snowball looked sure to win. Then Napoleon's puppies came forth, now as large and treacherous dogs, and they drove Snowball off the farm.

Napoleon established himself as leader, with the pack of dogs reinforcing his position. He said there would be no more meetings and no more debates. He and other pigs would decide everything. Three weeks later, Napoleon used Snowball's plans for the windmill and issued the order that work on the windmill was to begin.

To get necessary supplies, Napoleon began dealing with people. The other animals felt uneasy about it but could do nothing as Napoleon seemed above reproach and his guard dogs assured his position completely. The pigs moved into Jones's house and began sleeping in the beds. This was in direct opposition to one of the seven commandments, so the pigs began changing the commandments in order to fit their increasing status as masters of the farm. The windmill became the top priority, and whenever problems arose, they were always blamed on Snowball, who was supposedly lurking near the farm and causing every problem that existed. Food grew scarce. Napoleon told the animals that he would begin selling eggs to humans again, and the hens were required to lay eggs for this purpose. The hens believed this was murder of their chicks and refused, but Napoleon stopped their food rations until they complied with his demands. Soon after the hens' attempted refusal to comply with Napoleon, there was a mass murder, in which Napoleon's dogs killed every animal that had ever spoken against him. Squealer upheld the actions of Napoleon and convinced all the remaining animals that their lives were much better than they ever had been.

The seven commandments were abolished and the only slogan left was this: "All animals are equal but some animals are more equal than others." The pigs discovered alcohol and clothes, and invited humans over to inspect the farm. The people found it in excellent running order. The pigs came to look and act like people and treated the animals more horribly than Jones had.

Critical Evaluation:

Animal Farm was written soon after George Orwell resigned from the British Broadcasting Corporation in 1943, while he worked as the literary editor for the *Tribune*, in London. He had not written a novel during the three years he was with the BBC and was having an extremely hard time writing at all, with World War II in full force. *Animal Farm* was completed in four months. It was one year later that he found someone who would publish it and almost another year before it was finally offered to the public. *Animal Farm* and the book he wrote following it, *Nineteen Eighty-Four* (1949), are Orwell's most highly acclaimed works.

An anti-Soviet satire, the book was ahead of its time. The U.S.S.R. was fighting with the allied forces in World War II, and the book would be seen as an attack on the U.S.S.R. and Joseph Stalin. After World War II, the book was published. The political situation was different then, and *Animal Farm* appeared just as the Cold War was beginning.

Orwell called *Animal Farm* "the first . . . in which I tried, with full consciousness of what I was doing, to fuse political purpose and artistic purpose into one whole." *Animal Farm* was a huge success as soon as it was published. It was established as a modern classic almost immediately. A very short book, written simply and fluently, it is a drastic departure from anything else Orwell had or would produce.

Animal Farm abounds with allegory, beginning with Old Major, who recalls Karl Marx. Every character and event may be seen as symbolic of historical Russian figures and events between the years 1917 and 1943. Orwell said the book's purpose was "the destruction of the Soviet myth." The flag raised by the animals, with hoof and horn, is similar to the Russian flag of hammer and sickle. Napoleon is generally likened to Stalin, and the countenance and actions of Snowball are thought to resemble those of Leon Trotsky. The name "Snowball" recalls Trotsky's white hair and beard, and possibly too, that he crumbled under Stalin's opposition. The event in which Snowball is chased away from the farm is similar to the expulsion of Trotsky from Russia in 1929. The book is written with such sophistication and subtlety, however, that a reader unaware of Russian history might very well see it as an animal story only. Moreover, reading the book strictly to find reference to Russian history misses an important point: Orwell said the book "is intended as a satire on dictatorship in general." The name of the ruling pig, "Napoleon," is a reminder that there have been dictators outside Russia. Not Stalin in particular, but totalitarianism, is the enemy Orwell exposes.

The problem Orwell addresses is how to combine power with ideals. How do the oppressed who rise above their oppressors manage to keep from becoming like the oppressors? With this book, Orwell gives an instance of the slave coming to resemble the master after overthrowing him. There is not a happy ending. From the beginning of the story, the dogs are against the rats, thus foreshadowing an animal government in which social justice would not be acquired.

Beaird Glover

Bibliography:

Gardner, Averil. *George Orwell*. Boston: Twayne, 1987. Gives information on Orwell at the time of writing *Animal Farm* and a chapter-by-chapter synopsis of meaning and symbols as they apply to Russian history. Includes some criticism that *Animal Farm* received at its publication.

Hammond, J. R. *A George Orwell Companion*. New York: St. Martin's Press, 1982. Features pictures of Orwell spanning his career and gives an extended reference to characters and events of *Animal Farm* as they compare to historical Russia. Considers the evolution of Orwellian philosophy through his novels and essays.

Kalechofsky, Roberta. *George Orwell*. New York: Frederick Ungar, 1973. Has an extended section on *Animal Farm* about the corruption of the seven commandments of animalism and compares the themes of *Animal Farm* as similar to those of *Nineteen Eighty-Four*.

Meyers, Jeffrey. *A Reader's Guide to George Orwell*. Totowa, N.J.: Littlefield, Adams, 1977.

Gives a detailed account of the political allegory of *Animal Farm*, specifically with Russian history.

Williams, Raymond. *George Orwell*. New York: Viking Press, 1971. Includes several quotes from Orwell and the criticism he received for *Animal Farm*. Also explains the difficulties Orwell went through in trying to find a publisher.

ANNA CHRISTIE

Type of work: Drama
Author: Eugene O'Neill (1888-1953)
Type of plot: Social realism
Time of plot: Early twentieth century
Locale: Johnny the Priest's saloon, New York City, and Provincetown harbor
First performed: 1921; first published, 1923

> *Principal characters:*
> CHRIS CHRISTOPHERSON, captain of a barge
> ANNA, his daughter
> MAT BURKE, a stoker
> MARTHY OWEN, a prostitute

The Story:

Old Chris Christopherson looked upon the sea as the symbol of a malignant fate. True, he was now skipper of the coal barge, *Simeon Winthrop*, but in his younger days he had been an able seaman and boatswain on the old windjammers and had visited every port in the world. As far back as he knew, the men of his family in Sweden had followed the sea. His father died aboard ship in the Indian Ocean, and two of his brothers were drowned. Nor was the curse of the sea confined to the men in the family. After the news of her husband's and her sons' deaths, Chris's mother had died of a broken heart. Unable to bear the loneliness of being a sailor's wife, his own wife had brought their young daughter, Anna, to America to live with some cousins on a farm in Minnesota. Anna's mother had died, and the girl was brought up by her relatives.

Chris had not seen his daughter for almost twenty years. One day while he was having a drink at Johnny the Priest's saloon near South Street in New York City, he received a postcard from St. Louis telling him that Anna was on her way to New York. This news threw Chris into something of a panic, for living on the barge with him was a middle-aged prostitute named Marthy. Chris decided to get rid of the woman. Being a kind-hearted soul and genuinely fond of Marthy, he disliked the idea of turning her out, but Marthy said that Chris had always treated her decently, and she would move on to someone else. When Marthy caught a glimpse of Chris's daughter, she was shocked. Anna was twenty years old and pretty in a buxom sort of way, but her painted face and cheap showy clothes were telltale evidence of what she was—a prostitute. Marthy wondered what Chris's reaction was going to be.

In his eyes, however, Anna was the innocent child he had always imagined her to be, and he was even hesitant about ordering wine to celebrate their reunion. Life on the barge was an entirely new experience for Anna Christopherson. She came to love the sea and to respond to its beauty with the same intensity with which her father responded to its malignance. With the soothing effect of her new environment, and the presence of her father's gentleness and simplicity, Anna began to lose some of her hardness and to build some faith in men.

One night, while the *Simeon Winthrop* was anchored in the outer harbor of Provincetown, Massachusetts, Chris heard cries for help. He pulled aboard the barge four men who had been drifting for five days after the wreck of their ship. One of the men, an Irishman named Mat Burke, took an immediate fancy to Anna, and even in his weakened condition he made it clear that he intended to have Anna for his own. Mat Burke represented everything in life that Chris hated. In the first place, he was a stoker on a steamship, an occupation the old windjammer sailor regarded as beneath contempt. Second, Burke followed the sea and so was connected in

266

the old Swede's mind with inevitable tragedy. Last, and most important from Chris's viewpoint, Mat was obviously in love with Anna and wanted to take her away from him. To Anna, on the other hand, Mat represented all that she had always wanted in life. At first she was naturally suspicious of his Irish glibness, but she soon began to see that underneath his voluble exterior there were some genuine convictions, a basic core of integrity which gave her a sense of security, as well as, in the light of her own past, a gnawing fear.

Her father and Mat were mortal enemies from the start. This conflict reached its climax one day in the cabin when Chris, goaded on by the Irishman's taunts, came at Mat with a knife, intending to kill him. Anna came in as Mat overpowered the old man. She realized that they were fighting over her as if she were a piece of property which must belong to one or the other.

This situation was so close to her previous experience with men that she made them both listen to a confession of the truth about herself, of which apparently neither of them had been aware. She informed her father that his romantic picture of her idyllic life on the Minnesota farm was untrue from beginning to end, that she had been worked relentlessly by her relatives, and that at sixteen she had been seduced by one of her cousins. At last she had gone to St. Louis and entered a bawdy house, where her experience with men did not differ greatly from what she had known on the farm. She informed Mat that for the first time in her life she had realized what love might be. Mat, having neither intelligence nor imagination enough to appreciate Anna's sincerity, angrily called her names and left the barge in disgust. Chris followed him, and the two men proceeded to get drunk. Anna waited on the *Simeon Winthrop* for two days, hoping that Mat would return. Finally she prepared to go to New York and resume her old profession.

Her father was the first to return with the news that to save her from going back to the old life he had signed on the *Londonderry*, a steamer to Cape Town, Africa, and had made arrangements for his pay to be turned over to Anna. When Mat returned, Anna felt sure he had come back merely to kill her. He was bruised and bloody from waterfront fights. He too had signed on the *Londonderry*, and the irony of her father and Mat on the same boat struck Anna as funny. Finally she made Mat see that she had hated the men who had bought her and that all she wanted was the assurance of one man's love.

Chris was glad that Anna and Mat were reconciled, were going to be married and be happy, for he now realized that much of Anna's past misery was his own fault. At the same time, however, time he wondered what tricks the malignant sea would play on Anna and Mat in the future.

Critical Evaluation:

Anna Christie, which won a second Pulitzer Prize for Eugene O'Neill in 1922, was produced in an earlier version as *Chris*, about a veteran seaman reduced to the role of coal bargeman, who frequented O'Neill's favorite saloon. The final title of the play indicates O'Neill's shift of emphasis during numerous rewrites from the crusty old sea dog to his daughter Anna. Originally conceived of as a young woman carefully raised in England, Anna emerges as the title character in *Anna Christie*, a former prostitute tormented by her past. A realistic drama, with symbolic overtones, the play focuses upon the dynamics of the love-hate relationships of the three central figures, Chris, Anna, and Mat Burke, the Irish sailor tossed into their lives.

From one perspective, the plot of *Anna Christie* concerns the regeneration of a hardened prostitute as a result of her giving and receiving love, but this somewhat simplistic story is provided complexity through the development of the characters. As O'Neill has created them, they are human beings of passion and energy, people struggling against the forces of an impersonal universe.

The product of a brutal upbringing, Anna, a woman who is strong physically and mentally, mistrusts all men, and her dreams of love, home, and a sense of belonging are pitifully simple and small. Alienated and outcast, her position links her with the central figures of two of O'Neill's other early plays, Brutus Jones in *The Emperor Jones* (1921) and Yank in *The Hairy Ape* (1922). Like them, she is a victim of circumstances beyond her control. Unlike them, she is honest with herself and eventually is compelled to be honest with her father and lover. In the third act her outburst about the truth of her past is a proclamation of self not unlike Nora's declaration in Henrik Ibsen's *A Doll's House* (1879). In essence, she demands recognition and acceptance for herself. She may have sold herself to men in the past, but she refuses to be owned by them in the present. In contrast, Chris and Mat are weak and insensitive men. Chris is immature and deluded; he avoided responsibility as a father by sending Anna away as a child. He avoids responsibility for his woman Marthy by forcing her away when Anna arrives. He further tries to escape a truthful relationship with Anna by shipping out at the end of the play. Unwilling to examine his own motives, Chris hates and fears "dat ole davil" sea and blames it for all his misfortunes. Still, his efforts to protect Anna, although misguided, are understandable and human.

Mat, supremely confident in his youth and physical strength, as well as superstitious in his Catholicism, does not listen to Anna's doubts see her misgivings, believing that the power of his love will overcome whatever obstacles she might voice. Jealous of each other, both men would prefer to maintain the illusion that Anna is an innocent young woman in need of their masculine protection and guidance. Despite the fact that their sexual behavior as sailors has been equally promiscuous, the revelation of her sordid past hurts and enrages them, driving them off on two-day binges. Their sudden conversion to tolerance at the end of the play has concerned critics and audiences.

Certain elements, carefully integrated, lift the play above the realistic level. O'Neill uses the sea symbolically, as he does many times in his works, to represent the forces of life that are ineffable, uncontrolled, and sometimes cruel. Contrasted with the sea is the land. On land, there is the harshness of the farm of Anna's childhood, and the house she entered that brought her disease, and even Johnny the Priest's saloon, which is unfriendly to women of her kind. The vastness and power of the sea exhilarate Anna, who has been landlocked all her life. On the barge she feels cleansed, happy, as though she has found a home. Chris mistrusts the sea as Anna mistrusts men. He sees himself as its victim. The sea has deprived him of wife and family and he fears losing Anna to its spell. On the other hand, Mat, rescued by the barge, believes that the sea has brought him to Anna, and that the will of God operates within it. The sea is life, and the characters, however they respond to it, are at its mercy.

Another symbolic element is the fog, which represents the mystery of life and which sometimes clouds human understanding. Chris fears the fog for its ability to confuse and mislead; he considers it the worst of the tricks the sea can play. The fog of the first two acts allows Anna to be soothed and freed from the guilt of her past. When the fog lifts and the sun shines in Act III, she finds the strength to enlighten the men with the truth. When the fog returns at the end of the play, it carries a sense of foreboding for the future of the three characters.

Critics have faulted the last act, citing the neatness of the resolution as contrived, "a compromise with integrity." In its sense of inevitability, the play seems to promise a tragic ending. O'Neill responded that it is "just the sort of compromise those characters would have arranged for themselves in real life." In a letter he jokingly claimed that he had told his characters to die, but they insisted on living, which is "what most of us have to do." Another point of view sees the ending as far from happy, as the fog swirls in and old Chris mutters about the fog: "You can't see vhere you vas going, no. Only dat ole davil, sea—she knows!" Moreover, Anna is left landlocked and alone.

Written in the early 1920's, when O'Neill was producing startling experimental plays, *Anna Christie* appears to represent a return to more conventional drama for him. However, in the depth of the character delineation and the subtle integration of the symbolic material, O'Neill demonstrated his continued progress as a playwright.

"Critical Evaluation" by Joyce E. Henry

Bibliography:
Bogard, Travis. *Contour in Time: The Plays of Eugene O'Neill.* Rev. ed. New York: Oxford University Press, 1988. Argues for viewing the O'Neill canon as the playwright's autobiography. Contains a detailed comparison of the final version with earlier versions of *Anna Christie.*

Estrin, Mark W., ed. *Conversations with Eugene O'Neill.* Jackson: University Press of Mississippi, 1990. A fascinating collection of interviews with the playwright arranged chronologically from 1920 to 1948. Contains many of O'Neill's comments about the characters and creation of *Anna Christie.*

Floyd, Virginia. *The Plays of Eugene O'Neill: A New Assessment.* New York: Frederick Ungar, 1985. Chapters analyzing each of O'Neill's plays. Asserts that *Anna Christie* is a failure of character and plot.

Gelb, Arthur, and Barbara Gelb. *O'Neill.* Rev. ed. New York: Perennial Library, 1987. A monumental biography of almost one thousand pages with several sections of photographs. An excellent reference for details of the playwright's life and plays.

Houchin, John H., ed. *The Critical Response to Eugene O'Neill.* Westport, Conn.: Greenwood Press, 1993. A collection of critical opinions, including reviews of productions from periodicals and scholarly essays, three of which focus upon *Anna Christie.* The diversity of perspectives is useful.

ANNA KARÉNINA

Type of work: Novel
Author: Leo Tolstoy (1828-1910)
Type of plot: Social realism
Time of plot: Nineteenth century
Locale: Russia
First published: 1875-1877 (English translation, 1886)

> Principal characters:
> ANNA KARÉNINA
> ALEXEI KARÉNIN, her husband
> COUNT VRONSKY, her lover
> STEPAN OBLONSKY, her brother
> KITTY SHTCHERBATSKY, Stepan's sister-in-law
> KONSTANTINE LEVIN, Kitty's beloved

The Story:

Anna Karénina, the sister of Stepan Oblonsky, came to Moscow in an attempt to patch up a quarrel between her brother and his wife, Dolly. There she met the handsome young Count Vronsky, who was rumored to be in love with Dolly's younger sister, Kitty. Konstantine Levin, of an old Muscovite family, was also in love with Kitty, and his visit to Moscow coincided with Anna's. Kitty refused Levin, but to her chagrin she received no proposal from the count. Indeed, Vronsky had no intention of proposing to Kitty. His heart went out to Anna the first time he laid eyes on her, and when Anna returned to her home in St. Petersburg, he followed her.

Soon they began to be seen together at soirées and at the theater, apparently unaware of gossip which circulated about them. Karénin, Anna's husband, became concerned. A coldly ambitious and dispassionate man, he believed that his social position was at stake. One night, he discussed these rumors with Anna and pointed out the danger of her flirtation, as he called it. He forbade her to entertain Vronsky at home and cautioned her to be more careful. He was not jealous of his wife, only worried over the social consequences of her behavior. He reminded her of her duty to her young son, Seryozha. Anna said she would obey him, and there the matter rested.

Anna, however, was unable to conceal her true feelings when Vronsky was injured in a racetrack accident. Karénin upbraided her for her indiscreet behavior in public. He considered a duel, separation, and divorce, but rejected all these courses. When he finally decided to keep Anna under his roof, he reflected that he was acting in accordance with the laws of religion. Anna continued to meet Vronsky in secret.

Levin had returned to his country estate after Kitty had refused him, and he busied himself there in problems of agriculture and peasant labor. One day, he went into the fields and worked with a scythe along with the serfs. He felt that he was beginning to understand the old primitive philosophy of their lives. He planned new developments, among them a cooperative enterprise system. When he heard that Kitty was not married after all and that she had been ill but was soon returning to Moscow, he resolved to seek her hand in marriage once more. Secretly, he knew she loved him. His pride, as well as hers, had kept them apart. Accordingly, Levin made the journey to Moscow with new hope that soon Kitty would be his wife.

Against her husband's orders, Anna Karénina sent for Vronsky and told him that she was pregnant. Aware of his responsibilities to Anna, he begged her to petition Karénin for a divorce so that she would be free to marry him. Karénin informed her coldly that he would consider the child his and accept it so that the world should never know his wife's disgrace, but he refused to think of going through shameful divorce proceedings. Karénin reduced Anna to submission by warning her that he would take Seryozha away if she persisted in making a fool of herself.

The strained family relationship continued unbroken. One night, Karénin had planned to go out, and Anna persuaded Vronsky to come to the house. As he was leaving, Karénin met Vronsky on the front steps. Enraged, Karénin told Anna that he had decided to get a divorce and that he would keep Seryozha in his custody. Divorce proceedings, however, were so intricate, the scandal so great, the whole aspect of the step so disgusting to Karénin that he could not bring himself to go through with the process. As Anna's confinement drew near, he was still undecided. After winning an important political seat, he became even more unwilling to risk his public reputation.

At the birth of her child, Anna became deathly ill. Overcome with guilt, Vronsky attempted suicide but failed. Karénin was reduced to a state of such confusion that he determined to grant his wife any request, since he thought she was on her deathbed. The sight of Vronsky seemed to be the only thing that restored her. After many months of illness, she went with her lover and baby daughter to Italy, where they lived under strained circumstances. Meanwhile, Levin proposed once more to Kitty; after a flurry of preparations, they were married.

Anna Karénina and Vronsky returned to Russia and went to live on his estate. It was now impossible for Anna to return home. Although Karénin had not gone through with divorce proceedings, he considered himself separated from Anna and was everywhere thought to be a man of fine loyalty and unswerving honor, unjustly imposed upon by an unfaithful wife. Sometimes Anna stole into town to see Seryozha, but her fear of being discovered there by her husband cut these visits short.

After each visit, she returned bitter and sad. She became more and more demanding toward Vronsky, with the result that he spent less time with her. She took little interest in her child. Before long, she convinced herself that Vronsky was in love with another woman. One day, she could not stay alone in the house. She found herself at the railway station, and she bought a ticket. As she stood on the platform gazing at the tracks below, the thunder of an approaching train roared in her ears. Suddenly, she remembered a man run over in the Moscow railroad station on the day she and Vronsky met. Carefully measuring the distance, she threw herself in front of the approaching train.

After her death, Vronsky joined the army. He had changed from a handsome, cheerful man to one who welcomed death; his only reason for living had been Anna. For Levin and Kitty, life became a round of increasing daily work and mundane routine, which they shared with each other. At last, Levin knew the responsibility wealth imposed upon him in his dealings with the peasants. Kitty helped him to handle his responsibility. Although there were many questions he could never answer satisfactorily to himself, he was nevertheless aware of the satisfying beauty of life—its toil, leisure, pain, and happiness.

Critical Evaluation:

The span from the time when Leo Tolstoy first conceived of *Anna Karénina* to the time when he finished the novel covered seven years, the last four of which were spent in the actual task of writing. According to his wife Sonia's diary, the idea of writing a novel about adultery first occurred to Tolstoy in 1870. It was not until three years later, however, as Tolstoy remarked in a letter to a friend, that the impetus to begin work on the book was provided by Tolstoy's rereading of a fragment in Alexander Pushkin's *The Tales of Belkin* (1834). Tolstoy attributed the inspiration to a line which conjured in his imagination the scene of a reception in fashionable society—the scene manifests itself as Princess Betsy Tvershaya's party. Pushkin's influence, however, was perhaps greater than Tolstoy realized, for, in some aspects of character and appearance, Anna Karénina resembles Pushkin's protagonist Zinaida Volsky. Nevertheless, Tolstoy's work on the novel proceeded at an agonizingly slow pace, leaving the writer endlessly frustrated by what he described as a "block" which hampered his progress. Although the opening chapters appeared in 1875—the novel was first published in installments—the last chapters did not find their way into print until 1877. Tolstoy's perfectionism was such that he would allow nothing less than his best writing to be published, regardless of the personal anguish which the constant rewriting caused him.

The epigraph to *Anna Karénina*—a quotation from Romans 12:19, " 'Vengeance is mine: I will repay,' saith the Lord"—is suggestive of its theme, for Tolstoy, like his contemporary Fyodor Dostoevski, was deeply concerned with sin (or crime), guilt, punishment, and atonement. Moreover, the epigraph implies, along with its express prohibition of human retribution, that judgment, too, is a divine prerogative. It thus furnishes a key to Tolstoy's treatment of characters in the novel. He does not, for example, explicitly praise or condemn Anna, since such a value judgment would usurp a godly privilege. This is also true of the other characters. Tolstoy does not evaluate, he describes. Yet it is difficult to avoid drawing some conclusions because the plot revolves around adultery, an offense with both social and theological ramifications. Nevertheless, Tolstoy maintained that his intent was to show that all the adverse consequences of evil ultimately originated with God. In this context, then, Anna's ostracism from polite society, for example, would have to be understood as a manifestation of God's will—an interpretation consonant with Tolstoy's mystical religious beliefs. There is no doubt that Anna has sinned, and society's punishment of her appears to confirm God's guilty verdict. No matter how extenuating the circumstances, Tolstoy seems to say, God's punishment of sinners is inexorable.

In developing this theme in *Anna Karénina*, Tolstoy minimizes the purely secular interest that society has in suppressing adultery as an act disruptive of the social order, although this aspect of the problem has been dealt with by other novelists writing about adultery. Two examples will suffice here. In *The Scarlet Letter* (1850), Nathaniel Hawthorne depicts Hester Prynne's adultery as both a crime against society and a sin against God. Although Hester admits she is a sinner, she will not concede that she is a criminal. Thus, the spiritual strength that she derives from her admission of sinful guilt enables her to cope with her social isolation and ultimately to survive. Yet Hawthorne, despite portraying Hester in a sympathetic light, does not clearly exonerate her, for he sees value in society's standards, too. In effect, he declines to choose between the two. In *Madame Bovary* (1857), however, Gustave Flaubert presents Emma's adulteries strictly as transgressions against society; theological considerations are virtually nonexistent. Obsessed with romantic fantasies, Emma has no conception of the real-life strictures of society. Her multiple infidelities carry her deep into debt with gifts for her lovers and clothing, perfumes, and cosmetics for herself. When she is at last forced to accept the reality that she cannot pay her creditor, she is overwhelmed with guilt, remorse, despair, and the fear of discovery. She then takes arsenic and dies quickly but painfully, unable to face the punishment society is certain to exact. Flaubert thus underscores both the power and the primacy of society's norms.

These three well-known novels about adultery—*The Scarlet Letter, Madame Bovary,* and *Anna Karénina*—differ in their emphases, but their treatment of adultery is essentially similar. On the one hand, the emphasis in *The Scarlet Letter* is on the tension between the values of established society (religious and social) and individual values—in *Anna Karénina,* on the immanence of spiritual values and God's will. On the other hand, all three novels disapprove of adultery, although their reasons vary according to their biases, as revealed through their respective emphases.

In *Anna Karénina,* Tolstoy wrote a moving story of human emotional needs conflicting with the dominant social mores of the time. Given Tolstoy's religious mysticism combined with his incipient socialism, this elemental conflict could be resolved in no other way. The crucial factor in the equation revolves around what is usually characterized, euphemistically, as "the Russian soul," a quality lacking in Hawthorne and Flaubert. This nearly ineffable quality amalgamates religious mysticism and nationalism into almost divine zeal, the pressures of which eventually drive Anna to suicide, since her sense of betrayal of moral imperatives is nevertheless acute for her having betrayed them. She is thus uniquely representative of "the Russian soul." As such, she symbolizes Tolstoy's genuinely Russian insistence upon the marrying of eternal verities with modern conditions. For this reason, many critics believe that *Anna Karénina* stands not second to but equal with *War and Peace* (1866) in Tolstoy's corpus, offering a profound insight into the relationship between the individual and the surrounding society.

"Critical Evaluation" by Joanne G. Kashdan

Bibliography:
Bloom, Harold, ed. *Leo Tolstoy.* New York: Chelsea House, 1986. This book contains essays by R. P. Blackmur and Barbara Hardy. The former explores the way Tolstoy exposes his characters to ambiguity, studies their society and its manners, and discusses the nature of Anna's tragedy. The latter emphasizes Tolstoy's vivid realism, his superb handling of the flow of time, and the intricate and deft way he populates his novels with characters. Chronology and bibliography included.

Jones, Malcolm, ed. *New Essays on Tolstoy.* Cambridge, England: Cambridge University Press, 1978. In "Problems of Communication," Jones explores Tolstoy's amazing sense of physical presence and gesture and how previous critics have treated it.

Knowles, A. V., ed. *Tolstoy: The Critical Heritage.* Boston: Routledge & Kegan Paul, 1978. This book contains contemporary Russian reviews of the novel from 1875 to 1877. Includes a bibliography and an appendix with Russian literary and historical references.

Rowe, William W. *Leo Tolstoy.* Boston: Twayne, 1986. Chapter 5 treats the novel as Tolstoy's finest and traces how he developed the idea for it. Detailed discussion of structure. Separate sections on different themes and literary techniques in the novel, such as Anna's "guilt," Levin and Kitty, and foreshadowing. Chronology, notes, and bibliography included.

Wilson, A. N. *Tolstoy.* London: H. Hamilton, 1988. A full-scale biography. Chapter 12 delves into the gestation and development of the novel, its structural cohesiveness, and its scenes of intimacy. Notes and bibliography included.

ANNA OF THE FIVE TOWNS

Type of work: Novella
Author: Arnold Bennett (1867-1931)
Type of plot: Domestic realism
Time of plot: Late nineteenth century
Locale: The Potteries, England
First published: 1902

Principal characters:
 EPHRAIM TELLWRIGHT, a miser
 ANNA, his older daughter
 AGNES, his younger daughter
 HENRY MYNORS, Anna's suitor
 WILLIE PRICE, a man in love with Anna
 BEATRICE SUTTON, Anna's friend

The Story:

Ephraim Tellwright was a miser, one of the wealthiest men in any of the Five Towns, a group of small industrial towns joined by a single road. He was a former Methodist lay preacher and teacher, concerned more with getting congregations in sound financial shape than with their souls. Although he had married money and made more money from rentals and foreclosures, he lived in the most frugal way possible and gave his two daughters nothing but the barest essentials. Both of his wives had died, the first giving him his daughter Anna and the second producing Agnes before her death. Mr. Tellwright was usually taciturn. So long as his meals were on time, no money was wasted, and the house was never left alone and unguarded, he paid little attention to his daughters. Anna loved her father even though she could never feel close to him. Agnes, much younger, followed her sister's lead. The two girls were unusually close, having no one else in their lives.

On Anna's twenty-first birthday, her father called her into his office and told her that she would that day inherit almost fifty thousand pounds from her mother's estate. He had invested the original sum wisely, and it had grown to a fortune. Anna, who had never owned one pound to call her own, could not comprehend an amount so large. Accustomed to letting her father handle all business affairs, she willingly gave him control of her fortune. The income from the stocks and rentals was deposited in the bank in her name, but she gave her father her checkbook and signed only when she was instructed to do so. The money made little difference in Anna's life; it simply lay in the bank until her father told her to invest it.

One result of the money, however, created unhappiness for Anna. Among her properties was a run-down factory owned by Titus Price, who was also a Methodist and superintendent of the chapel's Sunday school. Because Price was continually behind in his rent, Mr. Tellwright forced Anna to keep demanding something on account. Knowing that the property would never rent to anyone else, the old miser never put Price out but kept hounding him for as much as the man could pay. Anna usually had to deal with Willie Price, the son, and she always left the interview with a feeling of guilt. Although the sight of Willie's embarrassment left her unhappy, she always demanded his money, because she was afraid to face her father without it.

A teacher in the Sunday school in which Anna taught was Henry Mynors, already at the age

274

of thirty a pillar in the chapel and a successful man in the community. Anna was attracted to him, and she tried to join in his religious fervor but could not quite bring herself to repent or to accept God publicly at the revival meetings. She felt that repentance should be a private matter. Henry was clearly in love with her. When the townspeople said that he was interested mainly in her money, Anna refused to believe the gossip. Henry began to call on her occasionally, combining his courtship with business with Mr. Tellwright. The miser persuaded Anna to invest some of her money in Henry's business after first arranging for a large share of the profits and a high interest.

After Anna had come into her fortune, she was invited for the first time to the house of Mrs. Sutton, the town's social leader. Mrs. Sutton's daughter Beatrice and Anna became friends. Rumors spread that Beatrice and Henry Mynors had once been engaged. The Suttons took Anna and Henry to the Isle of Man on a vacation, and Anna thought there could never again be such luxurious living. It had been necessary for her to take ten pounds of her own money to get clothes for the trip, but her father had berated her violently when she told him what she had done. Her time spent with Henry and the Suttons, however, helped her forget his anger. When the vacation was marred by Beatrice's serious illness, Anna won a permanent place in the Suttons' affection by her unselfish and competent nursing.

After Beatrice recovered, Anna and Henry returned home. Before they left the island, Henry proposed to Anna, and she accepted. Later her father gave his consent, because Henry knew the value of money. Young Agnes was enchanted by the romantic aspects of the courtship, and Anna was happy in her quiet love for Henry. The joy of her engagement, however, was immediately clouded by the news that old Mr. Price had hanged himself. Anna felt that she and her father were to blame, because they had hounded him for his rent. Henry assured her that Mr. Price was in debt to many people and that she need not feel guilty. Nevertheless, Anna worried a great deal about the suicide and about Willie, for whom she had quite maternal feelings.

Later, Willie confessed to her that a bank note he had given in payment had been forged. The confession seemed to reduce Willie to nothing. Anna realized that he and his father had been driven to desperation, and she tried to protect Willie and Mr. Price's reputation by taking the forged note from her father's office. When she told Mr. Tellwright that she had burned the note, he was furious with her and never forgave her.

Because Willie was planning to make a fresh start in Australia, Henry arranged to rent the Price house, intending that he and Anna would live there after they were married. Although Anna was sure she could never be happy in a house the miserable Prices had owned, she was docile and let Henry make all the arrangements. When Anna told her father that she needed one hundred pounds to pay for her linens and her wedding clothes, Mr. Tellwright denounced her for a spendthrift. Handing over the checkbook, he told her not to bother him again about her money. Henry, pleased at the turn of events, was full of plans for the use of Anna's fortune.

It became known that before his death, Mr. Price had defrauded the chapel of fifty pounds. Anna tried to keep the information from Willie, but someone told him just as he was ready to leave for Australia. When he told Anna good-bye, he looked like a whipped child. As Anna looked into his eyes for the last time, she knew suddenly that he loved her and that she loved him. She let him go, however, because she felt bound by her promise to Henry. She had been dutiful all her life; it was too late for her to change.

Willie was never heard from again. Had anyone in Five Towns happened to look into an abandoned pitshaft, the mystery of Willie would have been solved. The meek lad had found his only way to peace.

Critical Evaluation:

Anna of the Five Towns, Arnold Bennett's second novel, was the first that established the identity of the Five Towns, that area of the West Midlands devoted to the pottery industry and usually known as The Potteries. This was where Bennett himself had been brought up and where he entered his father's law business until moving to London. The Five Towns, as he called them (there are actually six or seven), served as the setting for many of his subsequent and more famous novels even though he never returned to live in the area.

The novel can to some extent be seen as a regional novel, as are Thomas Hardy's Wessex novels and some of George Eliot's works. Like Eliot's *Adam Bede* (1859), *Anna of the Five Towns* has a Midlands setting further defined by the various Methodist communities that flourished there in the mid- and late nineteenth century. Unlike Eliot's rural novel, however, *Anna of the Five Towns* can also be classified as an industrial novel. Bennett describes the details of the pottery manufacture knowledgeably, and he contrasts the best and worst practices in the works of Titus Price and Henry Mynors. This contrast echoes the larger contrast between Price's son, Willie, who works in his father's ramshackle workshop, and Mynors, whose efficiency in everything he does is exemplified in his modern factory.

In its Midlands setting, chapel culture, and industrial descriptions, *Anna of the Five Towns* also anticipates the novels of D. H. Lawrence. Like Lawrence, Bennett stresses the ugliness of industrialized urbanization, the ruination of the countryside, and the circumscribed, barren lives of many of the working class. Bennett, however, unlike Lawrence, does not attempt poetry in his style but veers toward the documentary. One feels there is some civic pride left in Bennett, just as civic pride continued among the inhabitants of The Potteries later in the century. More important, Bennett does not point toward a counterculture; spiritual life, insofar as it is still possible, is to be found in traditional interior modes of Christian self-examination as defined by the practices and traditions of Methodist spirituality.

In some ways, therefore, *Anna of the Five Towns* could also be called a religious novel: not in the traditional sense of the Victorian religious novel, but as a result of Bennett's taking the religious practices, beliefs, and spirituality of his characters seriously and analyzing them in a sympathetic way. Here again, Bennett is more akin to Eliot than to Hardy or Lawrence. Some critics have suggested that Bennett exposes the confining and even repressive atmosphere of nonconformity, but this is surely a prejudiced reading. Certain characters, among them Titus Price and Ephraim Tellwright, are exposed as hypocrites, yet their failings are portrayed in human terms. They are not the fault of Methodism. Ephraim's backsliding is part of his self-chosen dessication of spirit. He is based, if anything, on Honoré de Balzac's *Eugénie Grandet* (1833).

The faith of other characters, however, is genuine: Mrs. Sutton's is particularly attractive, but even Henry Mynor's is perfectly genuine. His Christian life may seem too perfect, but this is made to seem so by Bennett to underline Anna's unease with him and to explain why in fact she fell in love with Willie. His tentativeness and confessed failure awoke maternal protectiveness in her, an emotion that had survived the dessication of the Tellwright household.

In fact, Bennett has described very accurately not only the industrial state of The Potteries at the latter end of the nineteenth century, but also the state of nonconformist Protestantism, when the fires of the evangelical spirit were being replaced by duty and good works as an unspoken piety. Anna's spiritual odyssey mirrors this exactly: Unable to respond to the fervor of the revival meetings, she consciously chooses good works, obedience, and duty, and this she believes includes marriage to Henry, the epitome of the good Christian leader. Anna's choice is one of powerlessness. In feminist terms, she trades the control of father for that of husband.

Although the situation may be sanctioned by religion, Bennett does not see it as having been caused by it. The irony is that neither Anna's religion nor her money ever becomes a source of empowerment for her. She remains the poor little rich girl.

The literary success of *Anna of the Five Towns* lies in its being above all a novel of character. It is written from within Anna's experience and consciousness, and the inner psychological movements of her growth are as delicately described by Bennett as Hardy delineates Tess's development in *Tess of the D'Urbervilles* (1891). Anna's sympathies are those that remain with the reader, which is why her miserly and manipulative father retains some shreds of humanity and never becomes a Dickensian caricature. The scene in which Anna, on her twenty-first birthday, is presented with a list of documents to sign as the induction into her wealth is memorable because of the ambiguities of tone and sympathy with which the author surrounds this rite of passage. Bennett wisely understates the ironies of her shabby dress and yet polite treatment by moneyed society; he is more concerned with Anna's conscience and its dilemma. She technically owns the ramshackle Price works, and it is she who demands the rent, yet she is almost powerless not to do so, and so feels her guilt. The gesture of tearing up the forged note is poignant, as is, in its futility, the final, unused gift of a bank draft to Willie.

The novel's ending is, from the point of view of character, an anticlimax. Greater happiness could have been accorded to Anna, but Bennett is always a realist. Although she will have no great sorrows in her future life, she will have to rely on just those few memories of joy, epitomized in the Isle of Man holiday, to feed her spirit. Bennett is the sympathetic novelist of ordinary people, and *Anna of the Five Towns* a truly democratic novel.

Bennett's style and structures are economic and prefigure the growing economy of the twentieth century modernist novel, as opposed to the sprawling Victorian one. There is always sufficient detail to describe home, church, town, or factory; a sufficient variety of incidents within Anna's circumscribed life; and sufficient dialogue to balance the narrative. Everything unnecessary is pared away, however. The plot revolves around Henry's courtship of Anna, but as this is understated in itself, it allows Bennett a leisurely pace. His economies are not those of the miser but of the good housekeeper. The "slice of life" method of the French realists is the most powerful literary model, and what emerges is a novella.

"Critical Evaluation" by David Barratt

Bibliography:
Anderson, Linda R. *Bennett, Wells, and Conrad: Narrative in Transition.* London: Macmillan, 1988. Concentrates on the period 1890-1919 and concludes that each novelist was responding to a major redefining of the idea of the novel and of its relationship to reality. Also explores Bennett's refusal to distinguish between serious and popular literature. Analyzes *Anna of the Five Towns* in detail. Selected bibliography and index.

Bauer, H. P. "Spiritual Maternity and Self-Fulfillment in Arnold Bennett's *Anna of the Five Towns.*" In *The Anna Book: Searching for Anna in Literary History,* edited by Mickey Pearlman. Westport, Conn.: Greenwood Press, 1992. A historical, critical discussion of *Anna of the Five Towns* in a collection of essays that constitutes volume 46 of the series Contributions to the Study of World Literature.

Drabble, Margaret. *Arnold Bennett.* New York: Alfred A. Knopf, 1974. The most readable of the biographies on Bennett. Helps relate the complicated nexus that held him to the Five Towns, even when physically and culturally far removed. Bibliography and index, including a full list of Bennett's published works.

Lucas, John. *Arnold Bennett: A Study of His Fiction*. London: Methuen, 1974. A general overview of his fiction that includes a substantial section on *Anna of the Five Towns*. Praises Bennett's handling of Anna's relationship with Willie Price. Index.

Stone, Donald. "The Art of Arnold Bennett: Transmutation and Empathy in *Anna of the Five Towns* and *Riceyman Steps*." In *Modernism Reconsidered*, edited by Robert Kiely. Cambridge, Mass.: Harvard University Press, 1983. A comparative study of Bennett's two novels in the context of twentieth century English literature. Includes bibliographic references.

ANNALS

Type of work: History
Author: Cornelius Tacitus (c. 56-c. 120)
First transcribed: Ab excessu divi Augusti, c. 116 (English translation, 1698)

Principal personages:

TIBERIUS, Augustus Caesar's stepson and successor
GERMANICUS or NERO CLAUDIUS DRUSUS, Tiberius' brother
AGRIPPINA (MAJOR), Germanicus' wife and Caligula's mother
DRUSUS, Tiberius' son
DRUSUS, Germanicus' son
CALIGULA, Tiberius' successor
CLAUDIUS, Caligula's uncle and his successor
MESSALINA, Claudius' first wife
AGRIPPINA (MINOR), Claudius' niece and second wife
BRITANNICUS, Claudius' son, killed by Nero
NERO, Agrippina's son and Claudius' successor
POPPAEA, Nero's wife
AELIUS SEJANUS, Tiberius' favorite
PISO, leader of a conspiracy against Nero

By an accident of fate, works of Cornelius Tacitus are the only surviving histories of his day; all the writings of his contemporaries and immediate predecessors are lost. It may be that the fates were guided by standards of literary aesthetics rather than historical accuracy. Tacitus' facts and interpretations have from time to time been severely criticized, but he has always been admired for his lucid, morally charged narrative style. The *Annals* are not merely a skillful prose account of a half century of Roman history, but also a compassionate evaluation of the horrors of imperial despotism. In fact, the earliest extant manuscript is entitled *Ab excessu divi Augusti* (although in book 4, the writer refers to his work as *Annals*).

Tacitus saw in Roman history a gradual decline from a primitive golden age when no laws were necessary to times when laws became a necessity and, finally, an abominable evil. As the *Annals* proceed from the reign of Tiberius to those of Claudius and Nero (a section dealing with Caligula is lost, as are the last books) the tyranny becomes more cruel, the populace and patricians grow more submissive, the opportunists and informers become more despicable, and the dwindling number of virtuous people find themselves more helpless. In these matters, Tacitus is by no means taciturn; in fact, so great are the horrors depicted in the *Annals* that until the atrocities of twentieth century politics and war recapitulated them on a horrendously magnified scale, Tacitus' readers were inclined to view his account as grossly exaggerated, beyond the possible depths to which human nature could sink.

Tacitus is modest about his aims, though the grave irony of his remarks should not go unnoticed:

The matter upon which I am occupied is circumscribed, and unproductive of renown to the author—a state of undisturbed peace, or only interrupted in limited degree, the sad condition of affairs in the city, and a prince indifferent about extending the bounds of the empire. Not unprofitable, however, will it be to investigate matters which, though unimportant in a superficial view, frequently give the first impulse to events of magnitude. . . . I have only to record the mandates of despotism, incessant accusations, faithless friendships, the ruin of innocence; the one unvarying repetition of causes terminating in the same event, and presenting no novelty from their similarity and tiresome repetition. (4, 32-33)

In general, Tacitus presents not a sustained history, but a chronological depiction of selected events—some thoroughly detailed over several chapters and others sketched in lightly, continually referred to but not described extensively in any one place. It has been conjectured that the original *Annals* consisted of three hexads, the pattern employed by Vergil, Statius, Polynus, and Cicero; but there is no concrete evidence that there were two books written after book 16, and the loss of books 7-10 prevents scholars from being absolutely certain that those books fitted with books 11-12 to constitute a middle hexad. At any rate, the *Annals*, as they now stand, can be conveniently arranged by subject matter—the reign of Tiberius is the concern of the first six books, of Claudius in books 11-12, and of Nero in the final four books.

This is not to say that the focus of attention is concentrated on the three emperors. In dealing with Tiberius, for example, Tacitus devotes the opening forty-nine chapters to the first year (more space than to any other year of the entire history), beginning with the jockeying for power after the death of Augustus. Since Tiberius never led troops in battle after he became emperor, the narrative shifts to Tiberius' son Drusus (chapters 16-30) quelling the Pannonian mutiny and to Germanicus (most of chapters 31-71) campaigning on the Rhine. These two men, possible heirs to the throne, were the objects of the intrigues of the utterly unscrupulous Aelius Sejanus, Tiberius' favorite. Jealous of Germanicus' successes, Tiberius had him recalled and sent east as king in Armenia, where he died in 19 C.E., probably at the hands of Piso under orders from Tiberius. Piso's trial ended abruptly with his unexplained murder, although Tacitus hints that Tiberius arranged that as well. Drusus, then, dominated the sons of Germanicus as heir apparent, but Tiberius openly preferred Sejanus—"a stranger was called in as coadjutor in the government; nay, how little was wanting to his being declared colleague." Sejanus, "whose heart insatiably lusted for supreme domination," then dispatched Drusus with a slow poison that made him appear a victim of disease, and set out to marry Livia, his widow and the sister of Germanicus. There remained, however, Agrippina, widow of Germanicus, and her three sons. Sejanus contrived open enmity between Agrippina and Tiberius and skillfully arranged for the emperor to retire to Capri from Rome in 27 C.E. There, while Sejanus plotted his rise to power, Tiberius "indulged his cruel and libidinous disposition . . . in the secrecy of a retired situation." One of the most tantalizing lacunae of the *Annals* deals with Agrippina's hopeless struggle for the rights of her sons and the final conflict between Sejanus and the emperor, a struggle leading to Sejanus' execution.

The first hexad ends with Tiberius at the age of seventy-eight, at which age he had outlived all the intriguers who surrounded him and relinquished "nothing of his libidinous excesses." His end was dramatic, and Tacitus relishes the irony. Assured by Tiberius' physician that his death was imminent,

Caligula in the midst of a great throng of persons, paying their gratulations, was already going forth to make a solemn entrance on the sovereignty, when suddenly a notice came, "that Tiberius had recovered his sight and voice, and had called for some persons to give him food to restore him." The consternation was universal: the concourse about Caligula dispersed in all directions. . . . Caligula himself stood fixed in silence—fallen from the highest hopes, he now expected the worst. Macro [Caligula's right hand man], undismayed, ordered the old man to be smothered with a quantity of clothes. . . . (6, 51)

The dramatic technique is magnificent. Caligula is left as a monstrous legacy to Rome. The extant history resumes in book 11 with Claudius' succession to the purple. The new emperor is depicted as a cut above his predecessors: He dignified the theater, augmented the alphabet, restrained predatory creditors, increased the senate, and incorporated new provinces into the Empire. Intrigues, however, continued to flourish, centering upon Claudius' wife Messalina, who was concerned at the way in which freedmen (especially Narcissus and Pallas) had gained power. Messalina, knowing she was about to be murdered by Claudius' agents, committed suicide: "Tidings were then carried to Claudius 'that Messalina was no more'; without inquiring whether by her own or another's hand, [he] called for a cup of wine and proceeded in the feast." Tacitus brilliantly achieves a sense of horror at the moral corruption of the Empire with just such detail and understatement. Book 12 opens with the contest among the freedmen concerning the choice of a new wife for Claudius. Pallas prevailed with his suggestion of Agrippina, despite the fact that she was the daughter of Claudius' brother Germanicus. The horrendous narrative continues to delineate debauchery and chaos. Nero destroyed the emperor's son Britannicus, and Agrippina afterward poisoned Claudius in order to secure the succession for her own son, Nero. Book 13 tells of Agrippina's struggles for power, first against the freedwoman Acte and then against Poppaea, Nero's wife—murders and counter-murders and abortive palace revolts that went on while Nero engaged in his orgiastic debauches. Book 14 opens with Poppaea's vigorously dramatic reproach against Nero for his cowardice in not destroying his mother, who had desperately clung to life and power by incestuously lavishing her own body on her son. Tacitus handles Nero's attempts on Agrippina's life with almost grotesque comedy. First, she was put to sea in a faulty vessel, but she swam ashore while another woman, hoping to save herself by claiming to be the emperor's mother, was slain. Finally, brute force was resorted to and she was slain in bed: "to the centurion, as he was drawing his sword to dispatch her, she presented her womb, and with a loud voice, 'Strike your sword into my belly,' she cried, and was instantly dispatched." Thus, Tacitus vivifies an important dramatic scene with a stroke of realism.

Nero, struck with remorse and apparently unaware of the extent to which Roman society had degenerated to his own low level, feared to return to the capital. Matricide during the Republic would have seemed the destruction of morality's basis, the family. Nero's entry into Rome, however, was triumphant and he thenceforth "abandoned himself to all his inordinate passions which, though insufficiently controlled, had been somewhat checked by his reverence for his mother, such as it was." Throughout his career "Nero wallowed in all sorts of defilements, lawful and unlawful: and seemed to leave no atrocity which could add to his pollution," including one which Tacitus describes with great disgust—a mock-marriage "with all the solemnities of wedlock" to a homosexual. The height of his inhuman cruelty was the great fire of Rome, in which he madly reveled and from which he gained enormous profits. The most sustained episode of the final books concerns the conspiracy in 65 C.E. of Piso and eighteen other leaders to assassinate Nero and set up Piso as emperor.

Piso gave no promise of better government, since he was almost as addicted to sensuous pleasure as Nero himself, but some change was obviously necessary. The conspiracy had difficulty settling on a method, and before it could get under way the plot was inadvertently revealed when Epicharis, a freedwoman, attempted to solicit one of Nero's naval officers, Volusius Proculus, who alerted Nero. One of the rare cases of personal virtue was Epicharis' refusal to betray the conspirators, despite the horrible torture she endured. In their haste the conspirators betrayed themselves, and in panic Nero began wholesale slaughters. Chapters 37-70 constitute a steady series of death scenes—Epicharis, Seneca, Subrius Flavus, Lucan (who died reciting his verses), and others—each presented with vivid detail. Piso, himself, though urged to stir up a popular revolt, chose to sever his veins and "left a will full of odious flattery to Nero, in tenderness to his wife, a depraved woman and void of every recommendation but personal beauty."

The deaths of those close to Nero continued. Poppaea died "by a fit of passion in her husband, who gave her a violent blow with his foot when she was pregnant; for I cannot believe he poisoned her as some have stated." Her funeral was sumptuous; she was embalmed with spices rather than cremated as was the custom, but her death was "rejoiced at by those who recollected her . . . lewdness and cruelty." An account of the last two years of Nero's life is missing. The *Annals* end in mid-sentence, which indicates that this section was lost.

Such are the main lines of Tacitus' history, but the text abounds in frequent digressions tracing in close detail the fortunes of the Roman Empire and its provinces and outposts. This is done so vividly that some authorities suggest that Tacitus must have had a host of reliable sources in the form of autobiographies and diaries. The *Annals*, however, are in sum clearly the personal document of a writer with sincerity, intelligence, courage, and enormous artistry. In a very real sense, Tacitus was an existentialist in his manner of understanding the replacement of traditional morality with corruption. Convinced that human effort is absurd, he was sustained by a faith in human solidarity and unity in suffering. The gravity of his tragic vision is relieved by a deeply felt compassion for suffering, and he has left in the *Annals* one of the greatest histories of all time.

Bibliography:

Luce, T. J., and A. J. Woodman, eds. *Tacitus and the Tacitean Tradition*. Princeton, N.J.: Princeton University Press, 1993. Anthologizes important criticism by leading Tacitus scholars. Comments on the historian's influence as well as his achievement.

Mellor, Ronald. *Tacitus*. London: Routledge & Kegan Paul, 1993. Essential work on Tacitus. Portrays Tacitus as a moralist and psychologist whose observations of imperial Rome are of permanent relevance. Discusses how the portraits of the various emperors reflect the historian's biases and partialities.

Momigliano, Arnaldo. *Essays in Ancient and Modern Historiography*. Middletown, Conn.: Wesleyan University Press, 1977. Places Tacitus within the tradition of historiography. Authoritative.

Syme, Ronald. *Tacitus*. Oxford, England: Clarendon Press, 1958. Still an excellent sourcebook for the general reader. The most ambitious attempt to correlate Tacitus' history with documentary evidence on ancient Rome.

Velleius Paterculus. *The Tiberian Narrative, 2.94-131*. Edited by A. J. Woodman. Cambridge, England: Cambridge University Press, 1977. Comprehensive treatment of the portrait of Tiberius. Stresses the measure of qualified admiration within Tacitus' general contempt for the emperor.

ANNIE ALLEN

Type of work: Poetry
Author: Gwendolyn Brooks (1917-   )
First published: 1949

With the publication of her second book of poetry, *Annie Allen*, Chicago poet Gwendolyn Brooks became the first African American to win a Pulitzer Prize. The blackness-nourishing collection is arranged in three parts: "Notes from the Childhood and the Girlhood," "The Anniad" (which includes the long poem of that title and two short works as "Appendix to the Anniad"), and "The Womanhood." As the titles imply, each section of the book corresponds to a stage in the life of Annie Allen.

Brooks is securely anchored in the African American literary tradition. The poet's expertise with technical poetic forms is overshadowed only by her abiding and evident joy in words. Her work attests to an admiration for poet Langston Hughes, whose sharp comic irony matches her own. In the early 1940's, at their Chicago apartment located in the "very buckle of the Black belt," as Brooks describes it, she and her husband Henry Blakely gave a party for Hughes. Not long after, in 1945, Brooks's first book of poems *A Street in Bronzeville* was published by Harper & Row. Four years later, *Annie Allen* emerged to glowing reviews for its linguistic brilliance. While her first book emphasized community consciousness, the second focused on self-realization; the central character, Annie, moved from the security of her parents' home into city life, marriage, and motherhood. From her kitchenette above a real-estate agency, of which she says, "If you wanted a poem you had only to look out of a window," Brooks created the three-part poem that explores the artistic sensibility of a black woman not unlike herself.

Annie Allen begins with a dedication poem: "Memorial to Ed Bland," a soldier killed in World War II. Brooks and Bland were members of a Chicago poetry-writing workshop conducted by Inez Cunningham Stark. This first poem presents Brooks's central theme of an artistic life cut short and unfulfilled. Its structure underlines the truncated testimonial with lines of varying length and irregular rhymes and rhythms.

The first part, "Notes from the Childhood and the Girlhood," contains eleven poems. Beginning with "the birth in a narrow room," Brooks describes Annie's genesis in a "western country" and her early years of prancing with "gods and fairies," a romantic sensibility that permeates her life in the years before she sadly realizes "How pinchy is my room!" Poems 2 and 3, "Maxie Allen" and "the parents: people like our marriage: Maxie and Andrew," portray Annie's parents and illustrate the contrast between their stable, humble lives and her dreams of "something other." Halfway through the rhymed couplets of "Maxie Allen," however, Annie's mother shares some of her daughter's dissatisfaction with the moderate, dull life that has convinced them to settle for chicken and "shut the door."

Annie's innocent kindness comes through clearly in "Sunday chicken" (poem 4), eleven lines with three rhyming tercets and a concluding couplet. She dislikes killing the lovely "speckle-gray," "wild white," and "baffle-brown" chickens, comparing such actions to cannibalism. Poems 5 and 6 expose Annie once again to death and for the first time to white racism. Ironically, both poems have musical connections. In "old relative," structurally identical to poem 4, Annie grieves for the death of an elderly uncle and a resulting restriction on playing her favorite songs for the week-long mourning period. "[D]owntown vaudeville" introduces Annie to a black performer in a show attended by hostile whites:

> What was not pleasant was the hush that coughed
> when the Negro clown came on the stage and doffed
> His broken hat. The hush, first. Then the soft
> concatenation of delight and lift,
> And loud. The decked dismissal of his gift. . . .

If the first six poems in part 1 reflect Annie's childhood, poems 7 through 11 establish her as an adolescent dreamer hoping for a "gold half-god" to rescue her. Brooks believes in the power of the imagination and uses the ballad stanza in "the ballad of late Annie" and "throwing out the flowers" to introduce a mythical quality to the collection. Yet her flights of fancy are always tempered by harsh reality. The theme of life truncated is reiterated once more in the final stanza of "throwing out the flowers":

> Forgotten and stinking they stick in the can,
> And the vase breath's better and all, and all.
> And so for the end of our life to a man,
> Just over, just over and all.

Despite such ominous foreshadowing, the first part of *Annie Allen* ends with two positive affirmations and hints of the heroic "Anniad" to follow. In "pygmies are pygmies still, though percht on Alps," Annie celebrates the excellence and independence of pygmies who can see better and laugh at all the giants wallowing below. Poem 11, "my own sweet good," implies Annie's appreciation of her goodness and worth; yet it ends with her anticipation of a golden promise from a dimpled gold god.

Part 2, "The Anniad," is a forty-three-stanza mock heroic celebrating Annie's everyday life in a technically grand style. Unusual for modern poetry, the mock heroic provides Brooks with a means of social criticism that does not seem to take itself too seriously. "The Anniad" begins with

> Think of sweet and chocolate,
> Left to folly or to fate,
> Whom the higher gods forgot,
> Whom the lower gods berate;
> Physical and underfed
> Fancying on the featherbed
> What was never and is not.

She dreams of a knight who will rescue her from her parents' home. By the end of "The Anniad" Annie has been courted, she has married, been separated from her husband during the war, suffered his infidelity, and reconciled with him, and, finally, she has been deserted permanently Her "knight" loves neither her color nor her womanhood. He sees her as a mere trophy and "Leads her to a lowly room./ Which she makes a chapel of./ Where she genuflects to love."

"The Anniad's" self-conscious form and grandeur structurally convey Annie's satirical, lifesaving wit and imagination, while its content carries the daily frustrations, pain, and struggle. This contrast and resulting tension echo the earlier conflict between Annie's internal emotional complexity and her restrictive, "pinchy" room. When her "tan man" returns from war, he, like other black men, suffers from a lack of respect; he rejects her and pursues affairs with exotic, light-skinned women. While Annie tends the children at home, he revels with "wench and whiskey," trying to escape the overseas disease, tuberculosis, that stalks and finally kills him. The final stanza is a sad salute to Annie's survival and imagination:

> Think of almost thoroughly
> Derelict and dim and done.
> Stroking swallows from the sweat.
> Fingering faint violet.
> Hugging old and Sunday sun.
> Kissing in her kitchenette
> The minuets of memory.

The "Appendix to the Anniad" contains two poems, "leaves from a loose-leaf war diary" and "the sonnet-ballad," each challenging the romantic illusions created by "The Anniad." The first begins coldly with the line "thousands-killed in action" and goes on to suggest that to endure the horror of war and death ("untranslatable ice") people need superhuman powers. In the second stanza of the first poem, Brooks admits that the thought of heaven is no solace now. Instead, she longs for a return to life with all its sensual exuberance, "lips, lax wet and warm,/ Bees in the stomach,/ sweat across the brow. Now." Perhaps the second poem is most poignant, written without fantasy or myth, asking one simple postwar question: "oh mother, mother, where is happiness?"

"The Womanhood," Brooks final section of *Annie Allen*, returns to the ordinary yet important aspects of black life. Its first five-part poem, "the children of the poor," is a mother's dramatic monologue:

> People who have no children can be hard:
> Attain a mail of ice and insolence:
> Need not pause in the fire, and in no sense
> Hesitate in the hurricane to guard.

Brooks clearly echoes the frustration of women who want to help children survive in a hostile world but feel powerless: "What shall I give my children? who are poor,/ who are adjudged the leastwise of the land." She questions the power of prayer in part 3 and advises in part 4 that children be taught first to fight and then to fiddle. Other poems in this section express concern for children's physical and psychological safety. "Life for my child is simple and is good" shows daily dangers like "fingering an electric outlet" and simple joys like "throwing blocks out of a window," while "the ballad of the light-eyed little girl" tells of sweet Sally who starved her pet pigeon and then had to bury him "down and down."

The poems following "The Anniad" depart from the mock heroic's traditional rhyme and meter, employing free verse and irregular line breaks to illustrate Annie's move from romantic idealism to a clear-eyed response to social and racial injustice. Brooks confronts these issues gently but firmly in "I love those little booths at Benvenuti's" wherein an "old oaken waiter" looks amusedly at a group of whites who have ventured into a restaurant in Bronzeville expecting to be entertained. She reminds the reader "Nobody here will take the part of jester," a far cry from "downtown vaudeville" in the early part of the book.

One of Brooks's most powerful and black-affirming poems is "Beverly Hills, Chicago," faintly echoing the poetic style of T. S. Eliot in its narrative distance and list of objects and events. Annie's satirical remark, "We say ourselves fortunate to be driving by today" implies a clear sense of racial injustice, for she goes on to describe the privileged lives of the white-haired white people who live in the posh neighborhood with their "golden gardens":

We do not want them to have less.
But it is only natural that we should think we have not enough.
We drive on, we drive on.
When we speak to each other our voices are a little gruff.

Perhaps Brooks was prompted to include the beautiful poem "truth" immediately after "Beverly Hills, Chicago" because it reflects accurately the night years spent in the shade of white society. Brooks implies that blacks have waited too long to see the sun: "What if we wake one shimmering morning to/ Hear the fierce hammering/ Of his firm knuckles/ Hard on the door?" Of course, her implication is that the shock would be too much. The next poem, simply numbered "XI," refers to the "enormous business" of racism and inequality that makes blacks wonder "if one has a home."

The long poem "intermission" uses images of light and dark to convey Annie's self-affirming attitude, a sharp contrast to her earlier romantic desire for a gold god. In the third part of this poem she reflects, "there is silver under/ the veils of the darkness./ But few care to dig in the night/ For the possible treasure of stars." In the final poem of the book, Brooks calls for black and white unity: "Rise./ Let us combine. There are no magics or elves/ Or timely godmothers to guide us./ We are lost, must/ Wizard a track though our own screaming weed." Reading the entire collection brings the understanding that in *Annie Allen* Brooks has undertaken a struggle and a journey with life and with words. Like her character Annie, she has many lesions from her experience, but she has experienced some triumph too.

Carol F. Bender

Bibliography:
Brooks, Gwendolyn. *Report from Part One*. Detroit: Broadside Press, 1972. An essential work for students of Brooks, this autobiography illuminates her early years as a writer and traces the publication of *Annie Allen*. Useful authorial notes on poems in the appendix.
Evans, Mari. *Black Women Writers (1950-1980)*. Garden City, N.Y.: Doubleday, 1984. Three essays on Brooks's work, one written by Brooks herself. Excellent biographical chart and selected bibliographies.
Kent, George E. *A Life of Gwendolyn Brooks*. Lexington: University Press of Kentucky, 1990. The most comprehensive research and criticism on Gwendolyn Brooks's life and work. Kent devotes a good portion of the book to the details surrounding the publication of *Annie Allen*.
Milham, D. H. *Gwendolyn Brooks: Poetry and the Heroic Voice*. Lexington: University Press of Kentucky, 1987. An intense scholarly analysis of each of Brooks's major works. Includes an extensive technical study of the poetic forms of each poem in *Annie Allen*.
Mootry, Maria K., and Gary Smith. *A Life Distilled: Gwendolyn Brooks, Her Poetry and Fiction*. Chicago: University of Illinois Press, 1987. An impressive collection of eighteen essays discussing the range of Brooks's art. Contains an essential selected bibliography for serious scholars.

ANOTHER COUNTRY

Type of work: Novel
Author: James Baldwin (1924-1987)
Type of plot: Social realism
Time of plot: Mid-twentieth century
Locale: New York and France
First published: 1962

Principal characters:
RUFUS SCOTT, musician
IDA SCOTT, Rufus' sister
VIVALDO MOORE, aspiring writer
ERIC JONES, actor
RICHARD SILENSKI, writer
CASS SILENSKI, Richard's wife

The Story:
Rufus Scott, an African American musician, was in a desperate condition. He not only had no money, but also had fallen out of contact with his friends and his family. He had been out of touch for about a month and a half. Moreover, the most foreboding aspect of Rufus' condition was his total despair. This despair resulted primarily from his complete alienation from those who had formerly been close to him. As Rufus wandered the streets of New York, he remembered his relationships with people he loved. He realized that his love was often mixed with hostility. For example, months earlier, he had met a white Southern woman named Leona at a party. During the party, their affair began. Rufus realized that part of what he wanted from his relationship with Leona was to take out on her his rage against white people. This relationship was somewhat of a pattern with Rufus. He also had had an affair with a white Southern actor named Eric Jones. In his present desperate state, Rufus realized how he had abused both Eric and Leona, ultimately driving them away with his racist taunts and physical and psychological humiliation. Consequently, Rufus realized that he had used Eric's and Leona's love for him to abuse them and thereby vent his anger and frustrations. He had alienated himself from everyone to whom he had once been close. His once-close friend, aspiring writer Vivaldo Moore, who had become fed up with Rufus' inflicting his problems on him and others whom Vivaldo knew, Rufus had also driven away. After reflecting on his relationships and realizing how isolated he was, Rufus killed himself by jumping off of the George Washington Bridge.

Meanwhile, Ida, Rufus' sister, had been trying to find him. She went to the home of Richard Silenski, then a newly successful novelist, and his wife, Cass. Vivaldo was also present. One of Ida's chief characteristics—her anger against whites—became clear. She accused Rufus' friends of not caring about what happened to him, as all of them were white. Vivaldo felt especially guilty, recalling how he had failed to show up for his last scheduled meeting with Rufus. After Richard suggested checking with hospitals and the morgue, Rufus' friends learned the truth: Rufus was dead.

Ida's relationship with Rufus' circle of friends—Vivaldo, Richard, and Cass—continued. Vivaldo became attracted to Ida and the two became lovers, even though Ida, like Rufus, felt a simultaneous attraction to and repulsion from whites. Further complicating things was that Ida, an aspiring singer, decided to have an affair with white television producer Steve Ellis. Ida, believing that whites looked upon black women as promiscuous, decided to try to exploit this myth for the benefit of her career. She became involved with Ellis at the same time that she had a love affair with Vivaldo. Ida, Ellis, and Vivaldo became part of a triangle that mixed affection with hostility.

In addition to his affair with Ida, Vivaldo had other complications in his life. First, he had never been completely sure of his sexual orientation. He recalled being part of a gang that attacked a homosexual man, although he himself was sometimes attracted to men. Also, before meeting Ida, he had made frequent trips to Harlem to have sex with black women, something that made him feel exploitative, racist, and weak. He knew he was merely seeking thrills in his relationships with these women, and using them to try to hide from the emptiness of his own life. Complementing his indecisive feelings about his sexuality was Vivaldo's equally murky status as a writer. Vivaldo noted that he felt as distant from his characters as he did from himself. His novel would not crystallize in his imagination. In his relationship with Ida, in his former relationships with black women, in his confusion about his sexual orientation, and in his inertia as a writer—in fact, in his very identity—Vivaldo lived in a state of indecision and ignorance.

Eric Jones, once part of Rufus' circle, was currently an actor living in France. Eric planned to return to New York to look for acting jobs. This meant he would have to be separated temporarily from his male lover, Yves, with whom he had a committed relationship. Eric's impending return to the United States brought back memories of his coming-of-age in the South and accepting his sexual orientation as a young white man who was in love with a black man. In contrast to Vivaldo, Eric accepted his sexuality, even though he knew that much of society condemned his love for the black man, Henry. He also recalled his love and abuse at the hands of Rufus. Eric realized that in spite of the pain he experienced—in romantic relationships and at the hands of society—he needed to accept himself and to reject society's bigoted categorizations of homosexuals. On Eric's return to New York, he became the catalyst for important realizations by many of his circle of friends. For instance, in Cass's relationship with Eric, she realized the emptiness of her seemingly successful life as the wife of a successful novelist—who was also an unloving husband. In addition, Vivaldo realized that while he loved Eric as a friend, his sexual orientation made him need women in general and Ida in particular. Hence, Eric was an important vehicle for his friends' self-analysis.

The characters' coming to face themselves had important effects. In Vivaldo's case, for instance, he and Ida finally discussed the problems in their relationship, as Vivaldo was now ready to face the truth about many aspects of his life. They discussed their problems, including Ida's relationship with Ellis, which had failed to get her the career break she wanted. The affair had also resulted in her experiencing the humiliating disrespect of the black musicians with whom she worked. They knew of her plans to advance her career by having an affair with Ellis. After Eric played an instrumental part in the lives of others, he resumed his concentration on his own life with the impending arrival of Yves in New York. The novel ends with key characters having confronted painful truths about their identities and their lives.

Critical Evaluation:

James Baldwin has been widely acclaimed as America's greatest essayist as a result of his works *Notes of a Native Son* (1955) and *The Fire Next Time* (1963), among others. His novels also play a central role in American literary history. Like Ralph Ellison's *Invisible Man* (1952) and Baldwin's *Giovanni's Room* (1956), *Another Country* is an important landmark in the departure of African American literature from the tradition of the protest novel, best embodied by Richard Wright's *Native Son* (1940). The chief feature of the protest novel was a critique of race relations; in contrast, the aforementioned novels make a critique of society that goes beyond a condemnation of racism. *Another Country* examines such issues as personal responsibility, the formation of identity, and the need for honest self-reflection. Moreover, one can argue that a chief clue to Baldwin's interests in *Another Country* is contained in his early essay "Everybody's Protest Novel" in *Notes of a Native Son*. Particularly illuminating to readers of *Another Country* is the part of the essay that contains an attack on *Notes of a Native Son*. Baldwin states that the main tragedy in the life of the protagonist, Bigger Thomas, is that he accepts racists' labeling of him as subhuman, thus causing Baldwin to object that "the failure of the protest novel lies . . . in its insistence that it is his categorization alone that is real and can not be transcended." One could argue that in *Another Country* Rufus Scott's similar acceptance of conventional, prejudiced views of him is exactly why he commits suicide at the end of the first part of the book. The focus on him in the early part of the book would lead many readers to believe that he is the main character of the novel. That he is not may be seen as a subtle commentary on *Notes of a Native Son*. Rufus' death dramatizes Baldwin's belief in the destructive and life-negating consequences of internalization, self-condemnation, and self-alienation as represented in such characters as Rufus and his literary ancestor, Bigger Thomas. Rufus' death also jolts the reader into the realization that *Another Country* is not a protest novel, or the same kind of protest novel as *Notes of a Native Son*. Stylistically and thematically, *Another Country* broadens the scope of African American literature beyond the genre of the protest novel.

Another important aspect of *Another Country* is Baldwin's insistence that love, sexuality, and identity are intertwined and demand honest self-acceptance from the individual. Baldwin's statement in *The Fire Next Time* is essential for the reader to understand the centrality to Baldwin's vision of the aforementioned ideas. Baldwin writes: "Love takes off the masks we fear we cannot live without and know we cannot live within." One can say that this dilemma is represented in such characters as Eric and Vivaldo, whose sexuality is unmasked in their relationships and who must struggle for self-acceptance. They must accept what is revealed to them about themselves in their romantic and sexual relationships. Eric accepts his homosexuality. Vivaldo, more ambiguous than Eric, toward the end of the novel purports to accept his need for women in his romantic life. In Baldwin's presentation of the theme of love and the self-illumination it brings, another key idea of his works becomes apparent: honesty. To paraphrase a statement in *Another Country*, Baldwin makes clear in this novel and in other works that one must be honest with oneself about the life one has in order to attain the life one desires. In sum, truth, self-examination, and self-insight are intertwined in Baldwin's vision in *Another Country* and in his other works, novels, essays, and dramas.

Another important aspect of *Another Country* bears mentioning. *Giovanni's Room* and *Another Country* were among the first novels by a major American writer to deal frankly with the theme of homosexuality. Scholars on Baldwin have noted that American literature had treated the topic of homosexuality in a veiled way, sometimes as a subplot of a novel (for example, Wallace Thurman's *The Blacker the Berry*, 1929). Baldwin presents homosexuality frankly, which caused some critics at the time of the novel's publication to chastise him for the frankness of his themes and language. This aspect of the novel's reception makes clear how the novel was ahead of its time. Many readers would not find the novel shocking, though it is complex and honest in the portrayal of the importance of sexuality to one's sense of identity. *Another Country* is a very timely novel in that Baldwin uses it to grapple with issues that had not previously been given prominence in African American literature.

Another Country is an important American novel. Baldwin's complex vision provides a critique of individuals in particular and of society in general. Furthermore, for readers interested in examining central aspects of Baldwin's major thematic concerns, in his fiction and in his essays, *Another Country* is essential reading. The novel presents essential psychological issues about the formation and acceptance of identity. This thematic issue makes the novel engrossing; Baldwin ably presents the psychological growth, or lack thereof, of his characters. Baldwin also makes clear how central love is in one's psychological growth. The novel makes it evident that one cannot love others until one understands and accepts oneself. Baldwin thus shows his concern for the growth of the individual and for how that individual can connect in a meaningful way with society. This connection is essential. As in the case with Rufus Scott, self-alienation and isolation lead to death, in Baldwin's vision. Although Baldwin's *Another Country* is not in the genre of protest literature, Baldwin still uses the novel to make clear his concerns for society. *Another Country* engages central questions about life, and takes a central place in American literature.

Jane Davis

Bibliography:
Collier, Eugenia W. "The Phrase Unbearably Repeated." In *James Baldwin: A Critical Evaluation*, edited by Therman B. O'Daniel. Washington, D.C.: Howard University Press, 1977. Innovative essay on Baldwin's use of music to advance the themes of *Another Country*. Also discusses the use of music to advance characterization, to convey the need for love, and to show the characters' emotions.
Macebuh, Stanley. *James Baldwin: A Critical Study.* New York: Third Press, 1973. Intriguing discussion on love as the chief social theme of the novel and of Rufus as a major influence on the characters.
Newman, Charles. "The Lesson of the Master: Henry James and James Baldwin." In *James Baldwin*, edited by Harold Bloom. New York: Chelsea House, 1986. Creative discussion of the problem of identity in *Another Country* and the use of Rufus to make the white characters explore the inadequacy of their lives.
Rosenblatt, Roger. "Out of Control: *Go Tell It on the Mountain* and *Another Country*." In *James Baldwin*, edited by Harold Bloom. New York: Chelsea House, 1986. Imaginative discussion of the tensions among the characters, including the whites' guilt regarding Rufus' death and Eric as a liberating character.
Sylvander, Carolyn Wedin. *James Baldwin.* New York: Frederick Ungar, 1980. Perceptive discussion of Baldwin's presentation of the search for identity in *Another Country* and of the importance of Baldwin's honesty.

ANTIGONE

Type of work: Drama
Author: Jean Anouilh (1910-1987)
Type of plot: Tragedy
Time of plot: Antiquity
Locale: Thebes
First performed: 1944; first published, 1946 (English translation, 1946)

> *Principal characters:*
> ANTIGONE, younger daughter of Oedipus and Jocasta
> CREON, brother of Jocasta, acting king of Thebes
> THE CHORUS, played by a single actor/narrator
> HAEMON, son of Creon, engaged to Antigone
> ISMENE, Antigone's older sister

The Story:

King Oedipus died in exile, leaving the kingdom of Thebes to his two sons, Eteocles and Polynices, who were supposed to take turns as rulers. Instead, the two brothers fought over the prize; civil war ensued, and in the end both of them lay dead, each by the other's hand. Creon, surviving brother of the incestuous queen Jocasta, had assumed the role of king so as to restore order in Thebes, proclaiming a state funeral for his former ally Eteocles while ordering that the body of Polynices be left to rot in the sun as a negative example to his supporters. Antigone, younger daughter of Oedipus and Jocasta, defied Creon's edict by digging a grave for Polynices, an act of treason punishable by death.

Jean Anouilh, elaborating on the basic plot of the classical Greek play by Sophocles, begins his version with narration by the Chorus (initially known as the Prologue, and a single actor in Anouilh's play). As does the Chorus in Sophocles' version, as in other classical drama, Anouilh's dinner-jacketed narrator provides background information and running commentary to complement the action. The play is performed in modern dress with occasional deliberate anachronisms, such as the mention of nightclubs and sports cars.

Antigone, fully aware of the consequences of her deed, had already buried Polynices and was preparing herself for death, gradually separating herself from Haemon, from her sister, Ismene, from the elderly nursemaid who has cared for her since childhood, and even from her dog, to be left in the nursemaid's care. Creon, upon learning from his guards that Polynices has been buried, at first suspected political subversives but soon was forced to accept the fact of Antigone's guilt. Ever the pragmatic politician, Creon considered trying to cover up Antigone's crime, knowing the political troubles that would result from her martyrdom. Creon was prepared to have the guards who knew of Antigone's guilt put to death in order to assure their silence. Antigone, however, brought face-to-face with her uncle, refused to participate in a cover-up. She would not remain silent about her actions, insisting on her right to give her kin proper burial, even if the punishment she faced for doing so was death.

During their extended conversation, Creon tried to reason with Antigone, urging her to renounce her crime and assuring her of her total indemnity so that she could go on to marry Haemon as planned and, presumably, to lead a happy life. Antigone, however, would have none of Creon's proffered happiness, preferring to die rather than to take part in her uncle's political scheme. As in the Sophocles play, religion is the motive of Antigone's determination, since burial was a prerequisite to the afterlife. In Anouilh's version, however, the discussion centers upon the generation gap between Antigone and her uncle, pitting youthful idealism against experience and pragmatism. Still attempting to change Antigone's mind, Creon argued that the burial of Eteocles was no more than a matter of politics, of the need to choose one official hero among two scoundrels. Each brother, in fact, had plotted his father's assassination and had planned to sell Thebes to the highest bidder; what is more, the two bodies were in such condition that it was impossible to tell the brothers' remains apart.

Creon, for one, did not care which was which, so long as the burial served his political purpose. In accepting the throne, Creon agreed to accept matters as they were, not as they should be. Antigone, in refusing Creon's offer of compromise and pragmatism, in effect refused to accept things as they were, insisting rather on how they should be. She forced Creon to proceed with her execution. Although at the last minute she seemed to doubt her resolve, she ultimately allowed herself to be thrown in a pit, where she hanged herself with her belt. She was soon joined by Haemon, who, keeping Creon at bay with his sword, lay down beside her and stabbed himself to death. Haemon's mother, Creon's wife Eurydice, died a similar death upon learning what had happened to her son. Creon was thus left alone to look after his kingdom, attended by the guards and soldiers who had arrested Antigone.

Critical Evaluation:

From the early 1930's onward, thanks mainly to the plays of Jean Giraudoux (1882-1944), the topical rewriting of classical myth and drama became more the rule than the exception on the serious Paris stage, offering edification and entertainment in approximately equal portion. As the Greek writers had shown their inventiveness within rigid constraints of plot, so also the French playwrights of the period between World Wars I and II impressed their audiences with thoughtful, often witty variations on the familiar myths that most audience members had studied in school. Jean Anouilh, who came of age as a playwright during the decade of Giraudoux's prominence, achieved his first major success with *Le Voyageur sans bagage* (1937; *Traveller Without Luggage*, 1959), a dark comedy that, despite its contemporary setting, carries strong references to the Oedipus legend. By the time he addressed himself to Antigone, in the midst of World War II and the Nazi occupation of France, Anouilh had already treated the myth of Orpheus and Eurydice rather successfully on the stage, as he was later to do with that of Jason and Medea. In later years, as French taste moved away from the reworking of classical myth, Anouilh would move off in other directions, yet without ever forsaking the characteristic themes of youth and age, and realism and idealism, to be found in *Antigone*.

Among the more memorable and durable examples of its subgenre, outlasting even the better efforts of Jean Giraudoux, *Antigone* proved controversial throughout the 1940's and into the 1950's because of Anouilh's ambiguous portrayal of Antigone and Creon. For the initial spectators in 1944, there was little doubt that Antigone represented the indomitable, if weakened, spirit of free France, and Creon the expediency that involved collaboration with the Germans, if need be, in order to keep the country running. It seemed difficult to tell, however, which of the two characters was more sympathetically portrayed. There were those, for example, who saw Antigone's willful martyrdom as meaningless, outweighed by Creon's devotion to duty and to the maintenance of order. Such persons argued that Creon is the one who has the most to lose, which in a sense he does. Somewhat to his consternation, Anouilh, among the more resolutely theatrical of dramatists, found himself suddenly ranked with such contemporary thinker-playwrights as Albert Camus and Jean-Paul Sartre, who both, unlike himself, were aligned with the political Left. Anouilh, by contrast, preferred to think that his art lifted him above politics, a most difficult position to maintain in France during World War II and after. As if in reaction, Anouilh, for some years after *Antigone* was first performed, went out of his way to avoid any possible identification with thoughtful or literary theater, thus leaving himself open to a countercharge of playing to the crowds.

Ironically, more than fifty years after its initial productions, *Antigone* has proved to have survived the allegorical interpretations that seemed obvious to audiences during World War II, emerging instead as one of the more eloquent expressions of the generation gap to be found in the body of world theater. More closely related in theme and tone to Anouilh's earlier and later plays than was once commonly supposed, *Antigone* derives much of its dramatic strength from the author's unobtrusive, almost inadvertent lyricism, especially in those scenes in which Antigone evokes, for Ismene, the nursemaid, and Haemon the beauties of the life and world that she is about to forsake. Certain critics have heard in those lines a recollection of Emily's return from the dead in Thornton Wilder's *Our Town* (1938), an intertextual impression underscored by resemblances between Wilder's Stage Manager and the Chorus in *Antigone*. In any case, Antigone's lyrical speeches anticipate, and contrast with, the searing, searching rhetoric of her confrontation with Creon, in which she accuses him of selling out and in which she refuses any part of a world in which Haemon might grow to resemble his father. Of interest also, by way of comic relief tinged with social significance, is Anouilh's portrayal of Creon's guards as typical French soldiers with French names, by turns fawning and ferocious, who return to playing cards as soon as their part in the action is over.

During a long and generally distinguished career spanning more than fifty years and nearly as many performed plays, Anouilh consistently rejected traditional classifications, such as comedy and tragedy, for his efforts, preferring such personal, ironic categories as black plays, pink plays, and grating plays, the latter designed to set one's teeth on edge. Like the earlier *Traveller Without Luggage*, *Antigone* was labeled as a black play rather than a tragedy; in the absence of any substantial theory or criticism written by Anouilh, certain speeches of the Chorus in *Antigone* are often—and perhaps correctly—assumed to represent the author's views on tragedy as being too convenient, too comforting to represent real life. The Chorus' presence, as well as his lightly ironic approach to the action that he narrates, sets the concept of tragedy into a kind of relief, subject to the spectator's objective scrutiny as the familiar plot proceeds to run its course. Tragedy, suggests Anouilh through the Chorus, is for kings and princesses, while the rest of the world must contend with the more sordid details of reality.

David B. Parsell

Bibliography:
Falb, Lewis W. *Jean Anouilh*. New York: Frederick Ungar, 1977. A generally reliable overview of Anouilh's plays, prepared fairly late in his career. Somewhat more authoritative on the earlier works than on the later ones. Good discussion of *Antigone*.
Harvey, John. *Anouilh: A Study in Theatrics*. New Haven, Conn.: Yale University Press, 1964. Situates Anouilh's major work within the world dramatic tradition, showing how even in *Antigone*, playability takes precedence over ideas. Generally useful discussion of Anouilh's approach to stagecraft.
Howarth, William D. *Anouilh: Antigone*. London: Edward Arnold, 1983. Prepared for a British student audience, Howarth's volume provides useful background on Anouilh's career, the Antigone theme in world literature, and historical context of the play's first performances.

McIntyre, H. G. *The Theatre of Jean Anouilh*. London: Harrap, 1981. Although relatively brief, perhaps the most useful study of Anouilh's entire dramatic output, finding continuity and consistency where other critics have not. Interpretation of *Antigone* shows Creon as the more exemplary character without stressing implications of war allegory.

Pronko, Leonard C. *The World of Jean Anouilh*. Berkeley: University of California Press, 1961. Perhaps the strongest early study of Anouilh in English, prepared as Anouilh turned fifty, with his future direction still to be determined; good analysis of *Antigone*.

ANTIGONE

Type of work: Drama
Author: Sophocles (c. 496-406 B.C.E.)
Type of plot: Tragedy
Time of plot: Antiquity
Locale: Thebes
First performed: Antigonē, 441 B.C.E. (English translation, 1581)

>Principal characters:
>CREON, the king of Thebes
>ANTIGONE, the daughter of Oedipus
>ISMENE, her sister
>HAEMON, Creon's son
>TIRESIAS, a prophet

The Story:

Polynices and Eteocles, sons of the cursed family of King Oedipus, led two armies against each other before the gates of Thebes. Both brothers were killed in single combat with each other. Their uncle Creon, now the tyrant ruler of the city, ordered that Eteocles be given full funeral rites but that Polynices, who had attacked the city, be left unburied and unmourned. Anyone who broke this decree would be punished with death. Antigone and Ismene, the sisters of Polynices and Eteocles, discussed this order. With grief for the unburied brother tearing at her heart, Antigone asked Ismene to aid her in giving him burial. When Ismene refused to help in so dangerous a task, Antigone defiantly went alone to bury Polynices.

When Creon learned from a sentry that the body had been buried, he angrily ordered that the perpetrator be found. The sentry returned to the grave and uncovered the body. During a dust storm, Antigone came to look at the grave and, finding it open, filled the air with lamentation. Her cries attracted the attention of the sentry, who captured her and took her to Creon.

Questioned by Creon, she said that to bury a man was to obey the laws of the gods, even in those cases where it was against the laws of a man. Her reply angered Creon, and he decided that Antigone must die. Ismene tried to soften Creon's heart toward her sister by reminding him that Antigone was engaged to his son, Haemon, but Creon remained firm.

Haemon angered his father by arguing that there was popular sympathy for Antigone and that Creon should soften his cruel decree. When Creon said that he cared nothing for the ideas of the town, Haemon called his answer foolish. As punishment, Creon ordered that Antigone be killed before Haemon's eyes. Haemon fled with threats of revenge. Creon ordered that Antigone be walled up in a cave outside Thebes and left there to die for her crime against his law.

When Antigone was led out of the city, the people of Thebes followed her, lamenting her fate. She was thrust into the cave. All this while, Polynices' body lay unburied outside the walls. The prophet Tiresias warned Creon that the gods had not been pleased with his action and that the body should be buried. He foretold that before long Haemon would die if his father did not bury Polynices and rescue Antigone from the cave.

Creon, realizing that Tiresias' prophecies had never proved false, hurried to avert the fate the prophet had foretold. Quickly he ordered a tomb prepared for Polynices, and he himself set off to release Antigone. The will of the gods could not be changed so easily, however. When he reached the cave, he heard his son's voice within, crying out in grief. Creon entered and saw that Antigone had hanged herself with a rope made from her own dress. Haemon, sword in hand, rushed at his father as if to attack him but instead spat on the old man. He then fell on his sword and killed himself in sorrow over Antigone's death. News of these events quickly traveled back to the city, and Creon's wife, hearing of the many tragedies, died by her own hand.

On returning to Thebes with the body of his son, Creon learned of his wife's death. Realizing that his life could no longer have meaning, he had himself led out of the city into exile. He became the final victim of his own harsh tyranny.

Critical Evaluation:

Antigone is one of the finest, most moving tragedies ever written. It was very successful when it was first produced in 441 B.C.E., and according to tradition, Sophocles was made an Athenian general in the war against Samos because of it. Twentieth century audiences, too, find this play meaningful, particularly for the conflict it depicts between individual conscience and state policy. The fundamental issue of the play, however, goes deeper than that conflict, in that it probes the nature of suffering and finds in it a universal condition that exists at the very heart of the human experience.

Sophocles did not share Aeschylus' view that humans learn by pain, or the Christian idea that humans are purified by agony. Both opinions are ultimately optimistic because they are based on hope in a future vindication of misery. Sophocles faced the problem of pain without hope as an essential fact of life that no one could escape. Given this outlook, he was keenly attuned to the sadness and the tragedy inherent in life.

Ironically, Sophocles himself enjoyed the most fortunate life possible for a Greek. His life was crowned with honors from early manhood to the age of ninety, when he died. He was a skilled athlete and achieved public position. Most important, he had an extremely creative and successful dramatic career, writing more than 120 plays, 96 of which were awarded first place in the Athenian drama competitions. He was the foremost tragedian in Periclean Athens, an age of magnificent literary, artistic, and political genius. Moreover, he won a lasting reputation as one of the supreme playwrights of all time. *Antigone*, written when Sophocles was in his fifties, affords a penetrating look at his dramatic prowess.

The central theme of this play is the antithesis between Antigone and her uncle Creon. The issue of burying Polynices depends on a grasp of the Greek concept of death, in which an unburied body meant a soul condemned to torment. It was the profound obligation of the family to see that a body was properly inhumed. This was more than a matter of family loyalty; it was an act of piety demanded by the gods. Antigone undertakes that obligation even though it means treason to the state, rejection from her only sister Ismene, renunciation of her fiancé, and her own death. She is absolutely uncompromising despite knowing all the consequences beforehand.

Creon also has a valid stand when he believes that the traitor Polynices should be punished in death. A conscientious ruler, Creon is concerned about loyalty to the state, but in his position as king he confuses his own will with the good of Thebes. In pursuing his edict, which ordered that anyone who buries Polynices will be put to death, he changes from a good king into a tyrant because his vanity is involved: He will not allow a young woman or his son to put him in the wrong in front of the chorus of Theban elders. His flaw lies in a stubborn, self-righteous inflexibility when the tide of evidence turns against him. He angrily maintains his stand in the face of Antigone's martyrdom, his son's pleading, the sympathy of the townspeople for Antigone, and Tiresias' warnings. He relents only because of the fear he feels after Tiresias has prophesied doom for his family and the city, but his penitence comes too late to save him or the others.

Yet it is wrong to see Antigone as a perfect heroine or Creon as a willing malefactor. The same passion that goes into Antigone's heroic treason in burying her brother makes her unjustly cruel to her gentle sister Ismene, and she shows no thought whatever for Haemon, her fiancé. She is not only right but also unbearably self-righteous. Sophocles arouses sympathy for her when she laments that she will never have a husband or a child, but she made that choice freely and passionately. As far as character goes, there is no difference whatever between Antigone's self-righteousness and Creon's. Both are hard and unyielding.

The difference between the two lies in the principle by which they live. Antigone chooses to serve the gods, or divine law, while Creon makes the state his top priority. Both serve their principle with all the force of their being, but because Creon has chosen the lesser law, and because the state as he conceives it is indistinguishable from his own ego, he must bow in the end to the gods, who crush him. Ironically, he suffers the same fate he had meted out to Antigone: Just as he deprived her of the chance to have a husband and child, so is he left bereft of his wife and son.

Creon's fate is tragic because he blundered into it unwittingly, through stubbornly upholding a limited idea. The man lacked wisdom. Antigone's death is tragic because she voluntarily accepted it as the consequence of her heroism. For all her hardness, there is something truly grand and edifying in her fate. Suffering is a part of everyone's condition, but there is a vast difference in how different individuals accept it. People can stumble into suffering through ignorance and flaws of character, as Creon does, which is the normal human lot. Others freely choose suffering with open eyes by taking on a divine obligation. This way is intense and tragic, but it is the only path that can enlarge humanity. The greatness of *Antigone* lies in the clarity, poignancy, and integrity with which Sophocles presented these two sides of human suffering.

"Critical Evaluation" by James Weigel, Jr.

Bibliography:
Kitto, H. D. F. Greek Tragedy: A Literary Study. Garden City, N.Y.: Doubleday, 1954. Addresses types and elements of Greek tragedies, and compares Aeschylus, Sophocles, and Euripides. Discusses problems with the early exit of Antigone and argues that she is more than "mere antithesis to Creon" who is "more than the stubborn fool who kills her."

Melchinger, Siegfried. Sophocles. Translated by David A. Scrase. New York: Frederick Ungar, 1974. Provides a biography of Sophocles and explains Greek theater, chorus, staff, and actors, as well as each scene of *Antigone*.

Oudemans, Th. C. W., and A. P. M. H. Lardinois. *Tragic Ambiguity: Anthropology, Philosophy, and Sophocles' "Antigone."* New York: E. J. Brill, 1987. Applies Greek theology to *Antigone* and explains separative and harmonizing interpretations. One chapter explicates each episode of the play, another, the Greek tragic elements. A thorough study.

Segal, Charles Paul. "Sophocles' Praise of Man and the Conflicts of the *Antigone*." In *Sophocles: A Collection of Critical Essays*, edited by Thomas Woodward. Englewood Cliffs, N.J.: Prentice-Hall, 1966. Focuses on the individuality of Creon and Antigone instead of, as many other studies do, on their contrasts and conflicts. Identifies aspects of Athenian democracy in the play.

Winnington-Ingram, R. P. *Sophocles: An Interpretation*. New York: Cambridge University Press, 1980. Compares the common religious and political themes and plots of Sophocles' extant plays. Compares Antigone and Creon, assuming that all of Sophocles' plays focus on a hero who "suffers a wrong." Sees Antigone as "no reasoner."

THE ANTIQUARY

Type of work: Novel
Author: Sir Walter Scott (1771-1832)
Type of plot: Fiction of mannners
Time of plot: Late eighteenth century
Locale: Scotland
First published: 1816

Principal characters:

JONATHAN OLDBUCK OF MONKBARNS, the antiquary
LOVEL, an illegitimate son of unknown parents
SIR ARTHUR WARDOUR, a baronet and Oldbuck's friend
MISS ISABELLA WARDOUR, his daughter
EDIE OCHILTREE, a beggar
HECTOR M'INTYRE, Oldbuck's nephew
THE EARL OF GLENALLAN, the present head of a powerful family
DOUSTERSWIVEL, a magician

The Story:

When old Jonathan Oldbuck of Monkbarns first met young Lovel, he was impressed by the young man's good manners and conduct, but he was mystified by the little he could learn of Lovel's past. It was obvious that Lovel was not the boy's real name and that there was something in his history of which he was ashamed.

From his good friend Sir Arthur Wardour, Oldbuck at last learned that the young man was the illegitimate son of unknown parents. Although a benefactor had settled a large estate on him, he lived in solitude and disgrace because of his questionable ancestry. To make matters worse, he was in love with Sir Arthur's daughter, Isabella. Although the girl loved him, she would not accept him because she knew her father would not permit an alliance with a man of unknown and illegitimate origins. Even after Lovel had saved her life and that of her father when they were trapped by the tides, she gave him no more than the thanks due him for his bravery.

Sir Arthur was in serious financial straits, in debt to dozens of tradesmen and friends, among them Oldbuck. To restore his fortune, he had fallen into a plot prepared by Dousterswivel, an evil magician who had promised his aid in finding valuable minerals on Sir Arthur's property. Sir Arthur, forced to put up money before Dousterswivel would work his magic, had already borrowed one hundred pounds from Oldbuck, who accurately suspected that Dousterswivel was a crook.

Before the magician could attempt to work his magic, Oldbuck's nephew, Captain Hector M'Intyre, came home for a visit. A hotheaded young man, he accused Lovel of lying about the little he told of his past. Hector challenged Lovel to a duel, and although Lovel did everything he could to prevent it, the duel was fought. Having apparently wounded Hector fatally, Lovel was forced to flee the country on a boat provided by a friend. Hector actually did recover, but Lovel did not hear the news until much later. He had been aided in his flight by Edie Ochiltree, a beggar who knew all the secrets of the countryside. While Edie was hiding Lovel in a cave, they overheard Dousterswivel trying to convince Sir Arthur to put up more money to find buried treasure in the cave.

When Sir Arthur asked Oldbuck for another hundred pounds to give to Dousterswivel so that he would get the treasure from the cave, Oldbuck insisted that they themselves go to the cave and dig for the treasure. Although the magician tried to prevent the excursion, Oldbuck would not be denied. Everyone present was completely surprised when, after much digging, old Edie the beggar stuck a pick into the ground and hit a chest. When the chest was opened, the bewildered spectators found a fortune in coin; Sir Arthur was saved from disaster. Edie tricked Dousterswivel into digging for hours for more treasure that Edie said was also buried in the cave. He also arranged with a friend to have a specter appear and frighten the magician.

About the same time, an old woman in the neighborhood sent for the wealthy and powerful earl of Glenallan. Before she died, she wanted to clear her conscience of a terrible wrong she had done the earl. When he was a young man, he had been in love with a girl whom his mother hated. The earl had secretly married the girl before his mother, in a spiteful attempt to break up the romance, told her son that the girl was his own sister. Because of certain letters and the perjured testimony of servants, including the old woman telling the story, the earl had believed his mother's story. The young woman had taken her own life, but before she died, she had given birth to a male child. A servant had whisked the child away, and the old woman did not know whether he had lived or died. The earl, who had lived a life of misery because of the horrible crime he thought he had committed in marrying his own sister, was joyful at the old crone's information, though he grieved at the useless death of his wife. He told the story to Oldbuck and asked his help in determining whether the child had lived.

While Oldbuck and the earl of Glenallan were investigating, news came that the French were about to raid the Scottish coast. Hector, who was now fully recovered from the wound suffered at Lovel's hands, prepared to gather troops and meet Major Neville, an officer in charge of local defense. Lovel had not been heard from since the duel, and there were rumors that he had died at sea. Then old Edie brought the news that the ship carrying Lovel had put in to shore and that all aboard were safe. From his remarks to Oldbuck, the old gentleman learned that the money found in the cave on Sir Arthur's land had been buried there by Lovel and Edie after they had overheard the conversation between Dousterswivel and Sir Arthur. Lovel, hearing of Sir Arthur's financial difficulties, had chosen that way of helping Isabella's father without embarrassing the old gentleman by offering him money outright.

When Major Neville appeared to take charge of the garrison, everyone was amazed to see that he was in reality Lovel. He brought word that there would be no battle. A watchman had mistaken a bonfire for a signal that the French were coming. As they all stood talking, the earl of Glenallan noted the young man's marked resemblance to his dead wife. Through old papers and the words of old servants of the Glenallan family, the earl learned that Lovel was without doubt his son. While a baby, the boy had been cared for by the earl's brother and, unknown to the earl, he had inherited his uncle's fortune.

Lovel was restored to his rightful place, and within a month he and Isabella Wardour were married. From that time on, they all lived in peace, prosperity, and joy.

Critical Evaluation:

Sir Walter Scott's *The Antiquary*, the third in the Waverley series, is the novel most nearly contemporary to the author's own time. Although it is a love story, it is also a novel of manners. Scott admitted that, when necessary, he sacrificed the plot in order to describe more clearly the manners of the characters, particularly those of the lower social classes. His characterizations of the Scottish peasants are much more vivid than those of the upper classes.

The Antiquary met with unprecedented sales when it first appeared in 1816. Scott himself remarked that "it has been more fortunate than any of them . . . for six thousand went off in the first six days." It reached a fifth edition within two years and was translated during ensuing years into at least seven languages.

In spite of its being a potpourri of gothic elements, supernatural escapades among abbey ruins at night, scheming tricks of a charlatan magician, romantic rescues up sheer cliffs from a wild and sudden high tide, the usual genteel and static hero and heroine falling at the end into marriage as well as vast inherited wealth, the novel succeeded for other, more significant reasons.

Its lasting value is based on the scenes of Scottish village life and of the lower classes and their colorful dialogue. These scenes have wit and pathos and provide a sane balance to the unreal plot in which the upper-class characters are involved. The links between the two levels of the tale are the antiquary Jonathan Oldbuck of Monkbarns (who has much of Scott's interests and learning), and the wandering beggar Edie Ochiltree. These two characters move back and forth between the fishing village and country people and the nobility and their estates, providing connections between the two different worlds of the novel.

Scott drew the background of *The Antiquary* from the historical religious opposition of Catholics and Covenanters and the political conflict between England and France. These issues, however, form only a backdrop and do not affect the suspense and tension of the novel. Scenes such as that in the Fairport post office when the village gossips speculate about the newly arrived mail, or pathetic ones such as the Mucklebackit family's gathering in their cottage after their son Steenie's drowning, are remarkable because of their vividness. Such scenes constitute the core of the novel, its color and poetry. Moreover, Scott brings the characters in these scenes alive, perhaps because he drew them from individuals he had known from boyhood. Action and meaning belong to old Elspeth crooning her eerie ballads, Edie Ochiltree maintaining his pride and religious feeling though merely an "auld" beggar, Maggie haggling with Monkbarns over the price of fish, and Mucklebackit Senior trying to cope with his grief. Scott declared this to be a novel of lower-class manners; as such, it succeeds.

Bibliography:
Daiches, David. "Scott's Achievement as a Novelist." In *Scott's Mind and Art*, edited by A. Norman Jeffares. New York: Barnes & Noble Books, 1970. Clear analysis of Scott's depiction of character in *The Antiquary*, finding the portrayal of the merchant class more sympathetic than that of the nobility. Discusses the novel's unusual use of comic atmosphere.

Johnson, Edgar. *Sir Walter Scott: The Great Unknown.* 2 vols. New York: Macmillan, 1970. Extensively researched biography that explores Scott as a man and as a writer. Praises *The Antiquary*'s rich portrayal of life in Scotland and discusses the need to understand the past to live in the present. An excellent introductory source.

Millgate, Jane. *The Making of a Novelist.* Toronto: University of Toronto Press, 1984. Good introductory source that analyzes character and theme in *The Antiquary* and discusses the novel's structure and the importance of Oldbuck as a central figure. Compares the novel's treatment of past and present with *Guy Mannering* (1815).

Sutherland, John. *The Life of Walter Scott: A Critical Biography.* Oxford: Blackwell, 1995. Interesting literary analysis that characterizes *The Antiquary* as a middle-aged man's story, with Oldbuck a fictionalized portrait of Scott himself. Praises plot development in the first two volumes, but asserts that the third demonstrates rushed, conventional plotting.

Wagenknecht, Edward. *Sir Walter Scott.* New York: Continuum, 1991. Provides clear analysis of setting and character in *The Antiquary*, finding the novel most effective in its portrayal of the lower classes. Discusses the importance of the character of Elspeth.

ANTONY AND CLEOPATRA

Type of work: Drama
Author: William Shakespeare (1564-1616)
Type of plot: Tragedy
Time of plot: c. 30 B.C.E.
Locale: Egypt and parts of the Roman Empire
First performed: c. 1606-1607; first published, 1623

> *Principal characters:*
> MARK ANTONY,
> OCTAVIUS CAESAR, and
> LEPIDUS, triumvirs who ruled Rome
> ENOBARBUS and
> EROS, Antony's friends
> SEXTUS POMPEIUS, the leader of the party opposed to Octavius Caesar
> CLEOPATRA, the queen of Egypt
> OCTAVIA, Caesar's sister and Antony's wife
> CHARMIAN and
> IRAS, Cleopatra's attendants

The Story:

After the murder of Julius Caesar, the Roman Empire was ruled by the noble triumvirs Mark Antony, Lepidus, and Octavius (Caesar's nephew). Antony, having been given the Eastern sphere to rule, had gone to Alexandria and there he had seen and fallen passionately in love with Cleopatra, queen of Egypt. She was the flower of the Nile, but she had also been the mistress of Julius Caesar and many others. Antony was so enamored of her that he ignored his own counsel and the warnings of his friends. As long as he could he also ignored a request from Octavius Caesar that he return to Rome. Sextus Pompeius, son of Pompey the Great, and a powerful leader, was gathering troops to seize Rome from the rule of the triumvirs, and Octavius Caesar wished to confer with Antony and Lepidus. At last the danger of a victory by Sextus Pompeius, coupled with the news that his wife Fulvia was dead, forced Antony to leave Egypt and return to Rome.

Because Antony was a better general than either Lepidus or Octavius, Pompeius was confident of victory as long as Antony stayed in Egypt. When Pompeius heard that Antony was returning to Rome, he was reduced to hoping that Octavius and Antony would not mend their quarrels but continue to fight each other as they had in the past. Lepidus did not matter, since he sided with neither of the other two and cared little for conquest and glory. Pompeius was disappointed, however, for Antony and Octavius joined forces in the face of common danger. To seal their renewed friendship, Antony married Octavia, Octavius' sister, through whom each was bound to the other. Pompeius' scheme to keep Antony and Octavius apart had failed, but he still hoped that Antony's lust for Cleopatra would entice him back to Egypt. To stall for time, he sealed a treaty with the triumvirs. Antony, accompanied by his new wife, went to Athens to deal with matters relating to the Empire. There word reached him that Lepidus and Octavius had waged war in spite of the treaty they had signed and that Pompeius had been killed. Octavius next seized Lepidus on the pretext that he had aided Pompeius. Now the Roman world had but two rulers, Octavius and Antony.

Antony could not resist the lure of Cleopatra. Sending Octavia home from Athens, he hurried back to Egypt. By so doing, he ended all pretense of friendship between him and Octavius. Both prepared for a battle that would decide who was to be the sole ruler of the world. Cleopatra joined her forces with Antony's. Antony's forces were supreme on land, but Octavius ruled the sea and lured Antony to fight him there. Antony's friends and captains, particularly loyal Enobarbus, begged him not to risk his forces on the sea, but Antony was confident of victory and he prepared to match his ships with those of Octavius at Actium. In the decisive hour of the great sea fight, however, Cleopatra ordered her fleet to leave the battle and sail for home. Antony too left the battle, disregarding the duty he had toward his honor, and because he had set the example for desertion, many of his men went over to Octavius' forces.

Antony was sunk in gloom at the folly of his own actions, but he was drunk with desire for Cleopatra and sacrificed everything, even honor, to her. She protested that she had not known that he would follow her when she sailed away, but Antony had reason to know she lied. Yet he could not tear himself away.

Octavius sent word to Cleopatra that she might have anything she asked for if she would surrender Antony to him. Knowing that Octavius was likely to be the victor in the struggle, she sent him a message of loyalty and of admiration for his greatness. Antony, who saw her receive the addresses of Octavius' messenger, ranted and stormed at her for her faithlessness, but she easily dispelled his fears and jealousy and made him hers again. After his attempt to make peace with Octavius failed, Antony decided to march against his enemy again. At this decision, even the faithful Enobarbus left him and went over to Octavius, thinking Antony had lost his reason as well as his honor. Enobarbus was an honorable man, however, and shortly afterward he died of shame for having deserted his general.

On the day of the battle, victory was in sight for Antony despite overwhelming odds. Once again, though, the Egyptian fleet deserted him. With the defeat of Antony, Octavius became master of the world. Antony was like a madman and thought of nothing but avenging himself on the treacherous Cleopatra. When the queen heard of his rage, she had word sent to him that she was dead, killed by her own hand out of love for him. Convinced once more that Cleopatra had been true to him, Antony called on Eros, his one remaining follower, to kill him so that he could join Cleopatra in death, but Eros killed himself rather than his beloved general. Determined to die, Antony fell on his own sword. Even that desperate act was without dignity or honor, for he did not die immediately and could find no one who loved him enough to end his pain and misery. While he lay there, a messenger brought word that Cleopatra still lived. He ordered his servants to carry him to her. He died in her arms, each proclaiming eternal love for the other.

When Octavius Caesar heard the news of Antony's death, he grieved. Although he had fought and conquered Antony, he lamented the sorry fate of a great man turned weakling and ruined by his lust. He sent a messenger to assure Cleopatra that she would be treated royally, that she should be ruler of her own fate. The queen learned, however, as Antony had warned her, that Octavius would take her to Rome to march behind him in his triumphant procession, where she, a queen and mistress to two former rulers of the world, would be pinched and spat upon by rabble and slaves. To cheat him of his triumph, she put on her crown and all her royal garb, placed a poisonous asp on her breast, and lay down to die. Charmian and Iras, her loyal attendants, died the same death. Octavius Caesar, entering her chamber, saw her dead, as beautiful and desirable as in life. There was only one thing he could do for his onetime friend and the dead queen: He ordered their burial in a common grave, together in death as they had wished to be in life.

Critical Evaluation:

In his tragedies, William Shakespeare rose to dramatic heights seldom equaled. *Antony and Cleopatra* surely belongs to the greatest of his tragedies for its staggering scope, which covers the entire Roman Empire and the men who ruled it. Only a genius could apply such beauty of poetry and philosophy to match the powerful events: A man born to rule the world is brought to ruin by his weaknesses and desires; deserted by friends and subjects, he is denied a noble death and must attempt suicide, but bungles even that. The tragedy is grimly played out, and honor and nobility die as well as the man.

In *Antony and Cleopatra*, Shakespeare did not bind himself with the Aristotelian unities. He moves swiftly across the whole of the civilized world with a panorama of scenes and characters, creating a majestic expanse suitable to the broad significance of the tragedy. The play is Shakespeare's longest. It is broken up into small units, which intensify the impression of rapid movement. Written immediately after Shakespeare's four great tragedies—*Hamlet, Prince of Denmark* (c. 1600-1601), *Othello, the Moor of Venice* (1604), *King Lear* (c. 1605-1606), and *Macbeth* (1606)—it rivals them in tragic effect though it has no plot that Aristotle would recognize. Shakespeare took the story of *Antony and Cleopatra* from a translation of Plutarch but refashioned it into a complex rendering of a corruption that ennobles as it destroys. The play may lack the single, poignant representative character of the great tragedies, but it extends its significance by taking the whole world for its canvas.

As a tragic figure, Antony leaves much to be desired. His actions are little more than a series of vacillations between commitment to a set of responsibilities that are his by virtue of his person and office and submission to the overpowering passion that repeatedly draws him back to Cleopatra's fatal influence. His nobility is of an odd sort. He commands respect and admiration as one of the two omnipotent rulers of the world, but the audience is only told of his greatness; they do not see it represented in any of his actions. In fact, he does not really do anything until his suicide—and that he does not do efficiently. His nobility is attested by his past deeds and by his association with the glories of Rome, and Shakespeare frequently reminds the audience of it, but Antony does not demonstrate this quality in the play.

There is another impediment to Antony's tragic stature: He is too intelligent and aware of what he is doing. As Mark Van Doren has noted, he lives "in the full light of accepted illusion." He is not duped; Cleopatra is not Antony's Iago. Nor is there any self-deception; Antony does not pretend that his love for Cleopatra is more than it is.

Yet that love is sufficiently great to endow Antony with the nobility he salvages. It is not simply that he is a hero brought to disgrace by lust, although that much is true. Viewed from another angle, he is a hero set free from the limits of heroism by a love that frees him from a commitment to honor, allowing him instead to give his commitment to life. Of course, his liberation is also his humiliation and destruction. Both noble and depraved, both consequential and trivial, Antony finds new greatness in the intense passion that simultaneously lays him low.

Cleopatra is an equally complex character, but her complexity is less the result of paradox than of infinite variation. Throughout the first four acts she lies, poses, cajoles, and entices, ringing manifold changes on her powers to attract. Yet she is not a coarse temptress, not a personification of evil loosed upon a helpless victim. As her behavior in the last act reminds the audience, she is also an empress. Cleopatra too is swept along by overwhelming passion. She is not only a proud queen and conniving seducer but a sincere and passionate lover. Despite her tarnished past, her plottings in *Antony and Cleopatra* are dignified through the underlying love. Like Antony, she is not the sort of character who challenges the universe and transcends personal destruction. Rather, her dignity lies somewhere beyond, or outside, traditional heroism.

The complexity of Cleopatra is most apparent in the motivation for her suicide. Certainly one motive is the desire to avoid the humiliation of being paraded through Rome by the victorious Octavius Caesar. If that had been all, however, she would be nothing more than an egoistic conniver. More important, she is also motivated by her sincere unwillingness to survive Antony. The two motives become intertwined, since the humiliation of slavery would also extend to Antony, whose failures left her vulnerable, and taint his reputation. This mixture of motives is a model of the way in which the two lovers are at once each other's undoing and salvation. Their mutual destruction springs from the same love that provides both with their antiheroic greatness. Love is lower than honor in the Roman world, but it can generate an intensity that makes heroism irrelevant. Antony is too intelligent, Cleopatra too witty, and their love too intricate for ordinary tragedy.

The structure of the plot departs from the tragic norm. There is almost none of the complication and unraveling that are expected in tragedy. Rather, the action moves in fits and starts through the forty-two scenes of the play. Although the action of the play must extend over a long period of time, the quick succession of scenes suggests an unsteady hurtling toward the fatal conclusion. The helter-skelter quality is reinforced by the language of the play. Few speeches are long and there are many abrupt exchanges and quick, wide-ranging allusions. Shakespeare often uses feminine endings and spills the sense over the ends of lines in a metrical reflection of the nervous vitality of the play. Thus, plot and language spread the drama over the entire world and hasten its progress toward the inevitable conclusion.

"Critical Evaluation" by Edward E. Foster

Bibliography:
Bloom, Harold, ed. *Modern Critical Interpretations: William Shakespeare's "Antony and Cleopatra."* New York: Chelsea House, 1988. Bloom's concise anthology of major Shakespeare criticism of the 1970's and 1980's judiciously samples postmodernist, new historicist, feminist, and deconstructionist discussions of *Antony and Cleopatra*. See especially the essays by Jonathan Dollimore, Linda Bamber, and Laura Quinney.

Charney, Maurice. *Shakespeare's Roman Plays*. Cambridge, Mass.: Harvard University Press, 1961. Chapter 3, the centerpiece of Charney's influential book, brilliantly analyzes the imagery of *Antony and Cleopatra*; Charney gives particular attention to the imagery that clusters around the Egypt-Rome polarity, thereby constituting it as a complex central theme.

Granville-Barker, Harley. *Prefaces to Shakespeare*. Vol. 1. Princeton, N.J.: Princeton University Press, 1946. Granville-Barker's prefaces remain timeless monuments to a golden age of Shakespearean scholarship and theatrical performance. The preface to *Antony and Cleopatra* offers valuable insights into staging and characterization from the perspective of an influential stage director and critic.

Riemer, A. P. *A Reading of Shakespeare's "Antony and Cleopatra."* Sydney, Australia: Sydney University Press, 1968. A monograph-length, lucid introduction to the background of the play and its plot, characterization, and dramatic structure. Also contains a very useful chapter that discusses important criticism of the play during the early and mid-twentieth century.

Traversi, Derek. *Shakespeare: The Roman Plays*. Stanford, Calif.: Stanford University Press, 1963. In chapter 3 of this classic study, Traversi offers a methodical, analytical commentary on *Antony and Cleopatra*. Sees the play as a profound work of art that in its spaciousness, episodic form, and morally ambivalent valuations of Rome and Egypt escapes traditional definitions of tragedy.

APOLOGIA PRO VITA SUA

Type of work: Autobiography
Author: John Henry Newman (1801-1890)
First published: 1864

This long essay, also known as *History of My Religious Opinions*, is the famous reply written by John Henry Newman in answer to the attack upon him by Charles Kingsley. The years 1833-1841 had seen the publication of *Tracts for the Times*, to which Newman had been a contributor; these tracts, which gave their name to the Tractarian or Oxford Movement, were the spearhead of the great theological controversy of the middle years of the century. Newman and his friends were eager to return the Anglican church to something like its position during past centuries; they valued tradition and hierarchy, and wished to return to the severe, authoritarian faith of the past, from which they believed the Church of England had lapsed. They were the High Church party; and some idea of the rift that was created within the Church can be gleaned from Anthony Trollope's Barchester novels. In 1845, Newman left the Anglican church for the Roman; two years later he was ordained priest in that communion.

In January, 1864, Kingsley, an Anglican clergyman of what was known as the Broad Church party and a popular novelist, attacked Newman in a magazine article, in which he stated that "Truth, for its own sake, has never been a virtue with the Roman clergy. Father Newman informs us that it need not, and on the whole ought not to be." To this article, Newman replied in a pamphlet in February of that year, whereupon Kingsley wrote yet another pamphlet entitled "What, then, does Dr. Newman mean?" in which he accused Newman of having "gambled away" his reason, of having a "morbid" mind, and of not caring about "truth for its own sake." It was in answer to this pamphlet that Newman wrote *Apologia pro Vita Sua*.

Newman divided the work into chapters, each dealing with a crucial period in his life. The first gives the story of his youth and his education up to his thirty-second year, by which time he was a Fellow of Oriel College, Oxford, and had been ordained in the Anglican church. By his own account, he was an extraordinarily precocious lad who was preoccupied at a very early age with religious questions. He resembled, indeed, the hero of his own novel *Loss and Gain* (1848)—which phrase might be applied as a description of his career. Later readers may smile at Newman's decision, reached at the age of fifteen, that celibacy was the only course for him; yet his prodigious intellect shines through the account of his youth. He tells of his reading, but the decisive influences were his friends Hurrell Froude and the older John Keble. It was Froude, with his love for tradition and for the external beauty of the Roman church, who began to soften Newman's insular dislike of that institution.

The year 1830 was a momentous one for Newman. The revolution that deposed Charles X of France distressed him; the Whig victory in England distressed him even more. He had a violent dislike of Liberalism, which seemed everywhere triumphant, and the Tractarian Movement was largely a counterattack. Newman himself claimed that the movement had begun to stir as far back as 1828, when he was Vicar of St. Mary's, Oxford; but the date of its beginning is usually set in July, 1833, when Keble preached a famous sermon at Oxford against the errors of the Whig government in Church policy. In *Tracts for the Times*, Newman and his friends stated their position. As Newman saw it, the Whigs must be opposed and the Church of England returned to the position of authority it had held during the early seventeenth century. He considered himself as belonging to neither the High nor the Low Church party; he was merely anti-Liberal. He explained his position as based on dogma (he had no use for "religion as a mere sentiment" but thought there must be positive beliefs), a visible church with sacraments and rites and the Episcopal system, and anti-Romanism. Such was the general point of view of the Oxford Movement. Newman himself, incidentally, had very little to say about ritual, which is usually associated with the High Church position. He was interested in theology, not liturgies.

Newman admitted frankly that in the vast amount of writing he did during these years he did attempt to refute many of the tenets of Romanism. What he was seeking for himself was a basis in reason for his beliefs; for the Anglican church, he was seeking a theology of its own that would make it more than a *via media*, or "middle way." These investigations led him to a consideration of the common heritage of Romanism and Anglicanism and to the question of how much of the Roman belief could be accepted by an Anglican. He began to be convinced that in English history the real objection to Rome had been political rather than theological, and that Romanism and Anglicanism were, after all, not so far apart as was generally believed. Inevitably, he began to differentiate between Roman dogmas, which he could accept, and Roman practice, which he often could not. He confessed that, for a long time, the stumbling block had been the Roman veneration of the Virgin and prayers to the saints. Yet he was obviously drawing closer to Rome.

It was tract 90, published in 1841, that brought the storm on Newman's head and led to his final break with the Church of England. In this tract, he examined whether the Thirty-Nine Articles, on which the Church rests, were capable of a Roman interpretation. Immediately he was accused of everything from "traducing the Reformation" to planning to build a monastery near Oxford. He himself was feeling grave doubts about Anglicanism, derived mainly from his reading on the abstruse doctrines of the Monophysites. When he could no longer conscientiously maintain his clerical position, he resigned his living of St. Mary's in September, 1843. As he explains, he had spent the years from 1835 to 1839 trying, in his writings, to benefit the Church of England at the expense of the Church of Rome and the years from 1839 to 1843 trying to benefit the Church of England without prejudice to the Church of Rome. In 1843, he began to despair of the Church of England.

The years between 1843 and 1845 were spent in retirement. Newman had reached the crossroads but was still unable to make the ultimate decision. He had already retracted the "hard things" he had said against Rome, the things he had felt compelled to say in defense of the Anglican church. He made a point of seeing no Roman Catholics; his struggle was purely an inward one. Though he still believed that the Church of England was a branch of the true Church, though he still deplored the "Mariolatry" of Rome, he was convinced that Rome was more in accord with the early Church. His horror of Liberalism also played its part; he very genuinely believed that the spirit of Liberalism was the spirit of Antichrist. As he now saw the situation, on the one hand there was Liberalism leading inevitably to atheism; on the other, Anglicanism leading to Rome. He still remained in lay communion with the Church of England during this difficult period, but more and more often he found himself asking himself "Can I be saved in the English Church?" When he was convinced that the answer was negative, he made the great decision and was received into the Roman communion in 1845. Two years later, he was ordained priest.

In the concluding section of his essay, Newman defends himself against the insults hurled at him after his conversion. It was said that by submitting to Rome he had abdicated his power of personal judgment and that he was now compelled to accept dogmas that might be changed at any moment. His reply was that the Roman doctrines were not difficult for him, and that historically the Church had not suppressed freedom of intellect. He felt that an infallible Church had been intended by the Creator to preserve religion—especially in an age of increasing skepticism. Lastly—and this is the most famous part of the essay—he advanced the idea that a conflict between authority and private judgment is beneficial to the person whose ideas are being tested.

Though *Apologia pro Vita Sua* won for Newman a resounding victory over Kingsley, the work is not easy reading. The difficulty does not lie in the style, for no one writes more clearly and simply than he, but in the fact that he was writing for readers who were familiar with Church history and theological problems. Readers who lack the knowledge to grasp many of his arguments find the text impenetrable. Moreover, Newman's dilemma became more difficult to understand in later times. Yet the *Apologia pro Vita Sua* remains a powerful and sincere work. Some have seen in Newman, as Kingsley must have done, only a man whose habit of mind made him take refuge in an authoritarian Church that would solve his spiritual problems for him. Others would say that Newman's faith and intelligence serve as mutual checks, informing and enhancing each other.

Bibliography:

Harrold, Charles Frederick. *John Henry Newman: An Expository and Critical Study of His Mind, Thought, and Art.* New York: Longmans, Green, 1945. Authoritative and detailed. Chapter 12 discusses the Newman-Kingsley controversy and *Apologia pro Vita Sua.* Lengthy bibliography and index.

Houghton, Walter E. *The Art of Newman's "Apologia."* New Haven, Conn.: Yale University Press, 1945. Focuses on the artistic qualities of the work rather than on its historical or theological aspects. In-depth concentration on Newman's "principles of biography" and prose style. Includes diagrams of stylistic analysis.

Martin, Brian. *John Henry Newman: His Life and Work.* New York: Oxford University Press, 1982. An accessible and useful work for the beginning student. Discusses *Apologia pro Vita Sua* throughout, but particularly in chapter 8, "Literature and Religion." Discusses the book's influence on Newman's contemporaries.

Newman, John Henry. *Apologia pro Vita Sua.* Edited by David J. DeLaura. New York: W. W. Norton, 1968. A valuable source and overview. Contains the text of *Apologia pro Vita Sua* as well as basic texts of the Newman-Kingsley debate. Two further sections offer critical essays and early reactions to the work.

Ward, Wilfrid. *The Life of John Henry, Cardinal Newman: Based on His Private Journals and Correspondence.* 2 vols. New York: Longmans, Green, 1912. Early but definitive biography of Newman. Includes a thorough discussion of the background, sources, and effect of *Apologia pro Vita Sua.*

THE APOSTLE

Type of work: Novel
Author: Sholem Asch (1880-1957)
Type of plot: Historical
Time of plot: First century C.E.
Locale: Roman Empire
First published: 1943

> *Principal characters:*
> SAUL OF TARSHISH, later known as Paul
> JOSEPH BAR NABA OF CYPRUS, Saul's friend, an early convert
> REB ISTEPHAN, a famous Jewish preacher
> SIMON BAR JONAH, called Peter
> REB JACOB, Joseph's son

The Story:

It was seven weeks after the crucifixion of Yeshua (Jesus) of Nazareth by Pontius Pilate. All the poor of Jerusalem, who had found in Yeshua their Messiah, had gone into hiding, but the word was spreading. Little by little the story was told: of Yeshua who had come back after his death and of the Messiah who had appeared to his disciples. The matter was hotly argued on all sides. The pious Jews could not believe in a Messiah who had been killed; the Messianists devoutly affirmed their faith.

Saul of Tarshish and Joseph bar Naba came upon a street preacher, a rustic Galilean, who told with great conviction of Yeshua's return after he had been entombed. Cries of belief and of repugnance interrupted his talk. Saul himself spoke with great bitterness against this Messiah, for he had no patience with the gentle Yeshua who was crucified.

The agitation rapidly spread. One of the most vigorous upholders of Yeshua was Reb Istephan. He had a gift for moving people's souls, and more and more Jews became persuaded. Joseph bar Naba had known Yeshua in his lifetime, and when Joseph heard Reb Istephan, he was convinced. Joseph became a Messianist. This conversion disgusted Saul, and in sorrow and bitterness, he turned away from his friend Joseph.

Then a dramatic incident took place. Simon, the first of Yeshua's disciples, healed Nehemiah the cripple in the name of the Nazarene. Many were impressed by the cure, but others resented Simon's use of the Messiah's name. As a result, his enemies had their way, and Simon was imprisoned by the High Priest to await trial. Then another miracle happened. Simon and his follower Jochanan had been securely locked in a dungeon, but in the morning, they were walking the streets again. It was said that they had passed directly through the stone walls—with the help of Yeshua.

The resentment against the wild Galileans grew among the rulers, while the humble folk followed Simon with trust. The High Priest again brought Simon to trial, but Simon spoke so well in defense of his doctrine that he was freed. Now the tumult increased. The ignorant folk, seeing Simon released, concluded that there was official sanction for the new cult; hence, more joined the followers of Yeshua.

Saul was greatly incensed. He believed that the Messiah was yet to come and that the disciples were corrupting Jerusalem. He went to the High Priest and secured an appointment as official spy. In his new job, Saul tracked down the humble Messianists and sentenced them to the lash. Growing in power, Saul the Zealot finally took Reb Istephan prisoner for preaching the new faith. With grim pleasure, Saul led the way to the stoning pit and watched Istephan sink beneath the flung rocks. As he died, the preacher murmured a prayer forgiving his tormentors. Saul was vaguely troubled.

Then the Messianists were much heartened. Yeshua's younger brother, Reb Jacob ben Joseph, came to Jerusalem to head the humble cult, and Saul could do little against this pious and strict Jew. By chance, the High Priest heard of more Messianists in Damascus. Saul volunteered to investigate and hurried to his new field. En route, however, a vision appeared to him in which Yeshua said, "Saul, Saul, why dost thou persecute me?" Saul then recognized Yeshua as his Lord, and, as he was commanded, he went on to Damascus, although he was still blinded by the heavenly apparition. A follower of the new religion baptized him and restored his sight. The penitent Saul hurried away from the haunts of man. In all, he waited seven years for his mission.

Finally, as he prayed in his mother's house, the call came. Joseph bar Naba asked Saul to go with him to Antioch to strengthen the congregation there. At last, Saul was on the way to bring the word of the Messiah to others. He left for Antioch with Joseph and the Greek Titus, Saul's first convert.

Simon had founded the church at Antioch among the Greeks. The perplexing question was, could a devout Jew even eat with the Gentiles, let alone accept them into the church? In Jerusalem, Jacob held firmly to the law of the Torah: Salvation was only for the circumcised. Simon vacillated. In Jerusalem, he followed Jacob; among the Greeks he accepted Gentiles fully. Joseph had been sent by the elders of Jerusalem to Antioch to apply the stricter rule to the growing Messianic church.

Saul at first met with much suspicion. The Messianists remembered too well Saul the Zealot who had persecuted them. Little by little, the apostle won them over. Yeshua appeared to Saul several times, and he was much strengthened in the faith. At last, Saul found his true mission in the conviction that he was divinely appointed to bring the word of Yeshua to the Gentiles. He worked wonders at Antioch and built a strong church there, but his acceptance of Gentiles cost him Joseph's friendship. As a symbol of his new mission, Saul became Paul and began his years of missionary work.

Paul went to all the Gentiles—to Corinth, to Ephesus, to Cyprus. Everywhere, he founded a church, sometimes small but always zealous. Lukas, the Greek physician, went with him much of the time. Lukas was an able minister and a scholar who was writing the life of Yeshua.

The devout Jews in Jerusalem were greatly troubled by this strange preacher who accepted the Gentiles. Finally, they brought him up for trial. Paul escaped only by standing on his rights as a Roman citizen. As such, he could demand a trial before Caesar himself. Paul went to Rome as a captive, but he rejoiced, for he knew the real test of Christianity would be in Rome. Simon was already there, preaching to the orthodox Jews.

The evil Nero made Paul wait in prison for two years without a hearing and, even then, only the intervention of Seneca freed the apostle. For a short time, Simon and Paul worked together, one among the Jews and the other among the Gentiles. They converted many, and the lowly fervently embraced the promise of salvation.

To give himself an outlet for his fancied talents as an architect, Nero burned Rome and planned to rebuild a beautiful city. The crime, however, was too much, even for the Romans. To divert suspicion from himself, Nero blamed the Christians. He arrested thousands of them and, on the appointed day, opened the royal carnage. Jews and Christians, hour after hour, were gored by oxen, torn by tigers, and chewed by crocodiles. At the end of the third day, many Romans could no longer bear the sight, but still Nero observed the spectacle. It was so strange: The Christians died well, and with their last breaths, they forgave their persecutors.

Simon, a Jew, was crucified afterward; Paul, born a Roman citizen, was beheaded. Gabelus, the gladiator who had accepted Christianity, went with them to the execution. The deaths of Simon and Paul, however, were, in reality, the beginning. The martyrdom of the early Christians was the foundation stone of the Christian church.

Critical Evaluation:

During the four decades between his first ventures into short fiction and the publication of his novel *The Nazarene* (1939), Sholem Asch established himself as the most important Yiddish writer of his time, as well as a spokesperson and a crusader for his people. Although *The Nazarene* was a bestseller, it roused a storm of protest among Jews. Certainly, Asch's timing was unfortunate. Asch's story of the life of Christ appeared when Jews were facing the most wide scale persecutions in their history. It is hardly surprising that many embattled Jews viewed the book as evidence that Asch had left the faith and was urging others to follow his example or, alternatively, that he was an unprincipled opportunist, aiming at high sales among Christian readers or, perhaps, a Nobel Prize.

Asch was stunned by such accusations. His dedication to Judaism was as strong as ever. Moreover, the subject of *The Nazarene* did not mark a new departure in Asch's interests. As early as 1906, he had planned to write a book about Jesus, whom he regarded as one of the outstanding Jews in history. With this goal in mind, he had been collecting materials on primitive Christianity for some thirty years; during his numerous trips to the Holy Land, the subject had never been far from his mind. Asch's purpose in writing *The Nazarene, The Apostle,* and *Mary* (1949), the story of Jesus' mother, was not to glorify Christianity at the expense of Judaism, but to show his readers how deeply Christianity was rooted in Judaism and to remind them that adherents of the two faiths share the same ethical systems and worship the same God. In this way, he hoped, he could bring about a reconciliation between Christians and Jews.

Although most of his Jewish critics did not see it at the time, thematically, Asch's Christological novels were no different from his earlier works. Asch had always emphasized spiritual values. His heroes had always been Jewish leaders, often rabbis, who devoted themselves to God. Asch had often revealed his impatience with legalistic technicalities, especially when they served to separate human beings from their God, and he deplored factionalism, which so often sprang from an emphasis on the letter, rather than the spirit, of the law. Because of convictions like these, as well as his profound knowledge of those distant times, Asch respected the founders of the Christian church, including Jesus himself; Paul and the other apostles; and Mary, the mother of Jesus. As a deeply religious Jew, he understood these other devout Jews, even though he himself had no interest in adopting their faith.

In *The Apostle*, Saul is introduced as a person with just one aim in life: to serve his God. By nature, he is a fanatic. He cannot admit anything in his life that might distract him from his purpose. Therefore, he rejects the useful, respectable life his parents had intended for him, as a learned rabbi with a wife and a family. In order to avoid the sins of the flesh, he not only avoids women, but, from time to time, he even embraces the ascetic rules of the Nazarites; to avoid the sins of the intellect, Saul continually scrutinizes his ideas and those of others for any taint of heresy.

Ironically, Saul does not experience any uncertainties about his spiritual well-being until after he has become a Christian. From that time on, he is in constant conflict with himself. On one hand, he is as strong-willed as ever. On the other hand, he is mindful of Jesus' insistence on submitting to suffering rather than inflicting suffering upon others.

When Saul, or Paul, is sent to spread the gospel among the Gentiles, he does not feel threatened by paganism. It is clear that the pagan gods are dead. They serve merely to prop up the authority of the state or provide occasions for dissolute behavior. The Gentile world is more than ready for a faith that has some substance and offers some hope. What disturbs Paul is that the Gentiles who accept his news with such joy face rejection from his own people, the Jewish leaders of the new church, who insist that the only way into Christianity is through Judaism. For male Gentiles, that means circumcision. Paul understands that to Greeks, imbued with the ideal of physical beauty, circumcision is abhorrent. Because Christ always stressed the spirit, not the law, Paul is infuriated by the legalistic quibbling of the men in Jerusalem, who are making it difficult for him to fulfill his mission.

Unfortunately, Paul's increasing hostility toward the Jewish Christians has been misinterpreted as a reflection of Asch's own views, perhaps of some antipathy toward Judaism. In reality, although epic in scope and crowded with characters, *The Apostle* is primarily a character study. In Paul, Asch sees a great man, whose single-minded passion for God gives him the strength to do great deeds, while his inability to compromise produces conflicts with others and within himself. Paul's life illustrates how intolerance can damage an individual, while the history of the infant church shows how inflexibility can threaten an institution.

Both Christianity and Judaism continue to be troubled by factionalism. In Asch's novel, however, Paul finally learns to subdue his will and, in submission, he becomes whole. By thus identifying Paul's most important achievement as a spiritual one, Asch offers further proof of the kinship between Judaism and Christianity. As *The Apostle* shows, both great faiths are based on the assumption that human life is, above all, a spiritual matter.

"Critical Evaluation" by Rosemary M. Canfield Reisman

Bibliography:

Madison, Charles A. *Yiddish Literature: Its Scope and Major Writers*. New York: Frederick Ungar, 1968. Explains why Asch wrote his trilogy, in particular, the story of Paul, who has been regarded by many Jews as the founder of Christian anti-Semitism. A good discussion of a difficult subject.

Morgentaler, Goldie. "The Foreskin of the Heart: Ecumenism in Sholem Asch's Christian Trilogy." *Prooftexts: A Journal of Jewish Literary History* 8, no. 2 (May, 1988): 219-244. Explores the attitudes that underlie Asch's works, including *The Apostle*. Asserts that *The Apostle* is flawed by Asch's manipulation of history and Pauline theology to reflect his own beliefs.

Siegel, Ben. *The Controversial Sholem Asch: An Introduction to His Fiction*. Bowling Green, Ohio: Bowling Green University Popular Press, 1976. The first critical biography of Sholem Asch written in English. Siegel finds *The Apostle* to be vivid, but less effective than the other two works in the trilogy, and also dated. Includes a chronology, extensive notes, and useful bibliography.

"Talmud for the Acts." *Commonweal* 38, no. 24 (October 1, 1943): 588-589. A favorable review of *The Apostle*, reflecting contemporaneous Christian opinion. Admits that the book is fictional and sometimes not consistent with Catholic doctrine, but recommends it highly.

APPOINTMENT IN SAMARRA

Type of work: Novel
Author: John O'Hara (1905-1970)
Type of plot: Naturalism
Time of plot: 1930
Locale: Pennsylvania
First published: 1934

> *Principal characters:*
> JULIAN ENGLISH, a car dealer
> CAROLINE, his wife
> HARRY REILLY, a rich man
> AL GRECCO, the bootlegger's handyman

The Story:

Julian English was thirty years old, a congenial seller of cars and popular with the country club set. He had the right connections with Ed Charney, the local bootlegger, and consequently was always well supplied with liquor. He and Caroline had been married four years. Both natives of Gibbsville, they had an assured social position and no children.

Just before Christmas, they went to a party at the country club. As usual, Julian had too much to drink. He sat idly twirling his highball and listening to Harry Reilly's stories. Harry was a rich Irish Catholic and definitely a social climber. Julian disliked Harry, although Harry had lent him twenty thousand dollars the previous summer to bolster his Cadillac agency. That loan did not give Harry the right to make passes at Caroline, Julian thought darkly. Harry told stories in paragraphs. He always paused at the right time. Julian kept thinking how fitting it would be if he stopped the stories by throwing his drink in Harry's face. Julian grew bored. On impulse he did throw his drink in Harry's face. A big lump of ice hit Harry in the eye.

On the way home, Julian and Caroline quarreled furiously. Julian accused his wife of infidelity with Harry, among others. Caroline said that Julian always drank too much and chased women as well. More important, Harry had a mortgage on the car agency and a good deal of influence with the Catholics, and he was a man who could hold a grudge.

Al Grecco was a little man who, as Ed Charney's handyman, had a certain standing in the town. He liked Julian because Julian was the only one of the social set who was really friendly. Al had grown up on the wrong side of the tracks. Before he was finally sentenced to a year in prison, he had been arrested several times. When he got out, he worked in a poolroom for a while until his boss died. The widow wanted Al to stay on as manager, but he went to work for Charney. Now he delivered bootleg booze, ran errands, and kept an eye on Helene Holman, the torch singer at the Stage Coach, a country inn owned by Charney. Helene was Charney's girl, but Charney knew that if she were not carefully watched, she might, out of sheer good-heartedness, extend her favors to other men.

On Christmas Day, Julian woke up with a hangover. As was his custom, he quarreled with the cook. At Caroline's suggestion, he went to Harry Reilly's house to apologize. Although Reilly's sister was sympathetic, she brought down word that Harry would not see him; he had a black eye and was still perturbed.

Julian's father and mother came for Christmas dinner. The father, a staid, successful surgeon, was always looking for evidence of moral weakness in Julian, for his own father had committed suicide after embezzling a fortune. He was afraid that the English inheritance was stained. Dinner was a trying occasion.

Caroline and Julian had supper at the club. The usual crowd was there. Julian was unmercifully ribbed in the locker room. In a dismal mood, he sat drinking by himself while he waited for a chance to see Father Creedon and ask him to patch up his affair with Harry. The old priest was sympathetic and made light of the incident. After agreeing that Harry was a bore, he promised to send Julian some good Irish whiskey.

Ed Charney was a good family man who spent Christmas Day with his wife and son. He intended to go out to the Stage Coach only in the evening. Then his son became suddenly ill. It looked as if he would have to stay home. Mindful of Helene's weaknesses, he telephoned Al Grecco to go out to the inn to keep watch on her. It was Christmas night and she would be drinking too much. Al did not care for the assignment, but he dutifully went out to the inn and sat down with Helene.

The country club set began to drift in. Froggy Ogden, who was Caroline's one-armed cousin, was the oldest man there; he seemed to feel a responsibility for Julian, who was still drinking. In a spirit of bravado, Julian danced several times with Helene, even though Al warned him of Charney's anger. Finally, carried away by the music and too many drinks, Julian and Helene left the dance floor. Caroline and Froggy found Julian in a stupor in the back of a sedan and took him home.

The day after Christmas, Caroline went to her mother and announced her intention to divorce Julian. Her mother found it difficult to listen to her daughter. Caroline thought of herself as a heroine in an old-fashioned melodrama. She was determined not to go back to Julian. After meeting him on the street and quarreling with him again, she canceled the big party that they were to have given that very evening.

As he backed out of the garage with a case of Scotch, Al Grecco decided to kill Ed Charney. When Charney had phoned him, he had tried to excuse his lack of vigilance: He protested that he had only allowed Helene to dance. Ed, in a rage, had said some things that Al could not accept.

Determined to look businesslike, Julian went to his office at the automobile agency. He sat importantly at his desk and wrote figures on a piece of scratch paper. The only conclusion he could reach was that he needed more money. One of his salesmen came in to try to lay down the law. He asserted that Julian's difficulties were gossiped about in the little town of Gibbsville. The offense to Charney was particularly grave: He had been a good friend to the agency and had helped them sell cars to other bootleggers.

Julian left the office in no cheerful mood. He wandered into his club for lunch. Since it was the day after Christmas, the dining room was deserted except for some elderly lawyers and Froggy. Avoiding his wife's cousin, Julian sat down in a far corner of the room. After picking up his plate, Froggy followed him and began to reproach him for his conduct with the torch singer. He told Julian he had always distrusted him and had warned Caroline about his conduct many times. When Froggy invited him outside to fight, Julian refused because he could not hit a one-armed man. Froggy became more insulting, so that the lawyers came to their table to intervene. Julian was intensely angered when they seemed to side with Froggy. Turning quickly, he hit one of the lawyers in the mouth and dislodged his false teeth.

Julian went home and fell asleep. About ten o'clock, a society reporter awoke him when she came to get a story about the canceled party. After several drinks, he tried to seduce her but with no success. As soon as she left, Julian went to the garage, closed the door, and started the motor; his death was pronounced a suicide by the coroner.

Critical Evaluation:

John O'Hara was supreme in the art and craft of the short story. Perhaps because of his newspaper background, he was able to condense a tale to its fundamentals and produce tightly crafted and powerful short fiction. With his ear for speech and eye for effect, he was in two or three sentences able to bring to life a character from nearly any walk of life. This gift also marked his novels, in particular perhaps his first novel, *Appointment in Samarra*.

One of O'Hara's shortest and best-structured novels, *Appointment in Samarra* is the story of hubris in a modern setting. It takes place in 1930, after the crash of 1929 but before people understood just how bad the Depression would become. The hero of the novel, Julian English, has social status but destroys himself by not living up to it. Julian has two problems: people and alcohol, but both are revealed to be part of the inner problems that ultimately ruin him. There is much discussion in the book of who "belongs" and who does not, which clubs count in Gibbsville, what preparatory schools and colleges matter, and where one should be seen or not be seen. The laborer, mobster, and society man all think constantly about their position on the social ladder. Julian English thinks about it too much.

The novel presents an accurate picture of a broad cross section of Gibbsville society. Observing different kinds of people, from the secretary in the automobile agency and the ex-convict working for the gangland boss to the society matron, O'Hara achieved a new kind of fictional reporting, in the best sense of the term. The humor and fast pace of the novel and the clean, sure style give it a surface slickness that is almost misleading, for it is not a superficial novel. There is depth behind the meretricious glitter and hard-boiled sensual flavor. The book's racy language and sexual candor continued the pathbreaking trend begun only a short time earlier by Ernest Hemingway. The characters are concerned with superficialities, but that does not make them superficial. O'Hara is able to capture, especially in his dialogue, the nuances of tone that reveal the hidden depths.

Julian English, the central figure of the novel, is the most complex and interesting of the characters. He seems to burn with a compulsion toward self-destruction, yet however drunk he gets, part of his mind warns him when he is about to do something dangerous. Like many intelligent people, he observes himself as he moves through life. Yet, he recklessly plunges ahead, throwing the drink in Harry Reilly's face, dancing and going out to the car with Helene Holman at the roadhouse, getting deliberately drunk so that he will not care what happens. By the time he quarrels with Froggy Ogden at the club and fights with the lawyers in the dining room, he has given up hope and is as contemptuous of himself as he is of them. Rational action has ceased to have any meaning for him. Julian English is a direct forerunner of the existential heroes of Jean-Paul Sartre and Albert Camus a decade later, who were influenced by O'Hara and Hemingway and other writers of the American "hard-boiled" school of writing, and he toys with his fate with an almost objective curiosity. "If I do this," he seems to think, "will I get away with it?" Of course, he knows somewhere deep inside that he will not, that nobody ever gets away with anything. He is filled with "tremendous excitement" when he realizes that "he is in for it." Perhaps, as he contemplates his "unknown, well-deserved punishment," he is even slightly masochistic in his longing for pain and destruction.

Julian English's fatalism, and the fatalism that permeates the novel (and gives it its title) seem to be influenced in part by the novels and stories of Hemingway and F. Scott Fitzgerald, but O'Hara, while lacking the poetic vision and poetic style of Fitzgerald, avoids the hard-boiled prose of Hemingway and adds a poignant ruthlessness of his own. With economy and artistry, O'Hara draws the painful and engrossing portrait of a complex, fascinating, and doomed individual.

An inevitable progression, gaining in momentum like a ball rolling down a steep hill, takes over Julian English's fate. It would take a miracle to halt the inevitable doom that waits for him at the end, and as Julian knows, miracles do not happen for people like him. His death is early foreshadowed by the suicide of his grandfather. His own father frequently expresses fears that Julian's character is as weak as that of his grandfather, and Julian himself comes to believe that he has a defective character and is doomed by it. This belief numbs him and renders him helpless before the onrush of events.

Appointment in Samarra rises above O'Hara's other long works of fiction because it makes more of an attempt to deal with ideas and values. Often, the author's technique of recording action with the detachment of a photographer fails to establish a moral frame of reference; the reader does not know what the author's attitude toward the characters and events is. In this work, however, the character of Julian English is portrayed in compelling vitality. Also adding to the immediacy is O'Hara's custom of surrounding his dramatic action with historical exposition and long descriptions of the period: of its fashions, its horses and clubs, its automobiles, and the other transitory items that date a moment in history. In *Appointment in Samarra*, the precise documentation of social strata contributes to the story's realistic effect.

"Critical Evaluation" by Bruce D. Reeves

Bibliography:
Bier, Jesse. "O'Hara's *Appointment in Samarra*: His First and Only Real Novel." *College English* 25, no. 2 (November, 1963): 135-141. Compares O'Hara's first novel favorably with Ernest Hemingway's *The Sun Also Rises* (1926), but questions the importance of the rest of O'Hara's work.

Bruccoli, Matthew J. *The O'Hara Concern: A Biography of John O'Hara*. Pittsburgh, Pa.: University of Pittsburgh Press, 1995. A slightly expanded edition of the most complete biography of O'Hara, first published in 1975 and written with the cooperation of O'Hara's widow. Discusses the sources and background of *Appointment in Samarra* and argues that O'Hara is a major writer. Good bibliography.

Donaldson, Scott. "Appointment with the Dentist: O'Hara's Naturalistic Novel." *Modern Fiction Studies* 14, no. 4 (Winter, 1968-1969): 435-442. Argues that O'Hara was writing a naturalistic, as opposed to a didactic, novel and that this accounts for the novel's lukewarm acceptance.

Eppard, Philip B. *Critical Essays on John O'Hara*. New York: G. K. Hall, 1994. Includes reprints of the essays by Bier and Donaldson described here and provides further material on *Appointment in Samarra*.

Grebstein, Sheldon N. *John O'Hara*. New York: Twayne, 1966. The earliest and one of the most balanced book-length assessments of O'Hara's controversial career. Identifies the forces at work in *Appointment in Samarra* as fate, society, free will, self-knowledge, sex, and money.

Long, Robert Emmet. *John O'Hara*. New York: Frederick Ungar, 1983. A useful short study. Concludes that O'Hara is not a major writer, but calls *Appointment in Samarra* his "most nearly perfect novel."

THE ARABIAN NIGHTS' ENTERTAINMENTS

Type of work: Short fiction
Author: Unknown
Type of plot: Folklore
Time of plot: Legendary past
Locale: India, China, Persia, and Arabia
First published: Alf layla wa-layla, fifteenth century (English translation, 1706-1708)

Principal characters:
SHAHRIAR, the emperor of Persia and India
SCHEHERAZADE, his bride
THE FISHERMAN
THE KING OF THE BLACK ISLES, half man, half marble
SINDBAD THE SAILOR, a wanderer from Baghdad
THE SULTAN OF INDIA
HOUSSAIN,
ALI, and
AHMED, his sons
PERIEBANOU, Ahmed's wife
ALI BABA, a woodcutter in Persia
CASSIM, his brother
MORGIANA, his slave
ALADDIN, a good-for-nothing boy in China

The Stories:

Convinced by the treachery of his brother's wife and his own that all women were unfaithful, Shahriar, the emperor of Persia and India, vowed that he would marry a new wife every day and have her executed the next morning. Only Scheherazade, wise as well as beautiful, had the courage to try to save the young women of Persia. On the night of her marriage to Shahriar, she began to tell him a tale that fascinated him so much that he stayed her death for one night so that he could learn the end of the story. Eventually, Scheherazade told him stories for one thousand and one nights. Then, convinced of her worth and goodness, he bade her live and made her his consort.

One tale Scheherazade told was "The History of the Fisherman and the Genie": A poor fisherman drew from the sea in his nets a strange box with a seal on top. When he pried off the top, a huge genie appeared and threatened him with death, offering the poor man no more than his choice in the manner of his death. The fisherman begged for his life because he had done the genie a favor by releasing him, but the genie declared that he had vowed death to the man who opened the box. Finally, the fisherman exclaimed that he could not believe anything as huge and terrible as the genie could ever have been in a space so small. Dissolving into a cloud of smoke, the genie shrank until he could slip back into the box, whereupon the fisherman clamped on the lid. Throwing the box back into the sea, he warned all other fishermen to beware if it should ever fall into their nets.

Another story was "The History of the Young King of the Black Isles": A fisherman caught four beautiful fish, one white, one red, one blue, and one yellow. They were so choice that he took them to the sultan's palace. While the fish were being cooked, a beautiful girl suddenly appeared and talked to the fish, after which they were too charred to take to the sultan. When the same thing happened two days in a row, the sultan was called. After asking where the fish came from, he decided to visit the lake. Nearby, he found a beautiful, apparently deserted palace. As he walked through the beautiful halls, he found one in which a king was sitting on a throne. The king apologized for not rising, explaining that his lower half was marble.

He was the king of the Black Isles. When he had learned that his queen was unfaithful to him, he had nearly killed her black lover. In revenge, the queen had cast a spell over her husband, making him half marble. She whipped him daily and then had him dressed in coarse goat's hair over which his royal robes were placed. At the same time, while tending her lover, who remained barely alive, she had changed her husband's town and all its inhabitants into the lake full of fish.

The king told the sultan where the queen's lover was kept. There the sultan went, killed the lover, and put himself in the black man's place. The queen, overjoyed to hear speaking the one she had kept from death for so long, hastened to do all the voice commanded. She restored the king to his human form and the lake to its previous state as a populous town. The four colors of fish indicated the four different religions of the inhabitants.

When the queen returned to the sultan, whom she mistook for her lover, he killed her for her treachery. He took the king of the Black Isles home with him and rewarded the fisherman who had led him to the magic lake.

Shahriar was vastly entertained by "The History of Sindbad the Sailor": A poor porter in Baghdad, resting before the house of Sindbad, bewailed the fact that his lot was harder than that of Sindbad. Sindbad overheard him and invited the porter to dine with him. During the meal, he told of the hardships he had suffered to make his fortune.

On his first voyage to India by way of the Persian Gulf, Sindbad's ship was becalmed near a small green island. The sailors climbed onto the island, only to find that it was really a sea monster, which heaved itself up and swam away. Sindbad was the only man who did not get back to the ship. After days of clinging to a piece of driftwood, he landed on an island where some men were gathered. They led him to a maharajah, who treated Sindbad graciously. When he had been there some time, his own ship came into port, and he claimed his bales of goods, to the astonishment of the captain, who thought he had seen Sindbad killed at sea. Then Sindbad sailed home in the ship in which he had set out.

The porter was so impressed with the first tale that he came again to hear a second. On his second voyage, Sindbad was left asleep on an island where the sailors had rested. There he found a huge roc's egg. He waited, knowing that the parent bird would return to the nest at dusk. When it came, he used his turban to tie himself to the bird's leg. In the morning, the bird flew to a place surrounded by mountains. There Sindbad freed himself when the bird descended to pick up a serpent. The place seemed deserted, except for large serpents. Diamonds of great size were scattered throughout the valley.

Sindbad remembered that merchants were said to throw joints of meat into the diamond valley, from which big eagles carried the joints to their nests close to shore. At the nests, the merchants frightened away the birds and recovered diamonds that had stuck to the meat. Sindbad collected some large diamonds. With his turban, he fastened a piece of meat to his back and lay down. An eagle picked him up and carried him to its nest. When he was dropped into a nest, the merchant who claimed the nest was indignant and accused Sindbad of stealing his property. When Sindbad offered him some choice diamonds, the merchant was glad to take the adventurer back to civilization in return.

On his third voyage, Sindbad was wrecked on an island inhabited by cannibal dwarfs and huge black creatures, each with only one eye in the middle of its forehead. Sindbad and his friends blinded one black giant, but two others helped the blind one to chase the sailors. The giants and a large serpent overtook them, and only Sindbad was lucky enough to escape.

On his fourth voyage, Sindbad sailed from a port in Persia. He and his friends were shipwrecked on an island inhabited by cannibals, who fattened the sailors before killing them. Sindbad refused food, grew too thin to interest the cannibals, and finally found his way to the shore. There he met men who took him to their kingdom. To please the king, Sindbad made a fine saddle. In appreciation, the king married Sindbad to a beautiful girl. In that country, a man or woman was buried alive if the spouse died. When Sindbad's wife died, he was put in a tomb with a small amount of bread and water. As he ate the last of his food, he heard an animal snuffling, then running away. Following the sound, he found himself on the shore and hailed a ship that carried him home.

On his fifth voyage, Sindbad used his own ship. After his sailors had broken open a roc's egg, the parent rocs hurled tremendous stones on the ship and broke it to pieces. Sindbad came under the power of the Old Man of the Sea and escaped only after making the old man so intoxicated that he loosed his death grip on Sindbad. Again, Sindbad found a ship to take him home, and he did much profitable trading on the way.

On the sixth voyage, all of his companions succumbed on a beautiful but lifeless coast. Expecting to die, Sindbad built a raft that he put in an underground river to drift where it would. When he reached the kingdom of Serendib, he had to be revived. He found the country exceedingly rich and the people kind. When he asked to leave, the king sent him home with rich presents for Sindbad's ruler, the Caliph Harun-al-Rashid of Baghdad.

Sindbad made his seventh and final voyage to take gifts from the caliph to the king of Serendib. He carried them safely, but his return trip was delayed when corsairs seized his ship and sold the sailors into slavery. Sindbad was sold to an ivory merchant and was ordered to shoot an elephant a day. Annoyed at Sindbad's persistence, an elephant picked him up and took him to an elephant burial ground, to which Sindbad and his owner returned many times to gather ivory. As a reward, the merchant sent Sindbad home with rich goods.

Another diverting tale was "The History of Prince Ahmed": Houssain, Ali, and Ahmed, sons of the sultan of India, were all in love with the Princess Nouronnihar, their father's ward. To determine who should be the bridegroom, the sultan sent them out to find the most extraordinary things they could. Whoever brought back the rarest object would win the hand of the princess.

Houssain found a magic carpet that would transport him wherever he wished. Ali found an ivory tube containing a glass that would show any object he wished to see. Ahmed found an artificial apple, the odor of which would cure any illness.

The three princes met before they journeyed home. As they displayed their gifts, Houssain, looking through the tube, saw the princess apparently at the point of death. They all jumped on his magic carpet and were whisked to her bedroom, where Ahmed used his magic apple to revive her. The sultan could not determine which article was the most unusual, for all had been of use to effect the princess' recovery. He suggested an archery contest. Prince Ali shot farther than Houssain, but Ahmed's arrow could not be found. The sultan decided in favor of Ali. Houssain retired to become a dervish. Instead of attending the wedding, Ahmed went in search of his arrow, which he found at the foot of a mountain, much farther away than he could have shot. Looking around, he found a door into the mountain. When he passed through the door, he found a fairy called Periebanou, who pleased him so much that he married her.

When Ahmed went to visit his father, he refused to discuss where or how he lived, but he appeared to be so rich that the courtiers grew jealous and persuaded the sultan that it was dangerous to have his son so powerful a neighbor. The sultan asked Ahmed to perform unreasonable tasks, made possible only by Periebanou's help; but while Ahmed was fulfilling one request Periebanou's brother became so annoyed with the sultan that he killed him. Ahmed became sultan and afterward dealt kindly with his brothers.

Scheherazade also pleased her lord with "The History of Ali Baba and the Forty Thieves": Ali Baba was a Persian woodcutter. One day, to hide from a band of strange horsemen, he climbed a tree under which they had halted. When the leader cried, "Open, Sesame!" to a rock nearby, a door opened through which the men carried their heavy packs. After the men left, Ali Baba used the secret word to investigate the cave. He found such riches there that the gold he took could never be missed.

He and his wife were content with that amount, but his brother Cassim, to whom he had told his story, was greedy for more wealth. Without telling Ali Baba, Cassim went to the cave. He was so excited by the gold that he forgot the password and could not get out. When the robbers found him, they murdered him.

The robbers tried to find Ali Baba, intending to kill him and so keep the secret of their hoard. The leader brought his men, hidden in oil jars, to Ali Baba's house, but a beautiful slave, Morgiana, went in search of oil, discovered the ruse, and killed the bandits. Soon after, the robber captain, disguised as a merchant, entered the house, but again Morgiana came to her master's rescue, seeing through the robber's disguise and killing him.

To reward Morgiana, Ali Baba not only made her a free woman but also gave her to his son in marriage. After that, Ali Baba was the only one who knew the secret of the cave. He used the hidden wealth in moderation and passed the secret on to his children.

No less pleasing was "The History of Aladdin: Or, The Wonderful Lamp": Aladdin was a youthful vagabond who lived in China. An African magician, sensing that Aladdin would suit his plans and pretending to be the boy's rich uncle, took him to a secret place to get a magic lamp. Passing through halls stored with treasures, Aladdin filled his gown with so many things that he could not give the magician the lamp at the moment he wanted it, whereupon the magician sealed him up in the earth. By chance, Aladdin rubbed a ring the magician had given him. A genie appeared and escorted him home.

When Aladdin showed his mother the lamp, she tried to clean it to sell. As she rubbed, another genie appeared from whom Aladdin asked food. The food appeared on silver trays that Aladdin sold one by one to a peddler who swindled him. When an honest jeweler stopped Aladdin one day and asked to buy the silver, Aladdin began to realize the great riches he had at his disposal, enough to win him the sultan's daughter as his wife.

Because the grand vizier wanted his own son to marry the princess, he suggested that the sultan make many outrageous demands on Aladdin before he could be considered a suitor. The genies produced slaves, costumes, jewelry, gold, and chargers in such profusion, however, that the sultan gladly accepted Aladdin's suit. Overnight, Aladdin had the genie build a magnificent palace next to the sultan's.

Life went smoothly until one day, when Aladdin was away, the African magician persuaded the princess to trade the old lamp for a new one. Then the magician transported the great palace to Africa. When Aladdin came home, the sultan threatened him with arrest but allowed him forty days in which to find the palace and the princess. Rubbing his ring by chance and summoning its genie, Aladdin asked to be carried wherever his palace was. The princess was overjoyed to see him. After he had killed the magician by a ruse, he ordered the genie of the lamp to transport the palace back to China. There, after disposing of the magician's brother, who had followed them, Aladdin and the princess lived happily ever after.

Masterplots

Critical Evaluation:

The Arabian Nights' Entertainments is the title usually used in English to designate a group of tales more properly called *The Thousand and One Nights*. These stories, adapted and formalized by bazaar storytellers, had their origins in many lands throughout the East and were handed down by word of mouth for hundreds of years. Some present interesting parallels. In the story of "The Three Sisters," a baby is put in a basket to float down a river, a circumstance reminiscent of the biblical account of Moses in the bulrushes. In Sindbad's various journeys by sea, there are similarities to the wanderings of Ulysses as related by Homer; in one instance, there is a close parallel to the Cyclops story. Some of the characters have been drawn from history; but whether their source is folklore, religious tradition, or history, the tales have a timeless quality that has appealed from legendary times to the present to authors of every kind. Most scholars believe that the collection took its present form in Cairo in the fifteenth century; it was introduced to the Western world in a translation by Antoine Galland, published in Paris in 1704. Traditionally, there were a thousand and one stories told by Scheherazade to her emperor-husband, but in extant manuscripts the tales are not always the same. Practically all modern editions contain only a small portion of the complete collection. Those most frequently reprinted have become minor classics of the world's literature.

The older title of the work refers to the implied dramatic situation in which Scheherazade tells part of a story to Shahriar every night for the famous number of nights so as to forestall her death on the following morning. The tales are embedded in a frame-story, in the tradition of Giovanni Boccaccio's *Decameron* (1349-1351) and Geoffrey Chaucer's *Canterbury Tales* (1387-1400). Like the *Canterbury Tales*, *The Arabian Nights' Entertainments* includes some tales that are enriched by the situation of their framework. One of Scheherazade's first tales to her new husband and king, for example, is much more striking given the backdrop of Shahriar's repeated vow to kill his wife in the morning. "The History of the Fisherman and the Genie" also involves a powerful character, the genie, who has vowed to kill. In both cases, the vow is directed against one who has performed an act of charity or love. When the fisherman chastises the rebottled genie, predicting Allah's certain vengeance on him for killing, the humble man is in fact a mask through with Scheherazade is speaking to Shahriar.

"The History of the Young King of the Black Isles" alludes to Shahriar's motivation for his vow, which is rooted in his painful experience with an unfaithful wife; the fact that his brother's case paralleled his would indicate that the societies in which this book took form were preoccupied with a sense of inadequacy in sexual competition with blacks.

This racial, psychosexual problem amounts to the thematic focus of that story. The young king has likewise discovered his wife's infidelity and is greatly disturbed at her preference for a black lover. Throughout the story, black and white are pointedly juxtaposed. The king is described as extremely pale with only the smallest touch of black, a mole. His palace is black, perhaps an omen of his catastrophe. On the first two occasions of the spoiled fish (they are blackened), a fair lady comes out of the wall to upset the pan; on the third occasion, it is a black giant who performs the same act. The fact that the young king is turned to stone below the waist is part of the allegory, signifying his impotence upon having his male ego destroyed by his wife's preference for the slave. The sympathy and vengeance provided by the sultan are obviously designed to soothe Shahriar.

With "The History of Sindbad the Sailor," a smaller frame-story within the larger, readers come to the end of selections that contain pointed allusions to Shahriar's life and problems. All that can be said of the remaining selections' relationship to the framework is that they contain within their allegorical forms a wisdom about the ways of the world, which at one and the same time accords with Scheherazade's great learning and would no doubt impress Shahriar so much as to purge him of his unfortunate vision of all women as faithless and blind in their lust.

Sindbad, a wealthy man, tells his seven tales to a poor porter of the same name. The purpose of telling the tales is to justify the wealth of the rich Sindbad to the envious poor Sindbad. In each story, the wealth is justified by a different example of perils endured by the storyteller. Each of the seven stories follows a narrative pattern in which Sindbad sets out to sea to make money; loses everything in a catastrophe; undergoes a frightening experience (usually underground); escapes by means of his wits; and, finally, escapes with far greater riches than would ever have been possible by ordinary trading. The most frightening part of each episode is invariably a close brush with death, or a descent into the mythic world of the dead. Sindbad returns from each descent with treasures commensurate with the risks he had taken.

In "The History of Prince Ahmed," there is the familiar motif of trials undergone for the hand of a princess. In this case, however, there are two princesses, one mortal and one fairy. Ahmed and his brothers vie for the mortal princess, unaware of the fairy princess' love for Ahmed and of her having planned every detail of their adventures. The allegory involves Ahmed's being led unwittingly (and unwillingly) past the mortal princess and inexorably to the fairy princess (who is more beautiful and wise). The story points to the superiority of spiritual riches over material wealth. The sultan is depicted as foolish (and so deserving of his ultimate overthrow) when he ignores the superiority of Ahmed's magic apple, when he disqualifies Ahmed's archery for his arrow's being unrecoverable by ordinary mortal means, and when he demands material wealth of Ahmed.

"The History of Ali Baba and the Forty Thieves" depicts Ali Baba as a man who prospers through his lack of greed. He is contrasted with his brother Cassim in this; Cassim apparently married for money, while Ali Baba married a poor woman and was a woodcutter. When Ali Baba learns the magic formula for opening the door to wealth, he takes only as much as would not be missed. Cassim's greed, by contrast, causes him to become so excited by the wealth that he forgets the magic word and is killed. It is significant that Cassim, when he is trapped in the cave, has the entire treasure and, having it, has death along with it. When the threat of death for Ali Baba is resolved with the death of the thieves, the hero draws so temperately on his secret cache that it supports his family for many generations. (The fact that Ali Baba's life and fortunes are preserved by a clever woman, Morgiana, would not be lost on Shahriar.)

The next story too is an example of riches obtained by a successful descent into the underworld. In "The History of Aladdin: Or, The Wonderful Lamp," Aladdin is a naïve young man who is unaware of the great material value of the gold and silver trays and considers the food they had carried to be of greater importance. This sort of naïveté is the stuff of which wisdom is made, making him truly worthy of the sultan's daughter and of the powerful lamp.

It is helpful in understanding and enjoying *The Arabian Nights' Entertainments* to keep in mind the parallel symbolism of wealth, power, and beautiful women. All are symbolic of spiritual fulfillment. The omnipresence of the three in this book is one clear indication of the work's purpose: to teach a moral lesson as well as to entertain. It is a storehouse of wisdom couched in the terms all cultures know best, the terms of sight, smell, and touch, and of the delightful forms those sensations take in the imagination.

"Critical Evaluation" by John J. Brugaletta

Bibliography:
Bettelheim, Bruno. *The Uses of Enchantment: The Meaning and Importance of Fairy Tales.*

New York: Vintage Books, 1977. Offers detailed interpretations of the frame story and of the Sindbad stories and "The History of the Fisherman and the Genie." Compares them to Western fairy tales. Lacks a historical perspective but nevertheless a good demonstration of the psychoanalytic approach to *The Arabian Nights' Entertainments*.

Carpenter, Humphrey, and Mari Prichard. *The Oxford Companion to Children's Literature*. Oxford, England: Oxford University Press, 1984. Major entries on Aladdin, Ali Baba, and Sindbad, as well as references to the collection as a whole. Provides the stories' histories and their incorporation collectively and individually into Western children's literature.

Hamori, Andras. *On the Art of Medieval Arabic Literature*. Princeton, N.J.: Princeton University Press, 1974. Explores links between the tales of two of the collection's story cycles based on theme and literary motif, and demonstrates the tales' moral purpose connected to classical Islamic teaching about man's place in the universe.

Irwin, Robert. *The Arabian Nights: A Companion*. London: Allen Lane, 1994. An excellent source, which provides a variety of approaches and materials for study. Discusses translation, composition, and compilation of *The Arabian Nights' Entertainments*, explains the medieval Islamic life as the context of the tales, and makes comparisons to literary analogues in Arabic and other cultures.

Pinault, David. *Story-Telling Techniques in the "Arabian Nights."* Leiden: E. J. Brill, 1992. Detailed study of the tales' narrative structure, arguing for the persistence of oral methods of composition in the literary work as it exists, and analyzing the thematic and linguistic connections among the tales.

THE ARBITRATION

Type of work: Drama
Author: Menander (c. 342-c. 291 B.C.E.)
Type of plot: Comedy of manners
Time of plot: Fourth century B.C.E.
Locale: A suburb of Athens
First performed: After 304 B.C.E. (English translation, 1909)

> *Principal characters:*
> CHARISIUS, a young Athenian
> PAMPHILA, his wife
> SMICRINES, the miserly father of Pamphila
> ONESIMUS, Charisius' slave
> CHAERESTRATUS, Charisius' friend and neighbor
> SYRISCUS, a charcoal burner
> DAVUS, a goatherd
> HABROTONON, a pretty, harp-playing slave
> SOPHRONA, a nurse

The Story:

Pamphila, the daughter of a respected but miserly Athenian citizen, had been ravished by a drunken young man of ordinarily good behavior during the night festival of the Tauropolia. The only clue she had to his identity was a signet ring that he had left in her possession. A short time later, Pamphila was married to the young man, an Athenian named Charisius; Smicrines, her father, provided a good dowry for his idealistic but rather priggish son-in-law. Pamphila, who had soon begun to love her husband, gave birth to her child during his absence and, acting on the advice of her nurse Sophrona, exposed the infant and with the baby a pouch containing assorted tokens, including the ring. Charisius, learning of the birth from his servant Onesimus, decided that the child could not be his. Instead of repudiating Pamphila, however, he left home and began to waste his substance in rich feasts given at the home of his friend Chaerestratus, who lived next door. Pamphila was distracted because the husband she loved had deserted her for the company of hired dancing girls and harp players.

So matters stood when Smicrines came to investigate reports of Charisius' conduct; he had heard that his son-in-law was spending every night for a hired harp player a sum sufficient to feed a slave for a month. Just before his arrival a conceited, loud-mouthed cook named Carion, on his way to prepare a meal in the house of Chaerestratus, vainly questioned Charisius' servant Onesimus about his master; the cook also wanted to know why Charisius neglected his wife and paid twelve drachmas a night to be entertained by the lovely harp-playing slave Habrotonon. While Carion and Onesimus were talking, the musician was delivered by her master. The slave dealer managed to persuade the bemused Charisius that he owed money for several previous nights' entertainment. Charisius paid, but wily Onesimus recovered the overpayments for himself.

When Smicrines appeared, Onesimus managed to befuddle the anxious, angry father with the story that it was Chaerestratus who was giving the parties and that Charisius attended only to protect his friend's possessions and good name. After Smicrines had gone into his son-in-law's house, two of Chaerestratus' tenants appeared to pay their rent. They were Davus, a goat-herd, and Syriscus, a charcoal burner accompanied by his wife carrying a baby. While they waited they argued over another matter. A month earlier, Davus had come upon a baby exposed in the hills. His first impulse had been to adopt the foundling, but then, having calculated the cost of rearing a child, he began to think of returning the infant to the place where he had found it. Syriscus thereupon offered to adopt the baby in place of his own child, who had just died. When Syriscus had found that Davus intended to keep the trinkets left beside the baby, he claimed them because they might someday help to identify the child's parents. Davus refused to give up the tokens, but he had agreed to let someone else decide the matter. Smicrines, reappearing from the house of Charisius, was persuaded to listen to the story and give his decision. Deciding that the trinkets ought to go with the baby, he ordered Davus to give Syriscus the pouch.

While Syriscus and his wife were looking over the contents of the pouch, Onesimus recognized the signet ring that his master had lost at the time of the Tauropolia festival a year before. The slave borrowed it to show his master, then hesitated because to return it would be to accuse Charisius of having fathered the abandoned baby. Habrotonon came along about that time, saw the ring, heard the story, and concocted a scheme of her own. She would learn the truth by wearing the ring and seeing if Charisius recognized it. In that case, she would claim that she had been the girl he had ravished and so rescue the child from the life of a slave. Onesimus knew very well that her chief purpose was to win her own freedom.

Smicrines reappeared, determined to demand the return of his daughter and her dowry. The neighbors tried to dissuade him by saying that everything would turn out all right. As the party ended, broken up by Habrotonon and her claim that the child was hers, Onesimus infuriated the miserly Smicrines by congratulating him on bringing happiness to everybody by his arbitration.

Pamphila begged her father not to meddle with her marriage; she had no desire for another husband, she declared. If Charisius was infatuated with a harpist, that was only a temporary estrangement. At her father's announcement, however, that her husband's current love was the mother of his child, Pamphila fainted.

Regaining consciousness, she accused her nurse Sophrona of causing all the trouble by preventing her confession to Charisius after the birth of the child. While they argued, Habro-tonon happened by and recognized Pamphila as the girl who had been Charisius' companion one year earlier. She told the patrician so when he came to keep his promise to arrange for her freedom. At first, he regarded the story as another of her lies. To save himself, Onesimus also accused her of having invented the story. Habrotonon maintained stoutly that it was true, and she declared that she would rather see the child looked after properly than win her own freedom.

Chaerestratus, who had always admired the lovely slave, began questioning her about her own early history, but she remembered nothing of her infancy, not even her name. Then the sight of a small silver cup with an indecipherable inscription among the trinkets of Syriscus caused her to comment that she had once possessed a similar cup. Smicrines, seeing the cup for the first time, identified it as having once belonged to his oldest daughter, who had been kidnapped by the slave traders during the siege of the city some years before. Sophrona, recognizing the harp player as Smicrines' long-lost daughter Clearista, stirred the girl's recollection by using her baby name of "grasshopper."

Chaerestratus, who had loved the girl from the first, now asked to marry her, and when he showed miserly Smicrines how he could get his daughter back without spending money in court trials, he got both the girl and her father's blessing. Rascally Onesimus, instead of getting the beating he deserved, was probably given his freedom.

Critical Evaluation:

If Aristophanes was the greatest writer of the Old Comedy in fifth century Athens, Menander was certainly the finest practitioner of the New Comedy that flourished there a century later. The difference between those two kinds of theater is vast. The bawdiness and the fearless political and personal satire had given way, in the face of Macedonian military might, to the more timid and bourgeois comedy of manners, in which characters tend to be stock types. The poetic meters are simpler and the language is more colloquial. The chorus has been cut to a bare minimum, usually appearing as a band of revelers bearing no relation to the plot, and their songs are generally omitted from the manuscripts. New Comedy found its subject matter in domestic life and the complications of romance. It exploited sentiment, was given to moralizing, and used complex and improbable plots. Usually it lacked the exuberant vigor that marked the Old Comedy.

This theatrical development may be due, at least in part, to the fact that New Comedy was churned out at a prodigious rate. Menander himself was credited with having written more than a hundred plays, although he was not much older than fifty when he died. Dramatists vied with one another to give their plots ingenious twists as they reworked the same subject matter and the same stereotyped characters. Menander managed to individualize his characters more than his contemporaries, and he gained an international reputation in his lifetime. The Roman playwrights Plautus and Terence adapted Menander's comedies to suit Latin audiences. Through them Menander became the precursor of later Western drama and a direct ancestor of William Shakespeare and Molière.

Menander's own predecessor was the tragedian Euripides, who dealt with the theme of the foundling in *Ion* (c. 411 B.C.E.) and possibly other plays. It was a theme that would form a substantial part of the New Comedy. Euripides also handled romantic material that New Comedy writers adapted to their purpose, and he treated commonplace people in a way that suggested new developments in the theater. Further, Euripides developed a near colloquial diction that anticipated the later comedy. However, later dramatists eliminated the divine interventions that Euripides had staged, to concentrate on the element of coincidence in the resolution of human problems. It seems altogether fitting that Menander was buried beside Euripides.

The Arbitration is one of two plays by Menander to have survived nearly intact. Of the rest, there are no more than fragments and snippets. Even this would not be extant if papyrus manuscripts had not been found in Egypt late in the nineteenth century. As a result, the names of eighty of his plays have been ascertained, which show the extent to which the Roman dramatists borrowed from him.

In *The Arbitration*, Menander blends two common themes of New Comedy writing, those of the frustrated romance and of the foundling. He makes skillful use of dramatic irony by manipulating the plot so that the audience is fully aware of a situation to an understanding of which the characters must slowly grope their way. It is only when the characters grasp what the audience already knows that the solution to the problem occurs. The suspense lies in the author's devices to delay the solution. The audience is led logically into a maze where the end is what was stated in the prologue, and where a lot of cleverness has been spent in making the maze as complex as possible. It is clear from the outset that Charisius is the sole cause of the misery afflicting him and his wife Pamphila. The end of the play is not extant, but it is certain that Charisius must recognize his guilt and beg Pamphila's forgiveness before the comedy can end.

If the plot is more or less a pat formula, the characters are something more than pure types. Although they conform to stage patterns—Smicrines (small) is the tight-fisted father; Habro-

325

tonon (pretty thing) is the mistress with the heart of gold; Onesimus is the rascally servant; and Pamphila (wholly lovable) is the forgiving wife—they transcend their patterns in the natural way Menander has them react to their circumstances. Habrotonon's greatest desire is to gain her liberty, for which she resorts to deception, but when the welfare of a helpless infant is at stake, she is willing to expose her deception and sacrifice her liberty. This sacrifice is not made with any great theatrical flourish, but rather as an intrinsic part of her character. Menander even takes pains to individualize Davus the goatherd and Syriscus the charcoal-burner in the arbitration scene, where Smicrines unwittingly judges the fate of his own grandson.

The world of *The Arbitration* is one in which commoners are depicted as having dignity, in which slavery is altogether undesirable, and in which the most unlikely people might turn out to have respectable backgrounds. This is a sharp change from the aristocratic outlook of earlier Greek drama. The theme of the foundling, here developed in Pamphila's infant and in Habrotonon, mirrors a democratic view of society, not so much in politics but in morality. It stresses that everyone, regardless of their social position, has a right to be treated with consideration. Even though Menander had privileges of birth, wealth, and fame he subscribed to this outlook wholeheartedly, and *The Arbitration* is illuminated by it.

"Critical Evaluation" by James Weigel, Jr.

Bibliography:
Arnott, W. Geoffrey. *Menander, Plautus, Terence.* Oxford, England: Clarendon Press, 1975. Chapter on Menander discusses techniques in *The Arbitration* and other plays, placing the dramatist in the historical context of Greek dramatic art. Remarks on his use of traditional methods of dramaturgy to achieve comic effects.
Goldberg, Sander. *The Making of Menander's Comedy.* Berkeley: University of California Press, 1980. Comprehensive study of the dramatist's works. A chapter on *The Arbitration* provides careful explication of the plot and highlights Menander's various dramatic techniques.
Gomme, A. W., and F. H. Sandbach. *Menander: A Commentary.* London: Oxford University Press, 1973. Extensive, detailed, scholarly notes elucidating characters and scenes in *The Arbitration* and other plays. Comments on textual problems and highlights structural techniques used by the playwright.
Hunter, R. L. *The New Comedy of Greece and Rome.* Cambridge, England: Cambridge University Press, 1985. Uses *The Arbitration* as a principal example to illustrate techniques used by Menander and his contemporaries when they created their plots, analyzed relationships between the sexes, interjected philosophical issues into their plays, and used earlier works as sources for their dramas.
Webster, T. B. L. *Studies in Menander.* 2d ed. Manchester: Manchester University Press, 1960. Extensive commentary on the various extant fragments of the original play. Remarks on the insights this work provides into the playwright's chief concerns as a comic dramatist.

ARCADIA

Type of work: Novel
Author: Sir Philip Sidney (1554-1586)
Type of plot: Pastoral
Time of plot: Antiquity
Locale: Arcadia, Greece
First published: 1590; revised, 1593 as *The Countess of Pembroke's Arcadia*; revised, 1598

> *Principal characters:*
> PRINCE PYROCLES or ZELMANE, the son of Evarchus, king of Macedon
> PRINCE MUSIDORUS or DORUS, the duke of Thessalia, Pyrocles' friend, and
>   Evarchus' nephew
> BASILIUS, the duke of Arcadia
> GYNECIA, his wife
> PAMELA, his older daughter
> PHILOCLEA, his younger daughter
> PHILANAX, an Arcadian general and Basilius' friend
> DAMETAS, Basilius' chief herdsman
> MISO, his wife
> MOPSA, his daughter
> EVARCHUS, the king of Macedon

The Story:

Basilius was the powerful duke of Arcadia, a quiet and peaceful province of Greece. He ruled his faithful subjects happily and well. Overcome by an ungovernable curiosity to learn what the future held for him, his wife Gynecia, and his beautiful daughters Pamela and Philoclea, he went to consult the Oracle at Delphos. There he was told that his older daughter, Pamela, would be stolen from him; his younger daughter would engage in an unsuitable love affair; his wife would commit adultery; and a foreign ruler would sit upon his throne—all within a year.

Basilius repeated the prophecy to his friend Philanax, whom he left in charge of the country while he, in an effort to escape the destiny foretold by the Oracle, took his wife and daughters into a secluded part of the country to live for the year. Basilius lived in one of two lodges with his wife and Philoclea; in the other, he put Pamela under the care of Dametas, a rude shepherd of whose honesty Basilius had a high opinion.

Shortly after the duke's retirement, two young princes, Pyrocles and Musidorus, arrived in Arcadia. Reared together in close friendship, these young men of great courage, personal beauty, and integrity had been swept ashore at Lydia after experiencing a shipwreck and many strange adventures as well as performing many daring and honorable acts.

Pyrocles saw a picture of Philoclea, learned of her enforced retirement, and fell in love with her. Determined to see the princess face-to-face, he told Musidorus of his love and of his plan to disguise himself as a chivalric Amazon and to approach Philoclea in woman's guise. For a name, he took that of his lost lady Zelmane.

After a lengthy debate, in which Musidorus attempted to convince his friend of the folly of love, Pyrocles still remained firm in his intention; and the two princes traveled to the place of the duke's retirement with Pyrocles in his disguise as an Amazon. While Musidorus waited in a nearby wood, Pyrocles, now Zelmane, sat down and sang a melancholy song that awakened Dametas, who hastened to the duke's lodge to tell him of a strange woman who had arrived in the vicinity.

Basilius, upon seeing Pyrocles in his disguise, fell in love with the supposed Amazon. His true identity still unsuspected, Pyrocles was introduced to the duke's family and invited to remain with them for a while. Soon, a young shepherd appeared. He was Musidorus, who had fallen in love with Pamela on sight and assumed a disguise of his own. Musidorus, under the name Dorus, was taken by the chief herdsman as a servant after telling his contrived tale of being sent by a friend to serve Dametas.

Zelmane saved Philoclea from a savage lion, but in doing so, he was discovered to be a man by Gynecia, the duke's wife. She immediately fell in love with him. Dorus, meanwhile, saved Pamela from a bear. Before long, both princesses began to become enamored of the disguised princes.

The Arcadian shepherds, as was their custom, met and exchanged poetic songs for their own entertainment and that of the duke's family and his guests. The songs, often accompanied by dancing, chiefly concerned the gods and the human passions. This occasion only increased the intensity of the tangle of love relationships that had so rapidly developed.

After the pastoral festival, Gynecia and Basilius both declared their love for Zelmane, and Philoclea was puzzled greatly by the strange passion she felt for the person she thought a woman. In the meantime, Dorus pretended to be in love with Mopsa in order to be near Pamela, who in this manner became aware of his affection for her. He also managed to reveal his true station to her by means of subtle stories and poems.

Pyrocles, distressed by the advances of Basilius, revealed his true identity to Philoclea, who at first embraced him joyously but then became ashamed of her sudden show of affection. Gynecia, suspecting this attachment, was overcome with jealousy. While Gynecia, having sent Philoclea home from a meeting with Pyrocles, was starting to tell the disguised prince of the depth of her love, they were attacked by some roving ruffians. With the aid of some shepherds, Pyrocles, Basilius, and then Dorus drove off the attackers. This was only the prelude to an uprising by the citizens of a nearby Arcadian village, who had become enraged by the duke's seeming unconcern about his country. In an impassioned speech, however, Pyrocles convinced them of their error and stirred in them a renewed loyalty to Basilius. This triumph was celebrated by another pastoral entertainment, largely taken up with a poetic debate between Reason and Passion. Once more, the poems, dances, and stories served to increase the depth of the emotions felt by the royal party.

Dorus then told his friend of his moderate success with Pamela, whom he had urged to flee with him to Thessalia. Pyrocles, sharing Dorus' sorrow over their separation, decided to press his suit of Philoclea and to rid himself of the importunate demands of Basilius and Gynecia. When they renewed their entreaties, Pyrocles, still in his disguise and fearing to deny them outright, gave them hopeful but obscure answers.

Meanwhile, Dorus, having tricked Dametas and his family into leaving the lodge, had escaped with Pamela to a forest on the way to Thessalia. There they were set upon by a band of ruffians. The false Zelmane, hard pressed by Gynecia's declarations, was forced to pretend a deep passion for her, a situation which so distressed Philoclea that she kept to her room in the lodge in profound sorrow. In order to be free to execute a plan to be alone with Philoclea, Pyrocles moved from the lodge to a dark cave not far away. He then took the duke and his wife aside separately and made an assignation with each at the same time in the cave.

Gynecia, who had dressed like Zelmane, met Basilius in the cave; she was not recognized by her husband. Ashamed of her actions, she embraced him lovingly. Back at the lodge, Pyrocles, now in his own person, crept into Philoclea's room and, after a brief time, won her over and stayed the night.

Dametas, realizing that he had been tricked, began a search for Pamela. Entering the duke's lodge by a secret entrance, he discovered Philoclea and Pyrocles asleep. He left hastily to inform the local citizens of the treachery. Gynecia, angered at her husband's praise of Zelmane, revealed her identity in the cave. Basilius, ashamed, repented his weakness, pledged renewed love to his wife, and drank a long draught from a cup of a mysterious beverage standing close by. The liquid was a potion, believed by Gynecia to be a love philter, which the duchess had brought to give to Zelmane. After drinking it, Basilius fell to the ground and appeared to die. After the duke's death was discovered, Philanax and his troop of soldiers imprisoned Gynecia, Pyrocles, and Philoclea.

The rogues who had attacked Dorus and Pamela, the remnant of the rebellious band which had earlier caused much trouble, overwhelmed the lovers and captured them. While in captivity, Musidorus revealed his actual name and rank. A short time later, some of Philanax's soldiers were sent to search for Pamela and came upon the band and their prisoners. Recognizing the princess, the soldiers returned the entire group to Philanax, who put the lovers under restraint.

There was now a great turmoil, and many opinions and beliefs were exchanged as to the real guilt in the death of the duke and the disgrace of the princesses. Hearing that Evarchus, king of Macedon, had arrived in Arcadia to visit the duke, Philanax persuaded him to be the judge in the trial of the five people involved. Gynecia admitted her guilt and begged to be executed. Then Evarchus, not recognizing his son and his nephew because they had been away for such a long time, condemned the two princes to death and the princesses to milder punishments. Even after learning the true identity of the young men, Evarchus refused, from a deep sense of justice, to alter his verdict.

At that point Basilius, who had swallowed only a powerful sleeping potion, awoke. The young lovers and the duchess were promptly forgiven. Basilius pondered on how accurately the Oracle's prophecy had been fulfilled and how happily events had turned out. The princes and their loves soon wed and assumed the high stations for which their rank fitted them.

Critical Evaluation:

Sir Philip Sidney left two versions of his *Arcadia*, one incomplete and neither published during his lifetime. The first, referred to as the "old" *Arcadia*, is a complete pastoral romance in five books or "acts," as Sidney calls them. Although the work was known to Sidney's contemporaries, the manuscript of the old *Arcadia* disappeared until 1907, when it was rediscovered by Bertram Dobell. At some point during his short life, Sidney decided to revise the *Arcadia* in the form of a chivalric epic. This version, the incomplete new *Arcadia*, although it keeps the main story, amounts to a complete rewriting of the work, differing substantially from the first version in its narrative. The new version belongs to the epic genre and introduces many new characters in episodic digressions from the main plot. Sidney's recasting of the *Arcadia* ends midsentence in the middle of book three. Sidney had reached this far in his revision when he received orders from Queen Elizabeth to lead a company of soldiers into battle in The Netherlands, where he died from an infected wound. Four years later, in 1590, the incomplete new *Arcadia* was published by William Ponsonby. Then, in 1593, Ponsonby tacked the last half of the old *Arcadia* onto the new and published this complete although schizophrenic version as *The Countess of Pembroke's Arcadia*. This is the *Arcadia* known to generations of readers. A still later version, in 1598, includes Sidney's poems.

The study of Sir Philip Sidney's *Arcadia* leads to the consideration of a number of important biographical, literary, historical, and critical issues. A serious man who thought deeply about serious matters, Sidney led a short, complicated life. He was godson of a king, nephew to four earls, brother of an earl, uncle to three earls, grandson of a duke, and a special favorite of the queen and other powerful figures. He was endowed with a pleasing personality and a fine intellect. He received schooling at Oxford and on the Continent and was tutored by the remarkable scholar Hubert Languet. He died, however, in his early thirties with much promise unfulfilled and was mourned by the most influential men and women of his time.

The connection between Sidney's life and his work, as between the life and work of any important writer, must remain speculative to a degree, but some important links can be discerned. Sidney's connections and status allowed him the freedom to develop his talents. He was influenced by the medieval courtly love tradition, and this led him to consider, while in the environment of the court itself, the morality of human emotions, especially that of love, as a prime human concern. At the same time, his education permitted him access to the romances of later Greek civilization. Consequently, he was neither too burdened with official duties to take up the pen, nor so absorbed in the life of the court as to lose himself in its endless, petty intrigues. In short, the depth of his interests, the breadth of his literary background, the range of his activities as poet, soldier, and statesman, and the vigor of his expression mark him as a sort of exemplary figure of the English literary Renaissance.

Sidney became involved in two literary circles. One, which included Edmund Spenser and Edward Dyer, met at Leicester House in London during 1579 and 1580. The other group gathered at the home of his sister Mary, the Countess of Pembroke. If the Leicester group were more inclined to the romantic, the group that gathered at his sister's country estate was neoclassic in orientation, more concerned with the rules of literature than its reach, and more taken with the laws governing its dimensions than with love scenes in faraway lands; but it was at his sister's house (where he retreated after losing favor with the court), in a climate rather uncongenial for literary romance, that Sidney composed *Arcadia*. He wrote it, he said, for the entertainment of his sister. *Arcadia*, however, is more than mere entertainment.

There is a great variety of sources in Greek, Roman, Italian, and English literature from which Sidney draws his scenes, plot, ideas, and style. He has also woven together two traditions, the pastoral and the chivalric. The latter, derived partly from adventures related in later Greek literature and full of intrigues, disguises, and mysteries, appealed greatly to writers of the English Renaissance. Scenes and incidents were taken directly from *Ethiopica* (third century C.E.) by Heliodorus. There are also characters and incidents from Sir Thomas Malory's *Le Morte d'Arthur* (1485), a work filled with tales of chivalrous knights, which no doubt suggested scenes and events for *Arcadia*.

The contribution of earlier pastoral romances seems to have been largely, though not entirely, structural and organizational. The shape of the romance, its direction and main divisions, were determined by pastoral conventions. The world of *Arcadia* and of the pastoral is based on the creation of an artificial, rural setting populated by shepherds and shepherdesses. In this setting, it is possible for men and women to establish relationships and to discuss questions that would be impossible in the turmoil of the world at large. The postclassical pastoral writers were especially interested in having characters pursue the topic of love and having them establish more harmonious relations with the other sex and with nature, thus allowing them to move closer to God.

Sidney's *Arcadia* elaborates this pastoral convention and uses that elaboration to discuss ethics, politics, and theology. First, there is the tumultuous world outside Arcadia proper. This external world, including Asia Minor, and the homes of Pyrocles and Musidorus, stands in contrast to Arcadia itself. The second world, contained within the first, is the setting in which the two heroes fall in love. It is a transition between the outside chaos and the retreat within Arcadia that Basilius has chosen. This last and "purest" setting enables the process of love and its development toward perfection to occur.

Though modeled on an elaboration of the pastoral structure, Sidney's intention goes beyond the pastoral. First, there is a great variety of incidents, scenes, imagery, and concrete description ordinarily absent from the pastoral romance (for these images provide the basis for more extensive discussions than are usually found in pastoral works). Second, although the thematic content of *Arcadia* is centered in the Neoplatonic searching for love and the purification of romantic feelings, there are many political, ethical, and philosophical questions considered that are outside the customary range of the pastoral.

Despite Sidney's description of his work as mere entertainment, it clearly has rather large ambitions. As Fulke Greville, Sidney's friend and biographer, wrote in *The Life of the Renowned Sir Philip Sidney* (1652), the goal of *Arcadia* "was not vanishing pleasure alone, but moral Images and Examples, (as directing threds) to guide every man through the confused *Labyrinth* of his own desires, and life."

"Critical Evaluation" by Howard Lee Hertz

Bibliography:
Davis, Walter. "A Map of Arcadia: Sidney's Romance in Its Tradition." In *Sidney's "Arcadia."* New Haven, Conn.: Yale University Press, 1965. A thorough study of the work's complex background in Greek, Latin, and Spanish pastoral romance.
Lanham, Richard. "The Old *Arcadia*." In *Sidney's "Arcadia."* New Haven, Conn.: Yale University Press, 1965. The first close analysis of Sidney's prose style and its relation to classical modes of rhetoric; the starting point for discussion of Sidney's language.
Levao, Ronald. *Renaissance Minds and Their Fictions: Cusanus, Sidney, Shakespeare.* Berkeley: University of California Press, 1985. A brilliant discussion of the old *Arcadia* and how Sidney's narrative refuses to allow readers any stable reference point for judging the characters' moral dilemmas.
Raitiere, Martin N. *Faire Bitts: Sir Philip Sidney and Renaissance Political Theory.* Pittsburgh: Duquesne University Press, 1984. Places Sidney's work in the context of continental Protestant politics and elucidates Sidney's intellectual relations with his close friend, the French political theorist Hubert Languet. An important study.
Robertson, Jean, ed. *The Countess of Pembroke's Arcadia (The Old Arcadia).* Oxford: Clarendon Press, 1973. The first modern scholarly edition of the old *Arcadia*; Robertson's introduction provides an excellent starting point for study of the work.

AREOPAGITICA

Type of work: Essay
Author: John Milton (1608-1674)
First published: 1644

John Milton's classic defense of freedom of the press and religious liberty was his response to an ordinance of Parliament of June 14, 1643, requiring among other things that all books receive an official censor's approval prior to publication. Milton saw this act as a renewal of Stuart tyranny and of the Star Chamber decree of 1637, which had also denied freedom of the press. When this decree was abolished in 1640, a flood of political and religious pamphlets had followed, and for three years freedom of the press had prevailed in England. Milton viewed such intellectual and polemic activity as being healthy for the nation, and he deeply regretted the renewal of state control over printing. In his view, such control reflected the growing tendency of the Presbyterian Parliament to impose uniform religious practices on England and to oppose all political opposition. Milton's own Doctrine and Discipline of Divorce (1643), which supported more liberal divorce laws, had been printed without permission, and Parliament had sought to discover the author of this unlicensed work. In form, *Areopagitica* is a classical oration addressed to Parliament although it was not intended for oral delivery. Milton drew the title from a speech of Isocrates to the court of the Areopagus in Athens.

In the long opening section, Milton establishes a favorable view of the author and of the Parliament he is addressing. He characterizes Parliament as a strong defender of liberty that has already restored much lost freedom to the nation. Liberty, he adds, can exist only when complaints can be aired openly and considered wisely. He writes to Parliament equally as a passionate lover of liberty and as an ardent supporter of Parliament; beyond that he writes as a learned scholar representing the learned individuals of England.

The first argument in favor of freedom of the press begins with a long historical survey of this issue. Milton demonstrates that Greece and Rome valued this freedom highly and recognized atheism and libel as the only two reasons for censorship. Under the Christian Roman emperors, moreover, only following transcription were books examined, accepted, or judged heretical. Only with the Council of Trent and the Inquisition, "the most antichristian council and the most tyrannous inquisition that ever inquired," were books no more "as freely admitted into the world as any other birth." Milton points out to Parliament that the sources of their legislation were the tyrannical Council of Trent and the forces of tyranny that Parliament itself had once overthrown in the name of liberty.

Those who agree that the source of censorship is bad may still insist that it produces good results. To this contention Milton replies with his second major argument, that moral evil or good is a matter of rational choice and that virtue rests in temperance, in choosing between good and evil. God, Milton argues, left to the individual the exercise of a power of choice so that those who can distinguish between good and evil and who abstain from evil are the true Christians. Real virtue must face trial, must constantly be tested; to prohibit books, therefore, is to prohibit the testing of virtue and the confirming of truth. Censorship denies the efficacy of reason. To know evil through books and to reject it is a necessary condition for human virtue.

Proponents of censorship argue that circulating evil books produces undesirable results, including dissemination of evil thoughts among citizens, unnecessary exposure to temptation, and vain employment of time. Milton answers that all religious disputation would then have to be forbidden, for even the Bible and the church fathers often relate blasphemy, and, he continues, ignorant people are most often led astray not by learned books but by teachers of false doctrine who, even without books, are able to spread their doctrines. Prohibiting books, on the other hand, destroys learning and the ability to dispute evil; in addition, a good person may derive good even from evil while an evil one will be a fool with even the best book. As for unnecessary temptations and vain employment of time, since good people may find false doctrine useful in learning the truth, and bad people cannot be prevented forcibly from acquiring evil knowledge, censorship fails to perform its end.

Thus Milton leads to his third crucial argument, that censorship itself is an impractical gesture because it cannot accomplish its task of removing the sources of evil. Milton admits that Plato allowed censorship, but he adds that Plato also forbade music and dancing. Plato saw how impractical it was to forbid books alone, for to shut one gate against evil and leave open others is a fool's endeavor.

Another impracticality of censorship arises from the machinery required to carry out such a plan. Many hours would be required to read and approve all works ever published or yet to be published. Such a machinery would necessarily grow to resemble the abhorred Inquisition. Sects may flourish despite such efforts because they may persevere through oral tradition, as Christianity itself once did. Finally, how could the quality of the censor be ensured? Only a learned person should have this job, yet the tedium of reading so many books of little value would soon drive away all qualified individuals, leaving the job open to the base and ignorant. No matter what the quality of the censor, the very nature of the job ensures that only received knowledge, those truths already known and accepted by the age, would be allowed to pass.

Thus Milton passes to his next central argument, that censorship would bring harmful consequences. Censorship would discourage learning and the search for truth, dispossess scholars of respect, and undermine regard for the common people's ability to judge for themselves.

Milton's argument concludes with his fourth and most complex point, that licensing publications not only weakens the authority of the truth that England already possesses but also actively hinders the acquisition of new and higher truths. Milton's travels in Europe had shown him the horrible consequences of Inquisitional suppression and given him perspective on the relative freedoms permitted in England, but he saw that licensing in England would merely substitute the abuses of pre-Reformation England for a new tyranny of presbyters. Truth, he felt, must never stagnate; it must be believed and understood, not simply accepted from external authority. Without questioning and examination, doctrine becomes a matter of outward conformity.

Censorship is an obstacle to acquiring new and unknown truths, and although England through its reformation had advanced somewhat, she must not rest content with half measures. England would be able to boast of the light of her truth and present knowledge only by realizing that truth is given in order to pursue new wisdom. England must search "what we know not by what we know." England's great outburst of learning signifies that God regards the nation with special favor, indicating God's readiness to initiate some great new reformation. It would be wrong to use the terms "sect" or "schism" for this fervent search for wisdom that God inspires among England's people.

Milton believes that it is a good sign to see exercise of rational faculties in the midst of external threats to England's safety; such practice argues a healthy political body and confidence in the safe government Parliament provides, and it demonstrates the large portion of freedom allotted citizens by Parliament's mild yoke. Parliament cannot make English citizens less eager for knowledge and wisdom, Milton states, without first destroying their liberty. Of such tyranny Parliament once relieved this nation.

What is more likely to prohibit truth than the prohibition of new ideas? Because truth most often appears suspect to eyes accustomed only to received opinion, complacent disregard for the new frustrates further discovery of truth. Times such as these readily produce false prophets and true. Yet it is impossible to know whether they speak wisely unless they are heard. Defending such truth as is now possessed, people may find themselves persecuting new truths.

It does not matter, Milton avers, that false doctrine may exist under such freedom, for "Strong Truth" can conquer all error in "free and open encounter." If everyone were more charitable, people could tolerate and leave to individual conscience things that are indifferent and not fundamentally at odds with the "unity of Spirit" which truly binds everyone. Imposing strict conformity in matters best left to individual conscience converts truth to base outward conformity.

Bibliography:

Hanford, James Holly, and James G. Taaffe. *A Milton Handbook.* 5th ed. New York: Prentice-Hall, 1970. A wealth of information about Milton's life, works, and critical reputation. Offers synopses of individual works and comprehensive critical assessments. An excellent beginning source for the general reader and student.

Kranidas, Thomas. "Polarity and Structure in Milton's *Areopagitica.*" *English Literary Renaissance* 14 (1984): 175-190. A careful analysis of style and argumentative prose, especially informative on Milton's use of sources. Views Milton as a champion of Greek intellectual freedom, unlike the English prelates associated with historical religious repression and with the Roman Catholic Church.

Milton, John. *The Prose of John Milton.* Selected and edited by J. Max Patrick. Garden City, N.Y.: Doubleday, 1967. Includes the complete text of *Areopagitica.* Extensive introduction to the tract provides a critical analysis, an evaluation of previous scholarship, and a useful bibliography. Heavily annotated.

Whitaker, Juanita. " 'The Wars of Truth': Wisdom and Strength in *Areopagitica.*" *Milton Studies* 9 (1986): 7-38. Traces the themes of wisdom and strength in the tract and argues that Milton relates both to books, a principal metaphor of the argument. By promoting intellectual freedom, books contribute to political and civic strength.

Wolfe, Don M. *Milton in the Puritan Revolution.* New York: Humanities Press, 1963. Chapter on *Areopagitica* explains Milton's lines of argument. Places the work within its revolutionary milieu; compares Milton's pamphlet to other contemporary pamphlets advocating liberty.

ARIEL

Type of work: Poetry
Author: Sylvia Plath (1932-1963)
First published: 1965

The poems of *Ariel* were written in the last months of Sylvia Plath's life. In January of 1963, *The Bell Jar*, Plath's only novel, was published in England under the pseudonym Victoria Lucas. It was well received but Plath's life was too deep in the personal turmoil that is expressed in *Ariel* for her literary success to save her. She committed suicide on February 11, 1963. Many of the poems celebrate death, and death is what Plath chose for herself. The fact of her own death adds a seriousness to the work. The reader is aware, for better or for worse, not only that she wrote about death and suicide but also that she acquired it for herself at a young age, as her career as a writer was beginning. In reading *Ariel*, then, it is impossible not to try to imagine Plath's feelings about her own life and her thoughts of ending it. If there were any question that the poems were not genuinely from the poet's heart, these thoughts are vanquished by the knowledge of her death. Her life and death intrude, in a sense, on her art: The reader is not likely to experience *Ariel* in the same way that one might if the book's author had not committed suicide.

Plath's poetry has been categorized in what is known as the confessional school. Other poets from this school to whom Plath is often compared are Theodore Roethke, Robert Lowell, John Berryman, and Anne Sexton. Confessional poetry is characterized by experimentation in form and voice (often, use of free verse and of idiomatic and nonstandard English), use of metaphor that borders on private meaning or the surreal, and, most noticeably, frank discussion of the poet's own personal and private griefs. One of Plath's great achievements was her fusing of the emotional immediacy of the confessional style of poetry with the more distant, aesthetically rigorous formalism seen in the strictly structured poems of an earlier era. She manages to take her most emotional and sensuous feelings and use them objectively in terms of formal poetic devices. Her poems can capture the attention of the mind and the heart. It must be added that, while much of her poetry is in the confessional mode, it should not be assumed that every word is directly traceable to events in the poet's life. Even though the temptation is great to do otherwise, her poetry should be read as poetry, not as autobiography.

The poems of *Ariel* may be broken into four groups. These do not coincide with the order in which they are arranged in the book, but are the order in which they were written. "Elm," "The Moon and the Yew Tree," "The Rival," and "Berck-Plage" were written before July, 1962, and were inspired during Plath's stay at her husband Ted Hughes's home in Devon, England. The next group was written in October and November of 1962. These are the bee poems, including "The Bee Meeting," "The Arrival of the Bee Box," "Stings," "Wintering," and "The Swarm." Next followed the main body of the collection for *Ariel*, including "The Couriers," "Sheep in Fog," "The Applicant," "Lady Lazarus," "Cut," "The Night Dances," "Poppies in October," "Ariel," "Death & Co.," "Nick and the Candlestick," "Gulliver," "Getting There," "Medusa," "A Birthday Present," "Letter in November," "Daddy," and "Fever 103°." The last group of poems was written in January, 1963, in the last month of her life; these are "The Munich Mannequins," "Totem," and "Paralytic." Included in this last set are five others, which were written in the last week of Plath's life. They are "Balloons," "Contusion," "Kindness," "Edge," and "Words."

"Mary's Song," "Lesbos," and "The Swarm" appear in the American edition of *Ariel* but not in the original British edition. "The Swarm" belongs with the bee poems, and the other two are from the period in her life following the writing of the bee poems. This covers the time frame of the majority of the work in *Ariel*.

The main body of poems, from the later era of her life, read as a nightmare. Plath fuses her knowledge of poetic structure with Greek and biblical myths, in order to create her own place in the nightmare and create poetry that expresses her darkest fears and pains of life. This collection is a critically acclaimed masterpiece. The poems of *Ariel* differ from her earlier poems in that they are written in a simpler style, with a more economical use of words, more direct and pointed phrasing. They read in a more conversational tone than her earlier poems, and adhere less to formal meter and rhyme.

One exception to the general use of free verse in *Ariel* is the poem "Daddy," which is in anapestic trimeter. The rhyme scheme is based on the sound "oo," which is a grand use of a nursery-rhyme sound in discussing a fierce loathing for the character called "Daddy." Plath may have used and needed a strong sense of structure for this poem because it may be the most painful issue that she confronts in this volume. By using a rigid structure, she is more able to control her feelings over this delicate and very difficult subject matter. The poem alludes to the Holocaust and Nazis, and has raised much criticism. Some critics contend that she used those terms to accentuate her own personal experiences and in doing so trivialized the historical event. It is argued that using "Auschwitz" as a metaphor to explain personal tragedy not only demeans the Jews who suffered in that and other concentration camps during World War II, but also detracts from the writer's credibility, in that she is tampering with history. The poem's narrator compares herself with the Jews: "I began to talk like a Jew./ I think I may well be a Jew." Plath was criticized for stepping out of bounds in comparing her life to those imprisoned and slaughtered during World War II. It is argued in the poet's favor that her use of this emotion-laden subject served to broaden the parameters of the metaphor.

Themes of family life and marriage are prevalent throughout *Ariel*. "The Couriers" is composed of two groups of three two-line stanzas, then a final one-line stanza. The first group rejects ideas of domesticity and marriage, including this: "A ring of gold with the sun in it?/ Lies. Lies and a grief." The second group is an affirmation of symbols that are more to the poet's liking: "Frost on a leaf, the immaculate/ Cauldron talking and crackling." The final line "Love, love, my season" seems to show the poet loving in her own way, apart from the norms of society. She has risen above the rules and regulations imposed on a woman, who is meant to wed and have babies. She has discovered her own ability to love in the way that is most natural and comfortable, real to her. A very short poem, this one quickly defines the polarity of domestic love from the angle of what is expected versus what is a self-actualized woman's role in a relationship. Plath rejects the ideas she is handed and begins to build her own life.

Several of the poems of *Ariel* invoke this theme of the difficulties in living a free and unhampered life in the eye of societal expectations. Images of self are confident and positive while images of a self bound to another, or married, are doubting and unhappy. Plath's poems revel in her own self-sufficiency and self-expression.

The later poems continue the theme of "The Couriers," except that in them the woman is trapped and suffering. "The Applicant" falls into this group. The wife in that poem is a servant, a convenience to the husband, imprisoned by him. "A living doll, everywhere you look./ It can sew, it can cook,/ It can talk, talk, talk.// It works, there is nothing wrong with it." There is less of the freedom to love and the ability to do so by this point. The satisfaction, the "love, my season," that seems to be experienced by the speaker in "The Couriers" is completely absent in the lifeless "living doll" of "The Applicant."

"Nick and the Candlestick" depicts love for a child. This poem seems to concern Plath's second child, Nicholas Hughes. The first images are grisly and deathly and by the end, Nick has adopted the look of the Christ child. "Its first communion out of my live toes. . . . You are the baby in the barn." The poem hallucinates around the room of the child, finding the fish of the fishbowl to be "panes of ice,/ A vice of knives,/ A piranha/ Religion, drinking." The child sleeps and is solid, has no thought of his mother's desperate visions or her hostility.

At the time of her death, Plath had entered a phase in which she seemed to be relieving herself of the dramas and pains of her life through poetry. Perhaps she thought that if she died metaphorically in her poems, then she might experience a rebirth in life and revive her will to live. Some have argued that she had reached a state of transcendence and was therefore ready to die, but her poems sound much more sad and despairing than one who had achieved an inner sense of perfection, peace, and calmness.

Beaird Glover

Bibliography:
Hall, Caroline King Barnard. *Sylvia Plath*. Boston: Twayne, 1978. Contains a chronology and commentary on *The Bell Jar*, early poetry, transitional poetry, and later poetry. An excellent guide to Plath's life and body of work.
Lane, Gary, ed. *Sylvia Plath: New Views on the Poetry*. Baltimore: The Johns Hopkins University Press, 1979. Contains essays on the lasting value of Plath, her process of writing, and her influences. Sees Plath from personal and public contexts and considers the myth surrounding her.
Rose, Jacqueline. *The Haunting of Sylvia Plath*. London: Virago, 1991. Considers the life and work, with an entire chapter on the poem "Daddy" that includes references to other criticism. Considers Plath's use of fantasy and her process of writing, editing, and presenting her work.
Rosenblatt, Jon. *Sylvia Plath: The Poetry of Initiation*. Chapel Hill: University of North Carolina Press, 1979. Attentive to literary style and universal themes such as marriage and family life. Seeks to explain the work of Plath in terms other than strictly autobiographical. An excellent study of Plath for the general or the serious reader. Many poems from *Ariel* are discussed at length.
Wagner, Linda W., ed. *Sylvia Plath: The Critical Heritage*. London: Routledge & Kegan Paul, 1988. Contains essays from major literary magazines on personal encounters with Plath, and dozens of essays on her writings. This massive accumulation of criticism and reviews spans the years from 1960 to 1985.

DER ARME HEINRICH

Type of work: Poetry
Author: Hartmann von Aue (c. 1160/1165-c. 1210/1220)
Type of plot: Didactic
Time of plot: Late twelfth century
Locale: Germany
First transcribed: c. 1195

> *Principal characters:*
> HEINRICH VON AUE, a Swabian knight
> A PEASANT GIRL

The Story:

Heinrich von Aue, a Swabian knight, was a fortunate man. Wealthy and of noble birth, he was known throughout the land for his high standard of honor. His goal was to fulfill his obligations as a knight; nothing but purest virtue and upright truth marked his life. Suddenly, however, his life was blighted by disaster: Heinrich became leprous. As in the case of Job in ancient times, his physical appearance deteriorated rapidly, but he did not have the patience of Job. All his life seemed a curse to him, and his pride had left him without friends. His cheerfulness vanished, and he detested even the light of day. Only the hope of a cure for his terrible disease kept him alive.

Trying to find a cure for his malady, he sought out the most famous doctors in all Europe. The school of Montpellier was known for its able doctors, but when he went there, he learned that they knew of no medicine to heal him. Disappointed, he traveled to Salerno, where he talked to other skilled physicians. At last he met a master who told him that there was a cure, yet the cure itself was of such a nature that it would be impossible to achieve; therefore the doctor preferred not to talk about it. In desperation, Heinrich begged the doctor to reveal his remedy. After some hesitation the physician yielded and told the knight that he could be cured by the heart's blood of a virgin who would willingly, out of love for him, submit to a fatal operation.

Heinrich realized the hopelessness of his situation and returned sadly to Swabia. All his worldly belongings he gave to the poor and to the monks. Of his land and estates, he kept no more than a clearing in a wood where a poor but contented peasant lived with his family. Heinrich decided to join them in their house in the wood, and the peasant and his family did all they could to ease the suffering of the leprous man. They loved the knight and were concerned for his health because they realized that they would never find such a good master again. The peasant's young daughter, in particular, was deeply moved by Heinrich's suffering.

One day, the peasant asked why the doctors had been unable to help. Heinrich told him of the visit to Salerno and described the impossible cure of which the doctor had spoken. The young daughter overheard this tale. That night she woke her parents with her tears. By the next night she had decided that she wanted to be the virgin who could save their master's life. Her parents were horrified when they heard her request, and her father threatened physical punishment if she dared to mention the subject again. They listened in amazement as their daughter begged with heart-moving words to be allowed to gain the eternal life that would be assured her. She spoke also of the uncertainty her earthly life offered, and of the catastrophe that could befall the whole family if their master should die and a harsh ruler scourge the countryside. At

338

last she was able to convince her parents that her service to God and her master would be the most honorable thing she could do. Sorrowfully they gave their consent to her intended sacrifice.

Very early the next morning she told the unbelieving Heinrich of her willingness to help cure him. He warned her that she should not talk lightly about such a subject and assured her that she would soon forget her impulsive idea. After the parents confirmed the seriousness of their daughter's wish, Heinrich took a long time to consider her offer. Finally, he too yielded to her pleas.

Beautiful clothes and furs and a fine horse were bought for the young woman, and she and Heinrich set out on their journey to Salerno. When the doctor there heard from Heinrich that the young woman was willing to sacrifice herself in that fashion, he doubted the knight's words and took the girl aside to implore her to speak the truth by telling him whether she was ready of her own free will to face so horrible a fate. Impressed by her sincerity and beauty, the doctor declared that he would be much happier not to take her heart's blood. Still the woman remained steadfast and begged the doctor to proceed with the operation at once.

Sitting in a neighboring room, Heinrich heard the doctor sharpening his knife. The knight peered through a small hole in the wall and saw the girl tied to a table. For the first time he realized how beautiful she was, and he bitterly accused himself of trying to circumvent the judgment of God by sacrificing the girl's beauty to his ugliness. At the very last moment, before an incision had been made, he was able to stop the doctor. Although the young woman implored him not to be weak and even called him a coward and a man without the courage of a true knight, Heinrich disregarded her insults and left with her for home.

During the return journey, the grace of God touched Heinrich, and his leprosy disappeared, for he and the peasant girl had passed the test given to them by God. Heinrich looked younger and handsomer than ever before. The rumor of his miraculous cure having spread throughout the countryside, Heinrich's vassals came to meet the travelers three days before they arrived at their destination. The happy parents were the first to meet them, and all thanked God for her deliverance and the knight's cure. In spite of the peasant girl's low birth, the council of knights agreed that the hand of God had surely chosen her to become Heinrich's wife. All in the land, rich and poor, rejoiced when she and Heinrich were wed. After a long and happy life, they both entered the eternal kingdom of God.

Critical Evaluation:

Hartmann von Aue was one of the foremost German poets of the Middle Ages, and he is known to have been admired by his contemporary Gottfried von Strassburg for the clarity and purity of his "crystalline words." Beyond that encomium, information on Hartmann is limited to brief self-descriptions, as the one that begins *Der arme Heinrich*, in which he speaks of being a well-educated knight who could read several languages. We know approximately when his works were written, but his birth and death dates are uncertain, as is the location of the "Aue" where he was born. Several different towns lay claim to him, all with some justification. As with most medieval works, the original manuscript of *Der arme Heinrich* has been lost, and the work survived in only three complete manuscripts from the fourteenth century. Manuscript A, the best, was destroyed in Strassburg in 1870 in the war between the Germans and the French. Manuscripts B[a] and B[b], presumably copies of that source, are preserved in Heidelberg and Genf-Cologny, Hungary. There are also three fragments of the work, manuscripts C, D, and E (manuscript E, which contains verses 29 to 255, was discovered in 1965; its pages had been used to insulate organ pipes).

The reason for Hartmann's emphasis in the opening lines on his ability to read is that medieval audiences were interested above all in authenticity. Many of the famous German epics, including *Erek, Iwein, Parzifal,* and *Tristan,* were reworkings of British Arthurian legends as presented to European audiences by the French poet Chrétien de Troyes, and Hartmann's *Gregorius* was based on the Oedipus legend. Audiences first and foremost wanted to know the source of the story. It is all the more unusual therefore that no source has been found for the story of *Der arme Heinrich.* Since the main character, Heinrich, is said to come from the same "Aue" as the author, Hartmann, critics have speculated that Hartmann may have had a personal reason for writing this poem, namely to present in a positive light the marriage of one of his ancestors to a member of a lower class, a marriage that, without mitigating circumstances, would have defied the feudal class system. It is generally agreed that *Der arme Heinrich* was one of Hartmann's later works, written when his reputation was sufficiently established to allow his departing from convention.

Heinrich's sin, symbolically punished by the contraction of leprosy, was that presumption, *superbia.* He believed that he deserved his health, wealth, and the respect of others because he was a good man. Yet in concentrating on worldly pleasures—which Hartmann emphasizes by the repeated use of the adjective "worldly" in the opening pages—Heinrich was flouting the primary moral imperative of the Middle Ages, that of pleasing first God and then the world: "got unde der werlde."

People in medieval times were all too aware of the transience of worldly success and happiness. In their literature, the world is frequently personified as "Frau Welt," who when seen from the front is a seductively beautiful woman, but when seen from the back is rotting and riddled with worms. Heinrich's leprosy serves as a constant reminder of the ugly side of the world.

The conclusion of *Der arme Heinrich* has often been compared to a fairy tale. Heinrich's leprosy is cured, his youth and wealth are restored to him, he marries the girl, and the two of them live a long and happy life. Yet these are merely the external manifestations of the actual miracle, which is that of insight. For most of the story, Heinrich's way of thinking is worldly. He thinks he can buy favors: from the surgeon for a huge sum of money, from God for his gifts to the poor, and from the young woman for his gifts of ribbons and trinkets. He calculates his actions according to what others will think of him. Initially, he is afraid to accept the girl's offer not because it will cost her her life, but because he will look foolish in the eyes of others if the attempt fails. The miracle consists of his decision to stop the surgeon regardless of what others might say and to place his life entirely in the hands of God. Only when Heinrich has submitted fully to the will of God is he able to experience the grace of God.

The young woman, though nameless, plays easily as important a role as Heinrich in the work, for she is his counterpart. Heinrich needs to concentrate more on pleasing God, but the girl needs to concentrate more on pleasing the world, so that both of them in the end attain the medieval virtue of *mâze,* or moderation. Whereas the girl might at first appear to be saintly, her premature renunciation of the world is morally flawed, for her motive is not selfless. In believing that God will be obliged to reward her for her sacrifice by making her a queen in heaven, she is trying to force his hand.

The critic Ernst Rose has explained her death wish as a fearful overreaction against her awakening sexuality, a reaction that is not surprising given the fact that the man she loves is hideously deformed by leprosy. John Margetts makes even more explicit the sexual nature of the relationship between Heinrich and the girl by explaining Hartmann's brilliant use of double entendre in the scene where the girl lies bound and naked on the surgeon's table. Modern psychology has provided precise terminology for the human feelings accurately described in literature since the beginning of written record. The interpretation of *Der arme Heinrich* is enhanced by an understanding of the sexual element that is undeniably present. Heinrich's repeated reference to the girl as his *gemahel*, or wife, is evidence that he did not think of her as a child.

Der arme Heinrich is a short but intricately written tale that supports many levels of interpretation. The significance in the work of the number three, for example, is unmistakable. Like the Holy Trinity, three represents perfection and completion. The girl's parents consent to her sacrifice on the third day, but Hartmann gives the reader a numerological sign that their decision is too hasty by noting that the discussions leading up to the decision lasted only two nights.

"Critical Evaluation" by Jean M. Snook

Bibliography:

Fisher, Rodney W. "Hartmann's *Arme Heinrich*: The Classical Mediaeval Dilemma of *Ere*." In *Die Ehre als literarisches Motiv*, edited by August Obermayer. Dunedin, New Zealand: University of Otago, 1986. Fisher suggests metaphorical significance for the scene in Salerno. Compares Heinrich knocking on the door to Christ knocking at the door of the human heart.

Margetts, John. "Observations on the Representation of Female Attractiveness in the Works of Hartmann von Aue with Special Reference to *Der arme Heinrich*." In *Hartmann von Aue: Changing Perspectives*, edited by Timothy McFarland and Silvia Ranawake. Göttingen: Kümmerle, 1988. Draws on research into colloquial German vocabulary to demonstrate double entendre in the scene with the girl awaiting the surgeon's knife. Concludes that a sadomasochistic element is found in all of Hartmann's works, perhaps reflective of a repressive society.

Rose, Ernst. "Problems of Medieval Psychology as Presented in the 'Klein Gemahel' of *Heinrich the Unfortunate*." *The Germanic Review* 22, no. 3 (October, 1947): 182-187. An excellent article of enduring significance, which portrays the girl as precociously pubescent and afraid of her awakening sexuality. Her desire to be sacrificed is driven by unconscious masochism.

Swinburne, Hilda. "The Miracle in *Der arme Heinrich*." *German Life and Letters* 22, no. 3 (April, 1969): 205-209. A solid summary and analysis of the events surrounding the narrative turning point. Enumerates Heinrich's temptations and analyzes the situations in which both Heinrich and the maiden are tested by God.

Wallbank, Rosemary E. "The Salernitan Dimension in Hartmann von Aue's *Der arme Heinrich*." *German Life and Letters* 43, no. 2 (January, 1990): 168-176. Informative research into the respected medical schools in Montpellier and Salerno in the twelfth century and a discussion of their rigorous curricula and surgical practices.

THE ARMIES OF THE NIGHT
History as a Novel, the Novel as History

Type of work: Novel
Author: Norman Mailer (1923-   )
Type of plot: New journalism
Time of plot: October, 1967
Locale: Washington, D.C., Virginia, and New York
First published: 1968

> *Principal characters:*
> NORMAN MAILER, the author, a famous novelist
> MITCHELL GOODMAN, an author and political activist
> EDWARD DE GRAZIA, a lawyer and friend of Mailer
> DAVID DELLINGER, coordinator of the march on the Pentagon
> ROBERT LOWELL, a prominent American poet
> DWIGHT MACDONALD, a prominent American critic
> WILLIAM SLOANE COFFIN, JR., a Yale University chaplain
> BENJAMIN SPOCK, a pediatrician and antiwar activist
> WALTER TEAGUE, a Leninist organizer jailed with Mailer
> HIRSCHKOP, chief counsel for the demonstrators
> SCAIFE, U.S. commissioner who presides over Mailer's arraignment
> BEVERLY BENTLEY, Mailer's fourth wife

The Story:

On a September morning in 1967, Norman Mailer received a phone call from Mitchell Goodman, an old friend and a political activist, urging his participation in a demonstration the following month against the continuing Vietnam War. Mailer reluctantly agreed and, two days before the scheduled rally at the Pentagon, flew to Washington, D.C., from his home in New York.

Thursday evening, before going on to an assembly at the Ambassador Theater, Mailer attended a cocktail party at the home of a liberal academic couple. Discomfited by their bland benevolence, Mailer, who spent his time conversing with Dwight Macdonald, Robert Lowell, and Edward de Grazia, further offended the hostess by declining her food and walking away with her copy of his novel Why Are We in Vietnam? (1967). Arriving at the Ambassador Theater, where he was supposed to serve as master of ceremonies, Mailer first headed for the unlit men's room, where, spotted by a reporter for *Time* magazine, he inadvertently urinated onto the floor. On stage at last, furious that the proceedings had begun without him, Mailer wrested control of the microphone from de Grazia. Tipsy and inspired, he delivered an elaborate monologue about Vietnam and America in a manner that both engaged and enraged his audience.

On Friday, Mailer gathered at the Church of the Reformation for a ceremony in which thirty to forty young men affirmed their refusal of military service. In the company of people he found too nice and too principled, Mailer then walked a mile and a half to the Justice Department, where he, William Sloane Coffin, Jr., Mitchell Goodman, Benjamin Spock, Robert Lowell, and others gave speeches, and 994 draft cards were turned in to officials.

Following Saturday breakfast with Lowell and Macdonald, Mailer joined a crowd variously estimated at between 25,000 and 225,000 that was assembling near the Washington Monument.

He was piqued at not being asked to speak, but after speeches by numerous others, the throng proceeded across the Arlington Memorial Bridge toward the Pentagon in order to manifest opposition to the continuing war in Vietnam. Mailer was followed by a crew from the British Broadcasting Corporation, which was making a documentary about him. In the north parking lot, Mailer, seeking symbolic arrest and early release so that he could rejoin his wife in time for a party that evening in New York, was one of the first to cross the military police lines. Apprehended by a U.S. marshal and placed in a van for removal to the lockup, he had a hostile confrontation with a neo-Nazi also arrested during the demonstration. Mailer and dozens of other, mostly young, protesters were imprisoned in the U.S. post office in Alexandria.

While impatiently awaiting arraignment, Mailer telephoned his wife Beverly Bentley, an actress and a Southerner whose military father reminded him of some of the U.S. marshals. The prisoners were transported again, to a government workhouse twenty miles away, in Occaquam, Virginia. When a Leninist named Walter Teague lectured fellow prisoners on political tactics, Mailer, who considered himself a "Left Conservative," grew testy and helped defeat Teague's proposal that the imprisoned protesters send a collective letter critical of national mobilization leadership.

Mailer spent an uncomfortable night in custody and was not called to court until the following afternoon. He was represented by Hirschkop, chief counsel for the demonstrators, who argued strenuously with U.S. commissioner Scaife in order to keep his client from having to spend an additional night in jail. Pleading *nolo contendere*, Mailer was assessed a sentence of thirty days but was released on his own recognizance pending appeal and returned home to New York.

After reading distorted accounts of the demonstration and of his own role in it in *Time* magazine and *The Washington Post*, Mailer began to write his own version in two parts—a novelistic history of himself over four days, followed by a collective history consisting of his own ruminations on the historical context and the significance of the entire event. After recounting his personal experiences as a witness to and participant in the October, 1967, antiwar march, Mailer provided a more detached explanation of the context for the growing opposition to Pentagon policies. Criticizing the misperceptions and distortions of mainstream journalism, he offered an alternative overview of just what happened before, during, and after the incidents he described in the first section of his book. His experience culminated in the creation of *The Armies of the Night*, a hybrid of history and fiction that, for all of its critique of social disorder, concludes with a paean to America.

Critical Evaluation:

The Armies of the Night is not only a brilliant product of the countercultural ferment of the late 1960's; in common with contemporary works by Truman Capote, Tom Wolfe, Joan Didion, Hunter Thompson, and others, it is also an enduring attempt to challenge the categorical limits of nonfiction. With his first book, *The Naked and the Dead* (1948), a fiction that drew on his own combat experiences in the Pacific theater of World War II, Mailer was hailed as the most promising novelist of his generation. *Barbary Shore* (1951), *The Deer Park* (1955), *An American Dream* (1965), and *Why Are We in Vietnam?* did not fulfill the promise. Twenty years after his debut as a novelist, Mailer began to distinguish himself by endowing reportage with the power of imaginative fiction, by offering up dazzling verbal displays that bear the authority of actuality.

The Armies of the Night, Mailer's rendition of a 1967 march against the Pentagon, was soon followed by *Miami and the Siege of Chicago* (1968), an account of the Republican and Democratic national conventions of 1968, *Of a Fire on the Moon* (1970), a report on the American space program, *The Prisoner of Sex* (1971), Mailer's take on the women's movement, and *The Executioner's Song* (1979), the story of condemned murderer Gary Gilmore. Immersing himself in such salient issues of the day as the Vietnam War, electoral politics, feminism, sports, homicide, and aerospace, Mailer applied his novelistic gifts to depicting and ruminating over contemporary characters and events that he did not invent.

The *Armies of the Night* recounts its own genesis, in the inspired aftermath of a condensed, intense experience. The narrative derives power by concentrating its plot in a few abundant days and confining its composition to a few inspired weeks. Mailer began writing, rapidly, soon after returning from Washington that October, 1967, and the first fragment of his account, titled "The Steps of the Pentagon," appeared in print as early as March, 1968, in *Harper's Magazine*. The completed book, published a few months later, begins with an excerpt from *Time* magazine and concludes the first of its two sections with a report from *The Washington Post*. Much of the work stands in counterpoint to the reductive vision of reality that journalism, a dialect of what Mailer calls "technologese," would promulgate. Mailer, who flippantly makes himself the principal protagonist of the momentous events in Washington, sees himself in proud battle against totalitarianism, a depersonalizing power evident not only in a government that is conscripting young American men to devastate the people and places of southeast Asia but also in the regimentation of the liberal opposition. Mailer, who calls himself a Left Conservative, flaunts a flamboyant style and self to defeat the enemies of linguistic nuance and personal freedom. He mocks his own reputation and ambition while nevertheless affirming his distinctive powers of observation.

Compounding the comic arrogance of presuming to position himself at the epicenter of opposition to the war, Mailer refers to himself with a mock humble third-person pronoun "he," and at times with the grandiloquent epithet "The Novelist."

The *Armies of the Night* is stocked with Mailerisms, ostentatious phrases that dramatize the strain of literary creation and of individual life in the age of the corporation. Mailer playfully offers up virtuoso narrative set pieces, such as the liberal academic cocktail party, the assembly at the Ambassador Theater, and the hearing with a federal commissioner. He delights in cameo appearances by dissident celebrities such as Lowell, Macdonald, and Spock. As master of ceremonies at the Ambassador Theater, Mailer the protagonist dazzles, hectors, and beguiles his audience; as narrator, he delights in brazen epic similes featuring comparisons so prodigious as to leave the reader indignant and in awe. Mailer's self-conscious performance on stage as master of ceremonies, offering up an amalgam of charm and insult, is a miniature version of his activity as author. He celebrates and ridicules his own exhibition, whether on the stage of the Ambassador or in the pages of *The Armies of the Night*.

Book 1 of *The Armies of the Night* purports to be "History as a Novel" and book 2 "The Novel as History." The design of the work suggests a remarkable work of friction—between private and public realities, between Mailer and an impersonal system, between invention and chronicle. Mailer's point is that the first section, much the longer and the more compelling of the two, is, though anecdotal, idiosyncratic, jocular, and blatantly subjective, as reliable as the dispassionate, analytic section, an abstract meditation on the significance of the demonstration against the Department of Defense. Like conventional journalism, conventional history is inadequate for the mission of spiritual liberation that Mailer undertakes in marching against the machinery of war and, even more, in writing about that march.

The *Armies of the Night* begins with preparations for a coordinated defiance of authority and concludes with a paean of love to America. Like Walt Whitman, Mailer would be the epic bard who can speak for and to the entire nation, and his hybrid book, dedicated to a Southern wife whom he equates with the nation he embraces, is a self-conscious effort to alert his society about the dangers of suppressing the self. Convinced that jarring figures of speech affirm an author's liberty and the vitality of democracy, Mailer offers a tonic shock to the system, a repressive society that had become inured to the death it was inflicting. *The Armies of the Night* is an exuberant bravura performance, both a raucous call to arms and a passionate farewell to them.

Steven G. Kellman

Bibliography:
Bailey, Jennifer. *Norman Mailer: Quick-Change Artist.* New York: Barnes & Noble, 1979. Particularly attentive to Mailer's creation of personae, Bailey analyzes *The Armies of the Night* as his finest achievement in fictional journalism.
Bufithis, Philip H. *Norman Mailer.* New York: Frederick Ungar, 1978. In his lucid survey of Mailer's career, Bufithis pays particular attention to Mailer's characterization of himself and to the presences of Walt Whitman, Ralph Waldo Emerson, and Ernest Hemingway in *The Armies of the Night*, while praising the book as unmatched in drama, energy, and wit since Benjamin Franklin's *Autobiography.*
Kazin, Alfred. "The Trouble He's Seen." In *Critical Essays on Norman Mailer*, edited by J. Michael Lennon. Boston: G. K. Hall, 1986. Kazin's extended and enthusiastic review places Mailer's book within the context of his career and of American literature.
Merrill, Robert. *Norman Mailer.* Boston: Twayne, 1978. Focusing on the unique structure of what he argues is Mailer's most enduring work, Merrill examines its protagonist's experience as a rite of purification.
Solotaroff, Robert. *Down Mailer's Way.* Urbana: University of Illinois Press, 1974. Noting parallels to Henry Adams, Solotaroff offers insightful analysis of the style and the distance between author and protagonist in *The Armies of the Night.*

ARMS AND THE MAN
An Anti-Romantic Comedy

Type of work: Drama
Author: George Bernard Shaw (1856-1950)
Type of plot: Comedy
Time of plot: 1885-1886
Locale: Bulgaria
First performed: 1894; first published, 1898

Principal characters:
RAINA PETKOFF, an attractive young Bulgarian lady
CATHERINE, her mother
MAJOR PAUL PETKOFF, her father
MAJOR SERGIUS SARANOFF, her fiancé
CAPTAIN BLUNTSCHLI, a Swiss mercenary serving in the army
NICOLA, the Petkoffs' manservant
LOUKA, a young servant woman, Nicola's fiancée

The Story:

Raina was in her bedroom on the second floor of the Petkoff house in a small town in Bulgaria when her mother entered to tell her that Sergius had just led the Bulgarians to victory in battle with the Serbs. Raina rejoiced; her idealistic expectations of war and soldiers had been met. Louka entered to tell them that the army had ordered them to lock all the doors and windows while enemy stragglers were being pursued. Catherine and Louka left. Shots could be heard outside and a man stumbled into the room. He was a Serbian artillery officer, exhausted, nervous, and hungry. When soldiers appeared at the door, demanding to search the room, Raina on impulse hid the man and told them no one else was there.

Raina and the man talked. She expressed her contempt for his being a coward and for his stuffing his pockets with chocolate instead of ammunition. He tried to explain to her the realities of battle and identified her portrait of Sergius as the man who led the charge that won the battle; the Bulgarians had won only because the Serbians had had the wrong size ammunition. The man described Sergius as a romantic fool who had won by doing the professionally wrong thing. Raina objected strongly to this, but when the man decided to leave, Raina said she would save him and went in search of her mother; they returned to find him fast asleep on the bed.

Four months later, Nicola and Louka were arguing in the Petkoffs' garden. Nicola wanted Louka to be more polite to the Petkoffs because he intended to set up a shop and was counting on the Petkoffs as his principal customers. Major Petkoff returned from the war and was greeted by his wife, Catherine. Sergius was shown in. Bitter because the army refused to promote him, he declared his intention to resign. Sergius and Petkoff spoke of a tale they had heard of a Swiss officer being rescued by two Bulgarian women. At this point, Raina left, and when Louka entered, Sergius attempted to flirt with her. Louka told him that she knew a secret about Raina and a strange man. When they were alone, Raina and Catherine discussed the Swiss soldier. Raina left and Louka announced a Captain Bluntschli, who had come to return a coat Raina and Catherine had lent him. Catherine begged him not to reveal who it was who had helped him. Petkoff appeared and asked Bluntschli to stay to help with some transportation matters. When Raina entered, she managed to cover up her surprise at seeing Bluntschli.

After lunch that day, Petkoff and Sergius were in the library, writing orders for troop movements. Petkoff wanted his comfortable old coat and Catherine said it was in the closet (where she had put it after getting it back from Bluntschli). Nicola returned with the coat and all left except Raina and Bluntschli, who discussed lies, gratitude, and the differences between practicality and the false ideals of romanticism. Bluntschli saw through her pretense of noble ideals and Raina admitted that he had found her out. Raina told Bluntschli that she had put a photograph of herself in the pocket of the coat, but Bluntschli had never found it. He received mail that had collected for him, among which was the news that his father was dead and had left him a number of big hotels.

In a discussion between Louka and Nicola, Nicola suggested that it would be best if Louka and Sergius married and became his valued customers. Sergius entered and, after Nicola left, flirted again with Louka; he was still disillusioned about life and by his own inability to measure up to his ideals. Louka told him that Raina was sure to marry Bluntschli, so when Bluntschli entered, Sergius challenged him to a duel. Bluntschli agreed and, being a practical man, chose machine guns. Raina entered and wanted to know why they were going to fight; she suspected what had been going on with Louka and became disenchanted with Sergius, who concluded that life was a farce and that there was now no need for a duel. Raina said that Sergius should fight Nicola, since he was Louka's fiancé, information that disillusioned Sergius even more.

When Petkoff entered and wanted his coat again, Raina helped her father put it on and took the opportunity to slip the photograph out of the pocket. Her father had already found the picture, however, and wanted to know the meaning of the inscription "Raina, to her Chocolate Cream Soldier: a Souvenir." Thereupon, Bluntschli revealed that he was the chocolate cream soldier; Louka and Sergius became engaged; and Bluntschli lamented that despite his practicality he had always had a romantic streak—he had returned the coat in person, hoping to see Raina again. When he discovered that Raina was really twenty-three, not seventeen, as he had supposed, he proposed to her and was accepted. As Bluntschli left, Sergius supplied the final comment: "What a man! Is he a man!"

Critical Evaluation:

Arms and the Man, subtitled *An Anti-Romantic Comedy*, is most obviously an attack on the false ideals of warfare and the soldier's profession. Late nineteenth century British society, especially the aristocratic element, tended to see war as a noble undertaking and soldiers as brave, courageous, fearless, and honorable. Many military melodramas of the period upheld these ideals, but they were performed for a civilian audience. As George Bernard Shaw has Bluntschli make clear, soldiers themselves did not think this way. Although far from being a pacifist, Shaw demands that war be seen honestly: War makes men tired and hungry, afraid and nervous. In the person of Bluntschli and in his comments about battle, Shaw establishes the opposition with the archromantics of the play, Raina and Sergius. The satire of the play is aimed at the poetic view of war and soldiers and at the commonplace conjunction between soldiers, aristocracy, and love, the staples of the standard military melodrama of the period. When Raina chooses for her mate the practical, professional, middle-class Bluntschli, Shaw breaks the pattern in which only the brave deserve the fair.

Shaw's dramatic approach in *Arms and the Man* makes deliberate use of many of the oldest, stagiest of devices, ranging from the titillating circumstance of the strange man in the lady's boudoir to the appearance of an incriminating letter or photo. Shaw is reputed to have said that one cannot be too stagy on the stage. His main characters are taken from the stock military melodramas of the time: the noble soldier, the cowardly soldier, the beautiful lady, the comic servant. Shaw turns these stock characters to his own use, however: The beautiful lady does not end up in the arms of the noble soldier; the cowardly soldier is not really cowardly, just practical; the comic servant proves to be a man of considerable practical wisdom.

The key elements of the play are really contained in Sergius and Raina, rather than in Bluntschli. Bluntschli never changes in the course of the play; he is the standard against which the others are measured. Raina learns to divest herself of her impossible ideals, ideals that have no relation to real life, and thus becomes a fit partner for the cool and efficient Bluntschli. Sergius believes that he, and life generally, is to be despised because he finds himself unable to match his ideals. Sergius never does come to see the lesson taught by Bluntschli—that the problem is not an inability to live up to ideals but the acceptance of impossible ideals as reasonable and real.

From this point of view, *Arms and the Man* is a classic statement of the antiromantic view of life. Its commentary is not only directed at the military, however, for the play also presents a version of that common Shavian theme: the professional versus the amateur. The difference between the professional and the amateur is fundamentally one of attitude. Sergius' attitude marks him as an amateur. Romantic idealism makes folly of life because it is unreal and impossible to attain.

Shaw presents his ideas by using the old device of creating a closed unit—the Petkoff household—and then thrusting an outsider into its midst. The members of the Petkoff household had been perfectly content to live in its own small dreamworld (which the Bulgarian backwoods setting helps to emphasize), until their routines and values are suddenly called into question by the appearance of Bluntschli, who represents the "reality" of the outside world.

Shaw achieves the humor of the play with the old device of the descent from the sublime to the ridiculous: For each of Raina's and Sergius' noble utterances, Bluntschli has a deflating answer or response. Yet this is not merely a device to provoke laughter; rather, the repeated puncturing of poses lies at the heart of the play. The audience may laugh at Sergius and Raina, but both the audience and the characters are made to realize that it is their fake ideals and poses that are being called into question. The human inability to live up to ideals is a staple of comedy, but Shaw has elevated it from a simple comic device to a means of questioning a set of philosophical beliefs.

Arms and the Man was an important play for Shaw because it was the first of his plays to be a public success. In this play, Shaw made his first fairly direct attack upon false idealism, an attack aimed not so much at conscience as at attitudes. Certainly, the play elicited more laughter than any of Shaw's other plays, either before or after. In contrast to the other plays, the laughter in *Arms and the Man* tends to be more agreeable to many because Shaw is using so many of the traditional devices of comedy.

The play is also important because it marked the shift from Shaw's earlier propagandistic plays on social topics to more benign-seeming attacks on the romantic, idealistic follies of humankind. The social reformer of the earlier plays had shifted methods, though not goals, realizing that he must change attitudes before he can appeal to consciences. Whether propagandist or anti-idealist, however, Shaw did not simply want idle laughter. He maintained that it was easy to make people laugh—he wanted to make people think.

Gordon N. Bergquist

Bibliography:
Alexander, Nigel. *A Critical Commentary on Bernard Shaw's "Arms and the Man" and "Pygmalion."* London: Macmillan, 1968. A detailed critical exposition; includes an intro-

duction on "The Play of Ideas," discussion questions, and recommendations for further reading.

Bergquist, Gordon N. *The Pen and the Sword: War and Peace in the Prose and Plays of Bernard Shaw*. Salzburg, Austria: University of Salzburg, 1977. A detailed examination of the occurrence of soldiers and wars in Shaw's plays and of Shaw's thought on the military and related issues.

Carpenter, Charles A. *Bernard Shaw and the Art of Destroying Ideals: The Early Plays*. Madison: University of Wisconsin Press, 1969. A clear exposition of Shaw's methods in attacking idealism in *Arms and the Man* and other plays.

Crompton, Louis. *Shaw the Dramatist*. Lincoln: University of Nebraska Press, 1969. An excellent consideration of the social, philosophical, and historical background of *Arms and the Man*.

Dukore, Bernard F. *Bernard Shaw's "Arms and the Man": A Composite Production Book*. Carbondale: Southern Illinois University Press, 1982. Covers Shaw's directions and advice for four different productions of *Arms and the Man*. Includes Shaw's directorial notes, manuscript changes, and costume designs. Invaluable for preparing an actual staging of the play.

ARROWSMITH

Type of work: Novel
Author: Sinclair Lewis (1885-1951)
Type of plot: Social realism
Time of plot: Early twentieth century
Locale: United States and West Indies
First published: 1925

Principal characters:
MARTIN ARROWSMITH, a medical scientist
LEORA, his wife
DR. MAX GOTTLIEB, a scientist
GUSTAVE SONDELIUS, a scientist
TERRY WICKETT, Martin's friend
JOYCE LANYON, a young widow
DR. ALMUS PICKERBAUGH, a public health reformer

The Story:

Martin Arrowsmith was the descendant of pioneers in the Ohio wilderness. He grew up in the raw redbrick town of Elk Mills, in the state of Winnemac. A restless, lonely boy, he spent his odd hours in old Doc Vickerson's office. The village practitioner was a widower with no family of his own, and he encouraged Martin's interest in medicine.

At age twenty-one, Martin was a junior preparing for medical school at the University of Winnemac. Continuing on at the medical school, he was most interested in bacteriology, research, and the courses of Professor Max Gottlieb, a noted German scientist. After joining a medical fraternity, he made many lifelong friends. He also fell in love with Madeline Fox, a shallow pseudointellectual who was taking graduate work in English. To the young man from the prairie, Madeline represented culture. They became engaged.

Martin spent many nights in research at the laboratory, and he became the favorite of Professor Gottlieb. One day, Gottlieb sent him to the Zenith City Hospital on an errand. There Martin met an attractive nurse named Leora Tozer. He soon became so interested in Leora that he became engaged to her as well. Thus, young Martin Arrowsmith found himself engaged to two women at the same time. Unable to choose between them, he asked both Leora and Madeline to lunch with him. When he explained his predicament, Madeline stalked angrily from the dining room and out of his life. Leora remained, finding the situation amusing. Martin felt that his life had really begun.

Through his friendship with Gottlieb, Martin became a student instructor in bacteriology. Leora was called home to North Dakota. Leora's absence, trouble with the dean, and too much whiskey led to Martin's leaving school during the Christmas holidays. Traveling like a tramp, he arrived at Wheatsylvania, the town where Leora lived. In spite of the warnings of the dull Tozer family, Martin and Leora were married. Martin went back to Winnemac alone. A married man now, he gave up his work in bacteriology and turned his attention to general study. Later Leora joined him in Mohalis.

Upon completion of his internship, Martin set up an office in Wheatsylvania with money supplied by his wife's family. In the small prairie town, Martin made friends of the wrong sort, according to the Tozers, but he was fairly successful as a physician. He also made a number of enemies. Meanwhile, Martin and Leora moved from the Tozer house to their own home. When Leora's first child was born dead, they knew that they could never have another child.

Martin had again become interested in research. When he heard that the Swedish scientist Gustave Sondelius was to lecture in Minneapolis, Martin went to hear his lecture. In that way, Martin became interested in public health as a means of controlling disease. Back in Wheatsylvania, still under the influence of Sondelius, he became acting head of the Department of Public Health. Martin, in his official capacity, found a highly respected seamstress to be a chronic carrier of typhoid and sent her to the county home for isolation. He became generally unpopular. He therefore welcomed the opportunity to join Dr. Almus Pickerbaugh of Nautilus, Iowa, as the Assistant Director of Public Health, at a considerable increase in salary.

In Nautilus, he found Dr. Pickerbaugh to be a public-spirited evangelist with little knowledge of medicine or interest in scientific control of disease. The director spent his time writing health slogans in doubtful poetic meter, lecturing to clubs, and campaigning for health by means of Better Babies Week, Banish the Booze Week, and Tougher Teeth Week. Martin was gradually drawn under the influence of the flashy, artificial methods used by his superior. Although he tried to devote some time to research, the young doctor found that his job took all of his time. While Dr. Pickerbaugh was campaigning for election to Congress, Martin investigated the most sanitary and efficient dairy of the town. He found that the dairy was spreading disease through a streptococcus infection in the udders of the cows. Against the advice of Dr. Pickerbaugh, Martin closed the dairy and made many enemies for himself. Despite his act, however, he was made Acting Director of Public Health when Dr. Pickerbaugh was elected to Congress.

In his new capacity, Martin hired a competent assistant in order to have more time for research in bacteriology. Largely because he set fire to a block of tenements infested with tuberculosis, Martin was asked to resign. For the next year, he worked as staff pathologist of the fashionable Rouncefield Clinic in Chicago. Then publication of a scientific paper brought him again to the attention of his old friend and professor, Max Gottlieb, now located at the McGurk Institute in New York. Dr. Arrowsmith was glad to accept the position Gottlieb offered him.

At the McGurk Institute, Martin devoted his whole time to research, with Gottlieb as his constant friend and adviser. He worked on staphylococcus germs, producing first a toxin, then an antitoxin. Under the influence of Gottlieb and Terry Wickett, his colleague at McGurk, Martin discovered the X Principle, a bacterial infection that might prove to be a cure for disease. Although Martin wanted to postpone publication of his discovery until he was absolutely certain of its value, the directors of the institute insisted that he make his results public at once. Before his paper was finished, however, it was learned that the same principle had already been discovered at the Pasteur Institute, where it was called a bacteriophage. After that disappointment, Martin began work on the possibility of preventing and curing bubonic plague with the phage, as the new antitoxin was called.

Meanwhile, Gustave Sondelius had come to the McGurk Institute. He became so interested in Martin's work that he spent most of his time helping his young friend. When a plague broke out on St. Hubert, an island in the West Indies, Martin and Sondelius were asked to go there to help in the fight against the epidemic. Accompanied by Leora, they sailed for the island of St. Hubert. Before leaving, Martin had promised Gottlieb that he would conduct his experiment by deliberately refusing to treat some of the plague cases with phage. In this way, the effects of the treatment could be tabulated against a control group.

The plague spread daily on the tropical island. Sondelius was stricken, and he died. Martin was often away from his laboratory as he traveled between villages. During one of his trips,

Leora lighted a half-smoked cigarette that she had found on a table in his laboratory. The tobacco had been saturated with germs from an overturned test tube. Leora died of the plague before Martin's return.

Martin forgot to be the pure scientist. He gave the phage to all who asked for it. Although his assistant continued to take notes to carry on the research, Martin was no longer interested in the results. When the plague began to abate, he went back to New York. There, lonely and unhappy, he married Joyce Lanyon, a wealthy young widow whom he had met on St. Hubert. The marriage, however, was not a success. Joyce demanded more of his time than he was willing to take from research; he felt ill at ease among her rich and fashionable friends. When he was offered the assistant directorship of the McGurk Institute, he refused the position. In spite of Joyce's protests, he went off to join his old friend and colleague Terry Wickett at a rural laboratory in Vermont, where they intended to run experiments, searching for a cure for pneumonia. At last, Martin believed, his work and his life were really beginning.

Critical Evaluation:

In the 1920's, Sinclair Lewis hit his full stride as a novelist—during that time, he wrote *Main Street* (1920), *Babbitt* (1922), *Arrowsmith* (1925), and *Dodsworth* (1929), among other novels—and enjoyed both popular and critical acclaim. His considerable achievement in that decade earned for Lewis the Nobel Prize in Literature in 1930; he was the first American author to be thus distinguished. Even earlier, *Arrowsmith* was selected for the 1926 Pulitzer Prize. Lewis, however, objected to one of the criteria for awarding the prize, finding it incompatible with intellectual freedom; he therefore declined to accept. Such political bickering notwithstanding, *Arrowsmith* as a work of art is typical of Lewis' work at the peak of his literary productivity. It contains the fundamental elements of realism and satire that characterize Lewis' style at its best.

In *Arrowsmith*, as in other novels of this period, Lewis' realism is most obviously demonstrated in the generous use of detail. Almost in the fashion of a television documentary, Lewis embellishes the verisimilitude and credibility of his story with fact piled upon fact. As for satire, the ethical dilemmas of the medical profession still abound: The issues may change, but the controversy endures. Martin Arrowsmith, emotionally wracked by the deaths from bubonic plague of his colleague, Gustave Sondelius, and his wife, Leora, is no less obsessed and no less caught in ethical conflicts than today's practitioner dealing with a victim of cancer. The satiric view emerges from this double vision of life: pursue pure science or save whatever lives can be saved. To a certain extent, the dichotomy is artificial, for such either-or simplicity is not characteristic of medical decisions or any other decisions. In practical terms, however, it is very real: a choice between short-term and long-term benefits. Martin Arrowsmith chooses short-term benefits. He provides antitoxin for all, destroying the scientific validity of the tests that were to be conducted. The satiric flavor thus emerges as Martin's obligatory choice between two impossible alternatives.

Still, Martin himself is a somewhat ambiguous character. Are readers to admire him or despise him? Part of the reader's answer revolves around personal commitments to abstract "good" or immediate practical benefits. One may nonetheless view Dr. Arrowsmith as profoundly influenced by his mentors and professional colleagues; he does indeed strive for the best his fellows represent. If he falls short, Lewis would have readers believe that Arrowsmith's intentions are nevertheless worthy of respect.

A legitimate question remains, however: Does Professor Max Gottlieb (significantly, translated as "love of God") appear as a secret protagonist in the novel? Does Gottlieb represent the guiding force behind Martin Arrowsmith's actions? The answer is by no means definitive, but it is evident that Lewis himself was not at all clear on the issue of whether Arrowsmith or Gottlieb should triumph. By presenting a dilemma, rather than trying to solve it, Lewis established himself as a realist and a satirist, for he depicted an unvarnished human condition and portrayed the hazards of moral choice. His satire of medicine—like his satires of middle-class attitudes (*Babbitt*), of religious evangelism (*Elmer Gantry*, 1927), and of middle-class business (*Dodsworth*)—still rings true.

Bibliography:
Bucco, Martin, ed. *Critical Essays on Sinclair Lewis*. Boston: G. K. Hall, 1986. Begins with early interviews and goes on to contemporary critics. Articles include discussion of *Arrowsmith*; one article shows how the book developed from Lewis' unfinished novel about labor.
Dooley, D. J. *The Art of Sinclair Lewis*. Lincoln: University of Nebraska Press, 1967. Chapter 4 discusses the genesis, development, strengths, weaknesses, and reputation of *Arrowsmith*. Investigates the novel's central theme and characters.
Grebstein, Sheldon Norman. *Sinclair Lewis*. Boston: Twayne, 1962. Excellent chapter on the heroic Arrowsmith in the context of American society. Sees the novel as more artistic and inspired than its predecessors.
Griffin, Robert J., ed. *Twentieth Century Interpretations of "Arrowsmith."* Englewood Cliffs, N.J.: Prentice-Hall, 1968. Only book-length study of *Arrowsmith*. Includes early reviews and important essays by leading Lewis scholars.
Schorer, Mark. *Sinclair Lewis: An American Life*. New York: McGraw-Hill, 1961. Indispensable. Includes an examination of *Arrowsmith* from its beginnings to its critical reception. Also includes discussion of the men and women who were the prototypes for the character in *Arrowsmith*.

ARS POETICA

Type of work: Poetry
Author: Horace (Quintus Horatius Flaccus, 65-8 B.C.E.)
First published: c. 17 B.C.E. (English translation, 1640)

To Horace, this poem was the last of his epistles, but almost at once his contemporaries began referring to it as *Ars poetica* (the art of poetry), and by "poetry" they meant any field of literary composition. Horace addressed it to his friend Lucius Calpurnius Piso, famous for his battles in Thrace, and to his two sons. Apparently the older son yearned for a career as a dramatist or an epic poet. While not a formal treatise or an abstract discussion, like the similarly named composition of Aristotle, the 476 lines of this unsystematic letter in verse influenced Joachim du Bellay in writing the manifesto of the Pleiad, and a century later inspired Nicolas Boileau's *L'Art poétique* (1674) and Alexander Pope's *Essay on Criticism* (1711). Some of Horace's suggestions, like the classical five-act division of the drama, are no longer important, but today's writers still can learn much from the rest of the poem. The double purpose of literature, a mingling of "the useful with the sweet," has been quoted through the centuries in every literary movement.

One would be amused rather than impressed, begins Horace, by the painting of a creature with a horse's body and a man's head, with limbs from every sort of animal, adorned with feathers from a variety of birds. Yet poets combine just such outlandish elements, adding "purple patches" where they are entirely out of place in order to give color and brilliance to pompous openings in portions of their writing. Therefore he begins his *Ars poetica* with a plea for simplicity and unity.

Addressing Piso and his sons directly, Horace confesses that most poets are misled by what looks like truth. When striving for brevity, the poet becomes unintelligible. Attempts to write smoothly result in the loss of vigor and spirit. Aiming at grandeur, the poet becomes bombastic. Only when he or she is guided by art can a writer avoid some errors without committing worse ones. The remedy, therefore, is to select subjects equal to one's ability and to use appropriate language. Old words, properly used, seem new; new words, borrowed from the Greeks, may also have a place. People are admired for making over nature when they build harbors or drain marshes. Usage, then, should maintain or change the material and rules of speech.

Homer, according to Horace, shows the writer how to handle the deeds of kings and the sad tales of war. No one is sure who invented the elegiac couplet, but Archilochus devised the iambus, used in tragic and comic drama; and since it was born of rage, it is designed to record action. According to tradition, the Muses gave the lyric for singing about victories, lovers, and joyful banquets. All these meters have their specific uses, and the poets would do well to employ them only in their appropriate places, though sometimes a writer of comedy may borrow from other forms of poetic art or an author of tragedies set aside sesquipedalian words in favor of shorter ones to touch the hearts of his or her audience.

Horace continues by defining feeling as the true test of literary worth, for beauty of writing is not enough. Unless a writer feels, he or she cannot make the audience feel. One style of writing goes with a gloomy face; another sort goes with an angry one, or a playful one. Nature first makes one reveal one's feelings physically; then, with the tongue for an interpreter, she voices the emotions of the heart. There is also a difference in language between the gods and humanity, between old and young, between merchants and farmers, between Colchians, Assyrians, and Thebans.

Either follow tradition or be consistent in one's inventions, Horace advises. Achilles on the stage must be hot-tempered, appealing to the sword rather than to the law. Follow tradition and make Medea haughty, Ino tearful, and Ixion perjured. If the writer presents original characters, they must be consistent. One should not let them be too bombastic or promise too much out of prudent fear that the mountain in labor will bring forth no more than a ridiculous mouse.

If the writer wishes the applause of an audience, he or she must paint accurately the characteristics of the four ages of humankind. The young boy is unsettled and changing; the beardless youth is fond of horses and dogs, boastful, scornful of advice; in middle age, people are ambitious but cautious; and the elderly are surrounded by discomfort. One should not, in Horace's opinion, attribute the wrong qualities to a stage of human life.

In touching lightly on the rules laid down by classical dramatists, Horace believed in the superiority of showing action rather than telling about it. He does add that there are things too horrible to be seen. He comments on the number of actors—only three—and the place of the chorus. He comments on the rules and restraints of satyric drama. Then, after an appeal that Greek, not Roman, tastes be followed in selecting verse forms, he embarks on a history of the theater.

Slightly confused, he gives Thespis credit for inventing the tragedy, yet he describes him as traveling in a cart to put on plays in which the faces of actors were stained by dregs of wine. Then came Aeschylus, with the invention of the raised stage, the mask, and the buskins. Old comedy followed, soon to degenerate into license, and the chorus lost its role of criticism of the characters.

Roman playwrights, he continues, tried all forms of drama, but most were not successful because they were careless. Horace adjures his student reader to condemn any literary composition that has not been erased and amended. Even genius cannot discard rules. Characterizing himself, he says that he is too lazy to be a genius; he will perform his duty and criticize.

Answering the question of what to write, Horace declares that knowledge is the basis of good writing and that moral philosophy will supply matter. Life and manners should also occupy a writer's attention. The purposes of the poet should be to benefit and to entertain. "He has received the votes who has mingled the useful and the sweet, by instructing and delighting the reader at the same time."

Horace continues to advise hopeful poets that people do not always expect perfection from a poet. Some faults can be pardoned, for even Homer failed at times, though usually he excelled in his craft. Continued carelessness, however, is unforgivable, and eternally second-rate material cannot be tolerated. A person who cannot play the game should keep off the field unless he craves the jeers of the spectators. He advises Piso's son that, if he should write anything, he should let the censor of plays see it and then show it to his father and to Horace himself. Afterward, he should keep it in his desk for nine years. What one has not published, one can always destroy.

The final eighty lines of the poem deal with generalities. In the early days, says Horace, Orpheus represented the dignity of poets who, by their wisdom, distinguished between public and private property, divine and earthly things, lore and law. By their songs, they won honor. Homer and Tyrtaeus inspired men to battle; oracles guided men by their verses. It is still a question for debate whether a poet is born or made, but without both art and study even a genius will fail.

The best of writers need criticism, but they should avoid mere flatterers. One good critic used to mark, for improvement and reworking, lines in poems submitted to him, and if the would-be poet defended his mistakes, the critic had no more to do with him. The honest critic puts black marks before poor verses as Aristarchus did to Homer. Self-willed poets will not like such treatment, comments Horace, but in that case they are not worth trying to save. They are probably mad, each one, like a bear clawing at an innocent bystander. Such poets will be one's death, reading one their poetry.

Bibliography:
Armstrong, David. "The Addressees of the *Ars Poetica*: Herculaneum, the Pisones, and Epicurean Protreptic." *Materiali e Discussioni* 31 (1993): 185-230. This important article on the *Ars poetica* sheds fresh light on old problems. In particular, it discusses the specifics of the Epicurean use of free speech as therapy and its function as a model for Horace's *Ars poetica*.
Brink, Charles O. "Cicero's *Orator* and Horace's *Ars Poetica*." *Ciceroniana* 2 (1975): 97-106. An informative article clarifying issues on the relation, function, and sources of the two works.
_____. *Horace on Poetry.* Cambridge, England: Cambridge University Press, 1963-1982. The most comprehensive work on the *Ars poetica*. Its three volumes explore the sources of the poem and offer an edition of and extensive commentary on the text, accompanied by discussion of the poem's literary milieu. An annotated edition of Horace's other literary epistles complements his views on poetry.
Frischer, Bernard. *Shifting Paradigms: New Approaches to Horace's "Ars Poetica."* Atlanta: Scholars Press, 1991. This book reexamines the problems of genre, addressees, and date of the *Ars poetica*, reaching the innovative (but eccentric) conclusion that the poem is meant as a parody of pedantic criticism and not as a serious poetic treatise.

ART OF LOVE

Type of work: Didactic
Author: Ovid (Publius Ovidius Naso, 43 B.C.E.-17 C.E.)
First transcribed: Ars amatoria, c. 2 B.C.E. (English translation, 1612)

Art of Love is a set of entertaining and eminently practical instructions for successfully undertaking the game of love. The physical, not the philosophical, aspect of love is Ovid's sphere, and pleasure is its sole end. Two of the three books are addressed to young men, the third to young women. Together, they make up one of the earliest manuals of the type.

Choosing and winning the proper woman is the subject of the first book. Selection, Ovid encourages the potential lover, is easy: Rome is full of beautiful young women; one need only go where they are. He describes in detail the likeliest places: temples, law courts, the forum, the theater, the races, the baths, dinner parties. Once found, the woman must be brought to look favorably on the lover. Ovid's advice to this point is thorough and copious.

Be confident, he says, for all women want to be loved. Even if they do not want a lover, they will appreciate attention. Win over the lady's maid to advance your cause. A man should seduce the maid first, if he thinks it might help. He should write many letters; promise the beloved anything; plead eloquently; persist through constant refusals, and always be at her side. Advice on personal hygiene and fashion in dress is offered as well. Ovid tells of the usefulness of wine in warming hearts, and he explains how to handle a lady's husband. Weeping and pallor may gain a lady's pity, but timidity will never gain her favor. The man must take the initiative, and the woman will be glad of an excuse to give in. In short, a man should be adaptable and quick to seize any opportunity to win favor.

Book 2 consists of advice for holding the woman's love once it is won. Magic spells and potions will not work, Ovid assures his readers. To be loved, a man must be lovable. Physical beauty is good, but it fades in time. The mind and spirit must be cultivated. He advises the lover to learn tact, tolerance, gentleness, eloquence, humility. Never fight with a woman, for making up requires expensive gifts. Bear with her rages and unreasonableness. Let her win at games. Share her opinions and do all possible services for her. If a woman is ill, a man should be constantly in attendance.

A man should praise a woman elaborately and constantly. He should not let her find out about his other mistresses, unless he does so deliberately to make her jealous. If he knows she has other lovers, he should pretend not to know. He should not behave like a jealous husband. Never call attention to her imperfections or her age—mature women make better lovers, in any case. Finally, Ovid counsels, a man should learn the proper techniques in bed so that both partners may have the maximum of pleasure.

In Book 3, Ovid turns to advising women. He acknowledges that women also deserve some instruction in the art of love. He advises young women to taste love's delights now, before they grow too old to be desired by lovers.

Detailed advice is offered about improving one's appearance and dress, and how to enhance one's basic type. Cleanliness and cosmetics are discussed. A woman must learn to laugh, walk, talk, dance, and sing gracefully, play games well (but not too well), study some literature, and develop an even and pleasing temper. Women should make themselves available to lovers, Ovid says, by appearing in public places frequently. Beware of false or mercenary men, he warns, and do not believe everything a man says. Cultivate each man for his own particular talents and be especially pleasant to poets, for they can make a woman immortal in their verse.

A woman should not make it too easy for her lover, and should learn how to deceive her husband when necessary. She should not be violently jealous. She should make elaborate vows of love. Ovid also tells women what he has already told the men: learn to make love. Feign ecstasy even if you do not feel it. Be subtle and mysterious and desirable. Finally, when one is happy in love, one should remember to thank Ovid for showing the way.

Bibliography:

Binns, J. W. *Ovid*. London: Routledge & Kegan Paul, 1973. Includes A. S. Hollis' essay "The *Ars Amatoria* and *Remedia Amoris*," which uses close readings of selected passages to explore how Ovid combined material from traditional love elegies, didactic poetry, and Roman life.

Mack, Sara. *Ovid*. New Haven, Conn.: Yale University Press, 1988. Survey of Ovid's literary career, with a lengthy chapter on the love poetry. Asserts that Ovid creates a foolish speaker who uses his folly as a satire on Augustan values. Regards *Art of Love* as an assertion of poetic independence.

Myerowitz, Molly. *Ovid's Games of Love*. Detroit: Wayne State University Press, 1985. Discusses how love, like art, balances emotion and reason: Neither is natural; both are influenced by conventions. Love is a paradigm for the process of human culture, which liberates through a celebration of play but is constantly threatened by forces of nature.

Sharrock, Alison. *Seduction and Repetition in Ovid's "Ars Amatoria" 2*. Oxford, England: Clarendon Press, 1994. Connects the arts of love and poetry. Demonstrates that Ovid shows how one keeps the interest of the beloved and the reader. Examines Ovid's attitudes toward art and audience.

Wilkinson, L. P. *Ovid Surveyed; An Abridgement, for the General Reader, of Ovid Recalled.* Cambridge, England: Cambridge University Press, 1962. Good introduction to *Art of Love*. Notes its verbal subtleties and its relationship to the other poetry and the life of Augustan Rome.

THE ARTAMONOV BUSINESS

Type of work: Novel
Author: Maxim Gorky (Aleksey Maksimovich Peshkov, 1868-1936)
Type of plot: Family
Time of plot: c. 1863-1917
Locale: Russia
First published: Delo Artamonovykh, 1925 (English translation, 1927)

> *Principal characters:*
> ILYA ARTAMONOV, the father
> PYOTR ARTAMONOV, his oldest son
> NIKITA ARTAMONOV, his hunchbacked son
> ALEXEY ARTAMONOV, an adopted son
> NATALYA BAIMAKOV, Pyotr's wife
> ULIANA BAIMAKOV, the widow of the late mayor and Ilya's mistress
> ILYA, Pyotr's first son
> YAKOV, Pyotr's second son
> TIKHON VYALOV, a yardkeeper for the Artamonov factory

The Story:

About two years after the liberation of the Russian serfs, Ilya Artamonov arrived with his two sons, Pyotr and Nikita, and Alexey, his nephew and adopted son, in the little town of Dromov along the Vataraksha River. Ilya Artamonov had served as a bailiff to a prince, and the nobleman had recommended him highly to the authorities. Without giving the mayor of Dromov, Evgeny Baimakov, a chance for objections, Artamonov announced that he planned to build a linen factory and that he considered the mayor's daughter Natalya would make a good wife for his oldest son. Disregarding the resentment his dictatorial behavior provoked in the town, Artamonov went ahead with plans for the factory and preparations for Pyotr's marriage. The mayor, who died before the wedding, advised his wife Uliana to let Artamonov have his way. Pyotr's marriage to the mayor's daughter and the prospect of employment for many citizens did not, however, reduce the enmity felt toward the intruders.

When Uliana Baimakov became Ilya's mistress, she decided to live with the Artamonovs on the other side of the river, where the factory was located. Ilya tried to be a strict but humane superior to his men. Among his workers, Tikhon Vyalov was the ablest, although he begged not to be promoted because he did not want to supervise others. Meanwhile, Nikita, the hunchback, had fallen in love with Natalya, and when he overheard an unkind remark she made about him, he tried to hang himself. The attempt failed, and Nikita entered a monastery.

The factory developed rapidly under Ilya's direction. Pyotr was the second in charge. Alexey was unhappy at the factory and wanted to join the army, but Ilya refused to give him permission to enlist.

When Natalya bore her first child, the baby died after only five months. Another girl, Elena, followed. Then a much-desired son, also named Ilya, was born. Alexey married a woman nobody in the family liked or understood.

During the transportation of a heavy steam boiler, Ilya senior suffered a hemorrhage and died soon afterward. As time passed, Pyotr's only true happiness was his son. Against his wife's wishes, he let Ilya attend a good secondary school away from Dromov. While Pyotr devoted his time almost exclusively to the factory, Alexey made the necessary business trips to trade fairs and to Moscow. Although Natalya gave birth to a second boy, Yakov, Ilya remained Pyotr's favorite.

Despite all efforts to prepare Ilya as Pyotr's successor as the factory director, his son showed a completely different attitude. He liked to talk to Vyalov, the philosopher among the workers, whom Pyotr despised, and he also formed a close friendship with an uneducated child of a worker. After completing his schooling, Ilya announced his desire to become a historian. His father objected because he still wanted Ilya to take over the factory. Ilya refused and left Dromov without receiving any financial assistance from his father. Thereafter, Pyotr became an unhappy man; his wife could not please him, and he tried to find distraction with a local prostitute.

Often Pyotr had difficulty in controlling his temper, and one day he accidentally killed Ilya's former playmate. Vyalov, too, irritated him with philosophizing whenever he had a question to ask. Hoping to find some spiritual guidance, Pyotr finally decided to visit his brother Nikita in the monastery. Nikita explained that he had failed in his efforts to become a good monk. Although he considered himself unworthy, the monastery valued him highly because he was able to give visiting pilgrims some comfort with patient ears and empty phrases.

When Pyotr failed to find peace of mind with Nikita, he attended a trade fair in a nearby city. Alexey had told him so many exciting stories about city life that he hoped to find distraction there. After a series of extended drinking sprees and orgiastic behavior with prostitutes, he was finally discovered by Alexey, who had heard from a friend of the family about Pyotr's disgraceful behavior. Back home, Pyotr heard rumors that his son had become a member of a revolutionary extremist party. He also detected unusual new ideas in Alexey's son Miron. Only his younger son, Yakov, seemed unconcerned about the new ideas that were spreading among workers. Yakov was not good-looking; however, Pyotr considered his interests, mainly women, more normal than all the ideas expressed by the others, ideas which he believed a threat to the factory.

The rapid growth of the factory had brought a large settlement of workers to Dromov, along with many hardship cases. Pyotr tried to show his interest in his workers by building a new hospital or arranging a big party for them.

Alexey died suddenly. A telegram was sent to summon Nikita, but he had left the monastery. Only Vyalov knew his address. After the funeral, Nikita and Vyalov were seen together frequently. Pyotr's feelings grew against all people who did not think primarily of the factory, and when Nikita died four days before the outbreak of World War I, he had no kind word for his dying brother.

When Pyotr grew too old for most of the factory work and Yakov took over in his place, Yakov also became concerned over the growing signs of unrest among the workers. One worker, who spied for him in the factory, became his oppressor. Early in the war, many workers were drafted. Some returned, crippled, to the factory. Yakov's fear of being killed by his workers increased rapidly. He planned to go away with his mistress Pauline, a woman of easy virtue and expensive tastes. Trying to avoid suspicion, he let Pauline leave Dromov first. His own plan was to meet her in Moscow with all the money he could raise, but he never arrived in Moscow. Reports reached Dromov that he had been robbed, killed, and thrown from the train.

Pyotr, who had tried to ignore all rumors about uprisings and a new way of life for the workers, lived in a state of semicoma and asked constantly the whereabouts of Ilya and Yakov. He failed to realize what was going on around him until one day, he felt a sharp sense of hunger and realized that he was in his garden house. Outside he saw a soldier. When Pyotr called for his wife, only Vyalov came. He explained that Pyotr was a prisoner.

At first, Pyotr thought Vyalov was jeering at him. Later, he believed that he had been taken prisoner because someone had learned the truth about the death of Ilya's former playmate. Vyalov tried in vain to inform him about the revolution which had taken place and to explain that he was still alive only because of Ilya's influence. Pyotr thought Vyalov had gone mad. When Natalya arrived with a cucumber and a piece of bread, Pyotr considered himself insulted that she dared offer him such meager food when he was so hungry. Angrily, he threw the food away and with abusive words asked her to leave him alone.

Critical Evaluation:

In 1901, Maxim Gorky began to think about writing a novel tracing several generations of a Russian bourgeois family. It was more than twenty years before he actually published this work. In 1916, the publication of the novel was announced, only for Gorky to postpone writing it until after the October Revolution. Not until 1925, while living in Italy, did Gorky actually complete the novel, which depicts the beginning of industrial development in Russia, its brief flores-cence, and its downfall under the blows of the Bolshevik Revolution.

A former serf, Ilya Artamonov, the founder of the dynasty, is a typical representative of the newly born Russian merchant class. He builds a linen factory in a small provincial town of Dromov despite the hostility and apprehension of the townspeople. Energetic and self-confident, he neither looks back nor wastes his time. He goes forward destroying all obstacles to his goal and becomes the richest factory owner in his district. When Ilya dies, his sons take over and expand the business. Ultimately, however, the pattern is one of decline. Partly this is because of his sons' lack of vision, but mainly it is because of the impending revolution. Pyotr, as the oldest son, heads the factory, but lacks Ilya's enthusiasm or passion for work . He carries on the business as a heavy duty but does not really understand the purpose of his hard work. Although the factory prospers, Pyotr's alienation from his wife, children, and brothers grows. Trapped by the routines of life, unable to comprehend the political changes around him, he finds consolation in drinking and debauchery. His brother Nikita spends most of his life in the monastery telling beautiful lies to pilgrims who seek his advice. When he discovers that there is nothing spiritual or sacred even in the monastery, he returns home to die.

Unlike his brothers, Alexey Artamonov is full of energy and new ideas. He is interested in art and education, in the political and social life of the country. Always on the run, he is a real capitalist, a proprietor who believes in the power of millions of Russian men and in the possibility of creating a new Russian capitalist economy. His son Miron is also totally absorbed in the political and social issues of the day. He plans not only to become head of the business but to play an important political role in the renewed bourgeois Russia. Like other Russian bourgeois liberals, they try to turn Russian history in a new direction, toward industrialization, progress, and culture. Father and son symbolize the new Russian intelligentsia. They hold the future of Russia in their hands but are too weak and selfish to protect the country from the coming socialist revolution. The factory business born at the beginning of the novel dies with the arrival of the new era. The last pages of the book sound like an apocalypse—the end of the Artamonovs and their business, the end of all progressive beginnings. The finale is shocking. Pyotr Artamonov is dying, hungry, in his garden house, and the Red Army soldiers are patrol-ling his house. Only because his oldest son Ilya is a Bolshevik is Pyotr still alive. Gorky ends his novel with a revolution which brings neither triumph nor happiness, only bitterness and sadness.

Extraordinarily laconic yet amazingly full of depth, this novel imbues each detail with significance. Gorky describes with love and care the old Russian wedding ceremony, its traditions and rituals, brilliantly depicts several holiday celebrations and sprees at yearly merchant fairs, and sprinkles Russian proverbs, sayings, and folk poetry throughout. The action of the novel develops at different speeds. The first half of the book describes seven years of Ilya Artamonov's activities, which lay the foundation of his family business. The second half depicts the following forty-seven years in which not only the Artamonov dynasty but also the whole country flourishes and then collapses. Gorky masterfully uses real historical events of the first Russian Revolution of 1905, World War I, and the Revolution of 1917 as a background for portraying individual characters. He distances himself from the passing events and his heroes. Instead, it is the yardkeeper Tikhon Vyalov who survives all three generations of the Artamonovs as an independent witness and a secret judge. Ilya's grandchildren are born and then, like his sons, leave the stage; new characters appear, but Tikhon is still there. He watches everything, remembers everything, evaluating life and giving philosophical comments on the passing events. He is a symbol of the Russian people, a folk sage never precise about anything, who speaks in riddles and is an enigma himself.

Soviet critics praised *The Artamonov Business* for its truthful depiction of the growth of political activity of Russian working people and their fight against the bourgeoisie. They placed the novel among the best works in the traditions of Socialist Realism. With the collapse of communism and the Soviet empire, new Russian critics have rejected Gorky, blaming him for his direct call for terror and violence and for his justification of repression. The critical extremes of exaggerated praise and then equally exaggerated attacks are based on changing philosophical loyalties. Such criticism ignores the truly complex and contradictory personality of a great writer who was against any form of oppression and violence, who was for democracy and progress, who tried to depict life as it was and to understand what was going on in his beloved Russia. *The Artamonov Business* is a great proof of Gorky's quest to find the truth and to depict life as it was, with all its turmoil and injustice. The reader only has to look with open eyes devoid of political prejudice to see Gorky's honest attempt to capture social, political, and human complexities.

"Critical Evaluation" by Paulina L. Bazin

Bibliography:
Levin, Dan. *Stormy Petrel: The Life and Work of Maxim Gorky*. New York: Appleton-Century, 1965. The best interpretation of Gorky's life and literary activity. Chapter 34 gives a brief and very precise analysis of *The Artamonov Business* as a bitter statement about the Bolshevik Revolution of 1917.
Ovcharenko, Alexander. *Maxim Gorky and the Literary Quests of the Twentieth Century*. Moscow: Raduga, 1985. Gives a detailed analysis of Gorky's literary work. Chapter 3 gives a comprehensive analysis of *The Artamonov Business*, the history of its creation, the effect it had on world literature.
Scherr, Barry. *Maxim Gorky*. Boston: Twayne, 1988. Gives a brief biography of Maxim Gorky, literary analysis of his short stories, novels, plays, autobiographical writings, and essays on literature. Examines Gorky's depiction of historical changes in Russia by comparing *The Artamonov Business* with Gorky's last novel, *The Life of Klim Samgin* (1927-1936). A detailed bibliography is included.
Troyat, Henri. *Gorky*. Translated by Lowell Blair. New York: Crown, 1989. Gives the author's interpretation of Gorky's life and activity as a writer of the revolution, the founder of Socialist Realism. Brief reference to Gorky's literary canon, including *The Artamonov Business*.

Weil, Irwin. *Gorky: His Literary Development and Influence on Soviet Intellectual Life.* New York: Random House, 1966. An appreciation and evaluation of the social context and artistic merits of Gorky's works, including a brief and comprehensive analysis of *The Artamonov Business.*

AS I LAY DYING

Type of work: Novel
Author: William Faulkner (1897-1962)
Type of plot: Psychological realism
Time of plot: Early twentieth century
Locale: Mississippi
First published: 1930

> Principal characters:
> ADDIE BUNDREN, a dying old woman
> ANSE BUNDREN, her husband
> CASH,
> DARL,
> JEWEL, and
> VARDAMAN, their sons
> DEWEY DELL, their daughter

The Story:

Addie Bundren was dying. She lay in a bed in the Bundren farmhouse, looking out the window at her son Cash as he built the coffin in which she was to be buried. Obsessed with perfection in carpentry, Cash held up each board for her approval before nailing it in place. Dewey Dell, Addie's daughter, stood beside the bed, fanning her mother. In another room, Addie's husband, Anse, and two sons, Darl and Jewel, discussed the boys' plans to make a trip to sell a wagonload of lumber. Addie wished to be buried in Jefferson, the town where her relatives lay, and Anse was afraid that the boys might not get back in time to carry her body to the Jefferson graveyard. He finally approved the trip, however, and the boys set out.

Addie died while the two brothers were gone and before Cash could finish the coffin. When it was obvious that she was dying, a Dr. Peabody was summoned, but he came too late to help the sick woman. Vardaman, the youngest boy, arrived home with a fish he had caught, and his mother's death somehow became entangled in his mind with the death of the fish. Because Peabody was there when she died, Vardaman thought the doctor had killed her.

Meanwhile, a great rainstorm had arisen. Jewel and Darl were delayed on the road by a broken wagon wheel. Cash worked through the rain to finish the coffin. At last it was complete and Addie was placed in it, but the crazed Vardaman, who once had almost smothered in his crib, tried to let his mother out by boring holes through the top of the coffin.

After Jewel and Darl returned, neighbors gathered at the Bundren house for a funeral service conducted by Whitfield, the minister. Whitfield had once been Addie's lover and had fathered Jewel, the son whom she had seemed to favor.

Following the service, the family started out for Jefferson, but the rainstorm had so swollen the river that the bridge had been damaged and could not be crossed by wagon. After trying another bridge, which had also been washed out, they drove to an old ford near the first bridge. Anse, Dewey Dell, and Vardaman got across the river on the ruins of the bridge. Darl and Cash then attempted to drive the wagon across at the ford, with Jewel leading the way on his spotted horse, his one great possession. When the wagon was nearly across, a floating log upset it. Cash broke his leg and nearly died, and the mules were drowned; the coffin fell out and had to be dragged to the bank.

Anse refused to borrow mules, insisting that he must own the team that carried Addie to the grave. He made a trade in which he offered, without Jewel's consent, to give the spotted horse as part payment. When Jewel learned what his father had done, he rode off, apparently abandoning the group. Later, they discovered that he had put the spotted horse in the barn of Snopes, who was dickering with Anse. The family thus got new mules, and the trip continued.

By the time they arrived in Mottson, a town on the way to Jefferson, Addie had been dead so long that buzzards were following the wagon. They stopped to buy cement to strengthen Cash's broken leg, but the locals insisted that the wagon move on. The Bundrens, however, bought the cement and treated Cash's leg before they would budge. While they were in the town, Dewey Dell went to a drugstore to buy medicine that would abort the child she was carrying; she had become pregnant by a man with whom she had worked on the farm. The druggist refused to sell her the medicine.

Addie had been dead nine days and still was not buried. The family spent the last night before their arrival in Jefferson at the house of a Mr. Gillespie, who allowed them to put the malodorous coffin in his barn. During the night, Darl set fire to the barn. Jewel rescued the coffin by carrying it out on his back. Anse later turned Darl over to the authorities, who sent him to the asylum in Jackson.

Lacking a spade and shovel to dig Addie's grave, Anse stopped at a house in Jefferson and borrowed those tools. The burial finally took place. Afterward, Dewey Dell again tried to buy her medicine at a drugstore. One of the clerks pretended to be a doctor, gave her some innocuous fluid, and told her to come back that night for further treatment. The further treatment took the form of a seduction in the basement of the drugstore.

Cash's broken leg, encased in cement, had become so infected that Dr. Peabody said that Cash might not walk for a year. Before starting on the trip home, Anse bought himself a set of false teeth that he had long needed. He then returned the borrowed tools. When he got back to the wagon, he had acquired not only the new teeth but also a new Mrs. Bundren, the woman who lent him the tools.

Critical Evaluation:

Considered by many critics to be the greatest American fiction writer, William Faulkner was awarded the Nobel Prize in Literature in 1949, after a prolific career that included the production of nineteen novels and two volumes of poetry. Although his formal education had been limited, Faulkner read prodigiously, including the Greek and Roman classics, the Bible, and the works of William Shakespeare, the English Romantics, Joseph Conrad, James Joyce, and T. S. Eliot. After relatively undistinguished early attempts in poetry and prose, Sherwood Anderson advised Faulkner to concentrate on his "own postage stamp of native soil." This led to the saga of Yoknapatawpha County, a partly true regional history, based on Oxford, Mississippi, that merged imperceptibly into a coherent myth. Faulkner began the saga with *Sartoris* (1929) and continued it in *The Sound and the Fury* (1929) and *As I Lay Dying*.

In the Yoknapatawpha novels, Faulkner placed himself in the forefront of the avant-garde with his intricate plot organization, his bold experiments in the dislocation of narrative time, and his use of the stream-of-consciousness technique. His stylistic view of time was affected by his sense that past events continue into the present. As he once said, "There is no such thing as *was*; if *was* existed, there would be no grief or sorrow." These stylistic characteristics were undergirded by the development of a complex social structure that enabled Faulkner to explore the inherited guilt of the Southern past, the incapacity of the white aristocracy to cope with modern life, the relations between classes, and the relations between blacks and whites.

Starkly realistic, poignantly symbolic, grotesquely comic, and immensely complicated as an experiment in points of view, *As I Lay Dying* ranks with Faulkner's greatest novels. The relative simplicity of its style, characterized by staccato-like sentences and repetitive dialogue, enhances the tragicomic effect.

The novel's theme, in the very widest terms, is humanity's absurdly comic insistence on distinguishing between being and not-being. Peabody describes death as "merely a function of the mind—and that of the ones who suffer the bereavement." The theme is stated most clearly in the single chapter narrated from Addie's viewpoint: "I could just remember how my father used to say that the reason for living was to get ready to stay dead a long time." Addie has long since considered Anse dead, because she realizes that he, like most humans, cannot distinguish between the "thin line" of words that float upward into nothingness and the terrible reality of "doing [that] goes along the earth, clinging to it."

Nineteen of the fifty-nine chapters are narrated from Darl's viewpoint, making him the primary *persona* of the novel. His reference to his family's conglomerate madness sets the tone: "In sunset we fall into furious attitudes, dead gestures of dolls." The novel proceeds in a jerky, doll-like movement, as the narration passes through the viewpoints of fifteen different characters. Although Darl might be called the primary narrator, he is not the only interesting one. Vardaman, with ten chapters, displays a mentality reminiscent of Benjie's in *The Sound and the Fury*, showing the crazy events connected with the burial through the eyes of a confused and simple-minded child. The third chapter from his viewpoint consists of a single sentence: "My mother is a fish." Only three chapters present Anse's viewpoint, but that is enough to show that he is a bizarre combination of Darl's imagination, Vardaman's insanity, Cash's stubborn practicality, and Dewey Dell's earthiness.

Faulkner achieves his greatest artistic success with the least intrinsically interesting character, Cash. The first of the five chapters from Cash's viewpoint is an artistic coup. Until this point, the reader has repeatedly heard the steady buzzing of Cash's saw as he prepares his mother's coffin. Even through the rain and through the night, Cash will not cease his labor. In chapter 18, Cash speaks at last, saying "I made it on the bevel." Faulkner presents the carpenter's methodical mind in a straightforward list of his job-related preoccupations, beginning with "1. There is more surface for the nails to grip" and ending with "13. It makes a neater job." Cash's second chapter is a nine-line warning to his impatient father and brothers that the coffin is not "on a balance" in the wagon. After the tragedy in the river results from their ignoring his warning, Cash offers his laconic commentary in a chapter of only three lines. He remarks again that the coffin "wasn't on a balance" and does not even mention that his own leg has been broken. Cash's single-minded craftsmanship and superhuman patience become a reflection of the author's own technique.

"Critical Evaluation" by Kenneth John Atchity

Bibliography:

Bleikasten, André. *Faulkner's "As I Lay Dying."* Translated by Roger Little. Rev. ed. Bloomington: Indiana University Press, 1973. The only book-length study of Faulkner's novel. Lucid and comprehensive; an excellent starting point for serious study. Discusses Faulkner's manuscript and typescript and includes two facsimile pages.

Blotner, Joseph. *Faulkner: A Biography.* 2 vols. New York: Random House, 1974. An enormously detailed work. Begins with discussion of Faulkner's ancestors and traces the writer's development from precocious poet to preeminent novelist.

Cox, Dianne L., ed. *William Faulkner's "As I Lay Dying": A Critical Casebook*. New York: Garland, 1985. Contains a dozen essays examining such topics as the novel's chronology, language, and narrative design. Interesting individual chapters focus on the novel's debt to the Cubist movement and to the works of T. S. Eliot. Extensive annotated checklist of criticism.

Vickery, Olga W. *The Novels of William Faulkner*. Baton Rouge: Louisiana State University Press, 1959. A classic treatment of the Faulkner canon, still relevant despite years of subsequent scholarship. Asserts that the heart of *As I Lay Dying* is not the fulfillment of the burial promise but rather Addie herself and her effect on the Bundren family.

Volpe, Edmond L. *A Reader's Guide to William Faulkner*. New York: Noonday Press, 1964. An excellent beginner's source for discussion of Faulkner's works. Analyzes structure, themes, and characters and includes a useful appendix that clarifies the often-confusing chronologies and scene shifts of Faulkner's complex novels.

AS YOU LIKE IT

Type of work: Drama
Author: William Shakespeare (1564-1616)
Type of plot: Comedy
Time of plot: Middle Ages
Locale: Forest of Arden, France
First performed: c. 1599-1600; first published, 1623

Principal characters:
    THE BANISHED DUKE
    FREDERICK, his brother and usurper of his dominions
    OLIVER, the older son of Sir Rowland de Boys
    ORLANDO, the younger son of Sir Rowland de Boys
    ADAM, a servant to Oliver
    TOUCHSTONE, a clown
    ROSALIND, the daughter of the banished duke
    CELIA, the daughter of Frederick

The Story:

A long time ago, the elder and lawful ruler of a French province was deposed by his younger brother, Frederick. The old duke, driven from his dominions, fled with several faithful followers to the Forest of Arden. There he lived a happy life, free from the cares of the court and able to devote himself at last to learning the lessons nature had to teach. His daughter, Rosalind, had remained at court as a companion to her cousin Celia, the daughter of the usurping Duke Frederick. The two girls were inseparable, and nothing her father said or did would make Celia part from her dearest friend.

One day, Duke Frederick commanded the two girls to attend a wrestling match between the duke's champion, Charles, and a young man named Orlando, who was a special object of Duke Frederick's hatred because he was the son of Sir Rowland de Boys, who had been one of the banished duke's most loyal supporters. When Sir Rowland died, he had charged his oldest son, Oliver, with the task of looking after his younger brother's education, but Oliver had neglected his father's charge. The moment Rosalind laid eyes on Orlando she fell in love with him, and he with her. She tried to dissuade him from an unequal contest with a champion so much more powerful than he, but the more she pleaded the more determined Orlando was to distinguish himself in his lady's eyes. In the end he completely conquered his antagonist and was rewarded for his prowess by a chain from Rosalind's neck.

When Duke Frederick discovered his niece's interest in Sir Rowland's son, he immediately banished her from the court. Rosalind disguised herself as a boy and set out for the Forest of Arden, accompanied by Celia and the faithful Touchstone, the jester. Orlando had also found it necessary to flee because of his brother's harsh treatment. He was accompanied by the faithful servant Adam, an old man who willingly turned over his life savings of five hundred crowns for the privilege of following his young master.

Orlando and Adam set out for the Forest of Arden, but before they had traveled very far they were both weary and hungry. While Adam rested in the shade of some trees, Orlando wandered into that part of the forest where the old duke was, and came upon the outlaws at their meal. Desperate from hunger, Orlando rushed upon the duke with a drawn sword and demanded food.

The duke immediately offered to share the hospitality of his table, and Orlando blushed with shame over his rude manner. He would not touch a mouthful until Adam had been fed. When the old duke found that Orlando was the son of his friend, Sir Rowland de Boys, he took Orlando and Adam under his protection and made them members of his band of foresters.

Rosalind and Celia also arrived in the Forest of Arden, where they bought a flock of sheep and proceeded to live the life of shepherds. Rosalind passed as Ganymede, Celia, as her sister Aliena. They encountered real Arcadians—Silvius, a shepherd, and Phebe, a dainty shepherdess with whom Silvius was in love. The moment Phebe laid eyes on the disguised Rosalind, she fell in love with the supposed young shepherd and would have nothing further to do with Silvius. Disguised as Ganymede, Rosalind also met Orlando in the forest, and twitted him on his practice of writing verses in praise of Rosalind and hanging them on the trees. Touchstone displayed the same willfulness and whimsicality in the forest that he had shown at court, even in his love for Audrey, a country girl whose sole appeal was her unloveliness.

One morning, as Orlando was on his way to visit Ganymede, he saw a man lying asleep under an oak tree. A snake was coiled about the sleeper's neck, and a hungry lioness crouched nearby ready to spring. He recognized the man as his own brother, Oliver, and for a moment he was tempted to leave him to his fate. Then he drew his sword and killed the two animals. In the encounter, he himself was wounded by the lioness. Because Orlando had saved his life, Oliver repented and the two brothers were joyfully reunited.

His wound having bled profusely, Orlando was too weak to visit Ganymede, and he sent Oliver instead with a bloody handkerchief as proof of his wounded condition. When Ganymede saw the handkerchief, the supposed shepherd promptly fainted. The disguised Celia was so impressed by Oliver's concern for his brother that she fell in love with him, and they made plans to be married on the following day. Orlando was overwhelmed by this news and a little envious, but when Ganymede came to call upon Orlando, the young shepherd promised to produce the lady Rosalind the next day. Meanwhile Phebe came to renew her ardent declaration of love for Ganymede, who promised on the morrow to unravel the love tangle of everyone.

Duke Frederick, enraged at the flight of his daughter, Celia, had set out at the head of an expedition to capture his elder brother and put him and all his followers to death. On the outskirts of the Forest of Arden he met an old hermit who turned Frederick's head from his evil design. On the day following, as Ganymede had promised, with the banished duke and his followers as guests, Rosalind appeared as herself and explained how she and Celia had posed as the shepherd Ganymede and his sister Aliena. Four marriages took place that day with great rejoicing between Orlando and Rosalind, Oliver and Celia, Silvius and Phebe, and Touchstone and Audrey. Frederick had been so completely converted by the hermit that he resolved to take religious orders and straightway dispatched a messenger to the Forest of Arden to restore his brother's lands and those of all his followers.

Critical Evaluation:

William Shakespeare took most of the plot of *As You Like It* from a popular novel of the period, Thomas Lodge's *Rosalynde* (1590). What he added was dramatic characterization and wit. The play, a splendid comedy on love and life, is compounded of many elements, the whole set to some of Shakespeare's loveliest poetry. *As You Like It* more than fulfills the promise of its title. Its characters are, for the most part, wonderfully enamored of love, one another, and themselves. The play has freshness and vitality and, although adapted from an older story full of artifice, suggests a world of spontaneity and life.

As You Like It is often called a pastoral comedy because it employs the conventions of pastoral literature. Beginning in the third century B.C.E. and popular in the late sixteenth century, pastoral literature enabled poets, novelists, and dramatists to contrast the everyday world's fears, anxieties, disloyalties, uncertainties, and tensions with the imagined, mythical world where peace, longevity, contentment, and fulfillment reigned. Each age develops its own manner of describing lost happiness, far removed from the normal toil of human existence; the pastoral was the dominant vision in the late sixteenth century.

In the pastoral, the mythic, lost world is set in a simple, rural environment, which then becomes the image of all things desirable to honest people. *As You Like It* is typical of this convention and contains two contrasting worlds: the world of the court and the rural world—in this case the Forest of Arden. The court is inhabited by corrupt men such as Duke Frederick and Oliver. It is not significant that the gentle banished duke, Orlando, Rosalind, and Celia also once resided there. Rather, as the play develops, the court is the natural home of the wicked and ambitious. The audience is not shown the degeneration of Duke Frederick and Oliver; they are naturally wicked, and the court is their proper milieu.

The elder duke, Orlando, Rosalind, and Celia, on the other hand, are naturally good and the forest their natural milieu. If the court represents elaborate artifice, ambition, avarice, cruelty, and deception, the forest represents openness, tolerance, simplicity, and freedom. Rather than developing complex characters such as Hamlet, who like most humans has good and bad characteristics, pastorals apportion good and bad traits to separate characters, an allocation that imposes a necessary artifice upon the play and colors all actions, from falling in love to hating or helping a brother. A play such as *As You Like It* does not present natural behavior. On the other hand, by his adroit use of the conventions and artifice, Shakespeare achieved a remarkable exploration of love and its attendant values.

In the opening scene, Orlando, who has been denied an education and kept like an animal by his brother, is seen to be naturally good and decent. Talking to his brother Oliver, Orlando says, "You have train'd me like a peasant, obscuring and hiding from me all gentleman-like qualities. The spirit of my father grows strong in me, and I will no longer endure it: therefore allow me such exercises as may become a gentleman. . . ." Oliver, as naturally wicked as Orlando is naturally decent, says, "for my soul—yet I know not why—hates nothing more than he." Logic has no necessary place in this world. Love, however, does.

Love is a natural part of the pastoral world. Practically at first glance, Rosalind and Orlando are in love. Shakespeare's magic in *As You Like It* is to take the contrived love that is the expected part of the pastoral convention, and make of it a deeply felt experience that the audience can understand. Shakespeare manages this not only through the extraordinary beauty of his language but also through the structure of his play.

As You Like It is full of parallel actions. Orlando and Rosalind meet and immediately fall in love. Silvius and Phebe are in love. Touchstone meets Audrey in the forest, and they fall in love. At the end of the play Celia meets the reformed Oliver, and they fall in love just as quickly as Rosalind and Orlando had at the beginning of the play. The love match at the play's end nicely sets off the love match at the beginning.

Each love pairing serves a particular purpose. The focus of the play is primarily upon the Rosalind-Orlando match. Rosalind is the more interesting of the pair, for while she recognizes the silliness of the lover's ardor, she is as much a victim as those she scorns. In Act IV, while in boy's disguise, she pretends to Orlando that his Rosalind will not have him. He says, "Then . . . I die." Her response pokes fun at the expiring love: "No, faith, die by attorney. The poor world is almost six thousand years old, and in all this time there was not any man died in his own person, videlicet, in a love-cause. . . . Men have died from time to time and worms have eaten them, but not for love." She can toy with Orlando in her disguise as Ganymede, yet she is completely dominated by her strong passion, which is a part of the love experience. Rosalind's and Orlando's passion, however, is more refined than the passion the others experience.

Touchstone, in his quest for Audrey, exemplifies the earthier side of love. He at first wants to marry her out of church so that he can, once he tires of her, claim their marriage was invalid. The kind of love he represents is physical passion. The Phebe-Silvius pairing shows yet another face of love, that of the typical pastoral lover hopelessly in love with a fickle mistress. He sighs on his pillow and breaks off from company, forlornly calling out his mistress' name. Touchstone's and Silvius' kinds of love are extreme versions of qualities in Rosalind's love. In the comedies Shakespeare often used this device of apportioning diverse characteristics to multiple characters rather than building one complete character. Without Touchstone, love in the play might have been too sentimental to take seriously. Without Silvius, it might have been too crude. With both, love as exemplified by Rosalind and Orlando becomes a precious balance of substance and nonsense, spirituality and silliness.

Curious things happen in *As You Like It*. Good men leave the honorable forest to return to the wicked court. Wicked men who enter the forest are converted in their ways. At the end of the play, Oliver, who came to the Forest of Arden to hunt down his brother Orlando, gives his estate to Orlando and marries Celia, vowing to remain in the forest and live and die a shepherd. Duke Frederick came to the Forest of Arden in order to kill his brother. Meeting "an old religious man" in the forest, Duke Frederick "was converted/ Both from his enterprise and from the world." He too gives up his estate and his crown to his brother. The forest, the pastoral world, has the power to convert.

Why, then, do the elder duke, Orlando, and Rosalind elect to return to the court, home of wickedness? They do so because *As You Like It* is ultimately not a fairy tale but an expression of humanly felt experiences. The forest is a cleansing and regenerative experience, a place to which to retire to renew simplicity, honesty, and virtue. It is not, however, a permanent retreat. Good men stained by labor and trouble in their everyday world in the end must participate in that world. If they retreat to the pastoral world to renew themselves, they must return in the end to the community to take on the responsibilities all must face.

"Critical Evaluation" by Brian L. Mark

Bibliography:

Halio, Jay L., ed. *Twentieth Century Interpretations of "As You Like It."* Englewood Cliffs, N.J.: Prentice-Hall, 1968. Includes essays by Helen Gardner, John Russell Brown, Marco Mincoff (on Lodge's *Rosalynde* as the source), and the editor (on time and timelessness in Arden). Also includes an introduction and bibliography.

Jenkins, Harold. "*As You Like It.*" *Shakespeare Survey* 8 (1955): 40-51. Mainly concerned with the structure of the play, this essay notes the dearth of big theatrical scenes and causally linked events, which are replaced by a more complex design that emphasizes comic juxtapositions.

Knowles, Richard. "Myth and Type in *As You Like It.*" *English Literary History* 33 (1966): 1-22. Discusses the many mythical allusions in *As You Like It* that make the literal action reverberate beyond itself. Hercules is the dominant mythological figure, whom by analogy Orlando resembles. Biblical overtones are also discussed.

Leggatt, Alexander. *Shakespeare's Comedy of Love.* London: Methuen, 1974. Leggatt shows how the forest scenes provide an imaginative freedom to explore ideas and play roles.

Partisan laughter against any one character in the play is discouraged, for the audience is reminded of the partiality of any single perspective.

Young, David. *The Heart's Forest: A Study of Shakespeare's Pastoral Plays*. New Haven, Conn.: Yale University Press, 1972. Young reviews the pastoral tradition and its salient characteristics, so important in this play, and shows how Shakespeare explored and exploited the medium of pastoral drama in *As You Like It* and other plays, including *The Winter's Tale* (c. 1610-1611) and *The Tempest* (1611). A deliberate self-consciousness, he says, pervades *As You Like It*, whose atmosphere of artifice and hypothesis is fostered by extensive use of "if," and whose major theme is self-knowledge.

ASH WEDNESDAY

Type of work: Poetry
Author: T. S. Eliot (1888-1965)
First published: 1930

After the 1922 publication of *The Waste Land* had established his reputation as a major poet, T. S. Eliot wrote one important poem, "The Hollow Men" (1925), which seemed at that time to be a postlude to its predecessor but which now appears more as a prelude to *Ash Wednesday*. In any case, it should be read as a connecting link between the two longer poems. Its theme is the emptiness of modern intellectualism, which amounts only to "Shape, without form, shade without colour,/ Paralysed force, gesture without motion." It is another aspect of the Waste Land, desiccated and meaningless, inhabited only by the empty and futile hollow men.

Ash Wednesday marks an important point in the author's poetic development, for it sprang directly from his acceptance of the Anglo-Catholic faith. This biographical aspect of the poem, even more than its theme, influenced its reception by Eliot's former admirers and caused a schism among them that was unexpectedly revealing about the pre-World War II mind.

The tone of the poem is the humility appropriate to *Ash Wednesday*, the first day of the penitential season of Lent; its theme is the dilemma of human beings who want to believe and yet cannot bring themselves to do so because of their dry, sterile intellectualism. This theme is stated in the first of the six parts: the poet, turning his irony upon himself, describes this characteristically twentieth century predicament of a man caught in the web of his own intellectualizing who can yet know that he must

> . . . pray that I may forget
> These matters that with myself I too much discuss
> Too much explain,
>
> and that at this stage of religious experience the proper prayer is
>
> Teach us to sit still.

Throughout this opening section sound the echoes of the Penitential Office, "Turn thou us, O good Lord, and so shall we be turned," and of Guido Cavalcanti's sixteenth century poem, "In Exile at Sarzana."

The second part of *Ash Wednesday* is based on a reminiscence of the Valley of Dry Bones described by Ezekiel, whose language it echoes. Eliot once said in a lecture that the three white leopards could be taken as representing the World, the Flesh, and the Devil. They have fed on the body of the speaker, but Ezekiel was told to prophesy that these bones should live again, that "I [the Lord] shall put my spirit in you, and ye shall live, and I shall place you in your own land." There is also the figure of the Lady, who seems to play a role analogous to that of Dante Alighieri's Beatrice as an intermediary; she is dressed in white, the color of Faith. The speaker, having been stripped of everything, has learned resignation, but through the intercession of the Lady and the prophecy of Ezekiel he has found hope.

The third section, with its description of the spiral stairway, obviously recalls Dante's winding ascent of the Purgatorial Mount. There seems to be no direct connection with any particular canto of the *Purgatorio* of Dante's *The Divine Comedy* (c. 1320), only a linking of the journey of purgation with the penitential spirit of Lent. There is also the glimpse through the window of a scene suggestive of sensual pleasure that distracts the pilgrim from his journey. Dante is again recalled in the fourth section, this time by the Earthly Paradise and the Divine

Pageant at the end of the *Purgatorio*. Again there are echoes: of St. Paul's *Epistle to the Ephesians* and of the "Salve Regina."

For the fifth section, Eliot made use of a sermon by Lancelot Andrews that he had already quoted in an essay on the Bishop: ". . . the Word of an Infant? The Word and not be able to speak a word?"—an elaborate play upon the word (speech), the Word (the Logos, the most abstruse of Christian doctrines), and the Word made Flesh.

The last section, doubling back on the opening lines of the poem, suggests a scene in a confessional ("Bless me father") during which the beauty of the natural world intrudes into the mind of the speaker and distracts him from his proper meditation. Thus the world seeks to draw human beings back to itself. The poem ends, appropriately, with words taken (with one slight change) from the Penitential Office for Ash Wednesday in the Book of Common Prayer: "And let my cry come unto Thee."

Eliot's *Ash Wednesday* deals with various aspects of a certain stage in religious experience: "Lord, I am not worthy"; it is a poem of spiritual exile, as Cavalcanti's was one of physical exile. The dweller in the Waste Land who "cannot drink/ there, where trees flower, and springs flow" must find his way back through penitence with the humble prayer: "Suffer me not to be separated."

This is a simpler poem than *The Waste Land*, though Eliot used many of the same technical devices of ellipsis and echoes. *Ash Wednesday* rises to heights of verbal beauty unequaled in any other contemporary verse. Its reception, however, was curious and not without irony. To many readers of the 1920's, Eliot had become a voice for the disillusionment of the now famous "lost generation"—a statement that he himself characterized as "nonsense." The year 1930, with its Marxian enthusiasm for proletarian literature, probably saw the high point of the secular humanism of the twentieth century; Bertrand Russell's *A Free Man's Worship* was dominant. It was among the adherents of this way of thought that Eliot's greatest admirers were to be found. His becoming a member of the Anglican church and writing a poem with a deeply religious theme was to them a grievous shock. Some flatly refused to believe in his sincerity, and many considered his membership in the Church of England a pose, a kind of romantic, aesthetic Catholicism. To others, to whom religion was a retreat from reality, a "failure of nerve," he was a lost leader, a writer whose significant work had ended with "The Hollow Men." Yet there is some truth to the claim that the publication of *Ash Wednesday* marked the beginning of the intellectual swing in Western thought from the left to the right, with the consequent decline of the secular humanist attitude.

Bibliography:
Ackroyd, Peter. *T. S. Eliot: A Life*. New York: Simon & Schuster, 1984. A very readable biography that treats Eliot's life as an integral part of his work. Also examines the critical reception of *Ash Wednesday* and its relationship to Eliot's other works, as well as the author's indebtedness to the Bible and Dante.
Gardner, Helen. *The Art of T. S. Eliot*. New York: E. P. Dutton, 1950. Chapter 5 offers a fine analysis of *Ash Wednesday* as a transitional work reflecting Eliot's emerging understanding of Christianity. Gardner analyzes this poem in the context of Eliot's other prominent poems such as *The Waste Land* and *Four Quartets* (1943).
Hinchliffe, Arnold P. *"The Waste Land" and "Ash Wednesday": The Critics Debate*. Atlantic Highlands, N.J.: Humanities Press International, 1987. A useful review of the critical reception of these two poems since publication. A fine introduction to major critics and positions held by them, along with a succinct and helpful bibliography.

Smith, Grover Cleveland. *T. S. Eliot's Poetry and Plays: A Study in Sources and Meaning.* 2d ed. Chicago: University of Chicago Press, 1974. A standard critical work on Eliot's poetry. Includes a detailed exploration of Eliot's clever use of allusions and quotations to express his spiritual and philosophical concerns.

Southam, B. C., ed. *T. S. Eliot, "Prufrock," "Gerontion," "Ash Wednesday" and Other Shorter Poems: A Casebook.* London: Macmillan, 1978. A collection of excerpts from the criticism of prominent critics. Contains five essays on *Ash Wednesday.*

ASHES

Type of work: Novel
Author: Stefan Żeromski (1864-1925)
Type of plot: Historical
Time of plot: 1796-1812
Locale: Poland and Spain
First published: Popioły, 1904 (English translation, 1928)

Principal characters:
RAPHAEL OLBROMSKI
CHRISTOPHER CEDRO, his friend
HELEN, Raphael's beloved
PRINCE GINTULT, a nobleman
ELIZABETH, the prince's sister
NARDZEVSKI, Raphael's uncle

The Story:

When he was very young, Raphael Olbromski paid a short visit to the secluded estate of his uncle, Nardzevski, who was fond of his nephew and initiated him into the art of hunting. The fierce old man was a firm adherent to feudal times and treated his peasants as serfs. Casper, his huntsman, was his only intimate. Raphael's visit came to a sudden end after the arrival of an Austrian official who lectured Nardzevski severely on not having paid the new taxes and for his treatment of his peasants. The old man had no intention of submitting to the Austrians. To emphasize his defiance, he practiced his pistol marksmanship in the dining hall. He also ordered his steward to summon all the peasants in the morning and arrange for a public flogging of a miscreant. Raphael never learned what happened afterward, because early in the morning he was bundled into a sleigh and sent home.

A great sleighing party one winter attracted all the gentry. Raphael, mounted on a spirited horse, followed Helen's sleigh closely. The party stopped to dance at Raphael's house, and his aristocratic father staged a big celebration. During the affair, Raphael managed to tell Helen that he would come to her window some evening at midnight. The party lasted for two days, but Raphael missed much of it because he slept in a drunken stupor.

At school, Raphael was no student, but he was a leader. One evening, he and Christopher stole a rowboat and went out into the ice-packed Vistula. When they tried to land, the thin shore ice broke, and the boys were soaked. As they went on toward school, they sank into a bog. They were nearly frozen before Raphael took decisive measures. He tore off his wet clothes and those of the weakened Christopher, and the boys pummeled each other to get warm. Then, quite naked, they ran back to school, where they were caught as they tried to slip inside. Christopher fell ill with fever, and Raphael, as the leader, was chastised. When the beadle tried to carry out the punishment, however, Raphael drew a knife, wounded the beadle, and escaped.

When Raphael arrived home in disgrace, his father imprisoned him in a small room and forbade the family to speak to him. Later, he had to spend months working with the peasants. One night, Raphael took a fine mare from the barn and rode through a storm to Helen's house. When a watchman came upon them in an outbuilding, Helen got back to her bedroom safely, but Raphael barely escaped the fierce watchdogs.

A storm came up, and Raphael was followed by four wolves. When his horse stumbled, the wolves were on him. Three brought down the horse; Raphael killed the fourth with his hands. Gravely wounded, he was found by an old peasant, who took him home. When he recovered, his family cast him out and sent him to live with his older brother Peter, whom they had cast out years before.

Peter, in poor health from war wounds, lived quietly. Raphael spent delightful months in idleness until the arrival of Prince Gintult, his brother's old comrade. Peter and the prince had angry words on the treatment of peasants, however, and as the result of the quarrel, Peter had a hemorrhage and died. Having lost his home and melancholy with memories of Helen, who had been taken out of the country, Raphael went to stay with the prince.

In the noble household, Raphael was half family, half guest. The prince gave him money for clothes, and others gave him errands to run. Raphael was attracted to the prince's sister Elizabeth, a haughty young girl. One day, while they were riding in a group, Elizabeth's horse ran away. Raphael rescued her and made the mistake of kissing her as he held her in his arms. She slashed his face with her whip.

The prince suddenly departed on a voyage to Venice and Paris, after paying Raphael's lodging in a school for a year. Raphael studied fairly well and spent his time profitably. When he was forced to return home, his stern father outfitted him in work clothes, and for four years he worked on the farm. His release came with an offer of a position from Prince Gintult.

In Warsaw, Raphael served as secretary to the prince, who was writing a vague philosophical treatise on Freemasonry. In order to continue the work on the secret lodge, Raphael was taken into an order of the Masons; soon afterward, he was accepted in society. Through the lodge, he met Helen again.

Raphael and Helen fled to the country to enjoy their love. One night, they slept in a cave in the mountains. Although Raphael was armed, brigands overpowered him as he slept and bound him while they attacked Helen. She escaped their clutches at last and jumped over a cliff.

While he was searching for Helen's body and tracking the brigands, Raphael was arrested by a patrol. He did not dare give his correct name or mention Helen for fear of defiling her memory. While in prison, he had a long siege of fever. More than a year passed before he was released.

Penniless and tramping aimlessly about the country, Raphael fell in with his old friend Christopher. The reunited friends spent happy months on Christopher's estate. Then a soldier who had been with Napoleon for twelve years fired their imagination, and Raphael and Christopher decided to leave that Austrian-dominated part of Poland and join the emperor. Aided by Elizabeth, who was now married and living near the border, they made a daring escape across the frontier.

As an enlisted man, Christopher crossed Europe with Napoleon and took part in the Spanish campaign. His most vivid impressions were those of the siege of Saragossa, where he distinguished himself for valor and saved a young girl from soldiers who had sacked a convent and raped the nuns. He was thrilled when Napoleon abolished the Inquisition. After being wounded, he saw the emperor at close hand.

Raphael saw action in Poland, where the Austrian legions were too strong for Napoleon's forces. Once the Poles were preparing to demolish a church held by the enemy. Prince Gintult, fighting as a civilian, attempted to save the church by interfering with the cannoneers, and Raphael helped him. For his deed, the prince was cut down by an officer's sword. In the confusion, Raphael carried the wounded nobleman away to his father's house.

When the fighting died down, Raphael was discharged. He went to live at his uncle's old estate, and for a time he was happy there. He rebuilt the barns demolished by the soldiers, cleared land, and began building a house. Just as he was finishing, Christopher arrived. Invalided out of the army but well again, he was impatient for action. Reluctant to leave his home, Raphael objected at first; finally, however, he agreed to accompany his friend. In the middle of August, 1812, the Polish Corps was united with the Grand Army, and Raphael returned to serve the emperor. At Orsha, Napoleon reviewed his hordes of Polish, Dutch, Italian, and German soldiers.

Critical Evaluation:

The idealistic hero of this novel, Raphael Olbromski, questions the meaning of existence; and certainly, in the course of his life, he had reason to doubt the purpose of human suffering. Yet he has an idealism that centers in his love for Helen and in his patriotism.

The plot of *Ashes* is romantic and fanciful, although often embellished with a realistic covering of details and description. At times it suggests the picaresque tales of Henry Fielding and other eighteenth century novelists, but it also has a lushness and romanticism that are more German than English. Raphael is essentially passive, letting others work on him; his actions are unpremeditated and often foolish. His father, the prince, the brigands, and others send him hither and thither, changing the course of his existence, and because he has no particular ambitions, he obeys or yields to these forces. He is, for example, led to join the Masons, but through no convictions of his own. He is impressionable, impetuous, and naïve, and he often gets into trouble, as when he and Christopher return to school naked, when he runs away, when he kisses Elizabeth after rescuing her, and when he and Helen flee together. More than once, his character and his adventures come close to straining the reader's credulity.

Stefan Żeromski possesses a gift for describing action. The novel is filled with excellently drawn scenes, including the hunting scene that opens the book, the scene of the sleighs rushing between estates during holiday festivities, the scene of riding through snow on Baska to Helen's house, and the scene of Raphael and Baska chased by wolves. The characterization, too, is often fine; Żeromski can in a single detail encompass a whole personality, as in his description of the superior half-smile always on the faces of Prince Gintult and his sister, Elizabeth.

Raphael is torn between the shallow society of the cities and the life of the country. He is educated but not dedicated to books or intellectual pursuits, preferring to hunt and roam about in the woods and fields. For a long time, he exists on the fringes of the great world, barely aware of the momentous happenings occurring elsewhere. Then he is caught up in the wheel of history, and when his fortunes become so low that they could not sink any lower, his old friend Christopher Cedro appears to save him.

Raphael tries to rebuild his uncle's old estate, but again history and Christopher carry him away, and once more his fate is determined by forces outside himself. Perhaps Żeromski is suggesting through the life of his protagonist that it is futile for people to struggle against the forces of destiny and history.

Much of this work is in the German Romantic tradition. Żeromski describes nature in great detail and devotes long sections to philosophical speculations engendered by contemplation of nature. The tragic love affair of Helen and Raphael and the frequent unconnected sequences of action are reminiscent of Johann Wolfgang von Goethe. By contrast, the scenes that describe some of the Napoleonic campaigns are precise and realistic. *Ashes* ranks high as a historical novel, and Zeromski has been acknowledged as a master of the genre.

Bibliography:
Czerwinski, E. J., ed. *Dictionary of Polish Literature*. Westport, Conn.: Greenwood Press, 1994.

A survey of Żeromski's career, explaining his role in the Young Poland movement and commenting on the impact of his novels. Cites *Ashes* as one of his best, in which he speaks to his countrymen about their heroism during the Napoleonic era.

Kridl, Manfred. *A Survey of Polish Literature and Culture.* Translated by Olga Sherer-Virski. New York: Columbia University Press, 1956. Considers Żeromski the chief spokesperson for the Young Poland movement of the late nineteenth century. Provides a lengthy discussion of several important novels, including *Ashes.* Examines the structure of the book and comments on the significance of a number of themes.

Krzyżanowski, Julian. *A History of Polish Literature.* Translated by Doris Ronowicz. Warsaw: Polish Scientific Publishers, 1972. Outlines Żeromski's literary career and discusses the sociological influences that inspired much of his fiction. Notes that the novelist criticizes the Polish people during the Napoleonic period.

Kuk, Zenon M. "Tolstoy's *War and Peace* and Żeromski's *Ashes* as Historical Novels." *Folio: Essays on Foreign Languages and Literatures* 14 (December, 1982): 1-7. Comparative study of two novels about the Napoleonic Wars, explaining how each uses materials from history to create fiction with a didactic purpose.

Miłosz, Czesław. *The History of Polish Literature.* London: Macmillan, 1969. Sketches the novelist's career and comments briefly on his major fiction. Remarks on the significance of his choice of the Napoleonic era as the subject of *Ashes.* Notes his strengths in handling his story compassionately and in dealing with the historical tradition, but faults him for having "a penchant for melodrama."

THE ASPERN PAPERS

Type of work: Novella
Author: Henry James (1843-1916)
Type of plot: Psychological realism
Time of plot: Late nineteenth century
Locale: Venice
First published: 1888

> *Principal characters:*
> NARRATOR, a young literary scholar
> JULIANA BORDEREAU, a very old woman, once the mistress of Jeffrey
> Aspern
> TINA BORDEREAU, her spinster niece

The Story:

In the 1880's, a young American literary scholar heard that a woman who had long ago been the mistress of the famous American poet Jeffrey Aspern was still alive, in Venice. It was rumored that this old woman, Juliana Bordereau, had a cache of Jeffrey Aspern's papers, mostly letters. Frantic to lay his hands on the papers, the young man vowed to do whatever it took to get hold of them. Unfortunately, Juliana Bordereau, who was said to be close to death, never received visitors.

Even though there was no proof that the papers even existed, the young scholar decided to try to gain entrance to the Bordereau villa as a lodger. "Hypocrisy, duplicity are my only chance," he declared. "I'm sorry for it, but there's no baseness I wouldn't commit for Jeffrey Aspern's sake." He managed to convince Tina, the niece, that he was a writer who needed solitude. Tina then presented him to Juliana who, after listening to his lies, agreed to let him stay, but at an exorbitant price.

Weeks went by without the scholar getting any closer to the papers. At times he suspected that the women were on to him and were only out for the money. Meanwhile, there developed between him and the women a cat-and-mouse game in which the women tantalized him with vague hints as to the existence of the papers while he tried to conceal his motive for being there.

The more he convinced himself that the papers existed, the more determined he was to get to them, and the more difficult the women made it. Although he was not in the least attracted to Tina, he worked hard to ingratiate himself with her. Slowly he would bring the conversation around to certain rare items Juliana might possess. When he finally admitted that, yes, he was a Jeffrey Aspern scholar, Tina ran out of the room. Oddly enough, a day or so later Juliana asked to see him, but nothing was said about his interest in Jeffrey Aspern or the existence of any papers. Instead Juliana seemed more interested in pushing him on Tina.

The upshot was that the scholar and Tina had dinner together during which Tina revealed that Juliana did, after all, have a lot of Aspern's papers. Fearing that Juliana might destroy them, the scholar asked Tina to help him save them, and she promised to do what she could. In the days that followed, there was more game playing as Juliana dickered for higher rent while she hinted at an eventual reward. "She was such a subtle old witch," thought the young man at one point as she offered to sell him a small oval portrait of Jeffrey Aspern. When he feigned ignorance of the man's identity, she mocked him.

One day Tina came to the young man saying her aunt was ill and probably dying. She then told him that Aspern's papers had been removed from a green trunk and stuffed between Juliana's mattresses only to be removed again and stuffed in an ornate secretary just outside Juliana's bedroom. As he was passing by that room late one evening, the scholar could not resist checking out the contents of the secretary. At that very moment, Juliana appeared, her eyes blazing, and called him a "publishing scoundrel!"

Shaken, the scholar left the villa the next morning, but returned sometime later to learn that Juliana had died. Tina told him she now had the papers and hinted that he could have them if he would marry her. Again he fled the villa, but eventually his passion for the papers overcame any scruple and he returned prepared to agree to Tina's bargain. It was too late; in revenge for his rejection, Tina announced that she had destroyed all the papers, "one by one." "It took a long time," she said cruelly, "there were so many."

Earlier Tina had given the scholar the tiny portrait of Jeffrey Aspern that Juliana had tried to sell him for a thousand pounds. The scholar accepted it at face value, never suspecting that it might be worthless. At the end of the story, after being rejected by Tina, the scholar sent her a thousand pounds, telling her he had sold the portrait. In reality, however, he kept it for himself and thus never knew how duped he had been all along.

Critical Evaluation:

The term "vampirism" has been used to label those characters in Henry James's fiction who will stop at nothing to get what they want. Often it is a psychological sort of vampirism in which one person bullies another into submission. In *The Aspern Papers*, the vampirism is more substantive. The young scholar wants something that belongs to someone else—the papers— and he schemes to get them regardless of the consequences to their owner, the aging and infirm Juliana Bordereau, or her penniless niece, Tina. In his ruthless quest for these papers, he is not above lying, dissembling, flattering, even stealing. At the same time he lies to himself, rationalizing his duplicity, justifying his strategies as necessary in an effort to rescue valuable materials from a selfish old woman who does not appreciate their value.

As is the case with so much of James's fiction, no character in *The Aspern Papers* is above reproach. It is clear from the first encounter that the scholar has met his match in the crafty old Juliana when she charges him an outrageous rent, which he pays without batting an eye. At that moment, both recognize that they are adversaries, but Juliana has the upper hand because she has the papers (or so she lets him believe). She uses her age and eccentricity to her advantage. Likewise, Tina, though slow to catch on, soon enough sees how, by letting herself be used, she can play both ends against the middle. She becomes the go-between, deceiving both the scholar and her aunt. When her scheme backfires, she takes revenge on the scholar by telling him she has burnt the papers. It is exquisitely cruel revenge, all the more so if it is a lie and there never were any papers.

The irony is bitter in this story, for it is quite possible that time, energy, and cunning are expended over papers that either do not exist or do not amount to much. Tina's renunciation of the scholar—after she has burnt her bridges—is a moment of the most hollow triumph, for in winning the game with the scholar, she has lost even more than he has.

Much has been made of James's keen dramatic sense, and it is nowhere more evident than in *The Aspern Papers*. At select moments along the way, there are climactic scenes at the end of which a curtain seems to fall. There is, for example, the highly theatrical scene in which Juliana catches the scholar as he is about to pilfer the papers. Then there is the scene in which Tina drives the scholar away with her thinly veiled proposal of marriage. The most dramatic scene occurs when Tina, in a chilling turn, renounces the man who has rejected her and boasts of how methodically she destroyed the papers and how long it took because there were so many.

The moral world James's characters inhabit is a warped one in which perceptions are distorted and traditional values perverted. To begin with, there is the question of obsession. It is clear that the scholar and Juliana share a common obsession with Jeffrey Aspern. In her case, it has made her a mean-spirited recluse whose dependency on Tina has robbed her niece of a life of her own. Even more selfish and inconsiderate is the scholar whose interest in Aspern the poet has degenerated into his interest in Aspern the celebrity. He, too, is willing to exploit Tina in his determination to possess the papers.

There is also the curious question of renunciation, a common theme in the works of James. Ordinarily, renunciation is an act of contrition, but for Tina it becomes an act of revenge against a man who trifled with her affections and against an old woman who drained Tina's lifeblood to sustain the memory of an ancient passion. Tina destroys her inheritance when she destroys the papers. Thus, James presents the seemingly noble act of turning one's back on evil as an even subtler manifestation of evil.

It would be a mistake, no matter how serious the subject matter, to overlook the humor in *The Aspern Papers*. The characters in this story are not dealing in matters of great importance. The letters, if they do exist, could be mere drivel; at best, they would probably do little except add to the gossip surrounding a legendary literary figure. To the scholar, the papers are valuable, not because of what they contain (after all, he has not yet seen them), but merely because they exist (if, indeed, they do). He expends a ridiculous amount of time, money, and guile in the pursuit of something so uncertain and, as far as the world is concerned, unimportant. He cuts a ridiculous figure as he loses at his own game and never really realizes by how much he has lost. Tina may play a monstrous joke on him, but she too is more a comic than a tragic figure when the joke turns out to be on her.

Ultimately, the key to the brilliance of this story is to be found in James's decision to have the scholar narrate his own story. In "telling on himself," so to speak, the scholar reveals how naïve he is; he learns nothing from his experience. Instead, he remains a poor judge of what is going on. This is why, at the end, the scholar can only stare at the (probably worthless) picture of Jeffrey Aspern and write to Tina, "When I look at it, I can scarcely bear the loss—I mean of the precious papers."

In writing this story, James revealed the shameful side of scholarship. The novel condemns the use of any means, no matter how devious, to exploit the famous, especially invading their privacy and violating their personal effects. The irony is that James knew it would probably happen to him after he was gone (it did).

Thomas Whissen

Bibliography:
Bell, Millicent. "*The Aspern Papers:* The Unvisitable Past." In *Meaning in Henry James.* Cambridge, Mass.: Harvard University Press, 1991. Insightful examination of James's own "second thoughts" as revealed in a preface written twenty years later for a revised edition. Bell's examination of James's revisions is particularly enlightening.
Edel, Leon. *Henry James: A Life.* Rev. ed. New York: Harper & Row, 1985. An acclaimed James scholar's biographical criticism is original and pertinent.
Hocks, Richard A. *Henry James: A Study of the Short Fiction.* Boston: Twayne, 1990. Contains a challenging exposition of critic Dennis Pahl's "deconstruction" of *The Aspern Papers*, relatively free of critical jargon. Good discussion of the story's "framing device."

Neider, Charles, ed. *Short Novels of the Masters*. New York: Holt, Rinehart and Winston, 1966. A reliable introduction to the novella—sensible, concise, and literate.

Perosa, Sergio. "Henry James: *The Aspern Papers*." In *Leon Edel and Literary Art*, edited by Lyall H. Powers. Ann Arbor: University of Michigan Press, 1988. A unique perspective from an Italian professor of Anglo-American literature.

THE ASSISTANT

Type of work: Novel
Author: Bernard Malamud (1914-1986)
Type of plot: Social realism
Time of plot: 1930's
Locale: Brooklyn, New York
First published: 1957

Principal characters:
> MORRIS BOBER, a sixty-year-old immigrant Jewish grocer
> IDA BOBER, wife of Morris Bober
> HELEN BOBER, twenty-three-year-old daughter of Morris and Ida
> FRANK ALPINE, a young Italian man, a drifter

The Story:

Morris Bober, a sixty-year-old Jewish immigrant owner of a small Brooklyn grocery store, was slowly being driven out of business by a fancy delicatessen-grocery recently opened around the corner. Rising at six on a cold, windy autumn morning to sell a three-cent roll to a sour-faced Polish woman, Morris began his daily routine of drudgery and frustration. Working long hours in a dreary store, Morris barely made a living for himself, his wife Ida, and his daughter Helen, who desired to go to college and live a meaningful life. Every afternoon Morris escaped the gloom of the store by retreating to his upstairs apartment for a nap, his "one refreshment" for the day.

Morris was a decent man in an indecent and abusive world. He was a commercial failure surrounded by success. The harder he worked, the less he seemed to have. He extended credit indiscriminately, even in cases where he knew he would never be repaid. If he could serve the people who still did business at his store he would. Morris would not ignore the needs of another human being. He said it is the least one man can do for another.

Two holdup men appeared one night near closing time. Unwilling to believe that the thirteen dollars in Morris' cash drawer could be his entire take for the day, one of the men pistol-whipped him. Sick of his meager existence and filled with self-disgust, Morris bitterly denounced the years of failure and the false hope of success in America. He felt a profound sense of isolation and sadness. He wanted more for his wife and daughter, yet was unwilling to compromise his ideals.

A young Italian drifter named Frank Alpine entered the store. He was one of the men who had robbed Morris earlier. Frank worshiped the gentleness and goodness of Saint Francis. He began to hang around the store, helped Morris in small ways, finally asking to be taken in as an assistant in order to gain experience. When Morris stumbled across Frank asleep in the cellar and learned that Frank had lived for a week on a daily bottle of milk and two rolls stolen from the doorstep each morning, he gave in and hired Frank. Ida was distrustful of having a Gentile in her house, but when Morris' head wound reopened, Frank took it upon himself to run the store while Morris recovered. Business picked up as the Gentiles in the neighborhood felt more comfortable with one of their own behind the counter.

Ida was suspicious that Frank was up to no good and fearful that he would try to seduce her daughter. Her fears were realized when Frank first spied on Helen naked in the bathroom, and later on when he tried to lure her to his room. Helen, despite strong doubts, found herself falling in love with Frank, but refused his sexual advances. She sought a good man to escape the tragedy of the past, and Frank resolved to be the kind of person Helen wanted him to be.

Helen wanted to be more self-disciplined and told Frank he needed to be also. Frank emptied stolen cash from his wallet into the register and found joy that he now had control over his life. A moment later, however, after Helen called for him to meet her that evening in the park, Frank took back a dollar from the register in order to bring Helen home in a cab. The theft was discovered by Morris and, despite Frank's pleas, Morris exiled Frank from the store.

That evening Frank went to the park vowing to show his love to Helen. She arrived ahead of him. Ward Minoque, the man who earlier robbed and beat her father, attempted to rape her. She was saved from rape by Frank's intervention, was then raped by him, and cursed him as an "uncircumcised dog!"

During Frank's exile, the Bobers' fate became worse. They discovered that the previous increase in trade was attributable not so much to their assistant as to the illness of the grocer around the corner. The delicatessen closed, but a new, larger, self-service store opened that would surely drive Morris into bankruptcy. At this point, Morris "accidentally" left the gas to his bedroom heater turned on while forgetting to light it and was taken to the hospital. Frank saved his life, returned and again took over the store, explaining to Ida that he owed something to Morris.

When Morris returned, Frank confessed to him that he was one of the men who robbed him. Morris surprisingly replied that he already knew this, but that he could not forgive Frank for stealing from the store after he had been taken in. Morris sent Frank away once again. Not long after, Morris died of pneumonia after shoveling the spring snow from the sidewalk for the few customers he had left. At the funeral, Frank tumbled awkwardly into the grave and climbed out again, symbolically reborn.

Frank came to take over the store again and declared he was a changed man. He worked at an all-night coffee shop and returned to the store every morning in time to sell the Polish woman her roll. Declaring his love for Helen he offered to finance her college education. Helen accepted and realized that something in him had changed. She thanked him for running the store and supporting the family. One day in April Frank had himself circumcised and felt both "enraged and inspired" by the pain between his legs. "After Passover he became a Jew."

Critical Evaluation:

Bernard Malamud's second novel, *The Assistant* was an immediate success and within a few years of its publication attained the status of an American classic. Based upon his own experience working behind the counter in his immigrant father's grocery store, this novel established Malamud as a major American writer. Along with Saul Bellow and Philip Roth, Malamud was one of three Jewish American writers whose ascendance in American literature resulted from their portraits of the Jew as a persuasive symbol of Everyman. The problem of marginality, of alienation and living on the edge, is central to the Jewish experience, and in their fiction these authors present an ambiguous, complex universe in which Everyman is trying to survive.

Influenced by existentialism, Malamud uses Jewishness as an ethical symbol. In his works, the Jew becomes the metaphor for the universal good person who must endure great suffering while striving to withstand the dehumanizing pressures of the world. Malamud's central metaphor of Jewishness is the prison (the grocery store in *The Assistant*), a perfect symbol for the human and, most particularly, the Jewish condition.

A predominant theme in modern Jewish prose, Malamud's in particular, is that when one strives to accommodate oneself to the world, one loses oneself in the process. In his portrait of

Morris Bober in *The Assistant*, Malamud is concerned with self and its standing quarrel with an aggressively materialistic American culture. Malamud reverses the traditional American success story, as Morris and later Frank succeed morally only by virtue of their failure in society.

Morris possesses an ancient identity, and his relationship to this identity determines his moral and ethical development. At one point in the novel, Morris tells Frank that the "Jewish Law" is the basis of his behavior. Later, at Morris' burial, the rabbi dignifies Morris' life by stating that he was "a true Jew" who lived "the Jewish experience" and "with a Jewish heart." Morris suffers and endures, "but with hope."

Malamud's use of Jewish humor and irony help to explain his conflicting beliefs of optimism and pessimism and the balanced interplay of hope and despair in his art. Morris is a schlemiel, a character from Yiddish folk literature who is repeatedly knocked down by fortune but who always struggles to his feet to try his luck again. Hoping for the best but expecting the worst, Morris is constantly aware of the absurdity of his situation and his actions in the face of an unlucky fate. Malamud believes that "all men are Jews" because all people have the possibilities to be good. In a world of chaos and suffering, this moral code brings sanity and significance to one's life.

In *The Assistant*, Frank has the possibility of redemption. When Morris dies, the unwitting saint father makes way for the saint-elect prodigal son, the first life creating the pattern and possibility for the second. In continuing Morris' life, Frank fulfills the possibilities of the grocer's actual son, who died while still a child. In suffering for Morris and accepting responsibility, Frank achieves his own redemption, becoming at last an honest and good man. Although his struggle to survive and escape the tragedy of the past is, at the end of the novel, just beginning, Frank has the possibility to be human, to create meaning in life. His purification through pain and suffering and his struggle for rebirth through selfless love and ethical behavior represents Malamud's hope that people can prevail.

Malamud is an intensely moral writer who once said it was the writer's responsibility "to keep civilization from destroying itself." Malamud has consistently emphasized that he bases his writing on a belief in the nobility of the human spirit and that only readers who respect human beings can respect his work. His humane sensibility encompasses both human pain and human potential. He writes in defense of human beings. The humor and irony, tragic vision, and possibility for profound human decency that Malamud weaves throughout *The Assistant* stand as a testament to that defense.

In revealing the mystery of humankind in this brilliant work, Malamud shows faith and a sense of awe for the human capacity to endure. Malamud's work reflects his despair of the futility of humane values in the face of contemporary reality, yet he continues to fill his fictional world with love and beauty, compassion and hope, and to affirm life in spite of its ambiguities.

Milton S. Katz

Bibliography:
Alter, Isaka. "The Good Man's Dilemma: *The Natural, The Assistant*, and American Materialism." In *Critical Essays on Bernard Malamud*, edited by Joel Salzberg. Boston: G. K. Hall, 1987. Focuses perceptively on the social criticism in Malamud's fiction that most critics generally ignore.
Freedman, William. "From Bernard Malamud with Discipline and Love (*The Assistant* and *The Natural*)." In *Bernard Malamud: A Collection of Critical Essays*, edited by Leslie A. Field and Joyce W. Field. Rev. ed. Englewood Cliffs, N.J.: Prentice-Hall, 1975. Analyzes how

Frank Alpine, through submitting to the will of Morris Bober and his own conscience, undergoes a spiritual and psychic conversion. Frank is transformed from an "uncircumcised dog" to a "man of stern morality."

Helterman, Jeffrey. *Understanding Bernard Malamud*. Columbia: University of South Carolina Press, 1985. A highly readable guide. Chapter 3 discusses the themes, use of language, points of view, structure, and symbolism of *The Assistant*. The annotated bibliography is especially useful.

Hershinow, Sheldon J. *Bernard Malamud*. New York: Frederick Ungar, 1980. Offers a comprehensive analysis of *The Assistant*, discussing the themes of suffering and redemption, how Malamud relates to the American Dream of success, his use of Jewish humor and irony, and the skillful use of language in the novel.

Richman, Sidney. *Bernard Malamud*. Boston: Twayne, 1966. Chapter 3 provides an excellent, detailed analysis of *The Assistant*. The author concludes that *The Assistant* brought to literature a sense of awe for humanity's capacity to endure and for humanity's enigmatic powers of creation.

ASTROPHIL AND STELLA

Type of work: Poetry
Author: Sir Philip Sidney (1554-1586)
First published: 1591

Although itself an imitation of the much earlier Italian sonnets of Francesco Petrarca (1304-1374), better known as Petrarch, Sir Philip Sidney's sonnet sequence *Astrophil and Stella* helped create the vogue for that genre in late Elizabethan England. It was the first great Elizabethan sonnet sequence, predating William Shakespeare's by at least a decade. For the student of Sidney's life and poetry, it has additional interest for its autobiographical implications, reflecting Sidney's vain attempt to woo Penelope Devereux (1563-1607).

Born to an influential noble family, Sidney considered his most important role in English letters to be that of a patron rather than a poet. His support of poets Edward Dyer, Fulke Greville, and Edmund Spenser (whose *Shepheardes Calender* of 1579 was dedicated to Sidney) expressed his conviction that the English language could rival French and Italian in poetic beauty, a conviction he expressed in his posthumously published *Defence of Poesy* (1595). His own poetry was well known among Elizabethan noblemen but not published until after his death.

Although it is easy to exaggerate the autobiographical element in the *Astrophil and Stella* sonnets, there is little doubt about the identity of the two main characters of the title. "Stella" is Penelope Devereux, the beautiful daughter of the first earl of Essex. The earl's dying wish was for Penelope to marry Sidney, but at that time, in 1576, she was but thirteen, and there is little likelihood that Sidney had even met her. He probably did not meet her until the summer of 1581, and in November 1 of that year she married Robert, third Baron Rich.

By bestowing the pseudonym "Stella" on the object of his sonnets, Sidney was following the pattern in amorous poetry set by Petrarch, who in his sonnets celebrated his beloved under the name of "Laura." Yet with the name "Stella" Sidney is able to attain further significance, for as well as being a female name it is the Latin word for "star." The speaker of the sonnets, then, the lover of Stella, is aptly named "Astrophil," or "star-lover" in Greek; moreover, the "phil" coyly echoes Sidney's first name. There is no doubt about associating Astrophil with Sidney: In Sonnet 30 we are told that Astrophil's father was governor of Ireland, as was Philip Sidney's, and Sonnet 65 describes Astrophil's coat of arms, which is clearly that of the Sidney family. (Similarly, the Devereux coat of arms is described as Stella's in Sonnet 13.)

Sidney's sonnets, like Petrarch's, form a "sequence," a group of sonnets each of which is an artistic whole, yet which together develop a pattern of ideas. This pattern is not a "story" or "plot," for the form is not exactly narrative, but a development of character or emotions. Each sonnet explores a slightly different aspect of the love between Astrophil and his Stella, and from one sonnet to another their situation changes. Throughout the sequence, Stella is already married to another (an indication, though not proof, that they were all written after November, 1581); what changes is her treatment of Astrophil. Properly scornful of his advances at first, she gradually relents, giving him a kiss in Sonnet 74. Interspersed with the 108 sonnets are eleven "songs" in various meters, the last of which includes Stella's voice (which does not appear in the sonnets) debating with Astrophil. By that point—only four sonnets follow this last song—Stella regrets having given her heart to Astrophil, and he is constrained to leave.

Sidney shows amazing structural inventiveness in these sonnets and varies their rhyme schemes considerably. Petrarch's sonnets display the complex rhyming pattern that a rhyme-rich language such as Italian makes possible: It is basically a two-part pattern, in which the first eight lines or octave form a single unit and rhyme *abbaabba*, and the last six lines or sestet form another unit and rhyme variously but with never more than three rhyme sounds. To duplicate this pattern in English is more difficult, since there are fewer rhyming words for any given sound than in Italian. Yet Sidney does so in many of the sonnets: Even when he varies the *abba* pattern with alternating rhyme, he still uses only one rhyme sound—*abababab*—in the octave. Within the basic two-part structure of the Petrarchan sonnet, however, Sidney introduces an innovation that anticipates the Shakespearean form: The octave divides further into two quatrains, or sets of four lines, and the sestet is often yet another quatrain followed by a couplet (a rhymed pair).

The first *Astrophil and Stella* sonnet serves as an introduction to the whole, being a sort of sonnet on how to write a sonnet. Anxious to please Stella, the speaker decides to send her poetry but cannot decide how to go about writing any. After all his ideas are exhausted, the poet/lover finds his answer in the last line: " 'Fool,' said my Muse to me, 'look in thy heart and write.' " The second sonnet then flashes back, revealing the course of his love for Stella, which developed gradually, "Not at first sight." After a few more sonnets declaring his love for Stella, Astrophil admits in sonnet 5 that reason is better than love, that love is an illusion, that true beauty is the eternal beauty of virtue—and yet he still loves Stella.

The sixth sonnet is another sonnet about sonnets. Like the first, it contrasts the imitative nature of other love-poets with the honest simplicity of the heart that the muse advised Astrophil to consult in Sonnet 1. Sidney returns to this topic in Sonnet 15, where he lists types of bad poets and contrasts them to himself, whose only muse is Stella. The muses, or goddesses of inspiration in classical mythology, appear in seven of the sonnets (1, 3, 6, 55, 60, 77, and 84) and are contrasted to Stella, who is Astrophil's muse.

The fact that Stella is married, and thus that Astrophil's love for her is adulterous, was a long-standing Petrarchan tradition: It allowed for an idealization of the lady and of the love, which was usually presented as unconsummated. The troublesome husband is usually not acknowledged in Petrarchan sonnets. In *Astrophil and Stella* the husband is referred to directly in only three sonnets. All three, however, contain puns on the name of the lady Penelope's real-life husband, Lord Rich. In the first of these, Sonnet 24, "rich" is the first and the last word of the sonnet: "Rich fools there be," it opens, and after discussing rich fools in general, and the rich fool who happens to be married to Stella in particular, Astrophil curses the fate that made this fool rich in Stella's love, and cries in the last line, "Let him . . . grow in only folly rich." The pun on Lord Rich's name recurs in Sonnet 35 ("Fame/Doth grow ever rich, naming my Stella's name") and in 37, which laments that, though Stella is rich in everything, she "Hath no misfortune, but that Rich she is"—that is, that her name is Rich.

Despite these broad hints, the major conflict in the sonnet sequence is not between the two rivals for Stella's heart; since he is not much of a presence in the sonnets, the husband is not much of a threat to Astrophil there, whatever his status outside the world of the sonnets might be. What stands between Astrophil and Stella is not so much a real husband as the idea of a husband—or, to put it in the terms actually used in the sequence, the conflict is between Love and Virtue. Both Love and Virtue appear as allegorical characters, or personified abstractions. Love, in fact, appears under two names, Love and Cupid. Since Love is often referred to in *Astrophil and Stella* as the blind boy with the bow, we can properly consider them two names for the same character.

Love personified appears in 44 out of 108 of the sonnets, or more than 40 percent, and in 6 out of 11, or more than half of the songs. The characterization of Love as a supernatural person influencing Astrophil is one of Sidney's triumphs, and allows him to analyze and record the complex psychology of love in the poetry. Love is in turn a "Lieutenant" in the wars of passion (Sonnet 36), a military conqueror (42, 43), a scholar (46), and an eternal boy (Sonnet 73 and Song 2).

The conflict between Love and Virtue is the subject of Sonnet 52, but it appears explicitly in six other sonnets, 5, 25, 31, 48, 62, and 72. The first time Virtue and Love are mentioned together, the conflict is not seen: Virtue is embodied in Stella, who engenders Love in Astrophil. Yet the power of Virtue to make Astrophil "burn in love" (Sonnet 25) produces an irony: it is that very Virtue that will not allow Stella, while another man's wife, to return Astrophil's love. Yet Astrophil turns this moral irony into a sophistical seduction poem in Sonnet 52. He argues that, while Stella's "fair outside" belongs to Love, her soul belongs to Virtue. Until the final couplet, it sounds as if Astrophil is making the argument of traditional morality: The spiritual beauty that is the stuff of Virtue outweighs the merely physical beauty that is the stuff of Love. But then come the last two lines: "Let Virtue have that Stella's self; yet thus/ That Virtue yet that body grant to us." Thus Astrophil tries to have his cake and eat it too, to satisfy both Virtue and Love.

A memorable element of the *Astrophil and Stella* sonnets is the striking physical description of Stella. Not that description itself is unusual; the "vertical description" of the beloved, from head to toe, is a hallmark of the Petrarchan sonnet tradition. What is unusual is Sidney's departure from the Petrarchan cliché of the blue-eyed blonde as the feminine ideal to that of a dark beauty. The minor poet Henry Constable, to whom Lady Rich was later a patron, confirmed Astrophil/Sidney's description when he wrote of Penelope Rich's "black sparkling eyes."

In *Astrophil and Stella*, Sidney extended the range of the Petrarchan sonnet sequence and led the way for other English imitators of the Italian sonneteers. They transcended imitation by inverting many of the conventions and probing various psychological states of the lover. Moreover, they are the first English sonnets to include the voice of the woman, thereby forcing the character of the lover to display greater subtlety than had prevailed before in English verse.

John R. Holmes

Bibliography:
Hamilton, A. C. *Sir Philip Sidney: A Study of His Life and Works*. New York: Cambridge University Press, 1977. A critical biography based on original sources, which also analyzes Sidney's works in the probable order of their composition and provides insight into Sidney's development as a poet.
Kalstone, David. *Sidney's Poetry: Contexts and Interpretations*. Cambridge, Mass.: Harvard University Press, 1965. A specialized study focusing on the way Sidney reinvented the Italian poetic genres in English. Offers excellent analyses of the *Astrophil and Stella* sonnets in a form accessible to the general reader.
Kay, Dennis, ed. *Sir Philip Sidney: An Anthology of Modern Criticism*. Oxford, England: Clarendon Press, 1987. A collection of essays, mostly previously published, which concern all aspects of Sidney's writings, among them (previously available only in specialized literary journals) several dealing exclusively with the *Astrophil and Stella* sonnets.
Rudenstine, Neil L. *Sidney's Poetic Development*. Cambridge, Mass.: Harvard University Press, 1967. A chronological study of Sidney's poetic works, which includes a detailed discussion of the *Astrophil and Stella* sonnets.

Weiner, Andrew D. *Sir Philip Sidney and the Poetics of Protestantism*. Minneapolis: University of Minnesota Press, 1978. Provides helpful readings of Sidney's poetry, though limited by a critical theoretical approach, then in vogue, that connects sixteenth and seventeenth century theology and poetry. In the case of the *Astrophil and Stella* sonnets, this critical approach is quite illuminating, though a bit specialized for the general reader.

ATALA

Type of work: Novel
Author: François-Auguste-René de Chateaubriand (1768-1848)
Type of plot: Philosophical realism
Time of plot: Early eighteenth century
Locale: Louisiana
First published: 1801 (English translation, 1802)

> *Principal characters:*
> ATALA, an Indian maiden
> CHACTAS, the beloved of Atala
> FATHER AUBREY, a missionary

The Story:

Chactas was an old, blind, and wise Indian of the tribe of Natchez, whose hunting ground was in the territory of Louisiana. Because of his great age and deep wisdom gained through countless years of tragic misfortune, Chactas was the patriarch of the tribe. Thus it was that when a young Frenchman named René presented himself for membership in the tribe in the year 1725, it was Chactas who questioned him to determine his fitness to join the Natchez nation. Finding René fixed in his determination to become one of the tribe, Chactas accepted him. As the Indians prepared for a beaver hunt, Chactas—even though he was blind—was made the leader of the party. One night as they lay in their canoes, Chactas recited the story of his adventures to René.

When Chactas had lived but seventeen summers, his father was killed in battle and he himself was taken prisoner by the enemy and led away by the Spaniards to St. Augustine. There he was befriended by an old Castilian named Lopez and his sister. The two white people cared for the young man and tried to educate him as their son. After thirty moons had passed, however, Chactas tired of this civilized life and begged Lopez to allow him to return to his people. Lopez, knowing the dangers awaiting a lonely youth in the forests, at first tried to dissuade Chactas. At last, seeing that the youth was firm in his resolve, the old man sent him on his way with his blessing.

The warning given by the good Lopez soon proved correct. Chactas, having lost his way in the woods, was captured by an enemy tribe and taken to their village to await death by burning. Because of his youth and bravery, the women of the tribe took pity on him. One night, as he sat by the campfire, he heard a rustling and then felt the presence of a woman beside him. In low tones, she told him that she was Atala, daughter of the chief and his dead wife. She asked Chactas if he were a Christian, and when he told her that he had not forsaken the gods of his father, she departed.

For many days the tribe marched, taking Chactas with them, and each night Atala visited him by the fire. One night, after Chactas had been tied to a tree, Atala appeared and told his guard that she would watch the prisoner for a time. Since she was the daughter of the chief, the guard gladly gave her his place. She quickly untied the cords and gave Chactas his freedom, but, just as quickly, he placed the cords in her hand, telling her that he wanted to be chained to her forever. She cried out in anguish that their religions separated them. She also seemed to have some other terrible secret that she feared he would learn. Atala begged him to flee without her, but Chactas said that he would rather die by fire than leave her. Neither would change, and so Atala tied Chactas again, hoping that soon he would change his mind. Each night they slipped off into the woods together, but Chactas did not possess her, for her God helped her to deny her passion for Chactas. She prayed that the young man might give himself to her God so that one barrier to their love would be broken.

One night, her father's warriors discovered them together. Chactas was returned to the camp and placed under heavy guard. The tribe marched on and came at last to the place where Chactas was to be burned at the stake. Indians gathered from far and near to witness his torture and death at a Feast of the Dead. Chactas was prepared for his ordeal, his body painted and then laid on the ground with guards lying across the ropes so that they might feel the slightest movement of the prisoner's body. Despite the great precautions, however, Atala again freed him by a ruse, and they made their escape into the forest. Although they were pursued, the Indians were so drunk from celebrating the Feast of the Dead that the pursuit was only halfhearted, and the lovers had little trouble in eluding them.

Nevertheless, the wilderness almost conquered the fugitives, who were ill-prepared for the hardships they now had to endure. Their fates joined, Atala proclaimed her love for Chactas but said that they could never marry. Although she gave their differences in religion as the only reason, Chactas felt that there was more she feared to tell him. At last, upon his urging, she told him her secret. She was not the daughter of the chief, but the illegitimate child of a white man and the chief's wife. When Chactas learned that the white man was his old friend Lopez, he loved her as a sister as well as a lover. It was through Lopez that she had gained her Christian faith, transmitted to her by her mother.

A terrible storm drove them to the shelter of a tree, and while in that refuge, they saw a dog and an old hermit approaching. The hermit was a missionary, Father Aubry, who took them to his grotto and gave them food and shelter. Chactas feared to go, for he was not a Christian, but Father Aubry said that he was one of God's children and made him welcome. When he promised to instruct Chactas in Christianity so that he and Atala could be married, the girl paled at his words.

They learned that Father Aubry had spent almost his entire life among the natives, although he could have had a more comfortable life in Europe. A good man, he considered it a privilege and not a sacrifice to endure the hardships and dangers of the wilderness. Atala and Chactas became a part of the little community of Christian natives over whom the good priest presided. After a time, Chactas began to feel the spirit of God in his heart.

One day, returning from a pilgrimage with Father Aubry, Chactas found Atala apparently dying from a mysterious fever. Then they learned what her true secret had been. On her deathbed, Atala's mother had taken the girl's vow that she would always remain a virgin. Her own sin had made her want to protect her daughter, and Atala, knowing nothing of real love, had given her vow, which could never be broken. When Father Aubry told the lovers that the bishop in Quebec could release her from her vow, Chactas' heart grew light. In real anguish, Atala then told them that she had taken poison because she had believed Chactas was forever denied to her. There were no remedies for the poison. After receiving the blessing of the priest and the promise of Chactas that he would embrace the Christian religion so that they could be joined in heaven, the poor virgin died. With the priest's aid, Chactas buried his beloved. Then he said good-bye to Father Aubry and once more began his wanderings. Many years passed before he received baptism in the faith of his beloved Atala.

Many years more were to pass before the daughter of René, whom Chactas had adopted, took the bones of Atala and Father Aubry and Chactas to the land of the Natchez for burial. Chactas and Father Aubry had been killed by enemies. The daughter of René told a curious traveler that he should not grieve. The three friends were together with God.

Critical Evaluation:

A tale of passionate but pure love, *Atala* is another of the stories using the image of the noble savage, which began to find favor in the early nineteenth century. Against a background of the primitive American wilderness, the two lovers and the gentle priest wage a winning battle against sin and paganism. Simplicity and complexity of character are vividly contrasted, the two meeting in Christian faith in the goodness of God. *Atala* was the first of François-Auguste-René de Chateaubriand's romances to be published, and the book had a tremendous vogue in its own day. The novel was originally planned as part of a much longer work, *The Natchez*, based on Chateaubriand's travels on the American frontier and influenced by his Romantic philosophy.

Atala is one of the significant literary expressions of the Romantic movement which developed essentially in France, Germany, and England in the latter part of the eighteenth century and constituted a revolution in thinking about virtually every phase of life. The aspects of the movement given literary expression in *Atala* include an awareness of the distinction between the true nature of the human beings and the apparent or superficial nature which society imposes on them or which they adopt because of the expectations of those around them. The "true self" of Atala is that of a young woman with a natural warmth, compassion for the sufferings of others, and a readiness to love and to be loved. A vow that had societal but not natural force was imposed upon her by her mother; this and a misunderstanding of true religion make it impossible for her to be her natural self.

A second aspect of Romanticism—the "blue flower" concept expressed by Novalis in his *Heinrich von Ofterdingen* (1802)—is a recognition that sensitive people may catch glimpses of an ideal (often an ideal love) but that the full ideal is never completely attainable except through intuition or imagination. Love, then, may remain in a pure or ideal state only if it cannot become actual marriage. Chactas' love for Atala remains pure throughout his long life, colored by a tint of sadness for "what might have been," even while it remains more beautiful than it could have been in the realities of marriage, work, home, and children. It is somewhat in this vein that the noble savage is idealized; this image can be idealized by Europeans, because it is known to them almost exclusively through their imaginations.

With nature, it is not the same. European civilization had "tamed" nature. The Romantics (William Wordsworth and Chateaubriand are prime examples) discovered and deeply felt the beauties of uncontrolled nature, and *Atala* gives excellent testimony to the harmony of the receptive human spirit with that love of unspoiled nature, even with the hardships it may impose.

Chateaubriand does not represent the full range of Romantic thought; perhaps no single author incorporates all aspects of any literary period, but he is one of France's best prose representatives of European Romanticism.

Bibliography:
Hamilton, Jane F. "Ritual Passage in Chateaubriand's *Atala*." *Nineteenth Century French Studies* 15, no. 4 (Summer, 1987): 385-393. This article applies psychological theories about rites of passage and heroic development to *Atala*.

Porter, Charles A. *Chateaubriand: Composition, Imagination, and Poetry*. Saratoga, Calif.: Anma Libri, 1978. This brief monograph is published through Stanford French and Italian Studies. The text focuses on *Atala* and its companion piece, *René* (1802), in light of their portrayals of and interactions with Christianity.

Porter, Laurence M. "Writing Romantic Epiphany: Atala, Seraphita, Aurelia, Dieu." *Romance Quarterly* 34, no. 4 (November, 1987): 435-442. This article compares the heroine of *Atala* to characters in works by other French romantics, including Honoré de Balzac, Gérard de Nerval, and Victor Hugo.

Switzer, Richard. *Chateaubriand.* New York: Twayne, 1971. This book-length study approaches Chateaubriand's literary output from a primarily biographical position. It places *Atala* in the context of Chateaubriand's body of work, relating the text to trends in literature and thought.

Wang, Ben. "Inscribed Wilderness in Chateaubriand's *Atala.*" *Romance Notes* 33, no. 3 (Spring, 1993): 279-287. Discusses Chateaubriand's portrayals of nature and Native Americans in light of current ideas and literary theories.

ATALANTA IN CALYDON

Type of work: Poetry
Author: Algernon Charles Swinburne (1837-1909)
Type of plot: Tragedy
Time of plot: Antiquity
Locale: Greece
First published: 1865

Principal characters:
ŒNEUS, the king of Calydon
ALTHÆA, his wife
MELEAGER, their son
ATALANTA, a virgin hunter
CHORUS

The Story:

Œneus, father of Meleager, had offended Artemis, goddess of the hunt, by offering sacrifices to all the gods except her. As a punishment for his negligence, Artemis had sent into Calydon a wild boar that ravaged the land and the crops.

Althæa, embittered by the curse, refused to pay homage to Artemis and raged against the gods. Althæa was a woman of strong will and determination. Years before, when her son Meleager was born, she had had a strange dream concerning his birth. In the dream, three spinning women, the Fates, had visited Althæa and had promised that Meleager would have strength, good fortune, and a bounteous life, until the brand on the hearth burned completely. On hearing the last part of the prophecy, Althæa had sprung from her bed, grasped the burning brand, and beaten and trampled the heat from it with her bare hands and feet. Then, to guard Meleager's life, she had hidden the brand.

She also dreamed that the heatless brand burst into flame as a bud bursts into flower; with this strange phenomenon, Death had come to blow charred ash from the brand into her breast, but there Love had quenched the flame. The omen presaged for Althæa the security of her family; but in spite of her great pride, she was not unmindful of the lots that the gods might cast for mortals. These thoughts were in her mind as she went to arm Meleager for the boar hunt. Never had there been born so strong a man of royal birth as Meleager.

The Chorus, reviewing the life span of human beings, summed up this existence as a passing between a sleep and a sleep.

The warriors of Arcadia were to join the Calydonians in the hunt, and Meleager and Althæa discussed the qualities and characteristics of these men, among them the valiant sons of Leda, Althæa's sister. Meleager described Toxeus and Plexippus, Althæa's brothers, as undoing their deeds with too much talk. Althæa counseled her son against having too great pride in earthly accomplishments and advised him to submit his soul to fate. The Chorus admonished Meleager to follow his mother's counsel.

Meleager, recounting the many tumultuous battles he had experienced, pointed out to his mother that in all these frays he had never seen evidence of the infallible gods to whom she and the Chorus would have him submit. Œneus reported the coming of the Arcadians and said that among them was a woman armed for the hunt. Although Œneus wished to have this woman shown great respect because of her favor from the gods, he warned Meleager against becoming infatuated with her beauty. Althæa, recalling the prophecies of the Fates regarding Meleager's career, added to her husband's warning against earthly love. Again imploring her son to give himself to fate, she told him that he would not die as ordinary men die and that his death would be her death as well. Meleager declared his boundless love for his mother and expressed respect for her teaching. Ever faithful to Zeus, the sole determiner of things, he prepared for the hunt.

The Chorus, philosophizing on Love, saw her blind as a flame, covered by earth for hiding, and fronted by laughter to conceal the tears of desire. According to the portent of the Chorus, man and maid would go forth—the maid's name, Fate; the man's, Death. The Chorus lamented also the meagerness of life's span. This futility, an evil blossom born of sea foam and blood froth, had come into existence with Aphrodite, goddess of love. Before, there had been joy upon the earth, but Aphrodite's influence had resulted in suffering, evil, and devastation.

In the hunt, as predicted, Meleager met the Arcadian maiden. She was Atalanta, the virgin priestess of Artemis, whom Œneus had neglected in his sacrifices, and who had sent the wild boar to ravage Calydon. Atalanta invoked Artemis to favor Meleager that he might be victorious in the hunt. Meleager, confessing his love for Atalanta, was taunted by his uncles, Toxeus and Plexippus. Althæa pleaded for peace among her kinsmen lest words become snakes and poison them against each other.

The hunt proceeded. According to a message sent by Œneus to Althæa, the expedition demanded energy, courage, and hunting strategy. The boar, crazed by the chase and by the numerous wounds inflicted, charged Meleager, who with all daring and skill slew the animal, thereby ridding Calydon of its curse. Althæa offered praise to the gods. A messenger who had brought the message to Althæa added that pride in earthly accomplishments would bring about destruction.

The Chorus, chanting a song of thanksgiving to the gods, was hushed by the messenger, who ordered them to change their songs to wails of pity because Toxeus and Plexippus had been slain.

Althæa, lamenting the death of her brothers, found comfort in the thought that Meleager would avenge them. The messenger questioned whether her son should slay himself. When Althæa threatened him for his ambiguity, the messenger bluntly informed her that Meleager had slain his uncles.

After the boar had been killed, Toxeus and Plexippus had requested that the head and the hide be kept as a monument in Calydon; but Meleager, enamored of Atalanta, gave her the spoils of the hunt. Pleased with this token of his devotion, Atalanta laughed. The Calydonians construed her reaction as a taunt and sought to destroy her. In furious fighting to protect the maiden, Meleager killed his uncles. Althæa recalled her brothers' kindnesses in their childhood, anticipated her sister's scorn for Meleager's crime, and accepted her fate as a victim of many curses.

The Chorus, endeavoring to comfort Althæa in the loss of her brothers, was rebuked. Had Toxeus and Plexippus died in sacrifice or battle, Althæa maintained, their lives would not have been in vain; but knowing that they had been slain by her son, she could never become reconciled to their deaths or to his crime.

In Meleager's deed, caused by excessive earthly pride and undue desire for attainment, Althæa sensed her error in taking the burning brand from the fire at the time of his birth. Stoically, she thrust the brand into the fire that it might be consumed at last. Althæa suffered with torment and anguish as the Chorus described the burning, which resulted in Meleager's death after his return from the hunt.

Meleager reviewed his existence without remorse and besought Œneus and Althæa not to let his name die. He described his passing as an empty night harvest in which no man gathers fruit. Althæa died of sorrow. Atalanta, hailing Meleager's greatness, returned to Arcadia. Œneus ruled alone in Calydon.

Critical Evaluation:

Atalanta in Calydon was Algernon Charles Swinburne's first successful work. It was followed in 1866 by the first volume of his *Poems and Ballads*, which contains the shorter poems reckoned to be among his best. *Atalanta in Calydon* is a curiously anomalous work, whose form and manner seem to fly in the face of the aesthetic theories that had possessed Swinburne for five years previously: the theories of the Pre-Raphaelites, as explained to him by Dante Gabriel Rossetti and William Morris. Although it does not represent a frank refusal of the central doctrine of art for art's sake that the Pre-Raphaelites had imported from France, *Atalanta in Calydon* departs markedly from their ideas. As an exercise in classical pastiche, it seems to qualify as a deliberate step backward: a temporary but determined retreat toward artistic conservatism.

Swinburne adopted the story of Meleager from Ovid's *Metamorphoses* (before 8 C.E.). There is an older version briefly recounted in the *Iliad* (c. 800 B.C.E.), in which a war between the Calydonians and the Curetes is nearly lost because Meleager refuses to fight after being cursed by his mother, who had been angered by the loss in battle of her brother. In the version in the *Iliad*, there is no mention of Atalanta; Meleager is married to a woman named Cleopatra. He also is married in Ovid's version, in which his presentation of the boar's hide to Atalanta—after insisting that she be allowed to join the hunt, against his uncles' wishes—seems to be motivated by simple courtesy. Ovid also added the legend of the symbolic brand, of which Swinburne makes so much—Swinburne's version is shot through with images of life as a consuming fire that ultimately makes ashes of the flesh.

Swinburne did the bulk of the work on *Atalanta in Calydon* at Northcourt, the home of Mary Gordon, with whom he went riding in his spare time. When he returned to London following this interlude, he composed his finest poetry in a hectic rush, but also suffered a precipitous decline into alcoholism. Some of his biographers have speculated that he fell in love with Mary Gordon, and perhaps proposed to her, as a last desperate attempt at heterosexuality. After she decided to marry another man, he went rebounding back to the dissolute lifestyle that had scandalized London society.

However tempting it may be to assume that Swinburne's Atalanta is in some sense an image of Mary Gordon—that its powerful sense of tragedy is simply her rejection of his love—the text does not sustain such an interpretation. Although Swinburne's Meleager is unmarried and strongly attracted to Atalanta, he is determined to suppress his attraction in order to concentrate his mind on the hunt. There seems to be no real need for his father to warn him that the gods have designed Atalanta for celibacy and that she would not make a suitable wife, still less for his mother to complain that his pursuit of strange loves will be the death of her unless he gives it up. In fact, these passages raise the suspicion that in Swinburne's mind, if not in the literal wording of the poem, Atalanta might not be female.

Such a suspicion is intensified by the passage in which Plexippus and Toxeus attempt to bar Atalanta from the hunt. They seem to be ready enough to accept her masculinity; what they attack is the implied femininity of Meleager's fondness for her. Plexippus sneers at Meleager, calling him a "man grown girl" and "woman-tongued," although Meleager has already distinguished himself as one of the Argonauts. Atalanta closes the argument by insisting on her "iron maidenhood," winning the right to accompany Meleager on the hunt by insisting on her absolute celibacy. When the messenger describes how Meleager presented the spoils of the hunt to her, however, he describes her response in terms of an explicitly sexual metaphor.

If Atalanta were male in the private arena of Swinburne's imagination, then the anger of the uncles against her, and Althæa's wrath against Meleager, are cast in a different light. So is the dying Meleager's final speech, in which he demands that Atalanta "let no man/ Defile me or Despise me, saying, This man/ Died woman-wise, a woman's offering, slain/ Through female fingers in his woof of life,/ Dishonourable." He then begs her to kiss him once and twice.

The prime mover in this particular tragedy, as the Chorus loses no opportunity to remind the reader, is the sadistically insistent fate that has made both Atalanta and Meleager what they are. In an imitation Greek drama, Swinburne certainly would have the option of referring to this fate as Nemesis, or as the manifold gods of the classical pantheon, but he does not. In the remarkable passage that begins, "Who hath given man speech?" the Chorus concludes, after five full pages, with the final question, "Who makes desire, and slays desire with shame?" and the answer, "the supreme evil, God." It then proceeds to rage against that hateful God for three more pages. The Greek setting may have served to veil this calculated blasphemy from the eye of his critics, but Swinburne certainly seems to be addressing the God of the Victorians rather than the obsolete Zeus.

It is hard to see all this as the disappointment of a young man whose proposal to a female lover has been rejected; it makes more sense to construe it as the angry lamentation of a young man cursing the force of nature that forced upon him a pattern of desire that his society, and by extension his God, would not sanction. If this is so, the use of Greek myth and a form approximating that of Greek drama may be explicable in other terms than a temporary reconciliation of the poet with the aesthetic ideals of classicism that the Pre-Raphaelites so disliked. The Greeks were, after all, famed for their tolerance of homosexuality and for encoding homosexual ideals within their myths.

Whatever the reason, *Atalanta in Calydon* was the first work in which Swinburne found an authentic depth of feeling to energize his poetic fluency; it is a pity that the imaginative fuel it provided lasted only a few short years before Theodore Watts-Dunton took Swinburne in hand, putting the brake on his melodramatic self-assassination, and securing for him a long life of physical and creative impotence.

"Critical Evaluation" by Brian Stableford

Bibliography:
Cassidy, John A. *Algernon C. Swinburne*. New York: Twayne, 1964. A comprehensive study of Swinburne's life and work. Part 3 of chapter 5 posits that *Atalanta in Calydon* is a response to Mary Gordon's rejection of the marriage proposal that Swinburne may have made.
Henderson, Philip. *Swinburne: The Portrait of a Poet*. London: Routledge & Kegan Paul, 1974. Chapter 6 deals with various works, including *Atalanta in Calydon* and *Poems and Ballads*.
Louis, Margot Kathleen. *Swinburne and His Gods: The Roots and Growth of Agnostic Poetry*. Montreal: McGill-Queen's University Press, 1990. Tracks the changes in Swinburne's attitude to fate, in which context *Atalanta in Calydon* is a key work.
Rutland, William R. *Swinburne: A Nineteenth Century Hellene*. Oxford, England: Basil Blackwell, 1931. Proposes that Swinburne is an authentic tragedian in the classical tradition. Offers a comprehensive dissection of *Atalanta in Calydon*. Contains a useful appendix on various versions of the story of Meleager.
Thomas, Edward. *Algernon Charles Swinburne: A Critical Study*. London: Martin Secker, 1912. Chapter 1 opens this pioneering exercise in apologetics with a discussion of *Atalanta in Calydon*.

AUCASSIN AND NICOLETTE

Type of work: Fiction
Author: Unknown
Type of plot: Romance
Time of plot: Twelfth century
Locale: Provence, France
First published: Aucassin et Nicolette, early thirteenth century (English translation, 1880)

Principal characters:
COUNT GARIN DE BEAUCAIRE
AUCASSIN, his son
NICOLETTE, a slave

The Story:

Count Bougars de Valence and Count Garin de Beaucaire were at war. Count Garin had one son, Aucassin, who was so smitten by love that he would neither accept the duties of knighthood nor participate in his father's quarrel, unless his father consented to his love for Nicolette. She was a slave, bought by a captain of the town from the Saracens and reared as his own daughter. Count Garin agreed to the marriage of Aucassin to any daughter of a king or count but not to Nicolette. He went to see the captain and told him to send Nicolette away. The captain said that he would keep Nicolette out of sight, and she was imprisoned in the high chamber of a palace with an old woman to keep her company. Rumors sped through the countryside: Nicolette was lost; Nicolette had fled the country; Nicolette was slain by order of Count Garin.

Meanwhile, the war between the two counts grew more fierce, but Aucassin still refused to fight. Father and son then made a covenant; Aucassin would go into the battle, and if God willed that he should survive, the count must agree to allow him two or three words and one kiss from Nicolette. Aucassin rode into the fray, but thoughts of Nicolette so distracted him that he was captured. Then Aucassin reflected that if he were slain, he would have no chance at all to see Nicolette. Therefore, he laid his hand on his sword and began fighting with all of his strength. He killed ten knights, wounded seven, and took Count Bougars prisoner, but when Count Garin refused to keep the covenant, Aucassin released Count Bougars. Aucassin was cast into a dungeon.

Nicolette, knowing her companion to be asleep, escaped from her prison by a rope made of bed linen and went to the castle where Aucassin lay. While they exchanged lovers' vows, the guards came searching for Nicolette, as her escape had been discovered. A friendly sentinel, however, warned Nicolette of their coming. She leaped into the moat and, bruised and bleeding, climbed the outer wall.

Nicolette fell asleep in a thicket near the castle. The next day, she saw some shepherds eating their lunch at a fountain nearby. She asked them to take a message to Aucassin, saying there was a beast in the forest and that he should have this beast and not part with one of its limbs for any price. Nicolette built a lodge within the forest and waited to prove her lover's faith.

Aucassin was taken from his prison and allowed to attend a great feast, but he had no joy in it. A friendly knight offered his horse to Aucassin and suggested that he ride into the forest. Aucassin was only too happy for a chance to get away. He met the shepherds by the fountain and heard what Nicolette had told them. Aucassin prayed to God that he would find his quarry.

He rode in haste through the thorny forest. Toward evening, he began to weep because his search had been fruitless. He met a huge, ugly fellow, leaning on a terrible cudgel. Aucassin told him that he mourned for a white hound he had lost. The burly fellow scornfully replied that he had lost his best ox and had searched fruitlessly for three days without meat or drink. Aucassin gave the man twenty sols to pay for the beast. They parted and went their separate ways.

Aucassin found the lodge built by Nicolette and rested there that night. Nicolette heard Aucassin singing and came to him. The next day, they mounted Aucassin's horse and journeyed until they came to the seas. Aucassin and Nicolette embarked upon a ship. A terrible storm carried them to Torelore. First, Aucassin fought with the king of that strange land and then freed the king of his enemies. He and Nicolette lived happily in Torelore until Saracens besieged the castle and captured all within it. Aucassin was put in one ship and Nicolette in another. A storm scattered the ships, and that in which Aucassin was a prisoner drifted ashore at Beaucaire. He was now the Count of Beaucaire, since his parents had died.

Nicolette was in the ship bearing the king of Carthage, who was her true father. They did not recognize each other because Nicolette had been a small child when she was stolen. When she saw the walls of Carthage, however, memory came back to her, and she revealed her identity in a song. The king gave her great honor and desired to marry her to a king of the Saracens, but Nicolette remained steadfast in her love for Aucassin. She disguised herself as a minstrel and took ship for Provence, where she traveled from castle to castle until she came to Beaucaire.

In the great hall, Nicolette sang of her adventures. When Aucassin heard her song, he took her aside and inquired concerning Nicolette. He asked her to return to the land where Nicolette lived and to bring her to him. Nicolette returned to the captain's house, and there she clothed herself in rich robes and sent for Aucassin. At last, they were wedded and lived long years with great joy.

Critical Evaluation:

Aucassin and Nicolette is a unique text from roughly the first half of the thirteenth century. It can easily model as a textbook example of the generic transformation and experimentation that characterize thirteenth century French literature. Classified as a *chante-fable* or song-story, the work, whose author remains anonymous, advances the plot by alternating prose and assonanced, seven-syllabic verse passages. The prose sections of *Aucassin and Nicolette* primarily advance the plot, while the verse passages deliver material of more emotionally charged interest. In addition to the combination of prose and verse passages, the work embodies features from a wide variety of literary genres. It exhibits mainly the characteristics of the courtly romance and the chivalric epic, but it also includes elements borrowed from the *pastourelle*, the saint's life, the Byzantine adventure romance, troubadour lyric poetry, and the fabliau. Because of its compound nature, *Aucassin and Nicolette* is also referred to as a hybrid text. This composition was probably intended for public recital, possibly accompanied by musical instruments. While it is unique because it is the only existing example of this type of composition in French medieval literature, it was probably modeled after the Latin *prosimetrum* (prose-verse) tradition.

Besides its unique format, the text is curious in its treatment of subject matter and themes. While it is easily accessible and seemingly transparent, the intent of the author regarding his treatment of subject matter and themes remains rather elusive. The large number of differing interpretations brought forth by various scholars as to the underlying meaning of the work in general, and specific episodes such as the sojourn in Torelore, in particular, attest to this. It can safely be stated, however, that one of the most striking characteristics of *Aucassin and Nicolette* is the theme of reversal. The author has taken great delight in the reversal of the traditional chivalric romance elements, starting with the names of the protagonists: Aucassin, a French noble, carries a name that conjures up a Saracen theme, whereas his Carthaginian-born lover, Nicolette, has a French one. After both lovers have separately been incarcerated, it is not Aucassin, but Nicolette who succeeds in escaping in order to seek out her beloved, and it is her shrewdness and cunning that bring about their reunion in the woods. The reversal of roles and themes continues throughout the work, culminating with Nicolette's disguise as a male minstrel in order to effect her final reunion with Aucassin.

Aucassin and Nicolette parallels many other thirteenth century works in its experimentation with both form and content. The parodic treatment and literary subversion of traditional subjects such as war, duty, and love are found in many other contemporary romances. Nicolette's resourcefulness and proactive ways cast familiar echoes of other such heroines who surmount social constraints and who emerge as brave and adroit in obtaining their heart's desire. Lïenor, the female protagonist of the early thirteenth century *Le Roman de la rose: out, de guillaume de Dole* comes to mind. In this story, the young woman devises a trick in order to disprove a cowardly attack on her reputation. Through courage and a clever mind, she ensures that her marriage with the emperor Conrad be allowed to proceed.

Above all, *Aucassin and Nicolette* seems to indicate that the twelfth century literary models, whose generic codification and chivalric value system it subverts through the introduction of incongruous and farcical elements, do not correspond any longer to the reality or to the needs of the thirteenth century. It is this questioning and reworking of traditional subjects and structures that lies at the heart of *Aucassin and Nicolette*.

"Critical Evaluation" by Geert S. Pallemans

Bibliography:

Ferrante, Joan M. "Courtly Literature." In *Woman as Image in Medieval Literature: From the Twelfth Century to Dante*. New York: Columbia University Press, 1975. Describes *Aucassin and Nicolette* as a "parody romance" in which the usual role expectations of men and women are reversed.

Loomis, Laura Hibbard. Foreword to *Aucassin and Nicolete*. In *Medieval Romances*, edited by Roger Sherman Loomis and Laura Hibbard Loomis. New York: Random House, 1957. Emphasizes the dramatic and performance qualities of this *chante-fable*. Discusses the characterizations of Aucassin and Nicolette and the linkings of music to lyrics, lyrics to prose, and romance to fables.

Mason, Eugene. Introduction to *Aucassin and Nicolette and Other Medieval Romances and Legends*. New York: E. P. Dutton, 1951. Places *Aucassin and Nicolette* and the other romances within a historical perspective, emphasizing the contradictions inherent in an understanding of the Middle Ages and its literature.

Stevens, John. "Man and God: Religion and Romance." In *Medieval Romance: Themes and Approaches*. New York: W. W. Norton, 1973. In this chapter in his illuminating study of medieval romance, Stevens discusses the complex relationship between romantic and religious ideals. Posits that the author uses Aucassin's blasphemous speech about preferring Hell to Heaven as an illustration of the hyperbolic absurdity of young love.

Tattersall, Jill. "Shifting Perspectives and the Illusion of Reality in *Aucassin and Nicolette*." *French Studies* 38, no. 3 (July, 1984): 257-267. Describes how the author deliberately works against the audience's expectations by using a multiplicity of perspectives, switches in narrative viewpoints, and a variety of types of characterization.

AUGUST 1914

Type of work: Novel
Author: Aleksandr Solzhenitsyn (1918-   )
Type of plot: Historical realism
Time of plot: Early twentieth century
Locale: Russia
First published: Avgust chetyrnadtsatogo, 1971; expanded version, 1983 (English translation, 1972; expanded English translation, 1989, as *The Red Wheel*)

Principal characters:

SANYA, a young man in school
VARYA, a young woman
GENERAL SAMSONOV
COLONEL VOROTYNTSEV, a staff officer
ALINA, his wife
ARSENY BLAGODARYOV, an enlisted man
PYOTR STOLYPIN, the prime minister
DMITRI BOGROV, a police agent and assassin

The Story:

World War I had just begun for Russia. Sanya, a young student, boarded a train for Moscow to enlist in the army. Sanya had been inspired by Russia's monarch, the czar, who had become a hero to his country by declaring war on Germany and Austria. Filled with patriotism, Sanya rejected his former pacifism and secretly vowed to fight for his country. On the train to Moscow he met a former girlfriend, Varya, who since the days when Sanya knew her at school had become educated and grown into an intellectual. Armed with the radical opinions from speeches she had heard shouted on street corners, Varya questioned Sanya's patriotism and challenged his desire to join the army, saying that he denied his support to the common people's revolution in giving it to the wealthy czar and his family. Sanya, defeated by her arguments, could only say that he was headed for battle because "I feel sorry for Russia. . . ."

As the war began, Emperor Nicholas II paced up and down inside a room in his palace on a day in July, 1914, while his generals urged him, against his better judgment, to mobilize the Russian army. Nicholas lashed out at the generals and berated them for their incompetence. He wished that Stolypin, the prime minister, was still alive. Stolypin would have known what was best for Russia.

Stolypin had been murdered at a performance at the Kiev Opera House by a police agent and secret assassin named Dmitri Bogrov. Bogrov, who had come from a prominent and wealthy family, was a privileged and idle son intent on securing his place within the ruling class. Refusing to obey any agenda except his own, he had given his allegiance only to himself, even as he prepared for a career in the army. To further his career, Bogrov conspired with the czar's secret police to gain an entrance pass to the exclusive Kiev Opera House, and when the police intentionally overlooked the revolver hidden in his pocket, Bogrov was able to assassinate Stolypin and thereby halt the prime minister's program of modernization. Bogrov was thereupon betrayed by the police, who secretly tried and executed him to prevent his testifying.

Meanwhile on the battlefield at Tannenberg, Colonel Vorotyntsev, a graduate of a Russian military academy, and his friend Arseny Blagodaryov, an enlisted man, found themselves surrounded by advancing German troops. Rallying his men, Colonel Vorotyntsev led a successful charge through enemy lines.

The colonel's small victory grew out of his excellent training as a soldier and his devotion to the military. After eight years of marriage with his wife, Alina, he had become disenchanted with her and found himself troubled by dreams of adultery. In one dream, his wife turned down the covers of the bed they were to share and found another woman's nightgown under the covers. Haunted by this vision of dishonor, the colonel decided that a military life held more dignity than a domestic one.

Despite the colonel's break through enemy lines, the Russian army, betrayed by the incompetence of the czar's generals, was doomed. General Samsonov's Second Army was defeated by German General Hindenburg. Colonel Vorotyntsev retreated from the battlefield and reported to the Grand Duke, supreme commander of Russia's armies. The colonel told him that defeat was inevitable; old Russia would be destroyed, but the general staff refused to believe him and clung instead to the lie that the war could still be won.

Sanya reflected on the early days of the war and longed to return with Varya to the places they had known and loved when they were young. The war had aged them, however, and Sanya was too patriotic to waste his life indulging himself. Instead he would continue to serve the people of his mother Russia.

Critical Evaluation:

Aleksandr Solzhenitsyn, who was awarded the Nobel Prize in Literature for 1970, used his writing to confront the oppression of the former Soviet Union and the weight of its cruel bureaucracy, whereby individuals were lost and destroyed inside Siberian prisons, cancer wards, and insane asylums. Solzhenitsyn depicts simple human qualities and creates realistic portraits that bear witness to the incredible strength of the human spirit while undergoing intense suffering.

Best known for *One Day in the Life of Ivan Denisovich* (1962) and *The Gulag Archipelago, 1918-1956: An Experiment in Literary Investigation* (1973-1975), Solzhenitsyn was himself a prisoner. In 1941, after earning degrees in mathematics and physics, he had begun teaching, but by 1945 he was the commander of a Soviet army artillery battery. That was when he wrote a personal letter criticizing Communist leader, Joseph Stalin. The Soviet police and counterintelligence agents arrested Solzhenitsyn, and after a hasty trial he was found guilty of conspiring against the state and sentenced to a series of brutal prisons. It was during his confinement, in prison amid the frozen wasteland, where the petty theft of a slice of bread or a pair of work boots could mean death, that the author had the transformative experiences that were to form the core of *One Day in the Life of Ivan Denisovich*. His experiences included a diagnosis of cancer from which he miraculously recovered and which formed the basis of *The Cancer Ward*. Freed from exile in central Asia in 1956, Solzhenitsyn returned to Russia, but he was arrested again when *The Gulag Archipelago* was published in France. In 1974, the Soviet Union finally expelled Solzhenitsyn and forced him into exile in the United States, where he remained until his triumphant return to Russia following the collapse of the Soviet Union.

August 1914 is the first volume of *The Red Wheel*, a series of novels in which Solzhenitsyn intended to present a sweeping view of twentieth century Russia and to correct the falsifications imposed on Russian history by the Soviet regime. Borrowing different styles from fiction, journalism, and film, Solzhenitsyn conveys the intricacy of political movements by using every literary and rhetorical technique at his disposal to unravel what he sees as the grossly misinterpreted "knot" of Russian history.

On the political level, *August 1914* attacks czarism for its reliance on favoritism and for using a biased system of advancement, including bribery and nepotism, practices that led to the appointment of incompetent generals whose blunders cost the lives of thousands. Solzhenitsyn views the czar's weakness and corruption as the catalyst that started the terrible and bloody revolution that destroyed Russia's potential. In his books, Solzhenitsyn tried to explain why a great vision of Russia that included a well-developed and prosperous Siberia never materialized. For Solzhenitsyn, the dream died in the bloodbath of 1917, for which he sees two causes: the assassination in 1911 of prime minister Pyotr Stolypin, whose attempts to modernize Russia were cut short, and more specifically, the failure of General Samsonov, who represented traditional Russia—forthright and sincere but incapable and unable to adapt.

Solzhenitsyn splits the blame for Russia's economic and ethical poverty between two opposing camps, the backward-looking officials known as the Black Hundreds, who were drawn from the wealthy upper class, and the forward-looking revolutionaries known as the Red Hundreds, impoverished insurgents from the lower classes. According to the author, both groups prevented Russia from fulfilling her destiny and leading the world, for as the two sides attempted to vanquish each other, the country decayed around them and the dignity and the rights of people were needlessly sacrificed. This is the tragedy at the core of *August 1914*.

In 1983, Solzhenitsyn published an expanded edition of *August 1914* that included three hundred pages of additional text dealing with one of Communism's founders, Vladimir Lenin, and with Stolypin, the assassinated prime minister. Solzhenitsyn held that Stolypin's death stopped Russia's peaceful political development and removed a deterrent to the Bolshevik Revolution. Many historians and critics disagree, calling *August 1914* more of a personal political treatise than a serious dramatic novel.

In all his work, Solzhenitsyn advances his view of the human being as a noble animal, one capable of transcendence and dignity even in the most degrading and depersonalizing circumstances. Solzhenitsyn described his job as a writer by saying that he had "to treat universal and eternal themes: the mysteries of the heart and conscience, the collision between life and death, the triumph over spiritual anguish."

August 1914 is an example of a writer's use of the novel to rewrite history. By seducing the reader with the familiar devices of fiction—story, character, plot, and imagery—the author creates a reality in which events are seen from all sides, as opposed to the simplified, and biased, version provided in state-sanctioned textbooks. Accordingly, Solzhenitsyn describes his novel as a "fascicle," which he defines as a "dense, all-round exposition of the events of a brief time span."

While Solzhenitsyn may not be entirely accurate historically, he nevertheless establishes that the form in which history is presented—be it journalistic, cinematic, or fictive—is in large measure responsible for determining its "truth" for the people reading it. In this way, *August 1914* seeks to remedy the distortions of the past established by the Soviet regime.

Solzhenitsyn's thesis is that the suffering and endurance and triumph experienced by individuals at the hands of human institutions ought not to be forgotten or misinterpreted. As a result, *August 1914* stands as the author's testament to the continued vitality of what is past and to its relevance to the ongoing struggle for freedom and equality.

David Johansson

Bibliography:
Dunlop, John B., Richard Haugh, and Alexis Klimoff, eds. *Aleksandr Solzhenitsyn: Critical*

Essays and Documentary Materials. Belmont, Mass.: Nordland, 1973. A collection of critical essays that includes a bibliography of works by and about Solzhenitsyn.

Kelley, Donald R. *The Solzhenitsyn-Sakharov Dialogue: Politics, Society, and the Future.* Westport, Conn.: Greenwood Press, 1982. Examines the beliefs of Solzhenitsyn and Andrei Sakharov on the subject of what sort of political system ought to replace Communism in Russia.

Pontuso, James F. *Solzhenitsyn's Political Thought.* Charlottesville: University Press of Virginia, 1990. Examines the evolution of Solzhenitsyn's political thinking.

Venclova, Tomas. "War and Pieces." *The New Republic*, August 28, 1989, 33-37. Admires Solzhenitsyn's literary talent but faults his political stance in *August 1914*.

Wilson, Raymond J. "Solzhenitsyn's *August 1914* and *Lenin in Zurich*: The Question of Historical Determinism." *Clio* 14, no. 1 (Fall, 1984): 15-36. Examines Solzhenitsyn's views of history as portrayed in *August 1914*.

AURORA LEIGH

Type of work: Poetry and novel (verse novel)
Author: Elizabeth Barrett Browning (1806-1861)
Type of plot: Künstlerroman
Time of plot: Mid-nineteenth century
Locale: Italy and England
First published: 1856

> *Principal characters:*
> AURORA LEIGH, the protagonist, a poet
> ROMNEY LEIGH, her cousin
> LADY WALDEMAR, who wishes to marry Romney
> MARIAN ERLE, whom Romney wishes to marry

Aurora Leigh blends the genres of poetry and novel and is, at the same time, a *Bildungsroman* (a novel that traces the development of a young person to maturity) or, more properly, a *Künstlerroman*, in which a young artist struggles to create an artistic identity despite adverse conditions. It is innovative both in its blend of poetry and the novel and in its focus on a woman as an artist.

As befitting a developmental novelist, Barrett Browning proceeds chronologically, from Aurora's childhood in Italy to her triumph as a mature artist. The child of a British father and an Italian mother, who dies when Aurora is only four years old, she grows up bereft of a maternal nurturing that she pursues throughout her life. Her sorrowing father leaves Aurora to the care of a servant until his own death when she is thirteen. She is whisked away to "frosty" England, in contrast to the "green reconciling earth" of Italy, the latter country being, in all senses, her "motherland." She is placed with her father's sister, who lives a "caged life," a life which, in turn, encases Aurora. Her education now emphasizes useless facts and accomplishments such as "spinning glass" and the need to be "womanly," or submissive, as her aunt defined it. Aurora befriends her cousin, Romney Leigh, master of Leigh Hall, only a few years older than she. She escapes into her father's stored library and discovers poetry, finding her life's work by beginning to write poetry and to receive inspiration from England's natural world.

The narrative distance of book 1, which recalls Aurora's childhood, yields to the immediacy of the focus in book 2 on her twentieth birthday, a beautiful June day. Thrilled with her life among poets, Aurora crowns herself with ivy leaves and is embarrassed to be discovered by Romney, who is amused at her pretension. He has come to propose marriage (without any mention of love) because he assumes she will join him in his dedication to solving the problems of the poor. He derides her poetic ambitions and prophesies failure since, as a woman, she cannot "generalize." Women are "personal and passionate," fit to be "doting mothers and perfect wives." She refuses his offer by saying, "What you love,/ Is not a woman, Romney, but a cause." The two have contrasting views on bettering humanity. Romney wants to extend personal charity or espouse one of the current social schemes, such as that proposed by Charles Fourier (a system based on cooperation rather than on capitalism). Aurora insists that reform must come from within the individual and that "high-souled men . . . move masses." While poetry has excited her, he offers her only the chance to "sweep my barns and keep my hospitals." When her aunt dies shortly afterward, Aurora refuses a "bequest" that Romney invents, leaving for London to ensure independence in pursuing her career.

As book 3 opens, three years have passed, and Aurora has found lodging in Kensington, supporting herself with freelance prose writing. Lady Waldemar calls to enlist Aurora's aid in diverting Romney's plan to marry a seamstress, Marian Erle. Waldemar plans to marry Romney herself and insists that his gracious effort to save Marian from poverty will demean him. Aurora refuses to interfere and decides to visit Marian, allowing Barrett Browning to give her readers a glimpse of the wretched conditions that the poor endured. As the reader progresses into book 4, Marian describes her miserable past and her rescue by Romney; she is totally indebted to him and willing to be his "handmaid and wife." Romney still scorns love and insists that he and Marian will be partners in his work.

Aurora interrupts the narrative for a novelistic foreshadowing of events, regretting that she did not protect Marian or advance the wedding. In this way, Barrett Browning builds suspense for further developments. When the actual wedding day arrives, the reader gets a glimpse of hell, both in the author's description of the mob attending the wedding and in that of the languid upper-class guests gossiping about the mismatched couple. A riot breaks out with the announcement that Marian will not appear; Marian has sent Romney a letter explaining that she has become convinced (through her conversations with Lady Waldemar) that their marriage will discredit Romney.

Book 5 may seem a digression from the main narrative, but it is crucial to the development of Aurora's poetic career. Romney's last words to her made her feel inconsequential, so the meditations in this book encourage her to evaluate her commitment. She exhorts herself to be humble as she strains toward producing some epic work; she questions that her efforts can sustain the weight of inspiration. She has not been satisfied with her apprenticeship in poetry and wonders if the poet needs someone to approve her efforts. Does she need the approbation of a man? She refuses to accept her dependence and decides to "affect no compromise." Next she contemplates whether epic heroes are still to be found. Homer's heroes were not "twelve feet high"; they were simply human. Thus, her contemporary world could provide epic material; a poet can see heroes in her own age. Poets should work to "represent" their own era, "the full-veined, heaving, double-breasted Age," which serves as a nurturing bosom for future generations. Art requires sacrifice, chiefly that of commitment to one ideal; thus Barrett Browning allies herself to the Romantic concept that a poet cannot have both life and art, that art is "intellectual" and denies "feeling." Aurora is lonely; poignant lines describe her desolation: "How dreary 'tis for women to sit still/ On winter nights by solitary fires/ . . . [with] unkissed lips/ And eyes undried." She is "hungry" for love and approval, love and approval from her dead parents and from Romney. She resolves to ignore her pain and renews her commitment to poetry. When Aurora visits Lord Howe's home, she finds Lady Waldemar among the guests. Gossip reveals that Lady Waldemar has been assisting Romney in his work, particularly at Leigh Hall, and that the two will marry soon. Pained by the news, Aurora decides to leave for Italy, hailing it as a nurturing mother drawing her "home."

As book 6 opens, however, Aurora's journey has taken her through France, giving her the opportunity to locate Marian. In her bare lodgings, Marian reveals her secret, "a yearling creature," a baby boy. Aurora is sympathetic to the "fallen" Marian, who begins to tell of her journey through her own hell. Lady Waldemar had convinced Marian to leave Romney and emigrate to Australia, a trip which she would arrange. Instead of escorting Marian to a ship bound for Australia, however, Lady Waldemar's servant brought her to a brothel in Paris; Marian was raped and turned out on the streets when she went mad. Marian's saga continues into book 7, where she finds that she is pregnant and is taken in by a seamstress who allows her to work to support herself and her son. Moved by Marian's suffering, Aurora greets her as "sister" and offers to take her to Italy as her companion. She debates about writing to Romney about her discovery but is reluctant to ruin his supposed happiness. Calling upon "the man in me," she decides to write to Lord Howe and enclose a letter for Lady Waldemar, denouncing her evil machinations. The two travel on to Italy, but Aurora finds that she cannot recapture her childhood feelings for her "motherland." She also realizes that "The end of woman . . . / Is not a book"; she misses Romney and finds herself dissolving into "nothing" without love.

The last two books present the denouement; Aurora is surprised one evening to find that Romney has arrived. Because a letter went undelivered, she still assumes he has married Lady Waldemar; she also neglects to notice the signs that Romney is now blind. He admits that he has been wrong about his social programs and about her success as a poet. Aurora confesses that she is not the same person she was at twenty years old, and both agree that the Victorian principle, "Let us work," can solve their problems. Romney has experienced the death of his dreams for social reform and the loss of Leigh Hall in a fire set by a mob. He has come to make another grand gesture: marrying Marian to restore her reputation. He had never intended to marry Lady Waldemar, who has sent a letter to Aurora revealing her punishment for her treatment of Marian, her loss of Romney. She thinks she might have become a better person through this marriage and insists that she never meant Marian to be treated as she was. Marian now rejects Romney's proposal, revealing that she probably never loved him but instead was grateful for his generosity. She will not encumber him with "a bastard child/ And married harlot." She intends to dedicate her life to her child and may later help Romney in his work by caring for outcasts. Aurora finally realizes that Romney is blind and refuses to allow him to leave without telling him of her love. The two lovers agree to share their life's work; Aurora apparently succumbs to a compromise between art and life. She does, however, triumph; the marriage is based on her terms. She wins love, a poetic career, fame, independence, and power.

Following the acknowledged example of George Gordon, Lord Byron's *Don Juan* (1819-1824), Barrett Browning created an exuberant epic, monumental in size and in scope, incorporating discussions of class struggle, social programs, politics, religion, the status of women, poetic theory, the glories of nature, and contemporary life, among other topics. She uses epic conventions introduced by Homer and Vergil (announcement of theme, an elevated style through epic similes and antiquated word choice, formal speeches, descents into Hades, and an evil manipulator) and creates a significant heroine employed in a noble quest. Like her predecessors, Barrett Browning tried to establish a new society, based on the inspiration of poetry, giving women a respected citizenship.

Aurora Leigh's faults are the reversals of its virtues, since it crosses the genre boundaries of poetry (written entirely in blank verse and including brilliant imagery and careful word choice), the novel, and the epic. The novel's demands for "realism" and "real" dialogue are negated by an epic's large scope and, at times, long-winded, heroic speeches. However, the narrative structure remains intact: exposition, complication (her digressions help to build suspense), immediacy of action, and a welcome denouement. *Aurora Leigh*, extremely popular at its publication and newly restored by feminist critics to its proper status after years of neglect, is Barrett Browning's masterpiece.

Elizabeth R. Nelson

Bibliography:
Gilbert, Sandra, and Susan Gubar. *The Madwoman in the Attic*. New Haven, Conn.: Yale University Press, 1979. Feminist reading with emphasis on discussing Barrett Browning's

solution to the contemporary conflict between "woman" and "poet." Clarifies maternal imagery in the poem.

Kaplan, Cora. Introduction to *Elizabeth Barrett Browning: Aurora Leigh and Other Poems*. London: Women's Press, 1978. Provides an excellent starting point for comprehending the scope of the poem. The editor's comments are often cited to support other readings of the poem. Good notes and a bibliography of critical material available at the time.

Leighton, Angela. *Elizabeth Barrett Browning*. Bloomington: Indiana University Press, 1986. A useful reading of *Aurora Leigh* as feminist poem, especially in its defiance of patriarchal dominance of women and poetry.

Mermin, Dorothy. *Elizabeth Barrett Browning: The Origins of a New Poetry*. Chicago: University of Chicago Press, 1989. A biographical study emphasizing the female in *Aurora Leigh*, its position as a novel, maternal images, and its heroine's defiance of traditional attitudes toward women. Includes an excellent, comprehensive bibliography.

Moers, Ellen. *Literary Women*. Garden City, N.Y.: Doubleday, 1976. Focuses on the influence of Mme de Stael, George Sand, and Elizabeth Gaskell on Barrett Browning and her influence on later writers, especially Emily Dickinson. Moers suggests that Dickinson's poems be read in concert with *Aurora Leigh*. Cites epic features and establishes it as "*the* feminist poem."

THE AUTOBIOGRAPHY

Type of work: Autobiography
Author: Benvenuto Cellini (1500-1571)
First transcribed: 1558-1562; first published as *La vita di Benvenuto Cellini*, 1728 (English translation, 1771)

The Story:
At the age of fifty-eight, Benvenuto Cellini began to set down his memoirs. After relating a fictional version of the founding of Florence by his ancestors, he began the story of his life. Benvenuto was destined by his father to be a musician, and as a boy he was taught to play the flute and sing. His father's lessons in music failed to interest him, however, and at the age of fifteen Cellini apprenticed himself to a goldsmith. Cellini said of himself that he had a natural bent for the work and in a few months he had surpassed men long in the trade. As an apprentice and, later, as a journeyman goldsmith, Cellini traveled through Italy doing fine work and acting the part of a bravo. He became an excellent swordsman and handler of the poniard, as he proved when he killed an enemy in a street brawl.

In 1527, the constable of Bourbon marched on Rome and besieged Pope Clement VII in his fortress. Cellini, then in Rome and in sympathy with the pope, served the pontiff valiantly as an artillerist and as a goldsmith, having been commissioned by the besieged prelate to melt down jewelry and turn it into a more transportable form. Later, he boasted that during the siege he had killed the constable of Bourbon and wounded the prince of Orange.

After the siege was lifted and a truce declared, Cellini returned to Florence and killed the murderer of his brother. He later went to Mantua. Ill with fever in that city, he returned to Florence. When Pope Clement declared war on that city, however, Cellini left his shop and trade to enter the papal service. While in Rome he made a medallion of tremendous size for the papal cope, a work that was the beginning of his fortunes, for the splendid button greatly pleased the pontiff for whom it was made. From then on, during Clement's life, Cellini did much work for the papacy. His career under Pope Clement was nevertheless a stormy one. His fiery temper often caused him no end of trouble, as when he received the commission of the papal mint and then lost it because of his foolhardy and unmannerly actions. He killed an enemy in a quarrel but was lucky enough to be pardoned by his patron.

Cellini's greatest commission from Pope Clement was for a gold chalice. The chalice was never finished, for Clement died. During the last years of his life, however, the chalice was a matter of contention between the pope and his goldsmith. Cellini tended to work too slowly to suit the pope, and he, according to Cellini's account, often forgot that gold was needed to make the vessel.

Upon the accession of Cardinal Farnese as Pope Paul III, Cellini went into his service for a time. He was away from Rome a great deal, however, at one time taking service with Cosimo de' Medici, the duke of Florence. Upon his return to Rome, Cellini was imprisoned on a charge of homicide. The pope granted him a safe-conduct for a time, but eventually he was imprisoned. Only after many difficulties did he receive a pardon.

Cellini came to the notice of Emperor Charles V when that monarch visited Rome and was presented by the pope with a Book of Hours bound into a gold cover encrusted with jewels, the work of Cellini. A short time later, Cellini was sent for by Francis I, the king of France, but before he could leave Rome he was accused of theft and thrown into prison by the pope's *bargello*, or police force. Cellini cleared himself of the charge, but he had made so many enemies that he was kept in prison for many months and suffered, at times, cruel punishment.

Action on Cellini's behalf by King Francis only served to make his lot harder. At last, Cellini managed to escape by using bed sheets to lower himself from the prison tower and over the prison walls. Having broken his leg in flight, he was recaptured. Released after a long period of confinement, he found asylum with a French cardinal and, with the aid of Cardinal d'Este of Ferrara, made his way to France.

In France, with King Francis as his patron, the goldsmith and artist turned to sculpture. He executed an amazing statue of Jupiter for the king and also constructed the large statue of the nymph of Fontainebleau. However, Cellini made an enemy of Madame d'Étampes, the king's mistress, who made his career difficult and his life dangerous, and the cardinal of Ferrara did not fulfill the promises he had made. Cellini's amorous adventures also got him into many difficulties.

In desperation, and hoping for a better future, Cellini left France and returned to his native Florence in 1545, there to find protection under the patronage of Cosimo de' Medici. In Florence, he made an enemy of the duchess of Florence and a famous sculptor, Bandinello, whose work Cellini reviled in public and to the sculptor's face. As in France, a woman's enmity, the dislike of fellow artists, the pettifogging of minor officials, and small commissions used up Cellini's valuable time in Florence. Nevertheless, while there, in the years after 1545, Cellini did his greatest works, among them a bronze Perseus of which he was extremely proud. Following the completion of that statue, Cellini went to work on other pieces, including a tremendous crucifix with a mausoleum at its base to hold his body when he died.

While working in Florence for the duke, Cellini bought some farm land which, failing to bring him the revenues he had been promised, embroiled him in a long and upsetting litigation. That trouble, plus the enmity of the duchess, finally drove him from Florence. In 1562, while the duke and his family were away on a journey, Cellini left Florence and headed for Pisa. Cellini ended his memoirs with the departure for Pisa, though he lived for eight more years.

Critical Evaluation:

The Florentine Benvenuto Cellini—contemporary of Michelangelo, Titian, Tintoretto, and Jacopo Sansovino—was a completely natural man of his time. Utterly unself-conscious and uncritical, he presented himself through his *Autobiography* in the context of the Italian Renaissance, totally involved in its art, its politics, its religion, and its culture. His was the life *engagée*, and his *Autobiography* reflects what Italian Renaissance life was really like.

Characteristically, Cellini's temper and temperament were, by later standards, a mixture of extremes. He loved and he hated; he concentrated intensely and he wasted time. In his lifetime, he killed several men, yet he was at the same time tender, compassionate, and concerned about both men and women when he was convinced they were in need of succor. His love affairs were equally extravagant. He loved many women, produced at least six offspring out of wedlock (some of whom were legitimated), but married only once, from which union issued two legitimate children. He frequently offended powerful men in high position. As a consequence, he spent some time in prison and at other times was banished or exiled from his home, wherever it happened to be. At still other times, he was richly rewarded. He was obsessed with vengeance and honor. He killed his brother's murderer and revenged other outrages. He insisted upon maintaining his honor, regardless of how onerous the circumstances might be. In fact, honor and revenge were the key concepts in his life and, in turn, keys to the Renaissance mind.

This Renaissance fusion of apparent contradictions also delineates the versatility of the period. As a man of letters, he wrote his *Autobiography* (most of it dictated to a scribe), valuable treatises on goldsmithing and sculpture, and other discourses on art. Some of his letters and his petitions survived. He also produced some poetry, which has been largely ignored. He wrote in the lusty Tuscan dialect, more vital than other conventional modes of communication. He was best known, deservedly, as a goldsmith and a sculptor, but he was also an adept swordsman and a diligent soldier, and his engineering skills—particularly in the martial sphere—should not be underrated. This range of accomplishments was typical of cultured men of Cellini's time.

Despite his talents, Cellini was dependent upon patronage and relied for his livelihood upon commissions for artistic works from wealthy patrons. Hence, he executed vases and other vessels and plates as well as a variety of medals and jewelry for popes and prelates, royalty and nobles; busts and statuary for the Medici and for King Francis I of France; a crucifix for the Medici; and a famous salt cellar for Francis I, among other works. His irascible temper constantly brought him into conflict with his patrons, but Cellini was nevertheless honored, respected, and rewarded in his own time.

It was not necessary that an artist syncophantically cater to the tastes of his patron. Cellini thus conceived his ideas first and then convinced his patron that the ideas were worthy of support for their execution. Likewise, artists were not required to live morally or legally exemplary lives. They tended to live boisterous, disorderly lives in bohemian quarters wherever and whenever they congregated in urban centers. Their idiosyncrasies and eccentricities were tolerated by their patrons and by the general public because of their overriding contribution to culture. Rebellious religious and political activities were severely punished, however, as Cellini learned from his many imprisonments and exiles. Private immorality and public peculation were, however, more leniently viewed.

It was under such circumstances as these that Cellini produced his masterworks of art. Categorization is difficult. The sculptures have about them certain qualities of realism, even naturalism, yet they, like the goldsmithery, are more often placed by art critics in the mannerist school. In fact, such facile classification does injustice to precisely that quality which distinguishes Cellini's artistry, for Cellini was above all the epitome of the Renaissance man. His very versatility defies conventional classification. It is therefore more appropriate to say what he did and how he did it than to apply labels.

Among the goldsmithing works, the jewelry, always with gold settings that Cellini himself cast, was often enameled, encrusted with precious and semiprecious gems, and occasionally embellished with exquisitely intricate filigree work, which Cellini also used to decorate a variety of vessels and small casks. Other works—rings, medals, clasps, breviary covers, buckles, crucifixes—were done in gold leaf delicately beaten to form high- or low-relief designs or figures. Among the most famous of such works is the elegant salt cellar created for Francis I, a large vessel, nearly twelve inches high, featuring the figures of Neptune and Mother Earth set on an elaborately embossed base. Cellini also cast seals for the bulls of cardinals and for official documents of state, made dies for the stamping of coins, and struck medals. In addition, he designed plates for engraving and etching, and he produced larger metal works, both hammered and cast, such as ornate vases, chalices, and life-size cast figures.

As for sculpture, Cellini was adept in several media. He chiseled, for example, from white Carrara marble a life-size Christ crucified and set the figure upon a cross of black Carrara marble to create a tremendous sculpture, a study in contrasts between stark white and stark black. (This crucifix now hangs in the Church of San Lorenzo in the Escorial.) For the gateway to Francis I's palace at Fontainebleau, he cast in bronze a reclining nymph—now known as the Nymph of Fontainebleau—more than ten feet long, surrounded by animals and flanked by two figures symbolizing Victory. For sheer elegance, however, the Nymph is outshone by Cellini's silver Jupiter, also executed for Francis I, a gorgeous statue set on a gilded pedestal that conceals hard wooden ball bearings, allowing the statue to be moved with no more than a touch of the hand. A "colossus"—a sixty-foot statue of Mars—planned for Francis I's fountain at Fontainebleau was never brought to fruition. Yet it is the slightly larger than life-size cast bronze Perseus with the Head of Medusa—made for Cosimo de' Medici and still standing in the Loggia de' Lanzia—for which Cellini is best known and most admired. Using methods similar to those employed in creating the Nymph of Fontainebleau, he cast the figure of Perseus all in one piece, an amazing achievement of both art and craft. Cellini's description of the process forms one of the high points in his *Autobiography*.

"Critical Evaluation" by Joanne G. Kashdan

Bibliography:
Howarth, William. "Some Principles of Autobiography." In *Autobiography: Essays Theoretical and Critical*, edited by James Olney. Princeton, N.J.: Princeton University Press, 1980. Discusses Cellini's autobiography as one of several works that attempt in prose what painters do on canvas: the creation of a self-portrait. Claims Cellini provides a straightforward account of his life.
Pascal, Roy. "The Early History of Autobiography." In *Design and Truth in Autobiography*. Cambridge, Mass.: Harvard University Press, 1960. Includes a discussion of Cellini's *Autobiography* in a general assessment of works that emerged during the Renaissance. Believes that Cellini is truthful in the way he presents the facts of his life, and that he was confident of his greatness.
Pope-Hennessy, John W. *Cellini*. New York: Abbeville Press, 1985. Comprehensive biography of the artist. Uses the *Autobiography* as a principal source, but highlights the differences between Cellini's account of his life and the record of events in other sources. Profusely illustrated.
Symonds, J. A. Introduction to *The Life of Benvenuto Cellini*. 3d ed. New York: Liveright, 1889. Perceptive commentary about the style and veracity of Cellini's narrative, offering a balanced view of the *Autobiography* as a work of biography and history. Also comments on the various manuscripts and prior translations.
Weintraub, Karl Joachim. "Benvenuto Cellini: The Naïve Individuality." In *The Value of the Individual Self and Circumstance in Autobiography*. Chicago: University of Chicago Press, 1978. Excellent scholarly examination of the *Autobiography*; analyzes the themes of self-aggrandizement and Cellini's self-confident belief that the story of his life is worth telling. Claims the work is a significant document in the history of the development of the concept of human personality.

AUTOBIOGRAPHY

Type of work: Autobiography
Author: John Stuart Mill (1806-1873)
First published: 1873

The *Autobiography* is a unique and fascinating book, one of a handful likely to be read as long as nineteenth century Britain is remembered. It bears witness to the intellectual ferment that was part of the industrial and democratic revolutions of the time. Wider suffrage led to state-supported education in Britain and debate about its proper content. These circumstances supplied Mill's chief motives for recording his life. He wished to recount his own intellectual development and mission in a period of cultural transition and to describe his remarkable education.

Mill, better than anyone, articulated the outlook of nineteenth century liberalism, and so, more than any other intellectual, shaped thinking about politics and society in English-speaking countries in the twentieth century. His interests included political philosophy, ethics, economics, psychology, logic, the scientific method, religion, liberty, the prejudice suffered by women. His ordered, lucid prose helped guarantee that his books would long be read. Generous by nature and fair-minded in considering the views of others, he was, as British prime minister William Gladstone declared, a "saint of rationalism."

The book recounts in detail a truly remarkable instance of home schooling, through which Mill acquired by his middle teens knowledge and analytical skills far superior to those of most university graduates—to say nothing of a phenomenal capacity for work. Mill missed a real childhood, however, suffering emotional disabilities that led to a severe psychological crisis and lifelong insecurity. The *Autobiography* reveals and conceals the emotional dimension of a committed rationalist.

Mill's education was provided by his father, James Mill, a gifted Scotsman of modest birth who had been sponsored at university by a squire, John Stuart. Trained in the classics and living by his pen in London, James commenced his eldest son's education at the age of three with Greek. Beginning with *Aesop's Fables*, John later read the historian Herodotus, the philosopher Plato and numerous other works. Mill was tutored several hours each morning, then worked at his father's table, asking for definitions when necessary. He also read modern histories of Greece and Rome, typically—as he remembered it—on his own initiative, discussing them from his notes on long daily walks with his father. James gave explanations John was required to restate in his own words; this introduced him to the analysis of institutions and the biases of historians. He also studied math and wrote poetry.

He began Latin at eight, also teaching it to his sister. He also studied Greek and Latin poets, the historian Thucydides, and the philosopher Aristotle, and he commenced geometry, algebra, and calculus. His "private reading" was still mainly historical, and at eleven he wrote a long history of Roman government (his father did not intervene in any way). By this time he was reading Greek philosophers "with perfect ease," learning not just another language, but how to think critically. He was asked to explain and draw inferences. At about age ten he read aloud the entire manuscript of his father's ten-volume *History of British India* (1818), helping correct the proofs. At twelve he commenced logic with Aristotle and later writers. The heavily classical training raised no religious doubts: "I never threw off religion because I never had any."

Two friends of his father were important in his education. He learned economics from his father's exposition, on walks, of David Ricardo's thought. John took daily notes, which his father used when writing a book on political economy. John later made marginal summaries on the manuscript so the order of ideas could better be assessed. Philosopher Jeremy Bentham was James's mentor. Bentham took a strong interest in John, and, via James, shaped his philosophical outlook.

By age fourteen most of John's formal education was complete. He had no idea he was exceptional. When he learned otherwise, he judged his abilities average at best and credited his father. He spent a year, 1820-1821, in France with Bentham's brother's family. There he acquired excellent French, learned dancing and piano, and displayed little aptitude for fencing and riding. He learned to love mountain scenery and botany, studied at the University of Montpellier, and later described this breath of "free continental air" as the happiest year in his childhood.

James Mill's *History of British India* secured him a high bureaucratic position in the East India Company, which governed the colony of India. John studied law and German, and became the chief teacher of his eight siblings until he was forty-five. At eighteen he also began working for his father, and continued to do so for thirty-five years, seeking to achieve, as drafter of correspondence to India's administrators, beneficial government.

Mill, diligent and committed to ideas and reform, found time for another life in the world of ideas. While still a teenager he had edited Bentham's five-volume *Rationale of Judicial Evidence* (1825), a daunting task which required reconciling three complete manuscripts. And he continued to write, publishing more than fifty letters, reviews, and articles before reaching age twenty. He formed groups, including the Utilitarians (short-lived, but the group's name would come to denote a branch of philosophy), a self-study group, and a debating society. Though not eloquent, he impressed others with his precision and relentless logic. He was likened by a friend to a "great steam engine."

In his early twenties a mental crisis came that he judged a reaction to his intellectually rich but emotionally starved upbringing. Mill came to say that fear, not love, characterized the relationship between James and his older children. John became sunk in depression after realizing that even if he achieved all of his reform goals he would not be happy. Distraught, he concluded that the analytical emphasis of his father's teaching had stifled his emotional development. He seemed to take pleasure in nothing, not even long-cherished books. The pathos of a French playwright's description of his father's death brought tears and released Mill's pent-up feelings. The poetry of William Wordsworth, evoking pleasure in nature's beauty, was another source of emotional renewal.

The depression, which he thought fruitless to discuss with his father, led Mill to new friends and new ideas, all of which were part of the cultural reaction against the eighteenth century. Some, such as poet Samuel Taylor Coleridge, historian Thomas Carlyle, and their German mentors, emphasized feeling and intuition. Others, such as Auguste Comte, propounded something quite new to Mill: the notion that cultural history necessarily follows a particular pattern, from theological to metaphysical to positive (scientific) thinking.

One friendship was to prove especially significant for the emotionally fragile Mill—one with a beautiful, intelligent, intense young woman, Harriet Taylor (1807-1858). They met in 1830; he was twenty-five, she twenty-three. She was also a married mother of two, soon to be three, and divorce was not then accepted. What ensued was an ardent but platonic relationship beset by gossip, a shrinking circle of friends, and prolonged public embarrassment for all concerned. The pair saw each other frequently, even traveling together. This lasted two decades, until Mr. Taylor died and they could wed in 1851. Mill saw Harriet as his coworker and emotional lodestone. The *Autobiography*'s dumbfoundingly extravagant praise of her superiority in character, feeling, intellect, and judgment reveals by implication that he was dominated by her emotionally. She chilled his relations with his family. Mill, who lived at home until forty-five, the last fifteen years of which time he was the head of his dead father's household, makes no mention of his mother in the *Autobiography*. Equally strange was Harriet's failure to protest in the slightest his ludicrously exaggerated praise of her. One must look beyond the *Autobiography*, or read between the lines, to understand their relationship.

The unusual nature of Mill's private and emotional life, however, did not deflect him from his sense of mission, his commitment to enlightening the public and giving voice to liberal elements in Parliament. The *Autobiography* recounts his work in detail. *A System of Logic* (1843), his first major work, defends empiricism against intuitionism, which he saw as a bulwark for reactionary political and religious thinking. *Principles of Political Economy* (1848) defends free market production but holds that no economic laws determine how wealth is distributed; by concerted action workers can alter their share of the wealth labor creates. This view, expressed in the third edition of the book, contributed much to the rise of socialism in England. *On Liberty* (1859), a joint work with Harriet, defends free thought and the sovereignty of the individual, and proclaims the social value of letting people develop in diverse ways. It emphasizes—as had historian Alexis de Tocqueville's *Democracy in America* (1835-1840), a book Mill esteemed very highly—the danger of intolerant public opinion in a democracy. Mill hoped that *On Liberty* would be his most enduring work. *The Subjection of Women* (1869) combats the disenfranchisement of women.

Mill's liberalism is also evident in his numerous articles, many of which were later published as a book: *Dissertations and Discussions* (1859). His support for self-rule in Canada sped its achievement there. During America's Civil War he held that Union victory was vital to progress throughout the world and hoped it would destroy slavery, the "accursed thing" that violated America's constitution. He spoke for the exploited, be they landless Irish peasants or brutalized former slaves in Jamaica. His commitment to putting liberal ideas before the public is revealed not only by his many articles but also by his work as editor of the *London and Westminster Review* and his financial support of that and other journals.

In 1858, Parliament decided, over his able protest, to abolish the East India Company and rule directly. Mill received a generous position. He and Harriet planned a lengthy trip in southern Europe, but she suddenly died of consumption in Avignon, France. Much of his remaining fifteen years were spent living there, within sight of her grave. He continued to work productively, writing many of his books during the years in Avignon. Evidence of his apparent emotional need for a strong personality to fill the place first occupied by his father, then Harriet, is the fact that he elevated his stepdaughter Helen, who lived with him until his death in Avignon, to a similar position.

In the mid-1860's, Mill was asked to represent Westminster in Parliament. Though declaring that he would not campaign, he was victorious. His actions there were consistent with his principles. He sought land reform and the restoration of habeas corpus in Ireland, judicial action against those who violated the rights of Jamaicans, an end to election bribery, proportional representation for minorities, and enfranchisement of women. This last, surprisingly, was supported by eighty other members of Parliament, marking the effective beginning of the women's suffrage movement in England.

R. Craig Philips

Bibliography:

Borchard, Ruth. *John Stuart Mill, the Man.* London: Watts, 1957. A useful brief survey of Mill's life, though it draws heavily on the *Autobiography* itself.

Mill, John Stuart. *The Early Draft of John Stuart Mill's Autobiography.* Edited by Jack Stillinger. Champaign: University of Illinois Press, 1961. Reveals differences between early drafts and the published versions of the *Autobiography.*

_____. *John Stuart Mill and Harriet Taylor: Their Correspondence and Subsequent Marriage.* Edited by F. A. von Hayek. London: Routledge & Kegan Paul, 1951. A study of the most important relationship in Mill's adult years. Drastically alters the glowing image of Harriet Taylor created by the *Autobiography.*

Mazlish, Bruce. *James and John Stuart Mill, Father and Son in the Nineteenth Century.* New York: Basic Books, 1975. The material on James Mill adds much to one's understanding of his more famous son. The book has a strong "social science/psycho-history" perspective that is predicated on the validity of Freudian theory.

Packe, Michael. *The Life of John Stuart Mill.* New York: Macmillan, 1954. The standard biography. Comprehensive, intelligent, and elegantly written, setting many aspects of Mill's career in historical context.

THE AUTOBIOGRAPHY OF ALICE B. TOKLAS

Type of work: Novel
Author: Gertrude Stein (1874-1946)
Type of plot: Historical realism
Time of plot: 1903-1932
Locale: Paris, France
First published: 1933

> *Principal characters:*
> GERTRUDE STEIN, an artist
> ALICE B. TOKLAS, her companion

The Story:

The title of this book is misleading. The book is not an autobiography of Alice B. Toklas because she did not write it. The book is more the autobiography or memoirs of Alice B. Toklas and Gertrude Stein, as written by Gertrude Stein.

Alice was born in San Francisco, California. It was quite by accident that, shortly after the great San Francisco earthquake (April 18, 1906), Alice met Michael and Sarah Stein, Gertrude's older brother and his wife. They had just returned from Paris to tend to their real estate holdings damaged by the earthquake. Sarah had brought with her three small paintings by Henri Matisse. She showed them to Alice and her friends, told them about her exciting life in France, and invited them all to visit her in Paris. In less than a year Alice went to Paris and met Gertrude Stein.

Alice made her first visit to the already famous Saturday evening dinners at 27 rue de Fleurus, home of Gertrude Stein. Of greatest significance to Alice was what she saw and whom she met. She gave an account of the apartment and the extensive art collection, including paintings by Paul Cézanne, Pierre-Auguste Renoir, Matisse, and Pablo Picasso, with special attention given to Picasso's portrait of Gertrude Stein (which now hangs in New York's Metropolitan Museum). The list of the people in attendance on that and the many other Saturday evenings made up a veritable who's who of European art and American literature during the early decades of the twentieth century. The most important person Alice met that first evening was Pablo Picasso, the artist for whom Gertrude Stein had the greatest affinity.

Alice's arrival experiences continued on the next day and included her first vernissage— a preview of an art exhibition—where she was further introduced to the art and artists of Paris. The third instance of Alice's introduction was a walk with Gertrude through various artists' studios in Montmartre, then the artists' quarter of Paris.

In the following chapter, "Gertrude Stein in Paris: 1903-1907," Gertrude Stein spent her formative years as a writer and one involved in the development of modern art, with specific reference to Cézanne, Matisse, and Picasso. In 1903, Gertrude began writing *The Making of Americans*, an immense work that she regarded as her major literary accomplishment at that time. It was finished in 1911 but was not published until 1925. During these years she also wrote *Three Lives* (1909), her first published book.

In these years Gertrude and her brother Leo started buying the paintings that made up their vast and valuable art collection and, in this way, they met the major artists working in Paris. Of greatest consequence to Gertrude's writing were Matisse and Picasso, whose paintings were in many ways the visual counterparts of her literary style.

In the next chapter, "Gertrude Stein Before She Came to Paris," a few high points of her early life are recounted, such as her travels with her parents and brother, studying psychology with William James at Radcliffe, and studying medicine at The Johns Hopkins University. When she eventually lost interest in her medical studies she traveled with Leo in Europe and settled in London for a winter, spending most days reading English literature at the British Museum. Gertrude returned to America for a brief stay and wrote her first short novel (*Quod Erat Demonstrandum*, written 1903, "rediscovered" 1932, published as *Things as They Are*, 1950).

In "1907-1914," the story of Gertrude's and Alice's lives together begins again. The Saturday evenings at home continued on a regular basis, allowing further discussion about the famous artists, or those who were well known at the time. There were, however, also many minor figures, such as the maidservant Hélène, their Moroccan guide Mohammed, and a host of unnamed people. Virtually all these visitors became subjects of the portraits Gertrude Stein wrote during these years. One visitor was Carl Van Vechten, author and music critic for *The New York Times*. His early essay on Gertrude Stein included the quotation from her portrait "Sacred Emily" that was to become her most famous motto: "A rose is a rose is a rose is a rose."

Two important events in Gertrude Stein's life occurred during these years. In 1909, Alice B. Toklas moved to 27 rue de Fleurus and became Gertrude's lifelong companion. In 1913 Gertrude's brother Leo, who had been such an important influence on her early life, moved to Florence, Italy. They divided their art collection: She kept the Cézannes and Picassos and he took the Matisses and Renoirs.

"The War" reports the events that engaged Gertrude and Alice during World War I (1914-1918). In addition to continued writing, the two women performed volunteer work, driving a supply truck for the American Fund for the French Wounded.

The final chapter, "After the War: 1919-1932," describes a very different life. The exciting crowd from before the war had, by and large, disappeared from the Saturday evening gatherings. It was, however, replaced by a new group that Gertrude Stein labeled "the lost generation" of American writers. Among the best known were Sherwood Anderson, Ernest Hemingway, and F. Scott Fitzgerald. Gertrude Stein provided an extensive discussion of her relationship with Hemingway, suggesting that she not only influenced him to become a writer but also taught him how he should write.

The composer Virgil Thomson encouraged Stein to write the libretto for the opera *Four Saints in Three Acts* (written 1927-1928; first performed 1934). It included another famous Stein motto with Saint Ignatius and a chorus of saints singing "Pigeons on the grass alas."

Personally most satisfying for Gertrude Stein was the public recognition she received for her work in these years. The literary societies of Cambridge and Oxford universities invited her in 1926 to present her lecture "Composition as Explanation" to great acclaim. She realized then that she had become a writer of distinction.

The last page of the book answers the question of its authorship. It begins with Gertrude's effort to persuade Alice to write the book, but Gertrude finally admitted that the only way the autobiography would ever be written would be if she wrote it.

Critical Evaluation:

Gertrude Stein wrote more than two dozen books and plays, but most people have read only *The Autobiography of Alice B. Toklas* and, perhaps, *Three Lives*. Of course, many can quote "A rose is a rose is a rose is a rose," frequently forgetting the fourth rose, and "pigeons on the grass alas." As one of the preeminent authors of twentieth century American literature, she was the creator of a new literary style that has had a profound influence on many younger novelists, poets, and dramatists.

Even though Stein's writings at the time were known to only a small group of readers, the publication of *The Autobiography of Alice B. Toklas* made her an international celebrity. *The Autobiography of Alice B. Toklas* was a great success, even making the best-seller list. Following its publication she was persuaded to give lectures and readings throughout the United States, and she became one of the best-known writers of her day. Contributing to her renown was her association with the new school of contemporary painting in Paris—Picasso, Matisse, Cézanne, Renoir, and all the other Modernists.

Two types of readers were attracted to *The Autobiography of Alice B. Toklas*: the serious reader, who recognized it as a more accessible example of her unique literary style, and the general reader, who saw the book as a report on bohemian life in Paris. The latter took delight in a chatty, gossipy account of the lives of the more than four hundred people mentioned. Some of these people were to become famous artists of the twentieth century, others were well known at the time but soon faded into obscurity, while many belonged to neither group. Several people whose names appeared in *The Autobiography of Alice B. Toklas* objected to Stein's account of the Paris art scene and even wrote rejoinders trying to set the record straight.

The originality of Gertrude Stein's work can be observed in the way in which she transcribes banal daily speech, exactly as she hears it, into her literature. In her early study of psychology she observed that the brain does not always operate on a sequential or logical level and that conversation is frequently made up of repetitions reflecting digressing or associative thoughts. From the French Symbolist poets she learned how the imagination can create linguistic images without having the brain serve as mediator to establish logical order. She believed that the mind could assign meanings to words that are unrelated to their dictionary meaning, especially when dealing with words describing emotions or remembering specific sounds.

To appreciate Gertrude Stein's unique literary style the reader may wish to consider *The Autobiography of Alice B. Toklas* as a book of portraits. Stein wrote hundreds of portraits in her life, but these are unlike the traditional verbal or visual portraits found in art and literature. If one were to compare portraits written or painted in the eighteenth or nineteenth century with those, for example, painted by Picasso or Matisse in the early years of the twentieth century, one would note immediately that the former attempted to present a likeness that was as close as possible to the subject. In a Picasso or Matisse portrait, however, the painter does not strive for the representational correctness of a photograph and the viewer observes an abstract essence of the subject. In Picasso's *Portrait of a Young Girl*, for example, the subject has a head represented by numerous green shapes and a blue arm that seems to extend below the leg. Matisse's *Landscape at Collioure* is made up of no more than a series of different colored brushstrokes. Although painters can find such new and different ways to express themselves by varying colors and shapes, writers are much more limited by the boundaries of language.

In many of her portraits, Gertrude Stein rejects the use of traditional narrative prose with all its complicated grammar rules, conventions, and limitations. She also discards the artificial ways in which discourse has been recorded in written form over the centuries. What she does is to present a verbal portrait of an individual based on the way in which that person thinks and speaks, using words unique to the speaker, with variations and permutations. Speaking about language, Stein stated that "it does not make any difference to me what language I hear, I don't hear a language, I hear tones of voices and rhythms." Her portraits are as complicated and difficult to understand as the paintings of the modernist artists working in Paris at that time. *The Autobiography of Alice B. Toklas*, however, utilizes the least radical form of Stein's literary style. *The Autobiography of Alice B. Toklas* was written in the way in which Alice B. Toklas would have written or spoken the story. Even though the plot traces Gertrude's life from her birth until 1932, when she finished writing this book, the reader has more of an understanding of the essence of Gertrude Stein than an awareness or knowledge of her life. Gertrude has the character of Alice tell the story in her "rambling" speech, constantly interrupting herself to refer to a specific time, place, or person, and gradually painting the complete portrait as Gertrude Stein wants to be seen. References to artists or writers of her time, whether praising or blaming, ultimately serve only to complete that picture.

The last paragraph in *The Autobiography of Alice B. Toklas* provides an important statement. It suggests that the book is like Daniel Defoe's fictional biography of Robinson Crusoe— a complete literary work of fiction.

Thomas H. Falk

Bibliography:
Bridgman, Richard. *Gertrude Stein in Pieces*. New York: Oxford University Press, 1970. Scholars consider this to be the best book on Gertrude Stein. A well-written and carefully documented study, providing readers with a thorough insight into both Stein's life and work.
Greenfeld, Howard. *Gertrude Stein: A Biography*. New York: Crown, 1973. A brief introduction to Gertrude Stein, well suited for the general reader.
Hoffman, Michael J. *Gertrude Stein*. Boston: Twayne, 1976. A balanced, critical study identifying Stein's work as the most important source and influence on modernism.
Mellow, James R. *Charmed Circle: Gertrude Stein and Company*. New York: Praeger, 1974. A major and comprehensive study of Stein's life and work, providing many details in a very readable way.
Simon, Linda. *The Biography of Alice B. Toklas*. Garden City, N.Y.: Doubleday, 1977. A fine biography of Alice B. Toklas, especially for the reader interested in seeing the life and times from Alice's perspective. Can serve as a valuable companion volume to Stein's book.

THE AUTOBIOGRAPHY OF AN EX-COLOURED MAN

Type of work: Novel
Author: James Weldon Johnson (1871-1938)
Type of plot: Psychological realism
Time of plot: Early twentieth century
Locale: Southern United States, New York City, and Europe
First published: 1912

>   *Principal characters:*
>   ANONYMOUS NARRATOR, a mulatto who decides to pass for white
>   THE MILLIONAIRE, the narrator's patron

The Story:

Born in Georgia a few years after the Civil War, the narrator, in comparison with other blacks, lived in a comfortably furnished little house. Thinking her son superior to other children in his neighborhood, the narrator's mother was particular about his dress and his associates. Later, the narrator remembered scenarios of familial bliss that centered around a "tall man with a small, dark moustache" who visited them in the evenings several times a week. Because he admired the man's shiny boots and his gold watch and chain, the narrator developed a subconscious identification with the white man that helped give him a sense of freedom and self-confidence. He later learned that this man was his father. Whereas he identified with the tall, white man, the narrator's fondness for the black keys on the piano in his parlor represented his identification with that part of himself that was black. When he heard his mother playing old Southern songs on the piano, the narrator felt happiest. By the time he was seven, he could play all the songs his mother knew.

Eventually, the narrator and his mother moved from Georgia to Connecticut because the tall, white man was getting married and it would not have been appropriate for his black mistress and his illegitimate son to live in the same town with his white wife. In Connecticut, the narrator learned that he was black and what that meant. One day, the white students in his class were asked to stand. When he rose, his teacher asked him to wait and rise with the nonwhites. For the first time, the narrator recognized differences between himself and his classmates. He also noticed differences in the way he looked and the way his mother looked. He saw beauty in his features and defects in his mother's darker features. The narrator's heightened sense of difference forced him to adjust, temporarily, to the "dwarfing, warping, distorting influence" of America on the lives of blacks. After he became interested in reading the Bible and history books, the narrator's vicarious identification with heroic men of action like King David, Samson, and Robert the Bruce emphasized the narrator's early, intellectual separation from the masses of black people who were powerless in American society.

Despite his unassuming nature, the narrator was pleased with the applause he received after playing the piano at his graduation. Yet he wished to receive the even greater enthusiasm aroused by the speech given by Shiny, a dark-skinned classmate who was the class orator. What Shiny said and how he said it reflected not only upon himself but on the whole race of black people.

Not long after the narrator graduated, his mother died, and he decided to attend Atlanta University rather than Harvard, which would have been more expensive. The narrator never matriculated at Atlanta University because his money was stolen and he was too embarrassed to tell anyone at the school about his predicament. Instead, he caught a train for Jacksonville, Florida, where he earned money giving piano lessons and working in a cigar factory; where he earned the privileged position of "reader." Although he seemed relatively satisfied with his life in Jacksonville, the narrator longed to see the North again. When the cigar factory closed, he moved to New York City.

Enticed by the less than commendable features of the city's attractions, the narrator discovered a gambling-house where the clientele could drink, play pool, and shoot dice. Caught up in the heady experience of gambling, the narrator decided that this would be his occupation. Because his winning streaks were sporadic, however, he mastered the technique of playing ragtime music. A millionaire became his patron and introduced him to a world where rich, blasé, cynical whites paid him to entertain them with ragtime tunes. Attracted by the millionaire's "stamp of culture," the narrator agreed to play at dinners and parties. "Occasionally [the millionaire] 'loaned' me to some of his friends. And, too, I often played for him alone at his apartments."

Frightened out of New York by the prospect of being murdered by a jealous lover, the narrator accepted the millionaire's invitation to accompany him on an extended European tour. They spent weeks in London, Paris, Amsterdam, Luxembourg, Brussels, and Berlin, where the narrator's cosmopolitan sensibilities were refined. He discovered that the stereotyped descriptions of the natives of the different countries were false and that assumptions about an entire race or ethnic group could not be determined from generalizations. He enjoyed the freedom of not having to contend with constant reminders that he was a black man, and he learned something of the culture and languages of the different countries. His travels were rather aimless, however, until, while in Germany, he realized the artistic possibilities of making black music an accepted part of American culture. He decided to take ragtime music and make it classical. The millionaire argued against this resolve, but the narrator reasoned that he would have a better future as a composer.

As he made his way into the deep South, the narrator thought about the complexities of the race question. While making his musical notations, he noticed that "the Negroes themselves do not fully appreciate these old slave songs. The educated classes are rather ashamed of them and prefer to sing hymns from books." For all of its attractions and special cultural significance the South was chaotic. It defied all attempts to make it orderly. Already predisposed to choose the kind of life that would lift the burden of race from his shoulders, a lynching of a black man made the narrator finally decide to pass for white. As the narrator, transfixed, watched the horribly mechanical spectacle of the lynching, he did not identify with the man's predicament. The black man's fate could never be his own. The lynching forced the narrator to make a resolution he was able to keep. With his physical characteristics, speech patterns, and knowledge no one would believe he was black.

Critical Evaluation:

The Autobiography of an Ex-Coloured Man is the account of a mulatto who decides, after a series of experiences and revelations beginning in his childhood and stretching into adulthood, to "pass" for white. The mulatto narrator remains anonymous, and the tone of the book suggests that the story is based on fact. In the first paragraph the narrator professes to know his identity. He states that his autobiography was the complete expression of his "sort of savage and diabolical desire to gather up all the little tragedies of my life, and turn them into a practical joke on society."

When the novel was published anonymously in 1912, readers speculated about its verisimilitude. Anonymity, a common feature of the slave narratives that had lent support to the abolitionist movement, formed the foundation of the African American literary tradition. Just as anonymity had protected the identity of slaves and lessened the chance of reprisals from slave masters, it was not difficult to assume that this author chose anonymity to avoid answering questions or compromising his status. The book also revealed the trickster aspect of black-white relations: Readers could not be certain that what the narrator said was precisely what he was thinking.

Some critics judged the narrator to be a moral coward because he chose to live his life as a white man. This criticism makes the assumption that choosing to be black would have been better than choosing to be white. If, however, the making of money is not innately immoral, it does not follow that the narrator's decision to function as a white businessman necessarily means that he is a moral coward. The narrator is criticized because he looks to material comfort for self-aggrandizement rather than to Christianity for spiritual growth in suffering. Yet as a self-described agnostic, the narrator did not have any use for a religion that restricted people to emotionalism and numbed their impulse to strike back at avowed enemies. His willingness to suffer the millionaire's apparent ennui and homosexual overtures suggests an inability to demand respect when his physical comfort might be jeopardized.

Johnson explored the ambivalence that troubled mulattoes who have some of the "best" and some of the "worst" blood in the South coursing through their veins. More than once, the narrator decided to live as a black man and be an exemplar of his race, but he found he could not do it. He had not grown up with a reason to fight against social or economic injustices. He had had to develop an awareness of his ethnic relationship with black people and invent ways to give expression to his ethnicity. His intellectual attachment to biblical and historical figures provided a release for the psychological struggle that mirrored the plight of many light-skinned blacks, but he was physically detached from the majority of blacks.

Shamefully naïve about black folk culture, the narrator was repulsed by unkempt and loud lower-class blacks. For a short time, he appreciated the beauty of African American culture as lower-class blacks expressed it. His appreciation for black folk music waned, though, as he became aware that black music outside black society was not accepted as authentic art. The popular attitude of the time was that black people were fundamentally incapable of creating anything that could be considered artistic. The narrator adopted this view as his own.

Johnson's use of anonymity to reveal the novel's complexities accentuates the narrator's sense of isolation from himself and from others, whether black or white. Having the narrator pass through rural, urban, and international environments suggests that a cosmopolitan experience can stimulate the development of art forms. Yet the reaction to skin color, itself a rather ill-defined measure of personal identity, prevents the growth of artistic expression and an awareness of self.

Judith E. B. Harmon

Bibliography:
Bell, Bernard W. "James Weldon Johnson (1871-1938)." *The Afro-American Novel and Its Tradition.* Amherst: University of Massachusetts Press, 1987. The psychological impact of color and class has turned the mulatto narrator from the majority of black Americans and toward an identity with white Americans that subverts his self-worth.
Collier, Eugenia. "The Endless Journey of an Ex-Coloured Man." *Phylon* 32, no. 4 (Winter,

1971): 365-373. An analysis of the narrator's physical and psychological journeys that emphasizes the ambivalence of the dual heritage that characterizes African American life and letters.

Fleming, Robert E. "Irony as a Key to Johnson's *The Autobiography of an Ex-Coloured Man.*" *American Literature* 43, no. 1 (March, 1971): 83-96. Espouses the theory that to accept the unreliability of the narrator is essential to comprehending Johnson's novel.

Pisiak, Roxanna. "Irony and Subversion in James Weldon Johnson's *The Autobiography of an Ex-Coloured Man.*" *Studies in American Fiction* 21 (Spring, 1993): 83-96. This bibliographic essay cites numerous articles whose criticisms have focused on irony, one of the most interesting approaches to take to the novel.

Skerrett, Joseph T., Jr. "Irony and Symbolic Action in James Weldon Johnson's *The Autobiography of an Ex-Coloured Man.*" *American Quarterly* 32, no. 5 (Winter, 1980): 540-558. Discusses the complex duality that is revealed in the way Johnson developed the narrator's character and integrated aspects of his own history with the narrator's "fictional" history.

THE AUTOBIOGRAPHY OF BENJAMIN FRANKLIN

Type of work: Autobiography
Author: Benjamin Franklin (1706-1790)
First published: French translation, 1791 as *Mémoires de la vie privée*; English original, 1868

> *Principal personages:*
> BENJAMIN FRANKLIN
> JOSIAH FRANKLIN, his father
> JAMES FRANKLIN, his brother and first employer
> SIR WILLIAM KEITH, the governor of Pennsylvania
> MR. DENHAM, a merchant
> MR. MEREDITH, Franklin's partner in the print shop
> ALEXANDER HAMILTON
> GOUVERNEUR MORRIS

In Twyford, England, at the age of sixty-five, Benjamin Franklin began to set down reminiscences of his early days, which he addressed to his "Dear Son." For years he had been collecting information about his ancestors, who had lived in Ecton, Northamptonshire, as far back as 1555, the oldest date of the town records; and he thought that his son William Franklin (1731-1813) would someday be interested in the "circumstances" of his father's life, just as Franklin had delighted in anecdotes relating to his ancestors.

The work was composed in installments. The first section, dealing with Franklin's first twenty-four years, was the product of a week of leisure in England in 1771. Then, because of his political activities abroad and at home, he had no further opportunity to continue his task until friends persuaded him to resume his writing in 1783. The final section was probably written between November, 1789, and April, 1790. The work first appeared in France, and no complete English text appeared until 1868.

In spite of the lengthy period of composition, Franklin covered almost exclusively his life before July, 1757, adding only a few comments on his activities in the following years. The failure to complete his autobiography beyond his fifty-first year does not mean, however, that Franklin failed to write of his activities over the next thirty years. Some of his most important diplomatic missions are reported in individual compositions, such as the sample he showed to Jefferson of the "history of my life" that he said he was preparing. They include "Negotiations in London for Effecting a Reconciliation between Great Britain and the American Colonies" and the "Journal of the Negotiations for Peace with Great Britain from March 21st to July 1st, 1782."

Franklin, an indefatigable letter writer, also filled his correspondence (in many ways the most interesting part of his writing) with details and sketches. Some of the most complete are the letters to his wife, whom he addressed as "My dear Child." By combining the correspondence chronologically, a biographer can obtain Franklin's personal reactions to practically everything that happened to him. These letters show Franklin as the first American who stood apart from European influences.

The Franklin family, whose ancestors had lived in the Northamptonshire village of Ecton from the time they assumed a surname, which originally signified a middle-class landowner, was transplanted to Boston about 1682, when Benjamin's father Josiah brought his wife and several children to Massachusetts. After his wife's death, the older Franklin remarried. Benjamin, born of the second marriage, was the youngest son of seventeen children.

Fond of study and having quickly learned to read, Benjamin was initially destined for the ministry. However, after his father, a tallow-candler and soap-boiler by trade, calculated the cost of education and the pitiable salary received by most ministers, he took the boy out of school to learn a trade. Briefly he became his father's assistant; then, at the age of twelve, he was apprenticed to his half brother James, a printer. In his brother's shop, he saw his first writing in print, topical ballads written to be sold in the streets.

During this period he read *The Pilgrim's Progress* (1678/1684), Plutarch's *Parallel Lives* (105-115), and essays by Daniel Defoe, Sir Richard Burton, and Cotton Mather. A volume of the *Spectator*, acquired by chance, revealed to him the importance of style and, like Robert Louis Stevenson at a later date, he taught himself by rewriting and comparing sentences. From this printshop came the fifth—Franklin mistakenly says the second—newspaper in America, *The New England Courant*, to which Franklin became an anonymous contributor.

Quarrels with his brother eventually sent the seventeen-year-old apprentice to Philadelphia looking for employment. His arrival early in the morning, with three-pennyworth of rolls in his mouth and under his arms as he walked up Market Street past the home of Miss Read, whom he was later to marry, was Philadelphia's first sight of one of its most distinguished citizens.

Neither Bradford nor Keimer, the only printers in Philadelphia, was very advanced. After the boy found a place in Keimer's shop, his wide reading and his ability to talk and to listen brought him many friends. Eventually, Governor Keith offered to send him to England to buy type and equipment for a shop of his own. When he arrived in London, he learned that Keith, whose credit was not good, had provided nothing but promises. To support himself, Franklin found work in a printing house. After eighteen months, he was happy to accept the offer of a merchant who wanted him to take back to America a consignment of merchandise. Back in Philadelphia, he worked for a time in Keimer's shop; then he found a partner in the Welsh Pennsylvanian Hugh Meredith, and the two set up their own establishment. They prospered, and in 1729 Franklin became the sole proprietor when he bought out Meredith, whose drinking habits were distasteful to the temperate, frugal Franklin. He branched out as a stationer. In 1730, he founded *The Pennsylvania Gazette* and married Miss Read. At this point, the first section of *The Autobiography of Benjamin Franklin* ends.

In 1784, in Passy, France, Franklin picked up the story, this time addressing himself more generally to the reading public than to his son. With friends interested in scientific and intellectual matters, he had in 1743 founded a junto for their mutual exchange of ideas and intellectual improvement; this was later to become the American Philosophical Society, whose members sponsored a library for the use of the public.

Now that he had educated himself, Franklin sought moral perfection. He set down twelve virtues, then, at the suggestion of critical friends, added a thirteenth, pride. He did have reason to be proud. He had learned to speak fluent French, Spanish, and Italian. His civic spirit, born when he was appointed postmaster of Philadelphia, had induced him to reorganize the fire department, to start a movement to pave and light the streets, and to establish an academy that later became the University of Pennsylvania. The death of a son from smallpox led him to argue for inoculation against the disease. He invented an improved form of heating stove and offered it free for general use, only to learn later that he had made one stove manufacturer wealthy. Beginning in 1732, he published *Poor Richard's Almanack*, the usual collection of agricultural and astronomical data to which he added a compendium of practical wisdom and moral maxims. This venture brought him wealth and enabled him to retire from active business in 1748.

His thoughts about defense caused him to campaign for the establishment of a militia, but this man who so candidly confessed his "errata," or mistakes, was too well acquainted with himself to accept the appointment as their colonel. Other civic improvements, when initiated by others, needed his approval before his fellow citizens would adopt them. He extended his influence beyond his own city to the whole colony and to other colonies. Yale and Harvard awarded honorary degrees to this self-taught scholar, and he was elected to membership in cultural and scientific societies at home and abroad. Edward Braddock sought Franklin's advice in campaigning against the Indians, and when he disregarded it, it was with disastrous results.

After selling his shop to his foreman, Franklin occupied his time with philosophical concerns and scientific experiments, particularly those relating to electricity. His theories, when ignored or contradicted abroad, led to his experiments with lightning in 1752. Having represented Pennsylvania at the Albany Congress of 1754, he was chosen to represent it in protests to the English crown. His arrival in England, July 27, 1757, concludes his story of himself.

Bibliography:
Griffith, John. "The Rhetoric of Franklin's *Autobiography*." *Criticism* 13 (Winter, 1971): 77-94. A careful discussion of the strategies and aesthetics employed by Franklin in the execution of his literary designs. Emphasis is on literary analysis rather than on explication.
Jehlen, Myra. " 'Imitate Jesus and Socrates': The Making of a Good American." *South Atlantic Quarterly* 89, no. 3 (Summer, 1990): 501-524. General discussion of the moral and philosophical implications of Franklin's described regimen for acquiring the thirteen virtues that would bring perfection to one who possessed them.
Levin, David. "*The Autobiography of Benjamin Franklin*: The Puritan Experiment in Life and Art." In *Benjamin Franklin: A Collection of Critical Essays*, edited by Brian M. Barbour. Englewood Cliffs, N.J.: Prentice-Hall, 1979. Distinguishes between the character of Franklin's persona in the autobiography and the character of the writer himself; emphasis on Franklin's effort to resolve the Puritan dedication to virtue and the work ethic with the Enlightenment focus on rational inquiry.
Seavey, Ormond. *Becoming Benjamin Franklin: The Autobiography and the Life*. University Park: The Pennsylvania State University Press, 1988. A carefully documented and exhaustive two-part critical and psychological study of Franklin both as a writer with a rhetorical purpose and as a figure of the Enlightenment.
Shea, Daniel B., Jr. "Franklin and Spiritual Autobiography." In *Benjamin Franklin: A Collection of Critical Essays*, edited by Brian M. Barbour. Englewood Cliffs, N.J.: Prentice-Hall, 1979. Identifies Franklin's autobiography as a model in form and essence for the spiritual writings of Henry David Thoreau, Walt Whitman, and Emily Dickinson, among others.

THE AUTOBIOGRAPHY OF MALCOLM X

Type of work: Autobiography
Author: Malcolm X (1925-1965), edited by Alex Haley
First published: 1965

The Autobiography of Malcolm X, edited by Alex Haley, is an extended monologue by Malcolm X in which he recounts his life story, shares the dramatic changes that occurred in his life and thinking, and addresses the reader about the values he held as if he were a moral philosopher or a member of the clergy. Although the book is edited, it is written in the first person, communicating with readers as if no second party or editor interfered with Malcolm X's direct connection with his reading audience. The exception to this style is the epilogue which was written by the editor after Malcolm X's death. It is a record of the assassination of Malcolm X and reveals how the spirit of the man in life appears to continue after his death. It emphasizes the impact of Malcolm X's life and the number of people who have assessed his contribution, whether they agreed with his ideas or not. Malcolm X claimed that he would never live to see the *Autobiography* published; because he was killed before it was printed, the epilogue by the editor is important as a conclusion to the life story of Malcolm X and as an analysis of his impact.

The *Autobiography of Malcolm X* has been so widely read and the interest in Malcolm X as a leader in American life in the 1950's and 1960's is so broad that many authors have written about his life and his speeches. *Malcolm X: A Selected Bibliography*, published in 1984, includes more than one hundred pages of listings of works by other authors about Malcolm X, including dissertations and theses. Among all of his speeches and other writers' critiques, however, *The Autobiography of Malcolm X* remains the most complete and direct communication of his life experiences and changing ideas. It is in some ways a traditional conversion narrative, showing how a man alters his perceptions and values. It is in other ways an admonition to a general audience of that which Malcolm X considered to be wrong with his time and place. It is in still other ways an explanation by the author of how he, as one African American male, experienced rejection and found ways to address and repudiate the discrimination against him. Although Malcolm X's words often imply that he had a sense of contentment toward the end of his life and that he could share that completed sense of self with others, *The Autobiography of Malcolm X* also has a continuing theme of change. The author shows not only how he has changed throughout his life but also how he is open to further change toward the end of his life. Thus, it is a narrative told by, and about, a man "in process." The epilogue raises questions about the direction Malcolm's life took in his later years and whether these challenged earlier directions he had promoted.

Malcolm X was born Malcolm Little in 1925 in Omaha, Nebraska. From an early age, he had knowledge of both white discrimination against blacks and of black separatist reactions. His father was a Baptist minister and follower of the black nationalist Marcus Garvey. When the family moved to Mason, Michigan, his father was murdered by white supremacists. Malcolm's mother found the care of the dependent children such a strain that she was placed in a mental hospital, and Malcolm and his siblings were placed in foster homes. Malcolm succeeded, however, in his largely white environment and was elected president of his seventh-grade class. At the same time, however, his English teacher advised him not to attempt to become a lawyer but to be content with being a carpenter because he was black. The suggestion devastated Malcolm, and he moved to Boston to live with his half sister. He stopped attending school after the eighth grade, held some menial jobs, and became involved in illegal acts. He later moved to Harlem, where he was known as "Detroit Red" because he had a fair complexion and reddish hair. He had also become successful as a hustler, pimp, and drug dealer. By the time he was twenty-one years old, Malcolm had been sentenced to prison for ten years.

The autobiography becomes far more than a "slice of life" ethnic history of one man when Malcolm describes the changes in his thinking in prison. These changes were not just mental; his style of life was altered and became consistent with the new ideas he encountered and embraced while incarcerated. Some of his brothers and sisters had become followers of Elijah Muhammad, the leader of the Nation of Islam (sometimes named the "Black Muslims"), and they sent him literature by Muhammad. Malcolm wrote to this leader daily and, when he was released from prison in 1952, became a follower of Muhammad and took the name "Malcolm X" in place of his birth name, which he now rejected as a slave name. Malcolm embraced the ideas of the Nation of Islam: that the black race was the original race, that blacks must develop pride in themselves by separating themselves from whites, and that blacks would enter a new age in which their race would rule the world. Malcolm felt the appeal of this theology and value system for himself but, more important, believed that black men would find this thought acceptable because they had historically experienced the "devil-nature" of white people. Malcolm agreed with Muhammad that attempting to change a white-dominated society was useless and was not the mission of blacks. Instead, black people would always be victimized by the inferior whites, and their only recourse was to depend on themselves and their own community to realize their innate purity partly by disassociating from whites. In 1953, Malcolm X was appointed the assistant minister of Detroit's Temple Number One of the Nation of Islam and later became Muhammad's national representative. By 1954, Malcolm was the head of a major mosque in Harlem in New York City. He had become Muhammad's main spokesperson throughout the country.

The autobiography makes it clear that Malcolm revered Elijah Muhammad for giving him the greatest gift of all, a new identity. The name change symbolized what had happened to Malcolm's perspectives and values. He had become a full man, worshiping a relevant god, finally understanding the way out of his plight of oppression. He was obedient to the Nation of Islam's doctrines and morality, abstaining from liquor and drugs, refusing to exploit other blacks, honoring black women, and accepting full responsibility for the roles of husband and father in a secure family life. At the same time, Elijah Muhammad had found in the gifted Malcolm a spokesperson who would obediently follow Muhammad's direction and an appealing, articulate, but street-smart voice who could generate and maintain the interest of masses of black people in the ideas of the Nation of Islam. It appeared to be, and was for several years, a productive relationship between the leader and his main representative in which both found ways to meet the other's needs. Under Malcolm's skilled presentation, the Nation of Islam grew from a very small cult of several hundred persons to a major religious organization in the black community with thousands of followers in all fifty states.

Malcolm's successes, however, were not appreciated by some of Elijah Muhammad's other assistants and, eventually, Muhammad reprimanded Malcolm for remarks he had made about former president John Kennedy's assassination. Finally, Malcolm was removed from all responsibilities and expelled from the organization. This became one more decisive change in Malcolm's life and an opportunity to expand his own thinking further, beyond the strict ideologies of the Nation of Islam. He made a pilgrimage to Mecca, where he took the name El-Hajj Malik El-Shabazz and announced that he had altered his views on integration. This was partly because of his experience in Mecca of perceiving brotherhood among Muslims of many

431

nationalities, races, and ethnic groups. He also began working closely with Africans internationally who were seeking to unite blacks throughout the world. In order to process this work, he established a new organization, the Organization of Afro-American Unity, in the United States with headquarters in New York City.

Malcolm was assassinated while speaking to an audience of this organization in Harlem on February 21, 1965. Three persons were convicted of the crime, two of whom were members of the Nation of Islam. Malcolm had predicted his death through violence but had suspected that the action would require more than Black Muslim involvement, implying that other institutions such as governmental agencies would be part of the scheme.

The Autobiography of Malcolm X shows how Malcolm was a person always in transition and that the changes in his life were a series of dramatic conversions and reconversions. He was not content to keep fixed ideas for long periods of time without exploring options. Even as a member of the Nation of Islam, he applied thoughts he had read in the great works of Western culture from Georg Hegel, Immanuel Kant, and Friedrich Nietzsche. He also relied on traditional African American intellectuals including W. E. B. Du Bois, whom the Nation of Islam did not consider among its teachers. He could use philosophical images when speaking with the uneducated. He could also use the shrewdness, competitive instinct, and wariness of his ghetto experiences when talking with reporters. Malcolm had the ability to expand his own universe by expanding that of others, and the autobiography is an elongated sermon that takes the reader from small-town America to urban poverty through universal religion and, eventually, into international concepts and organizations. Each of his several conversions and new experiences broadened his world, and the readers of the book are compelled to make their own changes and transitions as they become excited by his story and thoughts.

Malcolm's autobiography is a document of spiritual growth and changing commitments that may encourage some to join in a similar journey. It appeals to both theologians and sociologists as a pilgrim's progress, a study of conversions. It is also a depiction of the emotional structure of a leader who had a great impact on twentieth century America. As such, it appeals to psychologists and literary critics. It conveys a continuing struggle of a charismatic figure whose words are meant to mold and direct readers' thoughts, even though this struggle is not finalized, not absolute, and part of an ongoing process. It is also a very personal testimony of a major player in the social revolutions of the mid-twentieth century United States, one who encouraged his readers to be converted to thinking about and acting out justice. Because of this encouragement, it appeals to many who remain dissatisfied with the status quo, although their plans for restructuring society may differ from those proposed by Malcolm X.

The epilogue by editor Alex Haley helps the reader to understand the ways in which Malcolm's life evolved and how unexpected the changes in his life were to many who knew him well, including the editor. It makes clear that this autobiography is no final testament but, rather, the words of a man whose evolution was never final. By the end of his life, Malcolm was questioning the earlier criticisms he had made of the 1960's Civil Rights movement. He was meeting cordially with Martin Luther King, Jr., whom he had earlier demeaned, and he was resistant to the authority of Elijah Muhammad, who had been his spiritual leader. He rejected the theology of a pure black race and expanded his commitment to the oppressed to include groups of all colors and ethnic backgrounds. He had evolved from a national leader to an international figure who was attempting to unite African and Third World peoples from all continents. The epilogue assesses Malcolm as a pilgrim who did not know what his future thoughts, acts, and commitments would be, but who remained open to more conversions and transitions.

The Autobiography of Malcolm X has sold millions of copies and has received critical acclaim by readers who sometimes take issue with Malcolm's philosophy. Nevertheless, it remains a great work as the testimony of a leader for social change whose appeal extends far beyond those groups which he formed or those people he directly represented. Many readers may be disturbed by some of the ideas he promoted, but all readers remain fascinated by the honesty, integrity, and humanity evidenced in this book.

William Osborne
Max Orezzoli

Bibliography:
Draper, Theodore. *The Rediscovery of Black Nationalism.* New York: Viking Press, 1969. The volume places Malcolm X in the larger environment of black nationalists, claiming that Malcolm attempted to relate African American liberation to more general African liberation, especially in the last year of his life. In so doing, Malcolm exceeded many fellow nationalists: He internationalized the African American struggle, becoming a proponent of a worldwide black revolutionary experience.

Essien-Udom, Essien Udosen. *Black Nationalism: A Search for a Black Identity in America.* New York: Dell, 1962. The author delineates the role of the Nation of Islam in the history of black nationalism and of its inheritance of values and ideologies consistent with earlier nationalists. Malcolm X's pivotal place in the promulgation of Nation of Islam ideas is assessed, his charismatic appeal critiqued, and his effectiveness in communicating with urban masses acknowledged.

Perry, Bruce. *Malcolm: The Life of a Man Who Changed Black America.* Barrytown, N.Y.: Station Hill Press, 1991. A detailed account of the life and acts of Malcolm, from parental relations to post-death analyses.

Rich, Andrea, and Arthur L. Smith. *Rhetoric of Revolution.* Durham, N.C.: Moore, 1970. One-third of the volume is devoted to Malcolm as the architect of black revolution in the last half of the twentieth century, emphasizing his motivation, style, and relations with other black leaders and organizations.

Wood, Joe, ed. *Malcolm X: In Our Own Image.* New York: St. Martin's Press, 1992. An anthology of writers such as Amiri Baraka and Angela Davis, each of whom addresses a subject related to Malcolm, such as black rage, philosophy, the allure of Malcolm, and *The Autobiography of Malcolm X.*

THE AUTOBIOGRAPHY OF MISS JANE PITTMAN

Type of work: Novel
Author: Ernest J. Gaines (1933-   )
Type of plot: Historical realism
Time of plot: Mid-1860's to early 1960's
Locale: Rural southern Louisiana
First published: 1971

Principal characters:

>MISS JANE PITTMAN, a black plantation worker
>CORPORAL BROWN, a Yankee soldier who inspires Jane to replace her
>   slave name
>NED DOUGLASS, Jane's adopted son
>JOE PITTMAN, Jane's common-law husband
>ROBERT SAMSON, SR., a plantation owner
>ROBERT "TEE BOB" SAMSON, JR., Robert's legitimate son
>TIMMY, Robert's illegitimate son
>MARY AGNES LEFABRE, the plantation schoolteacher Tee Bob loves
>JIMMY AARON, a young black civil rights leader

The Story:

Before Miss Jane Pittman agreed to give a tape-recorded account of her more than one hundred years of life—from before the end of slavery to the Civil Rights movement of the 1960's—the editor, a history teacher, had to convince her to do so in order to better teach African American history from the perspective of a black woman who had experienced it firsthand. Miss Jane's story began at the end of the Civil War on a southern Louisiana plantation, when she was about ten or eleven. While bringing Yankee soldiers a drink, Miss Jane, then called Ticey, befriended a Yankee named Corporal Brown, who influenced her to replace her slave name with that of Jane. Miss Jane decided to adopt the new name and the corporal's surname. Miss Jane revealed her pride for the first time when she refused to accept her old slave name ever again, although her mistress whipped her until she bled.

After the war ended a year later, Miss Jane, determined and proud, decided she was leaving the plantation for Ohio, in search of Corporal Brown, although she did not know the way or what she would eat along the way. When the two dozen other former slaves Miss Jane left with began their journey north, they decided to change their slave names, as Miss Jane had done, to declare their independence. They were soon to find out, however, that although they were legally free, they were to be treated no better and perhaps even worse than they had been during slavery. Soon after they left, they were brutally attacked by a group of patrollers and former Confederate soldiers, who used sticks to beat to death all of those in the group except Miss Jane and a young boy, Ned, who were undetected in the bushes.

The two children bravely continued on alone for what they thought was Ohio. The determined children journeyed until they eventually found themselves back on a southern Louisiana plantation that was very much like the one they had fled. On the plantation, Miss Jane worked in the field, lived in the old slave quarters, and took care of Ned as if he were her child. For a short time everything seemed to go well: The children and some adults were educated. White hate groups terrorized and killed blacks across the state, but the Yankee who temporarily owned the plantation had the plantation guarded by black troops to protect his workers. Soon, however, the original Confederate owner got his land back during the deals the North and South were making in an attempt to reunite the country. Life on the plantation returned much to the way it had been back in the days of slavery. The black politicians, troops, and teacher were all forced to leave, and the children were educated only a couple of months out of the year, when they could not be used in the fields. Racist hate groups terrorized and killed blacks more than ever.

Blacks fled the terrorism, leaving the South in droves. Miss Jane and Ned, however, decided to stay, and Ned matured into a political advocate of black rights. The Ku Klux Klan then began harassing him, so he left the plantation for Kansas. After Ned left, Miss Jane became the common-law wife of a widowed horse breaker, Joe Pittman. Joe soon found work on another plantation. He and Miss Jane had to borrow money and sell everything they owned to pay the plantation owner $150 plus $30 interest to leave the plantation. The money was what they supposedly owed for past protection against the Ku Klux Klan. Although the plantation owner was clearly embezzling their money, they paid out of fear. On the new plantation, Jane worked as a house servant, and the two lived there until Joe was killed while breaking a wild horse.

After twenty years of separation, Miss Jane reunited with Ned and his new family. Ned established a school to teach the local black children and preach the politics of Frederick Douglass, until a Cajun hit man, who had a contract out on Ned's life, killed him.

After Ned was murdered, Miss Jane moved to the Samson plantation to work in the fields and later in the house as a servant. The paternalistic owner, Robert Samson, treated the black employees well but did not see them as the equals of whites. He had two sons, one, Tee Bob, the legitimate son of his wife, Miss Amma Dean, and the other the illegitimate son of the black worker, Verda. He treated his illegitimate son, Timmy, better than most black employees living on the plantation, letting him get away with many boyish pranks and letting him become a close friend with his white half brother.

Eventually, however, Timmy was to learn his place would never be equal to that of whites in Louisiana during the 1920's. When a poor white man named Tom Joe decided to harass Timmy and accuse him of breaking his half brother's arm, Timmy disputed the charge, and when he refused to call the man "mister," Tom Joe beat him unconscious. Because this time Timmy had had a run-in with a white person, Robert would not defend him. Instead, Robert gave Timmy money and told him to move away for his own safety. No one on the plantation, including Robert, could explain to Tee Bob why his beloved half brother was being sent away when he had done nothing wrong. Robert accepted these double standards as "part of life, like the sun and rain was part of life," and he assumed "Tee Bob would learn them for himself when he got older." Tee Bob never did learn, however, to accept racial segregation. He fell in love with a beautiful mulatto Creole schoolteacher named Mary Agnes LeFabre, who looked white, but when he came to realize that the society in which he lived would never accept his marriage to her, he committed suicide.

Miss Jane Pittman's remembrances ended during the Civil Rights movement, with an episode in which a young black man named Jimmy was killed for his involvement in planning a protest against the arrest of a black woman for drinking out of the whites-only fountain. The novel ended on a defiant note when Miss Jane stood up to Robert Samson for the first time, leading the black community in protest against legal segregation: "Me and Robert looked at each other there a long time, then I went by him."

Critical Evaluation:

Ernest Gaines was one of the first authors to attempt to present African American history from the perspective of a black person. Until the 1970's, when it became popular to capture the lifestyle and dialect of the average black American in such novels as Alex Haley's *Roots* (1976), it was difficult to find fiction that presented African American history from the common person's perspective, especially from the perspective of a black woman. In *The Autobiography of Miss Jane Pittman*, Gaines uses the framing device of a history teacher who tape-records an interview. Although Miss Jane is actually a fictional character, she is based on the women who lived on the southern Louisiana plantation on which Gaines was raised. The novel depicts southern Louisiana plantation life, the dialect of the people, and history of the area accurately. Gaines, who was working as an English professor and not as a history teacher, accomplishes the fictional history teacher's goal of teaching black history more accurately through presenting it from the black perspective. The framing device is designed to make Miss Jane seem more real and make her autobiography more believable. It is not really important that she is fictional because her story is not fictional. Black women and men lived through the racism, hard labor, and poverty described in the novel. Thus, as the fictitious editor states in the introduction, "Miss Jane's story is all of their stories, and their stories are Miss Jane's."

In addition to re-creating a more personal depiction of African American history from a poor black woman's perspective, *The Autobiography of Miss Jane Pittman* also establishes two important themes: the determination and pride of African Americans in the face of seemingly unconquerable racism and the destructive effects of racism on all of society, including whites. Throughout the novel Miss Jane is a proud individual who has the courage to face the consequences of standing up for herself and others in a racist society. She endures a harsh whipping as a young adolescent in order to reject her slave name, and as a ninety-year-old woman stands up to her white employer and landlord, risking the loss of her home, source of income, and perhaps even her life in order to partake in a demonstration against segregation. Although Miss Jane clearly suffers in the novel, she and other blacks are not the only people who suffer from racial discrimination and social and legal segregation. The white plantation owner's son Tee Bob is deprived of a loving and productive marriage to a beautiful and intelligent woman simply because she is part black. He decides killing himself is a better alternative than living by the hypocritical standards of his father and his father's society.

Another important detail in the novel is the naming of Miss Jane. One way former slaves declared their independence from slavery and rejected the subservient status associated with slave names was by giving themselves new names. In the novel, former slaves decide to rename themselves after Frederick Douglass, Abraham Lincoln, and other abolitionists or Union soldiers who helped them obtain their freedom. Miss Jane not only names herself after a Yankee corporal who first acknowledges her worth as an individual by telling her to reject her slave name, but she also is referred to as Miss, which connotes her dignity as a lady. *The Autobiography of Miss Jane Pittman* is revolutionary in its presentation of a black woman who is a realistic, multidimensional individual who cannot be classified as a stereotype.

Suzanne Obenauer Shaut

Bibliography:

Babb, Valerie Melissa. *Ernest Gaines*. Boston: Twayne, 1991. A clear critical analysis that devotes one chapter to each of Gaines's major works, including a detailed chapter on *The Autobiography of Miss Jane Pittman* that discusses the novel's historical and cultural accuracy, use of oral history, themes, and character development.

Doyle, Mary Ellen. "Ernest Gaines' Materials: Place, People, Author." *Melus* 15 (Fall, 1988):

75-93. Discusses portrayals of Cajuns and Louisiana and includes a general criticism of Gaines's works, including *The Autobiography of Miss Jane Pittman*.

Gaines, Ernest. "Miss Pittman's Background." *The New York Times Book Review*, August 10, 1975, 23. A one-page article in which Gaines explains the extensive research that he put into writing the novel.

Gaudet, Marcia, and Carl Wooton. *Porch Talk with Ernest Gaines: Conversations on the Writer's Craft*. Baton Rouge: Louisiana State University Press, 1990. A brief introduction to Gaines's life and works and a lengthy series of interviews of Gaines, with a heavy emphasis on *The Autobiography of Miss Jane Pittman*.

Walker, Alice. "*The Autobiography of Miss Jane Pittman*." *The New York Times Book Review*, May 23, 1971, 6,12. A simple summary and insightful interpretation of the novel as significant for political reasons and complex character development.

THE AUTOBIOGRAPHY OF W. E. B. DU BOIS
A Soliloquy on Viewing My Life from the Last Decade
of Its First Century

Type of work: Autobiography
Author: W. E. B. Du Bois (1868-1963)
First published: Vospominaniia, 1962 (English translation, 1968)

The Autobiography of W. E. B. Du Bois: A Soliloquy on Viewing My Life from the Last Decade of Its First Century tells the impressive and inspiring story of an individual's struggles, defeats, and accomplishments, as well as his major ideas developed during ninety years of a life dedicated to promoting racial equality and the sociological study of African American realities in the United States. *The Autobiography of W. E. B. Du Bois* presents a view of American life distilled through the perceptive, analytical eyes of one who may have been the foremost African American intellectual. Progressing from the Reconstruction era at the end of the U.S. Civil War, through World Wars I and II, to the height of the Cold War and the atomic age, Du Bois' personal reflections provide a critical, panoramic sweep of American social history. *The Autobiography of W. E. B. Du Bois* is simultaneously a history of a personal and a social struggle, seen from the perspective of a central participant.

Du Bois was not simply an observer of the American scene. He contributed instrumentally to American history in his role as a leading architect of African American thought during the growth of the American Civil Rights movement in the twentieth century. Thus, *The Autobiography of W. E. B. Du Bois* is an important documentary piece of American history. From the inception of the National Association for the Advancement of Colored People (NAACP) in 1909, Du Bois was, as editor of its journal, *The Crisis*, its conscience and spokesperson. Du Bois opposed the influential policies of Booker T. Washington, creating a vital dialogue within the African American community. Much of Du Bois' vision of racial equality and African American achievement remains unfulfilled, and thus his autobiography is necessarily as much a blueprint for continued action as it is a historical narrative.

The chronological structure of the autobiography is purposefully transposed. Du Bois begins not with his childhood but with five brief chapters on his travels, starting in 1958, to Europe, the Soviet Union, and China. After seeing the accomplishments of socialist organization firsthand, Du Bois reaches the crowning ideological decision of his life: his conversion to communism. The remainder of the autobiography is fundamentally an embroidery on the question: How and why did Du Bois arrive at this crucial decision in the last years of his life? This chronological device focuses the entire work on Du Bois' inexorable move toward communist ideals in a way that starting simply with his birth and youthful years in Massachusetts could not accomplish.

Du Bois' chronicle of his childhood and early education is surprising precisely for its small-town conventionality and relative lack of racial conflict. Du Bois, it is crucial to remember, was born a northerner, in rural Massachusetts. Despite Du Bois' African American heritage and the close temporal proximity of his birth to the end of the U.S. Civil War, Du Bois neither came from a slave family nor had direct childhood experience with the aftermath of slavery that characterized the southern United States. Du Bois excelled in a predominantly white school and had white playmates. The strict norms of the time and region minimized opportunities for contacts with the opposite sex, black or white, and thus Du Bois not only grew up ignorant of sexual biology but also escaped the sanctions so ruthlessly imposed in

Southern states, where whites' exaggerated fears of miscegenation ran rampant.

The autobiography is replete with instances that illustrate Du Bois' hard work, thrift, diligent study, and persistent planning. Were it not for the fact that Du Bois' story ends with his expatriation, the narrative reads often like an African American version of a Horatio Alger story. Du Bois, ultimately, avoids the trap that captures the self-made man, asking instead: "Was I the masterful captain or the pawn of laughing sprites?" Du Bois did not trust his life to luck; he "just went doggedly to work" and let the consequences fall where they might.

Du Bois learned concretely about racial bigotry during his college years at Fisk University in Tennessee, prior to his return to Massachusetts, where he continued his academic studies at Harvard University. Du Bois learned from notable scholars (including William James) at Harvard, earned a second B.A. degree and, eventually, earned a Ph.D. in 1895. His doctoral program included a hiatus for two years of study in Germany, where Du Bois came to appreciate high standards of scholarship and listened to the stimulating lectures of the sociologist Max Weber. Following a year-long appointment at the University of Pennsylvania, where Du Bois completed a landmark sociological investigation, *The Philadelphia Negro: A Social Study*, he spent from 1897 to 1910 at Atlanta University as the nation's leading African American sociologist. If the black experience in America was to be investigated objectively and scientifi-cally, Du Bois observed, it must be studied by astute, well-trained, African American sociolo-gists such as himself.

As a result of the national importance of Du Bois' role in the NAACP, his considerable stature as an author and influential editor, and the problematic political legacy of the Du Bois-Washington debate—all of which are detailed in the autobiography and about which many critics and historians have commented—it is important to emphasize that a constant theme of the autobiography is Du Bois' work. Du Bois worked to initiate, foster, produce, and plan an ex- tended series of erudite, systematic sociological investigations of African American life. It is Du Bois' unrelenting drive to live an intellectual life, to teach the "talented tenth" of black America, and to destroy white myths and misapprehensions about African Americans by means of careful research that gives coherence to his autobiography and meaning to his accomplish-ments.

Du Bois' many trips from North to South, to Europe and beyond, stand as metaphors for his complex, ninety-year intellectual journey from naïve schoolboy to sage, idealistic communist. Along the way, Du Bois enriched the sociological vocabulary with insightful concepts, includ-ing "the color line," "the veil," "the talented tenth," "double consciousness," and many others. All find ready use and illustration in his autobiography. Du Bois reveled in the active, disci-plined application of the mind. Philosophically and organizationally, Du Bois accomplished what is beyond the grasp of most mortals. His grand sociological project was possible yet visionary; his communism was inclusive, liberating, and cooperative—never totalitarian or dictatorial. The temporary denial by the American government in 1951 of Du Bois' passport, ostensibly limiting his ability to travel outside the United States, propelled Du Bois toward a future unbounded by petty nationalisms, military-industrial excesses, or governmental oppres-sion of the citizenry.

Perhaps the most gripping and instructive section of the autobiography is Du Bois' straight-forward account of his indictment and persecution by the U.S. government on trumped-up charges, allegations infused with insinuations of treason and disloyalty. Du Bois' trial and acquittal in 1950 and 1951, for alleged failure to register as an agent of a foreign government, is a scary, sobering illustration of democratic institutions gone seriously awry. Du Bois was cleared of all charges, but the trial cost him his savings and his reputation. His fundamental faith in American institutions, already strained by years of racist oppression, crumbled completely. If Du Bois was sometimes angry, he often had justification.

Du Bois' autobiography is, from his perspective, a final reckoning and laying to rest of long-fought battles. Du Bois outlived most of his enemies and thereby won the satisfaction of the last word. It is on this personal level that the autobiography is least satisfying. The veracity of Du Bois' recollections concerning old animosities and interpersonal power struggles cannot be decided on the basis of his book alone. Du Bois leaves readers with selected, carefully crafted impressions of himself, his foes, and his intellectual journey. This book, he states with candor, is "a theory of my life"; it "is the Soliloquy of an old man on what he dreams his life has been . . . and what he would like others to believe."

Du Bois refers pointedly to his autobiography as a soliloquy. The soliloquy is a venerable technique in Western literature, especially in drama, reaching its classic form in William Shakespeare's plays and, more recently, in stream-of-consciousness writing typified by James Joyce's novel *Ulysses* (1922). Readers of Du Bois' autobiography will likely conclude, however, that Du Bois clearly speaks not to himself but rather to posterity.

Du Bois' choice of "soliloquy" to categorize his work reflects the political realities of 1960 more than it does a specific literary form. At the time Du Bois finished writing his autobiography, he had been persecuted by the American government, many of his well-educated African American friends had deserted him, and Du Bois lived in exile in the newly independent nation of Ghana. Thus, Du Bois had reasons for thinking that he was talking primarily to himself. He may well have wondered who, in the United States at least, would ever read his autobiography.

Deepening the possibility that few Americans might see or read his final autobiographical statement is the fact of its first publication not in English but in a 518-page translated edition in Russian, printed in Moscow. When the autobiography finally appeared, posthumously, in English in 1968, it was published by International Publishers, a publishing house well known for its Marxist and Soviet-oriented books. In 1991, *The Autobiography of W. E. B. Du Bois* enjoyed its eleventh printing, but it remains the least read of Du Bois' autobiographical works.

There are several reasons why Du Bois' autobiography still creates controversy in the United States. First, Du Bois enthusiastically endorses a radical, communist political perspective that many liberal and conservative Americans find unacceptable. Second, Du Bois levels stinging criticism at middle-class African Americans, who, in Du Bois' view, value their own economic security more highly than the worldwide struggle for racial equality and freedom of expression. Third, Du Bois praises the former Soviet Union for its opposition to organized religion. Finally, Du Bois transcends his previous, sharp critiques of whites, placing him at odds with separatist and some pluralist African American scholars who are more comfortable with Du Bois' earlier views. Nevertheless, W. E. B. Du Bois' autobiography is an engaging exposition in which Du Bois addresses his critics directly and usually with fairness, recounts his failures with dignity and humility, expounds his views with clarity and reason, and shares his hopes for a collective future with courage, conviction, and good will.

Michael R. Hill

Bibliography:
Butterfield, Stephen. *Black Autobiography in America*. Amherst: University of Massachusetts Press, 1974. Explicates the autobiographical works of Du Bois, Richard Wright, Langston Hughes, and others as concerted attempts to unite the pieces of divided selves. Concludes

that Du Bois' autobiographical works provide the most conscious and explicit examples in African American literature of this struggle.

Deegan, Mary Jo. "W. E. B. Du Bois and the Women of Hull-House: 1896-1899." *American Sociologist* 19 (Winter, 1988): 301-311. Deegan critically examines Du Bois' autobiographical omission of the pivotal influence of Jane Addams, Isabell Eaton, and other women scholars on the methodological foundation and concrete execution of Du Bois' classic sociological study, *The Philadelphia Negro: A Social Study*.

Duberman, Martin. *The Uncompleted Past*. New York: Random House, 1969. Praises the characterization of Du Bois' childhood, but dismisses—rather too curtly—Du Bois' discovery and embrace of communist principles. Emphasizes Du Bois' pursuit of what Duberman presents as conflicting goals.

Du Bois, W. E. B. *W. E. B. Du Bois: A Recorded Autobiography*. Interview by Moses Asch. New York: Folkways Records, 1961. Covers several of the major topics detailed in the autobiography, but more succinctly and conversationally. The recording enjoyably distills for listeners the incidents and accomplishments that Du Bois personally emphasized as important landmarks in his life.

Howe, Irving. *Celebrations and Attacks*. New York: Horizon Press, 1979. Presents a concise summary of Du Bois' autobiography and a useful discussion of the deeper complexities in his controversial debate with Booker T. Washington. Fails, however, to distinguish between totalitarian Stalinism and the broader democratic principles that Du Bois championed.

THE AUTOCRAT OF THE BREAKFAST-TABLE

Type of work: Essays
Author: Oliver Wendell Holmes (1809-1894)
First published: serial, 1857-1858; book, 1858

> *Principal characters:*
> THE AUTOCRAT
> THE SCHOOLMISTRESS,
> THE DIVINITY-STUDENT,
> THE OLD GENTLEMAN, and
> THE YOUNG FELLOW CALLED JOHN, the Autocrat's fellow boarders
> THE LANDLADY
> THE LANDLADY'S DAUGHTER
> BENJAMIN FRANKLIN, the Landlady's son
> THE PROFESSOR and
> THE POET, friends of the Autocrat who, though never present, contribute
> to the discussion

At one point in the recounting of his breakfast-table experiences, the Autocrat observed that, since medieval times, the reputation of Aristotle had passed through two stages and was just entering its third. First came the period of idolization, when everything attributed to the Greek sage was accepted not only as scientifically sound but as absolute and ultimate truth. Then came the period of critical examination, the stage at which his scientific inaccuracies were discovered and consequently all his ideas belittled and discredited. Finally, there was the third stage, the enlightened period when the scientific inaccuracies were excused, being viewed in historical perspective as unavoidable, and the value of his philosophical insights restored.

On a smaller time scale, the reputation of Oliver Wendell Holmes, along with that of his Cambridge-Boston group (as opposed to the Concord group), has gone through the first two of these stages but shows no signs, as yet, of entering the third. Although few, and certainly never Holmes himself, believed that Boston was the hub of the universe, Harvard Yard and the eastern end of Beacon Street (including the first eight doors on Arlington Street so as to take in the offices of the *Atlantic Monthly*) were for more than half a century regarded as the dual nerve center, the cerebrum and cerebellum, as it were, of American culture. A Cambridge-born Harvard professor of anatomy, a member of the Saturday Club, a resident of Beacon Street, Holmes did not merely share in such regard, he helped to create it. It was he, in fact, who coined the term "The Hub." (The original statement, however, as it appeared in chapter 6 of *The Autocrat of the Breakfast-Table*, was made not by a Bostonian but by an outlander who remarked, "Boston State-House is the hub of the solar system.") As lecturer, poet, novelist, biographer, and, most of all, perhaps, as the author of *The Autocrat of the Breakfast-Table* and, later, *The Professor at the Breakfast-Table* (1860) and *The Poet at the Breakfast-Table* (1872), Holmes helped to establish in the public mind a concept of Bostonian wit, sensibility, and culture.

Gradually—not suddenly as did the Wonderful One-Hoss Shay in chapter 11 of *The Autocrat of the Breakfast-Table*—the reputations of many of the New England writers became autumnal and dry, and a season of critical neglect set in before the situation reversed itself again. Nathaniel Hawthorne was resurrected by the New Critics; the cautiously radical Ralph Waldo

Emerson was turned into a spokesman for the Neoconservatives; and Henry David Thoreau, in conformist times, became a pet of nonconformists. The Concordians thus entered their third stage, but this did not happen with the Cambridge-Bostonians. Granted, their poetry is a mixture of neoclassic moralizing and a nostalgic and academic romanticism, but it should be remembered that Henry Wadsworth Longfellow had a gift for storytelling, that Robert Lowell was a sprightly satirist, and that Holmes possessed wit, urbanity, a background of knowledge, and a tolerant, all-encompassing view of life, the like of which has not appeared in English letters on either side of the Atlantic since his death.

It can be argued that in regard to Holmes such qualities did not produce the reputation but are deduced from it, that the alleged wit and urbanity are really provincial smugness, and that what passes for a tolerant and total worldview is in reality a carefully cultivated dilettantism. Such arguments have been made, but they neglect both the facts provided by history and the literary evidence provided by *The Autocrat of the Breakfast-Table*. The facts show that Holmes was learned in both science and humane letters and that he was one of the foremost advocates of technological progress in the nineteenth century United States. One English critic said that Holmes, rather than Emerson, deserves the title the "American Montaigne."

It is on an objective reading of *The Autocrat of the Breakfast-Table* that the case for Holmes must finally rest. The work appeared originally in the first twelve issues of the *Atlantic Monthly* (1857-1858) and was directly afterward published in book form. Its plan is simple: The Autocrat lives in a Beacon Hill boarding house; the essays are characterized as somewhat condensed reports, interlarded with the Autocrat's comments, of the conversations that take place each morning at the breakfast table around which a heterogeneous collection of boarders gathers. Each occasionally has a say but collectively their main purpose is to provide a sounding board for the wit and philosophizing of the Autocrat. There is conversation, but mostly there is monologue. The varied responses of the boarders allow Holmes's wit to play over a wide range of subjects, to jump easily from point to point, and to juxtapose ideas that have no apparent relevance.

The result may seem chaotic at first. The bubbling cleverness runs along easily enough but apparently to no particular place. The topics of the first chapter are, for example, in order of appearance: the algebraic classification of minds; the value of mutual admiration societies; the meaninglessness of brute fact; the typing of various kinds of speakers; the dangers of specialized learning; an attack on the use of puns (Holmes deplores the use of them here but cannot always resist them, as when he speaks of the landlady's economically minded poor relation as standing by her guns, "ready to repel boarders"); the poverty of pure logic as opposed to common sense; the foibles of young poets; the superiority of men of family over self-made men, "*other things being equal*" (Holmes's italics); and the rendering of a pair of poems. Holmes makes each of these points interesting, but there seems to be little connection between one and another. Gradually, however, it becomes evident that certain ideas recur; certain themes are announced and dropped but then repeated later with variations, and there are psychological connections in the apparently chance juxtapositions of ideas. The entirety develops in a geometric, not in an arithmetic, progression.

Holmes was a Bostonian, a Victorian American, and it has been said that his sympathies lay with the eighteenth century and that he was at heart a Neo-Johnsonian. If, however, his conscious affinities turned back one hundred years, his unconscious ones turned back even further. Andrew Lang noted "a fleeting resemblance to Sir Thomas Browne" based on "a community of professional studies," but this similarity between Holmes and the author of *Religio Medici* (1716) and *Urn Burial* (1658) is not explained simply by the fact that both were medical men. Holmes possessed the divided sensibility found also in the metaphysical school; and Browne, it is now acknowledged, was a metaphysical poet writing in prose. This division in Holmes, which is obscured by his neoclassical pose, is often neglected.

Holmes was divided along a different axis than was Browne, for he lived under different conditions. The religious division resulted from the fact that though Holmes had disavowed the Puritanism of his fathers, he never completely lost the scars of his youthful indoctrination. More important, perhaps, at least as far as its reflection in *The Autocrat of the Breakfast-Table* is concerned, is his divided allegiance between Brahminism on the one hand, which for him stood for all the deeply rooted elements of the good life, and on the other science, which meant technology and with it the unleashing of forces, both human and mechanical, that would destroy Brahminism. The division could not exercise itself in Holmes's poetry because the moralizing-romantic tradition was too binding. Yet when Holmes had at his disposal a form free from restrictions with which he could experiment as he wished, the essay, he was able to express his divided sensibility through the use of what closely resemble metaphysical techniques.

These techniques include the juxtaposition of topics, which is reflected most extremely in chapter 9. Here, anticipating the much later reflection of the metaphysical, Holmes presents a series of childhood reminiscences, the stuff of poems:

> Many times I have come bearing flowers such as my garden grew; but now I offer you this poor, brown, homely growth, you may cast it away as worthless. And yet—and yet—it is something better than flowers; it is a seed-capsule.

There is also the shift in prose style from the colloquial or scientific to the lofty and poetic, a device that hearkens back to the style of Browne. Most important, however, are the similitudes, the similes, metaphors, and extended analogies, which abound in *The Autocrat of the Breakfast-Table*. What is important here is that they are functional, not decorative; they are the very fabric of the work. Holmes uses them to bring into focus the two parts of his divided world. Science and beauty stand for the two parts of the central dichotomy, representing Holmes's own two alter egos as the professor and the poet, and they play their dual parts in all the analogies:

> We get beautiful effects from wit—all the prismatic colors—but never the object as it is in fair daylight. A pun, which is a kind of wit, is a different and much shallower trick in mental optics; throwing the shadows of two objects so that one overlies the other. Poetry uses the rainbow tints for special effects, but always keeps its essential object in the purest white light of truth.

Through the interplay of these two conflicting worlds and by means of analogy and opposition of character, Holmes brings out the themes of the work. They appear as questions, not as answers, for awareness of the divided world permits no dogmatic assertions. He asks what love is and what beauty is; how human communication and expression are achieved; what, after all, is really important; and how can that be found—whether it is by sculling beneath the bridges of the Charles, searching for seed capsules of poetry in one's memory, or counting the rings of an elm that stood when Shakespeare was a boy.

To bring out these questions in a meaningful way is a decided literary achievement. *The Autocrat of the Breakfast-Table* is not an entirely great literary work. Holmes does not maintain his metaphysical detachment, he becomes too concerned with his characters, and in the end he reduces the Autocrat and the Schoolmistress into the principal figures of a rather sentimental romance. These are weaknesses, but with respect to the strengths demonstrated in *The Autocrat of the Breakfast-Table* Holmes deserves to have his reputation advanced to the third stage.

Bibliography:

Grenander, M. E. "Doctors and Humanists: Transactional Analysis and Two Views of Man." *Journal of American Culture* 3, no. 3 (Fall, 1980): 470-479. Contends that Holmes paved the way for transactional analysis theory, for he discussed in *The Autocrat of the Breakfast-Table* the factors considered—consciously and subconsciously—by two people when they speak to each other.

Hoyt, Edwin P. *The Improper Bostonian: Dr. Oliver Wendell Holmes.* New York: William Morrow, 1979. Chapter 16 describes Holmes's relationship with Lowell, the editor of *The Atlantic Monthly,* and other notable Boston literati. Explains the appeal of *The Autocrat of the Breakfast-Table* to educated readers and delineates Holmes's literary prominence.

Mattson, J. Stanley. "Oliver Wendell Holmes and 'The Deacon's Masterpiece': A Logical Story?" In *New England Quarterly* 41, no. 1 (May, 1968): 104-114. Offers background on *The Autocrat of the Breakfast-Table* and analyzes the poem included in that work, "The Deacon's Masterpiece: The Wonderful One-Hoss Shay." Asserts that the poem is a satiric discussion of logic.

Small, Miriam Rossiter. *Oliver Wendell Holmes.* New York: Twayne, 1962. Chapter 3 of this biography, "The Breakfast-Table Series," discusses the style and theme of *The Autocrat of the Breakfast-Table* and obliquely compares it to Holmes's succeeding works. Asserts that readers of the essays derive pleasure from recognizing experience, thought, and emotions as they are couched in Holmes's apt and winning style.

Tilton, Eleanor M. *Amiable Autocrat: A Biography of Dr. Oliver Wendell Holmes.* New York: Henry Schuman, 1947. Reports the contemporary reception of *The Autocrat of the Breakfast-Table* and traces the essays from their serialized appearance to the publication in book form.

THE AWAKENING

Type of work: Novel
Author: Kate Chopin (1851-1904)
Type of plot: Psychological realism
Time of plot: Late nineteenth century
Locale: New Orleans and Grand Isle
First published: 1899

Principal characters:
    EDNA PONTELLIER, an upper-class housewife who is not satisfied to be
       someone's property
    LÉONCE PONTELLIER, her husband, a wealthy businessman
    ROBERT LEBRUN, a young man who becomes romantically involved with
       Edna
    ALCÉE AROBIN, an experienced playboy who seduces Edna
    ADÈLE RATIGNOLLE, Edna's friend
    MADEMOISELLE REISZ, a pianist who inspires Edna
    DOCTOR MANDELET, a physician and adviser to the Pontelliers

The Story:

The Pontelliers, residents of New Orleans, were vacationing at Grand Isle, a resort in the Gulf of Mexico. The Lebrun and Ratignolle families, also Creoles of New Orleans, were companions of Edna, who was unhappy with the limited role dictated to her by her husband Léonce. Madame Lebrun's caged parrot symbolized Edna's feeling of being trapped in a loveless marriage and in an economically oriented social system in which women were only wives and mothers. Her husband expected her to be like Adèle Ratignolle, who exemplified the type of submissive and sacrificial wife that Léonce expected and thought he deserved. Edna, however, was not willing to submit to such traditions or to sacrifice herself for the sake of her husband and their two sons.

When Léonce noticed that Edna had been sunburned after spending a time on the beach with Robert Lebrun, his main concern was that a "valuable piece of personal property" had "suffered some damage." In contrast to her husband's business-based value system, Robert offered her companionship and sympathy. She talked to him of her girlhood in Kentucky. Meanwhile, Léonce complained about her "habitual neglect of the children." Edna realized that she could never be a good mother like Adèle if it meant stifling her independence. "A certain light was beginning to dawn" in Edna that nurtured her dissatisfaction with her life and led her to recognize that her marriage to the forty-year-old businessman (twelve years her senior) was a mistake. She had been flattered by Léonce's devotion to her, but the violent opposition to the marriage by her father and her sister Margaret (because Léonce was a Catholic) may have been Edna's prime motive in marrying. Léonce belonged to another culture, a French American society quite different from the strict Presbyterian environment of Kentucky. One thing, however, was the same in both worlds. Women were regarded as necessary but inferior beings whose place was in the home.

Edna, who was interested in the arts, was introduced to Mademoiselle Reisz, a noted pianist. While the latter played, Edna envisioned a naked man in an attitude of resignation as he watched a bird fly away from him. The music inspired Edna to a sense of power, and, when the party moved to the beach, she overcame her fear of the water and learned to swim. Gaining confidence, Edna challenged her husband by refusing his sexual entreaty. By withholding herself sexually, she felt that she was in possession of her body.

One Sunday, Edna asked Robert to attend church with her on a neighboring island. During the service, however, she fled from the stifling atmosphere of the church, much like the time as a child in Kentucky when she ran away from the Presbyterian prayers that were "read in a spirit of gloom" by her father. She felt that the churches were part of the status quo that kept women in their places. At the end of the Grand Isle vacation, Robert went to Mexico. His departure depressed Edna, but it did not impair her rebellious nature. She told Mademoiselle Reisz that she would not sacrifice herself for anyone, even her children. When the family returned to New Orleans, Edna's first act of nonconformity was to ignore Reception Day. Léonce was amazed that his wife did not observe the tradition. It was not just a social convention, it was business. He angrily left to have dinner at his club. Edna threw her wedding ring on the carpet and broke a vase on the hearth. In a rebellious mood, Edna visited Mademoiselle Reisz. Edna discussed her attempt to paint, to become an artist. The pianist declared that an artist needed a courageous soul, a "soul that dared and defied."

Meanwhile, Léonce complained to Dr. Mandelet about the change in Edna, particularly her sexual withdrawal. She even refused to go to her sister's wedding. The doctor advised him to let Edna have her way for a while. Edna's father, a Kentucky colonel, arrived in New Orleans to buy a wedding present for Janet, his daughter. The real purpose for the visit was to coerce Edna into attending Janet's wedding, but Edna still refused to go. Fond of bourbon, of horses, and of women who knew their domestic duties, Edna's father angrily left. Soon after, Léonce left on one of his many business trips, and his mother took the children to Iberville. Edna was happy to be alone. For inspiration, she read Ralph Waldo Emerson, the famous champion of self-reliance and nonconformity. Edna, in a bold act of independence, decided to move out of her husband's house, ignoring his letter of disapproval in which he claimed he was "simply thinking of his financial integrity." Before she left, she had a dinner party. One of the guests, Alcée Arobin, began to court Edna. In the absence of Robert Lebrun, Edna responded to Arobin's sexual advances. She had not heard from Robert since he had gone to Mexico. When Robert returned, he avoided her. One day, they met accidentally, but he seemed distant and uninterested. Arobin, on the other hand, continued to visit her. Another chance meeting with Robert occurred, however, and he confessed that he loved her and that he had avoided her because she belonged to another. Edna said that she was no longer one of Mr. Pontellier's possessions. They made plans to meet again.

In the meantime, Edna helped Dr. Mandelet while Adèle was giving birth, an act that gave Edna a sense of dread. She explained to Mandelet that she wanted nothing but her own way, even if it meant trampling on the hearts and prejudices of others. He was unable to understand the depth of her commitment to finding a life of her own. Edna went to her little house, around the corner from the big house on Esplanade Street, expecting Robert to be there. Instead, she found a note: "I love you. Good-bye—because I love you." She realized that the man she loved was not as brave as she was. She also realized that she had another major decision to make. Grand Isle beckoned to Edna again. She walked to the beach, to the seductive voice of the sea. She saw a bird with a broken wing descend to the water. She thought about the courageous soul and about Robert's note and his failure to understand. Edna swam far into the ocean until her strength was gone. It was too late to go back.

Critical Evaluation:

When it was published in 1899, *The Awakening* was considered vulgar by most critics. The inferior social status of women was firmly entrenched, especially in the South. An accompanying concept was the assumed moral superiority of women, at least in sexual matters. Upper-class ladies like Edna Pontellier were ornaments, displays of their husbands' wealth. A book that challenged the traditional roles of women was likely to be controversial. The public was not ready to accept a liberated woman, even if she did commit suicide in the end. Kate Chopin disappeared from the literary world when her book was critically attacked and banned from libraries. Not all critics gave negative reviews. Willa Cather, later a famous novelist herself, praised *The Awakening*. Cather acclaimed the style of Chopin and also compared the protagonist to Emma Bovary and Anna Karenina, heroines of classic European fiction. From the mid-twentieth century on, critics, especially feminists, have raised the status of the novel to an American masterpiece. It has been celebrated as an important literary document in the history of women's rights and as an artistic success.

Kate Chopin tells Edna Pontellier's story without comment; the action and dialogue present ambiguities. Various schools of criticism have interpreted *The Awakening* from diverse views. Feminist critics have promoted it as a neglected text that should rightly be placed among the outstanding novels of the nineteenth century. It presented the plight of a woman who cannot accept the idea of being limited to a socially defined role. Edna rejects the economic and social success that her marriage to Léonce gives her in favor of working out her own destiny. She prefers to define her role actively rather than to be a passive object. Her awakening is sexual in part, but it is also a search for creativity, as suggested by her attempt to paint. She seeks the advice of the only artist she knows—Mademoiselle Reisz. She reads Emerson, the voice of individualism. From these sources, she gains the courage to challenge the authority of her husband. In her fight for independence, Edna Pontellier becomes a threat to the values of a society.

Feminist critics also recognize other elements of the book relating to psychoanalytic theory, mythology, linguistics, and cultural studies. Critics from different fields saw it as naturalistic, an extended work of local color, or as a conflict between Creole and American cultures. A major emphasis, however, was the consideration of the novel as a work of art, which often involved an examination of patterns of imagery that tie the novel together.

One example is how Chopin uses birds to help define Edna's situation. On the first page, the caged parrot suggests her feeling of being trapped by traditions. The mockingbird, on the other side of Madame Lebrun's door, further illustrates her passive role, in which a voice of her own was not expected. Edna, however, spoke for herself by moving out of Léonce's house into what she called her pigeon-house, suggestive of both a dependent domestic bird and a wild bird that has found its own nest. The advice that Edna got from the pianist included a reference to a bird that would have wings strong enough to fly above traditions and prejudices. Also, when the pianist played for Edna, the latter envisioned a naked man looking toward a distant bird in "hopeless resignation." Finally when Edna decided on suicide as a final act of free will, she watched a broken-winged bird descend into the sea. Edna Pontellier broke free from her cage, but she floundered in an alien environment. The story of her brief flight, however, has become a celebrated novel.

Noel Schraufnagel

Bibliography:
Chopin, Kate. *The Awakening*. Edited by Margaret Culley. New York: W. W. Norton, 1976. Contains fifteen essays or critical excerpts and ten 1899 reviews. Also contains background material on the situation of women in Chopin's time.

Fryer, Judith. *The Faces of Eve: Women in the Nineteenth Century Novel.* New York: Oxford University Press, 1976. A chapter describes Edna Pontellier as the first woman in American fiction who is a fully developed character.

Keesey, Donald, Comp. *Contexts for Criticism.* 2d ed. Mountain View, Calif.: Mayfield, 1994. Considers *The Awakening* from the perspectives of historical, formal, reader response, mimetic, intertextual, and poststructural criticism.

Ziff, Larzer. *The American 1890's: Life and Times of a Lost Generation.* New York: Viking Press, 1966. A social and literary history of the decade. Depicts Chopin as an artist and a pioneer in women's rights.

THE AWKWARD AGE

Type of work: Novel
Author: Henry James (1843-1916)
Type of plot: Social realism
Time of plot: 1890's
Locale: London and outlying estates
First published: 1899

Principal characters:

> FERNANDA BROOKENHAM (MRS. BROOK), the leader of a smart London set
> EDWARD BROOKENHAM, her husband and a government employee
> NANDA, their daughter
> HAROLD, their son
> MR. LONGDON, an elderly gentleman and a former suitor of Mrs. Brook's mother, Lady Julia
> GUSTAVUS VANDERBANK (VAN), a member of Mrs. Brook's circle and a government employee
> MR. MITCHETT (MITCHY), a wealthy young man who belongs to the circle
> THE DUCHESS (JANE), the widow of an Italian duke, also a member of the circle
> LITTLE AGGIE, her niece
> TISHY GRENDON, a young married woman and a friend of Nanda
> CARRIE DONNER, her sister
> MR. CASHMORE, Mrs. Donner's lover
> LADY FANNY CASHMORE, his wife
> LORD PETHERTON, Lady Fanny's brother and Mitchy's friend

The Story:

For the sophisticated conversationalists of Mrs. Brookenham's social set, innuendo and the hinted nuance had become a way of life. Indeed, their lives resided largely in talk. After Mr. Longdon spent his first evening at Mrs. Brookenham's, he had a long conversation with Gustavus Vanderbank, a remarkably handsome and imposing member of the set. Van had been taken with the older man, whose manner contrasted charmingly with that of the set, and Mr. Longdon, despite misgivings about that set, was similarly pleased. Mr. Longdon confided to Van that he had been a suitor to both Van's mother and Mrs. Brook's mother, Lady Julia, and that he had never forgotten his feelings for the latter, who was dramatically different from her daughter. Upon seeing a picture of Nanda, Mr. Longdon exclaimed on her similarity to Lady Julia. The conversation ended with Mr. Longdon's revealing that the conversational tone of Mrs. Brook's evening had indeed shocked him.

When she caught her son Harold in the act of stealing a five-pound note, Mrs. Brook had a colloquy with him. She was in her family mode, a studied and languorous melancholy quite at odds with her public manner, and her conversation turned on the problem of getting Harold invited to house parties and the family's financial straits. Harold left when the duchess entered, and the talk turned to Nanda, who was visiting her married friend Tishy Grendon. The duchess chided Mrs. Brook for allowing her daughter to mingle with such questionable associates; in the European manner, she was carefully sheltering her niece, Little Aggie, from any possible contaminations and preserving her as a perfect little *tabula rasa* until the time of her marriage.

She urged Mrs. Brook to snare Mitchy as a husband for Nanda, adding that his ugliness and his being the son of a shoemaker render him an impossible mate for Aggie. After a brief conversation between Mrs. Brook and her husband, Mitchy and Petherton entered the room. Despite his outrageous talk, Mrs. Brook attributed to Mitchy a gentleness and "niceness" lacking in the others. The duchess reentered the room, this time with Aggie, followed by Carrie Donner and Lady Fanny, and the talk turned to the erotic entanglements of the Grendon-Donner-Cashmore set. The duchess informed Mitchy that Nanda was her mother's source on the degree of intimacy between Mrs. Donner and Mr. Cashmore.

When they met, Nanda and Mr. Longdon sensed an immediate rapport. Mrs. Brook sounded Van on the subject of Mr. Longdon's fortune and what he might do for Nanda, and at the same time she indicated that she might possibly be in love with Van. At a weekend party given by Mitchy, Mr. Longdon urged Nanda to marry, but she confided to him that she would probably never marry. The duchess tried to persuade Mr. Longdon to settle a sum on Van that would allow him to marry Nanda, which would have left Mitchy free for Aggie, who was in love with him. Mr. Longdon made his offer to the uncertain Van, who requested time to consider the proposition and refused to allow his prospective benefactor to name a sum.

When Van revealed Mr. Longdon's generous offer to Mrs. Brook, that lady enigmatically hinted that he would refuse it. Against Van's wishes, Mrs. Brook told Mitchy what she had just learned and suggested that Van would pass up the chance to propose to Nanda rather than appear to have accepted a bribe. She justified passing on the information as being in accordance with that principle of openness and honesty that marks their society. When Nanda entered shortly after the departure of her mother's guests, Mrs. Brook questioned her about her relationship with Mr. Longdon and mentioned the possibility and advisability of his adopting her.

Later, at Mr. Longdon's house, Nanda told Mitchy, who she knew was in love with her, to marry Aggie. To please Nanda and to continue to enjoy at least the intimacy of sharing this plan with her, Mitchy acquiesced. He told Van of his intentions, indicating that he would no longer be a rival for Nanda. Van remained uncommitted and indecisive, however.

Several months later, everyone was gathered at Tishy Grendon's estate. Nanda had been Mr. Longdon's guest for several months; Harold had ably distracted Lady Fanny from her design to run off with another gentleman; and Little Aggie, having married and lost her innocence, had taken up with her aunt's lover, Petherton. In a tremendous scene in which she demanded Nanda's return from Mr. Longdon, Mrs. Brook had brought about public exposure of the group. She climaxed her performance with the revelation that Nanda had read a scabrous French novel, lent to her by Vanderbank, which was pronounced unfit even for the presumably far more experienced Tishy. As a result, Vanderbank learned the depths of knowledge already open to Nanda, depths in the unveiling of which he had been instrumental but which, with cruel irony, now made her an impossible choice to be his wife.

The scene at Tishy Grendon's estate destroyed the solidarity of the group. It was months before Van returned to Mrs. Brook's house, and though he had supposedly come to see Nanda, he ultimately avoided the chance to do so. Mrs. Brook interpreted this to mean that he had finally given Nanda up, and she enjoined Mitchy to tell Mr. Longdon. As she explained to her remarkably obtuse husband, her purpose in creating the scene at Tishy's had been simply to confirm Mr. Longdon's belief that she and her world were impossible for Nanda and to ensure his taking care of the girl.

Two weeks later, the overwrought and embarrassed Van made what was presumably his final visit to Nanda. Nanda, however, let the now awkward young man off easily by herself assuming the false position, and she generously entreated him not to desert her mother, a plea she also made to Mitchy. Once only Mr. Longdon remained, she broke down in the fullness of her suffering. They agreed that Vanderbank ought to have married Aggie. Only her kind of innocence could have met his measure, an innocence capable of becoming its own obverse at the first taste of experience. Even under such a circumstance, however, Mitchy would still have been totally out of the question for her; it was his fate, as it was Nanda's, to love only the person who is out of the question. Nanda's thoughts revolved around the suffering Mitchy as she made preparations for being taken away the following day by Mr. Longdon.

Critical Evaluation:

As he does in so much of his fiction, Henry James in *The Awkward Age* focuses his attention on the nature of social relationships in his adopted homeland, England. In this work, he does not, however, contrast the sophistication of European society with the more naïve, but at times morally superior, American scene. Instead, *The Awkward Age* is a scathing portrait of the hypocrisy and self-interest of British society, where young women, at that "awkward age" between girlhood and full-fledged adulthood, are especially vulnerable to the machinations of older women and men who wish to use them for their own purposes.

The unlikely hero of the story, Mr. Longdon, is not a member of the London society that James castigates. Well into middle age, Longdon returns to London from his country estate to reacquaint himself with the family of a woman he once loved deeply, whose memory he still cherishes though she is long dead. The society he finds is far different from the one he remembers from his youth. The contrast between past and present, and the loss Longdon feels for the values he holds sacred, is a theme James plays upon throughout the work. Longdon, too, is at an "awkward age," too old to pursue amorous relationships with women but young enough to be stirred by the beauty of a girl like Nanda. His solution is to become a kind of surrogate father for her, a knight who would rescue her from the metaphorical dungeon in which she is trapped by her scheming mother and the men who want her for all the wrong reasons.

Three women dominate the novel: Mrs. Brookenham, her daughter Nanda, and the shadow of Lady Julia. Longdon's reaction to each of them is a spur for what little action the novel contains. For the aging hero, the grace, poise, and moral rectitude he associates with Lady Julia has degenerated into Mrs. Brookenham's scheming and corruption. In Nanda, Longdon sees the reincarnation of her grandmother, and he believes it is his mission in life to save the young woman from the life she is destined to lead if she remains in the social circle dominated by her mother and her father's cousin, the duchess. These two femmes fatale, who are constantly working both as matchmakers and go-betweens for themselves and others in liaisons outside of marriage, strike the man from an earlier generation as reprehensible and as a violation of the principles that governed relations between the sexes in an earlier era.

From Longdon's efforts to wrest Nanda away from her mother, and from the efforts of Mrs. Brookenham and the duchess to guide various other characters into and out of relationships, a central theme of the novel emerges: power and control in social situations. For James, the question is not simply one of gender domination: The women in this novel seem to exercise as much power over men as men do over women. The unusual arrangement, which often blurs the line between traditional qualities associated with males and females, arises from all of the characters' acquiescence in the social strictures that, by common assumption, should govern the lives of people in the higher social sets. Those standards involve a view of marriage as a financial and social arrangement rather than as a bond between two individuals deeply in love. Hence, both men and women in the novel are constantly concerned with improving their status in society by seeking the partner who will bring them money or position or both. Because her fortune seems assured, the duchess' niece Aggie is a more attractive catch than Nanda. Even Longdon, whom James seems to intend as the moral arbiter in the work, places a monetary value on Nanda when he makes the proposal that if Vanderbank will marry Nanda, he will settle a small fortune on her to assure the couple's financial independence. What emerges from this web of posturing and negotiating is a portrait of society where genuine concern for human feelings is subordinate to self-interest.

Such attitudes are only suggested, however. James's fiction rarely states a moral position directly. Yet even within the James canon, *The Awkward Age* is a particularly difficult novel. Eschewing conventional methods of storytelling in fiction, James instead imposes dramatic principles on his story. Almost the entire novel is cast in the form of dialogue and conversation, and readers are left to discern characters' motives and moral qualities from the remarks they make about themselves and others. Often information is conflicting, even contradictory. It is never entirely clear whether such figures as Mrs. Brookenham and Vanderbank are simple seekers after pleasure or more complex personalities who recognize that living in the world of high society places extraordinary demands on individuals. It is never certain whether Mitchett is so devoted to Nanda that his marriage to Aggie is an act of self-sacrifice, or whether he is simply another of the dissolute men who populate Mrs. Brookenham's salon, willing to do whatever he is told rather than cause a scene. It is not even clear how Longdon and Nanda feel about each other when she agrees to leave her mother's home to live with him in the country. James has allowed readers to observe the characters and to listen to them for awhile. How to judge the characters, however, remains a constant enigma, akin to the situation everyone faces daily in trying to judge those who are only known through what they say and do.

"Critical Evaluation" by Laurence W. Mazzeno

Bibliography:
Edel, Leon. *Henry James: A Life.* 1st ed. New York: Harper & Row, 1985. Abridgment of Edel's definitive study of the novelist. Comments about the writing and publication of *The Awkward Age*; discusses James's handling of character development, especially that of the middle-aged Longdon and the two young women whose stories are central to the plot.
Gard, Roger, ed. *Henry James: The Critical Heritage.* London: Routledge & Kegan Paul, 1968. Includes excerpts from four reviews of *The Awkward Age* by James's contemporaries. Cites both British and American sources and records the mixed success of the work among nineteenth century readers.
Jones, Granville H. *Henry James's Psychology of Experience: Innocence, Responsibility, and Renunciation in the Fiction of Henry James.* Paris: Mouton, 1975. Uses *The Awkward Age* to explore "the position of innocence in the structure, form, style, and substance of James's fiction." Claims that the novel shows James's attempt to explore the ramifications of change and loss of innocence.
Macnaughton, William R. *Henry James: The Later Novels.* Boston: Twayne, 1987. A chapter on *The Awkward Age* provides commentary on the genesis of the novel, examines James's sources, and discusses the ambiguities created by the author's use of dramatic form for his story. Also explores the nature of James's development of central characters.
Sicker, Philip. *Love and the Quest for Identity in the Fiction of Henry James.* Princeton, N.J.: Princeton University Press, 1980. Studies the "evolving conception of romantic love" in James's fiction. Extended discussion of *The Awkward Age* focuses on the inability of the middle-aged protagonist to adjust to changes wrought by time.

BAAL

Type of work: Drama
Author: Bertolt Brecht (1898-1956)
Type of plot: Tragedy
Time of plot: c. 1911
Locale: Augsberg, Germany, and environs
First published: 1922; first performed, 1923; revised, 1926 (English translation, 1963)

Principal characters:
BAAL, a poet
ECKART, a composer
JOHANNES SCHMIDT, Baal's friend
JOHANNA REIHER, Johannes' fiancée
SOPHIE BARGER, Baal's lover
MECH, business man
EMILY MECH, his wife
DR. PILLER, a critic
MJURK, a nightclub owner

The Story:

A Brightly Lit Room. Dr. Piller brought Baal together with Mech and his wife Emily because Mech was interested in publishing Baal's poems. Baal was interested in the white arms of Mech's wife. He drunkenly insulted both Mech and Dr. Piller until they left in a rage.

Baal's Attic. Johannes confided to Baal that he had not seduced his seventeen-year old fiancée, Johanna, because of her innocence. He confessed that he believed the union of bodies was filthy, although he enjoyed making love to Johanna in his dreams. Baal extolled the ecstasies of love and proclaimed: "If love is too much for you, you vomit yourselves up," in pregnancy and bitterness. When asked, he advised Johannes not to seduce the girl.

Barroom. Baal was complaining to a group of teamsters about his affair with Emily Mech, and how he was tired of her hanging around, when Johannes and Johanna entered the bar. Emily came in and sat down with the three as they drank, and Baal flirted with the waitress Louise. The teamsters hailed Baal's song about an orgy until Eckart approached Baal and challenged him to join him in the woods to lead the life of free men. Baal declared it was too soon, and Eckart departed. As Baal continued to insult Emily, Johannes and Johanna withdrew, as did the teamsters, leaving Baal alone with a sobbing Emily whom he comforted and kissed.

Baal's Attic. After a night of lovemaking, Johanna felt guilty and refused to stay any longer with Baal. Asked if he still loved her, Baal declared he was "fed to the teeth." Johanna ran out of the door. Later in the day, two sisters, whom Baal had earlier seduced, came to his room and told him that a girl, Johanna Reiher, had drowned herself in the River Laach. Baal's landlady chased the girls out of his room. In the evening Baal, drunk on brandy, dragged Sophie Barger into his room because he needed a woman.

Whitewashed Houses and Brown Tree Trunks. Dark Bells. Baal carried on an elliptical conversation with a drunken bum about the bodies of dead trees and the bodies of dead women, Corpus Christi, Jesus, poetry, and religion.

A Night in May. Baal and Sophie made love in the woods although Sophie protested that she had been missing for three weeks and her mother believed that she had been drowned.

Night Cloud, a Night Spot. When Mjurk, the owner of the Night Cloud, refused to give Baal any more brandy, Baal created a riot in the café by singing a filthy song. He escaped retaliation by going through the toilet window.

Green Fields, Blue Plum Trees. In July, Baal and Eckart wandered through the cornfields and plum orchards and decided to soak in a pool of blue water.

Village Tavern. Baal conned a group of peasants into bringing all of their bulls to town the next evening. He wanted to create a divine spectacle for Eckart. He was thwarted in his intent because the village parson saw through his swindle and cleared up the matter. Somewhat amused by Baal, the parson sent him on his way and paid for his brandy.

Trees. A group of lumberjacks mourned over the death of their comrade Teddy. When one suggested that they drink to Teddy's memory with his barrel of brandy, Baal chided them for trying to steal the dead man's property. When they went to retrieve Teddy's brandy, they discovered that Baal had already drunk it all.

A Cabin. Rain. Eckart avoided answering any of Baal's questions about his life by changing the subject to Sophie's whereabouts. Immediately before she appeared at the door of the cabin, Baal complained that she was acting demented and hung around his neck like a stone.

The Plains. Sophie, pregnant with Baal's child, followed Eckart and Baal on their wanderings. When Eckart upbraided Baal for his treatment of Sophie, Baal accused Eckart of being willing to abandon Baal for Sophie: She would not, however, stay with Eckart. Eckart offered to take care of Sophie and take her home to her mother if she would renounce Baal. She refused, and the two men began to fight. As Baal declared their closeness during the battle to be better than that with a woman, he dragged Eckart off to camp in the woods, abandoning Sophie.

Room in an Inn. A family of sick and ugly beggars were playing cards in a hospital tavern, when Baal and Eckart burst in on them. The absurdist conversation sparked by Baal's champagne ended in the manifesto that they resided in the paradise of hell, that nothing lasted forever, and that the most beautiful thing of all is Nothing. Baal summoned Eckart away to wash themselves in the river.

Green Thicket of Leaves. Sitting on the bank of the river, Baal declared his love for Eckart and asserted he had no further need of women.

Highway. Baal, haunted by Johanna's death, awakened Eckart by singing to him a ballad of a drowned girl and asked Eckart if he had finished his Mass yet. Eckart declared himself to be too busy with a pale redhead.

Young Hazel Bushes. Baal met a young woman looking for Eckart and dragged her into the bushes for a quick seduction.

Maple in the Wind. Baal sang his newest poem, "Death in the Forest."

Barroom. Eight years later, Baal encountered his old acquaintances, who commented on his state of decline. He sang a song lamenting his birth and frantic life, and then in a sudden brawl over a waitress, he stabbed Eckart.

Forest. Baal headed north and sang about his own death.

Highway. As two rangers hunted for Baal, he overheard their conversation and learned that Eckart had died of the stab wound.

Log Cabin in the Forest. Dying, Baal was abandoned by drunken lumberjacks when the rain stopped and they returned to work. Baal crawled out the door to die on his Mother Earth.

Critical Evaluation:

The twenty-year-old Bertolt Brecht began writing *Baal* in 1918 as a response to Hans Johst's *The Lonely One* (1917), an expressionist drama about the nineteenth century poet Christian Dietrich Grabbe. Brecht had seen a production of Johst's play and discussed it in a seminar led by Arthur Kutschler at the Ludwig Maximilian University in Munich. Brecht despised the play for its idealism—the notion that artists are different from other people—and for its sentimentality. He set out to write an antithetical play, using as his models for the protagonist the fifteenth century French poet François Villon, the German expressionist balladeer and playwright Frank Wedekind, and Brecht's own bohemian experiences. Suggestions of the relationship between the French poets Paul Verlaine and Arthur Rimbaud also appear in the play. Brecht's first draft, written in 1918, closely follows the structure and episodes of Johst's play; later drafts move away from his antimodel, deemphasizing Johst's influence.

As Brecht's first mature play (he had written a short play during his school years), *Baal* is "indispensable reading for anyone who would understand Brecht's development," according to critic Ronald Speirs. The play is a heady brew of disparate influences and impulses that continued to be played out in many guises throughout Brecht's career. The tension of the play is dialectical; decay is linked to existence, destruction to productive energy, and Eros to Thanatos. Brecht allows no triumphant rebirth or transcendence.

The paganism implied in the protagonist's name is not simply a reflection of a naïve and innocent longing to return to nature. Baal was the Semitic-Phoenician fertility god, associated with storms and the figure of the bull. His attraction for Brecht, no doubt, in part derived from the knowledge that in the Judeo-Christian tradition, Baal was the embodiment of evil. Brecht's character has strong associations also with philosopher Friedrich Nietzsche's Dionysian principle and with Frank Wedekind's neopagan, antiheroine Lulu.

Although the action of the play takes place over a multiyear period, the essential movement is seasonal, as befits its roots in a mythic paganism. The play begins in spring with an emphasis on Baal's erotic desires. He successively seduces Emily, Johanna, and Sophie. The friendship between Eckart and Baal ripens throughout the summer until the autumnal harvest is signaled by Sophie's pregnancy. The fall's torrential rains drive Eckart and Baal from the woods into inns and taverns inhabited by worn-out social pariahs. Death marks the winter—first, Baal's enraged murder of Eckart and then, his own death, abandoned and alone, under the starry sky.

Baal himself is seduced by Nature, "that girl the world, who gives herself and giggles/ If you only let her crush you with her thighs,/ Shared with Baal who loved it, orgiastic wriggles," but he suffers no spiritual or metaphysical illusions. Nature will abandon him as easily as he abandons the lovers of which he has tired. Brecht's vision of nature incorporates a Darwinian materialism that does not deny the inevitability of death:

> In the dark womb of the earth the rotting Baal did lie.
> Huge as ever, calm, and pallid was the sky,
> Young and naked and immensely marvelous
> As Baal loved it when Baal lived among us.

As an amoral child of nature, Brecht's protagonist is lusting, romping, scratching after life, gobbling it up in great mouthfuls, all the while trying to survive in a world that is consuming and mad in itself. *Baal* also belongs to the satiric tradition, contemptuous of established institutions and sanctioned morality. Baal's lust is voracious and his teeth are sharp. When Baal insists that one must have teeth to reach love's ecstasy, "like biting into an orange when the juice squirts in your teeth," his friend Johannes observes, "Your teeth are the teeth of an animal: grayish-yellow, massive, uncanny."

Amidst a society rotted with corruption and offering no meaning, the poet exults in motiveless pranks. Baal's trickery may be illustrated by the episode with the peasants and their bulls—he desires to create a divine spectacle, but is thwarted by a well-intentioned and unimaginative parson. Baal celebrates life despite, or perhaps because of, being inextricably caught in the web of nature. This inevitability of death and decay is something that Brecht tried to overcome in his later plays. The atmosphere of *Baal* is one in which God is dead and nihilism is rampant. God is not dead in the medieval beast epic, to which *Baal* owes much, but God might as well be, for in such an epic, nature reigns, the Church is useless, and the court is incapable of dispensing justice. In both worlds—that of the medieval beast story or that of *Baal*—one has only oneself to depend upon or worry about. When asked if he believes in God, Baal answers: "I always believed in myself. But one *could* become an atheist."

Although the older Brecht, committed to the optimistic hope that the world could be improved through dedication to Marxism, repudiated the nihilism of his first play, it was from the writing of this play that many of the playwright's techniques and themes evolved. The method of welding together multiple sources fused with a heightened poetic lyricism became his standard procedure in crafting a drama, as did his reliance on multiple collaborators. In the case of *Baal*, he relied upon the illustrations of Caspar Neher for visual inspiration and scenic decoration, on playwright Lion Feuchtwanger for editing help in the second draft, and on the actors, including Oskar Homolka, in the 1926 revision was produced in Berlin and Vienna.

Baal was not produced again until the 1965 Off-Broadway production (in the 1963 English translation by Eric Bentley and Martin Esslin) with James Earl Jones as Eckart. Since that production it has often been revived in university and alternative theaters and occasionally even in more mainstream venues as a seminal work not only in the evolution of Brecht's theater but also in the development of contemporary drama.

Jane Anderson Jones

Bibliography:
Bentley, Eric. *"Baal."* In *The Brecht Commentaries 1943-1980.* New York: Grove Press, 1981. Describes Baal as a pleasure-seeker, part monster and part martyr in a world of nothingness. Suggests that the mythic elements in the play will become increasingly important to critical understanding of the play.
Hayman, Ronald. *Brecht: A Biography.* New York: Oxford University Press, 1983. Hayman intertwines a study of Brecht's life with a critical view of his work. Traces the inception of *Baal*, Brecht's collaboration with Caspar Neher, and the subsequent revisions of the play.
Hill, Claude. "Praise Ye the Cold, the Darkness, and Corruption!" In *Bertolt Brecht.* Boston: Twayne, 1975. In this chapter, discussing *Baal* and five other early works, Hill reveals the influences leading to Brecht's writing the play and points out that there were multiple drafts, resulting in three distinctly different versions.
Speirs, Ronald. *"Baal."* In *Critical Essays on Bertolt Brecht*, edited by Siegfried Mews. Boston: G. K. Hall, 1989. Speirs connects Baal with the cult of vitality and modern paganism as represented by the philosopher Friedrich Nietzsche's Dionysus and the playwright Frank Wedekind's Lulu. He explores how Baal experiences life's transience as both a threat of death and a source of pleasure.
Weideli, Walter. "To Live Here." In *The Art of Bertolt Brecht*, translated by Daniel Russell. New York: New York University Press, 1963. In *Baal* Weideli sees Brecht's dialectical intuition, which links decay to existence and attempts to convert destruction into productive energy. The play, rather than presenting an ideal, follows an example to its absurd conclusion.

BABBITT

Type of work: Novel
Author: Sinclair Lewis (1885-1951)
Type of plot: Social satire
Time of plot: 1920's
Locale: Zenith, a fictional Midwestern town
First published: 1922

> *Principal characters:*
> GEORGE F. BABBITT, a middle-aged real estate broker
> MYRA, his wife
> TED, their son
> VERONA, their daughter
> PAUL RIESLING, Babbitt's friend
> ZILLA, Paul's shrewish wife

The Story:

George F. Babbitt was proud of his house in Floral Heights, one of the most respectable residential districts in Zenith. Its architecture was standardized; its interior decorations were standardized; its atmosphere was standardized. Therein lay its appeal for Babbitt. He bustled about in a tile and chromium bathroom during his morning ritual of getting ready for another day. When he went down to breakfast, he was as grumpy as usual. It was expected of him. He read the dull real estate page of the newspaper to his patient wife, Myra. Then he commented on the weather, grumbled at his son and daughter, gulped his breakfast, and started for his office.

Babbitt was a real estate broker who knew how to handle business with zip and zowie. Having closed a deal whereby he forced a poor businessman to buy a piece of property at twice its value, he pocketed part of the money and paid the rest to the man who had suggested the enterprise. Proud of his acumen, he picked up the telephone and called his best friend, Paul Riesling, to ask him to lunch. Paul should have been a violinist, but he had gone into the tar-roofing business in order to support his shrewish wife, Zilla. Lately, she had made it her practice to infuriate doormen, theater ushers, or taxicab drivers, and then ask Paul to come to her rescue and fight them like a man. Cringing with embarrassment, Paul would pretend he had not noticed the incident. Later, at home, Zilla would accuse him of being a coward and a weakling.

So sad did Paul's affairs seem to Babbitt that he suggested a vacation to Maine together— away from their wives. Paul was skeptical, but with magnificent assurance, Babbitt promised to arrange the trip. Paul was humbly grateful. Back in his office, Babbitt refused a raise for one of his employees. When he got home, he and his wife decided to give a dinner party, with the arrangements taken from the contents of a woman's magazine, and everything edible disguised to look like something else.

The party was a great success. Babbitt's friends were exactly like Babbitt. They all became drunk on prohibition-period gin, were disappointed when the cocktails ran out, stuffed themselves with food, and went home to nurse headaches.

Some time later, Babbitt and Myra paid a call on the Rieslings. Zilla, trying to enlist their sympathy, berated her husband until he was goaded to fury. Babbitt finally told Zilla that she was a nagging, jealous, sour, and unwholesome wife, and he demanded that she allow Paul to go with him to Maine. Weeping in self-pity, Zilla consented. Myra sat calmly during the scene, but later she criticized Babbitt for bullying Paul's wife. Babbitt told her sharply to mind her own business. On the train, Babbitt and Paul met numerous businessmen who loudly agreed with one another that what this country needed was a sound business administration. They deplored the price of motor cars, textiles, wheat, and oil; they swore that they had not an ounce of race prejudice; they blamed communism and socialism for labor unions that got out of hand. Paul soon tired of the discussion and went to bed. Babbitt stayed up late, smoking countless cigars and telling countless stories.

Maine had a soothing effect upon Babbitt. He and Paul fished and hiked in the quiet of the north woods, and Babbitt began to realize that his life in Zenith was not all it should be. He promised himself a new outlook on life, a more simple, less hurried way of living.

Back in Zenith, Babbitt was asked to make a speech at a convention of real estate men, which was to be held in Monarch, a nearby city. He wrote a speech contending that real estate men should be considered professionals and called realtors. At the meeting, he declaimed loudly that real estate was a great profession, that Zenith was God's own country—the best little spot on earth—and to prove his statements, he quoted countless statistics on waterways, textile production, and lumber manufacture. The speech was such a success that Babbitt instantly won recognition as an orator.

Babbitt was made a precinct leader in the coming election. His duty was to speak to small labor groups about the inadvisability of voting for Seneca Doane, a liberal, in favor of a man named Prout, a solid businessman who represented the conservative element. Babbitt's speeches helped to defeat Doane. He was very proud of himself.

On a business trip to Chicago, Babbitt spied Paul Riesling sitting at dinner with a middle-aged and pretty woman. Later, in his hotel room, Babbitt indignantly demanded an explanation for Paul's lack of morality. Paul told Babbitt that he could no longer stand living with Zilla. Babbitt, feeling sorry for his friend, swore that he would keep Paul's secret from Zilla. Privately, Babbitt envied Paul's independence. Babbitt was made vice-president of the Booster's Club. He was so proud of himself that he bragged loudly when his wife called him at the office. It was a long time before he understood what she was trying to tell him; Paul had shot his wife. Zilla was still alive, and Paul was in prison.

Babbitt's world collapsed about him. Babbitt began to question his ideas about the power of the dollar. Paul was perhaps the only person Babbitt had ever loved. Myra had long since become a habit, and the children were too full of new ideas to be close to their father. Babbitt felt suddenly alone. He began to criticize the minister's sermons. He no longer visited the Athletic Club and rarely ate lunch with any of his business acquaintances. One day, the pretty widow Mrs. Judique came to his office and asked him to find her a flat. Babbitt joined her circle of Bohemian friends. He drank more than he had ever drunk in his life. He spent money wildly. Two of the most powerful men in town requested that he join the Good Citizen's League—or else. Babbitt refused to be bullied. For the first time in his life, he was a human being. He actually made friends with his archenemy, Seneca Doane, and discovered that he liked his liberal ideas. He praised Doane publicly. Babbitt's new outlook on life appealed to his children, who at once began to respect him as they never had before. Babbitt, however, became unpopular among his business-boosting friends. When he again refused to join the Good Citizen's League, he was snubbed in the streets. Gradually, Babbitt found that he had no real resources within himself. He was miserable.

When Myra became ill, Babbitt suddenly realized that he loved his colorless wife. He broke with Mrs. Judique and joined the Good Citizen's League. By the time Myra was well again, there was no more active leader in the town of Zenith than George F. Babbitt. Once more he announced his distrust of Seneca Doane. He became the best booster the club ever had. His last gesture of revolt was private approval of his son's elopement. Outwardly he conformed.

Critical Evaluation:

Zenith, "the Zip City—Zeal, Zest, and Zowie," is Sinclair Lewis' satirical composite picture of the typical progressive American "business city" of the 1920's, and middle-aged, middle-class Midwesterner George F. Babbitt is its average prosperous citizen. Everything about Zenith is modern. A few old buildings, ramshackle witnesses of the city's nineteenth century origins, are embarrassing, discordant notes amid the harmony of newness produced by shining sky-scrapers, factories, and railroads. One by one, the old buildings are surrounded and bulldozed. The thrust of all energies in the city is toward growth: One of Zenith's most booming businesses is real estate; one of its favorite occupations is the religious tallying and charting of population increase.

As Lewis presents his characters, however, the reader discovers that the prosperity and growth of Zenith are inversely proportional to the intellectual bankruptcy and spiritual stagnation of its inhabitants. They subscribe to the values of Zenith's culture, which are all based on the "Dollar Ethic"; Lewis' characters think in terms of production and consumption, judge people on the grounds of their purchasing power, and seek happiness in the earning and spending of money. This creed of prosperity permeates every aspect of society. It is evident not only in political and economic beliefs (discussion between Babbitt and his friends about government affairs is limited to the monotonous refrain, "What this country needs is a good, sound business administration") but in moral and religious attitudes as well. Thus, Dr. Drew attracts followers to his "Salvation and Five Percent" church with a combined cross-and-dollar-sign approach. Even more sinister is the facility with which the upright Babbitt carries through crooked deals in his real estate business. In one maneuver, he plots with a speculator to force a struggling grocer to buy the store building (which he has been renting for years) at a scalper's price. The money ethic is so elemental to Babbitt's conscience that he honestly feels nothing but delight and pride when the deal is completed; his only regret is that the speculator carries off nine thousand dollars while Babbitt receives a mere four hundred and fifty dollar commission. At the same time, Babbitt—with no inkling of his hypocrisy—discourses on his virtue to his friend Paul Riesling, touting his own integrity while denigrating the morality of his competitors.

The value placed on money also determines Zenith's aesthetic standards. There is no frivolity about the city's architecture; the most important structures are the strictly functional business buildings. Other structures, such as the Athletic Club—where the businessmen go to "relax" and discuss weighty matters of finance—are gaudy, unabashed copies of past styles; the Club's motley conglomeration includes everything from Roman to Gothic to Chinese. The culmination of literary talent in Zenith is the work of Chum Frink, whose daily newspaper lyrics are indistinguishable from his Zeeco car ads. He comes to Babbitt's dinner party fresh from having written a lyric in praise of drinking water instead of poison booze; with bootleg cocktail in hand, he identifies the American genius as the fellow who can run a successful business or the man who writes the Prince Albert Tobacco ads.

Most important, the prosperity ethic is at the heart of social norms in Zenith; it is the basis upon which each citizen judges his individual worth. Lewis' novel includes caricatures of men in every major field of endeavor: Howard Littlefield is the scholar; T. Cholmondeley Frink, the poet; Mike Monday, the popular preacher; Jake Offut, the politician; Vergil Gunch, the indus-trialist. Yet despite their various professions, these men are identical in their values; they are united in their complacent pride in their own success and in their scorn for those who have not "made it." A man is measured by his income and his possessions. Thus, Babbitt's car is far more than his means of transportation, and his acquisition of gimmicks like the nickel-plated cigar cutter more than mere whim; both car and cigar cutter are affirmations of competence and virility. The more Babbitt and his peers strive to distinguish themselves through ownership, however, the more alike they seem. Thus, the men of Zenith, since they are saturated day after day with the demands of the business life and its values, are even more alike than the women, who are not as immersed in the rat race as their husbands.

Mercilessly revealing and minutely detailed as the portrait of Zenith is, however, *Babbitt* would not be the excellent novel it is if Lewis had stopped at that. In addition to being an exposé of shallowness, the novel is the chronicle of one man's feeble and half-conscious attempt to break out of a meaningless and sterile existence. In the first half of the book, George Babbitt is the Zenithite par excellence; but in the realtor's sporadic bursts of discontent, Lewis plants seeds of the rebellion to come. Babbitt's complacency is occasionally punctured by disturbing questions: Might his wife be right that he bullied Zilla only to strut and show off his strength and virtue? Are his friends really interesting people? Does he really love his wife and enjoy his career? These nagging questions and the pressures in his life finally build sufficient tension to push Babbitt to the unprecedented step of taking a week's vacation in Maine without his wife and children. The trip relieves his tension and dissolves the questions, and he returns to another year in Zenith with renewed vigor and enthusiasm for Boosters, baseball, dinner parties, and real estate.

It takes the personal tragedy of his friend Paul Riesling to shock Babbitt out of his routine way of life; Paul's shooting of his wife and consequent imprisonment, which occur approximately midway in the novel, shake Babbitt to his foundations. The Babbitt of the first half of the story is a parody; the Babbitt of the second half, a weak and struggling human being. After Paul goes to prison, Babbitt, to all appearances, throws over his whole previous lifestyle: He drinks, smokes, and curses; he frequents wild parties, befriends the city's bohemian set, adopts radical opinions, and has a love affair. All these things are part of his rebellion against stifling circumstances and his attempt to escape into individuality. The attempt fails because he lacks the inner strength to be independent, and his revolt is ultimately little more than a teapot tempest. Whether preaching the philosophy of the Elks or rebelliously praising the radical politics of Seneca Doane, whether giving a dinner party with his wife or sneaking out to see Mrs. Judique, Babbitt never truly acts on his own.

Thus, by the end of the novel, Babbitt has "returned to the fold," joining the Good Citizen's League and redoubling his zeal in behalf of Zenith Booster activities. Even though Babbitt lacks the strength to break out of his mold, Lewis does not imply that he is unchanged by his experience. On the contrary, Babbitt rediscovers his love for his wife and learns something about himself. The Babbitt at the close of the novel has grown in awareness, even if he has proven himself incapable of essentially changing his life. If he has lost his own individuality, he is still able to hope for better things for his son, Ted, of whose elopement he secretly approves.

"Critical Evaluation" by Nancy G. Ballard

Bibliography:
Bucco, Martin, ed. *Critical Essays on Sinclair Lewis.* Boston: G. K. Hall, 1986. A collection of criticism on Sinclair Lewis. Begins with early interviews and goes on to contemporary

critics. Many articles include discussion of *Babbitt*; one article addresses the book exclusively.

Dooley, D. J. *The Art of Sinclair Lewis*. Lincoln: University of Nebraska Press, 1967. Discusses *Babbitt* as the first novel to represent what would become Lewis' characteristic method—the intensive study of a subject. Discusses the novel's strengths and weaknesses, and explores the significance of *Babbitt* in American life.

Grebstein, Sheldon Norman. *Sinclair Lewis*. Boston: Twayne, 1962. Makes a useful distinction between Lewis' novels, including *Babbitt*, which were written in the 1920's, and the rest of his work. Argues that *Babbitt* created an image of America that continues to be influential.

Love, Glen A. *Babbitt: An American Life*. Boston: Twayne, 1993. The only book-length study of *Babbitt*. Puts *Babbitt* into its historical and literary context. Chronology, critical analysis, bibliography.

Schorer, Mark. *Sinclair Lewis: An American Life*. New York: McGraw-Hill, 1961. Indispensable. Discusses *Babbitt* from its inception to its reviews, and includes an analysis of the novel, concluding that *Babbitt* was published with timing perfectly suited to match the national mood.

THE BACCHAE

Type of work: Drama
Author: Euripides (c. 485-406 B.C.E.)
Type of plot: Tragedy
Time of plot: Antiquity
Locale: Thebes, in Boeotia
First performed: Bakchai, c. 405 B.C.E. (English translation, 1781)

> *Principal characters:*
> DIONYSUS, the god of the vine
> PENTHEUS, the king of Thebes
> CADMUS, the grandfather of Pentheus and the former king
> TIRESIAS, a Theban seer
> AGAVE, Pentheus' mother

The Story:

Semele, the daughter of Cadmus, the king of Thebes, was visited by Zeus and conceived a child. While she was still carrying her unborn child, she prayed to see Zeus in all his splendor. Zeus accordingly appeared to her in the form of a bolt of lightning, and Semele was killed instantly. Zeus took the prematurely born child he had fathered and placed him within himself. At the proper time, the child was born again and was named Dionysus. When he grew up and became the god of revelry and wine, men established a cult for his worship. The cult of Dionysus spread throughout western Asia, but did not initially gain a real foothold in Europe. Dionysus, the god-man whom his devotees associated with the vine and with the ecstasies derived from the juice of the grape, decided that Thebes, home of his ancestors, would be the logical place to initiate his cult in the West. At first, Theban resistance to Dionysian behavior balked his efforts, and many Thebans refused to believe that he was a son of Zeus. Pentheus, the king of Thebes and grandson of Cadmus and cousin of Dionysus, dreaded the disorders and madness induced by the new cult, and he stubbornly opposed its mysteries, which were based on orgiastic and frenzied rites of nature.

A group of Eastern women, devotees of Dionysus, called on the Theban women to join them in the worship of their beloved god. During the ceremonies, blind Tiresias, an ancient Theban prophet, summoned old Cadmus, now withdrawn from public life, to the worship of Dionysus. While performing the frenzied rites, the two old men miraculously regained youthful vigor.

Pentheus, enraged when some of his people turned to the new religion, imprisoned all women who were seen carrying bacchic symbols such as wine, an ivy crown, or a staff. He rebuked his aged grandfather and accused Tiresias of spreading the cult in Thebes. Tiresias championed Dionysus, declaring that wine provided men with a temporary release from the harshness and miseries of life. The Theban maidens, he said, were exalted and purified by the bacchic ecstasies. Old Cadmus seconded the words of Tiresias and offered to place an ivy wreath on Pentheus' brow. Pentheus brushed it aside and ordered some of his soldiers to destroy Tiresias' house; others he directed to seize a mysterious stranger, a priest of Dionysus, who had a remarkable influence over Theban women.

When the stranger, Dionysus in disguise, was brought before the king, all the Theban women who had been jailed suddenly and mysteriously found themselves free in a forest, where they proceeded to worship Dionysus. Meanwhile, in the city, Pentheus asked the prisoner his name and his country. Dionysus refused to give his name but said that he was from Lydia, in Asia Minor, and that he and his followers had received their religion from Dionysus. When Pentheus asked to know more about the strange religion, Dionysus said that this knowledge was reserved for the virtuous only. Pentheus impatiently ordered a soldier to cut off Dionysus' curls, which the prisoner had said were dedicated to his god. Then Pentheus seized Dionysus' staff and ordered him to be imprisoned. Dionysus, calm in spite of these humiliations, expressed confidence in his own welfare and pity at the blindness of Pentheus. Before the guards took Dionysus to be imprisoned in the royal stables, he predicted catastrophe for Pentheus. The king, unmindful of this prophecy, directed that the female followers of Dionysus be put to practical womanly labors.

From his place of imprisonment, Dionysus called out encouragement to his devotees. Then he invoked an earthquake, which shook the foundations of Pentheus' fortress. Flames danced on Semele's tomb. Dionysus appeared, mysteriously freed from his prison, and rebuked his followers for any doubts and fears they had expressed. He cast a spell on Pentheus, who in his mad frenzy mistook a bull for Dionysus and chained the animal in its stall while the god-man looked on. Another earth tremor transformed the royal fortress into ruins.

Pentheus, enraged at seeing Dionysus free, ordered his guards to shut the gates of the city. A messenger reported that many Theban women, among them Pentheus' mother, Agave, were on nearby Mount Cithaeron observing Dionysian rites that combined a dignified and beautiful worship of nature with the cruel slaughter of cattle. A battle had taken place between the women and Boeotian peasants, but the frenzied women, although victorious over the peasants, did not harm them. Pentheus ordered the immediate suppression of the cult. Dionysus offered to lead the women back to the city, but he declared that if he did so the women would only grow more devoted to the man-god.

When Pentheus imperiously demanded that his orders be obeyed, Dionysus cast a spell over him that made the king express a desire to see the women at their worship. In a trance, he resisted only feebly when Dionysus dressed him in woman's clothes so that he might not be detected by the women, who were jealous of the secrecy of their cult. Pentheus, in fact, was almost overcome by Dionysus' charms as the god led him to Mount Cithaeron.

On the mountain, Pentheus complained that he could not see the rites because of the thick pine forest. Dionysus immediately bent a large pine tree to the ground, set Pentheus in its topmost branches, and gently let the tree return to its upright position. At that moment, the man-god disappeared, but his voice boomed out to his ecstatic devotees that a great enemy of the cult was hidden in the tall tree. The women, wild with fury, felled the tree with Pentheus in it. Agave, in a Dionysian frenzy, stood over her son. He frantically threw off his feminine dress and pleaded with her to recognize him, but in her bacchic trance she imagined him to be a lion. With prodigious strength she tore off his left arm at the shoulder. Her sisters, Ino and Autonoe, joined her and together the three women broke Pentheus' body to pieces. Agave placed his severed head on her wand and called upon the revelers to behold the desert-whelped lion's head she had taken.

Cadmus and his attendants carried the maimed body of Pentheus back to the city. The old man could only feel the deepest pity for his daughter in her blindness. When Agave awoke from her trance and recognized the head of her beloved son on her wand, she was bewildered and grief-stricken. Cadmus, mourning the violence that had occurred, urged all men to comply with the wishes of the Olympian deities.

Dionysus returned in his divine form and prophesied that Cadmus and his wife, Harmonia, transformed into dragons, would overcome many Grecian lands before they died. He showed no sympathy for Agave, who cried out that she had been guilty of sinning against him. He doomed her and her sisters to wander without respite until death overtook them.

Critical Evaluation:

The Bacchae, written in Macedonia after the author's voluntary exile from Athens and produced posthumously, is one of Euripides' most poetically beautiful as well as thematically difficult dramas. The play abounds in passages of nature description unsurpassed in any of the playwright's other works, and the lyrics of the chorus in praise of Dionysus and his gifts of wine and sensuality are particularly fine. The vivid descriptions of landscape and the hymns to bacchanalian pleasure in the first part of the play are so intriguing, in fact, that Pentheus seems a combined brute and prude for opposing the spread of the Dionysian cult in Thebes. In the second half of the play, Euripides' descriptive talent turns, with equal effectiveness, to a different purpose as he presents the grisly scene of Pentheus' slaughter by the revelers, terrifying in their mindless, maddened frenzy.

The fact that *The Bacchae* has been alternately interpreted as Euripides' approval of the Dionysian nature-worship cult and as his condemnation of religious excess attests the play's thematic complexity. Critics of the first persuasion cite the undeniable fact that the chorus, which traditionally functions as the upholder of moral values and mouthpiece of social standards, aligns itself with Dionysus and supports his attempt to introduce his cult into Thebes. Also a follower of the god-man is Tiresias, the familiar blind prophet of Greek tragedy, who vehemently exhorts Pentheus to accept the new cult and accompany him—along with Pentheus' grandfather, Cadmus—to the worship rites. Perhaps the strongest evidence that can be used to support this interpretation is that the doom foretold by the chorus for Pentheus, if he persists in opposing what they view as the unquestionable right of the gods to demand worship, comes true: The king of Thebes is killed by his own mother in a most savage and gruesome manner. Yet critics who feel that the play is Euripides' condemnation of excessive emotionalism and religious fanaticism can interpret the same event, Pentheus' cruel death, as the author's portrayal of the king as a victim of an unnecessary, unreasoning frenzy. This reading is also supported by the fact that Pentheus is not an evil character but a king who feels it is his duty to protect the city from disruptive social influences. This second interpretation would explain Agave's sentence of lifelong exile at the close of the play.

In view of Euripides' rational and humanistic stance in all his dramas, it would seem most likely that each interpretation contains some amount of truth but that both are oversimplified. It is true, for example, that Pentheus is not an evil king, but he is certainly unwise in his rejection of advice from his elders and in his total reliance on his own reason. His insistence that the cult be destroyed is a denial of one powerful aspect of human nature; Dionysus represents the animal nature in human beings, which is a strong force and must be reckoned with. It is also true that Agave is banished, but she is banished by Dionysus himself, against whom she has sinned not in worshiping him but in perverting her worship to such excessive lengths as to kill her own son. It would seem that in *The Bacchae*, as elsewhere, Euripides is arguing for moderation in all things: Pure reason that denies the animal element in human beings leads to destruction just as surely as does pure sensuality unleashed without reasonable control.

Bibliography:

Euripides. *The Bacchae of Euripides*. Translated by Geoffrey S. Kirk. New York: Cambridge University Press, 1979. Provides a translation and notes that are useful to anyone new to

Euripides' last complete play. Kirk provides a notable comparative text to other classic and ground-breaking versions of Euripides' play.

_____. *The Bacchae of Euripides*. Translated by C. K. Williams. New York: Farrar, Straus & Giroux, 1990. This version of the play is useful primarily for Martha Nussbaum's introduction, which presents an alternative view of the play and sets it in relief against another Greek tragedy.

Grene, David, and Richmond Lattimore, ed. *Greek Tragedies*. Vol. 3. Chicago, Ill.: University of Chicago Press, 1960. Richmond Lattimore is a scholar known for his work on Euripides. Arguably the most faithful translation and introduction to *The Bacchae* published to date. Includes contextual notes and a clear view to an understanding of Euripides at the end of his career.

Segal, Charles. *Dionysiac Poetics and Euripides' "Bacchae."* Princeton, N.J.: Princeton University Press, 1983. Provides contextual background for *The Bacchae* and explains why it is such a radical text. Also discusses other works that deal with Dionysus and speculates on Euripides' response to those texts.

Soyinka, Wole. *The Bacchae of Euripides: A Communion Rite*. New York: W. W. Norton, 1974. Nobel Prize-winning African author Wole Soyinka provides a new interpretation of *The Bacchae*, which brings to the fore important questions in the original text. Soyinka uses a communion rite to explain the death of Pentheus and the need to strew his body across the countryside.

THE BACHELORS

Type of work: Novel
Author: Muriel Spark (1918-   )
Type of plot: Social satire
Time of plot: Mid-twentieth century
Locale: London
First published: 1960

Principal characters:

RONALD BRIDGES, the assistant curator at a London museum of graphology and an epileptic

MARTIN BOWLES, a barrister

PATRICK SETON, a spiritualistic medium charged with fraudulent conversion

ALICE DAWES, his pregnant mistress and a diabetic waitress

ELSIE FORREST, her friend

MRS. FREDA FLOWER, a wealthy widow interested in spiritualism

MRS. MARLENE COOPER, the patron of a spiritualistic group

TIM RAYMOND, her nephew

EWART THORTON, a teacher

WALTER PRETT, an art critic

MATTHEW FINCH, the London correspondent of *The Irish Echo*

DR. MIKE GARLAND, a clairvoyant

FATHER T. W. SOCKETT, a spiritualistic clergyman ordained by Fire and the Holy Ghost

THE HONORABLE FRANCIS ECCLES, a British Council lecturer

MR. FERGUSON, a detective inspector of police

The Story:

London was home to many bachelors, including Ronald Bridges, a thirty-seven-year-old epileptic who worked as an assistant curator at a small handwriting museum. One Saturday morning, he met his friend Martin Bowles, a thirty-five-year-old lawyer. After completing some shopping, they stopped at a coffeehouse, where they spotted a thin, anxious-looking man of about fifty-five talking with a young girl. Martin told Ronald not to stare at the couple because next week he would be prosecuting the man, whose name was Patrick Seton. Patrick, a spiritualistic medium, had been charged with fraudulent conversion and forgery and was under orders to report to the police daily. Ronald looked slightly ill and said that he wanted to search for his newspaper, so Martin left. Actually, Ronald had thought he recognized Patrick from somewhere and was trying to assure himself that his epilepsy was not causing him to lose his memory. Experimental treatment in America had not been successful, but he had learned to control his attacks, even to the point of being able to order a beer when his bachelor friends Walter Prett, Matthew Finch, and Ewart Thorton gathered at a pub.

In addition to the legal charges, Patrick had personal problems. Alice, his girlfriend, was pregnant. Despite her friend Elsie's admonishments, she steadfastly defended Patrick's innocence and wanted him to divorce his wife and marry her before the baby was born. Alice was a very dependent person and felt that Patrick, by taking charge of her insulin injections, had only her best interests in mind.

The next evening, at a meeting of the spiritualist group where he was holding a séance, Patrick encountered more difficulties. Freda Flower, the wealthy widow who had charged him with having bilked her out of a sum of money by forging a letter, appeared for the séance. Tossing his body about and groaning, Patrick worked himself into a heavy trance and succeeded in contacting the spirit of Freda's husband despite the presence of another spiritual medium, Dr. Mike Garland, who tried to interrupt. It was a tricky situation, but with clever manipulations Patrick managed to get through the séance unscathed.

The competition between the two mediums polarized the group members and caused quite a stir among them. Several met over lunch to discuss the matter. Some planned to create an Inner Spiral of the most faithful members while others pursued less spiritual interests. After talking with Elsie about the beautiful Alice and her attachment to Patrick, Matthew spent the night with her. In his own rooms, Patrick thought over his statement to the police and his plan to get rid of Alice if he was acquitted. His discussion with Ferguson, the policeman, had not reassured him. To set up a potential alibi for himself, he went to see Dr. Lyte to get advice about giving insulin to Alice. At Alice's apartment, he convinced her of his solicitous nature.

To solidify the prosecution's case against Patrick, Martin elicited Ronald's handwriting expertise on the allegedly forged letter. He gave the letter to Ronald, who hid it in his apartment. In the coffeehouse later, Ronald and Matthew discussed the evidence with Alice, but she continued to believe Patrick innocent of everything, despite some very suspicious information on his background. Matthew, who loved Alice, was ready to sacrifice his longtime bachelor status to marry her. Ronald promised to get more information on the case to relieve her worries. All the talk about marriage appeared to trigger an epileptic fit. Luckily, Ronald had his medication with him and quickly recovered.

While these various people discussed his case, Patrick had not been idle. He returned to Dr. Lyte's office and reminded the doctor about a forgotten incident involving spiritualism and séances. He then demanded that the doctor lend him his chalet in the Alps so that he and Alice could go there for a secluded honeymoon. That was where he planned to implement his plan for Alice's demise. The doctor agreed and, feeling secure in his escape plans, Patrick confidently made his daily report to the police. He even gave Ferguson some details about the appearance and background of his rival, Garland.

When Ronald returned home, he discovered that the letter he was examining for forgery had been stolen from his apartment. Later, at a party, members of the group discussed the matter. Feelings ran high both for and against Patrick. Ronald suspected that it might have been Elsie who had pretended to be a cleaning lady and stolen the letter. Elsie sometimes did secretarial work for the Reverend T. W. Sockett, another of Patrick's rival spiritualists, and she believed that he would fall in love with her if she had something valuable to offer him. When she brought the letter to his apartment, however, she saw Mike Garland there dressed in women's clothes. Realizing that there was something going on between the two men, she took the letter and ran out. When she failed to appear at the café, Matthew, who had been hanging around Alice, began to understand what had happened. The next day, he told Ronald that Elsie did in fact have the letter but would give it to him only if he slept with her that night. At her apartment, Ronald managed to convince her to return the letter and to tell Alice what she had done. Alice, however, remained convinced of Patrick's spiritual claims and of his intentions to make a life for her and the baby. Meanwhile at the spiritualist group's meetings, gossip continued. Some thought Freda and Patrick might have been lovers and that maybe she really had written the letter. Father Sockett, learning that Mike Garland was a fake clairvoyant, went over to Patrick's side. At one meeting the group closely monitored Patrick's writhing to make sure he was really in a trance.

The next day, when the court case was to begin, several witnesses against him had left town, but the experts were ready with their testimony.

In court, Ronald, the star witness for the prosecution, as well as Freda Flower and others, gave testimony about Patrick's capabilities as a medium and a forger. In the middle of a debate over what constituted a genuine trance, Ronald had an epileptic attack in the courtroom. The defense brought in another graphologist, but Ronald had taken his medication and recovered. The surprise came when Father Sockett testified in favor of Patrick. The trial proceeded, with one witness discrediting the other. Through it all, Matthew stayed by Alice's side.

At the end of all the testimony, Patrick believed himself to be safe and envisioned himself away from London, giving Alice the fatal insulin injection in a remote region of the Alps. When the judge sentenced Patrick to no less than five years, even after he pleaded that he was about to become a father, the prosecution revealed his past as a con man. The next morning, as the sun rose over London and all the sleeping bachelors, Ronald pondered about it all and wondered when Matthew would marry Alice.

"The Story" by Louise M. Stone

Critical Evaluation:

There are times when the novels of Muriel Spark suggest a mildly hallucinatory card game in which the dealer declares the trump suit only after the last card has been played and then proceeds to take in all the tricks. This is not to say that she cheats or ignores the rules of the fictional game she is playing; however, she does add to her picture of the world some element of unearthly surprise, and she presents her people from an odd angle of vision so as to throw an oblique light on the troubled condition of human beings—and, since she is a Christian writer, on their relation to God or the devil. All of her novels deal in one degree or another with the problem of faith: the grace with which people accept it or the ways by which they try to evade it. The result is an original body of work that cannot be mistaken for that of anyone else.

Satire is the literary climate in which her lively art appears to flourish best. Yet satire, touched with fantasy or the supernatural, is always a risky business. It demands, among other things, a sharp wit and a spirited style. The reader must also be sufficiently involved in order to go along with the game of pretense, and the story must make its point if the reader is to accept the satire as an insightful comment on the absurdities of the material world or the mysteries of the soul.

Spark takes on the risks deliberately. Her first novel, *The Comforters* (1957), relied for much of its effect on ghostly presences and double identities. In one scene, a character heard the clatter of the author's typewriter at work on the book. *Robinson* (1958) brought into congruous relationship such disparate elements as a desert island, a murder, and a spiritual dilemma resolved in a rather bizarre fashion. *Memento Mori* (1959) was the novel in which Spark revealed to the fullest that audacity, altogether her own, which became the guiding principle of her fiction. In this book, Death is a disembodied voice on the telephone making calls to a group of old people and reminding them that they must die; what this chilling fable offers is a contrast between the selfish, trivial concerns of these people's lives and the inescapable fact of their mortality. *The Ballad of Peckham Rye* (1960) brings to the pubs and rooming houses of a London suburb a devil incarnate who provides the people of Peckham with opportunities to display humankind's natural capacity for error and evil. By means of devices such as these, Spark shows a critical and moral imagination at work among observations of the clutter and waste of the contemporary scene.

The Bachelors is more restrained. It contains no open struggle with otherworldly forces, whether of God or of the devil. The only touch of the supernatural comes when a quack spiritualistic medium does, apparently, establish communication with the dead in an episode so briefly presented that it gives little weight to Spark's swiftly paced and crowded narrative. In this novel, her focus is on bachelordom, the noncommunity of the unattached, uncommitted male. The bachelor's state is viewed as damnation, and for the ten examples presented, the writer provides an atmosphere of fearful reality. The lodgings in which they live, the pubs they frequent, the stores where they shop, their problems with meals, mothers, and women—all are images of the private hells of loneliness and trivial self-preoccupation in which each separately revolves. This vision is one that the more discerning of her bachelors share with their creator. Matthew Finch, who is Irish, Catholic, and plagued by sex, says that one's duty is to marry, to choose between Holy Orders and Holy Matrimony. Anything else—and he speaks from experience—is an unnatural life for a Christian. Ronald Bridges, a graphologist who is unable to fulfill his desire to become a priest because he is an epileptic, claims that he is a confirmed bachelor, but at the end of the novel he experiences a vision of the bachelor's selfish and uneasy life on the fringes of society: He imagines 17.1 bachelors in each of London's 38,500 streets, restless, awake, active with their bed partners, or asleep.

In this noncommunity, the solitary individuals try to find substitutes for solidarity and faith. Some, like Ronald Bridges, find another vocation. Others, like Martin Bowles, become social and moral hypocrites. Still others, like Walter Prett, revile the world out of drunken self-pity. A few, like Patrick Seton, prey on human credulity. Most, like Matthew Finch, simply struggle. His predicament, trapped between spirit and flesh, is amusing and nevertheless real.

The uses to which Spark puts her social outsiders are crafty and entertaining. Patrick Seton, the fraudulent medium, is charged with converting to his own needs two thousand pounds that Freda Flower, a rich widow, had given him for the work of The Wider Community, a spiritualistic group. Mrs. Flower and another patron of the circle, Mrs. Marlene Cooper, are already rivals for the place of leadership within the group, and the charge against Patrick further widens the split. Mrs. Cooper sees in the division an opportunity to direct the Inner Spiral, a secret group within The Wider Community; Freda Flower hopes to bring the members under the influence of Mike Garland, a clairvoyant of notorious reputation, and of his friend Father Sockett. Ronald Bridges becomes involved because he is the friend of Tim Raymond, Mrs. Cooper's nephew, and because as a handwriting expert, he has been asked to testify to the authenticity of a letter forged by Seton. Other complications include the fact that Martin Bowles, who is also Bridges' friend, is the prosecuting counsel against Patrick, and that Matthew Finch falls deeply in love with Alice. Through information innocently supplied by Matthew, Elsie Forrest, Alice's friend, is able to steal the letter from Bridges' lodgings. Meanwhile, Garland and Father Sockett are also after the letter for reasons of their own.

Spark handles this complicated material with skill and dash. After Patrick is convicted and sentenced, Matthew will marry Alice. Ronald Bridges will continue to suffer from the nightmares of his epileptic seizures. They are his cross, but because of them he has achieved a kind of wisdom and insight into the need of faith and the grace of compassion. This, the reader senses, is the meaning of Spark's conclusion, but she is too much an artist to flog a thesis or point to a moral. Her characters are good, foolish, sinister, and kind. They exist larger than life, and are illuminative of life, because they are self-contained in a world where sin and salvation coexist in precarious balance. It is a world where a man must earn the right to share commitment to his fellows or to God. This writer handles serious matters with a light but sure touch.

Spark's novels create an effect of wild improvisation, but actually the opposite is true. These works have been carefully planned and are cleanly structured and lucidly styled. Few writers have had a surer hold on the comic convention of the English novel, which brings the fantastic and the real together in a coherent whole.

Bibliography:
Bold, Alan, ed. *Muriel Spark: An Odd Capacity for Vision*. Totowa, N.J.: Barnes and Noble Books, 1984. A collection of essays by critics who investigate Spark's self-conscious style in portraying a sense of spiritual presence behind physical reality. Explores the novel as a sustained prose poem that uses poetic conventions in an unusual way.

Hynes, Joseph. *The Art of the Real: Muriel Spark's Novels*. London: Associated University Presses, 1988. An interesting source with a good bibliography and notes section. A long section on the novel explains its investigational motifs. Discusses how Spark's work conveys her unusual sense of reality.

Kemp, Peter. *Muriel Spark*. New York: Barnes and Noble Books, 1975. A long discussion of the novel's spiritual themes and the way it deals with materialism. Places the work within the perspective of Spark's other novels and themes.

Malkoff, Karl. *Muriel Spark*. New York: Columbia University Press, 1968. A discussion of Spark's use of poetic techniques in the novel to expose the commonplace from a transfigured point of view. Asserts that cataclysmic events force a reexamination of the ordinary. Analyzes the characters in terms of their solitary explorations to find new ways of knowing.

Stanford, Derek. *Muriel Spark*. Fontwell: Centaur Press, 1963. A memoir rather than a biography. Presents one person's image of Spark and her work. An interesting look at an unusual writer.

BACK TO METHUSELAH
A Metabiological Pentateuch

Type of work: Drama
Author: George Bernard Shaw (1856-1950)
Type of plot: Play of ideas
Time of plot: From the beginning of time to A.D. 31,920
Locale: The Garden of Eden, the Middle East, and Britain
First published: 1921; first performed, 1922

Principal characters:

Act I
ADAM, the first man
EVE, the first woman
CAIN, their son
THE SERPENT, not the traditional tempter

Act II
FRANKLYN BARNABAS, a former cleric
CONRAD BARNABAS, his brother, a biologist
A PARLORMAID in the Barnabas household
WILLIAM HASLAM, a young cleric
CYNTHIA BARNABAS (SAVVY), Franklyn's daughter
JOYCE BURGE, a British politician
LUBIN, a British politician

Act III
BURGE-LUBIN, president of the British Islands
BARNABAS, the accountant-general
CONFUCIUS, the chief secretary
WILLIAM HASLAM, the Archbishop of York
MRS. LUTESTRING, the domestic minister

Act IV
ELDERLY GENTLEMAN, a visitor to Ireland
ZOO, a young long-liver, his escort
GENERAL AUFSTEIG, a combination of Napoleon and Cain
AMBROSE BADGER BLUEBIN, the prime minister of the British Islands
ORACLE

Act V
CHLOE, a young girl entering adolescence
HE-ANCIENT, 800 years old
SHE-ANCIENT, a midwife
AMARYLLIS, the newly born
ARJILLAX, a sculptor
MARTELLUS, a sculptor
PYGMALION, a scientist
GHOST OF LILITH, the mother of creation

472

The Story:

Act I: In the Beginning. In Eden, Adam discovered a dead fawn; he and Eve now understood that death must come to them, but Adam was also bored by the idea of eternal life. Adam disposed of the fawn, and the Serpent awoke and told Eve that birth could overcome Death. She also told Eve of Lilith, who had given birth to Adam and Eve by tearing herself apart and that it took two to give birth. Adam left and the Serpent told Eve of the great secret of love and birth.

Several centuries later, in Mesopotamia, Adam was digging and Eve spinning. Cain entered and taunted Adam; Adam replied that Cain had murdered his brother. Cain wanted Eve to create more men so he could fight them. When Cain claimed that he was a higher thing than man, Eve said he was simply Anti-Man. Cain wanted martial glory and activity. Eve regarded Lua, Cain's wife, and her daughter as good-for-nothing. Eve worried that already her grandchildren were dying before they had learned to live, and she thought there must be something better than digging, spinning, and killing.

Act II: The Gospel of the Brothers Barnabas. After World War I, the brothers Barnabas discussed their theory of Creative Evolution and their belief that for humans to develop completely they needed to live at least three hundred years; they believed that nature would work on the imagination and will and accomplish this result. The brothers were joined by Franklyn's daughter and a young clergyman, and the parlormaid said that if she were to live several hundred years, she would hesitate to marry her fiancé, the cook.

The brothers were visited by two politicians who thought that the brothers had a scheme for winning the next election. They demonstrated their political stupidity and lost interest but still wished to exploit the theory. Haslam and Savvy were told that anyone might be the one to make this "evolutionary leap" yet have no idea that it was to happen. Haslam laughed at this.

Act III: The Thing Happens. Burge-Lubin, the president of the British Islands in 2170, wanted Barnabas to attend a film on a system for breathing under water. The state is really run by a wise Chinaman named Confucius. Barnabas saw the film of high officials who had drowned over the last several centuries and reported that four people from the past were the present Archbishop of York. He turned out to be Haslam, who looked to be forty-five years old but admitted to being 283 years old; he had been forced to stage "deaths" because of bureaucratic rules and pension problems. Mrs. Lutestring entered and turned out to be the Barnabas' parlor maid, now 275. She and Haslam realized that they could produce more long-livers and left to discuss marriage. The others now believed the theory.

Act IV: Tragedy of an Elderly Gentleman. In 3000, an Elderly Gentleman was on a visit to the lands of his ancestors on the Galway coast, accompanied by his son-in-law, the British prime minister, and General Aufsteig, who is much like both Cain and Napoleon. The Gentleman was warned by a long-liver that this was a dangerous place for short-livers because of the disease of discouragement. He was given a companion, Zoo, a young girl of 56; he was shocked when Zoo claimed that long-livers were superior; she believed short-livers should be killed, like bad children. Leading the Gentleman to the temple of the Oracle, she said that the prime minister only pretended to consult the Oracle. The general confronted the veiled Oracle and said that he was the Man of Destiny, a military genius who had no talent except for war. Since he would be dethroned if he went on making war, he asked the Oracle for a way out of this problem. Telling him he should die, she shot him—but missed.

The Gentleman arrived with the British Envoy. After talk with Zoo and others, the Gentleman became more discouraged. The Envoy wanted to know whether he should call an election in August or in the spring. The Oracle told him what she had told his predecessor fifteen years before: "Go home, poor fool." He left and decided to tell the people that he had gotten the exact same answer as his predecessor. The Gentleman was left alone and begged the Oracle for help; he wanted to stay. She killed him, saying that she could do nothing else for him.

Act V: As Far as Thought Can Reach. The children of A.D. 31,920, who were born at the age of eighteen and became adolescents four years later, were playing and making love. Chloe had just realized that art and pleasure no longer interested her and that she wished only to think of mathematics. Today was a Festival of the Arts and a birth. A He-Ancient of 800 years came by; the children were appalled at his way of life. A She-Ancient came and broke the giant egg shell and Amaryllis was born; she told Amaryllis that she would live long but eventually die accidentally.

Arjillax made statues of the Ancients, showing their maturity; the children disliked them. Martellus made two life-size statues, Man and Woman, for a scientist named Pygmalion, who managed to infuse them with life. Everyone was disgusted with them because they were like Man of thousands of years before. They died of discouragement, and the Ancients warned the children against making "dolls"; the only things they could really make were themselves. Eventually there would only be thought, not people.

Night came and the ghosts of Adam, Eve, Cain, and the Serpent appeared. The ghost of Lilith, the mother of creation, appeared and ended the play with a long speech about the constant attempts of the Life Force to create new and better forms of life.

Critical Evaluation:

Because *Back to Methuselah* is made up of five full-length plays, it is extremely difficult to produce. Its first full production was at the Garrick Theatre in New York, with Acts I and II being done on February 27, 1922, Acts III and IV on March 6, and Act V on March 13. This first production resulted in a deficit of $20,000. Obviously, a play that demands three long nights in the theater is unlikely to be produced often, both because of the expense and because of the demands on the audience.

The play presents the most complete representation of Shaw's mature thought. In addition to its main themes of Creative Evolution and the Life Force, the work embraces many other typically Shavian beliefs and themes. It is Shaw's most profound statement and at the same time often almost unactable.

The point of the play is simple enough: For humans to profit from their experience, they must learn to live longer and gain wisdom. Shaw believed that the human race had rarely, if ever, demonstrated that it had learned from the past or that it had made any progress in moving beyond the mundane passions of individuals. As a noted socialist, Shaw had spent many years on the public platform, written many pamphlets and books arguing for a socialist society, and composed many plays that presented the virtues of a socialist view of life and the vices of capitalism. Yet Shaw believed that socialism was only a short-term solution to such problems of life as evil, the organization of society, and equality. In *Back to Methuselah*, he does not deny socialism or give up on it, but turns instead to the possibility of a long-term solution. Socialism may be said to be a political solution, while Creative Evolution is a spiritual, even religious, solution. Socialism, Shaw believed, could prepare the way for the type of humans and society able to progress to the basic lessons of Creative Evolution.

The pattern presented in the play and reflected, for example, in the character of Eve in Act I, is that something higher is desired, taken into the imagination, and finally willed to happen. This pattern is Shaw's answer to Darwin, whose idea on the origin of species Shaw detested for its mindless mechanism and for its dependence on chance. In opposition to this, Shaw set up the centrality of the will.

In terms of Shaw's thought, the play should be read in conjunction with *Man and Superman* (1903) and *Saint Joan* (1923). Together, these three plays present Shaw's most concentrated efforts to supply humankind with a new creed and a new theology. *Man and Superman* presents the ideas of the Life Force (a force that has faith in itself though it may have no relation to humankind) and of Creative Evolution. The woman will, by nature, select the best mate for her children; woman is the huntress, man the quarry. In *Saint Joan*, the reader sees an advanced human (though she is not allowed to live long) who is superior to the ordinary desires and social practices of human life. Shaw believed in the force of will, in human ability to create a thing if it were willed hard enough.

Shaw's visionary fable must not be taken too literally. It is a myth or a metaphor, an imaginative vision of what might or could be, but it is not a literal plan or program for the future. Shaw's faith was in life, not necessarily in human beings. The specifics of the play are only imaginings, a way of suggesting possibilities, and an attempt to present to the audience the glorification of the will and of the Life Force. In each of the five acts, there is at least one spokesman for the Life Force: In Act I it is the Serpent; in Act II, the brothers Barnabas; in Act III the Archbishop (and Mrs. Lutestring); in Act IV, the Oracle (and Zoo); and in Act V, it is the Ancients (and Lilith).

Just as a number of the characters appear and reappear under various names and offices, so do a number of themes recur. The theme of war and the soldier occurs in Acts I, II, and IV, as Shaw makes some of the same points about military matters as in *Arms and the Man* (1894). The theme of discouragement reappears in Acts II and IV, after having been introduced by Eve in Act I. Discouragement, as Shaw sees it, is the recognition of a sense of futility in human life, and it is strong enough to kill. In Acts II, III, and IV, one can see political themes, but overriding all—in every part of the play—there is the triumph of life over death and matter. In the final act, the condition of the Ancients, who aspire to become pure thought (though they have not as yet done so), represents the triumph over matter, the ability to put aside the things of children such as art and pleasure and to arrive at mature contemplation.

Shaw's philosophy and dramatic practice do not always coincide, however. Shaw insists, for example, that humans can choose to live longer, yet in Acts II and III, where the first "leap" is made to long-living, it is the parlormaid and the Reverend William Haslam who think little of the idea of living longer, who become the first of the long-livers, apparently chosen by chance. Shaw always extolled the idea of living longer so that humans could accomplish better and more work, especially in social organization and politics. In the play, however, the state and any sort of social organization seems to have withered away. The Ancients do nothing but think, which issues in no more than a kind of self-gratification.

The play presents other dramatic difficulties. Act I seems to be the most dramatic and playable. The other parts are often dull, as Shaw admitted himself. Shaw was always known for the extended use of discussion in his plays, but there discussion seems to be indulged in for its own sake. Yet despite the frequent prosiness of the play, there are many entertaining comic scenes and acts, especially in the political commentary in Acts II, III, and IV, in the character of Eve in Act I, and in the confrontation of the short-livers with the long-livers in Act IV. The play has probably to be regarded more for its thought and content than for its innate dramatic qualities, but the final scene, where, on a darkened stage, Lilith in a poetic soliloquy delivers Shaw's summation of the past and future possibilities of humans, is a triumph of the fusion of thought and language.

Gordon N. Bergquist

Bibliography:

Crompton, Louis. *Shaw the Dramatist*. Lincoln: University of Nebraska Press, 1969. Includes an excellent chapter on *Back to Methuselah*, which discusses Shaw's debts to the thinkers and writers of his time.

Ervine, St. John. *Bernard Shaw: His Life, Work and Friends*. New York: William Morrow, 1956. An account that draws on personal knowledge of and correspondence with Shaw. The author often takes issue with Shaw's ideas.

Joad, C. E. M. "Shaw's Philosophy." In *George Bernard Shaw: A Critical Survey*, edited by Louis Kronenberger. New York: World Publishing, 1953. The best overall view of Shaw's ideas of Creative Evolution and the Life Force and their relations to other basic Shavian ideas.

Shaw, George Bernard. "Preface: The Infidel Half Century." In *Bernard Shaw: Collected Plays with Their Prefaces*. Vol. 5. New York: Dodd, Mead, 1972. Indispensable. Shaw's own lengthy and discursive discussion of the play, why he wrote it, and how it should be understood.

Whitman, Robert F. *Shaw and the Play of Ideas*. Ithaca, N.Y.: Cornell University Press, 1977. A discussion that emphasizes the way in which the play presents and resolves contradictions. Also deals with the importance of hope in the play and in the Shavian scheme of things.

BADENHEIM 1939

Type of work: Novel
Author: Aharon Appelfeld (1932-   )
Type of plot: Parable
Time of plot: 1939
Locale: Badenheim, Austria
First published: Badenheim, 'ir nofesh, 1975 (English translation, 1980)

> Principal characters:
> DR. PAPPENHEIM, the impresario
> MARTIN, the pharmacist
> TRUDE, his wife
> FRAU ZAUBERBLIT, a guest
> LEON SAMITZKY, one of the musicians
> PETER, the pastry shop owner
> MANDELBAUM, a performer
> SALLY, and
> GERTIE, prostitutes

The Story:

In early spring, the impresario Dr. Pappenheim returned to the Austrian resort town of Badenheim. As usual, he worried whether the performers, especially Mandelbaum, would appear as they had promised, and whether the festival would be successful. Soon, guests began to arrive. To Trude, the pharmacist's wife, they looked pale, like patients in a sanatorium. To her, everything looked "poisoned and diseased."

The next day, a sanitation department inspector visited the pharmacy. Although Martin, the pharmacist, did not know why the inspector was there, he felt guilty. All over Badenheim, investigators from the sanitation department measured things, erected fences, and put up flags. Porters unfolded rolls of barbed wire and put up cement pillars. People took off winter clothes and put on sportswear.

At April's end, the twins, who recited from the works of Rainer Maria Rilke, arrived. Dr. Shutz began following a schoolgirl. Frau Zauberblit, who had left a tubercular sanatorium, talked with Leon Samitzky, a musician who was homesick for Poland. Professor Fussholdt stayed in his room reading proofs of his latest book while his wife sunbathed and hunted for amorous adventures. The twins rehearsed. Dr. Pappenheim received a telegram announcing that Mandelbaum was ill and would not arrive.

In mid-May, an announcement demanded that all Jewish citizens register with the sanitation department before the end of the month. A rumor circulated that they were being sent to Poland. Samitzky was happy to be going to Poland. Dr. Pappenheim, however, explained that the sanitation department made the guests write their names in its "Golden Book" because it wanted a record of its attractiveness to tourists. Dr. Pappenheim, Frau Zauberblit, and Samitzky registered. Frau Zauberblit praised the sanitation department for "order and beauty."

The sanitation department began to look like a travel agency. Its posters carried such slogans as "Labor Is Our Life" and "The Air in Poland Is Fresher." The department stayed open at night. The band conductor carried his baptismal certificates in his pocket. Dr. Pappenheim told him that he could "join the Jewish order." When the conductor said that he did not believe in religion, Dr. Pappenheim invited him to become "a Jew without religion."

477

Frau Zauberblit's daughter arrived with a document that stated that her mother renounced her maternal rights; Frau Zauberblit signed it and her daughter left. That evening, the twins performed. They recited poems about death. They seemed to have "visited hell," of which they "were no longer afraid."

The long-awaited child prodigy arrived. Because his name was not on the hotel register, the doorman would not admit him. Dr. Pappenheim told the doorman to let him in, asking whether he could not see that the prodigy was a Jew? The half-Jewish waitress asked Samitzky if she could come to Poland, too, although she was not fully Jewish. Samitzky replied that even though both his parents had converted to Christianity, he would be going.

The sanitation department was now "the center," and it spread its nets in every direction. A barrier was erected to keep people from leaving or entering Badenheim. Milk was still being delivered, fruit was still being brought into town, and the band continued to play. However, the people were confined to the hotel, the pastry shop, and the swimming pool. At the sanitation department, Dr. Langmann was angry with Dr. Pappenheim. The people were registering for Poland. Dr. Pappenheim joked that it made no difference whether they were here or there.

A banquet was held to honor the child prodigy. The band conductor said that the people were going to their "native land." Dr. Langmann told Frau Milbaum that he was leaving the next day. She asked whether he had registered with the sanitation department. He replied that he felt he was "a free Austrian citizen" and that they could "send the Polish Jews to Poland; they deserve their country."

After midnight, the child prodigy sang in Yiddish. Sally, the prostitute, asked Dr. Pappenheim if she could come to Poland, too. He replied that "All the Jews and . . . everyone who wants to be a Jew" could come.

Summer arrived. The sanitation department closed the water supply. People who had spent their time swimming now stood on the tennis court. Dr. Pappenheim said that now everyone would have time to study. Swearing loyalty to "Dr. Pappenheim's Jewish Order," the half-Jewish waitress said that her thighs were Austrian meat, and she offered everyone a taste. She sawed on her legs with a knife and, bleeding, screamed that when they left for Poland they dare not go without her.

Letters stopped arriving. The weather got cold. Dr. Langmann asked the sanitation department to reexamine his case; he told them that he was an Austrian. When he was told that he was also a Jew, he asked what that meant.

The schoolgirl was pregnant. Dr. Shutz wrote his mother that he was getting married. He asked for money, but the post office was shut. Frau Zauberblit ran a temperature of 101.2° and spat blood. Samitzky drank steadily. In the pharmacy, Martin stopped two men from poisoning themselves. People started buying poisonous drugs. Martin locked the pharmacy, but people broke in and stole all the drugs.

Mandelbaum arrived. He said that where he had come from, the Jews had been put in quarantine, but a young officer had helped him escape so that he could get to the festival. Because Dr. Pappenheim had been trying to get Mandelbaum to come for years, he was happy.

The telephone lines were cut. The non-Jewish employees had left. Dr. Langmann called the Jews "an ugly people" and said that he could not see "any use" in them. Supplies did not arrive. The hotel owner opened the storeroom. The twins grew thin.

Summer ended. The hotel served golden cider. Usually, this was the time for leaving. Peter, the pastry shop owner, said, "Let Pappenheim emigrate, not us." Strangers filled the town. The two prostitutes, Sally and Gertie, offered them soup. Dr. Pappenheim told the strangers about Poland.

In the hotel, people stopped serving meals. People lined up for barley soup and dry bread. The old rabbi appeared in a wheelchair. Everyone had thought he was dead. A Christian lady had cared for him, he said, but suddenly she had left.

The musicians wanted to go home, but the roads were blocked. New supplies did not arrive. Stocks ran low. Peter vowed to kill Dr. Pappenheim. Dr. Pappenheim received a letter from the sanitation department requiring that the artists be placed "at their disposal." Delighted, he knew that a concert tour was coming.

The town ran out of cigarettes. People secretly swallowed drugs stolen from the pharmacy. The child prodigy performed only for boxes of candy and grew fat. The people wanted the festival to be held.

Two men came from the sanatorium to take Frau Zauberblit back. They told her that the Jewish patients were all emigrating; they told her that she needed to return before the patients could leave. She agreed to go. The pastry cook buried the dead at night at the back of the Luxembourg Gardens. Every day, more people died.

On the last night, the people celebrated Gertie's fortieth birthday. At the celebration, Dr. Pappenheim announced that the emigration procedures had been posted. Gertie apologized for having nothing to offer her guests. Dr. Pappenheim told them that they would hold a party later in Warsaw.

The next day, the Jews of Badenheim walked to the train station, but Peter refused to leave. As the people walked, they discussed things like wages in Poland, retirement, and vacations. Policemen walked behind, but they did not hurry the people. At the station, the people bought newspapers, lemonade, cigarettes, and sweets. Two armed policemen arrived, escorting Peter. An engine approached, pulling "four filthy freight cars." As everyone was sucked into the cars, Dr. Pappenheim remarked: "If the coaches are so dirty it must mean that we have not far to go."

Critical Evaluation:

Badenheim 1939 was originally published as a story in a collection entitled *Shanim Ve'shaot* (years and hours), but it was not published as a separate novel until 1980, when it appeared both in Hebrew and in English translation. The Hebrew title, literally "Badenheim, Resort Town," is less revealing of the novel's meaning than the English title, which indicates that the story occurs after the Nazis had taken over Austria. Aharon Appelfeld based the book, he said, on his experiences as a very young child at resorts to which his parents had taken him and on his personal knowledge of the Holocaust.

Appelfeld survived the Holocaust. At the age of eight, he escaped from the Transnistria labor camp in the Ukraine and survived for three years in forests and villages. He said that his blond hair and ability to speak Ukrainian helped him avoid capture. In 1944, he was liberated by the Red Army, after which he worked for them as a messenger boy. After a stay in Italy, he went to Israel in 1946.

The novel has been called a fable, a parable, and a comedy. Appelfeld uses dramatic irony, satire, and allegory, and the novel is alternately dreamlike, surrealistic, and nightmarish. The Holocaust is never mentioned. Appelfeld assumes that the readers have the necessary historical knowledge to recognize that the Holocaust is part of the story. Many critics feel that the omission of explicit references to the Holocaust adds to the book's power.

Critics often compare Appelfeld to the Jewish Austrian-Czech writer Franz Kafka, whose works have a similar nightmarish quality. In Kafka's works, the reader feels a vague anxiety that things are not what they seem and that all is not right. The same kind of feeling pervades *Badenheim 1939*. The vacationers and the workers at Badenheim, especially Dr. Pappenheim, expend tremendous energy denying the reality of their situation. Even when he sees the freight cars, Dr. Pappenheim does not accept the horror that awaits him.

The freight cars are the final symbol of the destruction awaiting the Jews of Badenheim. There are, however, many earlier signs that things are not as good as Dr. Pappenheim asserts, beginning with the fact that all Jews must register with the sanitation department. Putting up fences, unrolling barbed wire, and erecting cement columns could be interpreted as preparation for the festival, but in this context the preparations point to concentration camps. Trude's feeling that something is wrong with the guests foreshadows the moment when the guests are loaded into freight cars.

Badenheim 1939 depicts the assimilated Jews of Germany and Austria who, like the poet Rilke, whose works the twins recite, felt that they had become part of the culture of the nations in which they lived. Often, however, they still found themselves living, working, and vacationing almost exclusively among Jews. The novel captures the awakening that occurred to many of them when they discovered that no matter how assimilated they may have felt, the preponderance of the non-Jewish citizens of their nations did not consider them part of their culture. The Nazis decided that outright extermination was appropriate. Appelfeld's Austrian Jews, like Dr. Langmann and Peter, attribute their problems to such Polish Jews as Dr. Pappenheim. Appelfeld has created a terrifying novel about humankind's inhumanity and about people's inability to recognize that inhumanity, or its source, even when they are its victims.

Richard Tuerk

Bibliography:
Bernstein, Michael André. *Foregone Conclusions: Against Apocalyptic History*. Berkeley: University of California Press, 1994. Describes the way in which three historical periods— Austria before the Nazi rule, Austria during the Nazi rule, and the world after the Holocaust—are interrelated simultaneously in the novel.
Langer, Lawrence I. "Aharon Appelfeld and the Uses of Language and Silence." In *Remembering for the Future*, edited by Yehuda Bauer et al. 3 vols. Elmsford, N.Y.: Pergamon Press, 1989. Discusses Appelfeld's irony and ambiguity. The set also includes articles on Aharon Appelfeld by Nurit Govrin, A. Komem, Gila Ramraz-Raukh, and Lea Hamaoui.
Ramraz-Raukh, Gila. *Aharon Appelfeld: The Holocaust and Beyond*. Bloomington: Indiana University Press, 1994. Speaks of the novel's "cold horror." Sees the end as having been foreshadowed in the beginning.
Roth, Philip. "A Conversation with Philip Roth." In *Beyond Despair*, by Aharon Appelfeld, translated by Jeffrey M. Green. New York: Fromm International, 1994. First published in *The New York Review of Books*, February 28, 1988. Philip Roth, the American novelist, talks with Appelfeld about his life and works. Roth calls *Badenheim 1939* "vexing." The interview gives insight into the novel's autobiographical and historical background.
Wisse, Ruth R. "Aharon Appelfeld, Survivor." *Commentary* 76, no. 2 (August, 1983): 73-76. Discerns a "mood of predestination" in the novel. Emphasizes the self-deception of many of the characters.

THE BALD SOPRANO

Type of work: Drama
Author: Eugène Ionesco (1912-1994)
Type of plot: Absurdist
Time of plot: Mid-twentieth century
Locale: London
First performed: 1950; first published, 1954 as *La Cantatrice chauve* (English translation, 1956)

> *Principal characters:*
> MR. SMITH, the owner of the house where the play is set
> MRS. SMITH, his wife
> MR. MARTIN, their guest
> MRS. MARTIN, his wife
> MARY, the Smith's maid
> THE FIRE CHIEF

The Story:

After dinner, the Smiths sat down in the sitting room of their typically English home. Mr. Smith smoked his pipe and read the newspaper. Mrs. Smith, insisting that they were a typically English couple, spoke of what they had eaten and what the children had done. Mr. Smith clicked his tongue.

When Mrs. Smith remarked that Dr. Mackenzie-King had had his own liver removed before operating on Mr. Parker's liver, Mr. Smith argued that if Mackenzie-King had really been a good doctor, he should have taken his own life when Parker did not survive the liver operation; he asserted that a doctor should perish with a patient just as a captain has to go down with the ship. Mr. Smith then changed the subject, mentioning that he read that their friend Bobby Watson had died. The couple spoke about Bobby but quickly became lost in a confused conversation; because all of Bobby Watson's relatives were also named Bobby Watson, they were unable to figure out just who they were talking about, who had died, and who was still alive.

Mary, the Smiths' maid, returned from her day off and announced that the Martins, whom they had invited for dinner, had been waiting for a long time downstairs. The Smiths, before leaving the room, instructed her to bring them up. Mary showed the Martins into the sitting room, then left. As if they had never seen each other before, Mr. and Mrs. Martin began to question each other, wondering where and when they had previously met. Gradually, they were able to deduce that they had both taken the same train from Manchester and that they both lived in the same room and slept in the same bed. Moreover, both had a daughter who seemed to be the same child. Therefore, they concluded, the two of them must be married. As they kissed, thrilled to have found each other again, Mary came in and announced to the play's audience that Mr. and Mrs. Martin had reasoned incorrectly, that the daughter they thought they had in common was really two different children, and that they were not in fact husband and wife. Mary told the audience that she was Sherlock Holmes; then she left.

The Smiths returned, welcoming the Martins and yelling at them for having arrived so late. They sat and attempted to make conversation but were unable to say much. Mrs. Martin was prompted to describe an incident that had shocked her: She had seen a man on the street who had bent down to tie his shoe lace. Mr. Smith, in an attempt to outdo her, recounted a tale that they found even more bizarre, of a man on the subway who was reading a newspaper.

Their interchange was interrupted by the doorbell. When Mrs. Smith opened the door, there was no one there. Again the bell rang, Mrs. Smith went to the door, and no one was there. When the bell rang a third time, Mrs. Smith refused to answer the door because she had learned that when the bell rang, there was never anyone there. Mr. Smith disagreed, and the Martins joined the fight. Finally, Mr. Smith went to the door and opened it to discover the Fire Chief standing on their doorstep.

The Fire Chief, an old family friend, had played a prank by ringing the bell and hiding. He was looking for fires. Even though Mr. Smith insisted that there had not been a fire at their house for years, the Fire Chief was happy just to stay for a visit. They welcomed him in and asked him to join them in telling amusing stories. Although the stories they told sounded like fables, they were all meaningless, pointless, and nonsensical. The conversation was interrupted by Mary, who wanted to read them her own poem. Before she could begin, however, she and the Fire Chief recognized each other. They had been sweethearts once and were glad to meet again. She then began to recite her poem, which was about different things catching on fire. Mr. and Mrs. Smith pushed her out of the room.

The Fire Chief, very pleased with the poem, asked if anyone had heard of the bald soprano. For some reason, the Smiths and the Martins became very embarrassed. The Fire Chief then tactfully departed, and the Smiths and Martins began an angry discussion. Once again, what they said sounded as if it ought to make sense, but it did not. Nevertheless, they pursued the argument until their enraged chatter built to a climax, during which they threw words and sounds meaninglessly at each other. In the short scene that followed, the Martins appeared after dinner, sitting down in the same sitting room. Mr. Martin smoked his pipe and read the newspaper. Mrs. Martin, insisting that they were a typically English couple, spoke of what they had eaten. Mr. Martin clicked his tongue.

Critical Evaluation:

Eugène Ionesco was born in Romania and eventually moved to France, where he was educated and where he remained during World War I. With *The Bald Soprano*, his first play, and those that followed—including *The Lesson* (1951), *The Chairs* (1952), and *Rhinoceros* (1960)—he became internationally famous, and his plays were produced all over the world. Although his international success gradually declined, in France Ionesco continued to be highly respected, and his works are often revived there.

The name given to the style of Ionesco's plays (and to the plays of Samuel Beckett, Jean Genet, and Arthur Adamov) is absurdist. *The Bald Soprano*, which is frequently regarded as the first absurdist play, is typical of the theater of the absurd for its absence of plot and a circular trajectory that ends where it began. Absurdist characters tend to be broad, generalized, two-dimensional figures, while settings are nondescript and vague. Moreover, what the characters say is rather insignificant; they tend to communicate not through what they mean but through how they speak the words and how the reader or audience associates meanings with those words.

Little actually happens in an Ionesco play. Yet if readers and audiences feel that they can find little in *The Bald Soprano* that makes any sense, they have probably discovered an essential ingredient of this one-act absurdist classic. Long after the play had opened in Paris, Ionesco revealed that he got the idea of writing it when he tried learning English from an old textbook. The book, written in dialogue form, introduced members of a typical British family who conversed almost meaninglessly about themselves and the world in which they lived. This may be the strongest clue that the play is a satire of the British—and by extension, the middle-class—

way of life. With its parody of conventional characters and conventional settings, the play clearly also makes fun of middle-class theater. The recognition scene between Mr. and Mrs. Martin, which is highly reminiscent of nineteenth century melodrama, becomes comedic when the audience realizes that this married couple cannot remember that they share the same bed and that this is a fact they can only deduce intellectually. Ionesco called *The Bald Soprano* an anti-play, which is doubly appropriate because the piece is so deliberately unlike any plays that came before it and because it draws on traditional drama in order to make fun of it.

The fact that there is no conflict in the play reflects the nature of the people in the play: They want nothing and nothing can occur to them. These middle-class characters, the Smiths and the Martins, use language as a means not to communicate with each other but to compete and put down their adversaries. Language becomes a weapon for them. They are so far from being alive that when the Fire Chief comes looking for fires they laugh at the notion that anything could be warm and burning at their house. Mary's poem, which describes different objects going up in flames, suggests a passion alien to them, and they are so offended by her recitation that they shove her offstage. Unlike the Martins, who must reason who they are before they can recognize each other, Mary and the Fire Chief (both driven by fiery passion) know each other on sight.

The two middle-class couples—in contrast to the more easygoing working-class maid and fireman—are fierce defenders of their respectable way of life, but as Ionesco presents them, their lives are amazingly empty, their stories are nonsensical, and their words ultimately amount to nothing more than angry sounds. There is much to laugh at here, and the comedy in *The Bald Soprano* is brilliantly funny. Many of the fables that precede Mary's poem and the fractured clichés exchanged at the end of the play are such outrageously illogical parodies of familiar, everyday speech that the only way to respond to them is with laughter.

Kenneth Krauss

Bibliography:
Bradby, David. *Modern French Drama 1940-1990*. 2d ed. New York: Cambridge University Press, 1991. In his discussion of the New Theatre, which flourished in France after World War II, Bradby suggests that *The Bald Soprano* is the "ultimate form of audience aggression." Beautifully contextualizes the playwright's first effort with those of other absurdists.
Cohn, Ruby. *From "Desire" to "Godot": Pocket Theater of Postwar Paris*. Berkeley: University of California Press, 1989. In examining some of the great plays that opened in some of the tiniest theaters in Paris after World War II, Cohn describes the original production of *The Bald Soprano*, including curious and often funny backstage details. An illuminating appreciation of the script and its performance.
Dobrez, L. A. C. *The Existential and Its Exits: Literary and Philosophical Perspectives on the Works of Beckett, Ionesco, Genet, and Pinter*. New York: St. Martin's Press, 1986. Emphasizing the philosophical aspects of absurdist theater, the author explores Ionesco's most successful dramatic works. Addresses the play's peculiar mixture of tragedy and comedy.
Esslin, Martin. *The Theatre of the Absurd*. 3d ed. New York: Penguin, 1980. A pioneering critique that views Ionesco's work as basic to the absurdist repertory and provides fascinating information on how and why Ionesco wrote *The Bald Soprano*. A definitive work on absurdism; includes useful biographical and production data.
Lane, Nancy. *Understanding Eugene Ionesco*. Columbia: University of South Carolina Press, 1994. A reexamination of the playwright's career and works.

BAMBI
A Life in the Woods

Type of work: Novel
Author: Felix Salten (Siegmund Salzmann, 1869-1945)
Type of plot: Fable
Time of plot: Indeterminate
Locale: A forest
First published: Bambi: Eine Lebensgeschichte aus dem Walde, serial, 1922; book, 1923
(English translation, 1928)

Principal characters:
BAMBI, a deer
THE OLD PRINCE, a stag who befriends Bambi
BAMBI'S MOTHER
FALINE, Bambi's cousin
GOBO, her brother
HE or HIM, the enemy of forest creatures

The Story:
Bambi was born in a thicket in the woods. While he was still an awkward young fawn, his mother taught him that he was a deer. He learned that deer did not kill other animals nor did they fight over food as jaybirds did. He learned, too, that deer should venture from their hiding places to go to the meadow only in the early morning and late in the evening and that they must rely on the rustle of last year's dead leaves to give them warning of approaching danger. On his first visit to the meadow, Bambi had a conversation with a grasshopper and a close look at a butterfly.

One evening Bambi and his mother went to the meadow again. On his second visit, he was introduced to the hare, an animal with big, soft eyes and flopping ears. Bambi was not impressed. The little deer was considerably happier to meet his cousins, Gobo and Faline, and their mother, Ena. The two families were about to separate when two stags with spreading antlers on their heads came crashing out of the forest. Bambi's mother explained that the larger, statelier stag was Bambi's father.

As he grew older, Bambi learned the sounds and smells of the forest. Sometimes his mother went off by herself. Missing her one day, Bambi started out to look for her and came upon his cousins in the meadow. Faline suggested that both their mothers might have gone to visit their fathers. Bambi decided to continue his search by himself. As he stood at the edge of a clearing, he saw a creature he had never seen before. The creature raised what looked like a stick to its face. Terrified, Bambi ran back into the woods as fast as he could go. His mother appeared suddenly, and they both ran home to their glade. When he and his mother were safe again, Bambi learned that the creature he had seen was a man.

On another day, he began to call for his mother. Suddenly, a great stag stood before him. He coldly asked Bambi why he was crying and told him that he ought to be ashamed of himself. Then he was gone. The little deer did not tell his mother of his experience nor did he call her anymore. Later, he learned that he had met the Old Prince, the biggest and wisest stag in the forest. One morning Bambi was nibbling in the meadow with his mother when one of the stags came out of the forest. Suddenly, there was a crash. The stag leaped into the air and then fell dead. Bambi raced away after his mother. All he wanted was to go deeper and deeper into the forest until he could feel free of that new danger. He met the Old Prince again. When Bambi asked him who Man was, the stag only replied that he would find out for himself. Then he disappeared.

The forest gradually changed as summer passed into fall and then into winter. Snow fell, and grass was not easy to find. All the deer became more friendly during the cold months. They would gather to talk, and sometimes even one of the stags would join them. Bambi grew to admire the stags. He was especially interested in Ronno, the stag who had escaped after a hunter had wounded him in the foot. The constant topic of conversation was Man, for none of the deer could understand the black stick he carried. They all were afraid of it.

As the winter dragged on, the slaughter of the weaker animals in the forest began. A crow killed one of the hare's children, a squirrel raced around with a neck wound a ferret had given him, a fox murdered a pheasant. A party of hunters came into the woods with their noisemaking sticks and killed many of the animals. Bambi's mother and his cousin Gobo were not seen again.

That spring, Bambi grew his first pair of antlers. With his mother gone, he had to spend most of his time alone. The other stags drove him away when he tried to approach them, and Faline was shy with him. Deciding one day that he was not afraid of any of the stags, Bambi charged at what he thought was one of his tormentors in a thicket. The stag stepped aside, and Bambi charged past him. It was the Old Prince. Embarrassed, the young deer began to tremble when his friend came close to him. With an admonishment to act bravely, the older deer disappeared into the woods.

A year later, Bambi met Faline again, and once more they played as they had when they were very young. Then an older stag named Karus appeared and tried to block Bambi's way. When Bambi attacked him, Karus fled, as did the stag named Ronno, who had been pursuing Faline.

Faline and Bambi ventured into the meadow one day and there saw a stranger nibbling the grass. They were surprised when he came skipping up to them and asked if they did not know him. It was Gobo. Hunters had caught him and kept him until he was full-grown. Then he had been sent back to join his family in the forest. His mother was delighted to see him once more. Gobo explained his absence to an admiring audience and praised Man for his kindness. While he was talking, the Old Prince appeared and asked Gobo about the strip of horsehair around his neck. Gobo answered that it was a halter. The Old Prince remarked pityingly that he was a poor thing and vanished.

Gobo would not live as the other deer in the forest did. He insisted on going about during the day and sleeping at night. He had no fear about eating in the meadow, completely exposed. One day, when a hunter was in the woods, Gobo declared that he would go talk to him. He walked out into the meadow. Suddenly there was a loud report; Gobo leaped into the air and then dashed into the thicket, where he fell mortally wounded.

Bambi was alone when he met the Old Prince for the first time since Gobo's death. They were walking together when they found a hare caught in a noose. The Old Prince carefully managed to loosen the snare with his antlers. Then he showed Bambi how to test tree branches for a trap. Bambi realized for the first time that there was no time when Man was not in the woods. One misty morning, as Bambi stood at the edge of the clearing, a hunter wounded him. He raced madly for the forest and in its protection lay down to rest. Soon he heard a voice beside him, urging him to get up. It was the Old Prince. For an hour, the veteran led Bambi through the woods, crossing and recrossing the place where he had lain down, showing him the herbs which would stop his bleeding and clear his head. He stayed with Bambi until the wound had healed. Before he went off to die, the old stag showed Bambi a poacher who had been killed.

He explained that humans, like animals, must die. Bambi understood then that there is someone even more powerful than Him.

Walking through the forest one day, Bambi spied a brother and sister fawn crying for their mother. As the Old Prince had spoken to him so many years before, he asked them if they could not stay by themselves. Then, as his friend had done, he vanished into the forest.

Critical Evaluation:

The first widely acclaimed work by the Austrian novelist Felix Salten (born Siegmund Salzmann), *Bambi* has not only remained a classic of children's literature but has also earned the discriminating approval of writers such as John Chamberlain, Alfred Werner, and John Galsworthy. It has been reprinted often, even before Walt Disney's sentimentalized film version extended its popularity, and has been translated into most modern languages, including Hebrew and Chinese. Yet unlike many other children's favorites adapted by Disney, *Bambi* is a story of neither comfortable sentimentality nor whimsical humor. Instead, it is a touching, lyrical, sometimes gently melancholy romance of growth and developing awareness.

Possibly the melancholy of the novel springs in part from the writer's own childhood experiences. Salten suffered early in life from rootlessness and poverty. Until a relative discovered him destitute, friendless, and nearly famished and offered him employment, he despaired ever of surviving in a world of cruel indifference. To repay his benefactor, Salten, whose formal education was meager, began to write sketches at first, then longer pieces influenced by Guy de Maupassant and Gottfried Keller. The success of *Bambi* established for Salten a demand for more children's nature books that were to include, among his best, *Fifteen Rabbits* (1930) and *Perri* (1938). In addition to juvenile fiction, Salten wrote excellent criticism and travel literature, mostly revealing his appreciation for the United States (his adopted home after 1939) and Israel.

To the child's imagination, *Bambi* treats human experiences in the form of an animal fable. Young readers learn from the book the lessons of growing up, attaining independence, enduring the sorrows of loss, and meeting the challenges of change, from youth to maturity. Although many children's fairy tales resolve conflicts in the plot through wonderful interference, in *Bambi* life experiences are treated as natural, without the interference of magic or chance. On the contrary, the book deals honestly with two of the most terrible emotional crises a child can face: the estrangement of a father and the death of a mother. Bambi learns to become self-reliant, to earn from other forest creatures the respect deserved by the powerful and fully matured.

At the same time, Bambi comes to understand the weaknesses of his eternal enemy (Man); he masters his sexual rivals (Karus and Ronno), wins his mate Faline, and sires her young; and above all, he comes to terms with the Old Prince—the father-figure that has always protected and, from a distance, sustained him. Bambi learns the great lesson of resolute independence from the Old Prince. Whereas Gobo had tried to live with Man and died from his trusting mistake, the old stag has lived alone, true to the challenge he once gave Bambi: "Can't you stay by yourself?" Bambi learns to stay free, indifferent to comfort, even to friendship. He protects himself from dangers, yet he is sensitive to the need of protecting the weak who cannot defend themselves. Thus, he provides for children—and perhaps for their parents also—Salten's message of survival in a hostile world.

Bibliography:

Blount, Margaret. *Animal Land: The Creatures of Children's Fiction.* New York: William Morrow, 1975. Brief discussion of *Bambi* as a great example of "animal biography," avoiding its predecessors' and imitators' tendency to caricature. Poignant and poetic account of animal life and death compensates for novel's failings, chiefly its excessive anthropomorphism.

Cartmill, Matt. *A View to a Death in the Morning: Hunting and Nature Through History.* Cambridge, Mass.: Harvard University Press, 1993. Focuses primarily on Disney's film as a piece of antihunting propaganda, but discusses Salten's novel at greater length than most sources. The novel exudes violence and death, influenced by pessimism of post-World War I Austria and an intense misanthropy; the intrusion of human beings in the forest corrupts innocence and destroys life.

Egoff, Shirley A. *Thursday's Child: Trends and Patterns in Contemporary Children's Literature.* Chicago: American Library Association, 1981. Brief discussion of *Bambi* as the first significant European children's novel in the twentieth century. Novel was popular in its time, but the modern reader may find it overly sentimental; however, its negative view of humanity is quite modern and echoed by subsequent children's books about animals.

Meigs, Cornelia, et al. *A Critical History of Children's Literature.* Rev. ed. New York: Macmillan, 1969. Places *Bambi* as the most significant fact-based animal story in children's literature. Beautiful passages may appeal to reader despite sentimentality.

BARABBAS

Type of work: Novel
Author: Pär Lagerkvist (1891-1974)
Type of plot: Moral
Time of plot: First century C.E.
Locale: Palestine, the Near East, and Rome
First published: 1950 (English translation, 1951)

Principal characters:
BARABBAS, the robber freed in Christ's stead
A GIRL, unnamed, formerly intimate of Barabbas
SAHAK, a fellow slave of Barabbas and an Armenian Christian
THE ROMAN GOVERNOR
MARY
PETER
LAZARUS

The Story:

At Golgotha, Barabbas, watching the Crucifixion from which he had suddenly been saved, was startled by the words uttered by the figure on the cross: "My God, my God, why hast thou forsaken me?" Even stranger to him was the darkness that seemed to come over the world. As he was leaving the scene, he was also disturbed by the look of silent reproach directed at him by the dead man's mother.

Back in Jerusalem, he met and walked with a young girl, whom he had known before. The girl, who had a harelip, went with him to a dive where some of his low companions were gathered. Barabbas and the people there discussed Barabbas' rescue and the strange rabbi who had made such extreme claims and yet permitted himself to be crucified like a criminal. Barabbas was considerably relieved that the people in the café did not believe in the rabbi's divinity, although he was troubled that they had not noticed the darkness that had for a while hung over the land. After the young girl left the dive, Barabbas indulged, as a kind of escape from his worries, in a drunken debauch with one of the patrons of the café—a fat, crude woman.

Later, Barabbas met a red-bearded follower of Christ who expected Christ to rise from the dead the next day. He explained some of Christ's teachings to Barabbas but shamefacedly admitted that before the end he had denied Christ. The girl with the harelip, to whom Barabbas also talked about Christ, said that she had met Him. She was wilder in her predictions than was the red-bearded man; she expected the millennium and divine miracles at any moment. Superstition did not blur everything, however, for she told Barabbas that Christ's message was one of love. Barabbas thereupon went to the grave; he watched all night but saw nothing. The next day, however, the stone was gone from the entrance. He believed that the followers of Christ had taken the body; the girl thought He had risen.

Barabbas asked the followers of Christ about these events but found little satisfaction in their answers. He could not understand One who used His power by refraining from using it. Barabbas was later taken to a man who had been dead four days and had been raised again by this rabbi. This man told Barabbas that death was nothing; it was there, but it signified nothing. He added that after one had experienced death, life also was as nothing. As Barabbas further questioned the followers of Christ, it became clear that although they were believers, they were

488

quite confused as to the meaning of all of these happenings. When the followers learned Barabbas' identity, as sooner or later they did, they naturally hated him.

About this time, Barabbas became estranged from his fellows in the low life of Jerusalem—so much so that he resigned himself from sensual life. The fat woman, his sometime lover, thought that Christ's soul had possessed Barabbas. One day, by accident, Barabbas was present at a church meeting and heard a rather disappointing sermon by the red-bearded man who had denied Christ. He found the snuffling testimony of witness given by the harelipped girl even more distasteful. Later, when a blind man denounced the girl as a Christian, Barabbas nevertheless knifed the first person who stoned her. She died a humble martyr, but one who saw Christ as she died. Barabbas carried her body to the grave of a baby she had had; Barabbas had been the father of that child.

A short time later, Barabbas left Jerusalem and returned to the robber band that he had at one time led. The robbers were distressed by his seeming character change: Formerly the boldest of all, he had become apathetic. So bold had he been that years ago he had fought, killed, and supplanted the bandit leader; thus had he come by the scar on his face. What none of the characters knew was that Eliahu, whom Barabbas had killed, was his own father. Sensing that he no longer fitted in with the robber band, Barabbas silently stole away from the camp.

For an indeterminate period, Barabbas wandered the earth. Later, he was enslaved and put to mining for the Romans. There he met Sahak, a slave who was thrilled by the knowledge that Barabbas had seen Christ. Without revealing to Sahak the true nature of his relationship with Christ, Barabbas increased the details of Sahak's belief by telling him things about Christ. Some of these were lies, such as that he had seen an angel come down from the sky on the night that he had watched outside Christ's tomb. After a time, Barabbas apathetically suffered Sahak to enter into Christian observances with him. He even permitted Sahak to draw Christ's symbol on his slave's disk, and for a time he prayed with him. Years later, a new mine overseer, attracted to Christianity but mystified by its doctrine of love, noticed the two slaves, bound to each other by a chain. The overseer, having talked to them about Christianity, was moved to secure positions above ground for the two men. Although still slaves, Sahak and Barabbas were at least free of the deadly conditions of primitive mining.

Matters soon changed when the Roman governor of the territory learned through another slave that both men were Christians. Sahak refused to renounce his faith. Barabbas, who by this point would have liked to believe in Christ but could not, readily renounced his. He let the governor scratch through the sign that Sahak had put on his disk. He then had to witness Sahak's crucifixion. He was relieved when no miraculous occurrences accompanied the death of Sahak.

When the pagan but kindly Roman governor retired to Rome, he took Barabbas with him. Once, Barabbas went to the catacombs to see a Christian religious service, but no worshiper was there. In the darkness of the catacombs, he felt very much alone. He also felt that, as he had dreamed one night, he was still chained to Sahak, just as he had been during the days when he had pretended to believe.

After he had left the place of the dead, he smelled fire; flames were everywhere. He thought that Christ had returned to save the world, the first step of which would be to destroy Rome—for Rome felt that Christ was the enemy. Barabbas seized a burning brand and began to set everything afire that he could; he wildly thought that he was helping the Christians and his Savior.

Thrown into prison with the Christians, Barabbas learned that there had been no service in the catacombs because the followers had been forewarned that an attack was to be made on them. The fires were probably set by agents or spies to further discredit the Christians.

The Christians in the prison naturally denied that Barabbas, who had been caught in the act, was one of them. When they protested to the jailer, the man showed Barabbas' disk as evidence, which still had the Christian symbol dimly scratched on it. A venerable old man among the Christians turned out to be one whom Barabbas had met before, the man who had denied Christ. Now he explained to Barabbas that it was Caesar who had set the fires, not Christ; it had been Caesar, therefore, whom Barabbas had helped by trying to burn Rome. Christ's message was still that of love.

To the others, the old man added that they must not condemn Barabbas. He continued that Barabbas was unhappy and that he had to wear his crossed-out disk. The others were also weak and full of faults; their belief had come from God. They must not condemn a man who had no god in whom to believe. Soon the Christians were led out in pairs to be crucified, but Barabbas was taken alone. When death was coming, he spoke rather ambiguously into the darkness saying that he delivered up his soul "to thee."

Critical Evaluation:

The transformation of a soul is the subject of *Barabbas*. Pär Lagerkvist's novel has the tone and manner of an ancient, oft-told story, recounted simply but with feeling. The tale is told with an austerity that renders it all the more moving for being pared down to essentials. The poetic prose is precise and vivid, despite its leanness; at the end of the book, the reader realizes with amazement how clearly the author has pictured by means of a word here and a phrase there the ancient, biblical world. *Barabbas* is a superbly written, enigmatic novel, open to many possible interpretations. If it possesses any fault, it is only that occasionally the prose is almost self-consciously understated, that the sophistication underlying the simplicity of the narration seems to peek through; but this is a minor flaw and in no way detracts from the power of the book.

The question raised by *Barabbas* is that which haunts humanity, the question of what lies beyond life. Barabbas is compelled by his fate to question the universe in a manner that he does not understand or desire. Ordinarily such an uneducated thief would not have concerned himself with philosophical and moral issues, but the fact that he was acquitted and Jesus was crucified in his stead turns his world upside down. The book traces his wandering, both physically and spiritually, until his own end, also upon a cross. It is not the end that is important in this novel but rather the struggle. Lagerkvist leaves the ending ambiguous when he states that Barabbas' words were "as though" spoken to the darkness. The stages of this struggle are poignantly portrayed, from the initial confusion and wonderment through the denial to the final reassessment. Barabbas wants to believe, as so many human beings hunger for belief, but he cannot deceive himself; his belief must be hard-won, or it is meaningless and false.

The novel is rich with symbols, but the symbols never intrude; rather, they enrich the tale and serve to give it an added resonance. Most of the men and women who pass through the story are scarred, including Barabbas himself, who was at an early age scarred by his own father (whom he later unwittingly kills). These marked and deformed human beings seem to represent all of humanity, the battered multitudes who stare into the darkness, as does Barabbas, and wonder what is out there waiting for them. Love is the answer, Barabbas is told, but he finds it hard to believe. Yet the fat woman and the girl with the harelip both find momentary happiness because he seems briefly to love them. The slave's badge that he wears around his neck becomes a double symbol, representing both the bondage of humanity to the earth and its powers and, after it is engraved with the name of the Savior, possibilities of freedom and happiness. Christian symbols are woven into the narrative, but they seem to arise naturally from the gradually developing Christian religion, to appear as they are needed, to help the followers keep faith.

Although the short novel seems simple, it is amazingly intricate, probing the human mind and the human spirit. Like so much of the best literature, *Barabbas* can be read and appreciated on several different levels and reread from time to time with pleasure and profit. In 1951, shortly after the appearance of this novel, Lagerkvist was awarded the Nobel Prize in Literature.

Bibliography:

Gustafson, Alrik. *A History of Swedish Literature*. Minneapolis: University of Minnesota Press, 1961. Traces the evolution of Lagerkvist's prose style to its maturity in *Barabbas*. Examines the novel in terms of its author's search for expressive form and his grappling with the problem of evil.

Sjoberg, Leif. *Pär Lagerkvist*. New York: Columbia University Press, 1976. Argues that *Barabbas* is a modern rather than a historical novel. Relates the controversial ending to Lagerkvist's stated religious views.

Spector, Robert Donald. "*Barabbas*: The Bible as Modern Literature." In *Pär Lagerkvist*. New York: Twayne, 1973. Convincingly demonstrates how the novel reflects the dualism Lagerkvist saw in life. Spector's is the first full-length book in English devoted to Lagerkvist's work.

Swanson, Roy A. "Evil and Love in Lagerkvist's Crucifixion Cycle." *Scandinavian Studies* 38 (November, 1966): 302-317. Considers the novel's place in a series focusing on the event and significance of Jesus' crucifixion. Determines myth to be Lagerkvist's point of departure.

Weathers, Winston. "Death and Transfiguration: The Lagerkvist Pentalogy." In *The Shapeless God: Essays on Modern Fiction*, edited by Harry J. Mooney, Jr., and Thomas F. Staley. Pittsburgh: University of Pittsburgh Press, 1968. Assesses the novel as one of five by Lagerkvist that explore the meaning of death and the escape from death. Writing from a Christian perspective, he appraises the novel as a portrait of the secular person.

THE BARBER OF SEVILLE
Or, The Useless Precaution

Type of work: Drama
Author: Pierre-Augustin Caron de Beaumarchais (1732-1799)
Type of plot: Comedy
Time of plot: Eighteenth century
Locale: Seville, Spain
First performed: 1775; first published, 1775 as *Le Barbier de Séville: Ou, La Précaution inutile*,
    1775 (English translation, 1776)

Principal characters:
    FIGARO, the barber of Seville
    COUNT ALMAVIVA, a grandee of Spain
    BARTHOLO, a doctor
    ROSINE, his ward
    DON BAZILE, Rosine's singing-master

The Story:

    Count Almaviva was so much in love with Rosine, Dr. Bartholo's ward, that even though he had never spoken to her he had left Madrid and the pleasure of the court in order to be near her in Seville. Her guardian desired to marry her himself, however, and he kept the young girl locked in her room. To help him in his suit, the count enlisted the aid of Figaro, the barber and apothecary of Bartholo.

    A note Rosine threw from her window convinced the count that she returned his love. At Figaro's suggestion, the count disguised himself as a soldier seeking quarters for the night. He called himself Lindor, the name Figaro had used in telling Rosine of her unknown lover. When Bartholo, suspicious of everyone who might come near Rosine, refused to give the disguised count lodging, the count managed to slip a note to Rosine before Bartholo ordered him from the house. Bartholo forced Rosine to show him the note, but she cleverly tricked him into reading another note she had in her pocket. Nevertheless, his suspicions were not allayed.

    Figaro learned that Bazile was a party to Bartholo's plot to force Rosine to marry him the next day. The count thereupon disguised himself as a student and, calling himself Alonzo, told Bartholo that he had been sent by Don Bazile, Rosine's music teacher, who, so the count said, was ill and had asked Alonzo to take his place. The count thought that by pretending to help Bartholo he could be alone with Rosine and tell her his plans to rescue her from the old man. He gave Bartholo a letter that he claimed would help Bartholo in his suit. The letter implied that there was another woman with whom Lindor was in love. Bartholo refused to leave Rosine alone with the count until Figaro managed to trick him into leaving the room. Figaro took the opportunity to steal the key to Rosine's room from the old man's key ring. When Bartholo returned to the room, the music lesson seemed to be in progress. Suddenly Don Bazile was announced. It took all of Figaro's ingenuity to keep him from exposing the count as an impostor. Figaro and the count at last managed to get Don Bazile out of the house before Bartholo could learn the truth, but Bartholo, suspicious of everyone, sneaked behind the count and Rosine and overheard enough to make him decide to investigate Don Bazile's strange behavior and apparent bewilderment.

    Don Bazile confessed that he knew nothing of his supposed illness and had never before seen the so-called Alonzo. This confirmation of his suspicions made Bartholo uneasy. Although he feared that Alonzo was Lindor's friend, he did not suspect that Alonzo was Lindor himself. He told Don Bazile to arrange to have the notary come at once to perform his marriage with Rosine.

Immediately afterward he went to the young girl's room and showed her the letter the count had given him. Instead of helping the count, however, it worked against him, for Rosine believed Bartholo when he told her that her young lover would pretend to rescue her but was in reality planning to pass her on to Alonzo. Because Rosine did not know the real identity of the man she called Lindor, she believed Bartholo and promised to marry him at once. She also told him of Alonzo's plan to steal into her room that night and carry her off. Bartholo left her to arrange for the police to come and apprehend the kidnapper.

While Bartholo was gone, the count and Figaro climbed up a ladder and entered Rosine's room. Rosine accused the count of a plot to pass her on to someone else. The count then threw aside his disguise. He told her he was Count Almaviva and that in his love for her he had followed her hopelessly for the past six months. Rosine was so overcome that she fainted. When she was revived, she admitted that she had doubted him and that she had promised to marry Bartholo. She also told them that Bartholo knew of the plan to carry her away. Already the ladder had been removed from her window and the police were on the way.

When all looked blackest, Don Bazile appeared with a notary, as Bartholo had instructed him to do. The notary knew only that he was to perform a marriage here and another marriage at the home of Figaro. Here he was to marry Bartholo and a young lady named Rosine. At Figaro's home he was to marry Count Almaviva and a young lady named Rosine. By some clever and rapid talking, the count and Figaro were able to convince the notary that he was merely confused. Don Bazile was more difficult, but he finally decided the money the count slipped into his hand was more important than loyalty to Bartholo. He signed the marriage contract as a witness just before Bartholo burst into the room with many policemen and a justice of the peace.

Bartholo ordered the justice of the peace to arrest the count, but that civil servant was too much impressed with Count Almaviva's high position to risk offending him. Bartholo, anxious to marry his ward, then ordered the count out of the house. When he learned that the count and Rosine had just been married and that the contract was legally signed, he was infuriated and tried in vain to keep Rosine from leaving with her husband. By threatening Bartholo with a demand for an exact accounting of his ward's property, which Bartholo dared not allow, the justice of the peace was able to persuade the old man to sign the marriage certificate, which gave his consent to Rosine's marriage. Bartholo could not understand how his plans had failed. Figaro told him that youth and love could always defeat an old man's schemes.

Critical Evaluation:

Although the plot of *The Barber of Seville* has been used many times by dramatists and composers, Pierre-Augustin Caron de Beaumarchais took a fresh approach to the story. The play, fast-moving and brisk, has all the necessary ingredients for a sentimental comedy: intrigue, wit, clear-cut characterizations, satire, and a well-defined plot. Indeed, the plot is more important than the actors themselves, even though Figaro, the barber, has become famous in the literature of all countries.

Beaumarchais' *The Barber of Seville* displays wit, humor, and gaiety, and its structural ingenuity—the sheer fun of the piece—assures its immortality, just as in Gioacchino Antonio Rossini's opera of the same name and Wolfgang Amadeus Mozart's *The Marriage of Figaro*, which is based on Beaumarchais' sequel to the play.

Probability and depth of character are sacrificed to the plot, but the superbly constructed plot is well worth the sacrifice. It is a masterpiece of ingenuity and invention. Bartholo, the antagonist, and the protagonists Rosine, the count, and Figaro are expert in their attempts to outwit one another.

In the best tradition of farce, particularly French farce, the action never seems to flag. Even the catching songs that seemingly interrupt the action are, in fact, organic parts of it. Beginning somewhat slowly in the first act, much of which is necessary exposition, the action gathers momentum, twists and turns, moves from climax to higher climax, and ends abruptly in a quick denouement. The characters are confronted with one obstacle after another; there is withheld information revealed at crucial points in the play; and, finally, there is the big scene, or *scène à faire*.

Equally entertaining is the play's humor, which ranges from broad burlesque and farce to sophisticated comedy of manners. Slapstick is punctuated with brilliant wit and trenchant observations about people and society. Yet Beaumarchais' touch is always light. Though Bartholo is ridiculed as the stock jealous cuckold pursuing a lady young enough to be his daughter, the satire stops short of bitterness or vituperation. His only punishment is that he loses Rosine, whom he never possessed in the first place. Seriousness and heavy-handed moralizing is also averted. There is, of course, the underlying moral that youthful lovers can always outwit a foolish old man, but that moral is absorbed in the rollicking dialogue and madcap antics of Figaro and the count. Yet here the conquest of innocence is less offensive or cynical than in earlier neoclassical plays dealing with the same theme: Count Almaviva does not seduce Rosine but marries her. Not only love, but good will and lighthearted humor triumph.

Bibliography:

Cox, Cynthia. *The Real Figaro: The Extraordinary Career of Caron de Beaumarchais.* London: Longmans, 1962. Focuses mostly on Beaumarchais' many other activities, particularly diplomacy. Places *The Barber of Seville* in the context of Beaumarchais' traumatic trial. Provides much information on early performances, such as the one in which Marie-Antoinette played Rosine. Illustrations and bibliography.

Grendel, Frédéric. *Beaumarchais: The Man Who Was Figaro.* Translated by Roger Greaves. New York: Thomas Y. Crowell, 1977. Interprets the figure of Figaro as Beaumarchais' complete alter ego, the two having a similar ability to keep reinventing themselves for new situations. The complicated plot of *The Barber of Seville* demonstrates this ability at its best. Illustrations and selected bibliography.

Ratermanis, J. B., and W. R. Irwin. *The Comic Style of Beaumarchais.* New York: Greenwood Press, 1961. Interesting scene-by-scene analysis of *The Barber of Seville* and *The Marriage of Figaro* and discussion of what makes the comedy work on stage. Stresses that Figaro, as the central character, sets the plot of *The Barber of Seville* in motion without being affected by the consequences himself, unlike the situation in *The Marriage of Figaro*.

Sungolowsky, Joseph. *Beaumarchais.* New York: Twayne, 1974. Concise biography, including an account of the development of *The Barber of Seville* from a *parade* (brief comic sketches) through an *opera comique* to its present form. Stresses Beaumarchais' honing of his playwriting skills and his ability to reinvent comic traditions and character types.

Wood, John. Introduction to *"The Barber of Seville" and "The Marriage of Figaro."* London: Penguin, 1964. Excellent concise discussion of the plays and their social context. Sees *The Barber of Seville* as more concise and "manageable" than *The Marriage of Figaro*. Edition includes Beaumarchais' own notes on the characters and their costumes.

BARCHESTER TOWERS

Type of work: Novel
Author: Anthony Trollope (1815-1882)
Type of plot: Social satire
Time of plot: Mid-nineteenth century
Locale: "Barchester," a fictitious English cathedral town
First published: 1857

Principal characters:
BISHOP PROUDIE, the bishop of Barchester
MRS. PROUDIE, his wife
THE REVEREND OBADIAH SLOPE, his chaplain
THE REVEREND SEPTIMUS HARDING, a member of the cathedral chapter
MRS. ELEANOR BOLD, his daughter
DR. GRANTLY, the archdeacon of Barchester
CHARLOTTE STANHOPE, Mrs. Bold's friend
LA SIGNORA MADELINE VESEY NERONI, née STANHOPE, Charlotte's sister
ETHELBERT STANHOPE (BERTIE), Charlotte's brother
MR. QUIVERFUL, Mrs. Proudie's candidate for warden of Hiram's Hospital
THE REVEREND FRANCIS ARABIN, the vicar of St. Ewold's

The Story:

After the death of Bishop Grantly of Barchester, there was much conjecture as to his successor. Bishop Grantly's son, the archdeacon, was ambitious for the position, but his hopes were defeated when Dr. Proudie was appointed to the diocese. Bishop Proudie's wife was of Low Church propensities, as well as being a woman of extremely aggressive nature, who kept the bishop's chaplain, Obadiah Slope, in constant tow.

On the first Sunday of the new bishop's regime, Mr. Slope preached in the cathedral. His sermon was concerned with the importance of simplicity in the service and the consequent omission of chanting, intoning, and formal ritual. The cathedral chapter was aghast. For generations, the services in the cathedral had been chanted; the chapter could see no reason for discontinuing the practice. In counsel, it was decreed that Mr. Slope never be permitted to preach from the cathedral pulpit again.

The Reverend Septimus Harding, who had resigned from his position as warden of Hiram's Hospital because of moral scruples, now had several reasons to believe that he would be returned to his post, although at a smaller salary than that he had drawn before. Mr. Harding, however, was perturbed when Mr. Slope told him that he would be expected to conduct several services a week and to manage Sunday schools in connection with the asylum. Such duties would make arduous a preferment heretofore very pleasant and leisurely.

Another change of policy was effected in the diocese when the bishop announced, through Mr. Slope, that absentee clergymen should return and help in the administration of the diocese. For years, Dr. Vesey Stanhope had left his duties to his curates while he remained in Italy. Now he was forced to return, bringing with him an ailing wife and three grown children, spinster Charlotte, exotic Signora Madeline Vesey Stanhope Neroni, and ne'er-do-well Ethelbert. Signora Neroni, who was separated from her husband, was an invalid who passed her days lying on a couch. Bertie had studied art and had been at varying times a Christian, a Mohammedan, and a Jew. He had amassed sizable debts.

The Proudies held a reception in the bishop's palace soon after their arrival. Signora Neroni, carried in with great ceremony, captured the group's attention. She had a fascinating way with men and succeeded in almost devastating Mr. Slope. Mrs. Proudie disapproved and did her best to keep Mr. Slope and others away from the invalid.

When the living of St. Ewold's became vacant, Dr. Grantly made a trip to Oxford and saw to it that the Reverend Francis Arabin, a High Churchman, received the appointment. With Mrs. Proudie and Mr. Slope advocating Low Church practices, it was necessary to build up the strength of the High Church forces. Mr. Arabin was a bachelor of about forty years. The question arose as to what he would do with the parsonage at St. Ewold's.

Mr. Harding's widowed daughter, Mrs. Eleanor Bold, had a good income and was the mother of a baby boy. Mr. Slope attempted to interest her in the work of the Sunday schools. At the same time, he asked Mr. Quiverful of Puddingdale to take over the duties of the hospital. Mr. Quiverful's fourteen children were reason enough for his being grateful for the opportunity. Mrs. Bold, however, learned how her father felt about the extra duties imposed upon him, and she grew cold toward Mr. Slope. In the end, Mr. Harding decided that he simply could not undertake the new duties at his age, so Mr. Quiverful, a Low Churchman, was granted the preferment, much to Mrs. Proudie's satisfaction.

Mr. Slope was not the only man who was interested in Mrs. Bold. The Stanhope sisters, realizing that Bertie could never make a living for himself, decided that he should ask Mrs. Bold to be his wife. Meanwhile, Mr. Slope was losing favor with Mrs. Proudie. She was furious that he would throw himself at the feet of Signora Neroni, and his interest in Mr. Harding's daughter, who refused to comply with her wishes, was disgraceful.

At a large gathering one day at the Thornes of Ullathorne, an old and affluent family, Mrs. Bold found herself in the same carriage with Mr. Slope, whom by this time she greatly disliked. Later that day, as she was walking with him, he suddenly put his arm around her and declared his love. She rushed away and told Charlotte Stanhope, who suggested that Bertie should speak to Mr. Slope about his irregularity; but the occasion for this discussion never arose. Bertie himself told Mrs. Bold that his sister Charlotte had urged him to marry Mrs. Bold for her money. Naturally insulted, Mrs. Bold was angered at the entire Stanhope family. That evening, when Dr. Stanhope learned what had happened, he insisted that Bertie go away and earn his own living or starve. After Bertie had gone, Signora Neroni wrote a note asking Mrs. Bold to come to see her. When Mrs. Bold entered the Stanhope drawing room, Signora Neroni told her that she should marry Mr. Arabin. With calculating generosity, she had decided that he would make a good husband for Mrs. Bold.

The Dean of Barchester, who had suffered a stroke of apoplexy, was not expected to recover. It was understood that Dr. Grantly would not accept the deanship. Mr. Slope wanted the position, but Mrs. Proudie refused to consider him as a candidate. When the dean died, speculation ran high. Mr. Slope felt encouraged by the newspapers, which said that younger men should be admitted to places of influence in the church.

Mr. Slope had been sent off to another diocese, for Mrs. Proudie could no longer bear having him in Barchester. Mr. Arabin, through Oxford influences, was appointed to the deanship, which was a victory for the High Churchmen. With Mr. Slope gone, the Stanhopes felt safe in returning to Italy.

Miss Thorne asked Mrs. Bold to spend some time at Ullathorne. She also contrived to have Mr. Arabin there. It was inevitable that Mr. Arabin should fall in love with Mrs. Bold and ask her to be his wife. Dr. Grantly was satisfied. He had threatened to forbid the hospitality of Plumstead Episcopi to Mrs. Bold had she become the wife of a Low Churchman. In fact, Dr. Grantly was moved to such generosity that he furnished the deanery and gave wonderful gifts to the entire family, including a cello to his father-in-law, Mr. Harding.

Critical Evaluation:

As a young man, Anthony Trollope, son of a ne'er-do-well barrister of good family, seemed destined to continue the decline of the family. An undistinguished student in two distinguished public schools, he had no hopes for university or career. His mother persuaded a family friend to find work for him in the London Post Office, where his performance as a clerk was eventually rated as "worthless." Indeed, the burdens of supporting the family fell on his indefatigable mother, who converted a family business failure in Cincinnati, Ohio, into a literary career with her satiric study *Domestic Manners of Americans* (1832). Like his mother, the son found his path in life after a change of scenery. When the Post Office sent him to the south of Ireland to assist in a postal survey, his career in the postal service began to advance, he married happily, and he began to write.

Success as a writer came after the Post Office sent Trollope to survey southwest England. A midsummer visit to the beautiful cathedral town of Salisbury produced the idea for *The Warden* (1855) and, more important, furnished the outlines for a fictional county, Barsetshire, which became as impressive as Thomas Hardy's Wessex or William Faulkner's Yoknapatawpha. When Trollope returned to the same milieu in *Barchester Towers*, he achieved resounding acclaim. Later he wrote four more novels to create what became known as the Barsetshire Novels. This series was set in a chiefly agricultural county with its seat of Barchester, a quiet town in the West of England, which was noted for its beautiful cathedral and fine monuments rather than for any commercial prosperity. Thus at middle age began the career of one of the most prolific of the Victorian novelists, who also remained, until his last years, one of the most popular.

In his day, Trollope was admired as a realist. He was delighted with Nathaniel Hawthorne's appraisal that his novels were "just as real as if some giant had hewn a great lump out of the earth and put it under a glass case, with all its inhabitants going about their daily business, and not suspecting that they were being made a show of." Some have also viewed Trollope's series as comic works and his characters as being in the grip of a firmly controlled irony. The irony that Trollope perceives in the affairs of the people of Barchester arises from discrepancies between the ideals they uphold and the means by which they uphold those ideals. A lay person with no special knowledge of the Church of England, Trollope vividly depicts the internecine war between the party of the new bishop of Barchester and that of the former bishop's son, Archdeacon Grantly. Both parties intend to preserve the integrity of the Church. With the Church vested in buildings, furnishings, and livings, these clergymen end up fighting for power over the appurtenances and worldly forms of the Church.

Barchester Towers includes a number of subplots, all of which are related to the ecclesiastical power struggle. Since buildings, furnishings, and livings are occupied by human beings, the clerics who guard the Church must also dispose over the lives of human beings. Some of the characters—Mr. Harding and the Quiverfuls in the competition for wardenship of Hiram's Hospital or Eleanor Bold in the rivalry of two clergymen for her hand in marriage—become mere objects in the disputes over power. Episodes not directly related to the ecclesiastical battles serve to underscore them, as in the parallel between the rivalry of Mrs. Lookaloft and Mrs. Greenacre and the absurd ploys of the higher orders that abound in the novel.

The main conflicts of the novel are those that engage the high and mighty of Barchester. The strength of Trollope's satire lies in his refusal to oversimplify the motives of these Church worldlings or to deny them sincerity in their defense of the Church. Even as Slope genuinely believes Grantly and his type to be the enemies of religion, so also does the archdeacon honestly believe that Slope is the kind who could well ruin the Church of England.

One of Trollope's devices for deflating these militant clerics is to treat their wars in the mock-heroic vein. After the first meeting between the archdeacon and the Proudies, the author declares, "And now, had I the pen of a mighty poet, would I sing in epic verse the noble wrath of the archdeacon." In time, Mrs. Proudie is ironically compared to Juno, Medea, even Achilles, while the archdeacon's extravagance in celebrating Eleanor Bold's marriage to his champion, Arabin, is suggestive of a glorious warrior returning from the fields with his spoils.

The reduction of marital glory is furthered by a recurrent analogy with games, underscoring the truth that Barchester's leadership is really concerned with social rather than spiritual or moral issues. Slope's major defeats arise from his indecorous behavior with Madeline Neroni, who is alert to every possible move. Worse, he underestimates his opponent, Mrs. Proudie, and at the end discovers that "Mrs. Proudie had checkmated him."

Human strife is incongruous with the idealized setting of peaceful Barchester, its venerable church and close, and its rural villages round about, all endowed with a loveliness suggestive of the age-old pastoral tradition. The cathedral itself seems to judge the folly of its worldly champions. As the battles commence, Archdeacon Grantly looks up to the cathedral towers as if evoking a blessing for his efforts. However genial the comedy played out beneath the Barchester towers, the outcome is not without serious import, for the ultimate result is the further separation of human beings from their ideals. In the end, the bishop's wife finds that her "sphere is more extended, more noble, and more suited to her ambition than that of a cathedral city," and the bishop himself "had learnt that his proper sphere of action lay in close contiguity with Mrs. Proudie's wardrobe." As Mr. Slope makes his ignominious final departure from the city, "he gave no longing lingering look after the cathedral towers." As for the archdeacon, it is sufficient for him to "walk down the High Street of Barchester without feeling that those who see him are comparing his claims with those of Mr. Slope."

Despite the futility of its human strivings, *Barchester Towers* is a cheerful novel, not merely because the satire provokes laughter but also because occasionally, briefly, the real and the ideal meet. Mr. Harding is too peaceable, too naïve, too reticent to be effective in the world; nevertheless, when prompted by his dedication to simple justice, he personally introduces Mr. Quiverful to his own former charges at Hiram Hospital. This act, representing the union of his profession and practice, creates a consequence greater than the act would suggest, for it causes the Barchester world to treat Mr. Quiverful with more respect as he assumes his duties. Quite appropriately, Trollope brings the novel to its close with pastoral serenity by offering a word of Mr. Harding, who functions not as a hero and not as a perfect divine but as a good, humble man without guile.

"Critical Evaluation" by Catherine E. Moore

Bibliography:
Booth, Bradford A. *Anthony Trollope: Aspects of His Life and Art.* London: Edward Hulton, 1958. A study of Trollope's religious beliefs and their impact on *Barchester Towers.* Also examines the differences between high and low church clergy and the nature of the Church of England in general.

Clark, John W. *The Language and Style of Anthony Trollope*. London: André Deutsch, 1975. An excellent study of Trollope's use of language and his recourse in *Barchester Towers* to English dialects, foreign phrases, euphemisms, and church language.

Glendinning, Victoria. *Anthony Trollope*. New York: Alfred A. Knopf, 1993. The best late twentieth-century biography of Trollope. Provides interpretations of the characters of Bishop and Mrs. Proudie, Signora Neroni, and Mr. Slope. Also connects several scenes in the novel to events in Trollope's life.

Sadleir, Michael. *Trollope: A Commentary*. New York: Farrar, Straus, 1947. Uses Trollope family papers and letters as well as contemporary reviews of *Barchester Towers* to identify some of Trollope's sources and discuss the book's initial reception. Uses original documents to show the cuts in *Barchester Towers* that were demanded by the publisher.

Skilton, David. *Anthony Trollope and His Contemporaries: A Study in the Theory and Conventions of Mid-Victorian Fiction*. New York: St. Martin's Press, 1972. Discusses Trollope and *Barchester Towers* in the mid-Victorian context. Discusses the relationship between Trollope and such contemporary authors as Charles Dickens and William Thackeray.

BARNABY RUDGE
A Tale of the Riots of 'Eighty

Type of work: Novel
Author: Charles Dickens (1812-1870)
Type of plot: Historical
Time of plot: 1775-1780
Locale: England
First published: 1841

Principal characters:
  EMMA HAREDALE, an heiress
  GEOFFREY HAREDALE, her bachelor uncle
  EDWARD CHESTER, a young man in love with Emma
  JOHN CHESTER, his father
  JOHN WILLET, the landlord of the Maypole Inn
  JOE, his son
  GABRIEL VARDEN, a London locksmith
  DOLLY, his daughter
  SIMON TAPPERTIT, Varden's apprentice
  RUDGE, a fugitive from justice
  MRS. RUDGE, his wife
  BARNABY RUDGE, their half-witted son
  LORD GEORGE GORDON, a fanatic
  GASHFORD, his secretary
  HUGH, a hosteler at the Maypole Inn
  DENNIS, the hangman

The Story:

At twilight on a wild, windy day in March, 1775, a small group of men sat in the bar parlor of the Maypole Inn, an ancient hostelry situated in Chigwell parish on the borders of Epping Forest. Two guests in particular engaged the attention of John Willet, the proprietor. One was a well-dressed young gentleman who seemed preoccupied. The other, a traveler, sat huddled in an old riding coat, his hat pulled forward to hide his face from the landlord's curious gaze. After the young gentleman, Edward Chester, had left the inn, Joe Willet, the landlord's son, informed the others that Edward, whose horse had gone lame, intended to walk the twelve miles to London despite the stormy weather because he was hoping to see Emma Haredale at a masquerade she was attending in town.

The name Haredale seemed to interest the stranger, and he listened intently when Solomon Daisy, the parish clerk, told the story of a murder that had shocked the neighborhood twenty-two years before to the day. Mr. Reuben Haredale, Emma's father, was at that time owner of The Warren, a great house near the village. One morning, he was found murdered in his bedroom. His steward, a man named Rudge, and a gardener were missing. Several months later, Rudge's body, identified by the clothing he had been wearing, was recovered from a pond on the estate. There had been no trace of the gardener, and the mystery was still unsolved. Since her father's violent death, Emma Haredale had lived at The Warren with Mr. Geoffrey Haredale, her bachelor uncle.

The stranger called abruptly for his horse and galloped away, almost colliding with a chaise driven by Gabriel Varden, the Clerkenwell locksmith. By the light of a lantern, Varden saw the traveler's scarred, scowling face. On his way back to London that same night, Varden found Edward Chester lying wounded on the highway. About the fallen man capered the grotesque figure of Barnaby Rudge, son of the Rudge who had been Reuben Haredale's steward. The boy had been born half-witted on the day the murder was discovered. Helpless, loved, and pitied, he lived on a shabby street nearby with his mother and his tame, talking raven, Grip. Aided by Barnaby, Varden took the wounded man to the Rudge house and put him to bed.

The next morning, Varden told the story of his night's adventures to Dolly, his daughter, and Simon Tappertit, his apprentice. Dolly, who knew of Emma's affection for Edward Chester, was deeply concerned. When Varden went to the Rudge house to inquire about Edward, he found him greatly improved. While he was talking with Mrs. Rudge, whose face clearly revealed the troubles and sorrows of her life, a soft knocking sounded at the closed shutter. When she opened the door, Varden saw over her shoulder the livid face and fierce eyes of the horseman he had encountered the night before. The man fled, leaving the locksmith convinced that he was the highwayman who had attacked young Chester. Mrs. Rudge, visibly upset by the man's appearance on her doorstep, begged Varden to say nothing about the strange visitor.

John Chester, Edward's father, was a vain, selfish man with great ambitions for his son. Shortly after his son's mysterious attack, he and Geoffrey Haredale met by appointment in a private room at the Maypole. Although the two families had been enemies for years, Chester knew that they at last had a common interest in their opposition to a match between Emma and Edward. Chester confessed frankly that he wished his son to marry a Protestant heiress, not the niece of a Catholic country squire. Haredale, resenting Chester's superior airs, promised that he would do his best to change his niece's feelings toward Edward. The meeting of the two men caused great interest among the villagers gathered in the bar parlor of the inn.

The mysterious stranger came again to Mrs. Rudge's house. When permitted to enter, he demanded food and money. Frightened by the threats of the sinister blackmailer, she and her son moved secretly to a remote country village.

Haredale, true to his promise, refused Edward admittance to The Warren. When the young man confronted his father to demand an explanation for the agreement between him and Haredale, the older Chester sneered at his son for his sentimental folly and advised him not to let his heart rule his head. Edward, refusing to obey his father's commands, asked Dolly Varden to carry a letter to Emma, who entrusted Dolly with a return note. Hugh, the brutish hosteler at the Maypole, took the letter from Dolly by force and gave it to John Chester, who was using every means to keep the lovers apart. Before long, he had involved Mrs. Varden, Simon Tappertit, and John Willet in his schemes.

Joe Willet became resentful when his father, trying to keep Joe from acting as a go-between for the lovers, began to interfere with his son's liberties. Meanwhile, Joe had troubles of his own. He had apprenticed himself to the locksmith in order to be near Dolly, but Mrs. Varden favored Tappertit's suit. Joe, annoyed by what he considered Dolly's fickleness, trounced his rival and declared that he would go off to fight the rebels in America. Dolly wept bitterly when she heard of his enlistment.

Five years later, John Willet again presided over his bar parlor on the tempestuous nineteenth of March, the anniversary of Reuben Haredale's murder. Only Solomon Daisy was needed to make the gathering of cronies complete. When he appeared, he told the others that in the village churchyard he had seen one of the men believed murdered years before. Willet, disturbed by the clerk's story, carried it that same night to Geoffrey Haredale, who asked that the report be kept from his niece.

On the way home, Willet and the hosteler who had accompanied him on his errand were stopped by three horsemen. The travelers were Lord George Gordon, leader of an anti-Catholic crusade; Gashford, his secretary, and John Grueby, a servant. They stayed overnight at the Maypole.

Lord Gordon was a fanatic. Gashford, his sly, malevolent helper, was the true organizer of the No-Popery rioters, a rabble of the disaffected and lawless from the London slums. Haredale gained Gashford's enmity when he publicly revealed his past. John Chester, on the other hand, now a baronet, took an interest in the Gordon cause. Among Gashford's followers were Tappertit, Hugh from the Maypole, and Dennis, the public hangman.

By chance, Barnaby Rudge and his mother journeyed to London on the day the Gordon riots began. Separated from her by a yelling, roaming horde, Barnaby found himself pushed along in a mob led by Hugh and Tappertit. Catholic churches, public buildings, and the homes of prominent Papists were sacked and burned. Later, Barnaby was among those arrested and thrown into Newgate prison.

Gashford, wishing to be revenged on Haredale, sent part of the mob to destroy The Warren. On the way, the rioters, led by Tappertit, Dennis, and Hugh, plundered the Maypole and left the landlord bound and gagged. Haredale was not at home; he had gone to London in an attempt to learn the whereabouts of Barnaby and his mother. Fearing the destination of the mob headed toward Chigwell and alarmed for the safety of his niece and Dolly, her companion, he rode home as fast as he could. Solomon Daisy joined him on the way. Upon their arrival at the Maypole, they unbound Willet and heard his account of a strange face, which had peered through the window a short time before. Haredale and Daisy rode on to The Warren, a heap of smoking ruins. While they stirred among the ashes, they spied a man lurking in the old watchtower. Haredale threw himself upon the skulking figure. His prisoner was Rudge, the double murderer.

Haredale had Rudge locked in Newgate. A few hours later, rioters fired the prison and released the inmates. The mob was led by Hugh, who had learned of Barnaby's imprisonment from a one-armed stranger. The same armless man saved Varden from injury after the locksmith had refused to open the door of the prison. Tappertit and Dennis, meanwhile, had taken Emma and Dolly to a wretched cottage in a London suburb.

In an attempt to take refuge from the mob, Haredale went to the home of a vintner who he knew, but rioters attacked the house. Escaping through a secret passage, they encountered Edward Chester, just returned from abroad. With him was Joe Willet, who had lost an arm in the American war. Edward and Joe succeeded in taking Haredale and the vintner to a place of safety.

Betrayed by Dennis, Barnaby, his father, and Hugh were captured and sentenced to death. Having learned where the young women were being held, Edward and Joe led a party to rescue them. The riots had been quelled in the city, and Gashford, hoping to save himself, had betrayed Lord Gordon. Dennis was also under arrest. Tappertit, wounded and with his legs crushed, was discovered in the house where Emma and Dolly had been held. Mrs. Rudge vainly tried to get her husband to repent before he and Dennis died on the scaffold. Hugh, who was Sir John Chester's natural son, met the same end. After much effort, Varden was able to secure the release of innocent, feebleminded Barnaby.

Haredale withdrew all objections to a match between Edward and Emma. He planned to leave England, but before his departure, he revisited the ruins of The Warren. There he met Sir John Chester and killed his old enemy in a duel. He fled abroad that same night and died several years later in a religious institution. Gashford survived Lord Gordon and died at last by his own hand.

These grim matters were of little concern to Dolly, mistress of the Maypole, or to Joe, the beaming landlord; nor did they disturb the simple happiness of Barnaby Rudge, who lived many years on Maypole Farm, in company with his mother and Grip, his talking raven.

Critical Evaluation:

Barnaby Rudge was Dickens' first attempt at writing a historical novel, something he was to accomplish with greater success in *A Tale of Two Cities* (1859). *Barnaby Rudge* ambitiously treats such matters as parental relationships (especially father-son relationships) and complex political situations. Yet all too often, critics have ignored it or else attempted to excuse it as a misguided attempt at historical drama in the style popularized by Sir Walter Scott. Other criticisms of the novel have included unsatisfactorily developed female characters (a common criticism of Dickens' work) and the fact that so much of its purposes are enmeshed strongly with complex, contemporary political issues of Dickens' time.

Dickens' main subject in the novel is the Gordon Riots, which took place in the 1780's. The riots were a misguided movement, largely motivated by religious bigotry with no particular social grievance, and were one of the last great shows of anti-Catholic sentiment in England. When Dickens was writing *Barnaby Rudge*, he was perhaps motivated in part by his own fears about the potentially revolutionary situation existing in England at the time, a result of a clash between Chartism and Unionism. The novel's riots might be said to represent that most explosive of all political situations and the direst threat imaginable to Dickens and his middle-class audience: an alliance between the two political extremes, radical and reactionary. Yet in the novel, the riots are brought about more by the collision of various personal motives on the parts of its leaders than by any political or revolutionary motive. Each of the mob's leaders has his own differing personal motives, which are only momentarily submerged in a common cry, in this case "No Popery."

One of the great strengths of the novel is in the descriptions of its crowd scenes, as the mob sweeps from the pastoral landscape of the Maypole Inn to London's Newgate prison. The riot offered Dickens the opportunity to explore the way in which an explosive social situation can come into existence. He shows how intolerable social conditions can produce fuel for riot, destruction, and social chaos, believing that the social evil of the riots was primarily caused by those who saw no common human bond between themselves and those economically less fortunate. Dickens attributes much of the willful destruction of the existing order to selfish indifference or ignorance about the part on the past of such characters as Tappertit, Chester, Gashford, Hugh, and Barnaby. In some way or another, they all are alienated from an identity grounded in the social structure they want to smash.

Dickens uses the riots to expose a fundamental sickness in society, the mindless urge to destroy. He forces himself and his readers to confront the harsh realities of riot and revolution through the great detail in which he presents scenes of destruction. These scenes forcefully bring home to his readers, almost in a cautionary manner, the reality of what revolution actually means. The looting of The Warren, Haredale's home, for example, which takes place over the course of several pages in the novel, shows in its remorseless attention to detail how determined Dickens was that his readers be spared nothing of the pain of this destruction. Likewise, in his description of the destruction of the Maypole Inn, Dickens' prose takes on a note of recogniz-able rage at what he sees as an offense against nature. He is determined to show his readers that the average as well as the exceptional must suffer from revolution. The inn represents a modest way of life that is just as susceptible to the madness of revolution as the great house.

Barnaby Rudge presents the causes and conditions that made the riots possible through a series of dramatic oppositions. The most notable opposition that Dickens sets up is that of the influence of the past on the present, of the old order against the new. The pastoral world, represented by the Maypole Inn at Chigwell, just outside London, is an obvious image of a stable social order rooted in the past. Yet the opening sentences of the novel suggest that this is a way of life that has grown old and apparently deserves to die.

In part, in these opening scenes, Dickens seems to be implicating the landed aristocracy, which has given up its age-old responsibility to provide governance and guidance to its tenants. This is represented in the character of Sir John Chester, one of the driving background forces of the mob violence. Through Chester, Dickens also explores a familiar topic of great concern to him, that of parenthood, in this case the relationships between fathers and sons. By disowning his sons Edward and Hugh, Chester does not merely threaten his way of life by irresponsibility but actually brings about its downfall by the willful destruction of his lineage. His son Hugh is the final product of a way of life that has fallen into decay; allowed to live as an animal, he is quite willing to help destroy the society that has created and disowned him.

Barnaby Rudge, the title character, is similar to Hugh in that he too is the son of a wicked father. Simple-minded and ready to believe what people tell him without question, Barnaby is caught up in the riots as their revolutionary leader. Barnaby complements Hugh well, since the situation of the riots in which they both willingly participate is, in part, brought about by the actions of fathers such as theirs who selfishly destroy the traditional order of society. This selfishness damages the future, through their sons, as much as it destroys the past.

Barnaby is also an obvious image of the irrationality of violence, perhaps too obvious an image (although Dickens had originally planned to have three escapees from the Bedlam asylum lead the mob). Yet virtually no one connected with the riots has any more idea than Barnaby as to why he is where he is.

Often overlooked among Dickens' many novels, *Barnaby Rudge* certainly deserves more serious consideration. The novel is a complex treatment of the conditions that give rise to political disorder, coupled with a detailed treatment of one of Dickens' favorite themes, the relationships between parents and children.

"Critical Evaluation" by Craig A. Larson

Bibliography:

Adrian, Arthur A. *Dickens and the Parent-Child Relationship*. Athens: Ohio University Press, 1984. Explores the effect of the cruelty of parents who withhold their love and ignore their children's feelings. Views *Barnaby Rudge* as a study of "father-son friction."

Kincaid, James R. *Dickens and the Rhetoric of Laughter*. Oxford, England: Clarendon Press, 1971. Includes an excellent chapter on *Barnaby Rudge* that explores the nature of the humor in the novel. Suggests that Dickens wants the reader to laugh at tyranny.

Lindsay, Jack. "*Barnaby Rudge.*" In *Dickens and the Twentieth Century*, edited by John Gross and Gabriel Pearson. London: Routledge, 1962. Reconsiders *Barnaby Rudge*, treating the novel as a study of the nature of social change.

Newman, S. J. *Dickens at Play*. New York: St. Martin's Press, 1981. A good treatment of *Barnaby Rudge* that interprets the riots as a vision of the nature of anarchy. Focuses on the "unwilling collusion between madness and creativity" in the character of Lord Gordon.

Rice, Thomas J. "The Politics of *Barnaby Rudge.*" In *The Changing World of Charles Dickens*, edited by Robert Giddings. New York: Barnes & Noble, 1983. An excellent essay that firmly grounds the writing of *Barnaby Rudge* in the political situation of its time.

BARON MÜNCHAUSEN'S NARRATIVE
OF HIS MARVELLOUS TRAVELS AND CAMPAIGNS IN RUSSIA

Type of work: Novel
Author: Rudolf Eric Raspe (1737-1794)
Type of plot: Picaresque
Time of plot: Eighteenth century
Locale: The world and the moon
First published: 1785

> *Principal character:*
> HIERONYMUS VON MÜNCHAUSEN, a German nobleman

The Story:

Baron Münchausen related that he once set out on horseback on a journey to Russia in midwinter. He tied his horse to a stump projecting from the snow and went to sleep; when he woke up he found that the abundant snow had melted and that his horse was dangling from the weather-vane of a church steeple. He was subsequently pursued by a wolf that began to devour his horse as it fled; when he attacked it with his whip, it ate the entire horse and ended up in harness itself.

While waiting to receive a commission in the Russian army, the baron hurried from his bedroom to shoot at a flock of ducks, but he struck his head on the doorpost, which caused sparks to fly from his eyes. This experience proved useful when he found that he had lost the flint from his flintlock; he had only to raise the musket to his face and punch himself in the eye to bag sixteen birds. He was not so lucky with a stag that he tried to bring down by spitting a cherry stone at it, but he later encountered a fine specimen with a cherry tree growing between its antlers.

His aim was just as true when he threw two flints at a pursuing bear; they struck fire in the creature's stomach and blew it up. He had no such armaments when he encountered a wolf, so he thrust his arm into the beast's mouth, laid hold of its entrails, and turned it inside out. He dared not do the same to a rabid dog but threw his cloak over it instead; unfortunately, the cloak picked up the infection and passed it on to other suits in his wardrobe.

He possessed a greyhound so fast that it outran its own legs and had thereafter to be employed as a terrier. Another greyhound—a bitch—was determined to course even while heavily pregnant; one day when she chased a hare in a similar condition, the exertion led them both to give birth, and instinct led their respective offspring immediately to continue their mothers' chase.

Once the Russian army's campaign against the Turks began, the baron's horse suffered the indignity of being cut in two by a portcullis, but his farrier managed to sew the two halves together with sprigs of laurel that eventually sprouted to form a bower over the saddle. He was captured soon after and set to work as a slave to drive the sultan's bees to their pasture every day. One day, when he threw his silver hatchet at bears that were attacking a bee, the hatchet carried the bee all the way to the moon. To fetch it back, he had to climb a gigantic beanstalk; then while he was searching for it on the moon the sun dried up the beanstalk, whereupon he had to make a rope out of straw to climb back down to earth. He was still two miles up when he had to let go of the rope, and when he landed he made a hole nine fathoms deep.

Although the baron's original account of his adventures ended at this point, he—or someone

505

pretending to be him—continued to add more episodes to this remarkable career. After the war, he went to sea, where he had many adventures of a similarly preposterous but rather more complicated nature.

His adventures at the siege of Gibraltar involved the cunning use of colliding cannon balls, the total destruction of the British artillery, and the employment of a slingshot to cut down two prisoners-of-war from a scaffold. The sling in question was a family heirloom once used by Shakespeare for poaching deer and since employed in various other exploits, including the launching of a balloon. The baron saved other prisoners-of-war by making wings for them.

Later, the baron traveled to Ceylon, Sicily, the South Seas, and many other places, everywhere accomplishing extraordinary feats of ingenuity. He visited the moon again, this time as a passenger on a ship lifted up to it by a hurricane, but he found it to be very different from his first visit. Inside Mount Etna he conversed with the Roman god Vulcan. He and his companions were swallowed by a huge fish, and he was carried across the American continent by eagles.

His account continued to grow longer in subsequent versions, which became many and various. The most familiar English-language version continued with an expedition into the heart of Africa, a visit to an island of ice, a new expedition to Africa in the company of the Sphinx and the giants Gog and Magog, and an eventual triumphant return to England. These later adventures also involved him with Don Quixote. After other journeys to America and Russia he rediscovered the lost library of Alexandria, met the legendary magician Hermes Trismegistus, and eventually liberated France from its revolutionaries, freeing Marie Antoinette and her family from their imprisonment.

Critical Evaluation:

The first edition of *Baron Münchausen's Narrative of His Marvellous Travels and Campaigns in Russia* was a rather brief document, almost certainly written in English by Rudolf Eric Raspe, a German satirist forced to seek refuge in England in 1775 after allegedly stealing gems from an employer. He never formally admitted authorship of the work but was named as the original author by Gottfried Bürger, who translated the work into German. Its great success in England prompted the publisher to add more material to subsequent editions issued during 1786, which might have been by Raspe, although a marked difference in style makes it more probable that another writer was responsible.

Late in 1786, a new publisher, G. Kearsley, produced his own rival version of Münchausen's narrative. All the pirated material in this edition was considerably rewritten in a more pompous and cumbersome fashion, and much more of a similar stripe was added by an unknown hand. It is this text, originally titled *Gulliver Revived: Or, The Singular Travels, Campaigns, Voyages and Adventures of Baron Munikhouson, Commonly Called Münchausen*, that virtually all later editions follow in their early phases, although it ought properly to be regarded as a corrupt version of Raspe's text.

Kearsley added yet more new material to his text between 1786 and 1792, at which point a new rival issued *A Sequel to the Adventures of Baron Münchausen*, whose substance was quickly co-opted and added into Kearsley's text. The authorship of these new materials remains unknown, but it certainly was not Raspe. To add to the complications, editions of Münchausen issued in France and Germany were augmented by native writers, thus diverging markedly from the parent text. In effect, the baron became common property and was adopted as a source and an authority for all manner of tall tales. The real Baron Münchausen thus found himself briefly notorious, somewhat to his surprise and much to his chagrin. He did not take kindly to being made to look a fool, and deeply resented the fact that his reputation as a raconteur had been blackened by the utter absurdities and veiled obscenities favored by Raspe's successors.

Raspe's own version of the original anecdotes is much preferable to the Kearsley version. The improbabilities therein are modest enough to be amusing rather than appalling, and they are relayed in a delightfully laconic manner that suits their content very well. The writers who added to Raspe's work were decidedly inferior in both these respects, and they may fairly be said to have ruined his work, no matter how little damage they did to its salability. What survives their mutilations, however, is the idea of Münchausen: the comical, yet somehow towering, figure of the teller of tales who insists that the most astonishing improbabilities are records of actual events.

Münchausen is the incarnation of the power that stories have to grip and involve those who hear and read them, and the narrative draws on the remarkably rich "urban folklore" that is passed on by word of mouth, concerning events which—the tellers insist—actually happened to "a friend of a friend." However unlikely these made-up tales might be, there is something about them that seduces belief and generates passionate insistence if a subsequent teller is challenged. Münchausen's narrative is not a collection of such tales, for they are not of a kind that easily survives writing down, but Raspe's original jottings are a deft literary parody of them and of the manner of their telling.

The transformation and growth of the Münchausen narrative once it was out of Raspe's control is a curious phenomenon. The additional material is so bad, for the most part, that it is hard for later readers to understand how the book retained its popularity. The incidents became sillier and sillier and all topical material was soon outdated. Perhaps the work would have been forgotten, save as an example of eighteenth century grotesquerie, had it not been for several excellent film versions; the likelihood is, however, that it was sustained in spite of its inadequacies by the one great asset handed down by Raspe to his feeble imitators. Everyone understands Baron Münchausen and recognizes him because there is a little of Münchausen in everyone.

All human beings exaggerate when they relate the funny or horrible things that happened to them, all make their accomplishments slightly more marvellous, their escapes slightly more hairsbreadth, and their observations slightly more bizarre than they were in actual fact. This is a natural way of making the narratives of ordinary lives authentically dramatic. Baron Münchausen's narrative pokes fun at one of the absurd necessities of everyday social intercourse and points up the fact that although social life would not be possible without trust, the insistence that people tell the truth at all times makes it necessary that they constantly tell lies.

Brian Stableford

Bibliography:
Carswell, John. *The Prospector: Being the Life and Times of Rudolf Erich Raspe, 1737-1794.* London: Cresset Press, 1950. A useful biography of Raspe, including a commentary on his most famous invention.
Green, Roger Lancelyn. *Into Other Worlds.* New York: Abelard-Schuman, 1958. Cites Raspe's narrative in chapter 5, "A Lunatick Century," in the context of other fictional lunar voyages.
Raspe, R. E., et al. *Singular Travels, Campaigns and Adventures of Baron Münchausen.* London: Cresset Press, 1948. An edition of Raspe's original text and its earliest embellishments, together with the first version of the sequel that was later integrated with Kearsley's text. The introduction by John Carswell is an invaluable history of the text.
Rose, William, ed. Introduction to *The Travels of Baron Münchausen; Gulliver Revived: Or,*

The Vice of Lying Prophecy Exposed. London: G. Routledge & Sons, 1923. Provides a brief history of the work and a commentary on its genesis.

Welcher, Jeanne K., and George E. Bush, Jr. Introduction to *Gulliveriana IV*. Delmar, N.Y.: Scholars' Facsimiles & Reprints, 1973. Discusses the fifth edition (Kearsley's), which is here reproduced in facsimile, with particular reference to its contemporary critical reception.

BARREN GROUND

Type of work: Novel
Author: Ellen Glasgow (1873-1945)
Type of plot: Social realism
Time of plot: Late nineteenth and early twentieth centuries
Locale: Rural Virginia
First published: 1925

> *Principal characters:*
> DORINDA OAKLEY, the daughter of a poor white Virginia farmer
> JOSIAH and
> RUFUS, her brothers
> JASON GREYLOCK, the last member of an old Virginia family
> GENEVA ELLGOOD, who becomes Jason's wife
> NATHAN PEDLAR, a country farmer and merchant

The Story:

Late one cold winter day, Dorinda Oakley started to walk the four miles between Pedlar's Mill and her home at Old Farm. The land was bleak and desolate under a gray sky, and a few flakes of snow were falling. For almost a year, she had worked in Nathan Pedlar's store, taking the place of his consumptive wife. Her brisk walk carried her swiftly over the rutted roads toward her father's unproductive farm and the dilapidated Oakley house. On the way, she passed Green Acres, the fertile farm of James Ellgood, and the run-down farm of Five Oaks, owned by dissolute old Doctor Greylock, whose son, Jason, had given up his medical studies to take over his father's practice and to care for his drunken father.

As she walked, Dorinda thought of young Jason Greylock, who overtook her in his buggy before she reached Old Farm. During the ride to her home, she remembered the comment of old Matthew Fairlamb, who had told her that she ought to marry Jason. The young doctor was handsome and represented something different from the drab, struggling life Dorinda had always known. Her father and mother and her two brothers were unresponsive and bitter people. Mrs. Oakley suffered from headaches and tried to forget them in a ceaseless activity of work. At Old Farm, supper was followed by prayers, prayers by sleep.

Dorinda continued to see Jason. Taking the money she had been saving to buy a cow, she ordered a pretty dress and a new hat to wear to church on Easter Sunday. Her Easter finery, however, brought her no happiness. Jason sat in church with the Ellgoods and their daughter, Geneva, and afterward, he went home with them to dinner. Dorinda sat in her bedroom that afternoon and meditated on her unhappiness.

Later, Jason unexpectedly proposed, confessing that he too was lonely and unhappy. He spoke of his attachment to his father that had brought him back to Pedlar's Mill, and he cursed the tenant system, which he said was ruining the South. He and Dorinda planned to be married in the fall. When they met during the hot, dark nights that summer, he kissed her with half-angry, half-hungry violence.

Geneva Ellgood meanwhile told her friends that she was engaged to Jason Greylock. In September, Jason left for the city to buy surgical instruments. When he was overlong in returning, Dorinda began to worry. At last she visited Aunt Mehitable Green, an old black conjuring woman, in the hope that she would have heard some gossip from the Greylock servants concerning Jason. While there, Dorinda became ill and learned that she was to have a child. Distressed, she went to Five Oaks and confronted drunken old Dr. Greylock, who told her, as he cackled with sly mirth, that Jason had married Geneva Ellgood in the city. The old man intimated that Jason was white-livered and had been forced into the marriage by the Ellgoods. He added, leering, that Jason and his bride were expected home that night.

On the way home, Dorinda, herself unseen, saw the carriage that brought Jason and Geneva to Five Oaks. Late that night, she went to the Greylock house and tried to shoot Jason, who was frightened and begged for her pity and understanding. Despising him for his weakness and falseness, she blundered home through the darkness. Two days later, she packed her suitcase and left home. By accident, she took the northbound train rather than the one to Richmond, and so changed the course of her life.

Dorinda arrived in New York in October, frightened, friendless, and with no prospects of work. Two weeks later, she met a kindly middle-aged woman who took her in and gave her the address of a dressmaker who might hire her. On the way to the shop, however, Dorinda was knocked down by a cab. She awoke in a hospital. Dr. Faraday, a surgeon who had seen the accident, was able to save her life but not that of her baby. Dr. Faraday hired her to look after his office and children.

Dorinda lived in New York with the Faradays for two years. Then her father had a stroke, and she returned home. Her brother Josiah had married, and Mrs. Pedlar was dead. Dorinda had become a woman of self-confidence and poise. She saw Geneva Greylock, who already looked middle-aged, and had only pity for the woman who had married Jason. Her brother Rufus said Jason was drinking heavily and losing all his patients. Five Oaks Farm looked more run-down than ever. Determined to make the Oakley land productive once more, Dorinda borrowed enough money to buy seven cows. She found Nathan Pedlar helpful in many ways, for he knew good farming methods and gave her advice. When she saw Jason again, she wondered how she could ever have given herself to such a husk of a man.

After Mr. Oakley's death, Josiah and his wife Elvira went to live on their own land. Rufus, who hated the farm, wanted to go to the city, but before he could leave, he was accused of having murdered a neighboring farmer. Dorinda was convinced that he had committed the murder, but Mrs. Oakley swore under oath that her son had been at home with her at the time of the shooting. Her lie saved Rufus, but Mrs. Oakley's conscience began to torment her and she took to her bed. Her mind broken, she lived in dreams of her youth. When she died in her sleep, Dorinda wept. It seemed to her that her parents' lives had been futile and wasted.

During the next ten years, Dorinda worked hard. She borrowed more money to improve the farm and, although she had to save and scrimp, she was happy. Geneva Greylock was losing her mind. One day she told Dorinda that she had borne a child but that Jason had killed it and buried it in the garden. Geneva drowned herself the same day that Nathan Pedlar asked Dorinda to marry him.

Together Dorinda and Nathan prospered. She was now thirty-eight and still felt young. John Abner Pedlar, Nathan's crippled son, looked to her for help, and she gave it willingly. Nathan's other children meant less to her, and she was glad when they married and moved away. When Five Oaks was offered for sale, Dorinda and Nathan bought it for six thousand dollars. As Jason signed over the papers to her, Dorinda noticed that he was his dirty, drunken old father all over again.

Dorinda devoted the next few years to restoring Five Oaks. John Abner was still her friend and helper. There were reports that Jason was living in an old house in the pine woods and drinking heavily. Dorinda, busy with her house and dairy farm, had little time for neighborhood gossip. One day, Nathan took the train to the city to have a tooth pulled and to attend a lawsuit. The train was wrecked, and Nathan was killed while trying to save the lives of the other passengers. He was given a hero's funeral. The years following Nathan's death were Dorinda's happiest, for as time passed, she realized that she had regained, through her struggle with the land, her own integrity and self-respect.

One day, hunters found Jason sick and starving in the woods. Her neighbors assumed that Dorinda would take him in. Unwillingly, she allowed him to be brought to Old Farm, where she engaged a nurse to look after him. In a few months, Jason died. Many of the people at the funeral came only out of curiosity, and a pompous minister said meaningless things about Jason, whom he had never known. Dorinda felt nothing as she stood beside the grave, for her memories of Jason had outlived her emotions. She sensed that, for good or ill, the fervor and fever of her life, too, had ended.

Critical Evaluation:

Barren Ground is a disturbing novel because it represents the ways life can be lived under the most harrowing of circumstances. Ellen Glasgow writes about farmers faced with the difficulties of making an unwilling earth—a wasteland, in fact—yield a living. A few triumph against the odds; some do their best and barely survive; others give up and die early. All except those who give up work exceedingly hard. Glasgow believes, as she says in the 1933 preface to *Barren Ground*, that "the novel is experience illumined by imagination." In this novel, as in much of her work, she is faithful to her own experience in her native Virginia but colors that experience with a dark imagination that views human life as a constant struggle in which even the strong do not always survive. Those who do survive must adjust their idealism to fit reality.

The main theme of the novel is stated by its main character, Dorinda Oakley, who thinks that for the majority, life is "barren ground where they have to struggle to make anything grow." Dorinda has experienced more than the hardships of making a living from the soil of rural Virginia. At the age of twenty, she had the seed of love planted in her heart, only to have it uprooted by her lover's weakness. After that, as regards passion, her heart is indeed barren ground. Glasgow seems to suggest that Dorinda's life is also barren ground as far as happiness is concerned. To women, Glasgow writes, "love and happiness [are] interchangeable terms." After Jason jilts her, Dorinda spends the rest of her life distrusting men and building emotional, mental, physical, and financial walls to protect herself from them. She marries Nathan Pedlar only because she fears loneliness and because he is submissive to her and willing to live without physical intimacy. Dorinda becomes a cynic about love and marriage, believing that they seldom, if ever, go together; even when they do, the love does not endure.

Dorinda, like the characters of Thomas Hardy novels, is driven by forces beyond her control, by the "eternal purpose." She feels that the trivial incidents in life are the crucial ones. Those incidents—Nathan's train trip that results in his heroic death, her meeting with Jason in the road, her poor aim when the gun goes off, the particular place and moment when she falls on Fifth Avenue—changed the course of her life, yet none of them could have been foreseen or prevented. Dorinda believes that only once, in the hospital in New York, had the incident or device of fortune been in her favor. Much like Theodore Dreiser's Carrie Meeber or Hurstwood, she is "a straw in the wind, a leaf on a stream."

Glasgow, as she says in her preface, believes, however, that "character is fate," and that the individual destinies of her characters are partly determined by the nature they inherited, by, that is, their blood: Destiny is in the genes. The "vein of iron" that keeps Dorinda struggling (and that helps her to succeed) is a product of the "sense" of her great-grandfather, a member of the

Southern upper class, and the physical strength of her father, a member of the "poor white" class. Jason fails, like his father had, because of "bad blood." Even though unforeseen events control individual destiny, character determines what an individual does in the circumstances.

As an archetype, Dorinda is at first a Medea figure who falls in love with a Jason who will forsake her for another. She becomes, however, an Artemis or an Atalanta, the devouring female who remains estranged from the male physically and psychologically. In the final analysis, Glasgow shows that all individuals are always isolated from their fellow creatures. Beyond that, Dorinda is also, paradoxically, an Earth Mother, who causes the soil to be productive and who keeps the best cows in the state. Her maternal instinct is satisfied by this bond with the soil and by her adoption through marriage of Nathan's children, in particular John Abner. Although she is never psychologically a whole person, Dorinda does her best given her character and experience. She achieves a wholeness that most never achieve. Although she is a woman, she farms better than most of the men in her rural community. Her black hair symbolizes her relationship with the earth, as its opposite, the sky, is symbolized in her blue eyes. Her experiences are much like her mother's (an early separation from a lover, a loveless marriage), but she manages to combine her mother's habit of hard work with a contentment her morally repressed mother never had. Jason goes away to New York and comes back to a dying father just as Dorinda does. Yet Jason allows life to conquer him. Dorinda does not.

Bibliography:
Bond, Tonette. "Pastoral Transformations in *Barren Ground.*" *Mississippi Quarterly* 32 (Fall, 1979): 565-576. Discusses how Glasgow shows Dorinda's pastoral vision enabling her to re-create her internal and external landscapes. Relates Dorinda's spiritual revitalization to that of the defeated South; both need imagination, energy, and innovation to reclaim the Arcadian ideal.

Harrison, Elizabeth Jane. *Female Pastoral: Women Writers Re-Visioning the American South.* Knoxville: University of Tennessee Press, 1991. Considers Dorinda as a new type of pastoral heroine for her time. Suggests that she steals the role of hero from male characters in the novel and atones for this at the end.

Levy, Helen Fiddyment. *Fiction of the Home Place: Jewett, Cather, Glasgow, Porter, Welty, and Naylor.* Jackson: University Press of Mississippi, 1992. Discusses the place of *Barren Ground* in Glasgow's personal and literary development. Connects the author's rejection of her female destiny and her desire for the independence and achievement allowed males with her heroine's.

MacKethan, Lucinda H. *Daughters of Time: Creating Woman's Voice in Southern Story.* Athens: University of Georgia Press, 1990. Presents an alternative to the view of Dorinda Oakley as someone who is barren and cold and rejects her traditional female role. Relates Dorinda's life to the feminine through the Demeter myth that affirms nature, the life cycle, and female resiliency and strength.

Thiebaux, Marcelle. *Ellen Glasgow.* New York: Frederick Ungar, 1982. Discusses three themes developed in *Barren Ground:* the feminist theme of the protagonist's independent life; the Calvinist theme of her inheritance from her Scotch-Irish ancestors; and the agrarian theme of her attachment to the land.

BARRIO BOY
The Story of a Boy's Acculturation

Type of work: Autobiography
Author: Ernesto Galarza (1905-1984)
Type of plot: Historical
Time of plot: 1910-1920
Locale: Mexico and California
First published: 1971

> *Principal personages:*
> ERNESTO GALARZA, the narrator
> HENRIQUETA, his mother
> AUNT ESTHER, his guardian
> UNCLE JOSÉ, his closest companion
> UNCLE GUSTAVO

The Story:

Ernesto was born in an adobe in a small Mexican village that was hidden away in a mountainous region. It was so small that the town had only one street, no police, no fire department, and no mayor. The village belonged to everyone.

Ernesto's parents were divorced, so Ernesto lived with his mother, Henriqueta, as part of the property settlement. He also was reared by his Uncle Gustavo, his aunt Esther, and his Uncle José. Part of his daily chores was to watch over his pets: Coronel, his rooster; Nerón, his watchdog; and Relámpago, a burro who really did not belong to anyone.

Ernesto did not attend school so he did not know how to read or write well. Having a career was not as important as being able to prove his manhood through hard manual labor. Beginning at age seven, Ernesto learned that being a man meant working day and night without pay.

One summer day, a great hurricane showered the village. The street was flooded, and everyone worked together to save what was left of houses and corrals. Before the stories of the flood could be talked about, the *rurales*, special government police, entered the town looking for young men to be drafted in the army for the revolution. They did not allow anyone to leave. Fearing the worst, Henriqueta decided the family must escape for Tepic. The night before the family slipped away north, Halley's comet appeared in the sky. According to Don Cleofas, the oldest person in the village, this was an omen of something serious.

After a day and a half traveling on horseback, Ernesto and his family arrived in Tepic and settled in their new home. Life was different. Uncle Gustavo and José now worked for pay, and the marketplace became an adventure for Ernesto. He even began to be educated at home. The problems of the revolution his mother thought she left behind at the old village (which people called Jalco) followed them to Tepic. Good news, however, arrived in the form of jobs on the Southern Pacific Railroad. The family again traveled north to Acaponeta. Living there, close to the railroad station, often meant that revolutionaries came to the family's door. With every grace, Henriqueta served the men. Soon, a letter from Uncle Gustavo ordered them to leave Tepic for Urias and away from the violence. The stay in Urias did not last long, as the revolution soon entered Urias.

Ernesto and his family moved now further north to Leandro Valle, Mazatlán. Living there, Ernesto soon began to work, to earn money, and to become part of a gang. He also started first grade. However, life in Leandro Valle did not last long either, and they left for the United States.

After many weeks in Tucson, Ernesto and his mother traveled by train to Sacramento to meet with Uncle Gustavo and José. With his limited English, Ernesto and his mother found their way in Sacramento, where they lived in an apartment on 418 L Street. Ernesto encountered many mixed nationalities, including Japanese, Chinese, and Filipino. The stay in the United States was to remain permanent. Whether it be by season or not, José found work. Their homes in run-down places were always temporary.

Life in the United States was different for Ernesto. There were no marketplaces, no plazas, no close neighbors. Living in the United States also changed the way some Mexicans behaved. For Ernesto, who entered first grade and worked odd jobs, his English became better. Still, Ernesto and his family remained a Mexican family. *Pocho*, the unflattering name for an Americanized Mexican, was what Henriqueta jokingly called Ernesto.

With the remarriage of his mother, the family decided to move into a new house in Oak Park, a house outside the barrio surrounded by English-speaking neighbors. Ernesto made friends with a neighborhood boy, Roy, and soon bought a secondhand bicycle. He explored his new neighborhood and got a job as a carrier for the city's newspaper. Enrolled at Bret Harte School, Ernesto's knowledge of English developed quickly. His family was impressed by his education and a phone was installed for his use.

Homesickness became a problem for his family, but for Ernesto the problem was his responsibility of taking care of his younger sisters. This ordinary daily routine ended when an influenza epidemic spread into the city. Uncle Gustavo died, then Ernesto's mother.

With the advice of Mrs. Dodson, the landlady, José and Ernesto looked toward the future. They moved to a rented basement room on O Street, on the edge of the barrio. Ernesto continued his education and worked odd jobs with José. He was hired as a farmhand, and he learned how to drive a tractor. He worked as a drugstore clerk, then found a job as a delivery boy, then one as a Christmas card decorator.

During his summer vacation, Ernesto worked with other barrio people in the labor camps. He saw how the laborers were mistreated by the contractors, and he went to the state authorities for help. The laborers did not appreciate his efforts. Summer ended, so Ernesto returned home, biked his way to the high school, and thought of his future.

Critical Evaluation:

Barrio Boy is aptly subtitled *The Story of a Boy's Acculturation*. Ernesto Galarza recounts his immigration northward from a small village in Nayarit, Mexico, to the edge of the barrio in Sacramento, California. His adjustments in a new country, a new language, a new lifestyle bring many changes for Galarza. Small town life did not prepare Galarza for the differences he would encounter in the cities of Mazatlán and later Sacramento. Ernesto's tenacity and strength, however, allow him not only to survive but also to maintain his sense of identity as a Mexican. Acculturation, then, for Galarza, is not the process of abandoning one's culture but rather is the process of adaptation. This autobiography speaks to those who have traveled to the United States and who have faced the challenges of acculturation.

The autobiography is structured into five sections. Each part confronts Galarza's step-by-step process from being a Mexican to becoming a Mexican American. The first section, "In the Mountain Village," is a study in provincial Mexican life. Everyday mannerisms, traditions, and roles are poignantly played out. The lyrical description of the village and its people reads like a pastoral. One of the longest sections of the autobiography, the first section provides a clear and distinct portrait of Galarza's life before his move north.

When the family leaves the village, life becomes much less idyllic. Being able to settle down proves difficult during a revolution. "Peregrinations," the longest section of the book, tells this part of Galarza's story. Galarza also speaks sincerely of the struggles of the people, whether on burros or on foot, who move northward seeking refuge.

Realizing their best hope lies in emigrating to the United States, the family, in "North From Mexico," makes the decisive journey. Galarza details the train ride he and his mother endured. The train created in him a discomfort and an uneasiness toward the American people, whom he found both "agreeable and deplorable."

"Life in the Lower Part of Town" reflects the determination of Galarza and his family to benefit from the opportunities afforded to them. He begins his journey toward acculturation as he learns English and studies in school. He also acknowledges the differences in lifestyle between the Mexican and the Anglo American. He also points out his poverty.

The acculturation of Ernesto Galarza becomes complete in "On the Edge of the Barrio." Having to learn on his own, Galarza worked toward a promise of success. He participates, in his education, in society, and he becomes part of the American working class. His new identity as a Mexican American, because of his social participation, illustrates the positive balance Galarza maintained as a Mexican living in an Anglo American society.

With his life story set against the historical background of the Mexican Revolution, Galarza becomes a representative of his era. In essence, *Barrio Boy* offers him a forum to express, to share, and to educate his readers to undiscovered events in history on a personal level. In fact, Galarza seems to want his readers to participate fully in his journey, for he provides a glossary of the Spanish words he felt he could not translate.

Historically speaking, then, *Barrio Boy* is significant in three ways. First, in the recounting of his migratory travels, Galarza exemplifies the immigrant who is uprooted by a social or political event. The long journey to safety and rest is poignantly depicted in the actions of his uncles Gustavo and José. Second, *Barrio Boy* reveals the destitute conditions of the farm laborer. Galarza learned through personal experience the disgusting working conditions and inhumane treatment against migrant workers. Galarza allows his autobiography to become a voice for the oppressed farmworkers. Finally, to acknowledge that in his case the process of acculturation did not psychologically damage him illustrates Galarza's theme for his autobiography: To be able to maintain a cultural identity in a world that focuses on individuality is a social triumph. Certainly, many times in the narrative, Galarza notes homesickness and the comfort of being surrounded by people who speak his language. Yet, he is also able to participate outside the security of his barrio. Accordingly, then, *Barrio Boy* is more than just an immigrant story. Galarza demonstrates the potential of many immigrant Americans who seek new opportunities.

Carmen Carrillo

Bibliography:

Flores, Lauro. "Chicano Autobiography: Culture, Ideology and the Self." *The Americas Review* 18, no. 2 (Summer, 1990): 80-91. Explores the style, characterization, and structure of the autobiography. Asserts that *Barrio Boy* shows how society influences the individual.

Márquez, Antonio C. "Self and Culture: Autobiography as Cultural Narrative." *Bilingual Review* 14, no. 3 (September-December, 1987/1988): 57-63. Focusing on the theme of acculturation and adaptability, examines *Barrio Boy* as a celebration of individuality and culture. The themes of self-motivation and cultural pride are emphasized.

Robinson, Cecil. *Mexico and the Hispanic Southwest in American Literature*. Rev. ed. Tucson: University of Arizona Press, 1977. Offers an analysis of *Barrio Boy* as an autobiography and social commentary. The place and contribution of *Barrio Boy* to the Hispanic literary tradition is also examined.

Rocard, Marcienne. *The Children of the Sun: Mexican-Americans in the Literature of the United States*. Translated by Edward G. Brown, Jr. Tucson: University of Arizona Press, 1989. Analyzes the internal struggles and conflicts in *Barrio Boy* as well as other Hispanic novels and autobiographies. *Barrio Boy* is examined as the portrayal of acculturation from the immigrant's point of view. Also examines the politics of acculturation.

Saldívar, Ramón. "Ideologies of the Self: Chicano Autobiography." *Diacritics* 15, no. 3 (Fall, 1985): 25-34. Analyzing the language and characterization of *Barrio Boy*, examines individuality and the problems associated with moving from one culture to another. *Barrio Boy* is compared to other Chicano autobiographies.

BARRY LYNDON

Type of work: Novel
Author: William Makepeace Thackeray (1811-1863)
Type of plot: Picaresque
Time of plot: Eighteenth century
Locale: England, Ireland, and Europe
First published: serial, 1844; book, 1852

> *Principal characters:*
> REDMOND BARRY, a braggart and a bully
> LADY HONORIA LYNDON, his wife
> LORD BULLINGDON, her son

The Story:

Deprived of wealth and estates by relatives, Widow Barry devoted herself to the careful rearing of her son Redmond. Uncle Brady took a liking to the lad and asked the widow for permission to take the child to his ancestral home, Brady Castle. While there, Barry was treated kindly by his uncle. One of his cousins, Mick, persecuted him, however, and Mrs. Brady hated him. Aggressive by nature, Barry invited animosity; his landless pride in his ancestral heritage led him into repeated neighborhood brawls until he had fought every lad in the area and acquired the reputation of a bully. At age fifteen, he fell in love with twenty-four-year-old Nora Brady, who was in love with Captain John Quinn, an Englishman. Deeply in debt, Uncle Brady hoped that Nora would marry the captain, who had promised to pay some of the old man's debts. Thoroughly unscrupulous and lacking in appreciation for his uncle's kindness, Barry insulted Quinn in a fit of jealousy and wounded him in a duel.

Believing the captain dead, Barry hurriedly set out on the road to Dublin. On the way, he befriended a Mrs. Fitzsimons, the victim of a highway robbery. She took him to her castle where Barry spent some of his own money in a lavish attempt to create a good impression. When he had lost all his money through high living and gambling, Mrs. Fitzsimons and her husband were glad to see him leave.

Barry next took King George's shilling and enlisted for a military expedition in Europe. Boarding the crowded and filthy ship, he learned that Captain Quinn had not died after all but had married Nora Brady; the pistols had been loaded only with tow. Detesting service in the British army, Barry deserted to the Prussians. At the end of the Seven Years' War, he was garrisoned in Berlin. By that time, he was known as a thorough scoundrel and a quarrelsome bully. Sent by Frederick the Great to spy on the Chevalier Balibari, suspected of being an Austrian agent, Barry learned that the officer was his own father's brother, Barry of Ballybarry. This elderly gentleman actually made his way by gambling, rising and falling in wealth as his luck ran. When the gambler decided to leave Berlin, Barry, eager to escape from Prussian service, disguised himself and fled to Dresden. There he joined his uncle, who was high in favor at the Saxon court.

Barry, living like a highborn gentleman, supported himself by operating a gambling table. At the court of the Duke of X—, he pursued Countess Ida, one of the wealthiest heiresses in the duchy. Disliking the countess personally but greatly admiring her fortune, he ruthlessly set about to win her from her fiancé, the Chevalier De Magny. Gambling with the hapless man,

Barry won from him all he possessed. At last, De Magny agreed to play for the hand of Countess Ida and lost. Barry's scheme might have succeeded if he had not become involved in a court intrigue. He was forced to leave the duchy.

Roaming through all the famous cities of Europe, Barry acquired a wide reputation as a skillful gambler. At Spa, he met Lord Charles and Lady Honoria Lyndon who held the former Barry lands, and he decided to marry Lady Lyndon following the death of her sick husband. A year later, hearing that Lord Charles had died at Castle Lyndon in Ireland, he set out to woo Lady Honoria. Employing numerous underhanded devices, which included blackmail, bribery, dueling, and intimidation, Barry forced himself upon Lady Lyndon, who at first resisted his suit. Barry, however, pursued the lady relentlessly, bribing her servants, spying on her every move, paying her homage, and stealing her correspondence. When she fled to London to escape his persistent attentions, he followed her. At last, he overcame her aversion and objections, and she agreed to become his wife. Adding her name to his own, he became Barry Lyndon, Esq.

Although she was haughty and overbearing by nature, Lady Lyndon soon yielded to the harsh dominance of her husband, who treated her brutally and thwarted her attempts to control her own fortune. After a few days of marriage, the Lyndons went to Ireland, where he immediately assumed management of the Lyndon estates. Living in high fashion, he spent money freely in order to establish himself as a gentleman in the community. When Lady Lyndon attempted to protest, he complained of her ill temper; if she pleaded for affection, he called her a nag. The abuse he showered upon her was reflected in the way he used her son, Lord Bullingdon, who, unlike his mother, did not submit meekly to Barry's malice.

The birth of Bryan Lyndon added to Barry's problems. Since the estate was entailed upon Lord Bullingdon, young Bryan would have no rights of inheritance to Lady Lyndon's property. To provide for his son, Barry sold some of the timber on the estates over the protests of Lord Bullingdon's guardian. Barry gave the money obtained to his mother who used it to repurchase the old Barry lands, which Barry intended to bequeath to his son. Barry was actively despised in the community, but through foul means and cajolery, he won a seat in Parliament and used his victory to triumph over his enemies.

Barry made no attempt to disguise his contempt and disgust for his wife, who under his profligacy had become petulant. When she rebelled against his conduct, he threatened to remove Bryan from her; she was subdued many times in this manner. Little Bryan was completely spoiled by his father's indulgence. Barry also contrived to rid himself of his stepson, who finally obliged by running off to America to fight against the rebels. Barry's enemies used Lord Bullingdon's flight to slander the Irish upstart, and the young man's legal guardians continued their efforts to curb the wasteful dissipation of Lady Lyndon's wealth, which was dwindling under Barry's administration. In the end, Barry's unpopularity caused him to lose his seat in Parliament.

Heavily in debt, he retired to Castle Lyndon. When Lord Bullingdon was reported killed in America, young Bryan became heir to the estates. Soon afterward, the boy died when thrown from his horse. His death caused Lady Lyndon such anguish that a report spread that she was mad. Barry and his mother, now the mistress of Castle Lyndon, treated Lady Lyndon shabbily. Keeping her virtually a prisoner, spying on her every move, and denying her intercourse with her friends, they almost drove her mad. Under the necessity of signing some papers, she tricked Barry into taking her to London. There her indignant relatives and Lord George Poynings, Lady Lyndon's former suitor, gathered to free the unhappy woman from his custody; Barry was trapped.

Offered the alternative of going to jail as a swindler or of leaving the country with an annuity of three hundred pounds, he chose the latter. Later, he returned secretly to England and nearly succeeded in winning back his weak-willed wife. His attempt was foiled, however, by Lord Bullingdon, who reappeared suddenly after he had been reported dead. Barry was thrown into the Fleet Prison, where he died suffering from delirium tremens.

Critical Evaluation:

Published three years before *Vanity Fair* (1847-1848), William Makepeace Thackeray's *The Luck of Barry Lyndon: A Romance of the Last Century*, as it was titled in serial presentation, is a minor masterpiece of classic comedy, and it embodies many of the same concerns with sham, materialistic values, and egoism found in the later novel. Both novels feature the kind of antihero more familiar, perhaps, to later readers than to Thackeray's contemporaries. In fact, there are distinct resemblances between *Vanity Fair*'s picara, Becky Sharpe, whose sharp practices, manipulation, and emotional blackmail arouse ambivalent delight in readers, and Barry, the appealing rogue who, reprehensible as his values may be, is yet true to his own code. His autobiography, cast in the form of an adult's remembrance of about forty years of his life, shows Thackeray's skillful handling of time and his imaginative creation of picaresque episodes, in the course of which Barry ingenuously, naïvely, yet arrogantly reveals his vices and ambiguous virtues.

Thackeray is much more than a social historian in *Barry Lyndon*. The three-part arrangement of the novel shows Barry as an adolescent in Ireland, where he falls in love for the first time; then abroad in English and Prussian military service, gambling in Europe; and finally, upon his return to England, having become militarily and financially successful, making a marital conquest as well. In the tradition of Daniel Defoe, Tobias Smollett, and Henry Fielding, Thackeray presents a picaro who reveals the tawdriness of empire and gaming as well as reflecting the kinds of truths by which all people deceive themselves.

The tone of *Barry Lyndon*, with its combination of the conversational and the confessional, may not seem all that close to the tone of the author's mature fiction. However suited to the character the unself-conscious admissions of the narrative are, there is an air of levity and inconsequence about them that is missing from Thackeray's later works. Yet the reader will not have read very much of *Barry Lyndon* before realizing that the hero's unaffected air of candor and completeness is being used to highly ironic purposes by the author. The result is that the novel may be thought to consist of two narratives: that of the hero and that of the author. The latter undermines the former, and the causes of this disruption are the result of nothing more than the hero's excesses. This complicated narrative interplay has a number of noteworthy consequences.

On the one hand, it suggests that the author's intent is not to indulge his hero's narrative or to let it stand on its own account. Barry's amoral, improvised, opportunistic existence is not merely a colorful yarn or an episodic tissue of adventures. Its excesses produce their own moral counterpoint. This anticipates the situation in *Vanity Fair*, where Becky Sharpe's unprincipled behavior calls forth the author's most stringent moral irony. In that novel, Thackeray contrasts a world of dazzling extravagance and exploitation with the virtues of domesticity and conjugal love. Thackeray's moral vision is not yet as comprehensively laid out in *Barry Lyndon*, but its origins are clearly visible, lacking only a medium other than the author's implicit critique of his hero to articulate them.

The issue of tone and its implications are not confined to aesthetic considerations alone but pertain also to the question of genre. It is known from the publication of Thackeray's own nonfictional writings that he had a strong interest in English eighteenth century fiction and that one of his main interests was the manner in which he maintained lines of continuity with earlier novelistic practices.

It is a common critical practice to relate *Barry Lyndon* to Henry Fielding's *The Life of Jonathan Wild the Great* (1743). Fielding's novel, however, was a satirical adaptation of a popular genre literature of roguery. Works in this category depicted the brazen, criminal, and generally subversive careers of adventurers, men and women without attachment, commitment, or consistency, whose behavior represented a form of freedom as dangerous for the settled citizenry who came their way as for these protagonists themselves. This category owes much to picaresque fiction, one of the formative imaginative influences on the development of the novel. In *Barry Lyndon*, Thackeray reveals the intersection of an eighteenth century form with a nineteenth century sensibility, allowing on the one hand the protagonist's extemporaneous existence but ensuring on the other hand that such an existence is being depicted to exemplify a code of values that is the antithesis of those with which the protagonist identifies. Thackeray was by no means the only author of his day to adapt the literature of roguery to contemporary purposes— evidence of similar interests may be found in the work of Charles Dickens, and another contemporary of theirs, Harrison Ainsworth, made a successful career from the same practice.

Although Thackeray fully engages his moralizing imagination in *Barry Lyndon*, he appears also to distance himself from his own effects by permitting Barry to tell his own story—so that his own words will condemn him—and by conceiving his narrative in terms of an already existing genre. A further, and equally revealing, distancing tactic is the work's Irish dimension. If Thackeray were interested merely in drawing a moral lesson by depicting the counterproductive career of a picaresque hero, there would be no need to invoke an Irish element. The fact that one exists may be attributed to the commercial success achieved by Irish novelists in the early Victorian literary marketplace with their own picaresque works. Many of these works placed their protagonists in the setting of the Napoleonic wars, in which the improvisations and quirks of fortune endemic to the picaresque hero's career became identified with a positive, and even virtuous, historical outcome. In *Barry Lyndon*, Thackeray undoes such possibilities, for Barry's military service is not with the forces of the Crown. By this means, as well as by depicting Barry's empty social pretension and his generally amoral behavior, Thackeray presents him as retaining a stereotypical Irishness. Thackeray uses this ethnic label as a synonym for Barry's failure to integrate himself with the morality, decorum, laws of property, and codes of gentlemanliness which a responsible member of British society must observe. Thackeray ultimately presents the reader with an ideological and political judgment as well as a moral one.

"Critical Evaluation" updated by George O'Brien

Bibliography:
Altinal, A. Savkar. *Thackeray and the Problem of Realism.* New York: Peter Lang, 1986. Includes a chapter in which *Barry Lyndon* is discussed in the light of Thackeray's beginnings as a novelist. Discussion focuses mainly on the hero's character. Also discusses the novel's artistic achievements and its place in Thackeray's development.

Colby, Robert. "*Barry Lyndon* and the Irish Hero." *Nineteenth Century Fiction* 21 (September, 1966): 109-130. Locates the novel in the Thackeray canon and identifies sources for the story. Also discusses Thackeray's narrative method, as well as relevant contextual matters. The main emphasis is on the ways in which the novel reveals Thackeray's creative rereading of contemporary Irish fiction.

Hardy, Barbara. *Forms of Feeling in Victorian Fiction*. London: Peter Owen, 1985. Contains a chapter on Thackeray that makes a number of pertinent observations about *Barry Lyndon*. Analyzes the novel's comic character and the hero's emotional nature. Also notes the relation between these features and the novel's structure.

Miller, Mark Crispin. "*Barry Lyndon* Reconsidered." *Georgia Review* 30 (Winter, 1976): 827-853. Analyzes Stanley Kubrick's film adaptation of the novel, focusing on the director's vision. Evaluates the manner in which he deals with such themes as heritage and role-playing and assesses the differences between novel and film.

Parker, David. "Thackeray's *Barry Lyndon*." *Ariel* 6 (October, 1975): 68-80. Relates the novel to eighteenth century literature of roguery. Examines Thackeray's tonal and formal adaptations of that literary model, as well as his moralistic approach to his material.

BARTHOLOMEW FAIR

Type of work: Drama
Author: Ben Jonson (1573-1637)
Type of plot: Satire
Time of plot: Early seventeenth century
Locale: Smithfield, London
First performed: 1614; first published, 1631

> *Principal characters:*
> JOHN LITTLEWIT, a minor city official
> WIN-THE-FIGHT or WIN, his wife
> DAME PURECRAFT, her mother, a widow
> ZEAL-OF-THE-LAND BUSY, a Puritan, suitor of Dame Purecraft
> WINWIFE, Busy's rival, a London gallant
> QUARLOUS, Winwife's friend, a gamester
> BARTHOLOMEW COKES, a foolish young squire
> GRACE WELLBORN, Cokes's fiancée
> WASPE, Cokes's servant
> ADAM OVERDO, a justice of the peace
> DAME OVERDO, his wife
> URSULA, owner of a booth at Bartholomew Fair
> TROUBLE-ALL, a madman

The Story:

Winwife, a London gallant, came courting Dame Purecraft, a widow who lived with her daughter, Win-the-Fight, and her son-in-law, John Littlewit, a proctor. Littlewit disclosed to Winwife that Dame Purecraft had been told by fortune-tellers that she would marry, within a week, a madman. In this connection, Littlewit suggested to Winwife that he deport himself in the manner of his companion Tom Quarlous, a city madcap.

Quarlous, entering in search of Winwife, kissed Win-the-Fight several times until Winwife cautioned him to desist. Littlewit, who was not too acute, actually encouraged Winwife and Quarlous to be free with his wife. Littlewit also revealed to his visitors that Dame Purecraft had a new suitor, one Zeal-of-the-Land Busy, a Puritan from Banbury. Busy had taken lodgings in Littlewit's house.

Humphrey Waspe, the testy old servant of young Bartholomew Cokes, a foolish gentleman of the provinces, came to Littlewit to pick up a marriage license for his master. Soon afterward, Cokes appeared in company with two women. One was Mistress Overdo, his natural sister and the wife of Justice Adam Overdo; the other was Grace Wellborn, Cokes's fiancée and Overdo's ward. It was clear that Waspe was the servant of an extremely light-headed young man. Cokes declared his intention of squiring Grace to Bartholomew Fair before they returned to Middlesex. Waspe objected, but finally resigned himself to the inevitable. Winwife and Quarlous, sensing fun at hand, decided to go along. Not wishing to miss the fun, Littlewit declared that he would go too. Dame Purecraft and Busy both rationalized puritan strictures against attending fairs and gave the young couple permission to go so that Win might eat roast pig; Busy and the widow declared their intention of going with them to Bartholomew Fair.

In disguise and with a notebook in his pocket, Justice Overdo had gone to the fair to seek out criminals and to record lawlessness. Suspecting Ursula, a seller of beer and roast pig, Overdo stopped at her booth to test her. As he drank, various shady personalities entered the booth. He asked Mooncalf, Ursula's handyman, for information about them all, but Mooncalf's replies were always vague. Overdo conceived a feeling of sympathy for one Edgeworth, a young cutpurse, although not suspecting Edgeworth's profession. Overdo decided he should rescue the young man from such knavish company.

At Ursula's booth, where Winwife and Quarlous condescendingly stopped for a drink, Quarlous became involved in a fight with Knockem, a horse trader. Ursula, running from her kitchen to throw hot grease on Winwife and Quarlous, stumbled, and the grease burned her leg. Knockem declared that he would operate her booth while she sat by to oversee the business.

Cokes and his party arrived at the fair and made their way to Ursula's booth, where Overdo warned them against the evils of tobacco and ale. Edgeworth stole Cokes's purse and gave it to his confederate, Nightingale, a ballad monger. Mistress Overdo observed that Overdo, who was in disguise, spoke much in the manner of her own husband, Justice Adam Overdo. Missing his purse, Cokes declared indiscreetly that he had another one and that he defied cutpurses by placing it on his belt where the other one had been. Waspe, suspecting Overdo to be the cutpurse, thrashed the justice. As Overdo cried for help, Cokes and his party left Ursula's booth.

Busy led Littlewit, Win, and Dame Purecraft into the fair, after cautioning them to look neither to left nor right and to avoid the sinful booths as they marched toward Ursula's booth to get roast pig. While they waited to be served, Overdo reappeared, still determined to observe the goings on, but without preaching. Cokes and his party, burdened with trinkets, also returned to the booth. Waspe was miserable because Cokes was spending his money on every foolish article offered him. When a toyman and a gingerbread woman argued over customer rights, Cokes bought the wares of both and even retained the toyman to provide entertainment at the forthcoming marriage. Nightingale and Edgeworth feared that Cokes would spend all of his money before they could get at him again. Nightingale sang a ballad while Edgeworth lifted the second purse from the enchanted Cokes's belt. Winwife and Quarlous looked on with amusement. When Cokes realized his loss and cried out, Overdo, who was standing nearby, was seized as a suspect. Waspe, sure that Cokes would lose everything he possessed, took into his care a black box containing the marriage license.

Quarlous, meanwhile, disclosed to Edgeworth that he had been detected stealing Cokes's purse. In exchange for secrecy, Edgeworth promised to steal the contents of the black box.

Busy and his friends ate pork at Ursula's booth. Encountering the toyman and the gingerbread woman, Busy, in a moment of religious zeal, attempted to seize the wicked toys and upset the tray of gingerbread figures. The toyman called police officers, who took Busy, followed by Dame Purecraft, away to be put in the stocks. Littlewit and Win were now free to enjoy the fair as they chose.

Overdo, also in the stocks, overheard to his shame that he had a reputation for harshness in meting out justice. He did not reveal himself when the officers took him and Busy away to face Justice Overdo.

While Cokes was looking for the toyman and the gingerbread woman, in hopes of getting his money back from them, he was intercepted by Nightingale and Edgeworth, who tricked him out of his hat, jacket, and sword. Wretched Cokes began to understand at last that he was being grievously abused at the fair.

In another part of the fair, Winwife and Quarlous, who had attracted Grace away from her group, drew swords to decide a dispute as to who should have Cokes's attractive young fiancée. Grace bade them not to fight; at her suggestion, each wrote a word on a tablet. The first passerby was to choose the word he liked the better. The one whose word was thus chosen would win the hand of Grace, who had decided that Cokes was not the man for her. This business was interrupted, however, when Edgeworth urged both men to watch him steal the marriage license from Waspe, who was with the crowd in Ursula's booth.

Waspe and his companions, including Mistress Overdo, were drinking ale; all were quite intoxicated. When Waspe got into a scuffle with Knockem, Edgeworth took the license from the black box. Quarlous laughed at the drunken antics of one of the group and had to fight. Officers entered and seized Waspe for disturbing the peace.

Littlewit, who had written the story of the puppet show, left Win at Ursula's booth while he joined the puppeteers. While she waited, Win met Captain Whit, a bawd, who told her that he knew how she could live a life of endless pleasure and wealth.

Unable to find Justice Overdo at his lodgings, the officers returned their prisoners to the stocks. Waspe, brought to the stocks, managed to escape before his legs could be confined. When a madman engaged an officer in a scuffle, Overdo and Busy also escaped, the lock of the stocks having been left unclasped. Dame Purecraft suddenly fell in love with the madman Trouble-All, a lawyer who was distracted because of a past misunderstanding with Justice Overdo.

Later Quarlous, disguised as the madman and pursued by Dame Purecraft, returned to Winwife and Grace. Meanwhile, the real madman had chosen Winwife's word, "Palemon." Grace then declared that she would become Winwife's spouse. Overdo, disguised as a porter, came upon Quarlous. Anxious to help the man whom he had brought to distraction, Overdo gave him a seal and warrant for anything within reason that he might desire.

Cokes had found his way to the puppet theater, where he borrowed money from Littlewit. When Captain Whit, Knockem, and Edgeworth came to the theater, they had with them Win, masked, and Mistress Overdo, who was sick from too much ale. Captain Whit offered Win to Overdo for his pleasure. Waspe also came to the theater and joined his young master. The play was presented; it was an idiotic blending of the legends of Hero and Leander and Damon and Pythias. During the showing, Busy entered and threatened to break up the theater. Persuaded to argue the sinfulness of the puppet theater with one of the puppets, he was soundly defeated in the argument.

Quarlous, still disguised as the madman, came with Grace to the theater. Littlewit, who had gone in search of Win, returned without her. The true madman and Ursula entered. When all were together, Overdo declared his intention of punishing all who had engaged in rascality. When Quarlous questioned his judgment and revealed Edgeworth as a cutpurse and not an innocent youth, as the justice had supposed, Overdo decided there was such a thing as false judgment and that humanity was weak. Quarlous won the hand of Dame Purecraft. Being reassured that restitution would be made all around, Overdo invited everyone to his house for dinner.

Critical Evaluation:

Two years after the first performance of *Bartholomew Fair*, Ben Jonson published his accumulated plays in a folio volume entitled *Works*. Such an act was as unprecedented as it was audacious, because it implied both that Jonson considered himself worthy of serious attention as a writer and that the stage drama of the time should be considered an important part of literature.

Bartholomew Fair comes from Jonson's greatest period as a comic dramatist. It is one of Jonson's most direct defenses of drama (and art in general), a form that, although illusory, is a means to the truth. The play is also a clear portrayal of the reality of the world's evil and a plea for a sober appreciation of the depth of that evil. Like Jonson's *Volpone* (1605), *Epicœne* (1609), and *The Alchemist* (1610), *Bartholomew Fair* is characterized by a remarkable unity provided by a particular event or location. Plot and character are thus focused around a prevailing mania or social evil particular to that event or place. Jonson, in all these plays, makes an incisive analysis of the social scene and shows his opposition to humanity's acquisitive tendencies.

Bartholomew Fair teems with life and is probably unsurpassed for its delineation of English types—especially the low types—of the period. Jonson also held the society of his day up for criticism in such figures as Zeal-of-the-Land Busy, the Puritan; Adam Overdo, the zealous justice of the peace; and Bartholomew Cokes, the well-to-do simpleton from Middlesex. That no great evil is done in the play and that no one comes to any grief would indicate that Jonson, although a satirist, felt a real affection for all people in his beloved London.

Bartholomew Fair's main plot, if there can be said to be one, is the story, reminiscent of the *The Arabian Nights' Entertainments* of Harun-al-Rashid, of Adam Overdo's mingling, in disguise, among people to whom he metes out justice. The other plots are hinted at rather than developed. The play is framed by an "induction" given by the stagekeeper and the bookholder, in which the illusory character of drama as reality is raised for the audience's consideration. The induction includes an agreement between the audience and the author about what the audience can and cannot expect in the forthcoming drama, with a reminder that the audience should not look for real persons in the characters on stage, nor should it expect to see the Smithfield fair presented there. This disclaimer is ironic, because Jonson intends that his audience see itself in his characters. At the end of the play, the audience is invited to participate in the final celebration at Overdo's house, thus bringing the convention of life-as-drama full circle by drawing the audience into the world of the fair.

The puppet play that occurs in Act V is the center of Jonson's statement about drama and art. The puppet play is referred to in each act, since Littlewit has written the script and several characters look forward to attending the production. It is the climax of *Bartholomew Fair*; in the puppet play, the various characters' delusions are torn away. The range of possible aesthetic reactions to the illusion of drama is nicely detailed by the play-within-a-play. There is Cokes's naïve belief, Busy's Puritan denunciation of the theater, and Leatherhead's manipulation (as puppetmaster) of the audience's sensibilities. Grace, Winwife, and others in the audience not only watch the puppet show but also comment on Cokes's and Busy's comments, while Jonson's audience or reader observes those observers. Cokes worries about the injury one of the puppets may have received with a blow on the head and naïvely repeats all the puppets' lines as truth. Busy carries on the traditional Puritan argument against theater with the puppet Dionysius, charging that actors are unnatural since in theater, males dress up as females. The puppet answers that puppets are neither male nor female and lifts his garment to prove it. Busy, so gullible as to believe he was seriously arguing with a person, accepts the puppet's refutation.

The puppet show reduces the two greatest myths of Renaissance literature—the Hero and Leander ideal of love and the Damon and Pythias ideal of friendship—to the story of Hero the whore and the alehouse rowdies Damon and Pythias. The obscenities and scatological references in the puppet play are appropriate in the context, in which humanity is reduced to that most elemental level at which even sexual differences disappear, as in the puppets themselves.

The protagonist of the play is the fair itself, and Bartholomew Fair becomes a metaphor for the world. The two sets of characters—the respectable fairgoers and the disreputable fair employees—are seen to be essentially alike. They come together in the common acts of buying, drinking, and eating. Finally, there is no difference between them. The madness of the fair is the madness of the world. Certain words recur as motifs in the play, and the action comes to reflect these words: "vapours," meaning a game of arguing or irrational whims; "mad" and "madness"; "enormity"; and "warrant," meaning license. For Jonson, the whole world is regarded as mad, governed by follies and vapours, committing enormities of one sort or another, entirely governed by irrationalities, and seeking warrants of various kinds to justify its behavior.

Different characters refuse to accept the fair for what it is or to acknowledge the reality of the world's madness. Overdo disguises himself in order to catch troublemakers and mete out justice; instead, he is always too late and is mistaken for a criminal himself. Cokes is blinded by his innocent country origins and duped over and over again. Busy deceives himself by equating the fair not with the world but with sin. He reduces himself to an animal by closing his eyes to keep out the corruption of the fair and sniffing his way to Ursula's tent for roast pig. Dame Purecraft goes to the opposite extreme by embracing madness; falling in love with the madman Trouble-All is a way out of the madness of the world. As she says, "Mad do they call him! the world is mad in error, but he is mad in truth." Ursula is the only one who accepts her role without illusion or inhibition. She is a caricature of an earth mother—fat and gross, but honest.

Each of these characters, with the exception of Ursula, makes elaborate attempts to disguise from himself or herself the true nature of humanity; humanity's animal nature is fully expressed at the fair. Justice Adam Overdo is gently chastened at the end of the play by Quarlous with a line that can stand for Jonson's reminder to his audience: "Remember you are but Adam, flesh and blood." In *Bartholomew Fair*, Jonson does not try to change the world; instead he urges acceptance, without illusion, of the corruption of the world.

"Critical Evaluation" by Margaret McFadden-Gerber

Bibliography:
Barish, Jonas. *Ben Jonson and the Language of Prose Comedy.* Cambridge, Mass.: Harvard University Press, 1960. A masterful discussion of Jonson's comic language and an important starting point for study of Jonson's dramatic works. Convincingly argues for *Bartholomew Fair* as Jonson's masterpiece.

Barton, Anne. *Ben Jonson, Dramatist.* Cambridge, England: Cambridge University Press, 1984. Compelling discussion of Jonson's interests in chaos and order. Offers an important chapter on the use of names and naming—an obsessive interest of Jonson's across his career—in the context of discussions of names and language from Plato to historian William Camden, Jonson's contemporary and teacher.

Donaldson, Ian. *The World Upside Down.* Oxford, England: Clarendon Press, 1970. Views the play as festive in its forms and themes, and explores the anthropology of festivity. Excellent insights into the play's relevance to the court of James I.

Hamel, Guy. "Order and Judgement in *Bartholomew Fair.*" *University of Toronto Quarterly,* 43, no. 1 (Fall, 1973): 48-67. Discusses how the staging of the theatrically complex play reinforces Jonson's themes about justice in a complex world. An important essay for establishing Jonson's deliberate dramatic strategy for what was once considered the play's greatest flaw: its seemingly unwieldy theatrical structure.

Orgel, Stephen. *The Jonsonian Masque.* Cambridge, Mass.: Harvard University Press, 1965. Although mainly about Jonson's masques, Orgel's discussion is invaluable for his insights into Jonson's political use of costume, spectacle, and disguise, key elements of *Bartholomew Fair.*

BATOUALA

Type of work: Novel
Author: René Maran (1887-1960)
Type of plot: Social realism
Time of plot: c. 1910
Locale: Ubangi-Shari and French Equatorial Africa (present-day Central African Republic)
First published: Batouala, véritable roman nègre, 1921; definitive edition, 1938 (English
translation, 1922; definitive edition, 1972)

Principal characters:
BATOUALA, the chief of many villages
YASSIGUI'NDJA, the first and favorite of Batouala's nine wives
BISSIBI'NGUI, a handsome young man who seduces Batouala's wives
I'NDOUVOURA, another of Batouala's wives

The Story:
At the start of the day, the great chief Batouala arose at dawn to his usual morning ritual of
scratching himself, yawning, rubbing his eyes with the back of his hand, and making love to
his sleeping wife—all mundane acts he performed daily and mindlessly. His days consisted of
a morning smoke, his favorite pastime; breakfast with Yassigui'ndja, his first and favorite but
childless wife; and disdainful reflections on how the whites' way of life was different from his.
Because his thoughts and actions were tradition-inspired, he rejected anything that opposed
custom. He mused disdainfully on the ridiculousness of whites, the *boundjous,* who were "the
vilest and most perfidious of men" and therefore worthy of contempt. Their "witches' inventions"—from shoes and the radio to the telescope and bicycle—their proud claim of knowing
"everything and then some," their atrocities and exploitation of the natives in the name of
civilization, their paternalism and enslavement of the black people, and their "malignity and
omniscience" made them "terrifying." Unlike the Banda concept of life and work, the *boundjous'* concept of work meant fatigue without immediate or tangible remuneration. More
important to Batouala, the guardian of obsolete customs, the *boundjous* had robbed the villagers
of their dances and songs, their whole life. Batouala vowed that he would not tire of telling
about the *boundjous'* cruelty, duplicity, and greed until his last breath.

Batouala began his formal duties by summoning the villagers, among them Bissibi'ngui, to
remind them of the approaching feast of the Ga'nza, three days hence. Unbeknown to Batouala,
Bissibi'ngui, a young, handsome, muscular womanizer, popular among the village women, had
slept with eight of Batouala's nine wives. The exception was Yassigui'ndja, to whom Bissibi'ngui was attracted, but whom he had not yet seduced. Feeling young and "rich in unused
passion," particularly since Batouala was beginning to grow old and seemed most interested in
smoking his pipe, Yassigui'ndja was tempted to and did finally accept Bissibi'ngui's advances,
intimating through her musings that Batouala, although a good husband, no longer satisfied her
sexually.

Batouala's suspicions about Yassigui'ndja and Bissibi'ngui were aroused, and shortly thereafter confirmed, during the climax of the fertility dance of the Ga'nza ceremony, when "all
things are permitted, even perversions and sins against custom." Seized with the drunkenness
of the dance, Yassigui'ndja and Bissibi'ngui fell to the ground entwined, but they were soon
separated by the enraged, knife-wielding Batouala, who swore to skin his wife and emasculate

her seducer. The feverish festival of the Ga'nza ended abruptly, but not until Batouala's drunken father had died from a heavy dose of pernod, "foreign kene" (the white man's liquor). Because the villagers' dances and songs were forbidden by the colonial administration, Batouala's people were able to satisfy their customs only in the absence of the French commandant. At his approach, however, the drunken villagers fled, leaving behind the dead body of Batouala's father.

After the customary two-week ritual burial of Batouala's father, Batouala began planning his revenge on Bissibi'ngui. While the men were out burning the bush and arranging the nets for the great annual hunt, Yassingui'ndja and Bissibi'ngui pledged their desire to possess each other. The villagers held Yassigui'ndja responsible for the death of Batouala's father, and they threatened to ascertain her guilt by subjecting her to a series of violent tests. Bissibi'ngui agreed to leave the village and become a soldier, but not until after the great annual hunt. Joining Batouala and his hunting party, wily Bissibi'ngui began scheming to kill Batouala, the renowned hunter warrior. The hunt began, but not before a panther had bounded into their midst, causing confusion. Taking advantage of the pandemonium, Batouala aimed his lance at Bissibi'ngui, his *ouandja* (enemy), but missed. Disturbed by the confusion and Batouala's flying spear, the enraged panther mauled and disemboweled Batouala, the great chief and celebrated warrior, whose exploits in love and in war had been unparalleled.

Chaos prevailed for two weeks of exorcism, fetishes, and incantations, and the villagers finally gave up all hopes of saving their chief. While Batouala lay dying, the villagers plundered his belongings, raided his flock, and stole his weapons. In his delirium, Batouala reproached the whites. Emboldened, Yassigui'ndja and Bissibi'ngui made love in his hut. Suddenly, in one final defiant gesture, the chief rose from his bed and lunged at the pair, causing them to flee into the night. Batouala collapsed and died. The great chief had been felled by *Mourou*, the panther, and by the implacable witchcraft of *Do'ndorro*.

"The Story" by Pamela J. Olubunmi Smith

Critical Evaluation:

Batouala is important not as a story, although within its modest limits it provokes suspense and sustains interest in the affairs of its characters, but as a sensitive evocation of the experience of being an African native in the French Congo. René Maran, who was born in Martinique, served from 1909 until 1925 as a member of the diplomatic service of the French government in French Equatorial Africa. His novel, the result of six years of study and writing, is an attempt to render in a thoroughly objective manner the thoughts, beliefs, and attitudes of an African chief.

The attempt to be objective in the presentation of thoughts and attitudes necessarily involves the author's sympathetic extension of his imagination. Maran's work rings true not because he is a black man—for the knowledge of the temperament and customs of the black Africans is not inherited with skin color—but because he is concerned about the people of whose lives he writes and because, like them, he has come to love life and to condemn the French colonialism that did so much to destroy the values of life for the African natives.

The technique of the novel can be described as stream of consciousness, supplemented to some extent with descriptive passages that maintain the perspective of the African. At the same time, the persons whose experiences are being evoked are not of the same society as their author but removed, both spatially and in terms of culture, from the world of this stranger who is attempting to reconstruct the tenor of their days. To overcome the distance between himself and his subjects, Maran adopts a modification of the speech of the Africans; he writes as if their minds were speaking, and he retains their native phrasing. More important, he manages to express the smoldering, helpless anger that is part of the daily experience of Africans dominated by the white invaders. Such writing is objective in the sense that it communicates what is, in fact, part of someone's experience; but it is passionate and subjective because the reader can sense that the author shares the anger and, by sharing it, throws in his lot with that of his characters.

For a brief novel that does no more than tell how a young man's desire for the favorite wife of his chief is finally satisfied as the chief lies dying from the wound of a panther's bite, *Batouala* succeeds remarkably well in immersing the reader in a complete and foreign world. Considered didactically, the novel is powerfully effective because of its success as a representation of the experiences of the African.

Maran's indictment of the colonial administrators in the introduction to his novel speaks of the vileness of colonialization and of civilization built on corpses. He calls on his fellow writers to correct France's brutal policies. These remarks, however, impassioned as they are, do not compete in persuasive power with the sparse, bitter comments of the Africans themselves in the novel. The characters refer to the way they are treated like slaves, punished unreasonably, and used as police to keep their own brothers in line; the whites are indicted for lying, for believing lies, and for callously dismissing the suffering and death of the natives about them. One incident in the novel tells of the French commandant who, upon hearing of Batouala's imminent death, cheerfully replied that Batouala could rot to death and all the others with him.

The natives confuse conventions and objects they do not understand with magic, and in their reflections on that magic Maran depicts something of the natives' contempt for the white usurpers as well as something of their awe. In his reflections, Batouala thinks of white people's stench, particularly of their foul-smelling feet encased in skins; he marvels at the white people's ability to remove their teeth or even an eye; he thinks of white people who can look through tubes at objects far away, and he remembers the white "doctorro" who can make anyone urinate blue. At other moments, however, he remembers the colonials' drunkenness, their disregard for his children born of black women, and their promises—never kept.

If the novel expressed nothing more than the bitterness of a subjugated people, it would not be convincing and would fail to achieve its revolutionary intention. The main character, however, Batouala, is a living man and a convincing tribesman, not a mouthpiece for Maran. He knows the value of doing nothing and distinguishes between resting for the joy of it and sheer laziness. When he discovers that the young man, Bissibi'ngui, wants to possess his favorite wife, he does not accept the fact of desire, as most do in his tribe; he determines to pursue Bissibi'ngui and pounce on him like a panther, tearing him to bits. Bissibi'ngui had already been successful with eight of Batouala's nine wives, but his attempt to add Yassigui'ndja to his list of conquests is frustrated by Batouala's pride. Only an accident of the hunt, brought about by Batouala's act of hurling a javelin at Bissibi'ngui instead of at a charging panther, brings about his downfall and death. Ironically, the chief who would kill like the panther dies by the panther.

Not these events alone, but, more important, the characters' thoughts and responses intrigue the reader. While they are alive, they glory in life; the men think there is nothing better in all the world than to be strong, to run with the hunters, to be in danger, to kill the beasts that are hunted. They also delight in calling friends together, as in the circumcision ceremony, and the rhythm of their drumming conveys not only the invitation but also the spirit of it—the anticipatory joy of good food, drink, dancing, and riotous lovemaking. When a man dies from too much drink at the circumcision festival, however—as Batouala's father died—he is soon forgotten; he is no longer useful to anyone, and only convention prompts the mourning that extends over eight days in order to make sure that the man is truly dead, not merely sleeping. Death, to the native, is a sleep so profound that a man sleeping such a sleep never wakes again. The references to the gods are more conventional than pious; the concerns of the day, the joy and sorrow of it, are too compelling to leave time for either religion or metaphysics.

Batouala comes to a strange conclusion. The natives are not romanticized, they are not noble savages, but they are nevertheless noble in their direct acceptance of the needs and conventions of their lives. Even in their acceptance of superstition and in their giving way to the lust of the native dance they seem to relate themselves more honestly to the earth about them than do the white administrators who fortify their fancied superiority with alcohol, brutality, and disdain. The problem for the white colonials becomes that of using their knowledge and power to develop something more respectable than human meanness.

There is more than truth and power to *Batouala*; there is poetry, the rhythmical expression of jungle images and jungle emotions. This dimension of style gives the novel a beauty that makes the crime it depicts even more reprehensible. As long as the one people suffer under another, *Batouala* will continue to be not only a work of art but also an indictment.

Bibliography:
Cameron, Keith. *René Maran*. Boston: Twayne, 1985. A monograph of general criticism of Maran, an analysis of his fictional and nonfictional works, and an appraisal of the controversial French reception of *Batouala*. Chapter 1 provides a general background of Maran; chapter 2 sketches the genesis, structure, style, and reception of *Batouala*.

Irele, Abiola. *The African Experience in Literature and Ideology*. London: Heinemann, 1981. Contains a short but informative essay establishing *Batouala* as the likely precursor of French African prose and Maran as an important forerunner of the Negritude movement.

James, Charles. "*Batouala:* René Maran and the Art of Objectivity." *Studies in Black Literature* 4, no. 3 (1973): 19-23. Commemorates the fiftieth anniversary of Maran's 1921 Prix Goncourt for *Batouala*. Revisits its controversial reception and affirms the novel as "the very epitome of Maran's subtle and overt rebelliousness," noting its success in objectivity.

Ojo-Ade, Femi. *René Maran, the Black French Man: A Bio-Critical Study*. Washington, D.C.: Three Continents Press, 1984. Comprehensive, well-documented, critical study. Critiques Maran's passionate crusade to denounce victimization, injustice, and the evils of a colonial system. Questions the morality of Maran's stance and concludes that Maran's claim to "help the negro cause" is ambiguous and his reputation as "promoter of negro culture," paradoxical.

THE BAY OF SILENCE

Type of work: Novel
Author: Eduardo Mallea (1903-1982)
Type of plot: Existentialism
Time of plot: 1930's
Locale: Buenos Aires and Europe
First published: La bahía de silencio, 1940 (English translation, 1944)

> *Principal characters:*
> MARTÍN TREGUA, a young aspiring writer
> JIMÉNEZ, and
> ANSELMI, Martín's close friends
> MERCEDES MIRÓ, a rich woman
> GLORIA BAMBIL, a young librarian

The Story:

Martín Tregua was an aspiring writer in Buenos Aires who felt that he had to enjoy life to the fullest to improve his literary craft. Although he was an aloof young man and a newcomer to the city, he was constantly surrounded by young people who enjoyed the active night life of Buenos Aires as he did. His favorite pastime was to take long walks through the city, which exerted a passionate attraction over him that he could not understand.

Martín lived in a boardinghouse, where he had met his best friends: Jiménez, a government bureaucrat, and Anselmi, a law student. Another resident was Doctor Dervil, a well-read intellectual who engaged Martín in philosophical arguments on the purpose of life. Mercedes Miró was another close friend, a rich woman who gave Martín opportunities to meet interesting people from the Argentine upper classes.

Martín's life changed on the day he saw a woman come into a flower shop as he was finishing a purchase. He did not dare to speak to her, although her striking beauty and her absentminded manner caused him to remember having seen her thirteen years earlier, shortly after his arrival in Buenos Aires as a law student. On that day he had fallen in love with her beauty and had followed her to her home. Eventually he had found out her name and other information: She was well-born but had married a poor lawyer in rebellion against her family. Her husband became rich, however, through dubious financial arrangements with international investors.

Unable to concentrate on writing his novel but eager to keep busy, Martín joined Jiménez and Anselmi in publishing a newspaper for radical young people. Other young intellectuals joined the group, which became quite heterogeneous, and their newspaper, *El Navío* (the ship), achieved great success. The newspaper opened doors in the intellectual world of Buenos Aires to Martín. This came at a very good time because Mercedes Miró, with whom Martín had been in love, had asked that he stop seeing her. As a result, he had lost contact with the social class to which she had access.

Martín's fame was short-lived, however. Because of irreconcilable ideological differences, Martín's group decided to stop publication of *El Navío*. Even his close friends found themselves too busy with their personal problems to spend time with him. Jiménez had fallen in love with Inés Boll, a young woman who had taken a room in his boardinghouse in the hope of escaping the physical abuses of her husband. When Jiménez started dating her, he disappeared from Martín's life.

After the newspaper's demise, Martín's existentialist crisis became more acute. He could not stop thinking about the mysterious woman, who one night struck him with her car. Martín was not hurt. His monotony came to a sudden end the day that Jiménez was attacked by Inés' husband. The fight left Jiménez blind. In terror, Martín left for Europe.

His trip took him through several European countries. His final destination was Brussels, where his friend Ferrier was a physician. Ferrier was a well-read intellectual who, like Martín, enjoyed the night life of bars and nightclubs, and he introduced Martín to a number of interesting people. In Brussels, Martín seemed to recover from his depression; he started to enjoy life again and finally finished writing his novel. His knowledge of philosophy was enriched through his contact with political thinkers, vocal antifascists, and budding communists. Homesick for Buenos Aires, however, Martín returned to Argentina.

There Martín was depressed again for several months until he met Gloria Bambil. Gloria was a very reserved young librarian, but eventually she showed some interest in Martín. When he found that Gloria had read his first novel, he convinced her to go out with him. They became very dependent on each other, despite Gloria's insistence that she could not love anyone. Martín confronted her with his love, swearing that he could sense that they were in love. Gloria gave up and became his lover. She finally opened her heart to Martín and told him her personal background, including the fact that she had been abused by her father.

The mysterious woman came into Martín's life again. One night, as Gloria and Martín were having dinner, Gloria saw the woman and commented on her beauty. Martín, who had not forgotten the woman, remembered having read that she had recently lost one of her teenage sons in a riding accident. Several days later, he saw her in the same florist shop as twelve years before. As a tribute to her inexplicable influence on him, he decided to dedicate his story to her. That story is the plot of *The Bay of Silence*.

Critical Evaluation:

Eduardo Mallea is considered one of the promoters of vanguardism in Latin American literature. Extremely well read, he produces works that reflect multiple influences from European writers and intellectuals, especially from existentialist thinkers. In his own country, he was respected for his many articles as an editor of the literary section of *La Nación*, Argentina's major newspaper. It is said that his positive recommendation of a young writer resulted in that individual's immediate success.

Mallea's literary production reflects his strong inclination to the contemplative essay, in which he often explores two favorite themes: the purpose of human existence and Argentina's role in the twentieth century. Early in his career, with the publication in 1935 of *History of an Argentine Passion*, Mallea demonstrated interest in the existential quest in a systematic analysis of the history of Argentina in a worldwide context. In this autobiographical essay, Mallea brings forward issues relevant to pre-World War II society, such as social alienation and its related existential angst.

Unlike other existentialists, however, Mallea displays hope for the resolution of his characters' anguish. Following in the footsteps of the Spanish philosopher Miguel de Unamuno (1864-1936), Mallea offers in his philosophical analysis a new historical perspective by bringing a new point of view to the national history experienced by the common citizen. Mallea evaluates Argentine history by means of characters who, affected by everyday occurrences, take a closer look into those events that appear harmless but directly affect their existence. That untold history—what Mallea refers to as "the invisible Argentina"—is the core of Mallea's sociopolitical existentialism. His characters, true existential protagonists, accept the limitations of reason and view their experiences, however unimportant they may at first seem, as an intricate part of the natural or instinctual learning process. The protagonists soon learn that these experiences are not coincidental, and they start viewing them as part of the larger concept of life.

A novel of thesis, or *novela de conciencia* (novel of the conscience) to use Mallea's label, *The Bay of Silence* presents an intimate picture of the existential conflicts experienced by Martín Treba, an aspiring young writer. This strongly autobiographical novel is a fictional account of Martín's desire to document his existence, moved by an inexplicable need to address his memoirs to a mysterious woman, known throughout the novel simply as "you." Although a shadow character, the unnamed woman contributes to his existential crisis because the encounter triggers his exploration of his existential questioning. The unusual interpersonal dynamic of their casual meetings creates in Martín a feeling of aloofness or isolation, which leads him to leave the country.

The influence of the German *Bildungsroman* is obvious here. A young character feeling alienated from society leaves it for other environments and eventually returns home a mature adult. Unlike the traditional *Bildungsroman*, however, Mallea's work places the protagonist as the axis of the plot. Martín exemplifies the existentialist's efforts to use systematic analysis of his own experiences to articulate the essential isolation of the individual in a purposeless society. That fact is stressed by frequent interruption of the plot line by philosophical comments of a purely didactic nature. The lengthy novel subordinates the minimal action to the message, a constant attack on the dehumanizing influence of modern social structures.

Mallea is a literary figure, however, not a philosopher or a politician in the conventional sense. His interest in literature is evident in his vanguardist preference for spontaneous or unconscious thinking. The automatic thought, expressed in literature by means of stream of consciousness, verbalizes Martín's existentialist conflicts in a consciousness of existence. That consciousness conveys strong political convictions, that are related to Mallea's involvement in Argentine politics. After his existential crisis is over, Martín has gained a special knowledge, the so-called existential truth that affirms his natural freedom and his refusal to submit to repressive social structures.

Mallea's work may be considered a precursor of the highly experimental movement of the 1960's in Latin American literature. His literary style is an example of the influence of European literature in Latin America after World War II, a period that shaped later twentieth century literature. The fact that his characters are individuals who respond to human needs not necessarily limited to their Latin American locale makes Mallea one of the first Latin American writers of the twentieth century attractive to international readers. An intellectual with foreign connections, Mallea offers a production free of geographical boundaries. His work is the mature product of a threefold purpose of literature: personal, political, and aesthetic.

Rafael Ocasio

Bibliography:
Foster, David William, and Virginia Ramos Foster. "Mallea, Eduardo." In *Modern Latin American Literature*, edited by David William Foster and Virginia Ramos Foster. New York: Frederick Ungar, 1975. Surveys Mallea's production by providing excerpts from critical studies by various critics. A good introduction to Mallea's most famous works.
Gertel, Zunilda. "Mallea's Novel: An Inquiry into Argentine Character." In *Retrospect: Essays on Latin American Literature*, edited by Elizabeth Rogers and Timothy Rogers. York, S.C.:

Spanish Literature, 1987. A short analysis that concentrates on Mallea's oeuvre and indicates his contribution to the formation of contemporary Argentine society. Focuses on Mallea's literary and political importance.

Lewald, H. Ernest. *Eduardo Mallea*. Boston: Twayne, 1977. Excellent introduction to Mallea's life and works. Provides an overview of his works and gives strong biographical and historical background.

Mallea, Eduardo. *History of an Argentine Passion*. Translated by Myron Lichtblau. Pittsburgh, Pa.: Latin American Literary Review, 1983. Mallea's autobiographical accounts as they relate to the history of Buenos Aires and to his own literary works. Essential for readers interested in the influence of Mallea's autobiographical writings on his fictional works.

Polt, John Herman Richard. *The Writings of Eduardo Mallea*. Berkeley: University of California Press, 1981. In-depth analysis of Mallea's literary production. Places strong emphasis on contemporary literary theories. A good source for advanced readers of Mallea's works.

THE BEAUX' STRATAGEM

Type of work: Drama
Author: George Farquhar (1678?-1707)
Type of plot: Comedy of manners
Time of plot: Early eighteenth century
Locale: Lichfield, England
First performed: 1707; first published, 1707

Principal characters:
AIMWELL, a poor younger brother of Lord Aimwell
ARCHER, his friend
DORINDA, an heiress
LADY BOUNTIFUL, Dorinda's mother
MRS. SULLEN, Dorinda's sister-in-law
SULLEN, Dorinda's brother, a drunkard and a brute
FOIGARD, an Irishman disguised as a French priest

The Story:

Aimwell and Archer, two younger sons who were down to their last two hundred pounds, left London and traveled to Lichfield, where they hoped that Aimwell would marry an heiress and thus make their fortunes. Aimwell posed as his older brother, Lord Aimwell, and Archer assumed the livery of a servant. Arriving in Lichfield, they went to an inn, where the innkeeper at first mistook them for highwaymen traveling in disguise.

In Lichfield they learned that Dorinda, sister of Sullen, the local squire, was an heiress in her own right. Aimwell went to church on Sunday to call himself to her attention and to see her for himself. Back at the inn, Archer made advances to the innkeeper's daughter, Cherry. He found her ready to marry him and bring him a dower of two thousand pounds. Despite the fact that she was pretty and well-dowered, he could not, as a gentleman, make up his mind to marry her.

After church, Dorinda and her sister-in-law, Mrs. Sullen, talked about the gentleman they had seen at the service. Dorinda had already decided that she was in love with him. Citing her own unhappy marriage to the brutal and drunken Sullen, Mrs. Sullen urged her not to hurry into matrimony. Mrs. Sullen also disclosed that she was enjoying a flirtation with Bellair, a French officer held prisoner in Lichfield. Dorinda agreed to help Mrs. Sullen in her flirtation as long as Mrs. Sullen retained her honor.

At the inn, the landlord, who was in league with a gang of robbers, talked with the highwayman Gibbet about Aimwell and Archer. The evasiveness of Archer and Aimwell, when questioned, made the innkeeper and Gibbet even more certain that the two were also highwaymen. The innkeeper's daughter, overhearing the conversation, resolved to help Archer.

Meanwhile Dorinda and Mrs. Sullen tried to learn more about Aimwell. They had their servant invite his supposed servant, Archer, to the house so that they could question him about his master. While the two women made their plans, Gibbet introduced himself to Aimwell and tried to find out who Aimwell might be. They were both introduced to Foigard, who claimed to be a French priest but was actually an Irishman in disguise.

At the Sullen house, Dorinda and Mrs. Sullen questioned Archer about his master. Mrs. Sullen, seeing through his disguise as a servant, became infatuated with him. Dorinda and Mrs. Sullen later agreed that Aimwell and Archer must be hiding after a duel, since both of them were obviously gentlemen. Later in the day, Bellair came to the house. While he and Mrs. Sullen talked, Sullen entered and threatened to kill the Frenchman, even though the visitor bore no arms. Mrs. Sullen intervened, threatening her husband with a pistol.

Late in the afternoon, Aimwell pretended to be taken ill in front of the Sullen house. Carried inside for treatment, he took the opportunity to get better acquainted with Dorinda and her sister-in-law. Both Aimwell and Dorinda were soon convinced that they were in love, and Mrs. Sullen found herself more and more infatuated by Archer. While in the house, Archer discovered from the servants that Foigard, the pretended Frenchman, had plotted to introduce Bellair into Mrs. Sullen's bedroom that night.

On their return to the inn, Aimwell and Archer made Foigard acknowledge his plot against Mrs. Sullen. Rather than be taken to law, he agreed to help them. While they spoke, in another part of the inn, the landlord, Gibbet, and other highwaymen were plotting to rob the Sullen house that night. They planned to leave the country afterwards.

Early in the evening, Sir Charles Freeman, Mrs. Sullen's brother, arrived at the inn. Just returned to England, he was furious to learn that his sister had been married to Sullen. Sir Charles, knowing what a brute Sullen was, hoped to secure his sister's release from the marriage.

With the help of Foigard, Archer hid himself in Mrs. Sullen's bedroom. When he revealed himself to Mrs. Sullen, they talked until the robbers entered the house. Gibbet, entering Mrs. Sullen's room, was overpowered by Archer, who then went in pursuit of the other rogues. As he engaged two of them, Aimwell, who had been aroused by the innkeeper's daughter, arrived and aided his friend in subduing the robbers.

Archer, slightly wounded in the fray, was taken away and treated by Mrs. Sullen and her mother-in-law, Lady Bountiful. Aimwell proposed to Dorinda and was accepted. As Foigard was about to begin the impromptu ceremony, Aimwell became conscience-stricken at the thought of marrying the girl under false pretenses. When he revealed that he was not Lord Aimwell but only a poor younger brother, the ceremony was postponed.

Sir Charles Freeman arrived from the inn to visit his sister. Archer and Aimwell, who knew him well, realized that he would penetrate their disguises immediately. Dorinda put an end to their worries when she returned to tell Aimwell that his brother had died. He was now Lord Aimwell and a rich man. Aimwell could not believe the news until Sir Charles Freeman confirmed the story. Aimwell agreed quickly to give an amount equal to Dorinda's dower, ten thousand pounds, to Archer, who had helped him win her hand.

Sullen, entering on this scene of happiness, demanded to be told what Aimwell and Archer were doing in his home. He softened somewhat when told that they had rescued his family and property from robbers. Then Sir Charles questioned Sullen and discovered that he was as unhappy as Mrs. Sullen in their marriage. Sullen agreed to a separation, but he refused to give up her dower. Archer then produced some papers he had taken from the robbers, including the marriage documents and Sullen's titles to property, and gave them to Sir Charles Freeman. Faced with the loss of the documents, Sullen agreed to give up both his wife and her dower.

Everyone except Sullen joined hands and danced their celebration of the approaching marriage of Dorinda and Aimwell and Mrs. Sullen's separation from her husband. Sullen glumly sent for a drink of whiskey.

Critical Evaluation:

Restoration comedy has been condemned as immoral and superficial, but neither the moral indignation of its critics in centuries past nor the cool contempt of later commentators has diminished its appeal to audiences. Despite its carefree attitude toward moral conventions and its willingness to indulge in trivial humor, comedy written at the end of the seventeenth and in the very early eighteenth centuries continues to enjoy a theatrical and literary life.

George Farquhar's plays were written at a time when the early exuberance and rakish irreverence of Restoration comedy were beginning to give way to a more sentimental and moralized comedy. Farquhar's heart was with his Restoration masters, particularly Sir George Etherege, whose comedies from thirty years earlier reveled in cynicism, wit, and the ridicule of pretentious dandified behavior. Farquhar knew, however, that his audiences wanted to "feel" rather than to "think," so he curbed his natural bent toward wit and tried to develop a sentimental side. His Dorinda is compassionate enough, but one has the impression Farquhar would have preferred to make her more like Etherege's Harriet in *The Man of Mode* (1676)—a woman possessing no less charm and far more wit and worldly wisdom.

If Farquhar had to soften his satire, he managed to direct some of the energy that his precursors would have used for purposes of ridicule toward social criticism. It is one of the ironies of literary and dramatic history that a dramatist less comfortable with sentiment and feeling than with contempt and ridicule should have launched what we have come to know as the theater of social protest—ironic because ordinarily contempt is not associated with caring.

The cause that Farquhar championed was divorce. Here too there is delicious irony. The prevailing theme of Restoration comedy was seduction; its favorite butt, the cuckold. Infidelity was the fuel on which the cavalier engines ran. Happiness in marriage was as rare in fact as it was naïve in principle. For the famous Restoration rakes of Etherege and William Wycherley, marriage was a trap to be avoided at all cost; its greatest danger was that it exposed the husband to the risk of cuckoldry. (Sullen, at one point, even tells his wife "if you can contrive any way of being a whore without making me a cuckold, do it and welcome.") That is one danger a bachelor escaped. When Farquhar makes an eloquent case for Mrs. Sullen's liberation from marriage this is in one sense only to free her and her husband from the dangers of social embarrassment. Divorced, Mrs. Sullen is free to love Archer without cuckolding her husband.

Nevertheless, Farquhar's bid for divorce involves more than the oddity of Restoration manners. It is obvious that he has drifted far enough from Restoration cynicism to believe in the unnaturalness of a forced, unhappy marriage. Although he admired Restoration sophistication and the stylish cultivation of a studied and brilliant artificiality, Farquhar was enough of a child of the dawning age of sentiment to sympathize with the cry for nature and the plea for true sentiment. At the end of Act III, Mrs. Sullen is eloquent in her desperate assertions to Dorinda regarding the emotional suffering attendant on an unhappy marriage: Who can prove "the unaccountable disaffections of wedlock? Can a jury sum up the endless aversions that are rooted in our souls, or can a bench give judgment upon antipathies?" Such speeches open the floodgates to truly serious feeling, and they open the play's action to problems wit alone cannot solve. There is no clever answer—nor did Farquhar intend that there should be—to Mrs. Sullen's question, "Can radical hatreds ever be reconciled?" When she closes the act with the famous exclamation, "No, no sister, nature is the first lawgiver," we know that Farquhar has left the ranks of Restoration dramatists. That exclamation is followed by a rhymed closing epilogue that contrasts the harmony of the earth's elements with the agonizing disharmony of a bad marriage. Mrs. Sullen becomes reminiscent of Ulysses in William Shakespeare's *Troilus and Cressida* (1601-1602); when the perspicacious Greek hero analyzes the disunity of the Greeks, he makes similar allusions to the harmony of the spheres. There can be no victory for the Greeks unless each man and faction takes its proper place in the ranks of the Greek host. Mrs. Sullen sounds no less noble when she insists that without harmony and understanding between a husband and wife the marriage can have no center—nor tolerate a master: "Omnipotence is just, were man but wise."

The divorce theme is treated seriously, but Farquhar will not follow through on the sublime note of Mrs. Sullen's epilogue. Her husband finally agrees to a separation, but if Archer had not secured the papers from the robbers and placed them in Sir Charles Freeman's hands, Sullen would never have agreed to a divorce. He is tricked, then, in the spirit of Restoration foolery, into agreeing to the divorce on which Mrs. Sullen lavished so much sincere emotion. However, the charm of their brisk repartee at parting redeems the tone of Restoration theater. As the two adversaries shower barbs of polite insult in taking leave of each other, audiences have as their final impression the brilliance of Farquhar's benevolent satire.

Farquhar's closing tone is a reminder that he has been writing a Restoration comedy, not a sentimental domestic problem play. The happiness of the separated couple is as great as that of the united lovers, Dorinda and Aimwell. The Restoration rake-heroes, Archer and Aimwell, have out-thieved the thieves and stolen their way into the hearts, and fortunes, of their ladies. Mrs. Sullen has been freed by Archer's trickery only to fall into the hands of a fortune hunter, though a charming one. The wry note on which the play ends reestablishes the "way of the world" as Restoration comedy had conceived it. Farquhar may have tipped his hat to sentimental values, but the buttons of his costumes are firmly snapped by the same tailors who fashioned the theater of Etherege and Wycherley, Sir John Vanbrugh and William Congreve. The divorce theme lingers in the mind, but the antics of Archer and Aimwell, the disguises, the "catechisms" of love, and the farcical confrontation of Count Bellair and Sullen all distinguish Farquhar as the last of the Restoration comic dramatists.

"Critical Evaluation" by Peter A. Brier

Bibliography:

Berman, Ronald. "The Comedy of Reason." *Texas Studies in Literature and Language* 7 (Summer, 1965): 161-168. A brief discussion of *The Beaux' Stratagem* that sees the play as having a logic that is characteristic of Restoration comedy.

Burns, Edward. *Restoration Comedy: Crises of Desire and Identity*. New York: St. Martin's Press, 1987. Burns's central premise is that Restoration comedy was shaped by the pastoral mode so popular in sixteenth and seventeenth century literature. His treatment of individual plays and playwrights includes an interesting discussion of *The Beaux' Stratagem*.

Farquhar, George. *The Beaux' Stratagem*. Edited by Charles N. Fifer. Lincoln: University of Nebraska Press, 1977. The handiest modern edition of Farquhar's play. Fifer's introduction is concise and informative about the play's history and the comic traditions it embodies.

Milhous, Judith, and Robert D. Hume. *Producible Interpretation: Eight English Plays, 1675-1707*. Carbondale: Southern Illinois University Press, 1985. Two of the leading scholars in the field of Restoration and eighteenth century drama outline the production history of *The Beaux' Stratagem* and discuss interpretive problems. Given the scarcity of scholarship on Farquhar's most famous play, this is probably the best place to begin study of *The Beaux' Stratagem*.

Rothstein, Eric. *George Farquhar*. New York: Twayne, 1967. Farquhar has never attracted a great deal of critical attention. At the time of its publication, this was the best study of Farquhar and his work. Includes a short biographical sketch, followed by a solid discussion of the works, including a chapter on *The Beaux' Stratagem*.

THE BEAVER COAT

Type of work: Drama
Author: Gerhart Hauptmann (1862-1946)
Type of plot: Satire
Time of plot: Nineteenth century
Locale: The outskirts of Berlin
First performed: 1893; first published, 1893 as *Der Biberpelz* (English translation, 1912)

> *Principal characters:*
> FRAU WOLFF, a washerwoman and a seller of stolen goods
> JULIUS WOLFF, her husband, a poacher
> LEONTINE, their older daughter
> WULKOW, a buyer of stolen goods, a boatman
> KRÜGER, the well-to-do victim of the thieves
> DOCTOR FLEISCHER, his friend, a liberal
> VON WEHRHAHN, a justice of the peace
> MOTES, an informer

The Story:

To the suburban shack of the Wolff family, which Julius and Frau Wolff were paying off on the installment plan, their older daughter Leontine returned with complaints that her employers, the Krügers, had sent her out for wood late at night. Leontine had been hired out to the rich family in the neighborhood to earn enough money to start a stage career, because Frau Wolff thought that her appearance would assure her success. Although Julius wanted to send the girl back to the Krügers immediately, Frau Wolff seized the opportunity to devise a plan to steal the wood that her rebellious daughter had refused to carry. If the older daughter had delusions of grandeur, the younger one, Udelheid, did not.

Julius manufactured boats and ran the local ferry as a kind of front for his real profession, the illegal snaring of game. He had just returned with his shipwright's tools and oars, and Frau Wolff had just completed butchering a stag in preparation of the arrival of a boatman, Wulkow, who dealt in plundered goods. The family, which thrived by trickery, wit, and chance, just then had a supply of firewood and a stag ready for market.

Wulkow seemed very reluctant to pay more than thirteen shillings for the meat, but Frau Wolff, the real ringleader in the family dealings, bargained him up to seventeen. The important sale, however, was that Wulkow declared himself willing to pay sixty or seventy crowns for a good fur coat to relieve his rheumatism during the cold days on the barge. Frau Krüger had just bought such a coat for her husband's Christmas present. Their bargaining was interrupted by the appearance of Motes and his wife, who obtained eggs and bread from Frau Wolff in return for an uneasy truce over several snares they had found. Motes, who had lost an eye in a hunting accident and thereupon his job as a ranger, sometimes remedied his misfortunes by informing on poachers in the neighborhood.

After this encounter, Frau Wolff fortified her husband with whiskey for the midnight excursion to load wood. Their friend, the policeman who on his nightly rounds wheedled drinks, innocently helped the Wolffs prepare for the task ahead. He was several days late in delivering a message that Frau Wolff was to appear at Justice von Wehrhahn's house on the following morning.

In the justice's court the next day, Krüger lodged a complaint that his wood had been stolen, but the justice was not at all interested in the theft. He had heard that Krüger's friend and boarder, Doctor Fleischer, a notorious liberal democrat and freethinker, had said slanderous things about a certain official newly arrived in town, and von Wehrhahn was certain that he was the official referred to. He was therefore preoccupied with a plan to rig circumstantial evidence to press charges against Doctor Fleischer. When Krüger insisted that his hired girl be forced to return, Frau Wolff was brought in dripping from her work at the von Wehrhahn tubs to settle the dispute. She announced that she refused to send her daughter back to a house where she was forced to carry wood in the middle of the night. Krüger, who was partially deaf, became angry and accused the justice of shouting and the court of incompetency. As Frau Wolff returned with injured pride to her washing and Krüger stormed out, von Wehrhahn was left with Motes, who gave him reassurance.

Several days later, a beaver coat was delivered to Wulkow for ninety-nine crowns (when new, the coat had cost about one hundred crowns). Frau Wolff counted her money carefully, claiming that the boatman had cheated her of one crown. In spite of Julius' wish to pay the final installment on their house, his wife insisted on burying the money until things blew over. Udelheid, the younger daughter, busily building a fire of stolen wood, was sent to study confirmation verses for the coming celebratory season. Doctor Fleischer and his little boy, great favorites of the family, stopped by for a boat ride, a whimsical midwinter wish of the delicate child. Udelheid was taking them out when Krüger arrived with lamentations and apologies. He emphasized his lamentations by waving a stick of stolen wood and denouncing the security system for the loss of both his wood and his beaver coat. He apologized for the way he had treated Frau Wolff and pleaded that Leontine return to work at higher pay. Frau Wolff assured him that jail was the place for scoundrelly thieves.

In an effort to deceive the authorities, Frau Wolff declared that a waistcoat, a note, and a key had been found by her daughter near the railway station. Her theory was that the thief left them behind when he took the beaver coat to Berlin. Yet she seemed willing to believe that the thief might still be in the vicinity, all the more so after Wulkow appeared in the courtroom to register the birth of a daughter. So many petitioners showed up simultaneously that Justice von Wehrhahn could not get on with his plans to indict Doctor Fleischer for slander on the false testimony of Motes' landlady, who was quite gullible and ignorant of Motes' habit of avoiding any kind of payment whatsoever. Doctor Fleischer, however, had knowledge of a beaver coat. While out on the river he had seen a boatman—the unfortunate Wulkow, who could not get his boat free of the ice in time to get his wife to Berlin for the expected event—sitting on deck in a new fur coat. This evidence made no impression on von Wehrhahn; anyone could own a fur coat, he insisted, even a boatman. Wulkow assured him that boatmen could easily afford such a coat and that he himself had one. Krüger, not hearing all that was said, criticized the justice severely for not allowing the good washerwoman to present her daughter's evidence. He also rebuked the magistrate for consorting with Motes, a man who never paid his bills, who informed on others, and who was even now rigging false evidence. Doctor Fleischer presented documentary proof that Motes had extracted evidence from his landlady against himself. All this the justice waved aside.

Wulkow finally succeeded in registering the birth of his daughter. The incriminating evidence against him was thrown out, von Wehrhahn saying that he would have to search every house in the area—Frau Wolff suggested that he start with hers—if such flimsy stories were to be believed. Krüger stated that he would never rest until the coat and his stolen wood were found. Von Wehrhahn sent away Motes and his star witness. Frau Wolff, true to her sense of honor, refused to say anything good of Motes or anything bad of Doctor Fleischer, even though the justice was more than willing to hear such information. He admired her feelings but begged to differ with the honest lady, one whom everyone admired and with whom no one found fault. To his pronouncement that as sure as she was an honest woman, Doctor Fleischer was a thoroughly dangerous person, Frau Wolff said only that she did not know what to think.

Critical Evaluation:

The Beaver Coat is one of Gerhart Hauptmann's earliest comedies, written at a time when the young author was under the influence of such intellectual movements sweeping Europe as social determinism, which is epitomized in the writings of Karl Marx and Friedrich Engels, and naturalism, a literary movement begun in France and codified by Émile Zola. Although most of the works produced by naturalist authors, including those of Hauptmann, tend toward tragedy, *The Beaver Coat* is exceptional in that the playwright here applies the principles of naturalism to a decidedly comic plot. Hauptmann abandoned the strict demands of the well-made play, made popular in the nineteenth century by contemporary European writers and by the theories of Hauptmann's countryman Gustav Freytag, and relies instead on sharp characterization and the repetition of stock events to create humor and to mask the more serious social satire that the play embodies. Hauptmann's decision to cast his satire in the form of a comedy was fortuitous; despite a lackluster initial reception, *The Beaver Coat* came to be ranked with Gotthold Ephraim Lessing's *Minna von Barnhelm* (1767) and Heinrich von Kleist's *The Broken Jug* (1808) as one of the greatest comedies in German literature.

Central to the success of the drama is his depiction of the inventive and irrepressible Frau Wolff, whose attempts to outwit the officials of the Prussian government are the main source of comedy. She dominates both her family and friends, and she enlists their aid in outwitting the pompous justice of the peace who threatens her schemes for increasing the family's wealth. The other characters, often little more than types drawn from comic tradition as old as Aristophanes, allow playgoers to see the folly of a government so intent on rooting out political opposition that it permits criminal activity to occur right under the noses of the local magistrates.

Beneath its comic surface, *The Beaver Coat* offers a serious critique of nineteenth century Prussian society. Hauptmann achieves this by applying naturalism and realism to the play's comic conventions. Modeling his work on the theories of the naturalist movement most forcefully expounded by Zola, Hauptmann emphasizes details of everyday life and meticulously chronicles the speech and action of characters from the lower social classes. Using realistic techniques pioneered in drama by Henrik Ibsen, whom he greatly admired, Hauptmann in *The Beaver Coat* introduces a cast of characters from the working and criminal classes, presenting them sympathetically and with appreciation for their situation. This is no drawing-room comedy; instead, it shares many characteristics of the proletariat literature that had begun to appear in Europe during the final decades of the nineteenth century, inspired by the theories of Marx and Engels. The men and women in Hauptmann's comedy are engaged in a struggle that parallels the one described in the works of Charles Darwin and Herbert Spencer; their world clearly embodies the principle of "survival of the fittest." The animal imagery that dominates the play, especially in the naming of characters, reinforces this image. It should be no surprise to readers that the "wolf" (Frau Wolff) bests the blustering, militaristic "hen" (Wehrhahn). What is ironic, of course, is that the tables are turned in this portrait of society, and that the criminals are able to best the authorities even within the confines of the law.

Not surprisingly, Hauptmann was criticized by some of his contemporaries and by later audiences and readers because the comic resolution of *The Beaver Coat* leaves justice—at least legal justice—unserved and suggests that the criminal behavior of Frau Wolff and her family may be pardoned. The authorities in his own day found Hauptmann's treatment of government officials offensive; questions even arose regarding the way the playwright had been able to get his play passed by the government censor, who had judged the work to be so insignificant that it could not possibly have any adverse impact on audiences. In later years, when the aging Hauptmann became a darling of the Nazi regime, producers of *The Beaver Coat* found it necessary to sanitize the drama so that it would not lead German audiences to think ill of Hitler's regime.

That the play seems to condone immorality may be explained by appealing to the tradition Hauptmann is following. As a naturalist work, *The Beaver Coat* depicts, but does not judge, a slice of life the author knows well and presents without commentary. Hauptmann was quite familiar with both the characters and situations he dramatizes, and most of the men and women in *The Beaver Coat* are modeled on people he knew. Frau Wolff, for example, is a fictional portrait of his laundress, Marie Heinze; von Wehrhahn is drawn from Hauptmann's memories of an encounter with Oscar von Busse, who had harassed the young writer when he was living in Erkner, the town outside Berlin that serves as the setting for *The Beaver Coat*. Hauptmann is suggesting in his play that sometimes criminals do escape; sometimes justice is represented by people who do not uphold the concepts of law and equity in totally admirable ways. He makes no attempt to condone Frau Wolff's behavior or her cause, nor does he condemn it. Like all good practitioners of naturalism, Hauptmann is interested primarily in placing before his audience an accurate portrait of life among common people, whose struggle to get ahead in a society insensitive to their needs sometimes places them at odds with the law. Judgments are left to the audience, who may sympathize with the playwright's spunky and industrious heroine or condemn her for her actions as they see fit.

"Critical Evaluation" by Laurence W. Mazzeno

Bibliography:
Gassner, John. Introduction to *Five Plays by Gerhart Hauptmann*, translated by Theodore H. Lustig. New York: Bantam Publications, 1961. A general introduction that sketches Hauptmann's achievement as a dramatist, highlighting his contributions to the naturalist movement. Comments on the topicality of *The Beaver Coat*, but claims that it is an "outstanding character comedy" that transcends the limitations of the time and place of its initial production.
Maurer, Warren R. *Gerhart Hauptmann*. Boston: Twayne, 1982. Overview of Hauptmann's life and work intended for the nonspecialist. Organized chronologically, it shows the development of Hauptmann's theory of the drama. Discusses the principal themes of *The Beaver Coat*, highlights its politically charged undertone, and cites the author's use of imagery and dramatic structure.
_____. *Understanding Gerhart Hauptmann*. Columbia: University of South Carolina Press, 1992. Excellent overview of Hauptmann's works. Discussion of *The Beaver Coat* focuses on the comic aspects of the play and on the character of Mrs. Wolff.
Osborne, John. *The Naturalist Drama in Germany*. Totowa, N.J.: Rowman & Littlefield, 1971. Discusses *The Beaver Coat* as a naturalist comedy, citing various devices Hauptmann uses to achieve comic effect. Points out parallels to Molière's plays.
Sinden, Margaret. *Gerhart Hauptmann: The Prose Plays*. Toronto: University of Toronto Press, 1957. Studies the major dramas, including *The Beaver Coat*, which Sinden calls a work of great vigor. Discusses the play as an exploration of the impact of the modern era on a traditional rural settlement.

BECKET
Or, The Honor of God

Type of work: Drama
Author: Jean Anouilh (1910-1987)
Type of plot: Historical
Time of plot: Twelfth century
Locale: England, France, and Rome
First performed: Becket: Ou, L'Honneur de Dieu, 1959; first published, 1959 (English translation, 1960)

Principal characters:
THOMAS À BECKET, Archbishop of Canterbury
HENRY II PLANTAGENET, king of England
GILBERT FOLLIOT, Bishop of London
THE QUEEN, Eleanor of Aquitaine
THE QUEEN MOTHER
THE YOUNG MONK
GWENDOLINE, Becket's former mistress, a suicide

The Story:

King Henry was doing ritual penance for his suspected role in the assassination of Thomas à Becket, Archbishop of Canterbury, formerly his friend and chancellor of England. While the king wondered aloud where their friendship had gone wrong, Thomas' ghostly presence appeared before him, telling him to pray instead of talk. The scene then shifts to the early days of the two men's boon companionship. Henry made an impulsive appointment of Becket to the position of chancellor, a move intended to give the king more control of a rebellious clergy. Equally mistrusted by the bishops and by the king's own henchmen, Becket nevertheless performed his duties with grace and skill, earning the grudging respect of both sides.

The king, however, failed to understand his friend's true motivations. While riding through the woods shortly after Becket's appointment as chancellor, the two were caught in a downpour. The king's questions to Becket showed the king to be quite ignorant regarding his own subjects and the laws that governed them. The king then became enamored of the young peasant girl in the shack where they had taken cover. Becket pretended to want the girl for himself in order to parry the king's indiscretion. Becket soon thereafter lost his mistress to the king's misguided playfulness: The king decided that Becket should return the favor that the king had granted Becket in the shack. Specifically, the king should sleep with Becket's mistress. Becket, circumspect as ever, agreed to share Gwendoline's favors in exchange for those of the peasant girl. Gwendoline stabbed herself rather than sleep with the king. Henry, oblivious as ever, concluded that he had survived an assassination attempt on Gwendoline's part.

As chancellor, Becket found himself obliged to educate and civilize the king and his henchmen-barons, instructing them in manners and in enlightened self-interest, especially when dealing with conquered enemies such as France. Becket also perceived a growing domestic threat from the British clergy. Upon learning of the death of the Archbishop of Canterbury, Henry decided to move against that threat by naming his friend Becket to the post, much against Becket's wishes and better judgment. Becket, a former candidate for the priesthood, resolved to do, as usual, the best possible job of whatever was handed to him, giving away all of his possessions to the poor. The king, meanwhile, faced trouble in his household as well as in his reign. He was henpecked by his wife and mother, both of whom envied his friendship with Becket, and he was unable to control his adolescent sons.

Becket's resignation as chancellor, on the grounds that he could not serve God and king at once, drove the king to the desperate act of plotting against Becket with Gilbert Folliot, Bishop of London and chief among Becket's enemies within the church. Soon Becket, condemned on patently false charges of embezzlement and witchcraft, sought refuge, going first to France and then as far as Rome for an audience with the Pope. Becket then returned to France. The French, however, found him too worrisome a fugitive for permanent asylum. The king of France, seeking compromise, arranged for Becket to meet with King Henry on neutral ground in an effort to reconcile their differences. Both men still cared about each other, but neither would abandon his principles and the meeting failed. Returning from France, knowing his life to be in danger, Becket waited at Canterbury for the inevitable, a murderous assault by the henchmen of the king. The play's final scene, replicating the first, portrays the king's ritual flagellation for his part in the assassination plot. Such penance was in fact a deft political move, defusing a revolt mounted against the king by his own sons. The king was showing, in his deft statecraft, how much he had learned from Becket. A final irony was that Becket, from the grave, managed at last to transform Henry II from a petty tribal chieftain into a true monarch.

Critical Evaluation:

As in his earlier *L'Alouette* (1953; *The Lark*, 1955), about Joan of Arc, Anouilh, in *Becket*, treats the life and death of a martyred Christian saint through the eyes of a nonbeliever who is less concerned with faith than with human character and motivation. What matters to Anouilh is the legendary figure of Becket as recalled and reconstructed over the centuries in history and literature. As had the Greek myth that he had exploited earlier in his *Antigone* (1944; English translation, 1946), the lives of the saints provided context for psychological and social commentary. What Anouilh does in *Becket* is demystify the saint under consideration, presenting him to the audience in straightforward human terms.

The legend of Thomas à Becket has appealed frequently to playwrights, most notably T. S. Eliot, whose *Murder in the Cathedral* (1935) is still often revived. Eliot's play, however, takes the point of view of a believer, with emphasis on theological debate. Anouilh, well acquainted with Eliot's version, attempted some twenty-five years later to expand the scope of Eliot's inquiry, opening the exposition to include not only the outdoors (through the use of costly stage sets) but also a full range of European history and politics. For Eliot, Thomas' life was exemplary and inspirational; for Anouilh it was legendary and symbolic, illustrative of problems that continue to plague the human race. Borrowing freely from the conventions of murder mystery, spy fiction, and broad political satire, as well as from cinematic technique, Anouilh creates in *Becket* a highly convincing and entertaining portrayal of a close friendship in decline. The text of *Becket* often reads more like a screenplay than a stage play, with frequent flashbacks, rapid scene changes, and highly specific instructions about how a particular line is to be delivered. A 1964 film version, featuring Richard Burton as Becket and Peter O'Toole as the king, was extremely faithful to the text and remained in circulation for years afterward. By the time he addressed himself to Becket, Anouilh was well aware that the martyred bishop was no Saxon, as supposed by the historian Augustin Thierry (1795-1856), whose works Anouilh had read as a boy, but rather a Norman like the king himself. Thus deprived of a possible dramatic theme, Anouilh, in *Becket*, derives considerable rhetorical and dramatic effect at the level of character from the political interplay between the king and the pragmatic Becket (who did not, in fact, represent the compromising spirit of the conquered Saxon people). Inner-directed, secretive, at times seemingly heartless, Anouilh's Thomas is a shrewd political manipulator, yet it is impossible for him to believe in anything except the strict code of personal conduct that somehow, until the end, ensured his survival. In *Becket*, Anouilh continues an exposition, begun before *Antigone* and sustained through subsequent plays, of the inevitable conflict between idealism and realism. Antigone chooses death over compromise, but Thomas is a survivor, an unlikely candidate, until his last principled stand, for martyrdom. Forced, by his father's supposed collaboration with the occupying Norman army, to invent his own values, Thomas goes even so far as to deny his evident love for the unfortunate Gwendoline in favor of his newly contracted loyalty to the king. Still improvising, Becket becomes a martyr only when his contract to defend the "honor of God" as Archbishop conflicts with his previously sworn loyalty to the king.

Fifteen years after the first performances of *Antigone* and the subsequent liberation of France by Allied forces, the divided moral choices of World War II were still quite fresh in Anouilh's memory. No doubt he had also not forgotten the accusations of political ambiguity that had been leveled against *Antigone*. Thomas, at least as much a pragmatist as Antigone's antagonist, Creon, emerges as a more affirmative character than Creon or Antigone. Thomas substitutes in all of his actions an aesthetic standard for the religious conviction that he lacks. Even at the end, for Anouilh's Thomas, certain actions are simply more beautiful or appropriate than others. He shows, for example, an instinctive feel for the uses and abuses of political power, based upon his grasp of individual and group psychology. The king, a slow but generally receptive learner until the friendship goes sour, allows his cleverer, subtler friend ample opportunity to explain and to test his theories. At no point, however, does Anouilh allow content to intrude upon the play's intended entertainment value. His realized ambition, in Becket as in most of his other plays, is the creation of a playable, engrossing drama with a number of memorable lines and scenes.

Among Anouilh's best-known dramatic efforts (although expensive to mount and therefore seldom revived in production), *Becket* was written at the approximate midpoint of a distinguished, sometimes controversial dramatic career spanning more than fifty years and nearly as many plays. Among French playwrights of his generation, Anouilh was perhaps the most concerned with great theater rather than great ideas or great experiments. He shunned, however, such traditional classifications as comedy and tragedy, preferring to label his plays as black, pink, or grating, the last designed to set one's teeth on edge. Another of Anouilh's classifications is costume plays such as *Becket* and *The Lark*.

Many of the black plays are rich in comic elements, just as most pink plays carry tragic undertones beneath a comic surface. *Becket*, perhaps the most accomplished of the costume plays, combines comic and tragic elements in approximately equal portion, steering clear of melodrama in such scenes as that of Gwendoline's suicide. As a product of the author's full maturity, preceded by several lesser efforts, *Becket* displays a sure touch and a depth of vision absent from such earlier efforts as *Antigone*. At the same time, its monumental scope and glossy surface relate it closely to the commercial theater that Anouilh had long been accused of courting, especially by those who preferred to see him as a literary playwright. As Albert Camus had in his Caligula, Anouilh found in Becket a legendary historical figure subject to interpretation. Anouilh, following the lead of Jean Giraudoux and other French playwrights, found in classical mythology a rich context for the analysis of contemporary problems. Anouilh's Thomas emerges as a model hero for the latter half of the twentieth century. Unable or unwilling to believe in a higher power, Becket constantly improvises in search of values that might lead him toward himself.

David B. Parsell

Bibliography:

Della Fazia, Alba. *Jean Anouilh*. Boston: Twayne, 1969. A thoughtful examination of Anouilh's theater, with good consideration of the costume plays. Discussion of Becket is brief but perceptive.

Falb, Lewis W. *Jean Anouilh*. New York: Frederick Ungar, 1977. Good overview of Anouilh's theater, yet slights *Becket* in favor of *The Lark*.

Harvey, John. *Anouilh: A Study in Theatrics*. New Haven, Conn.: Yale University Press, 1964. Correctly distances Anouilh from the thinker-playwrights of his generation, situating him within the tradition of theatricality along with Molière and Shakespeare. Good analysis of the costume plays.

McIntyre, H. G. *The Theatre of Jean Anouilh*. London: Harrap, 1981. Prepared with Anouilh's life work all but complete, McIntyre's study is perhaps the most useful. It finds continuity where others have seen only confusion.

Pronko, Leonard C. *The World of Jean Anouilh*. Berkeley: University of California Press, 1961. Perhaps the strongest earlier study of Anouilh's theater, including the costume plays. Authoritative on theme and structure in the plays it covers.

THE BEDBUG
An Extravaganza in Nine Scenes

Type of work: Drama
Author: Vladimir Mayakovsky (1893-1930)
Type of plot: Satire
Time of plot: 1929 and 1979
Locale: Tambov, Soviet Union
First performed: Klop, 1929; first published, 1929 (English translation, 1931)

Principal characters:
IVAN PRISYPKIN, a former Party member and a worker
ELZEVIR DAVIDOVNA, a manicurist and cashier at a beauty parlor
ROSALIE PAVLOVNA, her mother
ZOYA BERYOZKINA, a working girl
OLEG BARD, a houseowner

The Story:

In a State Department store in Tambov, a central Russian town, in 1929, Ivan Prisypkin (otherwise known as Pierre Skripkin), a former Party member, former worker, and now the fiancé of Elzevir Davidovna Renaissance, accompanied her mother, Rosalie Pavlovna, and a neighboring houseowner, Oleg Bard, on a shopping spree in preparation for the wedding. Salespeople were hawking their wares, and Prisypkin was buying everything because his house had to be like a horn of plenty and his future children must be brought up to be refined. His future mother-in-law worried about splurging, while Oleg Bard supported Prisypkin's extravagance, pointing out, clearly in jest, that the triumph of the victorious proletarian class must be symbolized by a ravishing, elegant, and class-conscious wedding. Prisypkin came face-to-face with Zoya Beryozkina, his former girlfriend, who demanded an explanation for the shopping spree and, more important, for his abandoning her. "Our love is liquidated," he proclaimed, using a current official phrase mockingly, while Rosalie called her a pregnant slut. A militiaman finally broke up the confrontation.

In a hostel for young workers, there was a lively talk about Prisypkin's impending wedding and about the thorough change of his behavior. One of workers, looking for his boots, was told that Prisypkin had taken them—for the last time, he had sworn—to impress his fiancé. They all criticized Prisypkin's betrayal of his class, making fun of his awkward attempts to act like a member of high society. They also made fun of his mother-in-law, saying that her breasts weighed eighty pounds each. Some workers, however, chastised their colleagues for jealousy, noting that most of them would have done the same thing if they had had a chance.

Prisypkin showed up in brand-new shoes and tossed back the pair of worn-out boots he had "borrowed." The workers turned their backs to him, making all kinds of derisive gestures and performing mocking dances. Oleg Bard advised Prisypkin to ignore these vulgar manifestations, complaining that a man of great talent has no elbow room in Russia, what with capitalist encirclement and the building of socialism happening simultaneously in one country (again mocking common official phrases). Instead, he ought to learn more refined dances, like the foxtrot, and endeavor to rise above the riff-raff. As the workers continued to harass Prisypkin, he angrily retorted that they all had been fighting for a better life, after all. By bettering himself materially, he now firmly believed, he would raise the living standards of the whole proletariat. At that moment a voice announced that Zoya had tried to kill herself.

Undeterred, Prisypkin proceeded with the wedding, assisted ably by Oleg. The festivities took place with all the pomp of the rich. The wedding guests frolicked, uttered snide remarks, and acted according to their nature. When the ushers tried to calm them, a fire started, and many guests perished in the fire. The firemen found only charred corpses, with one person unaccounted for.

The scene shifts to an undetermined place fifty years later. In 1979, much had changed. There was an amphitheater set in modernistic surroundings. All persons were nameless, clad in sterile white attire, communicating with each other in a manner typical of a futuristic society. They were puzzled by a discovery of a frozen male body, and they had no idea who it might be. All they could see, after an X-ray examination, was that he had calloused hands. They decided to thaw the body out. It turned out that it was Ivan Prisypkin, the only person who had survived the wedding fire fifty years before. Doused by plenty of water, he had been able to survive half a century in a frozen state.

Prisypkin was bewildered by the people around him and by the state in which he found himself. He was filthy. His corner was like a pigsty, littered with cigarette butts and overturned bottles, recalling a carousing wedding celebration. The only person he could vaguely recognize now was Zoya Beryozkina, who had survived her suicide attempt. She brought him some books he had requested, but he rejected them as crude propaganda, wanting something "to pluck at his heartstrings." He finally found something to his liking, while Zoya remarked that she might have died for this skunk.

Because of enormous public curiosity about the discovery, Prisypkin was placed in a zoo cage. The spectacle was replete with musicians, spectators, and many reporters. When the cage was opened to view, the zoo director explained that they had found two bugs on the thawed-out body—*Bedbugus normalis* and *Bourgeoisius vulgaris*. The only difference was that the first gorges on a single human being, while the latter gorges on all of humanity. While the proletariat was writhing and scratching itself to rid itself of filth, its parasites built their nests and made their homes in the dirt. Prisypkin was used as an exhibit of the bygone era of filth. The era and the *Bourgeoisius vulgaris* were totally extinct. The signs on the cage, Caution—It Spits! No Unauthorized Entry! and Watch Your Ears—It Curses! delighted the crowd.

When Prisypkin looked at the audience, he began to express his bewilderment and to ask heart-rending questions, such as why he was alone and why he was suffering, calling upon the spectators to join him. To forestall possible harm to them, especially to children, the cage was covered again and the director calmed the spectators by explaining that the insect (Prisypkin) was tired and having hallucinations because of the lights. He would recover tomorrow and they could come and view him again.

Critical Evaluation:

Mayakovsky wrote *The Bedbug* as a satire on the Soviet society in the late 1920's. This is evident from many aspects of the play and from his biography. Mayakovsky was a staunch supporter of the communist system throughout his life. During the revolution he willingly lent his services to the revolutionary cause, "setting my heel on the throat of my own song," as he said in one of his poems. He was displeased with the New Economic Policy established by Vladimir Ilich Lenin in 1921 to bring Russia back from the ruins of the revolution and civil war. He was even more displeased with the First Five-Year Plan, instituted in 1928 by Joseph Stalin after the country had recovered economically. The worst aspect of that plan, according to Mayakovsky, was the establishment of a huge army of bureaucrats, who had always been a thorn in his side. It should be kept in mind that when the play was premiered in Moscow on

February 13, 1929, most of the audience consisted of exactly the kind of bureaucrats Maya-kovsky directed his satire against. The official reaction to the play was highly critical, and the author was accused of being against the state. Had he not committed suicide on April 14, 1930—caused in part by the "failure" of *The Bedbug* and other late works—many believe that he might have become a victim of the purges.

The main source of his disillusionment and bitterness was his fear that the proletariat, for whose sake the revolution had been fought, was being betrayed. The betrayal is embodied in the characters of Prisypkin and Elzevir Davidovna. Both belonged to the working class, but during the New Economic Policy they want to join the more affluent society that had been created by the freer economic policies. The couple pretends to belong still to the workers' union, which is Mayakovsky's way of criticizing the entire leadership. As a member of the victorious class, Prisypkin demands the benefits of victory ("what did I fight for?"): more and better material goods, a wife above a regular worker status, and "a horn of plenty." At the high point of his and Elzevir's rise, he changes his name to Pierre Skripkin (alluding to French culture and to a Russian name for a violin player) and adds Renaissance to Elzevir's last name. The wedding, opulent and ostentatious, mirrors their *nouveau riche* status. That almost all the wedding guests perish during the merrymaking is poetic justice.

The satire becomes more serious in the second half of the play. On the one hand, he criticizes the future Soviet society as sterile, nameless, devoid of love and compassion. On the other hand, the resurrected Prisypkin stands as a museum exhibit, filthy and utterly disoriented, to be feared and shunned in the advanced society for which he was supposed to have fought. Mayakovsky makes it clear that in such society there is no room for people of lower classes and workers. Prisypkin's painful cries "Where am I?" "Why am I alone in the cage?" and "Why am I suf-fering?" underscore the betrayal of the working class. Addressing the audience made up of the people who should have guaranteed the victory of the working class, Mayakovsky is posing a disturbing question about who the real traitors in the struggle are. Although one may call Mayakovsky an early dissident, it must be pointed out that he satirized his society not as an opponent but as an idealistic believer in the cause. He remained true to his belief; he was shunned and presumably would have been killed.

The play is written in a modernistic style, fashionable in the 1920's. It features fast-moving scenes instead of acts, a film technique of which Mayakovsky was fond. The characters are not individuals but types, expressing ideas and slogans rather than individual experience. Satire is the strongest thrust of the play. Mayakovsky uses satire unsparingly, often in a pungent, racy language that never misses its mark. As in his poetry, he frequently plays on words and phrases, always reaching for the strongest effect. For example, Oleg Bard, playing on Prisypkin's desire for his home to be a horn of plenty, solemnly declares that Comrade Prisypkin's "pants must be like a horn of plenty." That *The Bedbug* must have delighted many spectators the first time around, despite official disclaimers, is evident from the success of the play when it was staged again in the late 1950's and later, running simultaneously in two Moscow theaters.

Vasa D. Mihailovich

Bibliography:
Brown, Edward J. *Mayakovsky: A Poet in the Revolution*. Princeton, N.J.: Princeton University Press, 1973. A seminal study of Mayakovsky as a man and a writer by a leading American scholar of Soviet literature. Mayakovsky's role in the revolution, as reflected in his works, is emphasized.

Metchenko, Alexei, ed. *Vladimir Mayakovsky: Innovator*. Translated by Alex Miller. Moscow: Progress, 1976. Twenty-six articles, mostly by Russian scholars, about Mayakovsky's innovations in his poetry and plays. Of special interest is Valentin Pluchek's article, "The New Drama."

Shklovskii, Viktor B. *Mayakovsky and His Circle*. Edited and Translated by Lily Feiler. New York: Dodd, Mead, 1972. Recollections and critical remarks about Mayakovsky, including his plays, by one of the most respected modern Russian critics and Mayakovsky's contemporary.

Terras, Victor. *Vladimir Mayakovsky*. Boston: Twayne, 1983. Analysis of Mayakovsky's poetry and plays, as well as his role in literature and events of his time. The best brief English-language introduction to his works.

Woroszylski, Wiktor. *The Life of Mayakovsky*. Translated by Bolesław Taborski. New York: Orion Press, 1970. An objective biography by a contemporary Polish poet, based on documents and opinions of Mayakovsky's contemporaries. His contribution to theater and cinema is discussed at length.

THE BEGGAR'S OPERA

Type of work: Drama
Author: John Gay (1685-1732)
Type of plot: Social satire
Time of plot: Early eighteenth century
Locale: London
First performed: 1728; first published, 1728

> *Principal characters:*
> CAPTAIN MACHEATH, a highwayman
> MR. PEACHUM, a receiver of stolen goods and an informer
> POLLY PEACHUM, his daughter, who is in love with Macheath
> MR. LOCKIT, the warder of Newgate
> LUCY LOCKIT, his daughter, who is also in love with Macheath

The Story:

Mr. Peachum, who was reckoning up his accounts, declared that his was an honest employment. Like a lawyer, he acted both for and against thieves. That he should protect them was only fitting, since they afforded him a living. In a businesslike manner he was deciding who among some arrested rogues should escape punishment through bribes and who had been so unproductive as to deserve deportation or the gallows. Though Mrs. Peachum found a favorite of hers on his list, she made no effort to influence her husband's decision, for she knew that the weakness of her sex was to allow emotions to dominate practical considerations. She did say, however, that Captain Macheath, a highwayman, stood high in her regard, as well as in that—so she hinted to Mr. Peachum—of their daughter Polly. The news upset her spouse. If the girl were to marry, her husband might learn family secrets and gain power over them. Peachum ordered his wife to warn the girl that marriage and a husband's domination would mean her ruin. Consequently they were dismayed when Polly announced her marriage to Macheath. They predicted grimly that she would not be able to keep Macheath in funds for gambling and philandering, that there would not even be enough money to cause quarrels, that she might as well have married a lord.

The Peachums' greatest fear was that Macheath would have them hanged and so gain control of the fortune that was intended for Polly. They decided it would be best to dispose of him before he could do that, and they suggested to Polly that she inform on him. Widowhood, they told her, was a very comfortable state. The girl stubbornly asserted that she loved her dashing highwayman, and she warned Macheath of her parents' plan to have him arrested. They decided that he should go into hiding for a few weeks until, as Polly hoped, her parents should relent.

Parting from his love, Macheath met his gang at a tavern near Newgate to tell them that for the next week their rendezvous would have to be confined to their private hideout, so that Peachum would think the highwayman had deserted his companions. After his men left to go about their business, some street women and female pickpockets entered. Two of them covered Macheath with his own pistols as Peachum, accompanied by constables, rushed in to arrest him. When Macheath had been carried off to spend the night in Newgate, some of the women expressed indignation at not having been among those chosen to spring the trap and share in the reward Peachum had offered for the highwayman's capture.

Though Captain Macheath had funds to bribe his jailer to confine him with only a light pair of fetters, it was another matter to deal with Lucy Lockit, the jailer's daughter. As Macheath freely admitted, she was his wife but for the ceremony. Lucy had heard of his gallantry toward Polly Peachum and could only be convinced of his sincerity by his consenting to an immediate marriage.

Peachum and Lockit meanwhile agreed to split the reward for Macheath. As he went over his accounts, however, Peachum found cause to question his partner's honesty. One of his men had been convicted, although he had bribed Lockit to have the man go free. Peachum's informer, Mrs. Coaxer, had likewise been defrauded of information money. The quarrel between Peachum and Lockit was short-lived, however, as they were well aware that each had the power to hang the other. After his talk with Peachum, Lockit warned his daughter that Macheath's fate was sealed. He advised her to buy herself widow's weeds and be cheerful; since she could not have the highwayman and his money too, she might as well make use of the time that was left to extract what riches she could from him.

There was no clergyman to be found that day, but Lucy had so far softened toward her philandering lover as to agree to see if her father could not be bought off. She had just consented to help him when Polly appeared in search of her husband. Macheath managed to convince Lucy of his faithfulness by disowning Polly, who was carried off by the angry Peachum. After they had gone, Lucy agreed to steal her father's keys so that her lover might escape. Macheath, free once more, went to join two of his men at a gambling house. There he made arrangements to meet them again that evening at another den, where they would plan the next robbery.

Peachum and Lockit were discussing the disposal of assorted loot when they were joined by Mrs. Trapes, a procuress who innocently told them that Macheath was at that moment with one of her girls. While Peachum and Lockit went off to recapture him, Polly paid a visit to Lucy Lockit. Together they bewailed their common fate—Macheath's neglect. Lucy tried to give Polly a poisoned drink. When the suspicious girl refused to accept it, Lucy decided that perhaps Polly was too miserable to deserve to die.

When Macheath was brought back to prison once more by Peachum and Lockit, both girls fell on their knees before their fathers and begged that his life be spared. Neither parent was to be moved. Lockit announced that the highwayman would die that day. As he prepared to go to the Old Bailey, Macheath said that he was resigned to his fate, for his death would settle all disputes and please all his wives.

While Macheath in his cell reflected ironically that rich men can escape the gallows but the poor must hang, he was visited by two of his men. He asked them to make sure that Lockit and Peachum were hanged before they themselves were finally strung up. The thieves were followed by the distraught Polly and Lucy, come to bid Macheath farewell. When the jailer announced that four more of his wives, each accompanied by a child, had appeared to say good-bye, Macheath declared that he was ready to meet his fate.

The rabble outside, feeling that the poor should be allowed their vices just like the rich, raised so much clamor for Macheath's reprieve that charges were dropped and he was released in triumph. In the merrymaking that followed, he himself chose Polly as his partner, because, he gallantly announced, she was really his wife. From that time on he intended to give up the vices—if not the follies—of the rich.

Critical Evaluation:

The Beggar's Opera, one of the finest plays written in English in the early eighteenth century, follows in the satiric tradition of Jonathan Swift and Alexander Pope. John Gay's purpose was likewise to ridicule the corrupt politics of his day and the follies of polite society. His depiction of crime and vice in all strata of society and his shrewd, humorous characterizations give the play universality. *The Beggar's Opera* has remained popular since its first performances, both in its original version and in such reworkings as those by composers Benjamin Britten and Arthur Bliss; Bertolt Brecht's adaptation of the original with music by Kurt Weill, *The Threepenny Opera*; and a fine British film version made in 1953.

The Beggar's Opera was written as a satire of the government of King George II, represented by Macheath, and the Whig prime minister, Robert Walpole, represented by Peachum. Gay also satirizes the contrived but popular Italian operas and the simpler English alternative to them. The work features well-known English and Scottish ballads and airs to which Gay added his own lyrics.

Colley Cibber, whom Pope satirized in *The Dunciad* (1728) and who managed the Drury Lane Theatre, unwisely declined to produce *The Beggar's Opera* when Gay submitted it to him. At length a reluctant John Rich, of the Theatre Royal, agreed to produce the play. His fears of failure proved unwarranted, for the play became a great financial success. It was said at the time that *The Beggar's Opera* made Gay rich and Rich gay.

Gay's achievement and the reason for the play's continued success is the fact that the work can be enjoyed without a knowledge of the contemporary political and theatrical milieu that it satirizes. The tone is jocular and bawdy, but it never lapses into bitterness or mere vulgarity. The diction is simple, the satire sharp, but the message is neither overly subjective nor acidic. The play may itself be considered as one long song, for it has that lyrical, bell-like quality of its finest airs. The plot, unlike the comedies of manners, the burlesques, and the farces popular at the time, is extremely simple, with no complicated and intertwining subplots to divert attention.

Like a song or ballad, *The Beggar's Opera* has several refrains. One of these is the cynical view of love and marriage, a favorite theme of the comedy of manners. There is, too, the typical strain of antifeminism ("'Tis woman that seduces all mankind," sings Filch in Act I, scene ii). As Gay makes clear, however, neither sex is faultless when it comes to romance. "Love," says Lucy Lockit, "is so very whimsical in both sexes, that it is impossible to be lasting" (Act III, scene viii). That Macheath and Polly will at least attempt a lasting relationship is suggested by the song he sings to Polly in Act I, scene xiii:

> My heart was so free,
> It rov'd like the bee,
> 'Till Polly my passion requited;
> I sipt each flower,
> I chang'd ev'ry hour,
> But here ev'ry flower is united.

Not the least aspect of this song's effectiveness lies in its sexual imagery, which is typical of the play.

Two other refrains are the plays Gay makes on the words "duty" and "honor." Polly, say her parents, must have her husband "peach'd" (impeached, given to the authorities for reward money) because it is her "duty" thus to obey her parents—a subversion of the biblical commandment to honor one's parents. It is also the "duty" of the thieves to rob, of the whores to "love," and of Polly to stand by her husband, who is anything but faithful.

Another refrain, the pun on the word "honour," effectively criticizes the manners of the court. Thus the honor of the Peachums (that is, the Walpoles) is in question if Polly makes an unsuccessful marriage, one that is not remunerative. Yet Polly insists: "I did not marry him (as 'tis the fashion) coolly and deliberately for honour or money. But, I love him." The gang of thieves are "men of honour" in name only, just as are the courtiers, and Lockit, with heavy irony, declares to his fellow mobster, Peachum: "He that attacks my honour, attacks my livelyhood."

One of Lockit's songs advises: "When you censure the age,/ Be cautious and sage." Yet, subtle and sophisticated as his censure of the court and Walpole's government was, the prime minister saw through it and refused to allow the production of *Polly* (1729), Gay's sequel to *The Beggar's Opera*. By 1737, the Licensing Act was in effect and the theaters had been closed, ending dramatic criticism of the government. (*The Beggar's Opera* and the plays of Henry Fielding are in fact largely credited with having brought on the 1737 act.) Gay's masterpiece, however, not only survived but thrived.

"Critical Evaluation" by Clifton M. Snider

Bibliography:
Armens, Sven. *John Gay, Social Critic*. 1954. Reprint. New York: Octagon Books, 1966. This full-length critical examination of Gay and his work deals in depth with *The Beggar's Opera*.
Bronson, Bertrand H. *"The Beggar's Opera."* In *Studies in the Comic*. University of California Publications in English 8, no. 2. Los Angeles: University of California Press, 1941. A fine critical study of *The Beggar's Opera*, particularly valuable for placing the work in the context of its time and exploring the links to Italian opera that Gay so skillfully exploited.
Gay, John. *The Beggar's Opera*. Larchmont, N.Y.: Argonaut Books, 1961. This edition of the play, a reproduction of the 1729 version, contains the lyrics to all the tunes that Gay adapted.
Irving, William Henry. *John Gay: Favorite of the Wits*. Durham, N.C.: Duke University Press, 1940. Considered the best treatment of Gay's life and works.
Noble, Yvonne, ed. *Twentieth Century Interpretations of "The Beggar's Opera."* Englewood Cliffs, N.J.: Prentice-Hall, 1975. Comprises a series of nine critical and informative essays on Gay's masterpiece as well as an informative introduction by the editor.
Spacks, Patricia Meyer. *John Gay*. New York: Twayne, 1965. An excellent introduction to Gay's life and works.

BEING AND NOTHINGNESS

Type of work: Philosophy
Author: Jean-Paul Sartre (1905-1980)
First published: L'Être et le néant, 1943 (English translation, 1956)

The French philosopher Jean-Paul Sartre has become widely identified with twentieth century existentialism as its most popular and well-known proponent and as a lucid and gifted writer of both philosophy and literature. Although existentialist tenets had been expressed in the thought of such previous philosophers as Søren Kierkegaard and Martin Heidegger, the mood of alienation and despair evoked by existentialism found its greatest response in the post-World War II circumstances in which Sartre lived and worked. As the leading French intellectual movement of the era, Sartrean existentialism infiltrated virtually every form of thought and artistic achievement, including literature, the theater, the visual arts, and theology. *Being and Nothingness*, Sartre's major philosophical work, is considered to be one of the most influential texts of this movement, as well as being an important work in the history of philosophy as a whole.

Born in Paris in 1905, Sartre was educated at the École Normale Supérieure, where he graduated at the age of twenty-two with a major in philosophy. "Philosophy is absolutely terrific," he said later of his early educational experience. "You can learn the truth through it." In 1929, having completed his studies, Sartre began teaching in French secondary schools. Throughout this period (1929-1934), Sartre also traveled extensively in Greece, Italy, Egypt, and especially Germany, where he studied under the German philosophers Edmund Husserl and Martin Heidegger, both of whom greatly influenced his work. In 1935, Sartre began teaching at the Lycée Condorcet, where a following of young intellectuals soon gathered around him.

Although Sartre wrote throughout this time, his breakthrough to the larger world came in 1938 with the publication of *Nausea*, his first novel. A year later, he published a collection of short stories entitled *The Wall*. Both books emphasized the themes of loneliness, despair, and the anxiety of personal freedom, themes that recurred throughout all of Sartre's later work. In 1943, these themes were given large-scale, systematic philosophical expression with the publication of *Being and Nothingness*.

The book is divided into an introduction and four main parts. Sartre opens with a challenging discussion of pure Being, one of the central preoccupations of the metaphysical tradition of philosophy. Although he rejects the Kantian "thing-in-itself" (*das Ding an sich*), that aspect of pure Being that lies behind the phenomenal appearances of being, Sartre maintains that pure Being, when considered as a whole, always lies outside the realm of human perceptibility. The abundance of Being, in all its manifestations, cannot be specifically described or categorized by our consciousness of it. According to Sartre:

> Being is simply the condition of all revelation. It is being-for-revealing [*être-pour-dévoiler*] and not revealed being [*être dévoilé*]. . . Certainly I can pass beyond this table or this chair toward its being and raise the question of the being-of-the-table or the being-of-the-chair. But at that moment I turn my eyes away from the phenomenon of the table in order to concentrate on the phenomenon of being. [Being becomes] an appearance which, as such, needs in turn a being on the basis of which it can reveal itself.

This pure Being of which Sartre writes is manifested primarily as a *split* between "Being-in-itself" [*en-soi*] and "Being-for-itself" [*pour-soi*]. The examination of these two concepts forms the bulk of the first half of the book.

Being-in-itself may be described as that mode of being that is complete in itself, which does not choose what it may become. It corresponds to the realm of physical objects and phenomena, the universe of "things." Being-in-itself is causally predetermined by the nature of its own being; as Sartre writes, "Being-in-itself is never either possible or impossible. It *is*." Being-in-itself contains the realm of absolutes, the realm of "facticity" in which choice is impossible and Being simply exists without alternative.

On the other hand, Being-for-itself is not causally predetermined by anything. Being-for-itself may be defined as the realm of human consciousness, the realm of subjectivity and choice, and the realm of freedom within alternatives. It is the mode of being which cannot simply be, but must always be becoming; it can never be "complete in itself."

Being-in-itself is prior to Being-for-itself; that is, Being-for-itself depends on the existence of Being-in-itself for its own existence. As one of Sartre's more famous slogans has it, "Existence precedes essence." The existential choices a human makes every moment of life ("existence") determine that human's "essence," which Sartre defines simply as the past or what has already occurred in a person's life. These past occurrences or choices, taken together, make up the essential self, the Being-for-itself. Sartrean existentialism thus eliminates any idea of a human self or "human nature" imposed by God or by genetics; in Sartre's view, the essence of an individual human is only what he or she has chosen that essence to be.

Human consciousness itself exists only by the act of "nihilation" (*néantisation*), a word coined by Sartre: The consciousness causes a "nothingness" to arise between itself and the objects of consciousness, that Being-in-itself of which Being-for-itself is the consciousness. A wall of alienation or separation must always and necessarily exist between consciousness and its objects; since this separation distances us from Being itself, Sartre calls consciousness "a hole of being at the heart of Being," that is, a nothingness. Since Being-for-itself is indeterminate, unfixed, and always in the state of "becoming" rather than in the state of "being" possessed by Being-in-itself, human consciousness exists only by virtue of its incompleteness, its separation from Being-in-itself. Alienated from Being, consciousness must then be considered a "privation," or a form of nothing.

This condition irresistibly produces a deep and profound *anxiety* (another key Sartrean term) in the human aware of this alienated status, an anxiety that may be defined as "a continual awareness of one's own freedom." Humans are free to become, to choose. We are "condemned to be free," in Sartre's famous phrase. Humanity finds itself in an existence filled with alternatives, and must face these alternatives at every moment, choose, commit, and move on, without complete knowledge of the consequences of these choices. Humans themselves, then, not God, genetics, "human nature," or any other such predetermining factor, are responsible for their own being.

Although humanity knows this terrifying freedom to be its nature, its deepest desire lies in the realm of solidity and certainty, the realm of Being-in-itself. Being-for-itself seeks the impossible: to be united with Being-in-itself to form "Being-in-itself-for-itself," a state of being that is self-contained and self-existent, such as the state of Being-in-itself, but also self-conscious and free to choose, such as the state of Being-for-itself. Sartre calls this, humanity's deepest desire, the "Desire to Be God"; since this deepest desire of humanity is logically contradictory and so is inevitably frustrated, humanity is condemned to a tragic existence: "Man is a useless passion."

Because of this, human existence is revealed as "absurd" and meaningless. Life contains no external purpose or justification; our pitiful attempts to become God are directed toward an unattainable goal, the goal to exist simultaneously as free in choice (Being-for-itself) and absolute in nature (Being-in-itself).

In part 3, we find that Being-for-itself involves Being-for-others (*pour-autrui*) as well. This is the state of interpersonal relations, in which the Being-for-itself exists as an object for others. Conflict arises as the Being-for-itself seeks to recover its own being by making an object out of the others; however, the two (self and others) are inseparable, as the Being-for-itself can only know itself fully by means of Being-for-others.

What sort of life could be made out of such a seemingly gloomy philosophy? According to Sartre, humans are yet capable of "authentic existence"; this type of existence comes about by the willingness to stand by one's choices and face their consequences unflinchingly. This is the closest Sartre comes to an affirmation of human existence, thereby avoiding a complete abandonment to pessimism and despair: Humans may redeem themselves, at least from self-deception, by recognizing and acknowledging their position as "a quite unjustifiable creature in a groundless universe," to quote the critic Margaret Walker. By accepting complete responsibility for their own existence, people may "climb out of the abyss of despairing awareness to achieve some form of self-affirmation." This "authentic existence" is the goal of existential psychoanalysis, which is discussed in part 4 of the book.

Those who busy themselves with the day-to-day flurry of life merely to avoid facing the terrifying responsibility of choice exhibit what Sartre calls "bad faith" (*mauvaise foi*). Bad faith is a self-deception, in that the Being-for-itself seeks to objectify its own body as Being-in-itself; responsibility for actions or choices is thus evaded or postponed. Sartre gives the example of a woman who is being courted by a suitor. Her own desires are contradictory: She does not want to give in to his advances, nor does she want to reject him and possibly end the relationship. Therefore, she objectifies herself into a "thing," merely being acted upon rather than acting; if the suitor, for instance, holds her hand (and by doing so implicitly asks for a rational decision), she deceives herself into not noticing that he is holding her hand. Her hand, her body, become "objects"; she seeks to postpone her own existence as Being-for-itself by wrongfully seeing herself as Being-in-itself. This is a display of bad faith.

In the realm of Being-for-itself, bad faith is always a possibility. Sartre describes a waiter in a cafeteria to illustrate this point: By his overly precise and meticulous actions, the waiter seems robotlike; those who watch him realize that he is "playing at being" a waiter. The human consciousness, then, becomes an affectation of consciousness; bad faith becomes an ever-present possibility when it becomes clear that humans cannot simply "be who they are" apart from choice (Sartre's "principle of identity"), as this is possible only for Being-in-itself. The activity of consciousness is itself a choice, so any attempt to evade responsibility for one's existence is illusory.

No brief summary can do full justice to the complexity of Sartre's thorough and systematic treatise. *Being and Nothingness* must stand as one of the most ambitious and influential philosophical works of the twentieth century and certainly as Sartre's philosophical magnum opus. In his work, Sartre's existentialist concepts capture, probably to a greater degree than any other modern philosophy, the angst of the twentieth century mind.

Craig Payne

Bibliography:
Caws, Peter. *Sartre.* Boston: Routledge & Kegan Paul, 1979. Presents an overview of Sartre's philosophical writings. Chapters 4-6 discuss ideas from *Being and Nothingness* and examine

the concepts of being, negation, subjectivity, and "bad faith." Points out the roots of *Being and Nothingness* in Sartre's earlier writings, and especially highlights his ideas regarding interpersonal emotional relationships.

Danto, Arthur C. *Jean-Paul Sartre*. New York: Viking Press, 1975. Examines Sartre's relationship to other philosophers and in particular focuses on existentialism's relationship to analytic philosophy. Discusses Sartre's views on language, the analytic "philosophy of mind," and the structural representation of reality.

Grene, Marjorie G. *Sartre*. New York: New Viewpoints, 1973. Contains a helpful discussion of Sartre's philosophical predecessors and an analysis of his place among twentieth century thinkers. Chapters 4-5 specifically discuss the ideas of *Being and Nothingness*, which Grene calls "one of the treasure-houses" of philosophy. This view does not, however, prevent her from strongly criticizing the role of Cartesian dualities in Sartre's thinking such as the division of body and mind. Recommended for more advanced readers of Sartre.

Kern, Edith, ed. *Sartre: A Collection of Critical Essays*. Englewood Cliffs, N.J.: Prentice-Hall, 1962. Primarily discusses Sartre's fiction, but parts 5-6 contain evaluations of Sartre's contributions to philosophy and psychoanalysis.

Murdoch, Iris. *Sartre: Romantic Rationalist*. New Haven, Conn.: Yale University Press, 1959. A well-written introduction to Sartre's thought. Discusses *Being and Nothingness* thoroughly and, to a lesser degree, Sartre's fiction and politics. Critical of existentialism's "deficiencies," but presents Sartre's views fairly.

BEING AND TIME

Type of work: Philosophy
Author: Martin Heidegger (1889-1976)
First published: Sein und Zeit, 1927 (English translation, 1962)

Martin Heidegger exerted a strong influence on philosophy, theology, and politics. His most important works include *Was ist Metaphysik?* (1929; *What Is Metaphysics?*), a political treatise *Vom Wesen der Wahrheit* (1943; *The Truth from One Being*), and his collected essays, entitled *Wegmarken* (1967; *Pathmarks*). A complete edition of his work, published in 1975, consists of seventy volumes.

Martin Heidegger's *Being and Time* is a conception of philosophy based on Franz Brentano's *On the Manifold Meaning of Being According to Aristotle* (1862). The premise from which Heidegger analyzes the world around him, metaphysics, is a philosophy concerned with the study of the ultimate causes and the underlying nature of things. *Being and Time* is based on Aristotle's study of philosophy, which he wrote after his studies related to physics. The entire text provides a linguistic study of language meaning and usage, in the course of which Heidegger creates new words and assigns new meaning to existing words. His goal is to interpret the meaning of existence concretely in accordance with the way people live and with what influences them.

Being and Time is divided into two major parts. In the first part, Heidegger seeks to define the temporality of existence. In the second, he explores the idea of time as the transcendental limit for questioning the meaning of being.

Heidegger saw words as a metaphorical pathway that proceeds without our knowing where it came from or where it is going. In his view, the manner of questioning is an integral part of seeking answers. Depending on how questions are asked about a tree—for example, *What is that over there in the distance?* and *What is that which we call a tree?*—each question would evoke different answers even though both concern the same object. The essence of existence focuses on asking the correct questions. It is not enough merely to ask What?; one must also ask How?

Since no two human beings are totally alike and all question their existence individually, people learn to function in the world by communicating. Communication involves formulating meaningful questions and listening in order to formulate more questions. Heidegger labeled thoughts that were "self-evident" (*selbstaugenscheinlich*) as false-consciousness because those who stop asking questions acquire false notions.

Heidegger believed that language gives meaning to life. Humans were created by language, since humans are defined by consciousness. The bond between human beings and nature was broken by consciousness. Since animals and plants are part of each other in nature, consciousness and language are the alienation of nature. Speech and language produce dance, poetry, painting, and music, which are the foundation for culture within human society. Culture distances people from nature.

The experience of living suffices to enable people to understand the complex language of philosophers as well as the simple language of their contemporaries. Heidegger defines dialogue as "co-responding." According to Heidegger, it is irrelevant to know philosophy as long as people are in a dialogue with their own existence. In order to "co-respond," people should not answer, for when there are answers people stop listening. Philosophy is tuned co-respondence, in which vibrations from one thinker harmonize with the thinking of others.

Heidegger was the first to see that being with others (*Mitsein*) evoked a question of existence rather than a question of knowing.

In contrast to the existentialist thought prevalent in his time, Heidegger focused on considering ways in which humanity exists concretely. Extentialism centers on the analysis of existence and stresses freedom, responsibility, and usually the isolation of the individual. In metaphysics, however, in order to find meaning for self, people must look directly at humanity in the world. The only reality is concrete.

Metaphysics theorizes that the individual is the source of all values and responsible for his own development. In order to be part of humanity, individuals must be inseparable from the world. Being involves being "with"; however, individuals can learn about themselves even if they are not physically free. Espousing an affirmation of mystical self-liberation, Heidegger defines knowing as the ability to discuss the world.

Humankind has overemphasized knowing and become too technological. Heidegger criticizes science and technology, which he associates with nihilism. Knowing is grounded in existing. Being in the world is a necessary condition for knowing. Heidegger feels that people cannot learn anything they do not care about; without some type of fascination, there can be no knowledge.

Heidegger envisions the entire world as "being" or "existing," and he defines "existing" as that which is part of humanity's system of questioning. According to Heidegger, human beings are not physical structures but fluctuating series of possibilities (*Seinkönnen*) that constitute their existence.

Part of unconscious knowledge relates to an awareness of entities (*Zeug*). People are not necessarily conscious of their awareness. Heidegger defines "everydayness" (*Alltäglichkeit*) as the connection of humans with entities. The world is only authentically ready-to-hand as it "comes before us." People can form questions and listen for responses only as they experience life. It is the experience of individuals that offers development, not the body of historical knowledge that people have relied on before each individual experienced it.

When experiencing the world around the self, the primary concern is not what various things "are" but what they "do." Equipment is meaningless without knowing what the equipment can do. There are three areas, called deficient modes, that interfere with a person's ability to understand what things do in the world. The *conspicuous* mode relates to those situations in which an object cannot be used for its original purpose. In the *obtrusive* mode, understanding is interrupted when something is missing; when an item is needed and fails to be ready-at-hand, its obtrusiveness interferes with understanding. Last, in the *obstinate* mode, one item obstructs the ability to use another. If a lock on a box prevents someone from reaching a necessary object such as a hammer, the box is obstinate; a person who is obstinate cannot fully experience the world because the mind refuses to question what things do and dwells instead on what they are.

The concept of Being can be understood more fully when the relationship of Being and Being-there (*Dasein*) becomes disturbed. In order to see things ontologically, people must experience a disturbance. Heidegger claims that part of people's daily routine is filled with emptiness, which constitutes part of human suffering. Through experience with the deficient modes of concern, Heidegger circumvents understanding nature. With positive modes, people would never go beyond childhood concepts of concern that are rooted in nature. Existentialism is based on positive modes that, according to Heidegger, will lull people into ontological sleep. Heidegger views nature as a dark covering over the world that traps human beings into accepting answers without having voiced proper questions. Heidegger's approach to humanity's attempt to understand itself is through questioning and listening and further questioning.

The essence of the world has no meaning apart from humanity; therefore, understanding nature stops the thought process that Heidegger sees as a necessary manifestation of understanding people's place in the world.

Besides knowing their place in the world, human beings must also be involved with the world. While artists must accept their medium as it is, they are also deeply involved with their medium and must continue to question, observe, and listen to the medium's properties. Artists deal with the limits of their medium because in spite of the artist's involvement, the medium will go its own way. Artists are thus involved in the world by being active and participatory, according to Heidegger. Without such involvement, Being-there, or existence, becomes deficient. Being-there must give itself the task of understanding its Being-there.

The key to Heidegger's premise is his focus on humanity. Among the major points of Heidegger's concept of existence is its uniqueness. Existence is noncategorized, unstable, unpredictable, and therefore free. It is centered on the individual and has no specified behavior patterns, since it is in constant change. It is focused on potential. People are equated with their possibilities. Adventure, accomplished through constant questioning and the search for new pathways, is a key point to evolving. People continually challenge, question, and make their own decisions; however, humans can never truly know who they are, only who humanity was. People cannot project into the future, nor can human progress be scientifically measured.

Heidegger describes phenomena as the totality of what lies in the light of day or can be brought to light. The essence of humanity consists of its definition according to each individual and the freedom of mind of each individual. Humanity always precedes itself on the path to understanding. The origin or upheaval, as realized in the position of humanity, is the Heideggerian description of *eksistence*.

Annette M. Magid

Bibliography:
Kaelin, Eugene Francis. "Heidegger's *Being and Time*." *Journal of the American Academy of Religion* 58 (Winter, 1990): 715-716. Attempts to reinstate a philosophical connection with a theological premise, that is, to redefine the meaning of God within the humanity of self.

Martin, F. David. "Heidegger's Being of Things and Aesthetic Evaluation." *Journal of Aesthetic Education* 8 (July, 1974): 87-105. Brief interpretation of Heidegger's later thought with reference to the Being of things, aesthetic experience, and implications of aesthetic education.

Miles, Murray. "Fundamental Ontology and Existential Analysis in Heidegger's *Being and Time*." *International Philosophical Quarterly* 34 (September, 1994): 349-359. Provides a scholarly definition of the difference between existentialism and metaphysicalism.

Olafson, Frederick, A. Waugh, and J. M. Bell. "Heidegger and the Philosophy of Mind." *Southern Humanities Review* 23 (Summer, 1989): 293-294. Focuses on Heidegger's *Discourse on Thinking* (1969), which addresses the question of Being and gives background for understanding *Being and Time*.

Owensby, Jacob. "Some Roots of *Being and Time* in Life-Philosophy." *Research in Phenomenology* 19 (1989): 311-315. Relates the Greek philosophers Plato and Aristotle and the existentialist philosophers Immanuel Kant and Jean-Paul Sartre to the evolution of Heidegger's language exploration.

Scharff, Robert C. "Habermas on Heidegger's *Being and Time*." *International Philosophical Quarterly* 31 (June, 1991): 189-201. Clearly written analysis of Heidegger in terms of the philosophy of Jürgen Habermas.

BEL-AMI

Type of work: Novel
Author: Guy de Maupassant (1850-1893)
Type of plot: Naturalism
Time of plot: c. 1885
Locale: Paris and Cannes, France
First published: 1885 (English translation, 1889)

> *Principal characters:*
> GEORGES DUROY, later GEORGES DU ROY DE CANTEL, a newspaper man
> MADELEINE FORESTIER, the wife of Duroy's benefactor and later Duroy's wife
> CLOTILDE DE MARELLE, Duroy's mistress
> CHARLES FORESTIER, Duroy's former brother officer and the editor who befriends him
> MONSIEUR WALTER, the owner of the newspaper for which Duroy works
> BASILE WALTER, Monsieur Walter's wife
> SUZANNE WALTER, Monsieur Walter's daughter

The Story:

Georges Duroy, a former soldier, had only three francs in his pocket when he met his brother officer, Charles Forestier, in Paris one evening. Forestier, an editor of the daily newspaper, *La Vie Francaise*, unhesitatingly lent Duroy money to buy suitable clothes and invited him to come to dinner the following evening to meet the owner of the paper. The Forestiers' party was a success for Duroy. M. Walter hired him as a reporter to write a series of articles on his experiences in Algeria.

It was not easy for Duroy to adapt himself to his new job. His first article was due the day following the dinner party. Unable to write it in the proper form, he was forced to hurry to the Forestier home early in the morning to seek stylistic advice. Forestier, just leaving, referred Duroy to Mme Forestier for help. Together they turned out a successful piece. With her help, Duroy slowly built a reputation as a clever reporter, but his salary remained small.

Two months after the Forestiers' dinner party, Duroy called on Mme de Marelle, who had been among the guests that evening. Duroy's acquaintance with Mme de Marelle quickly developed into an intimate friendship. Because M. de Marelle was often away from home, his wife had ample time to see her lover, at his lodgings at first and then at an apartment that she rented. Duroy objected mildly to having Mme de Marelle bear this expense, but it was not long before he found himself regularly accepting small sums of money from her. It was Mme de Marelle's daughter Laurine who first called him "Bel-Ami," a nickname gradually adopted by most of his friends.

M. Forestier suffered from a bronchial ailment. As his health grew worse, his disposition became unbearable at the office. Duroy determined to avenge himself by attempting to seduce Mme Forestier. She gently rebuffed him but agreed that they could be friends. Duroy was brash enough to propose that she become his wife if she were ever widowed.

At Mme Forestier's suggestion, Duroy began to cultivate Mme Walter. The week following his first visit to her, he was appointed editor of the "Echoes," an important column. He had barely assumed this position when the editor of a rival newspaper, *La Plume*, accused him falsely of receiving bribes and suppressing news. To uphold the honor of *La Vie Francaise*,

562

Duroy was forced to challenge his disparager to a duel. Though neither man was injured, M. Walter was pleased with Duroy's spirit.

Duroy moved into the apartment that Mme de Marelle had rented for their meetings after promising that he would never bring anyone else there. Shortly afterward, Forestier became seriously ill, and Duroy received a telegram asking him to join the Forestiers in Cannes, where they had gone for the invalid's health. After Forestier's death, as he and Mme Forestier kept a vigil over the corpse, Duroy proposed once more. The widow made no promises, but the next day she told him that she might consider marrying him, though she warned him that she would have to be treated as an equal and her conduct left unquestioned.

Mme Forestier returned to Paris. A year later, she and Duroy, or Georges du Roy de Cantel, as he now called himself at his wife's suggestion, were married. They had agreed to spend their honeymoon with his parents in Normandy, but Mme de Cantel refused to spend more than one day with his simple, ignorant peasant family in their tiny home.

The newspaperman found in his wife a valuable ally who not only aided him in writing his articles but also, as the friend of influential men, helped him to find a place in political circles. Nevertheless, friction soon developed between them. After he had moved into his wife's home, de Cantel found that its comforts had been designed to please its old master and that he was expected to fill the niche his friend had occupied. Even the meals were prepared according to Forestier's taste. To pique his wife, de Cantel began to call Forestier "poor Charles," always using an accent of infinite pity when he spoke the name.

Not long after his marriage, de Cantel resumed his relationship with Mme de Marelle and at the same time began an affair with Mme Walter. He had briefly bemoaned the fact that he had not married wealthy young Suzanne Walter, but he soon became intrigued with the idea of seducing her mother, a pillar of dignity. His conquest was not a difficult one. Mme Walter began to meet her lover at his rooms and to shower so much affection and attentions upon him that he quickly became bored.

Among Mme de Cantel's political acquaintances was the foreign minister, Laroche-Mathieu, who supplied news of government activities to *La Vie Francaise*. Because the minister was also a close friend of M. Walter, it was not difficult for de Cantel's new lover to learn a state secret, namely that France would soon guarantee the Moroccan debt. Mme Walter planned to buy some shares of the loan with the understanding that de Cantel would receive part of the profit. While Mme Walter was carrying on her speculations, the de Cantels received a windfall in the form of a bequest from the late Count de Vaudrec, an old family friend of Mme de Cantel. De Cantel objected to the count's bequest of one million francs on the grounds that appearances would compromise her. He allowed her to accept the money only after she had agreed to divide it equally with him, so that it would seem to outsiders as if they had both received a share.

De Cantel profited handsomely when France assumed the Moroccan debt, but his gains were small compared to those of Laroche-Mathieu and M. Walter, who had become millionaires as a result of the intrigue. One evening, he and his wife were invited to view a painting in the Walters' magnificent new mansion. There de Cantel began a flirtation with Suzanne Walter; his own wife and Laroche-Mathieu had become intimates without attempting to conceal their friendship. That evening, de Cantel persuaded Suzanne to agree never to accept a proposal without first asking his advice. At home after the reception, he received with indifference the cross of the Legion of Honor that the foreign minister had given him. He felt that he was entitled to a larger reward for concealing news of the Moroccan affair from his readers. That spring, he surprised his wife and Laroche-Mathieu at a rendezvous. Three months later, he obtained a divorce, causing the minister's downfall by naming him corespondent.

A free man again, de Cantel was able to court Suzanne Walter. It was simple for him to persuade the girl to tell her parents she wished to marry him and to have her go away with him until they gave their consent to the match. Mme Walter was the only one at the magnificent church wedding to show any signs of sadness. She hated the daughter who had taken her lover, but she was powerless to prevent the marriage without compromising herself. M. Walter had managed to resign himself to having a conniving son-in-law and had, in fact, recognized his shrewdness by making him chief editor of the newspaper. Suzanne was innocently happy as she walked down the aisle with her father. Her new husband was also content. Greeting their well-wishers in the sacristy after the ceremony, he took advantage of the occasion to reaffirm, with his eyes, his feelings for Mme de Marelle. As he and his wife left the church, it seemed to him that it was only a stone's throw from that edifice to the chamber of deputies.

Critical Evaluation:

Bel-Ami is the story of an intriguer who climbs to a position of wealth and power by publishing the story of his first wife's disgrace and later cheating her of part of her fortune. The unscrupulous parvenu and the women he dupes are among the masterpieces of characterization produced by the French realistic school to which Guy de Maupassant belonged.

In the novel, Georges Duroy, who might be considered the male counterpart of William Makepeace Thackeray's Becky Sharp, represents the restlessness of a certain class at a time when the once-frozen class system slowly begins to thaw. He illustrates the morally debilitating nature of poverty. Although Maupassant scrupulously avoids comment, he seems to be suggesting that while it is easy enough to be moral with enough money in one's pocket, society should hesitate to condemn those who must use their wits to survive (and are not too particular about how they do it). Duroy automatically looks for prey (as he did when stationed in Africa) to help him get ahead, and if confronted he would have responded, what else could a man in his position do?

Duroy's essential laziness prevents him from taking advantage of all the opportunities that open before him, but a natural shrewdness and ruthlessness carry him along far enough to be within sight of his goal. He is a man who never can be satisfied. Neither his background nor his instincts have given him a moral base on which to conduct his life; to him, "honor" is a catchword, not a code that touches him to the core. In fact, nothing touches him deeply. Pleasure, for him, equals happiness.

Ambition and death alternate as themes in the novel, the latter showing the ultimate futility of the former. The long and painful death of Charles Forestier provides Duroy with a greater opportunity for advancing in the world with the aid of Madeleine Forestier, but it also foreshadows the end that awaits Duroy and everyone else. A sense of terror crushes Duroy when he sits by the body of Forestier, and he wonders what the difference is between flies who live a few hours and men who live a few years. He has no ideals, no purpose to his life other than temporary physical sensations, and he can even see how meaningless they are. He is not, however, a profound enough thinker to pursue this train of thought. Soon, he is back at his usual scheming and plotting. With superb understatement, Maupassant says at this point: "Duroy returned to all his old habits."

The young Maupassant considered himself a disciple of Gustave Flaubert. Certainly, the supple prose and carefully selected details, as well as the understated irony of the novel, are true to Flaubert's literary teachings. Maupassant also belonged to the circle of realists that included Émile Zola and Ivan Turgenev. He presents his characters in *Bel-Ami* with strict objectivity, noting always the word or gesture that betrays the essential personality of each one. Concise-ness and a rigorous economy of words and images underlie the art of the novel. He gives in *Bel-Ami* a true picture of the society of his time. Every detail is precise and factual, yet the view of humankind is powerfully universal.

Bibliography:

Donaldson-Evans, Mary. "The Harlot's Apprentice: Maupassant's *Bel-Ami.*" *The French Review: Journal of the American Association of Teachers of French* 60, no. 5 (April, 1987): 616-625. An examination of the hero and of sexual identity in Maupassant's novel. Discusses the novel in the context of nineteenth century naturalistic literature.

Hamilton, James F. "The Impossible Return to Nature in Maupassant's *Bel-Ami* or the Intellectual Heroine as Deviant." *Nineteenth-Century French Studies* 10, no. 3 (Spring/Summer, 1982): 326-339. Considers Maupassant's novel in terms of his conceptualization of female characters. The examinations of Madeleine Forestier and Clotilde de Marelle are rigorous and insightful. In dealing with the issue of heroine and intellect, the article elucidates Maupassant's use of naturalistic and realistic literary devices.

Lethbridge, Robert. "Maupassant's *Bel-Ami* and the Art of Illusion." In *Studies in French Fiction in Honour of Vivienne Milne*, edited by Robert Gibson. London: Grant & Cutler, 1988. Explores duplicity in the novel *Bel-Ami*. Also considers the work as an example of nineteenth century French literature.

Lloyd, Christopher. *Maupassant: "Bel-Ami."* London: Grant & Cutler, 1988. Examines the novel's philosophy and style and offers a thorough overview of the work as a study of social position and ambition.

Prince, Gerald. "*Bel-Ami* and Narrative as Antagonist." *French Forum* 11, no. 2 (May, 1986): 217-226. A study of the character of Georges Duroy in terms of Maupassant's development of narrative and of his construction of an antagonist.

BELINDA

Type of work: Novel
Author: Maria Edgeworth (1767-1849)
Type of plot: Social realism
Time of plot: Late eighteenth century
Locale: London and southern England
First published: 1801

Principal characters:
 BELINDA, a young woman
 LADY DELACOUR, a lady of fashion
 LORD DELACOUR, her husband
 HELENA DELACOUR, their daughter
 CLARENCE HERVEY, a wealthy young man
 VIRGINIA ST. PIERRE (RACHEL HARTLEY), his ward
 MR. VINCENT, Belinda's suitor
 MRS. SELINA STANHOPE, Belinda's aunt
 HARRIET FREKE, Lady Delacour's former friend
 MR. PERCIVAL and
 LADY ANNE PERCIVAL, friends to Helena and Belinda
 DR. X——, a physician

The Story:

Belinda's aunt, wishing Belinda to acquire a husband of wealth and social position, sent her to live with Lady Delacour, a leading figure in fashionable London. At first Belinda was dazzled by Lady Delacour's wit and elegance and by the glamour of her world. Quickly, however, Belinda became disgusted by the shallow frivolity that permeated this world and by the manipulative jockeying for social position that drove its players. In particular, she realized that Lady Delacour's social brilliance disguised a deeply unhappy woman who despised her husband and marriage, feared the aging of her body, and concealed a mysterious personal secret known only to her maid, Marriott.

Belinda's aunt hoped to match her with Clarence Hervey, who was not only wealthy but also the cleverest of London's eligible young men. Lady Delacour, too, encouraged Belinda's interest in Hervey, though she considered him one of her own admirers. To Belinda, Hervey initially seemed foppish and conceited, and Hervey was on his guard against Belinda because he assumed she shared the goals of her aunt, a notorious matchmaker. At a masked ball, a disguised Belinda overheard Hervey denigrating her before his male friends as a "composition of art and affectation." Belinda was mortified and resolved to take no interest in Hervey.

After the ball, Lady Delacour revealed to Belinda the real misery of her life. To hurt her husband, whom she thought an alcoholic fool, she had encouraged a beau, Colonel Lawless; Lord Delacour had shot Lawless in a duel, and Lady Delacour still suffered from guilt over his death. Motherhood meant little to her, and her surviving daughter, Helena, was someone she thought little about and seldom saw. She was obsessed by a rivalry with another London hostess, Mrs. Luttridge, and her best friend, Harriet Freke, had joined Mrs. Luttridge's camp. Finally, a breast injury she had received in a duel with another woman had, she thought, become a disease that was killing her, but she felt compelled to keep her sickness hidden from the world and continue her life of social gaiety as long as possible.

Belinda was both horrified by Lady Delacour's story and moved by it. She wanted to help Lady Delacour. Clarence Hervey, who soon revised his opinion of Belinda, wished this as well. They became friends in an effort to bring Lady Delacour closer to her daughter Helena. Helena had been cared for on school holidays by Mr. Percival and Lady Anne Percival, whom Hervey met when Mr. Percival saved him from drowning. Seeing Helena's longing for her mother, Hervey maneuvered a meeting between Helena and Belinda, and Hervey and Belinda arranged a visit from Helena to Lady Delacour. Lady Delacour was stirred by Helena's love and vowed to reform.

When Belinda attempted to reconcile Lady Delacour and her husband, Lady Delacour became suspicious that Belinda was pursuing Lord Delacour, so Belinda went to stay with the Percivals at Oakly-park, their country home. Before she left London, Belinda, who had rejected a proposal from the stupid and pretentious Sir Philip Baddely, had become more interested in Hervey, but when she saw a painting said to be a portrait of his mistress, she tried to stop thinking of him. At the Percivals' she met a new suitor, Mr. Vincent, heir to West Indian wealth. Belinda refused his first proposal, but she was influenced by Lady Anne's praise of his virtues to allow his continued courtship. Belinda also rejected Harriet Freke's efforts to alienate her from the Percivals and Lady Delacour, and she defeated the practical joke with which Freke tried to persuade Mr. Vincent's black servant, Juba, that he was haunted by a ghost.

Lady Delacour feared she was dying and summoned Belinda back to London. In the hope that an operation might save her, she revealed her disease to her husband. She was spared the operation when Dr. X—— informed her that her illness was caused not by breast disease but by the opium she had been taking.

Lady Delacour was convinced that Belinda still loved Hervey and tried to persuade her not to marry Mr. Vincent. Hervey, however, announced he would marry Virginia St. Pierre, the original of the portrait Belinda had seen earlier. Hervey had been the guardian of Virginia (then named Rachel Hartley, but renamed by Hervey) since her grandmother had died. He had planned to marry her and, influenced by the theories of the French philosopher Jean-Jacques Rousseau, had directed that she be kept as nearly as possible a "child of nature," protected from exposure to frivolous social sophistication. He preferred Belinda's strong, socially educated mind and character to Virginia's ignorance and passivity, but he thought that Virginia had fallen in love with him and he was obligated to marry her. On the verge of marrying Mr. Vincent, Belinda discovered he was a gambler (though he had been temporarily saved from ruin by the generous Hervey), and she ended the engagement. After further entanglements and disentanglements, Belinda and Hervey were free to marry each other.

Critical Evaluation:

During the first two decades of the nineteenth century, Maria Edgeworth was among the most popular and most critically admired of contemporary English novelists. Her reputation declined later in the century as standards of realism changed, although her novels had helped to develop such standards. The novels of Jane Austen and Sir Walter Scott came to eclipse Edgeworth's in the public eye, but Austen and Scott admired Edgeworth's fiction and were influenced by it.

Edgeworth herself came to dislike *Belinda*, particularly its title character, whom she called "cold" and "tame"; she preferred her novels with Irish settings, such as *Castle Rackrent* (1800) and *The Absentee* (1812). As a story about a young woman who must navigate social perils on her way to the choice of a suitable husband, *Belinda* is in many respects a conventional novel of its time. Its structure and manner show the influence of Fanny Burney and Elizabeth Inchbald, both well-regarded late eighteenth century novelists. Belinda is distinctive, though, in her combination of virtue and independent thought and in her refusal to submit to the authority of others. She can appreciate and act on wise advice from a friend, such as that of Lady Anne Percival, but she makes her own decisions. In the novel's last scene, the stage is set for Belinda's acceptance of Clarence Hervey, but she delays her acceptance, reinforcing the reader's sense that Belinda is as much her own woman at the end of the story as she was at the beginning.

Edgeworth emphasizes Belinda's independence by juxtaposing her against three other female characters, Harriet Freke, Lady Delacour, and Virginia St. Pierre. The outrageous Harriet Freke, cross-dressing, proclaiming women's superiority to men, and involving herself and Lady Delacour in an attempt to influence a political campaign, is a parody of a late eighteenth century feminist. She might have made a contemporary reader think of the scandals that had collected by 1801 around the pioneer feminist Mary Wollstonecraft. It had become known that Wollstone-craft, the author of *A Vindication of the Rights of Woman* (1792), had openly borne a child out of wedlock. Freke's characterization seems to support the most conservative patriarchal ideol-ogy of the period by illustrating the chaos produced by women who discard the rules of female propriety, are not subservient to men, and act in the public sphere. In fact, Edgeworth's thinking about women's intellectual and moral equality to men and the importance of educating women to develop their capacity for reasoned judgment was actually close to Wollstonecraft's.

Belinda comprises two major interpolated tales. One is about Lady Delacour, and the other is about Virginia St. Pierre. They serve as object lessons in the value of women's rights. Lady Delacour's life history is introduced near the beginning of the novel, Virginia St. Pierre's near the end. These histories develop perspectives, on the one hand, on the pitfalls of a woman's life that is apparently independent but in truth so out of control as to be prey to the whims of others, and, on the other hand, on the dangers of a woman's life subject to rigid control by protective guardians. Lady Delacour seeks worldly power and evades the dictates of a moral code that would have her obey her husband. Fearing the loss of worldly gratifications and subjection to her husband that may come if she admits her illness, she begins to be destroyed by the opium she takes to ameliorate the pain of her imagined breast disease. She becomes the prey of her own compulsions and of a quack doctor. Virginia St. Pierre, on the other hand, is the epitome of an overly sheltered young girl. During her childhood she was shielded from society because of her grandmother's fears about female vulnerability to seduction and unfaithful men, and as an adolescent she was kept isolated because of Clarence Hervey's enthusiasm for Jean-Jacques Rousseau's romantic ideas about the moral purity of a life close to nature. He also accepts uncritically Rousseau's ideas on the corrupting effects on women of an education that exposes them to worldly complexities. Whereas Lady Delacour is prey to her fears of loss of power and to the quack doctor's opium, the barely educated Virginia is prey to the fantasies encouraged by the romances to which she has become addicted. Neither is able to think clearly about her situation.

Set against these two interpolated tales as well as the dramatization of Harriet Freke, Belinda's story is Edgeworth's effort to define a mode of female behavior that is neither submissive to external authority nor willfully given over to excitements. Belinda's name recalls the vain, frivolous heroine of Alexander Pope's satire *The Rape of the Lock* (1712). Edgeworth's Belinda, however, is not frivolous; she can make her way toward reasoned judgments without depending on the guidance of a "superior" masculine vision.

That Belinda's character seemed dull to her author and that the more dramatic assertions of the unreformed Lady Delacour sometimes threaten to take over the novel suggest that for Edgeworth herself there were tensions between the domestic ideology her novel advocated and her own resistance to the restrictions it placed on women's lives. Nevertheless, the model of egalitarian marriage and devotion to family represented by the Percivals and the reformed Delacours points toward the dominant middle-class domestic ideal of the nineteenth century. *Belinda* shows clearly how Edgeworth believed this model to be empowering for women.

Anne Howells

Bibliography:
Butler, Marilyn. *Jane Austen and the War of Ideas.* Oxford, England: Clarendon Press, 1975. The chapter on Edgeworth is a good introduction to *Belinda*'s treatment of women's lives.

_____. *Maria Edgeworth: A Literary Biography.* Oxford, England: Clarendon Press, 1972. The best biography of Edgeworth. Has an extensive and thoughtful treatment of Edgeworth's relationship with her father, which was very influential on her writing. Discusses *Belinda*'s place in Edgeworth's canon.

Johnson, Claudia L. *Jane Austen: Women, Politics, and the Novel.* Chicago: University of Chicago Press, 1988. Places *Belinda* in the context of the politics of the 1790's and other novels of the period.

Kowaleski-Wallace, Elizabeth. *Their Fathers' Daughters: Hannah More, Maria Edgeworth, and Patriarchal Complicity.* New York: Oxford University Press, 1991. Investigates issues raised by Edgeworth's representation of women's rationality and irrationality and argues that her treatment of Lady Delacour and motherhood is the core of the novel.

Mellor, Anne K. *Romanticism and Gender.* New York: Routledge, Chapman & Hall: 1993. Reads *Belinda* as a presentation of "the new feminine Romantic ideology" of "balanced feminism." Extensive bibliography emphasizing women writers of the period, including Edgeworth.

A BELL FOR ADANO

Type of work: Novel
Author: John Hersey (1914-1993)
Type of plot: Social realism
Time of plot: 1943
Locale: Adano, Italy
First published: 1944

> *Principal characters:*
> MAJOR VICTOR JOPPOLO, the American military governor of Adano
> SERGEANT BORTH, Major Joppolo's subordinate
> CAPTAIN PURVIS, the head of the military police
> GENERAL MARVIN, the commander-in-chief of the American invasion troops and Major Joppolo's superior

The Story:

When the American army invaded Sicily, Major Victor Joppolo was placed in command of Adano. He set up his office in the city hall, rehired the janitor, and investigated the records left by the Fascist mayor, who had fled to the hills. Soon after his arrival, Major Joppolo summoned the leading citizens of the town and asked them, through Giuseppe, his interpreter, what they considered the most important thing to be done. Some answered that the shortage of food was the most pressing problem. Others insisted that what the town needed most was its bell, which had been removed by the Fascists. The bell, it seemed, had a soothing tone and it regulated the lives of Adano's residents. The major promised every effort to recover the bell. Meanwhile, the problem was to obtain food and to have produce brought into the town. In order that his directives would be understood and carried out, the major issued proclamations that the town crier, after being silent for so long, hastened to shout in the village.

On Sunday morning, when the major attended mass at one of the churches, he noticed a blonde girl sitting in front of him. When he later asked Giuseppe about her, the interpreter assumed that the American's interest had nothing to do with official business. Major Joppolo's primary interest, however, was the girl's father, Tomasino, owner of a fishing fleet. He had Giuseppe ask Tomasino to come to see him, but Tomasino, distrustful of authority, refused to come to the headquarters. The major therefore went to Tomasino, followed by practically all the townspeople. The old Italian was defiant, sure that the major had come to arrest him. Major Joppolo finally convinced him that he meant neither to arrest him nor to ask for a cut in the proceeds from the sale of the fish but rather wanted him to go out with his fishing fleet, despite the danger of mines.

The major and his policies had become the subject of much discussion among the people. The Fascist mayor provided a great deal of amusement because he had come out of hiding and been paroled into Sergeant Borth's custody. Every morning, the mayor had to go to Sergeant Borth and publicly confess a Fascist sin. Giuseppe was astonished to discover that the major meant what he said when he told him to report for work at seven in the morning. Gargano, the former Fascist policeman, learned that he could no longer force the others to make way for him when they stood in line at the bakery.

While driving through Adano one day, General Marvin found the road blocked by a mule cart. The driver, having had his daily quota of wine, was sleeping peacefully. When the mule refused to budge, the general ordered the vehicle thrown into the ditch. Reluctantly, the soldiers dumped the cart, mule, and sleeping driver. Swearing furiously, the general drove to the city hall, where he confronted Major Joppolo and ordered that all carts be forbidden to enter Adano.

The next day, a group of townspeople besieged the major to explain that the carts were essential, for they brought food and water into the town. Major Joppolo countermanded the general's order and telephoned Captain Purvis that he would accept full responsibility. Captain Purvis, anxious to keep out of trouble, ordered Lieutenant Trapani to make a memorandum and send it to General Marvin. The lieutenant, out of regard for Major Joppolo, put the memorandum among Purvis' papers in the hope that the captain, who rarely looked through his files, would never find it.

Major Joppolo's efforts to restore the bell were not successful, for it had been melted down by the Fascists. A young naval officer in charge of a nearby station promised to obtain a ship's bell for him.

In the meantime, Captain Purvis had gone through the papers on his desk and had found the memorandum for General Marvin. He ordered it forwarded at once. Lieutenant Trapani mailed it, but addressed it to the wrong person at headquarters in Algiers. From there, it was forwarded to the general's aide, Colonel Middleton. Every day the colonel met with General Marvin and went over important communications. Accordingly, he was halfway through Purvis' letter before he realized what it was. He tried to go on to the next letter, but it was too late. The general had heard Major Joppolo's name and that of Adano, and he remembered both.

The bell arrived in Adano. It was touched, prodded, sounded by the experts, and admired by everybody. When it pealed forth, the townspeople declared that its tone was even better than that of the old bell. The major was a hero. To show their appreciation and affection, the townspeople had him taken to a photographer. A local artist painted his portrait from the photograph. At the celebration that night, Sergeant Borth became very, very drunk. He refused to take orders from Major Joppolo, saying that the major was no longer in any position to give orders. Captain Purvis, said the sergeant, almost sobbing, had received a letter from General Marvin, ordering Major Joppolo back to Algiers. The next morning, the major said goodbye to Borth, who apologized for his conduct of the previous night. The major asked him to help his successor make the people happy. As he drove away from the town, he heard in the distance the tolling of a bell, the new bell for Adano.

Critical Evaluation:

John Hersey's *A Bell for Adano*, which was published in 1944 and for which the novelist was awarded the Pulitzer Prize the following year, achieved enormous popularity in its day and was seen as a classic war novel. Because Hersey had experienced the war as a correspondent, the novel was thought to be considerably more realistic than it actually is. With some qualifications, the work can, however, be placed in that genre of American fiction called realism.

The situation of an Italian-speaking American officer, Major Joppolo, serving as administrator of the small Sicilian village of Adano allows Hersey to set out his beliefs about the primacy of democracy over Fascism, the duty of leaders to serve the people, the need for administrative control, and the disasters that result when people are left to their own devices. These beliefs coincided with the opinions held by many Americans at the close of World War II. It was consequently the perfect reading material for Americans who needed to believe that war was necessary and that the United States was helping the rest of the world by occupying Italy. It was also pleasant to believe that amid the difficulties of war there could be moments of humor and that one could encounter good simple folk. The novel is optimistic, often comic in tone, and ultimately romantic in its conclusion: When Major Joppolo is ordered by General Marvin to leave the town, he stops for one final time to hear the ringing of the bell that his efforts had brought the people. "It was a fine sound on the summer air," the novel maintains, and the reader is left with the image of Joppolo as a decent man who has done his best. That the town has little future is immaterial; the residents of Adano will simply continue their bungling ways. The main conflict in the novel stems from the clashes between Major Joppolo, who believes in democracy and servant leadership, and General Marvin, whose selfishness and cruelty in shooting the mule and ordering carts out of the village make him the symbol of American arrogance and lack of consideration for the native population. There is additional conflict and satire in Joppolo's struggles with postwar bureaucracy; his reaction to his "Instructions to Civil Affairs Officers," which is to tear up the pages and use his own judgment, affords both humor and commentary on the unrealistic, theoretical approach to occupying a small town.

That General Marvin, who has the right to order Joppolo to leave Adano, is ultimately the victor, suggests that Hersey believes that it is important for individuals to do something good, even if it is only a small gesture. No one in the novel changes or develops; the soldiers continue to be superficial, the townspeople petty, the Army bureaucracy uncaring. Life goes on, but it is vital that individuals do good deeds and therein find satisfaction.

Most of the Italian villagers are depicted as foolish, nostalgic, and opportunistic. Hersey achieves some of his best humor at their expense, frequently using caricature and such tags as "lazy Fatta" and "formidable Margherita." Hersey also gives some of the townspeople dignity, however. Old Cacopardo's reproach of General Marvin's lack of appreciation of the antique mahogany table on which the general and his aide are playing mumblety-peg shows the clash of cultures and allows Hersey to point out the inability of most Americans to realize the richness of other histories and cultures. This same theme is echoed in the earliest conversations about the village bell when "small Zito" maintains that the bell will be of greater significance than additional food would be. Zito rejects a replica of the American Liberty Bell: "I do not think the people of Adano want any liberty that has a crack in it."

In his depictions of the soldiers Chuck and Polak, who seek only drink and sexual escapades and who destroy the art objects in the house where they are billeted, Hersey provides a biting commentary on the behavior of American soldiers abroad. Some reviewers in fact questioned Hersey's accuracy, particularly regarding the language he ascribed to the soldiers, which was considered shocking at the time.

The novel is more a series of vignettes than a complex narrative; there is little if any interior action. Hersey is at his best in depicting isolated incidents: Major Joppolo's arrival in Adano, the first visit with Tomasino and his family, the Hemingway-inspired dialogue between Chuck and Polak, the conversations about the crack in the American Liberty Bell, the final moments when Major Joppolo stops to hear the bell.

A Bell for Adano has an important history and keeps a secure place in American popular fiction and war literature. The novel eventually became both a Broadway play and a motion picture. Hersey's subsequent publication of *Hiroshima* (1946) further solidified the critical reputation of *A Bell for Adano* and gave it additional credibility.

"Critical Evaluation" by Katherine Hanley

Bibliography:
Bradbury, Malcolm. *The Modern American Novel*. New York: Oxford University Press, 1984. A helpful summary of twentieth century American fiction, which places *A Bell for Adano* in the mainstream of conventional realism and naturalism.

Gemme, Francis. *John Hersey's "A Bell for Adano," "Hiroshima," and Other Works: A Critical Commentary*. New York: Monarch Press, 1966. A brief survey for beginning students. Good cursory treatment of Hersey's works and an overview of the initial reception of his novels.

Huse, Nancy Lyman. *John Hersey and James Agee: A Reference Guide*. Boston: G. K. Hall, 1978. Extremely helpful compilation of materials for research. Includes reviews from the time of initial publication.

Sanders, David. *John Hersey*. New Haven, Conn.: College and University Press, 1967. Excellent overview of Hersey and his work; traces significant themes and beliefs. Good treatment of Hersey's life, with critical attention to his literary output.

_____. *John Hersey Revisited*. Boston: Twayne, 1990. A competent survey of Hersey's life and works, updating the previous information on the critical estimate of Hersey and of *A Bell for Adano*. Also includes bibliography.

THE BELL JAR

Type of work: Novel
Author: Sylvia Plath (as Victoria Lucas, 1932-1963)
Type of plot: Psychological realism
Time of plot: 1953
Locale: New York City and New England
First published: 1963

> *Principal characters:*
> ESTHER GREENWOOD, a college student
> DOREEN, a friend and guest editor
> MRS. GREENWOOD, Esther's widowed mother
> BUDDY WILLARD, a boyfriend of Esther
> DOCTOR NOLAN, a psychiatrist
> JOAN GILLING, Esther's colleague

The Story:

Esther Greenwood was in New York City the summer that Julius and Ethel Rosenberg were to be executed (1953). Ecstatic over having won a position as guest editor on the college board for a well-known magazine for young women, she was puzzled that she was not having the time of her life.

On the face of it, she had everything going for her. She was attractive, intelligent, and talented. She was a straight-A student. The magazine had arranged concerts, dances, celebrity interviews, fashion shows, and luncheons galore for the twelve college student women who had won positions as guest editors. Why was she feeling depressed? Esther's boyfriend Buddy was in a sanatorium recovering from tuberculosis. She was discovering that her feelings for him were lukewarm. She felt free to date other men, but somehow those dates were not turning out as well as she expected.

She and the eleven other young women from colleges across the United States were living in a hotel for women. Doreen, who was cynical and audacious, particularly appealed to Esther. One night on their way to a party, they let themselves be picked up by a disc jockey, Lenny Shepherd. After drinks he asked them to his apartment. After more drinks, Doreen and Lenny danced lasciviously. Esther was disgusted. She left Doreen and walked back to the hotel disillusioned with Doreen and later with herself for abandoning Doreen. Doreen was not the only reason Esther was disillusioned. The city glamour she had expected manifested itself as a series of shoddy episodes. Behind the glittery surfaces she saw a world of competition, meanness, fakery, and backbreaking work leading to some trivial end.

Esther and the other young women were invited to a "ladies' magazine" luncheon. Beautifully presented crabmeat salad was served, but later they were all violently sick. The crabmeat was tainted. Another event in New York City that was supposed to be wonderful was spoiled.

Another spoiled event for Esther was the work she was assigned at the magazine. She was a perfectionist, an overachiever, and always anxious about deadlines. Stress became apparent during a photography session. Esther, told to hold a paper rose and smile (to represent her dream to be a poet), burst into tears.

Later, however, she let Doreen talk her into going out on another date. It was another fiasco. Ripping Esther's dress and throwing her in the mud, calling her a slut, the "country-club gentleman" date, Marco, tried to rape her. She escaped and once again fled back to her hotel.

Her stint as guest editor over, in a gesture of her feelings, Esther threw all of her new clothes off the roof of the hotel. In the morning she left for home. Her mother met her at the train station. Esther hated their small house and the suburbs and planned to escape by attending a creative writing seminar at Harvard. She was not accepted. The rejection, in addition to her recent experiences, sent her into depression. She could not concentrate on writing her honors thesis. She tried to work on a novel, but disappointment and despondency locked her in lethargy. Esther's apathy worried her mother who, at her wits end, suggested they see a psychiatrist.

Unfortunately, the psychiatrist, Doctor Gordon, was the wrong doctor for Esther. She found him insensitive and patronizing. In addition, the shock treatments he prescribed for her not only frightened her but also sent her into a deeper depression. Esther began to dwell on suicide even though she made attempts to do normal things such as double-dating and hospital volunteer work.

One rainy day, after visiting the grave of her father, she returned home, left a note that she was going for a walk, took a bottle of sleeping pills and a glass of water, and went to the basement. Hiding herself in a crawl space behind some firewood, she swallowed the pills. She took too many, causing her to vomit, which saved her life. Now desperate, her mother sent Esther to a state mental institution.

At this point Esther's benefactress, Philomena Guinea, proposed that Esther should be sent to a private hospital. Philomena Guinea would finance it. At the new institution Esther began to improve. Dr. Nolan, her psychiatrist, an intuitive woman, gained Esther's trust. Intuitive people gained Esther's approval. Esther learned that it was all right to say that one hated one's mother. She also learned that her need to be sexually active was not only normal, but also feasible. Dr. Nolan prescribed birth control. Under compassionate supervision, and carefully conducted shock treatments, Esther began to improve.

One of Esther's college friends, Joan Gilling, was also at the hospital. Joan, like Esther, had tried to kill herself. Also, like Esther, Joan had dated Buddy Willard, but at the hospital Joan confessed that she preferred women to men. Initially disgusted with Joan's homosexuality, Esther nevertheless continued to befriend Joan. Eventually, Esther and Joan were allowed town and overnight privileges from the hospital. On one of these outings, Esther had her first sexual experience with a professor whom she had just met. Esther's experience was another misadventure. She began to hemorrhage. The professor, in a panic, took her to the apartment where Joan was staying. Joan, upset, took Esther to an emergency ward, and a doctor repaired the damage. One in a million, he said.

A few days later, Joan hanged herself. Doctor Nolan, worried that Joan's suicide would throw Esther back into despair, assured her that no one was to blame. A sign of Esther's newly gained stability was that neither her sexual misadventure nor Joan's suicide cast her into depression. Buddy Willard then visited Esther at the sanatorium and told her that she was no longer a suitable marriage prospect. Esther was not disturbed. In fact, his pompous announcement freed her. Buddy, from then on, was out of her life. It was another sign of her recovery that she responded in a healthy way to his announcement. Esther was well. She had the strength to face the panel of doctors, who, if she passed their examinations, would discharge her from the hospital. She would take charge, once again, of her destiny.

Critical Evaluation:

The Bell Jar is the only novel by Sylvia Plath, who is best known as a poet. Her novel was published in England in January, 1963, under the pseudonym Victoria Lucas. Plath committed suicide in February of the same year. Since its publication, *The Bell Jar* has received steady acclaim. Critics first viewed it as a fine first novel in the style of J. D. Salinger's *The Catcher in the Rye* (1951). *The Bell Jar* was published in the United States in 1971. Critics in the United States also praised the novel. It was a complex psychological portrayal of a young woman of the early 1950's. Esther Greenwood, in her search for self-determination, was a prototype heroine of the mid-century women's movement, a movement heralded by the publication of Betty Friedan's *The Feminine Mystique* in 1963.

Sylvia Plath had written a rough draft of *The Bell Jar* by 1960, and she won a grant to finish it from the Eugene F. Saxton Foundation. In a letter to her brother, she called the work a "pot-boiler." Her prose, however, took a turn from the mediocre to the remarkable; her poetry had already taken this turn. The poet Ted Hughes, Plath's husband, described Plath's rather sudden change from talent to genius as a "plunge into herself," into the subjective, the imaginary. That the novel contained so much of "herself" was her reason for publishing it under a pseudonym. She did not want to offend anyone she knew; the characters in the novel had their counterparts in life.

The protagonist, Esther Greenwood, is a young woman who sees life as if from within a bell jar. Her experiences are askew, not what they are supposed to be. There is always "a worm in the rose." She has a "perfect" boyfriend, but rather than finding him romantic she finds him dull, pilloried by mom's maxims. She watches a baby being born and instead of seeing a miracle, she sees brutality. She goes to New York City to have the time of her life, but the time of her life is overshadowed by the execution of the Rosenbergs. She discovers that the job of her dreams is contrived; she sees that the woman's world of fashion, romance, and domesticity is a sham.

What Plath learned when she wrote her honor's thesis, "The Magic Mirror: A Study of the Double in Two of Dostoevski's Novels," was "stuff about the ego as symbolized in reflections (mirror and water), shadows, twins." She wrote that "recognition of our various mirror images and reconciliation with them will save us from disintegration." *The Bell Jar* is, to some degree, a fictional account of this study. Throughout the novel, Plath shows the double, "the various mirror images" of the ego. Images of the double resonate throughout the narrative.

Esther's face is an example of the double. After traumatic episodes, Esther Greenwood sees her face mirrored as some kind of blotched, distorted, bloated image—an icon, she thinks, to her dark nature. Her "good" face is restored only after she undergoes a purging ritual, one that can be as simple as a hot bath, as radical as throwing her new clothes off the rooftop of a hotel, or as desperate as a suicide attempt. The double is not only associated with Esther's face; it is also associated with the faces of other people. The other face of Hilda, a guest editor, a young woman of high fashion, impeccably dressed, appears when she tells Esther that she is "so glad" the Rosenbergs are going to die. Out of her mouth echoes the voice of a demon. "Fashion" and "devil" are doubles of Hilda. Joan Gilling's suicide and lesbianism is the other side of the face of the privileged American girl. In addition to people, events also have double faces. A ladies' luncheon, put on by a glossy magazine epitomizing the glamorous "face" of feminine dreams, is elegantly presented, but the plates of crabmeat and avocado are poisonous.

The double motif exposes the hypocrisy that lies beneath the glamorous, glitzy surfaces of a mercantile society. The result is a densely packed, quickly paced novel, one that, in spite of its youthful tone, is complex. It describes the journey of a young woman undergoing trials and pitfalls in her search for an authentic life.

Alice L. Swensen

Bibliography:

Alexander, Paul. *Rough Magic*. New York: Penguin Books, 1991. As thorough a biography as one could wish.

Axelrod, Steven Gould. *Sylvia Plath: The Wound and the Cure of Wounds*. Baltimore, Md.: The Johns Hopkins University Press, 1990. An advanced work on the psychological underpinnings in Plath's fiction and poetry.

Macpherson, Pat. *Reflecting on "The Bell Jar."* London: Routlege & Kegan Paul, 1991. Focuses on the 1950's and what it was like to be a woman coming of age at that time.

Rose, Jacqueline. *The Haunting of Sylvia Plath*. Cambridge, Mass.: Harvard University Press, 1992. A psychoanalytical study focusing mainly on Plath's poetry, with a detailed account of the film of *The Bell Jar* and the lawsuit against it.

Wagner-Martin, Linda. *The Bell Jar: A Novel of the Fifties*. Boston: Twayne, 1992. An excellent analysis of the novel in the context of its times and of the author's life.

BELLEFLEUR

Type of work: Novel
Author: Joyce Carol Oates (1938-   )
Type of plot: Gothic
Time of plot: Mid-sixteenth to late twentieth centuries
Locale: Upstate New York
First published: 1980

Principal characters:
> JEAN PIERRE BELLEFLEUR, the American founder of the Bellefleur family
> LOUIS and
> JEDEDIAH, his sons
> RAPHAEL, Jedediah's son
> GIDEON, Jedediah's great-great-grandson
> LEAH, Gideon's first cousin and wife
> GERMAINE, daughter of Leah and Gideon

The Story:

Jean Pierre Bellefleur, banished from his native France and cast out by his father, a duke, settled in the Lake Noir region of the United States in the mid-1700's and became a powerful force in the area. Notorious for his drinking, gambling, and shady business deals, Jean Pierre was impeached from Congress during his second term for scandal and corruption. When his wife, Hilda, fled his house, to the neighbors' horror, he brought an Onondagan Indian woman, Antoinette, to live with him.

His son Louis married Germaine O'Hagan, a local woman, and had three children with her. Louis' family lived with Jean Pierre, and Louis participated in the family businesses with a disregard for the law that equaled that of his father.

Jedediah Bellefleur, the less business-minded son, went off to live in the nearby mountains to prove to himself that he could survive there for a year. The years began to multiply, and Jedediah did not return. He became a hermit, religiously zealous, suspicious of the occasional trappers and hunters he encountered on the mountain, and paranoid that his family would have him forcibly removed back to their home. His mission became to see the face of God.

After nineteen years on the mountain, Jedediah was persuaded to return to his family home; Jean Pierre, Louis, Antoinette, and Louis' children had been brutally murdered by vengeful neighbors. Only Germaine survived the midnight raid on the family home. In order to keep the family name alive, Jedediah married Germaine and they had three children, including Raphael, who dedicated himself to building the family fame and fortune.

In addition to running for governor and losing three times, helping to found the Republican Party in the area, and building up a hops empire from nothing, Raphael built Bellefleur Manor, a mammoth, Gothic castle that dominated the landscape in the Lake Noir region. There Raphael entertained numerous politicians, including senators, Supreme Court justices, a vice president, and dignitaries from overseas. He claimed to have offered refuge to Abraham Lincoln at the manor when Lincoln, depressed and anxiety-ridden, according to Raphael, hired an actor and staged his own murder. Raphael was best known for having a provision in his will that he be skinned upon his death. He ordered that the skin be stretched over a Civil War cavalry drum, that the drum forever reside in the Great Hall of Bellefleur Manor, and that it be "sounded each

578

day to announce meals, the arrival of guests, and other special events." The drum mainly was used by the Bellefleur children to scare each other and unsuspecting friends.

Subsequent generations of Bellefleurs were punctuated by such members of the family as Jean Pierre II, who was convicted of murdering eleven people in an area tavern; Hiram, an irrepressible sleepwalker; and Vernon, a poet; but most prominent were Gideon and Leah Bellefleur, who lived in the twentieth century.

Gideon and Leah were first cousins who married and had three children. They were beautiful, powerful, and extreme. Anything Gideon drove—a car, a horse, a plane—he drove fast. He raced for high stakes and always won. Leah took in and tamed strays: a large, ferocious cat; a child; a baby that she forcibly removed from its own mother's care; a dwarf. Her children believed she had the power of foresight. After a lengthy and inactive pregnancy with her third child, she set about to restore the Bellefleur fortune, which was a bit depleted, to its previous glory. For luck and inspiration in her business deals, Leah brought along her daughter Germaine, whom she believed had power of her own. Germaine was a quiet, precocious child who had been born with an extra torso and set of legs growing from her abdomen. These had been promptly cut off by her grandmother, but Germaine was characterized by a sadness that may have resulted from a sense of loss over the part of herself that had been removed, or may have resulted from the burden of knowing ahead of time what would happen to family members.

As Leah pursued her business interests and was away from home frequently, her relationship with Gideon, which once had been as passionate as all other aspects of their lives, began to sour. He had numerous affairs with tawdry, uneducated women, the antitheses of Leah, and eventually became obsessed with flying planes. Leah had a number of affairs of her own, which she used as a means to get business accomplished. They only bothered to fight over the affections of Germaine, each claiming to be a more devoted parent to her than the other was.

In an act that nullified not only the accumulating successes of Leah's business ventures, but also Bellefleur Manor and all but a few members of the family, Gideon crashed a plane loaded with explosives into the manor. Only Germaine, whom Gideon had safely deposited with a distant aunt, and the Bellefleurs who had long since fled the manor and never returned, were spared.

Critical Evaluation:

Joyce Carol Oates had published more than sixty works—including novels, plays, and collections of stories, poems, and essays—by the mid-1990's, making her one of the United States' most prolific writers. *Bellefleur*, which is generally acknowledged as her masterpiece, characterizes Oates's tremendous output through its abundance of events, characters, pages, even words per sentence. A huge, sprawling novel of 558 pages, *Bellefleur* covers seven generations and more than fifty members of the Bellefleur family, which dominated a region of the eastern United States that resembles upstate New York. In addition to elements of gothicism and Magical Realism, the novel is characterized by its nonchronological approach to relating the Bellefleur saga, its overabundance of specific details, and Oates's unusual habit of undercutting the story's tension by mentioning hints regarding the outcomes of various events before those events have even been related.

The Bellefleur family history parallels that of the United States, operating sometimes within the context of United States history and culture, but more often in the separate, parallel world of Bellefleur Manor. A sense of otherness is brought about largely by the massiveness of the manor and the miles of land surrounding it, including a range of mountains, all of which are owned or otherwise dominated by the Bellefleurs.

Increasing this sense of otherness is the fact that there are few details that reveal the particular time period of the novel's events. Oates does not provide birth and death dates for the characters beyond 1830 in the family tree found at the beginning of the novel. That readers are not able to pin a specific time to the events of the story makes the lives of the characters seem more fluid and adds to the novel's expansiveness. Not only do the Bellefleurs have an abundance of wealth, land, children, rooms in which to dwell, works of art, horses, and cars, they apparently live longer and more fully than the average human. The things that surround the Bellefleurs are carefully, specifically documented by Oates—one chapter is devoted to a history of the cars they have owned—but the timelessness of these items, their inability to date those surrounding them, increases the reader's sense of Bellefleur Manor as otherworldly and shows that the events of the past are inextricably bound up with the present.

Gothic elements, such as the stone castle with its several wings and towers and off-limits rooms, a would-be vampire, a family curse, and the vulture that steals a baby from the manor's garden, add an atmosphere of gloom and impending doom in the novel. Its elements of Magical Realism, however, create a sense of abundance and possibility that better capture the novel's feel. Young Raphael, whose only emotional connection is to a small, secluded pond, is absorbed into the pond that is, in turn, absorbed into the land. A deformed dwarf eventually straightens and grows tall after several years at the manor. One Bellefleur disappears into a mirror. The bigger-than-life passions of these characters have been so strong, they are transforming.

The sense of the possibility of the supernatural created by the Magical Realism pairs nicely with one of the novel's most striking characteristics, its nonchronological approach to the telling of the story. Despite elements of traditional, historic narratives in *Bellefleur*, Oates presents the events of the novel for effect. The frequent time shifting, which usually occurs at chapter breaks, enables Oates to juxtapose, for the sake of contrast, events from the past with events from the nearer present. The nonchronological approach adds to the reader's sense of the family as exerting a cumulative force on successive generations. The reader feels, along with the Bellefleurs, the power of their ancestry and the burden that is entailed in simply being born into the family. This burden is what drives many family members away and leads Gideon to finally destroy the family and the manor.

Oates's nonchronological approach is a useful device in another way: It allows her to hint at things to come, thereby undercutting any tension or suspense that might be building around certain events in the novel. Readers know ahead of time about the murders of Jean Pierre, Louis, and their families; about Raphael's being skinned; that Gideon will destroy the family; and other things. By undercutting much of the suspense or tension in the novel, Oates distances the reader from individual characters and maintains the focus on her more prevailing concern: the Bellefleur family. She uses the Bellefleurs to track both the ingenuity and potential that the United States represents, and the violence, lust, greed, and eventual destruction contained within the nation as well.

Bellefleur is a work remarkable in its scope, its vision, and its ability to work within, yet turn on, conventional storytelling devices. Events of the story are presented in waves, and the tension of the work is developed around seemingly insignificant events, while major plot points are frequently glossed over. At times, the reader is presented with pages-long lists of the things that surround the Bellefleurs. All these unconventional choices provide a multilayered, profound perspective on power and the American family.

Michelle Fredette

Bibliography:

Bender, Eileen T. "History as Woman's Game: '*Bellefleur*' as *Texte de Jouissance.*" *Soundings: An Interdisciplinary Journal* 76, nos. 2/3 (Summer/Fall, 1993): 369-381. Asserts that "unshapely, fueled by waves of ungratified desire, *Bellefleur* is an audacious and revisionary model of historical fiction."

Creighton, Joanne V. *Joyce Carol Oates: Novels of the Middle Years.* New York: Twayne, 1992. A critical analysis of Oates's novels and essays published between 1977 and 1990. Calls *Bellefleur* Oates's "most impressive reworking" of the nineteenth century gothic genre.

Cunningham, Valentine. "Counting up the Cost." *Times Literary Supplement*, March 20, 1981, 303. Describes *Bellefleur* as bloated with details and suffused with "peculiarly American" horrors.

Nodelman, Perry. "The Sense of Unending: Joyce Carol Oates's *Bellefleur* as an Experiment in Feminine Storytelling." In *Breaking the Sequence: Women's Experimental Fiction*, edited by Ellen G. Friedman and Miriam Fuchs. Princeton, N.J.: Princeton University Press, 1989. Argues that *Bellefleur*, in its nonchronological approach to storytelling, is especially feminine in its experimentation because it transcends "the limitations of both conventional and conventionally innovative forms of fiction" represented by the traditional narrative form of conflict, crisis, and resolution.

Oates, Joyce Carol. *(Woman) Writer: Occasions and Opportunities.* 1st ed. New York: E. P. Dutton, 1988. A collection of Oates's own musings on writing and the woman writer. Contains the preface to *Bellefleur*, in which Oates discusses the classification of the novel as gothic and reveals the one image from which the novel grew.

BELLS IN WINTER

Type of work: Poetry
Author: Czesław Miłosz (1911-   )
First published: 1978

Czesław Miłosz's *Bells in Winter* is a book of short lyric poems, an extended historical poem, and one long poem made up of six sections. The lyric poems are various, since some deal with nature and religion, and others with the social and historical losses of the mid-twentieth century. The long poem goes back to Miłosz's native Lithuania to attempt to come to terms with both the dislocations of the twentieth century and his own history. The earliest poems in the collection were written in 1936 and 1944 in the midst of the destruction of World War II in Eastern Europe. Miłosz is a poet who writes in Polish but was born in Lithuania, and he saw the destruction of his country and the slaughter of millions. So the context of history frames the rest of the poems, which were written in the 1970's.

The first poem in the collection is called "Encounter." It begins with a pastoral landscape with a hare and a man who perceives it. The poem then contrasts that pastoral scene with death and destruction. "Today neither of them is alive,/ Not the hare, nor the man who made the gesture." The speaker asks where are they going, but there is no answer. Instead, the sense of loss is modulated by placing it in another emotional context: "I ask not in sorrow, but in wonder." The poem was written in 1936, a time when the beginnings of World War II were becoming apparent. Wonder is the appropriate emotion to the cataclysm that was to take place; it is literally beyond sorrow.

In contrast, "A Frivolous Conversation," written in 1944, provides a positive vision which can come into being when "mutability ceases." The vision is of a blessed earth filled with marvels and "tranquil glory." However, the speaker of the poem only contemplates these wonders; he does not desire and is "content." The speaker is free from desire, and the time is free from the destruction that change brings. It is a rare moment of pure contemplation and stasis. Thus, the first two poems contrast and represent the dual vision on which Miłosz's art insists.

"Tidings" clearly contrasts to "A Frivolous Conversation." It seeks to define "earthly civilization," asking if it is "a system of colored spheres cast in smoked glass" or a "golden fleece,/ In a rainbow net." After such glorious but fantastical images, the answer is much different. "Or perhaps we'll say nothing of earthly civilization./ For nobody really knows what it was." This suggests that the various positive formulations of civilization are merely illusions, and the reality of human life is far different and more terrible.

"How It Was" also deals with civilization. The poem portrays a journey deep "into the mountains" where the speaker sees only "absence." There was "No eagle-creator," "protective spirits hid themselves in subterranean beds of bubbling ore." In this poem, there is no God the Father and no Son of God: "This time it was really the end of the Old and the New Testament." The poem ends with the speaker described as among those who "longed for the Kingdom" and took refuge "in the mountains to become the last heirs of a dishonored myth." Miłosz often writes about Christianity and its history. In this poem, the Christian era has come to an end and the poet-speaker is one of the few to remain loyal to a myth that no longer has the power to compel belief or reverence. Miłosz often sees the modern world as embracing nihilism; he understands its sources and context, but he can never give his assent to it.

"Not This Way" is a poem of self-accusation, one of many in the book. The poet-speaker describes himself as a "schemer" who uses language in a "childish" manner to transform "the sublime into the cordial." His voice "always lacked fullness." He desires a new language of the elements of "fire and water" to "render a new thanksgiving." In this vision, poetry must reduce itself to the essentials and to a language of utter simplicity in order to fulfill its mission.

"Study of Loneliness" portrays one man alone in the daily glories of nature who begins to question for whom those splendors exist. "For me alone?/ Yet it will be here long after I perish." Nature will go on, apparently indifferent to the fate of humanity. The resolution of the poem is a recognition that it is hopeless to complain: "And he knew there was no use in crying out, for none of them would save him." Salvation cannot come from humanity or from nature, even though Miłosz writes some of his most moving poems on the power within nature.

"A Felicitous Life" is one of the most interesting lyrics in the collection. It first portrays the blessed life of a man who dies in a time of peace without any disturbances in nature. He feels a pang of loss in his death: "It was bitter to say farewell to the earth so renewed." However, the resolution of the poem is very different. "Two days after his death a hurricane razed the coast." Dormant volcanos erupt "And war began with a battle in the islands." The regret at losing the world and beneficent nature is ironically reversed as the transitory nature of everything is revealed. Peace gives way to war and nature turns upon itself.

"Temptation" is another poem of self-accusation. The poet-speaker is seen as "taking a walk" with "the spirit of desolation." This spirit is telling the poet that he is "not necessary," others would have done what he did. The poem, however, reverses itself as the poet responds by rejecting that spirit of desolation. "It's not up to me to judge the calling of men./ And my merits, if any, I won't know anyway." Reputation is not the poet's business. He will be judged in time by others after he is dead. His job is simply to create and to do what he can. Desolation only impedes that creation as does concern with reputation.

"The Chronicles of the Town of Pornic" is a historical poem of four sections. In the first section, it is the site of Bluebeard's Castle. Giles de Laval had "too much freedom" and fell in with the "courtly Falstaffs" of his region. The judgment on his actions, however, is divided in the poem. He either "violated all divine and human rights," or he was put to death "out of greed for his land." Miłosz does not settle the problem but lets the opposite views stand simultaneously.

The next section of this poem is called "The Owners." It is now the time of revolution, when aristocrats are beheaded and the lower classes take over the castle. First, it is occupied by a blacksmith and later a merchant who pays off the debt. "The castle was then inherited by Joubert, manufacturer of cloth." The decline in the inhabitants is ironic as the common and ordinary replace the aristocrats. The "Vandeans" portrays the revenge of those who were temporarily displaced. They murder 215 persons in their social rage. Knowledge of this atrocity is retained only in the memory of a "very old woman" who witnessed it at the age of four.

The last section of the poem is "Our Lady of Recovery." The statue in the "granite chapel" represents a resolution to the murder that social change brings. Our Lady is there to create a longing to return to "the dear earth." The end of this section suggests that a new cycle is to begin, a fruitful and benign one. "Later they drank, grew boisterous, their women conceived./ Her smile meant that it was all according to her will." The will of the Virgin stands for the creative, in contrast to the destructive, impulse in humanity. She can help humankind overcome the seemingly endless destruction caused by class and history.

"Ars Poetica" is a manifesto on the art of poetry. Miłosz sees poetry as involuntary and controlled by a "daimonion." Such an activity is not pleasant, and no sane person would wish to become "a city of demons." The best poetry, according to Miłosz, is without "irony" and morbidity. Finally, he asserts, poetry "should be written rarely and reluctantly . . . and only with the hope/ that good spirits, not evil ones, choose us for their instrument." Miłosz consistently sees an important role for poetry if only the poet can suspend his pride and desire for rewards.

The last poem in the collection, "From the Rising of the Sun," is a long poem that is divided into six sections. The first section is clearly an introduction to the poem. It contrasts Miłosz's life in California along the Pacific coast with his childhood in Lithuania. In his early years, he was "cuddled like a vegetal baby in a seed." In America, "I write here in desolation/ Beyond the land and sea."

The second section returns to his early years in Poland where he was taught about nature by Stefan Baginski and Erazm Majewski. However, he turned away from "the profession of a traveler-naturalist." So now he makes a pilgrimage back to that earlier life and place. He returns to the chapel where a "wooden Madonna" is admired by art lovers. What is lost, however, can never be recovered again; his memory is "unfaithful." He hears ". . . no call./ And the holy had its abode only in denial." "Over Cities" returns to that early world, but the poet-speaker finds loss and absence again. "Everything taken away. Crossed out. All our treasures." He recalls scenes of instruction with "Sir Hieronymus," but neither he nor that world can return. "And where is Sir Hieronymus? Where did I go? Here there is no one."

"A Short Recess" deals with the guilt of Miłosz at leaving his native land to go to Paris, here called "Megalopolis." "I wanted glory, fame and power. . . . So I fled to countries." The decision to seek glory means that he must break pledges and oaths made in and to his land. The result is not glory but doubt and self-recrimination. "Who can tell what purpose is served by destinies/ And whether to have lived on earth means little/ Or much."

The last section of the poem, "Bells in Winter," returns triumphantly to the land that Miłosz abandoned for Paris and, later, California. He portrays a cold morning when he hears all of the church bells of the city peal "So that Lisbeth wrapped up in her cape could go to morning mass." (Lisbeth is an old servant woman who brought logs for the fireplace for the apartment that Miłosz occupied in his younger days.) He then contrasts that magical moment with the bells to his present residence in San Francisco and its "rusty fog." He sees, however, in this section, the possibility of restoration. "And the form of every single grain will be restored in glory./ I was judged for my despair because I was unable to understand this." The vision of the restoration of all things is evoked in the poem, even though the poet acknowledges that he has been unable to affirm it in his life.

James Sullivan

Bibliography:
Baranczak, Stanislaw. "Miłosz's Poetic Language: A Reconnaissance." *Language and Style* 18 (Fall, 1985): 319-333. Baranczak discusses the stylistic variety in Miłosz's poetry as being a way of dealing with the problem of being realistic and visionary at the same time.
Fuit, Aleksander. *The Eternal Moment: The Poetry of Czesław Miłosz.* Berkeley: University of California Press, 1990. The best extended study of Miłosz's poetry. Fuit discusses both the political and stylistic elements in the poetry.
Gordels, Nathan. "An Interview with Czesław Miłosz." *New York Review of Books* 33 (February 27, 1986): 34-35. The interview deals with the political issues of Poland and with Miłosz's attack on nationalism.

Grosholz, Emily. "Miłosz and the Moral Authority of Poetry." *Hudson Review* 39 (Summer, 1986): 251-270. Grosholz discusses Miłosz's critique of current social and scientific theories which claim the place religion once held.

Nathan, Leonard, and Arthur Quinn. *The Poet's Work: An Introduction to Czesław Miłosz.* Cambridge, Mass.: Harvard University Press, 1991. The book is the best available introduction to Miłosz's work. The authors provide contexts for the poetry and are especially good on the philosophical views that are such an important part of Miłosz's poetry.

BELOVED

Type of work: Novel
Author: Toni Morrison (1931-   )
Type of plot: Psychological realism
Time of plot: Nineteenth century
Locale: Cincinnati, Ohio
First published: 1987

> Principal characters:
> SETHE, a former slave
> BELOVED, her first daughter
> DENVER, her second daughter
> HALLE SUGGS, her deceased husband
> BABY SUGGS, her mother-in-law
> PAUL D GARNER, her lover
> HOWARD and
> BUGLAR, her sons

The Story:

In 1848, at the age of thirteen, Sethe was sold to Mr. Garner and his wife Lillian, who ran a plantation in northern Kentucky called Sweet Home. Intended to replace Baby Suggs, whose son Halle had purchased her freedom by renting out his labor on Sundays, Sethe married Halle, one of five male slaves (the "Sweet Home men") owned by the Garners, in 1849. Each of the other Sweet Home men, Paul A Garner, Paul D Garner, Paul F Garner, and Sixo, wanted Sethe for himself, but each accepted her choice and respected her position as Halle's wife.

Mr. Garner died in 1853, and his financially strapped, cancer-ridden widow sold Paul F and then brought her cruel brother-in-law, "schoolteacher," and his equally cruel nephews, to Sweet Home as overseers. Fearful that schoolteacher might sell them all, the remaining Sweet Home slaves began planning an escape in 1855. Before the plan could be effected, the pregnant Sethe was attacked by schoolteacher's two nephews. One held her down while the other sucked the milk from her breasts. Schoolteacher watched and took notes. Unknown to Sethe, her helpless husband saw the entire "mammary rape" from the hayloft, and the event destroyed his sanity. Determined to escape, Sethe sent her three children (Howard, age five; Buglar, age four; and Beloved, age nine months) to join the emancipated Baby Suggs in Cincinnati, planning to follow the next day. The four Sweet Home men failed to escape. Sixo was captured and burned alive, Paul A was hanged, Paul D was sold, and the broken Halle, who died soon after, had lost the will to escape. Only Sethe stumbled into the woods toward freedom.

Sethe nearly died of exposure, but she was found by a runaway white girl, Amy Denver, who doctored her torn feet and helped her to the Ohio River, where they found an abandoned, leaking boat. Before they could cross, Sethe's water broke and with Amy as midwife she gave birth prematurely to her second daughter, Denver, in the nearly swamped boat. Amy, also on the run, abandoned Sethe and Denver. Stamp Paid, a black riverman, found mother and daughter and ferried them across the Ohio to the Bodwins, Quaker conductors on the Underground Railroad. The Bodwins delivered Sethe and Denver to Baby Suggs's house on Bluestone Road outside Cincinnati, where Sethe was reunited with Howard, Buglar, and Beloved.

Sethe enjoyed twenty-eight glorious days of freedom before the slave catchers tracked her down. When the slave catchers approached, Sethe tried to kill her children rather than allow them to be returned to slavery. Three miraculously survived, but Beloved died. Sethe was arrested and sentenced to hang, but the Bodwins obtained a pardon for her and she was allowed to return to Bluestone Road. The ghost of the murdered Beloved also returned and haunted the house for eighteen years, during which it kept away all visitors, drove away Howard and Buglar in 1865, and broke the spirit of Baby Suggs, who took to her bed and died just months before the Civil War ended. Paul D Garner, after escaping from a Georgia chain gang and wandering through much of the eastern United States, found Sethe on Bluestone Road in 1873. He drove out the ghost and moved in with Sethe.

Just as Paul D, Sethe, and Denver began to bond into a family, a young black woman, calling herself Beloved, appeared from nowhere seeking sanctuary. Sethe took her in, and Beloved began disrupting the new family by insinuating herself into the affections of Sethe and Denver and seducing Paul D. In 1874, Stamp Paid told Paul D about Sethe's murder of her child nineteen years before, and Paul D left Sethe. Shunned by all as they had been since the murder in 1855, Sethe and Denver formed a family with Beloved.

The following year Sethe came to believe that Beloved was her own murdered child and gradually became obsessed with her, neglecting Denver as she tried desperately to make up for the murder. The diabolical Beloved soon consumed Sethe entirely. Sethe lost her job, and the starving Denver went begging for work. Through Denver the community learned of Beloved's presence and determined to help the Bodwins, who had rescued Sethe in 1855, rescue Denver from Sethe and Beloved. The women of the community began praying outside the house just as the elderly Mr. Bodwin arrived for Denver. The deranged Sethe, mistaking Mr. Bodwin for a slave catcher, tried to stab him with an ice pick. Denver and the other women stopped her, and Beloved disappeared. Broken in spirit by losing Beloved again, the twice bereaved Sethe took to her bed as the broken Baby Suggs had done in 1865. At the end of the novel Paul D, who had loved Sethe since she first arrived at Sweet Home twenty-five years before, returned to her. He refused to let Sethe die and began trying to heal her wounded heart.

Critical Evaluation:

In 1993, Toni Morrison became the first African American to receive the Nobel Prize in Literature. A great American novelist, Morrison has garnered numerous awards for her fiction, including a National Book Award nomination in 1975 for her second novel, *Sula*, the National Book Critics Circle Award in 1977 for her fourth novel, *Song of Solomon*, and the Pulitzer Prize in 1988 for *Beloved*. Morrison is responsible for helping bring African American literature and culture into the consciousness of the mainstream reader, not only through her fiction but also through an influential, best-selling volume of literary theory.

A modernist writer who has been compared to William Faulkner and James Joyce, Toni Morrison crafts novels that are complex and absorbing. They are also difficult to categorize. Multiple narrators in *Beloved* give the novel a veneer of realism. They reveal Sethe's story in fragments, a technique that closely emulates reality in the way in which people ordinarily learn about each other. On the other hand, the novel includes two ghosts as main characters, the infant Beloved and the adult Beloved. Some readers consider it a *Bildungsroman*, or coming-of-age novel, because at its close Sethe, with the help of Paul D, finally begins to discover a sense of self-worth. Still others consider it a historical novel because it is based on a historical incident, detailed in Middleton Harris' *The Black Book*, which Morrison edited in 1974, and because it examines the horrors of slavery and racism in excruciatingly frank detail.

Attempts to interpret Toni Morrison strictly within the Western literary tradition, however, fail because Morrison is intent on building an African American canon of literature, perhaps influenced by the Western tradition but always in rebellion against it. Differentiation between physical ownership and psychological possession are key themes; the characters in *Beloved*, particularly Sethe, must learn to judge themselves and each other according to their own values rather than those imposed on them by the dominant white culture. Few succeed. After Baby Suggs's feast, the community punishes her for being pretentious or "uppity," just as a white slave owner might have done, by refusing to warn her about the approaching slave-catchers. Stamp Paid, perhaps, is one who has been owned by the slavers but never possessed, who has performed their forced labor but has never internalized their forced values. Yet even Stamp Paid gives in to the values of white society when he reveals Sethe's crime to Paul D.

Those white values, in a sense, are represented by the poltergeist, the tantrum-throwing ghost of the murdered baby, Beloved, because neither white society nor its courts can understand Sethe's crime, which springs from her deep conviction that her children are better off dead than enslaved. Her guilt haunts the house on Bluestone Road and demands that Sethe and her family appease it. Buglar leaves home when the ghost has achieved such power that he can no longer look into a mirror without shattering it. Metaphorically, the African American past, dominated by subjection, has forced the African American to internalize the white judgment of black inferiority. Howard departs when the baby's handprints appear in a cake; the past taints even the spirit of celebration represented by the cake. Baby Suggs, who consecrated her emancipation by preaching self-love and pride to the other freed slaves, takes to her bed the day after Beloved's death, dying some time later in the belief that all her preaching has been a lie, that black people deserve neither love nor pride. Sethe must remain, appeasing the guilt, vivified as a ghost, that haunts her life.

When Paul D arrives in 1873, Sethe begins to experience love and hope for the first time since Beloved's death in 1855. Paul D drives away the ghost, but she returns several days later as a young woman of nineteen or twenty—the age Beloved would have been—and disrupts the bonding process that has nearly made a family of Sethe, Paul D, and Denver. Upon seeing her, Sethe runs to the outhouse but does not make it; she finds herself urinating on the ground in a scene reminiscent of her water breaking at Beloved's birth. This symbolic rebirth of Beloved destroys Sethe's chance at happiness. This new Beloved, threatening, demanding, controlling, destroying, eventually possesses Sethe, enslaving her again. Once again, she must be emancipated.

Perhaps the most striking example of Morrison's genius in this novel is her treatment of the adult ghost. The reader naturally is suspicious of this new Beloved, who may be Sethe's slain infant somehow brought to life, but the characters treat her as real. The reader experiences vicariously what Sethe experiences. Fear, guilt, shame, and self-loathing live in Sethe's mind and heart, and Beloved lives for the reader. The reader can never be sure, even after Beloved vanishes, if she is flesh or spirit, and so shares Sethe's self-doubt. Paul D's return reminds Sethe and the reader of that most Morrisonian of themes, self-affirmation as the key to life.

Craig A. Milliman

Bibliography:
Bloom, Harold, ed. *Toni Morrison: Modern Critical Views.* New York: Chelsea House, 1990.
Includes general essays on Morrison, plus Marilyn Sanders Mobley's essay identifying the source of Sethe's story and arguing that *Beloved*, rather than partaking of Western literary tradition, employs the "trope of memory to revise the genre of the slave narrative."

Gates, Henry Louis, Jr., and K. A. Appiah, eds. *Toni Morrison: Critical Perspectives Past and Present*. New York: Amistad Press, 1993. In a notable essay in this useful collection, Trudier Harris discusses physical ownership versus psychological possession. Most of the former slaves in the novel, Harris argues, were both owned and possessed, accepting the dominant white culture's evaluation of them rather than developing their own sense of self-worth.

Harding, Wendy, and Jacky Martin. *A World of Difference: An Inter-Cultural Study of Toni Morrison's Novels*. Westport, Conn.: Greenwood Press, 1994. Argues that Morrison's fiction should be analyzed at the "cultural interface," the territory where the dominant culture and the dominated collide and a new culture arises.

Harris, Trudier. *Fiction and Folklore: The Novels of Toni Morrison*. Knoxville: University of Tennessee Press, 1991. Harris argues that African American folklore, in part because of its "male-centered perspective," provides a useful framework for interpreting Morrison's fiction.

Samuels, Wilfred D., and Clenora Hudson-Weems. *Toni Morrison*. Boston: Twayne, 1990. Argues that *Beloved* is a historical novel that reshapes the slave narrative for a modern audience, omitting the conventional antislavery polemics, now unnecessary, and delving more deeply into the horrors of slavery than nineteenth century slave narrators dared.

BEN-HUR
A Tale of the Christ

Type of work: Novel
Author: Lew Wallace (1827-1905)
Type of plot: Historical
Time of plot: The time of Christ
Locale: Antioch and Jerusalem
First published: 1880

> *Principal characters:*
> BEN-HUR, a Roman-educated Jew
> BALTHASAR, an Egyptian
> SIMONIDES, a Jewish merchant and friend of Ben-Hur
> ESTHER, the daughter of Simonides
> IRAS, the daughter of Balthasar
> MESSALA, a Roman and an enemy of Ben-Hur

The Story:

In the Roman year 747, three travelers—an Athenian, a Hindu, and an Egyptian—met in the desert, where they had been led by a new bright star shining in the sky. After telling their stories to one another, they journeyed on, seeking the newborn child who was King of the Jews. In Jerusalem, their inquiries aroused the curiosity of King Herod, who asked that they be brought before him. Herod then asked them to let him know if they found the child, for he, too, wished to adore the infant whose birth had been foretold. Arriving at last in Bethlehem, the three men found the newborn child in a stable. Having been warned in a dream of Herod's evil intentions, however, they did not return to tell the king of the child's whereabouts.

At that time, there lived in Jerusalem three members of an old and eminent Jewish family named Hur. The father, who had been dead for some time, had distinguished himself in service to the Roman Empire and had, consequently, received many honors. The son, Ben-Hur, was handsome, and the daughter, Tirzah, was likewise beautiful. Their mother was a fervent nationalist who had implanted in their minds a strong sense of pride in their race and national culture.

When Ben-Hur was still a young man, his friend Messala returned from his studies in Rome. Messala had become arrogant, spiteful, and cruel. As Ben-Hur left Messala's home after their meeting, he was hurt, for he realized that Messala had so changed that their friendship must end.

A few days later, while watching a procession below him in the streets, Ben-Hur was implicated when a piece of tile, accidentally dislodged, fell on the Roman procurator. The Roman believed that the accident was an attempt on his life. Led by Messala, who had pointed out his former friend to the soldiers, the Romans arrested the Hur family and confiscated their property.

Ben-Hur was sent to be a galley slave. While he was being led away in chains, a young man took pity on him and gave him a drink. One day, while he was rowing at his usual place in the galley, Ben-Hur attracted the attention of Quintus Arrius, a Roman official. Later, during a sea battle, Ben-Hur saved the life of Quintus, who adopted the young Jew as his son. Educated as a Roman citizen, Ben-Hur inherited his foster father's wealth when Quintus died.

Ben-Hur went to Antioch, where he learned that his father's old servant, Simonides, was now a prosperous merchant. In effect, the wealth of Simonides was really the property of the Hur family, for he had been acting as agent for his dead master. Simonides assured himself that Ben-Hur was really the son of his old master and begged that he be allowed to serve the son as well. Ben-Hur was attracted to Simonides' daughter, Esther.

In company with a servant of Simonides, Ben-Hur went to see a famous well on the outskirts of Antioch. There an aged Egyptian was watering his camel, on which sat the most beautiful woman Ben-Hur had ever seen. While he looked, a chariot came charging through the people near the well. Ben-Hur seized the lead horse by the bridle and swerved the chariot aside. The driver was his false friend, Messala. The old Egyptian was Balthasar, one of the wise men who had traveled to Bethlehem. The beautiful woman was his daughter, Iras.

Learning that the arrogant Messala was to race his chariot in the games at Antioch, Ben-Hur wished to defeat and humiliate his former friend. He had Simonides and his friends place large wagers on the race, until Messala had staked his whole fortune. The day of the race came. At the turn, Messala suddenly struck with his whip at the horses of the chariot Ben-Hur was driving. Ben-Hur managed to keep his team under control, and then in the last lap around the arena, he drove his chariot so close to Messala's vehicle that the wheels locked. Messala was thrown under his horses and crippled for life. Messala had attempted foul play earlier in the race, so the judges allowed Ben-Hur to be proclaimed the winner. Messala was ruined.

From Balthasar, Ben-Hur learned that the King of the Jews to whom the Egyptian and his companions had paid homage some years before was not to be the king of a political realm, but of a spiritual one. Simonides, however, convinced Ben-Hur that the promised king would be a real deliverer who would lead the Jews to victory over the Romans.

From Antioch, Ben-Hur went to Jerusalem to search for his mother and sister. There he learned the part Messala had played in the ruin of his family. After Ben-Hur's arrest, his mother and sister had been thrown into prison, and Messala and the procurator had divided the confiscated property between them. Messala knew nothing of the fate of the two women after the procurator had ordered them confined to an underground cell. There they had contracted leprosy. When Pilate, the new procurator, arrived, he had ordered all political prisoners freed and so the two women had been set at liberty. There was no place for them to go except to the caves outside the city where the lepers were sent to die. A faithful old servant found them and carried food to them daily, under sacred oath never to reveal their names. When Ben-Hur met the old servant, she allowed him to believe that his mother and sister were dead.

Meanwhile, Simonides, acting for Ben-Hur, bought the Hur home. He, Esther, Balthasar, and Iras took possession of it. Ben-Hur himself could visit it only at night and in disguise. He was plotting to overthrow the Roman rule and was recruiting an army to follow the future King of the Jews. He went one day near the place where the lepers usually gathered on the hill beyond the city gates. On the way, he met a young man whom he recognized as the one who had given him a drink of water years before when he was being led away to slavery. The young man was the Nazarene. That day, the old servant had persuaded Tirzah and her mother to show themselves to the Nazarene as he passed. The women were cured, and Ben-Hur saw the two lepers transformed into his mother and sister.

Ben-Hur's attitude toward the King of the Jews was slowly changing. When he witnessed the crucifixion in company with Simonides and old Balthasar, any doubts that he might have had were removed. He was convinced then that Christ's kingdom was a spiritual one. From that day on, he and his family were Christians.

Some years later, in the beautiful villa at Misenum, Ben-Hur's wife, Esther, received a strange visit from Iras, the daughter of Balthasar. Iras told Esther that she had killed Messala for the misery he had brought her. When he learned of the visit, Ben-Hur was sure that on the day of the crucifixion, the day that Balthasar himself had died, Iras had deserted her father for Messala.

Ben-Hur was happy with Esther and their two children. He and Simonides devoted their fortunes to the Christian cause. When Nero began the persecution of the Christians in Rome, it was Ben-Hur who went there to build the catacombs under the city, so that those who believed in the Nazarene could worship in safety and peace.

Critical Evaluation:

Lew Wallace was a man of many vocations; in addition to writing several novels, he was, at one time or another during his life, a soldier, a lawyer, territorial governor of New Mexico, and minister to Turkey. His knowledge of and experience in the military, the law, government, and diplomacy developed in him an appreciation for history which enhanced the historical verisimilitude of his novels. It is that quality of evoking the spirit of the times which, in large part, accounts for the popular success of Wallace's two best novels, *The Fair God* (1873) and *Ben-Hur*. In fact, *Ben-Hur* is one of the all-time best-selling novels in English. The book has also been widely translated into several foreign languages.

Like Wallace's other books, *Ben-Hur* is a mainstream historical novel. Basic elements in the genre include a background of genuine historical events, which Wallace provides in his depictions of Roman decadence and the birth of Christianity. Also included are genuine historical figures in the narrative; Wallace uses King Herod, Balthasar, Pontius Pilate, Nero, and Jesus in cameo parts. The third element is a fictional protagonist whose deeds are not part of the historical record and whose actions and emotions can thus be manipulated at will by the novelist to suit the needs of his tale. Judah Ben-Hur is such a protagonist. Finally, the central focus of the plot is on events related to the personal and individual concerns of the protagonist, with historical matters relegated to the periphery of the action in the novel or used to highlight—sometimes ironically—the protagonist's role (usually a minor one) in the major affairs of his or her time. Thus, Wallace devotes most of his attention to the tribulations of the Jewish protagonist Ben-Hur and the perfidies of the Roman antagonist Messala, with historical events forming thematic parentheses around the central narrative.

It is interesting, moreover, that the final historical note in *Ben-Hur* depicts the protagonist—by then a convert to the Christian cause—building the Roman catacombs for the sheltering and the protection of persecuted Christians. *Hur* is the Hebrew word for "cave" or "cavern" (*ben* is a Hebrew prefix signifying son of). Surely, given Wallace's penchant for accurate details, his choice of a name for his protagonist was not accidental. In *Ben-Hur* Wallace has produced a classic historical novel.

Bibliography:

Gutjahr, Paul. "'To the Heart of the Solid Puritans': Historicizing the Popularity of *Ben-Hur*." *Mosaic* 26, no. 3 (Summer, 1993): 53-67. Offers reasons for *Ben-Hur*'s pleasing even readers mistrustful of novels. One reason mentioned is that the novel advocates feeling and faith to counter scientific challenges to the Bible and traditional Christianity.

Mayer, David, ed. *Playing Out the Empire: "Ben-Hur" and Other Toga Plays and Films, 1883-1908: A Critical Anthology.* Oxford, England: Clarendon Press, 1994. Includes introductory commentary and notes on Wallace's novel, William Young's 1899 play, and the 1907 Kalem Company film version.

Morsberger, Robert E., and Katharine M. Morsberger. *Lew Wallace: Militant Romantic.* New York: McGraw-Hill, 1980. Discusses sources of *Ben-Hur* and Wallace's method of composition. Summarizes the novel's plot; analyzes its themes and style. Comments on contemporary reviews of *Ben-Hur*, its popularity, and sales figures.

Quinn, Arthur Hobson. *American Fiction: An Historical and Critical Survey.* East Norwalk, Conn.: Appleton-Century-Crofts, 1936. Praises *Ben-Hur* for its magnificent opening, presentation of rival forces (Judaism, Christianity, Roman imperialism), key dramatic scenes (lepers' cell, naval battle, chariot race), absence of anti-Semitism, minor characters, and relation of all characters to Ben-Hur.

Thorp, Willard. "The Religious Novel as Best Seller in America." In *Religious Perspectives in American Culture*, edited by James Ward Smith and A. Leland Jamison. Princeton, N.J.: Princeton University Press, 1961. Places *Ben-Hur* in the context of novels concerning Christ. Accords it unique praise for presenting many varieties of life and for successfully using massive amounts of detail.

A BEND IN THE RIVER

Type of work: Novel
Author: V. S. Naipaul (1932-   )
Type of plot: Psychological realism
Time of plot: Early 1970's
Locale: The African interior
First published: 1979

Principal characters:

SALIM, a coastal Muslim who moves to the interior of Africa to open
a business
INDAR, his childhood friend
ALI (METTY), Salim's servant
NAZRUDDIN, the family friend who set up Salim in business
ZABETH, a woman from the bush
FERDINAND, her son
BIG MAN, the ruler of the Domain
RAYMOND, a white European who works for Big Man
YVETTE, his wife
FATHER HUISMANS, a teacher at the *lycée*

The Story:

Salim envied his well-to-do friend Indar, who informed him that he was going away to England to study at a famous university. Indar explained that one had to be strong to continue to live in Africa and that "We're not strong. We don't even have a flag." It is against such a backdrop of insecurity and fear that Salim decides to leave the coast and his Muslim community and head into the interior. "To stay with my community," Salim acknowledged, "to pretend that I had simply to travel along with them, was to be taken with them to destruction. I could be master of my fate only if I stood alone."

Nazruddin, a family friend, offered Salim his abandoned shop in the interior of Africa, at the bend of a river, in a settlement that had been half destroyed during the violence that preceded the area's political independence. Salim traveled to the interior, took over the small shop, and spent the next seven years attempting to establish himself before the violence and social chaos returned.

He befriended some Indian families, traded with a mysterious character named Zabeth, a magician from downriver, and agreed to look after her son, Ferdinand, who attended school at the local *lycée*. He soon acquired a living companion when his family, which had broken up and dispersed during a social revolution on the coast, sent him their slave, Ali, who took the new name of Metty (a name that means "someone of mixed race"). Salim later befriended a white couple, Raymond and Yvette. Raymond worked for the local ruler, Big Man (a character drawn after Joseph Mobutu, the king of Zaire); Big Man was the closest white personal friend of Raymond, who managed a university in the Domain, a group of new buildings in the town's former white suburb.

Father Huismans was a teacher at the *lycée*, where Ferdinand had enrolled as a student. Although the *lycée* was a remnant of the colonial period, Father Huismans possessed a genuine love for Africa and its traditions. He had amassed a large collection of African masks that were intended for specific religious purposes. Salim observed that, although Father Huismans knew a great deal about African religion, he did not seem concerned about the state of the country. During the subsequent revolution to purify Africa and cast off European influences, Father Huismans became a victim of his own purity, naïveté, and dedication to a religious-academic enterprise. His mutilated body was found among the thick water hyacinths that clotted the river. His head had been cut off and placed on a spike.

Ferdinand, schooled at the Domain, developed a powerful sense of self-importance and rebelled against Salim's more temperate influence. He became an idealist who committed his life to a new Africa under the leadership of Big Man and his flag of "authenticity." Salim came to realize that under the dictatorial powers of Big Man he was constantly surrounded by violence and by the threat of violence. The ancient tribes from the bush had been displaced by the new army, which drew its authority from Big Man.

Salim's life took a new turn when his childhood friend Indar came from his home in England as a guest of the government to teach at the Domain for one term. Indar introduced Salim to Raymond and Yvette, a meeting that changed the course of Salim's life. Indar's philosophy asserted that the past was a death trap: "You see that the past is something in your mind alone, that it doesn't exist in real life. You trample on the past, you crush it."

Salim maintained many ties with his past; these ties included his servant Metty and his obsession with the mystery and security of tribal life in the bush, which were embodied in the person of Zabeth. The past reflected Salim's dream of a peaceful world whose customs and rituals were barriers to the present disorder. Salim came to adopt Indar's philosophy, but he modified it to suit his own temperament. He concluded that he could not return to his home and that the idea was a deception that would weaken and destroy his reality. "We had to live in the world as it existed," he determined.

Salim's stoic philosophy had been shaped partly by his experience with Yvette, which opened up to him a powerful new vision of sexuality and romance. His sexual adventure with this fascinating, white European woman overwhelmed Salim with a sense of fulfillment and unappeased pleasure. Yet the romance soon gave way to bitter disillusionment and anger.

As the town and government experienced new insurrections, Raymond and Yvette realized that their comfortable life was coming to an end. In the last meeting with Yvette, Salim exploded in a rage and beat her to the floor. Although he accused her of seducing him with false promises, Salim's real contempt and anger were directed toward himself.

After he lost Yvette, Salim became increasingly frustrated with the moral and social decay of his violent surroundings. To escape the fate of those around him, he traveled to London, as Indar had done earlier. There, Salim became engaged to Nazruddin's daughter. When he returned to Africa, however, he got caught up in the corruption and was imprisoned for smuggling ivory. Ferdinand released him from prison and confessed to Salim his total disillusionment with the "new" Africa of Big Man. Salim finally came to the conclusion that the best he could hope for was to follow in the stoic but optimistic path of the successful Nazruddin, to return to England, and to start again in a world where there was a stable culture and where he could explore and learn to accept a new interior.

Critical Evaluation:

A Bend in the River is based on V. S. Naipaul's observations during a 1975 visit to Zaire, a new African nation that had formerly been the Belgian Congo. In Zaire, Naipaul encountered several worlds at once: the Congo of Joseph Conrad, a writer whose clear insights into that country and into human character had fascinated Naipaul since childhood; the Africa of the bush, seemingly eternal and indomitable, despite Arab and Belgian attempts to civilize it; and the new Africa, the so-called authentic Africa of Joseph Mobutu. Naipaul quickly saw through the rhetoric and propaganda of the new government and of the ostentatious façades of Zaire's new art and architecture, and he exposed Mobutu's kingship as a temporary reign of self-aggrandizement, greed, and terror. In creating his novel, *A Bend in the River*, Naipaul combined his experiences in Zaire (which he documented in his critical essay on Mobutu, "A New King for the Congo: Mobutu and the Nihilism of Africa," 1975) with his personal preoccupation with such themes as the mingling of different cultures and the deterioration of dreams, sexuality, and personal and cultural security.

The hero of the novel, Salim, comes from a coastal Muslim family that in its customs is closer to the Hindus of northwest India, from which it had come centuries earlier. As the narrator, he is established both as an African and as an outsider, for, as he points out, the coast is not truly African but rather an area settled by Arabs, Indians, Persians, and Portuguese. This cultural background helps to explain Salim's growing sense of dislocation and alienation as he attempts to come to grips with the bush (represented by Zabeth), the "new" Africa of Big Man, the philosophy of his friend, Indar, and his sexual and cultural fantasies that center upon Yvette.

Corruption pervades the novel. Big Man ruthlessly asserts his control over the "new" Africa by fear and violence. He commands respect because of his wealth and power, and he undermines the ancient culture of the African bush by his campaigns of terror. Despite the trappings of a new cultural identity and "authenticity," Big Man and his followers are no better than the cultures they have nationalized in the name of African unity. The sensitive and intelligent Ferdinand represents the bright young African who emerges from the bush and is seduced by the promises of Big Man, who promises a radicalized Africa. By the end of the novel, however, Ferdinand has become totally disillusioned by the movement's hypocrisy and use of terror. The novel ends with an impending revolution that may again bring about massive killings and, perhaps, even the destruction of Big Man himself. Ferdinand, filled with rage that all he has studied and worked for has come to nothing, warns Salim to flee the country.

None of the characters in this novel succeeds in finding his or her identity in this violent country. Indar flees to London, where he becomes a failure at his work and turns to living in a past he can never reassume. Yvette and Raymond, whom Big Man uses to advance his policies, are discarded once their usefulness is over. Father Huismans, another European, is murdered, despite his dedication to the religious culture of Africa. Ferdinand has lost his ideals and hope yet cannot return to the bush from which he had come.

Salim and Nazruddin come close to attaining a degree of independence and self-fulfillment, Nazruddin by exchanging his African past for a life in London, and Salim by seeking refuge in England from the social and psychic disorder of his fractured and radicalized homeland. Salim opens his story with words of wisdom that he achieved only after his painful experiences in the interior of Africa: "The world is what it is; men who are nothing, who allow themselves to become nothing, have no place in it." The idea of going home, the idea of the other place, is a fiction that comforts only to destroy those who believe in it. There are no places to escape in this changing, dangerous, and disillusioning world, and this is especially true of people like Salim. He discovers that he must live in the world as it is, and that even his passage to England and his relationship with Nazruddin and his daughter will offer no more than a temporary respite from the relentless disorder that has shaped him.

Richard Kelly

Bibliography:
Kelly, Richard. *V. S. Naipaul*. New York: Continuum, 1989. Analyzes Naipaul's novels, short stories, essays, and travel books through *The Enigma of Arrival* (1988).
King, Bruce. *V. S. Naipaul*. Basingstoke, England: Macmillan, 1993. A thorough introduction to Naipaul's work.
McSweeney, Kerry. *Four Contemporary Novelists*. Montreal: McGill-Queen's University Press, 1983. Includes one chapter on Naipaul's novels, which provides an excellent discussion of the major themes in the writer's oeuvre.
Nixon, Rob. *London Calling: V. S. Naipaul, Postcolonial Mandarin*. New York: Oxford University Press, 1992. Examines Naipaul's cultural conflicts as they are reflected in his fiction.
Ramchand, Kenneth. *The West Indian Novel and Its Background*. New York: Barnes & Noble Books, 1970. An invaluable source of information about the cultural background that shaped Naipaul's thinking.
Updike, John. "Un Pé Pourrie." *The New Yorker*, May 21, 1979, 141-144. An insightful review of *A Bend in the River* by a novelist who has also written about Africa.

BENITO CERENO

Type of work: Novella
Author: Herman Melville (1819-1891)
Type of plot: Adventure
Time of plot: 1799
Locale: Harbor of St. Maria, off the coast of Chile, and Lima, Peru
First published: 1856

> *Principal characters:*
> AMASA DELANO, an American sea captain
> DON BENITO CERENO, a Spanish sea captain
> BABO, an African slave

The Story:

Captain Amasa Delano was commander of an American ship called *Bachelor's Delight*, which was anchored in the harbor of St. Maria, on an island off the coast of southern Chile. While there, he saw a ship apparently in distress, and thinking it carried a party of monks, he set out in a whaleboat to board the vessel and supply it with food and water. When he came aboard, he found that the ship, the *San Dominick*, was a Spanish merchant ship carrying slaves. The crew was parched and moaning; the ship itself was filthy; the sails were rotten. Most deplorable of all, the captain, the young Don Benito Cereno, seemed barely able to stand or to talk coherently. Aloof and indifferent, Cereno seemed ill both physically (he coughed constantly) and mentally. He was attended by Babo, his devoted slave.

Delano sent the whaleboat back to his ship to get additional water, food, and extra sails for the *San Dominick*, while he remained aboard the desolate ship. He tried to talk to Cereno, but the captain's fainting fits kept interrupting the conversation. The Spaniard seemed reserved and sour, in spite of Delano's attempts to assure the man that he was now out of danger. Delano finally assumed that Cereno was suffering from a severe mental disorder. The captain did, with great difficulty and after frequent private talks with Babo, manage to explain that the *San Dominick* had been at sea for 190 days. They had, Cereno explained, started out as a well-manned and smart vessel sailing from Buenos Aires to Lima but had encountered several gales around Cape Horn, lost many officers and men, and then had run into dreadful calms and the ravages of plagues and scurvy. Most of the Spanish officers and all the passengers, including the slave owner, Don Alexandro Aranda, had died of fever. Delano, who knew that the weather in recent months had not been as extreme as Cereno described it, simply concluded that the Spanish officers had been incompetent and had not taken the proper precautions against disease. Cereno continually repeated that only the devotion of his slave, Babo, had kept him alive.

Numerous other circumstances on the *San Dominick* began to make the innocent Delano more suspicious. Although everything was in disorder and Cereno was obviously ill, he was dressed perfectly in a clean uniform. Six black men were sitting in the rigging holding hatchets, although Cereno said they were only cleaning them. Two were beating up a Spanish boy, but Cereno explained that this deed was simply a form of sport. The slaves were not in chains; Cereno claimed they were so docile that they did not require chains. This notion pleased the humane Delano, although it also surprised him.

Every two hours, as they awaited the expected wind and the arrival of Delano's whaleboat, a large African man in chains was brought before Cereno, who would ask him if he, Cereno, could be forgiven. The man would answer, "No," and be led away. At one point, Delano began to fear that Cereno and Babo were plotting against him, for they moved away from him and whispered together. Cereno then asked Delano about his ship, requesting the number of men and the strength of arms aboard the *Bachelor's Delight*. Delano thought they might be pirates.

Nevertheless, Delano joined Cereno and Babo in Cereno's cabin for dinner. Throughout the meal, Delano alternately gained and lost confidence in Cereno's story. He tried, while discussing a means of getting Cereno new sails, to get Babo to leave the room, but the man and the master were apparently inseparable. After dinner, Babo, while shaving his master, cut his cheek slightly despite the warning that had been given. Babo left the room for a second and returned with his own cheek cut in a curious imitation of his master's. Delano thought this episode curious and sinister, but he finally decided that the man was so devoted to Cereno that he had punished himself for inadvertently cutting his master.

At last, Delano's whaleboat returned with more supplies. Delano, about to leave the *San Dominick*, promised to return with new sails the next day. When he invited Cereno to his own boat, he was surprised at the captain's curt refusal and his failure to escort the visitor to the rail. Delano was offended at the Spaniard's apparent lack of gratitude. As the whaleboat was about to leave, Cereno appeared suddenly at the rail. He expressed his gratitude profusely and then, hastily, jumped into the whaleboat. At first Delano thought that Cereno was about to kill him; then he saw Babo at the rail brandishing a knife. In a flash, he realized that Babo and the other slaves had been holding Cereno a captive. Delano took Cereno back to the *Bachelor's Delight*. Later they pursued the fleeing slaves. The slaves, having no guns, were easily captured by the American ship and brought back to shore.

Cereno later explained that the slaves, having mutinied shortly after the ship set out, had committed horrible atrocities and killed most of the Spaniards. They had murdered the mate, Raneds, for a trifling offense and had committed atrocities on the dead body of Don Alexandro Aranda, whose skeleton they placed on the masthead.

On his arrival in Lima, Don Benito Cereno submitted a long testimony, recounting all the cruelties the slaves had committed. Babo was tried and hanged. Cereno felt enormously grateful to Delano, recalling the strange innocence that had somehow kept the slaves from harming him, when they had the chance, aboard the *San Dominick*. Don Benito Cereno planned to enter a monastery; however, broken in body and spirit, he died three months after he completed his testimony.

Critical Evaluation:

Originally serialized in *Putnam's Monthly* in 1855, *Benito Cereno* first appeared, slightly revised, in book form as the first story in Herman Melville's *Piazza Tales* in 1856. It was not reprinted until 1924, when interest in Melville's writings was revived. Since then, it has often been praised as not only one of Melville's best fictional works but also one of the finest short novels in American literature.

Benito Cereno is Melville's version of a true story he had read in Amasa Delano's *Narrative of Voyages and Travels in the Northern and Southern Hemispheres* (1817). Melville freely adapts Delano's account to his own fictional purposes. The court depositions, which make up a considerable part of the latter half of *Benito Cereno*, have been shown to be close to those in Delano's account, though Melville omitted some of the court material. In contrast, the creation of atmosphere, the building of suspense, the development of the three main characters—Delano, Cereno, and Babo—and the extended use of symbolism are among Melville's chief contributions to the original story. Also, the thematically important conversation between Delano and Cereno at the end of *Benito Cereno* was added by Melville.

The remarkable third paragraph of *Benito Cereno* illustrates Melville's careful combining of atmospheric detail, color symbolism, and both dramatic and thematic foreshadowing.

> The morning was one peculiar to that coast. Everything was mute and calm; everything grey. The sea, though undulated into long roods of swells, seemed fixed, and was sleeked at the surface like waved lead that has cooled and set in the smelter's mould. The sky seemed a grey surtout. Flights of troubled grey vapours among which they were mixed, skimmed low and fitfully over the waters, as swallows over meadows before storms. Shadows present, foreshadowing deeper shadows to come.

The description, with its repeated use of the color grey and the word "seemed," is important in setting the scene for a story the action of which will be, as seen through Delano's eyes, ambiguous and deceptive until the light of truth suddenly blazes upon the American captain's mind. Until that time, he will be seeing both action and character through a mist. The grey is symbolically significant also because Delano's clouded vision will cause him to misjudge both the whites and blacks aboard the *San Dominick*. In the light of the final revelations of the story, the grey has a moral symbolism too, perhaps for Melville and surely for the modern reader, since Cereno and Delano are not morally pure good, nor is Babo all bad. The Spaniard is a slaver, and the American appears to condone the trade though he is not a part of it; the slave is certainly justified in seeking an escape from captivity for himself and his fellow slaves, though one cannot justify some of the atrocities consciously committed by Babo and his followers. The closing sentence of this mist-shrouded paragraph, "Shadows present, foreshadowing deeper shadows to come," not only looks forward to the mystery that so long remains veiled but also anticipates the final words of the two captains, words that partly suggest the great difference in their characters. Delano says, "You are saved: what has cast such a shadow upon you?" Cereno replies, "The negro."

In reading *Benito Cereno*, one is caught up in the same mystery that Captain Delano cannot penetrate, and one longs for a final release of the suspense, a solution to the strange puzzle. Melville's hold upon the reader until the flash of illumination in the climax is maintained by his use of Delano's consciousness as the lens through which scene, character, and action are viewed. The revelation is so long delayed because of Delano's being the kind of man he is. His heart is benevolent, but his mind is slow to perceive through the dragging hours from his boarding the *San Dominick* until he is finally shocked into recognition of the truth when Babo prepares to stab Don Benito with the dagger he had concealed in his hair. Delano is alternately repelled by Don Benito's manner or suspicious of his intentions and then inclined to acquit Cereno of seeming rudeness because of his frail health or condemn himself for his suspicions with the excuse that "the poor invalid scarcely knew what he was about."

Just as Melville may have intended to portray Delano as representing a type of American— good-hearted, friendly, and helpful but rather slow-witted and naïve—so he may have delineated Don Benito as emblematic of eighteenth century Spanish aristocracy—proud, enfeebled, and, finally, troubled in conscience over such moral crimes as slave trading. To Delano, he first appears as "a gentlemanly, reserved-looking, and rather young man . . . dressed with singular richness, but bearing plain traces of recent sleepless cares and disquietudes." Later, Don Benito's manner "conveyed a sort of sour and gloomy disdain [which] the American in charity ascribed to the harassing effects of sickness." Further observation leads Delano to conclude that Don Benito's "singular alternations of courtesy and ill-breeding" are the result of either "innocent lunacy, or wicked imposture." He is finally undeceived and apologizes for having suspected villainy in Don Benito toward the end of the danger-filled encounter with the slaves.

Delano is lighthearted and eager to dismiss the affair when the danger is over and his suspicions have been erased. Don Benito's mind, however, is of a different cast. He broods on the results in human experience of the confusing of appearance and reality. "[Y]ou were with me all day," he says to Delano, "stood with me, sat with me, looked at me, ate with me, drank with me, and yet, your last act was to clutch for a monster, not only an innocent man, but the most pitiable of all men. To such degree may malign machinations and deceptions impose. So far may ever the best man err, in judging the conduct of one with the recesses of whose condition he is not acquainted."

The horrors resulting from the slave mutiny and the tensions and terror that followed Delano's kind offer to aid a ship in apparent distress, leave an already ill man a dejected and broken one. The shadow of "the negro" has been cast forever upon him. He retires to the monastery on the symbolically named Mount Agonia and, three months later, is released from his sufferings, in death.

Babo, the third major character in *Benito Cereno*, is unforgettable, one of the first important black characters in American fiction (Harriet Beecher Stowe's Uncle Tom had preceded him by only four years). He is one of the most striking of Melville's "masked" men who appear in his work from beginning to end, hiding their true selves behind the semblance they present to the world. Captain Delano is completely deceived in his first sight of Babo with Don Benito. "By his side stood a black of small stature, in whose rude face, as occasionally, like a shepherd's dog, he mutely turned it up into the Spaniard's, sorrow and affection were equally blended." His attentiveness makes him seem "less a servant than a devoted companion" to Don Benito. Though he speaks little, his few brief speeches suggest the intelligence that enables him to lead the revolt on the *San Dominick*. He is capable of irony when Benito explains that it is to Babo that he owes his preservation and that Babo pacified "his more ignorant brethren, when at intervals tempted to murmurings." "Ah, master," he sighs, ". . . what Babo has done was but duty." The remark is as masked as Babo's bowed face, and the American is so completely taken in that, "As master and man stood before him, the black upholding the white, Captain Delano could not but bethink him of the beauty of that relationship which could present such a spectacle of fidelity on the one hand and confidence on the other."

With its many ironies—an aristocratic Spanish slaver captured by his slaves, a murderous man posing as a faithful servant, a naïve American protected from violent death through his own innocence and uncovering villainy by accident—*Benito Cereno* may be read as a magnificently contrived parable of limited, rational, well-ordered humanity struggling against evil in the social and natural universe and achieving at least a partial victory.

"Critical Evaluation" by Henderson Kincheloe

Bibliography:
Bloom, Harold, ed. *Herman Melville's "Billy Budd," "Benito Cereno," "Bartleby the Scrivener," and Other Tales.* New York: Chelsea House, 1987. Collects the best in late twentieth century views of Melville's tale, with emphasis on postmodernist approaches to the interweaving of fiction and history and to the different types of documentation represented in the narrative.
Burkholder, Robert E., ed. *Critical Essays on Herman Melville's "Benito Cereno."* New York: G. K. Hall, 1992. Contains indispensable essays on *Benito Cereno* in relation to nineteenth century expansionism, slavery, and other topics.
Gross, Seymour, ed. *A "Benito Cereno" Handbook.* Belmont, Calif.: Wadsworth, 1965. Still

one of the most comprehensive texts for understanding Melville's short novel. Reprints Melville's source, a chapter in the travel narrative of the eighteenth century ship captain Amasa Delano, as well as eleven critical articles offering historical points of view and discussions of narrative mode, style, symbolism, and theme.

Newman, Lea Bertani Vozar. *A Reader's Guide to the Short Stories of Herman Melville*. Boston: G. K. Hall, 1986. The section on *Benito Cereno* is indispensable, with sections on publication history, sources and influences, relationship to Melville's other works, a summary of criticism, and a comprehensive bibliography of related works.

Runden, John P. *Melville's "Benito Cereno": A Text for Guided Research*. Boston: D. C. Heath, 1965. An overview of responses to the story from early reviews to mid-twentieth century interpretations. Includes discussion of Melville's source in a biography of Charles V. Text of *Benito Cereno* is reprinted with original pagination.

BEOWULF

Type of work: Poetry
Author: Unknown
Type of plot: Epic
Time of plot: Sixth century
Locale: Denmark, southern Sweden (land of the Geats)
First transcribed: c. 1000

Principal characters:
BEOWULF, a Geat hero
HROTHGAR, the king of the Danes
UNFERTH, a Danish warrior
WIGLAF, a loyal noble of Beowulf's court

The Story:

Once, long ago in Hrothgar's kingdom, a monster named Grendel roamed the countryside at night. Rising from his marshy home, Grendel would stalk to the hall of the king, where he would seize fifteen of Hrothgar's sleeping warriors and devour them. Departing, he would gather fifteen more into his huge arms and carry them back to his watery lair. For twelve years this slaughter continued.

Word of the terror spread. In the land of the Geats, ruled over by Hygelac, lived Beowulf, a man of great strength and bravery. When he heard the tale of Hrothgar's distress, he set sail for Denmark to rid the land of its fear. With a company of fourteen men he came ashore and asked a coast watcher to lead him to Hrothgar's high hall. There he was feasted in great honor while the mead cup went around the table. Unferth reminded Beowulf of a swimming contest which Beowulf was said to have lost. Beowulf said only that he had more strength and that he had also slaughtered many deadly monsters in the sea. At the close of the feast, Hrothgar and his warriors went to their rest, leaving Beowulf and his band in the hall. Then the awful Grendel came to the hall and seized one of the sleeping warriors. He was fated to kill no more that night, for Beowulf without shield or spear seized the dreaded monster and wrenched off his right arm. Thus maimed, Grendel fled back to his marshland home. His bloody arm was hung in Hrothgar's hall.

The next night Grendel's mother came to avenge her son. Bursting into the great hall, she seized one of the warriors, Aeschere, Hrothgar's chief counselor, and fled with him into the night. She also took with her the prized arm of Grendel. Beowulf was asleep in a house removed from the hall, and not until morning did he learn of the monster's visit. Then, with Hrothgar leading the way, a mournful procession approached the dire marsh. At its edge they sighted the head of the ill-fated Aeschere and saw the stain of blood on the water. Beowulf prepared for a descent to the home of the foe. Unferth offered Beowulf the finest sword in the kingdom, and thus forfeited his own chance of brave deeds.

As Beowulf sank beneath the waters of the marsh, he was beset on every hand by prodigious monsters. After a long swim he came to the lair of Grendel's mother. Failing to wound her with Unferth's sword, he seized the monster by the shoulder and threw her to the ground. During a grim hand-to-hand battle, in which Beowulf was being worsted, he sighted a famous old sword of the giants, which he seized and thrust at Grendel's mother, who fell in helpless death throes. Then Beowulf turned and saw Grendel himself lying weak and maimed on the floor of the lair. Quickly he swung the sword and severed Grendel's head from his body. As he began to swim back up to the surface of the marsh, the sword with which he had killed his enemies melted until only the head and hilt were left. On his return, the Danes rejoiced and feted him with another high feast. He presented the sword hilt to Hrothgar and returned Unferth's sword without telling that it had failed him.

The time came for Beowulf's return to his homeland. He left Denmark in great glory and sailed toward the land of the Geats. Once more at the court of his lord Hygelac, he was held in high esteem and was rewarded with riches and position. After many years, Beowulf himself became the king of the Geats. One of the Geats accidentally discovered an ancient hoard of treasure and, while its guardian dragon slept, carried away a golden goblet which he presented to Beowulf. The discovery of the loss caused the dragon to rise in fury and to devastate the land. Old man that he was, Beowulf was determined to rid his kingdom of the dragon's scourge. Daring the flames of the dragon's nostrils, he smote his foe with his sword, but without effect. Once more Beowulf was forced to rely on the grip of his mighty hands. Of all his warriors only Wiglaf stood by his king; the others fled. The dragon rushed at Beowulf and sank its teeth deeply into his neck, but Wiglaf smote the dragon with his sword, and Beowulf with his war-knife gave the dragon its death blow.

Weak from loss of blood, the old hero was dying. His last act was to give Wiglaf a king's collar of gold. The other warriors now came out of hiding and burned with pagan rites the body of their dead king. From the dragon's lair they took the treasure hoard and buried it in the great mound they built over Beowulf's ashes. Then with due ceremony they mourned the passing of the great and dauntless Beowulf.

Critical Evaluation:

Beowulf is the earliest extant heroic poem in any modern European language. The poem has come down through the centuries in a single manuscript, which was damaged and almost destroyed in the 1731 fire in the Cotton Library. Although the manuscript dates from the tenth century, the poem was probably composed in the eighth century and deals with sixth century events, before the migration of the Germanic tribes to Britain.

The poem was composed and performed orally. Old English bards, or scops, most likely began by piecing together traditional short songs, called heroic lays; they then gradually added to that base until the poem grew to its present size. The verse form is the standard Old English isochronic in that each line contains four stresses; there is a strong caesura in the middle of the lines, and the resultant half lines are bound together by alliteration. Although little Old English poetry survives, *Beowulf*'s polished verse and reflective, allusive development suggest that it is part of a rich poetic tradition.

Besides having unusual literary merit, *Beowulf* also provides information about and insight into the social, political, and ethical systems of Anglo-Saxon culture. There is a strong emphasis on courage in battle, fidelity to one's word, and loyalty to kinsmen. This is a violent but highly principled society in which struggle is everywhere and honor is everything. The hero, bound by family ties, by his own word, and by a strict code of revenge, is surrounded by his comitatus, his band of devoted comrades in arms. Judeo-Christian elements enter into the poem and into the society, but these aspects of the poem bear more resemblance to the philosophical systems of the Old Testament, stressing justice rather than love. There is controversy about whether these elements are intrinsic or are interpolations by a tenth century monastic scribe. In any case, it does not much resemble the Christianity of the High Middle Ages or of the modern world. Frequently the poem seems a reflection on the traditional pagan value system from the moral point of view of the new, incompletely assimilated Christianity.

Despite the fact that the heroic poem centers on valorous exploits, *Beowulf* contains curiously little action. The plot is embedded in a mass of other materials which some critics have seen as irrelevant or peripheral. However, the poem is basically reflective and ruminative, and the digressive materials provide the context in which the action of the poem is to be seen and interpreted. Consequently, *Beowulf* contains historical information, ceremonial descriptions, lengthy genealogies, elaborate speeches, and interspersed heroic songs which reveal much about the world in which *Beowulf* is set. For example, it is important that the action is entwined in a historical sequence of events, because complex loyalties and responsibilities are thereby implied. Beowulf helps Hrothgar because of the past links between their families, and, much later, when Beowulf succumbs to the dragon, it is clear that the future of his whole people is in jeopardy. In addition, the songs of the scop at Hrothgar's court indicate the value of poetry as a means of recording the past and honoring the brave. In like manner, the genealogies dignify characters by uniting them with revered ancestors, and the ceremonies underscore the importance of present deeds and past worth. Through these apparently extrinsic materials, the poet builds a continuity between past and present and extends the significance of his poem and characters to the whole of society.

In this context, Beowulf meets a series of challenges embodied in the poem's three monsters. That Beowulf battles imposing monsters rather than human adversaries suggests that his actions bear larger meanings. The hero arrives at the court of Hrothgar at the height of his youthful abilities. Not a neophyte, he has already fought bravely and demonstrated his preternatural power and charisma. He has no doubts or hesitancies as he prepares to fight. Grendel, a descendant of the line of Cain, is hateful to God, a lonely and vicious outcast, who hates light and joy and exacts bloody vengeance on man. All the more fearful because of his vague but imposing physique, Grendel is a representative of the physical evil which was so present in the lives and imaginations of the Anglo-Saxons. Beowulf confronts that physical evil and, bolstered by lineage and loyalty, routs the inimical force with which all people must contend.

However, Grendel, mortally wounded, escapes to his undersea lair, a submerged area devoid of light and appropriate to his joyless evil. Beowulf must, as a result, trace evil to its source if he is to be truly victorious. He ultimately returns with Grendel's head as a sign of victory, but to do that he must descend to the depths and exterminate the source of evil figured in Grendel's mother. This battle is more difficult and ominous: Beowulf doubts his capacities and his men almost give up on him. Naturally this battle is more arduous, because he is facing the intellectual or moral evil which is at the root of the physical evil that threatens human life and joy. The poem is not a moral allegory in which Beowulf roots evil out of the world, but an exemplum of how each person must face adversity.

One greater challenge remains for Beowulf, and it is significant that it is separated by space and years from these youthful encounters. As a young warrior, Beowulf faced evil in vigorous foreign exploits; as an old king in his own country, he faces the dragon, the ultimate test of his courage. The dragon is at once less horrible (he does not have a distorted human form) and more fearsome. Beowulf, as the representative of his society, must enter the battle in which he knows he will die. The nonhuman dragon is a figure of the metaphysical evil which is woven into the fabric of the universe. Physical and moral evil can be challenged and overcome, but the ultimate evil (perhaps, at its extremity, age and death) cannot be avoided. Beowulf slays his antagonist and transcends his own death. By dying as he lived, he is a model for triumph in the last struggle every human must face.

"Critical Evaluation" by Edward E. Foster

Bibliography:

Brodeur, Arthur G. *The Art of "Beowulf."* Berkeley: University of California Press, 1960. From the starting point of belief in a singular author having written *Beowulf*, this volume provides a structural and thematic criticism of the work. It discusses diction, unity, setting, and Christian elements. A landmark reference.

Goldsmith, Margaret E. *The Mode and Meaning of "Beowulf."* London: Athlone Press, 1970. This book revises earlier discussions of Christian allegory in *Beowulf*. An attempt is made to prove the text to be an extended Christian allegory. A classic examination of the manuscript's Christian hero pitted against evil.

Nicholson, Lewis E. *An Anthology of "Beowulf" Criticism.* Notre Dame, Ind.: University of Notre Dame Press, 1963. This early volume saves hours of searching through scholarly journals by presenting a comprehensive collection of widely recognized articles. It covers over two dozen aspects of the text from allegory to zoology.

Ogilvy, Jack D. A., and Donald C. Baker. *Reading "Beowulf."* Norman: University of Oklahoma Press, 1983. This work provides a modern and thorough view of the poem. After providing the historical background for the piece, it focuses on a two-part summary of the story and a subsequent analysis of theme, versification, and style. It includes an extensive annotated bibliography as well as many illustrations.

Whitelock, Dorothy. *The Audience of "Beowulf."* Oxford, England: Clarendon Press, 1951. A transcription of a series of lectures that concentrates on the poet and audience of *Beowulf* in their context of early Christianity. There are several references to other scholarly works as well as translations of the actual text. It contains an extensive index.

BÉRÉNICE

Type of work: Drama
Author: Jean Baptiste Racine (1639-1699)
Type of plot: Tragedy
Time of plot: 79 C.E.
Locale: Rome
First performed: 1670; first published, 1671

> *Principal characters:*
> TITUS, the emperor of Rome
> BÉRÉNICE, the queen of Palestine
> ANTIOCHUS, the king of Comagene
> PAULIN, Titus' confidant
> ARSACE, Antiochus' friend and confidant
> PHÉNICE, Bérénice's confidante

The Story:

The period of official mourning for the Emperor Vespasian had ended. His son Titus was to succeed to the throne, and the rumor was that he would marry Bérénice, the queen of Palestine, with whom he had long been in love. Antiochus, the war companion of Titus and a close friend, was also Bérénice's faithful friend. Although he had been in love with her for five years, she had never responded to his feeling.

Antiochus, who had hoped that Titus would not marry Bérénice, went to see her for the last time before he left Rome. He gave orders to his confidant Arsace to prepare everything for his departure. Arsace was surprised that Antiochus should be preparing to leave when Titus was rising to great honor and would, in all probability, want his friend close by.

Bérénice, confident that the rumor of her marriage with Titus was true, was expecting a confirmation at any moment. When Antiochus appeared to bid her farewell, she cruelly reproached him for declaring his love at that time. She declared that she had enjoyed his friendship and was depending on him to stay as a witness to her happiness.

Titus, aware that his love for Bérénice was a cause of concern to the Roman Empire, asked Paulin, a faithful confidant, his opinion of the emperor's suit. Paulin said frankly that the court would approve anything Titus might do, but that the Roman people would never be willing to have Bérénice as their empress. Although Titus realized this fact only too well, he tried desperately to cling to his hope that somehow he could make her his wife without arousing public indignation and protest. Meanwhile, he sent for Antiochus and asked him to take Bérénice back to her own country.

When Bérénice arrived, full of love and joy and believing that she would soon marry Titus, the emperor, unable to tell her the truth, blamed his father's death for the restrictions imposed upon him. She misunderstood him, however, and with all her passion reaffirmed her love, saying that he could never miss his father as she would miss him if he did not love her. Overwhelmed, Titus found it impossible to tell her that he could not make her his empress.

Left alone with Phénice, Bérénice showed some concern over Titus' actions and speech. Then, remembering that Titus was to see Antiochus, she imagined that he was jealous of Antiochus and therefore really in love with her, and that soon everything would be all right.

When Antiochus arrived, Titus asked him to talk to Bérénice in his place, as a friend, and to assure her that Titus was sacrificing their love only out of the demands of duty. Left alone with Arsace, Antiochus did not know whether to rejoice for himself or grieve for his friend. Although his heart was filled with renewed hope, he did not want to be the one to tell Bérénice of Titus' decision. In spite of his reluctance Bérénice persuaded him to reveal what Titus had told him. On hearing his story she refused to believe him and said that she would see Titus herself. In a painful interview she declared that she would kill herself. Paulin had a difficult time keeping Titus from following her when she left. Antiochus, alarmed, came to beg Titus to save her life.

Titus met with the representatives of the Senate. Meanwhile, he asked Antiochus to reassure Bérénice of his love. Arsace came looking for Antiochus with the news that Bérénice, about to leave Rome, had written a letter to Titus. Antiochus announced that he was going to commit suicide and left. Bérénice, coming out of her apartment, met Titus and told him she was leaving immediately. When Titus declared that he loved her now more than ever, she pleaded with him to show mercy and love her less when he ordered her to leave. He found the letter, which announced her decision to die since she could not stay with him. Saying that he could not let her go, he called for Antiochus. When Bérénice collapsed, Titus, in despair, assured her that he loved her to such a degree that he would be willing to give up the empire for her sake, even though he knew that she would be ashamed of him if he were to do so. If she would not promise to stay alive, he declared, he would kill himself. When Antiochus arrived, Titus told him to be a witness of how weak love had made his friend. Antiochus replied that he had always loved Bérénice and that he had been preparing to commit suicide when Titus called him back.

Moved by so much grief on all sides, Bérénice accepted Titus' decision. Leaving, she asked Antiochus to pattern his decision on theirs. The three went their different ways.

Critical Evaluation:

In his preface to *Bérénice*, Racine writes about the originality of this powerful tragedy, in which the plot is very limited. Racine explains that a tragedy need not include death. He argues that it is the "majestic sadness" expressed by the three principal characters in *Bérénice* which creates all the aesthetic pleasure for theatergoers and readers alike. Racine understands that readers of tragedies are moved to tears by the restrained dignity and the profound sentiments expressed by characters—and not by the deaths of sympathetic characters. In *Bérénice*, no one dies, but readers are moved by the self-sacrifice and humanity shown by Emperor Titus and Queen Bérénice.

Bérénice was the fifth of eleven tragedies that Racine wrote between 1664 and 1691. It stands out from his other tragic masterpieces because of the stark simplicity of plot and the small number of principal characters. In *Bérénice*, the only major characters are the Roman emperor Titus, his fiery queen Bérénice from Palestine, and King Antiochus from the Middle Eastern kingdom of Comagena. Many years before, Antiochus had fallen in love with Bérénice, but as this tragedy begins, Antiochus realizes that Bérénice loves only Titus. Unlike many of his tragedies, *Bérénice* has no villains.

The tragic conflict in *Bérénice* is quite simple. The newly crowned Roman emperor Titus and the Palestinian queen Bérénice have loved each other for several years, and they wish to get married. In his preface, Racine stresses that their mutual love is so pure that they have not yielded to the temptation to make love before marriage. There is little or nothing in *Bérénice* that could offend the moral or religious sensitivities of a reader. The passion that Titus and Bérénice feel for each other has become more intense because they have not yet consummated their love. Although Titus and Bérénice are kind and moral characters, there is an insurmountable obstacle to their happiness: Roman law does not permit an emperor to marry a woman who is not Roman, or a woman who is a queen. Many Roman historians have explained that Rome was ruled by tyrannical kings before the creation of the Roman Republic. No real difference existed between the absolute power of Roman emperors and that of Roman kings. It was only a question of terminology. Racine suggests throughout this tragedy that xenophobia is the only possible explanation for the Roman tradition that prevents an emperor from marrying a foreigner. When Jean Racine wrote *Bérénice*, King Louis XIV of France was married to Queen Maria Teresa of Spain. No one in France would have dared to criticize the king's decision to marry a foreigner; such criticism would have been viewed as unacceptable interference with the king's freedom of action. Despite the irrational nature of his subjects' hatred of foreigners and queens, Titus knows that he would have to resign if he were to marry Bérénice, and he believes that it would be dishonorable for him to resign from his position. Fate weighs heavily on the three principal characters as they come to understand that none of them can ever attain true happiness in life. As this tragedy begins, however, Bérénice has not yet discovered this. Bérénice tells Antiochus of her profound love for Titus; she considers Antiochus to be a countryman and a friend. Although she and Antiochus were once attracted to each other, she believes that neither still feels any passion for the other.

She is, however, mistaken. When Antiochus tells her that he still loves her, Bérénice restrains herself and tells him that she can love only Titus. In her mind, she is not free to love anyone other than her fiancé, Titus. Titus is also so emotionally committed to Bérénice that he could never love another woman.

Titus and Bérénice try to persuade themselves that Romans will not oppose their marriage. No one of the three wants to recognize that social prejudice has doomed his or her love to failure. Titus tries to believe that it will somehow be possible for him to reconcile his passion for Bérénice with his duty to uphold Roman laws and traditions, but he soon realizes that no such compromise exists. In many scenes in this tragedy, Titus and Bérénice agonize about what they should do, and they ask themselves whether they possess the inner strength to renounce their personal happiness in order to ensure peace and tranquillity in Rome. Bérénice becomes very angry and questions the sincerity of Titus' passion for her. At first, she cannot believe that Titus, who had claimed to love her, could decide not to marry her because of political pressure, but she comes to realize that his decision not to marry indicates, paradoxically, the depth of his passion for her. If he were to resign as emperor, Bérénice would someday be unable to respect a man who had shown so little respect for his social duty. The profound psychological insights into the nature of passion and the exquisite quality of the poetry in *Bérénice* continue to move readers and theatergoers centuries after its first performance.

"Critical Evaluation" by Edmund J. Campion

Bibliography:
Abraham, Claude. *Jean Racine*. Boston: Twayne, 1977. An excellent general introduction to Racine's plays as well as an annotated bibliography of important critical studies. Examines the psychological depth of *Bérénice* and develops the not totally convincing argument that Bérénice is a "self-centered" and "arrogant" character.
Barthes, Roland. *On Racine*. Translated by Richard Howard. New York: Hill & Wang, 1964. Examines the importance of love, violence, and heroism in Racine's tragedies. Argues persuasively that Bérénice is consumed with her love for Titus, whereas the emperor is unwilling to accept the dominance of passion in his life.

Cloonan, William J. *Racine's Theatre: The Politics of Love*. University, Miss.: Romance Monographs, 1977. Examines the political motivation for Titus' decision not to marry Bérénice and suggests that the emperor no longer loves Bérénice as passionately as he once did. Argues that Bérénice is a much more sympathetic character than Titus.

Knapp, Bettina L. *Jean Racine: Mythos and Renewal in Modern Theater*. University: University of Alabama Press, 1971. Contains a fascinating Jungian interpretation of Racine's tragedies. Describes and extraordinary psychological complexity of Titus and Bérénice.

Weinber, Bernard. *The Art of Jean Racine*. Chicago: University of Chicago Press, 1963. Analyzes the evolution of Racine's skill as a tragic playwright. The chapter on *Bérénice* explores the evocative power of Racine's refined verse and his artistry in using a simple plot.

BERLIN ALEXANDERPLATZ

Type of work: Novel
Author: Alfred Döblin (1878-1957)
Type of plot: Social realism
Time of plot: 1928-1929
Locale: Berlin
First published: Berlin Alexanderplatz: Die Geschichte vom Franz Biberkopf, 1929 (English translation, 1931)

Principal characters:
FRANZ BIBERKOPF, an ex-convict
EMILIE (MEIZE) PARSUNKE, his girlfriend
REINHOLD, his betrayer
EVA, his ex-girlfriend
HERBERT WISCHOW, Eva's pimp
FATTY PUMS, criminal overlord
OSKAR FISCHER, member of Pums's gang

The Story:
Franz Biberkopf was released from Tegel prison, where he had served four years for killing his girlfriend in a drunken rage. Back in Berlin, he decided to go straight. He began to peddle bow ties on a street corner and drifted into selling other merchandise. At the same time, he started an affair with Polish Lina and got involved fleetingly with a bewildering series of political movements, ranging from homosexual rights to the Nazi Party. His wearing of the Nazi armband angered his worker friends, who expelled him from his favorite pub. However, his real troubles began after he entered on a partnership with Otto Lüders. After Lüders robbed and assaulted one of his customers, to whose apartment he had gained access by using Franz's name, Biberkopf was forced to flee to an obscure part of the city to avoid complications.

A few weeks later, Franz returned to his usual haunts and took up a job as a newspaper vendor. He also began to consort with the flashy miscreant Reinhold. Reinhold was adept at making women fall in love with him, but he tired quickly of each new conquest and devised a system for Franz to help him. Each time Reinhold tired of a girlfriend, Franz would throw off his current mistress and take Reinhold's latest cast-off. When Franz became sincerely attached to Cissy, one of Reinhold's rejects, he refused to comply further. Indeed, he told Reinhold's girlfriend how things stood. This infuriated Reinhold, though he pretended to acquiesce in Franz's attempt to reform him.

Through a mixup, Franz was recruited by Fatty Pums, a so-called fruit vendor, who wanted his men to collect some "produce." It soon became clear that Pums headed a criminal gang, which included Reinhold. The gang was closely pursued as they drove away from a robbery, and Reinhold, given to psychotic rages and remembering Franz's interference with his social life, pushed him from the speeding automobile. Franz was run over by the chasing car.

He awoke in a hospital, missing one arm. As a bed-ridden invalid, he was taken in by the pimp Herbert Wischow and his companion Eva, friends from his criminal days. Once Franz felt better, Eva set him up with the young prostitute named Emilie (Meize) Parsunke, who began to support him. With time on his hands, Franz started dropping in for friendly chats with Reinhold. At first, the members of Pums's gang had feared the crippled Franz, thinking he would betray them to the police. When they found that he bore them no grudge—though his forbearance was inexplicable—they included him in a few jobs. Reinhold did not trust Franz, however, and decided to push him away by taking Meize away from him. Meize had been secretly seeing another gang member, Oskar Fischer, to learn more about the gang's activities so that she could protect Franz. Oskar passed her to Reinhold, after the couple met him "by chance" at a pleasure resort. Reinhold and Meize thereupon went for a walk in the woods and Reinhold turned on his charm. He was on the point of seducing her when he tactlessly began running down her lover. This made Meize's blood boil and she broke away. Reinhold, mad with lust, dragged her to the earth and, attempting to rape her, ended by killing her. He got Oskar to help him bury the body.

When Meize did not return, Franz was distraught. Reinhold was not afraid of retribution because he had concealed his crime well. Oskar, who had decided to rob without the gang, was arrested. Because he believed, erroneously, that Reinhold had warned the police, he tried to retaliate by confessing to being an accessory to Reinhold's murder of Meize. Reinhold had, however, moved the corpse, putting it in a trunk that he had asked Franz to buy in a conspicuous manner. When the body was found in its new berth, both Reinhold and Franz were suspected. The police put out a dragnet for them.

Franz learned of Meize's death and the hunt for him through the newspapers. Disguised with a false arm, he set off to track down Reinhold. For a while, he was protected by two talkative good angels—one of the novel's many brief departures from realism. Eventually, tired and confused, Franz wandered into a nightclub that was in the process of being raided by the police. He was arrested. Reinhold, who had gotten himself jailed under an assumed name, thinking prison was an ideal hiding place, was betrayed by a young man he had befriended.

Franz had a mental breakdown and was placed in the Buch Asylum where he lay as if dead. In his mind, he was undergoing a violent confrontation with Death, who recalled to Franz his misdeeds and charged him to start a new life. When he came out of his stupor, he had changed. After he was released, he quietly became a gatekeeper, refused to incriminate Reinhold at the killer's trial, and avoided any bad associations. From then on, he was known by the new name Franz Karl Biberkopf, for he was a remade man.

Critical Evaluation:

Berlin Alexanderplatz was an unusual twentieth century, avant-garde novel in being both a popular and a critical success. Readers liked the book's cynical, acid portrayal of Berlin's underworld as well as its happy ending, and the critics were enthusiastic about Döblin's use of montage techniques to create an electrifying portrait of a metropolis.

The breezy, hard-boiled tone, which characterizes much of the book, is a hallmark of Berlin's interwar writing. Germany's premier playwright of the time, Bertolt Brecht, perfected this tone in such works as *The Three Penny Opera* (1928). Works of this type depicted the world of small-time criminals, shysters, prostitutes, and other outcasts and deviants. Their lives, like those of gamblers, were filled with abrupt rises and falls. Relationships were unstable and unpredictable, passions hot, and loyalties only for the short term. To these characters, highly industrialized, modernized Berlin seemed to be governed not by rational procedures but by a whimsical, inscrutable fate. The only way to live in such a world was with a shield of knowing cynicism. In Döblin's book, characters such as Herbert and Eva have adopted this cynical attitude, and Franz acquires it in modified form at the conclusion. He learns about the mysteriousness of fate when he is repeatedly laid low by such unexpected disasters as Meize's disappearance.

However, Franz's outlook at the end is not purely cynical but includes a more positive element. This element, which accompanies the book's fatalism throughout, is the celebration of primal, resilient vitality. Döblin reflects this vitality both in the ongoing nascence of the city— a city that is constantly being demolished and reconstructed—and in the ingenuity of its inhabitants, who invent innumerable dodges to survive and strive in the difficult conditions. In his 1924 essay "The Spirit of the Naturalistic Age," Döblin asserted that the twentieth century would produce improved humans, who would arise from the energy of people living in giant collectives. The massification of humans, which many writers deplored, represented for Döblin the staging ground for the emergence of a happier, more fraternal, humanity. In *Berlin Alexanderplatz*, he pointed to this new spirit by frequently departing from his narrative to present a collage of the components of urban life that testify to the vitality of the metropolis and in his description of Franz's regeneration. In the asylum, Franz feels his body dissolve and flow out to take sustenance from the age's massed energy. This leads him to a nondenominational religious exaltation wherein he is healed through connection to the inner principle of his age.

Critical enthusiasm for *Berlin Alexanderplatz* focused on the author's use of montage, that is, the juxtaposition of heterogeneous materials. While working on his book, Döblin had been reading the Irish novelist James Joyce's *Ulysses* (1922), in which the montage method is extensively utilized. However, where Joyce deployed a different battery of devices in each major section of his text, Döblin took the single tool of montage and used it in various ways for varied effects. One of his uses was to interrupt his narrative by a cascade of facts and observations about Berlin life. He quotes advertisements and public notices, catalogs streetcar stops and the departments in a giant corporation, and chronicles the weather and stock market prices. The cumulative effect of such information is to lend immediacy to the novel's setting, Berlin. A second type of montage uses the thumbnail sketch. When Franz is hiding out after the Lüders disaster, for example, Döblin goes through his apartment building, room by room, and briefly describes each resident. Each life holds a spark of interest, and this is another indication of the city's fertility. Lastly, Döblin mixes in tales taken from the Bible and heroic sagas to deepen the novel's perspective. In *Ulysses*, Joyce uses the parallels between his story and the Greek myth referred to in his title to cast a dual light on his characters and to suggest both that they are degraded in relation to the classical prototypes and that their survival in the city demands a degree of heroic mettle. By contrast, when Döblin compares his protagonist's betrayal by Reinhold to the classical precedent of Orestes, who was betrayed by his mother, he does not use the parallel to imply connections between the times. Instead, the author explicitly declares that the Greek tale could no longer have anything but picturesque value once the classical style of life was surpassed.

James Feast

Bibliography:
Berman, Russell A. *The Rise of the Modern German Novel: Crisis and Charisma.* Cambridge, Mass.: Harvard University Press, 1986. Concludes that Weimar literature often ties political progressivism to a mystical faith in humanity, a linkage the author considers central to Döblin's masterpiece, *Berlin Alexanderplatz.*
Boa, Elizabeth, and J. H. Reid. *Critical Strategies: German Fiction in the Twentieth Century.* Montreal: McGill-Queen's University Press, 1972. In this survey of twentieth century German literature, Döblin's book is discussed as regards its plastic rendering of space and its thematic insistence on the inseparability of the individual and an individual's milieu.

Dollenmayer, David B. *The Berlin Novels of Alfred Döblin: "Wadzek's Battle with the Steam Turbine," "Berlin Alexanderplatz," "Men Without Mercy," and "November 1918."* Berkeley: University of California Press, 1988. Indicates how *Berlin Alexanderplatz* was quite a departure for Döblin who until then had focused on intellectual protagonists and usually set his books in earlier times or in foreign lands.

Durrani, Osman. *Fictions of Germany.* Edinburgh: Edinburgh University Press, 1994. A quarter of this 200-page book is devoted to *Berlin Alexanderplatz*, concentrating especially on Döblin's masterful use of Berlin slang and on his montage techniques.

Kort, Wolfgang. *Alfred Döblin.* New York: Twayne, 1974. Includes a valuable chapter on the author's thoughts on the twentieth century epic, noting that Döblin considered *Berlin Alexanderplatz* an epic, not a novel. Kort argues that the book calls into play the creative power of the reader, who must help construct the text.